"There can be no doubt that this is the best text of the history of philosophy now available in English."

—*The Historical Bulletin*

". . . a comprehensive survey of ancient philosophy . . . in a fresh and interesting as well as an accurate and authoritative manner."

—*The Catholic Historical Review*

". . . should be valuable not merely as a textbook but as an introduction to Christian philosophy for the general reader."

—*Pax*

". . . broad-minded and objective, comprehensive and scholarly, unified and well-proportioned . . . We cannot recommend too highly the adoption of Father Copleston's book as a manual in Catholic seminaries, colleges and universities."

—*Thought*

". . . a skillful, discerning analysis of the interplay of philosophical currents in Christian thought over eleven centuries."

—*America*

". . . a stimulating, informative, and interesting contribution to an appreciation of the medieval world-view with all its philosophical complexity."

—*Catholic Literary World*

". . . marked by solid learning, breadth of view, scientific objectivity and shrewd common sense."

—*The* (London) *Tablet*

"Father Copleston's work will rank as the most authoritative and outstanding study in this field by a Catholic scholar and second to none as a book of general reference on the subject."

—*Homiletic and Pastoral Review*

A HISTORY OF PHILOSOPHY

VOLUME I:
GREECE AND ROME

VOLUME II:
AUGUSTINE TO SCOTUS

VOLUME III:
OCKHAM TO SUAREZ

by
Frederick Copleston, S.J.

A DIVISION OF DOUBLEDAY & COMPANY, INC.
GARDEN CITY, NEW YORK

Image Books editions of Volumes I, II, III of A HISTORY OF PHILOSOPHY first published 1962 and 1963 by special arrangement with The Newman Press.

This Image edition, published April 1985, consists of Volumes I, II, III in one book.

VOL. I
DE LICENTIA SUPERIORUM ORDINIS:
Franciscus Mangan, S.J., Praep. Prov. Angliae

NIHIL OBSTAT:
C. Lattey, S.J., Censor Deputatus

IMPRIMATUR:
✠ Thomas, Archiepiscopus Birmingamiensis
Die 17 Martii 1944

VOL. II
DE LICENTIA SUPERIORUM ORDINIS:
Martinus D'Arcy, S.J., Praep. Prov. Angliae

NIHIL OBSTAT:
T. Corbishley, S.J., Censor Deputatus

IMPRIMATUR:
✠ Joseph, Archiepiscopus Birmingamiensis
Die 24 Aprilis 1948

VOL. III
DE LICENTIA SUPERIORUM ORDINIS:
E. Helsham, S.J.
Praep. Prov. Angliae

NIHIL OBSTAT:
J. L. Russell, S.J.
Censor Deputatus

IMPRIMATUR:
✠ Joseph, Archiepiscopus Birmingamiensis
Birmingamiae die 4 Januarii 1952

ISBN: 0-385-23031-1

Library of Congress Catalog Card Number

Printed in the United States of America

PREFACE

THERE are so many histories of philosophy already in existence that it seems necessary to give some explanation why one has added to their number. My chief motive in writing this book, which is designed to be the first volume of a complete history of philosophy, has been that of supplying Catholic ecclesiastical seminaries with a work that should be somewhat more detailed and of wider scope than the text-books commonly in use and which at the same time should endeavour to exhibit the logical development and inter-connection of philosophical systems. It is truc that there are several works available in the English language which (as distinct from scientific monographs dealing with restricted topics) present an account, at once scholarly and philosophical, of the history of philosophy, but their point of view is sometimes very different from that of the present writer and of the type of student whom he had in mind when writing this book. To mention a "point of view" at all, when treating of the history of philosophy, may occasion a certain lifting of the eyebrows; but no true historian can write without some point of view, some standpoint, if for no other reason than that he must have a principle of selection, guiding his intelligent choice and arrangement of facts. Every conscientious historian, it is true, will strive to be as objective as possible and will avoid any temptation to distort the facts to fit a preconceived theory or to omit the mention of certain facts simply because they will not support his preconceived theory; but if he attempts to write history without any principle of selection, the result will be a mere chronicle and no real history, a mere concatenation of events or opinions without understanding or *motif*. What would we think of a writer on English history who set down the number of Queen Elizabeth's dresses and the defeat of the Spanish Armada as facts of equal importance, and who made no intelligent attempt to show how the Spanish venture arose, what events led to it and what its results were? Moreover, in the case of an historian of philosophy, the historian's own personal philosophical outlook is bound to influence his selection and presentation of facts or, at least, the emphasis that he lays on certain facts or aspects. To take a simple example. Of two historians of ancient philosophy, each may make an equally objective study of the facts, e.g. of the history of Platonism and Neo-Platonism; but if the one man is convinced that all "transcendentalism" is sheer folly, while the other firmly believes in the reality of the transcendental, it is hardly conceivable that their presentation of the Platonic tradition should be exactly the same. They may both narrate the opinion of the Platonists objectively and conscientiously; but the former will probably lay little emphasis on Neo-Platonic metaphysics, for instance, and will indicate the fact that he regards Neo-Platonism as a sorry ending to Greek philosophy, as a relapse into "mysticism" or "orientalism," while the other may emphasise the syncretistic aspect of Neo-Platonism and its importance for Christian thought. Neither will have distorted the facts, in the sense of attributing to philosophers opinions they did not hold or suppressing certain of their tenets or neglecting chronology or logical interconnection, but all the same their pictures of Platonism and Neo-Platonism will be unmistakably different. This being so, I have no hesitation in claiming the right to compose a work on the history of philosophy from the standpoint of the scholastic philosopher. That there may be mistakes or misinterpretations due to ignorance, it would be presumptuous folly to deny; but I do claim that I have striven after objectivity, and I claim at the same time that the fact that I have written from a definite standpoint is an advantage rather than a disadvantage. At the very least it enables one to give a fairly coherent and meaningful account of what might otherwise be a mere jumble of incoherent opinions, not as good as a fairy-tale.

From what has been said, it should be clear that I have written not for scholars or specialists, but students of a certain type, the great majority of whom are making their first acquaintance with the history of philosophy and who are studying it concomitantly with systematic scholastic philosophy, to which latter subject they are called upon to devote the greater part of their attention for the time being. For the readers I have primarily in mind (though I should be only too glad if my book should prove of any use to others as well) a series of learned and original monographs would be of less use than a book which is frankly designed as a text-book, but which may, in the case of some students, serve as an incentive to the study of the original philosophical texts and of the commentaries and treatises on those texts by celebrated scholars. I have tried to bear this in mind, while writing the present work, for *qui vult finem, vult etiam media*. Should the work, therefore, fall into the hands of any readers who are well acquainted with the literature on the history of ancient philosophy, and cause them to reflect that this idea is founded on what Burnet or Taylor say, that idea on what Ritter or Jaeger or Stenzel or Praechter have said, let me remind them that I am possibly quite well aware of this myself, and that I may not have agreed uncritically or unthinkingly with what the scholar in question says. Originality is certainly desirable when it means the discovery of a truth not hitherto revealed, but to pursue originality for the sake of originality is not the proper task of the historian. I willingly acknowledge my debt, therefore, to those men who have shed lustre on British and Continental scholarship, to men like Professor A. E. Taylor, Sir David Ross, Constantin Ritter, Werner Jaeger and others. In fact, it is one of my excuses for writing this book that some of the manuals which are in the hands of those for whom I am writing have paid but scant attention to the results of modern specialist criticism. For my own part, I should consider a charge of making insufficient use of such sources of light a more reasonable ground for adverse criticism, than a charge of making too much use of them.

Grateful thanks are due to the Encyclopaedia Britannica Co., Ltd., for permission to use diagrams taken from Sir Thomas Little Heath's article on Pythagoras (14th edit.); to Professor A. E. Taylor (and Messrs. Macmillan & Co., Ltd.) for his generous permission to utilise so freely his study on Forms and Numbers in Plato (reprinted from *Mind in Philosophical Studies*); to Sir David Ross and Messrs. Methuen & Co. for kind permission to incorporate his table of the moral virtues according to Aristotle (from *Aristotle*, p. 203); to Messrs. George Allen & Unwin, Ltd., for permission to quote a passage from the English translation of Professor Nicolai Hartmann's *Ethics* and to utilise a diagram from that work; to the same publishers and to Dr. Oscar Levy to make some quotations from the authorised English translation of Nietzsche's works (of which Dr. Levy is editor); to Messrs. Charles Scribner's Sons (U.S.A.) for permission to quote the translation of Cleanthes' Hymn to Zeus by Dr. James Adam (from Hicks' *Stoic and Epicurean*); to Professor E. R. Dodds and the S.P.C.K. for permission to utilise translations found in *Select Passages Illustrating Neo-platonism* (S.P.C.K. 1923); and to

Messrs. Macmillan & Co., Ltd., for permission to quote from R. L. Nettleship's *Lectures on the Republic of Plato.*

References to the pre-Socratic philosophers are given according to the fifth edition of Diels' *Vorsokratiker* (D. in text). Some of the fragments I have translated myself, while in other cases I have (with the kind permission of Messrs. A. & C. Black, Ltd.) adopted the English translation given by Burnet in his *Early Greek Philosophy*. The title of this work is abbreviated in reference to E.G.P., and *Outlines of the History of Greek Philosophy*, by Zeller—Nestle—Palmer, appear generally as *Outlines*. Abbreviations for the titles of Platonic dialogues and the works of Aristotle should be sufficiently obvious; for the full titles of other works referred to recourse may be had to the first Appendix at the end of the volume, where the abbreviations are explained. I have mentioned a few works, by way of recommendation, in the third Appendix, but I do so simply for the practical convenience of the type of student for whom I have primarily written; I do not dignify the short list of books with the title of bibliography and I disclaim any intention of giving a bibliography, for the simple reason that anything approaching a full bibliography (especially if it took into account, as it ought to do, valuable articles in learned periodicals) would be of such an enormous size that it would be quite impracticable to include it in this work. For a bibliography and a survey of sources, the student can turn to e.g. Ueberweg-Praechter's *Die Philosophie des Altertums.*

AUTHOR'S FOREWORD TO REVISED EDITION

My thanks are due to the Rev. T. Paine, S.J., the Rev. J. Woodlock, S.J., and the Reader of Messrs. Burns Oates and Washbourne, Ltd., for their valuable assistance in the correction of misprints and other errors of form which disfigured the first impression, and for their suggestions in regard to the improvement of the index. Some slight additions to the text have been made, as on p. 126, and for these I am entirely responsible.

CONTENTS

Part IV

ARISTOTLE

Part V

POST-ARISTOTELIAN PHILOSOPHY

APPENDICES

CHAPTER I

INTRODUCTION

I. *Why Study the History of Philosophy?*

I. We would scarcely call anyone "educated" who had no knowledge whatsoever of history; we all recognise that a man should know something of the history of his own country, its political, social and economic development, its literary and artistic achievements—preferably indeed in the wider setting of European and, to a certain extent, even World history. But if an educated and cultured Englishman may be expected to possess some knowledge of Alfred the Great and Elizabeth, of Cromwell and Marlborough and Nelson, of the Norman invasion, the Reformation, and the Industrial Revolution, it would seem equally clear that he should know something at least of Roger Bacon and Duns Scotus, of Francis Bacon and Hobbes, of Locke, Berkeley and Hume, of J. S. Mill and Herbert Spencer. Moreover, if an educated man is expected to be not entirely ignorant of Greece and Rome, if he would be ashamed to have to confess that he had never even heard of Sophocles or Virgil, and knew nothing of the origins of European culture, he might equally be expected to know something of Plato and Aristotle, two of the greatest thinkers the world has ever known, two men who stand at the head of European philosophy. A cultured man will know a little concerning Dante and Shakespeare and Goethe, concerning St. Francis of Assisi and Fra Angelico, concerning Frederick the Great and Napoleon I: why should he not be expected also to know something of St. Augustine and St. Thomas Aquinas, Descartes and Spinoza, Kant and Hegel? It would be absurd to suggest that we should inform ourselves concerning the great conquerors and destroyers, but remain ignorant of the great creators, those who have really contributed to our European culture. But it is not only the great painters and sculptors who have left us an abiding legacy and treasure: it is also the great thinkers, men like Plato and Aristotle, St. Augustine and St. Thomas Aquinas, who have enriched Europe and her culture. It belongs, therefore, to a cultured education to know something at least of the course of European philosophy, for it is our thinkers, as well as our artists and generals, who have helped to make our time, whether for good or ill.

Now, no one would suppose that it is waste of time to read the works of Shakespeare or contemplate the creations of Michelangelo, for they have intrinsic value in themselves which is not diminished by the number of years that have elapsed between their deaths and our own time. Yet no more should it be considered a waste of time to study the thought of Plato or Aristotle or St. Augustine, for their thought-creations abide as outstanding achievements of the human spirit. Other artists have lived and painted since the time of Rubens, but that does not lessen the value of Rubens' work: other thinkers have philosophised since the time of Plato, but that does not destroy the interest and beauty of his philosophy.

But if it is desirable for all cultured men to know something of the history of philosophic thought, so far as occupation, cast of mind and need for specialisation permit, how much more is this not desirable for all avowed students of philosophy. I refer especially to students of the Scholastic Philosophy, who study it as the *philosophia perennis*. That it is the *philosophia perennis* I have no wish to dispute; but it did not drop down from Heaven, it grew out of the past; and if we really want to appreciate the work of St. Thomas Aquinas or St. Bonaventure or Duns Scotus, we should know something of Plato and Aristotle and St. Augustine. Again, if there is a *philosophia perennis*, it is only to be expected that some of its principles should be operative in the minds even of philosophers of modern times, who may seem at first sight to stand far from St. Thomas Aquinas. And even if this were not so, it would be instructive to observe what results follow from false premisses and faulty principles. Nor can it be denied that the practice of condemning thinkers whose position and meaning has not been grasped or seen in its true historic setting is greatly to be deprecated, while it might also be borne in mind that the application of true principles to all spheres of philosophy was certainly not completed in the Middle Ages, and it may well be that we have something to learn from modern thinkers, e.g. in the field of Aesthetic theory or Natural Philosophy.

2. It may be objected that the various philosophical systems of the past are merely antique relics; that the history of philosophy consists of "refuted and spiritually dead systems, since each has

killed and buried the other."[1] Did not Kant declare that Metaphysic is always "keeping the human mind in suspense with hopes that never fade, and yet are never fulfilled," that "while every other science is continually advancing," in Metaphysic men "perpetually revolve round the same point, without gaining a single step"?[2] Platonism, Aristotelianism, Scholasticism, Cartesianism, Kantianism, Hegelianism—all have had their periods of popularity and all have been challenged: European Thought may be "represented as littered with metaphysical systems, abandoned and unreconciled."[3] Why study the antiquated lumber of the chamber of history?

Now, even if all the philosophies of the past had been not only challenged (which is obvious) but also refuted (which is not at all the same thing), it still remains true that "errors are always instructive,"[4] assuming of course that philosophy is a possible science and is not *of itself* a will-o'-the-wisp. To take an example from Mediaeval Philosophy, the conclusions to which Exaggerated Realism lead on the one hand and those to which Nominalism lead on the other hand indicate that the solution of the problem of universals is to be sought in a mean between the two extremes. The history of the problem thus serves as an experimental proof of the thesis learnt in the Schools. Again, the fact that Absolute Idealism has found itself incapable of providing any adequate explanation of finite selves, should be sufficient to deter anyone from embarking on the monistic path. The insistence in modern philosophy on the theory of knowledge and the Subject-Object relation should, despite all the extravagances to which it has led, at any rate make it clear that subject can no more be reduced to object than object to subject, while Marxism, notwithstanding its fundamental errors, will teach us not to neglect the influence of technics and man's economic life on higher spheres of human culture. To him especially who does not set out to learn a given system of philosophy but aspires to philosophise *ab ovo*, as it were, the study of the history of philosophy is indispensable, otherwise he will run the risk of proceeding down blind alleys and repeating the mistakes of his predecessors, from which a serious study of past thought might perhaps have saved him.

3. That a study of the history of philosophy may tend to

[1] Hegel, *Hist. Phil.*, I, p. 17.
[2] *Proleg.*, p. 2 (Mahaffy).
[3] A. N. Whitehead, *Process and Reality*, p. 18. Needless to say, the anti-historical attitude is not Professor Whitehead's own attitude.
[4] N. Hartmann, *Ethics*, I, p. 119.

induce a sceptical frame of mind is true, but it must be remembered that the fact of a succession of systems does not prove that any one philosophy is erroneous. If *X* challenges the position of *Y* and abandons it, that does not by itself prove that the position of *Y* is untenable, since *X* may have abandoned it on insufficient grounds or have adopted false premisses, the development of which involved a departure from the philosophy of *Y*. The world has seen many religions—Buddhism, Hinduism, Zoroastrianism, Christianity, Mohammedanism, etc., but that does not prove that Christianity is not the true Religion; to prove that, a thorough refutation of Christian Apologetics would be necessary. But just as it is absurd to speak as if the existence of a variety of Religions *ipso facto* disproved the claim of any one religion to be the true Religion, so it is absurd to speak as though the succession of philosophies *ipso facto* demonstrated that there is no true philosophy and can be no true philosophy. (We make this observation, of course, without meaning to imply that there is no truth or value in any other religion than Christianity. Moreover, there is this great difference between the true (revealed) Religion and the true philosophy, that whereas the former, as revealed, is necessarily true in its totality, in all that is revealed, the true philosophy may be true in its main lines and principles without reaching completion at any given moment. Philosophy, which is the work of the human spirit and not the revelation of God, grows and develops; fresh vistas may be opened up by new lines of approach or application to new problems, newly discovered facts, fresh situations, etc. The term "true philosophy" or *philosophia perennis* should not be understood to denote a static and complete body of principles and applications, insusceptible of development or modification.)

II. *Nature of the History of Philosophy*

1. The history of philosophy is certainly not a mere congeries of opinions, a narration of isolated items of thought that have no connection with one another. If the history of philosophy is treated "only as the enumeration of various opinions," and if all these opinions are considered as of equal value or disvalue, then it becomes "an idle tale, or, if you will, an erudite investigation."[1] There is continuity and connection, action and reaction, thesis and antithesis, and no philosophy can really be understood fully

[1] Hegel, *Hist. Phil.*, I, p. 12.

unless it is seen in its historical setting and in the light of its connection with other systems. How can one really understand what Plato was getting at or what induced him to say what he did, unless one knows something of the thought of Heraclitus, Parmenides, the Pythagoreans? How can one understand why Kant adopted such an apparently extraordinary position in regard to Space, Time and the Categories, unless one knows something of British empiricism and realises the effect of Hume's sceptical conclusions on the mind of Kant?

2. But if the history of philosophy is no mere collection of isolated opinions, it cannot be regarded as a continual progress or even a spiral ascent. That one can find plausible instances in the course of philosophic speculation of the Hegelian triad of thesis, antithesis and synthesis is true, but it is scarcely the task of a scientific historian to adopt an *a priori* scheme and then to fit the facts into that scheme. Hegel supposed that the succession of philosophic systems "represent the necessary succession of stages in the development" of philosophy, but this can only be so if the philosophic thought of man is the very thinking of the "World-Spirit." That, practically speaking, any given thinker is limited as to the direction his thought will take, limited by the immediately preceding and the contemporary systems (limited also, we might add, by his personal temperament, his education, the historical and social situation, etc.) is doubtless true; none the less he is not determined to choose any particular premisses or principles, nor to react to the preceding philosophy in any particular way. Fichte believed that his system followed logically on that of Kant, and there is certainly a direct logical connection, as every student of modern philosophy is aware; but Fichte was not *determined* to develop the philosophy of Kant in the particular way he did. The succeeding philosopher to Kant might have chosen to re-examine Kant's premisses and to deny that the conclusions which Kant accepted from Hume were true conclusions; he might have gone back to other principles or excogitated new ones of his own. Logical sequence there undoubtedly is in the history of philosophy, but not *necessary* sequence in the strict sense.

We cannot, therefore, agree with Hegel when he says that "the final philosophy of a period is the result of this development, and is truth in the highest form which the self-consciousness of spirit affords of itself."[1] A good deal depends, of course, on how you

[1] *Hist. Phil.*, III, p. 552.

divide the "periods" and what you are pleased to consider the final philosophy of any period (and here there is ample scope for arbitrary choice, in accordance with preconceived opinion and wishes); but what guarantee is there (unless we first adopt the whole Hegelian position) that the final philosophy of any period represents the highest development of thought yet attained? If one can legitimately speak of a Mediaeval period of philosophy, and if Ockhamism can be regarded as the final main philosophy of that period, the Ockhamist philosophy can certainly not be regarded as the supreme achievement of mediaeval philosophy. Mediaeval philosophy, as Professor Gilson has shown,[1] represents a *curve* rather than a straight line. And what philosophy of the present day, one might pertinently ask, represents the synthesis of all preceding philosophies?

3. The history of philosophy exhibits man's search for Truth by the way of the discursive reason. A Neo-Thomist, developing St. Thomas' words, *Omnia cognoscentia cognoscunt implicite Deum in quolibet cognito,*[2] has maintained that the judgment always points beyond itself, always contains an implicit reference to Absolute Truth, Absolute Being.[3] (We are reminded of F. H. Bradley, though the term "Absolute" has not, of course, the same meaning in the two cases.) At any rate we may say that the search for truth is ultimately the search for Absolute Truth, God, and even those systems of philosophy which appear to refute this statement, e.g. Historical Materialism, are nevertheless examples of it, for they are all seeking, even if unconsciously, even if they would not recognise the fact, for the ultimate Ground, the supremely Real. Even if intellectual speculation has at times led to bizarre doctrines and monstrous conclusions, we cannot but have a certain sympathy for and interest in the struggle of the human intellect to attain Truth. Kant, who denied that Metaphysics in the traditional sense were or could be a science, none the less allowed that we cannot remain indifferent to the objects with which Metaphysics profess to deal, God, the soul, freedom;[4] and we may add that we cannot remain indifferent to the human intellect's search for the True and the Good. The ease with which mistakes are made, the fact that personal temperament, education and other apparently "fortuitous" circumstances may so often

[1] Cf. *The Unity of Philosophical Experience.* [2] *De Verit.*, 22, 2, ad 1.
[3] J. Maréchal, S.J., *Le Point de Départ de la Metaphysique*: *Cahier V*.
[4] Pref. to 1st Ed. of *Critique of Pure Reason*.

lead the thinker up an intellectual cul-de-sac, the fact that we are not pure intelligences, but that the processes of our minds may frequently be influenced by extraneous factors, doubtless shows the need for religious Revelation; but that should not cause us to despair altogether of human speculation nor make us despise the *bona-fide* attempts of past thinkers to attain Truth.

4. The present writer adheres to the Thomistic standpoint that there is a *philosophia perennis* and that this *philosophia perennis* is Thomism in a wide sense. But he would like to make two observations on this matter: (*a*) To say that the Thomist system is the perennial philosophy does not mean that that system is closed at any given historical epoch and is incapable of further development in any direction. (*b*) The perennial philosophy after the close of the Mediaeval period does not develop merely alongside of and apart from "modern" philosophy, but develops also in and through modern philosophy. I do not mean to suggest that the philosophy of Spinoza or Hegel, for instance, can be comprehended under the term Thomism; but rather that when philosophers, even if they would by no means call themselves "Scholastic," arrive by the employment of true principles at valuable conclusions, these conclusions must be looked on as belonging to the perennial philosophy.

St. Thomas Aquinas certainly makes some statements concerning the State, for example, and we have no inclination to question his principles; but it would be absurd to expect a developed philosophy of the modern State in the thirteenth century, and from the practical point of view it is difficult to see how a developed and articulate philosophy of the State on scholastic principles could be elaborated in the concrete, until the modern State had emerged and until modern attitudes towards the State had shown themselves. It is only when we have had experience of the Liberal State and of the Totalitarian State and of the corresponding theories of the State, that we can realise all the implications contained in the little that St. Thomas says on the State and develop an elaborated Scholastic political philosophy applicable to the modern State, which will expressly contain all the good contained in the other theories while renouncing the errors. The resultant State-philosophy will be seen to be, when looked at in the concrete, not simply a development of Scholastic principle in absolute isolation from the actual historical situation and from intervening theories, but rather a development of these principles in the light of the historical situation, a development achieved in and through opposing theories of the State. If this point of view be adopted, we shall be enabled to maintain the idea of a perennial philosophy without committing ourselves, on the one hand, to a very narrow outlook whereby the perennial philosophy is confined to a given century, or, on the other hand, to an Hegelian view of philosophy, which necessarily implies (though Hegel himself seems to have thought otherwise—inconsistently) that Truth is never attained at a given moment.

III. *How to Study the History of Philosophy*

1. The first point to be stressed is the need for seeing any philosophical system in its historical setting and connections. This point has already been mentioned and does not require further elaboration: it should be obvious that we can only grasp adequately the state of mind of a given philosopher and the *raison d'être* of his philosophy if we have first apprehended its historical *point de départ.* The example of Kant has already been given; we can understand his state of mind in developing his theory of the *a priori* only if we see him in his historical situation *vis-à-vis* the critical philosophy of Hume, the apparent bankruptcy of Continental Rationalism and the apparent certainty of mathematics and the Newtonian physics. Similarly, we are better enabled to understand the biological philosophy of Henri Bergson if we see it, for example, in its relation to preceding mechanistic theories and to preceding French "spiritualism."

2. For a profitable study of the history of philosophy there is also need for a certain "sympathy," almost the psychological approach. It is desirable that the historian should know something of the philosopher as a man (this is not possible in the case of *all* philosophers, of course), since this will help him to feel his way into the system in question, to view it, as it were, from inside, and to grasp its peculiar flavour and characteristics. We have to endeavour to put ourselves into the place of the philosopher, to try to see his thoughts from within. Moreover, this sympathy or imaginative insight is essential for the Scholastic philosopher who wishes to understand modern philosophy. If a man, for example, has the background of the Catholic Faith, the modern systems, or some of them at least, readily appear to him as mere bizarre monstrosities unworthy of serious attention, but if he succeeds, as far as he can (without, of course, surrendering

his own principles), in seeing the systems from within, he stands much more chance of understanding what the philosopher meant.

We must not, however, become so preoccupied with the psychology of the philosopher as to disregard the truth or falsity of his ideas taken in themselves, or the logical connection of his system with preceding thought. A *psychologist* may justly confine himself to the first viewpoint, but not an *historian* of philosophy. For example, a purely psychological approach might lead one to suppose that the system of Arthur Schopenhauer was the creation of an embittered, soured and disappointed man, who at the same time possessed literary power and aesthetic imagination and insight, and *nothing more*; as though his philosophy were simply the manifestation of certain psychological states. But this viewpoint would leave out of account the fact that his pessimistic Voluntaristic system is largely a reaction to the Hegelian optimistic Rationalism, as it would also leave out of account the fact that Schopenhauer's aesthetic theory may have a value of its own, independent of the *kind of man* that propounded it, and would also neglect the whole problem of evil and suffering which is raised by Schopenhauer's system and which is a very real problem, whether Schopenhauer himself was a disappointed and disillusioned man or not. Similarly, although it is a great help towards the understanding of the thought of Friedrich Nietzsche if we know something of the personal history of the man, his ideas can be looked at in themselves, apart from the man who thought them.

3. To work one's way into any thinker's system, thoroughly to understand not only the words and phrases as they stand, but also the shade of meaning that the author intended to convey (so far as this is feasible), to view the details of the system in their relation to the whole, fully to grasp its genesis and its implications, all this is not the work of a few moments. It is but natural, then, that specialisation in the field of the history of philosophy should be the general rule, as it is in the fields of the various sciences. A specialist knowledge of the philosophy of Plato, for instance, requires besides a thorough knowledge of Greek language and history, a knowledge of Greek mathematics, Greek religion, Greek science, etc. The specialist thus requires a great apparatus of scholarship; but it is essential, if he is to be a true historian of philosophy, that he should not be so overwhelmed with his scholarly equipment and the details of learning, that he fails

to penetrate the spirit of the philosophy in question and fails to make it live again in his writings or his lectures. Scholarship is indispensable but it is by no means enough.

The fact that a whole lifetime might well be devoted to the study of one great thinker and still leave much to be done, means that anyone who is so bold as to undertake the composition of a continuous history of philosophy can hardly hope to produce a work that will offer anything of much value to specialists. The author of the present work is quite conscious of this fact, and as he has already said in the preface, he is not writing for specialists but rather utilising the work of specialists. There is no need to repeat again here the author's reasons for writing this work; but he would like once more to mention that he will consider himself well repaid for his work if he can contribute in some small degree, not only to the instruction of the type of student for whom the work is primarily designed, but also to the broadening of his outlook, to the acquirement of a greater understanding of and sympathy with the intellectual struggle of mankind, and of course to a firmer and deeper hold on the principles of true philosophy.

IV. *Ancient Philosophy*

In this volume we treat of the philosophy of the Greeks and Romans. There can scarcely be much need for dwelling on the importance of Greek culture: as Hegel says, "the name of Greece strikes home to the hearts of men of education in Europe."[1] No one would attempt to deny that the Greeks left an imperishable legacy of literature and art to our European world, and the same is true in regard to philosophic speculation. After its first beginnings in Asia Minor, Greek philosophy pursued its course of development until it flowered in the two great philosophies of Plato and Aristotle, and later, through Neo-Platonism, exercised a great influence on the formation of Christian thought. Both in its character as the first period of European speculation and also for its intrinsic value, it cannot but be of interest to every student of philosophy. In Greek philosophy we watch problems come to light that have by no means lost their relevance for us, we find answers suggested that are not without value; and even though we may discern a certain *naïveté*, a certain over-confidence and precipitation, Greek philosophy remains one of the glories of European achievement. Moreover, if the philosophy of the

[1] *Hist. Phil.*, I, p. 149.

Greeks must be of interest to every student of philosophy for its influence on subsequent speculation and for its own intrinsic value, still more should it be of interest to students of Scholastic philosophy, which owes so much to Plato and to Aristotle. And this philosophy of the Greeks was really their own achievement, the fruit of their vigour and freshness of mind, just as their literature and art were their own achievement. We must not allow the laudable desire of taking into account possible non-Greek influence to lead us to exaggerate the importance of that influence and to underestimate the originality of the Greek mind: "the truth is that we are far more likely to underrate the originality of the Greeks than to exaggerate it."[1] The tendency of the historian always to seek for "sources" is, of course, productive of much valuable critical investigation, and it would be folly to belittle it; but it remains true that the tendency can be pushed too far, even to lengths when criticism threatens to be no longer scientific. For instance, one must not assume *a priori* that every opinion of every thinker is borrowed from a predecessor: if this is assumed, then we should be logically compelled to assume the existence of some primeval Colossus or Superman, from whom all subsequent philosophic speculation is ultimately derived. Nor can we safely assume that, whenever two succeeding contemporary thinkers or bodies of thinkers hold similar doctrines, one must have borrowed from the other. If it is absurd, as it is, to suppose that if some Christian custom or rite is partially found in Asiatic Eastern religion, Christianity must have borrowed that custom or rite from Asia, so it is absurd to suppose that if Greek speculation contains some thought similar to that appearing in an Oriental philosophy, the latter must be the historical source of the former. After all, the human intellect is quite capable of interpreting similar experiences in a similar way, whether it be the intellect of a Greek or an Indian, without its being necessary to suppose that similarity of reaction is an irrefutable proof of borrowing. These remarks are not meant to depreciate historical criticism and research, but rather to point out that historical criticism must rest its conclusions on historical proofs and not deduce them from *a priori* assumptions, garnishing them with a pseudo-historical flavour. Legitimate historical criticism would not, as yet at least, seem to have seriously impaired the claim to originality made on behalf of the Greeks.

[1] Burnet, *G.P.*, I, p. 9.

Roman philosophy, however, is but a meagre production compared with that of the Greeks, for the Romans depended in large part on the Greeks for their philosophic ideas, just as they depended on the Greeks in art and, to a great extent at least, in the field of literature. They had their own peculiar glory and achievements (we think at once of the creation of Roman Law and the achievements of Roman political genius), but their glory did not lie in the realm of philosophical speculation. Yet, though the dependence of Roman Schools of philosophy on Greek predecessors is undeniable, we cannot afford to neglect the philosophy of the Roman world, since it shows us the sort of ideas that became current among the more cultured members of the class that was Master of the European civilised world. The thought of the later Stoa, for example, the teaching of Seneca, Marcus Aurelius and Epictetus, affords in many respects an impressive and noble picture which can hardly fail to arouse admiration and esteem, even if at the same time we are conscious of much that is lacking. It is desirable too that the Christian student should know something of the best that paganism had to offer, and should acquaint himself with the various currents of thought in that Greco-Roman world in which the Revealed Religion was implanted and grew. It is to be regretted if students should be acquainted with the campaigns of Julius Caesar or Trajan, with the infamous careers of Caligula or Nero, and yet should be ignorant of the philosopher-Emperor, Marcus Aurelius, or the influence at Rome of the Greek Plotinus, who though not a Christian was a deeply religious man, and whose name was so dear to the first great figure of Christian philosophy, St. Augustine of Hippo.

PART I

PRE-SOCRATIC PHILOSOPHY

CHAPTER II

THE CRADLE OF WESTERN THOUGHT: IONIA

THE birthplace of Greek philosophy was the sea-board of Asia Minor and the early Greek philosophers were Ionians. While Greece itself was in a state of comparative chaos or barbarism, consequent on the Dorian invasions of the eleventh century B.C., which submerged the old Aegean culture, Ionia preserved the spirit of the older civilisation,[1] and it was to the Ionian world that Homer belonged, even if the Homeric poems enjoyed the patronage of the new Achaean aristocracy. While the Homeric poems cannot indeed be called a philosophical work (though they are, of course, of great value through their revelation of certain stages of the Greek outlook and way of life, while their educational influence on Greeks of later times should not be underestimated), since the isolated philosophical ideas that occur in the poems are very far from being systematised (considerably less so than in the poems of Hesiod, the epic writer of mainland Greece, who portrays in his work his pessimistic view of history, his conviction of the reign of law in the animal world and his ethical passion for justice among men), it is significant that the greatest poet of Greece and the first beginnings of systematic philosophy both belong to Ionia. But these two great productions of Ionian genius, the poems of Homer and the Ionian cosmology, did not merely follow on one another; at least, whatever view one holds of the authorship, composition and date or dates of the Homeric poems, it is clear enough that the society reflected in those poems was not that of the period of the Ionian cosmology, but belonged to a more primitive era. Again, the society depicted by Hesiod, the later of the "two" great epic poets, is a far cry from that of

[1] "It was in Ionia that the new Greek civilisation arose: Ionia in whom the old Aegean blood and spirit most survived, taught the new Greece, gave her coined money and letters, art and poesy, and her shipmen, forcing the Phoenicians from before them, carried her new culture to what were then deemed the ends of the earth." Hall, *Ancient History of the Near East*, p. 79.

the Greek *Polis*, for between the two had occurred the breakdown of the power of the noble aristocracy, a breakdown that made possible the free growth of city life in mainland Greece. Neither the heroic life depicted in the *Iliad* nor the domination of the landed nobility depicted in the poems of Hesiod was the setting in which Greek philosophy grew up: on the contrary, early Greek philosophy, though naturally the work of individuals, was also the product of the City and reflected to a certain extent the reign of law and the conception of law which the pre-Socratics systematically extended to the whole universe in their cosmologies. Thus in a sense there is a certain continuity between the Homeric conception of an ultimate law or destiny or will governing gods and men, the Hesiodic picture of the world and the poet's moral demands, and the early Ionian cosmology. When social life was settled, men could turn to rational reflection, and in the period of philosophy's childhood it was Nature as a whole which first occupied their attention. From the psychological standpoint this is only what one would expect.

Thus, although it is undeniable that Greek philosophy arose among a people whose civilisation went back to the pre-historic times of Greece, what we call early Greek philosophy was "early" only in relation to subsequent Greek philosophy and the flowering of Greek thought and culture on the mainland; in relation to the preceding centuries of Greek development it may be looked on rather as the fruit of a mature civilisation, marking the closing period of Ionian greatness on the one hand and ushering in on the other hand the splendour of Hellenic, particularly of Athenian, culture.[1]

We have represented early Greek philosophic thought as the ultimate product of the ancient Ionian civilisation; but it must be remembered that Ionia forms, as it were, the meeting-place of West and East, so that the question may be raised whether or not Greek philosophy was due to Oriental influences, whether, for instance, it was borrowed from Babylon or Egypt. This view has been maintained, but has had to be abandoned. The Greek philosophers and writers know nothing of it—even Herodotus, who was so eager to run his pet theory as to the Egyptian origins of Greek religion and civilization—and the Oriental-origin theory is due mainly to Alexandrian writers, from whom it was taken

[1] For what Julius Stenzel calls *Vortheoretische Metaphysik* cf. Zeller, *Outlines*, Introd. ss 3; Burnet, *E.G.P.*, Introd.; Ueberweg-Praechter, pp. 28–31; Jaeger, *Paideia*; Stenzel, *Metaphysik des Altertums*, I, pp. 14 ff., etc.

over by Christian apologists. The Egyptians of Hellenistic times, for instance, interpreted their myths according to the ideas of Greek philosophy, and then asserted that their myths were the origin of the Greek philosophy. But this is simply an instance of allegorising on the part of the Alexandrians: it has no more objective value than the Jewish notion that Plato drew his wisdom from the Old Testament. There would, of course, be difficulties in explaining *how* Egyptian thought could be transmitted to the Greeks (traders are not the sort of people we would expect to convey philosophic notions), but, as has been remarked by Burnet, it is practically waste of time to inquire whether the philosophical ideas of this or that Eastern people could be communicated to the Greeks or not, unless we have first ascertained that the people in question really possessed a philosophy.[1] That the Egyptians had a philosophy to communicate has never been shown, and it is out of the question to suppose that Greek philosophy came from India or from China.[2]

But there is a further point to be considered. Greek philosophy was closely bound up with mathematics, and it has been maintained that the Greeks derived their mathematics from Egypt and their astronomy from Babylonia. Now, that Greek mathematics were influenced by Egypt and Greek astronomy by Babylon is more than probable: for one thing, Greek science and philosophy began to develop in that very region where interchange with the East was most to be expected. But that is not the same as saying that Greek scientific mathematics *derive* from Egypt or their astronomy from Babylon. Detailed arguments left aside, let it suffice to point out that Egyptian mathematics consisted of empirical, rough and ready methods of obtaining a practical result. Thus Egyptian geometry largely consisted of practical methods of marking out afresh the fields after the inundation of the river Nile. Scientific geometry was not developed by them, but it was developed by the Greeks. Similarly Babylonian astronomy was pursued with a view to divination: it was mainly astrology, but among the Greeks it became a scientific pursuit. So even if we grant that the practical gardener-mathematics of the Egyptians and the astronomical observations of Babylonian

[1] *E.G.P.*, pp. 17–18.

[2] "*Nel sesto secolo A.C. ci si presenta, in Grecia, uno dei fenomeni meravigliosi della coltura umana. La Scuola di Mileto crea la ricerca scientifica: e le linee fondamentali, stabilite in quei primi albori, si perpetuano attraverso le generazioni e i secoli.*" Aurelio Covotti, *I Presocratici* p. 31 (Naples, 1934).

astrologers influenced the Greeks and supplied them with preliminary material, this admission is in no way prejudicial to the originality of the Greek genius. Science and Thought, as distinct from mere practical calculation and astrological lore, were the result of the Greek genius and were due neither to the Egyptians nor to the Babylonians.

The Greeks, then, stand as the uncontested original thinkers and scientists of Europe.[1] They first sought knowledge for its own sake, and pursued knowledge in a scientific, free and unprejudiced spirit. Moreover, owing to the character of Greek religion, they were free from any priestly class that might have strong traditions and unreasoned doctrines of their own, tenaciously held and imparted only to a few, which might hamper the development of free science. Hegel, in his history of philosophy, dismisses Indian philosophy rather curtly, on the ground that it is identical with Indian religion. While admitting the presence of philosophical *notions*, he maintains that these do not take the form of *thought*, but are couched in poetical and symbolic form, and have, like religion, the practical purpose of freeing men from the illusions and unhappiness of life rather than knowledge for its own sake. Without committing oneself to agreement with Hegel's view of Indian philosophy (which has been far more clearly presented to the Western world in its purely philosophic aspects since the time of Hegel), one can agree with him that Greek philosophy was from the first *thought* pursued in the spirit of free science. It may with some have tended to take the place of religion, both from the point of view of belief and conduct; yet this was due to the inadequacy of Greek religion rather than to any mythological or mystical character in Greek philosophy. (It is not meant, of course, to belittle the place and function of "Myth" in Greek thought, nor yet the tendency of philosophy at certain times to pass into religion, e.g. with Plotinus. Indeed as regards myth, "In the earlier cosmologies of the Greek physicists the mythical and the rational elements interpenetrate in an as yet undivided unity." So Professor Werner Jaeger in *Aristotle, Fundamentals of the History of His Development*, p. 377.)

Professor Zeller emphasises the impartiality of the Greeks as they regarded the world about them, which in combination with

[1] As Dr. Praechter points out (p. 27), the religious conceptions of the Orient, even if they had been taken over by the Greeks, would not explain the peculiar characteristic of Greek philosophy, free speculation on the essence of things. As for Indian philosophy proper, it would not appear to be earlier than the Greek.

their sense of reality and power of abstraction, "enabled them at a very early date to recognise their religious ideas for what they actually were—creations of an artistic imagination."[1] (This, of course, would scarcely hold good for the Greek people at large—the non-philosophical majority.) From the moment when the proverbial wisdom of the Wise Men and the myths of the poets were succeeded by the half-scientific, half-philosophic reflections and investigations of the Ionian cosmologists, art may be said to have been succeeded (logically, at any rate) by philosophy, which was to reach a splendid culmination in Plato and Aristotle, and at length in Plotinus to reach up to the heights where philosophy is transcended, not in mythology, but in mysticism. Yet there was no abrupt transition from "myth" to philosophy; one might even say that the Hesiodic theogony, for example, found a successor in Ionian cosmogonic speculation, the myth-element retreating before growing rationalisation yet not disappearing. Indeed it is present in Greek philosophy even in post-Socratic times.

The splendid achievement of Greek thought was cradled in Ionia; and if Ionia was the cradle of Greek philosophy, Miletus was the cradle of Ionian philosophy. For it was at Miletus that Thales, the reputedly earliest Ionian philosopher, flourished. The Ionian philosophers were profoundly impressed with the fact of change, of birth and growth, decay and death. Spring and Autumn in the external world of nature, childhood and old age in the life of man, coming-into-being and passing-away—these were the obvious and inescapable facts of the universe. It is a great mistake to suppose that the Greeks were happy and careless children of the sun, who only wanted to lounge in the porticoes of the cities and gaze at the magnificent works of art or at the achievements of their athletes. They were very conscious of the dark side of our existence on this planet, for against the background of sun and joy they saw the uncertainty and insecurity of man's life, the certainty of death, the darkness of the future. "The best for man were not to have been born and not to have seen the light of the sun; but, if once born (the second best for him is) to pass through the gates of death as speedily as may be," declares Theognis,[2] reminding us of the words of Calderón (so dear to Schopenhauer), "*El mayor delito del hombre, Es haber nacido.*" And the words of Theognis are re-echoed in the words of Sophocles

[1] *Outlines of the History of Greek Philosophy*, by Eduard Zeller, 13th edit., revised by Nestle, translated by L. R. Palmer, pp. 2–3.

[2] 425–7.

in the *Oedipus Coloneus*, "Not to have been born exceeds every reckoning" . . . μὴ φῦναι τὸν ἅπαντα νικᾷ λόγον.[1]

Moreover, although the Greeks certainly had their ideal of moderation, they were constantly being lured away from it by the will to power. The constant fighting of the Greek cities among themselves, even at the heyday of Greek culture, and even when it was to their obvious interest to unite together against a common foe, the constant uprisings within the cities, whether led by an ambitious oligarch or a democratic demagogue, the venality of so many public men in Greek political life—even when the safety and honour of their city was at stake—all manifest the will to power which was so strong in the Greek. The Greek admired efficiency, he admired the ideal of the strong man who knows what he wants and has the power to get it; his conception of ἀρετή was largely that of ability to achieve success. As Professor De Burgh remarks, "The Greek would have regarded Napoleon as a man of pre-eminent aretê."[2] For a very frank, or rather blatant, acknowledgment of the unscrupulous will to power, we have only to read the report that Thucydides gives of the conference between the representatives of Athens and those of Melos. The Athenians declare, "But you and we should say what we really think, and aim only at what is possible, for we both alike know that into the discussion of human affairs the question of justice only enters where the pressure of necessity is equal, and that the powerful exact what they can, and the weak grant what they must." Similarly in the celebrated words, "For of the Gods we believe, and of men we know, that by a law of their nature wherever they can rule they will. This law was not made by us, and we are not the first who have acted upon it; we did but inherit it, and shall bequeath it to all time, and we know that you and all mankind, if you were as strong as we are, would do as we do."[3] We could hardly ask for a more unashamed avowal of the will to power, and Thucydides gives no indication that he disapproved of the Athenian conduct. It is to be recalled that when the Melians eventually had to surrender, the Athenians put to death all those who were of military age, enslaved the women and children, and colonised the island with their own settlers—and all this at the zenith of Athenian splendour and artistic achievement.

[1] 1224. [2] *The Legacy of the Ancient World*, p. 83, note 2.
[3] From Benjamin Jowett's translation of Thucydides (Oxford Un. Press).

In close connection with the will to power stands the conception of ὕβρις. The man who goes too far, who endeavours to be and to have more than Fate destines for him, will inevitably incur divine jealousy and come to ruin. The man or the nation who is possessed by the unbridled lust for self-assertion is driven headlong into reckless self-confidence and so to destruction. Blind passion breeds self-confidence, and overweening self-confidence ends in ruin.

It is as well to realise this side of the Greek character: Plato's condemnation of the "Might is Right" theory becomes then all the more remarkable. While not agreeing, of course, with Nietzsche's valuations, we cannot but admire his perspicacity in seeing the relation between the Greek culture and the will to power. Not, of course, that the dark side of Greek culture is the only side—far from it. If the drive of the will to power is a fact so is the Greek ideal of moderation and harmony a fact. We must realise that there are two sides to the Greek character and culture: there is the side of moderation, of art, of Apollo and the Olympian deities, and there is the side of excess, unbridled self-assertion, of Dionysian frenzy, as seen portrayed in the *Bacchae* of Euripides. As beneath the splendid achievements of Greek culture we see the abyss of slavery, so beneath the dream-world of Olympian religion and Olympian art we see the abyss of Dionysian frenzy, of pessimism and of all manner of lack of moderation. It may, after all, not be entirely fanciful to suppose, inspired by the thought of Nietzsche, that there can be seen in much of the Olympian religion a self-imposed check on the part of the Dionysian Greek. Driven on by the will to power to self-destruction, the Greek creates the Olympian dream-world, the gods of which watch over him with jealousy to see that he does not transgress the limits of human endeavour. So does he express his consciousness that the tumultuous forces in his soul would be ultimately ruinous to him. (This interpretation is not of course offered as an account of the origin of the Greek Olympian religion from the scientific viewpoint of the historian of religion: it is only meant to suggest psychological factors—provisions of "Nature," if you like—that may have been operative, even if unconsciously, in the soul of the Greek.)

To return from this digression. In spite of the melancholic side of the Greek, his perception of the constant process of change, of transition from life to death and from death to life, helped to lead him, in the person of the Ionian philosophers, to a beginning of philosophy; for these wise men saw that, in spite of all the change and transition, there must be something permanent. Why? Because the change is from something into something else. There must be something which is primary, which persists, which takes various forms and undergoes this process of change. Change cannot be merely a conflict of opposites; thoughtful men were convinced that there was something behind these opposites, something that was primary. Ionian philosophy or cosmology is therefore mainly an attempt to decide what this primitive element or *Urstoff*[1] of all things is, one philosopher deciding for one element, another for another element. What particular element each philosopher decided on as his *Urstoff* is not so important as the fact that they had in common this idea of Unity. The fact of change, of motion in the Aristotelian sense, suggested to them the notion of unity, though, as Aristotle says, they did not explain motion.

The Ionians differed as to the character of their *Urstoff*, but they all held it to be material—Thales plumping for water, Anaximenes for air, Heraclitus for fire. The antithesis between spirit and matter had not yet been grasped; so that, although they were *de facto* materialists—in that they assigned a form of matter as the principle of unity and primitive stuff of all things—they can scarcely be termed materialists in our sense of the word. It is not as though they conceived a clear distinction between spirit and matter, and then denied it; they were not fully conscious of the distinction, or at least they did not realise its implications.

One might be tempted, therefore, to say that the Ionian thinkers were not philosophers so much as primitive scientists, trying to account for the material and external world. But it must be remembered that they did not stop short at *sense*, but went beyond appearance to *thought*. Whether water or air or fire be assigned as the *Urstoff*, it certainly does not *appear* as such, i.e. as the ultimate element. In order to arrive at the conception of any of these as the ultimate element of all things it is necessary to go beyond appearance and sense. And they did not arrive at their conclusions through a scientific, experimental approach, but by means of the speculative reason: the unity posited is indeed a

[1] The German word *Urstoff* is here employed, simply because it expresses the notion of primitive element or substrate or "stuff" of the universe in one short word.

material unity, but it is a unity posited by thought. Moreover, it is abstract—abstracting, that is to say, from the data of appearance—even if materialist. Consequently we might perhaps call the Ionian cosmologies instances of *abstract materialism*: we can already discern in them the notion of unity in difference and of difference as entering into unity: and this is a philosophic notion. In addition the Ionian thinkers were convinced of the reign of law in the universe. In the life of the individual ὕβρις, the overstepping of what is right and proper for man, brings ruin in its train, the redressing of the balance; so, by extension to the universe, cosmic law reigns, the preservation of a balance and the prevention of chaos and anarchy. This conception of a law-governed universe, a universe that is no plaything of mere caprice or lawless spontaneity, no mere field for lawless and "egoistic" domination of one element over another, formed a basis for a scientific cosmology as opposed to fanciful mythology.

From another point of view, however, we may say that with the Ionians science and philosophy are not yet distinguished. The early Ionian thinkers or wise men pursued all sorts of scientific considerations, astronomical for instance, and these were not clearly separated from philosophy. They were Wise Men, who might make astronomical observations for the sake of navigation, try to find out the one primary element of the universe, plan out feats of engineering, etc., and all without making any clear distinction between their various activities. Only that mixture of history and geography, which was known as ἱστορίη, was separated off from the philosophico-scientific activities, and that not always very clearly. Yet as real philosophic notions and real speculative ability appear among them, as since they form a stage in the development of the classical Greek philosophy, they cannot be omitted from the history of philosophy as though they were mere children whose innocent babblings are unworthy of serious attention. The first beginnings of European philosophy cannot be a matter of indifference to the historian.

CHAPTER III

THE PIONEERS: EARLY IONIAN PHILOSOPHERS

1. *Thales*

THE mixture of philosopher and practical scientist is seen very clearly in the case of Thales of Miletus. Thales is said to have predicted the eclipse of the sun mentioned by Herodotus[1] as occurring at the close of the war between the Lydians and the Medes. Now, according to the calculations of astronomers, an eclipse, which was probably visible in Asia Minor, took place on May 28th, 585 B.C. So if the story about Thales is true, and if the eclipse which he foretold is the eclipse of 585, then he must have flourished in the early part of the sixth century B.C. He is said to have died shortly before the fall of Sardis in 546/5 B.C. Among other scientific activities ascribed to Thales are the construction of an almanac and the introduction of the Phoenician practice of steering a ship's course by the Little Bear. Anecdotes narrated about him, which may be read in the life of Thales by Diogenes Laërtius, e.g. that he fell into a well or ditch while star-gazing, or that, foreseeing a scarcity of olives, he made a corner in oil, are probably just tales of the type easily fathered on a Sage or Wise Man.[2]

In the *Metaphysics* Aristotle asserts that according to Thales the earth is superimposed upon water (apparently regarding it as a flat floating disc). But the most important point is that Thales declared the primary stuff of all things to be water . . . indeed, that he raised the question of the One at all. Aristotle conjectures that observation may have led Thales to this conclusion, "getting the notion perhaps from seeing that the nutriment of all things is moist, and that heat itself is generated from the moist and kept alive by it (and that from which they come to be is a principle of all things). He got his notion from this fact, and from the fact that the seeds of all things have a moist nature, and water is the origin of the nature of moist things."[3] Aristotle also suggests, though with diffidence, to be sure, that Thales was influenced by the older theologies, wherein water—as the Styx of the poets—was the object of adjuration among the gods. However

[1] *Hist.*, I, 74. [2] Diog. Laërt, *Lives of the Philosophers*, 1, 22–44.
[3] *Metaphysics* (trans. by J A. Smith and W. D. Ross)

this may be, it is clear that the phenomenon of evaporation suggests that water may become mist or air, while the phenomenon of freezing might suggest that, if the process were carried further, water could become earth. In any case the importance of this early thinker lies in the fact that he raised the question, what is the ultimate nature of the world; and not in the answer that he actually gave to that question or in his reasons, be they what they may, for giving that answer.

Another statement attributed to Thales by Aristotle, that all things are full of gods, that the magnet has a soul because it moves iron,[1] cannot be interpreted with certainty. To declare that this statement asserts the existence of a world-soul, and then to identify this world-soul with God[2] or with the Platonic Demiurge[3] —as though the latter formed all things out of water—is to go too far in freedom of interpretation. The only certain and the only really important point about Thales' doctrine is that he conceived "things" as varying forms of one primary and ultimate element. That he assigns *water* as this element is his distinguishing historical characteristic, so to speak, but he earns his place as the First Greek philosopher from the fact that he first conceives the notion of Unity in Difference (even if he does not isolate the notion on to the logical plane), and, while holding fast to the idea of unity, endeavours to account for the evident diversity of the many. Philosophy naturally tries to understand the plurality that we experience, its existence and nature, and to understand in this connection means, for the philosopher, to discover an underlying unity or first principle. The complexity of the problem cannot be grasped until the radical distinction between matter and spirit has been clearly apprehended: before this has been apprehended (and indeed even after its apprehension, if, once "apprehended," it is then denied), *simpliste* solutions of the problem are bound to suggest themselves: reality will be conceived as a material unity (as in the thought of Thales) or as Idea (as in certain modern philosophies). Justice can be done to the complexity of the problem of the One and the Many only if the essential degrees of reality and the doctrine of the analogy of being are clearly understood and unambiguously maintained: otherwise the richness of the manifold will be sacrificed to a false and more or less arbitrarily conceived unity.

[1] *De Anima*, A 5, 411 a 7; 2, 405 a 19. [2] So Aëtius, I, 7, XI (D. 11 A 23).
[3] Cicero: *De Nat. D.*, I, 10, 25 (D *ibid.*).

It is indeed possible that the remark concerning the magnet being alive, attributed by Aristotle to Thales, represents the lingering-on of a primitive animism, in which the concept of the anima-phantasma (the shadowy double of a man that is perceived in dreams) came to be extended to sub-human organic life, and even to the forces of the inorganic world; but, even if this is so, it is but a relic, since in Thales we see clearly the transition from myth to science and philosophy, and he retains his traditional character as initiator of Greek philosophy, ἀλλὰ Θαλῆς μὲν ὁ τῆς τοιαύτης ἀρχηγὸς φιλοσοφίας.[1]

II. *Anaximander*

Another philosopher of Miletus was Anaximander. He was apparently a younger man than Thales, for he is described by Theophrastus as an "associate" of Thales.[2] Like him, Anaximander busied himself with practical scientific pursuits, and is credited with having constructed a map—probably for the Milesian sailors on the Black Sea. Participating in political life, as so many other Greek philosophers, he led a colony to Apollonia.

Anaximander composed a prose-work on his philosophical theories. This was extant in the time of Theophrastus, and we are indebted to the latter for valuable information as to the thought of Anaximander. He sought, like Thales, for the primary and ultimate element of all things; but he decided that it could not be any one particular kind of matter, such as water, since water or the moist was itself one of the "opposites," the conflicts and encroachments of which had to be explained. If change, birth and death, growth and decay, are due to conflict, to the encroachment of one element at the expense of another, then—on the supposition that everything is in reality water—it is hard to see why the other elements have not long ago been absorbed in water. Anaximander therefore arrived at the idea, the primary element, the *Urstoff*, is indeterminate. It is more primitive than the opposites, being that out of which they come and that into which they pass away.[3]

This primary element (ἀρχή) was called by Anaximander—and, according to Theophrastus, he was the first so to call it—the material cause. "It is neither water nor any other of the so-called

[1] *Metaph.*, 983 b 18.
[2] *Phys. Opin.*, fr. 2 (D. 12 A 9). Cf. Ps. Plut. *Strom.*, 2 (D. 12 A 10).
[3] Frag. 1.

elements, but a nature different from them and infinite, from which arise all the heavens and worlds within them." It is τὸ ἄπειρον, the substance without limits. "Eternal and ageless" it "encompasses all the worlds."[1]

The encroachments of one element on another are poetically represented as instances of injustice, the warm element committing an injustice in summer and the cold in winter. The determinate elements make reparation for their injustice by being absorbed again into the Indeterminate Boundless.[2] This is an instance of the extension of the conception of law from human life to the universe at large.

There is a plurality of co-existent worlds which are innumerable.[3] Each is perishable, but there seems to be an unlimited number of them in existence at the same time, the worlds coming into being through eternal motion. "And in addition there was an eternal motion in which the heavens came to be."[4] This eternal motion seems to have been an ἀπόκρισις or "separating off," a sort of sifting in a sieve, as we find in the Pythagorean doctrine represented in the *Timaeus* of Plato. Once things had been separated off, the world as we know it was formed by a vortex movement or δίνη—the heavier elements, earth and water, remaining in the centre of the vortex, fire going back to the circumference and air remaining in between. The earth is not a disc, but a short cylinder "like the drum of a pillar."[5]

Life comes from the sea, and by means of adaptation to environment the present forms of animals were evolved. Anaximander makes a clever guess as to the origin of man. ". . . he further says that in the beginning man was born from animals of another species, for while other animals quickly find nourishment for themselves, man alone needs a lengthy period of suckling, so that had he been originally as he is now, he could never have survived."[6] He does not explain—a perennial difficulty for evolutionists—how man survived in the transition stage.

The Doctrine of Anaximander shows an advance, then, on that of Thales. He proceeds beyond the assignation of any one determinate element as primary to the conception of an Indeterminate Infinite, out of which all things come. Moreover, he makes

[1] Frags. 1–3.
[2] Frag. 1.
[3] D. 12 A 17. Simpl. *Phys.*, 1121, 5: Aët. II, 1, 3: Cic. *De Nat. D.*, 1, 10, 25: Aug. *C.D.*, viii, 2.
[4] Cf. Hippol., *Ref.*, 16, 2 (D. 12 A 11).
[5] Frag. 5. Ps. Plut. *Strom.*, 2 (D. 12 A 10).
[6] Ps. Plut. *Strom.*, fr. 2 (D. 12 A 10).

some attempt at least to answer the question *how* the world developed out of this primary element.

III. *Anaximenes*

The third philosopher of the Milesian School was Anaximenes. He must have been younger than Anaximander—at least Theophrastus says that he was an "associate" of Anaximander. He wrote a book, of which a small fragment has survived. According to Diogenes Laërtius, "he wrote in the pure unmixed Ionic dialect."

The doctrine of Anaximenes appears, at first sight at any rate, to be a decided retrogression from the stage reached by Anaximander, for Anaximenes, abandoning the theory of τὸ ἄπειρον, follows Thales in assigning a determinate element as the *Urstoff*. This determinate element is not water, but *Air*. This may have been suggested to him by the fact of breathing, for man lives so long as he breathes, and it might easily appear that air is the principle of life. In fact, Anaximenes draws a parallel between man and nature in general. "Just as our soul, being air, holds us together, so do breath and air encompass the whole world."[1] Air then is the *Urstoff* of the world, from which the things that are and have been and shall be, the gods and things divine, arose, while other things come from its offspring."[2]

But there is obviously a difficulty in explaining how all things came from air, and it is in his proffered solution to this difficulty that Anaximenes shows a trace of genius. In order to explain how concrete objects are formed from the primitive element, he introduces the notion of condensation and rarefaction. Air in itself is invisible, but it becomes visible in this process of condensation and rarefaction, becoming fire as it is dilated or rarefied; wind, cloud, water, earth and finally stones, as it is condensed. And indeed this notion of condensation and rarefaction suggests another reason why Anaximenes fixed on air as the primary element. He thought that, when air becomes rarefied, it becomes warmer and so tends to fire; while when it becomes condensed, it grows colder and tends towards the solid. Air then stands midway between the circumambient ring of flame and the cold, moist mass within it, and Anaximenes fixes on air as a sort of half-way house. The important point in his doctrine, however, may be said to be his attempt to found all quality on quantity—for that

[1] Frag. 2. [2] Hippol. *Ref.*, i, 7 (D. 13 A 7).

is what his theory of condensation and rarefaction amounts to in modern terminology. (We are told that Anaximenes pointed out that when we breathe with the mouth open, the air is warm; while when we breathe with the mouth shut, the air is cold—an experimental proof of his position.)[1]

As with Thales, the earth is conceived as flat. It floats on the air like a leaf. In the words of Professor Burnet, "Ionia was never able to accept the scientific view of the earth, and even Democritus continued to believe it was flat."[2] Anaximenes gave a curious explanation of the rainbow. It is due to the sun's rays falling on a thick cloud, which they cannot penetrate. Zeller remarks that it is a far cry from Iris, Homer's living messenger of the gods, to this "scientific" explanation.[3]

. . . . .

With the fall of Miletus in 494, the Milesian School must have come to an end. The Milesian doctrines as a whole came to be known as the philosophy of Anaximenes, as though in the eyes of the ancients he was the most important representative of the School. Doubtless his historical position as the last of the School would be sufficient to explain this, though his theory of condensation and rarefaction—the attempt to explain the properties of the concrete objects of the world by a reduction of quality to quantity—was probably also largely responsible.

In general we may once more repeat that the main importance of the Ionians lies in the fact that they raised the question as to the ultimate nature of things, rather than in any particular answer which they gave to the question raised. We may also point out that they all assume the eternity of matter: the idea of an absolute beginning of this material world does not enter into their heads. Indeed for them *this* world is the only world. It would scarcely be correct, however, to regard the Ionian cosmologists as dogmatic materialists. The distinction between matter and spirit had as yet not been conceived, and, until this happened, there could hardly be materialists in our sense. They were materialists in the sense that they tried to explain the origin of all things out of some material element: but they were not materialists in the sense of deliberately denying a distinction between matter and spirit, for the very good reason that the distinction had not been so clearly conceived that its formal denial was possible.

[1] (Plut., *De prim. frig.*, 947 f.), Frag. 1. [2] *G.P.*, I, p. 9. [3] *Outlines*, p. 31.

It scarcely needs to be indicated that the Ionians were "dogmatists," in the sense that they did not raise the "critical problem." They assumed that we could know things as they are: they were filled with the *naïveté* of wonder and the joy of discovery.

CHAPTER IV

THE PYTHAGOREAN SOCIETY

It is important to realise that the Pythagoreans were not merely a crowd of disciples of Pythagoras, more or less independent and isolated from one another: they were members of a religious society or community, which was founded by Pythagoras, a Samian, at Kroton in South Italy in the second half of the sixth century B.C. Pythagoras himself was an Ionian, and the earlier members of the School spoke the Ionic dialect. The origins of the Pythagorean Society, like the life of the founder, are shrouded in obscurity. Iamblichus, in his life of Pythagoras, calls him "leader and father of divine philosophy," "a god, a 'demon' (i.e. a superhuman being), or a divine man." But the Lives of Pythagoras by Iamblichus, Porphyry and Diogenes Laërtius, can hardly be said to afford us reliable testimony, and it is doubtless right to call them romances.[1]

To found a school was probably not new in the Greek world. Although it cannot be proved definitely, it is highly probable that the early Milesian philosophers had what amounted pretty well to Schools about them. But the Pythagorean School had a distinguishing characteristic, namely, its ascetic and religious character. Towards the end of the Ionian civilisation there took place a religious revival, attempting to supply genuine religious elements, which were catered for neither by the Olympian mythology nor by the Milesian cosmology. Just as in the Roman Empire, a society verging towards its decline, its pristine vigour and freshness lost, we see a movement to scepticism on the one hand and to "mystery religions" on the other hand, so at the close of the rich and commercial Ionian civilisation we find the same tendencies. The Pythagorean Society represents the spirit of this religious revival, which it combined with a strongly marked scientific spirit, this latter of course being the factor which justifies the inclusion of the Pythagoreans in a history of philosophy. There is certainly common ground between Orphicism and Pythagoreanism, though it is not altogether easy to determine the precise relations of the one to the other, and the degree of

[1] *"Ben, invero, possono dirsi romanzi, le loro 'Vite.'"* Covotti, *I Presocratici*, p. 66.

influence that the teaching of the Orphic sect may have had on the Pythagoreans. In Orphicism we certainly find an organisation in communities bound together by initiation and fidelity to a common way of life, as also the doctrine of the transmigration of souls—a doctrine conspicuous in Pythagorean teaching—and it is hard to think that Pythagoras was uninfluenced by the Orphic beliefs and practices, even if it is with Delos that Pythagoras is to be connected, rather than with the Thracian Dionysian religion.[1]

The view has been held that the Pythagorean communities were *political* communities, a view, however, that cannot be maintained, at least in the sense that they were essentially political communities—which they certainly were not. Pythagoras, it is true, had to leave Kroton for Metapontum on the instance of Cylon; but it seems that this can be explained without having to suppose any specifically political activities on the part of Pythagoras in favour of any particular party. The Pythagoreans did, however, obtain political control in Kroton and other cities of Magna Graecia, and Polybius tells us that their "lodges" were burnt down and they themselves subjected to persecution —perhaps about 440–430 B.C.,[2] though this fact does not necessarily mean that they were an essentially political rather than a religious society. Calvin ruled at Geneva, but he was not primarily a politician. Professor Stace remarks: "When the plain citizen of Crotona was told not to eat beans, and that under no circumstances could he eat his own dog, this was too much"[3] (though indeed it is not certain that Pythagoras prohibited beans or even all flesh as articles of food. Aristoxenus affirms the very opposite as regards the beans.[4] Burnet, who is inclined to accept the prohibitions as Pythagorean, nevertheless admits the possibility of Aristoxenus being right about the taboo on beans).[5] The Society revived after some years and continued its activities in Italy, notably at Tarentum, where in the first half of the fourth century B.C. Archytas won for himself a reputation. Philolaus and Eurytus also worked in that city.

As to the religious-ascetic ideas and practices of the Pythagoreans, these centred round the idea of purity and purification, the doctrine of the transmigration of souls naturally leading to the promotion of soul-culture. The practice of silence, the influence

[1] Cf. Diog. Laërt., 8, 8. [2] Polybius, ii, 39 (D. 14, 16).
[3] Stace, *Critical History of Greek Philosophy*, p. 33.
[4] ap. Gell., iv, II, 5 (D. 14, 9). [5] *E.G.P.*, p. 93, note 5.

of music and the study of mathematics were all looked on as valuable aids in tending the soul. Yet some of their practices were of a purely external character. If Pythagoras really did forbid the eating of flesh-meat, this may easily have been due to, or at least connected with, the doctrine of metempsychosis; but such purely external rules as are quoted by Diogenes Laërtius as having been observed by the School can by no stretch of the imagination be called philosophical doctrines. For example, to abstain from beans, not to walk in the main street, not to stand upon the parings of your nails, to efface the traces of a pot in the ashes, not to sit down on a bushel, etc. And if this were all that the Pythagorean doctrines contained, they might be of interest to the historian of religion, but would hardly merit serious attention from the historian of philosophy. However, these external rules of observance by no means comprise all that the Pythagoreans had to offer.

(In discussing briefly the theories of the Pythagoreans, we cannot say how much was due to Pythagoras himself, and how much was due to later members of the School, e.g. to Philolaus. And Aristotle in the *Metaphysics* speaks of the Pythagoreans rather than of Pythagoras himself. So that if the phrase, "Pythagoras held . . ." is used, it should not be understood to refer necessarily to the founder of the School in person.)

In his life of Pythagoras, Diogenes Laërtius tells us of a poem of Xenophanes, in which the latter relates how Pythagoras, seeing somebody beating a dog, told him to stop, since he had recognised the voice of a friend in the yelping of a dog. Whether the tale be true or not, the ascription to Pythagoras of the doctrine of metempsychosis may be accepted. The religious revival had brought to fresh life the old idea of the power of the soul and its continued vigour after death—a contrast to the Homeric conception of the gibbering shades of the departed. In such a doctrine as that of the transmigration of souls, the consciousness of personal identity, self-consciousness, is not held in mind or is not regarded as bound up with soul, for in the words of Dr. Julius Stenzel: "*. . . die Seele wandert von Ichzustand zu Ichzustand, oder, was dasselbe ist, von Leib zu Leib; denn die Einsicht, dass zum Ich der Leib gehort, war dem philosophischen Instinkt der Griechen immer selbstverständlich.*"[1] The theory of the soul as the harmony of the body, which is proposed by Simmias in Plato's *Phaedo* and

[1] *Metaphysik des Altertums, Teil I*, p. 42.

attacked by Plato, would hardly fit in with the Pythagorean view of the Soul as immortal and as undergoing transmigration; so the ascription of this view to the Pythagoreans (Macrobius refers expressly to Pythagoras and Philolaus)[1] is at least doubtful. Yet, as Dr. Praechter points out, it is not out of the question if the statement that the soul was harmony of the body, or *tout simple* a harmony, could be taken to mean that it was the principle of order and life in the body. This would not necessarily compromise the soul's immortality.[2]

(The similarity in several important points between Orphicism and Pythagoreanism may be due to an influence exerted by the former on the latter; but it is very hard to determine if there actually was any direct influence, and if there was, how far it extended. Orphicism was connected with the worship of Dionysus, a worship that came to Greece from Thrace or Scythia, and was alien to the spirit of the Olympian cult, even if its "enthusiastic" and "ecstatic" character found an echo in the soul of the Greek. But it is not the "enthusiastic" character of the Dionysian religion which connects Orphicism with Pythagoreanism; rather is it the fact that the Orphic initiates, who, be it noted, were organised in communities, were taught the doctrine of the transmigration of souls, so that for them it is the soul, and not the imprisoning body, which is the important part of man; in fact, the soul is the "real" man, and is not the mere shadow-image of the body, as it appears in Homer. Hence the importance of soul-training and soul-purification, which included the observance of such precepts as avoidance of flesh-meat. Orphicism was indeed a religion rather than a philosophy—though it tended towards Pantheism, as may be seen from the famous fragment Ζεὺς κεφαλή, Ζεὺς μέσσα, Διὸς δ' ἐκ πάντα τέτυκται[3]; but, in so far as it can be called a philosophy, it was a *way of life* and not mere cosmological speculation, and in this respect Pythagoreanism was certainly an inheritor of the Orphic spirit.)

To turn now to the difficult subject of the Pythagorean mathematico-metaphysical philosophy. Aristotle tells us in the *Metaphysics* that "the Pythagoreans, as they are called, devoted themselves to mathematics, they were the first to advance this study, and having been brought up in it they thought its principles were the principles of all things . . ."[4] They had the enthusiasm

[1] *Somn. Scip.*, I, 14, 19 (D. 44 A 23).
[2] Ueberweg-Praechter, p. 69.
[3] D. 21 a.
[4] *Metaph.*, 985, b 23–6.

of the early students of an advancing science, and they were struck by the importance of number in the world. All things are numerable, and we can express many things numerically. Thus the relation between two related things may be expressed according to numerical proportion: order between a number of ordered subjects may be numerically expressed, and so on. But what seems to have struck them particularly was the discovery that the musical intervals between the notes on the lyre may be expressed numerically. Pitch may be said to depend on number, in so far as it depends on the lengths, and the intervals on the scale may be expressed by numerical ratios.[1] Just as musical harmony is dependent on number, so it might be thought that the harmony of the universe depends on number. The Milesian cosmologists spoke of a conflict of opposites in the universe, and the musical investigations of the Pythagoreans may easily have suggested to them the idea of a solution to the problem of the "conflict" through the concept of number. Aristotle says: "since they saw that the attributes and the ratios of the musical scales were expressible in numbers; since then all other things seemed in their whole nature to be modelled after numbers, and numbers seemed to be the first things in the whole of nature, and the whole heaven to be a musical scale and a number."[2]

Now Anaximander had produced everything from the Unlimited or Indeterminate, and Pythagoras combined with this notion that of the Limit, or τὸ πέρας, which gives form to the Unlimited. This is exemplified in music (in health too, where the limit is the "tempering," which results in the harmony that is health), in which proportion and harmony are arithmetically expressible. Transferring this to the world at large, the Pythagoreans spoke of the cosmical harmony. But, not content with stressing the important part played by numbers in the universe, they went further and declared that things *are* numbers.

This is clearly not an easy doctrine to understand, and it is a hard saying that all things are numbers. What did the Pythagoreans mean by this? First of all, what did they mean by numbers, or how did they think of numbers? This is an

[1] It seems certain that the Pythagorean acoustic ratios were ratios of lengths and not of frequencies, which the Pythagoreans would hardly be in a position to measure. Thus the longest harpstring was called ἡ ὑπάτη, though it gave our "lowest" note and frequency, and the shortest was called ἡ νεάτη, though it gave our "highest" note and frequency.

[2] *Metaph.*, 985, b 31–986 a 3.

important question, for the answer to it suggests one reason why the Pythagoreans said that things are numbers. Now, Aristotle tells us that (the Pythagoreans) hold that the elements of number are the even and the odd, and of these the former is unlimited and the latter limited; and the I proceeds from both of these (for it is both even and odd), and number from the I; and the whole heaven, as has been said, is numbers."[1] Whatever precise period of Pythagorean development Aristotle may be referring to, and whatever be the precise interpretation to be put on his remarks concerning the even and the odd, it seems clear that the Pythagoreans regarded numbers spatially. One is the point, two is the line, three is the surface, four is the solid.[2] To say then that all things are numbers, would mean that "all bodies consist of points or units in space, which when taken together constitute a number."[3] That the Pythagoreans regarded numbers in this way is indicated by the "tetraktys," a figure which they regarded as sacred.

.
. .
. . .
. . . .

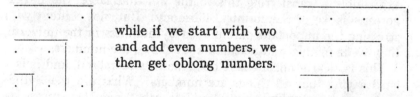

This figure shows to the eye that ten is the sum of one, two, three and four; in other words, of the first four integers. Aristotle tells us that Eurytus used to represent numbers by pebbles, and it is in accord with such a method of representation that we get the "square" and the "oblong" numbers.[4] If we start with one and add odd numbers successively in the form of "gnomons," we get square numbers,

. . .
. . .
. . .

while if we start with two and add even numbers, we then get oblong numbers.

. . . .
. . . .
. . . .

This use of figured numbers or connection of numbers with geometry clearly makes it easier to understand how the Pythagoreans regarded things as being numbers, and not merely as

[1] *Metaph.*, 986 a 17–21.
[2] Cf. art. *Pythagoras,*, Enc. Brit., 14th edit., by Sir Thos. Little Heath.
[3] Stöckl, *Hist. Phil.*, I, p. 48 (trans. by Finlay, 1887).
[4] *Metaph.*, 1092, b 10–13.

being numerable. They transferred their mathematical conceptions to the order of material reality. Thus "by the juxtaposition of several points a line is generated, not merely in the scientific imagination of the mathematician, but in external reality also; in the same way the surface is generated by the juxtaposition of several lines, and finally the body by the combination of several surfaces. Points, lines and surfaces are therefore the real units which compose all bodies in nature, and in this sense all bodies must be regarded as numbers. In fact, every material body is an expression of the number Four (τετρακτύς), since it results, as a fourth term, from three constituent elements (Points, Lines, Surfaces)."[1] But how far the identification of things with numbers is to be ascribed to the habit of representing numbers by geometrical patterns, and how far to an extension to all reality of Pythagorean discoveries in regard to music, it is extremely difficult to say. Burnet thinks that the original identification of things with numbers was due to an extension of the discovery that musical sounds can be reduced to numbers, and not to an identification of numbers with geometrical figures.[2] Yet if objects are regarded—as the Pythagoreans apparently regarded them—as sums of material quantitative points, and if, at the same time, numbers are regarded geometrically as sums of points, it is easy to see how the further step, that of identifying objects with numbers, could be taken.[3]

Aristotle, in the above-quoted passage, declares that the Pythagoreans held that "the elements of number are the even and the odd, and of these the former is unlimited and the latter limited." How do the limited and the unlimited come into the picture? For the Pythagoreans the limited cosmos or world is surrounded by the unlimited or boundless cosmos (air) which it "inhales." The objects of the limited cosmos are thus not pure limitation, but have an admixture of the unlimited. Now, the Pythagoreans, regarding numbers geometrically, considered that they also (composed of the even and the odd) are products of the limited and the unlimited. From this point of view too, then, it is but an easy step to the identification of numbers with things, the even being identified with the unlimited and the odd with the limited. A contributory explanation may be seen in the fact that the odd gnomons (cf. figures) conserve a fixed quadratic

[1] Stöckl, *Hist. Phil.*, I, pp. 43–9.
[2] *E.G.P.*, p. 107.
[3] Philolaus (as we learn from the fragments) insisted that nothing could be known, nothing would be clear or perspicuous, unless it had or was number.

shape (limited), while the even gnomons present a continually changing rectangular shape (unlimited).[1]

When it came to assigning definite numbers to definite things, scope was naturally allowed for all manner of arbitrary caprice and fancy. For example, although we may be able to see more or less why justice should be declared to be four, it is not so easy to see why καιρός should be seven or animation six. Five is declared to be marriage, because five is the product of three—the first masculine number, and two—the first feminine number. However, in spite of all these fanciful elements the Pythagoreans made a real contribution to mathematics. A knowledge of "Pythagoras' Theorem" as a geometrical fact is shown in Sumerian computations: the Pythagoreans, however, as Proclus remarked,[2] transcended mere arithmetical and geometrical facts, and digested them into a deductive system, though this was at first, of course, of an elementary nature. "Summing up the Pythagorean geometry, we may say that it covered the bulk of Euclid's Books i, ii, iv, vi (and probably iii), with the qualification that the Pythagorean theory of proportion was inadequate in that it did not apply to incommensurable magnitudes."[3] The theory which did solve this last arose under Eudoxus in the Academy.

To the Pythagoreans, not only was the earth spherical,[4] but it is not the centre of the universe. The earth and the planets revolve—along with the sun—round the central fire or "hearth of the Universe" (which is identified with the number One). The world inhales air from the boundless mass outside it, and the air is spoken of as the Unlimited. We see here the influence of Anaximenes. (According to Aristotle—*De Caelo*, 293, a 25–7—the Pythagoreans did not deny geocentricism in order to explain phenomena, but from arbitrary reasons of their own.)

The Pythagoreans are of interest to us, not only because of their musical and mathematical investigations; not only because of their character as a religious society; not only because through their doctrine of transmigration of souls and their mathematical metaphysic—at least in so far as they did not "materialise"

[1] Cf. Arist. *Physics*, 203 a 10–15.

[2] *In Eukleiden*, Friedlein, 65, 16–19.

[3] Heath, *art. cit.*

[4] Cf. the words of the Russian philosopher, Leo Chestov: "It has happened more than once that a truth has had to wait for recognition whole centuries after its discovery. So it was with Pythagoras' teaching of the movement of the earth. Everyone thought it false, and for more than 1,500 years men refused to accept this truth. Even after Copernicus savants were obliged to keep this new truth hidden from the champions of tradition and of sound sense." Leo Chestov, *In Job's Balances*, p. 168 (trans. by C. Coventry and Macartney).

numbers[1]—they tended to break away from the *de facto* materialism of the Milesian cosmologists; but also because of their influence on Plato, who was doubtless influenced by their conception of the soul (he probably borrowed from them the doctrine of the tripartite nature of the soul) and its destiny. The Pythagoreans were certainly impressed by the importance of the soul and its right tendance, and this was one of the most cherished convictions of Plato, to which he clung all his life. Plato was also strongly influenced by the mathematical speculations of the Pythagoreans—even if it is difficult to determine the precise extent of his debt to them in this respect. And to say of the Pythagoreans that they were one of the determining influences in the formation of the thought of Plato, is to pay them no mean tribute.

[1] As a matter of fact the Pythagorean mathematisation of the universe cannot really be regarded as an "idealisation" of the universe, since they regarded number geometrically. Their identification of things and numbers is thus not so much an idealisation of things as a materialisation of numbers. On the other hand, in so far as "ideas," such as justice, are identified with numbers, one may perhaps speak with justice of a tendency towards idealism. The same theme recurs in the Platonic idealism.

It must, however, be admitted that the assertion that the Pythagoreans effected a geometrisation of number would scarcely hold good for the later Pythagoreans at least. Thus Archytas of Tarentum, a friend of Plato, was clearly working in the very opposite direction (cf. Diels, B 4), a tendency to which Aristotle, believing in the separation and irreducible character of both geometry and arithmetic, firmly objected. On the whole it might be better perhaps to speak of a Pythagorean discovery (even if incompletely analysed) of *isomorphisms* between arithmetic and geometry rather than of an interreduction.

CHAPTER V

THE WORD OF HERACLITUS

HERACLITUS was an Ephesian noble and flourished, according to Diogenes, about the 69th Olympiad, i.e. *c.* 504–501 B.C.; his dates cannot be accurately determined. The office of *Basileus* was hereditary in his family, but Heraclitus relinquished it in favour of his brother. He was, we gather, a melancholy man, of aloof and solitary temperament, who expressed his contempt for the common herd of citizens, as also for the eminent men of the past. "The Ephesians," he said of the citizens of his own city, "would do well to hang themselves, every grown man of them, and leave the city to beardless lads; for they have cast out Hermodorus, the best man among them, saying, "We will have none who is best among us; if there be any such, let him be so elsewhere and among others."[1] Again he comments: "In Priene lived Bias, son of Teutamas, who is of more account than the rest." (He said: "Most men are bad.")[2]

Heraclitus expresses his opinion of Homer in the saying: "Homer should be turned out of the lists and whipped, and Archilochus likewise." Similarly he observed: "The learning of many things does not teach understanding, otherwise it would have taught Hesiod and Pythagoras, and again Xenophanes and Hecataeus." As for Pythagoras, he "practised scientific inquiry beyond all other men, and making a selection of these writings, claimed for his own wisdom what was but a knowledge of many things and an imposture."[3]

Many of Heraclitus' sayings are pithy and pungent in character, if somewhat amusing on occasion. For example: "Physicians who cut, burn, stab and rack the sick, demand a fee for it which they do not deserve to get"; "Man is called a baby by God, even as a child by man"; "Asses prefer straw to gold"; "Man's character is his fate."[4] In regard to Heraclitus' attitude to religion, he had little respect for the mysteries, and even declares that "The mysteries practised among men are unholy mysteries."[5] Moreover, his attitude towards God was pantheistic, in spite of the religious language he employed.

[1] Frag. 121. [2] Frag. 39. [3] Frags. 42, 40, 129 (latter doubtful, acc. to D).
[4] Frags. 58, 79, 9, 119. [5] Frag. 14.

The style of Heraclitus seems to have been somewhat obscure for he gained in later time the nickname of ὁ σκοτεινός. This practice appears to have been not altogether unintentional: at least we find among the fragments sentences such as: "Nature loves to hide"; "The lord whose is the oracle by Delphi neither utters not hides its meaning, but shows it by a sign." And of his own message to mankind he says: "Men are as unable to understand it when they hear it for the first time, as before they have heard it at all."[1] Burnet points out that Pindar and Aeschylus possess the same prophetic tone, and attributes it in part to the contemporary religious revival.[2]

Heraclitus is known to many for the famous saying attributed to him, though apparently not his own: "All things are in a state of flux, πάντα ῥεῖ. Indeed this is all that many people know about him. This statement does not represent the kernel of his philosophic thought, though it does indeed represent an important aspect of his doctrine. Is he not responsible for the saying: "You cannot step twice into the same river, for fresh waters are ever flowing in upon you"?[3] Moreover, Plato remarks that "Heraclitus says somewhere that all things pass and nought abides; and comparing things to the current of a river, he says you cannot step twice into the same stream."[4] And Aristotle describes Heraclitus' doctrine as affirming that "All things are in motion, nothing steadfastly is."[5] In this respect Heraclitus is a Pirandello in the ancient world, crying out that nothing is stable, nothing abides, proclaiming the unreality of "Reality."

It would be a mistake, however, to suppose that Heraclitus meant to teach that there is nothing which changes, for this is contradicted by the rest of his philosophy.[6] Nor is the proclamation of change even the most important and significant feature of his philosophy. Heraclitus lays stress on his "Word," i.e. on his special message to mankind, and he could scarcely feel himself justified in doing this if the message amounted to no more than the truth that things are constantly changing; a truth seen by the other Ionian philosophers and hardly bearing the character of novelty. No, Heraclitus' original contribution to philosophy is

[1] Frags. 123, 93, 1 (cf. 17, 34). Cf. Diog. Laërt., 9, 6. [2] *E.G.P.*, p. 132.
[3] Cf. Frags. 12 and 91. [4] *Crat.* 402 a. [5] *De Caelo*, 298 b 30 (III, i).
[6] Heraclitus does indeed teach that Reality is constantly changing, that it is its essential nature to change; but this should not be interpreted as meaning that for him there is no changing Reality at all. Heraclitus has often been compared to Bergson, but Bergson's thought too has, not infrequently, been grossly, if understandably, misinterpreted.

to be found elsewhere: it consists in the conception of unity in diversity, difference in unity. In the philosophy of Anaximander, as we have seen, the opposites are regarded as encroaching on one another, and then as paying in turn the penalty for this act of injustice. Anaximander regards the war of the opposites as something disorderly, something that ought not to be, something that mars the purity of the One. Heraclitus, however, does not adopt this point of view. For him the conflict of opposites, so far from being a blot on the unity of the One, is essential to the being of the One. In fact, the One only exists in the tension of opposites: this tension is essential to the unity of the One.

That Reality is One for Heraclitus is shown clearly enough by his saying: "It is wise to hearken, not to me, but to my Word, and to confess that all things are one."[1] On the other hand, that the conflict of opposites is essential to the existence of the One is also shown clearly by such statements as: "We must know that war is common to all and strife is justice, and that all things come into being and pass away through strife,"[2] and Homer was wrong in saying: "Would that strife might perish from among gods and men!" He did not see that he was praying for the destruction of the universe, for, if his prayer were heard, all things would pass away.[3] Again, Heraclitus says positively: "Men do not know how what is at variance agrees with itself. It is an attunement of opposite tensions, like that of the bow and the lyre."[4]

For Heraclitus, then, Reality is One; but it is many at the same time—and that not merely accidentally, but essentially. It is essential to the being and existence of the One that it should be one and many at the same time; that it should be Identity in Difference. Hegel's assignment of Heraclitus' philosophy to the category of Becoming is therefore based on a misconception—and also errs by putting Parmenides earlier than Heraclitus, for Parmenides was a critic as well as a contemporary of Heraclitus, and must be the later writer.[5] The philosophy of Heraclitus corresponds much more to the idea of the concrete universal, the One existing in the many, Identity in Difference.

But what is the One-in-many? For Heraclitus, as for the Stoics of later times, who borrowed the notion from him, the essence of all things is Fire. Now, it might seem at first sight that Heraclitus is merely ringing the changes on the old Ionian theme—as

[1] Frag. 50. [2] Frag. 80.
[3] Numenius. Frag. 16, apud Chalcidium, c. 297 (D. 22 A 22).
[4] Frag. 51. [5] Hegel, *Hist. Phil.*, vol. I.

though because Thales made Reality to be Water and Anaximenes Air, Heraclitus, simply in order to find something different from his predecessors, fixed on Fire. Naturally, the wish to find a different *Urstoff* may have operated to a certain extent, but there was something more in his choice of Fire than that: he had a positive reason, and a very good reason for fixing on Fire, a reason bound up with the central thought of his philosophy.

Sense-experience tells us that fire lives by feeding, by consuming and transforming into itself heterogeneous matter. Springing up, as it were, from a multitude of objects, it changes them into itself, and without this supply of material it would die down and cease to exist. The very existence of the fire depends on this "strife" and "tension." This is, of course, a sensual symbolism of a genuine philosophic notion, but it clearly bears a relation to that notion that water or air will not so easily bear. Thus Heraclitus' choice of Fire as the essential nature of Reality was not due simply to arbitrary caprice on his part, nor merely to the desire for novelty, to the necessity of differing from his predecessors, but was suggested by his main philosophic thought. "Fire," he says, "is want and surfeit"—it is, in other words, all things that are, but it is these things in a constant state of tension, of strife, of consuming, of kindling and of going out.[1] In the process of fire Heraclitus distinguished two paths—the upward and the downward paths. "He called change the upward and the downward path and said that the cosmos comes into being in virtue of this. When fire is condensed it becomes moist, and under compression it turns to water; water being congealed is turned to earth, and this he calls the downward path. And, again, the earth is itself liquefied and from it water comes, and from that everything else; for he refers almost everything to the evaporation from the sea. This is the upward path."[2]

However, if it be maintained that all things are fire, and are consequently in a constant state of flux, it is clear that some explanation must be offered of what appears at least to be the stable nature of things in the world. The explanation offered by Heraclitus is in terms of measure: the world is "an ever-living Fire, with measures of it kindling and measures going out."[3] So if Fire takes from things, transforming into itself by kindling, it also gives as much as it takes. "All things are an exchange for Fire, and Fire for all things, even as wares for gold and gold for

[1] Frag. 65. [2] Diog. Laërt., 9, 8–9. [3] Frag. 30.

wares."[1] Thus, while the substance of each kind of matter is always changing, the aggregate quantity of that kind of matter remains the same.

But it is not only the relative stability of things that Heraclitus tries to explain, but also the varying preponderance of one kind of matter over another, as seen in day and night, summer and winter. We learn from Diogenes that Heraclitus explained the preponderance of different elements as due to "the different exhalations." Thus "the bright exhalation, when ignited in the circle of the sun, produced day; and the preponderance of the opposite exhalation produced night. The increase of warmth proceeding from the bright exhalation produced summer; and the preponderance of moisture from the dark exhalation produced winter."[2]

There is, as we have seen, constant strife in the universe, and there is also a relative stability of things, due to the different measures of Fire, kindling or going out in more or less equal proportions. And it is the fact of this measure, of the balance of the upward and downward paths, which constitutes what Heraclitus calls the "hidden attunement of the Universe," and which he declares is "better than the open."[3] "Men," says Heraclitus in an already-quoted fragment, "do not know how what is at variance agrees with itself. It is an attunement of opposite tensions, like that of the bow and the lyre."[4] The One, in short, is its differences, and the differences are themselves one, they are different aspects of the one. Neither of the aspects, neither the upward nor the downward path, can cease: if they were to cease, then the One itself would no longer exist. This inseparability of opposites, the essential character of the different moments of the One, comes out in such sayings as: "The way up and the way down is the same," and "It is death to souls to become water, and death to water to become earth. But water comes from earth, and from water, soul."[5] It leads, of course, to a certain relativism, as in the statements that "Good and ill are one"; "The sea is the purest and the impurest water. Fish can drink it and it is good for them: to men it is undrinkable and destructive"; "Swine wash in the mire, and barnyard fowls in the dust."[6] However, in the One all tensions are reconciled, all differences harmonised: "To God all things are fair and good and right, but men hold some

[1] Frag. 90. [2] Diog. Laërt., 9, 11. [3] Frag. 54. [4] Frag. 51.
[5] Frags. 60, 36. [6] Frags. 58, 61, 37.

things wrong and some right."[1] This is, of course, the inevitable conclusion of a pantheistic philosophy—that everything is justified *sub specie aeternitatis*.

Heraclitus speaks of the One as God, and as wise: "The wise is one only. It is unwilling and willing to be called by the name of Zeus."[2] God is the universal Reason (Λόγος), the universal law immanent in all things, binding all things into a unity and determining the constant change in the universe according to universal law. Man's reason is a moment in this universal Reason, or a contraction and canalisation of it, and man should therefore strive to attain to the viewpoint of reason and to live by reason, realising the unity of all things and the reign of unalterable law, being content with the necessary process of the universe and not rebelling against it, inasmuch as it is the expression of the all-comprehensive, all-ordering Λόγος or Law. Reason and consciousness in man—the fiery element—are the valuable element: when the pure fire leaves the body, the water and earth which are left behind are worthless, a thought which Heraclitus expresses in the saying: "Corpses are more fit to be cast out than dung."[3] A man's interest, then, is to preserve his soul in as dry a state as possible: "The dry is the wisest and best."[4] It may be pleasure to souls to become moist, but all the same "it is death to soul to become water."[5] Souls should strive to rise above the private worlds of the 'sleeping" to the common world of the "waking," i.e. to the common world of thought and reason. This thought is of course the Word of Heraclitus. There is, then, one immanent law and Reason in the universe, of which human laws should be the embodiment, though at best they can be but its imperfect and relative embodiment. By stressing universal law and man's participation in Reason, Heraclitus helped to pave the way for the universalist ideals of Stoicism.

This conception of universal, all-ordering Reason appears in the system of the Stoics, who borrowed their cosmology from Heraclitus. But we are not entitled to suppose that Heraclitus regarded the One, Fire, as a *personal* God, any more than Thales or Anaximenes regarded Water or Air as a personal God: Heraclitus was a pantheist, just as the Stoics in later times were pantheists. It is, however, true that the conception of God as the immanent, ordering Principle of all things, together with the moral attitude of acceptance of events as the expression of divine

[1] Frag. 102. [2] Frag. 32. [3] Frag. 96. [4] Frag. 118. [5] Frags. 77, 36.

Law, tends to produce a psychological attitude that is at variance with what would seem to be logically demanded by the theoretical identification of God with the cosmic unity. This discrepancy between psychological attitude and the strict demands of theory became very clear in the Stoic School, the members of which so often betray a mental attitude and employ language that would suggest a theistic conception of God, rather than the pantheistic conception logically demanded by the cosmological system—a discrepancy which was aggravated among the later Stoics especially, owing to their increasing concentration on ethical questions.

Did Heraclitus teach the doctrine of a universal conflagration recurring periodically? As the Stoics certainly held this doctrine, and as they borrowed from Heraclitus, the doctrine of the periodic and universal conflagration has been attributed to Heraclitus too; but, for the following reasons, it does not seem possible to accept this attribution. In the first place, Heraclitus, as we have seen, insisted on the fact that the tension or conflict of opposites is essential to the very existence of the One. Now, if all things were periodically to relapse into pure fire, the fire itself should logically cease to exist. In the second place, does not Heraclitus expressly say that the "sun will not go beyond his measures; otherwise the Erinyes, the handmaids of Justice, will find him out,"[1] and "this world was ever, is now, and ever shall be an ever-living Fire, with measures of it kindling and measures going out"? In the third place, Plato contrasts Heraclitus and Empedocles on the ground that, according to Heraclitus, the One is always Many, while, according to Empedocles, the One is many and one by turns.[2] When Professor Zeller says: "It is a contradiction which he, and probably Plato too, has not observed," he is making an unwarrantable supposition. Of course, if it were clear from certain evidence that Heraclitus actually did teach the doctrine of a periodic general conflagration, then we should indeed have to conclude that the contradiction involved was unobserved by both Heraclitus himself and by Plato; but as evidence goes to show that Heraclitus did not teach this doctrine, we cannot reasonably be called upon to attribute a mistake to Plato in this matter. Moreover, it was apparently the Stoics who first stated that Heraclitus maintained the doctrine of a general conflagration;[3] and even the Stoics are divided on the subject. Does not Plutarch

[1] Frag. 94. [2] *Soph.*, 242 d. [3] Cf. *E.G.P.*, pp. 159–60.

make a character say: "I see the Stoic conflagration spreading over the poems of Hesiod, just as it does over the writings of Heraclitus and the verses of Orpheus"?[1]

What are we to say of the doctrine of Heraclitus, the notion of unity in difference? That there is a many, a plurality, is clear enough. But at the same time the intellect constantly strives to conceive a unity, a system, to obtain a comprehensive view to link things up; and this goal of thought corresponds to a real unity in things: things *are* interdependent. Even man, with his immortal soul, depends on the rest of creation. His body depends, in a very real sense, on the whole past history of the world and of the human race: he depends on the material universe for life—bodily life through air, food, drink, sunlight, etc.—for his intellectual life too, through sensation as the starting-point of knowledge. He depends also for his cultural life on the thought and culture, the civilisation and development of the past. But though man is right in seeking a unity, it would be wrong to assert unity to the detriment of plurality. Unity, the only unity that is worth having, is a unity in difference, identity in diversity, a unity, that is to say, not of poverty, but of richness. Every material thing is a unity in diversity (consisting of molecules, atoms, electrons, etc.), every living organism also—even God Himself, as we know by Revelation, is Unity in Distinction of Persons. In Christ there is unity in diversity—unity of Person in diversity of Natures. The union of the Beatific Vision is a union in distinction—otherwise it would lose its richness (apart of course, from the impossibility of a "simple" unity of identification between God and creature).

Can we look on the created universe as a unity? The universe is certainly not a substance: it comprises a plurality of substances. It is, however, a totality in our idea of it, and if the law of the conservation of energy be valid, then it is in a sense a physical totality. The universe, then, may to a certain degree be considered a unity in diversity; but we may perhaps go further and suggest with Heraclitus that the conflict of opposites—change—is necessary to the existence of the material universe.

(i) As far as inorganic matter is concerned, change—at the very least in the sense of locomotion—is necessarily involved, at any rate if modern theories of the composition of matter, the theory of light, etc., are to be accepted.

[1] *De def. orac.*, 415 f.

(ii) This, too, is clear, that if there is to be finite, materially-conditioned life, then change is essential. The life of a bodily organism must be sustained by respiration, assimilation, etc., all of which processes involve change, and so the "conflict of opposites." The preservation of specific life on the planet involves reproduction, and birth and death may well be termed opposites.

(iii) Would it be possible to have a material universe in which there was no conflict of opposites, absolutely no change at all? In the first place, there could be no life in such a universe, for embodied life, as we have seen, involves change. But would it be possible to have a material universe—in which there was no life—that was entirely static, entirely without change and movement? If matter be regarded in terms of energy, it is very hard to see how there could be any such purely static material universe. But, prescinding from all physical theories, even if such a universe were physically possible, could it be rationally possible? We could at least discover no possible function for such a universe—without life, without development, without change, a sort of primitive chaos.

A purely material universe seems, then, to be inconceivable not only *a posteriori* but also *a priori*. The idea of a material universe, in which organic life is present, demands change. But change means diversity on the one hand, for there must be a *terminus a quo* and a *terminus ad quem* of the change, and stability on the other hand, for there must be *something which changes*. And so there will be identity in diversity.

We conclude, then, that Heraclitus of Ephesus conceived a genuine philosophic notion, even though he pursued the same way of sensual symbolism as his Ionian predecessors, and this notion of the One as essentially many can be clearly discerned beneath all the sensual symbolism. Heraclitus did not indeed rise to the conception of substantial thought, the νόησις νοήσεως of Aristotle, nor did he sufficiently account for the element of stability in the universe as Aristotle tried to do; but, as Hegel says, "if we wish to consider fate so just as always to preserve to posterity what is best, we must at least say of what we have of Heraclitus, that it is worthy of this preservation."[1]

[1] *Hist. Phil.*, I, pp. 297–8.

CHAPTER VI

THE ONE OF PARMENIDES AND MELISSUS

THE reputed founder of the Eleatic School was Xenophanes. However, as there is no real evidence that he ever went to Elea in Southern Italy, it is unlikely that he is to be accounted anything more than a tutelary founder, a patron of the School. It is not difficult to see why he was adopted as a patron by the School that held fast to the idea of the motionless One, when we consider some of the sayings attributed to him. Xenophanes attacks the anthropomorphic Greek deities: "If oxen and horses or lions had hands, and could paint with their hands, and produce works of art as men do, horses would paint the forms of the gods like horses, and oxen like oxen, and make their bodies in the image of their several kinds":[1] and substitutes in their place, "One god, the greatest among Gods and men, neither in form like unto mortals, nor in thought," who "abideth ever in the selfsame place, moving not at all; nor doth it befit him to go about now hither now thither."[2] Aristotle tells us in the *Metaphysics* that Xenophanes, "referring to the whole world, said the One was god."[3] Most probably, then, he was a monist and not a monotheist, and this interpretation of his "theology" would certainly be more compatible with the Eleatic attitude towards him than a theistic interpretation. A really monotheistic theology may be a familiar enough notion to us, but in the Greece of the period it would have been something exceptional.

But whatever the opinions of Xenophanes may have been, the real founder of the Eleatic School from a philosophical and historical viewpoint was undoubtedly Parmenides, a citizen of Elea. Parmenides seems to have been born towards the close of the sixth century B.C., since round about 451–449 B.C., when 65 years old, he conversed with the young Socrates at Athens. He is said to have drawn up laws for his native city of Elea, and Diogenes preserves a statement of Sotion to the effect that

[1] Frag. 15. One might compare the words of Epicharmus (Frag. 5): "For the dog seems to the dog to be the most beautiful creature, and the ox to the ox, the donkey to the donkey, and the swine to the swine."

[2] Frags. 23 and 26.

[3] *Metaph.*, A 5, 986 b 18.

Parmenides began by being a Pythagorean, but afterwards abandoned that philosophy in favour of his own.[1]

Parmenides wrote in verse, most of the fragments we possess being preserved by Simplicius in his commentary. His doctrine in brief is to the effect that Being, the One, *is*, and that Becoming, change, is illusion. For if anything comes to be, then it comes either out of being or out of not-being. If the former, then it already is—in which case it does not come to be; if the latter, then it is nothing, since out of nothing comes nothing. Becoming is, then, illusion. Being simply *is* and Being is One, since plurality is also illusion. Now, this doctrine is obviously not the type of theory that rises immediately to the mind of the man in the street, and so it is not surprising to find Parmenides insisting on the radical distinction between the Way of Truth and the Way of Belief or Opinion. It is very probable that the Way of Opinion exposed in the second part of the poem, represents the cosmology of the Pythagoreans; and since the Pythagorean philosophy would itself scarcely occur to the man who went *merely* by sense-knowledge, it should not be maintained that Parmenides' distinction between the two Ways has all the formal generality of Plato's later distinction between Knowledge and Opinion, Thought and Sense. It is rather the rejection of one definite philosophy in favour of another definite philosophy. Yet it is true that Parmenides rejects the Pythagorean philosophy—and, indeed, every philosophy that agrees with it on the point—because it admits change and movement. Now change and movement are most certainly phenomena which appear to the senses, so that in rejecting change and movement, Parmenides is rejecting the way of sense-appearance. It is, therefore, not incorrect to say that Parmenides introduces the most important distinction between Reason and Sense, Truth and Appearance. It is true, of course, that even Thales recognised this distinction to a certain extent, for his supposed truth, that all is Water, is scarcely perceptible immediately to the senses: it needs reason, which passes beyond appearance, in order to be conceived. The central "truth" of Heraclitus is, again, a truth of reason and far exceeds the common opinion of men, who trust in everything to sense-appearance. It is also true that Heraclitus even makes the distinction partly explicit, for does he not distinguish between mere common sense and his Word? Yet it is Parmenides who first lays great and

[1] Diog. Laërt., 9, 21.

explicit stress on the distinction, and it is easy enough to understand why he does so, when we consider the conclusions to which he came. In the Platonic philosophy the distinction became of cardinal importance, as indeed it must be in all forms of idealism.

Yet though Parmenides enunciates a distinction which was to become a fundamental tenet of idealism, the temptation to speak of him as though he were himself an idealist is to be rejected. As we shall see, there is very good reason for supposing that in Parmenides' eyes the One is sensual and material, and to turn him into an objective idealist of the nineteenth-century type is to be guilty of an anachronism: it does not follow from the negation of change that the One is Idea. We may be called upon to follow the way of thought, but it does not follow that Parmenides regarded the One, at which we arrive by this way, as actually being Thought itself. If Parmenides had represented the One as self-subsistent Thought, Plato and Aristotle would hardly have failed to record the fact, and Socrates would not have found the first sober philosopher in Anaxagoras, with his concept of Mind or Nous. The truth really seems to be that though Parmenides does assert the distinction between Reason and Sense, he asserts it not to establish an idealist system, but to establish a system of Monistic Materialism, in which change and movement are dismissed as illusory. Only Reason can apprehend Reality, but the Reality which Reason apprehends is material. This is not idealism but materialism.

To turn now to the doctrine of Parmenides on the nature of the world. His first great assertion is that "It is." "It," i.e. Reality, Being, of whatever nature it may be, is, exists, and cannot not be. It is, and it is impossible for it not to be. Being can be spoken of and it can be the object of my thought. But that which I can think about and speak of can be, "for it is the same thing that can be thought and that can be." But if "It" *can* be, then it *is*. Why? Because if it could be and yet were not, then it would be nothing. Now, nothing cannot be the object of speech or thought, for to speak about nothing is not to speak, and to think about nothing is the same as not thinking at all. Besides, if it merely *could be*, then, paradoxically, it could never come to be, for it would have to come out of nothing, and out of nothing comes nothing and not something. Being, then, Reality, "It" was not first possible, i.e. nothing, and then existent: it was always existent—more accurately, "It is."

Why do we say "more accurately, It is?" For this reason: If something comes into being, it must arise either out of being or out of not-being. If it arises out of being, then there is no real arising, no coming-to-be; for if it comes out of being, it already is. If, however, it arises out of not-being, then not-being must be already something, in order for being to be able to arise out of it. But this is a contradiction. Being therefore, "It" arises neither out of being nor out of not-being: it never came into being, but simply *is*. And as this must apply to all being, nothing ever becomes. For if anything ever becomes, however trifling, the same difficulty always recurs: does it come out of being or out of not-being? If the former, then it already is; if the latter, then you fall into a contradiction, since not-being is nothing and cannot be the source of being. Change, therefore, becoming and movement are impossible. Accordingly "It is." "One path only is left for us to speak of, namely, that *It is.* In this path are very many tokens that what is, is uncreated and indestructible, for it is complete, immovable and without end."[1]

Why does Parmenides say that "It" is complete, i.e. one Reality, which cannot be added to? Because if it is not one but divided, then it must be divided by something other than itself. But Being cannot be divided by something other than itself, for besides being there is nothing. Nor can anything be added to it, since anything that was added to being would itself be being. Similarly, it is immovable and continuous, for all movement and change, forms of becoming, are excluded.

Now, of what nature is this "It," Being, according to Parmenides? That Parmenides regarded Being as material, seems to be clearly indicated by his assertion that Being, the One, is finite. Infinite for him must have meant indeterminate and indefinite, and Being, as the Real, cannot be indefinite or indeterminate, cannot change, cannot be conceived as expanding into empty space: it must be definite, determinate, complete. It is temporarily infinite, as having neither beginning nor end, but it is spatially finite. Moreover, it is equally real in all directions, and so is spherical in shape, "equally poised from the centre in every direction: for it cannot be greater or smaller in one place than in another."[2] Now, how could Parmenides possibly think of Being as spherical, unless he thought of it as material? It would seem, then, that Burnet is right when he aptly says: "Parmenides is

[1] Frag. 8. [2] Frag. 8.

not, as some have said, 'the father of idealism'; on the contrary, all materialism depends on his view of reality."[1] Professor Stace has to admit that "Parmenides, Melissus and the Eleatics generally did regard Being as, in some sense, material"; but he still tries to make out that Parmenides was an idealist in that he held the "cardinal thesis of idealism," "that the absolute reality, of which the world is a manifestation, consists in thought, in concepts."[2] It is perfectly true that the Being of Parmenides can be grasped only by thought, but so can the reality of Thales or Anaximenes be grasped only by thought, in concepts. But to equate "being grasped in thought" with "being thought" is surely a confusion.

As an historical fact, then, it would seem that Parmenides was a materialist and nothing else. However, that does not prevent there being an unreconciled contradiction in Parmenides' philosophy, as affirmed by Professor Stace,[3] so that, though a materialist, his thought contains also the germs of idealism, or would at any rate form the *point de départ* for idealism. On the one hand Parmenides asserted the unchangeability of Being, and, in so far as he conceived of Being as material, he asserted the indestructibility of matter. Empedocles and Democritus adopted this position and used it in their atomistic doctrine. But while Parmenides felt himself compelled to dismiss change and becoming as illusion, thus adopting the very opposite position to that of Heraclitus, Democritus could not reject what appears to be an inescapable fact of experience, which needs more explanation than a curt dismissal. Democritus, therefore, while adopting Parmenides' thesis that being can neither arise nor pass away—the indestructibility of matter—interpreted change as due to the aggregation and separation of indestructible particles of matter. On the other hand, it is an historical fact that Plato seized on the thesis of Parmenides concerning the unchangeability of Being, and identified the abiding being with the subsistent and objective Idea. To that extent, therefore, Parmenides may be called the father of idealism, in that the first great idealist adopted a cardinal tenet of Parmenides and interpreted it from an idealistic standpoint. Moreover, Plato made great use of Parmenides' distinction between the world of reason and the world of sense or appearance. But if in that historical sense Parmenides may rightly be described as the father of idealism, through his undoubted influence on Plato, it must be understood at the same

[1] *E.G.P.*, p. 182. [2] *Crit. Hist.*, pp. 47 and 48. [3] *Crit. Hist.*, pp. 49–52.

time that Parmenides himself taught a materialistic doctrine, and that materialists like Democritus were his legitimate children.

Heraclitus, in his theory of the πάντα ῥεῖ, laid stress on *Becoming*. As we have seen, he did not assert Becoming to the total exclusion of Being, saying that there is becoming, but nothing which becomes. He affirmed the existence of the One—Fire, but held that change, becoming, tension, are essential to the existence of the One. Parmenides, on the other hand, asserted Being even to the exclusion of Becoming, affirming that change and movement are illusory. Sense tells us that there is change, but truth is to be sought, not in sense, but in reason and thought. We have, therefore, two tendencies exemplified in these two philosophers, the tendency to emphasise Becoming and the tendency to emphasise Being. Plato attempted a synthesis of the two, a combination of what is true in each. He adopts Parmenides' distinction between thought and sense, and declares that sense-objects, the objects of sense-perception, are not the objects of true knowledge, for they do not possess the necessary stability, being subject to the Heraclitean flux. The objects of true knowledge are stable and eternal, like the Being of Parmenides; but they are not material, like the Being of Parmenides. They are, on the contrary, ideal, subsistent and immaterial Forms, hierarchically arranged and culminating in the Form of the Good.

The synthesis may be said to have been worked out further by Aristotle. Being, in the sense of ultimate and immaterial Reality, God, is changeless, subsistent Thought, νόησις νοήσεως. As to material being, Aristotle agrees with Heraclitus that it is subject to change, and rejects the position of Parmenides, but Aristotle accounts better than Heraclitus did for the relative stability in things by making Plato's Forms or Ideas concrete, formal principles in the objects of this world. Again, Aristotle solves the dilemma of Parmenides by emphasising the notion of potentiality. He points out that it is no contradiction to say that a thing is X actually but Y potentially. It *is* X, but is going to be Y in the future in virtue of a potentiality, which is not simply nothing, yet is not actual being. Being therefore arises, not out of not-being nor out of being precisely as being *actu*, but out of being considered as being *potentia*, δύναμει. Of the second part of the poem of Parmenides, *The Way of Belief*, it is unnecessary to say anything, but it is as well to say a few words concerning Melissus, as he supplemented the thought of his master, Parmenides.

Parmenides had declared that Being, the One, is spatially finite; but Melissus, the Samian disciple of Parmenides, would not accept this doctrine. If Being is finite, then beyond being there must be nothing: being must be bounded or limited by nothing. But if being is limited by nothing, it must be infinite and not finite. There cannot be a void outside being, "for what is empty is nothing. What is nothing cannot be."[1]

Aristotle tells us that the One of Melissus was conceived as material.[2] Now, Simplicius quotes a fragment to prove that Melissus did *not* look upon the One as corporeal, but as incorporeal. "Now, if it were to exist, it must needs to be one; but if it is one, it cannot have body; for if it had body, it would have parts, and would no longer be one."[3] The explanation seems to be indicated by the fact that Melissus is speaking of an hypothetical case. Burnet, following Zeller, points out the similarity of the fragment to an argument of Zeno, in which Zeno is saying that if the ultimate units of the Pythagoreans existed, then each would have parts and would not be one. We may suppose, therefore, that Melissus, too, is speaking of the doctrine of the Pythagoreans, is trying to disprove the existence of their ultimate units, and is not talking of the Parmenidean One at all.

[1] Frag. 7. [2] *Metaph.*, 986 b 18–21. [3] Frag. 9. (Simplic. *Phys.*, 109, 34).

CHAPTER VII

THE DIALECTIC OF ZENO

ZENO is well known as the author of several ingenious arguments to prove the impossibility of motion, such as the riddle of Achilles and the tortoise; arguments which may tend to further the opinion that Zeno was no more than a clever riddler who delighted in using his wits in order to puzzle those who were less clever than himself. But in reality Zeno was not concerned simply to display his cleverness—though clever he undoubtedly was—but had a serious purpose in view. For the understanding of Zeno and the appreciation of his conundrums, it is therefore essential to grasp the character of this purpose, otherwise there is danger of altogether misapprehending his position and aim.

Zeno of Elea, born probably about 489 B.C., was a disciple of Parmenides, and it is from this point of view that he is to be understood. His arguments are not simply witty toys, but are calculated to prove the position of the Master. Parmenides had combated pluralism, and had declared change and motion to be illusion. Since plurality and motion seem to be such evident data of our sense-experience, this bold position was naturally such as to induce a certain amount of ridicule. Zeno, a firm adherent of the theory of Parmenides, endeavours to prove it, or at least to demonstrate that it is by no means ridiculous, by the expedient of showing that the pluralism of the Pythagoreans is involved in insoluble difficulties, and that change and motion are impossible even on their pluralistic hypothesis. The arguments of Zeno then are meant to refute the Pythagorean opponents of Parmenides by a series of clever *reductiones ad absurdum*. Plato makes this quite clear in the *Parmenides*, when he indicates the purpose of Zeno's (lost) book. "The truth is that these writings were meant to be some protection to the arguments of Parmenides against those who attack him and show the many ridiculous and contradictory results which they suppose to follow from the affirmation of the one. My writing is an answer to the partisans of the many and it returns their attack with interest, with a view to showing that the hypothesis of the many, if examined sufficiently in detail, leads to even more ridiculous results than the hypothesis of the

One."[1] And Proclus informs us that "Zeno composed forty proofs to demonstrate that being is one, thinking it a good thing to come to the help of his master."[2]

1. *Proofs against Pythagorean Pluralism*

1. Let us suppose with the Pythagoreans that Reality is made up of units. These units are either with magnitude or without magnitude. If the former, then a line for example, as made up of units possessed of magnitude, will be infinitely divisible, since, however far you divide, the units will still have magnitude and so be divisible. But in this case the line will be made up of an infinite number of units, each of which is possessed of magnitude. The line, then, must be infinitely great, as composed of an infinite number of bodies. Everything in the world, then, must be infinitely great, and *a fortiori* the world itself must be infinitely great. Suppose, on the other hand, that the units are without magnitude. In this case the whole universe will also be without magnitude, since, however many units you add together, if none of them has any magnitude, then the whole collection of them will also be without magnitude. But if the universe is without any magnitude, it must be infinitely small. Indeed, everything in the universe must be infinitely small.

The Pythagoreans are thus faced with this dilemma. Either everything in the universe is infinitely great, or everything in the universe is infinitely small. The conclusion which Zeno wishes us to draw from this argument is, of course, that the supposition from which the dilemma flows is an absurd supposition, namely, that the universe and everything in it are composed of units. If the Pythagoreans think that the hypothesis of the One is absurd and leads to ridiculous conclusions, it has now been shown that the contrary hypothesis, that of the many, is productive of equally ridiculous conclusions.[3]

2. If there is a many, then we ought to be able to say *how many* there are. At least, they should be numerable; if they are not numerable, how can they exist? On the other hand, they cannot possibly be numerable, but must be infinite. Why? Because between any two assigned units there will always be other units, just as a line is infinitely divisible. But it is absurd to say that the many are finite in number and infinite in number at the same time.[4]

[1] *Parmen.*, 128 b.
[2] Procl., *in Parmen.*, 694, 23 (D. 29 A 15).
[3] Frags. 1, 2.
[4] Frag. 3.

3. Does a bushel of corn make a noise when it falls to the ground? Clearly. But what of a grain of corn, or the thousandth part of a grain of corn? It makes no noise. But the bushel of corn is composed only of the grains of corn or of the parts of the grains of corn. If, then, the parts make no sound when they fall, how can the whole make a sound, when the whole is composed only of the parts?[1]

II. *Arguments against the Pythagorean Doctrine of Space*

Parmenides denied the existence of the void or empty space, and Zeno tries to support this denial by reducing the opposite view to absurdity. Suppose for a moment that there is a space in which things are. If it is nothing, then things cannot be in it. If, however, it is something, it will itself be in space, and *that* space will itself be in space, and so on indefinitely. But this is an absurdity. Things, therefore, are not in space or in an empty void, and Parmenides was quite right to deny the existence of a void.[2]

III. *Arguments Concerning Motion*

The most celebrated arguments of Zeno are those concerning motion. It should be remembered that what Zeno is attempting to show is this: that motion, which Parmenides denied, is equally impossible on the pluralistic theory of the Pythagoreans.

1. Let us suppose that you want to cross a stadium or race-course. In order to do so, you would have to traverse an infinite number of points—on the Pythagorean hypothesis, that is to say. Moreover, you would have to travel the distance in finite time, if you wanted to get to the other side at all. But how can you traverse an infinite number of points, and so an infinite distance, in a finite time? We must conclude that you *cannot* cross the stadium. Indeed, we must conclude that no object can traverse any distance whatsoever (for the same difficulty always recurs), and that all motion is consequently impossible.[3]

2. Let us suppose that Achilles and a tortoise are going to have a race. Since Achilles is a sportsman, he gives the tortoise a start. Now, by the time that Achilles has reached the place from which the tortoise started, the latter has again advanced to

[1] Arist., *Phys.*, H, 5,250 a 19; Simplic., 1108, 18 (D. 29 A 29).
[2] Arist., *Phys.*, Δ 3,210 b 22; 1,209 a 23. Eudem., *Phys.*, Frag. 42 (D. 29 A 24)
[3] Arist., *Phys.*, Z 9,239 b 9; 2,233 a 21; *Top.*, Θ 8,160 b 7.

another point; and when Achilles reaches *that* point, then the tortoise will have advanced still another distance, even if very short. Thus Achilles is always coming nearer to the tortoise, but never actually overtakes it—and never *can* do so, on the supposition that a line is made up of an infinite number of points, for then Achilles would have to traverse an infinite distance. On the Pythagorean hypothesis, then, Achilles will never catch up the tortoise; and so, although they assert the reality of motion, they make it impossible on their own doctrine. For it follows that the slower moves as fast as the faster.[1]

3. Suppose a moving arrow. According to the Pythagorean theory the arrow should occupy a given position in space. But to occupy a given position in space is to be at rest. Therefore the flying arrow is at rest, which is a contradiction.[2]

4. The fourth argument of Zeno, which we know from Aristotle[3] is, as Sir David Ross says, "very difficult to follow, partly owing to use of ambiguous language by Aristotle, partly owing to doubts as to the readings."[4] We have to represent to ourselves three sets of bodies on a stadium or race-course. One set is stationary, the other two are moving in opposite directions to one another with equal velocity.

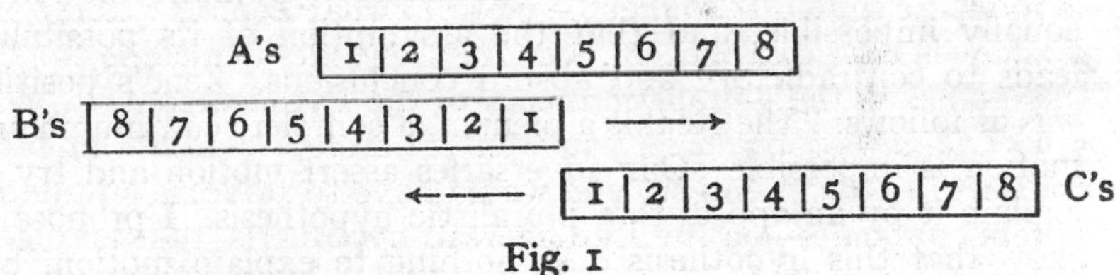

Fig. 1

The A's are stationary; the B's and C's are moving in opposite directions with the same velocity. They will come to occupy the following position:

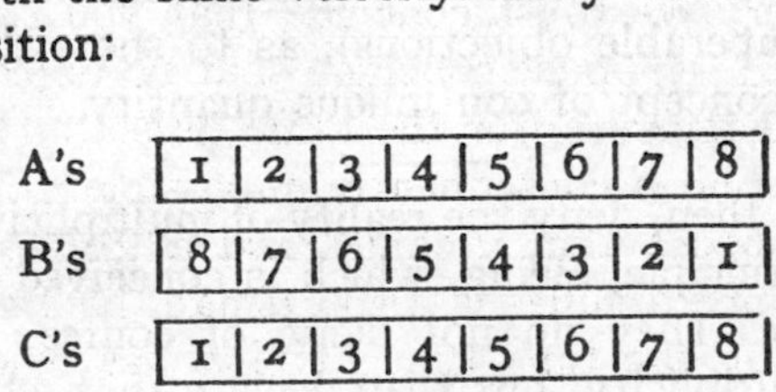

A's	1	2	3	4	5	6	7	8
B's	8	7	6	5	4	3	2	1
C's	1	2	3	4	5	6	7	8

Fig. 2

[1] Arist., *Phys.*, Z 9,239 b 14.
[2] Arist., *Phys.*, Z 9,239 b 30.
[3] Arist., *Phys.*, Z 9,239 b 33.
[4] Ross, *Physics*, p. 660.

In attaining this second position the front of B1 has passed four of the A's, while the front of C1 has passed all the B's. If a unit of length is passed in a unit of time, then the front of B1 has taken half the time taken by the front of C1 in order to reach the position of Fig. 2. On the other hand the front of B1 has passed all the C's, just as the front of C1 has passed all the B's. The time of their passage must then be *equal*. We are left then with the absurd conclusion that the half of a certain time is equal to the whole of that time.

How are we to interpret these arguments of Zeno? It is important not to let oneself think: "These are mere sophistries on the part of Zeno. They are ingenious tricks, but they err by supposing that a line is composed of points and time of discrete moments." It may be that the solution of the riddles is to be found in showing that the line and time are continuous and not discrete; but, then, Zeno was not concerned to hold that they are discrete. On the contrary, he is concerned to show the absurd consequences which flow from supposing that they are discrete. Zeno, as a disciple of Parmenides, believed that motion is an illusion and is impossible, but in the foregoing arguments his aim is to prove that even on the pluralistic hypothesis motion is equally impossible, and that the assumption of its possibility leads to contradictory and absurd conclusions. Zeno's position was as follows: "The Real is a plenum, a complete continuum and motion is impossible. Our adversaries assert motion and try to explain it by an appeal to a pluralistic hypothesis. I propose to show that this hypothesis does nothing to explain motion, but only lands one in absurdities." Zeno thus reduced the hypothesis of his adversaries to absurdity, and the real result of his dialectic was not so much to establish Parmenidean monism (which is exposed to insuperable objections), as to show the necessity of admitting the concept of continuous quantity.

The Eleatics, then, deny the reality of multiplicity and motion. There is one principle, Being, which is conceived of as material and motionless. They do not deny, of course, that we *sense* motion and multiplicity, but they declare that what we sense is illusion: it is mere appearance. True being is to be found, not by sense but by thought, and thought shows that there can be no plurality, no movement, no change.

The Eleatics thus attempt, as the earlier Greek philosophers attempted before them, to discover the one principle of the world. The world, however, as it presents itself to us, is clearly a pluralistic world. The question is, therefore, how to reconcile the one principle with the plurality and change which we find in the world, i.e. the problem of the One and the Many, which Heraclitus had tried to solve in a philosophy that professed to do justice to both elements through a doctrine of Unity in Diversity, Identity in Difference. The Pythagoreans asserted plurality to the practical exclusion of the One—there are many ones; the Eleatics asserted the One to the exclusion of the many. But if you cling to the plurality which is suggested by sense-experience, then you must also admit change; and if you admit change of one thing into another, you cannot avoid the recurring problem as to the character of the common element in the things which change. If, on the other hand, you start with the doctrine of the One, you must—unless you are going to adopt a one-sided position like that of the Eleatics, which cannot last—deduce plurality from the One, or at least show how the plurality which we observe in the world is consistent with the One. In other words, justice must be done to both factors—the One and the Many, Stability and Change. The one-sided doctrine of Parmenides was unacceptable, as also was the one-sided doctrine of the Pythagoreans. Yet the philosophy of Heraclitus was also unsatisfactory. Apart from the fact that it hardly accounted sufficiently for the stable element in things, it was bound up with materialistic monism. Ultimately it was bound to be suggested that the highest and truest being is immaterial. Meanwhile it is not surprising to find what Zeller calls "compromise-systems," trying to weld together the thought of their predecessors.

Note on "Pantheism" in pre-Socratic Greek Philosophy

(i) If a Pantheist is a man who has a subjective religious attitude towards the universe, which latter he identifies with God, then the Pre-Socratics are scarcely to be called pantheists. That Heraclitus speaks of the One as Zeus is true, but it does not appear that he adopted any religious attitude towards the One—Fire.

(ii) If a pantheist is a man who, while denying a Transcendent Principle of the universe, makes the universe to be ultimately *Thought* (unlike the materialist, who makes it Matter alone), then the Pre-Socratics again scarcely merit the name of pantheists, for they conceive or speak of the One in material terms (though it is true that the spirit-matter distinction had not yet been so clearly conceived that they could deny it in the way that the modern materialistic monist denies it).

(iii) In any case the One, the universe, could not be identified with the Greek gods. It has been remarked (by Schelling) that there is no supernatural in Homer, for the Homeric god is part of nature. This remark has its application in the present question. The Greek god was finite and anthropomorphically conceived; he could not possibly be identified with the One, nor would it occur to anyone to do so literally. The *name* of a god might be sometimes transferred to the One, e.g. Zeus, but the one is not to be thought of as identified with the "actual" Zeus of legend and mythology. The suggestion may be that the One is the only "god" there is, and that the Olympian deities are anthropomorphic fables; but even then it seems very uncertain if the philosopher ever *worshipped* the One. Stoics might with justice be called pantheists; but, as far as the early Pre-Socratics are concerned, it seems decidedly preferable to call them monists, rather than pantheists.

CHAPTER VIII

EMPEDOCLES OF AKRAGAS

EMPEDOCLES was a citizen of Akragas, or Agrigentum, in Sicily. His dates cannot be fixed, but it appears that he visited the city of Thurii shortly after its foundation in 444–43 B.C. He took part in the politics of his native city, and seems to have been the leader of the democratic party there. Stories were later circulated about Empedocles' activities as magician and wonder-worker, and there is a story that he was expelled from the Pythagorean Order for "stealing discourses."[1] Apart from thaumaturgic activities, Empedocles contributed to the growth of medicine proper. The death of the philosopher has been made the subject of several entertaining fables, the best known being that he jumped into the crater of Etna in order to make people think that he had gone up to heaven and esteem him as a god. Unfortunately, he left one of his slippers on the brink of the volcano, and, as he used to wear slippers with brazen soles, it was easily recognised.[2] Diogenes, however, who recounts this story, also informs us that "Timaeus contradicts all these stories, saying expressly that he departed into Peloponnesus, and never returned at all, on which account the manner of his death is uncertain."[3] Empedocles, like Parmenides and unlike the other Greek philosophers, expressed his philosophical ideas in poetical writings, more or less extensive fragments of which have come down to us.

Empedocles does not so much produce a new philosophy, as endeavour to weld together and reconcile the thought of his predecessors. Parmenides had held that Being is, and that being is material. Empedocles not only adopted this position, but also the fundamental thought of Parmenides, that being cannot arise or pass away, for being cannot arise from not-being, nor can being pass into not-being. Matter, then, is without beginning and without end; it is indestructible. "Fools!—for they have no far-reaching thoughts—who deem that what before was not comes into being, or that aught can perish and be utterly destroyed. For it cannot be that aught can arise from what in no way is, and

[1] Diog. Laërt., 8, 54.
[2] Diog. Laërt., 8, 69.
[3] Diog. Laërt., 8, 71. (The great Germanic classical poet Hölderlin wrote a poem on the legendary death of Empedocles, also an unfinished poetic play.)

it is impossible and unheard of that what *is* should perish, for it will always *be*, wherever one may keep putting it."[1] And again: "And in the All there is naught empty and naught too full," and "In the All there is naught empty. Whence, then, could aught come to increase it?"[2]

So far, then, Empedocles agrees with Parmenides. But on the other hand, change is a fact which cannot be denied, and the dismissal of change as illusory could not long be maintained. It remained, then, to find a way of reconciling the fact of the existence of change and motion with the principle of Parmenides, that Being—which, be it remembered, is material according to Parmenides—neither comes into being nor passes away. This reconciliation Empedocles tried to effect by means of the principle that objects as wholes begin to be and cease to be—as experience shows they do—but that they are composed of material particles, which are themselves indestructible. There is "only a mingling and interchange of what has been mingled. Substance (Φυσις) is but a name given to these things by men."[3]

Now, though Thales had believed all things to be ultimately water and Anaximenes air, they believed that one kind of matter can become another kind of matter, at least in the sense that, e.g., water becomes earth and air becomes fire. Empedocles, however, interpreting Parmenides' principle of the unchangeability of being in his own way, held that one kind of matter cannot become another kind of matter, but that there are fundamental and eternal kinds of matter or elements—earth, air, fire and water. The familiar classification of the four elements was therefore invented by Empedocles, though he speaks of them, not as elements but as "the roots of all."[4] Earth cannot become water, nor water, earth: the four kinds of matter are unchangeable and ultimate particles, which form the concrete objects of the world by their mingling. So objects come into being through the mingling of the elements, and they cease to be through the separation of the elements: but the elements themselves neither come into being nor pass away, but remain ever unchanged. Empedocles, therefore, saw the only possible way of reconciling the materialistic position of Parmenides with the evident fact of change, the way of postulating a multiplicity of ultimate material particles, and may thus be called a mediator between the system of Parmenides and the evidence of the senses.

[1] Frag. 11. [2] Frag. 14. [3] Frag. 8. [4] Frag. 7 (ἀγένητα i.e. στοιχεῖα).

Now the Ionian philosophers had failed to explain the process of Nature. If everything is composed of air, as Anaximenes thought, how do the objects of our experience come into being? What force is responsible for the cyclical process of Nature? Anaximenes assumed that air transforms itself into other kinds of matter through its own inherent power; but Empedocles saw that it is necessary to postulate active forces. These forces he found in Love and Hate, or Harmony and Discord. In spite of their names, however, the forces are conceived by Empedocles as physical and material forces, Love or Attraction bringing the particles of the four elements together and building up, Strife or Hate separating the particles and causing the cessation of the being of objects.

According to Empedocles the world-process is circular, in the sense that there are periodic world-cycles. At the commencement of a cycle the elements are all mixed up together—not separated out to form concrete objects as we know them—a general mixture of particles of earth, air, fire and water. In this primary stage of the process Love is the governing principle, and the whole is called a "blessed god." Hate, however, is round about the sphere, and when Hate penetrates within the sphere the process of separation, the disuniting of the particles, is begun. Ultimately the separation becomes complete: all the water particles are gathered together, all the fire particles, and so on. Hate reigns supreme, Love having been driven out. Yet Love in turn begins its work, and so causes gradual mingling and uniting of the various elements, this process going on until the element-particles are mixed up together as they were in the beginning. It is then the turn of Hate to start its operations anew. And so the process continues, without first beginning and without last end.[1]

As to the world as we know it, this stands at a stage half-way between the primary sphere and the stage of total separation of the elements: Hate is gradually penetrating the sphere and driving out Love as it does so. As our earth began to be formed out of the sphere, air was the first element to be separated off; this was followed by fire, and then came earth. Water is squeezed out by the rapidity with which the world rotates. The primary sphere, i.e. primary in the cyclical process, not primary in an absolute sense, is described in what appear to us somewhat

[1] This theme of an unending cyclic process reappears in the philosophy of Nietzsche under the name of the Eternal Recurrence.

amusing terms. "There" (i.e. in the sphere) "are distinguished neither the swift limbs of the sun; no, nor the shaggy earth in its might, nor the sea—so fast was the god bound in the close covering of Harmony, spherical and round, rejoicing in his circular solitude."[1] The activity of Love and Strife is illustrated in various ways. "This" (i.e. the contest between them) "is manifest in the mass of mortal limbs. At one time all the limbs that are the body's portion are brought together by Love in blooming life's high season; at another, severed by cruel Strife, they wander each alone by the breakers of life's sea. It is the same with plants and the fish that make their homes in the waters, with the beasts that have their lairs on the hills and the seabirds that sail on wings."[2]

The doctrine of transmigration of souls is taught by Empedocles in the book of the Purifications. He even declares: "For I have already been in the past a boy and a girl, a shrub and a bird and a fish which lives in the sea."[3] It can scarcely be said, however, that this doctrine fits in well with the cosmological system of Empedocles, since, if all things are composed of material particles which separate at death, and if "the blood round the heart is the thought of men,"[4] there is little room left for immortality. But Empedocles may not have realised the discrepancy between his philosophical and religious theories. (Among the latter are certainly some very Pythagorean-sounding prescriptions, such as: "Wretches, utter wretches, keep your hands from beans!")[5]

Aristotle remarks that Empedocles made no distinction between thought and perception. His actual theory of vision is given by Theophrastus, a theory used by Plato in the *Timaeus.*[6] In sense-perception there is a meeting between an element in us and a similar element outside us. All things are constantly giving off effluences, and when the pores of the sense-organs are the right size, then these effluences enter in and perception takes place. In the case of vision, for example, effluences come to the eyes from things; while, on the other hand, the fire from inside the eye (the eye is composed of fire and water, the fire being sheltered from the water by membranes provided with very small pores, which prevent water getting through, but allow fire to get out) goes out to meet the object, the two factors together producing sight.

[1] Frag. 27. [2] Frag. 20. [3] Frag. 117. [4] Frag. 105. [5] Frag. 141.
[6] Arist., *De An.*, 427 a 21. Theoph., *de sensu*, 1 ff. Plat., *Tim.*, cf. 67 c ff. (D. 31 A 86).

In conclusion, we may remind ourselves that Empedocles tried to reconcile the thesis of Parmenides, that being can neither come to be nor pass away, with the evident fact of change by postulating ultimate particles of the four elements, the mingling of which forms the concrete objects of this world and the separation of which constitutes the passing-away of such objects. He failed, however, to explain how the material cyclic process of Nature takes place, but had recourse to mythological forces, Love and Hate. It was left to Anaxagoras to introduce the concept of Mind as the original cause of the world-process.

CHAPTER IX

THE ADVANCE OF ANAXAGORAS

ANAXAGORAS was born at Clazomenae in Asia Minor about 500 B.C., and, although a Greek, he was doubtless a Persian citizen, for Clazomenae had been reduced after the suppression of the Ionian Revolt; and it may even be said that he came to Athens in the Persian Army. If this is so, it would certainly explain why he came to Athens in the year of Salamis, 480/79 B.C. He was the first philosopher to settle in the city, which was later to become such a flourishing centre of philosophic study.[1]

From Plato[2] we learn that the young Pericles was a pupil of Anaxagoras, an association which afterwards got the philosopher into trouble, for after he had resided about thirty years in the city, Anaxagoras was brought to trial by the political opponents of Pericles, i.e. about 450 B.C. Diogenes tells us that the charges were those of impiety (he refers to Sotion) and Medism (referring to Satyros). As to the first charge, Plato relates, it was based on the fact that Anaxagoras taught that the sun is a red-hot stone and the moon is made of earth.[3] These charges were doubtless trumped up, mainly in order to get a hit at Pericles through Anaxagoras. (Pericles' other teacher, Damon, was ostracised.) Anaxagoras was condemned, but was got out of prison, probably by Pericles himself, and he retired to Ionia where he settled at Lampsacus, a colony of Miletus. Here he probably founded a school. The citizens erected a monument to his memory in the market-place (an altar dedicated to Mind and Truth), and the anniversary of his death was long observed as a holiday for school children, at his own request, it is said.

Anaxagoras expressed his philosophy in a book, but only fragments of this remain, and these appear to be confined to the first part of the work. We owe the preservation of the fragments we possess to Simplicius (A.D. sixth century).

. . . . .

Anaxagoras, like Empedocles, accepted the theory of Parmenides that Being neither comes into being nor passes away,

[1] Anax. is said to have had property at Claz. which he neglected in order to follow the theoretic life. Cf. Plato, *Hipp. M.*, 283 a.

[2] *Phaedrus*, 270 a.

[3] *Apol.*, 26 d.

but is unchangeable. "The Hellenes do not understand rightly coming into being and passing away, for nothing comes into being or passes away, but there is a mingling and a separation of things which are" (i.e. persist).[1] Both thinkers, then, are in agreement as to the indestructibility of matter, and both reconcile this theory with the evident fact of change by positing indestructible material particles, the mingling of which forms objects, the separation of which explains the passing away of objects. But Anaxagoras will not agree with Empedocles that the ultimate units are particles corresponding to the four elements—earth, air, fire and water. He teaches that everything which has parts qualitatively the same as the whole is ultimate and underived. Aristotle calls these wholes, which have qualitatively similar parts, τὰ ὁμοιομερῆ; τὸ ὁμοιομερές being opposed to τὸ ἀνομοιομερές. This distinction is not difficult to grasp if one takes an example. If we suppose that a piece of gold is cut in half, the halves are themselves gold. The parts are thus qualitatively the same as the whole, and the whole can be said to be ὁμοιομερές. If, however, a dog, a living organism, be cut in half, the halves are not themselves two dogs. The whole is in this case therefore ἀνομοιομερές. The general notion is thus clear, and it is unnecessary to confuse the issue by introducing considerations from modern scientific experiment. Some things have qualitatively similar parts, and such things are ultimate and underived (as regards *kind*, that is to say, for no given conglomeration of particles is ultimate and underived). "How can hair come from what is not hair, or flesh from what is not flesh?" asks Anaxagoras.[2] But it does not follow that everything which seems to be ὁμοιομερές is really so. Thus it is related by Aristotle that Anaxagoras did not hold Empedocles' elements—earth, air, fire and water—to be really ultimate; on the contrary, they are mixtures composed of many qualitatively different particles.[3]

In the beginning, particles—there is no indivisible particle, according to Anaxagoras—of all kinds were mingled together. "All things were together, infinite both in number and in smallness; for the small too was infinite. And, when all things were together, none of them could be distinguished for their smallness."[4] "All things are in the whole." The objects of experience arise, when ultimate particles have been so brought together that

[1] Frag. 17.
[2] Frag. 10.
[3] *De Gen. et corr.*, Γ, 1, 314 a 24. *De Caelo*, Γ, 3, 302 a 28.
[4] Frag. 1

in the resulting object particles of a certain kind predominate. Thus in the original mixture particles of gold were scattered about and mixed with all sorts of other particles; but when particles of gold have been so brought together—with other particles—that the resultant visible object consists predominantly of gold-particles, we have the gold of our experience. Why do we say "with other particles"? Because in concrete objects of experience there are, according to Anaxagoras, particles of *all* things; yet they are combined in such a way that one kind of particle predominates and from this fact the whole object gets its denomination. Anaxagoras held the doctrine that "in everything there is a portion of everything,"[1] apparently because he did not see how he could otherwise explain the fact of change. For instance, if grass becomes flesh, there must have been particles of flesh in the grass (for how can "flesh" come "from what is not flesh"?), while on the other hand in the grass the grass-particles must predominate. Grass, therefore, consists predominantly of grass, but it also contains other kinds of particles, for "in everything there is a portion of everything," and "the things that are in one world are not divided nor cut off from one another with a hatchet, neither the warm from the cold nor the cold from the warm."[2] In this way Anaxagoras sought to maintain the Parmenidean doctrine concerning being, while at the same time adopting a realist attitude towards change, not dismissing it as an illusion of the senses but accepting it as a fact, and then trying to reconcile it with the Eleatic theory of being. Later on Aristotle would attempt to solve the difficulties raised by the doctrine of Parmenides in regard to change by means of his distinction between potency and act.

Burnet does not think that Anaxagoras considered, as the Epicureans supposed him to, "that there must be minute particles in bread and water which were like the particles of blood, flesh and bones."[3] In his opinion it was of the opposites, the warm and the cold, the dry and the moist, that everything contained a portion according to Anaxagoras. Burnet's view has certainly much to support it. We have already seen the fragment in which Anaxagoras declares that "the things that are in one world are not cut off from one another with a hatchet, neither the warm from the cold, nor the cold from the warm." Moreover, since according to Anaxagoras, there are no indivisible particles, there

[1] Frag. 11. [2] Frag. 8. [3] *G.P.*, I., pp. 77–8.

cannot be any ultimate particles in the sense of what cannot be further divided. But it would not seem to follow necessarily from the indivisibility of the particles that, in the philosopher's opinion, there were no ultimate *kinds* which could not be qualitatively resolved. And does not Anaxagoras explicitly ask how hair can come from what is not hair? In addition to this we read in fragment 4 of the mixture of all things—"of the moist and the dry, and the warm and the cold, and the bright and the dark, and of much earth that was in it, and a multitude of innumerable seeds in no way like each other. For none of the other things either is like any other. And these things being so, we must hold that all things are in the whole." This fragment scarcely gives the impression that the "opposites" stand in any peculiar position of privilege. While admitting, therefore, that Burnet's view has much to be said for it, we prefer the interpretation already given in the text.[1]

So far Anaxagoras' philosophy is a variant from Empedocles' interpretation and adaptation of Parmenides, and offers no particularly valuable features. But when we come to the question of the power or force that is responsible for the forming of things out of the first mass, we arrive at the peculiar contribution of Anaxagoras to philosophy. Empedocles had attributed motion in the universe to the two physical forces of Love and Strife, but Anaxagoras introduces instead the principle of Nous or Mind. 'With Anaxagoras a light, if still a weak one, begins to dawn, because the understanding is now recognised as the principle."[2] "Nous," says Anaxagoras, "has power over all things that have life, both greater and smaller. And Nous had power over the whole revolution, so that it began to revolve at the start. . . . And Nous set in order all things that were to be, and all things that were and are now and that will be, and this revolution in which now revolve the stars and the sun and the moon and the air and the aether which are separated off. And the revolution itself caused the separating off, and the dense is separated off from the rare, the warm from the cold, the bright from the dark, and the dry from the moist. And there are many portions in many things. But no thing is altogether separated off from anything else except Nous. And all Nous is alike, both the greater and the smaller; but nothing else is like anything else, but each

[1] Cf. Zeller, *Outlines*, p. 62; Stace, *Crit. Hist.*, pp. 95 ff.; Covotti, *I Presocratici*, ch. 21.

[2] Hegel, *Hist. Phil.*, I, p. 319.

single thing is and was most manifestly those things of which there are most in it."[1]

Nous "is infinite and self-ruled, and is mixed with nothing, but is alone, itself by itself."[2] How then did Anaxagoras conceive of Nous? He calls it "the finest of all things and the purest, and it has all knowledge about everything and the greatest power . . ." He also speaks of Nous being "there where everything else is, in the surrounding mass."[3] The philosopher thus speaks of Nous or Mind in material terms as being "the thinnest of all things," and as occupying space. On the strength of this Burnet declares that Anaxagoras never rose above the conception of a corporeal principle. He made Nous purer than other material things, but never reached the idea of an immaterial or incorporeal thing. Zeller will not allow this, and Stace points out how "all philosophy labours under the difficulty of having to express non-sensuous thought in language which has been evolved for the purpose of expressing sensuous ideas."[4] If we speak of a mind as "clear" or as someone's mind as being "greater" than that of another, we are not on that account to be called materialists. That Anaxagoras conceived of Nous as occupying space is not sufficient proof that he would have declared Nous to be corporeal, had he ever conceived the notion of a sharp distinction between mind and matter. The non-spatiality of the mind is a later conception. Probably the most satisfactory interpretation is that Anaxagoras, in his concept of the spiritual, did not succeed in grasping clearly the radical difference between the spiritual and the corporeal. But that is not the same as saying that he was a *dogmatic* materialist. On the contrary, he first introduces a spiritual and intellectual principle, though he fails to understand fully the essential difference between that principle and the matter which it forms or sets in motion.

Nous is present in all living things, men, animals and plants, and is the same in all. Differences between these objects are due, then, not to essential differences between their souls, but to differences between their bodies, which facilitate or handicap the fuller working of Nous. (Anaxagoras, however, does not explain the human consciousness of independent selfhood.)

Nous is not to be thought of as *creating* matter. Matter is eternal, and the function of Nous seems to be to set the rotatory movement or vortex going in part of the mixed mass, the action

[1] Frag. 12. [2] Frag. 12. [3] Frag. 14. [4] *Crit. Hist.*, p. 99.

of the vortex itself, as it spreads, accounting for the subsequent motion. Thus Aristotle, who says in the *Metaphysics* that Anaxagoras "stood out like a sober man from the random talkers that had preceded him,"[1] also says that "Anaxagoras uses Mind as a *deus ex machina* to account for the formation of the world; and whenever he is at a loss to explain why anything necessarily is, he drags it in. But in other cases he makes anything rather than Mind the cause."[2] We can easily understand, then, the disappointment of Socrates who, thinking that he had come upon an entirely new approach when he discovered Anaxagoras, found "my extravagant expectations were all dashed to the ground when I went on and found that the man made no use of Mind at all. He ascribed no causal power whatever to it in the ordering of things, but to airs, and aethers, and waters, and a host of other strange things."[3] Nevertheless, though he failed to make full use of the principle, Anaxagoras must be credited with the introduction into Greek philosophy of a principle possessed of the greatest importance, that was to bear splendid fruit in the future.

[1] *Metaph.*, A 3, 984 b 15–18. [2] *Metaph.*, A 4, 985 a 18–21.
[3] *Phaedo*, 97 b 8.

CHAPTER X

THE ATOMISTS

THE founder of the Atomist School was Leucippus of Miletus. It has been maintained that Leucippus never existed,[1] but Aristotle and Theophrastus make him to be the founder of the Atomist philosophy, and we can hardly suppose that they were mistaken. It is not possible to fix his dates, but Theophrastus declares that Leucippus had been a member of the School of Parmenides, and we read in Diogenes' *Life of Leucippus* that he was a disciple of Zeno (οὗτος ἤκουσε Ζήνωνος). It appears that the *Great Diakosmos*, subsequently incorporated in the works of Democritus of Abdera, was really the work of Leucippus, and no doubt Burnet is quite right when he compares the Democritean *corpus* with the Hippocritean, and remarks that in neither case can we distinguish the authors of the various component treatises.[2] The whole *corpus* is the work of a School, and it is most unlikely that we shall ever be in a position to assign each work to its respective author. In treating of the Atomist philosophy, therefore, we cannot pretend to distinguish between what is due to Leucippus and what is due to Democritus. But since Democritus is of considerably later date and cannot with historical accuracy be classed among the Pre-Socratics, we will leave to a later chapter his doctrine of sense-perception, by which he attempted to answer Protagoras, and his theory of human conduct. Some historians of philosophy, indeed, treat of Democritus' views on these points when dealing with the Atomist philosophy in the section devoted to the Pre-Socratics, but in view of the undoubtedly later date of Democritus, it seems preferable to follow Burnet in this matter.

The Atomist philosophy is really the logical development of the philosophy of Empedocles. The latter had tried to reconcile the Parmenidean principle of the denial of the passage of being into not-being or vice versa, with the evident fact of change by postulating four elements which, mixed together in various proportions, form the objects of our experience. He did not, however, really work out his doctrine of particles, nor did he

[1] Epicurus, for instance, denied his existence, but it has been suggested that this denial was due to Epicurus' determination to claim originality.

[2] *E.G.P.*, p. 331.

carry the quantitative explanation of qualitative differences to its logical conclusion. The philosophy of Empedocles formed a transitional stage to the explanation of all qualitative differences by a mechanical juxtaposition of material particles in various patterns. Moreover, Empedocles' forces—Love and Strife—were metaphorical powers, which would have to be eliminated in a thorough-going mechanical philosophy. The final step to complete mechanism was attempted by the Atomists.

According to Leucippus and Democritus there are an infinite number of indivisible units, which are called atoms. These are imperceptible, since they are too small to be perceived by the senses. The atoms differ in size and shape, but have no quality save that of solidity or impenetrability. Infinite in number, they move in the void. (Parmenides had denied the reality of space. The Pythagoreans had admitted a void to keep their units apart, but they identified it with the atmospheric air, which Empedocles showed to be corporeal. Leucippus, however, affirmed at the same time the non-reality of space and its existence, meaning by non-reality, non-corporeity. This position is expressed by saying that "what is not" is just as much real as "what is." Space, then, or the void, is not corporeal, but it is as real as body.) The later Epicureans held that the atoms all move downwards in the void through the force of *weight*, probably influenced by Aristotle's idea of absolute weight and lightness. (Aristotle says that none of his predecessors had held this notion.) Now Aëtius expressly says that while Democritus ascribed size and shape to the atoms, he did not ascribe to them weight, but that Epicurus added weight in order to account for the movement of the atoms.[1] Cicero relates the same, and also declares that according to Democritus there was no "top" or "bottom" or "middle" in the void.[2] If this is what Democritus held, then he was of course quite right, for there is no absolute up or down; but how in this case did he conceive the motion of the atoms? In the *De Anima*[3] Aristotle attributes to Democritus a comparison between the motions of the atoms of the soul and the motes in a sunbeam, which dart hither and thither in all directions, even when there is no wind. It may be that this was also the Democritean view of the original motion of the atoms.

However, in whatever way the atoms originally moved in the

[1] Aët., i, 3, 18 and 12, 6 (D. 68 A 47).
[2] *De Fato*, 20, 46 and *De Fin.*, i, 6, 17 (D. 68 A 47 and 56).
[3] *De An.*, A, 2, 403 b 28 ff.

void, at some point of time collisions between atoms occurred, those of irregular shape becoming entangled with one another and forming groups of atoms. In this way the vortex (Anaxagoras) is set up, and a world is in process of formation. Whereas Anaxagoras thought that the larger bodies would be driven farthest from the centre, Leucippus said the opposite, believing, wrongly, that in an eddy of wind or water the larger bodies tend towards the centre. Another effect of the movement in the void is that atoms which are alike in size and shape are brought together as a sieve brings together the grains of millet, wheat and barley, or the waves of the sea heap up together long stones with long and round with round. In this way are formed the four "elements"—fire, air, earth and water. Thus innumerable worlds arise from the collisions among the infinite atoms moving in the void.

It is at once noticeable that neither Empedocles' forces, Love and Strife, nor the Nous of Anaxagoras appear in the Atomist philosophy: Leucippus evidently did not consider any moving force to be a necessary hypothesis. In the beginning existed atoms in the void, and that was all: from that beginning arose the world of our experience, and no external Power or moving Force is assumed as a necessary cause for the primal motion. Apparently the early cosmologists did not think of motion as requiring any explanation, and in the Atomist philosophy the eternal movement of the atoms is regarded as self-sufficient. Leucippus speaks of everything happening ἐκ λόγου καὶ ὑπ' ἀνάγκης[1] and this might at first sight appear inconsistent with his doctrine of the unexplained original movement of the atoms and of the collisions of the atoms. The latter, however, occur necessarily owing to the configuration of the atoms and their irregular movements, while the former, as a self-sufficient fact, did not require further explanation. To us, indeed, it may well seem strange to deny chance and yet to posit an eternal unexplained motion—Aristotle blames the Atomists for not explaining the source of motion and the kind of motion[2]—but we ought not to conclude that Leucippus meant to ascribe the motion of the atoms to *chance*: to him the eternal motion and the continuation of motion required no explanation. In our opinion, the mind boggles at such a theory and cannot rest content with Leucippus' ultimate; but it is an interesting

[1] Frag. 2 (Aët., I, 25, 4).
[2] *Phys.*, Θ i, 252 a 32; *De Caelo*, Γ 2, 300 b 8; *Metaph.*, A, 4, 985 b 19–20.

historical fact, that he himself was content with this ultimate and sought no "First Unmoved Mover."

It is to be noted that the atoms of Leucippus and Democritus are the Pythagorean monads endowed with the properties of Parmenidean being—for each is as the Parmenidean One. And inasmuch as the elements arise from the various arrangements and positions of the atoms, they may be likened to the Pythagorean "numbers," if the latter are to be regarded as patterns or "figurate numbers." This can be the only sense to be attached to Aristotle's dictum that "Leucippus and Democritus virtually make all things number too and produce them from numbers."[1]

In his detailed scheme of the world, Leucippus was somewhat reactionary, rejecting the Pythagorean view of the spherical character of the earth and returning, like Anaxagoras, to the view of Anaximenes, that the earth is like a tambourine floating in the air. But, though the details of the Atomist cosmology do not indicate any new advance, Leucippus and Democritus are noteworthy for having carried previous tendencies to their logical conclusion, producing a purely mechanical account and explanation of reality. The attempt to give a complete explanation of the world in terms of mechanical materialism has, as we all know, reappeared in a much more thorough form in the modern era under the influence of physical science, but the brilliant hypothesis of Leucippus and Democritus was by no means the last word in Greek philosophy: subsequent Greek philosophers were to see that the richness of the world cannot in all its spheres be reduced to the mechanical interplay of atoms.

[1] *De Caelo*, Γ 4, 303 a 8.

CHAPTER XI

PRE-SOCRATIC PHILOSOPHY

1. It is often said that Greek philosophy centres round the problem of the One and the Many. Already in the very earliest stages of Greek philosophy we find the notion of unity: things change into one another—therefore there must be some common substratum, some ultimate principle, some unity underlying diversity. Thales declares that water is that common principle, Anaximenes air, Heraclitus fire: they choose different principles, but they all three believe in one ultimate principle. But although the fact of change—what Aristotle called "substantial" change—may have suggested to the early Cosmologists the notion of an underlying unity in the universe, it would be a mistake to reduce this notion to a conclusion of physical science. As far as strict scientific proof goes, they had not sufficient data to warrant their assertion of unity, still less to warrant the assertion of any particular ultimate principle, whether water, fire or air. The fact is, that the early Cosmologists leapt beyond the data to the intuition of universal unity: they possessed what we might call the power of metaphysical intuition, and this constitutes their glory and their claim to a place in the history of philosophy. If Thales had contented himself with saying that out of water earth is evolved, "we should," as Nietzsche observes, "only have a scientific hypothesis: a false one, though nevertheless difficult to refute." But Thales went beyond a mere scientific hypothesis: he reached out to a metaphysical doctrine, expressed in the metaphysical doctrine, that *Everything is One.*

Let me quote Nietzsche again. "Greek philosophy seems to begin with a preposterous fancy, with the proposition that *water* is the origin and mother-womb of all things. Is it really necessary to stop there and become serious? Yes, and for three reasons: Firstly, because the proposition does enunciate something about the origin of things; secondly, because it does so without figure and fable; thirdly and lastly, because in it is contained, although only in the chrysalis state, the idea—Everything is one. The first-mentioned reason leaves Thales still in the company of religious and superstitious people; the second, however, takes him out of this company and shows him to us as a natural philosopher; but by virtue of the third, Thales becomes the first Greek philosopher."[1] This holds true of the other early Cosmologists; men like Anaximenes and Heraclitus also took wing and flew above and beyond what could be verified by mere empirical observation. At the same time they were not content with any mythological assumption, for they sought a real principle of unity, the ultimate substrate of change: what they asserted, they asserted in all seriousness. They had the notion of a world that was a whole, a system, of a world governed by law. Their assertions were dictated by reason or thought, not by mere imagination or mythology; and so they deserve to count as philosophers, the first philosophers of Europe.

2. But though the early Cosmologists were inspired by the idea of cosmic unity, they were faced by the fact of the Many, of multiplicity, of diversity, and they had to attempt the theoretical reconciliation of this evident plurality with the postulated unity —in other words, they had to account for the world as we know it. While Anaximenes, for example, had recourse to the principle of condensation and rarefaction, Parmenides, in the grip of his great theory that Being is one and changeless, roundly denied the facts of change and motion and multiplicity as illusions of the senses. Empedocles postulated four ultimate elements, out of which all things are built up under the action of Love and Strife, and Anaxagoras maintained the ultimate character of the atomic theory and the quantitative explanation of qualitative difference, thus doing justice to plurality, to the many, while tending to relinquish the earlier vision of unity, in spite of the fact that each atom represents the Parmenidean One.

We may say, therefore, that while the Pre-Socratics struggled with the problem of the One and the Many, they did not succeed in solving it. The Heraclitean philosophy contains, indeed, the profound notion of unity in diversity, but it is bound up with an over-assertion of Becoming and the difficulties consequent on the doctrine of Fire. The Pre-Socratics accordingly failed to solve the problem, and it was taken up again by Plato and Aristotle, who brought to bear on it their outstanding talent and genius.

3. But if the problem of the One and the Many continued to exercise Greek philosophy in the Post-Socratic period, and received much more satisfactory solutions at the hands of Plato

[1] *Philosophy during the Tragic Age of the Greeks*, in sect. 3.

and Aristotle, it is obvious that we cannot characterise Pre-Socratic philosophy by reference to that problem: we require some other note of characterisation and distinction. Where is it to be found? We may say that Pre-Socratic philosophy centres round the external world, the Object, the not-self. Man, the Subject, the self, is of course not excluded from consideration, but the interest in the not-self is predominant. This can be seen from the question which the successive Pre-Socratic thinkers set themselves to answer: "Of what is the world ultimately composed?" In their answers to this question the early Ionian philosophers certainly went beyond what the empirical data warranted, but, as already remarked, they tackled the question in a philosophic spirit and not in the spirit of weavers of mythological fancies. They had not differentiated between physical science and philosophy, and combined "scientific" observations of a purely practical character with philosophic speculations; but it must be remembered that a differentiation between physical science and philosophy was hardly possible at that early stage—men wanted to know something more about the world, and it was but natural that scientific questions and philosophical questions should be mingled together. Since they were concerned with the *ultimate* nature of the world, their theories rank as philosophical; but since they had not yet formed any clear distinction between spirit and matter, and since their question was largely prompted by the fact of material change, their answer was couched for the most part in terms and concepts taken from matter. They found the ultimate "stuff" of the universe to be some kind of matter—naturally enough—whether the water of Thales, the Indeterminate of Anaximander, the air of Anaximenes, the fire of Heraclitus, or the atoms of Leucippus, and so a large part of their subject-matter would be claimed by physical scientists of to-day as belonging to their province.

The early Greek philosophers are then rightly called Cosmologists, for they were concerned with the nature of the Cosmos, the object of our knowledge, and man himself is considered in his objective aspect, as one item in the Cosmos, rather than in his subjective aspect, as the subject of knowledge or as the morally willing and acting subject. In their consideration of the Cosmos, they did not reach any final conclusion accounting for all the factors involved; and this apparent bankruptcy of Cosmology, together with other causes to be considered presently, naturally led to a swing-over of interest from Object to Subject, from the Cosmos to Man himself. This change of interest, as exemplified in the Sophists, we will consider in the following section of this book.

4. Although it is true that Pre-Socratic philosophy centres round the Cosmos, the external world, and that this cosmological interest is the distinguishing mark of Pre-Socratic as contrasted with Socratic philosophy, it must also be remarked that one problem at any rate connected with man as the knowing subject was raised in Pre-Socratic philosophy, that of the relation between sense-experience and reason. Thus Parmenides, starting with the notion of the One, and finding himself unable to explain coming-to-be and passing-away—which are given in sense-experience—set aside the evidence of the senses as illusion, and proclaimed the sole validity of reason, which alone is able to attain the Real and Abiding. But the problem was not treated in any full or adequate manner, and when Parmenides denied the validity of sense-perception, he did so because of a metaphysical doctrine or assumption, rather than from any prolonged consideration of the nature of sense-perception and the nature of non-sensuous thought.

5. Since the early Greek thinkers may justly be termed philosophers, and since they proceeded largely by way of action and reaction, or thesis and antithesis (e.g. Heraclitus over-emphasising Becoming and Parmenides over-stressing Being), it was only to be expected that the germs of later philosophical tendencies and Schools would already be discernible in Pre-Socratic philosophy. Thus in the Parmenidean doctrine of the One, when coupled with the exaltation of Reason at the expense of sense-perception, we can see the germs of later idealism; while in the introduction of Nous by Anaxagoras—however restricted his actual use of Nous may have been—we may see the germs of later philosophical theism; and in the atomism of Leucippus and Democritus we may see an anticipation of later materialistic and mechanistic philosophies which would endeavour to explain all quality by quantity and to reduce everything in the universe to matter and its products.

6. From what has been said, it should be clear that Pre-Socratic philosophy is not simply a pre-philosophic stage which can be discounted in a study of Greek thought—so that we should be justified in starting immediately with Socrates and Plato. The Pre-Socratic philosophy is *not* a pre-philosophic stage, but is the

first stage of Greek philosophy: it may not be pure and unmixed philosophy, but it is philosophy, and it deserves to be studied for the sake of its own intrinsic interest as the first Greek attempt to attain a rational understanding of the world. Moreover, it is not a self-contained unit, shut off from succeeding philosophic thought in a watertight compartment; rather is it preparatory to the succeeding period, for in it we see problems raised which were to occupy the greatest of Greek philosophers. Greek thought develops, and though we can hardly over-estimate the native genius of men like Plato and Aristotle, it would be wrong to imagine that they were uninfluenced by the past. Plato was profoundly influenced by Pre-Socratic thought, by the Heraclitean, Eleatic and Pythagorean systems; Aristotle regarded his philosophy as the heir and crown of the past; and both thinkers took up philosophic problems from the hands of their predecessors, giving, it is true, original solutions, but at the same time tackling the problems in their historic setting. It would be absurd, therefore, to start a history of Greek philosophy with a discussion of Socrates and Plato without any discussion of preceding thought, for we cannot understand Socrates or Plato—or Aristotle either—without a knowledge of the past.

We must now turn to the next phase of Greek philosophy, which may be considered the antithesis to the preceding period of Cosmological speculation—the Sophistic and Socratic period.

PART II

THE SOCRATIC PERIOD

CHAPTER XII

THE SOPHISTS

THE earlier Greek philosophers had been chiefly interested in the Object, trying to determine the ultimate principle of all things. Their success, however, did not equal their philosophic sincerity, and the successive hypotheses that they advanced easily led to a certain scepticism as to the possibility of attaining any certain knowledge concerning the ultimate nature of the world. Add to this that doctrines such as those of Heraclitus and Parmenides would naturally result in a sceptical attitude in regard to the validity of sense-perception. If being is static and the perception of movement is an illusion, or if, on the other hand, all is in a state of constant change and there is no real principle of stability, our sense-perception is untrustworthy, and so the very foundations of Cosmology are undermined. The systems of philosophy hitherto proposed excluded one another: there was naturally truth to be found in the opposing theories, but no philosopher had yet arisen of sufficient stature to reconcile the antitheses in a higher synthesis, in which error should be purged away and justice done to the truth contained in rival doctrines. The result was bound to be a certain mistrust of cosmologies. And, indeed, a swing-over to the Subject as point of consideration was necessary if real advance was to be made. It was Plato's consideration of thought that made possible a truer theory in which justice should be done to the facts of both stability and mutability; but the reaction from Object to Subject, which made possible the advance, first appears among the Sophists, and was largely an effect of the bankruptcy of the older Greek philosophy. In face of the dialectic of Zeno, it might well appear doubtful if advance in the study of cosmology was really possible.

Another factor besides the scepticism consequent on the former Greek philosophy, which directed attention to the Subject, was the growing reflection on the phenomena of culture and civilisation, due in large part to extended acquaintance on the part of the Greeks with foreign peoples. Not only did they know something of the civilisations of Persia, Babylon and Egypt, but they had also come into contact with people of a much less advanced stage, such as the Scythians and Thracians. This being so, it was but natural that a highly intelligent people like the Greeks should begin to ask themselves questions; e.g. Are the various national and local ways of life, religious and ethical codes, merely conventions or not? Was Hellenic culture, as contrasted with non-Hellenic or barbarian cultures, a matter of νόμος, man-made and mutable, existing νόμῳ, or did it rest on Nature, existing Φύσει? Was it a sacred ordinance, having divine sanction, or could it be changed, modified, adapted, developed? Professor Zeller points out in this connection how Protagoras, most gifted of the Sophists, came from Abdera, "an advanced outpost of Ionic culture in the land of the Thracian barbarian."[1]

Sophism,[2] then, differed from the older Greek philosophy in regard to the matter with which it dealt, namely, man and the civilisation and customs of man: it treated of the microcosm rather than the macrocosm. Man was becoming self-conscious: as Sophocles says, "Miracles in the world are many, there is no greater miracle than man."[3] But Sophism also differed from previous Greek philosophy in its *method*. Although the method of the older Greek philosophy by no means excluded empirical observation, yet it was characteristically deductive. When a philosopher had settled on his general principle of the world, its ultimate constituent principle, it then remained to explain particular phenomena in accordance with that theory. The Sophist, however, sought to amass a wide store of particular observations and facts; they were Encyclopaedists, Polymaths. Then from these accumulated facts they proceeded to draw conclusions, partly theoretical, partly practical. Thus from the store of facts they accumulated concerning differences of opinion and belief, they might draw the conclusion that it is impossible to have any certain knowledge. Or from their knowledge of various nations and ways of life, they might form a theory as to the origin of civilisation or the beginning of language. Or again they might

[1] *Outlines*, p. 76.

[2] In using the term "Sophism" I do not mean to imply that there was any Sophistic system: the men whom we know as the Greek Sophists differed widely from one another in respect both of ability and of opinions: they represent a trend or movement, not a school.

[3] *Antigone*, 332 ff.

draw practical conclusions, e.g. that society would be most efficiently organised if it were organised in this or that manner. The method of Sophism, then, was "empirico-inductive."[1]

It is to be remembered, however, that the practical conclusions of the Sophists were not meant to establish objective norms, founded on necessary truth. And this fact points to another difference between Sophism and the older Greek philosophy, namely, difference of end. The latter was concerned with objective truth: the Cosmologists wanted to find out the objective truth about the world, they were in the main disinterested seekers after truth. The Sophists, on the other hand, were not primarily intent on objective truth: their end was practical and not speculative. And so the Sophists became instruments of instruction and training in the Greek cities, aiming at teaching the art and control of life. It has been remarked that while a band of disciples was more or less accidental for the Pre-Socratic philosophers—since their primary aim was *finding out* the truth—it was essential for the Sophists, since they aimed at *teaching*.

In Greece, after the Persian Wars, political life was naturally intensified, and this was particularly the case in democratic Athens. The free citizen played some part, at any rate, in political life, and if he wanted to get on he obviously had to have some kind of training. The old education was insufficient for the man who wished to make his way in the State; the old aristocratic ideal was, whether intrinsically superior to the new ideals or not, incapable of meeting the demands made on leaders in the developing democracy: something more was needed, and this need was met by the Sophists. Plutarch says that the Sophists put a theoretical training in the place of the older practical training, which was largely an affair of family tradition, connection with prominent statesmen, practical and experiential training by actual participation in political life. What was now required was courses of instruction, and the Sophists gave such courses in the cities. They were itinerant professors who travelled about from city to city, thus gathering a valuable store of knowledge and experience, and they gave instruction on various themes—grammar, the interpretation of poets, the philosophy of mythology and religion, and so on. But, above all, they professed to teach the art of *Rhetoric*, which was absolutely necessary for political life. In the Greek city-state, above all at Athens, no one could hope to make

[1] Zeller, *Outlines*, p. 77.

his mark as a politician unless he could speak, and speak well. The Sophists professed to teach him to do so, training him in the chief expression of political "virtue," the virtue of the new aristocracy of intellect and ability. There was, of course, nothing wrong in this in itself, but the obvious consequence—that the art of rhetoric might be used to "get across" a notion or policy which was not disinterested or might be definitely harmful to the city or merely calculated to promote the politician's career—helped to bring the Sophists into bad repute. This was particularly the case with regard to their teaching of Eristic. If a man wanted to make money in the Greek democracy, it had to be done mainly by lawsuits, and the Sophists professed to teach the right way of winning these lawsuits. But clearly that might easily mean in practice the art of teaching men how to make the unjust appear the just cause. Such a procedure was obviously very different from the procedure of the old truth-seeking attitude of the philosophers, and helps to explain the treatment meted out to the Sophists at the hands of Plato.

The Sophists carried on their work of instruction by the education of the young and by giving popular lectures in the cities; but as they were itinerant professors, men of wide experience and representative of a, as yet, somewhat sceptical and superficial reaction, the idea became current that they gathered together the young men from their homes and then pulled to pieces before them the traditional ethical code and religious beliefs. Accordingly the strict adherents of tradition regarded the Sophists with some suspicion, though the young were their enthusiastic supporters. Not that the levelling-out tendencies of the Sophists were all weakening to Greek life: their breadth of view generally made them advocates of Panhellenism, a doctrine sorely needed in the Greece of the city-state. But it was their sceptical tendencies that attracted most attention, especially as they did not put anything really new and stable in place of the old convictions which they tended to unsettle. To this should be added the fact that they took payment for the instruction which they imparted. This practice, however legitimate in itself, was at variance with the practice of the older Greek philosophers, and did not agree with the Greek opinion of what was fitting. It was abhorrent to Plato, while Xenophon says that the Sophists speak and write to deceive for their gain, and they give no help to anyone.[1]

[1] Xen., *Cyneg.*, 13, 8 (D. 79, 2 a).

From what has been said, it is clear that Sophism does not deserve any sweeping condemnation. By turning the attention of thinkers to man himself, the thinking and willing subject, it served as a transition stage to the great Platonic-Aristotelian achievement. In affording a means of training and instruction, it fulfilled a necessary task in the political life of Greece, while its Panhellenistic tendencies certainly stand to its credit. And even its sceptical and relativist tendencies, which were, after all, largely the result of the breakdown of the older philosophy on the one hand, and of a wider experience of human life on the other, at least contributed to the raising of problems, even if Sophism itself was unable to solve these problems. It is not fanciful to discern the influence of Sophism in the Greek drama, e.g. in Sophocles' hymn to human achievement in the *Antigone* and in the theoretical discussions contained in plays of Euripides, and in the works of the Greek historians, e.g. in the celebrated Melian dialogue in the pages of Thucydides. The term Σοφιστής took some time to acquire its disparaging connotation. The name is applied by Herodotus to Solon and Pythagoras, by Androtion to the Seven Wise Men and to Socrates, by Lysias to Plato. Moreover, the older Sophists won for themselves general respect and esteem, and, as historians have pointed out, were not infrequently selected as "ambassadors" of their respective cities, a fact which hardly points to their being or being regarded as charlatans. It was only secondarily that the term "Sophist" acquired an unsavoury flavour—as in Plato; and in later times the term seems to have reacquired a good sense, being applied to the professors of rhetoric and prose writers of the Empire, without the significance of quibbler or cheat. "It is particularly through the opposition to Socrates and Plato that the Sophists have come into such disrepute that the word now usually signifies that, by false reasoning, some truth is either refuted and made dubious, or sometning false is proved and made plausible."[1]

On the other hand, the relativism of the Sophists, their encouragement of Eristic, their lack of stable norms, their acceptance of payment, and the hair-splitting tendencies of certain later Sophists, justify to a great extent the disparaging signification of the term. For Plato, they are "shopkeepers with spiritual wares";[2] and when Socrates is represented in the *Protagoras*[3] as asking Hippocrates, who wanted to receive instruction from

[1] Hegel, *Hist. Phil.*, I, p. 354. [2] *Protag.*, 313 c 5–6. [3] *Protag.*, 312 a 4–7.

Protagoras, "Wouldn't you be ashamed to show yourself to the Greeks as a Sophist?", Hippocrates answers: "Yes, truly, Socrates, if I am to say what I think." We must, however, remember that Plato tends to bring out the bad side of the Sophists, largely because he had Socrates before his eyes, who had developed what was good in Sophism beyond all comparison with the achievements of the Sophists themselves.

CHAPTER XIII
SOME INDIVIDUAL SOPHISTS

1. *Protagoras*

PROTAGORAS was born, according to most authors, about 481 B.C., a native of Abdera in Thrace,[1] and seems to have come to Athens about the middle of the century. He enjoyed the favour of Pericles, and we are told that he was entrusted by that statesman with the task of drawing up a constitution for the Panhellenic colony of Thurii, which was founded in 444 B.C. He was again in Athens at the outbreak of the Peloponnesian War in 431 and during the plague in 430, which carried off two of Pericles' sons. Diogenes Laërtius relates the story that Protagoras was indicted for blasphemy because of his book on the gods, but that he escaped from the city before trial and was drowned on the crossing to Sicily, his book being burnt in the market-place. This would have taken place at the time of the oligarchic revolt of the Four Hundred in 411 B.C. Burnet is inclined to regard the story as dubious, and holds that if the indictment did take place, then it must have taken place before 411. Professor Taylor agrees with Burnet in rejecting the prosecution story, but he does so because he also agrees with Burnet in accepting a much earlier date for the birth of Protagoras, namely 500 B.C. The two writers rely on Plato's representation of Protagoras in the dialogue of that name as an elderly man, at least approaching 65, in about the year 435. Plato "must have known whether Protagoras really belonged to the generation before Socrates, and could have no motive for misrepresentation on such a point."[2] If this is correct, then we ought also to accept the statement in the *Meno* that Protagoras died in high repute.

The best-known statement of Protagoras is that contained in his work, 'Αλήθεια ἤ Καταβάλλοντες (λόγοι), to the effect that "man is the measure of all things, of those that are that they are, of those that are not that they are not."[3] There has been a considerable controversy as to the interpretation which should be put on this famous saying, some writers maintaining the view that by "man" Protagoras does not mean the individual man,

[1] *Protag.*, 309 c; *Rep.*, 600 c; Diog. Laërt., 9, 50 ff.
[2] *Plato*, p. 236, note.
[3] Frag. 1.

but man in the specific sense. If this were so, then the meaning of the dictum would not be that "what appears to you to be true is true for you, and what appears to me to be true is true for me," but rather that the community or group or the whole human species is the criterion and standard of truth. Controversy has also turned round the question whether things—Χρήματα—should be understood exclusively of the objects of sense-perception or should be extended to cover the field of values as well.

This is a difficult question and it cannot be discussed at length here, but the present writer is not prepared to disregard the testimony of Plato in the *Theaetetus*, where the Protagorean dictum, developed it is true, as Plato himself admits, is certainly interpreted in the individualistic sense in regard to sense-perception.[1] Socrates observes that when the same wind is blowing, one of us may feel chilly and the other not, or one may feel slightly chilly and the other quite cold, and asks if we should agree with Protagoras that the wind is cold to the one who feels chilly and not to the other. It is quite clear that in this passage Protagoras is interpreted as referring to the individual man, and not at all to man in the specific sense. Moreover, it is to be noted that the Sophist is not depicted as saying that the wind merely *appears* chilly to the one and not to the other. Thus if I have come in from a run in the rain on a cold day, and say that the water is warm; while you, coming from a warm room, feel the same water as cold, Protagoras would remark that neither of us is mistaken—the water *is* warm in reference to my sense-organ, and *is* cold in reference to your sense-organ. (When it was objected to the Sophist that geometrical propositions are constant for all, Protagoras replied that in actual concrete reality there are no geometrical lines or circles, so that the difficulty does not arise.[2])

Against this interpretation appeal is made to the *Protagoras* of Plato, where Protagoras is not depicted as applying the dictum in an individualistic sense to ethical values. But even granting that Protagoras must be made consistent with himself, it is surely not necessary to suppose that what is true of the objects of sense-perception is *ipso facto* true of ethical values. It may be pointed out that Protagoras declares that man is the measure of πάντων χρημάτων (*all* things), so that if the individualistic interpretation be accepted in regard to the objects of sense-perception, it should also be extended to ethical values and judgments, and

[1] *Theaet.*, 151 e, 152 a. [2] Arist., *Metaph.*, B 2, 997 b 32–998 a 6.

that, conversely, if it is not accepted in regard to ethical values and judgments, it should not be accepted in regard to the objects of sense-perception: in other words, we are forced to choose between the *Theaetetus* and *Protagoras*, relying on the one and rejecting the other. But in the first place it is not certain that πάντων χρημάτων is meant to include ethical values, and in the second place it might be well that the objects of the special senses are of such character that they *cannot* become the subject of true and universal knowledge, while on the other hand ethical values are of such a kind that they *can* become the subject of true and universal knowledge. This was the view of Plato himself, who connected the Protagorean saying with the Heraclitean doctrine of flux, and held that true and certain knowledge can only be had of the supersensible. We are not trying to make out that Protagoras held the Platonic view on ethical values, which he did not, but to point out that sense-perception and intuition of values do not *necessarily* stand or fall together in relation to certain knowledge and truth for all.

What, then, was Protagoras' actual teaching in regard to ethical judgments and values? In the *Theaetetus* he is depicted as saying both that ethical judgments are relative ("For I hold that whatever practices seem right and laudable to any particular State are so for that State, so long as it holds by them") and that the wise man should attempt to substitute sound practices for unsound.[1] In other words, there is no question of one ethical view being true and another false, but there is question of one view being "sounder," i.e. more useful or expedient, than another. "In this way it is true both that some men are wiser than others and that no one thinks falsely." (A man who thinks that there is no absolute truth, is hardly entitled to declare absolutely that "no one thinks falsely.") Now, in the *Protagoras*, Plato depicts the Sophist as maintaining that αἰδώς and δίκη, have been bestowed on *all* men by the gods, "because cities could not exist if, as in the case of other arts, few men only were partakers of them." Is this at variance with what is said in the *Theaetetus*? It would appear that what Protagoras means is this: that Law in general is founded on certain ethical tendencies implanted in all men, but that the individual varieties of Law, as found in particular States, are relative, the law of one State, without being "truer" than that of another State, being perhaps "sounder" in the sense

[1] *Theaet.*, 166 ff.

of more useful or expedient. The State or city-community would be the determiner of law in this case and not the individual, but the relative character of concrete ethical judgments and concrete determinations of Nomos would be maintained. As an upholder of tradition and social convention, Protagoras stresses the importance of education, of imbibing the ethical traditions of the State, while admitting that the wise man may lead the State to "better" laws. As far as the individual citizen is concerned, he should cleave to tradition, to the accepted code of the community —and that all the more because no one "way" is truer than another. αἰδώς and δίκη incline him to this, and if he has no share in these gifts of the gods and refuses to hearken to the State, the State must get rid of him. While at first sight, therefore, the "relativistic" doctrine of Protagoras might seem intentionally revolutionary, it turns out to be used in support of tradition and authority. No one code is "truer" than another, therefore do not set up your private judgment against the law of the State. Moreover, through his conception of αἰδώς and δίκη Protagoras gives at least some hints of the unwritten or natural law, and in this respect contributed to the broadening of the Greek outlook.

In a work, Περὶ θεῶν, Protagoras said· "With regard to the gods, I cannot feel sure either that they are or that they are not, nor what they are like in figure; for there are many things that hinder sure knowledge, the obscurity of the subject and the shortness of human life."[1] This is the only fragment of the work that we possess. Such a sentence might seem to lend colour to the picture of Protagoras as a sceptical and destructive thinker, who turned his critical powers against all established tradition in ethics and religion; but such a view does not agree with the impression of Protagoras which we receive from Plato's dialogue of that name, and would doubtless be mistaken. Just as the moral to be drawn from the relativity of particular codes of law is that the individual should submit himself to the traditional education, so the moral to be drawn from our uncertainty concerning the gods and their nature is that we should abide by the religion of the city. If we cannot be certain of absolute truth, why throw overboard the religion that we inherit from our fathers? Moreover, Protagoras' attitude is not so extraordinary or destructive as the adherents of a dogmatic religion might naturally suppose, since, as Burnet remarks, Greek religion did not consist

[1] Frag. 4.

"in theological affirmations or negations" but in worship.[1] The effect of the Sophists, it is true, would have been to weaken men's trust in tradition, but it would appear that Protagoras personally was conservative in temper and had no intention of educating revolutionaries; on the contrary, he professed to educate the good citizen. There are ethical tendencies in all men, but these can develop only in the organised community: if a man is to be a good citizen, therefore, he must absorb the whole social tradition of the community of which he is a member. The social tradition is not absolute truth, but it is the norm for a good citizen.

From the relativistic theory it follows that on every subject more than one opinion is possible, and Protagoras seems to have developed this point in his Ἀντιλογίαι. The dialectician and rhetorician will practise himself in the art of developing different opinions and arguments, and he will shine most brightly when he succeeds τὸν ἥττω λόγον κρείττω ποιεῖν. The enemies of the Sophists interpreted this in the sense of making the *morally worse* cause to prevail,[2] but it does not necessarily possess this morally destructive sense. A lawyer, for example, who pleaded with success the just cause of a client who was too weak to protect himself or the justice of whose cause it was difficult to substantiate, might be said to be making the "weaker argument" prevail, though he would be doing nothing immoral. In the hands of unscrupulous rhetoricians and devotees of eristic, the maxim easily acquired an unsavoury flavour, but there is no reason to father on Protagoras himself a desire to promote unscrupulous dealing. Still, it cannot be denied that the doctrine of relativism, when linked up with the practice of dialectic and eristic, very naturally produces a desire to succeed, without much regard for truth or justice.

Protagoras was a pioneer in the study and science of grammar. He is said to have classified the different kinds of sentence[3] and to have distinguished terminologically the genders of nouns.[4] In an amusing passage of the *Clouds* Aristophanes depicts the Sophist as coining the feminine ἀλεκτρύαινα from the masculine ἀλεκτρυών (cock).[5]

II. *Prodicus*

Prodicus came from the island of Ceos in the Aegean. The

[1] *G.P.*, I, p. 117. [2] Aristoph., *Clouds*, 112 ff., 656–7. [3] Diog. Laërt., 9, 53 ff. [4] Arist., *Rhet.*, 5, 1407 b 6. [5] *Clouds*, 658 ff., 847 ff.

inhabitants of this island were said to be pessimistically inclined, and Prodicus was credited with the tendencies of his countrymen, for in the pseudo-Platonic dialogue *Axiochus* he is credited with holding that death is desirable in order to escape the evils of life. Fear of death is irrational, since death concerns neither the living nor the dead—the first, because they are still living, the second, because they are not living any more.[1] The authenticity of this quotation is not easy to establish.

Prodicus is perhaps chiefly remarkable for his theory on the origin of religion. He held that in the beginning men worshipped as gods the sun, moon, rivers, lakes, fruits, etc.—in other words, the things which were useful to them and gave them food. And he gives as an example the cult of the Nile in Egypt. This primitive stage was followed by another, in which the inventors of various arts—agriculture, viniculture, metal work, and so on—were worshipped as the gods Demeter, Dionysus, Hephaestus, etc. On this view of religion prayer would, he thought, be superfluous, and he seems to have got into trouble with the authorities at Athens.[2] Prodicus, like Protagoras, was noted for linguistic studies,[3] and he wrote a treatise on synonyms. He seems to have been very pedantic in his forms of expression.[4]

(Professor Zeller says:[5] "Although Plato usually treats him with irony, it nevertheless speaks well for him that Socrates occasionally recommended pupils to him (*Theaet.*, 151b), and that his native city repeatedly entrusted him with diplomatic missions (*Hipp. Maj.*, 282 c)." As a matter of fact, Zeller seems to have missed the point in the *Theaetetus* passage, since the young men that Socrates has sent to Prodicus are those who, he has found, have not been "pregnant" with thoughts when in his company. He has accordingly sent them off to Prodicus, in whose company they have ceased to be "barren.")

III. *Hippias*

Hippias of Elis was a younger contemporary of Protagoras and was celebrated particularly for his versatility, being acquainted with mathematics, astronomy, grammar and rhetoric, rhythmics and harmony, history and literature and mythology—in short, he was a true Polymath. Not only that, but when present at a certain Olympiad, he boasted that he had made all his own

[1] 366 c ff. [2] Frag. 5. [3] Cf. *Crat.*, 384 b. [4] Cf. *Protag.*, 337 a f.
[5] *Outlines*, pp. 84–5.

clothes. His list of the Olympic victors laid the foundation for the later Greek system of dating by means of the Olympiads (first introduced by the historian Timaeus).[1] Plato, in the *Protagoras*, makes him say that "law being the tyrant of men, forces them to do many things contrary to nature."[2] The point seems to be that the law of the city-state is often narrow and tyrannical and at variance with the natural laws (ἄγραφοι νόμοι).

IV. *Gorgias*

Gorgias of Leontini, in Sicily, lived from about 483 to 375 B.C., and in the year 427 he came to Athens as ambassador of Leontini, in order to ask for help against Syracuse. On his travels he did what he could to spread the spirit of Panhellenism.

Gorgias seems to have been at first a pupil of Empedocles, and to have busied himself with questions of natural science, and may have written a book on Optics. He was led, however, to scepticism by the dialectic of Zeno and published a work entitled *On Not-being or Nature* (Περὶ τοῦ μὴ ὄντος ἢ περὶ Φύσεως), the chief ideas of which can be gathered from Sextus Empiricus and from the pseudo-Aristotelian writing *On Melissus, Xenophanes and Gorgias*. From these accounts of the contents of Gorgias' work it is clear that he reacted to the Eleatic dialectic somewhat differently to Protagoras, since while the latter might be said to hold that everything is true, Gorgias maintained the very opposite. According to Gorgias, (i) Nothing exists, for if there were anything, then it would have either to be eternal or to have come into being. But it cannot have come into being, for neither out of Being nor out of Not-being can anything come to be. Nor can it be eternal, for if it were eternal, then it would have to be infinite. But the infinite is impossible for the following reason. It could not be in another, nor could it be in itself, therefore it would be nowhere. But what is nowhere, is nothing. (ii) If there were anything, then it could not be known. For if there is knowledge of being, then what is thought must be, and Not-being could not be thought at all. In which case there could be no error, which is absurd. (iii) Even if there were knowledge of being, this knowledge could not be imparted. Every sign is different from the thing signified; e.g. how could we impart knowledge of colours by word, since the ear hears tones and not colours? And how could the same representation of being

[1] Frag. 3.

[2] 337 d, 2–3.

be in the two persons at once, since they are different from one another?[1]

While some have regarded these astonishing ideas as expressing a seriously meant philosophical Nihilism, others have thought that the doctrine constitutes a joke on the part of Gorgias, or, rather, that the great rhetorician wanted to show that rhetoric or the skilful use of words was able to make plausible even the most absurd hypothesis. (*Sic* H. Gomperz.) But this latter view hardly agrees with the fact that Isocrates sets Gorgias' opinions besides those of Zeno and Melissus, nor with the writing Πρὸς τὰ Γοργίου, which treats Gorgias' opinions as worth a philosophical criticism.[2] In any case a treatise on Nature would scarcely be the place for such rhetorical *tours de force*. On the other hand, it is difficult to suppose that Gorgias held in all seriousness that nothing exists. It may be that he wished to employ the Eleatic dialectic in order to reduce the Eleatic philosophy to absurdity.[3] Afterwards, renouncing philosophy, he devoted himself to rhetoric.

Rhetorical art was regarded by Gorgias as the mastery of the art of persuasion, and this necessarily led him to a study of practical psychology. He deliberately practised the art of suggestion (ψυχαγωγία), which could be used both for practical ends, good and bad, and for artistic purposes. In connection with the latter Gorgias developed the art of justifiable deception (δικαία 'απάτη), calling a tragedy "a deception which is better to cause than not to cause; to succumb to it shows greater powers of artistic appreciation than not to."[4] Gorgias' comparison of the effects of tragedy to those of purgatives reminds us of Aristotle's much-discussed doctrine of the κάθαρσις.

The fact that Plato places the might-is-right doctrine in the mouth of Callicles,[5] while another disciple, Lycophron, asserted that nobility is a sham and that all men are equal, and that the law is a contract by which right is mutually guaranteed,[6] while yet another disciple demanded the liberation of slaves in the name of natural law,[7] we may ascribe with Zeller to Gorgias' renunciation of philosophy, which led him to decline to answer questions of truth and morality.[8]

Other Sophists whom one may briefly mention are Thrasymachus

[1] Cf. Frags. 1, 3. [2] Aristotle or Theophrastus? [3] Cf. Zeller, *Outlines*, p. 87.
[4] Frag. 23 (Plut., *de gloria Athen.*, 5, 348 c).
[5] *Gorgias*, 482 e ff. [6] Frags. 3 and 4.
[7] Alcidamas of Elaea. Cf. Aristot., *Rhet.*, III, 3, 1406 b; 1406 a. Schol. on I 13, 1373 b. [8] *Outlines*, p. 88.

of Chalcedon, who is presented in the *Republic* as the brutal champion of the rights of the stronger,[1] and Antiphon of Athens, who asserts the equality of all men and denounces the distinction between nobles and commons, Greeks and barbarians, as itself a barbarism. He made education to be the most important thing in life, and created the literary *genre* of Τέχνη ἀλυπίας λόγοι παραμυθητικοί, declaring that he could free anyone from sorrow by oral means.[2]

v. *Sophism*

In conclusion I may observe again that there is no reason for ascribing to the great Sophists the intention of overthrowing religion and morality; men like Protagoras and Gorgias had no such end in view. Indeed, the great Sophists favoured the conception of a "natural law," and tended to broaden the outlook of the ordinary Greek citizen; they were an educative force in Hellas. At the same time it is true that "in a certain sense every opinion is true, according to Protagoras; every opinion is false, according to Gorgias."[3] This tendency to deny the absolute and objective character of truth easily leads to the consequence that, instead of trying to *convince* anyone, the Sophist will try to *persuade* him or talk him over. Indeed, in the hands of lesser men Sophism soon acquired an unpleasant connotation—that of "Sophistry." While one can only respect the cosmopolitanism and broad outlook of an Antiphon of Athens, one can only condemn the "Might-is-Right" theory of a Thrasymachus on the one hand and the hair-splitting and quibbling of a Dionysodorus on the other. The great Sophists, as we have said, were an educative force in Hellas; but one of the chief factors in the Greek education which they fostered was rhetoric, and rhetoric had its obvious dangers, inasmuch as the orator might easily tend to pay more attention to the rhetorical presentation of a subject than to the subject itself. Moreover, by questioning the absolute foundations of traditional institutions, beliefs and ways of life, Sophism tended to foster a relativistic attitude, though the evil latent in Sophism lay not so much in the fact that it raised problems, as in the fact that it could not offer any satisfactory intellectual solution to the problems it raised. Against this relativism Socrates and Plato reacted, endeavouring to establish the sure foundation of true knowledge and ethical judgments.

[1] *Rep.*, 338 c.
[2] Cf. Plut., apud Diels. Frag. 44 and 87 A 6.
[3] Ueberweg-Praechter, p. 122.

CHAPTER XIV

SOCRATES

1. *Early Life of Socrates*

THE death of Socrates fell in the year 399 B.C., and as Plato tells us that Socrates was seventy years old or a little more at the time of his death, he must have been born about 470 B.C.[1] He was the son of Sophroniscus and Phaenarete of the Antiochid tribe and the *deme* of Alopecae. Some have said that his father was a worker in stone,[2] but A. E. Taylor thinks, with Burnet, that the story was a misunderstanding which arose from a playful reference in the *Euthyphro* to Daedalus as the ancestor of Socrates.[3] In any case, Socrates does not seem to have himself followed his father's trade, if it was his father's trade, and the group of Graces on the Akropolis, which were later shown as the work of Socrates, are attributed by archaeologists to an earlier sculptor.[4] Socrates cannot, however, have come from a very poor family, as we find him later serving as a fully-armed hoplite, and he must have been left sufficient patrimony to enable him to undertake such a service. Phaenarete, Socrates' mother, is described in the *Theaetetus*[5] as a midwife, but even if she was, this should not be taken to imply that she was a professional midwife in the modern sense, as Taylor points out.[6] Socrates' early life thus fell in the great flowering of Athenian splendour. The Persians had been defeated at Plataea in 479 and Aeschylus had produced the *Persae* in 472: Sophocles and Euripides were still boys.[7] Moreover, Athens had already laid the foundation of her maritime empire.

In Plato's *Symposium* Alcibiades describes Socrates as looking like a satyr or Silenus,[8] and Aristophanes said that he strutted

[1] *Apol.*, 17 d.

[2] Cf. Diog. Laërt. (Thus Praechter says roundly: *Der Vater des Sokrates war Bildhauer*, p. 132.)

[3] *Euthyphro*, 10 c.

[4] Diog. Laërt. remarks that "Some say that the Graces in the Akropolis are his work."

[5] *Theaet.*, 149 a.

[6] Taylor, *Socrates*, p. 38.

[7] "All the great buildings and works of art with which Athens was enriched in the Periclean age, the Long Walls which connected the city with the port of Peiraeus, the Parthenon, the frescoes of Polygnotus, were begun and completed under his eyes." *Socr.*, p. 36.

[8] *Sympos.*, 215 b 3 ff.

like a waterfowl and ridiculed his habit of rolling his eyes.[1] But we also know that he was possessed of particular robustness of body and powers of endurance. As a man he wore the same garment winter and summer, and continued his habit of going barefoot, even on a winter campaign. Although very abstemious in food and drink, he could drink a great deal without being any the worse for it. From his youth upwards he was the recipient of prohibitory messages or warnings from his mysterious "voice" or "sign" or *daimon*. The *Symposium* tells us of his prolonged fits of abstraction, one lasting the whole of a day and night—and that on a military campaign. Professor Taylor would like to interpret these abstractions as ecstasies or rapts, but it would seem more likely that they were prolonged fits of abstraction due to intense mental concentration on some problem, a phenomenon not unknown in the case of some other thinkers, even if not on so large a scale. The very length of the "ecstasy" mentioned in the *Symposium* would seem to militate against its being a real rapture in the mystico-religious sense,[2] though such a prolonged fit of abstraction would also be exceptional.

When Socrates was in his early twenties, thought, as we have seen, tended to turn away from the cosmological speculations of the Ionians towards man himself, but it seems certain that Socrates began by studying the cosmological theories of East and West in the philosophies of Archelaus, Diogenes of Apollonia, Empedocles and others. Theophrastus asserts that Socrates was actually a member of the School of Archelaus, the successor of Anaxagoras at Athens.[3] In any case Socrates certainly suffered a disappointment through Anaxagoras. Perplexed by the disagreement of the various philosophical theories, Socrates received a sudden light from the passage where Anaxagoras spoke of Mind as being the cause of all natural law and order. Delighted with the passage, Socrates began to study Anaxagoras, in the hope that the latter would explain how Mind works in the universe, ordering all things for the best. What he actually found was that Anaxagoras introduced Mind merely in order to get the vortex-movement going. This disappointment set Socrates on his own line of investigation, abandoning the Natural Philosophy which seemed to lead nowhere, save to confusion and opposite opinions.[4]

[1] *Clouds*, 362 (cf. *Sympos.*, 221).

[2] It is true, however, that the history of mysticism does record instances of prolonged ecstatic states. Cf. Poulain, *Grâces d' oraison*, p. 256.

[3] *Phys. Opin.*, fr. 4.

[4] *Phaedo*, 97–9.

A. E. Taylor conjectures that on Archelaus' death, Socrates was to all intents and purposes his successor.[1] He tries to support this contention with the aid of Aristophanes' play, *The Clouds*, where Socrates and his associates of the notion-factory or Φροντιστήριον are represented as addicted to the natural sciences and as holding the air-doctrine of Diogenes of Apollonia.[2] Socrates' disclaimer, therefore, that he ever took "pupils"[3] would, if Taylor's conjecture be correct, mean that he had taken no paying pupils. He had had ἑταῖροι, but had never had μαθηταί. Against this it may be urged that in the *Apology* Socrates expressly declares: "But the simple truth is, O Athenians, that I have nothing to do with physical speculations."[4] It is true that at the time when Socrates was depicted as speaking in the *Apology* he had long ago given up cosmological speculation, and that his words do not necessarily imply that he *never* engaged in such speculations; indeed, we know for a fact that he *did*; but it seems to the present writer that the whole tone of the passage militates against the idea that Socrates was ever the professed head of a School dedicated to this kind of speculation. What is said in the *Apology* certainly does not prove, in the strict sense, that Socrates was not the head of such a School before his "conversion," but it would seem that the natural interpretation is that he never occupied such a position.

The "conversion" of Socrates, which brought about the definite change to Socrates the ironic moral philosopher, seems to have been due to the famous incident of the Delphic Oracle. Chaerephon, a devoted friend of Socrates, asked the Oracle if there was any man living who was wiser than Socrates, and received the answer "No." This set Socrates thinking, and he came to the conclusion that the god meant that he was the wisest man because he recognised his own ignorance. He then came to conceive of his mission as being to seek for the stable and certain truth, true wisdom, and to enlist the aid of any man who would consent to listen to him.[5] However strange the story of the Oracle may appear, it most probably really happened, since it is unlikely that Plato would have put a mere invention into the mouth of Socrates in a dialogue which obviously purports to give an historical account of the trial of the philosopher, especially as the *Apology* is of early date, and many who knew the facts were still living.

Socrates' marriage with Xanthippe is best known for the stories

[1] *Socr.*, p. 67. [2] *Clouds*, 94. [3] *Apol.*, 19. [4] *Apol.*, 19. [5] *Apol.*, 20 ff.

about her shrewish character, which may or may not be true. Certainly they are scarcely borne out by the picture of Socrates' wife given in the *Phaedo*. The marriage probably took place some time in the first ten years of the Peloponnesian War. In this war Socrates distinguished himself for bravery at the siege of Potidaea, 431/30, and again at the defeat of the Athenians by the Boeotians in 424. He was also present at the action outside Amphipolis in 422.[1]

II. *Problem of Socrates*

The problem of Socrates is the problem of ascertaining exactly what his philosophical teaching was. The character of the sources at our disposal—Xenophon's Socratic works (*Memorabilia* and *Symposium*), Plato's dialogues, various statements of Aristotle, Aristophanes' *Clouds*—make this a difficult problem. For instance, were one to rely on Xenophon alone, one would have the impression of a man whose chief interest was to make good men and citizens, but who did not concern himself with problems of logic and metaphysics—a popular ethical teacher. If, on the other hand, one were to found one's conception of Socrates on the Platonic dialogues taken as a whole, one would receive the impression of a metaphysician of the highest order, a man who did not content himself with questions of daily conduct, but laid the foundations of a transcendental philosophy, distinguished by its doctrine of a metaphysical world of Forms. Statements of Aristotle, on the other hand (if given their natural interpretation), give us to understand that while Socrates was not uninterested in theory, he did not himself teach the doctrine of subsistent Forms or Ideas, which is characteristic of Platonism.

The common view has been that though Xenophon's portrayal is too "ordinary" and "trivial," mainly owing to Xenophon's lack of philosophical ability and interest (it has indeed been held, though it seems unlikely, that Xenophon deliberately tried to make Socrates appear more "ordinary" than he actually was and than he knew him to be, for apologetic purposes), we cannot reject the testimony of Aristotle, and are accordingly forced to conclude that Plato, except in the early Socratic works, e.g. the *Apology*, put his own doctrines into the mouth of Socrates. This view has the great advantage that the Xenophontic and the Platonic

[1] *Apol.*, 28 e. Burnet suggests that the fighting at the foundation of Amphipolis (some fifteen years earlier) may be referred to.

Socrates are not placed in glaring opposition and inconsistency (for the shortcomings of Xenophon's picture can be explained as a result of Xenophon's own character and predominant interests), while the clear testimony of Aristotle is not thrown overboard. In this way a more or less consistent picture of Socrates is evolved, and no unjustified violence (so the upholders of the theory would maintain) is done to any of the sources.

This view has, however, been challenged. Karl Joel, for example, basing his conception of Socrates on the testimony of Aristotle, maintains that Socrates was an intellectualist or rationalist, representing the Attic type, and that the Xenophontic Socrates, a *Willensethiker*, representing the Spartan type, is unhistorical. According to Joel, therefore, Xenophon gave a Doric colouring to Socrates and misrepresented him.[1]

Döring, on the contrary, maintained that we must look to Xenophon in order to obtain our historical picture of Socrates. Aristotle's testimony simply comprises the summary judgment of the Old Academy on Socrates' philosophical importance, while Plato used Socrates as a peg on which to hang his own philosophical doctrines.[2] Another view has been propagated in this country by Burnet and Taylor. According to them the historic Socrates is the *Platonic* Socrates.[3] Plato no doubt elaborated the thought of Socrates, but, all the same, philosophical teaching which is put into his mouth in the dialogues substantially represents the actual teaching of Socrates. If this were correct, then Socrates would himself have been responsible for the metaphysical theory of Forms or Ideas, and the statement of Aristotle (that Socrates did not "separate" the Forms) must be either rejected, as due to ignorance, or explained away. It is most unlikely, say Burnet and Taylor, that Plato would have put his own theories into the mouth of Socrates if the latter had never held them, when people who had actually known Socrates and knew what he really taught, were still living. They point out, moreover, that in some of the later dialogues of Plato, Socrates no longer plays a leading part, while in the *Laws* he is left out altogether—the inference

[1] *Der echte und der Xenophontische Sokrates*, Berlin, 1893, 1901.

[2] *Die Lehre des Sokrates als sozialesreform system. Neuer Versuch zur Lösung des Problems der sokratischen Philosophie.* München, 1895.

[3] "While it is quite impossible to regard the Socrates of Aristophanes and the Socrates of Xenophon as the same person, there is no difficulty in regarding both as distorted images of the Socrates we know from Plato. The first is legitimately distorted for comic effect, the latter, not so legitimately, for apologetic reasons." Burnet, *G.P.*, I, p. 149.

being that where Socrates *does* play the leading part, it is his own ideas, and not simply Plato's, that he is giving, while in the later dialogues Plato is developing independent views (independent of Socrates at least), and so Socrates is allowed to drop into the background. This last argument is undoubtedly a strong one, as is also the fact that in an "early" dialogue, such as the *Phaedo*, which deals with the death of Socrates, the theory of Forms occupies a prominent place. But, if the Platonic Socrates is the historic Socrates, we ought logically to say that in the *Timaeus*, for example, Plato is putting into the mouth of the chief speaker opinions for which he, Plato, did not take the responsibility, since, if Socrates does not stand for Plato himself, there is no compelling reason why Timaeus should do so either. A. E. Taylor indeed does not hesitate to adopt this extreme, if consistent, position; but not only is it *prima facie* extremely unlikely that we can thus free Plato from responsibility for most of what he says in the dialogues, but also, as regards the *Timaeus*, if Taylor's opinion is true, how are we to explain that this remarkable fact first became manifest in the twentieth century A.D.?[1] Again, the consistent maintenance of the Burnet-Taylor view of the Platonic Socrates involves the ascription to Socrates of elaborations, refinements and explanations of the Ideal Theory which it is most improbable that the historic Socrates really evolved, and which would lead to a complete ignoring of the testimony of Aristotle.

It is true that much of the criticism levelled against the Ideal Theory by Aristotle in the *Metaphysics* is directed against the mathematical form of the theory maintained by Plato in his lectures at the Academy, and that in certain particulars there is a curious neglect of what Plato says in the dialogues, a fact which might appear to indicate that Aristotle only recognised as Platonic the unpublished theory developed in the Academy; but it certainly would not be adequate to say that there was a complete dichotomy between the version of the theory that Aristotle gives (whether fairly or unfairly) and the evolving theory of the dialogues. Moreover, the very fact that the theory undergoes evolution, modification and refinement in the dialogues would imply that it represents, in part at least, Plato's own reflections on his position. Later writers of Antiquity certainly believed that we can look to

[1] Cf. pp. 245–7 of this book; *v.* also Cornford's *Plato's Cosmology,* where he discusses Professor Taylor's theory.

the dialogues for Plato's own philosophy, though they differ concerning the relation of the dialogues to the teaching of Socrates, the earlier among them believing that Plato introduced much of his own thought into the dialogues. Syrianus contradicts Aristotle, but Professor Field observes that his reasons appear to be "his own sense of what was fitting in the relation of teacher and disciple."[1]

An argument in favour of the Burnet-Taylor hypothesis is constituted by the passage in the second Letter, where Plato affirms that what he has said in writing is nothing but Socrates "beautified and rejuvenated."[2] In the first place, however, the genuineness of the passage, or even of the whole letter, is not certain, while in the second place it could be perfectly well explained as meaning that the dialogues give what Plato considered the metaphysical superstructure legitimately elaborated by himself on the basis of what Socrates actually said. (Field suggests that it might refer to the application of the Socratic method and spirit to "modern" problems.) For no one would be so foolish as to maintain that the dialogues contain nothing of the historic Socrates. It is obvious that the early dialogues would naturally take as their point of departure the teaching of the historic Socrates, and if Plato worked out the epistemological and ontological theories of succeeding dialogues through reflection on this teaching, he might legitimately regard the results attained as a justifiable development and application of Socrates' teaching and method. His words in the Letter would gain in point from his conviction that while the Ideal Theory as elaborated in the dialogues might, without undue violence, be regarded as a continuation and development of the Socratic teaching, this would not be equally true of the mathematical form of the theory given in the Academy.

It would, of course, be ridiculous to suggest that a view sponsored by such scholars as Professor Taylor and Professor Burnet could be lightly dismissed, and to make any such suggestion is very far from the mind of the present writer; but in a general book on Greek philosophy it is impossible to treat of the question at any considerable length or to give the Burnet-Taylor theory the full and detailed consideration that it deserves. I must, however, express my agreement with what Mr. Hackforth, for

[1] *Plato and his Contemporaries*, p. 228, Methuen, 1930. Cf. Field's summary of the evidence on the Socratic question, pp. 61–3.

[2] 314 c, καλοῦ καὶ νέου γεγονότος.

example, has said[1] concerning the lack of justification for ignoring the testimony of Aristotle that Socrates did not separate the Forms. Aristotle had been for twenty years in the Academy and interested as he was in the history of philosophy, can scarcely have neglected to ascertain the origin of such an important Platonic doctrine as the theory of Forms. Add to this the fact that the extant fragments of the Dialogues of Aeschines give us no reason to differ from the view of Aristotle, and Aeschines was said to have given the most accurate portrait of Socrates. For these reasons it seems best to accept the testimony of Aristotle, and, while admitting that the Xenophontic Socrates is not the complete Socrates, to maintain the traditional view, that Plato did put his own theories into the mouth of the Master whom he so much reverenced. The short account of Socrates' philosophical activity now to be given is therefore based on the traditional view. Those who maintain the theory of Burnet and Taylor would, of course, say that violence is thereby done to Plato; but is the situation bettered by doing violence to Aristotle? If the latter had not enjoyed personal intercourse with Plato and his disciples over a long space of time, we might have allowed the possibility of a mistake on his part; but in view of his twenty years in the Academy this mistake would appear to be ruled out of court. However it is unlikely that we shall ever obtain absolute certainty as to the historically accurate picture of Socrates, and it would be most unwise to dismiss all conceptions save one's own as unworthy of consideration. One can only state one's reasons for accepting one picture of Socrates rather than another, and leave it at that.

(Use has been made of Xenophon in the following short account of Socrates' teaching: we cannot believe that Xenophon was either a nincompoop or a liar. It is perfectly true that while it is difficult—sometimes, no doubt, impossible—to distinguish between Plato and Socrates, "it is almost as hard to distinguish between Socrates and Xenophon. For the *Memorabilia* is as much a work of art as any Platonic dialogue, though the manner is as different as was Xenophon from Plato."[2] But, as Mr. Lindsay points out, Xenophon wrote much besides the *Memorabilia*, and consideration of his writings in general may often show us what is Xenophon, even if it does not always show us what is Socrates.

[1] Cf. article by R. Hackforth on Socrates in *Philosophy* for July 1933.
[2] A. D. Lindsay in Introd. to *Socratic Discourses* (Everyman), p. viii.

The *Memorabilia* gives us the impression that Socrates made on Xenophon, and we believe that it is in the main trustworthy, even if it is always as well to remember the old scholastic adage, *Quidquid recipitur, secundum modum recipientis recipitur.*)

III. *Philosophical Activity of Socrates*

1. Aristotle declares that there are two improvements in science which we might justly ascribe to Socrates—his employment of "inductive arguments and universal definitions" (τούς τ'ἐπακτικούς λόγους καὶ τὸ ὁρίζεσθαι καθόλου).[1] The last remark should be understood in connection with the following statement, that "Socrates did not make the universals or the definitions exist apart; his successor, however, gave them separate existence, and this was the kind of thing they called Ideas."

Socrates was therefore concerned with universal definitions, i.e. with the attaining of fixed concepts. The Sophists propounded relativistic doctrines, rejecting the necessarily and universally valid. Socrates, however, was struck by the fact that the universal concept remains the same: particular instances may vary, but the definition stands fast. This idea can be made clear by an example. The Aristotelian definition of man is "rational animal." Now, individual men vary in their gifts: some are possessed of great intellectual gifts, others not. Some guide their lives according to reason: others surrender without thought to instinct and passing impulse. Some men do not enjoy the unhampered use of their reason, whether because they are asleep or because they are "mentally defective." But all animals who possess the gift of reason—whether they are actually using it or not, whether they can use it freely or are prevented by some organic defect—are men: the definition of man is fulfilled in them, and this definition remains constant, holding good for all. If "man," then "rational animal"; if "rational animal," then "man." We cannot now discuss the precise status or objective reference of our generic and specific notions: we simply want to illustrate the contrast between the particular and the universal, and to point out the constant character of the definition. Some thinkers have maintained that the universal concept is purely subjective, but it is very difficult to see how we could form such universal notions, and why we should be compelled to form them, unless there was a foundation for them in fact. We shall have to return later to the question of

[1] *Metaph.*, M. 1078 b 27–9.

the objective reference and metaphysical status of universals: let it suffice at present to point out that the universal concept or definition presents us with something constant and abiding that stands out, through its possession of these characteristics, from the world of perishing particulars. Even if all men were blotted out of existence, the definition of man as "rational animal" would remain constant. Again, we may speak of a piece of gold as being "true gold," implying that the definition of gold, the standard or universal criterion, is realised in this piece of gold. Similarly we speak of things as being more or less beautiful, implying that they approach the standard of Beauty in a greater or less degree, a standard which does not vary or change like the beautiful objects of our experience, but remains constant and "rules," as it were, all particular beautiful objects. Of course, we might be mistaken in supposing that we knew the standard of Beauty, but in speaking of objects as more or less beautiful we imply that there *is* a standard. To take a final illustration. Mathematicians speak of and define the line, the circle, etc. Now, the perfect line and the perfect circle are not found among the objects of our experience: there are at best only approximations to the definitions of the line or the circle. There is a contrast, therefore, between the imperfect and changeable objects of our everyday experience on the one hand and the universal concept or definition on the other hand. It is easy to see, then, how Socrates was led to attach such importance to the universal definition. With a predominant interest in ethical conduct, he saw that the definition affords a sure rock on which men could stand amidst the sea of the Sophist relativistic doctrines. According to a relativistic ethic, justice, for example, varies from city to city, community to community: we can never say that justice is this or that, and that this definition holds good for all States, but only that justice in Athens is this and in Thrace that. But if we can once attain to a universal definition of justice, which expresses the innermost nature of justice and holds good for all men, then we have something sure to go upon, and we can judge not only individual actions, but also the moral codes of different States, in so far as they embody or recede from the universal definition of justice.

2. To Socrates, says Aristotle, may rightly be ascribed "inductive arguments." Now, just as it is a mistake to suppose that in occupying himself with "universal definitions" Socrates was concerned to discuss the metaphysical status of the universal, so it

would be a mistake to suppose that in occupying himself with "inductive arguments" Socrates was concerned with problems of logic. Aristotle, looking back on Socrates' actual practice and method, sums it up in logical terms; but that should not be taken to imply that Socrates developed an explicit theory of Induction from the standpoint of a logician.

What was Socrates' practical method? It took the form of "dialectic" or conversation. He would get into conversation with someone and try to elicit from him his ideas on some subject. For instance, he might profess his ignorance of what courage really is, and ask the other man if he had any light on the subject. Or Socrates would lead the conversation in that direction, and when the other man had used the word "courage," Socrates would ask him what courage is, professing his own ignorance and desire to learn. His companion had used the word, therefore he must know what it meant. When some definition or description had been given him, Socrates would profess his great satisfaction, but would intimate that there were one or two little difficulties which he would like to see cleared up. Accordingly he asked questions, letting the other man do most of the talking, but keeping the course of the conversation under his control, and so would expose the inadequacy of the proposed definition of courage. The other would fall back on a fresh or modified definition, and so the process would go on, with or without final success.

The dialectic, therefore, proceeded from less adequate definitions to a more adequate definition, or from consideration of particular examples to a universal definition. Sometimes indeed no definite result would be arrived at;[1] but in any case the aim was the same, to attain a true and universal definition; and as the argument proceeded from the particular to the universal, or from the less perfect to the more perfect, it may truly be said to be a process of induction. Xenophon mentions some of the ethical phenomena which Socrates sought to investigate, and the nature of which he hoped to enshrine in definitions—e.g. piety and impiety, just and unjust, courage and cowardice.[2] (The early dialogues of Plato deal with the same ethical values—the *Euthyphron* with piety (no result); the *Charmides* with temperance (no result); the *Lysis* with friendship (no result).) The investigation

[1] The early dialogues of Plato, which may safely be considered "Socratic" in character, generally end without any determinate and positive result having been attained.

[2] *Mem.*, I, I, 16.

is, for instance, concerning the nature of injustice. Examples are brought forward—to deceive, to injure, to enslave, and so on. It is then pointed out that it is only when these things are done to friends that they are unjust. But the difficulty arises that if one, for example, steals a friend's sword when he is in a passing state of despair and wishes to commit suicide, no injustice is committed. Nor is it unjust on a father's part if he employs deception in order to induce his sick son to take the medicine which will heal him. It appears, therefore, that actions are unjust only when they are performed ***against friends with the intention of harming them.***[1]

3. This dialectic might, of course, prove somewhat irritating or even disconcerting or humiliating to those whose ignorance was exposed and whose cocksureness was broken down—and it may have tickled the fancy of the young men who congregated round Socrates to hear their elders being "put in the sack"—but the aim of Socrates was not to humiliate or to disconcert. His aim was to discover the truth, not as matter of pure speculation, but with a view to the good life: in order to act well, one must know what the good life is. His "irony," then, his profession of ignorance, was sincere; he did not know, but he wanted to find out, and he wanted to induce others to reflect for themselves and to give real thought to the supremely important work of caring for their souls. Socrates was deeply convinced of the value of the soul, in the sense of the thinking and willing subject, and he saw clearly the importance of knowledge, of true wisdom, if the soul is to be properly tended. What are the true values of human life which have to be realised in conduct? Socrates called his method "midwifery," not merely by way of playful allusion to his mother, but to express his intention of getting others to produce true ideas in their minds, with a view to right action. This being so, it is easy to understand why Socrates gave so much attention to definition. He was not being pedantic, he was convinced that a clear knowledge of the truth is essential for the right control of life. He wanted to give birth to true ideas in the clear form of definition, not for a speculative but for a practical end. Hence his preoccupation with ethics.

4. I have said that Socrates' interest was predominantly ethical. Aristotle says quite clearly that Socrates "was busying himself about ethical matters."[2] And again, "Socrates occupied

[1] *Mem.*, 4, 2, 14 ff.

[2] *Metaph.*, A 987 b 1–3.

himself with the excellences of character, and in connection with them became the first to raise the problem of universal definitions."[1] This statement of Aristotle is certainly borne out by the picture of Socrates given by Xenophon.

Plato in the *Apology* relates the profession of Socrates at his trial, that he went where he could do the greatest good to anyone, seeking "to persuade every man among you that he must look to himself, and seek virtue and wisdom before he looks to his private interests, and look to the State before he looks to the interests of the State; and that this should be the order which he observes in all his actions."[2] This was the "mission" of Socrates, which he regarded as having been imposed upon him by the god of Delphi, to stimulate men to care for their noblest possession, their soul, through the acquisition of wisdom and virtue. He was no mere pedantic logician, no mere destructive critic, but a man with a mission. If he criticised and exposed superficial views and easy-going assumptions, this was due not to a frivolous desire to display his own superior dialectical acumen, but to a desire to promote the good of his interlocutors and to learn himself.

Of course it is not to be expected in a member of a Greek City state that an ethical interest should be completely severed from a political interest, for the Greek was essentially a citizen and he had to lead the good life within the framework of the city. Thus Xenophon relates that Socrates inquired τί πόλις, τί πολιτικός τί ἀρχὴ ἀνθρώπων, τὶ ἀρχηγὸς ἀνθρώπων, and we have seen Socrates' statement in the *Apology* about looking to the State itself before looking to the interests of the State.[3] But, as the last remark implies, and as is clear from Socrates' life, he was not concerned with party politics as such, but with political life in its ethical aspect. It was of the greatest importance for the Greek who wished to lead the good life to realise what the State is and what being a citizen means, for we cannot care for the State unless we know the nature of the State and what a good State is. Knowledge is sought as a means to ethical action.

5. This last statement deserves some development, since the Socratic theory as to the relation between knowledge and virtue is characteristic of the Socratic ethic. According to Socrates knowledge and virtue are one, in the sense that the wise man, he who *knows* what is right, will also *do* what is right. In other

[1] *Metaph.*, M 1,078 b 17–19. [2] *Apol.*, 36.
[3] Xen., *Mem.*, 1, 1, 16; *Apol.*, 36.

words, no one does evil knowingly and of set purpose; no one chooses the evil *as such*.

This "ethical intellectualism" seems at first sight to be in blatant contradiction with the facts of everyday life. Are we not conscious that we ourselves sometimes deliberately do what we know to be wrong, and are we not convinced that other people act sometimes in the same way? When we speak of a man as being responsible for a bad action, are we not thinking of him as having done that act with knowledge of its badness? If we have reason to suppose that he was not culpably ignorant of its badness, we do not hold him to be morally responsible. We are therefore inclined to agree with Aristotle, when he criticises the identification of knowledge and virtue on the ground that Socrates forgot the irrational parts of the soul and did not take sufficient notice of the fact of moral weakness, which leads a man to do what he knows to be wrong.[1]

It has been suggested that, as Socrates was himself singularly free from the influence of the passions in regard to moral conduct, he tended to attribute the same condition to others, concluding that failure to do what is right is due to ignorance rather than to moral weakness. It has also been suggested that when Socrates identified virtue with knowledge or wisdom he had in mind not any sort of knowledge but a real personal conviction. Thus Professor Stace points out that people may go to church and say that they believe the goods of this world to be worth nothing, whereas they *act* as if they were the only goods they valued. This is not the sort of knowledge Socrates had in mind: he meant a real personal conviction.[2]

All this may well be true, but it is important to bear in mind what Socrates meant by "right." According to Socrates that action is right which serves man's true utility, in the sense of promoting his true happiness (εὐδαιμονία). Everyone seeks his own good as a matter of course. Now, it is not every kind of action, however pleasant it may appear at the time, which promotes man's true happiness. For instance, it might be pleasant to a man to get drunk constantly, especially if he is suffering from some overwhelming sorrow. But it is not to the true good of man. Besides injuring his health, it tends to enslave him to a habit, and it goes counter to the exercise of man's highest possession, that

[1] *Eth. Nic.*, 1145 b.

[2] *Crit. Hist.*, pp. 147–8. Professor Stace considers, however, that "Aristotle's criticism of Socrates is unanswerable."

which differentiates him from the brute—his reason. If a man constantly gets drunk, believing this to be his true good, then he errs from ignorance, not realising what his true good is. Socrates would hold that if he knew that it was to his own true good and conducive to his happiness *not* to get drunk, then he would not get drunk. Of course we would remark with Aristotle that a man might well know that to contract a habit of drunkenness is not conducive to his ultimate happiness, and yet still contract the habit. This is doubtless true; it does not seem that Aristotle's criticism can be gainsaid; but at this point we might observe (with Stace) that if the man had a *real personal conviction* of the evil of the habit of drunkenness, he would not contract it. This does not dispose of Aristotle's objection, but it helps us to understand how Socrates could say what he did. And, as a matter of fact, is there not a good deal in what Socrates says, when viewed from the psychological standpoint? A man might know, intellectually, that to get drunk is not conducive to his ultimate happiness and dignity as a man, but when the impulse comes upon him, he may turn his attention away from this knowledge and fix it on the state of intoxication as seen against the background of his unhappy life, until this state and its desirability engage all his attention and take on the character of a true good. When the exhilaration has worn off, he recalls to mind the evil of drunkenness and admits: "Yes, I did wrong, knowing it to be wrong." But the fact remains, that at the moment when he surrendered to the impulse, that knowledge had slipped from the field of his mental attention, even if culpably.

Of course, we must not suppose that the utilitarian standpoint of Socrates envisages the following of whatever is pleasurable. The wise man realises that it is more advantageous to be self-controlled, than to have no self-control; to be just, rather than to be unjust; courageous, rather than cowardly—"advantageous" meaning what is conducive to true health and harmony of soul. Socrates certainly considered that pleasure is a good, but he thought that true pleasure and lasting happiness attend the moral rather than the immoral man, and that happiness does not consist in having a great abundance of external goods.

While we cannot accept the over-intellectualist attitude of Socrates, and agree with Aristotle that ἀκρασία or moral weakness is a fact which Socrates tended to overlook, we willingly pay tribute to the ethic of Socrates. For a rational ethic must be founded on human nature and the good of human nature as such. Thus when Hippias allowed ἄγραφοι νόμοι, but excepted from their number laws which varied from State to State, remarking that the prohibition of sexual intercourse between parents and children is not a universal prohibition, Socrates rightly answered that racial inferiority which results from such intercourse justifies the prohibition.[1] This is tantamount to appealing to what we would call "Natural Law," which is an expression of man's nature and conduces to its harmonious development. Such an ethic is indeed *insufficient*, since the Natural Law cannot acquire a morally binding force, obligatory in conscience—at least in the sense of our modern conception of "Duty"—unless it has a metaphysical basis and is grounded in a transcendental Source, God, Whose Will for man is expressed in the Natural Law; but, although insufficient, it enshrines a most important and valuable truth which is essential to the development of a rational moral philosophy. "Duties" are not simply senseless or arbitrary commands or prohibitions, but are to be seen in relation to human nature as such: the Moral Law expresses man's true good. Greek ethics were predominantly eudaemonological in character (cf. Aristotle's ethical system), and though, we believe, they need to be completed by Theism, and seen against the background of Theism, in order to attain their true development, they remain, even in their incomplete state, a perennial glory of Greek philosophy. Human nature is constant and so ethical values are constant, and it is Socrates' undying fame that he realised the constancy of these values and sought to fix them in universal definitions which could be taken as a guide and norm in human conduct.[2]

6. From the identification of wisdom and virtue follows the unity of virtue. There is really only one virtue, insight into what is truly good for man, what really conduces to his soul's health and harmony. A more important consequence, however, is the teachability of virtue. The Sophists, of course, professed to teach the art of virtue, but Socrates differed from them, not only in the fact that he declared himself to be a learner, but also in the fact that his ethical inquiries were directed to the discovery of universal

[1] Xen., *Mem.*, IV, 4, 19 ff.

[2] Not all thinkers have been willing to admit that human nature *is* constant. But there is no real evidence to show that "primitive" man differed essentially from modern man; nor have we justification for supposing that a type of man will arise in the future who will be *essentially* different from the man of to-day.

and constant moral norms. But though Socrates' method was dialectic and not lecturing, it necessarily follows from his identification of virtue with knowledge that virtue can be taught. We would make a distinction: intellectual knowledge of what virtue is can be imparted by instruction, but not virtue itself. However, if wisdom as real personal conviction is stressed, then *if* such wisdom can be taught, perhaps virtue could be taught too. The chief point to remark is that "teaching" for Socrates did not mean mere notional instruction, but rather leading a man to a real insight. Yet although such considerations undoubtedly render Socrates' doctrine of the teachability of virtue more intelligible, it remains true that in this doctrine the over-intellectualism of his ethic is again apparent. He insisted that as, e.g., the doctor is the man who has learnt medicine, so the just man is he who has learnt what is just.

7. This intellectualism was not likely to make Socrates particularly favourable to democracy as practised at Athens. If the doctor is the man who has learnt medicine, and if no sick man would entrust himself to the care of one who had no knowledge of medicine, it is unreasonable to choose public officials by lot or even by vote of the inexperienced multitude.[1] True rulers are those who know how to rule. If we would not appoint as pilot of a vessel a man devoid of all knowledge of the pilot's art and of the route to be traversed, why appoint as ruler of the State one who has no knowledge of ruling and who does not know what is to the good of the State?

8. In regard to religion, Socrates seems to have spoken generally of "gods" in the plural and to have meant thereby the traditional Greek deities; but one can discern a tendency towards a purer conception of Deity. Thus, according to Socrates, the knowledge of the gods is not limited, they are everywhere present and know all that is said and done. As they know best what is good, man should simply pray for the good and not for particular objects like gold.[2] Occasionally belief in one God comes to the fore,[3] but it does not appear that Socrates ever paid much attention to the question of monotheism or polytheism. (Even Plato and Aristotle find a place for the Greek gods.)

Socrates suggested that as man's body is composed of materials gathered from the material world, so man's reason is a part of the universal Reason or Mind of the world.[4] This notion was to be

[1] *Mem.*, 1, 2, 9; 3, 9, 10. [2] *Mem.*, 1, 3, 2. [3] *Mem.*, 1, 4, 5, 7. [4] *Mem.*, 1, 4, 8.

developed by others, as was also his teaching on teleology, anthropocentric in character. Not only are sense-organs given to man in order to enable him to exercise the corresponding senses, but anthropocentric teleology is extended to cosmic phenomena. Thus the gods give us the light without which we cannot see, and Providence is displayed in the gifts of food made to man by the earth. The sun does not approach so near the earth as to wither up or to scorch man, nor is it set so far away that he cannot be warmed thereby. These and suchlike considerations are natural in a man who studied in the School of the Cosmologists and was disappointed at the little use that Anaxagoras made of his principle of Mind; but Socrates was not a Cosmologist or a Theologian, and though he may be called "the real founder of Teleology in the consideration of the world,"[1] he was, as we have seen, primarily interested in human conduct.[2]

9. The picture that Aristophanes gives of Socrates in the *Clouds* need not detain us.[3] Socrates had been a pupil of the old philosophers, and he had admittedly been influenced by the teaching of Anaxagoras. As to the "Sophistic" flavouring imparted to his character in the *Clouds*, it is to be remembered that Socrates like the Sophists, concentrated his attention on the Subject, on man himself. He was a public and familiar figure, known to all the audience for his dialectical activity, and to some he undoubtedly seemed to be "rationalistic," critically destructive and anti-traditionalist in tendency. Even if it were to be assumed that Aristophanes himself realised the difference that existed between Socrates and the Sophists—which is not at all clear—it would not necessarily follow that he would express this realisation before a public audience. And Aristophanes is known to have been a traditionalist and an opponent of the Sophists.

IV. *Trial and Death of Socrates*

In 406 B.C. Socrates showed his moral courage by refusing to agree to the demand that the eight commanders who were to be impeached for their negligence at Arginusae should be tried together, this being contrary to the law and calculated to evoke a hasty sentence. He was at this time a member of the Committee

[1] Ueb.-Praechter, p. 145; *der eigentliche Begründer der Teleologie in der Betrachtung der Welt.*

[2] Cf. e.g. *Mem.*, I, 1, 10–16.

[3] It is, as Burnet observes, a caricature which—like any caricature, if it is to have point—possesses a foundation in fact.

of the πρυτάνεις or Committee of the Senate. His moral courage was again shown when he refused, at the demand of the Thirty in 404/3, to take part in the arrest of Leon of Salamis, whom the Oligarchs intended to murder, that they might confiscate his property. They wished to incriminate as many prominent citizens as possible in their doings, doubtless with a view to the eventual day of reckoning. Socrates, however, simply refused to take any part in their crimes, and would probably have paid for his refusal with his life, had not the Thirty fallen.

In the year 400/399 Socrates was brought to trial by the leaders of the restored democracy. Anytus, the politician who remained in the background, instigated Meletus to carry on the prosecution. The indictment before the court of the King Archon is recorded as follows[1]: "Meletus, son of Miletus, of the deme of Pitthus, indicts Socrates, son of Sophroniscus, of the deme of Alopecae, on his oath, to the following effect. Socrates is guilty (i) of not worshipping the gods whom the State worships, but introducing new and unfamiliar religious practices; (ii) and, further, of corrupting the young. The prosecutor demands the death penalty."

The first charge was never explicitly defined, the reason seeming to be that the prosecutor was relying on the jury's recollection of the reputation of the old Ionian cosmologists and perhaps of the profanation of the mysteries in 415, in which Alcibiades had been involved. But no reference could be made to the profanation in view of the Amnesty of 404/3, of which Anytus had himself been the chief promoter. The second charge, that of corrupting the young, is really a charge of infusing into the young a spirit of criticism in regard to the Athenian Democracy. At the back of it all was doubtless the thought that Socrates was responsible for having "educated Alcibiades and Critias—Alcibiades, who had for a time gone over to Sparta and who led Athens into such straits, Critias, who was the most violent of the Oligarchs. This again could not be explicitly mentioned because of the Amnesty of 404/3, but the audience would have grasped easily enough what was meant. That is why Aeschines could say, some fifty years later: "You put Socrates the Sophist to death, because he was shown to have educated Critias."[2]

The accusers no doubt supposed that Socrates would go into voluntary exile without awaiting trial, but he did not. He remained for trial in 399 and defended himself in court. In the

[1] Diog. Laërt., 2, 40. [2] i, 173.

trial Socrates might have made much of his military service and of his defiance of Critias in the time of the Oligarchy, but he merely brought the facts in, coupling them with his defiance of the democracy in the matter of the trial of the commanders. He was condemned to death by a majority of either 60 or 6 votes by a jury of 500 or 501.[1] It then rested with Socrates to propose an alternative penalty, and it was obviously the wisest course to propose a sufficiently substantial penalty. Thus if Socrates had proposed exile, this alternative to the death penalty would doubtless have been accepted. Socrates, however, proposed as his proper "reward" free meals in the Pryntaneum, after which he consented to propose a small fine—and all this without any attempt to influence the jury, as was usual, by bringing a weeping wife and children into court. The jury was annoyed at Socrates' cavalier behaviour, and he was sentenced to death by a larger majority than the one that had found him guilty.[2] The execution had to be delayed for about a month, to await the return of the "sacred boat" from Delos (in memory of Theseus' deliverance of the city from the tribute of seven boys and girls imposed by Minos of Knossos), and there was plenty of time to arrange an escape, which the friends of Socrates did in fact arrange. Socrates refused to avail himself of their kind offers, on the ground that such a course would be contrary to his principles. Socrates' last day on earth is recounted by Plato in the *Phaedo*, a day that was spent by Socrates in discoursing on the immortality of the soul with his Theban friends, Cebes and Simmias.[3] After he had drunk the hemlock and lay dying, his last words were: "Crito, we owe a cock to Aesculapius; pay it, therefore, and do not neglect it." When the poison reached his heart there was a convulsive movement and he died, "and Crito, perceiving it, closed his mouth and eyes. This, Echecrates, was the end of our friend, a man, we should say, who was the best of all his time that we have known, and, moreover, the most wise and just."[4]

[1] Cf. *Apol.*, 36 a (the reading of which is not absolutely certain), and Diog. Laërt., 2, 41. Burnet and Taylor, understanding Plato as saying that Socrates was condemned by a majority of 60 votes, suppose that the voting was 280 to 220, out of a jury of 500.

[2] Diog. Laërt (2, 42) says that the majority was 80 votes in excess of the first majority. According to Burnet and Taylor, the second voting would thus be 360 in favour of the death penalty as against 140.

[3] This remark is not meant to prejudice my view that the theory of Forms is not to be ascribed to Socrates.

[4] *Phaedo*, 118.

CHAPTER XV

MINOR SOCRATIC SCHOOLS

THE term "Minor Socratic Schools" should not be taken to indicate that Socrates founded any definite School. He hoped, no doubt, that others would be found to carry on his work of stimulating men's minds, but he did not gather round him a band of disciples to whom he left a patrimony of definite doctrine. But various thinkers, who had been disciples of Socrates to a greater or less extent, emphasised one or other point in his teaching, combining it also with elements culled from other sources. Hence Dr. Praechter calls them *Die einseitigen Sokratiker*, not in the sense that these thinkers only ***reproduced*** certain sides of Socrates' teaching, but in the sense that each of them was a *continuation* of Socratic thought in a particular direction, while at the same time they modified what they took from earlier philosophising, in order to harmonise it with the Socratic legacy.[1] In some ways, then, the use of a common name, Minor Socratic Schools, is unfortunate, but it may be used, if it is understood that the connection of some of these thinkers with Socrates is but slender.

1. *The School of Megara*

Euclid of Megara (not to be confused with the mathematician) seems to have been one of the earliest disciples of Socrates, as—if the story be genuine—he continued his association with Socrates in spite of the prohibition (of 431/2) of Megarian citizens entering Athens, coming into the city at dusk dressed as a woman.[2] He was present at the death of Socrates in 400/399, and after that event Plato and other Socratics took refuge with Euclid at Megara.

Euclid seems to have been early acquainted with the doctrine of the Eleatics, which he so modified under the influence of the Socratic ethic as to conceive of the One as the Good. He also regarded virtue as a unity. According to Diogenes Laërtius, Euclid asserted that the One is known by many names, identifying the One with God and with Reason.[3] The existence of a

[1] Ueberweg-Praechter, p. 155.
[2] Gell, *Noct. Att.*, 6, 10.
[3] Diog. Laërt., 2, 106.

principle contrary to the Good he naturally denied, as that principle would be multiplicity, which is illusory on the Eleatic view. We may say that he remained an adherent of the Eleatic tradition, in spite of the Socratic influence that he underwent.

The Megaric philosophy, particularly under the influence of Eubulides, developed into an Eristic which concocted various ingenious arguments, designed to disprove a position through a *reductio ad absurdum*. For example, the famous difficulty: "One grain of corn is not a heap: add a grain and there is yet no heap: when does the heap begin?" was designed to show that plurality is impossible, as Zeno wanted to show that motion was impossible. Another conundrum is that ascribed by some to Diodorus Cronus, another Megaric: "That which you have not lost, you still have; but you have not lost horns; therefore you still have horns." Or again: "Electra knows her brother, Orestes. But Electra does not know Orestes (who stands before her, disguised). Therefore Electra does not know what she knows."[1]

Another philosopher of the Megaric School, Diodorus Cronus (mentioned above), identified the actual and the possible: only the actual is possible. His argument was as follows: The possible cannot become the impossible. Now, if of two contradictories one has actually come to pass, the other is impossible. Therefore, if it had been possible before, the impossible would have come out of the possible. Therefore it was not possible before, and only the actual is possible; (e.g. "The world exists," and "The world does not exist," are contradictory propositions. But the world actually exists. Therefore it is impossible that the world does not exist. But if it were ever possible that the world should not exist a possibility has turned into an impossibility. This cannot be so. Therefore it was never possible that the world should not exist.) This proposition has been taken up in recent times by Professor Nicolai Hartmann of Berlin, who has identified the actual with the possible on the ground that what actually happens depends on the totality of given conditions, and—given those conditions—nothing else could have happened.[2]

A noted adherent of the School was Stilpo of Megara, who taught at Athens about 320, but was afterwards banished. He applied himself chiefly to ethics, developing the point of self-sufficiency in a theory of "apathy." When asked what he had lost in the plundering of Megara, he replied that he had not seen

[1] Cf. Diog. Laërt., 2, 108. [2] *Möglichkeit und Wirklichkeit*, Berlin, 1938.

anyone carrying off wisdom or knowledge.[1] Zeno (the Stoic) was a pupil of Stilpo.

II. *The Elean-Eretrian School*

This School was named after Phaedo of Elis (the Phaedo of Plato's Dialogue) and Menedemus of Eretria. Phaedo of Elis seems to have resembled the Megarians in his use of dialectic, while Menedemus was chiefly interested in ethics, holding the unity of virtue and knowledge.

III. *The Early Cynic School*

The Cynics, or disciples of the dog, may have got their name from their unconventional mode of life or from the fact that Antisthenes, the founder of the School, taught in the gymnasium known as the *Kynosarges*. Perhaps both factors had something to do with the nickname.

Antisthenes (*c.* 445–*c.* 365) was born of an Athenian father and of a Thracian slave mother.[2] This might explain why he taught in the *Kynosarges*, which was reserved for those who were not of pure Athenian blood. The Gymnasium was dedicated to Heracles, and the Cynics took the hero as a sort of tutelary god or patron. One of Antisthenes' works was named after Heracles.[3]

At first a pupil of Gorgias, Antisthenes afterwards became an adherent of Socrates, to whom he was devoted. But what he chiefly admired in Socrates was the latter's independence of character, which led him to act in accordance with his convictions, no matter what the cost. Neglecting the fact that Socrates had been independent of earthly riches and the applause of men only in order to obtain the greater good of true wisdom, Antisthenes set up this independence and self-sufficiency as an ideal or end in itself. Virtue in his eyes was simply independence of all earthly possessions and pleasures: in fact, it was a negative concept—renunciation, self-sufficiency. Thus the negative side of Socrates' life was changed by Antisthenes into a positive goal or end. Similarly, Socrates' insistence on ethical knowledge was exaggerated

[1] Diog. Laërt., 2, 115. Senec., *Ep.*, 9, 3. [2] Diog. Laërt., 6, 1.

[3] It has been suggested that it was Diogenes who founded the Cynic School or "Movement," and not Antisthenes: Arist. refers to the followers of Antisthenes as Ἀντισθένειοι (*Metaph.*, 1043 b 24). But the nickname of "Cynics" seems to have been accepted, only in the time of Diogenes and Arist.'s use of the term Ἀντισθένειοι would not appear to prove anything against Antisthenes having been the real fountain-head of the Cynic School.

by Antisthenes into a positive contempt for scientific learning and art. Virtue, he said, is sufficient by itself for happiness: nothing else is required—and virtue is the absence of desire, freedom from wants, and complete independence. Socrates, of course, had been independent of the opinion of others simply because he possessed deep convictions and principles, the surrender of which, to satisfy popular opinion, he regarded as treason to the Truth. He did not, however, set out to flout popular opinion or public convictions simply for the sake of doing so, as the Cynics, particularly Diogenes, seem to have done. The philosophy of the Cynics was thus an exaggeration of one side of Socrates' life and attitude, and that a negative one or at least one consequent on a much more positive side. Socrates was ready to disobey the Oligarchy at the risk of his life, rather than commit an act of injustice; but he would not have lived in a tub like Diogenes merely to flaunt his disregard for the ways of men.

Antisthenes was strongly opposed to the theory of Ideas, and maintained that there are only individuals. He is said to have remarked: "O Plato, I see a horse, but I do not see horseness."[1] To each thing only its own name should be applied: e.g. we can say "Man is man" or "The good is good," but not "The man is good." No predicate should be attributed to a subject other than the subject itself.[2] With this goes the doctrine that we can only predicate of an individual its own individual nature; one cannot predicate of it membership of a class. Hence the denial of the theory of Ideas. Another logical theory of Antisthenes was that of the impossibility of self-contradiction. For if a man says different things, he is speaking of different objects.[3]

Virtue is wisdom, but this wisdom consists principally in "seeing through" the values of the majority of mankind. Riches, passions, etc., are not really good, nor are suffering, poverty, contempt, really evil: independence is the true good. Virtue, then, is wisdom and it is teachable, though there is no need of long reasoning and reflection in order to learn it. Armed with this virtue, the wise man cannot be touched by any so-called evil of life, even by slavery. He stands beyond laws and conventions, at least those of the State that does not recognise true virtue. The ideal state or condition of life in which all would live in

[1] Simplic. in Arist., *Categ.*, 208, 29 f.; 211, 17 f.
[2] Plat., *Soph.*, 251 b; Arist., *Metaph.*, Δ 29, 1024 b 32–25 a 1.
[3] Arist., Top., A xi, 104 b 20; *Metaph.*, Δ 29, 1024 b 33–4.

independence and freedom from desire, is of course incompatible with wars.[1]

Socrates had, indeed, placed himself in opposition on occasion to the authority of the Government, but he was so convinced of the rightness of the State's authority as such and of the Law, that he would not take advantage of the opportunity presented to him of escape from prison, but preferred to suffer death in accordance with the Law. Antisthenes, however, with his usual one-sided exaggeration denounced the historic and traditional State and its Law. In addition he renounced the traditional religion. There is only one God; the Greek pantheon is only a convention. Virtue is the only service of God: temples, prayers, sacrifices, etc., are condemned. "By convention there are many gods, but by nature only one."[2] On the other hand, Antisthenes interpreted the Homeric myths allegorically, trying to get moral applications and lessons out of them.

Diogenes of Sinope (d. *c.* 324 B.C.) thought that Antisthenes had not lived up to his own theories and called him a "trumpet which hears nothing but itself."[3] Banished from his country, Diogenes spent most of his life in Athens, though he died in Corinth. He called himself the "Dog," and held up the life of animals as a model for mankind. His task was the "recoining of values,"[4] and to the civilisation of the Hellenic world he opposed the life of animals and of the barbaric peoples.

We are told that he advocated community of wives and children and free love, while in the political sphere he declared himself a citizen of the world.[5] Not content with Antisthenes' "indifference" to the external goods of civilisation, Diogenes advocated a positive asceticism in order to attain freedom. Connected therewith is his deliberate flouting of convention, doing in public what it is generally considered should be done in private—and even what should not be done in private.

Disciples of Diogenes were Monimus, Onesicritus, Philiscus, Crates of Thebes. The latter presented his considerable fortune to the city, and took up the Cynic life of mendicancy, followed by his wife Hipparchia.[6]

[1] Cf. Vita Antisth., apud Diog. Laërt.
[2] Cf. Cic., *De Nat.*, 1, 13, 32; Clem. Alex., *Protrep.*, 6, 71, 2; *Strom.*, 5, 14, 108, 4.
[3] Dion. Chrys., 8, 2. [4] Diog. Laërt., 6, 20. [5] Diog. Laërt., 6, 72.
[6] Diog. Laërt., *Lives of Crates and Hipparchia.*

IV. *The Cyrenaic School*

Aristippus of Cyrene, founder of the Cyrenaic School, was born about 435 B.C. From 416 he was in Athens, from 399 in Aegina, from 389/388 with Plato at the court of the elder Dionysius, and then again after 356 in Athens. But these dates and order of events cannot be regarded as beyond dispute, to say the least of it.[1] It has even been suggested that Aristippus never founded the Cyrenaic "School" at all, but was confused with his grandson, a later Aristippus. But in view of the statements of Diog. Laërt., Sotion and Panaetius (cf. D.L., 2, 84 f.), it does not seem possible to accept the statement of Sosicrates and others (D.L.) that Aristippus wrote nothing at all, while the passage in Eusebius' *Praeparatio Evangelica* (14, 18, 31) can be explained without having to suppose that Aristippus never laid a foundation for the Cyrenaic philosophy.

In Cyrene Aristippus seems to have become acquainted with the teaching of Protagoras, while afterwards at Athens he was in relation with Socrates. The Sophist may have been largely responsible for Aristippus' doctrine, that it is our sensations alone that give us certain knowledge:[2] of things in themselves they can give us no certain information, nor about the sensations of others. Subjective sensations, then, must be the basis for practical conduct. But if my individual sensations form the norm for my practical conduct, then, thought Aristippus, it follows as a matter of course that the end of conduct is to obtain pleasurable sensations.

Aristippus declared that sensation consists in movement. When the movement is gentle, the sensation is pleasurable; when it is rough, there is pain; when movement is imperceptible or when there is no movement at all, there is neither pleasure nor pain. The rough movement cannot be the ethical end. Yet it cannot consist in the mere absence of pleasure or pain, i.e. be a purely negative end. The ethical end must, therefore, be pleasure, a positive end.[3] Socrates had indeed declared that virtue is the one path to happiness, and he held out happiness as a motive for the practice of virtue, but he did not maintain that pleasure is the end of life. Aristippus, however, seized on the one side of the Socratic teaching and disregarded all the rest.

[1] Dates from Heinrich von Stein's *De philos. Cyrenaica*, part I, *De Vita Aristippi*, Gött, 1858.

[2] Cf. Sext. Emp. *adv. mathemat.*, 7, 191 ff.

[3] Diog. Laërt., 2, 86 ff.

Pleasure, then, according to Aristippus, is the end of life. But what kind of pleasure? Later on for Epicurus it would be rather painlessness, negative pleasure, that is the end of life; but for Aristippus it was positive and present pleasure. Thus it came about that the Cyrenaics valued bodily pleasure above intellectual pleasure, as being more intense and powerful. And it would follow from their theory of knowledge that the quality of the pleasure does not come into account. The consequential following-out of this principle would obviously lead to sensual excesses; but, as a matter of fact, the Cyrenaics, no doubt adopting the hedonistic elements in Socrates' doctrine, declared that the wise man will, in his choice of pleasure, take cognisance of the future. He will, therefore, avoid unrestrained excess, which would lead to pain, and he will avoid indulgence that would occasion punishment from the State or public condemnation. The wise man, therefore, needs judgment in order to enable him evaluate the different pleasures of life. Moreover, the wise man in his enjoyments will preserve a certain measure of independence. If he allows himself to be enslaved, then to that extent he cannot be enjoying pleasure, but rather is he in pain. Again, the wise man, in order to preserve cheerfulness and contentment, will limit his desires. Hence the saying attributed to Aristippus, ἔχω (Λαΐδα), καὶ οὐκ ἔχομαι ἐπεὶ τὸ κρατεῖν καὶ μὴ ἡττᾶσθαι ἡδονῶν ἄριστον, οὐ τὸ μὴ χρῆσθαι.[1]

This contradiction in the teaching of Aristippus between the principle of the pleasure of the moment and the principle of judgment, led to a divergence of views—or an emphasis on different sides of his doctrine—among his disciples. Thus *Theodorus the Atheist* declared indeed that judgment and justness are goods (the latter only because of the external advantages of a just life), and that individual acts of gratification are indifferent, the contentment of the mind being true happiness or pleasure, but he asserted too that the wise man will not give his life for his country and that he would steal, commit adultery, etc., if circumstances allowed it. He also denied the existence of any god at all.[2] *Hegesias* also demanded indifference towards individual acts of gratification, but he was so convinced of the miseries of life and of the impossibility of attaining happiness, that he emphasised a negative concept of the end of life, namely, absence of pain and sorrow.[3] Cicero and other sources tell us that Hegesias'

[1] Diog. Laërt., 2, 75.

[2] Diog. Laërt., 2, 97; Cic., *De Nat. D.*, 1, 1, 12.

[3] Diog. Laërt., 2, 94–6.

lectures at Alexandria led to so many suicides on the part of his hearers, that Ptolemy Lagi forbade their continuance![1] *Anniceris*, on the other hand, stressed the positive side of Cyrenaicism, making positive pleasure and, indeed, individual acts of gratification the end of life. But he limited the logical conclusions of such a view by giving great weight to love of family and country, friendship and gratitude, which afford pleasure even when they demand sacrifice.[2] In the value he placed on friendship he differed from Theodorus, who declared (D.L.) that the wise are sufficient for themselves and have no need of friends.

Diogenes Laërtius clearly implies that these philosophers had their own peculiar disciples: for example, he speaks of "Hegesiakoi," though he also classes them together as "Cyrenaics." Thus, while Aristippus the Cyrenaic laid the foundation of the"Cyrenaic" or pleasure-philosophy (*v. sup.*), he can hardly be said to have founded a closely-knit philosophical School, comprising Theodorus, Hegesias, Anniceris, etc., as members. These philosophers were part-heirs of Aristippus the elder, and represent a philosophical tendency rather than a School in the strict sense.

[1] Cic., *Tusc.*, 1, 34, 83.
[2] Diog. Laërt., 2, 96 f.; Clem. Alex., *Strom.*, 2, 21, 130, 7 f.

CHAPTER XVI

DEMOCRITUS OF ABDERA

THIS would seem to be the right place to say something of the epistemological and ethical theories of Democritus of Abdera. Democritus was a disciple of Leucippus and, together with his Master, belongs to the Atomist School; but his peculiar interest for us lies in the fact that he gave attention to the problem of knowledge raised by Protagoras and to the problem of conduct which relativistic doctrines of the Sophists had rendered acute. Nowhere named by Plato, Democritus is frequently mentioned by Aristotle. He was head of a School at Abdera, and was still alive when Plato founded the Academy. The reports of his journeys to Egypt and Athens cannot be accepted with certainty.[1] He wrote copiously, but his writings have not been preserved.

1. The account of sensation given by Democritus was a mechanical one. Empedocles had spoken of "effluences" from objects which reach the eye, for example. The Atomists make these effluences to be atoms, images (δείκελα, εἴδωλα), which objects are constantly shedding. These images enter through the organs of sense, which are just passages (πόροι) and impinge on the soul, which is itself composed of atoms. The images, passing through the air, are subject to distortion by the air; and this is the reason why objects very far off may not be seen at all. Differences of colour were explained by differences of smoothness or roughness in the images, and hearing was given a like explanation, the stream of atoms flowing from the sounding body causing motion in the air between the body and the ear. Taste, smell and touch were all explained in the same way. (Secondary qualities would, therefore, not be objective.) We also obtain knowledge of the gods through such εἴδωλα; but gods denote for Democritus higher beings who are not immortal, though they live longer than men. They are δύσφθαρτα but not ἄφθαρτα. Strictly speaking, of course, the Atomist system would not admit of God, but only of atoms and the void.[2]

Now, Protagoras the Sophist, a fellow-citizen of Democritus, declared all sensation to be equally true for the sentient subject:

[1] Diog. Laërt., 9, 34 f. Cf. Burnet, *G.P.*, I, p. 195.

[2] According to Diog. Laërt. (9, 35), quoting Favorinus, Democritus ridiculed the assertions of Anaxagoras concerning Mind.

thus an object might be truly sweet for X, truly bitter for Y. Democritus, however, declared that all the sensations of the special senses are false, for there is nothing real corresponding to them outside the subject. "Νόμῳ there is sweet, νόμῳ there is bitter; νόμῳ there is warm and νόμῳ there is cold; νόμῳ there is colour. But ἐτεῇ there are atoms and the void."[1] In other words, our sensations are purely subjective, though they are caused by something external and objective—the atoms, namely—which, however, cannot be apprehended by the special senses. "By the senses we in truth know nothing sure, but only something that changes according to the disposition of the body and of the things that enter into it or resist it."[2] The special senses, then, give us no information about reality. Secondary qualities, at least, are not objective. "There are two forms of knowledge (γνώμη), the trueborn (γνησίη) and the bastard (σκοτίη). To the bastard belong all these: sight, hearing, smell, taste, touch. The trueborn is quite apart from these."[3] However, as the soul is composed of atoms, and as all knowledge is caused by the immediate contact with the subject of atoms coming from the outside, it is evident that the "trueborn" knowledge is on the same footing as the "bastard," in the sense that there is no absolute separation between sense and thought. Democritus saw this, and he comments: "Poor Mind, it is from us" (i.e. from the senses), "thou hast got the proofs to throw us with. Thy throw is a fall."[4]

2. Democritus' theory of conduct, so far as we can judge from the fragments, did not stand in scientific connection with his atomism. It is dominated by the idea of happiness or εὐδαιμονίη, which consists in εὐθυμίη or εὐεστώ. Democritus wrote a treatise on cheerfulness (Περὶ εὐθυμίης), which was used by Seneca and Plutarch. He considers that happiness is the end of conduct, and that pleasures and pain determine happiness; but "happiness dwelleth not in herds nor in gold; the soul is the dwelling-place of the 'daimon.' "[5] "The best thing for a man is to pass his life so as to have as much joy and as little trouble as may be."[6] However, just as sense-knowledge is not true knowledge, so the pleasures of sense are not true pleasures. "The good and the true are the same for all men, but the pleasant is different for different people."[7] We have to strive after well-being (εὐεστώ) or cheerfulness (εὐθυμίη), which is a state of soul, and the attainment of

[1] Frag. 9. [2] Frag. 9. [3] Frag. 11. [4] Frag. 125.
[5] Frag. 171. (Almost "fortune.") [6] Frag. 189. [7] Frag. 69.

which requires a weighing, judging and distinguishing of various pleasures. We should be guided by the principle of "symmetry" or of "harmony." By the use of this principle we may attain to calm of body—health, and calm of soul—cheerfulness. This calm or tranquillity is to be found chiefly in the goods of the soul. "He who chooses the goods of the soul, chooses the more divine; he who chooses the goods of the tabernacle (σκῆνος), chooses the human."[1]

3. It appears that Democritus exercised an influence on later writers through a theory of the evolution of culture.[2] Civilisation arose from need (χρέια) and prosecution of the advantageous or useful (σύμφερον), while man owes his arts to the imitation of nature, learning spinning from the spider, house-building from the swallow, song from the birds, etc. Democritus also (unlike Epicurus) emphasised the importance of the State and of political life, declaring that men should consider State affairs more important than anything else and see to it that they are well managed. But that his ethical ideas postulated freedom, whereas his atomism involved determinism, apparently did not occur to Democritus in the form of a problem.

4. It is clear from what has been said that Democritus, in carrying on the cosmological speculation of the older philosophers (in his philosophic atomism he was a follower of Leucippus), was hardly a man of his period—the Socratic period. His theories concerning perception, however, and the conduct of life, are of greater interest, as showing at least that Democritus realised that some answer was required to the difficulties raised by Protagoras. But, although he saw that some answer was required, he was personally unable to give any satisfactory solution. For an incomparably more adequate attempt to deal with epistemological and ethical problems, we have to turn to Plato.

[1] Frag. 37. [2] Frag. 154.

PART III

PLATO

CHAPTER XVII

LIFE OF PLATO

PLATO, one of the greatest philosophers of the world, was born at Athens (or Aegina), most probably in the year 428/7 B.C., of a distinguished Athenian family. His father was named Ariston and his mother Perictione, sister of Charmides and niece of Critias, who both figured in the Oligarchy of 404/3. He is said to have been originally called Aristocles, and to have been given the name Plato only later, on account of his robust figure,[1] though the truth of Diogenes' report may well be doubted. His two brothers, Adeimantus and Glaucon, appear in the *Republic*, and he had a sister named Potone. After the death of Ariston, Perictione married Pyrilampes, and their son Antiphon (Plato's half-brother) appears in the *Parmenides*. No doubt Plato was brought up in the home of his stepfather; but although he was of aristocratic descent and brought up in an aristocratic household, it must be remembered that Pyrilampes was a friend of Pericles, and that Plato must have been educated in the traditions of the Periclean régime. (Pericles died in 429/8.) It has been pointed out by various authors that Plato's later bias against democracy can hardly have been due, at any rate solely, to his upbringing, but was induced by the influence of Socrates and still more by the treatment which Socrates received at the hands of the democracy. On the other hand, it would seem possible that Plato's distrust of democracy dated from a period very much earlier than that of the death of Socrates. During the later course of the Peloponnesian War (it is highly probable that Plato fought at Arginusae in 406) it can hardly have failed to strike Plato that the democracy lacked a truly capable and responsible leader, and that what leaders there were were easily spoiled by the necessity of pleasing the populace. Plato's final abstention from home politics no doubt dates from the trial and condemnation of his Master; but the

[1] Diog. Laërt., 3, 4.

formulation of his conviction that the ship of State needs a firm pilot to guide her, and that he must be one who *knows* the right course to follow, and who is prepared to act conscientiously in accordance with that knowledge, can hardly fail to have been laid during the years when Athenian power was passing to its eclipse.

According to a report of Diogenes Laërtius, Plato "applied himself to the study of painting, and wrote poems, dithyrambics at first, and afterwards lyric poems and tragedies."[1] How far this is true, we cannot say; but Plato lived in the flourishing period of Athenian culture, and must have received a cultured education. Aristotle informs us that Plato had been acquainted in his youth with Cratylus, the Heraclitean philosopher.[2] From him Plato would have learnt that the world of sense-perception is a world of flux, and so not the right subject-matter for true and certain knowledge. That true and certain knowledge is attainable on the conceptual level, he would have learnt from Socrates, with whom he must have been acquainted from early years. Diogenes Laërtius indeed asserted that Plato "became a pupil of Socrates" when twenty years old,[3] but as Charmides, Plato's uncle, had made the acquaintance of Socrates in 431,[4] Plato must have known Socrates at least before he was twenty. In any case we have no reason for supposing that Plato became a "disciple" of Socrates, in the sense of devoting himself wholly and professedly to philosophy, since he tells us himself that he originally intended to embark on a political career—as was natural in a young man of his antecedents.[5] His relatives in the Oligarchy of 403–4 urged Plato to enter upon political life under their patronage; but when the Oligarchy started to pursue a policy of violence and attempted to implicate Socrates in their crimes, Plato became disgusted with them. Yet the democrats were no better, since it was they who put Socrates to death, and Plato accordingly abandoned the idea of a political career.

Plato was present at the trial of Socrates, and he was one of the friends who urged Socrates to increase his proposed fine from one to thirty *minae*, offering to stand security;[6] but he was absent from the death-scene of his friend in consequence of an illness.[7] After the death of Socrates, Plato withdrew to Megara and took shelter with the philosopher Euclid, but in all probability he soon returned to Athens. He is said by the biographers to have

[1] Diog. Laërt., 3, 5. [2] *Metaph.*, A 6, 987 a 32–5. [3] Diog. Laërt., 3, 6.
[4] At least, this is what the reference to Potidaea (*Charmides*, 153) implies.
[5] *Ep.*, 7, 324 b 8–326 b 4. [6] *Apol.*, 34 a 1, 38 b 6–9. [7] *Phaedo*, 59 b 10.

travelled to Cyrene, Italy and Egypt, but it is uncertain what truth there is in these stories. For instance, Plato himself says nothing of any visit to Egypt. It may be that his knowledge of Egyptian mathematics, and even of the games of the children, indicate an actual journey to Egypt; on the other hand, the story of the journey may have been built up as a mere conclusion from what Plato has to say about the Egyptians. Some of these stories are obviously legendary in part; e.g. some give him Euripides as a companion, although the poet died in 406. This fact makes us rather sceptical concerning the reports of the journeys in general; but all the same, we cannot say with certainty that Plato did *not* visit Egypt, and he may have done so. If he did actually go to Egypt, he may have gone about 395 and have returned to Athens at the outbreak of the Corinthian wars. Professor Ritter thinks it very probable that Plato was a member of the Athenian force in the first years of the wars (395 and 394).

What is certain, however, is that Plato visited Italy and Sicily, when he was forty years old.[1] Possibly he wished to meet and converse with members of the Pythagorean School: in any case he became acquainted with Archytas, the learned Pythagorean. (According to Diogenes Laërtius, Plato's aim in undertaking the journey was to see Sicily and the volcanoes.) Plato was invited to the court of Dionysius I, Tyrant of Syracuse, where he became a friend of Dion, the Tyrant's brother-in-law. The story goes that Plato's outspokenness excited the anger of Dionysius, who gave him into the charge of Pollis, a Lacedaemonian envoy, to sell as a slave. Pollis sold Plato at Aegina (at that time at war with Athens), and Plato was even in danger of losing his life; but eventually a man of Cyrene, a certain Anniceris, ransomed him and sent him to Athens.[2] It is difficult to know what to make of this story, as it is not mentioned in Plato's *Epistles*: if it really happened (Ritter accepts the story) it must be dated 388 B.C.

On his return to Athens, Plato seems to have founded the Academy (388/7), near the sanctuary of the hero Academus. The Academy may rightly be called the first European university, for the studies were not confined to philosophy proper, but extended over a wide range of auxiliary sciences, like mathematics, astronomy and the physical sciences, the members of the School joining in the common worship of the Muses. Youths came to the Academy, not only from Athens itself, but also from abroad;

[1] *Ep.*, 7, 324 a 5–6. [2] Diog. Laërt., 3, 19–20.

and it is a tribute to the scientific spirit of the Academy and a proof that it was not simply a "philosophical-mystery" society, that the celebrated mathematician Eudoxus transferred himself and his School from Cyzicus to the Academy. It is as well to lay stress on this scientific spirit of the Academy, for though it is perfectly true that Plato aimed at forming statesmen and rulers, his method did not consist in simply teaching those things which would be of immediate practical application, e.g. rhetoric (as did Isocrates in his School), but in fostering the disinterested pursuit of science. The programme of studies culminated in philosophy, but it included as preliminary subjects a study of mathematics and astronomy, and no doubt harmonics, in a disinterested and not purely utilitarian spirit. Plato was convinced that the best training for public life is not a merely practical "sophistic" training, but rather the pursuit of science for its own sake. Mathematics, apart of course from its importance for Plato's philosophy of the Ideas, offered an obvious field for disinterested study, and it had already reached a high pitch of development among the Greeks. (The studies seem also to have included biological, e.g. botanical, researches, pursued in connection with problems of logical classification.) The politician so formed will not be an opportunist time-server, but will act courageously and fearlessly in accordance with convictions founded on eternal and changeless truths. In other words, Plato aimed at producing statesmen and not demagogues.

Besides directing the studies in the Academy, Plato himself gave lectures and his hearers took notes. It is important to notice that these lectures were not published, and that they stand in contrast to the dialogues, which were published works meant for "popular" reading. If we realise this fact, then some of the sharp differences that we naturally tend to discern between Plato and Aristotle (who entered the Academy in 367) disappear, at least in part. We possess Plato's popular works, his dialogues, but not his lectures. The situation is the exact opposite in regard to Aristotle, for while the works of Aristotle that are in our hands represent his lectures, his popular works or dialogues have not come down to us—only fragments remain. We cannot, therefore, by a comparison of Plato's dialogues with Aristotle's lectures, draw conclusions, without further evidence, as to a strong opposition between the two philosophers in point of literary ability, for instance, or emotional, aesthetic and "mystical" outlook. We are told that Aristotle used to relate how those who came to hear Plato's lecture on the Good, were often astonished to hear of nothing but arithmetic and astronomy, and of the limit and the One. In *Ep.* 7, Plato repudiates the accounts that some had published of the lecture in question. In the same letter he says: "So there is not, and may there never be, any treatise by me at least on these things, for the subject is not communicable in words, as other sciences are. Rather is it that after long association in the business itself and a shared life that a light is lit in the soul, kindled, as it were, by a leaping flame, and thenceforward feeds itself." Again, in *Ep.* 2: "Therefore I have never myself written a word on these matters, and there neither is nor ever shall be any written treatise of Plato; what now bears the name belongs to Socrates, beautified and rejuvenated."[1] From such passages some draw the conclusion that Plato had not much opinion of the value of books for really educative purposes. This may well be so, but we should not put undue emphasis on this point, for Plato, after all, *did* publish books—and we must also remember that the passages in question may not be by Plato at all. Yet we must concede that the Ideal Theory, in the precise form in which it was taught in the Academy, was not given to the public in writing.

Plato's reputation as teacher and counsellor of statesmen must have contributed to bringing about his second journey to Syracuse in 367. In that year Dionysius I died, and Dion invited Plato to come to Syracuse in order to take in hand the education of Dionysius II, then about thirty years old. Plato did so, and set the Tyrant to a course of geometry. Soon, however, Dionysius' jealousy of Dion got the upper hand, and when Dion left Syracuse, the philosopher after some difficulty managed to return to Athens, whence he continued to instruct Dionysius by letter. He did not succeed in bringing about a reconciliation between the Tyrant and his uncle, who took up residence at Athens, where he consorted with Plato. In 361, however, Plato undertook a third journey to Syracuse at the earnest request of Dionysius, who wished to continue his philosophical studies. Plato apparently hoped to draft a constitution for a proposed confederation of Greek cities against the Carthaginian menace, but opposition proved too strong: moreover, he found himself unable to secure the recall of Dion, whose fortune was confiscated by his nephew.

[1] *Ep.* 7, 341 c 4–d 2; *Ep.* 2, 314 c 1–4.

In 360, therefore, Plato returned to Athens, where he continued his activities in the Academy until his death in the year 348/7.[1] (In 357 Dion succeeded in making himself master of Syracuse, but he was murdered in 353, to the great grief of Plato, who felt that he had been disappointed in his dream of a philosopher-king.)

[1] *Uno et octogesimo anno scribens est mortuus.* Cic., *De Senect.*, 5, 13.

CHAPTER XVIII

PLATO'S WORKS

A. *Genuineness*

In general it may be said that we possess the entire corpus of Plato's works. As Professor Taylor remarks: "Nowhere in later antiquity do we come on any reference to a Platonic work which we do not still possess."[1] We may suppose, then, that we possess all Plato's published dialogues. We do not, however, as already remarked, possess a record of the lectures that he delivered in the Academy (though we have more or less cryptic references in Aristotle), and this would be all the more to be regretted if those are right who would see in the dialogues popular work designed for the educated laymen, to be distinguished from the lectures delivered to professional students of philosophy. (It has been conjectured that Plato lectured without a manuscript. Whether this be the fact or not, we have not got the manuscript of any lectures delivered by Plato. All the same, we have no right to draw an oversharp distinction between the doctrines of the dialogues and the doctrine delivered within the precincts of the Academy. After all, not all the dialogues can easily be termed "popular" work, and certain of them in particular show evident signs that Plato is therein groping after the clarification of his opinions.) But to say that we most probably possess all the dialogues of Plato, is not the same as to say that all the dialogues that have come down to us under the name of Plato are actually by Plato himself: it still remains to sift the genuine from the spurious. The oldest Platonic MSS. belong to an arrangement attributed to a certain Thrasyllus, to be dated round about the beginning of the Christian era. In any case this arrangement, which was by "tetralogies," seems to have been based on an arrangement in "trilogies" by Aristophanes of Byzantium in the third century B.C. It would appear, then, that the thirty-six dialogues (reckoning the Epistles as one dialogue) were generally admitted by scholars of that period to be the work of Plato. The problem can thus be reduced to the question: "Are the thirty-six dialogues all genuine or are some of them spurious; and, if so, which?"

[1] *Plato*, p. 10.

Doubts were cast upon some of the dialogues even in antiquity. Thus from Athenaeus (*flor. c.* 228 B.C.) we learn that some ascribed the *Alcibiades II* to Xenophon. Again, it would seem that Proclus not only rejected the *Epinomis* and *Epistles*, but even went so far as to reject the *Laws* and *Republic*. The assigning of spurious works was carried much further, as might be expected, in the nineteenth century, especially in Germany, the culmination of the process being reached under Ueberweg and Schaarschmidt. "If one includes the attacks of ancient and modern criticism, then of the thirty-six items of the tetralogies of Thrasyllus, only five have remained free from all attack."[1] Nowadays, however, criticism runs in a more conservative direction, and there is general agreement as to the genuineness of all the important dialogues, as also a general agreement as to the spurious character of certain of the less important dialogues, while the genuineness of a few of the dialogues remains a matter of dispute. The results of critical investigation may be summed up as follows:

(i) Dialogues which are generally rejected are: *Alcibiades II*, *Hipparchus*, *Amatores* or *Rivales*, *Theages*, *Clitophon*, *Minus*. Of this group, all except the *Alcibiades II* are probably contemporary fourth-century work, not deliberate forgeries but slighter works of the same character as the Platonic dialogues; and they may be taken, with some degree of justification, as contributing something to our knowledge of the conception of Socrates current in the fourth century. The *Alcibiades II* is probably later work.

(ii) The genuineness of the following six dialogues is disputed: *Alcibiades I*, *Ion*, *Menexenus*, *Hippias Maior*, *Epinomis*, *Epistles*. Professor Taylor thinks that the *Alcibiades I* is the work of an immediate disciple of Plato[2] and Dr. Praechter, too, thinks that it is probably not the authentic work of the Master.[3] Praechter considers the *Ion* to be genuine, and Taylor remarks that it "may reasonably be allowed to pass as genuine until some good reason for rejecting it is produced."[4] The *Menexenus* is clearly taken by Aristotle to be of Platonic origin, and modern critics are inclined to accept this view.[5] The *Hippias Maior* is most probably to be taken as the genuine work of Plato, as it seems to be alluded to, though not by name, in the *Topics* of Aristotle.[6] As to the *Epinomis*, though Professor Jaeger ascribes it to Philippus of

[1] Ueberweg-Praechter, p. 195. Dr. Praechter's invaluable work does not, of course, represent the hypercritical fashion of the time of Ueberweg.
[2] *Plato*, p. 13. [3] Ueberweg-Praechter, p. 199. [4] *Plato*, p. 13.
[5] Arist., *Rhet.*, 1415 b 30. [6] *Topics* A 5, 102 a 6; E 5, 135 a 13; Z 6, 146 a 22.

Opus,[1] Praechter and Taylor deem it authentic. Of the *Epistles*, 6, 7 and 8 are generally accepted and Professor Taylor thinks that the acceptance of these *Epistles* leads logically to the acceptance of all the rest, except 1 and possibly 2. It is true that one would not like to relinquish the *Epistles*, as they give us much valuable information concerning Plato's biography; but we must be careful not to let this very natural desire influence unduly our acceptance of *Epistles* as genuine.[2]

(iii) The genuineness of the remaining dialogues may be accepted; so that the result of criticism would seem to be that of the thirty-six dialogues of the tetralogies, six are generally rejected, six others may be accepted until proved unauthentic (except probably *Alcibiades I* and certainly *Epistle I*), while twenty-four are certainly the genuine work of Plato. We have, therefore, a very considerable body of literature on which to found our conception of the thought of Plato.

B. *Chronology of Works*

1. *Importance* of determining the chronology of the works.

It is obviously important in the case of any thinker to see how his thought developed, how it changed—if it did change—what modifications were introduced in the course of time, what fresh ideas were introduced. The customary illustration in this connection is that of the literary production of Kant. Our knowledge of Kant would scarcely be adequate, if we thought that his Critiques came in his early years and that he later reverted to a "dogmatic" position. We might also instance the case of Schelling. Schelling produced several philosophies in the course of his life, and for an understanding of his thought it is highly desirable that one should know that he began with the standpoint of Fichte, and that his theosophical flights belong to his later years.

2. Method of determining the chronology of the works.[3]

(i) The criterion that has proved of most help in determining the chronology of the works of Plato is that of *language*. The argument from language is all the surer in that, while differences of content may be ascribed to the conscious selection and purpose of the author, development of linguistic style is largely

[1] *Aristotle*, e.g. p. 132. Cf. Diog. Laërt., 3, 37. Taylor (*Plato*, p. 497) thinks that Diog. only means that Philippus transcribed the *Epinomis* from wax tablets.

[2] Ritter accepts Epistles 3 and 8 and the main narrative of 7.

[3] Cf. Ueberweg-Praechter, pp. 199–218.

unconscious. Thus Dittenberger traces the frequent use of τί μήν; and the growing use of γε μήν and ἀλλὰ μήν, as formula of agreement, to the first Sicilian journey of Plato. The *Laws* certainly belong to Plato's old age,[1] while the *Republic* belongs to an earlier period. Now, not only is there a decreased vigour of dramatic power visible in the *Laws*, but we can also discern points of linguistic style which Isocrates had introduced into Attic prose and which do not appear in the *Republic*. This being so, we are helped in assessing the order of the intervening dialogues, according to the degree in which they approach the later style of writing.

But while the use of linguistic style as a criterion for determining the chronology of the dialogues has proved to be the most helpful method, one cannot, of course, neglect to make use of other criteria, which may often decide the matter at issue when the linguistic indications are doubtful or even contradictory.

(ii) One obvious criterion for assessing the order of the dialogues is that afforded by the direct testimony of the ancient writers, though there is not as much help to be had from this source as might perhaps be expected. Thus while Aristotle's assertion that the *Laws* were written later than the *Republic* is a valuable piece of information, the report of Diogenes Laërtius to the effect that the *Phaedrus* is the earliest of the Platonic dialogues cannot be accepted. Diogenes himself approves of the report, but it is evident that he is arguing from the subject-matter (love—in the first part of the dialogue) and from the poetic style.[2] We cannot argue from the fact that Plato treats of love to the conclusion that the dialogue must have been written in youth, while the use of poetic style and myth is not in itself conclusive. As Taylor points out, we should go far wrong were we to argue from the poetical and "mythical" flights of the second part of Faust to the conclusion that Goethe wrote the second part before the first.[3] A similar illustration might be taken from the case of Schelling, whose theosophical flights, as already mentioned, took place in his advanced age.

(iii) As for references within the dialogues to historical persons and acts, these are not so very many, and in any case they only furnish us with a *terminus post quem*. For example, if there were a reference to the death of Socrates, as in the *Phaedo*, the dialogue must clearly have been composed after the death of Socrates, but that does not tell us *how long after*. However, critics

[1] Arist., *Pol.*, B 6, 1264 b 27. [2] Diog. Laërt., 3, 38. [3] *Plato*, p. 18.

have obtained some help from this criterion. For instance, they have argued that the *Meno* was probably written when the incident of the corruption of Ismenias of Thebes was still fresh in people's memory.[1] Again, if the *Gorgias* contains a reply to a speech of Polycrates against Socrates (393/2), the *Gorgias* would probably have been written between 393 and 389, i.e. before the first Sicilian journey. It might, naïvely, be supposed that the age ascribed to Socrates in the dialogues is an indication of the date of composition of the dialogue itself. but to apply this criterion as a universal rule is clearly going too far. For instance, a novelist might well introduce his detective-hero as a grown man and as an already experienced police officer in his first novel, and then in a later novel treat of the hero's first case. Moreover, though one may be justified in supposing that dialogues dealing with the personal fate of Socrates were composed not long after his death, it would be clearly unscientific to take it for granted that dialogues dealing with the last years of Socrates, e.g. the *Phaedo* and the *Apology*, were all published at the same time.

(iv) References of one dialogue to another would obviously prove a help in determining the order of the dialogues, since a dialogue that refers to another dialogue must have been written after the dialogue to which it refers; but it is not always easy to decide if an apparent reference to another dialogue really *is* a reference. However, there are some cases in which there is a clear reference, e.g. the reference to the *Republic* that is contained in the *Timaeus*.[2] Similarly, the *Politicus* is clearly the sequel to the *Sophistes* and so must be a later composition.[3]

(v) In regard to the actual content of the dialogue, we have to exercise the greatest prudence in our use of this criterion. Suppose for instance, that some philosophical doctrine is found in a short summary sentence in dialogue X, while in dialogue Y it is found treated at length. A critic might say: "Very good, in dialogue X a preliminary sketch is given, and in dialogue Y the matter is explained at length." Might it not be that a short summary is given in dialogue X precisely because the doctrine has already been treated at length in dialogue Y? One critic[4] has maintained that the negative and critical examination of problems precedes the positive and constructive exposition. If this be taken as a criterion, then the *Theaetetus*, the *Sophistes*, the *Politicus*, the

[1] *Meno*, 90 a. [2] 17 ff. [3] *Polit.*, 284 b 7 ff., 286 b 10.
[4] K. Fr. Hermann.

Parmenides, should precede in date of composition the *Phaedo* and the *Republic*, but investigation has shown that this cannot be so.

However, to say that the content-criterion has to be used with prudence, is not to say that it has no use. For example, the attitude of Plato towards the doctrine of Ideas suggests, that the *Theaetetus*, *Parmenides*, *Sophistes*, *Politicus*, *Philebus*, *Timaeus*, should be grouped together, while the connection of the *Parmenides*, *Sophistes* and *Politicus* with the Eleatic dialectic suggests that these dialogues stand in a peculiarly close relation with one another.

(vi) Differences in the artistic construction of the dialogues may also be of help in determining their relation to one another in regard to order of composition. Thus in certain dialogues the setting of the dialogue, the characterisation of the personages who take part in it, are worked out with great care: there are humorous and playful allusions, vivid interludes and so on. To this group of dialogues belongs the *Symposium*. In other dialogues, however, the artistic side retreats into the background, and the author's attention is obviously wholly occupied with the philosophic content. In dialogues of this second group—to which the *Timaeus* and the *Laws* would belong—form is more or less neglected: content is everything. A probably legitimate conclusion is that the dialogues written with more attention to artistic form are earlier than the others, as artistic vigour flagged in Plato's old age and his attention was engrossed by the theoretic philosophy. (This does not mean that the use of poetic *language* necessarily becomes less frequent, but that the power of conscious artistry tends to decrease with years.)

3. Scholars vary in their estimate of the results obtained by the use of criteria such as the foregoing; but the following chronological schemes may be taken as, in the main, satisfactory (though it would hardly be acceptable to those who think that Plato did not write when he was directing the Academy in its early years).

I. *Socratic Period*

In this period Plato is still influenced by the Socratic intellectual determinism. Most of the dialogues end without any definite result having been attained. This is characteristic of Socrates' "not knowing."

i. *Apology*. Socrates' defence at his trial.

ii. *Crito*. Socrates is exhibited as the good citizen who, in spite of his unjust condemnation, is willing to give up his life in obedience to the laws of the State. Escape is suggested by Crito and others, and money is provided; but Socrates declares that he will abide by his principles.

iii. *Euthyphron*. Socrates awaits his trial for impiety. On the nature of piety. No result to the inquiry.

iv. *Laches*. On courage. No result.

v. *Ion*. Against the poets and rhapsodists.

vi. *Protagoras*. Virtue is knowledge and can be taught.

vii. *Charmides*. On temperance. No result.

viii. *Lysis*. On friendship. No result.

ix. *Republic*. Bk. I. On justice.

(The *Apology* and *Crito* must obviously have been written at an early date. Probably the other dialogues of this group were also composed before the first Sicilian journey from which Plato returned by 388/7.)

II. *Transition Period*

Plato is finding his way to his own opinions.

x. *Gorgias*. The practical politician, or the rights of the stronger versus the philosopher, or justice at all costs.

xi. *Meno*. Teachability of virtue corrected in view of ideal theory.

xii. *Euthydemus*. Against logical fallacies of later Sophists.

xiii. *Hippias* I. On the beautiful.

xiv. *Hippias* II. Is it better to do wrong voluntarily or involuntarily?

xv. *Cratylus*. On the theory of language.

xvi. *Menexenus*. A parody on rhetoric.

(The dialogues of this period were probably composed before the first Sicilian journey, though Praechter thinks that the *Menexenus* dates from after the journey.)

III. *Period of Maturity*

Plato is in possession of his own ideas.

xvii. *Symposium*. All earthly beauty is but a shadow of true Beauty, to which the soul aspires by Eros.

xviii. *Phaedo*. Ideas and Immortality.

xix. *Republic*. The State. Dualism strongly emphasised, i.e. metaphysical dualism.

xx. *Phaedrus*. Nature of love: possibility of philosophic rhetoric.
Tripartition of soul, as in *Rep*.
(These dialogues were probably composed between the first and second Sicilian journeys.)

IV. *Works of Old Age*

xxi. *Theaetetus*. (It may be that the latter part was composed *after* the *Parmenides*.) Knowledge is not sense-perception or true judgment.

xxii. *Parmenides*. Defence of ideal theory against criticism.

xxiii. *Sophistes*. Theory of Ideas again considered.

xxiv. *Politicus*. The true ruler is the *knower*. The legal State is a makeshift.

xxv. *Philebus*. Relation of pleasure to good.

xxvi. *Timaeus*. Natural science. Demiurge appears.

xxvii. *Critias*. Ideal agrarian State contrasted with imperialistic sea-power, "Atlantis."

xxviii. *Laws* and *Epinomis*. Plato makes concessions to real life, modifying the Utopianism of the *Republic*.
(Of these dialogues, some may have been written between the second and third Sicilian journeys, but the *Timaeus*, *Critias*, *Laws* and *Epinomis* were probably written after the third journey).

xxix. Letters 7 and 8 must have been written after the death of Dion in 353.

Note

Plato never published a complete, nicely rounded-off and finished philosophical system: his thought continued to develop as fresh problems, other difficulties to be considered, new aspects of his doctrine to be emphasised or elaborated, certain modifications to be introduced, occurred to his mind.[1] It would, therefore, be desirable to treat Plato's thought genetically, dealing with the different dialogues in their chronological order, so far as this can be ascertained. This is the method adopted by Professor A. E. Taylor in his outstanding work, *Plato, the Man and his Work*.

[1] Cf. the words of Dr. Praechter, *Platon ist ein Werdender gewesen sein Leben lang*. Ueberweg-Praechter, p. 260.

In a book such as this, however, such a course is scarcely practicable, and so I have thought it necessary to divide up the thought of Plato into various compartments. None the less, in order to avoid, as much as can be, the danger of cramming together views that spring from different periods of Plato's life, I will attempt not to lose sight of the gradual genesis of the Platonic doctrines. In any case, if my treatment of Plato's philosophy leads the reader to turn his attention to the actual dialogues of Plato, the author will consider himself amply rewarded for any pains he has taken.

CHAPTER XIX

THEORY OF KNOWLEDGE

PLATO'S theory of knowledge cannot be found systematically expressed and completely elaborated in any one dialogue. The *Theaetetus* is indeed devoted to the consideration of problems of knowledge, but its conclusion is negative, since Plato is therein concerned to refute false theories of knowledge, especially the theory that knowledge is sense-perception. Moreover, Plato had already, by the time he came to write the *Theaetetus*, elaborated his theory of degrees of "knowledge," corresponding to the hierarchy of being in the *Republic*. We may say, then, that the positive treatment preceded the negative and critical, or that Plato, having made up his mind what knowledge is, turned later to the consideration of difficulties and to the systematic refutation of theories which he believed to be false.[1] In a book like the present one, however, it seems best to treat first of the negative and critical side of the Platonic epistemology, before proceeding to consider his positive doctrine. Accordingly, we propose first of all to summarise the argument of the *Theaetetus*, before going on to examine the doctrine of the *Republic* in regard to knowledge. This procedure would seem to be justified by the exigencies of logical treatment, as also by the fact that the *Republic* is not primarily an epistemological work at all. Positive epistemological doctrine is certainly contained in the *Republic*, but some of the *logically prior* presuppositions of that doctrine are contained in the later dialogue, the *Theaetetus*.

The task of summarising the Platonic epistemology and giving it in systematic form is complicated by the fact that it is difficult to separate Plato's epistemology from his ontology. Plato was not a critical thinker in the sense of Immanuel Kant, and though it is possible to read into his thoughts an anticipation of the Critical Philosophy (at least, this is what some writers have endeavoured to do), he is inclined to assume that we can have knowledge and to be primarily interested in the question what

[1] We do not thereby mean to imply that Plato had not made up his mind as to the status of sense-perception long before he wrote the *Theaetetus* (we have only to read the *Republic*, for instance, or consider the genesis and implications of the Ideal Theory): we refer rather to systematic consideration in published writings.

is the true object of knowledge. This means that ontological and epistemological themes are frequently intermingled or treated *pari passu*, as in the *Republic*. We will make an attempt to separate the epistemology from the ontology, but the attempt cannot be wholly successful, owing to the very character of the Platonic epistemology.

1. *Knowledge is not Sense-perception*

Socrates, interested like the Sophists in practical conduct, refused to acquiesce in the idea that truth is relative, that there is no stable norm, no abiding object of knowledge. He was convinced that ethical conduct must be founded on knowledge, and that that knowledge must be knowledge of eternal values which are not subject to the shifting and changing impressions of sense or of subjective opinion, but are the same for all men and for all peoples and all ages. Plato inherited from his Master this conviction that there can be knowledge in the sense of objective and universally valid knowledge; but he wished to demonstrate this fact theoretically, and so he came to probe deeply into the problems of knowledge, asking what knowledge is and of what.

In the *Theaetetus* Plato's first object is the refutation of false theories. Accordingly he sets himself the task of challenging the theory of Protagoras that knowledge is perception, that what appears to an individual to be true is true for that individual. His method is to elicit dialectically a clear statement of the theory of knowledge implied by the Heraclitean ontology and the epistemology of Protagoras, to exhibit its consequences and to show that the conception of "knowledge" thus attained does not fulfil the requirements of true knowledge at all, since knowledge must be, Plato assumes, (i) infallible, and (ii) of what *is*. Sense-perception is neither the one nor the other.

The young mathematical student Theaetetus enters into conversation with Socrates, and the latter asks him what he thinks knowledge to be. Theaetetus replies by mentioning geometry, the sciences and the crafts, but Socrates points out that this is no answer to his question, for he had asked, not *of* what knowledge is, but *what* knowledge is. The discussion is thus meant to be epistemological in character, though, as has been already pointed out, ontological considerations cannot be excluded, owing to the very character of the Platonic epistemology.

Moreover, it is hard to see how in any case ontological questions can be avoided in an epistemological discussion, since there is no knowledge *in vacuo*: knowledge, if it is knowledge at all, must necessarily be knowledge of something, and it may well be that knowledge is necessarily related to some particular type of object.

Theaetetus, encouraged by Socrates, makes another attempt to answer the question proposed, and suggests that "knowledge is nothing but perception,"[1] thinking no doubt primarily of vision, though in itself perception has, of course, a wider connotation. Socrates proposes to examine this idea of knowledge, and in the course of conversation elicits from Theaetetus an admission of Protagoras' view that perception means appearance, and that appearances vary with different subjects. At the same time he gets Theaetetus to agree that knowledge is always of something that *is*, and that, as being knowledge, it must be infallible.[2] This having been established, Socrates next tries to show that the objects of perception are, as Heraclitus taught, always in a state of flux: they never *are*, they are always *becoming*. (Plato does not, of course, accept Heraclitus' doctrine that *all* is becoming, though he accepts the doctrine in regard to the objects of sense-perception, drawing the conclusion that sense-perception cannot be the same as knowledge.) Since an object may appear white to one at one moment, grey at another, sometimes hot and sometimes cold, etc., "appearing to" must mean "becoming for," so that perception is always of that which is in process of becoming. My perception is true for me, and if I know what appears to me, as I obviously do, then my knowledge is infallible. So Theaetetus has said well that perception is knowledge.

This point having been reached, Socrates proposes to examine the idea more closely. He raises the objection that if knowledge is perception, then no man can be wiser than any other man, for I am the best judge of my own sense-perception as such. What, then, is Protagoras' justification for setting himself up to teach others and to take a handsome fee for doing so? And where is our ignorance that makes us sit at his feet? For is not each one of us the measure of his own wisdom? Moreover, if knowledge and perception are the same, if there is no difference between seeing and knowing, it follows that a man who has come to know (i.e. see) a thing in the past and still remembers it, does not know it—although he remembers it—since he does not see it.

[1] 151 e 2–3. [2] 152 c 5–7.

Conversely, granted that a man can remember something he has formerly perceived and can *know* it, even while no longer perceiving it, it follows that knowledge and perception cannot be equated (even if perception were a kind of knowledge).

Socrates then attacks Protagoras' doctrine on a broader basis, understanding "Man is the measure of all things," not merely in reference to sense-perception, but also to all truth. He points out that the majority of mankind believe in knowledge and ignorance, and believe that they themselves or others can hold something to be true which in point of fact is not true. Accordingly, anyone who holds Protagoras' doctrine to be false is, according to Protagoras himself, holding the truth (i.e. if the man who is the measure of all things is the individual man).

After these criticisms Socrates finishes the claims of perception to be knowledge by showing (i) that perception is not the whole of knowledge, and (ii) that even within its own sphere perception is not knowledge.

(i) Perception is not the whole of knowledge, for a great part of what is generally recognised to be knowledge consists of truths involving terms which are not objects of perception at all. There is much we know about sensible objects, which is known by intellectual reflection and not immediately by perception. Plato gives existence or non-existence as examples.[1] Suppose that a man sees a mirage. It is not immediate sense-perception that can inform him as to the objective existence or non-existence of the mirage perceived: it is only rational reflection that can tell him this. Again, the conclusions and arguments of mathematics are not apprehended by sense. One might add that our knowledge of a person's character is something more than can be explained by the definition, "Knowledge is perception," for our knowledge of a person's character is certainly not given in bare sensation.

(ii) Sense-perception, even within its own sphere, is not knowledge. We cannot really be said to know anything if we have not attained truth about it, e.g. concerning its existence or non-existence, its likeness to another thing or its unlikeness. But truth is given in reflection, in the judgment, not in bare sensation. The bare sensation may give, e.g. one white surface and a second white surface, but in order to judge the similarity between the two, the mind's activity is necessary. Similarly, the

[1] 185 c 4–e 2.

railway lines *appear* to converge: it is in intellectual reflection that we know that they are really parallel.

Sense-perception is not, therefore, worthy of the name of knowledge. It should be noted how much Plato is influenced by the conviction that sense-objects are not proper objects of knowledge and cannot be so, since knowledge is of what is, of the stable and abiding, whereas objects of sense cannot really be said to *be*—*qua* perceived, at least—but only to *become*. Sense-objects are objects of apprehension in some sort, of course, but they elude the mind too much to be objects of real knowledge, which must be, as we have said, (i) infallible, (ii) of what *is*.

(It is noteworthy that Plato, in disposing of the claim of perception to be the whole of knowledge, contrasts the private or peculiar objects of the special senses—e.g. colour, which is the object of vision alone—with the "common terms that apply to everything," and which are the objects of the mind, not of the senses. These "common terms" correspond to the Forms or Ideas which are, ontologically, the stable and abiding objects, as contrasted with the particulars or *sensibilia*).

II. *Knowledge is not simply "True Judgment"*

Theaetetus sees that he cannot say that judgment *tout simple* is knowledge, for the reason that false judgments are possible. He therefore suggests that knowledge is true judgment, at least as a provisional definition, until examination of it shows whether it is correct or false. (At this point a digression occurs, in which Socrates tries to find out how false judgments are possible and come to be made at all. Into this discussion I cannot enter at any length, but I will mention one or two suggestions that are made in its course. For example, it is suggested that one class of false judgments arises through the confusion of two objects of different sorts, one a present object of sense-perception, the other a memory-image. A man may judge—mistakenly—that he sees his friend some way off. There is someone there, but it is not his friend. The man has a memory-image of his friend, and something in the figure he sees recalls to him this memory-image: he then judges falsely that it is his friend who is over there. But, obviously, not all cases of false judgment are instances of the confusion of a memory-image with a present object of sense-perception: a mistake in mathematical calculation can hardly be reduced to this. The famous simile of the "aviary" is introduced, in an attempt to show how other kinds of false judgment may arise, but it is found to be unsatisfactory; and Plato concludes that the problem of false judgment cannot be advantageously treated until the nature of knowledge has been determined. The discussion of false judgment was resumed in the *Sophistes*.)

In the discussion of Theaetetus' suggestion that knowledge is true judgment, it is pointed out that a judgment may be true without the fact of its truth involving knowledge on the part of the man who makes the judgment. The relevance of this observation may be easily grasped. If I were to make at this moment the judgment, "Mr. Churchill is talking to President Truman over the telephone," it *might* be true; but it would not involve knowledge on my part. It would be a guess or random shot, as far as I am concerned, even though the judgment were objectively true. Similarly, a man might be tried on a charge of which he was actually not guilty, although the circumstantial evidence was very strong against him and he could not prove his innocence. If, now, a skilful lawyer defending the innocent man were able, for the sake of argument, so to manipulate the evidence or to play on the feelings of the jury, that they gave the verdict "Not guilty," their judgment would actually be a true judgment; but they could hardly be said to *know* the innocence of the prisoner, since *ex hypothesi* the evidence is against him. Their verdict would be a true judgment, but it would be based on persuasion rather than on knowledge. It follows, then, that knowledge is not simply true judgment, and Theaetetus is called on to make another suggestion as to the right definition of knowledge.

III. *Knowledge is not True Judgment plus an "Account"*

True judgment, as has been seen, may mean no more than true belief, and true belief is not the same thing as knowledge. Theaetetus, therefore, suggests that the addition of an "account" or explanation (λόγος) would convert true belief into knowledge. Socrates begins by pointing out that if giving an account or explanation means the enumeration of elementary parts, then these parts must be known or knowable: otherwise the absurd conclusion would follow that knowledge means adding to true belief the reduction of the complex to unknown or unknowable elements. But what does giving an account mean?

1. It cannot mean merely that a correct judgment, in the

sense of true belief, is expressed in words, since, if that were the meaning, there would be no difference between true belief and knowledge. And we have seen that there is a difference between making a judgment that happens to be correct and making a judgment that one *knows* to be correct.

2. If "giving an account" means analysis into elementary parts (i.e. knowable parts), will addition of an account in this sense suffice to convert true belief into knowledge? No, the mere process of analysing into elements does not convert true belief into knowledge, for then a man who could enumerate the parts which go to make up a wagon (wheels, axle, etc.) would have a scientific knowledge of a wagon, and a man who could tell you what letters of the alphabet go to compose a certain word would have a grammarian's scientific knowledge of the word. (N.B. We must realise that Plato is speaking of the mere enumeration of parts. For instance, the man who could recount the various steps that lead to a conclusion in geometry, simply because he had seen them in a book and had learnt them by heart, without having really grasped the necessity of the premisses and the necessary and logical sequence of the deduction, would be able to enumerate the "parts" of the theorem; but he would not have the scientific knowledge of the mathematician.)

3. Socrates suggests a third interpretation of "plus account." It may mean "being able to name some mark by which the thing one is asked about differs from everything else."[1] If this is correct, then to know something means the ability to give the distinguishing characteristic of that thing. But this interpretation too is disposed of, as being inadequate to define knowledge.

(*a*) Socrates points out that if knowledge of a thing means the addition of its distinguishing characteristic to a correct notion of that thing, we are involved in an absurd position. Suppose that I have a correct notion of Theaetetus. To convert this correct notion into knowledge I have to add some distinguishing characteristic. But unless this distinguishing characteristic were *already* contained within my correct notion, how could the latter be called a *correct* notion? I cannot be said to have a correct notion of Theaetetus, unless this correct notion includes Theaetetus' distinguishing characteristics: if these distinguishing characteristics are not included, then my "correct notion" of Theaetetus

[1] 208 c 7–8.

would equally well apply to all other men; in which case it would *not* be a correct notion of Theaetetus.

(*b*) If, on the other hand, my "correct notion" of Theaetetus includes his distinguishing characteristics, then it would also be absurd to say that I convert this correct notion into knowledge by adding the *differentia*, since this would be equivalent to saying that I convert my correct notion of Theaetetus into knowledge by adding to Theaetetus, as already apprehended in distinction from others, that which distinguishes him from others.

N.B. It is to be noted that Plato is not speaking here of *specific* differences, he is speaking of individual, sensible objects, as is clearly shown by the examples that he takes—the sun and a particular man, Theaetetus.[1] The conclusion to be drawn is not that no knowledge is attained through definition by means of a difference, but rather that the individual, sensible object is indefinable and is not really the proper object of knowledge at all. This is the real conclusion of the dialogue, namely, that true knowledge of sensible objects is unattainable, and—by implication—that true knowledge must be knowledge of the universal and abiding.

IV. *True Knowledge*

1. Plato has assumed from the outset that knowledge is attainable, and that knowledge must be (i) infallible and (ii) of the *real*. True knowledge must possess both these characteristics, and any state of mind that cannot vindicate its claim to both these characteristics cannot be true knowledge. In the *Theaetetus* he shows that neither sense-perception nor true belief are possessed of both these marks; neither, then, can be equated with true knowledge. Plato accepts from Protagoras the belief in the relativity of sense and sense-perception, but he will not accept a universal relativism: on the contrary, knowledge, absolute and infallible knowledge, is attainable, but it cannot be the same as sense-perception, which is relative, elusive and subject to the influence of all sorts of temporary influences on the part of both subject and object. Plato accepts, too, from Heraclitus the view that the objects of sense-perception, individual and sensible particular objects, are always in a state of becoming, of flux, and so are unfit to be the objects of true knowledge. They come into being and pass away, they are indefinite in number, cannot be clearly grasped in

[1] 208 c 7–e 4.

definition and cannot become the objects of scientific knowledge. But Plato does not draw the conclusion that there are no objects that are fitted to be the objects of true knowledge, but only that sensible particulars cannot be the objects sought. The object of true knowledge must be stable and abiding, fixed, capable of being grasped in clear and scientific definition, which is of the *universal*, as Socrates saw. The consideration of different states of mind is thus indissolubly bound up with the consideration of the different objects of those states of mind.

If we examine those judgments in which we think we attain knowledge of the essentially stable and abiding, we find that they are judgments concerning *universals*. If, for example, we examine the judgment "The Athenian Constitution is good," we shall find that the essentially stable element in this judgment is the concept of goodness. After all, the Athenian Constitution might be so changed that we would no longer qualify it as good, but as bad. This implies that the concept of goodness remains the same, for if we term the changed Constitution "bad," that can only be because we judge it in reference to a fixed concept of goodness. Moreover, if it is objected that, even though the Athenian Constitution may change as an empirical and historical fact, we can still say "The Athenian Constitution is good," if we mean the particular form of the Constitution that we once called good (even though it may in point of fact have since been changed), we can point out in answer that in this case our judgment has reference, not so much to the Athenian Constitution as a given empirical fact, as to a certain *type* of constitution. That this type of constitution happens at any given historical moment to be embodied in the Athenian Constitution is more or less irrelevant: what we really mean is that this universal type of constitution (whether found at Athens or elsewhere) carries with it the universal quality of goodness. Our judgment, as far as it attains the abiding and stable, really concerns a universal.

Again, scientific knowledge, as Socrates saw (predominantly in connection with ethical valuations), aims at the definition, at crystallising and fixing knowledge in the clear and unambiguous definition. A scientific knowledge of goodness, for instance, must be enshrined in the definition "Goodness is . . . ," whereby the mind expresses the essence of goodness. But definition concerns the universal. Hence true knowledge is knowledge of the universal. Particular constitutions change, but the concept of goodness remains the same, and it is in reference to this stable concept that we judge of particular constitutions in respect of goodness. It follows, then, that it is the universal that fulfils the requirements for being an object of knowledge. Knowledge of the highest universal will be the highest kind of knowledge, while "knowledge" of the particular will be the lowest kind of "knowledge."

But does not this view imply an impassable gulf between true knowledge on the one hand and the "real" world on the other—a world that consists of particulars? And if true knowledge is knowledge of universals, does it not follow that true knowledge is knowledge of the abstract and "unreal"? In regard to the second question, I would point out that the essence of Plato's doctrine of Forms or Ideas is simply this: that the universal concept is not an abstract form devoid of objective content or references, but that to each true universal concept there corresponds an objective reality. How far Aristotle's criticism of Plato (that the latter hypostatised the objective reality of the concepts, imagining a transcendent world of "separate" universals) is justified, is a matter for discussion by itself: whether justified or unjustified, it remains true that the essence of the Platonic theory of Ideas is not to be sought in the notion of the "separate" existence of universal realities, but in the belief that universal concepts have objective reference, and that the corresponding reality is of a higher order than sense-perception as such. In regard to the first question (that of the gulf between true knowledge and the "real" world), we must admit that it was one of Plato's standing difficulties to determine the precise relation between the particular and the universal; but to this question we must return when treating of the theory of Ideas from the ontological viewpoint: at the moment one can afford to pass it over.

2. Plato's positive doctrine of knowledge, in which degrees or levels of knowledge are distinguished according to objects, is set out in the famous passage of the *Republic* that gives us the simile of the Line.[1] I give here the usual schematic diagram, which I will endeavour to explain. It must be admitted that there are several important points that remain very obscure, but doubtless Plato was feeling his way towards what he regarded as the truth; and, as far as we know, he never cleared up his precise meaning

[1] *Rep.*, 509 d 6–511 e 5.

in unambiguous terms. We cannot, therefore, altogether avoid conjecture.

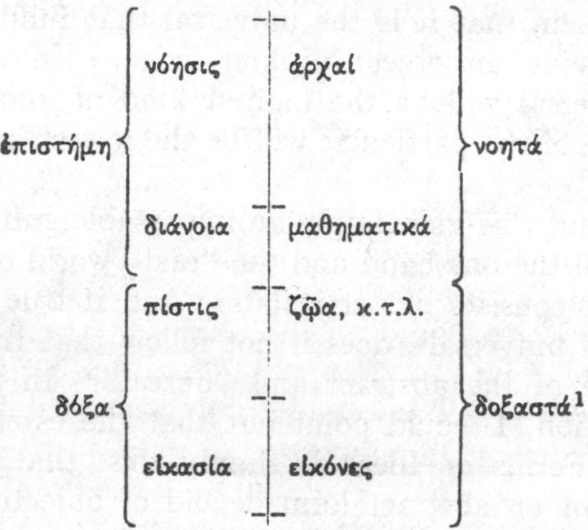

The development of the human mind on its way from ignorance to knowledge, lies over two main fields, that of δόξα (opinion) and that of ἐπιστήμη (knowledge). It is only the latter that can properly be termed knowledge. How are these two functions of the mind differentiated? It seems clear that the differentiation is based on a differentiation of object. δόξα (opinion), is said to be concerned with "images," while ἐπιστήμη, at least in the form of νόησις, is concerned with originals or archetypes, ἀρχαί. If a man is asked what justice is, and he points to imperfect embodiments of justice, particular instances which fall short of the universal ideal, e.g. the action of a particular man, a particular constitution or set of laws, having no inkling that there exists a principle of absolute justice, a norm and standard, then that man's state of mind is a state of δόξα: he sees the images or copies and mistakes them for the originals. But if a man has an apprehension of justice in itself, if he can rise above the images to the Form, to the Idea, to the universal, whereby all the particular instances must be judged, then his state of mind is a state of knowledge, of ἐπιστήμη or γνῶσις. Moreover, it is possible to progress from one state of mind to the other, to be "converted," as it were; and when a man comes to realise that what he formerly took to be originals are in reality only images or copies, i.e. imperfect embodiments of the

[1] On the left side of the line are states of mind: on the right side are corresponding objects. In both cases the "highest" are at the top. The very close connection between the Platonic epistemology and the Platonic ontology is at once apparent.

ideal, imperfect realisations of the norm or standard, when he comes to apprehend in some way the original itself, then his state of mind is no longer that of δόξα, he has been converted to ἐπιστήμη.

The line, however, is not simply divided into two sections; each section is subdivided. Thus there are two degrees of ἐπιστήμη and two degrees of δόξα. How are they to be interpreted? Plato tells us that the lowest degree, that of εικασία, has as its object, in the first place, "images" or "shadows", and in the second place "reflections in water and in solid, smooth, bright substances, and everything of the kind."[1] This certainly sounds rather peculiar, at least if one takes Plato to imply that any man mistakes shadow and reflections in water for the original. But one can legitimately extend the thought of Plato to cover in general images of images, imitations at second hand. Thus we said that a man whose only idea of justice is the embodied and imperfect justice of the Athenian Constitution or of some particular man, is in a state of δόξα in general. If, however, a rhetorician comes along, and with specious words and reasonings persuades him that things are just and right, which in reality are not even in accord with the empirical justice of the Athenian Constitution and its laws, then his state of mind is that of εἰκασία. What he takes for justice is but a shadow or caricature of what is itself only an image, if compared to the universal Form. The state of mind, on the other hand, of the man who takes as justice the justice of the law of Athens or the justice of a particular just man is that of πίστις.

Plato tells us that the objects of the πίστις section are the real objects corresponding to the images of the εἰκασία section of the line, and he mentions "the animals about us, and the whole world of nature and of art."[2] This implies, for instance, that the man whose only idea of a horse is that of particular real horses, and who does not see that particular horses are imperfect "imitations" of the ideal horse, i.e. of the specific type, the universal, is in a state of πίστις. He has not got knowledge of the horse, but only opinion. (Spinoza might say that he is in a state of *imagination*, of inadequate knowledge.) Similarly, the man who judges that external nature is true reality, and who does not see that it is a more or less "unreal" copy of the invisible world (i.e. who does not see that sensible objects are imperfect realisations of the specific type) has only πίστις. He is not so badly off as the

[1] *Rep.*, 509 e 1–510 a 3. [2] *Rep.*, 510 a 5–6.

dreamer who thinks that the images that he sees are the real world (εἰκασία), but he has not got ἐπιστήμη: he is devoid of real scientific knowledge.

The mention of art in the above quotation helps us to understand the matter a little more clearly. In the tenth book of the *Republic*, Plato says that artists are at the third remove from truth. For example, there is the specific form of man, the ideal type that all individuals of the species strive to realise, and there are particular men who are copies or imitations or imperfect realisations of the specific types. The artist now comes and paints a man, the painted man being an imitation of an imitation. Anyone who took the painted man to be a real man (one might say anyone who took the wax policeman at the entrance of Madame Tussaud's to be a real policeman) would be in a state of εἰκασία, while anyone whose idea of a man is limited to the particular men he has seen, heard of or read about, and who has no real grasp of the specific type, is in a state of πίστις. But the man who apprehends the ideal man, i.e. the ideal type, the specific form of which particular men are imperfect realisations, has νόησις.[1] Again, a just man may imitate or embody in his actions, although imperfectly, the idea of justice. The tragedian then proceeds to imitate this just man on the stage, but without knowing anything of justice in itself. He merely imitates an imitation.

Now, what of the higher division of the line, which corresponds in respect of object to νοητά, and in respect of state of mind to ἐπιστήμη? In general it is connected, not with ὁρατά or sensible objects (lower part of the line), but with ἀορατά, the invisible world, νοητά. But what of the subdivision? How does νόησις in the restricted sense differ from διάνοια? Plato says that the object of διάνοια is what the soul is compelled to investigate by the aid of the imitations of the former segments, which it employs as images, starting from hypothesis and proceeding, not to a first principle, but to a conclusion.[2] Plato is here speaking of mathematics. In geometry, for instance, the mind proceeds from hypotheses, by the use of a visible diagram, to a conclusion. The geometer, says Plato, assumes the triangle, etc., as known, adopts these "materials" as hypotheses, and then, employing a visible diagram, argues to a conclusion, being interested, however, not in the diagram itself (i.e. in this or that particular triangle or particular square or particular diameter). Geometers thus employ

[1] Plato's theory of art is discussed in a later chapter. [2] *Rep.*, 510 b 4–6.

figures and diagrams, but "they are really endeavouring to behold those objects which a person can only see with the eye of thought."[1]

One might have thought that the mathematical objects of this kind would be numbered among the Forms or ἀρχαί, and that Plato would have equated the scientific knowledge of the geometer with νόησις proper; but he expressly declined to do so, and it is impossible to suppose (as some have done) that Plato was fitting his epistemological doctrines to the exigencies of his simile of the line with its divisions. Rather must we suppose that Plato really meant to assert the existence of a class of "intermediaries," i.e. of objects which are the object of ἐπιστήμη, but which are all the same inferior to ἀρχάι, and so are the objects of διάνοια and not of νόησις.[2] It becomes quite clear from the close of the sixth book of the *Republic*[3] that the geometers have not got νοῦς or νόησις in regard to their objects; and that because they do not mount up above their hypothetical premisses, "although taken in connection with a first principle these objects come within the domain of the pure reason."[4] These last words show that the distinction between the two segments of the upper part of the line is to be referred to a distinction of state of mind and not only to a distinction of object. And it is expressly stated that understanding or διάνοια is intermediate between opinion (δόξα) and pure reason (νόησις).

This is supported by the mention of hypotheses. Nettleship thought that Plato's meaning is that the mathematician accepts his postulates and axioms as if they were self-contained truth: he does not question them himself, and if anyone else questions them, he can only say that he cannot argue the matter. Plato does not use the word "hypothesis" in the sense of a judgment which is taken as true while it *might* be untrue, but in the sense of a judgment which is treated as if it were self-conditioned, not being seen in its ground and in its necessary connection with being.[5] Against this it might be pointed out that the examples of "hypotheses" given in 510 c are all examples of entities and not of judgments, and that Plato speaks of destroying hypotheses rather than of reducing them to self-conditioned or self-evident propositions. A further suggestion on this matter is given at the close of this section.

[1] *Rep.*, 510 e 2–511 a 1.
[2] Cf. W. R. F. Hardie, *A Study in Plato*, p. 52 (O.U.P., 1936).
[3] *Rep.*, 510 c.
[4] *Rep.*, 511 c 8–d 2.
[5] *Lectures on the Republic of Plato* (1898), pp. 252 f.

In the *Metaphysics*,[1] Aristotle tells us that Plato held that mathematical entities are "between forms and sensible things." "Further, besides sensible things and forms, he says there are the objects of mathematics, which occupy an intermediate position, differing from sensible things in being eternal and unchangeable, from Forms in that there are many alike, while the Form itself is in each case unique." In view of this statement by Aristotle, we can hardly refer the distinction between the two segments of the upper part of the line to the state of mind alone. There must be a difference of object as well. (The distinction would be drawn between the states of mind exclusively, if, while τὰ μαθηματικά belonged *in their own right* to the same segment as αἱ ἀρχαί, the mathematician, acting precisely as such, accepted his "materials" hypothetically and then argued to conclusions. He would be in the state of mind that Plato calls διάνοια, for he treats his postulates as self-conditioned, without asking further questions, and argues to a conclusion by means of visible diagrams; but his reasoning would concern, not the diagrams as such but ideal mathematical objects, so that, if he were to take his hypotheses "in connection with a first principle," he would be in a state of νόησις instead of διάνοιά, although the true object of his reasoning, the ideal mathematical objects, would remain the same. This interpretation, i.e. the interpretation that would confine the distinction between the two segments of the upper part of the line to states of mind, might well seem to be favoured by the statement of Plato that mathematical questions, when "taken in connection with a first principle, come within the domain of the pure reason"; but Aristotle's remarks on the subject, if they are a correct statement of the thought of Plato, evidently forbid this interpretation, since he clearly thought that Plato's mathematical entities were supposed to occupy a position between αἱ ἀρχαί and τὰ ὁρατά.)

If Aristotle is correct and Plato really meant τὰ μαθηματικά to constitute a class of objects on their own, distinct from other classes, in what does this distinction consist? There is no need to dwell on the distinction between τὰ μαθηματικά and the objects of the lower part of the line, τὰ ὁρατά, since it is clear enough that the geometrician is concerned with ideal and perfect objects of thought, and not with empirical circles or lines, e.g. cart-wheels or hoops or fishing-rods, or even with geometrical diagrams as such, i.e. as sensible particulars. The question, therefore, resolves

[1] 987 b 14 ff. Cf. 1059 b 2 ff.

itself into this: in what does the distinction between τὰ μαθηματικά, as objects of διάνοια, and αἱ ἀρχαί, as objects of νόησις, really consist?

A natural interpretation of Aristotle's remarks in the *Metaphysics* is that, according to Plato, the mathematician is speaking of intelligible particulars, and not of sensible particulars, nor of universals. For example, if the geometer speaks of two circles intersecting, he is not speaking of the sensible circles drawn nor yet of circularity as such—for how could circularity intersect circularity? He is speaking of intelligible circles, of which there are many alike, as Aristotle would say. Again, to say that "two and two make four" is not the same as to say what will happen if twoness be added to itself—a meaningless phrase. This view is supported by Aristotle's remark that for Plato "there must be a first 2 and 3, and the numbers must not be addable to one another."[1] For Plato, the integers, including 1, form a series in such a way that 2 is *not* made up of two 1's, but is a unique numerical form. This comes more or less to saying that the integer 2 is twoness, which is not composed of two "onenesses." These integer numbers Plato seems to have identified with the Forms. But though it cannot be said of the integer 2 that there are many alike (any more than we can speak of many circularities), it is clear that the mathematician who does not ascend to the ultimate formal principles, does in fact deal with a plurality of 2's and a plurality of circles. Now, when the geometer speaks of intersecting circles, he is not treating of sensible particulars, but of intelligible objects. Yet of these intelligible objects there are many alike, hence they are not real universals but constitute a class of intelligible particulars, "above" sensible particulars, but "below" true universals. It is reasonable, therefore, to conclude that Plato's τὰ μαθηματικά are a class of intelligible particulars.

Now, Professor A. E. Taylor,[2] if I understand him correctly, would like to confine the sphere of τὰ μαθηματικά to ideal spatial magnitudes. As he points out, the properties of e.g. curves can be studied by means of numerical equations, but they are not themselves numbers; so that they would not belong to the highest section of the line, that of αἱ ἀρχαί or Forms, which Plato identified with Numbers. On the other hand, the ideal spatial magnitudes, the objects which the geometrician studies, are not sensible

[1] *Metaph.*, 1083 a 33–5.
[2] Cf. *Forms and Numbers, Mind*, Oct. 1926 and Jan. 1927. (Reprinted in *Philosophical Studies*.)

objects, so that they cannot belong to the sphere of τὰ ὁρατά. They therefore occupy an intermediate position between Number-Forms and Sensible Things. That this is true of the objects with which the geometer deals (intersecting circles, etc.) I willingly admit; but is one justified in excluding from τὰ μαθηματικά the objects with which the arithmetician deals? After all, Plato, when treating of those whose state of mind is that of διάνοια, speaks not only of students of geometry, but also of students of arithmetic and the kindred sciences.[1] It would certainly not appear from this that we are justified in asserting that Plato confined τὰ μαθηματικά to ideal spatial magnitudes. Whether or not we think that Plato ought to have so confined the sphere of mathematical entities, we have to consider, not only what Plato *ought* to have said, but also what he *did* say. Most probably, therefore, he understood, as comprised in the class of τὰ μαθηματικά, the objects of the arithmetician as well as those of the geometer (and not only of these two, as can be inferred from the remark about "kindred sciences"). What, then, becomes of Aristotle's statement that for Plato numbers are not addable (ἀσυμβλητόι)? I think that it is certainly to be accepted, and that Plato saw clearly that numbers as such are unique. On the other hand, it is equally clear that we add groups or classes of objects together, and speak of the characteristic of a class as a number. These we add, but they stand for the classes of individual objects, though they are themselves the objects, not of sense but of intelligence. They may, therefore, be spoken of as intelligible particulars, and they belong to the sphere of τὰ μαθηματικά, as well as the ideal spatial magnitudes of the geometer. Aristotle's own theory of number may have been erroneous, and he may thus have misrepresented Plato's theory in some respects; but if he definitely stated, as he did, that Plato posited an intermediate class of mathematical entities, it is hard to suppose that he was mistaken, especially as Plato's own writings would seem to leave no reasonable doubt, not only that he actually posited such a class, but also that he did not mean to confine this class to ideal spatial magnitudes.

(Plato's statement that the hypotheses of the mathematicians —he mentions "the odd and the even and the figures and three kinds of angles and the cognates of these in their several branches of science"[2]—when taken in connection with a first principle, are

[1] *Rep.*, 510 c 2 ff.

[2] *Rep.*, 510 c 4-5.

cognisable by the higher reason, and his statement that the higher reason is concerned with first principles, which are self-evident, suggest that he would welcome the modern attempts to reduce pure mathematics to their logical foundations.)

It remains to consider briefly the highest segment of the line. The state of mind in question, that of νόησις, is the state of mind of the man who uses the hypotheses of the διάνοια segment as starting-points, but passes beyond them and ascends to first principles. Moreover, in this process (which is the process of Dialectic) he makes no use of "images," such as are employed in the διάνοια segment, but proceeds in and by the ideas themselves,[1] i.e. by strictly abstract reasoning. Having clearly grasped the first principles, the mind then descends to the conclusions that follow from them, again making use only of abstract reasoning and not of sensible images.[2] The objects corresponding to νόησις are αἱ ἀρχάι, the first principles or Forms. They are not merely epistemological principles, but also ontological principles, and I will consider them more in detail later; but it is as well to point out the following fact. If it were merely a question of seeing the ultimate principles of the hypotheses of the διάνοια section (as e.g. in the modern reduction of pure mathematics to their logical foundations), there might be no very great difficulty in seeing what Plato was driving at; but he speaks expressly of dialectic as "destroying the hypotheses," ἀναιροῦσα τὰς ὑποθέσεις,[3] which is a hard saying, since, though dialectic may well show that the postulates of the mathematician need revision, it is not so easy, at first sight at least, to see how it can be said to destroy the hypotheses. As a matter of fact, Plato's meaning becomes clearer if we consider one particular hypothesis he mentions—the odd and the even. It would appear that Plato recognised that there are numbers which are neither even nor odd, i.e. irrational numbers, and that in the *Epinomis*[4] he demands the recognition of quadratic and cubic "surds" as *numbers*.[5] If this is so, then it would be the task of dialectic to show that the traditional hypotheses of the mathematician, that there are no irrational numbers, but that all numbers are integers and are either even or odd, is not strictly true. Again, Plato refused to accept the Pythagorean idea of the point-unit and spoke of the point as "the beginning of a line,"[6] so that the point-unit, i.e. the point as having magnitude of its

[1] *Rep.*, 510 b 6–9. [2] *Rep.*, 511 b 3–c 2. [3] *Rep.*, 533 c 8.
[4] *Epin.*, 990 c 5–991 b 4. [5] Cf. Taylor, *Plato*, p. 501 [6] *Metaph.*, 992 a 20 ff.

own, would be a fiction of the geometer, "a geometrical fiction,"[1] an hypothesis that needs to be "destroyed."

3. Plato further illustrated his epistemological doctrine by the famous allegory of the Cave in the seventh book of the *Republic.*[2] I will briefly sketch the allegory, since it is valuable as showing clearly, if any further proof be needed, that the ascent of the mind from the lower sections of the line to the higher is an epistemological progress, and that Plato regarded this process, not so much as a continuous process of evolution as a series of "conversions" from a less adequate to a more adequate cognitive state.

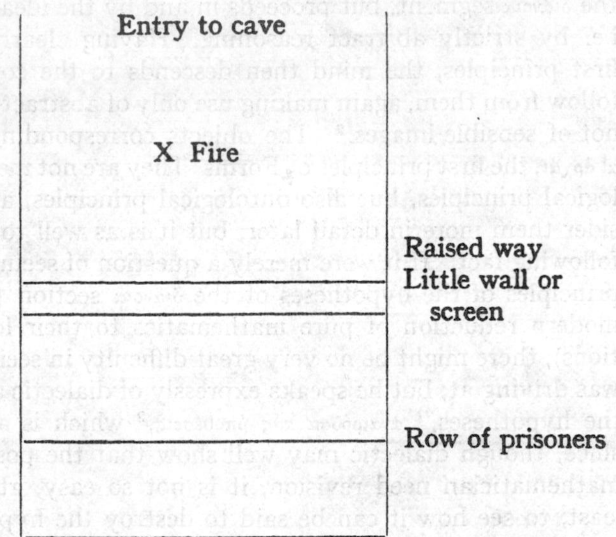

Plato asks us to imagine an underground cave which has an opening towards the light. In this cave are living human beings, with their legs and necks chained from childhood in such a way that they face the inside wall of the cave and have never seen the light of the sun. Above and behind them, i.e. between the prisoners and the mouth of the cave, is a fire, and between them and the fire is a raised way and a low wall, like a screen. Along this raised way there pass men carrying statues and figures of animals and other objects, in such a manner that the objects they carry appear over the top of the low wall or screen. The

[1] *Metaph.*, 992 a 20–1. [2] *Rep.*, 514 a 1–518 d 1.

prisoners, facing the inside wall of the cave, cannot see one another nor the objects carried behind them, but they see the shadows of themselves and of these objects thrown on to the wall they are facing. They see only shadows.

These prisoners represent the majority of mankind, that multitude of people who remain all their lives in a state of εἰκασία, beholding only shadows of reality and hearing only echoes of the truth. Their view of the world is most inadequate, distorted by "their own passions and prejudices, and by the passions and prejudices of other people as conveyed to them by language and rhetoric."[1] And though they are in no better case than children, they cling to their distorted views with all the tenacity of adults, and have no wish to escape from their prison-house. Moreover, if they were suddenly freed and told to look at the realities of which they had formerly seen the shadows, they would be blinded by the glare of the light, and would imagine that the shadows were far more real than the realities.

However, if one of the prisoners who has escaped grows accustomed to the light, he will after a time be able to look at the concrete sensible objects, of which he had formerly seen but the shadows. This man beholds his fellows in the light of the fire (which represents the visible sun) and is in a state of πίστις, having been "converted" from the shadow-world of εἰκόνες, prejudices and passions and sophistries, to the real world of ζῷα, though he has not yet ascended to the world of intelligible, non-sensible realities. He sees the prisoners for what they are, namely prisoners, prisoners in the bonds of passion and sophistry. Moreover, if he perseveres and comes out of the cave into the sunlight, he will see the world of sun-illumined and clear objects (which represent intelligible realities), and lastly, though only by an effort, he will be able to see the sun itself, which represents the Idea of the Good, the highest Form, "the universal cause of all things right and beautiful—the source of truth and reason."[2] He will then be in a state of νόησις. (To this Idea of the Good, as also to the political considerations that concerned Plato in the *Republic*, I shall return in later chapters.)

Plato remarks that if someone, after ascending to the sunshine, went back into the cave, he would be unable to see properly because of the darkness, and so would make himself "ridiculous"; while if he tried to free another and lead him up to the light, the

[1] Nettleship, *Lectures on the Republic of Plato*, p. 260. [2] *Rep.*, 517 b 8–c 4.

prisoners, who love the darkness and consider the shadows to be true reality, would put the offender to death, if they could but catch him. Here we may understand a reference to Socrates, who endeavoured to enlighten all those who would listen and make them apprehend truth and reason, instead of letting themselves be misled by prejudice and sophistry.

This allegory makes it clear that the "ascent" of the line was regarded by Plato as a progress, though this progress is not a continuous and automatic process: it needs effort and mental discipline. Hence his insistence on the great importance of *education*, whereby the young may be brought gradually to behold eternal and absolute truths and values, and so saved from passing their lives in the shadow-world of error, falsehood, prejudice, sophistical persuasion, blindness to true values, etc. This education is of primary importance in the case of those who are to be statesmen. Statesmen and rulers will be blind leaders of the blind, if they dwell in the spheres of εἰκασία or πίστις, and the wrecking of the ship of State is a more terrible thing than the wreck of anyone's individual barque. Plato's interest in the epistemological ascent is thus no mere academic or narrowly critical interest: he is concerned with the conduct of life, tendance of the soul and with the good of the State. The man who does not realise the true good of man will not, and cannot, lead the truly good human life, and the statesman who does not realise the true good of the State, who does not view political life in the light of eternal principles, will bring ruin on his people.

The question might be raised, whether or not there are religious implications in the epistemology of Plato, as illustrated by the simile of the Line and the allegory of the Cave. That the conceptions of Plato were given a religious colouring and application by the Neo-Platonists is beyond dispute: moreover, when a Christian writer, such as the Pseudo-Dionysius, traces the mystic's ascent to God by the *via negativa*, beyond visible creatures to their invisible Source, the light of which blinds by excess of light, so that the soul is in a state of, so to speak, luminous obscurity, he certainly utilises themes which came from Plato *via* the Neo-Platonists. But it does not necessarily follow that Plato himself understood the ascent from a religious viewpoint. In any case this difficult question cannot be profitably touched on until one has considered the ontological nature and status of Plato's Idea of the Good; and even then one can scarcely reach definitive certainty.

CHAPTER XX

THE DOCTRINE OF FORMS

In this chapter I propose to discuss the theory of Forms or Ideas in its ontological aspect. We have already seen that in Plato's eyes the object of true knowledge must be stable and abiding, the object of intelligence and not of sense, and that these requirements are fulfilled by the universal, as far as the highest cognitive state, that of νόησις, is concerned. The Platonic epistemology clearly implies that the universals which we conceive in thought are not devoid of objective reference, but we have not yet examined the important question, in what this objective reference consists. There is indeed plenty of evidence that Plato continued to occupy himself throughout his years of academic and literary activity with problems arising from the theory of Forms, but there is no real evidence that he ever radically changed his doctrine, still less that he abandoned it altogether, however much he tried to clarify or modify it, in view of difficulties that occurred to him or that were suggested by others. It has sometimes been asserted that the mathematisation of the Forms, which is ascribed to Plato by Aristotle, was a doctrine of Plato's old age, a relapse into Pythagorean "mysticism,"[1] but Aristotle does not say that Plato *changed* his doctrine, and the only reasonable conclusion to be drawn from Aristotle's words would appear to be that Plato held more or less the same doctrine, at least during the time that Aristotle worked under him in the Academy. (Whether Aristotle misinterpreted Plato or not is naturally another question.) But though Plato continued to maintain the doctrine of Ideas, and though he sought to clarify his meaning and the ontological and logical implications of his thought, it does not follow that we can always clearly grasp what he actually meant. It is greatly to be regretted that we have no adequate record of his lectures in the Academy, since this would doubtless throw great light on the interpretation of his theories as put forward in the dialogues, besides conferring on us the inestimable benefit of knowing what Plato's "real" opinions were, the opinions that he transmitted only through oral teaching and never published.

[1] Cf. Stace, *Critical History*, p. 191.

In the *Republic* it is assumed that whenever a plurality of individuals have a common name, they have also a corresponding idea or form.[1] This is the universal, the common nature or quality which is grasped in the concept, e.g. beauty. There are many beautiful things, but we form one universal concept of beauty itself: and Plato assumed that these universal concepts are not merely subjective concepts, but that in them we apprehend objective essences. At first hearing this sounds a peculiarly naïve view, perhaps, but we must recall that for Plato it is thought that grasps reality, so that the object of thought, as opposed to sense-perception, i.e. universals, must have reality. How could they be grasped and made the object of thought unless they were real? We *discover* them: they are not simply invented by us. Another point to remember is that Plato seems first to have concerned himself with moral and aesthetic universals (as also with the objects of mathematical science), as was only natural, considering the main interest of Socrates, and to think of Absolute Goodness or Absolute Beauty existing in their own right, so to speak, is not unreasonable, particularly if Plato identified them, as we believe that he did. But when Plato came to turn his attention more to natural objects than he had formerly done, and to consider class-concepts, such as those of man or horse, it was obviously rather difficult to suppose that universals corresponding to these class-concepts existed in their own right as objective essences. One may identify Absolute Goodness and Absolute Beauty, but it is not so easy to identify the objective essence of man with the objective essence of horse: in fact, to attempt to do so would be ludicrous. But some principle of unity had to be found, if the essences were not to be left in isolation one from another, and Plato came to devote attention to this principle of unity, so that all the specific essences might be unified under or subordinated to one supreme generic essence. Plato tackles this problem from the logical viewpoint, it is true, inquiring into the problem of logical classification; but there is no real evidence that he ever abandoned the view that universals have an ontological status, and he doubtless thought that in settling the problem of logical classification, he was also settling the problem of ontological unification.

To these objective essences Plato gave the name of Ideas or Forms (ἰδέαι or εἴδη), words which are used interchangeably.

[1] *Rep.*, 596 a 6–7; cf. 507 ab.

The word εἶδος in this connection appears suddenly in the *Phaedo*.[1] But we must not be misled by this use of the term "Idea." "Idea" in ordinary parlance means a subjective concept in the mind, as when we say: "That is only an idea and nothing real"; but Plato, when he speaks of Ideas or Forms, is referring to the objective content or reference of our universal concepts. In our universal concepts we apprehend objective essences, and it is to these objective essences that Plato applied the term "Ideas." In some dialogues, e.g. in the *Symposium*, the word "Idea" is not used, but the *meaning* is there, for in that dialogue Plato speaks of essential or absolute Beauty (αὐτο ὃ ἔστι καλόν), and this is what Plato would mean by the Idea of Beauty. Thus it would be a matter of indifference, whether he spoke of the Absolute Good or of the Idea of the Good: both would refer to an objective essence, which is the source of goodness in all the particular things that are truly good.

Since by Ideas or Forms Plato meant objective essences, it becomes of paramount importance for an understanding of the Platonic ontology to determine, as far as possible, precisely how he regarded these objective essences. Have they a transcendental existence of their own, apart from particular things, and, if so, what is their relation to one another and to the concrete particular objects of this world? Does Plato duplicate the world of sense-experience by postulating a transcendental world of invisible, immaterial essences? If so, what is the relation of this world of essences to God? That Plato's language often implies the existence of a separate world of transcendental essences cannot be denied, but it must be remembered that language is primarily designed to refer to the objects of our sense-experience, and is very often found inadequate for the precise expression of metaphysical truths. Thus we speak, and cannot well help speaking, of "God foreseeing," a phrase that, as it stands, implies that God is in time, whereas we know that God is not in time but is eternal. We cannot, however, speak adequately of the eternity of God, since we have no experience of eternity ourselves, and our language is not designed to express such matters. We are human beings and have to use human language—we can use no other: and this fact should make us cautious in attaching too much weight to the mere language or phrases used by Plato in dealing with abstruse, metaphysical points. We have to endeavour to

[1] *Phaedo*, 102 b 1.

get at the meaning behind those phrases. By this I do not mean to imply that Plato did not believe in the subsistence of universal essences, but simply to point out that, if we find that he did in fact hold this doctrine, we must beware of the temptation to put that doctrine in a ludicrous light by stressing the phrases used by Plato, without due consideration of the meaning to be attached to those phrases.

Now, what we might call the "vulgar" presentation of the Platonic theory of Ideas has generally been more or less as follows. In Plato's view the objects which we apprehend in universal concepts, the objects with which science deals, the objects corresponding to universal terms of predication, are objective Ideas or subsistent Universals, existing in a transcendental world of their own—somewhere "out there"—apart from sensible things, understanding by "apart from" practically spatial separation. Sensible things are copies or participations in these universal realities, but the latter abide in an unchanging heaven of their own, while sensible things are subject to change, in fact are always becoming and can never truly be said to *be*. The Ideas exist in their heaven in a state of isolation one from another, and apart from the mind of any Thinker. Plato's theory having been thus presented, it is pointed out that the subsistent universals either *exist* (in which case the real world of our experience is unjustifiably duplicated) or they do not exist, but have independent and *essential reality* in some mysterious way (in which case a wedge is unjustifiably driven between existence and essence.) (The Thomist School of Scholastic philosophers, be it remarked in passing, admit a "real distinction" between essence and the act of existence in created being; but, for them, the distinction is *within* the creature. Uncreated Being is Absolute Existence and Absolute Essence in identity.) Of the reasons which have led to this traditional presentation of the doctrine of Plato one may enumerate three.

(i) Plato's way of speaking about the Ideas clearly supposes that they exist in a sphere apart. Thus in the *Phaedo* he teaches that the soul existed before its union with the body in a transcendental realm, where it beheld the subsistent intelligible entities or Ideas, which would seem to constitute a plurality of "detached" essences. The process of knowledge, or getting to know, consists essentially in recollection, in remembering the Ideas which the soul once beheld clearly in its state of pre-existence.

(ii) Aristotle asserts in the *Metaphysics*[1] that Plato "separated" the Ideas, whereas Socrates had not done so. In his criticism of the theory of Ideas he constantly supposes that, according to the Platonists, Ideas exist apart from sensible things. Ideas constitute the reality or "substance" of things; "how, therefore," asks Aristotle, "can the Ideas, being the substance of things, exist apart?"[2]

(iii) In the *Timaeus* Plato clearly teaches that God or the "Demiurge" forms the things of this world according to the model of the Forms. This implies that the Forms or Ideas exist apart, not only from the sensible things that are modelled on them, but also from God, Who takes them as His model. They are therefore hanging in the air, as it were.

In this way, say the critics, Plato—

(*a*) Duplicates the "real" world;
(*b*) Posits a multitude of subsistent essences with no sufficient metaphysical ground or basis (since they are independent even of God);
(*c*) Fails to explain the relation between sensible things and the Ideas (except by metaphorical phrases like "imitation" or "participation"); and
(*d*) Fails to explain the relation of the Ideas to one another, e.g. of species to genus, or to find any real principle of unity. Accordingly, if Plato was trying to solve the problem of the One and the Many, he failed lamentably and merely enriched the world with one more fantastic theory, which was exploded by the genius of Aristotle.

It must be left to an examination of Plato's thought in more detail to show what truth there is in this presentation of the theory of Ideas; but we would point out at once that these critics tend to neglect the fact that Plato saw clearly that the plurality of Ideas needs some principle of unity, and that he tried to solve this problem. They also tend to neglect the fact that we have indications not only in the dialogues themselves, but also in the allusions of Aristotle to Plato's theory and Plato's lectures, *how* Plato tried to solve the problem, namely, by a new interpretation, and application of the Eleatic doctrine of the One. Whether Plato actually solved the problems that arise out of his theories is a matter for dispute, but it will not do to speak as though he

[1] *Metaph.*, A, 987 b 1–10; M, 1078 b 30–32. [2] *Metaph.*, A, 991 b 2–3.

never saw any of the difficulties that Aristotle afterwards brought against him. On the contrary, Plato anticipated some of the very objections raised by Aristotle and thought that he had solved them more or less satisfactorily. Aristotle evidently thought otherwise, and he may have been right, but it is unhistorical to speak as though Aristotle raised objections which Plato had been too foolish to see. Moreover, if it is an historical fact, as it is, that Plato brought difficulties against himself, one should be careful in attributing to him an opinion that is fantastic—unless, of course, we are compelled by the evidence to believe that he held it.

Before going on to consider the theory of Ideas as presented in the dialogues, we will make some preliminary observations in connection with the three reasons that we enumerated in support of the traditional presentation of Plato's Ideal Theory.

(i) It is an undeniable fact that Plato's way of speaking about the Ideas very often implies that they exist "apart from" sensible things. I believe that Plato really did hold this doctrine; but there are two cautionary observations to be made.

(*a*) If they exist "apart from" sensible things, this "apart from" can only mean that the Ideas are possessed of a reality independent of sensible things. There can be no question of the Ideas being in a place, and, strictly speaking, they would be as much "in" as "out of" sensible things, for *ex hypothesi* they are incorporeal essences and incorporeal essences cannot be in a place. As Plato had to use human language, he would naturally express the essential reality and independence of the Ideas in spatial terminology (he could not do anything else); but he would not *mean* that the Ideas were spatially separate from things. Transcendence in this connection would mean that the Ideas do not change and perish with sensible particulars: it would no more mean that they are in a heavenly place of their own than God's transcendence implies for us that God is in a place, different from the places or spaces of the sensible objects He has created. It is absurd to speak as though the Platonic Theory involved the assumption of an Ideal Man with length, breadth, depth, etc., existing in the heavenly place. To do so is to make the Platonic theory gratuitously ridiculous: whatever the transcendence of the Ideas might mean, it could not mean *that*.

(*b*) We should be careful not to place too much weight on doctrines such as that of the pre-existence of the soul and the process of "recollection." Plato sometimes, as is well known, makes use of "Myth," giving a "likely account," which he does not mean to be taken with the same exactitude and seriousness as more scientifically argued themes. Thus in the *Phaedo* "Socrates" gives an account of the soul's future life, and then expressly declares that it does not become a man of sense to affirm that these things are exactly as he has described them.[1] But while it is clear enough that the account of the soul's future life is conjectural and admittedly "mythical" in character, it appears altogether unjustifiable to extend the concept of "myth" to include the whole doctrine of immortality, as some would do, for in the passage alluded to in the *Phaedo* Socrates declares that, though the picture of the future life is not to be understood literally or positively affirmed, the soul is "certainly immortal." And, as Plato couples together immortality after death with pre-existence, it hardly seems that one is warranted in dismissing the whole conception of pre-existence as "mythical." It may possibly be that it was no more than an hypothesis in Plato's eyes (so that, as I said, we should not attach too much weight to it); but, all things considered, we are not justified in simply asserting that it actually is myth, and, unless its mythical character can be demonstrated satisfactorily, we ought to accept it as a seriously-meant doctrine. Yet even if the soul pre-existed and contemplated the Forms in that state of pre-existence, it would *not* follow that the Forms or Ideas are in any *place*, save metaphorically. Nor does it even necessarily follow that they are "detached" essences, for they might all be included in some ontological principle of unity.

(ii) In regard to the statements of Aristotle in the *Metaphysics* it is as well to point out at once that Aristotle must have known perfectly well what Plato taught in the Academy and that Aristotle was no imbecile. It is absurd to speak as though Aristotle's insufficient knowledge of contemporary mathematical developments would necessarily lead to his essentially perverting Plato's doctrine of the Forms, at least in its non-mathematical aspects. He may or may not have fully understood Plato's mathematical theories: it does not follow from this alone that he made an egregious blunder in his interpretation of the Platonic ontology. If Aristotle declares that Plato "separated" the Forms, we cannot pass over this statement as mere ignorant criticism.

[1] *Phaedo*, 114 d 1–2.

All the same, we have to be careful not to assume *a priori* what Aristotle meant by "separation," and in the second place we have to inquire whether Aristotle's criticism of the Platonic theory necessarily implies that Plato himself drew the conclusions that Aristotle attacks. It *might* be that some of the conclusions attacked by Aristotle were conclusions that he (Aristotle) considered to be logical consequences of the Platonic theory, although Plato may not have drawn those conclusions himself. If this were the case, then we should have to inquire whether the conclusions really did flow from Plato's premisses. But as it would be impracticable to discuss Aristotle's criticism until we have seen what Plato himself said about the Ideas in his published works, it is best to reserve till later a discussion of Aristotle's criticism, although it is true that, since one has to rely largely on Aristotle for knowledge of what Plato taught in his lectures, one cannot help drawing upon him in an exposition of the Platonic doctrine. It is, however, important (and this is the burden of these preliminary remarks) that we should put out of our heads the notion that Aristotle was an incompetent fool, incapable of understanding the true thought of the Master.[1] Unjust he may have been, but he was no fool.

(iii) It can scarcely be denied that Plato in the *Timaeus* speaks as though the Demiurge, the Efficient Cause of order in the world, fashions the objects of this world after the pattern of the Forms as Exemplary Cause, thus implying that the Forms or Ideas are quite distinct from the Demiurge, so that, if we call the Demiurge "God," we should have to conclude that the Forms are not only "outside" the things of this world, but also "outside" God. But though Plato's language in the *Timaeus* certainly implies this interpretation, there is some reason, as will be seen later, to think that the Demiurge of the *Timaeus* is an *hypothesis* and that Plato's "theism" is not to be over-stressed. Moreover, and this is an important fact to remember, Plato's doctrine, as given in his lectures, was not precisely the same as that given in the dialogues: or it might be better to say that Plato developed aspects of his doctrine in his lectures that scarcely appear in the dialogues. The remarks of Aristotle concerning Plato's lecture on the Good, as recorded by Aristoxenus, would seem to indicate

[1] It is indeed the opinion of the writer that Aristotle, in his criticism of the Ideal Theory, scarcely does justice to Plato, but he would ascribe this to the polemical attitude Aristotle came to adopt towards the theory rather than to any supposed imbecility.

that in dialogues such as the *Timaeus*, Plato revealed some of his thoughts only in a pictorial and figurative way. To this question I return later: we must now endeavour to ascertain, as far as possible, what Plato's doctrine of Ideas actually was.

1. In the *Phaedo*, where the discussion centres round the problem of immortality, it is suggested that truth is not to be attained by the bodily senses, but by reason alone, which lays hold of the things that "really are."[1] What are the things that "really are," i.e. that have true being? They are the essences of things, and Socrates gives as examples justice itself, beauty itself, and goodness itself, abstract equality, etc. These essences remain always the same, while particular objects of sense do not. That there really exist such essences is assumed by Socrates: he lays it down "as an hypothesis that there is a certain abstract beauty, and goodness, and magnitude," and that a particular beautiful object, for instance, is beautiful because it partakes of that abstract beauty.[2] (In 102 b the word Idea is applied to these essences; they are termed εἴδη.) In the *Phaedo* the existence of these essences is used as an aid in the proof of immortality. It is pointed out that the fact that a man is able to judge of things as more or less equal, more or less beautiful, implies knowledge of a standard, of the essence of beauty or equality. Now, men do not come into the world and grow up with a clear knowledge of universal essences: how is it, then, that they can judge of particular things in reference to a universal standard? Is it not because the soul pre-existed before its union with the body, and had knowledge of the essences in its state of pre-existence? The process of learning would thus be a process of reminiscence, in which particular embodiments of the essence acted as reminders of the essences previously beheld. Moreover, since rational knowledge of essences in this life involves transcending the bodily senses and rising to the intellectual plane, should we not suppose that the soul of the philosopher beholds these essences after death, when he is no longer hampered and shackled by the body?

Now, the natural interpretation of the doctrine of the Ideas as given in the *Phaedo* is that the Ideas are subsistent universals; but it is to be remembered that, as already mentioned, the doctrine is put forward tentatively as an "hypothesis," i.e. as a premiss which is assumed until connection with an evident first principle either justifies it or "destroys" it, or shows that it stands

[1] *Phaedo*, 65 c 2 ff. [2] *Phaedo*, 100 b 5–7.

in need of modification or correction. Of course, one cannot exclude the possibility that Plato put forward the doctrine tentatively because he (Plato) was not yet certain of it, but it would appear legitimate to suppose that Plato makes Socrates put forward the doctrine in a tentative fashion precisely because he knew very well that the historical Socrates had not reached the metaphysical theory of the Ideas, and that in any case he had not arrived at Plato's final Principle of the Good. It is significant that Plato allows Socrates to divine the Ideal Theory in his "swan-song," when he becomes "prophetic."[1] This might well imply that Plato allows Socrates to divine a certain amount of his (i.e. Plato's) theory, but not all. It is also to be noted that the theory of pre-existence and reminiscence is referred, in the *Meno*, to "priests and priestesses,"[2] just as the sublimest part of the *Symposium* is referred to "Diotima." Some have concluded that these passages were avowedly "Myths" in Plato's eyes, but it might equally well be the case that these hypothetical passages (hypothetical for *Socrates*) reveal something of Plato's own doctrine, as distinct from that of Socrates. (In any case we should not use the doctrine of reminiscence as an excuse for attributing to Plato an explicit anticipation of Neo-Kantian theory. The Neo-Kantians may think that the *a priori* in the Kantian sense is the truth that Plato was getting at or that underlies his words, but they cannot be justified in fathering the explicit doctrine on to Plato, without much better evidence than they can offer.) I conclude, then, that the theory of Ideas, as put forward in the *Phaedo*, represents but a part of Plato's doctrine. It should not be inferred that for Plato himself the Ideas were "*detached*" subsistent universals. Aristotle clearly stated that Plato identified the One with the Good; but this unifying principle, whether already held by Plato when he composed the *Phaedo* (as is most probable) or only later elaborated, certainly does not appear in the *Phaedo*.

2. In the *Symposium*, Socrates is represented as reporting a discourse made to him by one Diotima, a "Prophetess," concerning the soul's ascent to true Beauty under the impulse of Eros. From beautiful forms (i.e. bodies), a man ascends to the contemplation of the beauty that is in souls, and thence to science, that he may look upon the loveliness of wisdom, and turn towards the "wide ocean of beauty" and the "lovely and majestic forms

[1] Cf. *Phaedo*, 84 e 3–85 b 7. [2] *Meno*, 81 a 5 ff.

which it contains," until he reaches the contemplation of a Beauty that is "eternal, unproduced, indestructible; neither subject to increase nor decay; not partly beautiful and partly ugly; not at one time beautiful and at another time not; not beautiful in relation to one thing and deformed in relation to another; not here beautiful and there ugly; not beautiful in the estimation of some people and deformed in that of others. Nor can this supreme beauty be figured to the imagination like a beautiful face, or beautiful hands, or any other part of the body, nor like any discourse, nor any science. Nor does it subsist in any other thing that lives or is, either in earth, or in heaven, or in any other place; but it is eternally self-subsistent and monoeidic with itself. All other things are beautiful through a participation of it, with this condition, that although they are subject to production and decay, it never becomes more or less, or endures any change." This is the divine and pure, the monoeidic beautiful itself.[1] It is evidently the Beauty of the *Hippias Maior*, "from which all beautiful things derive their beauty."[2]

The priestess Diotima, into whose mouth Socrates puts his discourse on Absolute Beauty and the ascent thereto under the impulse of Eros, is represented as suggesting that Socrates may not be able to follow her to such sublime heights, and she urges him to strain all his attention to reach the obscure depth of the subject.[3] Professor A. E. Taylor interprets this to mean that Socrates is too modest to claim the mystical vision for himself (although he has really experienced it), and so represents himself as but reporting the words of Diotima. Taylor will have nothing to do with the suggestion that the speech of Diotima represents *Plato's* personal conviction, never attained by the historical Socrates. "Much unfortunate nonsense has been written about the meaning of Diotima's apparent doubt whether Socrates will be able to follow her as she goes on to speak of the 'full and perfect vision . . .' It has even been seriously argued that Plato is here guilty of the arrogance of professing that he has reached philosophical heights to which the 'historical' Socrates could not ascend."[4] That such a procedure would be indicative of arrogance on Plato's part might be true, if there were question of a mystical vision, as Taylor apparently thinks there is; but it is by no means certain that there is any question of religious mysticism in the

[1] *Sympos.*, 210 e 1–212 a 7.
[2] *Hippias Maior*, 289 d 2–5.
[3] *Sympos.*, 209 e 5–210 a 4. Cf. 210 e 1–2.
[4] *Plato*, p. 229, note i.

speech of Socrates, and there seems no real reason why Plato should not be able to claim a greater philosophic penetration in regard to the ultimate Principle than Socrates, without thereby laying himself open to any justifiable charge of arrogance. Moreover, if, as Taylor supposes, the opinions put into the mouth of Socrates in the *Phaedo* and the *Symposium* are those of the historic Socrates, how does it come about that in the *Symposium* Socrates speaks as though he had actually grasped the ultimate Principle, the Absolute Beauty, while in the *Phaedo* the theory of Ideas (in which abstract beauty finds a place) is put forward as a tentative hypothesis, i.e. in the very dialogue that purports to give Socrates' conversation before his death? Might we not be justified in expecting that if the historic Socrates had really apprehended the final Principle for certain, some sure indication of this would have been given in his final discourse? I prefer, then, the view that in the *Symposium* the speech of Diotima does not represent the certain conviction of the historic Socrates. In any case, however, this is an academic point: whether the report of Diotima's words represents the conviction of the historic Socrates or of Plato himself, the evident fact remains that some hint (at the very least) of the existence of an Absolute is therein given.

Is this Beauty in itself, the very essence of Beauty, a subsistent essence, "separate" from beautiful things, or is it not? It is true that Plato's words concerning science might be taken to imply a scientific appreciation of the mere universal concept of Beauty which is embodied in varying degrees in various beautiful objects; but the whole tenor of Socrates' discourse in the *Symposium* leads one to suppose that this essential Beauty is no mere concept, but has objective reality. Does this imply that it is "separate?" Beauty in itself or Absolute Beauty is "separate" in the sense that it is real, subsistent, but not in the sense that it is in a world of its own, spatially separate from things. For *ex hypothesi* Absolute Beauty is spiritual; and the categories of time and space, of local separation, simply do not apply in the case of that which is essentially spiritual. In the case of that which transcends space and time, we cannot even legitimately raise the question, *where* it is. It is nowhere, as far as local presence is concerned (though it is not nowhere in the sense of being unreal). The Χωρισμός or separation would thus seem to imply, in the case of the Platonic essence, a reality beyond the subjective reality of the abstract concept—a subsistent reality, but not a local separation. It is, therefore, just as true to say that the essence is immanent, as that it is transcendent: the great point is that it is *real* and independent of particulars, unchanged and abiding. It is foolish to remark that if the Platonic essence is real, it must be somewhere. Absolute Beauty, for instance, does not exist outside us in the sense in which a flower exists outside us—for it might just as well be said to exist inside us, inasmuch as spatial categories simply do not apply to it. On the other hand, it cannot be said to be inside us in the sense that it is purely subjective, is confined to us, comes into being with us, and perishes through our agency or with us. It is both transcendent and immanent, inaccessible to the senses, apprehensible only by the intellect.

To the means of ascent to Absolute Beauty, the signification of Eros, and the question whether a mystical approach is implied, we must return later: at the present I wish simply to point out that in the *Symposium* indications are not wanting that Absolute Beauty is the ultimate Principle of unity. The passage[1] concerning the ascent from different sciences to one science—the science of universal Beauty—suggests that "the wide ocean of intellectual beauty," containing "lovely and majestic forms," is subordinate to or even comprised in the ultimate Principle of Absolute Beauty. And if Absolute Beauty is a final and unifying Principle, it becomes necessary to identify it with the Absolute Good of the *Republic*.

3. In the *Republic* it is clearly shown that the true philosopher seeks to know the essential nature of each thing. He is not concerned to know, for example, a multiplicity of beautiful things or a multiplicity of good things, but rather to discern the essence of beauty and the essence of goodness, which are embodied in varying degrees in particular beautiful things and particular good things. Non-philosophers, who are so taken up with the multiplicity of appearances that they do not attend to the essential nature and cannot distinguish, e.g. the essence of beauty from the many beautiful phenomena, are represented as having only opinion (δόξα) and as lacking in scientific knowledge. They are not concerned with not-being, it is true, since not-being cannot be an object of "knowledge" at all, but is completely unknowable; yet they are no more concerned with true being or reality, which is stable and abiding: they are concerned with fleeting phenomena or appearances, objects which are in a state of *becoming*,

[1] *Sympos.*, 210 a 4 ff.

constantly coming to be and passing away. Their state of mind is thus one of δόξα and the object of their δόξα is the phenomenon that stands half-way between being and not-being. The state of mind of the philosopher, on the other hand, is one of knowledge, and the object of his knowledge is Being, the fully real, the essential, the Idea or Form.

So far, indeed, there is no direct indication that the essence or Idea is regarded as subsistent or "separate" (so far as the latter term is applicable at all to non-sensual reality); but that it *is* so regarded may be seen from Plato's doctrine concerning the Idea of the Good, the Idea that occupies a peculiar position of pre-eminence in the *Republic*. The Good is there compared to the sun, the light of which makes the objects of nature visible to all and so is, in a sense, the source of their worth and value and beauty. This comparison is, of course, but a comparison, and as such should not be pressed: we are not to suppose that the Good exists as an object among objects, as the sun exists as an object among other objects. On the other hand, as Plato clearly asserts that the Good gives being to the objects of knowledge and so is, as it were, the unifying and all-comprehensive Principle of the essential order, while itself excelling even essential being in dignity and power,[1] it is impossible to conclude that the Good is a mere concept or even that it is a non-existent end, a teleological principle, as yet unreal, towards which all things are working: it is not only an epistemological principle, but also—in some, as yet, ill-defined sense—an *ontological* principle, a principle of being. It is, therefore, real in itself and subsistent.

It would seem that the Idea of the Good of the *Republic* must be regarded as identical with the essential Beauty of the *Symposium*. Both are represented as the high-peak of an intellectual ascent, while the comparison of the Idea of the Good with the sun would appear to indicate that it is the source not only of the goodness of things, but also of their beauty. The Idea of the Good gives being to the Forms or essences of the intellectual order, while science and the wide ocean of intellectual beauty is a stage on the ascent to the essentially beautiful. Plato is clearly working towards the conception of the Absolute, the absolutely Perfect and exemplary Pattern of all things, the ultimate ontological Principle. This Absolute is immanent, for phenomena embody it, "copy" it, partake in it, manifest it, in their varying degrees;

[1] *Rep.*, 509 b 6–10.

but it is also transcendent, for it is said to transcend even being itself, while the metaphors of participation (μέθεξις) and imitation (μίμησις)[1] imply a distinction between the participation and the Partaken of, between the imitation and the Imitated or Exemplar. Any attempt to reduce the Platonic Good to a mere logical principle and to disregard the indications that it is an ontological principle, necessarily leads to a denial of the sublimity of the Platonic metaphysic—as also, of course, to the conclusion that the Middle Platonist and Neo-Platonist philosophers entirely misunderstood the essential meaning of the Master.

At this point in the discussion there are two important observations to be made:

(i) Aristotle in the *Eudemian Ethics*[2] says that Plato identifies the Good with the One, while Aristoxenus, recalling Aristotle's account of Plato's lecture on the Good, tells us that the audience, who went to the lecture expecting to hear something about human goods, such as wealth, happiness, etc., were surprised when they found themselves listening to a discourse on mathematics, astronomy, numbers and *the identity of the good and one.* In the *Metaphysics*, Aristotle says that "Of those who maintain the existence of the unchangeable substances, some say that the one itself is the good itself, but they thought its substance lay mainly in its unity."[3] Plato is not mentioned by name in this passage, but elsewhere[4] Aristotle distinctly says that, for Plato, "the Forms are the cause of the essence of all other things, and the One is the cause of the essence of the Forms." Now, in the *Republic*,[5] Plato speaks of the ascent of the mind to the first principle of the whole, and asserts that the Idea of the Good is inferred to be "the universal author of all things beautiful and right, parent of light and of the lord of light in this world, and the *source of truth and reason* in the other." Hence it would seem only reasonable to conclude that the One, the Good and the essential Beauty are the same for Plato, and that the intelligible world of Forms owes its being in some way to the One. The word "emanation" (so dear to the Neo-Platonists) is nowhere used, and it is difficult to form any precise notion how Plato derived the Forms from the One; but it is clear enough that the One is the unifying Principle. Moreover, the One itself, though immanent in the Forms, is also transcendent, in that it cannot

[1] These phrases occur in the *Phaedo*. [2] 1218 a 24. [3] *Metaph.*, 1091, b 13–15. [4] *Metaph.*, 988 a 10–11. [5] 517 b 7–c 4.

be simply equated with the single Forms. Plato tells us that "the good is not essence, but far exceeds essence in dignity and power," while on the other hand it is "not only the source of intelligibility in all objects of knowledge, but also of their being and essence,"[1] so that he who turns his eye towards the Good, turns it towards "that place where is the full perfection of being."[2] The implication is that the Idea of the Good may rightly be said to transcend being, since it is above all visible and intelligible objects, while on the other hand, as the Supremely Real, the true Absolute, it is the Principle of being and essence in all things.

In the *Timaeus*, Plato says that "It is hard to find the maker and father of the universe, and having found him, it is impossible to speak of him to all."[3] That the position occupied by the Demiurge in the *Timaeus* suggests that these words apply to him, is true; but we must remember (*a*) that the Demiurge is probably a symbol for the operation of Reason in the universe, and (*b*) that Plato explicitly said that there were subjects on which he refused to write,[4] one of these subjects being without doubt his full doctrine of the One. The Demiurge belongs to the "likely account."[5] In his second letter, Plato says that it is a mistake to suppose that any of the predicates we are acquainted with apply to the "king of the universe,"[6] and in his sixth letter he asks his friends to swear an oath of loyalty "in the name of the God who is captain of all things present and to come, and of the Father of that captain and cause."[7] Now, if the "Captain" is the Demiurge, the "Father" cannot be the Demiurge too, but must be the One; and I think that Plotinus was right in identifying the Father with the One or Good of the *Republic*.

The One is thus Plato's ultimate Principle and the source of the world of Forms, and Plato, as we have seen, thinks that the One transcends human predicates. This implies that the *via negativa* of Neo-Platonist and Christian philosophers is a legitimate approach to the One, but it should not be immediately concluded that the approach to the One is an "ecstatic" approach, as in Plotinus. In the *Republic* it is definitely asserted that the approach is *dialectical*, and that a man attains the vision of the Good by "pure intelligence."[8] By dialectic the highest principle of the soul is raised "to the contemplation of that which is best in existence."[9] To this subject we must return later.

[1] *Rep.*, 509 b 6–10.
[2] *Rep.*, 526 e 3–4.
[3] *Tim.*, 28 c 3–5.
[4] Cf. *Ep.* 2, 314 b 7–c 4.
[5] *Tim.*, 30 b 6–c 1.
[6] *Ep.* 2, 312 e ff.
[7] *Ep.* 6, 323 d 2–6.
[8] *Rep.* 532 a 5–b 2.
[9] *Rep.*, 532 c 5–6.

(ii) If the Forms proceed from the One—in some undefined manner—what of particular sensible objects? Does not Plato make such a rift between intelligible and visible worlds that they can be no longer interconnected? It would appear that Plato, who in the *Republic*[1] appears to condemn empirical astronomy, was forced by the progress of empirical science to modify his views, and in the *Timaeus* he himself considers nature and natural questions. (Moreover, Plato came to see that the dichotomy between an unchanging, intelligible world of reality and a changing world of unreality is hardly satisfactory. "Shall we be easily persuaded that change and life and soul and wisdom are not really present to what completely is, that it is neither living nor intelligent but is something awful and sacred in its thoughtless and static stability?")[2] In the *Sophist* and *Philebus* it is implied that διάνοια and αἴσθησις (which belong to different segments of the Line) unite together in the scientific judgment of perception. Ontologically speaking, the sensible particular can become the object of judgment and knowledge only in so far as it is really subsumed under one of the Ideas, "partaking" in the specific Form: in so far as it is a class-instance, it is real and can be known. The sensible particular *as such*, however, considered precisely in its particularity, is indefinable and unknowable, and is not truly "real." To this conviction Plato clung, and it is obviously an Eleatic legacy. The sense-world is, therefore, not wholly illusion, but it contains an element of unreality. Yet it can hardly be denied that even this position, with its sharp distinction between the formal and material elements of the particular, would leave the problem of the "separation" of the intelligible world from the sensible world really unresolved. It is this "separation" that Aristotle attacked. Aristotle thought that determinate form and the matter in which it is embodied are inseparable, both belonging to the real world, and, in his opinion, Plato simply ignored this fact and introduced an unjustifiable separation between the two elements. The real universal, according to Aristotle, is the *determined* universal, and the determined universal is an inseparable aspect of the real: it is a λόγος ἔνυλος or definition embodied in matter. Plato did not see this.

(Professor Julius Stenzel made the brilliant suggestion[3] that when Aristotle criticised Plato's "separation," he was criticising Plato for his failure to see that there is no genus alongside the

[1] *Rep.*, 529–30. [2] *Sophist*, 248 e 6–249 a 2. [3] *Zahl und Gestalt*, pp. 133 ff.

species. He appeals to *Metaph.*, 1037 b 8 ff., where Aristotle attacks Plato's method of logical division for supposing that in the resulting definition the intermediate *differentiae* must be recapitulated, e.g. Plato's method of division would result in our defining man as a "two-footed animal." Aristotle objects to this on the ground that "footedness" is not something alongside "two-footedness." Now, that Aristotle objected to this method of division is true; but his criticism of the Platonic theory of Forms on the ground of the Χωρισμός it introduces, cannot be reduced to the criticism of a logical point, for Aristotle is not criticising Plato merely for putting a generic form alongside the specific form, but for putting Forms in general alongside particulars.[1] It may well be, however, that Aristotle considered that Plato's failure to see that there is no genus alongside the species, i.e. no merely determinable universal, helped to conceal from him the Χωρισμός he was introducing between Forms and particulars—and here Stenzel's suggestion is valuable; but the Χωρισμός attacked by Aristotle cannot be confined to a logical point. That is clear from the whole tenor of Aristotle's criticism.)

4. In the *Phaedrus* Plato speaks of the soul who beholds "real existence, colourless, formless and intangible, visible only to the intelligence" (ἡ ἀχρωματός τε καὶ ἀσχημάτιστος καὶ ἀναφὴς οὐσία ὄντως οὖσα, ψυχῆς, κυβερνήτῃ μόνῳ θεατὴ νῷ),[2] and which sees distinctly "absolute justice, and absolute temperance, and absolute science; not such as they appear in creation, nor under the variety of forms to which we nowadays give the name of realities, but the justice, the temperance, the science, which exist in that which is real and essential being" (τὴν ἐν τῷ ὅ ἐστιν ὂν ὄντως ἐπιστήμην οὖσαν). This would seem to me to imply that these Forms or *Ideals* are comprised in the Principle of Being, in the One, or at least that they owe their essence to the One. Of course, if we use the imagination and try to picture to ourselves absolute justice or temperance existing on its own account in a heavenly world, we shall no doubt think Plato's words childishly naïve and ludicrous; but we should ask ourselves what Plato *meant* and should beware of attributing hastily to him such an extraordinary conception. Most probably Plato means to imply, by his figurative account, that the Ideal of Justice, the Ideal of Temperance, etc., are objectively grounded in the Absolute Principle of Value, in the Good, which "contains" within itself the ideal of human nature

[1] Cf. Hardie, *A Study in Plato*, p. 75. [2] *Phaedrus*, 247 c 6–8.

and so the ideal of the virtues of human nature. The Good or Absolute Principle of Value has thus the nature of a τέλος; but it is not an unrealised τέλος, a non-existent end-to-be-achieved; it is an existent τέλος, an ontological Principle, the Supremely Real, the perfect Exemplary Cause, the Absolute or One.

5. It is to be noted that at the beginning of the *Parmenides* the question is raised what Ideas Socrates is prepared to admit.[1] In reply to Parmenides, Socrates admits that there are Ideas of "likeness" and "of the one and many," and also of "the just and the beautiful and the good," etc. In answer to a further question, he says that he is often undecided, whether he should or should not include Ideas of man, fire, water, etc.; while, in answer to the question whether he admits Ideas of hair, mud, dirt, etc., Socrates answers, "Certainly not." He admits, however, that he sometimes gets disturbed and begins to think that there is nothing without an Idea, though no sooner has he taken up this position than he "runs away," afraid that he "may fall into a bottomless pit of nonsense and perish." He returns, therefore, "to the Ideas of which I was just now speaking."

Julius Stenzel uses this discussion in an attempt to prove that εἶδος had at first for Plato a definitely valuational connotation, as was but natural in the inheritor of Socrates. It was only later that the term came to be extended to cover all class-concepts. I believe that this is, in the main, correct, and that it was largely this very extension of the term Idea (i.e. *explicit* extension, since it already contained an implicit extension) which forced on Plato's attention difficulties of the type considered in the *Parmenides*. For, as long as the term εἶδος is "laden with moral and aesthetic qualities,"[2] as long as it has the nature of a valuational τέλος, drawing men under the impulse of Eros, the problem of its internal unity or multiplicity does not so obviously arise: it is the Good and the Beautiful in One. But once Ideas of man and other particular objects of our experience are explicitly admitted, the Ideal World threatens to become a Many, a reduplication of this world. What is the relation of the Ideas to one another, and what is their relation to particular things? Is there any real unity at all? The Idea of the Good is sufficiently remote from sensible particulars not to appear as an unwelcome reduplication of the latter; but if there is an Idea of man, for instance, "separate"

[1] 130 a 8 ff.

[2] *Plato's Method of Dialectic*, p. 55 (Trs. D. J. Allan, Oxford, Clarendon Press 1940.)

from individual men, it might well appear as a mere reduplication of the latter. Moreover, is the Idea wholly present in every individual man, or is it only partially present in every individual man? Again, if it is legitimate to speak of a likeness between individual men and the Idea of Man, must you not postulate a τρίτος ἄνθρωπος, in order to account for this resemblance and so proceed on an infinite regress? This type of objection was brought against the Ideal Theory by Aristotle, but it was already anticipated by Plato himself. The difference is, that while Plato (as we shall see later) thought that he had answered the objections, Aristotle did not think that Plato had answered them.

In the *Parmenides*, therefore, the question of the relation of individual objects to the Idea is discussed, objections being raised to the Socratic explanation. According to Socrates the relation may be described in two ways: (i) As a participation (μέθεξις, μετέχειν) of the particular object in the Idea; (ii) as an imitation (μίμησις) of the Idea by the particular object, the particular objects being ὁμοιώματα and μιμήματα of the Idea, the latter being the exemplar or παράδειγμα. (It does not seem possible to refer the two explanations to different periods of Plato's philosophical development—at least, not in any rigid way—since both explanations are found together in the *Parmenides*,[1] and both thoughts occur in the *Symposium*.)[2] The objections raised by Parmenides against these Socratic theories are, no doubt, intended to be serious criticism—as, indeed, they are—and not a mere *jeu d'esprit*, as has been suggested. The objections are real objections, and it would appear that Plato tried to develop his theory of Ideas in an attempt to meet some such criticisms as that which he puts into the mouths of the Eleatics in the *Parmenides*.

Do particular objects participate in the whole Idea or only in part of it? This is the dilemma proposed by Parmenides as a logical consequence of the participation-explanation of the relation between Ideas and particular objects. If the first of the alternatives be chosen, then the Idea, which is one, would be entirely in each of many individuals. If the second of the alternatives be chosen, then the Form or Idea is unitary and divisible (or many) at the same time. In either case a contradiction is involved. Moreover, if equal things are equal by the presence of a certain amount of equality, then they are equal by what is less than

[1] *Parm.*, 132 d 1 ff.

[2] *Sympos.*, 211 b 2 (μετέχοντα). In 212 a 4, sense-objects are spoken of as εἴδωλα, which implies "imitation."

equality. Again, if something is big by participation in bigness it is big by possessing that which is less than bigness—which seems to be a contradiction. (It is to be noted that objections of this kind suppose that the Ideas are what amount to individual objects on their own account, and so they serve to show the impossibility of regarding the Idea in this way.)

Socrates suggests the imitation-theory, that particular objects are copies of the Ideas, which are themselves patterns or exemplars; the resemblance of the particular objects to the Idea constitutes its participation in it. Against this Parmenides argues that, if white things are like whiteness, whiteness is also like white things. Hence, if the likeness between white things is to be explained by postulating a Form of whiteness, the likeness between whiteness and white things should also be explained by postulating an archetype, and so on indefinitely. Aristotle argued in much the same way, but all that really follows from the criticism is that the Idea is not simply another particular object, and that the relation between the particular objects and the Idea cannot be the same as that between different particular objects.[1] The objection, then, is to the point as showing the necessity for further consideration of the true relations, but this does not show that the Ideal Theory is totally untenable.

The objection is also raised that on Socrates' theory the Ideas would be unknowable. Man's knowledge is concerned with the objects of this world, and with the relations between individual objects. We can, for example, know the relation between the individual master and the individual slave, but this knowledge is insufficient to inform us as to the relationship between absolute mastership (the Idea of Mastership) and absolute slavery (the Idea of Slavery). For that purpose we should require absolute knowledge and this we do not possess. This objection, too, shows the hopelessness of regarding the Ideal World as merely parallel to this world: if we are to know the former, then there must be some objective basis in the latter which enables us to know it. If the two worlds are merely parallel, then, just as we would know the sensible world without being able to know the Ideal World, so a divine intelligence would know the Ideal World without being able to know the sensible world.

[1] Proclus pointed out that the relation of a copy to its original is a relation not only of resemblance, but also of derivation-from, so that the relation is not symmetrical. Cf. Taylor, *Plato*, p. 358: "My reflection in the glass is a reflection of my face, but my face is not a reflection of it."

The objections raised are left unanswered in the *Parmenides*, but it is to be noticed that Parmenides was not concerned to deny the existence of an intelligible world: he freely admits that if one refuses to admit the existence of absolute Ideas at all, then philosophic thinking goes by the board. The result of the objections that Plato raises against himself in the *Parmenides* is, therefore, to impel him to further exact consideration of the nature of the Ideal World and of its relation to the sensible world. It is made clear by the difficulties raised that some principle of unity is required which will, at the same time, not annihilate the many. This is admitted in the dialogue, though the unity considered is a unity in the world of Forms, as Socrates "did not care to solve the perplexity in reference to visible objects, but only in reference to thought and to what may be called ideas."[1] The difficulties are, therefore, not solved in the *Parmenides*; but the discussion must not be regarded as a destruction of the Ideal Theory, for the difficulties simply indicate that the theory must be expounded in a more satisfactory way than Socrates has expounded it hitherto.

In the second part of the dialogue Parmenides himself leads the discussion and undertakes to exemplify his "art," the method of considering the consequences which flow from a given hypothesis and the consequences which flow from denying that hypothesis. Parmenides proposes to start from the hypothesis of the One and to examine the consequences which are seen to flow from its assertion and its denial. Subordinate distinctions are introduced, the argument is long and complicated and no satisfactory conclusion is arrived at. Into this argument one cannot enter in a book like the present one, but it is necessary to point out that this second part of the *Parmenides* is no more a refutation of the doctrine of the One than the first part was of the Ideal Theory. A real refutation of the doctrine of the One would certainly not be put into the mouth of Parmenides himself, whom Plato greatly respected. In the *Sophist* the Eleatic Stranger apologises for doing violence to "father Parmenides,"[2] but, as Mr. Hardie aptly remarks, this apology "would hardly be called for if in another dialogue father Parmenides had done violence to himself."[3] Moreover, at the end of the *Parmenides* agreement is voted as to the assertion that, "If One is not, then nothing is." The participants may not be sure of the status of the many or

[1] 135 e 1–4. [2] 241 a. [3] *A Study in Plato*, p. 106.

of their relation to the One or even of the precise nature of the One; but they are at least agreed that there *is* a One.

6. In the *Sophist* the object before the interlocutors is to define the Sophist. They have a notion, of course, what the Sophist is, but they wish to *define* the Sophist's nature, to pin him down, as it were, in a clear formula (λόγος). It will be remembered that in the *Theaetetus* Socrates rejected the suggestion that knowledge is true belief plus an account (λόγος); but in that dialogue the discussion concerned particular sensible objects, while in the *Sophist* the discussion turns on class-concepts. The answer which is given to the problem of the *Theaetetus* is, therefore, that knowledge consists in apprehending the class-concept by means of genus and difference, i.e. by *definition*. The method of arriving at definition is that of analysis or division (διαίρεσις, διαιρεῖν κατ'εἴδη), whereby the notion or name to be defined is subsumed under a wider genus or class, which latter is then divided into its natural components. One of these natural components will be the notion to be defined. Previous to the division a process of synthesis or collecting (συνάγειν εἰς ἕν, συναγωγή) should take place, through which terms that are at least *prima facie* interrelated are grouped together and compared, with a view to determining the genus from which the process of division is to start. The wider class chosen is divided into two mutually-exclusive sub-classes, distinguished from one another by the presence or absence of some peculiar characteristic; and the process is continued until the *definiendum* is finally tracked down and defined by means of its genus and differences. (There is an amusing fragment of Epicrates, the comic poet, describing the classification of a pumpkin in the Academy.)

There is no need to enter either upon the actual process of tracking down the Sophist, or upon Plato's preliminary example of the method of division (the definition of the angler); but it must be pointed out that the discussion makes it clear that the Ideas may be one and many at the same time. The class-concept "Animal," for example, is one; but at the same time it is many, in that it contains within itself the sub-classes of "Horse," "Fox," "Man," etc. Plato speaks as though the generic Form pervades the subordinate specific Form or is dispersed throughout them, "blending" with each of them, yet retaining its own unity. There is a communion (κοινωνία) between Forms, and one Form partakes of (μετέχειν) another (as in "Motion exists" it is implied that

Motion blends with Existence); but we should not suppose that one Form partakes of another in the same sense in which the individual partakes of the specific Form, for Plato would not speak of the individual blending with the specific Form. The Forms thus constitute a hierarchy, subordinate to the One as the highest and all-pervading Form; but it is to be remembered that for Plato the "higher" the Form is, the richer it is, so that his point of view is the opposite to that of the Aristotelian, for whom the more "abstract" the concept, the poorer it is.

There is one important point to be noticed. The process of division (Plato, of course, believed that the logical division detects the grades of real being) cannot be prolonged indefinitely, since ultimately you will arrive at the Form that admits of no further division. These are the *infimae species* or ἄτομα εἴδη. The Form of Man, for instance, is indeed "many" in this sense, that it contains the genus and all relative differences, but it is not many in the sense of containing further subordinate specific classes into which it could be divided. On the contrary, below the ἄτομον εἶδος Man there stand *individual men.* The ἄτομα εἴδη, therefore, constitute the lowest rung of the ladder or hierarchy of Forms, and Plato very probably considered that by bringing down the Forms, by the process of division, to the border of the sensible sphere, he was providing a connecting link between τὰ ἀορατά and τὰ ὁρατά. It may be that the relation between the individuals and the *infimae species* was to be elucidated in the *Philosopher,* the dialogue which, it is conjectured, was once intended by Plato to follow the *Statesman* and which was never written; but it cannot be said that the chasm was ever satisfactorily bridged, and the problem of the Χωρισμός remained. (Julius Stenzel put forward the suggestion that Plato adopted from Democritus the principle of dividing until the atom is reached, which, in Plato's hands, becomes the intelligible "atomic Form." It is certainly significant that geometrical shape was a feature of the atom of Democritus, while geometrical shapes play an important part in Plato's picture of the formation of the world in the *Timaeus*; but it would seem that the relation of Plato to Democritus must always remain conjectural and something of a puzzle.)[1]

I have mentioned the "blending" of the Forms, but it is also to be noticed that there are Forms which are incompatible, at least in their "particularity," and will not "blend," e.g. Motion

[1] Cf. Chapter X, *Democritus,* in *Plato's Method of Dialectic.*

and Rest. If I say: "Motion does not rest," my statement is true, since it expresses the fact that Motion and Rest are incompatible and do not blend: if, however, I say: "Motion is Rest," my statement is false, since it expresses a combination that is not objectively verified. Light is thus thrown on the nature of false judgment which perplexed Socrates in the *Theaetetus*; though more relevant to the actual problem of the *Theaetetus* is the discussion of false statement in 262 e ff. of the *Sophist*. Plato takes as an example of a true statement, "Theaetetus sits," and as an example of a false statement, "Theaetetus flies." It is pointed out that Theaetetus is an existent subject and that Flying is a real Form, so that false statement is not a statement about *nothing*. (Every significant statement is about *something*, and it would be absurd to admit non-existent facts or objective falsehoods.) The statement has a meaning, but the relation of participating between the actual "sitting" of Theaetetus and the different Form "Flying" is missing. The statement, therefore, has a meaning, but the statement as a whole does not correspond with the fact as a whole. Plato meets the objection that there can be no false statement because there is nothing for it to mean, by an appeal to the Theory of Forms (which does not appear in the *Theaetetus*, with the consequence that in that dialogue the problem could not be solved). "We can have discourse only through the weaving together of Forms."[1] It is not meant that all significant statements must concern Forms exclusively (since we can make significant statements about singular things like Theaetetus), but that every significant statement involves the use of at least one Form, e.g. "Sitting" in the true statement, "Theaetetus sits."[2]

The *Sophist* thus presents us with the picture of a hierarchy of Forms, combining among themselves in an articulated complex; but it does not solve the problem of the relation of the particulars to the "atomic Forms." Plato insists that there are εἴδωλα or things which are not non-existent, but which at the same time are not fully real; but in the *Sophist* he realises that it is no longer possible to insist on the completely unchanging character

[1] *Soph.*, 259 e 5–6.

[2] To postulate Forms of Sitting and Flying may be a logical application of Plato's principles, but it obviously raises great difficulties. Aristotle implies that the upholders of the Ideal Theory did not go beyond postulating Ideas of natural substances (*Met.* 1079 a). He also asserts that according to the Platonists there are no Ideas of Relations, and implies that they did not believe in Ideas of Negation.

of all Reality. He still holds that the Forms are changeless, but somehow or other spiritual motion must be included in the Real. "Life, soul, understanding" must have a place in what is perfectly real, since, if Reality as a whole excludes all change, intelligence (which involves life) will have no real existence anywhere at all. The conclusion is that "we must admit that what changes and change itself are real things,"[1] and that "Reality or the sum of things is both at once—all that is unchangeable and all that is in change."[2] Real being must accordingly include life, soul and intelligence, and the change implied by them; but what of the εἴδωλα, the purely sensible and perpetually changing, mere becoming? What is the relation of this half-real sphere to Real Being? This question is not answered in the *Sophist*.

7. In the *Sophist*[3] Plato clearly indicates that the whole complex of Forms, the hierarchy of genera and species, is comprised in an all-pervading Form, that of Being, and he certainly believed that in tracing out the structure of the hierarchy of Forms by means of διαίρεσις he was detecting, not merely the structure of logical Forms, but also the structure of ontological Forms of the Real. But whether successful or not in his division of the genera and species, was it of any help to him in overcoming the Χωρισμός, the separation between the particulars and the *infimae species*? In the *Sophist* he showed how division is to be continued until the ἄτομον εἶδος is reached, in the apprehension of which δόξα and αἴσθησις are involved, though it is λόγος alone that determines the "undetermined" plurality. The *Philebus* assumes the same, that we must be able to bring the division to an end by setting a limit to the unlimited and comprehending sense-particulars in the lowest class, so far as they can be comprehended. (In the *Philebus* Ideas are termed ἑνάδες or μονάδες). The important point to notice is that for Plato the sense-particulars *as such* are the unlimited and the undetermined: they are limited and determined only in so far as they are, as it were, brought within the ἄτομον εἶδος. This means that the sense-particulars in so far as they are not brought within the ἄτομον εἶδος and cannot be brought within it, are not true objects at all: they are not fully real. In pursuing the διαίρεσις as far as the ἄτομον εἶδος Plato was, in his own eyes, comprehending all Reality. This enables him to use the words: "But the form of the infinite must not be brought near to the many until one has observed its full number,

[1] 249 b 2–3. [2] 249 d 3–4. [3] Cf. 253 b 8 ff.

the number between the one and the infinite; when this has been learnt, each several individual thing may be forgotten and dismissed into the infinite."[1] In other words, the division must be continued until particulars in their intelligible reality are comprehended in the ἄτομον εἶδος: when this has been done, the remainder, i.e. the sense-particulars, in their non-intelligible aspect, as impenetrable to λόγος, may be dismissed into the sphere of what is fleeting and only semi-real, that which cannot truly be said to *be*. From Plato's own point of view, therefore, the problem of the Χωρισμός may have been solved; but from the point of view of anyone who will not accept his doctrine of sense-particulars, it is very far from being solved.

8. But though Plato may have considered that he had solved the problem of the Χωρισμός, it still remained to show how the sense-particulars come into existence at all. Even if the whole hierarchy of Forms, the complex structure comprised in the all-embracing One, the Idea of Being, or the Good is an ultimate and self-explanatory principle, the Real and the Absolute, it is none the less necessary to show how the world of appearance, which is not simply not-being, even if it is not fully being, came into existence? Does it proceed from the One? If not, what is its cause? Plato made an attempt to answer this question in the *Timaeus*, though I can here only summarise very briefly his answer, as I shall return later to the *Timaeus* when dealing with the physical theories of Plato.

In the *Timaeus* the Demiurge is pictured as conferring geometrical shapes upon the primary qualities within the Receptacle or Space, and so introducing order into disorder, taking as his model in building up the world the intelligible realm of Forms. Plato's account of "creation" is most probably not meant to be an account of creation in time or *ex nihilo*: rather is it an analysis, by which the articulate structure of the material world, the work of a rational cause, is distinguished from the "primeval" chaos, without its being necessarily implied that the chaos was ever actual. The chaos is probably primeval only in the logical, and not in the temporal or historic sense. But if this is so, then the non-intelligible part of the material world is simply assumed: it exists "alongside of" the intelligible world. The Greeks, it would seem, never really envisaged the possibility of creation out of nothing (*ex nihilo sui et subiecti*). Just as the logical process of

[1] *Philebus*, 16 d 7–e 2.

διαίρεσις stops at the ἄτομον εἶδος and Plato in the *Philebus* dismisses the merely particular εἰς τὸ ἄπειρον, so in the physical analysis of the *Timaeus* the merely particular, the non-intelligible element (that which, logically considered, cannot be comprehended under the ἄτομον εἶδος) is dismissed into the sphere of that which is "in discordant and unordered motion,"[1] the factor that the Demiurge "took over." Therefore, just as, from the viewpoint of the Platonic logic, the sense-particulars as such cannot be deduced, cannot be rendered fully intelligible (did not Hegel declare that Herr Krug's pen could not be deduced?), so, in the Platonic physics, the chaotic element, that into which order is "introduced" by Reason, is not explained: doubtless Plato thought that it was inexplicable. It can neither be *deduced* nor has it been *created out of nothing*. It is simply there (a fact of experience), and that is all that we can say about it. The Χωρισμός accordingly remains, for, however "unreal" the chaotic may be, it is not not-being *tout simple*: it is a factor in the world, a factor that Plato leaves unexplained.

9. I have exhibited the Ideas or Forms as an ordered, intelligible structure, constituting in their totality a One in Many, in such a way that each subordinate Idea is itself one in many, as far as the ἄτομον εἶδος, below which is τὸ ἄπειρον. This complex of Forms is the Logical-Ontological Absolute. I must now raise the question, whether Plato regarded the Ideas as the Ideas of God or as independent of God. For the Neo-Platonists, the Ideas were the Thoughts of God: how far can such a theory be ascribed to Plato himself? If it could be so ascribed, it would clearly go a long way towards showing how the "Ideal World" is at once a unity and a plurality—a unity as contained in the Divine Mind, or Nous, and as subordinated to the Divine Plan, a plurality as reflecting the richness of the Divine Thought-content, and as only realisable in Nature in a multitude of existent objects.

In the tenth book of the *Republic*[2] Plato says that God is the Author (Φυτουργός) of the ideal bed. More than that, God is the Author of all other things—"things" in the context meaning other essences. From this it might appear that God created the ideal bed by *thinking* it, i.e. by comprising within His intellect the Idea of the world, and so of man and of all his requirements. (Plato did not, of course, imagine that there was a material ideal bed.) Moreover, since Plato speaks of God as "king" and "truth"

[1] *Tim.*, 30 a 4-5. [2] *Rep.*, 597 b 5-7.

(the tragic poet is at the third remove ἀπὸ βασιλέως καὶ τῆς ἀληθείας), while he has already spoken of the Idea of the Good as κυρία ἀλήθειαν καὶ νοῦν παραχομένη[1] and as Author of being and essence in intelligible objects (Ideas),[2] it might well appear that Plato means to Identify God with the Idea of the Good.[3] Those who wish to believe that this was really Plato's thought, and who proceed to interpret "God" in a theistic sense, would naturally appeal to the *Philebus*,[4] where it is implied that the Mind that orders the universe is possessed of soul (Socrates certainly says that wisdom and mind cannot exist without soul), so that God would be a living and intelligent being. We should thus have a personal God, Whose Mind is the "place" of Ideas, and Who orders and rules the universe, "king of heaven and earth."[5]

That there is much to be said for this interpretation of Plato's thought, I would not deny: moreover, it is naturally attractive to all those who desire to discover a tidy system in Plato and a theistic system. But common honesty forces one to admit the very serious difficulties against this tidy interpretation. For example, in the *Timaeus* Plato pictures the Demiurge as introducing order into the world and forming natural objects according to the model of the Ideas or Forms. The Demiurge is probably a symbolic figure representing the Reason that Plato certainly believed to be operative in the world. In the *Laws* he proposes the institution of a Nocturnal Council or Inquisition for the correction and punishment of atheists. Now, "atheist" means, for Plato, first and foremost the man who denies the operation of Reason in the world. Plato certainly admits that soul and intelligence belong to the Real, but it does not seem possible to assert with certainty that, in Plato's view, the Divine Reason is the "place" of the Ideas. It might, indeed, be argued that the Demiurge is spoken of as desiring that "all things should come as near as possible to being like himself," and that "all things should be good"[6]—phrases which suggest that the separation of the Demiurge from the Ideas is a Myth and that, in Plato's real thought, he is the Good and the ultimate Source of the Ideas. That the *Timaeus* never says that the Demiurge created the Ideas or is their Source, but pictures them as distinct from him (the

[1] *Rep.*, 517 c 4.
[2] *Rep.*, 509 b 6–10.
[3] The fact that Plato speaks of God as "king" and "truth," while the Idea of the Good is "the source of truth and reason," suggests that God or Reason is *not* to be identified with the Good. A Neo-Platonic interpretation is rather implied.
[4] *Phil.*, 30 c 2–e 2.
[5] *Phil.*, 28 c 6 ff.
[6] *Tim.*, 29 e 1–30 a 7.

Demiurge being depicted as Efficient Cause and the Ideas as Exemplary Cause), does not seem to be conclusive evidence that Plato did *not* bring them together; but it should at least make us beware of asserting positively that he *did* bring them together. Moreover, if the "Captain" and God of the sixth letter is the Demiurge or Divine Reason, what of the "Father"? If the "Father" is the One, then it would not look as though the One and the whole hierarchy of the Ideas can be explained as thoughts of the Demiurge.[1]

But if the Divine Reason is not the ultimate, is it possible that the One is the ultimate, not only as ultimate Exemplary Cause, but also as ultimate Productive Cause, being itself "beyond" mind and soul as it is "beyond" essence? If so, can we say that the Divine Reason proceeds in some way (timelessly, of course) from the One, and that this Reason either contains the Ideas as thoughts or exists "alongside" the Ideas (as depicted in the *Timaeus*)? In other words, can we interpret Plato on Neo-Platonic lines?[2] The remark about the "Captain" and the "Father" in the sixth letter might be understood in support of this interpretation, while the fact that the Idea of the Good is never spoken of as a *soul* might mean that the Good is beyond soul, i.e. more than soul, not less than soul. The fact that in the *Sophist* Plato says, through the mouth of the Eleatic Stranger, that "Reality or the sum of things" must include soul, intelligence and life,[3] implies that the One or total Reality (the Father of *Ep.* 6) comprises not only the Ideas but also mind. If so, what is the relation of Mind to the World-soul of the *Timaeus*? The World-soul and the Demiurge are distinct in that dialogue (for the Demiurge is depicted as "making" the World-soul); but in the *Sophist* it is said that intelligence must have life, and that both these must have soul "in which they reside."[4] It is, however, possible that the making of the World-soul by the Demiurge is not to be taken literally at all, especially as it is stated in the *Phaedrus* that soul is a beginning and uncreated,[5] and that the World-soul and the Demiurge represent together the Divine Reason immanent in the world. If this were so, then we should have the One, the Supreme Reality, embracing and in some sense the Source (though not the Creator in time) of the Divine Reason (=Demiurge=

[1] Though in *Timaeus*, 37 c, the "Father" means the Demiurge.

[2] The Neo-Platonists held that the Divine Reason was not ultimate, but proceeded from the One.

[3] *Soph.*, 248 e 6–249 d 4. [4] 249 a 4–7. [5] 245 c 5–246 a 2.

World-soul) and the Forms. We might then speak of the Divine Reason as the "Mind of God" (if *we* equated God with the One) and the Forms as Ideas of God; but we should have to bear in mind that such a conception would bear a closer resemblance to later Neo-Platonism than to specifically Christian philosophy.

That Plato had some idea of what he meant hardly needs to be stressed, but in view of the evidence at our disposal we must avoid dogmatic pronouncements as to what he *did* mean. Therefhre, although the present writer is inclined to think that the second interpretation bears some resemblance to what Plato actually thought, he is very far from putting it forward as certainly the authentic philosophy of Plato.

10. We must now touch briefly on the vexed question of the mathematical aspect of the Ideal Theory.[1] According to Aristotle,[2] Plato declared that:

(i) The Forms are Numbers;
(ii) Things exist by participation in Numbers;
(iii) Numbers are composed of the One and the great-and-small or "indeterminate duality" (ἀόριστος δυάς) instead of, as the Pythagoreans thought, the unlimited (ἄπειρον) and limit (πέρας);
(iv) τὰ μαθηματικά occupy an intermediate position between Forms and things.

With the subject of τὰ μαθηματικά or the "intermediates" I have already dealt when treating of the Line: it remains, therefore, to consider the following questions:

(i) Why did Plato identify Forms with Numbers and what did he mean?
(ii) Why did Plato say that things exist by participation in numbers?
(iii) What is meant by composition from the One and the great-and-small?

With these questions I can only deal very briefly. Not only would an adequate treatment require a much greater knowledge of mathematics, both ancient and modern, than the present writer possesses; but it is also doubtful if, with the material at our disposal, even the mathematically-gifted specialist could give a really adequate and definitive treatment.

[1] My debt to Professor Taylor's treatment of the topic will be obvious to all those who have read his articles in *Mind* (Oct. 1926 and Jan. 1927). Cf. Appendix to *Plato*.

[2] *Metaph.*, A, 6, 9; M and N.

(i) Plato's motive in identifying Forms with Numbers seems to be that of rationalising or rendering intelligible the mysterious and transcendental world of Forms. To render intelligible in this case means to find the *principle of order*.

(ii) Natural objects embody the principle of order to some extent: they are, for example, instances of the logical universal and tend towards the realisation of their form: they are the handiwork of intelligence and exhibit design.

(*a*) This truth is expressed in the *Timaeus* by saying that the sensible characters of bodies are dependent on the geometrical structure of their corpuscles. This geometrical structure is determined by that of their faces, and that of their faces by the structure of the two types of triangles (isosceles right-angled and right-angled scalene) from which they are built up. The ratios of the sides of the triangles to one another may be expressed numerically.

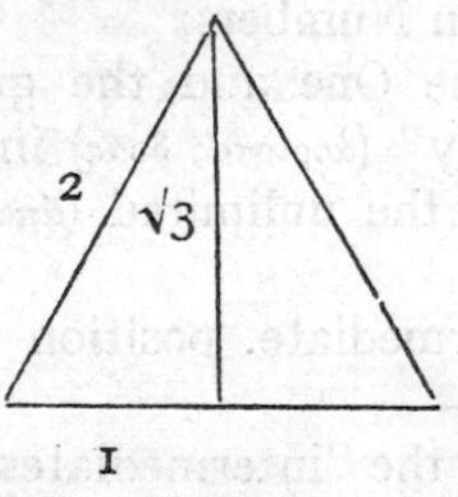

Half-equilateral or right-angled scalene.

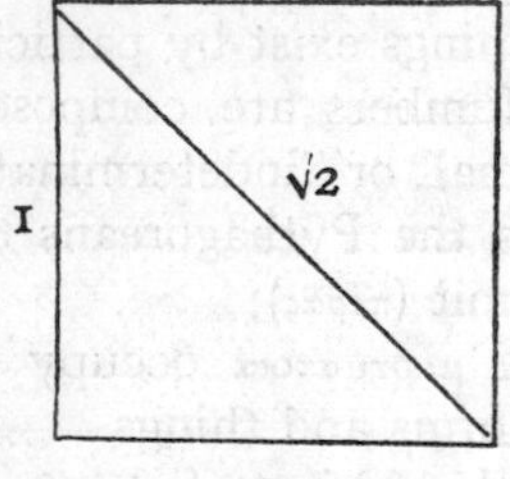

Half-square or right-angled isosceles.

(*b*) Another expression of the same truth is the doctrine of the *Epinomis* that the apparently mazy movements of the heavenly bodies (the primary objects of official cult) really conform to mathematical law and so express the wisdom of God.[1]

(*c*) Natural bodies, therefore, embody the principle of order and may, to a greater or less extent, be "mathematicised." On the other hand, they cannot be entirely "mathematicised"—they are not Numbers—for they embody also contingency, an irrational element, "matter." They are thus not said to *be* Numbers, but to *participate* in Numbers.

(iii) This partly irrational character of natural objects gives us the key to the understanding of the "great and the small."

(*a*) The triplet of numbers which gives the ratio of the sides to one another is, in the case of the isosceles right-angled triangle,

[1] 990 c 5–991 b 4.

1, 1, $\sqrt{2}$, and in the case of the right-angled scalene, 1, $\sqrt{3}$, 2. In either case, then, there is an irrational element which expresses the *contingency* in natural objects.

(*b*) Taylor points out that in a certain sequence of fractions—nowadays derived from a "continual fraction," but actually alluded to by Plato himself[1] and by Theo of Smyrna[2]—alternate terms converge upwards to $\sqrt{2}$ as limit and upper bound, while alternate other terms converge downwards to $\sqrt{2}$ as limit and lower bound. The terms of the whole sequence, therefore, in their original order, are in consequence alternately "greater and less" than $\sqrt{2}$, while jointly converging to $\sqrt{2}$ as their unique limit. We have, then, the characteristics of the great and the small or the indeterminate duality. The "endlessness" of the continued fraction, the "irrationality," seems to be identified with the material element, the element of non-being, *in all that becomes*. It is a mathematical expression of the Heraclitean flux-character of natural entities.

This may seem fairly clear as regards natural bodies. But what are we to make of Aristotle's dictum that "from the great and the small, by participation in the One, come the Forms, i.e. the Numbers"?[3] In other words, how can we explain the extension of the form-matter composition to the integers themselves?

If we take the series $1 + \frac{1}{2} + \frac{1}{4} + \frac{1}{8} + \ldots + \frac{1}{2n} + \ldots$ we have a series that converges to the number 2. It is clear, then, that an infinite series of rational fractions may converge towards a rational limit, and examples could be given in which the μέγα καὶ μικρόν are involved. Plato would seem to have extended this composition from the μέγα καὶ μικρόν to the integers themselves, passing over, however, the fact that 2 as the limit of convergence cannot be identified with the integer 2, since the integers are *presupposed* as a series from which the convergents are formed. In the Platonic Academy the integers were derived or "educed" from One by the help of the ἀόριστος δυάς, which seems to have been identified with the *integer* 2, and to have been given the function of "doubling." The result is that the integers are derived in a non-rational series. On the whole we may say that, pending new light from philologically exact mathematical history, the theory of the composition of the integers from the One and the great-and-small will continue to look like a puzzling excrescence on the Platonic theory of Ideas.

[1] *Rep.*, 546 c. [2] *Expositio*, ed. Hiller, 43, 5–45, 8. [3] *Metaph.*, 987 b 21–2.

11. In regard to the whole tendency to pan-mathematisation I cannot but regard it as unfortunate. That the real is rational is a presupposition of all dogmatic philosophy, but it does not follow that the whole of reality can be rationalised by us. The attempt to reduce all reality to mathematics is not only an attempt to rationalise all reality—which is the task of philosophy, it may be said—but presupposes that all reality can be rationalised *by us*, which is an assumption. It is perfectly true that Plato admits an element in Nature that cannot be submitted to mathematisation, and so to rationalisation, but his attempt to rationalise reality and the extension of this attempt to the spiritual sphere has a flavour about it which may well remind us of Spinoza's deterministic and mechanistic view of reality (expressed in his *Ethica more geometrico demonstrata*) and of Hegel's attempt to comprehend the inner essence of ultimate Reality or God within the formulae of logic.

It may at first sight appear strange that the Plato who composed the *Symposium*, with its ascent to Absolute Beauty under the inspiration of Eros, should have been inclined to pan-mathematicism; and this apparent contrast might seem to support the view that the Socrates of the Platonic dialogues does not give Plato's opinions, but his own, that while Socrates invented the Ideal Theory as it appears in the dialogues, Plato "arithmetised" it. Yet, apart from the fact that the "mystical" and predominantly religious interpretation of the *Symposium* is very far from having been demonstrated as the certain interpretation, the apparent contrast between the *Symposium*—assuming for the moment that the "ascent" is a religious and mystical one—and Plato's mathematical interpretation of the Forms, as related to us by Aristotle, would hardly seem to be a compelling argument for the view that the Platonic Socrates is the historic Socrates, and that Plato reserved most of his personal views for the Academy, and, in the dialogues, for expression by other *dramatis personae* than the figure of Socrates. If we turn to Spinoza, we find a man who, on the one hand, was possessed by the vision of the unity of all things in God, and who proposed the ideal intuition of the *amor intellectualis Dei*, and who, on the other hand, sought to extend the mechanical aspect of Physics to all reality. Again, the example of Pascal should be sufficient to show us that mathematical genius and a deeply religious, even mystical, temperament are not at all incompatible.

Moreover, pan-mathematicism and idealism might even be held to lend support to one another. The more Reality is mathematicised, the more, in a sense, it is transferred on to an ideal plane, while, conversely, the thinker who desires to find the true reality and being of Nature in an ideal world might easily grasp the proffered hand of mathematics as an aid in the task. This would apply especially in the case of Plato, since he had before him the example of the Pythagoreans, who combined not only an interest in mathematics, but also a trend towards pan-mathematicism with religious and psychological interests. We are, therefore, in no way entitled to declare that Plato *could not* have combined in himself religious and transcendentalist tendencies with a tendency to pan-mathematicism, since, whether incompatible or not from the abstract viewpoint, history has shown that they are not incompatible from the psychological standpoint. If the Pythagoreans were possible, if Spinoza and Pascal were possible, then there is no reason why we should say, i.e. *a priori*, that Plato could not have written a mystical book and delivered the lecture on the Good in which, we learn, he spoke of arithmetic and astronomy and identified the One and the Good. But, though we cannot assert this *a priori*, it still remains to inquire whether in actual fact Plato meant such a passage as the speech of Socrates in the *Symposium* to be understood in a religious sense.

12. By what process does the mind arrive at the apprehension of the Ideas, according to Plato? I have already spoken briefly of the Platonic dialectic and method of διαίρεσις, and nobody will deny the importance of dialectic in the Platonic theory; but the question arises whether Plato did or did not envisage a religious, even a mystical, approach to the One or Good. *Prima facie* at least the *Symposium* contains mystical elements, and, if we come to the dialogue with our minds full of the interpretation given it by Neo-Platonist and Christian writers, we shall probably find in it what we are seeking. Nor can this interpretation be set aside *ab initio*, for certain modern scholars of great and deserved repute have lent their powerful support thereto.

Thus, referring to Socrates' speech in the *Symposium*, Professor Taylor comments: "In substance, what Socrates is describing is the same spiritual voyage which St. John of the Cross describes, for example, in the well-known song, *En una noche oscura*, which opens his treatise on the *Dark Night*, and Crashaw hints at more obscurely all through his lines on *The Flaming Heart*, and

Bonaventura charts for us with precision in the *Itinerarium Mentis in Deum*."[1] Others, however, will have none of this; for them Plato is no mystic at all, or if he does display any mystical leanings, it is only in the weakness of old age that he does so. Thus Professor Stace declares, that "the Ideas are rational, that is to say, they are apprehended through reason. The finding of the common element in the manifold is the work of inductive reason, and through this alone is the knowledge of the Ideas possible. This should be noted by those persons who imagine that Plato was some sort of benevolent mystic. The imperishable One, the absolute reality, is apprehended, not by intuition or in any kind of mystic ecstasy, but only by rational cognition and laborious thought."[2] Again, Professor C. Ritter says that he would like "to direct a critical remark against the recent attempts, oft repeated, to stamp Plato as a mystic. These are wholly based on forged passages of the *Epistles*, which I can only consider as inferior achievements of a spiritual poverty which seeks to take refuge in occultism. I am astonished that anyone can hail them as enlightened wisdom, as the final result of Platonic philosophising."[3] Professor Ritter is, needless to say, perfectly well aware that certain passages in the certainly authentic works of Plato lend themselves to interpretation in the mystical sense; but, in his view, such passages are not only poetical and mythical in character, but were understood as such by Plato himself. In his earlier works Plato throws out suggestions, is feeling his way, as it were, and sometimes clothes his half-formed thoughts in poetical and mythical language; but when, in later dialogues, he applies himself to a more scientific treatment of his epistemological and ontological doctrines, he no longer brings in priestesses or uses poetic symbolism.

It would seem that, if we regard the Good predominantly in its aspect as Ideal or τέλος, Eros might well be understood as simply the impulse of man's higher nature towards the good and virtue (or, in the language of the doctrine of pre-existence and reminiscence, as the natural attraction of man's higher nature towards the Ideal which he beheld in the state of pre-existence). Plato, as we have seen, would not accept a merely relativistic ethic: there are absolute standards and norms, absolute ideals. There is thus an ideal of justice, an ideal of temperance, an ideal

[1] *Plato*, p. 225. [2] *Critical Hist.*, pp. 190–1.
[3] *The Essence of Plato's Philosophy*, p. 11.

of courage, and these ideals are real and absolute, since they do not vary but are the unchanging standards of conduct. They are not "things," for they are ideal; yet they are not merely subjective, because they "rule," as it were, man's acts. But human life is not lived out atomistically, apart from Society and the State, nor is man a being entirely apart from nature; and so we can arrive at the apprehension of an all-embracing Ideal and τέλος, to which all particular Ideals are subordinate. This universal Ideal is the Good. It is apprehended by means of dialectic, i.e. *discursively*; but in man's higher nature there is an attraction towards the truly good and beautiful. If man mistakenly takes sensible beauty and good, e.g. the beauty of physical objects, as his true good, then the impulse of attraction of Eros is directed towards these inferior goods, and we have the earthly and sensual man. A man may, however, be brought to see that the soul is higher and better than the body, and that beauty of soul is of more value than beauty of body. Similarly, he may be brought to see the beauty in the formal sciences[1] and the beauty of the Ideals: the power of Eros then attracts him "towards the wide ocean of intellectual beauty" and "the sight of the lovely and majestic forms which it contains."[2] Finally, he may come to apprehend how all the particular ideals are subordinate to one universal Ideal or τέλος, the Good-in-itself, and so to enjoy "the science" of this universal beauty and good. The rational soul is akin to the Ideal,[3] and so is able to contemplate the Ideal and to delight in its contemplation once the sensual appetite has been restrained.[4] "There is none so worthless whom Love cannot impel, as it were by a divine inspiration, towards virtue."[5] The true life for man is thus the philosophic life or the life of wisdom, since it is only the philosopher who attains true universal science and apprehends the rational character of Reality. In the *Timaeus* the Demiurge is depicted as forming the world according to the Ideal or Exemplary Pattern, and as endeavouring to make it as much like the Ideal as the refractory matter at his disposal will permit. It is for the philosopher to apprehend the Ideal and to endeavour to model his own life and that of others according to the Pattern. Hence the place accorded to the Philosopher-King in the *Republic*.

Eros or Love is pictured in the *Symposium*[6] as "a great god," holding an intermediate place between the divine and the mortal.

[1] Cf. *Philebus*, 51 b 9–d 1.
[2] *Sympos.*, 210 d 3–5.
[3] Cf. *Phaedo*.
[4] Cf. *Phaedrus*.
[5] *Sympos.*, 179 a 7–8.
[6] 201 d 8 ff.

Eros, in other words, "the child of Poverty and plenty," is *desire*, and desire is for what is not yet possessed, but Eros, though poor, i.e. not yet possessing, is the "earnest desire for the posession of happiness and that which is good." The term "Eros" is often confined to one species of Eros—and that by no means the highest—but it is a term of wider connotation than physical desire, and is, in general, "the desire of generation in the beautiful, both with relation to the body and the soul." Moreover, since Eros is the desire that good be for ever present with us, it must of necessity be also the desire for immortality.[1] By the lower Eros men are compelled to seek immortality through the production of children: through a higher Eros poets like Homer and statesmen like Solon leave a more enduring progeny "as the pledges of that love which subsisted between them and the beautiful." Through contact with Beauty itself the human being becomes immortal and produces true virtue.

Now all this might, it seems, be understood of a purely intellectualist, in the sense of discursive, process. None the less, it is true that the Idea of the Good or the Idea of Beauty is an ontological Principle, so there can be no *a priori* reason why it should not itself be the object of Eros and be apprehended intuitively. In the *Symposium* the soul at the summit of the ascent is said to behold Beauty "on a sudden," while in the *Republic* the Good is asserted to be seen last of all and only with an effort—phrases which might imply an intuitional apprehension. What we might call the "logical" dialogues may give little indication of any mystical approach to the One; but that does not necessarily mean that Plato never envisaged any such approach, or that, if he ever envisaged it, he had rejected it by the time he came to write the *Parmenides*, the *Theaetetus* and the *Sophist*. These dialogues deal with definite problems, and we have no right to expect Plato to present all aspects of his thought in any one dialogue. Nor does the fact that Plato never proposes the One or the Good as the object of official religious cult necessarily militate against the possibility of his admitting an intuitional and mystical approach to the One. In any case we would scarcely expect Plato to propose the radical transformation of the popular Greek religion (though in the *Laws* he does propose its purification, and hints that true religion consists in a virtuous life and recognition of Reason's operation in the universe, e.g. in the movements of the heavenly

[1] 206 a 7–207 a 4.

bodies); while, if the One is "beyond" being and soul, it might never occur to him that it could be the object of a popular cult. After all, Neo-Platonists, who certainly admitted an "ecstatic" approach to the One, did not hesitate to lend their support to the traditional and popular religion.

In view of these considerations, it would appear that we are forced to conclude that (*a*) we are certain as to the *dialectical* approach, and (*b*) we are uncertain as to any mystical approach, while not denying that some passages of Plato's writings could be understood as implying such an approach, and may *possibly* have been meant by Plato to be so understood.

13. It is evident that the Platonic Theory of Forms constitutes an enormous advance on pre-Socratic Philosophy. He broke away from the *de facto* materialism of the pre-Socratics, asserting the existence of immaterial and invisible Being, which is not but a shadow of this world but is real in a far deeper sense than the material world is real. While agreeing with Heraclitus, that sensible things are in a state of flux, of becoming, so that they can never really be said to *be*, he saw that this is but one side of the picture: there is also true Being, a stable and abiding Reality, which can be known, which is indeed the supreme object of knowledge. On the other hand, Plato did not fall into the position of Parmenides, who by equating the universe with a static One, was forced to deny all change and becoming. For Plato the One is transcendent, so that becoming is not denied but is fully admitted in the "created" world. Moreover, Reality itself is not without Mind and life and soul, so that there is spiritual movement in the Real. Again, even the transcendent One is not without the Many, just as the objects of this world are not entirely without unity, for they participate in or imitate the Forms and so partake in order to some extent. They are not fully real, but they are not mere Not-being; they have a share in being, though true Being is not material. Mind and its effect, order, are present in the world: Mind or Reason permeates, as it were, this world and is not a mere *Deus ex machina*, like the Nous of Anaxagoras.

But if Plato represents an advance on the pre-Socratics, he represents an advance also on the Sophists and on Socrates himself. On the Sophists, since Plato, while admitting the relativism of bare αἴσθησις, refused, as Socrates had before him, to acquiesce in the relativity of science and moral values. On Socrates himself, since Plato extended his investigations beyond the sphere of ethical standards and definitions into those of logic and ontology. Moreover, while there is no certain indication that Socrates attempted any systematic unification of Reality, Plato presents us with a Real Absolute. Thus while Socrates and the Sophists represent a reaction to the foregoing systems of cosmology and to the speculations concerning the One and the Many (though in a true sense Socrates' pre-occupation with definiteness concerns the One and the Many), Plato took up again the problems of the Cosmologists, though on a much higher plane and without abandoning the position won by Socrates. He may thus be said to have attempted the synthesis of what was valuable, or appeared to him valuable, in the pre-Socratic and Socratic philosophies.

It must, of course, be admitted that the Platonic Theory of Forms is unsatisfactory. Even if the One or Good represents for him the ultimate Principle, which comprises all the other Forms, there remains the Χωρισμός between the intelligible and the purely sensible world. Plato may have thought that he had solved the problem of the Χωρισμός from the epistemological standpoint, by his doctrine of the union of λόγος, δόξα and αἴσθησις in the apprehension of the ἄτομα εἴδη; but, ontologically speaking, the sphere of pure Becoming remains unexplained. (It is, however, doubtful if the Greeks *ever* "explained" it.) Thus Plato does not appear to have cleared up satisfactorily the meaning of μέθεξις and μίμησις. In the *Timaeus*[1] he says explicitly that the Form never enters "into anything else anywhere," a statement which shows clearly that Plato did *not* regard the Form or Idea as an intrinsic constituent of the physical object. Therefore, in view of Plato's own statements, there is no point in trying to delete the difference between him and Aristotle. Plato may well have apprehended important truths to which Aristotle failed to do justice, but he certainly did not hold the same view of the universal as that held by Aristotle. Consequently, "participation" for Plato should not be taken to mean that there is an "ingredience" of "eternal objects" into "events." "Events" or physical objects are thus, for Plato, no more than imitations or mirror-images of the Ideas, and the conclusion is inescapable that the sensible world exists "alongside" the intelligible world, as the latter's shadow and fleeting image. The Platonic Idealism is a grand and sublime philosophy which contains much truth (for the purely sensible world is indeed neither the only world nor yet the

[1] 52 a 1-4

highest and most "real" world); but, since Plato did not claim that the sensible world is mere illusion and not-being, his philosophy inevitably involves a Χωρισμός, and it is useless to attempt to slur over the fact. After all, Plato is not the only great philosopher whose system has landed him in difficulties in regard to "particularity," and to say that Aristotle was right in detecting the Χωρισμός in the Platonic philosophy is not to say that the Aristotelian view of the universal, when taken by itself, obviates all difficulties. It is far more probable that these two great thinkers emphasised (and perhaps over-emphasised) different aspects of reality which need to be reconciled in a more complete synthesis.

But, whatever conclusions Plato may have arrived at, and whatever imperfections or errors there may be in his Theory of Ideas, we must never forget that Plato meant to establish ascertained truth. He firmly held that we can, and do, apprehend essences in thought, and he firmly held that these essences are not purely subjective creations of the human mind (as though the ideal of justice, for instance, were purely man's creation and relative in character): we do not create them, we discover them. We judge of things according to standards, whether moral and aesthetic standards or generic and specific types: all judgment necessarily implies such standards, and if the scientific judgment is objective, then these standards must have objective reference. But they are not found, and cannot be found, in the sense-world as such: therefore they must be transcendent of the fleeting world of sense-particulars. Plato really did not raise the "critical problem," though he undoubtedly believed that experience is inexplicable, unless the objective existence of the standards is maintained. We should not attribute to Plato the position of a Neo-Kantian, for even if (which we do not mean to admit) the truth underlying the doctrines of pre-existence and reminiscence is the Kantian *a priori*, there is no evidence that Plato himself used these "myths" as figurative expressions for the doctrine of a purely subjective *a priori*. On the contrary, all the evidence goes to show that Plato believed in the truly objective reference of concepts. Reality can be known and Reality is rational; what cannot be known is not rational, and what is not fully real is not fully rational. This Plato held to the last, and he believed that if our experience (in a wide sense) is to be explained or rendered coherent, it can only be explained on the basis of his theory. If he was no Kantian, he was, on the other hand, no mere romancer or mythologist: he was a *philosopher*, and the theory of Forms was put forward as a philosophic and rational theory (a philosophic "hypothesis" for the explanation of experience), not as an essay in mythology or popular folklore, nor as the mere expression of the longing for a better world than this one.

It is, then, a great mistake to change Plato into a poet, as though he were simply an "escapist" who desired to create a supercorporeal world, an ideal world, wherein he could dwell away from the conditions of daily experience. If Plato could have said with Mallarmé, "La chair est triste, hélas! et j'ai lu tous les livres, Fuir! là-bas fuir . . . ,"[1] it would have been because he believed in the *reality* of a supersensual and intelligible world, which it is given to the philosopher to *discover*, not to create. Plato did not seek to transmute "reality" into dream, creating his own poetical world, but to rise from this inferior world to the superior world of the pure Archetypal Ideas. Of the subsistent reality of these Ideas he was profoundly convinced. When Mallarmé says: "Je dis: une fleur, et hors de l'oubli où ma voix relègue aucun contour, en tant que quelque chose d'autre, que les calices sus, musicalement se lève, idée même et suave, l'absente de tous bouquets," he is thinking of the creation of the ideal flower, not of the discovery of the Archetypal Flower in the Platonic sense. Just as in a symphony the instruments may transmute a landscape into music, so the poet transmutes the concrete flowers of experience into idea, into the music of dream-thought. Moreover, in actual practice Mallarmé's emptying-out of particular circumstances served rather the purpose of widening the associative, evocative and allusive scope of the idea or image. (And because these were so personal, it is so difficult to understand his poetry.) In any case, however, all this is foreign to Plato, who, whatever his artistic gifts may have been, is primarily a philosopher, not a poet.

Nor are we entitled to regard Plato's aim as that of transmuting reality in the fashion of Rainer Maria Rilke. There may be truth in the contention that we build up a world of our own by clothing it, as it were, from within ourselves—the sunlight on the wall may mean more to us than it means "in itself," in terms of atoms and electrons and light-waves, because of our subjective impressions, and the allusions, associations, overtones and undertones

[1] Stéphane Mallarmé, *Poems*. (Trans. by Roger Fry. Chatto & Windus, 1936.)

that we supply—but Plato's effort was not to enrich, beautify and transmute this world by subjective evocations, but to pass beyond the sensible world to the world of thought, the Transcendental Reality. Of course, it still remains open to us, if we are so inclined, to discuss the psychological origins of Plato's thought (it *might* be that he was psychologically an escapist); but, if we do so, we must at the same time remember that this is not equivalent to an interpretation of what Plato meant. Whatever "subconscious" motives he may or may not have had, he certainly meant to pursue a serious, philosophic and scientific inquiry.

Nietzsche accused Plato of being an enemy to this world, of setting up a transcendental world out of enmity to this world, of contrasting a "There" with a "Here" out of dislike of the world of experience and of human life and out of moral presuppositions and interests. That Plato was influenced by disappointments in actual life, e.g. by the political conduct of the Athenian State or by his disappointment in Sicily, is probably true; but he was not actively hostile to this world; on the contrary, he desired to train statesmen of the true type, who would, as it were, carry on the work of the Demiurge in bringing order into disorder. He was hostile to life and this world, only in so far as they are disordered and fragmentary, out of harmony with or not expressing what he believed to be stable realities and stable norms of surpassing value and universal significance. The point is not so much what influences contributed to the formation of Plato's metaphysic, whether as causes, conditions or occasions, as the question: "Did Plato prove his position or did he not?"—and with this question a man like Nietzsche does not concern himself. But we cannot afford to dismiss *a priori* the notion that what there is of order and intelligibility in this world has an objective foundation in an invisible and transcendent Reality, and I believe that Plato not only attained a considerable measure of truth in his metaphysic, but also went a long way towards showing that it *was* the truth. If a man is going to talk at all, he is certain to make valuational judgments, judgments which presuppose objective norms and standards, values which can be apprehended with varying degrees of insight, values which do not "actualise" themselves but depend for their actualisation on the human will, co-operating with God in the realisation of value and the ideal in human life. We have, of course, no direct intuition of the Absolute, as far as natural knowledge is concerned (and in so far as the Platonic theory implies such a knowledge it is inadmissible, while in so far as it identifies true knowledge with direct apprehension of the Absolute it might seem to lead, unwittingly, to scepticism), but by rational reflection we can certainly come to the knowledge of objective (and indeed transcendentally-grounded) values, ideals and ends, and this after all is Plato's main point.

CHAPTER XXI

THE PSYCHOLOGY OF PLATO

1. PLATO in no way fell a victim to the crude psychology of the former Cosmological Schools, in which the soul was reduced to air or fire or atoms: he was neither materialist nor epiphenomenalist, but an uncompromising spiritualist. The soul is clearly distinct from the body; it is man's most valuable possession, and the true tendance of the soul must be its chief concern. Thus at the close of the *Phaedrus*, Socrates prays: "Beloved Pan, and all ye other Gods who here are present, grant me to be beautiful in the inner man, and all I have of outer things to be consonant with those within. May I count the wise man only rich. And may my store of gold be such none but the temperate man can bear."[1] The reality of the soul and its pre-eminence over the body finds emphatic expression in Plato's psychological dualism, which corresponds to his metaphysical dualism. In the *Laws*[2] Plato defines the soul as "self-initiating motion" (τὴν δυναμένην αὐτὴν κινεῖν κίνησιν) or the "source of motion." This being so, the soul is prior to the body in the sense that it is superior to the body (the latter being moved without being the source of motion) and must rule the body. In the *Timaeus* Plato says that "the only existing thing which properly possesses intelligence is soul, and this is an invisible thing, whereas fire, water, earth and air are all visible bodies";[3] and in the *Phaedo* he shows that the soul cannot be a mere epiphenomenon of the body. Simmias suggests that the soul is only the harmony of the body and perishes when the body, of which it is the harmony, perishes; but Socrates points out that the soul can rule the body and its desires, whereas it is absurd to suppose that a mere harmony can rule that of which it is the harmony.[4] Again, if the soul were a mere harmony of the body, it would follow that one soul could be more of a soul than another (since a harmony will admit of increase or diminution), which is an absurd supposition.

But although Plato asserts an essential distinction between sou and body, he does not deny the influence that may be exercised on the soul by or through the body. In the *Republic* he includes

[1] 279 b 8–c 3. [2] 896 a 1–2. [3] 46 d 5–7. [4] 85 e 3–86 d 4, 93 c 3–95 a 2.

physical training among the constituents of true education, and he rejects certain types of music because of the deleterious effect they have on the soul. In the *Timaeus*, again, he admits the evil influence that can be wrought by bad physical education and by bodily habits of vice, which may even bring about an irremediable state in which the soul is enslaved,[1] and in the *Laws* he stresses the influence of heredity.[2] In fact, a defective constitution inherited from the parents and a faulty education or environment are responsible for most of the soul's ills. "No one is willingly bad; the bad man becomes bad because of some faulty habit of body and a stupid upbringing, and these are unwelcome evils that come to any man without his choice."[3] Even if, therefore, Plato speaks on occasion as though the soul merely dwelt in the body and used it, we must not represent him as denying any interaction of soul and body on one another. He may not have *explained* interaction, but this is a most difficult task in any case. Interaction is an obvious fact, and has to be accepted: the situation is certainly not bettered by denying interaction, because one cannot fully explain it, or by reducing soul to body in order to do away with the necessity of giving any explanation at all or of confessing that one has not got one to give.

2. In the *Republic* we find the doctrine of the tripartite nature of the soul,[4] a doctrine which is said to have been borrowed from the Pythagoreans.[5] The doctrine recurs in the *Timaeus*, so we can hardly be justified in supposing that Plato ever abandoned it.[6] The soul consists of three "parts"—the rational "part" (τὸ λογιστικόν), the courageous or spirited "part" (τὸ θυμοειδές) and the appetitive "part" (τὸ ἐπιθυμητικόν). The word "part" may justifiably be used in this connection, since Plato himself employs the term μέρος; but I put it just now in inverted commas in order to indicate that it is a metaphorical term and should not be taken to mean that the soul is extended and material. The word μέρος appears in 444 b 3 of the fourth book of the *Republic*, and before this Plato uses the word εἶδος, a word that shows that he regarded the three parts as forms or functions or principles of action, not as parts in the material sense.

τὸ λογιστικόν is what distinguishes man from the brute, and is the highest element or formality of the soul, being immortal and

[1] *Tim.*, 86 b ff. [2] Laws, 775 b ff. [3] *Tim.*, 86 d 7–e 3. [4] Bk. 4.
[5] Cf. Cic., *Tusc. Disp.*, 4, 5, 10. (In this passage Cicero refers to *two* parts, the rational and the non-rational parts.)
[6] *Tim.*, 69 d 6–70 a 7.

akin to the divine. The two other formalities, τὸ θυμοειδές and τὸ ἐπιθυμητικόν, are perishable. Of these the spirited part is the nobler (in man more akin to moral courage), and is, or should be, the natural ally of reason, though is is found in animals. τὸ ἐπιθυμητικόν refers to bodily desires, for the rational part of the soul has its own desires, e.g. the passion for truth, Eros, which is the rational counterpart of the physical Eros. In the *Timaeus*[1] Plato locates the rational part of the soul in the head, the spirited part in the breast, and the appetitive part below the midriff. The location of the spirited element in heart and lungs was an ancient tradition, going back to Homer; but whether or not Plato understood these locations literally, it is hard to say. He may have meant that these locations are the points of interaction on the body of the several principles of the soul: did not Descartes (who certainly believed in the spirituality of the soul) locate the point of interaction in the pineal gland? But it is difficult to believe that Plato ever worked out his psychology systematically, as may be seen from the following considerations.

Plato declared that the soul is immortal, and the *Timaeus* certainly teaches that only the rational part of the soul enjoys this privilege.[2] But if the other parts of the soul are mortal and perishable, then they must be separable from the rational part in some mysterious way or they must form a different soul or souls. The apparent insistence on the simplicity of the soul in the *Phaedo* might be referred to the rational part; but in the Myths (e.g. of the *Republic* and the *Phaedrus*) it is implied that the soul survives in its totality, at least that it preserves memory in the state of separation from the body. I do not mean to suggest that all that is contained in the Myths is to be taken literally, but only to point out that their evident supposition that the soul after death retains memory and is affected by its previous life in the body, whether for good or evil, implies the possibility of the soul surviving in its totality and retaining at least the remote potentiality of exercising the spirited and appetitive functions, even though it could not exercise them actually in the state of separation from the body. However, this remains no more than a possible interpretation, and in view of Plato's own express statements and in view of his general dualistic position, it would seem probable that for him only τὸ λογιστικόν survives, and that the other parts of the soul perish entirely. If the conception of the

[1] *Tim., ibid.*

[2] *Tim.*, 69 c 2–e 4.

three elements of the souls as three μέρη conflicts with the conception of three εἴδη, then that is simply a proof that Plato never fully elaborated his psychology or worked out the implications of the statements he made.

3. Why did Plato assert the tripartite nature of the soul? Mainly owing to the evident fact of the conflict within the soul. In the *Phaedrus* occurs the celebrated comparison in which the rational element is likened to a charioteer, and the spirited and appetitive elements to two horses.[1] The one horse is good (the spirited element, which is the natural ally of reason and "loves honour with temperance and modesty"), the other horse is bad (the appetitive element, which is "a friend to all riot and insolence"); and, while the good horse is easily driven according to the directions of the charioteer, the bad horse is unruly and tends to obey the voice of sensual passion, so that it must be restrained by the whip. Plato, therefore, takes as his *point de départ* the fact of experience that there are frequently rival springs of action within man; but he never really discusses how this fact can be reconciled with the unity of consciousness, and it is significant that he expressly admits that "to explain what the soul is, would be a long and most assuredly a godlike labour," whereas "to say what it resembles is a shorter and a human task."[2] We may conclude, then, that the tendency to regard the three principles of action as principles of one unitary soul and the tendency to regard them as separable μέρη remain unreconciled in Plato's psychology.

Plato's main interest is, however, evidently the ethical interest of insisting on the right of the rational element to rule, to act as charioteer. In the *Timaeus* the rational part of the soul, the immortal and "divine" element, is said to be made by the Demiurge out of the same ingredients as the World-Soul, while the mortal parts of the soul, together with the body, are made by the celestial gods.[3] This is doubtless a mythical expression of the fact that the rational element of the soul is the highest and is born to rule, has a natural right to rule, because it is more akin to the divine. It has a natural affinity with the invisible and intelligible world, which it is able to contemplate, whereas the other elements of the soul are bound up essentially with the body, i.e. with the phenomenal world, and have no direct part in reason and rational activity and cannot behold the world of Forms.

[1] 246 a 6 ff. [2] 246 a 4–6. [3] 41 c 6–42 e 4, 69 b 8–c 8.

This dualistic conception reappears in Neo-Platonism, in St. Augustine, in Descartes, etc.[1] Moreover, in spite of the adoption of the Peripatetic doctrine of the soul by St. Thomas Aquinas and his School, the Platonic *way of speaking* remains and must always remain the "popular" way of speaking among Christians, since the *fact* that influenced Plato's thought, the fact of the interior conflict in man, naturally looms large in the minds of all those who support the Christian Ethic. It should, however, be noted that the fact that we feel this conflict *within ourselves* demands a more unified view of the soul than is afforded by the Platonic psychology. For, if there were a plurality of souls within man—the rational and irrational—then our consciousness of the conflict as taking place within ourselves and the consciousness of moral responsibility would be inexplicable. I do not mean to imply that Plato was entirely blind to the truth, but rather to suggest that he laid such stress on one aspect of the truth that he tended to neglect the other aspect, and so failed to give any really satisfactory rational psychology.

4. That Plato asserted the immortality of the soul is clear enough. From his explicit assertions it would appear, as we have seen, that this is confined to one part of the soul, τὸ λογιστικόν, though it is just possible that the soul survives in its totality, although it cannot, obviously enough, exercise its lower functions in a state of separation from the body. It is true, however, that the latter position might appear to lead to the conclusion that the soul is more imperfect and worse off in a state of separation from the body than it is in this mortal life—a conclusion which Plato would certainly refuse to accept.

Complete rejection of the Platonic Myths would seem to be prompted, to a certain extent at least, by the desire to get rid of any notion of sanctions after death, as if a doctrine of rewards and punishments were irrevelant—and even hostile—to morality. But is it fair or in accordance with principles of historical criticism to father this attitude on Plato? It is one thing to admit that the details of the Myths are not meant to be taken seriously (all admit this), and quite another thing to say that the conception of a future life, the character of which is determined by conduct in this life, is itself "mythical." There is no real evidence that Plato himself regarded the Myths in their entirety as mere moonshine:

[1] Cf. St. Aug.: *Homo anima rationalis est mortali atque terreno utens corpore.* (*De moribus Ecc. cath.*, I, 27.)

if he did, why did he put them forward at all? It seems to the present writer that Plato was by no means indifferent to the theory of sanctions, and that this was one of the reasons why he postulated immortality. He would have agreed with Leibniz that "in order to satisfy the hope of the human race, it must be proved that the God Who governs all is just and wise, and that He will leave nothing without recompense and without punishment. These are the great foundations of ethics."[1]

How did Plato attempt to prove immortality?

(i) In the *Phaedo*[2] Socrates argues that contraries are produced from contraries, as "from stronger, weaker," or "from sleeping, awaking, and from awaking, sleeping." Now, life and death are contraries, and from life is produced death. We must, therefore, suppose that from death life is produced.

This argument rests on the unproved assumption of an eternal cyclic process: it also supposes that a contrary is produced from a contrary, as the matter out of which it proceeds or is made. The argument would hardly satisfy us: besides, it says nothing of the condition of the soul in its state of separation from the body, and would, by itself, lead to the doctrine of the wheel of rebirth. The soul in one "period" on earth might have no conscious remembrance of any former period on earth, so that all that is "proved" is that the soul survives, not that the individual survives *qua* individual.

(ii) The next argument adduced in the *Phaedo*[3] is that from the *a priori* factor in knowledge. Men have a knowledge of standards and absolute norms, as is implied in their comparative judgments of value. But these absolutes do not exist in the sense-world: therefore man must have beheld them in a state of pre-existence. Similarly, sense-perception cannot give us knowledge of the necessary and universal. But a youth, even one who has had no mathematical education, can, by a process of questioning alone, without teaching, be induced to "give out" mathematical truths. As he has not learnt them from anybody and cannot get them from sense-perception, the implication is that he apprehended them in a state of pre-existence, and that the process of "learning" is simply a process of reminiscence (cf. *Meno*, 84 ff.).

As a matter of fact, the process of questioning employed by Socrates in the *Meno* is really a way of teaching, and in any case

[1] Letter to unknown correspondent about 1680, Duncan, *Philosophical Works of Leibniz*, p. 9.
[2] 70 d 7–72 e 2
[3] 72 e 3–77 d 5

a certain amount of mathematical knowledge is tacitly presupposed. However, even if the mathematical science cannot be accounted for by "abstraction," mathematics could still be an *a priori* science, without our being compelled to postulate pre-existence. Even supposing that mathematics could, theoretically at least, be worked out entirely *a priori* by the slave boy of *Meno*, that would not necessitate his having pre-existed: there is always an alternative on Kantian lines.[1]

Simmias points out[2] that this argument proves no more than that the soul existed before its union with the body: it does not prove that the soul survives death. Socrates accordingly observes that the argument from reminiscence must be taken in conjunction with the preceding argument.

(iii) The third argument in the *Phaedo* (or second, if the two previous arguments are taken together) is from the uncompounded and deiform nature of the soul—from its spirituality, as we would say.[3] Visible things are composite and subject to dissolution and death—and the body is of their number. Now, the soul can survey the invisible and unchanging and imperishable Forms, and by coming thus into contact with the Forms, the soul shows itself to be more like them than it is to visible and corporeal things, which latter are mortal. Moreover, from the fact that the soul is naturally destined to rule the body, it appears to be more like the divine than the mortal. The soul, as we may think, is "divine"—which for the Greeks meant immortal and unchanging.

(This argument has developed into the argument from the higher activities of the soul and the spirituality of the concept to the spiritual and uncompounded nature of the soul.)

(iv) Another argument of the *Phaedo* occurs in Socrates' answer to the objections of Cebes. (To Socrates' refutation of the "epiphenomenalism" suggested by Simmias, I have referred earlier.) Cebes suggests[4] that the expenditure of energy which is undergone by the soul in its successive bodily lives may "wear it out," so that in the end it will "perish altogether in some one of the deaths." To this Socrates replies with another proof of immortality.[5] The existence of Forms is admitted. Now, the presence of one Form will not admit of the presence of a contrary

[1] I do not mean to imply an acceptance of the Kantian Critique, but simply to point out that, even on Plato's assumption, his conclusion is not the only one possible.

[2] 77. [3] 78 b 4–80 e 1. [4] 86 e 6–88 b 8. [5] 103 c 10–107 a 1.

Form, nor will a thing that is what it is by virtue of its participation in one Form admit of the simultaneous presence of a contrary Form, e.g. though we cannot say that fire is *warmth*, it is *warm*, and will not admit of the opposite predicate "cold" simultaneously. Soul is what it is by virtue of its participation in the Form of Life: therefore it will not admit of the presence of the contrary Form, "death." When, therefore, death approaches, the soul must either perish or withdraw. That it does not perish is assumed. Strictly speaking, then, this argument should not be termed an argument for the imperishability of the soul, once granted its spirituality. Cebes is understood by Socrates to accept the spirituality of the soul, but to be arguing that it might wear itself out. Socrates' answer practically comes to this, that a spiritual principle cannot wear itself out.

(v) In the *Republic*[1] Socrates assumes the principle that a thing cannot be destroyed or perish except through some evil that is inherent in it. Now, the evils of the soul are "unrighteousness, intemperance, cowardice, ignorance"; but these do not destroy it, for a thoroughly unjust man may live as long or longer than a just man. But if the soul is not destroyed by its own internal corruption, it is unreasonable to suppose that it can be destroyed by any external evil. (The argument evidently supposes dualism.)

(vi) In the *Phaedrus*[2] it is argued that a thing which moves another, and is moved by another, may cease to live as it may cease to be moved. The soul, however, is a self-moving principle,[3] a source and beginning of motion, and that which is a beginning must be uncreated, for if it were not uncreated, it would not be a beginning. But if uncreated, then indestructible, for if soul, the beginning of motion were destroyed, all the universe and creation would "collapse and come to a standstill."

Now, once granted that the soul is the principle of motion, it must always have existed (if motion is from the beginning), but obviously this does little to prove personal immortality. For all this argument shows, the individual soul might be an emanation from the World-Soul, to which it returns at bodily death. Yet on reading the *Phaedo* in general and the Myths of the *Phaedo*, *Gorgias* and *Republic*, one cannot avoid the impression that Plato believed in real personal immortality. Moreover, passages such as that in which Socrates speaks of this life as a preparation for

[1] 608 d 3–611 a 2. [2] 245 c 5 ff. [3] Cf. *Laws*, 896 a 1–b 3.

eternity,[1] and remarks like that made by Socrates in the *Gorgias*,[2] that Euripides might be right in saying that life here is really death and death really life (a remark which has an Orphic ring about it), can hardly permit one to suppose that Plato, in teaching immortality, meant to affirm a mere persistence of τὸ λογιστικόν without any personal consciousness or continued self-identity. It is far more reasonable to suppose that he would have agreed with Leibniz when the latter asks: "Of what use would it be to you, sir, to become king of China on condition of forgetting what you have been? Would it not be the same as if God at the same time that he destroyed you, created a king in China?"[3]

To consider the Myths in detail is not necessary, for they are but pictorial representations of the truth that Plato wished to convey, namely, that the soul persists after death, and that the soul's life hereafter will be in accordance with its conduct on this earth. How far Plato seriously intended the doctrine of successive reincarnations, which is put forward in the Myths, is uncertain: in any case it would appear that there is a hope for the philosophic soul of escaping from the wheel of reincarnation, while it would also appear that there may be incurable sinners who are flung for ever into Tartarus. As already mentioned, the presentation of the future life in the Myths is hardly consonant with Plato's assertion that only τὸ λογιστικόν survives, and in this sense I should agree with Ritter when he says: "It cannot be maintained with certainty that Plato was convinced of the immortality of the soul, as that is taught in the Myths of the *Gorgias*, the *Phaedo* and the *Republic*."[4]

Plato's psychological doctrine is, therefore, not a systematically elaborated and consistent body of "dogmatic" statements: his interest was undoubtedly largely ethical in character. But this is not to say that Plato did not make many acute psychological observations, which may be found scattered throughout the dialogues. We have only to think of the illustrations he gives in the *Theaetetus* of the process of forgetting and remembering, or the distinction between memory and recollection in the *Philebus*.[5]

[1] *Rep.*, 498 b 3–d 6. [2] 492 e 8–11. [3] Duncan, p. 9. [4] *Essence*, p. 282.
[5] *Theaet.*, 191 c 8 and ff.; *Phil.*, 33 c 8–34 c 2.

CHAPTER XXII
MORAL THEORY

1. *The Summum Bonum*

PLATO'S ethic is eudaemonistic, in the sense that it is directed towards the attainment of man's highest good, in the possession of which true happiness consists. This highest good of man may be said to be the true development of man's personality as a rational and moral being, the right cultivation of his soul, the general harmonious well-being of life. When a man's soul is in the state it ought to be in, then that man is happy. At the beginning of the *Philebus* two extreme positions are taken up by Protarchus and Socrates *causa argumenti*. Though they are both agreed that the good must be a state of soul, Protarchus is prepared to maintain that the good consists in *pleasure*, while Socrates will maintain that the good consists in *wisdom*. Socrates proceeds to show that pleasure as such cannot be the true and sole human good, since a life of unmixed pleasure (bodily pleasure is understood), in which neither mind nor memory nor knowledge nor true opinion had any share, "would be, not a human life, but that of a *pulmo marinus* or an oyster."[1] Not even Protarchus can think such a life desirable for a human being. On the other hand, a life of "unmixed mind," which was destitute of pleasure, could not be the sole good of man; even if intellect is the highest part of man and intellectual activity (especially the contemplation of the Forms) is man's highest function, man is not pure intellect. Thus the good life for man must be a "mixed" life, neither exclusively the life of the mind nor yet exclusively the life of sense-pleasure. Plato, therefore, is prepared to admit those pleasures which are not preceded by pain, e.g. the intellectual pleasures,[2] but also pleasures which consist in the satisfaction of desire, provided that they are innocent and are enjoyed in moderation. Just as honey and water must be mixed in due proportion in order to make a pleasing drink, so pleasant feeling and intellectual activity must be mixed in due proportion in order to make the good life of man.[3]

First of all, Plato says, the good life must include all knowledge

[1] 21 c 1–8. [2] Cf. 51. [3] 61 b 4 ff.

of the truer type, the exact knowledge of timeless objects. But the man who was acquainted only with the exact and perfect curves and lines of geometry, and had no knowledge at all of the rough approximations to them which we meet with in daily life, would not even know how to find his way home. So second-class knowledge, and not only the first-class variety, must be admitted into the mixture: it will do a man no harm, provided that he recognises the second-class objects for what they are, and does not mistake the rough approximations for the exact truth. In other words, a man need not turn his back completely on this mortal life and the material world in order to lead the truly good life, but he must recognise that this world is not the only world, nor yet the highest world, but a poor copy of the ideal. (Music, says Protarchus, must be admitted, "if human life is to be a life at all," in spite of the fact that it is, according to Socrates, "full of guesswork and imitation" and "wanting in purity."[1])

All the "water" having thus been admitted to the mixing-bowl, the question arises, how much "honey" to put in. The deciding vote in this question, how much pleasure to admit, rests with knowledge. Now, knowledge, says Plato, would claim kinship with the class of "true" and "unmixed" pleasures; but, as to the rest, knowledge will accept only those which accompany health and a sober mind and any form of goodness. The pleasures of "folly and badness" are quite unfit to find a place in the blend.

The secret of the blend which forms the good life is thus measure or proportion: where this is neglected, there exists, not a genuine mixture, but a mess. The good is thus a form of the beautiful, which is constituted by measure and proportion, and συμμετρία, καλόν and ἀλήθεια will be the three forms or notes found in the good. The first place goes to "seasonableness," τὸ καίριον, the second to proportion or beauty or completeness (τὸ σύμμετρον καὶ καλόν καὶ τὸ τέλεον καὶ ἱκανον), the third to νοῦς καὶ φρόνησις, the fourth to ἐπιστῆμαι καὶ τέχναι καὶ δόξαι ὀρθαί, the fifth to the pleasures which have no pain mixed with them (whether involving actual sensation or not), and the sixth to the moderate satisfaction of appetite when, of course, this is harmless. Such, then, is man's true good, the good life, εὐδαιμονία, and the compelling motive in the search for it is Eros, the desire or longing for good or happiness.

[1] 62 c 1-4.

Man's *summum bonum* or happiness includes, of course, knowledge of God—obviously so if the Forms are the Ideas of God; while, even if the *Timaeus* were taken literally and God were supposed to be apart from the Forms and to contemplate them, man's own contemplation of the Forms, which is an integral constituent of his happiness, would make him akin to God. Moreover, no man could be happy who did not recognise the Divine operation in the world. Plato can say, therefore, that the Divine happiness is the pattern of man's happiness.[1]

Now, happiness must be attained by the pursuit of virtue, which means becoming as like to God as it is possible for man to become. We must become "like the divine so far as we can, and that again is to become righteous with the help of wisdom."[2] "The gods have a care of anyone whose desire is to become just and to be like God, as far as man can attain to the divine likeness, by the pursuit of virtue."[3] In the *Laws* Plato declares that "God is the measure of all things, in a sense far higher than any man, as they say, can ever hope to be." (He thus answers Protagoras.) "And he who would be dear to God, must as far as possible be like Him and such as He is. Wherefore the temperate man is the friend of God, for he is like Him. . . ." He goes on to say that to offer sacrifice to the gods and pray to them is "the noblest and best of all things, and also the most conducive to a happy life," but points out that the sacrifices of the wicked and impious are unacceptable to the gods.[4] Worship and virtue belong, therefore, to happiness, so that although the pursuit of virtue and the leading of a virtuous life is the means of attaining happiness, virtue itself is not external to happiness, but is integral to it. Man's good is a condition of soul primarily, and it is only the truly virtuous man who is a truly good man and a truly happy man.

II. *Virtue*

1. In general we may say that Plato accepted the Socratic identification of virtue with knowledge. In the *Protagoras*[5] Socrates shows, as against the Sophist, that it is absurd to suggest that justice can be impious or piety unjust, so that the several virtues cannot be entirely disparate. Furthermore, the intemperate man is one who pursues what is really harmful to man while the temperate

[1] *Theaet.*, 176 a 5–e 4. [2] *Theaet.*, 176 b 1–3. [3] *Rep.*, 613 a 7–b 1.
[4] *Laws*, 715 e 7–717 a 3. [5] *Protag.*, 330 c 3 ff.

man pursues what is truly good and beneficial. Now, to pursue what is truly good and beneficial is wise, while to pursue what is harmful is foolish. Hence temperance and wisdom cannot be entirely disparate. Again, true valour or courage means, e.g. standing your ground in battle when you know the risks to which you are exposed; it does not mean mere foolhardiness. Thus courage can no more be separated from wisdom than can temperance. Plato does not, of course, deny that there are distinct virtues, distinguished according to their objects or the parts of the soul of which they are the habits; but all these distinct virtues form a unity, inasmuch as they are the expressions of the same knowledge of good and evil. The distinct virtues are, therefore, unified in prudence or the knowledge of what is truly good for man and of the means to attain that good. It is made clear in the *Meno* that *if* virtue is knowledge or prudence, it can be taught, and it is shown in the *Republic* that it is only the philosopher who has true knowledge of the good for man. It is not the Sophist, content with "popular" notions of virtue, who can teach virtue, but only he who has exact knowledge, i.e. the philosopher. The doctrine that virtue is knowledge is really an expression of the fact that goodness is not a merely relative term, but refers to something that is absolute and unchanging: otherwise it could not be the object of knowledge.

To the idea that virtue is knowledge and that virtue is teachable, Plato seems to have clung, as also to the idea that no one does evil knowingly and willingly. When a man chooses that which is *de facto* evil, he chooses it *sub specie boni*: he desires something which he imagines to be good, but which is, as a matter of fact, evil. Plato certainly allowed for the headstrong character of appetite, which strives to carry all before it, sweeping the charioteer along with it in its mad onrush to attain that which appears to it as a good; but if the bad horse overpowers the resistance of the charioteer, it can, on Plato's principles, only be because either the charioteer has no knowledge of the true good or because his knowledge of the good is obscured for the time being by the onrush of passion. It might well seem that such a doctrine, inherited from Socrates, conflicts with Plato's obvious admission of moral responsibility, but it is open to Plato to reply that a man who knows what is truly good may allow his judgment to be so obscured by passion, at least temporarily, that the apparent good appears to him as a true good, although he is responsible for having allowed passion so to darken reason. If it be objected that a man may deliberately choose evil because it is evil, Plato could only answer that the man has said: "Evil, be thou my good." If he chooses what is really evil or harmful, knowing it to be ultimately such, that can only be because he, in spite of his knowledge, fixes his attention on an aspect of the object which appears to him as good. He may indeed be responsible for so fixing his attention, but, if he chooses, he can only choose *sub ratione boni*. A man might very well know that to murder his enemy will be ultimately harmful to him, but he chooses to do it all the same, since he fixes his attention on what appears to be the immediate good of satisfying his desire for revenge or of obtaining some benefit by the elimination of his enemy. (It might be remarked that the Greeks needed a clearer view of *Good* and *Right* and their relation to one another. The murderer may know very well that murder is wrong, but he chooses to commit it as being, *in some respects*, a *good*. The murderer who knew that murder was wrong might also know, of course, that "wrong" and "ultimately harmful or evil" were inseparable, but that would not take away the aspect of "goodness" (i.e. usefulness or desirability) attaching to the act. When we use the word "evil," we often mean "wrong," but when Plato said that no one willingly chooses to do what he knows to be evil, he did not mean that no one chooses to do what he knows to be wrong, but that no one deliberately chooses to do what he knows to be in all respects harmful to himself.)

In the *Republic*[1] Plato considers four chief or cardinal virtues —wisdom (Σοφία), courage or fortitude ('Ανδρεία), temperance (Σωφροσύνη) and justice (Δικαιοσύνη). Wisdom is the virtue of the rational part of the soul, courage of the spirited part, while temperance consists in the union of the spirited and appetitive parts under the rule of reason. Justice is a general virtue consisting in this, that every part of the soul performs its proper task in due harmony.

2. In the *Gorgias* Plato argues against the identification of good and evil with pleasure and pain, and against the "Superman" morality propounded by Callicles. Against Polus, Socrates has tried to show that to do an injustice, e.g. to play the part of the tyrant, is worse than to suffer injustice, since to do injustice makes one's soul worse, and this is the greatest evil that a man

[1] *Rep.*, Bk. 4.

can suffer. Moreover, to do injustice and then to get off scot-free is the worst thing of all, because that only confirms the evil in the soul, whereas punishment may bring reformation. Callicles breaks in on the discussion in order to protest that Socrates is appealing "to the popular and vulgar notions of right, which are not natural, but only conventional":[1] to do evil may be disgraceful from the conventional standpoint, but this is simply herd-morality. The weak, who are the majority, club together to restrain "the stronger sort of men," and proclaim as *right* the actions that suit them, i.e. the members of the herd, and as *wrong* the actions that are harmful to them.[2] Nature, however, shows among both men and animals that "justice consists in the superior ruling and having more than the inferior."[3]

Socrates thanks Callicles for his frankness in openly stating his opinion that Might is Right, but he points out that if the weak majority do in fact tyrannise over the "strong," then they are actually the stronger and also are justified, on Callicles' own admission. This is not a mere verbal quibble, for if Callicles persists in maintaining his rejection of conventional morality, he must now show how the strong, the ruthless and unscrupulous individualist, is qualitatively "better" than the herd-man, and so has the right to rule. This Callicles tries to do by maintaining that his individualist is wiser than "the rabble of slaves and nondescripts," and so ought to rule and have more than his subjects. Irritated by Socrates' observation that, in this case, the physician should have more to eat and drink than anybody else, and the cobbler larger shoes than anybody, Callicles affirms that what he means is that those who are wise and courageous in the administration of the State ought to rule the State, and that justice consists in their having more than their subjects. Goaded by Socrates' question, whether the ruler should rule himself as well, Callicles roundly asserts that the strong man should allow his desires and passions full play. This gives Socrates his chance, and he compares Callicles' ideal man to a leaky cask: he is always filling himself with pleasure but never has enough: his life is the life of a cormorant not of a man. Callicles is prepared to admit that the scratcher who is constantly relieving his itch has a happy life, but he boggles at justifying the life of the

[1] *Gorgias*, 482 e 3-5.
[2] The resemblance to the opinions of Nietzsche is obvious, though Nietzsche's idea was very far from being that of the political and licentious tyrant.
[3] 483 d 5-6.

catamite, and in the end is driven to admit a *qualitative* difference in pleasures. This leads to the conclusion that pleasure is subordinate to the good, and that reason must, therefore, be judge of pleasures and admit them only in so far as they are consonant with health and harmony and order of soul and body. It is thus not the intemperate man but the temperate man who is truly good and happy. The intemperate man does evil to himself, and Socrates drives home his point by the "Myth" of the impossibility of escaping judgment after death.[1]

3. Plato expressly rejects the maxim that one should do good to one's friends and evil to one's enemies. To do evil can never be good. In the first Book Polemarchus puts forward the theory that "it is just to do good to our friend if he is a good man, and to hurt our enemy if he is a bad man."[2] Socrates (understanding by "to hurt" to do real harm, and not simply to punish—which he regarded as remedial) objects that to hurt is to make worse, and, in respect of human excellence, that means less just, so that, according to Polemarchus, it pertains to the just man to make the unjust man worse. But this is obviously rather the work of the unjust man than of the just man.

[1] *Gorgias*, 523 ff. [2] *Rep.*, 335 a 7–8.

CHAPTER XXIII
THE STATE

PLATO'S political theory is developed in close connection with his ethics. Greek life was essentially a communal life, lived out in the City-State and unthinkable apart from the City, so that it would not occur to any genuine Greek that a man could be a perfectly good man if he stood entirely apart from the State, since it is only in and through Society that the good life becomes possible for man—and Society meant the City-State. The rational analysis of this experimental fact results in the doctrine that organised Society is a "natural" institution, that man is essentially a social animal—a doctrine common to both Plato and Aristotle: the theory that Society is a necessary evil and results in the stunting of man's free development and growth would be entirely foreign to the genuine Greek. (It would, of course, be foolish to represent the Greek consciousness according to the analogy of the ant-heap or the beehive, since individualism was rife, showing itself both in the internecine wars between States and in the factions within the Cities themselves, e.g. in attempts on the part of an individual to establish himself as Tyrant; but this individualism was not a rebellion against Society as such—rather did it presuppose Society as an accepted fact.) For a philosopher like Plato, then, who concerned himself with man's happiness, with the truly good life for man, it was imperative to determine the true nature and function of the State. If the citizens were all morally bad men, it would indeed be impossible to secure a good State; but, conversely, if the State were a bad State, the individual citizens would find themselves unable to lead the good life as it should be lived.

Plato was not a man to accept the notion that there is one morality for the individual and another for the State. The State is composed of individual men and exists for the leading of the good life: there is an absolute moral code that rules all men and all States: expediency must bow the knee to Right. Plato did not look upon the State as a personality or organism that can or should develop itself without restraint, without paying any attention to the Moral Law: it is not the arbiter of right and wrong, the source of its own moral code, and the absolute justification of its own actions, be the latter what they may. This truth finds clear expression in the *Republic*. The interlocutors set out to determine the nature of justice, but at the close of the first Book Socrates declares that "I know not what justice is."[1] He then suggests in the second Book[2] that if they consider the State they will see the same letters "written larger and on a larger scale," for justice in the State "will be larger and more easily discernible." He proposes, therefore, that "we inquire into the nature of justice and injustice as appearing in the State first, and secondly in the individual, proceeding from the greater to the lesser and comparing them." The obvious implication of this is that the principles of justice are the same for individual and State. If the individual lives out his life as a member of the State, and if the justice of the one as of the other is determined by ideal justice, then clearly neither the individual nor the State can be emancipated from the eternal code of justice.

Now, it is quite obvious that not every actual Constitution or every Government embodies the ideal principle of Justice; but Plato was not concerned to determine what empirical States *are* so much as what the State *ought* to be, and so, in the *Republic*, he sets himself to discover the Ideal State, the pattern to which every actual State ought to conform itself, so far as it can. It is true that in the work of his old age, the *Laws*, he makes some concessions to practicability; but his general purpose remained that of delineating the norm or ideal, and if empirical States do not conform to the ideal, then so much the worse for the empirical States. Plato was profoundly convinced that Statesmanship is, or should be, a science; the Statesman, if he is to be truly such, must know what the State is and what its life ought to be; otherwise he runs the risk of bringing the State and its citizens to shipwreck and proves himself to be not a Statesman but a bungling "politician." Experience had taught him that actual States were faulty, and he turned his back on practical political life, though not without the hope of sowing the seeds of true statesmanship in those who entrusted themselves to his care. In the seventh Letter Plato speaks of his sad experience, first with the Oligarchy of 404 and then with the restored Democracy, and adds: "The result was that I, who had at first been full of eagerness for a public career, as I gazed upon the whirlpool of public life and

[1] 354 c 1. [2] 368 e 2–369 a 3.

saw the incessant movement of shifting currents, at last felt dizzy . . . and finally saw clearly in regard to all States now existing that without exception their system of government is bad. Their constitutions are almost without redemption, except through some miraculous plan accompanied by good luck. Hence I was forced to say in praise of the correct philosophy that it affords a vantage-point from which we can discern in all cases what is just for communities and for individuals; and that accordingly the human race will not be free of evils until either the stock of those who rightly and truly follow philosophy acquire political authority, or the class who have power in the cities be led by some dispensation of providence to become real philosophers."[1]

I shall outline Plato's political theory, first as it appears in the *Republic*, and then as it appears in the *Statesman* and the *Laws*.

I. *The Republic*

I. The State exists in order to serve the wants of men. Men are not independent of one another, but need the aid and co-operation of others in the production of the necessaries of life. Hence they gather associates and helpers into one dwelling-place "and give this joint dwelling the name of City."[2] The original end of the city is thus an economic end, and from this follows the principle of the division and specialisation of labour. Different people have different natural endowments and talents and are fitted to serve the community in different ways: moreover, a man's work will be superior in quality and also in quantity if he works at one occupation alone, in accordance with his natural gifts. The agricultural labourer will not produce his own plough or mattock, but they will be produced for him by others, by those who specialise in the production of such instruments. Thus the existence of the State, which at present is being considered from the economic viewpoint, will require the presence of husbandmen, weavers, shoemakers, carpenters, smiths, shepherds, merchants, retail traders, hired labourers, etc. But it will be a very rude sort of life that is led by these people. If there is to be a "luxurious" city, something more will be required, and musicians, poets, tutors, nurses, barbers, cooks, confectioners, etc., will make their appearance. But with the rise of population consequent on the growing luxury of the city, the territory will be insufficient for the city's needs, and some of the neighbour's

[1] *Ep.*, 7, 325 d 6–326 b 4.

[2] *Rep.*, 369 c 1–4.

territory will have to be annexed. Thus Plato finds the origin of war in an economic cause. (Needless to say, Plato's remarks are not to be understood as a justification of aggressive war: for his remarks on this subject see the section on war under the heading of the *Laws*.)

2. But, if war is to be pursued, then, on the principle of the division and specialisation of labour, there will have to be a special class of guardians of the State, who will devote themselves exclusively to the conduct of war. These guardians must be spirited, gifted with the θυμοειδές element; but they must also be philosophic, in the sense of knowing who the true enemies of the State are. But if the exercise of their task of guardianship is to be based on knowledge, then they must undergo some process of education. This will begin with music, including narrative. But, says Plato, we will scarcely permit the children of the State to receive into their minds at their most impressionable age opinions the reverse of those which they should entertain when they are grown to manhood.[1] It follows, then, that the legends about the gods, as retailed by Hesiod and Homer, will not be taught to children or indeed admitted into the State, since they depict the gods as indulging in gross immorality, taking various forms, etc. Similarly, to assert that the violation of oaths and treaties was brought about by the gods is intolerable and not to be admitted. God is to be represented, not as the author of all things, whether good or bad, but only of such things as are good.[2]

It is to be noted in all this how, though Socrates starts off the discussion by finding the origin of the State in the need of supplying the various natural wants of man and asserts the economic origin of the State, the interest soon shifts to the problem of education. The State does not exist simply in order to further the economic needs of men, for man is not simply "Economic Man," but for their happiness, to develop them in the good life, in accordance with the principles of justice. This renders education necessary, for the members of the State are rational beings. But it is not any kind of education that will do, but only education to the true and the good. Those who arrange the life of the State, who determine the principles of education and allot the various tasks in the State to its different members, must have knowledge of what is really true and good—in other words, they must be philosophers. It is this insistence on truth that leads Plato to

[1] 377 a 12–c 5.

[2] 380 a 5–c 3.

the, as it appears to us, rather extraordinary proposal to exclude epic poets and dramatists from the ideal State. It is not that Plato is blind to the beauties of Homer or Sophocles: on the contrary, it is just the fact that the poets make use of beautiful language and imagery which renders them so dangerous in Plato's eyes. The beauty and charm of their words are, as it were, the sugar which obscures the poison that is imbibed by the simple. Plato's interest is primarily ethical: he objects to the way the poets speak about the gods, and the way in which they portray immoral characters, etc. In so far as the poets are to be admitted at all into the ideal State, they must set themselves to produce examples of good moral character, but, in general, epic and dramatic poetry will be banished from the State, while lyric poetry will be allowed only under the strict supervision of the State authorities. Certain harmonies (the Ionian and Lydian) will be excluded as effeminate and convivial. (We may think that Plato exaggerated the bad results that would follow from the admission of the great works of Greek literature, but the principle that animated him must be admitted by all who seriously believe in an objective moral law, even if they quarrel with his particular applications of the principle. For, granted the existence of the soul and of an absolute moral code, it is the duty of the public authorities to prevent the ruin of the morality of the members of the State so far as they can, and so far as the particular acts of prevention employed will not be productive of greater harm. To speak of the absolute rights of Art is simply nonsense, and Plato was quite justified in not letting himself be disturbed by any such trashy considerations.)

Besides music, gymnastics will play a part in the education of the young citizens of the State. This care of the body, in the case of those who are to be guardians of the State and athletes of war, will be of an ascetic character, a "simple, moderate system," not calculated to produce sluggish athletes, who "sleep away their lives and are liable to most dangerous illnesses if they depart, in ever so slight a degree, from their customary regimen," but rather "warrior athletes, who should be like wakeful dogs, and should see and hear with the utmost keenness."[1] (In these proposals for the State education of the young, both physically and mentally, Plato is anticipating what we have seen realised on a great scale, and which, we recognise, may be used for bad

[1] 403 e 11–404 b 8.

ends as well as for good. But that, after all, is the fate of most practical proposals in the political field, that while they may be used for the benefit of the State, i.e. its true benefit, they may also be abused and applied in a way that can only bring harm to the State. Plato knew that very well, and the selection of the rulers of the State was a matter of great concern to him.)

3. We have then so far two great classes in the State—the inferior class of artisans and the superior class of guardians. The question arises, who are to be the rulers of the State. They will, says Plato, be carefully chosen from the class of guardians. They are not to be young: they must be the best men of their class, intelligent and powerful, and careful of the State, loving the State and regarding the State's interests as identical with their own—in the sense, needless to say, of pursuing the true interests of the State without thought of their own personal advantage or disadvantage.[1] Those, then, who from childhood up have been observed to do that which is best for the State, and never to have deserted this line of conduct, will be chosen as rulers of the State. They will be the perfect guardians, in fact the only people who are rightly entitled to the name of "guardian": the others, who have hitherto been termed guardians, will be called "auxiliaries," having it as their office to support the decisions of the rulers.[2] (Of the education of the rulers I shall treat shortly.)

The conclusion is, therefore, that the ideal State will consist of three great classes (excluding the slave class, of whom more later), the artisans at the bottom, the Auxiliaries or military class over them, and the Guardians or Guardian at the top. However, though the Auxiliaries occupy a more honourable position than the artisans, they are not to be savage animals, preying on those beneath them, but even if stronger than their fellow-citizens, they will be their friendly allies, and so it is most necessary to ensure that they should have the right education and mode of life. Plato says that they should possess no private property of their own, but should receive all necessaries from their fellow-citizens. They should have a common mess and live together like soldiers in a camp: gold and silver they should neither handle nor touch. "And this will be their salvation and the salvation of the State."[3] But if they once start amassing property, they will very soon turn into tyrants.

4. It will be remembered that Plato set out at the beginning

[1] 412 c 9–413 c 7. [2] 414 b 1–6. [3] 417 a 5–6.

of the dialogue to determine the nature of justice, and that having found the task difficult, the suggestion was made that they might be able to see more clearly what justice is if they examined it as it exists in the State. At the present point of the discussion, when the different classes of the State have been outlined, it becomes possible to behold justice in the State. The wisdom of the State resides in the small class of rulers or Guardians, the courage of the State in the Auxiliaries, the temperance of the State consists in the due subordination of the governed to the governing, the justice of the State in this, that everyone attends to his own business without interfering with anyone else's. As the individual is just when all the elements of the soul function properly in harmony and with due subordination of the lower to the higher, so the State is just or righteous when all the classes, and the individuals of which they are composed, perform their due functions in the proper way. Political injustice, on the other hand, consists in a meddling and restless spirit, which leads to one class interfering with the business of another class.[1]

5. In the fifth Book of the *Republic* Plato treats of the famous proposal as to "community" of wives and children. Women are to be trained as men: in the ideal State they will not simply stay at home and mind the baby, but will be trained in music and gymnastics and military discipline just like men. The justification of this consists in the fact that men and women differ simply in respect to the parts they play in the propagation of the species. It is true that woman is weaker than man, but natural gifts are to be found in both sexes alike, and, as far as her nature is concerned, the woman is admissible to all pursuits open to man, even war. Duly qualified women will be selected to share in the life and official duties of the guardians of the State. On eugenic principles Plato thinks that the marriage relations of citizens, particularly of the higher classes of the State, should be under the control of the State. Thus the marriages of Guardians or Auxiliaries are to be under the control of the magistrates, with a view not only to the efficient discharge of their official duties, but also to the obtaining of the best possible offspring, who will be brought up in a State nursery. But be it noted that Plato does not propose any complete community of wives in the sense of promiscuous free love. The artisan class retains private property and the family: it is only in the two upper classes that

[1] 433 a 1 and ff.

private property and family life is to be abolished, and that for the good of the State. Moreover, the marriages of Guardians and Auxiliaries are to be very strictly arranged: they will marry the women prescribed for them by the relevant magistrates, have intercourse and beget children at the prescribed times and not outside those times. If they have relations with women outside the prescribed limits and children result, it is at least hinted that such children should be put out of the way.[1] Children of the higher classes, who are not suitable for the life of those classes, but who have been "legitimately" born, will be relegated to the class of the artisans.

(Plato's proposals in this matter are abhorrent to all true Christians. His intentions were, of course, excellent, for he desired the greatest possible improvement of the human race; but his good intentions led him to the proposal of measures which are necessarily unacceptable and repugnant to all those who adhere to Christian principles concerning the value of the human personality and the sanctity of human life. Moreover, it by no means follows that what has been found successful in the breeding of animals, will also prove successful when applied to the human race, for man has a rational soul which is not intrinsically dependent on matter but is directly created by Almighty God. Does a beautiful soul always go with a beautiful body or a good character with a strong body? Again, if such measures were successful—and what does "successful" mean in this connection?—in the case of the human race, it does not follow that the Government has the right to apply such measures. Those who to-day follow, or would like to follow, in the footsteps of Plato, advocating, e.g. compulsory sterilisation of the unfit, have not, be it remembered, Plato's excuse, that he lived at a period anterior to the presentation of the Christian ideals and principles.)

6. In answer to the objection that no city can, in practice, be organised according to the plans proposed, "Socrates" replies that it is not to be expected that an ideal should be realised in practice with perfect accuracy. Nevertheless he asks, what is the smallest change that would enable a State to assume this form of Constitution? and he proceeds to mention one—which is neither small nor easy—namely, the vesting of power in the hands of the philosopher-king. The democratic principle of government is, according to Plato, absurd: the ruler must govern in virtue of

[1] 461 c 4–7.

knowledge, and that knowledge must be knowledge of the truth. The man who has knowledge of the truth is the genuine philosopher. Plato drives home his point by the simile of the ship, its captain and crew.[1] We are asked to imagine a ship "in which there is a captain who is taller and stronger than anyone else in the ship, but he is a little deaf and is short-sighted, and his knowledge of navigation is not much better." The crew mutiny, take charge of the ship and, "drinking and feasting, they continue their voyage with such success as might be expected of them." They have, however, no idea of the pilot's art or of what a true pilot should be. Thus Plato's objection to democracy of the Athenian type is that the politicians really do not know their business at all, and that when the fancy takes the people they get rid of the politicians in office and carry on as though no special knowledge were required for the right guidance of the ship of State. For this ill-informed and happy-go-lucky way of conducting the State, he proposes to substitute rule by the philosopher-king, i.e. by the man who has real knowledge of the course that the ship of State should take, and can help it to weather the storms and surmount the difficulties that it encounters on the voyage. The philosopher will be the finest fruit of the education provided by the State: he, and he alone, can, as it were, draw the outline of the concrete sketch of the ideal State and fill up that outline, because he has acquaintance with the world of Forms and can take them as his model in forming the actual State.[2]

Those who are chosen out as candidates or possible rulers will be educated, not only in musical harmony and gymnastics, but also in mathematics and astronomy. They will not, however, be trained in mathematics merely with a view to enabling them to perform the calculations that everyone ought to learn to perform, but rather with a view to enabling them to apprehend intelligible objects—not "in the spirit of merchants or traders, with a view to buying or selling," nor only for the sake of the military use involved, but primarily that they may pass "from becoming to truth and being,"[3] that they may be drawn towards truth and acquire the spirit of philosophy.[4] But all this will merely be a prelude to Dialectic, whereby a man starts on the discovery of

[1] 488 a 1–489 a 2.

[2] Plato, like Socrates, considered the "democratic" practice of choosing magistrates, generals, etc., by lot or according to their rhetorical ability, irrational and absurd.

[3] 525 b 11–c 6.

[4] 527 b 9–11.

absolute being by the light of reason only, and without any assistance of the senses, until he "attains at last to the absolute good by intellectual vision and therein reaches the limit of the intellectual world."[1] He will thus have ascended all the steps of the "Line." The chosen rulers of the State, therefore, or rather those who are chosen as candidates for the position of Guardians, those who are "sound in limb and mind" and endowed with virtue, will be gradually put through this course of education, those who have proved themselves satisfactory by the time they have reached the age of thirty being specially selected for training in Dialectic. After five years spent in this study they will "be sent down into the den and compelled to hold any military or other office which the young are qualified to hold," in order that they may get the necessary experience of life and show whether, when confronted with various temptations, "they will stand firm or flinch."[2] After fifteen years of such probation those who have distinguished themselves (they will then be fifty years old) will have reached the time "at which they must raise the eye of the soul to the universal light which lightens all things, and behold the absolute good; for that is the pattern according to which they are to order the State and lives of individuals, and the remainder of their own lives too, making philosophy their chief pursuit; but when their turn comes, toiling also at politics and ruling for the public good, not as if they were doing some great thing, but of necessity; and when they have brought up others like themselves and left them in their place to be governors of the State, then they will depart to the Islands of the Blest and dwell there; and the city will give them public memorials and sacrifices and honour them, if the Pythian oracle consent, as demi-gods, and at any rate as blessed and divine."[3]

7. In the eighth and ninth Books of the *Republic* Plato develops a sort of philosophy of history. The perfect State is the aristocratic State; but when the two higher classes combine to divide the property of the other citizens and reduce them practically to slavery, aristocracy turns into timocracy, which represents the preponderance of the spirited element. Next the love of wealth grows, until timocracy turns into oligarchy, political power coming to depend on property qualifications. A poverty-stricken class is thus developed under the oligarchs, and in the end the poor expel the rich and establish democracy. But the

[1] 532 a 7–b 2. [2] 539 e 2–540 a 2. [3] 540 a 7–c 2.

extravagant love of liberty, which is characteristic of democracy, leads by way of reaction to tyranny. At first the champion of the common people obtains a bodyguard under specious pretences; he then throws off pretence, executes a *coup d'état* and turns into a tyrant. Just as the philosopher, in whom reason rules, is the happiest of men, so the aristocratic State is the best and happiest of States; and just as the tyrannical despot, the slave of ambition and passion, is the worst and most unhappy of men, so is the State ruled by the tyrant the worst and most unhappy of States.

II. *The Statesman* (*Politicus*)

1. Towards the close of the *Statesman*, Plato shows that the science of politics, the royal and kingly science, cannot be identical with e.g. the art of the general or the art of the judge, since these arts are ministerial, the general acting as minister to the ruler, the judge giving decisions in accordance with the laws laid down by the legislator. The royal science, therefore, must be superior to all these particular arts and sciences, and may be defined as "that common science which is over them all, and guards the laws, and all things that there are in the State, and truly weaves them all into one."[1] He distinguishes this science of the monarch or ruler from tyranny, in that the latter rests merely on compulsion, whereas the rule of the true king and statesman is "the voluntary management of voluntary bipeds."[2]

2. "No great number of persons, whoever they may be, can have political knowledge or order a State wisely," but "the true government is to be found in a small body, or in an individual,"[3] and the ideal is that the ruler (or rulers) should legislate for individual instances. Plato insists that laws should be changed or modified as circumstances require, and that no superstitious regard for tradition should hamper an enlightened application to a changed condition of affairs and fresh needs. It would be just as absurd to stick to obsolete laws in the face of new circumstances, as it would be for a doctor to insist on his patient keeping to the same diet when a new one is required by the changed conditions of his health. But as this would require divine, rather than human, knowledge and competence, we must be content with the second-best, i.e. with the reign of *Law*. The ruler will administer the State in accordance with fixed Law. The Law must be

[1] 305 e 2–4. [2] 276 e 10–12 [3] 297 b 7–c 2.

absolute sovereign, and the public man who violates law should be put to death.[1]

3. Government may be government by one, by few, or by many. If we are speaking of well-ordered governments, then that of the one, monarchy, is the best (leaving out of account the ideal form, in which the monarch legislates for individual cases), that of the few the second-best, and that of the many the worst. If, however, we are speaking of lawless governments, then the worst is government by the one, i.e. tyranny (since that can do the most harm), the second-worst that by the few, and the least bad that by the many. Democracy is thus, according to Plato, "the worst of all lawful governments, and the best of all lawless ones," since "the government of the many is in every respect weak and unable to do either any great good or any great evil when compared with the others, because in such a State the offices are parcelled out among many people."[2]

4. What Plato would think of demagogic Dictators is clear from his remarks on tyrants, as also from his observations on the politicians who are devoid of knowledge and who should be called "partisans." These are "upholders of the most monstrous idols, and themselves idols; and, being the greatest imitators and magicians, they are also Sophists *par excellence*."[3]

III. *The Laws*

1. In the composition of the *Laws* Plato would seem to have been influenced by personal experiences. Thus he says that perhaps the best conditions for founding the desired Constitution will be had if the enlightened Statesman meets with an enlightened and benevolent tyrant or sovereign, since the despot will be in a position to put the suggested reforms into practice.[4] Plato's (unhappy) experience at Syracuse would have shown him at least that there was a better hope of realising the desired constitutional reforms in a city ruled over by one man than in a democracy such as Athens. Again, Plato was clearly influenced by the history of Athens, its rise to the position of a commercial and maritime empire, its fall in the Peloponnesian war. For in Book Four of the *Laws* he stipulates that the city shall be about eighty stadia from the sea—although even this is too near—i.e. that the State should be an agrarian, and not a commercial State, a producing, and not an importing, community. The Greek prejudice against

[1] 297 e 1–5. [2] 303 a 2–8. [3] 303 b 8–c 5. [4] 709 d 10–710 b 9.

trade and commerce comes out in his words, that "The sea is pleasant enough as a daily companion, but has a bitter and brackish quality; for it fills the streets with merchants and shopkeepers, and begets in the souls of men unfaithful and uncertain ways—making the State unfaithful and unfriendly both to her own citizens and also towards the rest of men."[1]

2. The State must be a true Polity. Democracy, oligarchy and tyranny are all undesirable because they are class-States, and their laws are passed for the good of particular classes and not for the good of the whole State. States which have such laws are not real polities but parties, and their notion of justice is simply unmeaning.[2] The government is not to be entrusted to any one because of considerations of birth or wealth, but for personal character and fitness for ruling, and the rulers must be subject to the law. "The State in which the law is above the rulers, and the rulers are the inferior of the law, has salvation and every blessing which the gods can confer." Plato here re-emphasises what he has already said in the *Statesman*.

The State exists, then, not for the good of any one class of men, but for the leading of the good life, and in the *Laws* Plato reasserts in unambiguous terms his conviction as to the importance of the soul and the tendance of the soul. "Of all the things which a man has, next to the gods, his soul is the most divine and the most truly his own," and "all the gold which is under or upon the earth is not enough to give in exchange for virtue."[3]

3. Plato had not much use for enormous States, and he fixes the number of the citizens at the number 5,040, which "can be divided by exactly fifty-nine divisors" and "will furnish numbers for war and peace, and for all contracts and dealings, including taxes and divisions."[4] But although Plato speaks of 5,040 citizens, he also speaks of 5,040 houses, which would imply a city of 5,040 families rather than individuals. However that may be, the citizens will possess house and land, since, though Plato expressly clings to communism as an ideal, he legislates in the *Laws* for the more practical second-best. At the same time he contemplates provisions for the prevention of the growth of a wealthy and commercial State. For example, the citizens should have a currency that passes only among themselves and is not accepted by the rest of mankind.[5]

[1] 705 a 2–7. [2] 715 a 8–b 6. [3] 726 a 2–3, 728 a 4–5.
[4] 737 e 1–738 b 1. [5] 742 a 5–6.

4. Plato discusses the appointment and functions of the various magistrates at length: I will content myself with mentioning one or two points. For example, there will be thirty-seven guardians of the law (νομοφύλακες), who will be not less than fifty years old when elected and will hold office up to their seventieth year at the latest. "All those who are horse or foot soldiers, or have taken part in war during the age for military service, shall share in the election of magistrates."[1] There shall also be a Council of 360 members, also elected, ninety from each property-class, the voting being designed apparently in such a way as to render unlikely the election of partisans of extreme views. There will be a number of ministers, such as the ministers who will have care of music and gymnastics (two ministers for each, one to educate, the other to superintend the contests). The most important of the ministers, however, will be the minister of education, who will have care of the youth, male and female, and who must be at least fifty years old, "the father of children lawfully begotten, of both sexes, or of one at any rate. He who is elected, and he who is the elector, should consider that of all the great offices of the State this is the greatest"; the legislator should not allow the education of children to become a secondary or accidental matter.[2]

5. There will be a committee of women to superintend married couples for ten years after marriage. If a couple have not had any children during a period of ten years, they should seek a divorce. Men must marry between the ages of thirty and thirty-five, girls between sixteen and twenty (later eighteen). Violations of conjugal fidelity will be punishable. The men will do their military service between the ages of twenty and sixty; women after bearing children and before they are fifty. No man is to hold office before he is thirty and no woman until she is forty. The provisions concerning the superintendence of married relations by the State are hardly acceptable to us; but Plato doubtless considered them the logical consequence of his conviction that "The bride and bridegroom should consider that they are to produce for the State the best and fairest specimens of children which they can."[3]

6. In Book Seven Plato speaks of the subject of education and its methods. He applies it even to infants, who are to be rocked frequently, as this counteracts emotions in the soul and

[1] 753 b 4–7. [2] 765 d 5–766 a 6. [3] 783 d 8–e 1.

produces "a peace and calm in the soul."[1] From the age of three to the age of six boys and girls will play together in the temples, supervised by ladies, while at the age of six they will be separated, and the education of the two sexes will be conducted in isolation, though Plato does not abandon his view that girls should have more or less the same education as boys. They will be educated in gymnastics and music, but the latter will be carefully watched over, and a State anthology of verse will be composed. Schools will have to be built, and paid teachers (foreigners) will be provided: children will attend daily at the schools, where they will be taught not only gymnastics and music, but also elementary arithmetic, astronomy, etc.

7. Plato legislates for the religious festivals of the State. There will be one each day, that "one magistrate at least will sacrifice daily to some god or demigod on behalf of the city and citizens and their possessions."[2] He legislates, too, on the subject of agriculture and of the penal code. In regard to the latter Plato insists that consideration should be paid to the psychological condition of the prisoner. His distinction between βλαβή and ἀδικία[3] amounts pretty well to our distinction between a civil action and a criminal action.

8. In the tenth Book Plato lays down his famous proposals for the punishment of atheism and heresy. To say that the universe is the product of the motions of corporeal elements, unendowed with intelligence, is atheism. Against this position Plato argues that there must be a source of motion, and that ultimately we must admit a self-moving principle, which is soul or mind. Hence soul or mind is the source of the cosmic movement. (Plato declares that there must be more than one soul responsible for the universe, as there is disorder and irregularity as well as order, but that there may be more than two.)

A pernicious heresy is that the gods are indifferent to man.[4] Against this Plato argues:

(*a*) The gods cannot lack the power to attend to small things.

(*b*) God cannot be too indolent or too fastidious to attend to details. Even a human artificer attends to details.

(*c*) Providence does not involve "interference" with law. Divine justice will at any rate be realised in the succession of lives.

[1] 790 c 5–791 b 2. [2] 828 b 2–3. [3] 861 e 6 ff. [4] 899 d 5–905 d 3.

A still more pernicious heresy is the opinion that the gods are venal, that they can be induced by bribes to condone injustice.[1] Against this Plato argues that we cannot suppose that the gods are like pilots who can be induced by wine to neglect their duty and bring ship and sailors to ruin, or like charioteers who can be bribed to surrender the victory to other charioteers, or like shepherds who allow the flock to be plundered on condition that they share in the spoils. To suppose any of these things is to be guilty of blasphemy.

Plato suggests penalties to be inflicted on those proved guilty of atheism or heresy. A morally inoffensive heretic will be punished with at least five years in the House of Correction, where he will be visited by members of the "Nocturnal Council," who will reason with him on the error of his ways. (Presumably those guilty of the two graver heresies will receive a longer term of imprisonment.) A second conviction will be punished with death. But heretics who also trade on the superstition of others with a view to their own profits, or who found immoral cults, will be imprisoned for life in a most desolate part of the country and will be cast out unburied at death, their families being treated as wards of the State. As a measure of safety Plato enacts that no private shrines or private cults are to be permitted.[2] Plato observes that before proceeding to prosecute an offender for impiety, the guardians of the law should determine "whether the deed has been done in earnest or only from childish levity."

9. Among the points of law dwelt on in Books Eleven and Twelve we may mention the following as of interest:

(*a*) It would be an extraordinary thing, says Plato, if any well-behaved slave or freeman fell into the extremes of poverty in any "tolerably well-ordered city or government." There will, therefore, be a decree against beggars, and the professional beggar will be sent out of the country, "so that our country may be cleared of this sort of animal."[3]

(*b*) Litigiousness or the practice of conducting lawsuits with a view to gain, and so trying to make a court a party to injustice, will be punishable by death.[4]

(*c*) Embezzlement of public funds and property shall be punished by death if the offender is a citizen, since, if a man who has had the full benefit of the State-education behaves in this way, he is incurable. If, however, the

[1] 905 d 3–907 d 1. [2] 909 d 7–8. [3] 936 c 1–7. [4] 937 d 6–938 c 5.

offender is a foreigner or a slave, the courts will decide the penalty, bearing in mind that he is probably not incurable.[1]

(*d*) A Board of εὔθυνοι will be appointed to audit the accounts of the magistrates at the end of their terms of office.[2]

(*e*) The Nocturnal Council (which is to meet early in the morning before the business of the day begins) will be composed of the ten senior νομοφύλακες, the minister and ex-ministers of education, and ten co-opted men between the ages of thirty and forty. It will consist of men who are trained to see the One in the Many, and who know that virtue is one (i.e. they will be men trained in Dialectic) and who have also undergone training in mathematics and astronomy, that they may have a firmly-grounded conviction as to the operation of divine Reason in the world. Thus this Council, composed of men who have a knowledge of God and of the ideal pattern of goodness, will be enabled to watch over the Constitution and be "the salvation of our government and of our laws."[3]

(*f*) In order to avoid confusion, novelties and restlessness, no one will be permitted to travel abroad without sanction of the State, and then only when he is over forty years of age (except, of course, on military expeditions). Those who go abroad will, on their return, "teach the young that the institutions of other States are inferior to their own."[4] However, the State will send abroad "spectators," in order to see if there is anything admirable abroad which might with profit be adopted at home. These men will be not less than fifty or more than sixty years old, and on their return they must make a report to the Nocturnal Council. Not only will visits of citizens to foreign countries be supervised by the State, but also visits of travellers from abroad. Those who come for purely commercial reasons will not be encouraged to mix with the citizens, while those who come for purposes approved of by the Government will be honourably treated as guests of the State.[5]

10. *Slavery*. It is quite clear from the *Laws* that Plato accepted the institution of slavery, and that he regarded the slave as the property of his master, a property which may be alienated.[6] Moreover, while in contemporary Athens the children of a

[1] 941 c 4–942 a 4. [2] 945 b 3–948 b 2. [3] 960 e 9 ff. [4] 951 a 2–4. [5] 949 e 3 ff. [6] Cf. 776 b 5–c 3.

marriage between a slave woman and a freeman seem to have been considered as free, Plato decrees that the children always belong to the master of the slave woman, whether her marriage be with a freeman or a freedman.[1] In some other respects, too, Plato shows himself severer than contemporary Athenian practice, and fails to give that protection to the slave that was accorded by Athenian law.[2] It is true that he provides for the protection of the slave in his public capacity (e.g. whoever kills a slave in order to prevent the latter giving information concerning an offence against the law, is to be treated as though he had killed a citizen),[3] and permits him to give information in murder cases without being submitted to torture; but there is no explicit mention of permission to bring a public prosecution against a man guilty of ὕβρις against his slave, which was permitted by Attic law. That Plato disliked the free-and-easy way in which the slaves behaved in democratic Athens appears from the *Republic*,[4] but he certainly did not wish to advocate a brutal treatment of the slave. Thus in the *Laws*, although he declares that "slaves ought to be punished as they deserve, and not admonished as if they were freemen, which will only make them conceited," and that "the language used to a servant ought always to be that of command, and we ought not to jest with them, whether they are females or males"; he expressly says that "we should tend them carefully, not only out of regard to them, but yet more out of respect to ourselves. And the right treatment of slaves is not to maltreat them, and to do them, if possible, even more justice than those who are our equals; for he who really and naturally reverences justice and really hates injustice, is discovered in his dealings with that class of man to whom he can easily be unjust."[5] We must, therefore, conclude that Plato simply accepted the institution of slavery, and, in regard to the treatment of slaves, that he disliked Athenian laxity on the one hand and Spartan brutality on the other.

11. *War*. In the first Book of the *Laws*, Cleinias the Cretan remarks that the regulations of Crete were designed by the legislator with a view to war. Every city is in a natural state of war with every other, "not indeed proclaimed by heralds, but everlasting."[6] Megillus, the Lacedaemonian, agrees with him. The Athenian Stranger, however, points out (*a*) that, in regard to

[1] 930 d 1–e 2.
[2] Cf. *Plato and Greek Slavery*, Glenn R. Morrow, in *Mind*, April 1939, N.S. vol. 48, No. 190.
[3] 872 c 2–6.
[4] *Rep.*, 563.
[5] 776 d 2–718 a 5.
[6] 626 a 2–5.

civil or internal war, the best legislator will endeavour to prevent it occurring in his State, or, if it does arise, will endeavour to reconcile the warring factions in an abiding friendship, and (*b*), that in regard to external or international war, the true statesman will aim at the best. Now, the happiness of the State, secured in peace and goodwill, is the best. No sound legislator, therefore, will ever order peace for the sake of war, but rather, if he orders war it will be for the sake of peace.[1] Thus Plato is not at all of the opinion that Policy exists for the sake of War, and he would scarcely sympathise with the virulent militarists of modern times. He points out that "many a victory has been and will be suicidal to the victors, but education is never suicidal."[2]

12. When man reflects on human life, on man's good and on the good life, as Plato did, he clearly cannot pass by man's social relations. Man is born into a society, not only into that of the family but also into a wider association, and it is in that society that he must live the good life and attain his end. He cannot be treated as though he were an isolated unit, living to himself alone. Yet, although every thinker who concerns himself with the humanistic viewpoint, man's place and destiny, must form for himself some theory of man's social relations, it may be well that no theory of the State will result, unless a somewhat advanced political consciousness has gone before. If man feels himself as a passive member of some great autocratic Power—the Persian Empire, for example—in which he is not called upon to play any active role, save as taxpayer or soldier, his political consciousness is scarcely aroused: one autocrat or another, one empire or another, Persian or Babylonian, it may make very little difference to him. But when a man belongs to a political community in which he is called upon to shoulder his burden of responsibility, in which he has not only duties but also rights and activities, then he will become politically conscious. To the politically unconscious man the State may appear as some thing set over against him, alien if not oppressive, and he will tend to conceive his way of salvation as lying through individual activity and perhaps through co-operation in other societies than that of the reigning bureaucracy: he will not be immediately stimulated to form a theory of the State. To the politically conscious man, on the other hand, the State appears as a body in which he has a

[1] 628 c 9–e 1. [2] 641 c 2–7.

part, as an extension in some sort of himself, and so will be stimulated—the reflective thinker, that is to say—to form a theory of the State.

The Greeks had this political consciousness in a very advanced degree: the good life was to them inconceivable apart from the Πόλις. What more natural, then, than that Plato, reflecting on the good life in general, i.e. the good life of man as such, should reflect also on the State as such, i.e. the ideal Πόλις? He was a philosopher and was concerned, not so much with the ideal Athens or the ideal Sparta, as with the ideal City, the Form to which the empirical States are approximations. This is not, of course to deny that Plato's conception of the Πόλις was influenced to a great extent by the practice of the contemporary Greek City-State—it could not be otherwise; but he discovered principles which lie at the basis of political life, and so may truly be said to have laid the foundations of a *philosophical* theory of the State. I say a "philosophical" theory of the State, because a theory of immediate reform is not general and universal, whereas Plato's treatment of the State is based on the nature of the State as such, and so it is designed to be universal, a character which is essential for a philosophic theory of the State. It is quite true that Plato dealt with reforms which he thought to be necessitated by the actual conditions of the Greek States, and that his theory was sketched on the background of the Greek Πόλις; but since he meant it to be universal, answering to the very nature of political life, it must be allowed that he sketched a philosophical theory of the State.

The political theory of Plato and Aristotle has indeed formed the foundation for subsequent fruitful speculation on the nature and characteristics of the State. Many details of Plato's *Republic* may be unrealisable in practice, and also undesirable even if practicable, but his great thought is that of the State as rendering possible and as promoting the good life of man, as contributing to man's temporal end and welfare. This Greek view of the State, which is also that of St. Thomas, is superior to the view which may be known as the liberal idea of the State, i.e. the view of the State as an institution, the function of which is to preserve private property and, in general, to exhibit a negative attitude towards the members of the State. In practice, of course, even the upholders of this view of the State have had to abandon a completely *laissez-faire* policy, but their theory remains barren, empty and negative in comparison with that of the Greeks.

However, it may well be that individuality was insufficiently stressed by the Greeks, as even Hegel notes. ("Plato in his *Republic* allows the rulers to appoint individuals to their particular class, and assign to them their particular tasks. In all these relations there is lacking the principle of subjective freedom." Again, in Plato "the principle of subjective freedom does not receive its due.")[1] This was brought into strong light by the theorists of the modern era who stressed the Social Contract theory. For them men are naturally atoms, separate and disunited, if not mutually antagonistic, and the State is merely a contrivance to preserve them, so far as may be, in that condition, while at the same time providing for the maintenance of peace and the security of private property. Their view certainly embodies truth and value, so that the individualism of thinkers like Locke must be combined with the more corporate theory of the State upheld by the great Greek philosophers. Moreover, the State which combines both aspects of human life must also recognise the position and rights of the supernatural Society, the Church. Yet we have to be careful not to allow insistence on the rights of the Church and the importance of man's supernatural end to lead us to minimise or mutilate the character of the State, which is also a "perfect society," having man's temporal welfare as its end.

[1] Hegel, *The Philosophy of Right*, sect. 299 and sect. 185. Trans. Professor S. W. Dyde. (George Bell & Sons, 1896.)

CHAPTER XXIV

PHYSICS OF PLATO

1. THE physical theories of Plato are contained in the *Timaeus*, Plato's only "scientific" dialogue. It was probably written when Plato was about seventy years old, and was designed to form the first work of a trilogy, the *Timaeus*, the *Critias*, and the *Hermocrates*.[1] The *Timaeus* recounts the formation of the material world and the birth of man and the animals; the *Critias* tells how primitive Athens defeated the invaders from mythical Atlantis, and then was itself overwhelmed by flood and earthquake; and it is conjectured that the *Hermocrates* was to deal with the rebirth of culture in Greece, ending with Plato's suggestions for future reform. Thus the Utopian State or Socratic Republic[2] would be represented in the *Critias* as something realised in the past, while practical reforms for the future would be proposed in the *Hermocrates*. The *Timaeus* was actually written, the *Critias* breaks off before completion, and was left unfinished, while the *Hermocrates* was never composed at all. It has been very reasonably suggested that Plato, conscious of his advancing age, dropped the idea of completing his elaborate historical romance and incorporated in the *Laws* (Books 3 ff.) much of what he had wanted to say in the *Hermocrates*.[3]

The *Timaeus* was thus written by way of preface to two politico-ethical dialogues, so that it would be hardly correct to represent Plato as having suddenly conceived an intense interest in natural science in his old age. It is probably true that he was influenced by the growing scientific interest in the Academy, and there can be little doubt that he felt the necessity of saying something about the material world, with a view to explaining its relation to the Forms; but there is no real reason for supposing that the centre of Plato's interest underwent a radical shift from ethical, political and metaphysical themes to questions of natural science. As a matter of fact, he says expressly in the *Timaeus* that an account of the material world cannot be more than "likely," that we should not expect it to be exact or even altogether

[1] Cf. *Tim.*, 27 ab.
[2] 26 c 7–e 5.
[3] See Introd. to Professor Cornford's edition of *Timaeus*.

self-consistent,[1] phrases which clearly indicate that in Plato's eyes Physics could never be an exact science, a science in the true sense. Nevertheless, some account of the material universe was called for by the peculiar character of the Platonic theory of Ideas. While the Pythagoreans held that things are numbers, Plato held that they participate in numbers (retaining his dualism), so that he might justly be expected to proffer some explanation from the physical standpoint of how this participation comes to be.

Plato doubtless had another important reason for writing the *Timaeus*, namely to exhibit the organised Cosmos as the work of Intelligence and to show that man partakes of both worlds, the intelligible and the sensible. He is convinced that "mind orders all things," and will not agree "when an ingenious individual (Democritus?) declares that all is disorder":[2] on the contrary, soul is "the oldest and most divine of all things," and it is "mind which ordered the universe."[3] In the *Timaeus*, therefore, Plato presents a picture of the intelligent ordering of all things by Mind, and exhibits the divine origin of man's immortal soul. (Just as the entire universe comprises a dualism of the intelligible and eternal on the one hand, and the sensible and fleeting on the other, so man, the microcosm, comprises a dualism of eternal soul, belonging to the sphere of Reality, and body which passes and perishes.) This exhibition of the world as the handiwork of Mind, which forms the material world according to the ideal pattern constitutes an apt preface to the proposed extended treatment of the State, which should be rationally formed and organised according to the ideal pattern and not left to the play of irrational and "chance" causes.

2. If Plato thought of his physical theories as a "likely account" (εἰκότες λόγοι), are we thereby compelled to treat the whole work as "Myth"? First of all, the theories of Timaeus, whether myth or not, must be taken as Plato's theories: the present writer entirely agrees with Professor Cornford's rejection of Professor A. E. Taylor's notion that the *Timaeus* is a "fake" on Plato's part, a statement of "fifth-century Pythagoreanism," "a deliberate attempt to amalgamate Pythagorean religion and mathematics with Empedoclean biology,"[4] so that "Plato was not likely to feel himself responsible for the details of any of his speaker's

[1] Cf. 27 d 5–28 a 4 and 29 b 3–d 3. This was a consequence of the epistemological and ontological dualism, which Plato never abandoned.

[2] *Philebus*, 28 c 6–29 a 5.

[3] *Laws*, 966 d 9–e 4.

[4] *A Commentary on Plato's Timaeus*, pp. 18–19.

theories." Apart from the inherent improbability of such a fake on the part of a great and original philosopher, already advanced in years, how is it that Aristotle and Theophrastus and other ancients, as Cornford points out, have left us no hint as to the faked character of the work? If this was its real character, they cannot all have been ignorant of the fact; and can we suppose that, if they were aware of such an interesting fact, they would all have remained absolutely silent on the point? It is really too much to ask us to believe that the true character of the *Timaeus* was first revealed to the world in the twentieth century. Plato certainly borrowed from other philosophers (particularly the Pythagoreans), but the theories of Timaeus are Plato's own, whether borrowed or not.

In the second place, although the theories put into the mouth of Timaeus are Plato's own theories, they constitute, as we have seen, a "likely account," and should not be taken as meant to be an exact and scientific account—for the very simple fact that Plato did not consider such an exact scientific account to be possible. He not only says that we should remember that we "are only human," and so should accept "the likely story and look for nothing further"[1]—words which might imply that it is just human frailty which renders true natural science impossible; but he goes further than that, since he expressly refers this impossibility of an exact natural science to "the nature of the subject." An account of what is only a likeness "will itself be but likely": "what becoming is to being, that is belief to truth."[2] The theories are put forward, therefore, as "likely" or probable; but that does not mean that they are "mythical" in the sense of being consciously designed to symbolise a more exact theory that, for some reason or other, Plato is unwilling to impart. It may be that this or that feature of the *Timaeus* is conscious symbolism, but we have to argue each case on its own merits, and are not justified in simply dismissing the whole of the Platonic Physics as Myth. It is one thing to say: "I do not think an exact account of the material world possible, but the following account is as likely or more likely than any other"; and it is another thing to say: "I put forward the following account as a mythical, symbolic and pictorial expression of an exact account which I propose to keep to myself." Of course, if we care to call a confessedly "probable" account "Myth," then the *Timaeus* is certainly Myth; but it is

[1] *Tim.*, 29 d 1–3. [2] *Tim.*, 29 c 1–3.

not Myth (in its entirety at least) if by "Myth" you mean a symbolic and pictorial representation of a truth clearly perceived by the author but kept to himself. Plato means to do the best he can, and says so.

3. Plato sets out to give an account of the generation of the world. The sensible world is becoming, and "that which becomes must necessarily become through the agency of some cause."[1] The agent in question is the divine Craftsman or Demiurge. He "took over"[2] all that was in discordant and unordered motion, and brought it into order, forming the material world according to an eternal and ideal pattern, and fashioning it into "a living creature with soul and reason"[3] after the model of the ideal Living Creature, i.e. the Form that contains within itself the Forms of "the heavenly race of gods, the winged things which fly through the air, all that dwells in the water, and all that goes on foot on the dry earth."[4] As there is but one ideal living Creature, the Demiurge made but one world.[5]

4. What was the motive of the Demiurge in so acting? The Demiurge is good and "desired that all things should come as near as possible to being like himself," judging that order is better than disorder, and fashioning everything for the best.[6] He was limited by the material at his disposal, but he did the best he could with it, making it "as excellent and perfect as possible."

5. How are we to regard the figure of the Demiurge? He must at least represent the divine Reason which is operative in the world; but he is not a Creator-God. It is clear from the *Timaeus* that the Demiurge "took over" a pre-existing material and did his best with it: he is certainly not said to have created it out of nothing. "The generation of this cosmos," says Plato, "was a mixed result of the combination of Necessity and Reason,"[7] Necessity being also called the Errant Cause. The word "Necessity" naturally suggests to us the reign of fixed law, but this is not precisely what Plato meant. If we take the Democritean or Epicurean view of the universe, according to which the world is built up out of atoms without the aid of Intelligence, we have an example of what Plato meant by Necessity, i.e. the *purposeless*, that which was not formed by Intelligence. If we also bear in mind that in the Atomistic System the world owes its origin to the "chance" collision of atoms, we can more easily see how Plato

[1] 28 c 2–3. [2] 30 a 3–4. [3] 30 b 1–c 1. [4] 39 e 3–40 a 2. [5] 31 a 2–b 3. [6] 29 e 3–30 a 6. [7] 47 e 5–48 a 2.

could associate Necessity with Chance or the Errant Cause. For us these may seem to be opposed notions, but for Plato they were akin, since they both denote that in which Intelligence and conscious Purpose have no share. Thus it is that in the *Laws* Plato can speak of those who declare that the world originated "not by the action of mind, or of any God, or from art, but by nature and chance" (φύσει καὶ τύχῃ) or of necessity (ἐξ' ἀνάγκης).[1] Such a view of the universe is characterised by Aristotle[2] as the ascription of the world to Spontaneity (τὸ αὐτόματον), though inasmuch as motion is due to the previous motion of another atom, one could also say that the universe is due to Necessity. Thus the three notions of "spontaneously" and "by chance" and "of necessity" were allied notions. The elements, if considered as left to themselves, as it were, proceed spontaneously or by chance or necessarily, according to the point of view taken; but they do not subserve *purpose* unless the operation of Reason is introduced. Plato can, therefore, speak of Reason "persuading" necessity, i.e. making the "blind" elements subserve design and conscious purpose, even though the material is partly intractable and cannot be fully subordinated to the operation of Reason.

The Demiurge was, then, no Creator-God. Moreover, Plato most probably never thought of "chaos" as ever existing in actual fact, in the sense of there having been an historical period when the world was simply a disorderly chaos. At any rate this was the tradition of the Academy with but very few dissentient voices (Plutarch and Atticus). It is true that Aristotle takes the account of the world's formation in the *Timaeus* as an account of formation in time (or at least criticises it as so interpreted), but he expressly mentions that the members of the Academy declared that in describing the world's formation they were merely doing so for purposes of exposition, in order to understand the universe, without supposing that it ever really came into existence.[3] Among Neo-Platonists Proclus gave this interpretation[4] and Simplicius.[5] If this interpretation is correct, then the Demiurge is still less like a Creator-God: he is a symbol of the Intelligence operative in the world, the King of heaven and earth of the *Philebus*.[6] Moreover, it is to be noted that in the *Timaeus* itself Plato asserts that "it is hard to find the maker and father of the universe, and having found him it is impossible to speak of him

[1] *Laws*, 889 c 4–6. [2] *Physics*, B. 4, 196 a 25. [3] *De Caelo*, 279 b 33.
[4] i, 382; iii, 273. [5] *Phys.*, 1122, 3. [6] 28 c 7–8.

to all."[1] But if the Demiurge is a symbolic figure, it may also be that the sharp distinction implied in the *Timaeus* between the Demiurge and the Forms is only a pictorial representation. In treating of the Forms I inclined towards what might be called a Neo-Platonic interpretation of the relation between Mind, the Forms and the One, but I admitted that it *might* be that the Forms were Ideas of Mind or Intelligence. In any case it is not necessary to suppose that the picture of the Demiurge as a Divine Craftsman outside the world and also entirely distinct from the Forms is to be taken literally.

6. What did the Demiurge "take over"? Plato speaks of the "Receptacle—as it were, the nurse—of all Becoming."[2] Later he describes this as "Space, which is everlasting, not admitting destruction; providing a situation for all things which come into being, but itself apprehended without the senses by a sort of bastard reasoning, and hardly an object of belief."[3] It appears, therefore, that Space is not that out of which the primary elements are made, but that *in which* they appear. It is true that Plato makes a comparison with gold out of which a man moulds figures;[4] but he goes on to say that Space "never departs at all from its own character. For it is ever receiving all things, and never in any way whatsoever takes on any character which is like any of the things that enter it."[5] It is probable, then, that Space or the Receptacle is not the matter out of which the primary qualities are made, but that in which they appear.

Plato remarks that the four elements (earth, air, fire and water) cannot be spoken of as substances, since they are constantly changing: "for they slip away and do not wait to be described as 'that' or 'this' or by any phrase that exhibits them as having permanent being."[6] They are rather to be termed *qualities*, which make their appearance in the Receptacle, "in which (ἐν ᾧ) all of them are always coming to be, making their appearance and again vanishing out of it."[7] The Demiurge thus "took over" (*a*) the Receptacle, "a kind of thing invisible and characterless, all-receiving, partaking in some very puzzling way of the intelligible and very hard to apprehend,"[8] and (*b*) the primary qualities, which appear in the Receptacle and which the Demiurge fashions or builds up after the model of the Forms.

7. The Demiurge proceeds to confer geometrical shapes on the

[1] 28 c 3–5. [2] 49 a 5–6. [3] 52 a 8–b 2. [4] 50 a 5–b 5.
[5] 50 b 7–c 2. [6] 49 e 2–4. [7] 49 e 7–50 a 1. [8] 51 a 7–b 1.

four primary elements. Plato only takes things as far back as triangles, choosing the right-angled isosceles (half-square) and the right-angled scalene or half-equilateral, from which are to be built up the square and equilateral faces of the solids.[1] (If anyone asks why Plato makes a beginning with triangles, he answers that "the principles yet more remote, God knows and such men as are dear to Him."[2] In the *Laws*[3] he indicates that it is only when the third dimension is reached that things become "perceptible to sense." It is sufficient, therefore, for purposes of exposition to start with the surface or second dimension, and leave the remoter principles alone.) The solids are then constructed, the cube being assigned to earth (as the most immobile or hard to move), the pyramid to fire (as the "most mobile," having "the sharpest cutting edges and the sharpest points in every direction"), the octahedron to air, and the icosahedron to water.[4] These bodies are so small that no single one of them is perceptible by us, though an aggregate mass is perceptible.

The elementary solids or particles may be, and are, transformed into one another, since water, for example, may be broken down into its constituent triangles under the action of fire, and these triangles may recombine in Space into the same figure or into different figures. Earth, however, is an exception because, although it may be broken up, its constituent triangles (isosceles or half-square, from which the cube is generated) are peculiar to it alone, so that earth-particles "can never pass into any other kind."[5] Aristotle objects to this exception made in favour of earth, on the ground that it is unreasonable and unsupported by observation.[6] (The particles are spoken of as "motions or powers,"[7] and in the state of separation they have "some vestiges of their own nature."[8] Thus Ritter says that "Matter may be defined as that which acts in space."[9]) From the primary elements come substances as we know them: e.g. copper is "one of the bright and solid kinds of water," containing a particle of earth, "which, when the two substances begin to be separated again by the action of time," appears by itself on the surface as verdigris.[10] But Plato observes that to enumerate the genesis and nature of substances is not much more than a "recreation," a "sober and sensible pastime" that affords innocent pleasure.[11]

8. The Demiurge is depicted as creating the World-Soul

[1] Cf. 53 c 4 ff. [2] 53 d 6–7. [3] 894 a 2–5. [4] 55 d 6 ff. [5] 56 d 5–6. [6] *De Caelo*, 306 a 2. [7] 56 c 4. [8] 53 b 2. [9] *Essence*, p. 261. [10] 59 c 1–5. [11] 59 c 5–d 2.

(though it is unlikely that Plato meant this to be taken literally, for in the *Phaedrus* it is stated that soul is uncreated[1]), which is a mixture composed of (*a*) Intermediate Existence (i.e. intermediate between the Indivisible Existence of the Forms and the Divisible Existence or Becoming of purely sensible things); (*b*) Intermediate Sameness; and (*c*) Intermediate Difference.[2] As immortal souls are also fashioned by the Demiurge from the same ingredients as the World-Soul,[3] it follows that the World-Soul and all immortal souls share in both worlds—in the unchanging world, inasmuch as they are immortal and intelligible, and in the changing world, inasmuch as they are themselves living and changing. The stars and planets have intelligent souls which are the celestial gods,[4] made by the Demiurge and having assigned to them the office of fashioning the mortal parts of the human soul and the human body.[5] It would appear from the *Phaedrus* that human souls never really had a beginning, and Proclus interprets Plato in this sense, though it is true that in the *Laws* the question seems to be left open.[6]

As to the traditional Greek deities, whose genealogies were narrated by the poets, Plato remarks that "to know and to declare their generation is too high a task for us"; it is best to "follow established usage."[7] Plato seems to have been agnostic as regards the existence of the anthropomorphic deities,[8] but he does not reject them outright, and in the *Epinomis*[9] the existence of invisible spirits (who were to play a large part in post-Aristotelian Greek philosophy), in addition to that of the celestial gods, is envisaged. Plato, therefore, upholds the traditional worship, though he places little reliance on the stories of the generation and genealogy of the Greek deities, and was probably doubtful if they really existed in the form in which the Greeks popularly conceived them.

9. The Demiurge, having constructed the universe, sought to make it still more like its pattern, the Living Creature or Being. Now, the latter is eternal, but "this character it was not possible to confer completely on the generated things. But he took thought to make a certain moving likeness of eternity; and, at the same time that he ordered the Heaven, he made, of eternity that abides in unity, an everlasting likeness moving according to number—that

[1] 246 a 1–2. [2] 35 a 1 ff. Cf. *Proclus*, ii, 155, Cornford's *Timaeus*, pp. 59 ff.
[3] 41 d 4 ff. [4] 39 e 10–42 a 1. [5] Cf. 41 a 7–d 3, 42 d 5–e 4.
[6] 781 e 6–782 a 3. [7] *Tim.*, 40 d 6–41 a 3. [8] Cf. *Phaedrus*, 246 c 6–d 3.
[9] 984 d 8–e 3.

which we have named Time."[1] Time is the movement of the sphere, and the Demiurge gave man the bright Sun to afford him a unit of time. Its brightness, relative to that of the other celestial bodies, enables man to differentiate day and night.

10. One cannot enter into details concerning the formation of the human body and its powers, or of the animals, etc. It must suffice to point out how Plato stresses finality, as in his quaint observation that "the gods, thinking that the front is more honourable and fit to lead than the back, gave us movement for the most part in that direction."[2]

The conclusion of the whole account of the formation of the world is that "having received its full complement of living creatures, mortal and immortal, this world has thus become a visible living creature embracing all things which are visible, an image of the intelligible, a perceptible god, supreme in greatness and excellence, in beauty and perfection, this Heaven, one and single in its kind."[3]

[1] *Tim.*, 37 d 3–7. [2] *Tim.*, 45 a 3–5. [3] *Tim.*, 92 c 5–9.

CHAPTER XXV

ART

1. *Beauty*

1. Had Plato any appreciation of natural beauty? There is not an abundance of material from which to form an opinion. However, there is a description of natural scenery at the beginning of the *Phaedrus*,[1] and there are some similar remarks at the beginning of the *Laws*,[2] though in both cases the beauty of the scene is appreciated rather from a utilitarian standpoint, as a place of repose or as a setting for a philosophic discussion. Plato had, of course, an appreciation of human beauty.

2. Had Plato any real appreciation of Fine Art? (This question only arises because of his dismissal of dramatists and epic poets from the Ideal State on moral grounds, which might he held to imply that he lacked any real appreciation of literature and art.) Plato dismissed most of the poets from the *Republic* owing to metaphysical and, above all, moral considerations; but there certainly are not wanting indications that Plato was quite sensible of the charm of their compositions. While the words at the beginning of *Republic* 398 would not appear to be entirely sarcastic, in No. 383 of the same dialogue Socrates affirms that "although we praise much in Homer, this we shall not praise, the sending by Zeus of a lying dream to Agamemnon." Similarly, Plato makes Socrates say: "I must speak, although the love and awe of Homer, which have possessed me from youth, deter me from doing so. He seems to be the supreme teacher and leader of this fine tragic band, but a man should not be reverenced before the truth and I must needs speak out."[3] Again, "We are ready to acknowledge that Homer is the greatest of poets and first of tragedy writers; but we must recognise that hymns to the gods and praises of the good are the only poetry which ought to be admitted into our State."[4] Plato expressly says that if only poetry and the other arts will prove their title to be admitted into a well-ordered State, "we shall be delighted to receive her, knowing that we ourselves are very susceptible of her charms; but we may not on that account betray the truth."[5]

Bearing these points in mind, it seems impossible to write Plato

[1] 230 b 2 ff. [2] 625 b 1–c 2. [3] 595 b 9–c 3. [4] 607 a 2–5. [5] 607 c 3–8.

down as a Philistine in regard to the arts and literature. And if it be suggested that his tributes of appreciation to the poets are but the grudging tributes of convention, we may point to Plato's own artistic achievement. If Plato himself had shown in no degree the spirit of the artist, it might be possible to believe that his remarks concerning the charms of the poets were due simply to convention or were even sarcastic in tone; but when we consider that it is the author of the *Symposium* and the *Phaedo* who speaks, it is really too much to expect anyone to believe that Plato's condemnation, or at least severe restriction, of art and literature was due to aesthetic insensibility.

3. What was Plato's theory of Beauty? That Plato regarded beauty as objectively real, is beyond all question. Both in the *Hippias Maior* and in the *Symposium* it is assumed that all beautiful things are beautiful in virtue of their participation in the universal Beauty, Beauty itself. So when Socrates remarks "Then beauty, too, is something real," Hippias replies, "Real, why ask?"[1]

The obvious consequence of such a doctrine is that there are degrees of beauty. For if there is a real subsistent Beauty then beautiful things will approximate more or less to this objective norm. So in the *Hippias Maior* the notion of relativity is introduced. The most beautiful ape will be ugly in comparison with a beautiful man, and a beautiful porridge-pot will be ugly in comparison with a beautiful woman. The latter in turn will be ugly in comparison with a god. Beauty itself, however, in virtue of a participation in which all beautiful things are beautiful, cannot be supposed to be something which "may just as well be called ugly as beautiful."[2] Rather is it "not partly beautiful and partly ugly; not at one time beautiful and at another time not; not beautiful in relation to one thing and deformed in relation to another; not here beautiful and there ugly, not beautiful in the estimation of some people and deformed in that of others; . . . but . . . eternally self-subsistent and monoeidic with itself."[3]

It follows also that this supreme Beauty, as being absolute and the source of all participated beauty, cannot be a beautiful *thing*, and so cannot be material: it must be supersensible and immaterial. We can see at once, then, that if true Beauty is supersensible, beautiful works of art or literature will, apart from

[1] *H.M.*, 287 c 8–d 2. [2] *H.M.*, 289 c 3–5. [3] *Sympos.*, 211 a 2–b 2.

any other consideration, necessarily occupy a comparatively low step on the ladder of beauty, since they are material, whereas Beauty itself is immaterial; they appeal to the senses, while absolute Beauty appeals to the intellect (and indeed to the rational will, if we bring into consideration the Platonic notion of Eros). Now, no one will wish to question the sublimity of Plato's idea of the ascent from the things of sense to the "divine and pure, the monoeidic beautiful itself"; but a doctrine of supersensible beauty (unless it is purely analogical) makes it very difficult to form any definition of beauty which will apply to the beautiful in all its manifestations.

The suggestion is offered in the *Hippias Maior*[1] that "whatever is useful is beautiful." Thus efficiency will be beauty: the efficient trireme or the efficient institution will be beautiful in virtue of its efficiency. But in what sense, then, can the Supreme Beauty be thought of as useful or efficient? It ought, if the theory is to be consistent, to be Absolute Usefulness or Efficiency—a difficult notion to accept, one might think. Socrates, however, introduces a qualification. If it is the useful or efficient which is beautiful, is it that which is useful for a good or for a bad purpose or for both? He will not accept the idea that what is efficient for an evil purpose is beautiful, and so it must be that the useful for a good purpose, the truly profitable, is the beautiful. But if the beautiful is the profitable, i.e. that which *produces* something good, then beauty and goodness cannot be the same, any more than the cause and its product can be the same. But since Socrates is unable to accept the conclusion that what is beautiful is not at the same time good, he suggests that the beautiful is that which gives pleasure to the eye or ear—e.g. beautiful men and colour-patterns and pictures and statues, beautiful voices and music and poetry and prose. This definition is, of course, not quite consistent with the characterisation of supreme Beauty as immaterial, but, quite apart from that fact, it is involved in another difficulty. That which gives pleasure through sight cannot be beautiful simply because it comes through *sight*, for then a beautiful tone would not be beautiful: nor can a tone be beautiful precisely because it gives pleasure to the sense of *hearing*, since in that case a statue, which is seen but not heard, would not be beautiful. The objects, therefore, which cause aesthetic pleasure of sight or hearing must share some common character which makes them beautiful, which

[1] 295 C I ff.

belongs to them both. What is this common character? Is it perhaps "Profitable pleasure," since the pleasures of sight and hearing are "the most harmless and the best of pleasures?" If this be so, then, says Socrates, we are back in the old position that beauty cannot be good nor the good beautiful.

If anything like the foregoing definition of beauty were maintained, it would be inconsistent with Plato's general metaphysical position. If Beauty is a transcendental Form, how can it possibly be that which gives pleasure to the senses of sight and hearing? In the *Phaedrus*[1] Plato declares that beauty alone, in distinction from wisdom, has the privilege of manifesting itself to the senses. But does it manifest itself through what is itself beautiful or not? If the latter, how can there be a real manifestation? If the former, then do the sensible manifesting beauty and the supersensible manifested beauty unite in a common definition or not? And if so, in what definition? Plato does not really offer any definition that will cover both types of beauty. In the *Philebus* he speaks of true pleasure as arising from beautiful shapes and colours and sounds and goes on to explain that he is referring to "straight lines and curves" and to "such sounds as are pure and smooth and yield a single pure tone." These "are not beautiful relatively to anything else but in their own proper nature."[2] In the passage in question Plato distinguishes between the pleasure attaching to the perception of beauty and beauty itself, and his words must be read in connection with his statement[3] that "measure and symmetry everywhere pass into beauty and virtue," which implies that beauty consists in μετριότης καὶ συμμετρία. Perhaps this is as near as Plato ever comes to offering a definition of beauty that would apply to sensible and to supersensible beauty (he certainly assumed that there are both, and that the one is a copy of the other); but if we take into account the remarks on beauty scattered about in the dialogues, it is probable that we must admit that Plato wanders "among so many conceptions, among which it is just possible to say that the identification of the Beautiful with the Good prevails,"[4] though the definition offered in the *Philebus* would seem to be the most promising.

[1] 250 d 6–8. [2] 51 b 9–c 7. [3] *Phil.*, 64 e 6–7.
[4] *Aesthetic*, by Benedetto Croce, pp. 165–6. (2nd edit., trs. by Douglas Ainslie, Macmillan, 1929.)

II. *Plato's Theory of Art*

1. Plato suggests that the *origin* of art is to be sought in the natural instinct of expression.[1]

2. In its metaphysical aspect or its essence, art is *imitation*. The Form is exemplary, archetypal; the natural object is an instance of μίμησις. Now, the painting of a man, for example, is the copy or imitation of a natural, particular man. It is, therefore, the imitation of an imitation. Truth, however, is to be sought properly in the Form; the work of the artist accordingly stands at two removes from the truth. Hence Plato, who was above all things interested in truth, was bound to depreciate art, however much he might feel the beauty and charm of statues, painting or literature. This depreciatory view of art comes out strongly in the *Republic*, where he applies it to the painter and the tragic poet, etc.[2] Sometimes his remarks are a little comical, as when he observes that the painter does not even copy objects accurately, being an imitator of appearance and not of fact.[3] The painter who paints a bed, paints it only from one point of view, as it appears to the senses immediately: the poet portrays healing, war and so on, without any real knowledge of the things of which he is speaking. The conclusion is that "imitative art must be a long way from truth."[4] It is "two grades below reality, and quite easy to produce without any knowledge of the truth—for it is mere semblance and not reality."[5] The man who gives up his life to producing this shadow of reality has made a very bad bargain.

In the *Laws* there appears what is perhaps a somewhat more favourable judgment concerning art, though Plato has not altered his metaphysical position. When saying that the excellence of music is not to be estimated merely by the amount of sense-pleasure it occasions, Plato adds that the only music which has real excellence is the kind of music "which is an imitation of the good."[6] Again, "those who seek for the best kind of song and music, ought not to seek for that which is pleasant, but for that which is true; and the truth of imitation consists, as we were saying, in rendering the thing imitated according to quantity and quality."[7] He thus still clings to the concept of music as imitative ("everyone will admit that musical compositions are all imitative

[1] Cf. *Laws*, 653–4, 672 b 8–c 6. [2] *Rep.*, 597 c 11 and ff. [3] *Rep.*, 597 e 10 ff.
[4] *Rep.*, 598 b 6. [5] *Rep.*, 598 e 6–599 a 3. [6] *Laws*, 668 a 9–b 2.
[7] *Laws*, 668 b 4–7.

and representative"), but admits that imitation may be "true" if it renders the thing imitated as best as it can in its own medium. He is ready to admit music and art into the State, not only for educative purposes, but also for "innocent pleasure";[1] but he still maintains the imitation-theory of art, and that Plato's idea of imitation was somewhat narrow and literal must be clear to anyone who reads the second Book of the *Laws* (though it must be admitted, I think, that to make *music* imitative implies a widening of imitation to include symbolism. That music is imitative is, of course, a doctrine common to both the *Republic* and the *Laws*.) It is through this concept of imitation that Plato arrives at the qualities of a good critic, who must (*a*) know of what the imitation is supposed to be; (*b*) know whether it is "true" or not; and (*c*) know whether it has been well executed in words and melodies and rhythms.[2]

It is to be noted that the doctrine of μίμησις would indicate that for Plato art definitely has its own sphere. While ἐπιστήμη concerns the ideal order and δόξα the perceptible order of natural objects, εἰκασία concerns the imaginative order. The work of art is a product of imagination and addresses itself to the emotional element in man. It is not necessary to suppose that the imitative character of art maintained by Plato *essentially* denoted mere photographic reproduction, in spite of the fact that his words about "true" imitation indicate that this is what he was often thinking of. For one thing, the natural object is not a photographic copy of the Idea, since the Idea belongs to one order and the perceptible natural object belongs to another order, so that we may conclude by analogy that the work of art need not necessarily be a mere reproduction of the natural object. It is the work of imaginative creation. Again, Plato's insistence on the imitative character of music makes it very difficult, as I have mentioned, to suppose that imitation meant essentially mere photographic reproduction. It is rather imaginative symbolism, and it is precisely because of this fact that it does not assert truth or falsehood, but is imaginative and symbolic and wears the glamour of beauty, that it addresses itself to the emotional in man.

Man's emotions are varied, some being profitable, others harmful. Reason, therefore, must decide what art is to be admitted and what is to be excluded. And the fact that Plato definitely admits forms of art into the State in the *Laws* shows that art

[1] *Laws*, 670 d 6–7. [2] *Laws*, 669 a 7–b 3.

occupies a particular sphere of human activity, which is irreducible to anything else. It may not be a high sphere, but it is a sphere. This is borne out by the passage in which Plato, after referring to the stereotyped character of Egyptian art, remarks that "if a person can only find in any way the natural melodies, he should confidently embody them in a fixed and legal form."[1] It must, however, be admitted that Plato does not realise—or, if he does realise, does not sufficiently exhibit—the specifically disinterested character of aesthetic contemplation in itself. He is much more concerned with the educational and moral effects of art, effects which are irrelevant, no doubt, to aesthetic contemplation as such, but which are none the less real, and which must be taken into account by anyone who, like Plato, values moral excellence more than aesthetic sensibility.[2]

3. Plato recognises that the popular view of art and music is that they exist to give pleasure, but it is a view with which he will not agree. A thing can only be judged by the standard of pleasure when it furnishes no utility or truth or "likeness" (reference to imitation), but exists solely for the accompanying charm.[3] Now, music, for instance, is representative and imitative, and good music will have "truth of imitation":[4] therefore music, or at least good music, furnishes a certain kind of "truth," and so cannot exist solely for the sake of the accompanying charm or be judged of by the standard of sense-pleasure alone. The same holds good for the other arts. The conclusion is that the various arts may be admitted into the State, provided that they are kept in their proper place and subordinated to their educative function, this function being that of giving *profitable* pleasure. That the arts do not, or should not, give pleasure, Plato by no means intends to assert: he allows that in the city there should be "a due regard to the instruction and amusement which the Muses give,"[5] and even declares that "every man and boy, free and slave, both sexes, and the whole city, should never cease charming themselves with the strains of which we have spoken, and that there should be every sort of change and variation of them in order to take away the effect of sameness, so that the singers may always have an appetite for their hymns and receive pleasure from them."[6]

[1] 657 b 2–3.

[2] For further treatment of Plato's philosophy of art, see e.g. Professor R. G. Collingwood's article, "Plato's Philosophy of Art," in *Mind* for April 1925.

[3] *Laws*, 667 d 9–e 4. [4] 668 b 4–7. [5] 656 c 1–3. [6] 665 c 2–7.

But though Plato in the *Laws* allows for the pleasurable and recreative functions of art, the "innocent pleasure"[1] that it affords, he most certainly stresses its educative and moral function, its character of providing profitable pleasure. The attitude displayed towards art in the *Laws* may be more liberal than that shown in the *Republic*, but Plato's fundamental attitude has not changed. As we have seen when treating of the State, a strict supervision and censorship of art is provided for in both dialogues. In the very passage in which he says that due regard should be paid to the instruction and amusement given by the Muses, he asks if a poet is to be allowed to "train his choruses as he pleases, without reference to virtue or vice."[2] In other words, the art admitted into the State must have that remote relation to the Form ("truth of imitation" *via* the natural object) which is possible in the creations of the imagination. If it has not got that, then the art will be not only unprofitable but also bad art, since good art must have this "truth of imitation," according to Plato. Once more, then, it becomes clear that art has a function of its own, even if not a sublime one, since it constitutes a rung on the ladder of education, fulfils a need of man (expression) and affords recreation and innocent amusement, being the expression of a definite form of human activity—that of the creative imagination (though "creative" must be understood in connection with the doctrine of imitation). Plato's theory of art was doubtless sketchy and unsatisfactory, but one can hardly be justified in asserting that he had no theory at all.

Note on the Influence of Plato

1. The example of Plato is an influence by itself. His life was one of utter devotion to truth, to the attainment of abiding, eternal and absolute truth, in which he firmly and constantly believed, being ready to follow, as Socrates was, wherever reason might lead. This spirit he endeavoured to stamp upon the Academy, creating a body of men who, under the ascendency of a great teacher, would devote themselves to the attainment of Truth and Goodness. But though he was a great speculative philosopher, devoted to the attainment of truth in the intellectual sphere, Plato, as we have seen, was no mere theorist. Possessed of an intense moral earnestness and convinced of the reality of absolute moral values and standards, he urged men to take

[1] 670 d 7. [2] 656 c 5–7.

thought for their dearest possession, their immortal soul, and to strive after the cultivation of true virtue, which alone would make them happy. The good life, based on an eternal and absolute pattern, must be lived both in private and in public, realised both in the individual and in the State: as relativistic private morality was rejected, so was the opportunist, superficial, self-seeking attitude of the sophistic "politician" or the theory that "Might is Right."

If man's life *ought* to be lived under the dominion of reason according to an ideal pattern, in the world as a whole we must acknowledge the actual operation of Mind. Atheism is utterly rejected and the order in the world is ascribed to Divine Reason, ordering the cosmos according to the ideal pattern and plan. Thus that which is realised in the macrocosm, e.g. in the movements of heavenly bodies, should also be realised in man, the microcosm. If man does follow reason and strives to realise the ideal in his life and conduct, he becomes akin to the Divine and attains happiness in this life and the hereafter. Plato's "other-worldliness" did not spring from a hatred of this life, but was rather a consequence of his convinced belief in the reality of the Transcendent and Absolute.

2. Plato's personal influence may be seen from the impression he made on his great pupil, Aristotle. Witness the latter's verses to the memory

> Of that unique man
> Whose name is not to come from the lips of the wicked.
> Theirs is not the right to praise him—
> Him who first revealed clearly
> By word and by deed
> That he who is virtuous is happy.
> Alas, not one of us can equal him.[1]

Aristotle gradually separated himself from some of the Platonic doctrines that he had held at first; but, in spite of his growing interest in empirical science, he never abandoned metaphysics or his belief in the good life culminating in true wisdom—in other words, he never abandoned altogether the legacy of Plato, and his philosophy would be unthinkable apart from the work of his great predecessor.

3. Of the course of Platonism in the Academy and in the Neo-Platonic School I shall speak later. Through the Neo-Platonists

[1] Arist., Frag. 623. (Rose, 1870.)

Platonism made its influence felt on St. Augustine and on the formative period of mediaeval thought. Indeed, although St. Thomas Aquinas, the greatest of the Schoolmen, adopted Aristotle as "the Philosopher," there is much in his system that can be traced back ultimately to Plato rather than to Aristotle. Moreover, at the time of the Renaissance, the Platonic Academy of Florence endeavoured to renew the Platonic tradition, while the influence of the Platonic Republic may be seen in St. Thomas More's *Utopia* and Campanella's *City of the Sun*.

4. In regard to modern times, the influence of Plato may not be at first sight so obvious as it is in Antiquity and in the Middle Ages; but in reality he is the father or grandfather of all spiritualist philosophy and of all objective idealism, and his epistemology, metaphysics and politico-ethics have exercised a profound influence on succeeding thinkers, either positively or negatively. In the contemporary world we need only think of the inspiration that Plato has afforded to thinkers like Professor A. N. Whitehead or Professor Nicolai Hartmann of Berlin.

5. Plato, who stands at the head of European philosophy, left us no rounded system. That we do not possess his lectures and a complete record of his teaching in the Academy, we naturally regret, for we would like to know the solution of many problems that have puzzled commentators ever since; but, on the other hand, we may in a real sense be thankful that no cut and dried Platonic system (if ever there was such) has come down to us, a system to be swallowed whole or rejected, for this fact has enabled us to find in him, more easily perhaps than might otherwise be the case, a supreme example of the philosophic spirit. If he has not left us a complete system, Plato has indeed left us the example of a way of philosophising and the example of a life devoted to the pursuit of the true and the good.

CHAPTER XXVI

THE OLD ACADEMY

THE Platonic philosophy continued to exercise a profound influence throughout Antiquity; we must, however, distinguish various phases in the development of the Platonic School. The old Academy, which consisted of disciples and associates of Plato himself, held more or less to the dogmatic content of the Master's philosophy, though it is noticeable that it was the "Pythagorean" elements in the thought of Plato that received particular attention. In the Middle and New Academies an anti-dogmatic sceptical tendency is at first predominant, though it later gives way before a return to dogmatism of an eclectic type. This eclecticism is very apparent in Middle Platonism, which is succeeded at the close of the period of ancient philosophy by Neo-Platonism, an attempt at a complete synthesis of the original content of Platonism with those elements which had been introduced at various times, a synthesis in which those traits are stressed which are most in harmony with the general spirit of the time.

The Old Academy includes, together with men like Philippus of Opus, Heraclides Ponticus, Eudoxus of Cnidus, the following successors to Plato in the headship of the School at Athens: Speusippus (348/7–339/8), Xenocrates (339/8–315/4), Polemon (315/4–270/69) and Crates (270/69–265/4).

Speusippus, Plato's nephew and immediate successor as Scholarch, modified the Platonic dualism by abandoning the Ideas as distinct from τὰ μαθηματικά and making Reality to consist in mathematical numbers.[1] The Platonic Number-Ideas were thus dismissed, but the essential χωρισμός remained. By his admission of scientific perception (ἐπιστημονικὴ αἴσθησις) Speusippus is sometimes said to have given up the Platonic dualism of knowledge and perception,[2] but it must be remembered that Plato had himself gone some way towards admitting this, inasmuch as he allowed that λόγος and αἴσθησις co-operate in the apprehension of the atomic idea.

It is difficult to tell exactly what the members of the Old

[1] Frag. 42, a–g.

[2] So Praechter, p. 343.

Academy taught, since (unless Philippus of Opus wrote the *Epinomis*) no whole work of theirs has come down to us, and we have only the remarks of Aristotle and the testimony of other ancient writers to rely on. But apparently Speusippus held that substances proceed from the One and the absolute Many, and he placed the Good or τελεία ἕξις at the end of the process of becoming and not at the beginning, arguing from the development of plants and animals. Among the animate beings that proceed from the One is the invisible Reason or God,[1] which he probably also identified with the World-Soul. (Possibly this might afford an argument in favour of a "Neo-Platonic" interpretation of Plato.) As for human souls, these are immortal in their entirety. We may note that Speusippus interpreted the account of "creation" in the *Timaeus* as a mere form of exposition and not as meant to be an account of an actual creation in time: the world has no beginning in time. The traditional gods he interpreted as physical forces, and thus brought upon himself a charge of atheism.[2]

Xenocrates of Chalcedon, who succeeded Speusippus as Scholarch, identified the Ideas with mathematical numbers, and derived them from the One and the Indeterminate Duality (the former being Νοῦς or Zeus, the father of the gods, the latter being the feminine principle, the mother of the gods).[3] The World-Soul, produced by the addition of the Self and the Other to number, is a self-moved number. Distinguishing three worlds—the sublunar, the heavenly, and the super-celestial—Xenocrates filled all three worlds with "demons," both good and bad. This doctrine of evil demons enabled him to explain the popular myths, in which evil actions are ascribed to "gods," and the existence of immoral cults, by saying that the evil actions were the acts of evil demons, and that the immoral cults were directed to these demons and not to the gods.[4] In company with his predecessor, Xenocrates held that even the irrational parts of the soul (which was not created in time) survive after death, and, together with his successor, Polemon, he deprecated the consumption of flesh-meat on the ground that this might lead to the dominion of the irrational over the rational. Like Speusippus and Crantor (and in opposition to Aristotle), Xenocrates understood the priority of the simple over the composite in the *Timaeus* to be a logical and

[1] Frag. 38–9. [2] Cic., *De Nat. D.*, 1, 13, 32. [3] Frag. 34 ff. [4] Frag. 24 ff.

not a temporal priority.[1] (The Περὶ ἀτόμων γραμμῶν, attributed to Aristotle, was directed against Xenocrates' hypothesis of tiny invisible lines, which he employed as an aid in the deduction of dimensions from numbers.)

Heraclides Ponticus adopted from the Pythagorean Ecphantus the theory that the world is composed of particles which he called ἄναρμοι ὄγκοι, probably meaning that they are separated from one another by space. From these material particles the world was composed through the operation of God. The soul is therefore corporeal (consisting of aether, an element added to the others by Xenocrates). While asserting the diurnal revolution of the earth on its axis, Heraclides also held that Mercury and Venus revolve round the sun, and he seems to have suggested that the earth may do likewise.

One of the most celebrated mathematicians and astronomers of Antiquity is *Eudoxus* (*c.* 497–355 B.C.). Philosophically speaking, he is noteworthy for having held (*a*) that the Ideas are "mixed" with things,[2] and (*b*) that pleasure is the highest good.[3]

The first commentary on Plato's *Timaeus* was written by *Crantor* (*c.* 330–270), in which he interpreted the account of "creation" as a timeless and not as a temporal event. It is depicted as taking place in time simply for the purpose of logical schematism. In this interpretation Crantor was in accord, as we have seen, with both Speusippus and Xenocrates. In his Περὶ πένθους Crantor upheld the doctrine of the moderating of the passions (Metriopathy) in opposition to the Stoic ideal of Apathy.[4]

[1] Frag. 54. [2] *Metaph.*, A 9, 991 a 8–19. [3] *Eth. Nic.*, 1101 b 27 ff.; 1172 b 9 ff.
[4] Cic., *Acad.*, 2, 44, 135; *Tusc.*, 3, 6, 12.

PART IV

ARISTOTLE

CHAPTER XXVII

LIFE AND WRITINGS OF ARISTOTLE

ARISTOTLE was born in 384/3 B.C. at Stageira in Thrace, and was the son of Nicomachus, a physician of the Macedonian king, Amyntas II. When he was about seventeen years old Aristotle went to Athens for purposes of study and became a member of the Academy in 368/7 B.C., where for over twenty years he was in constant intercourse with Plato until the latter's death in 348/7 B.C. He thus entered the Academy at the time when Plato's later dialectic was being developed and the religious tendency was gaining ground in the great philosopher's mind. Probably already at this time Aristotle was giving attention to empirical science (i.e. at the time of Plato's death), and it may be that he had already departed from the Master's teaching on various points; but there can be no question of any radical break between Master and pupil as long as the former was still alive. It is impossible to suppose that Aristotle could have remained all that time in the Academy had he already taken up a radically different philosophical position to that of his Master. Moreover, even after Plato's death Aristotle still uses the first person plural of the representatives of the Platonic doctrine of Ideas, and soon after Plato's death Aristotle eulogises him as the man "whom bad men have not even the right to praise, and who showed in his life and teachings how to be happy and good at the same time."[1] The notion that Aristotle was in any real sense an opponent of Plato in the Academy and that he was a thorn in the side of the Master, is scarcely tenable: Aristotle found in Plato a guide and friend for whom he had the greatest admiration, and though in later years his own scientific interests tended to come much more to the fore, the metaphysical and religious teaching of Plato had a lasting influence upon him. Indeed, it was this side of Plato's teaching that would have perhaps a special

[1] Frag. 623. (Rose, *Aristotelis Fragmenta*. Berlin, 1870 edit.)

value for Aristotle, as offsetting his own bent towards empirical studies. "In fact, this myth of a cool, static, unchanging and purely critical Aristotle, without illusions, experiences, or history, breaks to pieces under the weight of the facts which up to now have been artificially suppressed for its sake."[1] As I shall briefly indicate, when considering Aristotle's writings, the Philosopher developed his own personal standpoint only gradually; and this is, after all, only what one would naturally expect.

After Plato's death Aristotle left Athens with Xenocrates (Speusippus, Plato's nephew, had become head of the Academy, and with him Aristotle did not see eye to eye; in any case he may not have wished to remain in the Academy in a subordinate position under its new head), and founded a branch of the Academy at Assos in the Troad. Here he influenced Hermias, ruler of Atarneus, and married his niece and adopted daughter, Pythias. While working at Assos, Aristotle no doubt began to develop his own independent views. Three years later he went to Mitylene in Lesbos, and it was there that he was probably in intercourse with Theophrastus, a native of Eresus on the same island, who was later the most celebrated disciple of Aristotle. (Hermias entered into negotiations with Philip of Macedon, who conceived the idea of an Hellenic defeat of the Persians. The Persian general, Mentor, got hold of Hermias by treachery and carried him off to Susa, where he was tortured but kept silence. His last message was: "Tell my friends and companions that I have done nothing weak or unworthy of philosophy." Aristotle published a poem in his honour.[2])

In 343/2 Aristotle was invited to Pella by Philip of Macedon to undertake the education of his son Alexander, then thirteen years old. This period at the court of Macedon and the endeavour to exercise a real moral influence on the young prince, who was later to play so prominent a part on the political stage and to go down to posterity as Alexander the Great, should have done much to widen Aristotle's horizon and to free him from the narrow conceptions of the ordinary Greek, though the effect does not seem to have been so great as might have been expected: Aristotle never ceased to share the Greek view of the City-State as the centre of life. When Alexander ascended the throne in 336/5, Aristotle left Macedon, his pedagogical activity being now presumably at an

[1] Werner Jaeger, *Aristotle. Fundamentals of the History of His Development*, p. 34. (Trans. R. Robinson. Clarendon Press, 1934.)

[2] Diog. Laërt. 5, 7 and 8.

end, and probably went for a time to Stageira, his native city, which Alexander rebuilt as payment of his debt to his teacher. After a time the connection between the philosopher and his pupil became weaker: Aristotle, though approving to a certain extent of Macedonian politics, did not approve of Alexander's tendency to regard Greeks and "barbarians" as on an equal footing. Moreover, in 327, Callisthenes, nephew of Aristotle, who had been taken into the service of Alexander on Aristotle's recommendation, was suspected of taking part in a conspiracy and was executed.

In 335/4 Aristotle had returned to Athens, where he founded his own School. Apart from the fact of his absence from Athens for some years, the development of his own ideas no doubt precluded any return to the Athenian Academy. The new School was in the north-east of the city, at the Lyceum, the precincts of Apollo Lyceus. The School was also known as the Περίπατος, and the members as οἱ Περιπατητικοί, from their custom of carrying on their discussions while walking up and down in the covered ambulatory or simply because much of the instruction was given in the ambulatory. The School was dedicated to the Muses. Besides educational and tuitional work the Lyceum seems to have had, in a more prominent way than the Academy, the character of a union or society in which mature thinkers carried on their studies and research: it was in effect a university or scientific institute, equipped with library and teachers, in which lectures were regularly given.

In 323 B.C. Alexander the Great died, and the reaction in Greece against Macedonian suzerainty led to a charge of ἀσέβεια against Aristotle, who had been so closely connected with the great leader in his younger days. Aristotle withdrew from Athens (lest the Athenians should sin against philosophy for the second time, he is reported to have said) and went to Chalcis in Euboea, where he lived on an estate of his dead mother. Shortly afterwards, in 322/1 B.C., he died of an illness.

The Works of Aristotle

The writings of Aristotle fall into three main periods, (i) the period of his intercourse with Plato; (ii) the years of his activity at Assos and Mitylene; (iii) the time of his headship of the Lyceum at Athens. The works fall also into two groups or kinds, (i) the exoteric works—ἐξωτερικοί, ἐκδεδομένοι λόγοι—which were written for the most part in dialogue form and intended for general publication; and (ii) the pedagogical works—ἀκροαματικοὶ λόγοι, ὑπομνήματα, πραγματεῖα—which formed the basis of Aristotle's lectures in the Lyceum. The former exist only in fragments, but of the latter kind we possess a large number. These pedagogical works were first made known to the public in the edition of Andronicus of Rhodes (*c.* 60–50 B.C.), and it is these works which have earned for Aristotle a reputation for baldness of style unembellished by literary graces. It has been pointed out that, though a great inventor of philosophical terms, Aristotle was neglectful of style and of verbal beauty, while his interest in philosophy was too serious to admit of his employing metaphor instead of clear reason or of relapsing into myth. Now, this is true of the pedagogical works—that they lack the literary graces, but it is also true that the works which Aristotle himself published, and of which we possess only fragments, did not disdain the literary graces: their fluent style was praised by Cicero,[1] and even myths were occasionally introduced. They do, however, represent Aristotle's earlier work, when he was under direct Platonic influence or working his way towards his own independent position.

(i) In Aristotle's *first period* of literary activity he may be said to have adhered closely to Plato, his teacher, both in content and, in general at least, in form, though in the Dialogues Aristotle seems to have appeared himself as the leader of the conversation. "*. . . sermo ita inducitur ceterorum, ut penes ipsum sit principatus.*" (So Cic. *Ad Att.* 13, 19, 4.) It is most probable that in the Dialogues Aristotle held the Platonic philosophy, and only later changed his mind. Plutarch speaks of Aristotle as changing his mind (μετατίθεσθαι).[2] Moreover, Cephisodorus, pupil of Isocrates, saddles Aristotle with Plato's theories, e.g. concerning the Ideas.[3]

(*a*) To this period belongs the dialogue of *Eudemus*, or *On the Soul*, in which Aristotle shares Plato's doctrine of recollection and the apprehension of the Ideas in a state of pre-existence, and is in general dominated by the Master's influence. Aristotle argues for the immortality of the soul on lines suggested by the *Phaedo*—the soul is not a mere harmony of the body. Harmony has a contrary, namely, disharmony. But the soul has no contrary. Therefore the soul is not a harmony.[4] Aristotle supposes

[1] Cf. *De Orat.*, I, xi, 49.
[2] *De virt. mor.*, c. 7.
[3] Euseb. *Prep. Evang.*, XIV, 6, following Numenius.
[4] Frag. 41. (Rose.)

pre-existence and the substantiality of the soul—also Forms. Just as men who fall ill may lose their memories, so the soul, on entering this life, forgets the state of pre-existence; but just as those who recover health after sickness remember their suffering, so the soul after death remembers this life. Life apart from the body is the soul's normal state (κατὰ φύσιν); its inhabitation of the body is really a severe illness.[1] This is a very different view from that afterwards put forward by Aristotle when he had taken up his own independent position.

(*b*) The *Protrepticus* also belongs to this period of Aristotle's development. This appears to have been an epistle to Themison of Cyprus and not a dialogue. In this work the Platonic doctrine of Forms is maintained, and the philosopher is depicted as one who contemplates these Forms or Ideas and not the imitations of them (αὐτῶν γὰρ ἐστι θεατής ἀλλ' οὐ μιμημάτων).[2] Again Phronesis retains the Platonic signification, denoting metaphysical speculation, and so having a theoretical meaning and not the purely practical significance of the *Nicomachean Ethics*. In the *Protrepticus* Aristotle also emphasises the worthlessness of earthly goods, and depicts this life as the death or tomb of the soul, which enters into true and higher life only through bodily death. This view certainly indicates direct Platonic influence, for in the *Nicomachean Ethics* Aristotle insists on the necessity of earthly goods, in some degree at least, for the truly happy life, and so even for the philosopher.

(*c*) It is probable that the oldest parts of the Logical Works, of the *Physics*, and perhaps also of the *De Anima* (book Γ) date back to this period. Thus if a preliminary sketch of the *Metaphysics* (including book A) dates back to Aristotle's *second* period, it is to be supposed that *Physics* (book 2) dates back to his *first* period, since in the first book of the *Metaphysics* there is a reference to the *Physics*, or at least the setting-out of the theory of the causes is presupposed.[3] It is probable that the *Physics* fall into two groups of monographs, and the first two books and book 7 are to be ascribed to the earliest period of Aristotle's literary activity.

(ii) In his *second period* Aristotle began to diverge from his former predominantly Platonic position and to adopt a more

[1] Frag. 35. (Rose.)
[2] Iambl., *Protr.*, assuming that chapters 6–12 of Iamblichus' work consist of passages from Aristotle's *Protrepticus*. (Cf. Jaeger, *Aristotle*, pp. 60 ff.)
[3] *Metaph.*, A, 983 a 33–4.

critical attitude towards the teaching of the Academy. He still looked on himself as an Academician apparently, but it is the period of criticism or of growing criticism in regard to Platonism. The period is represented by the dialogue *On Philosophy*, Περὶ φιλοσοφίας, a work which combines clear Platonic influence with a criticism of some of Plato's most characteristic theories. Thus although Aristotle represents Plato as the culmination of previous philosophy (and indeed as regards pre-Aristotelian philosophy, Aristotle always held this idea), he criticises the Platonic theory of Forms or Ideas, at least under its later form of development at Plato's hands. "If the Ideas were another kind of number, and not the mathematical, we should have no understanding of it. For who understands another kind of number, at any rate among the majority of us?"[1] Similarly, although Aristotle adopts more or less Plato's stellar theology, the concept of the Unmoved Mover makes its appearance,[2] though Aristotle has not yet adopted the multitudinous movers of his later metaphysics. He applies the term visible god—τοσοῦτον ὁρατὸν θεόν—to the Cosmos or Heaven, a term which is of Platonic derivation.

It is interesting that the argument for the existence of the Divine drawn from the gradations of perfections is found in this dialogue. "In general, wherever there is a better there is also a best. Now, since among the things that are one is better than another, there is also a best thing, and this would be the divine." Aristotle supposes apparently the gradation of real forms.[3] The subjective belief in God's existence is derived by Aristotle from the soul's experience of ecstasies and prophecies in e.g. the state of sleep, and from the sight of the starry heavens, though such recognition of occult phenomena is really foreign to Aristotle's later development.[4] In this dialogue, then, Aristotle combines elements that can have no other source than Plato and his circle with elements of criticism of the Platonic philosophy, as when he criticises the Platonic theory of Ideas or the doctrine of "creation" as given in the *Timaeus*, asserting the eternity of the world.[5]

It appears that a first sketch of the *Metaphysics* goes back

[1] Frag. 11. (Rose.)

[2] Frag. 21. (Rose.) It must be admitted that this fragment implies that Aristotle had not yet definitely stated the existence of the First Mover or broken with his former views.

[3] Frag. 15. (Rose.) Professor Jaeger thinks that the dialogue contained also the proofs from motion and causality.

[4] Frags. 12 and 14. (Rose.) Cf. *Laws*, 966 d 9–967 a 5.

[5] Cf. Frag. 17. (Rose.)

to this second period in Aristotle's development, the period of transition. This would comprise Book A (the use of the term "we" denoting the transitional period), Book B, Book K, 1–8, Book Λ (except C 8), Book M, 9–10, Book N. According to Jaeger the attack in the original *Metaphysics* was directed mainly against Speusippus.[1]

The *Eudemian Ethics* are sometimes thought to belong to this period, and to date from Aristotle's sojourn at Assos. Aristotle still holds to the Platonic conception of Phronesis, though the object of philosophic contemplation is no longer the Ideal World of Plato but the transcendent God of the *Metaphysics*.[2] It is also probable that an original *Politics* dates from this second period, including Books 2, 3, 7, 8, which deal with the Ideal State. Utopias on the style of the Platonic Republic are criticised by Aristotle.

The writings *De Caelo* and *De Generatione et Corruptione* (Περὶ οὐρανοῦ and Περὶ γενέσεως καὶ φθορᾶς) are also ascribed to this period with probability.

(iii) Aristotle's *Third Period* (335–322) is that of his activity in the Lyceum. It is in this period that there appears Aristotle the empirical observer and scientist, who is yet concerned to raise a sure philosophical building upon a firm foundation sunk deep in the earth. We cannot but marvel at the power of organising detailed research in the provinces of nature and history that is shown by Aristotle in this last period of his life. There had, indeed, been in the Academy a practice of classification, mainly for logical purposes, that involved a certain amount of empirical observation, but there was nothing of the sustained and systematic investigation into details of nature and history that the Lyceum carried out under the direction of Aristotle. This spirit of exact research into the phenomena of nature and history really represents something new in the Greek world, and the credit for it must undoubtedly go to Aristotle. But it will not do to represent Aristotle as merely a Positivist in the last phase of his life, as is sometimes done, for there is really no evidence to show that he ever abandoned metaphysics, in spite of all his interest in exact, scientific research.

Aristotle's lectures in the School formed the basis of his "pedagogical" works, which were circulated among the members of the School, and were, as already mentioned, first given to the

[1] Jaeger, *Aristotle*, p. 192. [2] Cf. *Eud. Eth.*, 1249 b.

public by Andronicus of Rhodes. Most of the pedagogical works belong to this period, except, of course, those portions of works which are probably to be ascribed to an earlier phase. These pedagogical works have offered many difficulties to scholars, e.g. because of the unsatisfactory connections between books, sections that appear to break the logical succession of thought, and so on. It now appears probable that these works represent lectures of Aristotle which were equivalently published—so far as the School was concerned—by being given as lectures. But this does not imply that each work represents a single lecture or a continuous course of lectures: rather are they different sections or lectures which were later put together and given an external unity by means of a common title. This work of composition can have been only in part accomplished by Aristotle himself: it continued in the following generations of the School and was first completed by Andronicus of Rhodes, if not later.

These works of Aristotle's third period may be divided into:

(*a*) *Logical Works* (combined in Byzantine times as the *Organon*). The *Categories* or κατηγορίαι (Aristotelian in content at least), the *De Interpretatione* or Περὶ ἑρμενείας (on proposition and judgment), the *Prior Analytics* or Ἀναλυτικὰ Πρότερα (two books on inference), the *Posterior Analytics* or Ἀναλυτικὰ ὕστερα (two books on proof, knowledge of principles, etc.), the *Topics* or Τοπικά (eight books on dialectic or probable proof), the Sophistical Fallacies or Περὶ σοφιστικῶν ἐλέγκων.

(*b*) *Metaphysical Works.*
The *Metaphysics*, a collection of lectures of different dates, so called from its position in the Aristotelian Corpus, probably by a Peripatetic before the time of Andronicus.

(*c*) Works on Natural Philosophy, Natural Science, Psychology, etc. The *Physics* or φυσικὴ ἀκρόασις or φυσικά or τὰ περὶ φύσεως. This work consists of eight books, of which the first two must be referred to Aristotle's Platonic period. *Metaphysics* A 983 a 32–3 refers to the *Physics*, or rather presupposes explicitly the setting-out of the theory of causes in *Physics* 2. Book 7 of the *Physics* probably belongs also to the earlier work of Aristotle, while Book 8 is really not part of the *Physics* at all, since it quotes the *Physics*, with the remark "as we have previously shown in the *Physics*."[1] The total work would then appear to have consisted originally of a

[1] *Physics*, VIII, 251 a 9, 253 b 8, 267 b 21.

number of independent monographs, a supposition borne out by the fact that the *Metaphysics* quotes as "Physics" the two works *De Caelo* and *De Generatione et Corruptione.*[1]

The *Meteorology* or Μετεωρολογικά or Περὶ μετεώρων (four books).

The *Histories of Animals* or Περὶ τὰ ζῷα ἱστορίαι (ten books on comparative anatomy and physiology, of which the last is probably post-Aristotelian).

The Ἀνατομαί in seven books, which is lost.

The *De Incessu Animalium* or Περὶ ζῴων πορείας (one book) and the *De Motu Animalium* or Περὶ ζῴων κινήσεως (one book).

The *De Generatione Animalium* or Περὶ ζῴων γενέσεως (five books).

The *De Anima* or Περὶ ψυχῆς, Aristotle's Psychology in three books.

The *Parva Naturalia*, a number of smaller treatises dealing with such subjects as perception (Περὶ αἰσθήσεως καὶ αἰσθητῶν), memory (Περὶ μνήμης καὶ ἀναμνήσεως), sleep and waking (Περὶ ὕπνου καί ἐγρηγόρσεως), dreams (Περὶ ἐνυπνίων), long life and short life (Περὶ μακροβιότητος καὶ βραχυβιότητος), life and death (Περὶ ζωῆς καὶ θανάτου, breathing (Περὶ ἀναπνοῆς), divination in sleep (Περὶ τῆς καθ' ὕπνον μαντικῆς).

The *Problemata* (Προβλήματα) seems to be a collection of problems, gradually formed, which grew up round a nucleus of notes or jottings made by Aristotle himself.

(*d*) *Works on Ethics and Politics.*

The *Magna Moralia* or Ἠθικὰ μεγάλα, in two books, which would seem to be a genuine work of Aristotle, at least so far as the content is concerned.[2] Part would appear to date from a time when Aristotle was still more or less in agreement with Plato.

The *Nicomachean Ethics* (Ἠθικὰ Νικομάχεια) in ten books, a work which was edited by Aristotle's son Nicomachus after the philosopher's death.

The *Politics* (Πολιτικά), of which books 2, 3, 7, 8, would appear to date from the second period of Aristotle's literary activity. Books 4–6 were, thinks Jaeger, inserted before the first book was prefixed to the whole, for Book 4 refers to 3 as the beginning of the work—'εν τοῖς πρώτοις λόγοις. "The contents of 2 are merely negative."[3]

[1] *Metaph.*, 989 a 24.

[2] Cf. H. von Arnim, *Die drei arist. Ethiken.* (Sitz. Wien. Ak, 2 Abl., 1924.)

[3] Jaeger, *Aristotle*, p. 273.

Collection of Constitutions of 158 States. That of Athens was found in papyrus in 1891.

(*e*) *Works on Aesthetics, History and Literature.*

The *Rhetoric* (Τέχνη ῥητορική) in three books.

The *Poetics* (Περὶ ποιητικῆς), which is incomplete, part having been lost.

Records of dramatic performances at Athens, collection of Didascalia, list of victors at Olympic and Pythian games. Aristotle was engaged on a work concerning the Homeric problem, a treatise on the territorial rights of States (Περὶ τῶν τόπων δικαιώματα πόλεων), etc.

There is no need to suppose that all these works, for example the collection of the 158 Constitutions, were by Aristotle himself, but they would have been initiated by him and carried out under his superintendence. He entrusted others with the compilation of a history of natural philosophy (Theophrastus), of mathematics and astronomy (Eudemus of Rhodes), and medicine (Meno). One can but marvel at the catholicity of his interests and the scope of his aims.

The mere list of Aristotle's works shows a rather different spirit to that of Plato, for it is obvious that Aristotle was drawn towards the empirical and scientific, and that he did not tend to treat the objects of this world as semi-illusory or as unfitted to be objects of knowledge. But this difference in tendency, a difference which was no doubt accentuated as time went on, has, when coupled with consideration of such facts as the Aristotelian opposition to the Platonic theory of Ideas and to the Platonic dualistic psychology, led to the popular conception of a radical contrast between the two great philosophers. There is, of course, truth in this view, since there are clear cases of opposition between their tenets and also a general difference in atmosphere (at least if we compare Plato's exoteric works—and we have no other—with Aristotle's pedagogical works), but it can easily be exaggerated. Aristotelianism, historically speaking, is not the opposite of Platonism, but its development, correcting one-sided theories—or trying to do so—such as the theory of Ideas, the dualistic psychology of Plato, etc., and supplying a firmer foundation in physical fact. That something of value was omitted at the same time is true, but that simply shows that the two philosophies should not be considered as two diametrically opposed systems, but as two complementary philosophical spirits and bodies of doctrine. A synthesis was later attempted in Neo-Platonism, and mediaeval philosophy shows the same synthetic spirit. St. Thomas, for instance, though speaking of Aristotle as "the Philosopher," could not, and would not have wished to, cut himself off entirely from the Platonic tradition, while in the Franciscan School even St. Bonaventure, who awarded the palm to Plato, did not disdain to make use of Peripatetic doctrines, and Duns Scotus carried much further the impregnation of the Franciscan spirit with Aristotelian elements.

And it should not be supposed that Aristotle, in his enthusiasm for facts and his desire to set a firm empirical and scientific foundation, was lacking in systematic power or ever renounced his metaphysical interest. Both Platonism and Aristotelianism culminate in metaphysics. Thus Goethe can compare Aristotle's philosophy to a pyramid rising on high in regular form from a broad basis on the earth, and that of Plato to an obelisk or a tongue of flame which shoots up to heaven. Nevertheless, I must admit that, in my opinion, the direction of Aristotle's thought was increasingly directed away from the Platonic position to which he at first adhered, while the results of his new orientation of thought do not always combine harmoniously with those elements of the Platonic legacy which he seems to have retained to the last.

CHAPTER XXVIII

LOGIC OF ARISTOTLE

1. ALTHOUGH Aristotle divides philosophy systematically in different ways on different occasions,[1] we may say that the following is his considered view of the matter.[2] (i) *Theoretical* Philosophy,[3] in which knowledge as such is the end in view and not any practical purpose, is divided into (*a*) Physics or Natural Philosophy, which has to do with material things which are subject to motion; (*b*) Mathematics, which has to do with the unmoved but unseparated (from matter); (*c*) Metaphysics, which has to do with the separated (transcendent) and unmoved. (Metaphysics would thus include what we know as Natural Theology.[4]) (ii) *Practical* Philosophy (πρακτική) deals principally with Political Science, but has as subsidiary disciplines Strategy, Economics and Rhetoric, since the ends envisaged by these disciplines are subsidiary to and depend on that of Political Science.[5] (iii) *Poetical* Philosophy (ποιητική) has to do with production and not with action as such, as in the case with Practical Philosophy (which includes ethical action in the wider or political sense), and is to all intents and purposes the Theory of Art.[6]

2. The Aristotelian Logic is often termed "formal" logic. Inasmuch as the Logic of Aristotle is an analysis of the forms of thought (hence the term *Analytic*), this is an apt characterisation; but it would be a very great mistake to suppose that for Aristotle logic concerns the forms of human thinking in such an exclusive way that it has no connection with external reality. He is chiefly concerned with the forms of proof, and he assumes that the conclusion of a scientific proof gives certain knowledge concerning reality. For example, in the syllogism "All men are mortal, Socrates is a man, therefore Socrates is mortal," it is not merely that the conclusion is deduced correctly according to the

[1] Cf. *Top.*, A 14, 105 b 19 ff.

[2] Cf. *Top.*, Z 6, 145 a 15 ff. *Metaph.*, E 1, 1025 b 25.

[3] Cf. *Metaph.*, K 7, 1064 b 1 ff.

[4] Cf. *Metaph.*, E 1, 1026 a 10 ff.

[5] Cf. *Eth. Nic.*, A 1, 1094 a 18 ff.

[6] Determining the rank of the branches of philosophy according to the rank of their object, Aristotle gives the palm to "Theology." Cf. *Metaph.*, K 7, 1064 b 1 ff. It has been argued that the threefold division has no adequate warrant in Aristotle's own words and that he conceived the *Poetics*, not as a philosophical aesthetic theory, but simply as a practical manual.

formal laws of logic: Aristotle assumes that the conclusion is verified in reality. He presupposes, therefore, a realist theory of knowledge and for him logic, though an analysis of the forms of thought, is an analysis of the thought that thinks reality, that reproduces it conceptually within itself, and, in the true judgment, makes statements about reality which are verified in the external world. It is an analysis of human thought in its thought about reality, though Aristotle certainly admits that things do not always exist in extramental reality precisely as they are conceived by the mind, e.g. the universal.

This may be clearly seen in his doctrine of the Categories. From the logical viewpoint the Categories comprise the ways in which we think about things—for instance, predicating qualities of substances—but at the same time they are ways in which things actually exist: things are substances and actually have accidents. The Categories demand, therefore, not only a logical but also a metaphysical treatment. Aristotle's Logic, then, must not be likened to the Transcendental Logic of Kant, since it is not concerned to isolate *a priori* forms of thought which are contributed by the mind alone in its active process of knowledge. Aristotle does not raise the "Critical Problem": he assumes a realist epistemology, and assumes that the categories of thought, which we express in language, are also the objective categories of extramental reality.

3. In the *Categories* and in the *Topics* the number of Categories or Praedicamenta is given as ten: οὐσία or τί ἐστι (man or horse); ποσόν (three yards long;) ποιόν (white); πρός τι (double); ποῦ (in the market-place); πότε (last year); κεῖσθαι (lies, sits); ἔχειν (armed, with shoes); ποιεῖν (cuts); πάσχειν (is cut or burnt). But in the *Posterior Analytics* they appear as eight, κεῖσθαι or *Situs* and ἔχειν or *Habitus* being subsumed under the other categories.[1] Aristotle, therefore, can hardly have looked upon the deduction of the Categories as definitive. Nevertheless, even if the tenfold division of the Categories was not looked upon as definitive by Aristotle, there is no reason to suppose that he regarded the list of Categories as a haphazard list, devoid of structural arrangement. On the contrary, the list of the Categories constitutes an orderly arrangement, a classification of concepts, the fundamental types of concepts governing our scientific knowledge. The word κατηγορεῖν means to predicate, and in the *Topics* Aristotle considers

[1] Cf. e.g. *Anal. Post.*, A 22, 83 a 21 ff., b 15 ff.

the Categories as a classification of predicates, the ways in which we think of being as realised. For example, we think of an object either as a substance or as a determination of substance, as falling under one of the nine categories that express the way in which we think of substance as being determined. In the *Categories* Aristotle considers the Categories rather as the classification of genera, species and individuals from the *summa genera* down to individual entities. If we examine our concepts, the ways in which we represent things mentally, we shall find, for example, that we have concepts of organic bodies, of animals (a subordinate genus), of sheep (a species of animal); but organic bodies, animals, sheep, are all included in the category of substance. Similarly, we may think of colour in general, of blueness in general, of cobalt; but colour, blueness, cobalt, all fall under the category of quality.

The Categories, however, were not in Aristotle's mind simply modes of mental representation, moulds of concepts: they represent the actual modes of being in the extramental world, and form the bridge between Logic and Metaphysics (which latter science has Substance as its chief subject).[1] They have, therefore, an ontological as well as a logical aspect, and it is perhaps in their ontological aspect that their orderly and structural arrangement appears most clearly. Thus, in order that being may exist, substance must exist: that is, as it were, the starting-point. Only singulars actually exist outside the mind, and for a singular to exist independently in this way it must be a substance. But it cannot exist merely as a substance, it must have accidental forms. For instance, a swan cannot exist unless it has some colour, while it cannot have colour unless it has quantity, extension. At once, then, we have the first three Categories—substance, quantity, quality, which are intrinsic determinations of the object. But the swan is the same in specific nature as other swans, is equal in size or unequal in size to other substances; in other words, it stands in some relation to other objects. Moreover, the swan as a physical substance, must exist in a certain *place* and at a certain *period*, must have a certain *posture*. Again, material substances, as belonging to a cosmic system, *act* and are *acted upon*. Thus some of the Categories belong to the object considered in itself, as its *intrinsic* determinations, while others belong to it as *extrinsic* determinations, affecting it as standing in relation to other material objects. It will be seen, therefore, that even if the

[1] *Metaph.*, 1017 a 23–4. ὁσαχῶς γὰρ λέγεται, τοσαταυχῶς τὸ εἶναι σημαίνει.

number of the Categories could be reduced by subsuming certain Categories under others, the principle whereby the Categories are deduced is by no means merely a haphazard principle.

In the *Posterior Analytics* (in connection with definition) and in the *Topics*, Aristotle discusses the ***Predicables*** or various relations in which universal terms may stand to the subjects of which they are predicated. They are ***genus*** (γένος), ***species*** (εἶδος), ***difference*** (διαφορά), ***property*** (ἴδιον), ***accident*** (συμβεβηκός). In the *Topics* (I, c. 8), Aristotle bases his division of the predicables on the relations between subject and predicate. Thus if the predicate is co-extensive with the subject, it either gives us the essence of the subject or a property of the subject; while if it is not co-extensive with the subject, it either forms part of the attributes comprised in the definition of the subject (when it will be either a genus or a difference) or it does not do so (in which case it will be an accident).

Essential definitions are strict definitions by genus and difference, and Aristotle considered definition as involving a process of division down to the ***infimae species*** (cf. Plato).[1] But it is important to remember that Aristotle, aware that we are by no means always able to attain an essential or real definition, allows for nominal or descriptive definitions,[2] even though he had no high opinion of them, regarding as he did essential definitions as the only type of definition really worthy of the name. The distinction, however, is of importance, since in point of fact, we have to be content, in regard to the natural objects studied by physical science, with distinctive or characteristic definitions, which even if they approach the ideal more closely than Aristotle's nominal or descriptive definition, do not actually attain it.

(Some writers have emphasised the influence of language on philosophy. For instance, because we speak of the rose as being red (and this is necessary for purposes of social life and communication), we are naturally inclined to think that in the actual objective order there is a quality or accident, "redness," which inheres in a thing or substance, the rose. The philosophical categories of substance and accident can thus be traced back to the influence of words, of language. But it should be remembered that language follows thought, is built up as an expression of thought, and this is especially true of philosophical terms. When Aristotle laid down the ways in which the mind thinks about

[1] *Anal. Post.*, B 13. [2] *Anal. Post.*, B 8 and 10.

things, it is true that he could not get away from language as the medium of thought, but the language follows thought and thought follows things. Language is not an *a priori* construction.)

4. Scientific knowledge *par excellence* means for Aristotle, deducing the particular from the general or the conditioned from its cause, so that we know both the cause on which the fact depends and the necessary connection between the fact and its cause. In other words, we have scientific knowledge when we know the cause on which the fact depends, as the cause of that fact and of no other, and further, that the fact could not be other than it is."[1]

But though the premisses are prior to the conclusion from the logical viewpoint, Aristotle clearly recognises that there is a difference between logical priority or priority *in se* and epistemological priority *quoad nos*. He expressly states that " 'prior' and 'better known' are ambiguous terms, for there is a difference between what is prior and better known in the order of being and what is prior and better known to man. I mean that objects nearer to sense are prior and better known to man; objects without qualification prior and better known are those further from sense."[2] In other words, our knowledge starts from sense, i.e. from the particular, and ascends to the general or universal. "Thus it is clear that we must get to know the primary premisses by induction; for the methods by which even sense-perception implants the universal is inductive."[3] Aristotle is thus compelled to treat not only of deduction, but also of induction. For instance, in the aforementioned syllogism the major premiss, "All men are mortal," is founded on sense-perception, and Aristotle has to justify both sense-perception and memory, since both are involved. Hence we have the doctrine that the senses *as such* never err: it is only the judgment which is true or false.

Thus if a patient who is suffering from *delirium tremens* "sees" pink rats, the senses as such do not err; error arises when the patient judges that the pink rats are "out there," as real extramentally-existing objects. Similarly, the sun *appears* smaller than the earth, but this is not an error on the part of the senses; indeed if the sun appeared as *larger* than the earth, the senses would be out of order. Error arises when, through a lack of

[1] *Anal. Post.*, I 2, 71 b.
[2] *Anal. Post.*, 71 b–72 a.
[3] *Anal. Post.*, II 19, 100 b.

astronomical knowledge, a man *judges* that the sun is objectively smaller than the earth.

5. In the *Analytics*, therefore, Aristotle treats, not only of scientific proof, demonstration or deduction, but also of induction (ἐπαγωγή). Scientific induction means for him *complete* induction, and he expressly states that "induction proceeds through an enumeration of all the cases."[1] *Incomplete* induction is of use especially to the orator. Aristotle used experiment but did not elaborate a scientific methodology of induction and the use of hypothesis. Although he admits that "syllogism through induction is clearer to us,"[2] his ideal remains that of deduction, of syllogistic demonstration. The analysis of deductive processes he carried to a very high level and very completely; but he cannot be said to have done the same for induction. This was no doubt only natural in the Ancient World, where mathematics was so much more highly developed than natural science. Nevertheless, after stating that sense-perception as such cannot attain the universal, Aristotle points out that we may observe groups of singulars or watch the frequent recurrence of an event, and so, by the use of the abstract reason, attain to knowledge of a universal essence or principle.[3]

6. In the *Prior Analytics* Aristotle inquires into the forms of inference, and he defines the syllogism as "discourse in which certain things being stated, something other than what is stated follows of necessity from their being so."[4] He discusses the three figures of the syllogism, etc.:

(i) The Middle Term is Subject in one premiss and Predicate in the other. Thus: M is P, S is M, therefore S is P. Every animal is a substance. Every man is an animal. Therefore every man is a substance.

(ii) The Middle Term is Predicate in both premisses. P is M, S is not M, therefore S is not P.
Every man is risible. But no horse is risible. Therefore no horse is a man.

(iii) The Middle Term is Subject in both premisses. Thus: M is P, M is S, therefore S is P.
Every man is risible. But every man is an animal. Therefore some animals are risible.

In the *Topics*[5] Aristotle distinguishes *demonstrative* reasoning

[1] *Anal. Priora*, II 23, 68 b. [2] *Anal. Priora*, II, 23, 68 b. [3] *Anal. Post.*, I, 31.
[4] *Anal. Priora*, I, 1, 24 b. [5] I, 100 a b.

(i.e. "when the premisses from which the reasoning starts are true and primary, or are such that our knowledge of them has originally come through premisses which are primary and true") from *dialectical* reasoning (i.e. reasoning "from opinions that are generally accepted," i.e. "by all, or by the majority, or by the most notable and illustrious of them"). He adds a third kind of reasoning, eristic or "contentious" reasoning (which "starts from opinions that seem to be generally accepted, but are not really such"). This third is dealt with at length in the *De Sophisticis Elenchis*, where Aristotle examines, classifies and solves the various kinds of fallacy.

7. Aristotle saw clearly that the premisses in deduction themselves need proof, while on the other hand if *every* principle needs proof, we shall be involved in a *processus in infinitum* and *nothing* will be proved. He held, therefore, that there are certain principles which are known intuitively and immediately without demonstration.[1] The highest of these principles is the *principle of contradiction.* Of these principles no proof can be given. For example, the logical form of the principle of contradiction—"Of two propositions, one of which affirms something and the other denies the same thing, one must be true and the other false"—is not a proof of the principle in its metaphysical form—e.g. "The same thing cannot be an attribute and not an attribute of the same subject at the same time and in the same way." It simply exhibits the fact that no thinker can question the principle which lies at the basis of all thinking and is presupposed.[2]

We have, therefore, (i) first principles, perceived by νοῦς; (ii) what is derived necessarily from first principles, perceived by ἐπιστήμη; and (iii) what is contingent and could be otherwise, the subject of δόξα. But Aristotle saw that the major premiss of a syllogism, e.g. All men are mortal, cannot be derived immediately from the first principles: it depends also on induction. This involves a realist theory of universals, and Aristotle declares that induction exhibits the universal as implicit in the clearly known particular.[3]

8. In a book of this nature it would scarcely be desirable to enter upon a detailed exposition and discussion of the Aristotelian logic, but it is necessary to emphasise the very great contribution that Aristotle made to human thought in this branch of science,

[1] Cf. *Anal. Post.*, I 3, 72 b.
[2] Cf. *Metaph.*, 1005 b 35 ff.
[3] *Anal. Post.*, A 1, 71 a.

especially in regard to the syllogism. That logical analysis and division had been pursued in the Academy, in connection with the theory of Forms, is quite true (one has only to think of the discussions in the *Sophist*); but it was Aristotle who first constituted logic ("Analytics") as a separate science, and it was Aristotle who discovered, isolated and analysed the fundamental form of inference, namely, the syllogism. This is one of his lasting achievements, and even if it were his only positive achievement, it would still be one for which his name would rightly be held in lasting memory. One could not justifiably assert that Aristotle made a complete analysis of all deductive processes, for the classical syllogism supposes (i) three propositions, each in subject and predicate form; (ii) three terms, from which each proposition takes both subject and predicate, and, given this situation, determines the cases in which two of the propositions entail the third in virtue, either (*a*) of logical form only, or (*b*) of an adjoined existence assertion, as with *Darapti*. Aristotle, for instance, did not consider that other form of inference discussed by Cardinal Newman in his *Grammar of Assent*, when the mind derives conclusions, not from certain propositions but from certain concrete facts. The mind considers these facts and, after forming a critical estimate of them, infers a conclusion, which is not a general proposition (as in induction proper), but a particular conclusion such as, e.g. "The prisoner is innocent." It is certainly true that general propositions are implied (e.g. evidence of a certain type is compatible, or incompatible, with the innocence of an accused man), but the mind is not actually concerned to elicit the implication of presupposed propositions so much as to elicit the implications of a number of concrete facts. St. Thomas Aquinas recognised this type of reasoning, and attributed it to the *vis cogitativa*, also called *ratio particularis*.[1] Moreover, even in regard to that form of inference which Aristotle analysed, he did not really consider the question, whether these general principles from which it starts are simply formal principles or have ontological import. The latter view seems to be assumed for the most part.

But it would be absurd to criticise Aristotle adversely for not having made a complete study of all the forms of inference, and for not having clearly raised and solved all the questions that might be raised in connection with the forms of human thought:

[1] Ia, 78, 4. Cf. IIa, IIae, 2, 1.

the task that he did undertake to accomplish, he accomplished very well, and the group of his logical treatises (later termed the *Organon*) constitute a masterpiece of the human mind. It is not without reason, we may be sure, that Aristotle represents himself as being a pioneer in logical analysis and systematisation. At the close of the *De Sophisticis Elenchis* he remarks, that while much had been said by others before him on the subject of Rhetoric, for instance, he had no anterior work to speak of on the subject of reasoning, which he might have used as a foundation, but was compelled to break what was practically new ground. It was not the case that systematic analysis of the reasoning-processes had been already completed in part: nothing at all existed in this line. The professors of rhetoric had given their pupils an empirical training in "contentious arguments," but they never worked out a scientific methodology or a systematic exposition of the subject: he had had to start from the beginning by himself. Aristotle's claim in reference to the particular subject-matter of the *De Sophisticis Elenchis* is doubtless substantially just in regard to the discovery and analysis of the syllogism in general.

Occasionally one hears people speak as though modern logical studies had deprived the traditional Aristotelian logic of all value, as though one could now relegate the traditional logic to the lumber-room of museum pieces, of interest only to the philosophical antiquarian. On the other hand, those who have been brought up according to the Aristotelian tradition may be tempted to display a mistaken loyalty to that tradition by attacking, e.g. modern symbolic logic. Either extreme is in fact unwarranted, and it is necessary to adopt a sane and balanced position, recognising indeed the incompleteness of the Aristotelian logic and the value of modern logic, but at the same time refusing to discredit the Aristotelian logic on the ground that it does not cover the whole province of logic. This sane and balanced position is the position maintained by those who have made a deep study of logic, a point that needs to be emphasised lest it be thought that it is only Scholastic philosophers, speaking *pro domo sua*, who in the present age still attach any value to the logic of Aristotle. Thus, while affirming, and rightly affirming, that "it is no longer possible to regard it as constituting the whole subject of deduction," Susan Stebbing admits that "the traditional syllogism retains its value";[1] while Heinrich Scholz declares that "the

[1] Susan Stebbing, *A Modern Introd. to Logic*, p. 102. (London, 1933.)

Aristotelian *Organon* is to-day still the most beautiful and instructive introduction to logic ever written by man."[1] Modern symbolic logic may be an addition, and a very valuable addition, to the logic of Aristotle, but it should not be regarded as a completely opposite counter thereto: it differs from non-symbolic logic by its higher degree of formalisation, e.g. by the idea of propositional functionality.

9. This necessarily brief and curtailed treatment of the Aristotelian logic may profitably be concluded by a summary of a *few characteristic topics* discussed in the *Organon*, a summary from which will appear the wide range of the Aristotelian logical analysis. In the *Categories*, Aristotle treats of the range of variability of Subject and *Predicate*, in the *De Interpretatione* of the opposition of propositions, modal and assertoric, which leads him into an interesting discussion of excluded middle in Chapters 7 and 10. In the first book of the *Prior Analytics* he discusses the conversion of pure propositions and of necessary and contingent propositions, analyses the syllogisms in the three figures, and gives rules for constructing or discovering syllogisms dealing with, e.g. oblique inference (Ch. 36), negation (Ch. 46), proofs *per impossibile* and *ex hypothesi* (Chs. 23 and 44). In the second book Aristotle deals with the distribution of truth and falsity between premisses and conclusion, the defects in the syllogism, induction in a narrow sense, through "enumeration of all the cases" (Ch. 23), the enthymeme, etc.

The first book of the *Posterior Analytics* treats of the structure of a deductive science and its logical starting-point, the unity, diversity, distinction and logical ranking of sciences, ignorance, error and invalidity; while the second book is concerned with definitions, essential and nominal, the difference between definition and demonstration, the indemonstrability of the essential nature, the way in which basic truths become known, etc. The *Topics* is concerned with the predicables, definition, the technique of proof or the practice of dialectic, the *De Sophisticis Elenchis* with the classification of fallacies and their solutions.

[1] *Geschichte der Logik*, p. 27. (Berlin, 1931.)

CHAPTER XXIX

THE METAPHYSICS OF ARISTOTLE

1. "ALL men by nature desire to know."[1] So does Aristotle optimistically begin the *Metaphysics*, a book, or rather collection of lectures, which is difficult to read (the Arabian philosopher Avicenna said that he had read the *Metaphysics* of Aristotle forty times without understanding it), but which is of the greatest importance for an understanding of the philosophy of Aristotle, and which has had a tremendous influence on the subsequent thought of Europe.[2] But though all men desire to know, there are different degrees of knowledge. For example, the man of *mere experience*, as Aristotle calls him, may know that a certain medicine had done good to X when he was ill, but without knowing the reason for this, whereas the man of *art* knows the reason, e.g. he knows that X was suffering from fever, and that the medicine in question has a certain property which abates fever. He knows a universal, for he knows that the medicine will tend to cure all who suffer from that complaint. Art, then, aims at production of some kind, but this is not Wisdom in Aristotle's view, for the highest Wisdom does not aim at producing anything or securing some effect—it is not utilitarian—but at apprehending the first principles of Reality, i.e. at knowledge for its own sake. Aristotle places the man who seeks for knowledge for its own sake above him who seeks for knowledge of some particular kind with a view to the attainment of some practical effect. In other words, that science stands higher which is desirable for its own sake and not merely with a view to its results.

This science, which is desirable for its own sake, is the science of first principles or first causes, a science which took its rise in wonder. Men began to wonder at things, to desire to know the explanation of the things they saw, and so philosophy arose out

[1] *Metaph.*, A, 980 a 1.

[2] The name *Metaphysics* simply refers to the position of the *Metaphysics* in the Aristotelian Corpus, i.e. as coming after the *Physics*. But the book is metaphysical also in the sense that it concerns the first and highest principles and causes, and so involves a higher degree of abstraction than does the *Physics*, which deals predominantly with a particular type of being—that which is subject to motion. Still, it is true to say that if we wish to know Aristotle's doctrine on the themes treated of to-day under the heading *Metaphysics*, we must consult not only the *Metaphysics* itself but also the *Physics*.

of the desire of understanding, and not on account of any utility that knowledge might possess. This science, then, is of all sciences to be called free or liberal, for, like a free man, it exists for its own sake and not for the sake of someone else. Metaphysics is thus, according to Aristotle, Wisdom *par excellence*, and the philosopher or lover of Wisdom is he who desires knowledge about the ultimate cause and nature of Reality, and desires that knowledge for its own sake. Aristotle is therefore a "dogmatist" in the sense that he supposes that such knowledge is attainable, though he is not of course a dogmatist in the sense of advancing theories without any attempt to prove them.

Wisdom, therefore, deals with the first principles and causes of things, and so is universal knowledge in the highest degree. This means that it is the science which is furthest removed from the senses, the most abstract science, and so is the hardest of the sciences as involving the greatest effort of thought. "Sense-perception is common to all and therefore easy and no mark of Wisdom."[1] But, though it is the most abstract of the sciences, it is, in Aristotle's view, the most *exact* of the sciences, "for those which involve fewer principles are more exact than those which involve additional principles, e.g. arithmetic than geometry."[2] Moreover, this science is in itself the most knowable, since it deals with the first principles of all things, and these principles are in themselves more truly knowable than their applications (for these depend on the first principles, and not vice versa), though it does not follow that they are the most knowable in regard *to us*, since we necessarily start with the things of sense and it requires a considerably effort of rational abstraction to proceed from what is directly known to us, sense-objects, to their ultimate principles.

2. The causes with which Wisdom or philosophy deals are enumerated in the *Physics* and are four in number: (i) the substance or essence of a thing; (ii) the matter or subject; (iii) the source of motion or the efficient cause; and (iv) the final cause or good. In the first book of the *Metaphysics* Aristotle investigates the views of his predecessors, in order, he says, to see if they discussed any other kind of cause besides the four he has enumerated. In this way he is led to give a brief sketch of the history of Greek philosophy up to his time, but he is not concerned to catalogue all their opinions, whether relevant or irrelevant to his purpose, for he wishes to trace the evolution of the notion of the

[1] *Metaph.*, 982 a 11–12. [2] *Metaph.*, 982 a 26–8.

four causes, and the net result of his investigation is the conclusion, not only that no philosopher has discovered any other kind of cause, but that no philosopher before himself has enumerated the four causes in a satisfactory manner. Aristotle, like Hegel, regarded previous philosophy as leading up to his own position; there is none of the paraphernalia of the dialectic in Aristotle, of course, but there is the same tendency to regard his own philosophy as a synthesis on a higher plane of the thought of his predecessors. There is certainly some truth in Aristotle's contention, yet it is by no means completely true, and he is sometimes far from just to his predecessors.

Thales and the early Greek philosophers busied themselves with the material cause, trying to discover the ultimate substratum of things, the principle that is neither generated nor destroyed, but from which particular objects arise and into which they pass away. In this way arose, e.g. the philosophies of Thales, Anaximenes, Heraclitus, who posited one material cause, or Empedocles, who postulated four elements. But even if elements are generated from one material cause, why does this happen, what is the source of the movement whereby objects are generated and destroyed? There must be some cause of the becoming in the world, even the very facts themselves must in the end impel the thinker to investigate a type of cause other than the material cause. Attempted answers to this difficulty we find in the philosophies of Empedocles and Anaxagoras. The latter saw that no material element can be the reason why objects manifest beauty and goodness, and so he asserted the activity of Mind in the material world, standing out like a sober man in contrast with the random talk of his predecessors.[1] All the same, he uses Mind only as a *deus ex machina* to explain the formation of the world, and drags it in when he is at a loss for any other explanation: when another explanation is at hand, he simply leaves Mind out.[2] In other words, Anaxagoras was accused by Aristotle of using Mind simply as a cloak for ignorance. Empedocles, indeed, postulated two active principles, Friendship and Strife, but he used them neither sufficiently nor consistently.[3] These philosophers, therefore, had succeeded in distinguishing two of Aristotle's four causes, the material cause and the source of movement; but they had not worked out their conceptions systematically or elaborated any consistent and scientific philosophy.

[1] *Metaph.*, 984 b 15–18. [2] *Metaph.*, 985 a 18–21. [3] *Metaph.*, 985 a 21–3.

After the philosophy of the Pythagoreans, who cannot be said to have contributed very much, came the philosophy of Plato, who evolved the doctrine of the Forms, but placed the Forms, which are the cause of the essence of things (and so, in a sense, the cause), apart from the things of which they are the essence. Thus Plato, according to Aristotle, used only two causes, "that of the essence and the material cause."[1] As to the final cause, this was not explicitly, or at least not satisfactorily, treated by previous philosophers, but only by the way or incidentally.[2] As a matter of fact, Aristotle is not altogether just to Plato, since the latter, in the *Timaeus*, introduces the concept of the Demiurge who serves as an efficient cause, and also makes use of the star-gods, besides maintaining a doctrine of finality, for the final cause of becoming is the realisation (in the sense of imitation) of the Good. Nevertheless, it is true that Plato, through the *chorismos*, was debarred from making the realisation of its immanent form or essence the final cause of the concrete substance.

3. After stating some of the main problems of philosophy in Book three (B) of the *Metaphysics*, Aristotle declares at the beginning of Book four (Γ) that metaphysical science is concerned with being as such, is the study of being *qua* being. The special sciences isolate a particular sphere of being, and consider the attributes of being in that sphere; but the metaphysician does not consider being of this or that particular characteristic, e.g. as living or as quantitative, but rather being itself and its essential attributes as being. Now, to say that something is, is also to say that it is *one*: unity, therefore, is an essential attribute of being, and just as being itself is found in all the categories, so unity is found in all the categories. As to goodness, Aristotle remarks in the *Ethics* (*E.N.* 1096) that it also is applicable in all the categories. Unity and goodness are, therefore, transcendental attributes of being, to use the phraseology of the Scholastic philosophers, inasmuch as, applicable in all the categories, they are not confined to any one category and do not constitute genera. If the definition of man is "rational animal," animal is the genus, rational the specific difference; but one cannot predicate animality of rationality, the genus of the specific difference, though one can predicate being of both. Being, therefore, cannot be a genus, and the same holds good of unity and goodness.

The term "being," however, is not predicated of all existent

[1] *Metaph.*, 988 a 8–10. [2] *Metaph.*, 988 b 6–16.

things in precisely the same sense, for a substance is, possesses being, in a way that a quality, for instance, which is an affection of substance, cannot be said to be. With what category of being, then, is metaphysics especially concerned? With that of substance, which is primary, since all things are either substances or affections of substances. But there are or may be different kinds of substances, and with which kind does first philosophy or metaphysics deal? Aristotle answers that, if there is an unchangeable substance, then metaphysics studies unchangeable substance, since it is concerned with being *qua* being, and the true nature of being is shown in that which is unchangeable and self-existent, rather than in that which is subject to change. That there is at least one such unchangeable being which causes motion while remaining itself unmoved, is shown by the impossibility of an infinite series of existent sources of movement, and this motionless substance, comprising the full nature of being, will have the character of the divine, so that first philosophy is rightly to be called theology. Mathematics is a theoretical science indeed and deals with motionless objects, but these objects, *though considered in separation from matter*, do not exist separately: physics deals with things that are both inseparable from matter and are subject to movement: it is only metaphysics that treats of that which both exists in separation from matter and is motionless.[1]

(In Book *E* of the *Metaphysics* Aristotle simply divides substances into changeable and unchangeable substances, but in Book Λ he distinguishes three kinds of substances, (i) sensible and perishable, (ii) sensible and eternal, i.e. the heavenly bodies, (iii) non-sensible and eternal.)

Metaphysical science is, therefore, concerned with being, and it studies being primarily in the category of substance, not "accidental being," which is the object of no science,[2] nor being as truth, since truth and falsity exist in the judgment, not in things.[3] (It also establishes the first principles or axioms, especially the principle of contradiction, which, though not of course deducible, is the ultimate principle governing all being and all knowledge.[4]) But, if metaphysics studies substance, non-sensible substance, it is obviously of importance to determine what non-sensible substances there are. Are the objects of mathematics substances, or

[1] *Metaph.*, 1026 a 6–32. Cf. 1064 a 28–b 6.

[2] *Metaph.*, VI (E) 2. E.g. a confectioner aims at giving pleasure; if his productions produce health, that is "accidental."

[3] *Metaph.*, VI (E), 4.

[4] *Metaph.*, IV (Γ), 3 ff.

universals, or the transcendental ideas of being and unity? No, replies Aristotle, they are not: hence his polemic against the Platonic theory of ideas, of which a summary will now be given.

4. (i) The argument for Plato's theory that it makes scientific knowledge possible and explains it, proves, says Aristotle, that the universal is real and no mere mental fiction; but it does not prove that the universal has a subsistence apart from individual things. And, indeed, on Plato's theory, strictly applied, there should be Ideas of negations and relations. For if, whenever we conceive a common concept in relation to a plurality of objects, it is necessary to postulate a Form, then it follows that there must be Forms even of negations and relations. "Of the ways in which we prove that the Forms exist, none is convincing, for from some no inference necessarily follows, and from some it follows that there are Forms of things of which we think there are no Forms."[1]

(ii) The doctrine of Ideas or Forms is *useless*.

(*a*) According to Aristotle, the Forms are only a purposeless doubling of visible things. They are supposed to explain why the multitude of things in the world exist. But it does not help simply to suppose the existence of another multitude of things, as Plato does. Plato is like a man who, unable to count with a small number, thinks that he will find it easier to do so if he doubles the number.[2]

(*b*) The Forms are useless for our knowledge of things. "They help in no wise towards the knowledge of the other things (for they are not even the substance of these, else they would have been in them.[3])" This seems to be an expression of Aristotle's interest in the visible universe, whereas Plato was not really concerned with the things of this world for their own sake, but as stepping-stones to the Forms; though, by getting to know the Types, at which phenomena are, as it were, aiming or which they are trying to realise, we can, inasmuch as we are efficient causes, contribute to this approximate realisation. To this consideration Plato attached very considerable importance. For example, by coming to know the ideal Type of the State, to which actual States are, in a greater or less degree, approximations, we are enabled to contribute to the elevation of the actual State—for we know the goal.

(*c*) The Forms are useless when it comes to explaining the movement of things. Even if things exist in virtue of the Forms,

[1] *Metaph.*, 990 b 8–11. [2] *Metaph.*, 990 a 34–b 8. [3] *Metaph.*, 991 a 12–13.

how do the latter account for the movement of things and for their coming-to-be and passing-away? "Above all one might discuss the question what on earth the Forms contribute to sensible things, either to those that are eternal or to those that come into being and cease to be."[1] The Forms are motionless, and the objects of this world, if they are copies of the Forms, should be motionless too; or, if they move, as they do, whence their motion?

Aristotle would not seem to be altogether just to Plato in pursuing this line of criticism, since Plato fully realised that the Forms are not moving causes, and it was precisely on this account that he introduced the concept of the Demiurge. The latter may be a more or less mythological figure, but, however that may be, it is clear that Plato never considered the Forms to be principles of motion and that he made an attempt to account for the dynamism of the world on other lines.

(*d*) The Forms are supposed to explain sensible objects. But they will themselves be sensible: the Ideal Man, for instance, will be sensible, like Socrates. The Forms will resemble the anthropomorphic gods: the latter were only eternal men, and so the Forms are only "eternal sensibles."[2]

This is not a very telling criticism. If the Ideal Man is conceived as being a replica of concrete man on the ideal plane, in the common sense of the word "ideal," as being actual man raised to the highest pitch of development, then of course Ideal Man will be sensible. But is it at all likely that Plato himself meant anything of this kind? Even if he may have implied this by the phrases he used on certain occasions, such an extravagant notion is by no means essential to the Platonic theory of Forms. The Forms are subsistent concepts or Ideal Types, and so the subsistent concept of Man will contain the idea of corporeality, for instance, but there is no reason why it should itself be corporeal: in fact, corporeality and sensibility are *ex hypothesi* excluded when it is postulated that the Ideal Man means an *Idea*. Does anybody suppose that when later Platonists placed the Idea of man in the Divine Mind, they were positing an actual concrete man in God's Mind? The objection seems really to be a debating point on Aristotle's part, i.e. so far as it is supposed to touch Plato personally, and that not a particularly fair one. It would be conclusive against a very gross rendering of the theory of

[1] *Metaph.*, 991 a 8–10. [2] *Metaph.*, 997 b 5–12

Forms; but it is useless to read into Plato the most gross and crude interpretation possible.

(iii) The theory of Ideas or Forms is an *impossible* theory.

(*a*) "It must be held to be impossible that the substance, and that of which it is the substance, should exist apart; how, therefore, can the Ideas, being the substance of things, exist apart?"[1] The Forms contain the essence and inner reality of sensible objects; but how can objects which exist apart from sensibles contain the essence of those sensibles? In any case, what is the relation between them? Plato tries to explain the relation by the use of terms such as "participation" and "imitation," but Aristotle retorts that "to say that they (i.e. sensible things) are patterns and the other things share in them, is to use empty words and poetical metaphors."[2]

This criticism would certainly be a very serious one if separation meant local separation. But does separation, in the case of the Forms, necessarily imply local separation? Does it not rather mean independence? Literal local separation would be impossible if the Forms are to be looked on as subsistent concepts or Ideas. It seems that Aristotle is arguing from the point of view of his own theory, according to which the form is the immanent essence of the sensible object. He argues that participation can mean nothing, unless it means that there is a real immanent form, co-constitutive of the object with matter—a conception not admitted by Plato. Aristotle rightly points out the inadequacy of the Platonic theory; but, in rejecting Platonic exemplarism, he also betrays the inadequacy of his own (Aristotle's) theory, in that he provides no real transcendental ground for the fixity of essences.

(*b*) "But, further, all things cannot come from the Forms in any of the usual senses of 'from'."[3] Here Aristotle again touches on the question of the relation of the Forms to that of which they are said to be Forms, and it is in this connection that he objects that the explanatory phrases used by Plato are merely poetical metaphors. This is of course one of the crucial points of the Platonic theory, and Plato himself seems to have felt the inadequacy of the attempted explanation. He cannot be said to have cleared up in any satisfactory manner what he actually meant by the metaphors he used and what the relation of sensible

[1] *Metaph.*, 991 b 1–3. [2] *Metaph.*, M, 1079 b 24–6; A, 991 a 20–2.
[3] *Metaph.*, A, 991 a 19–20.

objects to the Forms really is. But it is curious that Aristotle, in his treatment of the Platonic theory in the *Metaphysics*, neglects the Demiurge altogether. One might suggest as a reason for this neglect, that the ultimate cause of motion in the world was, for Aristotle, a *Final* Cause. The notion of a super-terrestrial *efficient* Cause was for him unacceptable.

(*c*) The Forms will be individual objects like those other objects of which they are the Forms, whereas they should be not individuals but *universals*. The Ideal Man, for instance, will be an individual like Socrates. Further, on the supposition that when there is a plurality of objects possessing a common name, there must be an eternal pattern or Form, we shall have to posit a third man (τρίτος ἄνθρωπος), whom not only Socrates imitates, but also the Ideal Man. The reason is that Socrates and the Ideal Man have a nature in common, therefore there must be a subsistent universal beyond them. But in this case the difficulty will always recur and we shall proceed to infinity.[1]

This criticism of Aristotle would hold good if Plato held that the Forms are things. But did he? If he held them to be subsistent concepts, they do not turn into individual objects in the same sense that Socrates is an individual object. Of course they are individual concepts, but there are signs that Plato was trying to systematise the whole world of concepts or Ideas, and that he envisaged them as forming one articulated system—the rational structure of the world, as we might say, that the world, to speak metaphorically, is always trying to embody, but which it cannot fully embody, owing to the contingency which is inevitable in all material things. (We are reminded of Hegel's doctrine of the universal Categories in relation to the contingent objects of Nature.)

(iv) Against the theory that the Forms are Numbers.

(*a*) It scarcely seems necessary to treat of Aristotle's objections and criticisms in detail, since the Form-Number theory was perhaps an unfortunate adventure on Plato's part. As Aristotle remarks, "mathematics has come to be the whole of philosophy for modern thinkers, though they say that it should be studied for the sake of other things."[2]

For Aristotle's general treatment of number and pertinent questions, one should see *Metaphysics* A, 991 b 9 to 993 a 10 and M and N.

[1] *Metaph.*, A, 990 b 15–17; K, 1059 b 8–9. [2] *Metaph.*, 992 a 32–b 1.

(*b*) If the Forms are Numbers, how can they be causes?[1] If it is because existing things are other numbers (e.g. "one number is man, another is Socrates, another Callias"), then why "are the one set of numbers causes of the other set"? If it is meant that Callias is a numerical ratio of his elements, then his Idea will also be a numerical ratio of elements, and so neither will be, properly speaking, a number. (Of course, for Plato the Forms were exemplary causes, but not efficient causes.)

(*c*) How can there be two kinds of numbers?[2] If besides the Form-numbers it is also necessary to posit another kind of numbers, which are the mathematical objects, then what is the basis of differentiation between the two kinds of numbers? We only know one kind of numbers, thinks Aristotle, and that is the kind of numbers with which the mathematician deals.

(*d*) But whether there are two classes of numbers, i.e. Forms and mathematical objects (Plato) or simply one class, i.e. mathematical numbers existing, however, apart from sensible objects (Speusippus), Aristotle objects (i) that if the Forms are numbers, then they cannot be unique, since the elements of which they are composed are the same (as a matter of fact, the Forms were not supposed to be unique in the sense that they were without inner relation to one another); and (ii) that the objects of mathematics "cannot in any way exist separately."[3] One reason for the latter assertion is that a *processus in infinitum* will be unavoidable if we accept the separate existence of mathematical objects, e.g. there must be separate solids corresponding to the sensible solids, and separate planes and lines corresponding to the sensible planes and lines. But there must also be other separate planes and lines corresponding to the planes and lines of the separate solid. Now, "the accumulation becomes absurd, for we find ourselves with one set of solids apart from the sensible solids; three sets of planes apart from the sensible planes—those which exist apart from the sensible planes, and those in the mathematical solids, and those which exist apart from those in the mathematical solids; four sets of lines; and five sets of points. With which of these, then, will the mathematical sciences deal?"[4]

(*e*) If the substance of things is mathematical, then what is the source of movement? "If the great and the small are to *be* movement, evidently the Forms will be moved; but if they are not,

[1] *Metaph.*, 991 b 9 ff. [2] *Metaph.*, e.g. 991 b 27–31. [3] *Metaph.*, b 1077 –1214. [4] *Metaph.*, 1076 b 28–34.

whence did movement come? If we cannot answer this, the whole study of Nature has been annihilated."[1] (As already remarked, Plato tried to provide a source of movement other than the Forms themselves, which are motionless.)

(v) Some of what Aristotle has to say on the subject of Plato's mathematical objects and the Form-numbers implies a rather crude interpretation of Platonic doctrine, as though for example Plato imagined that mathematical objects or the Forms are things. Moreover, Aristotle has himself to meet the great difficulty against the abstraction theory of mathematics (for Aristotle the geometrician, for instance, considers, not separate mathematical objects but sensible things abstractly, i.e. according to one particular point of view), namely, that we cannot abstract e.g. the perfect circle from nature, since there is no perfect circle in nature which we could abstract, while on the other hand it is difficult to see how we could form the idea of a perfect circle by "correcting" the imperfect circles of nature, when we should not know that the circles of nature *were* imperfect unless we *previously* knew what a perfect circle was. To this Aristotle might answer either that, though perfect circles are not given really, i.e. as regards measurement, in nature, yet they are given *quoad visum*, and that this is sufficient for the abstraction of the idea of the perfect circle, or that mathematical figures and axioms are more or less arbitrary hypotheses, so that the cardinal requisite in mathematics is to be consistent and logical, without its being necessary to suppose that e.g. every type of geometry will fit the "real" world, or, on the other hand, that it has an ideal world corresponding to it, of which it is the mental reflection or perception.

In general, we would point out that we cannot well dispense with either Plato or Aristotle, but that the truth in both of them has to be combined. This the Neo-Platonists attempted to do. For example, Plato posited the Forms as Exemplary Causes: the later Platonists placed them in God. With due qualifications, this is the correct view, for the Divine Essence is the ultimate Exemplar of all creatures.[2] On the other hand, Plato assumes that we

[1] *Metaph.*, A, 992 b 7–9.

[2] St. Thomas Aquinas, who quotes St. Augustine as to the Divine Ideas, teaches that there is a plurality of ideas in the Divine Mind (*S.T.*, I, 15, 2), rejecting the opinion of Plato that they are "outside" the Divine Mind (cf. *S.T.*, I, 15, 1, ad 1). He explains that he does not mean that there is a plurality of accidental *species* in God, but that God, knowing perfectly His Essence, knows it as imitable (or *participabilis*) by a plurality of creatures.

have, or can have, direct knowledge of the Forms. Now, we certainly have not got a direct knowledge of the Divine Ideas, as Malebranche supposed we have. We have direct knowledge only of the expressed universal, and this expressed universal exists externally, i.e. as universal, only in the particulars. We have therefore the external exemplary Idea in God, the foundation in the particular object, i.e. its specific essence, and the abstract universal in our minds. From this point of view Aristotle's criticism of Plato would seem to be justified, for the universal, of which we have direct knowledge, simply is the nature of the individual thing. It would appear, therefore, that we require both Plato and Aristotle in order to form anything like a complete philosophical view. Plato's Demiurge must be identified with the Aristotelian νόησις νοήσεως, the eternal Forms must be referred to God, and Aristotle's doctrine of the concrete universal must be accepted, together with the Aristotelian doctrine of abstraction. Neither of these two great thinkers can be accepted precisely as he stands, and while it is right to value Aristotle's criticism of the Platonic theory of Forms, it is a great mistake to suppose that that theory was a mass of crude absurdity, or that it can be dispensed with altogether. The Augustinian philosophy was, through Neo-Platonism, strongly impregnated with the thought of Plato.

Although it has been admitted that Aristotle's fundamental criticism of the Platonic theory of Forms, that the theory involves the *chorismos*, is justified, and that the Platonic theory cannot stand by itself but needs to be supplemented by Aristotle's doctrine of the immanent Form (which we consider abstractly in its universality), we have not given an altogether sympathetic treatment of Aristotle's criticisms. "How, then," it might be asked, "can you say that Aristotle's statements concerning what Plato taught must be taken seriously? If Aristotle's account of what Plato taught is correct, then his criticisms of the Platonic theory were perfectly justified, while if his criticisms misrepresent the Platonic theory, then he either deliberately misrepresented that theory or he did not understand it."

First of all, it must be admitted that Aristotle was attacking, in his own mind at least, the theory of Plato himself, and not merely that of some Platonists as distinct from Plato: a careful reading of the *Metaphysics* hardly permits any other supposition. Secondly, it must be admitted that Aristotle, though primarily perhaps attacking the form of the Platonic theory that was taught in the Academy, was perfectly well acquainted with the content of the published dialogues, and knew that some of his own criticisms had already been raised in the *Parmenides*. Thirdly, there is no real reason for supposing that the Platonic theory as taught in the Academy involved a retraction or rejection of the theory developed in the published works of Plato: if this had been the case, we might reasonably have expected Aristotle to make some reference to the fact; while conversely, if he makes no reference to such a change of view on Plato's part, we have no right to affirm such a change without better evidence than can be offered. The mathematical form of the theory was probably meant to be a supplement to the theory, or, rather, a speculative justification and elucidation of it, an 'esoteric' version of it (if one may use a word with somewhat unfortunate associations, without at the same time wishing to imply that the mathematical version was *another* and *different* theory). Aristotle, therefore, was attacking, under both its aspects, what he regarded as the *Platonic* theory of Ideas. (It must, however, be remembered that the *Metaphysics* is not a continuous book, written for publication, and that we cannot assume without more ado that all the objections raised against the Platonic theory in Aristotle's lectures were regarded with equal seriousness by Aristotle himself. A man may say things in his lectures that he would not say, in the same form at least, in a work intended for publication.)

It would seem, then, that we are faced by an awkward dilemma. Either Plato, in spite of the difficulties that he himself saw and proposed in the *Parmenides*, held the theory in the exact form under which it was attacked by Aristotle (in which case Plato appears in a foolish light), or Aristotle grossly misunderstood the Platonic theory (in which case it is Aristotle who appears as the fool). Now, we are not willing to admit that either Plato or Aristotle was a fool, and any treatment of the problem that necessarily involves either supposition is to our mind thereby ruled out of court. That Plato on the one hand never really solved satisfactorily the problem of the *chorismos*, and that Aristotle on the other hand was not perfectly *au fait* with contemporary higher mathematics, does not show either of them to be a fool and can easily be admitted; but this admission obviously does not dispose of the difficulty involved by Aristotle's criticisms, that the Platonic theory is therein depicted as excessively naïve, and that

Aristotle makes little reference to the dialogues and is silent as to the Demiurge. But perhaps a way out of the difficulty can be found. Aristotle, well aware that Plato had not satisfactorily solved the problem of the *chorismos*, had broken away from his Master's theory and adopted a quite different standpoint. When he regarded the theory *from that standpoint*, it could not but appear to him as extravagant and bizarre under any form: he might, therefore, have easily considered himself justified in attempting to put this bizarre character of the theory in an exaggerated light for polemical purposes. One might cite as a parallel the case of Hegel. To one who believes that the Hegelian system is a mere intellectual *tour de force* or an *extravaganza*, nothing is easier than to overstate and even to misrepresent the undoubtedly weak elements in that system for polemical purposes, even though the critic, believing the system to be fundamentally false, could not be justly accused of deliberate misrepresentation. We would wish that the critic had acted otherwise in the interests of historical accuracy, but we could hardly dub him an imbecile because he had chosen to overdo the rôle of critic. While refusing to believe that Aristotle felt towards Plato any of the animus that Schelling and Schopenhauer felt towards Hegel, I would suggest that Aristotle overdid the rôle of critic and exaggerated weak points in a theory that he considered false. As to his silence concerning the Demiurge, that can be explained, in part at least, if we remember that Aristotle was criticising Plato from his own (i.e. Aristotle's) standpoint, and that the conception of the Demiurge was unacceptable to him: he did not take it seriously. If, in addition, Aristotle had reason to believe that the actual Demiurge of the *Timaeus* was largely a symbolic figure, and *if* Plato never worked out thoroughly, even in the Academy, the precise nature or status of Mind or Soul, then it is not so difficult to understand how Aristotle, who did not believe in any formation of the world *a tergo*, could neglect the figure of the Demiurge altogether in his criticism of the Ideal Theory. He may have been unjustified in neglecting it to the extent that he did, but the foregoing considerations may make it easier to understand how he could do so. The suggestions we have made may not be altogether satisfactory, and no doubt remain open to serious criticism, but they have at least this advantage, that they make it possible for us to escape from the dilemma of holding either Plato or Aristotle to have been a fool. And after all, Aristotle's root criticism of

Plato's theory is perfectly justified, for by using the terms "imitation" and "participation," Plato clearly implies that there is some formal element, some principle of comparative stability, in material things, while on the other hand, by failing to provide a theory of substantial form, he failed to explain this immanent formal element. Aristotle rightly provided this element, but, seeing (rightly again) that the Platonic Forms, being "separate," *could not* account for this element, he unfortunately went too far by rejecting the Platonic exemplarism altogether: looking on the Platonic theory from the point of view of a *biologist* primarily (with a biologist's insistence on the immanent entelechy) and from the theological standpoint envisaged in the *Metaphysics* (xii), he had no use for Platonic exemplarism, Platonic mathematicism and the Platonic Demiurge. Thus, when regarded in the light of his own system, Aristotle's attitude towards Plato's theory is quite understandable.

5. But although Aristotle passes an adverse criticism on the Platonic theory of separate Ideas or Forms, he is in full agreement with Plato that the universal is not merely a subjective concept or a mode of oral expression (*universale post rem*), for to the universal in the mind there corresponds the specific essence in the object, though this essence does not exist in any state of separation *extra mentem*: it is separated only in the mind and through the mind's activity. Aristotle was convinced, as Plato was, that the universal is the object of science: it follows, then, that if the universal is in no way real, if it has no objective reality whatsoever, there is no scientific knowledge, for science does not deal with the individual as such. The universal is real, it has reality not only in the mind but also in the things, though the existence in the thing does not entail that formal universality that it has in the mind. Individuals belonging to the same species are real substances, but they do not partake in an objective universal that is numerically the same in all members of the class. This specific essence is numerically different in each individual of the class, but, on the other hand, it is specifically the same in all the individuals of the class (i.e. they are all alike in species), and this objective similarity is the real foundation for the abstract universal, which has numerical identity in the mind and can be predicated of all the members of the class indifferently. Plato and Aristotle are, then, at one as to the character of true science, namely, that it is directed to the universal element in things, i.e.

to the specific similarity. The scientist is not concerned with individual bits of gold as individual, but with the essence of gold, with that specific similarity which is found in all individual bits of gold, i.e. supposing that gold is a species. "Socrates gave the impulse to this theory" (i.e. the Platonic theory) "by means of his definitions, but he did not separate them" (i.e. the universals) "from the particulars; and in this he thought rightly in not separating them. This is plain from the results, for without the universal it is not possible to get knowledge, but the separation is the cause of the objections that arise with regard to the Ideas."[1] *Strictly* speaking, therefore, there is no objective Universal for Aristotle, but there is an objective foundation in things for the subjective universal in the mind. The universal "horse" is a subjective concept, but it has an objective foundation in the substantial forms that inform particular horses.

The individuals are truly substance (οὐσία). Are the universals substances, i.e. is the specific element, the formal principle, that which places the individual in its specific class, to be called substance? No, says Aristotle, except in a secondary and derived sense. It is the individual alone which is the subject of predication and is itself not predicated of others. The species may, however, be called substance in a secondary sense and it has a claim to this title, since the essential element has a higher reality than the individual *qua* individual and is the object of science. Aristotle, therefore, terms the individuals πρῶται οὐσίαι and the species δεύτεραι οὐσίαι.[2] In this way Aristotle has brought upon himself the charge of contradiction. The alleged contradiction consists in this, that if only the individual is truly substance and if science is concerned with the οὐσία, it necessarily follows that the individual is the true object of science, whereas Aristotle teaches in point of fact the very opposite, namely, that science is not concerned with the individual as such but with the universal. In other words, Aristotle teaches that science is concerned with substance and that the individual is substance in the primary sense, while on the other hand he teaches that the universal is of

[1] *Metaph.*, M, 1086 b 2–7. We may compare K, 1059 b 25–6 ("every formula and every science is of universals") and Z 1036 a 28–9 ("definition is of the universal and of the form").

[2] *Categ.* 5. It is to be noted that the terms *first* and *second* in this respect are not valuations but mean first or second *in regard to us*, πρὸς ἡμᾶς. We come to know the individuals first and the universals only secondarily by abstraction, but Aristotle does not depart from his view that the universal is an object of science and has a higher reality than the individual as such.

superior quality and is the true object of science, which would seem to be the exact opposite of what he should teach on his premisses.

In answer to this accusation of self-contradiction, we might answer two things. (i) There is no real contradiction, if we consider what Aristotle *means*. When he says that the individual is truly substance and that it alone is truly substance, he means to reject Plato's doctrine that the universal is a separate substance on its own, but he does not mean to deny that the universal, in the sense of the formal or specific element in things, is real. The individual is truly substance, but that which makes it a substance of this or that kind, that which is the chief element in the thing and is the object of science, is the universal element, the form of the thing, which the mind abstracts and conceives in formal universality. So when he says that the universal is the object of science he is not contradicting himself, for he has not denied that the universal has some objective reality but only that it has a separate existence. It is real in the individual: it is not transcendent, if considered in its objective reality, but immanent, the concrete universal. The individual alone is substance in the true sense, but the individual sensible thing is compound, and the intellect, in scientific knowledge, goes straight to the universal element, which is really there, though existing only concretely, *as an element of the individual*. Aristotle was no doubt influenced by the fact that individuals perish, while the species persists. Thus individual horses perish, whereas the nature of horses remains the same (specifically, though not numerically) in the succession of horses. It is the nature of horses that the scientist considers, and not merely Black Beauty or any other individual horse. (ii) Nor does Aristotle really contradict himself even in terminology, for he expressly distinguishes the two meanings of οὐσία or substance. Substance in the primary sense is the individual substance, composed of matter *and* form: substance in the secondary sense is the formal element or specific essence that corresponds to the universal concept. πρῶται οὐσίαι are objects which are not predicated of another, but of which something else (i.e. accident or τὸ συμβεβηκός) is predicated. Substances in the secondary sense (δεύτεραι οὐσίαι) are the nature, in the sense of specific essence, that which corresponds to the universal concept, ἡ κατὰ τὸν λόγον οὐσία. Moreover, when Aristotle speaks of primary and secondary substances, he does not mean primary and secondary in nature, dignity, or time, but primary and secondary in regard to us.[1]

The individual substance, οὐσία αἰσθητή, is a compound (σύνολον) of the subject or substratum (ὑποκείμενον or ὕλη) and the essence of form. To the individual substance belong the conditions (πάθη) and the relations (πρός τι), which are distinguished according to the nine accidental categories. The universal becomes pre-eminently the object of science, because it is the essential element and so has reality in a higher sense than what is *merely* particular. The universal certainly exists only in the particular, but from this it follows, not that we are unable to make the universal an object of science in its universality, but that we cannot apprehend the universal except through apprehension of the individual.

Is it true, as Aristotle thinks it is true, that universals are necessary for science? (i) If by science is meant knowledge of the universal, the answer is obvious. (ii) If by science is meant Wisdom in the sense in which Aristotle uses the term, then it is perfectly true to say that the philosopher is not concerned with the particular as particular. If, for example, the philosopher is arguing about contingent being, he is not thinking of this or that particular contingent being as such, but with contingent being in its essential nature, even if he uses particular contingent beings as an illustration. If he were confined to the particular contingent beings that have actually been experienced, either by himself or by others whose testimony he could trust, then his conclusion would be limited to those particular beings, whereas he desires as philosopher to reach a universal conclusion which will apply to all possible contingent beings. (iii) If by science is meant "science" in the sense in which we use the term generally to-day, then we must say that, although knowledge of the true universal essence of a class of beings would certainly be desirable and remains the ideal, it is hardly *necessary*. For example, botanists can get along very well in their classification of plants without knowing the essential definition of the plants in question. It is enough for them if they can find phenomena which will suffice to

[1] Professor Zeller remarks: "It is, of course, a contradiction to attribute a higher reality to form, which is always a universal, in comparison to that which is a compound of form and matter, and at the same time to assert that only the universal is the object of knowledge which is in itself the prior and better known. The results of this contradiction are to be observed throughout the whole Aristotelian system." (*Outlines*, p. 274.) This is scarcely a fortunate statement of the alleged contradiction.

delimit and define a species, irrespective of whether the real specific essence is thereby defined or not. It is significant that when Scholastic philosophers wish to give a definition which is representative they so often say "Man is a rational animal." They would scarcely take it upon themselves to give an essential definition of the cow or the buttercup. We frequently have to be content with what we might call the "nominal" essence as opposed to the real essence. Yet even in this case knowledge of *some* universal characteristics is necessary. For even if you cannot assign the difference of some species, yet you have got to define it, if you define it at all, in function of some universal characteristics possessed by the whole class. Suppose that "Rational Animal" is the real definition of man. Now, if you could not attain this definition but had to describe man as e.g. a featherless significantly-speaking biped, you imply a knowledge of the universals "featherlessness" and "significantly-speaking." So even classification or description by accidental characteristics would seem to imply a discerning of the universal in some way, for one discerns the type even if one cannot adequately define it. It is as though one had a dim realisation of the universal, but could not adequately define or grasp it clearly. Universal definition, in the sense of real essential definition, would thus remain the ideal at any rate, even if in practice empirical science can get along without attaining the ideal, and Aristotle is of course speaking of science in its ideal type. He would never agree with the empiricist and nominalist views of e.g. J. S. Mill, although he would doubtless admit that we often have to content ourselves with description instead of true definition.

6. Aristotle, therefore, refuses to admit that the objects of mathematics or universals are substances. In the *Metaphysics*, where he wishes to refute the Platonic theory, he simply denies flatly that they are substances, though in the *Categories*, as we have seen, he called them secondary substances or substances in a secondary and derived sense. In any case, it is the individual that is truly substance, and only the individual. There is, however, this further point to be observed. According to Aristotle,[1] the sensible individuals cannot be defined owing to the material element in them, which renders them perishable and makes them obscure to our knowledge. On the other hand, substance is primarily the definable essence or form of a thing, the principle

[1] *Metaph.*, VII (Z), 15.

in virtue of which the material element is some definite concrete object.[1] It follows from this that substance is primarily form which is, in itself, immaterial, so that if Aristotle begins by asserting that individual sensible objects are substances, the course of his thought carries him on towards the view that pure form alone is truly and primarily substance. But the only forms that are really independent of matter are God, the Intelligences of the spheres and the active intellect in man, so that it is these forms which are primarily substance. If metaphysics studies substance, then, it is easily seen that it is equivalent to "theology." It is certainly not unreasonable to discern here the influence of Platonism, since, in spite of his rejection of the Platonic theory of Ideas, Aristotle evidently continued to look on matter as the element which is impenetrable to thought and on pure form as the intelligible. It is not suggested that Aristotle was wrong in thinking this, but, right or wrong, it is clearly a legacy of Platonism.

7. Aristotle, as we have seen, gives four principles: ἡ ὕλη or matter, τὸ εἶδος or the form, τὸ ὅθεν ἡ κίνησις—the source of movement or the efficient cause, and τὸ οὗ ἕνεκα or the final cause. Change or motion (i.e. motion in the general sense of the term, which includes every passage from a *terminus a quo* to a *terminus ad quem*, such as the change of the colour of a leaf from green to brown) is a fact in the world, in spite of the dismissal of change as illusory by Parmenides, and Aristotle considered this fact of change. He saw that several factors are involved, to each of which justice must be done. There must, for example, be a substratum of change, for in every case of change which we observe there is something that changes. The oak comes from the acorn and the bed from the wood: there is something which is changed, which receives a new determination. First of all, it is in potentiality (δύναμις) to this new determination; then under the action of some efficient cause (τὸ ὅθεν ἡ κίνησις) it receives a new actualisation (ἐντελέχεια). The marble upon which the sculptor works is in potency to receiving the new form or determination which the sculptor gives it, namely, the form of the statue.

Now, when the marble receives the form of the statue, it is indeed changed, but this change is only accidental, in the sense that the substance is still marble, but the shape or figure is

[1] *Ibid.*, 17.

different. In some cases, however, the substance by no means remains the same: thus when the cow eats grass, the grass is assimilated in the process of digestion and takes on a new substantial form. And since it would seem that, absolutely speaking, anything might ultimately change into anything else, it would appear that there is an ultimate substratum which has no definite characteristics of its own, but is simply potentiality as such. This is what Aristotle means by ἡ πρώτη ἑκάστῳ ὑποκειμένη ὕλη[1]—the *materia prima* of the Scholastics—which is found in all material things and is the ultimate basis of change. Aristotle is, of course, perfectly aware that no efficient agent ever acts directly on prime matter as such: it is always some definite thing, some already actualised substratum, that is acted upon. For example, the sculptor works upon the marble; this is his matter, the substratum of the change which he initiates: he does not act upon prime matter as such. Similarly, it is grass which becomes cow, and not prime matter as such. This means that prime matter never exists precisely as such—as bare prime matter, we might say—but always exists in conjunction with form, which is the formal or characterising factor. In the sense that prime matter cannot exist by itself, apart from all form, it is only logically distinguishable from form; but in the sense that it is a real element in the material object, and the ultimate basis of the real changes that it undergoes, it is really distinguishable from form. We should not, therefore, say that prime matter is the simplest body in the material universe, for it is not a body at all, but an element of body, even of the simplest body. Aristotle teaches in the *Physics*[2] that the apparently simplest bodies of the material sublunary world, the four elements, earth, air, fire and water, themselves contain contraries and can be transmuted into one another. But if they can change, then they presuppose composition of potentiality and act. Air, for instance, *is* air, but *can become* fire. It has the form or *actuality* of air, but has also the *potentiality* of becoming fire. But it is logically necessary to

[1] Cf. *Physics*, 193 a 29 and 191 a 31–2. λέγω γάρ ὕλην τὸ πρῶτον ὑποκείμενον ἑκάστῳ, ἐξ οὗ γίγνεταί τι ἐνυπάρχοντος μὴ κατὰ συμβεβηκός.

One might also approach prime matter from this point of view. Take any material substance and think away all its definite characteristics, all that it possesses in common with other substances—colour, shape, etc. You are ultimately left with a substratum that is absolutely formless, characterless, that cannot exist by itself, but is logically to be presupposed. This is prime matter. Cf. Stace, *Critical History*, p. 276.

[2] Cf. e.g. *Physics*, I, 6; III, 5.

presuppose, prior to the potentiality of becoming fire or any other particular and definite kind of thing, a potentiality of becoming at all, i.e. a bare potentiality.

Now, change is the development of a previously existing body, not precisely as that definite body, but as a body capable of becoming something else, though as not yet that something else. It is the actualisation of a potentiality; but a potentiality involves an actual being, which is not yet that which it could be. Steam, for example, does not come from nothing, it comes from water. But it does not come from water precisely as water: water precisely as water is water and nothing else. Steam comes from water, which could be steam and "demands" to be steam, having been heated to a certain temperature, but is not yet steam, which is as yet "deprived" of the form of steam—not merely in the sense that it has not got the form of steam, but in the sense that it could have the form of steam and ought to have it but has not yet got it. There are, then, three, and not merely two, factors in change, since the product of change contains two positive elements—form and matter—and presupposes a third element—privation (στέρησις). Privation is not a positive element in the same sense that matter and form are positive elements, but it is, nevertheless, necessarily presupposed by change. Aristotle accordingly gives three presuppositions of change, matter, form and privation or exigency.[1]

8. The concrete sensible substance is thus an individual being, composed of matter and form. But the formal element in such a being, that which makes it this definite thing, is specifically the same in all the members of an *infima species*. For instance, the specific nature or essence of man is the same (though not, of course, numerically the same) in Socrates and in Plato. This being so, it cannot be that the formal element renders the concrete sensible substance this individual, i.e. form cannot be the principle of individuation in sensible objects. What is the individuating principle according to Aristotle? It is matter. Thus Callias and Socrates are the same in form (i.e. the human form or nature), but they are different in virtue of the different matter that is informed.[2] This view of the principle of individuation was adopted by St. Thomas Aquinas, but seeing the difficulty involved in holding that completely characterless prime matter is the principle of individuation, he said that it is *materia signata*

[1] *Physics*, I, 7 ff. [2] *Metaph.*, 1034 a 5–8.

quantitate which individualises matter considered as having an anticipatory exigency for the quantity that it will afterwards actually possess in virtue of its union with form. This theory, that it is matter that individualises, would appear to be a consequence or legacy of Platonism, according to which Form is the universal.

From this theory it logically follows that each pure form must be the only member of its species, must exhaust the possibilities of its species, since there is no matter which can act as a principle of individuation within the species. St. Thomas Aquinas drew this conclusion, and did not hesitate to say (a point in which he was at variance with St. Bonaventure) that the pure intelligences or angels constitute so many species, that there cannot be a plurality of angels or immaterial forms belonging to one species. This conclusion was one that had already occurred to Aristotle himself, for, after observing that plurality depends on matter, he goes on to comment that the immovable first mover, having no matter, must be numerically one, and not only one in formula or definition.[1] It is true that the passage in question seems to be by way of objection against Aristotle's theory of a plurality of unmoved movers, but it at least clear that he was not unaware of the consequence that follows from his doctrine of matter as principle of individuation within the species.

There is a further and a more serious consequence, which would appear to follow from this doctrine. According to Aristotle, matter is at once the principle of individuation and unknowable in itself. Now, from this it appears to follow, that the individual concrete thing is not fully knowable. Moreover, Aristotle, as has been mentioned, explicitly stated that the individual cannot be defined, whereas science is concerned with the definition or essence. The individual as such, therefore, is not the object of science and is not fully knowable. Aristotle does indeed remark[2] concerning individual intelligible (i.e. mathematical circles) and sensible circles (e.g. of bronze or wood) that, though they cannot be defined, they are apprehended by intuition (μετὰ νοήσεως) or perception (αἰσθήσεως); but he did not elaborate this hint or work out any theory of the intuition of the individual. Yet such a theory is surely necessary. For example, we are fully convinced that we can and do know an individual person's character, but we do not arrive at the knowledge by discursive and scientific

[1] *Metaph.*, 1074 a 33–8. [2] *Metaph.*, 1036 a 2–6.

reasoning. In fact, one can hardly avoid the impression that Aristotle's exaltation of scientific definition, of knowledge of substance in the sense of specific essence, and his depreciation of knowledge of the sensible individual, were little more than a relic of his Platonic education.

9. In the ninth book of the *Metaphysics* Aristotle discusses the notions of potency and act. This is an extremely important distinction, as it enables Aristotle to admit a doctrine of real development. The Megaric School had denied potentiality, but, as Aristotle remarks, it would be absurd to say that the builder who is not actually building cannot build. It is true, of course, in one sense, that he cannot build when he is not actually building, i.e. if "cannot build" be understood as "cannot be actually building" (that is an obvious application of the principle of contradiction); but he has a potentiality for building, a power to build, even when he is not actually employing that power. That potentiality is not simply the negation of actuality can be shown by a simple illustration. A man in a state of deep sleep or coma is not actually thinking, but, being a man, he has the potentiality of thinking, whereas a stone, though it is not actually thinking, has no potentiality for thinking. A natural object is in potency in regard to the full realisation of its form, e.g. an acorn or a small tree in regard to its full development. This potency may be the power to effect a change in another or it may be a power of self-realisation: in either case it is something real, something between not-being and actuality.

Actuality, says Aristotle, is prior to potency.[1] The actual is always produced from the potential, the potential is always reduced to act by the actual, that which is already in act, as man is produced by man. In this sense the actual is *temporally* prior to the potential. But the actual is also prior to the potential *logically*, in principle, since the actuality is the end, that for the sake of which the potency exists or is acquired. Thus, although a boy is temporally prior to his actualisation as man, his manhood is logically prior, since his boyhood is for the sake of his manhood. Moreover, that which is eternal is prior in substance to that which is perishable; and that which is eternal, imperishable, is in the highest sense actual. God, for example, exists necessarily, and that which exists necessarily must be fully actual: as the eternal Source of movement, of the reduction of potentiality to act, God

[1] *Metaph.*, 1049 b 5.

must be full and complete actuality, the Unmoved First Mover. Eternal things, says Aristotle,[1] must be good: there can be in them no defect or badness or perversion. Badness means defect or perversion of some kind, and there can be no defect in that which is fully actual. It follows that there can be no separate bad principle, since that which is without matter is pure form. "The bad does not exist apart from bad things."[2] It is clear from this that God, in the thought of Aristotle, took on something of the character of Plato's Idea of the Good, and indeed he remarks that the cause of all goods is the good itself.[3] The First Unmoved Mover, being the source of all movement, as *final* cause, is the ultimate cause why potentiality is actualised, i.e. why goodness is realised.

It is through the distinction between potency and act that Aristotle answers Parmenides. Parmenides had said that change is impossible, because being cannot come out of not-being (out of nothing comes nothing), while equally it cannot come from being (for being already *is*). Thus fire could not come out of air, since air is air and not fire. To this Aristotle would reply that fire does not come out of air as air, but out of air which can be fire and is not yet fire, that has a potentiality to become fire. Abstractly put, a thing comes into being from its privation. If Parmenides were to object that this is tantamount to saying that a thing comes into being from not-being, Aristotle would answer that it does not come into being from its privation merely (i.e. from bare privation), but from its privation *in a subject*. Were Parmenides to retort that in this case a thing comes into being from being, which is a contradiction, Aristotle could answer that it does not come into being from being precisely as such, but from being which is also not-being, i.e. not the thing which it comes to be. He thus answers the Parmenidean difficulty by recourse to the distinction between form, matter and privation, or (better and more generally), between act, potency and privation.[4]

10. The distinction of potency and act leads to the doctrine of the hierarchy or scale of existence, for it is clear that an object which is in act as regards its own *terminus a quo* may be in potency as regards a further *terminus ad quem*. To use a hackneyed illustration, the hewn stone is in act as regards the unhewn stone—in respect to the latter's potentiality of being hewn—but in potency

[1] *Metaph.*, 1051 a 20–1. [2] *Metaph.*, 1051 a 17–18. [3] *Metaph.*, 985 a 9–10.
[4] For a discussion of potentiality and act, cf. *Metaph.*, Δ, 12 and Θ.

as regards the house, in respect to the part it will play in the house that is yet to be built. Similarly, the soul or ψυχή, i.e. the soul in its sensitive aspect and functions, is act in regard to the body, but potency in respect to the higher function of νοῦς. At the bottom of the ladder, so to speak, is prime matter, in itself unknowable and never actually existing apart from form. In union with the contraries, with heat or cold and with dryness or wetness, it forms the four bodies—earth, air, water and fire. These relatively, though not absolutely, simple bodies form in turn inorganic bodies, such as gold, and the simple tissues of living beings (both together called homoemerous bodies). Anomoemerous beings, organisms, are formed of homoemerous bodies as their material. Thus the rungs of the ladder are gradually ascended, until we come to the active intellect of man, unmixed with matter, the separate intelligence of the spheres and finally God. (The doctrine of the scale of existence should not, of course, be understood as involving "evolution." Pure forms do not evolve out of matter. Moreover, Aristotle held that species are eternal, though individual sensible objects perish.)

11. How is change initiated? Stone that is unhewn remains unhewn so far as the stone itself is concerned: it does not hew itself. No more does hewn stone build itself into a house. In both cases an external agent, source of the change or movement, is required. In other words, besides the formal and material causes an *efficient* cause is requisite, τὸ ὅθεν ἡ κίνησις. But this is not necessarily *external* to the thing that undergoes the change: for instance, according to Aristotle, each of the four elements has a natural movement towards its own proper place in the universe (e.g. fire goes "up"), and the element in question will move in accord with its natural motion unless it is hindered. It belongs to the form of the element to tend towards its natural region,[1] and thus the formal and efficient causes coincide. But this does not mean that the efficient cause is always identical with the formal cause: it is identical in the case of the soul, formal principle of the organism, regarded as initiator of movement; but it is not identical in the case of the builder of the house, while in that of the generation of the human being, for example, the efficient cause, the father, is only specifically, and not numerically, the same as the formal cause of the child.

12. It will be remembered that Aristotle thought of himself as

[1] *De Caelo*, 311 a 1–6.

being the first thinker to give real consideration to the final cause, τὸ οὗ ἕνεκα. But though he lays great stress on finality, it would be a mistake to suppose that finality, for Aristotle, is equivalent to *external* finality, as though we were to say, for instance, that grass grows in order that sheep may have food. On the contrary, he insists much more on internal or immanent finality (thus the apple tree has attained its end or purpose, not when the fruit forms a healthy or pleasant food for man or has been made into cider, but when the apple tree has reached that perfection of development of which it is capable, i.e. the perfection of its form), for in his view the formal cause of the thing is normally its final cause as well.[1] Thus the formal cause of a horse is the specific form of horse, but this is also its final cause, since the individual of a species naturally strives to embody as perfectly as may be the specific form in question. This natural striving after the form means that the final, formal and efficient causes are often the same. For example, in the organic substance the soul or ψυχή is the formal cause or determining element in the *compositum*, while at the same time it is also the efficient cause, as source of movement, and final cause, since the immanent end of the organism is the individual embodiment of the specific form. Thus the acorn, in the whole process of its development into a full-grown tree, is tending towards the full realisation of its final cause. In Aristotle's view it is the final cause itself which moves, i.e. by attraction. In the case of the oak tree its final cause, which is also its formal cause, causes the development of the acorn into the oak-tree by drawing up, as it were, the acorn towards the term of its process of development. It might of course be objected that the final cause, the perfected form of the oak, does not as yet exist and so cannot cause, while on the other hand it cannot cause as conceived in the mind (as the idea of the picture in the artist's mind is said to have a causal action), since the acorn is without mind and power of reflection. He would answer, no doubt, by recalling the fact that the form of the acorn is the form of the oak in germ, that it has an innate and natural tendency towards its own full evolution. But difficulties might arise for Aristotle if one were to continue asking questions.

(Of course, in spite of the tendency to run the causes together, Aristotle does not deny that the causes may be physically distinct from one another. For instance, in the building of a house, the

[1] *Metaph.*, H, 1044 a 36–b 11. Cf. *Physics*, B, 7, 198 a 24 ff.

formal cause of the house—so far as one can talk of the formal cause of a house—is not only conceptually but also physically distinct from the final cause, the idea or plan of the house in the architect's mind, as also from the efficient cause or causes. In general, however, one can say that the efficient, final, formal and material causes tend to melt, into two, that Aristotle inclines to reduce the four causes to two, namely, the formal cause and the material cause (though in our modern use of the term "cause" we naturally think first of all of efficient causality, and then perhaps of final causes).

This emphasis on finality does not mean that Aristotle excludes all mechanical causality, and this in spite of the anthropomorphic language he uses concerning teleology in nature, e.g. in his famous saying that "Nature does nothing in vain, nothing superfluous,"[1] language which is scarcely consistent with the theology of the *Metaphysics* at least. Sometimes finality and mechanism combine, as in the fact that light cannot but pass through the lantern, since its own particles are finer than those of the horn, though it thereby serves to preserve us from stumbling;[2] but in other cases there may be, he thinks, only mechanical causality at work (as in the fact that the colour of the eyes of the animal has no purpose, but is due simply to circumstances of birth).[3] Moreover, Aristotle says explicitly that we must not always look for a final cause, since some things have to be explained only by material or efficient causes.[4]

13. Every motion, every transit from potentiality to act, requires some principle in act, but if every becoming, every object in movement, requires an actual moving cause, then the world in general, the universe, requires a First Mover.[5] It is important, however, to note that the word "First" must not be understood temporally, since motion, according to Aristotle, is necessarily eternal (to initiate it or cause it to disappear would itself require motion). Rather is it to be understood as meaning *Supreme*: the First Mover is the eternal source of eternal motion. Moreover, the First Mover is not a Creator-God: the world existed from all eternity without having been created from all eternity. God forms the world, but did not create it, and He forms the world, is

[1] *De Caelo*, A 4, 271 a 33.
[2] *Anal. Post.*, 94 b 27–31. Cf. *De Gen. An.*, 743 b 16 f.
[3] *De Gen. An.*, 778 a 16-b 19; 789 b 19 f. *De Part. An.*, 642 a 2; 677 a 17–19
[4] *Metaph.*, 1049 b 24 ff.
[5] For First Mover, see *Metaph.*, Δ and *Physics*, Θ, 6, 258 b 10 f.

the source of motion, by *drawing* it, i.e. by acting as *final* cause. In Aristotle's view, if God caused motion by efficient physical causation—"shoving" the world, as it were—then He Himself would be changed: there would be a reaction of the moved on the mover. He must act, therefore, as Final Cause, by being the object of desire. To this point we shall return in a moment.

In *Metaphysics*, Λ 6 ff., Aristotle shows that this moving Principle must be of such a kind that it is pure act, ἐνέργεια, without potentiality. Presupposing the eternity of the world (if time could come into being there would, he thinks, be a time before time was—which is contradictory—and since time is essentially connected with change, change too must be eternal) he declares that there must be a First Mover which causes change without itself being changed, without having any potentiality, for if, for instance, it could cease from causing motion, then motion or change would not be necessarily eternal—which it is. There must accordingly be a First Mover which is pure act, and if it is pure act, then it must be immaterial, for materiality involves the possibility of being acted upon and changed. Moreover, experience, which shows that there exists the ceaseless, circular motion of the heavens, confirms this argument, since there must be a First Mover to move the heavens.

As we have seen, God moves the universe as Final Cause, as being the object of desire. Apparently God is conceived as moving directly the first heaven, causing the daily rotation of the stars round the earth. He moves by inspiring love and desire (the desirable and the intelligible are the same in the immaterial sphere), and so there must be an Intelligence of the first sphere, and other Intelligences in the other spheres. The Intelligence of each sphere is spiritual, and the sphere desires to imitate the life of its Intelligence as closely as may be. Not being able to imitate it in its spirituality, it does the next best thing by performing a circular movement. In an earlier period Aristotle maintained the Platonic conception of star souls, for in the Περὶ Φιλοσοφίας the stars themselves possess souls and move themselves; but he abandoned the conception in favour of that of the Intelligences of the spheres.

It is a curious fact that Aristotle does not seem to have had any very definite conviction as to the *number* of unmoved movers. Thus in the *Physics* there are three passages which refer to a plurality of unmoved movers,[1] while in the *Metaphysics* a plurality also appears.[2] According to Jaeger, chapter eight of *Metaphysics*, Λ is a later addition on Aristotle's part. In chapters seven and nine (continuous and forming part of the "original" *Metaphysics*) Aristotle speaks of the One Unmoved Mover. But in chapter eight the fifty-five transcendent movers make their appearance. Plotinus afterwards objected that the relation of these to the First Mover is left wholly obscure. He also asks how there can be a plurality of them, if matter is the principle of individuation—as Aristotle held it to be. Now, Aristotle himself saw this last objection, for he inserts the objection in the middle of chapter eight without giving a solution.[3] Even in Theophrastus' time some Aristotelians clung to *one* Unmoved Mover —not seeing how the independent movements caused by the plurality of movers could be harmonised.

It was ultimately due to this notion of a plurality of movers that mediaeval philosophers supposed there were Intelligences or Angels that move the spheres. By making them subordinate to and dependent on the First Mover or God, they were taking up the only possible position, since, if any harmony is to be achieved, then the other movers must move in subordination to the First Mover and should be related by intelligence and desire to Him, whether directly or indirectly, i.e. hierarchically. This the Neo-Platonists saw.

The First Mover, being immaterial, cannot perform any bodily action: His activity must be purely spiritual, and so intellectual. In other words, God's activity is one of thought. But what is the object of His thought? Knowledge is intellectual participation of the object: now, God's object must be the best of all possible objects, and in any case the knowledge enjoyed by God cannot be knowledge that involves change or sensation or novelty. God therefore knows Himself in an eternal act of intuition or self-consciousness. Aristotle, then, defines God as "Thought of Thought," νόησις νοήσεως.[4] God is subsistent thought, which eternally thinks itself. Moreover, God cannot have any object of thought outside Himself, for that would mean that He had an end outside Himself. God, therefore, knows only Himself. St.

[1] *Physics*, 258 b 11; 259 a 6–13; 259 b 28–31. (Jaeger thinks that these three passages are later additions, but as it is only in the third passage that A. assumes the actual existence of a plurality of unmoved movers, Ross (*Physics*, pp. 101–2) reasonably concludes that this passage alone was added after the completion of *Metaph.*, Λ).

[2] *Metaph.*, Λ 8. [3] *Metaph.*, 1074 a 31–8. [4] *Metaph.*, Λ 9, 1074 b 33–5.

Thomas[1] and others, e.g. Brentano, have tried to interpret Aristotle in such a way as not to exclude knowledge of the world and the exercise of Divine Providence; but, though St. Thomas is right as to the true view of God, it does not follow that this was the view of Aristotle. "Aristotle has no theory either of divine creation or of divine providence."[2] He does indeed speak in rather a different strain on occasion, as when he speaks of God as the captain of an army who brings about order in the army, or says that God provides for the continuance of generation in the case of those beings which, unlike the stars, are incapable of permanent existence: but such remarks should hardly be pressed in view of his treatment of the First Mover.[3]

Is the God of Aristotle a Personal God? Aristotle sometimes speaks of God as the First Unmoved Mover (τὸ πρῶτον κινοῦν ἀκίνητον), sometimes as ὁ θεός,[4] while in the *Nicomachean Ethics* he also speaks about οἱ θεοί.[5] Like most Greeks, Aristotle does not seem to have worried much about the number of the gods, but if we are to say that he was definitely and exclusively monotheist, then we would have to say that his God is personal. Aristotle may not have spoken of the First Mover as being personal, and certainly the ascription of anthropomorphic personality would be very far indeed from his thoughts, but since the First Mover is Intelligence or Thought, it follows that He is personal in the philosophic sense. The Aristotelian God may not be personal *secundum nomen*, but He is personal *secundum rem*. We should add, however, that there is no indication that Aristotle ever thought of the First Mover as an object of worship, still less as a Being to Whom prayers might profitably be addressed. And indeed, if Aristotle's God is entirely self-centred, as I believe Him to have been, then it would be out of the question for men to attempt personal intercourse with Him. In the *Magna Moralia* Aristotle says expressly that those are wrong who think that there can be a friendship towards God. For (*a*) God could not return our love, and (*b*) we could not in any case be said to *love* God.[6]

[1] *In Met.*, xii, lect. xi: *Nec tamen sequitur quod omnia alia a se ei sunt ignota; nam intelligendo se intelligit omnia alia.*

[2] Ross, *Aristotle*, p. 184.

[3] *In De Caelo*, A 4, 271 a 33. Aristotle says that God and nature do nothing in vain, but he had not yet elaborated his theory of the Unmoved Mover.

[4] *Metaph.* Λ 7.

[5] *Eth. Nic.*, e.g. 1170 b 8 ff. and 1179 a 24–5. Cf. *Eth. Nic.*, 1179 a 24–5.

[6] *M.M.*, 1208 b 26–32.

14. Other arguments for the existence of God are found in rudimentary form in Aristotle's works. Thus in the fragments of the Περὶ Φιλοσοφίας he pictures men who behold for the first time the beauty of the earth and sea and the majesty of the heavens, and conclude that they are the work of gods. This is an adumbration of the teleological argument.[1] In the same work Aristotle hints at least at a line of argument which was later to develop into the "fourth way" of St. Thomas Aquinas (through various intermediaries, of course). Aristotle there argues that "where there is a better, there is a best; now, among existing things one is better than another, therefore there is a best, which must be the divine."[2] This line of argument leads directly only to a *relatively* best: in order to arrive at the absolutely best, or the Perfect, it is necessary to introduce the idea of causality, arguing that all finite perfections ultimately spring from or are "participations" in Absolute Perfection, which is the fount of all finite perfections. This St. Thomas does, referring to a passage in the *Metaphysics*,[3] and even making use of Aristotle's illustration of fire, which is said to be the hottest of all things, inasmuch as it is the cause of the heat of all other things.[4] As far as Aristotle himself is concerned, the use of the degrees of perfection in order to prove God's existence would seem to be confined to his earlier period, when he is still strongly under Platonic influence: in the *Metaphysics* he does not use this line of argument in reference to the existence of the divine. In general, we must say that Aristotle, when he came to compose the *Metaphysics*, had moved a good way from the popular religious conceptions that appear, for example, in the fragments of the Περὶ Φιλοσοφίας. He continued on occasion to use language that hardly fits the conceptions of *Metaphysics*, Λ; but in any case we would not expect Aristotle to avoid all popular language, expressions and notions with an absolute and rigorous consistency, while it is also extremely probable that he never really attempted any final systematisation of his doctrine concerning God or to harmonise the expressions he sometimes employs implying Divine Providence and activity in the world with the speculations of the *Metaphysics*.

15. From what has been said, it should be apparent that Aristotle's notion of God was far from satisfactory. It is true that he shows a clearer apprehension of the ultimate Godhead

[1] Frag. 14. (Rose.) [2] Frag. 15. (Rose.)
[3] *Metaph.*, 993 b 23–31. Cf. 1008 b 31–1009 a 5.
[4] St. Thomas, *Summa Theologica*, Ia, q., 2, art. 3, in corp.

than Plato does, but in Book Λ of the *Metaphysics* at least, Aristotle leaves out of account that Divine operation in the world which was so insisted on by Plato, and which is an essential element in any satisfactory rational theology. The Aristotelian God is efficient Cause *only* by being the final Cause. He does not know this world and no Divine plan is fulfilled in this world: the teleology of nature can be nothing more than unconscious teleology (at least this is the only conclusion that will really fit in with the picture of God given in the *Metaphysics*). In this respect, therefore, the Aristotelian metaphysic is inferior to that of Plato. On the other hand, while not a few of Aristotle's doctrines must be traced to a Platonic origin, he certainly succeeded, by his doctrine of immanent teleology, of the movement of all concrete sensible objects towards the full realisation of their potentialities, in establishing the reality of the sensible world on a firmer foundation than was possible for his great predecessor, and at the same time attributed a real meaning and purpose to becoming and change, even if in the process he abandoned valuable elements of Plato's thought.

CHAPTER XXX

PHILOSOPHY OF NATURE AND PSYCHOLOGY

1. NATURE is the totality of objects which are material and subject to movement. As a matter of fact, Aristotle does not really define what he means by nature, but it is clear from what he writes in the *Physics*[1] that he regards Nature as the totality of natural objects, i.e. of objects which are capable of initiating change and of bringing it to an end, of objects which have an inner tendency to change. Artificial objects, a bed for instance, have not the power of self-movement. The "simple" bodies of which the bed is composed have this power of initiating change or movement, but they do so as natural bodies, not as components of a bed as such. This position has, of course, to be qualified by the doctrine that the passage of lifeless bodies from a state of rest to a state of movement must be initiated by an external agent. But, as we have seen, when the agent removes an obstacle, e.g. makes a hole in the bottom of a cauldron, the water responds with a movement of its own, its natural downward motion. This may seem a contradiction, namely, that natural objects are spoken of as having in themselves a principle of movement; while, on the other hand, Aristotle makes use of the maxim, that whatever is moved is moved in virtue of the action of an external agent.[2] Aristotle, however, holds that the apparent initiation of movement by animals, e.g. when an animal goes for food, is not an absolute initiation, for there would be no movement were the food not an external attractive agent. Similarly, when the water falls through the hole in the cauldron, this downward movement may indeed be spoken of as though it were a natural movement of the element, yet it is incidentally caused

[1] *Physics*, B 1, 192 b 13 ff.

[2] Aristotle's words in *Physics*, H 1, 241 b 39 ff. and Θ 4, 254 b 7 ff., may seem to be somewhat ambiguous. He says that whatever is moved is moved by something, either by itself or by something else, not that every moving thing is moved by something else; but the discussion that follows these words, when understood in the light of his principle of the priority of act to potency and in the light of his arguments for the existence of the Unmoved Mover shows clearly enough that in his eyes no moving thing can be the *absolute* initiator of motion. Whatever initiates motion *absolutely* must be itself *unmoved*. Whether there is a plurality of unmoved movers or not is, of course, another question. The principle, however, is clear.

by the external agent who makes the hole and so removes the obstacle to the natural motion of the water, while it is directly caused by that which generated the water and made it heavy, presumably by the primary contraries, hot or cold. Aristotle expresses the matter by saying that inanimate bodies have in themselves "a beginning of being moved" but not "a beginning of causing movement."[1]

2. Movement in the wider sense is divided into coming-to-be and passing-away on the one hand, and κίνησις or movement in the narrower sense on the other. This latter (κίνησις) is to be divided into its three kinds—qualitative movement (κίνησις κατὰ τὸ ποιόν or κατὰ πάθος), quantitative movement (κατὰ τὸ ποσόν or κατὰ μέγεθος) and local movement (κίνησις κατὰ τὸ ποῦ or κατὰ τόπον). The first is ἀλλοίωσις or qualitative change, the second αὔξησις καὶ φθίσις or quantitative change, the third φορά or motion in our ordinary sense of the word.[2]

3. Presuppositions of local motion, and indeed of all motion, are Place and Time. That Place (τόπος) exists is proved[3] (*a*) by the fact of displacement, e.g. by the fact that where there is water, there may come to be air; and (*b*) by the fact that the four elements have their natural places. These distinctions of natural place are not simply relative to us but exist independently: for instance "up" is the place whither fire moves and "down" the place whither earth moves. Place, therefore, exists and it is defined by Aristotle as τὸ τοῦ περιέχοντος πέρας ἀκίνητον πρῶτον,[4] the *Terminus continentis immobilis primus* of the Scholastics. Aristotle's τόπος, then, is the limit within which a body is, a limit considered as immobile. If this definition is adopted then obviously there can be no empty place nor any place outside the universe or world, for place is the inner limit of the containing body. But Aristotle distinguished between the vessel or container of a body and its place. In the case of a boat carried down by a stream, the stream—itself moving—is the vessel rather than the place of the boat. Place, then, is the first unmoved limit of the container, reckoning outwards. In the actual case in point the whole river, according to Aristotle, is the place of the boat and of whoever is in the boat, on the ground that the whole river is at rest, ὅτι ἀκίνητον ὁ πᾶς.[5] Everything in the physical universe

[1] *Physics*, 254 b 33–256 a 3. Cf. *De Caelo*, 311 a 9–12.
[2] *Physics*, E 2, 226 a 24 ff.; Θ 7, 260 a 26 ff.
[3] *Physics*, Δ 1, 208 a 27 ff. [4] *Physics*, Δ 4, 212 a 20 ff.
[5] *Physics*, Δ 4, 212 a 19–20.

is thus in a place, while the universe itself is not. Since, therefore, motion occurs through change of place, the universe itself cannot move *forwards*, but only by turning.

4. According to Aristotle a body can only be moved by a present mover in contact with the moved. What, then, are we to say of projectiles?[1] The original mover communicates to the medium, e.g. air or water, not only motion but also the power of moving. The first particles of air moved move other particles *and* the projectiles. But this power of moving decreases in proportion to the distance, so that in the end the projectile comes to rest irrespective of opposing forces. Aristotle is thus no believer in the law of inertia: he thought of compulsory movement as tending to decelerate, whereas "natural" movement tends to accelerate. (Cf. *Physics*, 230 a 18 ff.) In this he was followed by e.g. St. Thomas, who rejected the *impetus* theory of Philoponus, Al Bitrogi, Olivi, etc.

5. In regard to Time, Aristotle points out that it cannot be simply identified with movement or change, for movements are many, while time is one.[2] However, time is clearly connected with movement and change: if we are unaware of change, we are also unaware of time. The definition of time given by Aristotle is ὁ χρόνος ἀριθμός ἐστι κινήσεως κατὰ τὸ πρότερον καὶ ὕστερον.[3] He does not refer in this definition to pure number but to number in the sense of that which is numbered, i.e. to the numerable aspect of movement. Time, however, is a *continuum*, as movement is a continuum: it does not consist of discrete points.

Only things which are in movement or at rest in such a way that they are capable of movement, are in time: what is eternal *and* immobile is not in time. (Movement is eternal but obviously it is not immobile: therefore it is in time, and it necessarily follows that time also is eternal, in the sense that it never first began and will never end.) It is to be noted that the movement referred to is not of necessity local motion, for Aristotle expressly allows that the recognition even of a change in one's own state of mind may enable us to recognise a lapse of time. As to Aristotle's assertion that time is that in movement which is *counted*, it is not meant to be understood as though we could count the *nows* involved in change, as though the period of change were made up of discrete points of time: he means that, when one is conscious of time, one

[1] *Physics*, 215 a 14 ff.; 266 b 27 ff. [2] *Physics*, Δ 10–11, 218 a 30 ff.
[3] *Physics*, Δ 11, 219 b 1–2 ff.; 220 a 24–5 ff.

is recognising plurality, i.e. a plurality of phases. Time, then, is that aspect of element of change or movement, which makes it possible for the mind to recognise a plurality of phases.[1]

If we are to measure time, we must have a standard of measurement. According to Aristotle, movement in a straight line is not satisfactory for this purpose, for it is not uniform. If it is natural movement, it accelerates; if it is unnatural, it decelerates. What movement, then, is both natural and uniform? In Aristotle's view movement in a circle is naturally uniform, and the rotation of the heavenly spheres is a natural movement. So it is thus the best suited for our purpose—and telling time by the sun will be justified.[2]

Aristotle raises the question,[3] though he does not treat it at length, whether there would be time if there were no mind. In other words, as time is the measure of movement or movement *qua* countable, would there be any time if there were no mind to count? He answers that there would be no time, properly speaking, though there would be the substratum of time. Professor Ross comments that this position is consistent with Aristotle's general account of the *continuum*.[4] In the continuum there are no actual parts, but only potential parts. These are brought into actual existence when some event breaks up the *continuum*. So with time or duration. The "nows" within duration are brought into actual existence by a mind which distinguishes the "nows" within that duration. The difficulty that time may have existed when there were as yet no minds in existence, is at first sight no difficulty for Aristotle, since he thought of animals and men as having always existed. But a more pertinent difficulty is that counting is not the creation of parts, but the recognition of parts already there.[5] In any case, how could there be change if there were no time? We might suggest in answer that since, according to Aristotle, time is not really distinguished from the *prius* and *posterius* of motion, time exists independently of the mind, because motion does, though it receives a complement, as it were, from mind. "Parts" of time are potential in the sense that they are not formally distinguished from one another save by the "counting" mind; but they are not potential in the sense that they have no real existence apart from mind. Aristotle's position is not that of Kant, nor does it, of itself, lead to the position of Kant.

[1] Cf. Ross, *Physics*, p. 65.
[2] *Physics*, 223 a 29–224 a 2.
[3] *Physics*, 223 a 21–9.
[4] Ross, *Physics*, p. 68.
[5] Ross, *Physics*, p. 69.

6. Aristotle raises the question of the possibility of the infinite.

(*a*) An infinite body, he says, is impossible,[1] since every body is bounded by a surface, and no body which is bounded by a surface can be infinite. He also proves the impossibility of an existent actually infinite body by showing that it could be neither composite nor simple. For example, if it is supposed to be composite, the elements of which it is composed are themselves either infinite or finite. Now, if one element is infinite and the other element or elements finite, then the latter are deleted by the first, while it is impossible for both elements to be infinite, since one infinite element would equal the whole body. As to finite elements, composition of such elements would certainly not form one actually infinite body. Aristotle also considered that the existence of absolute "up," "down," etc., which he accepted, shows that there cannot be an existent actually infinite body, for such distinctions would be meaningless in the case of an infinite body. Nor can there be an actual infinite number, since number is that which can be numbered, whereas an infinite number could not be numbered.[2]

(*b*) On the other hand, though Aristotle rejected an existent actually infinite body or number, he admitted the infinite in another sense.[3] The infinite exists potentially. For example, no spatial extension is an actual infinite, but it is potentially infinite in the sense that it is infinitely divisible. A line does not consist of an actual infinite of points, for it is a *continuum* (it is in this way that Aristotle attempts, in the *Physics*, to meet the difficulties raised by Zeno the Eleatic), but it is infinitely divisible, though this potentially infinite division will never be completely realised in actuality. Time, again, is potentially infinite, since it can be added to indefinitely; but time never exists as an actual infinite, for it is a *successive continuum* and its parts never coexist. Time, therefore, resembles spatial extension in being infinitely divisible (though no actual infinity is ever realised), but is also potentially infinite by way of addition, and in this it differs from extension, since extension, according to Aristotle, has a maximum, even if it has no minimum. A third potential infinity is that of Number, which resembles time in being potentially infinite by way of addition, since you cannot count up to a number beyond which all counting and addition is impossible. Number, however, differs

[1] *Physics*, 5, 204 a 34–206 a 7. [2] *Physics*, 204 b 7–10. [3] *Physics*, 206 a 9 ff.

from both time and extension in being insusceptible of infinite division, for the reason that it has a minimum—the unit.

7. According to Aristotle, all natural motion is directed towards an end.[1] What is the end that is sought in nature? It is the development from a state of potentiality to one of actuality, the embodiment of form in matter. With Aristotle, as with Plato, the teleological view of nature prevails over the mechanical, even if it is difficult to see how Aristotle could logically admit any conscious teleology in regard to nature in general. The teleology is not, however, all-pervasive and all-conquering, since matter sometimes obstructs the action of teleology (as, for instance, in the production of monsters, which must be ascribed to defective matter.[2]) Thus the working of teleology in any particular instance may suffer interference from the occurrence of an event which does not serve the end in question at least, but the occurrence of which cannot be avoided owing to certain circumstances. This is τὸ αὐτόματον or the "fortuitous," consisting of those events which are "by nature," though not "according to nature," e.g. the production of a monster by generation. Such occurrences are undesirable and are distinguished by Aristotle from luck (τύχη), which denotes the occurrence of a desirable event, e.g. which might be the willed end of a purposive agent, as in the case of the finding of a treasure in a field.[3]

With what justification does Aristotle speak of "Nature" as having ends? Plato had made use of the conceptions of a World-Soul and of the Demiurge, and so was enabled to speak of ends in nature, but Aristotle talks as though there were some teleological activity inherent in nature itself. He does indeed speak on occasion of ὁ θεός, but he never gives any satisfactory treatment of the relation of nature to God, and what he says about God in the *Metaphysics* would seem to preclude any purposive activity in nature on the part of God. Probably it is true to say that Aristotle's increasing interest in empirical science led him to neglect any real systematisation of his position, and even lays him open to a justified accusation of inconsistency with his metaphysical presuppositions. While having no wish to reject or question Aristotle's view that there is teleology in nature, we are, it seems, compelled to admit that Aristotle's metaphysical system, his theology, gives him little justification for speaking of nature,

[1] *De Caelo*, A 4, 217 a 33. ὁ θεός καὶ ἡ φύσις οὐδὲν μάτην ποιοῦσιν.
[2] *De Gen. An.*, 767 b 13–23. [3] *Physics*, B, 4–6. Cf. *Metaph.*, E, 2–3.

as he not infrequently does, as though it were a consciously operating and organising principle. Such language bears an unmistakably Platonic flavour.

8. According to Aristotle the universe consists of two distinct worlds—the superlunary and the sublunary. In the superlunary world are the stars, which are imperishable and undergo no change other than that of local motion, their motion being circular and not rectilinear, as is the natural movement of the four elements. Aristotle concludes that the stars are composed of a different material element, *aether*, which is the fifth and superior element, incapable of any change other than change of place in a circular movement.

Aristotle maintained the view that the earth, spherical in shape, is at rest in the centre of the universe, and that round it lie the layers, concentric and spherical, of water, air and fire or the warm (ὑπέκκαυμα). Beyond these lie the heavenly spheres, the outermost of which, that of the fixed stars, owes its motion to the First Mover. Accepting from Calippus the number thirty-three as the number of spheres which must be presupposed in order to explain the actual motion of the planets, Aristotle assumed also twenty-two backward-moving spheres, interposed between the other spheres, in order to counteract the tendency of a sphere to disturb the motion of the planet in the next encompassed sphere. He thus obtained fifty-five spheres, excluding the outermost sphere; and this is the explanation of his suggestion in the *Metaphysics* that there are fifty-five unmoved movers, in addition to the First Mover that moves the outermost sphere. (He remarks that if the computation of Eudoxus be accepted instead of that of Calippus, then the number will be forty-nine).[1]

9. Particular things in this world come into being and pass away, but species and genera are eternal. There is, therefore, no evolution in the modern sense to be found in the system of Aristotle. But although Aristotle cannot develop any theory of temporal evolution, an evolution of species, he can and does develop a theory of what may be called "ideal" evolution, namely, a theory concerning the structure of the universe, a theory of the scale of being, in which form is ever more predominant as the scale is ascended. At the bottom of the scale comes inorganic matter, and above this organic matter, the plants being less perfect than the animals. Nevertheless, even the plants possess

[1] Cf. *Metaph.*, Λ, 8.

soul, which is the principle of life, and which Aristotle defines as "the entelechy of a natural body endowed with the capacity of life" or as "the first entelechy of a natural organic body." (So in *De Anima* B 1, 412 a 27–b 4, ψυχή ἐστιν ἐντελέχεια ἡ πρώτη σώματος φυσικοῦ δυνάμει ζωὴν ἔχοντος· τοιοῦτο δέ, ὃ ἂν ᾖ ὀργανικόν, or ἐντελέχεια ἡ πρώτη σώματος φυσικοῦ ὀργανικοῦ.) Being the act of the body, the soul is at the same time form, principle of movement, and end. The body is for the soul, and every organ has its purpose, that purpose being an activity.

At the beginning of the *De Anima* Aristotle points out the importance of an investigation concerning the soul, for the soul is, as it were, the vital principle in living things.[1] This problem is, however, he says, a difficult one, for it is not easy to ascertain the right method to be employed: but he insists—and how wisely—that the speculative philosopher and the naturalist have different standpoints, and so frame their definitions differently. It is not every thinker that has recognised that different sciences have their different methods, and that because a particular science cannot employ the method of the chemist or the natural scientist, it does not follow that all its conclusions must necessarily be vitiated.[2]

The composite substance, says Aristotle,[3] is a natural body endowed with life, the principle of this life being called the soul (ψυχή). Body cannot be soul, for body is not life but what has life. (In the first book of the *De Anima*, where Aristotle gives a history of Psychology, he remarks, apropos of the views of different philosophers concerning the soul, that "the most far-reaching difference is that between the philosophers who regard the elements as corporeal and those who regard them as incorporeal." Aristotle ranges himself with the Platonists as against the followers of Leucippus and Democritus.) The body, then, must be as matter to the soul, while the soul is as form or act to the body. Hence Aristotle, in his definition of the soul, speaks of it as the entelechy or act of the body that possesses life in potency —"potentiality of life," as he remarks, not referring to a thing which has become dispossessed of soul, but to that which possesses it. The soul is thus the realisation of the body and is inseparable from it (though there may be—as Aristotle held there were—parts which can be separated, because they are not precisely realisations of the body). The soul is thus the cause and principle

[1] *De An.*, 402 a 1–9. [2] *De An.*, 402 a 10 ff. [3] *De An.*, 412 a.

of the living body, (*a*) as source of movement,[1] (*b*) as final cause, and (*c*) as the real substance (i.e. formal cause) of animate bodies.

The different types of soul form a series of such a kind that the higher presupposes the lower, but not vice versa. The lowest form of soul is the nutritive or vegetative soul, τὸ θρεπτικόν, which exercises the activities of assimilation and reproduction. It is found, not only in plants, but also in animals; yet it can exist by itself, as it does in plants. In order that any living thing should continue to exist, these functions are necessary: they are found, therefore, in all living things, but in plants they are found alone, without the higher activities of soul. For plants sensation is not necessary, for they do not move but draw their nourishment automatically. (The same holds good, indeed, of motionless animals.) But animals endowed with the power of movement must have sensation, for it would be useless for them to move after their food, if they could not recognise it when they found it.

Animals, then, possess the higher form of soul, the sensitive soul, which exercises the three powers of sense-perception (τὸ αἰσθητικόν), desire (τὸ ὀρεκτικόν), and local motion (τὸ κινητικόν κατὰ τόπον).[2] Imagination (φαντασία) follows on the sensitive faculty, and memory is a further development of this.[3] Just as Aristotle has pointed out the necessity of nutrition for the preservation of life at all, so he shows the necessity of touch in order that an animal should be able to distinguish its food, at least when it is in contact with it.[4] Taste, whereby that which is food attracts the animal, and what is not food repels it, is also necessary. The other senses, though not strictly necessary, are for the well-being of the animal.

10. Higher in the scale than the merely animal soul is the human soul. This soul unites in itself the powers of the lower souls, τὸ θρεπτικόν, τὸ αἰσθητικόν, τὸ ὀρεκτικόν, τὸ κινητικόν κατὰ τόπον, but has a peculiar advantage in the possession of νοῦς, τὸ διανοητικόν. The latter is active in two ways, as the power of scientific thought (λόγος, νοῦς θεωρητικός = τὸ ἐπιστημονικόν) and as the power of deliberation (διάνοια πρακτική = λογιστικόν). The former has truth as its object, truth for its own sake, while the latter aims at truth, not for its

[1] Aristotle insists that the soul is badly defined if it is assigned motion as its characteristic. The soul moves actively but does not itself move. This is against the Platonic doctrine of the soul as a self-moving entity. Cf. *De An.*, A, 3.

[2] *De An.*, B 3.

[3] *De An.*, 3, 427 b 29 ff.; *Rhet.*, A 11, 1370 a 28–31; *De Mem.*, 1; *Anal. Post.*, B 19, 99 b 36 ff.

[4] *De An.*, 3, 12. Cf. *De Sensu*, 1.

own sake but for practical and prudential purposes. All the powers of the soul, with the exception of νοῦς, are inseparable from the body and perishable: νοῦς, however, pre-exists before the body and is immortal. λείπεται δὲ τὸν νοῦν μόνον θύραθεν ἐπεισιέναι καὶ θεῖον εἶναι μόνον.[1] This νοῦς, however, which enters into the body, requires a potential principle—a *tabula rasa*, on which it may imprint forms; and so we have the distinction between the νοῦς ποιητικός and the νοῦς παθητικός. (Aristotle speaks himself of τὸ ποιοῦν: the phrase νοῦς ποιητικός is first found in Alexander Aphrodisiensis, *c.* A.D. 220). The active intellect abstracts forms from the images or *phantasmata*, which, when received in the passive intellect, are actual concepts. (Aristotle considered that the use of imagery is involved in all thinking.) Only the active intellect is immortal. οὗτος ὁ νοῦς χωριστὸς καὶ ἀπαθὴς καὶ ἀμιγὴς τῇ οὐσίᾳ ὢν ἐνέργεια, ἀεὶ γὰρ τιμιώτερον τὸ ποιοῦν τοῦ πάσχοντος καὶ ἡ ἀρχὴ τῆς ὕλης . . . καὶ τοῦτο μόνον ἀθάνατον καὶ ἀΐδιον, . . . ὁ δὲ παθητικὸς νοῦς φθαρτός.[2] To this point I shall return in a moment.

11. If we leave out of account the question of the νοῦς ποιητικός, it is clear that Aristotle does not uphold the Platonic dualism in the *De Anima*, for he makes soul to be the entelechy of the body, so that the two form one substance. Altogether Aristotle allows a much closer union between soul and body than did the Platonists: the tendency to look on the body as the tomb of the soul is not that of Aristotle. Rather is it for the good of the soul to be united with the body, since only so can it exercise its faculties. This was the view adopted by the mediaeval Aristotelians, such as St. Thomas, although many great Christian thinkers had spoken and continue to speak, in language very reminiscent of the Platonic tradition—we have only to think of St. Augustine. Aristotle insisted that the Platonic School failed to give any satisfactory explanation of the soul's union with the body. They seem, he says, to suppose that any soul can fit itself into any body. This cannot be true, for every body appears to have a distinct form and character.[3] "A notion like that of Descartes, that the existence of the soul is the first certainty and the existence of matter a later inference, would have struck Aristotle as absurd. The whole self, soul and body alike, is something given and not questioned."[4] Needless to say, if Aristotle would have opposed the Cartesian view, he would also have opposed the

[1] *De Gen. et Corrupt.*, B 3, 738 b 27 ff.
[2] *De An.*, 3, 5, 430 a 17 ff.
[3] *De An.*, 414 a 19 ff.
[4] Ross, *Aristotle*, p. 132.

position of those who would reduce the whole human soul and all its activities to the condition of an epiphenomenon of the body, making the highest activity of human thought a mere efflorescence of the brain, though the direction of Aristotle's psychology, as it developed, would seem to have been towards a position suspiciously resembling an epiphenomenalist position, especially if one is right in supposing that the active intellect of man was not, in Aristotle's eyes, an individualised principle, which persisted after death as the individual mind of, e.g. Socrates or Callias. The absence of a doctrine of historical organic evolution would, however, naturally preclude Aristotle from accepting epiphenomenalism in the modern sense.

12. The well-worn question arises, "What was Aristotle's precise doctrine as to the Active Intellect?" Aristotle's *precise* doctrine one cannot give: it is a matter of interpretation, and different interpretations have been advanced both in the ancient and in the modern world. What Aristotle says in the *De Anima* is as follows: "This Nous is separable and impassible and unmixed, being essentially an actuality. For the active is always of higher value than the passive, and the originative principle than the matter. Actual knowledge is identical with its object; potential knowledge is prior in time in the individual, but in general it is not temporally prior; but Nous does at one time function and at another not. When it has been separated it is that only which it is in essence, and this alone is immortal and eternal. We do not remember, however, because active reason is impassible, but the passive reason is perishable, and without the active reason nothing thinks."[1]

Of this much-disputed passage various interpretations have been given. Alexander of Aphrodisias (*flor. c.* A.D. 220) identified "reason," i.e. the Active Intellect, with God, being followed in this by Zabarella (end of sixteenth and early seventeenth century A.D.), who would make God's function in the soul to be the illumination of the potentially known, as the sun's light makes what is visible to be actually seen. Now, although, as Sir David Ross points out,[2] it would not be necessarily inconsistent on Aristotle's part to speak of God's immanence in the *De Anima*, while speaking of His transcendence in the *Metaphysics*, while on the other hand it might be possible for the two books to represent divergent views of God, the interpretation of Alexander of Aphrodisias and

[1] *De An.*, 3, 5, 430 a 17 ff. [2] *Aristotle*, p. 153.

Zabarella, as Ross allows, is most unlikely. For is it probable that Aristotle, having described God as the Unmoved Mover Whose causal activity is one of attraction—as *Finis*—and as knowing only Himself, should go on, in another book, to depict God as immanent in man in such a way as actually to impart knowledge to him?

If the Active Intellect is not to be identified with God, is it to be regarded as individual and particular in each single man or as an identical principle in all men? Aristotle's words, "We do not remember," when taken together with his assertion[1] that memory and loving and hating perish at death, as belonging to the whole man and not to Reason, which is "impassable," seem to indicate that the Active Intellect in its separate existence has no memory. Although this does not prove with certainty that the Active Intellect of each man is not individual in its state of separation, it does seem to raise a difficulty in accepting such an interpretation. Moreover, when Aristotle asserts that "potential knowledge is prior in time in the individual, but in general it is not temporally prior, but Nous does not at one time function and at another not," he seems to be drawing a distinction between the individual, who at one time knows and at another not, and the Active Intellect, which is an essentially active principle. Perhaps, then, Aristotle regarded the Active Intellect as a principle which is identical in all men, an Intelligence that has above it the hierarchy of the other separate Intelligence, that enters into man and functions within him, and that survives the death of the individual. If this were correct, then the conclusion would necessarily follow that the individualised human soul perishes with the matter it informed.[2] (Yet, even if one is inclined to such an interpretation, one must admit that there is very considerable difficulty in supposing that, in Aristotle's opinion, the active intellect of Plato was numerically the same as that of Socrates. All the same, if he believed in the individual character of the active intellect in each single man, what did he mean when he said that it came "from outside"? Was this simply a relic of Platonism?)

[1] *De An.*, 408 b 24–30.

[2] St. Thomas Aquinas, in his Commentary on Aristotle's *De Anima* (3, lect. 10), does not interpret Aristotle in the Averroistic sense, i.e. as denying individual immortality. The active intellect is essentially and only an *active* principle: hence it is unaffected by passions and emotions and is not retentive of *species*. The separated human reason cannot, therefore, function as it does in the state of union with the body, and the mode of its functioning after death is not treated by Aristotle in the *De Anima*; but this omission does not mean that Aristotle denied individual immortality or condemned the separated intellect to a state of enforced and absolute inactivity.

CHAPTER XXXI

ARISTOTLE'S ETHICS

1. THE Ethics of Aristotle are frankly teleological. He is concerned with action, not as being right in itself irrespective of every other consideration, but with action as conducive to man's good. What conduces to the attainment of his good or end will be a "right" action on man's part: the action that is opposed to the attainment of his true good will be a "wrong" action.

"Every art and every inquiry, every action and choice, seems to aim at some good; whence the good has rightly been defined as that at which all things aim."[1] But there are different goods, corresponding to different arts or sciences. Thus the doctor's art aims at health, seamanship at a safe voyage, economy at wealth. Moreover, some ends are subordinate to other and more ultimate ends. The end of giving a certain medicine might be to produce sleep, but this immediate end is subordinate to the end of health. Similarly, the making of bits and reins for cavalry horses is the end of a certain craft, but it is subordinate to the wider and more comprehensive end of conducting warlike operations efficiently. These ends, therefore, have further ends or goods in view. But if there is an end which we desire for its own sake and for the sake of which we desire all other subordinate ends or goods, then this ultimate good will be the best good, in fact, *the* good. Aristotle sets himself to discover what this good is and what the science corresponding to it is.

As to the second question, Aristotle asserts that it is political or social science which studies the good for man. The State and the individual have the same good, though this good as found in the State is greater and nobler.[2] (Here we see an echo of the *Republic*, that in the ideal State we see justice writ large.) Ethics, then, are regarded by Aristotle as a branch of political or social science: we might say that he treats first of individual ethical science and secondly of political ethical science, in the *Politics*.

As to the question what is the good of man, Aristotle points out that it cannot be answered with the exactitude with which

[1] *E.N.*, 1094 a 1–3. [2] *E.N.*, 1094 a 27–b 11. Cf. *M.M.*, 1181 a and b.

a mathematical problem can be answered, and that owing to the nature of the subject-matter, for human action is the subject-matter of ethics, and human action cannot be determined with mathematical exactitude.[1] There is also this big difference between mathematics and ethics, that while the former starts from general principles and argues to conclusions, the latter starts with the conclusions. In other words, in ethics we start from the actual moral judgments of man, and by comparing, contrasting and sifting them, we come to the formulation of general principles.[2] This view presupposes that there are natural tendencies implanted in man, the following of which in a general attitude of consistent harmony and proportion, i.e. recognising relative importances and unimportances, is the ethical life for man. This view affords a basis for a natural as opposed to an arbitrary ethic, but considerable difficulties arise as to the theoretical establishment of moral *obligation*, especially in a system such as that of Aristotle, who cannot link up his ethic of human action with the Eternal Law of God, as Christian philosophers of the Middle Ages, who accepted so much from Aristotle, tried to do. However, in spite of such defects, Aristotle's ethic is eminently common-sense for the most part, founded as it is on the moral judgments of the man who was generally looked upon as a good and virtuous man. Aristotle intended his ethic to be a justification and supplementation of the natural judgments of such a man, who is, he says, best qualified to judge in matters of this kind.[3] It may be thought that the taste of the intellectual and professor comes out strongly in his picture of the ideal life, but one can scarcely accuse Aristotle of attempting a purely *a priori* and deductive ethic, or an *Ethica more geometrico demonstrata*. Moreover, although we can discern evidence of contemporary Greek taste in matters of human conduct, e.g. in Aristotle's account of the moral virtues, the philosopher certainly considered himself to be dealing with human nature as such, and to be founding his ethic on the universal characteristics of human nature—in spite of his opinion of the "barbarians." If he were alive to-day and had to answer, e.g. Friedrich Nietzsche, he would no doubt insist on the basic universality and constancy of human nature and the necessity

[1] *E.N.*, 1094 b 11–27. Cf. *E.E.*, I, 6.

[2] In the *Eudemian Ethics* Aristotle says that we start with "true but obscure judgments" (1216 b 32 ff.) or "the first confused judgments" (1217 a 18 ff.), and go on to form clear ethical judgments. In other words Aristotle starts with the ordinary moral judgments of men as the basis of argument.

[3] *E.N.*, 1094 b 27 ff.

of constant valuations, which are not merely relative but are founded in nature.

What do people generally view as the end of life? Happiness, says Aristotle, and he, like a true Greek, accepts this view. But obviously this does not take us very far by itself, for different people understand very different things by happiness. Some people identify it with pleasure, others with wealth, others again with honour, and so on. More than that, the same man may have different estimations of what happiness is at different times. Thus when he is ill he may regard health as happiness, and when he is in want he may regard wealth as happiness. But pleasure is rather an end for slaves than freemen, while honour cannot be the end of life, for it depends on the giver and is not really our own. Honour, moreover, seems to be aimed at assuring us of our virtue (hence, perhaps, the Victorian attachment to "respectability"); so perhaps moral virtue is the end of life. No, says Aristotle, for moral virtue can go with inactivity and misery; and happiness, which is the end of life, that at which all aim, must be an activity and excludes misery.[1]

Now, if happiness is an activity and an activity of man, we must see what activity is peculiar to man. It cannot be the activity of growth or reproduction, nor yet of sensation, since these are shared by other beings below man: it must be the activity of that which is peculiar to man among natural beings, namely, the activity of reason or activity in accordance with reason. This is indeed an activity of virtue—for Aristotle distinguished, besides the moral virtues, the intellectual virtues—but it is not what people ordinarily mean when they say that happiness consists in being virtuous, since they are generally thinking of moral virtues, such as justice, temperance, etc. In any case, happiness, as the ethical end, could not consist simply in virtue as such: it consists rather in activity according to virtue or in virtuous activity, understanding by virtue both the intellectual and the moral virtues. Moreover, says Aristotle, it must, if it really deserves the name of happiness, be manifested over a whole life and not merely for brief periods.[2]

But if happiness is essentially activity in accordance with virtue, Aristotle does not mean by this simply to exclude all the common notions about happiness. For instance, the activity to which virtue is the tendency is necessarily accompanied by

[1] *E.N.*, A 4 and ff. [2] *E.N.*, 1100 a 4 ff.; 1101 a 14–20.

pleasure, since pleasure is the natural accompaniment of an unimpeded and free activity. Again, without some external goods a man cannot well exercise that activity—an Aristotelian view to which the Cynics took exception, for the most part at least.[1] The character of happiness as an activity, and an activity peculiar to man, is therefore preserved without at the same time having to sacrifice or exclude pleasure and external prosperity. Once more Aristotle shows the common-sense character of his thought, and that he is not "over-transcendental" or hostile to this earth.

This being established, Aristotle goes on to consider, first the general nature of good character and good action, then the leading moral virtues, the virtues of that part of man which can follow the plan laid down by reason, then the virtues of the intellect. At the end of the *Nicomachean Ethics* he considers the ideal life, or the ideal life of activity in accordance with virtue, which life will be the truly happy life for man.

2. As to goodness of character in general, Aristotle says that we start by having a capacity for it, but that it has to be developed by practice. How is it developed? By doing virtuous acts. At first sight this looks like a vicious circle. Aristotle tells us that we become virtuous by doing virtuous acts, but how can we do virtuous acts unless we are already virtuous? Aristotle answers[2] that we begin by doing acts which are objectively virtuous, without having a reflex knowledge of the acts and a deliberate choice of the acts as good, a choice resulting from an habitual disposition. For instance, a child may be told by its parents not to lie. It obeys without realising perhaps the inherent goodness of telling the truth, and without having yet formed a habit of telling the truth; but the acts of truth-telling gradually form the habit, and as the process of education goes on, the child comes to realise that truth-telling is right in itself, and to choose to tell the truth for its own sake, as being the right thing to do. It is then virtuous in this respect. The accusation of the vicious circle is thus answered by the distinction between the acts which *create* the good disposition and the acts which *flow from* the good disposition once it has been created. Virtue itself is a disposition which has been developed out of a capacity by the proper exercise

[1] Aristotle remarks that the truly happy man must be sufficiently equipped with external goods. He thus rejects extreme Cynicism, but he warns us (cf. *E.E.*, 1214 b 25 f.) not to mistake indispensable conditions of happiness for essential elements of happiness.

[2] *E.N.*, B 1, 1103 a 14–b 26; B 4, 1105 a 17–b 18.

of that capacity. (Further difficulties might arise, of course, concerning the relation between the development of moral valuations and the influence of social environment, suggestion of parents and teachers, etc., but with these Aristotle does not deal.[1])

3. How does virtue stand to vice? It is a common characteristic of all good actions that they have a certain order or proportion, and virtue, in Aristotle's eyes, is a mean between two extremes, the extremes being vices, one being a vice through excess, the other being a vice through defect.[2] Through excess or defect of what? Either in regard to a feeling or in regard to an action. Thus, in regard to the feeling of confidence, the excess of this feeling constitutes rashness—at least when the feeling issues in action, and it is with human actions that ethics are concerned—while the defect is cowardice. The mean, then, will be a mean between rashness on the one hand and cowardice on the other hand: this mean is courage and is the virtue in respect to the feeling of confidence. Again, if we take the action of giving of money, excess in regard to this action is prodigality—and this is a vice—while defect in regard to this action is illiberality. The virtue, liberality, is the mean between the two vices, that of excess and that of defect. Aristotle, therefore, describes or defines moral virtue as "a disposition to choose, consisting essentially in a mean relatively to us determined by a rule, i.e. the rule by which a practically wise man would determine it."[3] Virtue, then, is a disposition, a disposition to choose according to a rule, namely, the rule by which a truly virtuous man possessed of moral insight would choose. Aristotle regarded the possession of practical wisdom, the ability to see what is the right thing to do in the circumstances, as essential to the truly virtuous man, and he attaches much more value to the moral judgments of the enlightened conscience than to any *a priori* and merely theoretical conclusions. This may seem somewhat naïve, but it must be remembered that for Aristotle the prudent man will be the man who sees what is truly good for a man in any set of circumstances: he is not required to enter upon any academic preserve, but to see what truly befits human nature in those circumstances.

When Aristotle speaks of virtue as a mean, he is not thinking

[1] Aristotle thus insists that a completely right action must be not only "externally" the right thing to do in the circumstances, but also done from a right motive, proceeding from a moral agent acting precisely as a moral agent. (Cf. *E.N.*, 1105 b 5 ff.).

[2] *E.N.*, B, 6 ff.

[3] *E.N.*, 1106 b 36–1107 a 2.

of a mean that has to be calculated arithmetically: that is why he says in his definition "relatively to us." We cannot determine what is excess, what mean and what defect by hard-and-fast, mathematical rules: so much depends on the character of the feeling or action in question: in some cases it may be preferable to err on the side of excess rather than on that of defect, while in other cases the reverse may be true. Nor, of course, should the Aristotelian doctrine of the mean be taken as equivalent to an exaltation of mediocrity in the moral life, for as far as excellence is concerned virtue is an extreme: it is in respect of its essence and its definition that it is a mean. One may illustrate this important point by a diagram given in the *Ethics* of Professor Nicolai Hartmann of Berlin,[1] in which the horizontal line at the bottom of the figure represents the ontological dimension, and the vertical line the axiological dimension.

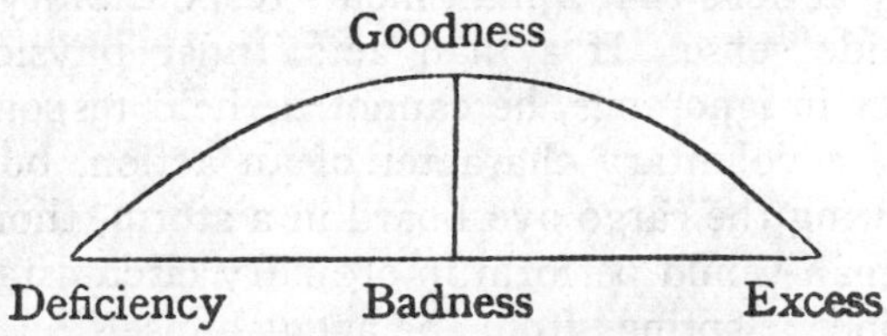

This diagram illustrates the important point that virtue (ἀρετή) has a double position. (i) As regards the ontological dimension, it is a mean (μεσότης); as regards the axiological dimension, it is an excellence or extreme (ἀκρότης). It is not as though virtue were a composition of vices from a valuational point of view, since, from this point of view, it stands in opposition to both vices; but it is nevertheless a mean from the ontological viewpoint, since it combines in itself both the good points which, run to excess, constitute vices. For example, courage is not boldness alone, nor is it cool foresight alone, but a synthesis of both—this character of a synthesis preventing courage from degenerating into the daring of the foolhardy man on the one hand or the prudence of the coward on the other hand. "What Aristotle so strongly felt in the lower moral values, without being able to formulate it, was just this, that all valuational elements, taken in isolation, have in them a point beyond which they are dangerous, that they are tyrannical, and that for the true fulfilment

[1] *Ethics*, by Nicolai Hartmann, vol. 2, p. 256. (Trans., Dr. Stanton Coit. George Allen & Unwin, Ltd.)

of their meaning in their real carrier there is always a counterweight. Because of this profoundly justified feeling, he assigned virtue to no one of these elements but to their synthesis. It is precisely in their synthesis that the danger in values is diminished, their tyranny in consciousness paralysed. In this matter Aristotle's procedure is a model for every further treatment of the problem of contrasts."[1]

One must, however, admit that Aristotle's treatment of the virtues betrays the fact that he was under the influence of the predominantly *aesthetic* attitude of the Greek towards human conduct, a fact that appears in a clear light in his treatment of the "great-souled" man. The notion of a crucified God would have been abhorrent to him: it would most probably have seemed in his eyes at once unaesthetic and irrational.

4. A presupposition of moral action is Freedom, since it is only for voluntary actions that a man incurs responsibility, i.e. voluntary in a wide sense. If a man acts under physical external compulsion or in ignorance, he cannot be held responsible. Fear may lessen the voluntary character of an action, but an action such as throwing the cargo overboard in a storm, though not one that a sane man would perform in ordinary circumstances, is yet voluntary, since it springs from the agent himself.[2]

In regard to ignorance Aristotle certainly makes some pertinent observations, as when he points out that while a man who acts in rage or under the influence of drink may be said to act *in* ignorance, he cannot be said to act *from* ignorance, for that ignorance is itself due to rage or drink.[3] However, his assertion that an action done through ignorance is involuntary if it is subsequently regretted by the agent, non-voluntary if not subsequently regretted, can scarcely be accepted, for although the agent's subsequent attitude may reveal his general character, i.e. whether he is on the whole a good or bad man, it cannot serve to differentiate between unwilling and merely involuntary acts.[4]

In regard to the Socratic position that no man acts against knowledge, Aristotle does on occasion show that he is alive to the reality of the moral struggle[5] (he was too good a psychologist to disregard the point), but when he is treating formally of the question, in reference to continence and incontinence,[6] he tends

[1] Hartmann, *Ethics*, 2, p. 424.
[2] *E.N.*, Γ 1, 1100 a 8–19.
[3] *E.N.*, Γ1, 1110 b 24–7.
[4] *E.N.*, Γ 1110 b 18 ff.
[5] *E.N.*, e.g. 1102 b 14 ff.
[6] *E.N.*, H.

to overlook this and to emphasise the view that the man who does a wrong act does not know at the moment of action that the act is wrong. This may certainly happen sometimes, e.g. in the case of actions done under the stress of passion, but Aristotle does not allow sufficiently for the truth that a man may do deliberately what he knows to be wrong, and, moreover, what he knows to be wrong at the moment that he does it. It might be remarked that, owing to what might be called the strictly human character of Aristotle's ethic, by which "right" is explained in terms of "good," he could answer that even the incontinent man acts *sub ratione boni*. This is true, but all the same the incontinent man may know well enough that the action he performs is morally wrong. In fact, Aristotle, while professedly rejecting the Socratic theory, was none the less dominated by it to a certain extent. He lacked a proper concept of duty, though in this he seems to have been at one with other Greek theorists before the rise of the Stoics, with certain reservations in the case of Plato. An action may be good or contributory to good without thereby being strictly obligatory, a duty, and Aristotle's ethical theory does not account for this distinction.

5. Aristotle, like Plato before him, had no really distinct concept of will, but his description or definition of choice as "desireful reason" or "reasonable desire"[1] or as "the deliberate desire of things in our power,"[2] shows that he had some idea of will, for he does not identify preferential choice (προαίρεσις) with either desire by itself or with reason by itself. His description of it would seem to indicate that he regarded it as substantially *sui generis*. (Aristotle does indeed declare that προαίρεσις has to do with means and not with ends, but in his use of the word, both in the *Ethics* itself and also elsewhere, he is not consistent.[3])

Aristotle's analysis of the moral process is as follows. (i) The agent desires an end. (ii) The agent deliberates, seeing that B is the means to A (the end to be obtained), C the means to B, and so on, until (iii) he perceives that some particular means near to the end or remote from it, as the case may be, is something that he can do here and now. (iv) The agent chooses this means that presents itself to him as practicable *hic et nunc*, and (v) does the act in question. Thus a man might desire happiness (in fact, he always does, Aristotle thought). He then sees that health is a

[1] *E.N.*, 1139 b 4–5. [2] *E.N.*, 1113 a 9–11.
[3] *E.N.*, e.g. 1111 b 26 ff. But cf. e.g. 1144 a 20 ff.

means to happiness, and that exercise is a means to health. He then perceives that to go for a walk is something that he can do here and now. He chooses this act and does it, i.e. takes the walk. This analysis may be a very good statement of the way in which we fix on actions in view of an end: the difficulty is to allow for any real moral obligation in Aristotle's system, at least if considered in itself and without any of the supplementary treatment that later philosophers have given it.

From the doctrine that virtuous activity is voluntary and in accordance with choice, it follows that virtue and vice are in our power, and that Socrates' doctrine is false. True, a man may have formed a bad habit of such strength that he cannot cease to perform the intrinsically bad actions that naturally flow from that habit, but he could have refrained from contracting that habit in the first place. A man may have so blinded his conscience that he fails now to discern the right, but he is himself responsible for his blindness and for bringing about his ignorance. This may be said to be the general thought of Aristotle, though, as we have seen, in his formal treatment of the Socratic position he does not do sufficient justice to moral weakness and to sheer wickedness.

6. Aristotle's treatment of the moral virtues is often enlightening and shows his common-sense moderation and clear judgment. For example, his characterisation of courage as a mean between rashness or foolhardiness and cowardice, seems, when developed, to set the true nature of courage in relief and to distinguish it from forms of pseudo-courage. Similarly, his description of the virtue of temperance as a mean between profligacy and "insensibility," serves to bring out the truth that temperance or self-control in regard to the pleasures of touch does not of itself involve a puritanical attitude towards sense and the pleasures of sense. Again, his insistence that the mean is a mean "relatively to us" and cannot be arithmetically determined, brings out his practical, empirical and common-sense outlook. As he pertinently remarks, "If ten pounds of food are too much for a man and two are too little, the trainer in gymnastics will not order six pounds, for this may be too much or too little for the special case: for a Milo it may be too little, but for one who is beginning to train it may be too much."[1]

It can hardly be denied, however (and who would expect anything else?) that his treatment of the virtues is, to a certain

[1] *E.N.*, 1106 a 36-b 4.

extent, determined by contemporary Greek taste.[1] Thus his view that the "great-souled" and self-respecting man will be ashamed of receiving benefits and so putting himself in the position of an inferior, while on the contrary he will always pay back benefits received with greater ones in order to make his friend his debtor, may be in accordance with Greek taste (or with those of Nietzsche), but will scarcely be acceptable in all quarters. Again, Aristotle's pictures of the "great-souled" man as slow in step, deep in voice and sedate in speech is largely a matter of aesthetic taste.[2]

7. In Book Five of the *Ethics* Aristotle treats of Justice. Under Justice he understands (*a*) what is lawful and (*b*) what is fair and equal. (τὸ μὲν δίκαιον ἄρα τὸ νόμιμον καὶ τὸ ἴσον, τὸ δ' ἄδικον τὸ παράνομον καὶ τὸ ἄνισον (*E.N.*, 1129 a 34)). The first kind of justice, "universal" justice, is practically equivalent to obedience to law, but since Aristotle envisages the law of the State—ideally, at least—as extending over the whole of life and enforcing virtuous actions in the sense of materially virtuous actions (since of course law cannot enforce virtuous actions, formally or subjectively considered), universal justice is more or less coterminous with

[1] The conception of a man claiming honour from others as a due to his "virtue" and nobility is somewhat repugnant to us, but it was a lineal descendant of the Homeric hero's expectation of honour as due to his ἀρετή.

[2] *E.N.*, 1124 b 9–1125 a 16.
Sir David Ross gives the following tabulation of the moral virtues as treated by Aristotle. (*Aristotle*, p. 203.)

Feeling	*Action*	*Excess*	*Mean*	*Defect*
Fear		Cowardice	Courage	Unnamed
Confidence		Rashness	Courage	Cowardice
Certain pleasures of touch		Profligacy	Temperance	Insensibility
(Pain arising from desire of such pleasures)	Giving of money	Prodigality	Liberality	Illiberality
	Taking of money	Illiberality	Liberality	Prodigality
	Giving of money on large scale	Vulgarity	Magnificence	Meanness
	Claiming of honour on large scale	Vanity	Self-respect	Humility
	Pursuit of honour on small scale	Ambition	Unnamed	Unambition
Anger		Irascibility	Gentleness	Unirascibility
Social Intercourse	Telling truth about oneself	Boastfulness	Truthfulness	Self-depreciation
	Giving of pleasure: By way of amusement	Buffoonery	Wittiness	Boorishness
	in life generally	Obsequiousness	Friendliness	Sulkiness
Shame		Bashfulness	Modesty	Shamelessness
Pains at good or bad fortune of others		Envy	Righteous Indignation	Malevolence

virtue, looked at in its social aspect at any rate. Aristotle, like Plato, is firmly convinced of the positive and educative function of the State. This is diametrically opposed to theories of the State, such as those of Herbert Spencer in England and Schopenhauer in Germany, who rejected the positive functions of the State and confined the functions of law to the defence of personal rights, above all the defence of private property.

"Particular" justice is divided into (*a*) Distributive Justice, whereby the State divides goods among its citizens according to geometrical proportions, i.e. according to merit (as Burnet says, the Greek citizen regarded himself as a shareholder in the State, rather than as a taxpayer), and (*b*) Remedial Justice. This latter is subdivided into two types, (i) that dealing with voluntary transactions (Civil Law), and (ii) that dealing with involuntary transactions (Criminal Law). Remedial Justice proceeds according to arithmetical proportion. Aristotle added to these two main divisions of particular justice Commercial or Commutative Justice.

According to Aristotle, Justice is a mean between acting unjustly and being unjustly treated.[1] But this is hardly acceptable and is obviously asserted merely in order to bring justice into line with the other virtues already discussed. For the business man, for instance, who is just in his dealings, is the man who chooses to give the other fellow his due and to take exactly his own share without further extortion, rather than to give the other man less than his due or to take for himself more than what is owing to him. To give the other fellow more than his share or to accept for himself less than his own due, is scarcely a vice—or even, necessarily, to be unjustly treated. However, Aristotle goes on to say, rather more happily, that justice is not really a mean as the other virtues are, but is a mean in the sense that it produces a state of affairs that stand midway between that in which A has too much and that in which B has too much.[2]

Finally[3] Aristotle draws the very valuable distinction between various types of action that are materially unjust, pointing out that to do an action which results in damage to another, when the damage was not foreseen or intended—and still more if the damage would not ordinarily result from that action—is very different from doing an action which would naturally result in

[1] *E.N.*, 1133 b 30–2. [2] *E.N.*, 1133 b 32 ff.
[3] *E.N.*, E, 8, 1135 a 15–36 a 9. Cf. *Rhet.*, 1374 a 26–b 22.

damage to another, particularly if that damage was foreseen and intended. The distinctions drawn afford room for equity as a type of justice superior to legal justice, the latter being too general for application to all particular cases. καὶ ἔστιν αὕτη ἡ φύσις ἡ τοῦ ἐπιεικοῦς, ἐπανόρθωμα νόμου, ᾗ ἐλλείπει διὰ τὸ καθόλου.[1]

8. Discussing the intellectual virtues Aristotle divides them according to the two rational faculties, (i) the scientific faculty—τὸ ἐπιστημονικόν, by which we contemplate objects that are necessary and admit of no contingency, and (ii) the calculative faculty—τὸ λογιστικόν, or faculty of opinion, which is concerned with objects that are contingent. The intellectual virtues of the scientific faculty are ἐπιστήμη, "the disposition by virtue of which we demonstrate,"[2] and which has regard to proof, and νοῦς or intuitive reason, whereby we grasp a universal truth after experience of a certain number of particular instances and then see this truth or principle to be self-evident.[3] The union of νοῦς and ἐπιστήμη is theoretical wisdom or σοφία, and it is directed to the highest objects—probably including not only the objects of Metaphysics, but also those of Mathematics and Natural Science. The contemplation of these objects belongs to the ideal life for man. "Wisdom or philosophy may be defined as the combination of intuitive reason and science, or as scientific knowledge of the most precious things, with the crown of perfection, so to speak, upon it." Knowledge is dignified by its object, and Aristotle remarks that it would be absurd to call political science the highest type of knowledge, unless indeed men were the highest of all beings—and that he did not believe.[4] "There are other things in the universe of a nature far more divine than his, as, for example, the starry heavens of which the universe is built. From all of which it is clear that wisdom is a combination of science and the speculative reason, directed to the noblest objects in creation."[5]

The virtues of τὸ λογιστικόν are τέχνη or art, "the disposition by which we make things by the aid of a true rule,"[6] and practical wisdom or φρόνησις, "a true disposition towards action, by the aid of a rule, with regard to things good or bad for men."[7] φρόνησις is subdivided according to the objects with which it is concerned. (i) As concerned with the individual's good, it is φρόνησις in the narrow sense. (ii) As concerned with the family, with household

[1] *E.N.*, 1137 b 26–7. [2] *E.N.*, 1139 b 31–2. [3] *E.N.*, Z, 6, 1140 b 31–1141 a 8.
[4] *E.N.*, 1141 a 9–2. [5] *E.N.*, 1141 a 33–b 3. [6] *E.N.*, 1140 a 9–10, 20–21.
[7] *E.N.*, 1140 b 4–6.

management, it is called Economics (οἰκονομία). (iii) As concerned with the State, it is called Political Science in the wider sense. This latter, Politics in a wide sense, is again subdivided into (*a*) the Architectonic or Legislative faculty, Politics in the narrower sense, and (*b*) the Subordinate or Administrative faculty. The last again subdivides into (α) Deliberative and (β) Judicial. (It is important to note that, in spite of these divisions, it is really the same virtue that is called practical wisdom in connection with the individual and Politics in connection with the good of the State.)

Practical wisdom, says Aristotle, is concerned with the practical syllogism, e.g. A is the end, B is the means, therefore B should be done. (If Aristotle were confronted with the difficulty that this only gives us an hypothetical imperative and not a categorical imperative, he might answer that in ethical matters the end is happiness, and as happiness is an end that all seek and cannot help seeking, that they seek by nature, the imperative that bears on our choice of means to this end is different from the imperatives that bear on the means to some freely-chosen end, and that while the latter are hypothetical, the former is a categorical imperative.) But Aristotle, with his customary good sense, expressly recognises that some people may have knowledge of the right action to do from their experience of life, although they have not got a clear idea of the general principles. Hence it is better to know the conclusion of the practical syllogism, without the major premiss, than to know the major premiss without knowing the conclusion.[1]

In reference to Socrates' view that all virtue is a form of prudence, Aristotle declares that Socrates was partly right and partly wrong. "He was wrong in holding that all virtue is a form of prudence, but right in holding that no virtue can exist without prudence."[2] Socrates held that all the virtues were forms of reason (as being forms of knowledge), but Aristotle declares that the truth is rather that they are all *reasonable*. "Virtue is not only the right and reasonable attitude, but the attitude which leads to right and reasonable choice, and right and reasonable choice in these matters is what we mean by prudence."[3] Prudence, therefore, is necessary for the truly virtuous man, (*a*) as being "the excellence of an essential part of our nature," and (*b*) inasmuch as "there can be no right choice without both prudence

[1] *E.N.*, 1141 b 14–22. [2] *E.N.*, 1144 b 19–21. [3] *E.N.*, 1144 b 26–8.

and virtue, seeing that the latter secures the choice of the right end, and the former the choice of the right means to its attainment."[1] But prudence or practical wisdom is not the same thing as cleverness (δεινότης). Cleverness is the faculty by which a man is enabled to find the right means to any particular end, and a rogue may be very clever in discovering the right means to attain his ignoble end. Mere cleverness is, then, different from prudence, which presupposes virtues and is equivalent to moral insight.[2] Prudence cannot exist without cleverness, but it cannot be reduced to cleverness, for it is a moral virtue. In other words, prudence is cleverness as dealing with the means that lead to the attainment, not of any sort of end, but of the true end of man, what is best for man, and it is moral virtue that enables us to choose the right end, so that prudence presupposes moral virtue. Aristotle is quite well aware that it is possible for a man to do what is right, what he ought to do, without being a good man. He is good only if his action proceeds from moral choice and is done because it is good.[3] For this prudence is necessary.

Aristotle admits that it is possible to have "natural" virtues in separation from one another (e.g. a child might be naturally courageous, without being at the same time gentle), but in order to have a moral virtue in the full sense, as a reasonable disposition, prudence is necessary. Moreover, "given the single virtues of prudence, all the virtues necessarily follow from it."[4] Socrates was then right in holding that no virtue can exist without prudence, though he was wrong in supposing that all virtues are forms of prudence. In the *Eudemian Ethics*[5] Aristotle remarks that for Socrates all the virtues were forms of knowledge, so that to know what justice is, for example, and to be just would come simultaneously, just as we are geometers from the moment we have learned geometry. In reply Aristotle says that it is necessary to distinguish between theoretical science and productive science. "We do not wish to know what bravery is but to be brave, nor what justice is but to be just." Similarly, he observes in the *Magna Moralia*[6] that "any one who knows the essence of justice is not forthwith just," while in the *Nicomachean Ethics* he compares those who think they will become good by mere theoretical knowledge, to patients who listen attentively to what the doctor says, but carry out none of his orders.[7]

[1] *E.N.*, 1145 a 2–6. [2] *E.N.*, 1144 a 23 ff. [3] *E.N.*, 1144 a 13 ff.
[4] *E.N.*, 1144 b 32–45 a 2. [5] *E.E.*, 1216 b 3–26. [6] *M.M.*, 1183 b 15–16.
[7] *E.N.*, 1105 b 12–18.

9. Aristotle refuses to admit that pleasures as such are bad. Pleasure cannot indeed be *the* good, as Eudoxus thought, for pleasure is the natural accompaniment of an unimpeded activity (as a sort of colouring attached to the activity), and it is the activity that should be aimed at, not the accompanying pleasure. We ought to choose certain activities, even if no pleasure resulted from them.[1] Nor is it true to say that all pleasures are desirable, for the activities to which certain pleasures are attached are disgraceful.

But if pleasure is not *the* good, we must not fall into the opposite extreme and say that all pleasure is wrong because some pleasures are disgraceful. As a matter of fact, says Aristotle, we might really say that disgraceful pleasures are not really pleasant, just as what appears white to a man with bad eyes, may not be really white. This observation is perhaps not very convincing: more convincing is Aristotle's remark that the pleasures themselves may be desirable, but not when obtained in such a way: and still more convincing is his suggestion that pleasures differ specifically according to the activities from which they are derived.[2]

Aristotle will not allow that pleasure is simply a replenishment, i.e. that pain represents a falling-short in the natural state, and that pleasure is a replenishment of the deficiency. It is true, indeed, that where there is replenishment there is pleasure, and that where there is exhaustion there is pain, but we cannot say universally of pleasure that it is a replenishment after antecedent pain. "The pleasures of mathematics, among the pleasures of sense those of smell as well as many sights and sounds, lastly, hopes and memories, are instances of pleasure which involve no antecedent pain."[3]

Pleasure, then, is something positive, and its effect is to perfect the exercise of a faculty. Pleasures differ specifically according to the character of the activities to which they are attached, and the good man must be our standard as to what is truly pleasant and unpleasant. (Aristotle remarks on the importance of training children to delight in and dislike the proper things, for which purpose the educator uses pleasure and pain "as a species of rudder."[4]) Some pleasures are pleasant only to those whose nature is corrupt: the true pleasures for man are those that accompany the activities that are proper to man. "All others, like the activities which they accompany, are so only in a partial and secondary sense."[5]

[1] *E.N.*, 1174 a 7–8. [2] *E.N.*, 1173 b 20–31. [3] *E.N.*, 1173 b 16–19. [4] *E.N.*, 1172 a 19–25. [5] *E.N.*, 1176 a 22–9.

In all this discussion of Pleasure, Aristotle's good sense and psychological insight are evident. He may be thought by some to over-emphasise the pleasures of theoretical and purely intellectual activity, but he sedulously avoids all extreme positions, refusing to agree with Eudoxus on the one hand that pleasure is *the* good, or with Speusippus on the other hand that all pleasures are bad.

10. Aristotle devotes Books Eight and Nine of the *Ethics* to the subject of Friendship. Friendship, he says, "is one of the virtues, or at any rate implies virtue. Moreover, it is one of the prime necessities of life."[1] Aristotle tends to give a somewhat self-centred picture of friendship. Thus he emphasises our need for friends at different periods of our life, and suggests that in friendship a man is loving himself—at first hearing a rather egoistic viewpoint. But he attempts the reconciliation of egoism and altruism by pointing out that it is necessary to distinguish the uses of the term "self-loving." Some men seek to get as much as possible for themselves of money, honour or the pleasures of the body, and these we call self-loving by way of reproach: others, i.e. good men, are anxious to excel in virtue and noble actions, and these, though "self-loving," we do not blame as such. The latter type of man "will give away money in order that his friend may have more. For the money goes to the friend, but the noble deed to himself, and in this way he appropriates the greater good. Similarly with regard to honours and offices."[2] The picture of a man relinquishing money or office to his friend in order that he himself may have the noble action to his credit, is not altogether pleasing; but Aristotle is doubtless right in observing that there can be a good type of self-love as well as a bad type. (Indeed we are bound to love ourselves and to make ourselves as good as possible.) A happier thought is Aristotle's saying that a man's relations to his friend are the same as his relations to himself, since the friend is a second self.[3] In other words, the concept of the self is capable of extension and may grow to include friends, whose happiness or misery, success or failure, become as our own. Moreover, incidental observations, such as "friendship consists in loving rather than in being loved,"[4] or that "men wish well to their friends for their sake,"[5] show that his view of friendship was not so egoistic as his words would sometimes lead one to suppose.

[1] *E.N.*, 1155 a 3–5. [2] *E.N.*, 1169 a 27–30. [3] *E.N.*, 1166 a 30–2.
[4] *E.N.*, 1159 a 27–8. [5] *E.N.*, 1157 b 31–2.

That Aristotle's concept of friendship was a very wide one can be seen from the divisions that he makes between different types of friendship. (i) On the lowest level are friendships of utility, in which men do not love their friends for what they are in themselves, but only for the advantage which they receive from them.[1] Such friendships are necessary to man, since man is not economically self-sufficient. A business friendship would be of this type. (ii) Friendships of pleasure. These are founded on the natural delight that men take in the society of their fellow-men, and are characteristic of the young, for "young people live by feeling, and have a main eye to their own pleasure and to the present moment."[2] But both these types of friendship are unstable, for when the motive of the friendship—utility or pleasure—is gone, the friendship also is destroyed. (iii) Friendships of the good. This type of friendship is perfect friendship and endures as long as both retain their character—"and virtue," says Aristotle, "is a lasting thing."

As we would expect, Aristotle makes not a few observations on the subject of friendship, which, if not profound, are shrewd and to the point, and which are applicable not only to natural friendship, but also to supernatural friendship with Christ Our Lord. For example, he observes that friendship differs from affection in that the latter is a feeling, the former a trained habit of mind,[3] and that "the wish for friendship is of rapid growth, but friendship itself is not."[4]

11. "If happiness is activity in accordance with virtue, it is reasonable that it should be in accordance with the highest virtue, and this will be that of the best thing in us."[5] The faculty, the exercise of which constitutes perfect happiness, is, according to Aristotle, the contemplative faculty, by which he means the faculty of intellectual or philosophic activity, thus showing the intellectualist standpoint which he shared with Plato. The precise relation of moral action to the highest type of human happiness is left obscure, but of course Aristotle makes it quite clear in the *Ethics* that without moral virtue true happiness is impossible.

Aristotle gives several reasons for saying that man's highest happiness consists in τὸ θεωρῆσαι.[6] (i) Reason is the highest faculty

[1] *E.N.*, 1156 a 10–12. [2] *E.N.*, 1156 a 31–3. [3] *E.N.*, 1157 b 28–31.

[4] *E.N.*, 1156 b 31–2.

God, says Aristotle, does not need a friend, since "the deity is his own well-being," but we need a friend or friends, since "with us welfare involves a something beyond us." (*E.E.*, 1245 b 14–19.)

[5] *E.N.*, 1177 a 12–13. [6] *E.N.*, K, 7.

of man, and theoretic contemplation is the highest activity of reason. (ii) We can keep up this form of activity longer than any other, e.g. than bodily exercise. (iii) Pleasure is one of the elements of happiness, and "philosophy is admittedly the pleasantest of the activities in which human excellence manifests itself." (The last remark may have seemed a trifle unusual even to Aristotle himself, for he adds, "the pleasures of philosophy at least appear to be wonderfully pure and reliable, nor indeed is it surprising if the life of him who knows is pleasanter than that of the learner.") (iv) The philosopher is more self-sufficient than any other man. He cannot indeed dispense with the necessaries of life any more than others can (and Aristotle considered that the philosopher needs external goods in moderation and friends); but all the same "the thinker is able to pursue his studies in solitude, and the more of a thinker he is, the more capable he is of doing so." The co-operation of others is a great assistance to him, but if it be wanting, the thinker is better able than other men to get along without it. (v) Philosophy is loved for its own sake and not for the sake of any results that accrue from it. In the field of practical activity, it is not the action itself that is desirable, but some result to be attained by means of the activity. Philosophy is no mere means to a further end. (vi) Happiness would seem to imply leisure. Now, "the practical virtues find the field of their exercise in war or politics, which cannot be said to be leisurely employments, least of all war."

It is in the exercise of reason, then, and in the exercise of that reason concerning the noblest objects, that man's complete happiness is found, provided that it is extended over "a complete term of years." Such a life expresses the divine element in man, but we shall refuse to listen to those who advise us, being human and mortal, to mind things that are human and mortal. On the contrary, as far as possible, we ought to try to put off our mortality and do all we can to live the life to which the highest element in us points. For though it be but a small part of us, yet in power and value it far surpasses all the others. Moreover, it would seem to be the real self in each of us, since it is sovereign over all and better than all. And accordingly it would be strange if we were not to choose the life of our own true selves, but of something other than ourselves.[1]

What objects does Aristotle include among the objects of

[1] *E.N.*, 1177 b 26–1178 a 8.

theoretic contemplation? He certainly includes the invariable objects of metaphysics and mathematics, but does he include the objects of natural science? Probably only so far as they are non-contingent, since the highest activity of man is, as we have already seen, concerned with objects that are not contingent. In the *Metaphysics*[1] Aristotle makes physics a branch of theoretic wisdom, though in another place in the *Metaphysics*[2] he implies that it is also the study of contingent events. Physics therefore can belong to "contemplation" only in so far as it studies the invariable or necessary element in the contingent events that constitute the object of physics.

The highest object of metaphysics is God, but in the *Nicomachean Ethics* Aristotle does not expressly include the religious attitude expressed in the definition of the ideal life contained in the *Eudemian Ethics*, namely, "the worship and contemplation of God."[3] Whether Aristotle meant this attitude of religious adoration to be understood in the picture of the ideal life given in the *Nicomachean Ethics*, or had come to lose sight of this earlier religious attitude, we cannot well decide. In any case his treatment of contemplation exercised a great influence on posterity, not least on Christian philosophers, who naturally found it well adapted to their purpose. The intellectualist attitude of Aristotle finds its echo in the teaching of St. Thomas Aquinas, that the essence of the Beatific Vision consists in the act of the intellect rather than in the will's act, on the ground that the intellect is the faculty by which we *possess*, the will the faculty by which we enjoy the object already possessed by the intellect.[4]

[1] *Metaph.*, 1005 b 1–2, 1026 a 18–19.
[2] Cf. e.g. *Metaph.*, 1069 a 30 ff., where Aristotle says that physics has to do not only with eternal objects, but also with perishable sensible objects.
[3] *E.E.*, 1249 b 20. I have already mentioned (when treating of Aristotle's metaphysics) the philosopher's dictum in the *Magna Moralia* (1208 b 26–32) that there can be no question of friendship towards God, since, even if it were possible for us to love Him, He could not return our love.
[4] Cf. e.g. *Summa Theologica*, Ia, q. 26, art. 2.

CHAPTER XXXII

POLITICS

1. The State (and by State Aristotle is thinking of the Greek City-State), like every other community, exists for an end. In the case of the State this end is the supreme good of man, his moral and intellectual life. The family is the primitive community that exists for the sake of life, for the supply of men's everyday wants,[1] and when several families join together and something more than the mere supply of daily needs is aimed at, the village comes into existence. When, however, several villages are joined together to form a larger community that is "nearly or quite self-sufficing,"[2] there comes into existence the State. The State comes into existence for the bare ends of life, but it continues in existence for the sake of the good life, and Aristotle insists that the State differs from family and village, not merely quantitatively but qualitatively and specifically.[3] It is only in the State that man can live the good life in any full sense, and since the good life is man's natural end, the State must be called a natural society. (The Sophists were therefore wrong in thinking that the State is simply the creation of convention.) "It is evident that the State is a creature of nature, and that man is by nature a political animal. And he who by nature and not by mere accident is without a State, is either above humanity or below it."[4] Man's gift of speech shows clearly that nature destined him for social life, and social life in its specifically complete form is, in Aristotle's view, that of the State. The State is prior to the family and to the individual in the sense that, while the State is a self-sufficing whole, neither the individual nor the family are self-sufficient. "He who is unable to live in society, or who has no need because he is sufficient for himself, must be either a beast or a god."[5]

The Platonic-Aristotelian view of the State as exercising the positive function of serving the end of man, the leading of the good life or the acquisition of happiness, and as being *natura prior* (to be distinguished from *tempore prior*) to the individual and the family, has been of great influence in subsequent philosophy.

[1] *Pol.*, 1252 b 13–14. [2] *Pol.*, 1252 b 28 ff. [3] *Pol.*, 1252 a 8–23.
[4] *Pol.*, 1253 a 1–4. [5] *Pol.*, 1253 a 27–9.

Among Christian mediaeval philosophers it was naturally tempered by the importance they rightly attached to individual and family, and by the fact that they accepted another "perfect society," the Church, whose end is higher than that of the State (also by the fact that the nation-State was comparatively undeveloped in the Middle Ages); but we have only to think of Hegel in Germany and of Bradley and Bosanquet in England, to realise that the Greek conception of the State did not perish along with Greek freedom. Moreover, though it is a conception that can be, and has been, exaggerated (especially where Christian truth has been absent and so unable to act as a corrective to one-sided exaggeration), it is a richer and truer conception of the State than that of, e.g. Herbert Spencer. For the State exists for the temporal well-being of its citizens, i.e. for a positive and not merely for a negative end, and this positive conception of the State can quite well be maintained without contaminating it with the exaggerations of Totalitarian State mysticism. Aristotle's horizon was more or less bounded by the confines of the Greek City-State (in spite of his contacts with Alexander), and he had little idea of nations and empires; but all the same his mind penetrated to the essence and function of the State better than did the *laissez-faire* theorists and the British School from Locke to Spencer.

2. In the *Politics*, as we have it, Aristotle's treatment of the family is practically confined to discussion of the master-slave relationship and to the acquisition of wealth. Slavery (the slave, according to Aristotle, is a living instrument of action, i.e. aid to his master's life) is founded on nature. "From the hour of their birth, some are marked out for subjection, others for rule."[1] "It is clear that some men are by nature free, and others slaves, and that for these slavery is both expedient and right."[2] This view may well seem to us monstrous, but it must be remembered that the essence of Aristotle's doctrine is that men differ in intellectual and physical capacities and are thereby fitted for different positions in society. We regret that Aristotle canonised the contemporary institution of slavery, but this canonisation is largely an historical accident. Stripped of its historic and contemporary accidentals, what is censurable in it is not so much the recognition that men differ in ability and in adaptability (the truth of this is too obvious to need elaboration), but the over-rigid

[1] *Pol.*, 1254 a 23–4.

[2] *Pol.*, 1255 a 1–3.

dichotomy drawn between two types of men and the tendency to regard the "slave-nature" as something almost less than human. However, Aristotle tempered his acceptance and rationalisation of slavery by insisting that the master should not abuse his authority, since the interests of master and slave are the same,[1] and by saying that all slaves should have the hope of emancipation.[2] Moreover, he admitted that the child of a natural slave need not himself be a natural slave, and rejected slavery by right of conquest on the ground that superior power and superior excellence are not equivalent, while on the other hand the war may not be a just war.[3] Nevertheless, regarded in itself, this rationalisation of slavery is regrettable and betrays a limited outlook on the part of the philosopher. In fact, Aristotle rejected the legitimacy of the historical origin of slavery (conquest), and then proceeded to give a philosophic rationalisation and justification of slavery!

3. There are, in general, two distinct modes of acquiring wealth, and an intermediate mode.[4]

(i) The "natural" mode consists in the accumulation of things needed for life by, e.g. grazing, hunting, agriculture. Man's needs set a natural limit to such accumulation.

(ii) The intermediate mode is that of barter. In barter a thing is used apart from its "proper use," but in so far as it is employed for the acquisition of the needs of life, barter may be called a natural mode of acquiring wealth.

(iii) The second, and "unnatural," mode of acquiring wealth is the use of money as a means of exchange for goods. It seems very odd to us that Aristotle should condemn retail trade, but his prejudice is largely determined by the ordinary Greek attitude towards commerce, which was regarded as illiberal and unfit for the free man. Of importance is Aristotle's condemnation of "usury," the breeding of money out of money, as he calls it. "Money was intended to be used in exchange, but not to increase at interest." This, literally taken, would condemn all taking of interest on money, but Aristotle was probably thinking of the practice of money-lenders, or usurers in our sense, who make victims of the needy, credulous and ignorant: though he certainly found a rationalisation of his attitude in his doctrine about the

[1] *Pol.*, cf. 1255 b 9–15, 1278 b 33–8. (In 1260 b 5–7 Aristotle criticises Plato's notion that masters should not converse with their slaves.)

[2] *Pol.*, 1330 a 32–3.

[3] *Pol.*, 1254 b 32–4, 1255 a 3–28.

[4] *Pol.*, 1256 a ff. (A, 8–11).

"natural" purpose of money. Cows and sheep have a natural increase, as have fruit-trees, but money has no such natural increase: it is meant to be a means of exchange and nothing else. To serve as a means of exchange is its natural purpose, and if it is used to get more wealth merely by a process of lending it, without any exchange of goods for money and without any labour on the part of the lender, then it is being used in an unnatural way. Needless to say, Aristotle did not envisage modern finance. If he were alive to-day, we cannot say how he would react to our financial system, and whether he would reject, modify or find a way round his former views.

4. Aristotle, as one might expect, refused to allow himself to be carried away by Plato's picture of the ideal State. He did not think that such radical changes as Plato proposed were necessary; nor did he think that they would all, if feasible, be desirable. For instance, he rejected the Platonic notion of the crèche for the children of the Guardian-class, on the ground that he who is a child of all is a child of none. Better to be a real cousin than a Platonic son![1] Similarly, he criticised the notion of communism, on the ground that this would lead to disputes, inefficiency, etc. The enjoyment of property is a source of pleasure, and it is of no use for Plato to say that the State would be made happy if the Guardians were deprived of this source of happiness, for happiness is either enjoyed by individuals or it is not enjoyed at all.[2] In general, Plato aimed at excessive unification. Aristotle had no sympathy for the accumulation of wealth as such; but he saw that there is a need, not so much of equalising all property as of training citizens not to desire excessive wealth and, if any are incapable of being trained, then of preventing them acquiring it.

5. The qualifications of citizenship are taken by Aristotle from the practice of the Athenian democracy, which was not the same as the modern democracy with its representative system. In his view all the citizens should take their share in ruling and being ruled by turn,[3] and the minimum of citizen-rights is the right to participate in the Assembly and in the administration of justice. A citizen, therefore, is he ᾧ ἐξουσία κοινωνεῖν ἀρχῆς βουλευτικῆς καὶ κριτικῆς.[4]

The fact that Aristotle considered it essential for the citizen to sit in the Assembly and in the Law Courts, led him to exclude

[1] *Pol.*, 1262 a 13–14.
[2] Pol., 1264 b 15–23.
[3] *Pol.*, cf. 1277 b.
[4] *Pol.*, 1275 b 18–19.

the class of mechanics and artisans from the citizenship, for they had not got the necessary leisure. Another reason is that manual toil deliberalises the soul and makes it unfit for true virtue.[1]

6. Discussing various types of Constitution Aristotle divides governments into those which aim at the common interest and those which aim at their own private interest.[2] Each of these broad divisions has three subdivisions, so that there are three good types of Constitution and three wrong or deviation-types of Constitution. To the right form Kingship corresponds the deviation-form Tyranny, to Aristocracy Oligarchy, and to Polity Democracy, and in his treatment of the comparative merits of the various Constitutions appears Aristotle's political sense. For him the ideal is that one man should so transcend all the other citizens individually and in the mass in respect of excellence that he would be the natural monarch and ruler. But in point of fact the perfect man does not appear, and, in general, pre-eminent heroes are found only among primitive peoples. This being so, aristocracy, i.e. the rule of many good men, is better than monarchy. Aristocracy is the best form of government for a body of people who can be ruled as freemen by men whose excellence makes them capable of political command. However, Aristotle recognises that even Aristocracy is perhaps too high an ideal for the contemporary State, and so he advocates "Polity," in which "there naturally exists a warlike multitude able to obey and to rule in turn by a law which gives office to the well-to-do according to their desert."[3] This is practically equivalent to rule by the middle-class, and is more or less a half-way house between Oligarchy and Democracy, since in a Polity it is indeed a multitude that rules—in distinction from Oligarchy—yet it is not a propertyless mob, as in Democracy, for ability to serve as a warrior, i.e. as a heavily-armed hoplite, presupposes a certain amount of property. Aristotle is probably thinking—though he does not refer to it—of the Constitution at Athens in 411 B.C., when power rested with the Five Thousand who possessed heavy armour and the system of payment for attendance at meetings had been abolished. This was the Constitution of Theramenes.[4] Aristotle admired this type of Constitution, but his contention that the middle-class is the most stable, since both rich and poor are more likely to trust the middle-class than one another (so that the middle-class need

[1] *Pol.*, cf. 1277 a 33–1278 a 15, 1328 b 33–1329 a 21. [2] *Pol.*, 1279 a 17–21.
[3] *Pol.*, 1288 a 12–15. [4] Cf. *Athen. Polit.*, 28 and 33.

fear no coalition against it) may not sound so convincing to us as it did to him, though there is doubtless some truth in the view.[1]

7. Aristotle treats acutely of the various kinds and degrees of revolution which tend to occur under different Constitutions, of their causes and the means of preventing them; and, owing to his great historical knowledge, he was able to give apt historical illustrations of the points he wished to make.[2] He points out, for instance, that the revolutionary state of mind is largely brought about by one-sided notions of justice—democrats thinking that men who are equally free should be equal in everything, oligarchs thinking that because men are unequal in wealth they should be unequal in everything. He emphasises the fact that rulers should have no opportunity of making money for themselves out of the offices they hold, and stresses the requisites for high office in the State, namely, loyalty to the Constitution, capacity for administrative work and integrity of character. Whatever be the type of Constitution, it must be careful not to go to extremes; for if either democracy or oligarchy is pushed to extremes the ensuing rise of malcontent parties will be sure to lead in the end to revolution.

8. In Books Seven and Eight of the *Politics* Aristotle discusses his positive views of what a State should be.

(i) The State must be large enough to be self-sufficing (of course Aristotle's notion of what a self-sufficing community actually is would be altogether inadequate for modern times), but not so large that order and good government are rendered impracticable. In other words, it must be large enough to fulfil the end of the State and not so large that it can no longer do so. The number of citizens requisite for this purpose cannot of course be arithmetically determined *a priori*.[3]

(ii) Similarly with the territorial extent of the State. This should not be so small that a leisured life is impossible (i.e. that culture is impracticable) nor yet so large that luxury is encouraged. The city should not aim at mere wealth, but at importing her needs and exporting her surplus.[4]

(iii) Citizens. Agricultural labourers and artisans are necessary, but they will not enjoy citizen rights. Only the third class, that of the warriors, will be citizens in the full sense. These will be warriors in youth, rulers or magistrates in middle-age and priests

[1] *Pol.*, 1295 b 1–1296 a 21. [2] *Pol.*, Bk. 5. [3] Pol., 1325 b 33–1326 b 24.
[4] *Pol.*, 1326 b 25–1327 b 18.

in old age. Each citizen will possess a plot of land near the city and another near the frontier (so that all may have an interest in the defence of the State). This land will be worked by the non-citizen labourers.[1]

(iv) Education. Aristotle, like Plato, attached great importance to education and, again like Plato, he considered it to be the work of the State. Education must begin with the body, since the body and its appetites develop earlier than the soul and its faculties; but the body is to be trained for the sake of the soul and the appetites for the sake of the reason. Education is therefore, first and foremost, a moral education—the more so because the citizen will never have to earn his living by work as husbandman or artisan, but will be trained to be, first a good soldier, and then a good ruler and magistrate.[2] This emphasis on moral education shows itself in Aristotle's views concerning pre-natal care and the games of the children. The Directors of Education will take all these matters very seriously, and will not consider the games of the children and the stories that are told them as things too insignificant for them to attend to. (In regard to musical education Aristotle makes the amusing remark, that "The rattle is a toy suited to the infant mind, and musical education is a rattle or toy for children of a larger growth."[3])

As the *Politics* is unfortunately incomplete—the sections dealing with education in science and philosophy being missing—we cannot say what precise directions Aristotle would have given in regard to the higher education of the citizens. One thing, however, is obvious, that both Plato and Aristotle had a lofty and noble conception of education and of the ideal of the citizen. They would have but scant sympathy with any scheme of education that laid the emphasis on technical and utilitarian training, since such a scheme leaves the higher faculties of the soul untended and so fails to fit man to attain his proper end, which is the purpose of education. For although it may sometimes look as though Aristotle wanted to educate men merely to be cogs in the State machine, this is really not the case: in his eyes the end of the State and the end of the individual coincide, not in the sense that the individual should be entirely absorbed in the State but in the sense that the State will prosper when the individual citizens are good, when they attain their own proper end. The only real guarantee of the stability and prosperity of the State is

[1] *Pol.*, 1328 b 2–1331 b 23. [2] *Pol.*, 1332 b–1333 a 16. [3] *Pol.*, 1340 b 29–31.

the moral goodness and integrity of the citizens, while conversely unless the State is good and the system of its education is rational, moral and healthy, the citizens will not become good. The individual attains his proper development and perfection through his concrete life, which is a life in Society, i.e. in the State, while Society attains its proper end through the perfection of its members. That Aristotle did not consider the State to be a great Leviathan beyond good and evil is clear from the criticism he passes on the Lacedaemonians. It is a great mistake, he says, to suppose that war and domination are the be-all and end-all of the State. The State exists for the good life, and it is subject to the same code of morality as the individual. As he puts it, "the same things are best for individuals and states."[1] Reason and history both show that the legislator should direct all his military and other measures to the establishment of peace. Military States are safe only in wartime: once they have acquired their empire, they rust away like iron and fall. Both Plato and Aristotle, in their preoccupation with the fostering of a truly cultural political life, set their faces against imperialist dreams of military aggrandisement.

[1] *Pol.*, 1333 b 37.

CHAPTER XXXIII

AESTHETICS OF ARISTOTLE

I. *Beauty*

I. ARISTOTLE distinguishes the beautiful from the merely pleasant. For example, in the *Problemata*[1] he contrasts sexual preference with aesthetic selection, thus distinguishing real objective beauty from "beauty" that has reference only to desire. Again in the *Metaphysics*[2] he says that the mathematical sciences are not unrelated to the beautiful. The beautiful, therefore, for him cannot be the merely pleasant, that which pleasantly stimulates the senses.

2. Does Aristotle distinguish beauty from the good? He would seem not to have been very clear on this point.

(*a*) In the *Rhetoric*[3] he states that "the beautiful is that good which is pleasant because it is good," a definition which would not seem to admit of any real distinction between the beautiful and the moral. (Professor W. Rhys Roberts translates τὸ καλόν as Noble, cf. *Oxford Trans.*, Vol. XI.)

(*b*) In the *Metaphysics*, however, he expressly states that "the good and the beautiful are different (for the former always implies conduct as its subject, while the beautiful is found also in motionless things)."[4] This statement seems to differentiate between the beautiful and the moral at least, and may be taken to imply that the beautiful as such is not simply the object of desire. This should allow of a doctrine of aesthetic contemplation and of the *disinterested* character of such contemplation—as stated by e.g. Kant and Schopenhauer.

3. A further definition or description—and a more satisfactory one—is found in the *Metaphysics*[5] where Aristotle says that "the chief forms of beauty are order and symmetry and definiteness." It is the possession of these three properties that confers on mathematics a certain diagnostic value in regard to beautiful objects. (Aristotle seems to have been conscious of his obscurity, for he goes on to promise a more intelligible treatment, though, if the promise was ever fulfilled, its fulfilment is not extant.)

[1] 896 b 10–28. [2] 1078 a 31–b 6. [3] 1366 a 33–6. [4] 1078 a 31–2. [5] 1078 a 36–b 1.

Similarly in the *Poetics*[1] Aristotle says that "beauty is a matter of size and order" or consists in size and order. Thus he declares that a living creature, in order to be beautiful, must present a certain order in its arrangement of parts and also possess a certain definite magnitude, neither too great nor too small. This would tally more or less with the definition in the *Metaphysics* and would imply that the beautiful is the object of contemplation and not of desire.

4. It is interesting to note that Aristotle in the *Poetics*[2] makes the subject-matter of Comedy to be the ridiculous, "which is a species of the ugly." (The ridiculous is "a mistake or deformity not productive of pain or harm to others.") This would imply that the ugly may be employed in a work of art, subordinated to the total effect. Aristotle does not, however, treat expressly of the relation of the ugly to the beautiful nor of the question, how far the "ugly" may become a constitutive element of the beautiful.[3]

II. *Fine Art in General*

1. Morality aims at conduct itself (πράττειν), Art at producing something, not at activity itself. But Art in general (τέχνη) must be subdivided[4] into:

(*a*) Art that aims at completing the work of nature, e.g. producing tools, since nature has provided man only with his hands.

(*b*) Art that aims at *imitating* nature. This is Fine Art, the essence of which Aristotle, like Plato, finds in imitation. In other words, in art an imaginary world is created which is an imitation of the real world.

2. But "imitation" has not, for Aristotle, the rather contemptuous colouring that it has for Plato. Not believing in Transcendental Concepts, Aristotle would naturally not make art a copy of a copy, at the third remove from truth. In fact, Aristotle inclines to the opinion that the artist goes rather to the ideal or the universal element in things, translating it into the medium of whatever art is in question. He says[5] that Tragedy makes its personages better, Comedy worse, than the "men of the present

[1] 1450 b 40–1.

[2] 1449 a 32–4.

[3] Cf. "Beautiful art shows its superiority in this, that it describes as beautiful things which may be in nature ugly or displeasing." Kant, *Critique of Judgment*, I. 1, 48.

[4] *Physics*, B 8, 199 a 15 ff.

[5] *Poetics*, 1448 a 16–18.

day." According to Aristotle, Homer's personages are better than we are. (Homer, it will be remembered, came in for some very hard knocks at the hands of Plato.)

3. Imitation, Aristotle insists, is natural to man, and it is also natural for man to delight in works of imitation. He points out that we may delight to view artistic representations of what is, in reality, painful to us to see.[1] (Cf. Kant, in passage already quoted in footnote.) But the explanation of this fact he seems to find in the purely intellectual pleasure of recognising that this man in the picture, for example, is someone we know, e.g. Socrates. This pleasure in recognition is no doubt a fact, but it hardly goes far towards constructing a theory of art: in fact, it is really irrelevant.

4. Aristotle expressly states that poetry "is something more philosophic and of graver import than history, since its statements are of the nature rather of universals, whereas those of history are singulars."[2] He goes on to explain that by a singular statement he means what e.g. Alcibiades did or had done to him, and by an universal statement "what such or such a kind of man will probably or necessarily say or do." The poet's function is, therefore, "to describe, not the thing that has happened, but a kind of thing that might happen, i.e. what is possible as being probable or necessary." It is in this that Aristotle finds the distinction between poet and historian, not in the one writing verse and the other prose. As he remarks: "you might put the work of Herodotus into verse, and it would still be a species of history."

On this theory, then, the artist deals rather with *types*, which are akin to the universal and ideal. An historian might write the life of Napoleon, telling what the historic figure Napoleon said and did and suffered: the poet, however, though he called the hero of his epic Napoleon, would rather portray universal truth or "probability." Adherence to historic fact is of minor importance in poetry. The poet may indeed take a subject from real history, but if what he describes is in—to use Aristotle's words—"the probable and possible order of things," he is none the less a poet. Aristotle even says that it is much better for the poet to describe what is probable but impossible than what is possible but improbable. This is simply a way of emphasising the universal character of poetry.

5. It is to be noted that Aristotle says that the statements of

[1] *Poetics*, 1448 b 10–19. [2] *Poetics*, 1451 b 5–8.

poetry are of the nature *rather* of universals. In other words, poetry is not concerned with the abstract universal: poetry is not philosophy. Aristotle accordingly censures didactic poetry, for to give a system of philosophy in verse is to write versified philosophy; it is not to produce poetry.

6. In the *Poetics* Aristotle confines himself to a consideration of Epic, Tragedy and Comedy, particularly Tragedy: painting and sculpture and music are only mentioned incidentally, as when he tells us[1] that the painter Polygnotus portrayed personages "better than we are," Pauson worse, and Dionysius "just like ourselves." But what he does have to say on the subject of the other arts is important for his theory of imitation.

Thus *Music* (which is treated more or less as an accompaniment to the drama) was declared by Aristotle to be the most imitative of all the arts. Pictorial art only indicates mental or moral moods through external factors such as gesture or complexion, whereas musical tunes contain *in themselves* imitations of moral moods. And in the *Problemata*[2] he asks, "Why does what is heard alone of the objects of sense possess emotional import?" Aristotle would seem to be thinking of the direct stimulative effect of music which, though a fact, is hardly an aesthetic fact; yet the theory that music is the most imitative of the arts would none the less seem to extend the concept of imitation so far as to include *symbolism*, and to open the way to the romantic conception of music as a direct embodiment of spiritual emotion. (In the *Poetics* Aristotle remarks that "rhythm alone, without harmony, is the means in the dancer's imitations; for even he, by the rhythms of his attitudes, may represent men's characters, as well as what they do and suffer."[3])

7. In the *Politics*[4] Aristotle observes that drawing is useful in the education of the young, to acquire a "more correct judgment of the works of artists," and he argues also[5] that "music has a power of forming the character, and should therefore be introduced into the education of the young." It might seem, then, that Aristotle's interest in Fine Art is mainly educational and moral; but, as Bosanquet remarks, "to introduce aesthetic interest into education is not the same as to introduce educational interest into aesthetic."[6] Aristotle certainly regarded both music and the drama as having as one of their functions that of moral

[1] 1448 a 5–6. [2] 919 b 26. [3] 1447 a 26–8. [4] 1338 a 17–19.
[5] 1340 b 10–13. [6] *A History of Aesthetic*, p. 63.

education; but it does not necessarily follow that a person who recognises this function thereby makes the moral effect of an art a characteristic of its essence.

But though Aristotle dwells on the educational and moral aspect of art, that does not mean that he was blind to its recreative nature or effect.[1] If by allowing to music and the drama a recreative function he had referred merely to sense-pleasure or a tickling of the fancy, this would have been irrelevant to aesthetic; but higher recreation might well mean something more.

III. *Tragedy*

1. Aristotle's famous definition of tragedy is as follows:[2] "A tragedy—is the imitation of an action that is serious (σπουδαίας) and also, as having magnitude, complete in itself; in language with pleasurable accessories, each kind brought in separately in the parts of the work; in a dramatic, not in a narrative form; with incidents arousing pity and fear, wherewith to accomplish its catharsis (κάθαρσις) of such emotions."

I may add in explanation one or two points:

(i) "Serious," "noble," "good," indicate the character of the content of tragedy. This it shares with Epic poetry, and by it both are distinguished from Comedy and Satire, which deal with the inferior or ugly or ridiculous.

(ii) "Complete in itself," i.e. having beginning, middle and—being an organic whole. This *unity of plot* or organic unity of structure is the only unity strictly demanded by Aristotle.

In the *Poetics*[3] Aristotle does indeed observe that tragedy, in distinction from epic poetry, "endeavours to keep as far as possible within a single circuit of the sun or something near that"; but this is simply a statement of fact and he does not expressly state a demand for Unity of Time. As for Unity of Place, it is not mentioned. It is incorrect, therefore, to say that Aristotle demanded the three Unities in drama.

(iii) "Language with pleasurable accessories." Aristotle tells us himself that he means "with rhythm and harmony or song superadded."

[1] Aristotle certainly regarded the giving of enjoyment as one of the functions of tragedy. The question is, how far was this enjoyment specifically aesthetic in character?

[2] *Poetics*, 1449 b 25–9.

[3] 1449 b 12–14.

(iv) "Each kind brought in separately," i.e. "some portions are worked out with verse only, and others in turn with song." Aristotle is naturally thinking of Greek tragedy with its alternations of spoken verse and choral songs.

(v) "In a dramatic, not in a narrative form." This distinguishes tragedy from epic poetry.

(vi) Catharsis. This states the psychological end or aim of tragedy, and I shall return to it presently.

2. Aristotle enumerates six formative elements of tragedy . . . fable or plot, characters, diction, thought, spectacle and melody.[1]

(i) The most important of these elements, in Aristotle's opinion, is the Plot, which is "the end and purpose of the tragedy." It is more important than Character, for "in a play—they do not act in order to portray the characters; they include the characters for the sake of action." Aristotle gives his reason for this somewhat strangely sounding dictum. "Tragedy is essentially an imitation not of persons but of action and life, of happiness and misery. All human happiness or misery takes the form of action; the end for which we live is a certain kind of activity, not a quality. Character gives us qualities, but it is in our actions—what we do—that we are happy or the reverse—a tragedy is impossible without action, but there may be one without Character."[2] (It is true perhaps that we can enjoy a good story in which the character-drawing is defective better than one in which the character-drawing is good but the plot is ridiculous.)

(ii) Aristotle, however, does not mean to belittle the importance of character-delineation in the drama: he admits that a tragedy without it is a defective tragedy and esteems it the most important element after the Plot.

(iii) "Thirdly comes the element of Thought, i.e. the power of saying whatever can be said, or what is appropriate to the occasion." Aristotle is thinking here, not of speech as revealing character directly but of speech "on a purely indifferent subject," i.e. Thought shown "in all they say when proving or disproving some particular point, or enunciating some universal proposition." Euripides certainly used tragedy as an opportunity for discussions on

[1] *Poetics*, 1450 a 4–16. [2] *Poetics*, 1450 a 17–26.

various topics; but we may well feel that the drama is scarcely the place for Socratic disquisitions.

(iv) Diction, i.e. the verse and prose. This is important, but, as Aristotle wisely remarks, "one may string together a series of characteristic speeches of the utmost finish as regards Diction and Thought, and yet fail to produce the true tragic effect."

(v) Melody is "the greatest of the pleasurable accessories of Tragedy."

(vi) The Spectacle is indeed an attraction; but it is "the least of all the parts, and has least to do with the art of poetry." The getting-up of the *mise en scène* is "more a matter for the costumier than for the poet." It is a pity that Aristotle's words on this matter have not been heeded in later times. Elaborate scenery and spectacular effect are poor substitutes for plot and character-drawing.

3. Aristotle demands, as we have seen, unity of plot, in the sense of organic, structural unity. The plot must be neither so vast that it cannot be taken in at once by the memory nor so short that it is small and insignificant. But he points out that unity of plot "does not consist, as some suppose, in its having one man as its subject," nor in describing everything that happens to the hero. The ideal is that the several incidents of the plot should be so connected "that the transposal or withdrawal of any one of them will disjoin and dislocate the whole. For that which makes no perceptible difference by its presence or absence is no real part of the whole." The incidents must follow one another, not "episodically" but with probability or necessity. As Aristotle observes, "there is a great difference between a thing happening *propter hoc* and *post hoc*" (διὰ τάδε ἢ μετὰ τάδε).

4. Aristotle thought of Tragedy (complex, at least) as involving Peripety or Discovery, or both: (i) Περιπέτεια is the change from one state of things to the opposite, e.g. when the Messenger reveals the secret of Oedipus' birth, the whole state of affairs is changed within the play, for Oedipus realises that he has, unwittingly committed incest, (ii) Αναγνώρισις is "a change from ignorance to knowledge, and thus to either love or hate, in the personages marked for good or evil fortune."[1] In the case of Oedipus the Discovery is of course attended by Peripety, and this is, according to Aristotle, the finest form of Discovery.

[1] *Poetics*, 1451 b 32–5.

Thus is attained the tragic effect, the arousing of pity and fear.

5. Since tragedy is an imitation of actions arousing pity and fear, there are three forms of plot that must be avoided:

(i) A good man must not be seen passing from happiness to misery, as this is, in Aristotle's opinion, simply odious and will distract our minds by such disgust and horror that the tragic effect will not be realised.

(ii) A bad man must not be seen passing from misery to happiness. This is quite "untragic," appealing neither to our pity nor to our fear.

(iii) An extremely bad man must not be seen falling from happiness to misery. This may arouse human feeling but neither pity nor fear, for pity is occasioned by undeserved misfortune and fear by the misfortune of one like ourselves.

It remains, then, that tragedy should portray an "intermediate" type of person passing through misfortune, brought about by some error of judgment and not by vice or depravity. Aristotle accordingly refuses to agree with critics who censured Euripides for giving an unhappy ending to many of his plays, for this is the proper thing for tragedy, though not for Comedy. (Though there were occasional comic interludes in Greek tragedies, the tendency was to have unmixed tragedy or unmixed comedy, and Aristotle's views rather reflect this tendency.)

6. Tragic pity and fear should be aroused by the plot itself, and not by extraneous elements, e.g. by the portrayal of a brutal murder on the stage. (Aristotle would of course thoroughly approve of the way in which the murder of Agamemnon took place behind the scenes. Presumably he would censure the murder of Desdemona on the stage.)

7. We come now to the consideration of the psychological aim of tragedy, the arousing of pity and fear for the κάθαρσις of these emotions. The exact meaning to be attached to this famous doctrine of the κάθαρσις has been a subject of constant discussion: as Professor Ross says, "a whole library has been written on this famous doctrine."[1] The solution of the difficulty is rendered all the harder by the fact that the second book of the *Poetics* is missing—in which, it is conjectured, Aristotle explained what he meant by *catharsis* (and probably also treated of Comedy).

[1] Ross, *Aristotle*, p. 282. On this subject see e.g. *Aristotle's Theory of Poetry and Fine Art*, by S. H. Butcher (Macmillan); *Aristotle on the Art of Poetry*, by Ingram Bywater (Oxford).

Two main lines of explanation have been defended. (i) The catharsis in question is a *purification* of the emotions of pity and fear, the metaphor being drawn from ceremonial purification (the view of Lessing); (ii) the catharsis is a *temporary elimination* of the emotions of pity and fear, the metaphor being drawn from medicine (the view of Bernays). This latter view is the one that is most acceptable, i.e. from the exegetic standpoint, and now generally holds the field. According to this view the proximate object of tragedy, in Aristotle's eyes, is to arouse the emotions of pity and fear, i.e. pity for the past and actual sufferings of the hero, fear for those which loom before him. The ulterior object of tragedy then would be to relieve or purge the soul of these emotions through the harmless and pleasurable outlet afforded by the medium of art. The implication is that these emotions are undesirable, or rather that they are undesirable when in excess, but that all men, or at any rate most men, are subject to them, some in an excessive degree, so that it is a healthy and beneficial practice for all—necessary in the case of some—to give them a periodic opportunity of excitation and outlet through the medium of art, the process being at the same time a pleasurable one. This would be Aristotle's answer to Plato's criticism of tragedy in the *Republic*: tragedy has not a demoralising effect but is a harmless pleasure. How far Aristotle recognised an intellectual element in this recreation, is a question we cannot answer with only a truncated *Poetics* before us.

That Aristotle had in mind a purgative effect and not a moral purificative effect seems to be borne out by the *Politics*.

(i) According to Aristotle the flute has an exciting, and not an ethical effect, and should be left to professionals and kept for times when the hearing of music is a κάθαρσις rather than a form of education.[1] The inference is that catharsis is connected, not with ethical effect but with emotional effect.

(ii) Aristotle admits the "enthusiastic" harmonies in a well-ordered State, because they restore those who are subject to fits of enthusiasm to the normal condition. He then goes on to enumerate three purposes for which music should be studied: (*a*) "education," (*b*) "purification" ("the word 'purification' we use at present without explanation, but when hereafter we speak of poetry, we will treat the subject

[1] *Pol.*, 1341 a 17 ff.

with more precision"), (*c*) "for intellectual enjoyment, for relaxation and for recreation after exertion." From this enumeration alone one might suppose, applying what is said to tragedy, that the tragic effect might be ethical and purgative at the same time. But Aristotle proceeds to make a distinction. "In education ethical melodies are to be performed, but we may listen to the melodies of action and passion when they are performed by others. For feelings such as pity and fear, or again, enthusiasm, exist very strongly in some souls, and have more or less influence over all. Some persons fall into a religious frenzy whom we see disenthralled by the use of mystic melodies, which bring healing and purification to the soul. Those who are influenced by pity or fear and every emotional nature have a like experience, others in their degree are stirred by something which specially affects them, and all are in a manner purified and their souls lightened and delighted. The melodies of purification likewise give an innocent pleasure to mankind."[1] From this it would appear that the catharsis of pity and fear, though an "innocent pleasure," is not looked upon by Aristotle as ethical in character; and if it is not ethical in character, then "purification" should not be interpreted as purification in an ethical sense, but in a non-ethical sense, i.e. as a metaphor from medicine.

This interpretation is not acceptable to all. Thus Professor Stace declares that "The theory of certain scholars, based upon etymological grounds, that it means that the soul is purged, not *through*, but *of* pity and terror, that by means of a diarrhoea of these unpleasant emotions we get rid of them and are left happy, is the thought of men whose scholarship may be great, but whose understanding of art is limited. Such a theory would reduce Aristotle's great and illuminating criticism to the meaningless babble of a philistine."[2] The question, however, is not what is the *right* view of tragedy, but what was *Aristotle's* view. In any case, even the upholders of the "diarrhoea" theory could agree with Stace's own interpretation of Aristotle's meaning ("the representation of truly great and tragic sufferings arouses in the beholder pity and terror which purge his spirit, and render it serene and pure"), provided that "pure" is not understood as the term of an educational process.

[1] *Pol.*, 1342 a 1–16. [2] *Crit. Hist.*, p. 331.

IV. *Origins of Tragedy and Comedy*

1. According to Aristotle,[1] tragedy began with "improvisation" on the part of the leader of the Dithyramb, no doubt between the two halves of the chorus. In origin, therefore, it would be connected with the worship of Dionysus, just as the renaissance of the drama in Europe was connected with the mediaeval mystery plays.

2. Comedy began in a parallel manner, from the phallic songs, "which still survive as institutions in many of our cities." He thought no doubt of the leader coming to improvise some scurrilous piece.

3. The most significant thing in the development of the drama is for Aristotle the increasing importance of the actor. Aeschylus first increased the number of actors to two, curtailing the business of the Chorus. Sophocles added a third actor and scenery.

4. When spoken parts were introduced, the iambic metre was brought in as "the most speakable of metres." ("The reason for their original use of the trochaic tetrameter was that their poetry was satyric and more connected with dancing than it now is.")

Discussion of the highly problematic question of the origins of tragedy and comedy scarcely belongs to the history of philosophy; so I will content myself with the foregoing brief indication of the view of Aristotle, which bristles with difficulties (i) as to interpretation, (ii) as to its correctness.

Note on the Older Peripatetics

The old Academy continued the mathematical speculation of Plato: the older Peripatetics continued Aristotle's empirical trend, while adhering closely to the general philosophical position of their Master, though they made slight modifications and developments, e.g. in the field of logic. Thus both Theophrastus and Eudemus of Rhodes adhered pretty faithfully to the metaphysical and ethical tenets of Aristotle, this being especially true of Eudemus who was termed by Simplicius the γνησιώτατος of Aristotle's disciples.[2] Theophrastus ardently defended the Aristotelian doctrine of the eternity of the world against Zeno the Stoic.

Theophrastus of Eresus in Lesbos succeeded Aristotle as head of the Peripatetic School in 322/1 and continued in that office until his death in 288/7 or 287/6.[3] He is chiefly remarkable for

[1] *Poetics*, 1449 a 9–30. [2] Simplic. *Phys.*, 411, 14. [3] Diog. Laërt., 5, 36.

his continuation of Aristotle's work in the field of empirical science. Applying himself particularly to Botany, he left works on that subject which made him the botanical authority up to the end of the Middle Ages, while through his zoological studies he seemed to have grasped the fact that changes of colour in the animal world are partly due to "adaptation to environment." A scholar of wide interests, like Aristotle himself, Theophrastus also composed a history of philosophy (the famous φυσικῶν δόξαι) and works on the history and nature of religion, Περὶ θεῶν, Περὶ εὐσεβείας and Περὶ τὸ θεῖον ἱστορία.. Of these works only part of the history of philosophy has come down to us, while Porphyry has preserved some of the Περὶ εὐσεβείας.[1] Believing that all living beings are akin, Theophrastus rejected animal-sacrifices and the eating of flesh-meat and declared that *all* men are related to one another and not merely the fellow-members of a nation. One may also mention his celebrated work, the *Characters*, a study of thirty types of character.

Aristoxenus of Tarentum brought with him into the Peripatetic School certain of the later Pythagorean theories, e.g. the doctrine that the soul is the harmony of the body, a doctrine that led Aristoxenus to deny the soul's immortality.[2] He thus championed the view suggested by Simmias in the *Phaedo* of Plato. But he followed in the footsteps of Aristotle by his empirical work on the nature and history of music.

Aristoxenus' theory of the soul was shared by Dicaearchus of Messene,[3] who composed a βίος Ἑλλάδος, in which he traced the civilisation of Greece through the stages of primitive savagery, nomadic life and agriculture. He differed from Aristotle in that he accorded the practical life the preference over the theoretical.[4] In his Τριπολιτικός he declared that the best constitution is a mixture of the three types of government, monarchy, aristocracy and democracy, and considered that this type of mixed constitution was realised at Sparta.

Demetrius of Phaleron, a pupil of Theophrastus, and a prolific writer[5] is remarkable for his political activity (he was head of the government at Athens from 317 until 307) and for having urged Ptolemy Soter to found the library and School of Alexandria (whither Demetrius betook himself about 297). As this project

[1] Porph., Περὶ ἀποχῆς ἐμψύχων.
[2] Cic., *Tusc.*, 1, 10, 19.
[3] Cic., *Tusc.*, 1, 10, 21; 31, 77.
[4] Cic., *Ad Att.*, 2, 16, 3
[5] Diog. Laërt., 5, 80–1.

was realised by Ptolemy Philadelphus, the successor of Ptolemy Soter, shortly after 285, Demetrius furnished the link between the work of the Peripatos at Athens and the scientific and research work of the Greeks at Alexandria, the city which was to become a celebrated centre of scholarship and learning.

CHAPTER XXXIV

PLATO AND ARISTOTLE

PLATO and Aristotle are, without a shadow of doubt, not only the two greatest Greek philosophers, but also two of the greatest philosophers the world has seen. They had much in common with one another (how should it not be so, when Aristotle was for many years a pupil of Plato and began from the Platonic standpoint?); but there is also a marked difference of outlook between them, which, if one prescinds from the very considerable common element, enables one to characterise their respective philosophies as standing to one another in the relation of thesis (Platonism) to antithesis (Aristotelianism), a thesis and an antithesis which need to be reconciled in a higher synthesis, in the sense that the valuable and true elements in both need to be harmoniously developed in a more complete and adequate system than the single system of either philosopher taken in isolation. Platonism may be characterised by reference to the idea of Being, in the sense of abiding and steadfast reality, Aristotelianism by reference to the idea of Becoming; but, if unchanging being is real, so also are change and becoming real, and to both aspects of reality must justice be done by any adequate system of philosophy.

To characterise the philosophy of Plato by reference to the idea of Being and that of Aristotle by reference to the idea of Becoming, is to be guilty of a generalisation, a generalisation which does not, of course, represent the whole truth. Did not Plato treat of Becoming, did he not propound a theory of teleology, it may be asked with justice; did he not recognise the material world as the sphere of change and did he not even explicitly admit that change or movement (so far as this is involved by the nature of life or soul) must belong to the sphere of the real? On the other hand, did not Aristotle find a place, and a very important place, for unchanging being, did he not, even in the changing, material world, discover an element of stability, of fixity, did he not declare that the sublimest occupation of man is the contemplation of unchanging objects? One cannot but give an affirmative answer to these questions; yet the truth of the generalisation is not disposed of, since it refers to what is peculiarly characteristic in each system, to its general tone or flavour, to the general orientation of the philosopher's thought. I will attempt briefly to justify this generalisation, or at least to indicate the lines along which I should attempt to justify it in detail, did space permit.

Plato, like Socrates, assumed the validity of ethical judgments; like Socrates again, he attempted to reach a clear apprehension of ethical values dialectically, to enshrine their nature in definition, to crystallise the ethical idea. He came to see, however, that if ethical concepts and ethical judgments are objective and universally valid, these concepts must possess some objective foundation. Obviously enough moral values are ideals, in the sense that they are not concrete things like sheep or dogs: they are what ought to be realised in the concrete world, or what it is desirable to realise in the concrete world, through human conduct: hence the objectivity attaching to values cannot be the same kind of objectivity that attaches to sheep or dogs, but must be an ideal objectivity or an objectivity in the ideal order. Moreover, material things in this world change and perish, whereas moral values, Plato was convinced, are unchanging. He concluded, therefore, that moral values are ideal, yet objective, essences, apprehended intuitively at the end of a process of dialectic. These moral values, however, have a common share in goodness or perfection, so that they are rightly said to participate in, to derive their goodness or perfection from, the supreme ideal essence, absolute goodness or perfection, the Idea of the Good, the "sun" of the ideal world.

In this way Plato elaborated a metaphysic on the basis of the Socratic ethic, and, being based on the thought of Socrates, it could, without undue propriety, be put into the mouth of Socrates. But, in the course of time, Plato came to apply his dialectic, not only to moral and aesthetic values, but to the common concept in general, maintaining that, just as good things participate in goodness, so individual substances participate in the specific essence. This new viewpoint cannot be said to constitute a radical break in Plato's thought, inasmuch as the theory of values itself rested to a certain extent on a logical foundation (that the common name must have an objective reference), it is rather an extension of the theory; but the new viewpoint forced Plato to consider more closely, not only the relation between the Ideas themselves, but also between sensible objects and the Ideas or exemplary essences. He thus developed his theory of the hierarchic noetic structure and the "communion" between the Ideas and explained participation as imitation, with the result that, in place of pure values on the one hand and bearers of values on the other, there was substituted the dichotomy between true essential Reality, the objective noetic structure and sensible particulars, between the original and the mirrored or "copy." This division came to have the force of a division between Being on the one hand and Becoming on the other, and there can be no question on which side of the dividing line Plato's chief interest lay.

It may be objected that Plato regarded the specific essence of e.g. man as an ideal and that the true meaning of Becoming is to be sought in the gradual approximation to and realisation of the ideal in the material world, in human personality and society, a realisation which is the task of God and of God's human co-operators. This is perfectly true, and I have not the slightest wish to belittle the importance of teleology in the Platonic philosophy; but none the less, the emphasis was most decidedly placed by Plato on the sphere of Being, of true Reality. Through his doctrine of teleology he certainly admitted some relation between the changing world and the unchanging world of Being; but becoming as such and particularity as such were to him the irrational, the factor that must be dismissed into the sphere of the indeterminate. How could it be otherwise for a thinker to whom logic and ontology are one, or at least parallel? Thought is concerned with the universal and thought apprehends Being: the universal, then, is Being and the particular as such is not Being. The universal is unchanging, so that Being is unchanging, the particular changes, becomes, perishes, and in so far as it changes, becomes, perishes, it is not Being. Philosophical activity or dialectic is an activity of thought and is thus concerned with Being primarily and only secondarily with Becoming, in so far as it "imitates" Being, so that Plato, as philosopher, was primarily interested in essential and unchanging Being. He was also interested, it is true, in the moulding of the world according to the pattern of Being; but the emphasis is placed unmistakably on Being rather than on Becoming.

It might seem that much of what I have said in regard to Plato would apply equally well, perhaps even better, to Aristotle, who asserted that the metaphysician is concerned with being as being, who referred change and becoming to the final causality of the unmoved First Mover, who taught that man's highest activity is the theoretic contemplation of unchanging objects, of those beings which are *par excellence* being, actuality, form. Nevertheless, this very real side of the Aristotelian philosophy represents rather the Platonic legacy, even if elaborated and developed by Aristotle himself. I do not intend for a moment to question the fact that Aristotle attributed great importance to this aspect of his philosophy or the fact that Aristotle accomplished a great deal in this line of speculation, e.g. by bringing out clearly the intellectual and immaterial nature of pure form and so making a contribution of tremendous value to natural theology; but I wish to inquire into the character of Aristotle's peculiar contribution to philosophy in so far as he deviated from Platonism, to ask what was the antithesis that Aristotle set over against the Platonic thesis.

What was Aristotle's chief objection against the Platonic theory of Ideas? That it left an unbridged chasm between sensible objects and the Ideas. As the sensible objects were said to imitate or participate in the Ideas, one would expect to find Plato admitting some internal essential principle, some formal cause within the object itself, placing it in its class, constituting it in its essence, whereas in point of fact Plato did not allow for an interior formal principle of this sort, but left a dualism of pure universal and pure particular, a dualism which resulted in depriving the sensible world of most of its reality and meaning. What was Aristotle's answer to this objection? While admitting the general Platonic position that the universal element, or essential form, is the object of science, of rational knowledge, he identified this universal element with the immanent essential form of the sensible object, which, together with its matter, constitutes the object and which is the intelligible principle in the object. This formal principle realises itself in the activity of the object, e.g. the formal principle in an organism, its entelechy, expresses itself in organic functions, unfolds itself in matter, organises, moulds and shapes matter, tends towards an end, which is the adequate manifestation of the essence, of the "idea," in the phenomenon. All nature is conceived as a hierarchy of species, in each of which the essence tends towards its full actualisation in a series of phenomena, drawn, in some rather mysterious way, by the ultimate final causality of the supreme Unmoved Mover, which is itself complete actuality, pure immaterial Being or Thought, self-subsistent and self-contained. Nature is thus a dynamical process of self-perfection or self-development, and the series of phenomena has meaning and value.

From this brief statement of Aristotle's position it should be quite clear that his philosophy is not simply a philosophy of Becoming. Being may truly be predicated of something in so far as it is actual, and that which is *par excellence* Being is also *par excellence* Actuality, unmixed with potency; the world of becoming, being a world of realisation, of reduction of potency to act, is a world in which actuality or being is being constantly realised in matter, in phenomena, under the final attraction of ultimate Actuality or Being; so that the explanation of Becoming is to be found in Being, for Becoming is for the sake of Being, which is always logically, even when it is not temporally, prior. If I say, then, that Aristotle was possessed by the concept of Becoming, that his philosophy, as peculiarly his, may justly be characterised by reference to his doctrine of Becoming, I do not mean to deny that Being was, for him as for Plato, of supreme importance or that he gave a metaphysic of Being which was, in some respects, greatly superior to that of Plato: what I mean is, that Aristotle, through his theory of the entelechy, the immanent substantial form, which tends to its realisation in the processes of nature, was enabled to attach a meaning and reality to the sensible world which are missing in the philosophy of Plato and that this particular contribution to philosophy gives a characteristic tone and flavour to Aristotelianism as distinct from Platonism. Aristotle said that the end of man is an activity, not a quality, whereas one has the impression that for Plato quality would take precedence of activity: Plato's "Absolute" was not the immanent activity of Aristotle's "self-thinking Thought" and Plato's "Absolute" was the supreme Exemplar. (That Aristotle's characterisation of matter tended to diminish the reality and intelligibility of the material world is no objection against my main thesis, since his doctrine of matter was very largely an effect of his Platonic education, and my main thesis is concerned with Aristotle's *peculiar* contribution to the philosophy of nature.)

Aristotle thus made a most important contribution to the philosophy of nature and he certainly regarded himself as having broken fresh ground. In the first place, he regarded his doctrine of the *immanent* essence as an antithesis to, or correction of, Plato's doctrine of the transcendental essence, and, in the second place, his remarks concerning the emergence of the idea of finality in philosophy, even if those remarks are to some extent patently unjust to Plato, show clearly that he regarded his theory of immanent teleology as something new. But though Aristotle provided a needed correction or antithesis to Platonism in this respect, he discarded much that was of value in the process of correcting his predecessor. Not only was Plato's conception of Providence, of Divine Reason immanent in the world and operating in the world, discarded by Aristotle, but also Plato's conception of exemplary causality. Plato may have failed to work out a systematised view of Absolute Being as exemplary Cause of essences, as Ground of value; he may have failed to realise, as Aristotle realised, that the immaterial form is intelligent, that supreme Actuality is supreme Intelligence; he may have failed to bring together and identify the supreme Efficient, Exemplary and Final Causes; but, in his opposition to Plato's inadequate view of the concrete object of this world, Aristotle allowed himself to miss and pass over the profound truth in the Platonic theory. Each thinker, then, has his high-points, each made an invaluable contribution to philosophy, but neither thinker gave the complete truth, even so far as that is attainable. One may be drawn towards either Plato or Aristotle by temperamental affinity, but one would not be justified in rejecting Aristotle for Plato or Plato for Aristotle: the truths contained in their respective philosophies have to be integrated and harmoniously combined in a complete synthesis, a synthesis which must incorporate and build upon that cardinal tenet, which was held in common by both Plato and Aristotle, namely, the conviction that the fully real is the fully intelligible and the fully good, while utilising also the peculiar contributions of each philosopher, in so far as these contributions are true and so compatible.

In the pages devoted to Neo-Platonism we shall witness an attempt, successful or unsuccessful as the case may be, to accomplish such a synthesis, an attempt which has been repeated in the course of both mediaeval and modern philosophy; but it might be as well to point out that, if such a synthesis is possible, it is made possible largely through the Platonic elements which are contained in Aristotelianism. Let me give one example, to illustrate my meaning. If Aristotle, in correcting what he considered to be the excessively dualistic character of the Platonic anthropology (I refer to the soul-body relationship), had explicitly rejected the supersensible character of the rational principle in man and had reduced thought, for example, to matter in motion, he would indeed have posited an antithesis to the Platonic theory, but this antithesis would have been of such a character that it could not combine with the thesis in a higher synthesis. As it was, however, Aristotle never, as far as we know, rejected the presence of a supersensible principle in man—he affirms it in his *De Anima* —even though he insisted that the soul cannot inhabit *any* body but is the entelechy of a particular body. A synthesis was, therefore, rendered possible, which would include the Aristotelian idea of the soul as the form of the body, while allowing, with Plato, that the *individual* soul is more than the body and survives death in individual self-identity.

Again, it might appear perhaps at first sight that the Aristotelian God, the Thought of Thought, constitutes an incompatible antithesis to the Platonic Idea of the Good, which, though intelligible, is not depicted as intelligent. Yet, since pure form is not only the intelligible but also the intelligent, the Platonic Absolute Good cried out, as it were, to be identified with the Aristotelian God, an identification which was accomplished in the Christian synthesis at least, so that both Plato and Aristotle contributed different, though complementary, facets of theism.

(In the foregoing remarks I have spoken of a synthesis of Platonism and Aristotelianism; but one is entitled to speak of he necessity of a synthesis only when there is question of two 'antithetical" theories, each of them being more or less true in what it affirms and false in what it denies. For example, Plato was correct in affirming exemplarism, wrong in neglecting immanent substantial form, while Aristotle was correct in asserting his theory of the immanent substantial form, wrong in neglecting exemplarism. But there are other aspects of their philosophies in regard to which one can hardly speak of the necessity for a synthesis, since Aristotle himself accomplished the synthesis. For instance, the Aristotelian logic, that marvellous creation of genius, does not need to be synthesised with the Platonic logic, owing to the simple fact that it was a tremendous advance on Plato's logic (or what we know of it, at least) and itself comprised what was valuable in the Platonic logic).

PART V

POST-ARISTOTELIAN PHILOSOPHY

CHAPTER XXXV

INTRODUCTORY

1. With the reign of Alexander the Great the day of the free and independent Greek City-State had really passed away. During his reign and that of his successors, who fought with one another for political power, any freedom that the Greek cities possessed was but nominal—at least it depended on the goodwill of the paramount sovereign. After the death of the great Conqueror in 323 B.C. we must speak rather of Hellenistic (i.e. in opposition tc National-Hellenic) than of Hellenic civilisation. To Alexander the sharp distinction between Greek and "Barbarian" was unreal: he thought in terms of Empire, not in terms of the City: and the result was, that while the East was opened up to the influence of the West, Greek culture on its side could not remain uninfluenced by the new state of affairs. Athens, Sparta, Corinth, etc.—these were no longer free and independent units, united in a common feeling of cultural superiority to the barbarian darkness round about them: they were merged in a larger whole, and the day was not far distant when Greece was to become but a Province of the Roman Empire.

The new political situation could not be without its reaction on philosophy. Both Plato and Aristotle had been men of the Greek City, and for them the individual was inconceivable apart from the City and the life of the City: it was in the City that the individual attained his end, lived the good life. But when the free City was merged in a greater cosmopolitan whole, it was but natural that not only cosmopolitanism, with its ideal of citizenship of the world, as we see it in Stoicism, but also individualism should come to the fore. In fact these two elements, cosmopolitanism and individualism, were closely bound together. For when the life of the City-State, compact and all-embracing, as Plato and Aristotle had conceived it, had broken down and citizens were merged in a much greater whole, the individual was inevitably cast adrift by himself, loosed from his moorings in the City-State. It w but to be expected, then, that in a cosmopolitan society philosopl should centre its interest in the individual, endeavouring to me his demand for guidance in life, which he had to live out in great society and no longer in a comparatively small City-family and so displaying a predominantly ethical and practical trend—as in Stoicism and Epicureanism. Metaphysical and physical speculation tend to drop into the background: they are of interest not for their own sake but as providing a basis and preparation for ethics. This concentration on the ethical makes it easy to understand why the new Schools borrowed their metaphysical notions from other thinkers, without attempting fresh speculation on their own. Indeed it is to the pre-Socratics that they return in this respect, Stoicism having recourse to the Physics of Heraclitus and Epicureanism to the Atomism of Democritus. More than that, the post-Aristotelian Schools returned to the pre-Socratics, at least in part, even for their ethical ideas or tendencies, the Stoics borrowing from Cynic ethics and the Epicureans from the Cyrenaics.

This ethical and practical interest is particularly marked in the development of the post-Aristotelian Schools in the Roman period, for the Romans were not, like the Greeks, speculative and metaphysical thinkers; they were predominantly men of practice. The old Romans had insisted on *character*—speculation was somewhat foreign to them—and in the Roman Empire, when the former ideals and traditions of the Republic had been swamped, it was precisely the philosopher's task to provide the individual with a code of conduct which would enable him to pilot his way through the sea of life, maintaining a consistency of principle and action based on a certain spiritual and moral independence. Hence the phenomenon of philosopher-directors, who performed a task somewhat analogous to that of the spiritual director as known to the Christian world.

This concentration on the practical, the fact that philosophy took as its office the provision of standards of life, naturally led to a wide diffusion of philosophy among the cultured classes of the Hellenistic-Roman world and so to a kind of Popular Philosophy. Philosophy in the Roman period became more and more part of the regular course of education (a fact which demanded its presentation in an easily apprehended form), and it was in this way that philosophy became a rival to Christianity, when the new Religion began to lay claim to the allegiance of the Empire. Indeed one may say that philosophy, to a certain extent at least, offered to satisfy the religious needs and aspirations of man. Disbelief in the popular mythology was common, and where this disbelief reigned—among the educated classes—those who were not content to live without religion at all had either to attach themselves to one of the many cults that were introduced into the Empire from the East and which were definitely more calculated to satisfy man's spiritual aspirations than the official State religion with its businesslike attitude, or to turn to philosophy for the satisfaction of those needs. And so it is that we can discern religious elements in such a predominantly ethical system as Stoicism, while in Neo-Platonism, the last flower of Ancient Philosophy, the syncretism of religion and philosophy reaches its culmination. More than that, we may say that in Plotinian Neo-Platonism, in which the mystical flight of the spirit or ecstasy is made the final and highest point of intellectual activity, philosophy tends to pass over into religion.

Insistence on ethics alone leads to an ideal of spiritual independence and self-sufficiency such as we find in both Stoicism and Epicureanism, while insistence on religion tends rather to assert dependence on a Transcendental Principle and to ascribe the purification of the self to the action of the Divine, an attitude that we find in a mystery-cult like that of Mithras. It is to be noted, however, that both tendencies, the tendency to insist on the ethical, the self-sufficient perfection of the personality or the acquisition of a true moral personality, and the tendency to insist on the attitude of the worshipper towards the Divine or the need of the non-self-sufficient human being to unite himself with God, contributed to meet the same want, the want of the individual in the Greco-Roman world to find a sure basis for his individual life, since the religious attitude too brought with it a certain independence *vis-à-vis* the secular Empire. In practice, of course, the two attitudes tended to coalesce, the emphasis being placed sometimes on the ethical (as in Stoicism), sometimes on the religious factor (as in the mystery-cults), while in Neo-Platonism there was an attempt at a comprehensive synthesis, the ethical being subordinated to the religious, but without losing its importance.

2. In the development of the Hellenistic-Roman philosophy it is usual to distinguish several phases:[1]

[1] Cf. Ueberweg-Praechter, pp. 32–3.

(i) The first phase or period extends from about the end of the fourth century B.C. to the middle of the first century B.C. This period is characterised by the founding of the Stoic and Epicurean philosophies, which place the emphasis on conduct and the attainment of personal happiness, while harking back to pre-Socratic thought for the cosmological bases of their systems. Over against these "dogmatic" systems stands the Scepticism of Pyrrho and his followers, to which must be added the sceptical vein in the Middle and New Academies. The interaction between these philosophies led to a certain Eclecticism, which showed itself in a tendency on the part of the Middle Stoa, the Peripatetic School and the Academy to eclectic assimilation of one another's doctrines.

(ii) Eclecticism on the one hand and Scepticism on the other hand continue into the second period (from about the middle of the first century B.C. to the middle of the third century A.D.), but this period is characterised by a return to philosophical "orthodoxy." Great interest is taken in the founders of the Schools, their lives, works and doctrines, and this tendency to philosophical "orthodoxy" is a counterpart to the continuing eclecticism. But the interest in the past was also fruitful in scientific investigation, e.g. in editing the works of the old philosophers, commenting on them and interpreting them. In such work the pre-eminence belongs to the Alexandrians.

This scientific interest is not, however, the sole characteristic of the second period. Over against the scientific interest we find the tendency to religious mysticism, which becomes ever stronger. It has been pointed out (e.g. Praechter, p. 36) that this tendency has a common root with the scientific tendency, namely, the disappearance of productive speculation. While the latter factor might lead to scepticism or to devotion to scientific pursuits, it might equally result in a tendency to religious mysticism. This tendency was of course favoured by the growing religious consciousness of the time and by acquaintance with religions of eastern origin. Western philosophers, e.g. the Neo-Pythagoreans, endeavoured to incorporate these religious-mystical elements into their speculative systems, while eastern thinkers, e.g. Philo of Alexandria, tried to systematise their religious conceptions in a philosophic framework. (Thinkers like Philo were, of course, also influenced by the desire to win over the Greeks for their un-Greek doctrines by presenting the latter in philosophic guise.)

(iii) The third period (from about the middle of the third

century A.D. to the middle of the sixth century A.D.—or, in Alexandria, to the middle of the seventh century) is that of Neo-Platonism. This final speculative effort of Ancient Philosophy attempted to combine all the valuable elements in the philosophic and religious doctrines of East and West in one comprehensive system, practically absorbing all the philosophic Schools and dominating philosophical development for a number of centuries, so that it cannot justifiably be overlooked in a history of philosophy or be relegated to the dustbin of esoteric mysticism. Moreover, Neo-Platonism exercised a great influence on Christian speculation: we have only to think of names like those of St. Augustine and the Pseudo-Dionysius.

3. A feature of the Hellenistic world that must not be passed over is the increased cultivation of the special sciences. We have seen how philosophy and religion tended to become united: with regard to philosophy and the special sciences the opposite holds good. Not only had the domain of philosophy become more sharply delineated than it was in the early days of Greek thought, but the different sciences had themselves reached such a pitch of development that they required special treatment. Moreover, the improvement in the external conditions for research and study, though itself largely an outcome of specialisation, reacted in turn on the cultivation of the sciences, promoting an intensification of departmental work and research. The Lyceum had, of course, greatly contributed to the growth and development of the sciences, but in the Hellenistic age there arose scientific Institutes, Museums and Libraries in the great capital cities of Alexandria, Antioch, and Pergamon, with the result that philological and literary research, mathematical, medical and physical studies, were enabled to make great strides. Thus according to Tzetzes, the "outer" library at Alexandria contained 42,800 volumes, while the main library in the Palace contained some 400,000 "mixed" and some 90,000 "unmixed" or "simple" volumes, the latter being probably small papyrus rolls while the former were bigger rolls. Later on the larger volumes, divided into books, were reduced to "simple" volumes. We are told that when Antony presented Cleopatra with the Pergamene library, he gave her 200,000 "simple" volumes.

It may be, of course, that the influence of philosophy on the special sciences was not always favourable to their advance, for speculative assumptions sometimes took a place which did not belong to them and led to hasty and precipitate conclusions, when experiment and exact observation should have exercised the decisive rôle. On the other hand, however, the special sciences were helped by being given a philosophical foundation, for they were thereby rescued from crude empiricism and from an exclusively practical and utilitarian orientation.

CHAPTER XXXVI

THE EARLY STOA

1. THE founder of the Stoic School was Zeno, who was born about 336/5 B.C. at Citium in Cyprus and died about 264/3 at Athens. He seems to have at first followed his father in commercial activity.[1] Coming to Athens about 315–313 he read the *Memorabilia* of Xenophon and the *Apology* of Plato and was filled with admiration for Socrates' strength of character. Thinking that Crates the Cynic was the man who most resembled Socrates, he became his disciple. From the Cynics he seemed to have turned to Stilpo,[2] though Zeno is also reported to have listened to Xenocrates and, after Xenocrates' death, to Polemon. About the year 300 B.C. he founded his own philosophic School, which takes its name from the Στοὰ Ποικίλη, where he lectured. He is said to have taken his own life. Of his writings we possess only fragments.

Zeno was succeeded in the leadership of the School by Cleanthes of Assos (331/30–233/2 or 231) and Cleanthes by Chrysippus of Soloi in Cilicia (281/278–208/205), who was called the second founder of the School because of his systematisation of the Stoic doctrines. Εἰ μὴ γὰρ ἦ Χρύσιππος, οὐκ ἂν ἦν Στόα.[3] He is said to have written more than 705 books and was famed for his dialectic, though not for his style of composition.

Among Zeno's pupils were Ariston of Chios, Herillus of Carthage, Dionysius of Heracleia, Persion of Citium. A pupil of Cleanthes was Sphairus of the Bosphorus. Chrysippus was succeeded by two pupils, Zeno of Tarsus and Diogenes of Seleucia. The latter came to Rome in 156/5 B.C., together with other philosophers, as ambassadors of Athens in an attempt to obtain remission of the fine. The philosophers gave lectures in Rome, which excited admiration among the youth of the City, though Cato thought that such philosophical interests were not consonant with the military virtues and he advised the Senate to get rid of the embassy as soon as possible.[4] Diogenes was succeeded by Antipater of Tarsus.

[1] Diog. Laërt., 7, 2 and 31. [2] Diog. Laërt., 7, 2. [3] Diog. Laërt., 7, 183. [4] Plut., *Cat. Mai.*, 22.

11. *Logic of the Stoa*

Logic was divided by the Stoics into Dialectic and Rhetoric, to which some added the Theory of Definitions and the Theory of the Criteria of Truth.[1] Something will be said here of the Stoic epistemology, omitting their account of formal logic, though we may note the fact that the Stoics reduced the ten Categories of Aristotle to four, namely, the substrate (τὸ ὑποκείμενον), the essential constitution (τὸ ποιόν or τὸ ποιὸν ὑποκείμενον), the accidental constitution (τὸ πῶς ἔχον or τὸ πῶς ἔχον ποιὸν ὑποκείμενον) and the relative accidental constitution (τὸ πρός τι πῶς ἔχον, τὸ πρός τι πῶς ἔχον ποιὸν ὑποκείμενον). A further feature of the formal logic of the Stoa may also be mentioned. Propositions are simple if their terms are non-propositions, otherwise compound. The compound proposition, "if X, then Y" (τὸ συνημμένον), is declared to be (i) true, if X and Y are both true; (ii) false, if X is true and Y is false; (iii) true, if X is false and Y is true; (iv) true, if X and Y are both false. Thus our "material" implication is separated from our "formal" implication and our "strict" implication, and from entailment by ontological necessitation.[2]

The Stoics rejected not only the Platonic doctrine of the transcendental universal, but also Aristotle's doctrine of the concrete universal. Only the individual exists and our knowledge is knowledge of particular objects. These particulars make an impression on the soul (τύπωσις—Zeno and Cleanthes—or ἑτεροίωσις—Chrysippus), and knowledge is primarily knowledge of this impression. The Stoics adopted, therefore, the opposite position to that of Plato, for, while Plato depreciated sense-perception, the Stoics founded all knowledge on sense-perception. They would doubtless re-echo the words of Antisthenes, to the effect that he saw a horse but not "horseness." (Zeno, as we have seen, became a pupil of Crates the Cynic.) The soul is originally a *tabula rasa*, and, in order for it to know, there is need of perception. The Stoics did not of course deny that we have knowledge of our interior states and activities, but Chrysippus reduced this knowledge, too, to perception, which was rendered all the easier in that these states and activities were considered to consist of material processes. After the act of perception a memory (μνήμη) remains behind, when the actual object is no longer there, and experience arises from a plurality of similar recollections (ἐμπειρία).

[1] Diog. Laërt., 7, 41–2. [2] Sext. Emp., *Pyrr. Hyp.*, 2, 105; *Adv. Math.*, 8, 449.

The Stoics were therefore Empiricists, even "Sensualists"; but they also maintained a Rationalism which was scarcely consistent with a thoroughly empiricist and nominalist position. For although they asserted that reason (λόγος, νοῦς) is a product of development, in that it grows up gradually out of perceptions and is formed only about the fourteenth year, they also held, not only that there are deliberately-formed general ideas, but also that there are general ideas (κοιναὶ ἔννοιαι or προλήψεις), which are apparently antecedent to experience (ἔμφυτοι προλήψεις) in that we have a natural predisposition to form them—virtually innate ideas, we might call them. What is more, it is only through Reason that the system of Reality can be known.

The Stoics devoted a good deal of attention to the question of the criterion of truth. This they declared to be the φαντασία καταληπτική, the apprehensive perception or representation. The criterion of truth lies, therefore, in the perception itself, namely, in the perception that compels the assent of the soul, i.e. to all intents and purposes in clear perception. (This is scarcely consistent with the view that it is science alone that gives us certain knowledge of Reality.) However, the difficulty arose that the soul can withhold assent from what is objectively a true perception. Thus when the dead Alcestis appeared to Admetus from the underworld, her husband had a clear perception of her, yet he did not assent to this clear perception because of subjective hindrances, namely, the belief that dead people do not rise again, while on the other hand there may be deceptive apparitions of the dead. In view of this sort of objection the later Stoics, as Sextus Empiricus tells us, added to the criterion of truth, "which has no hindrance." Objectively speaking, the perception of the dead Alcestis has the value of a criterion of truth—for it is objectively a καταληπτικὴ φαντασία—but subjectively speaking, it cannot act as such, because of a belief which acts as a subjective hindrance.[1] This is all very well, but the difficulty still remains of ascertaining when there is such a hindrance and when there is not.

III. *Cosmology of the Stoa*

In their cosmology the Stoics had recourse to Heraclitus for the doctrine of the Logos and of Fire as the world-substance; but elements are also present which are borrowed from Plato and

[1] Sext. Emp., *Adv. Math.*, 7, 254 ff.

Aristotle. Thus the λόγοι σπερματικοί seem to be a transposition on to the material plane of the ideal theory.

According to the Stoics there are two principles in Reality, τὸ ποιοῦν and τὸ πάσχον. But this is not dualism as we find it in Plato, since the active principle, τὸ ποιοῦν, is not spiritual but material. In fact it is hardly dualism at all, since the two principles are both material and together form one Whole. The Stoic doctrine is therefore a monistic materialism, even if this position is not consistently maintained. It is uncertain what Zeno's view was, but Cleanthes and Chrysippus would seem to have regarded the two factors as ultimately one and the same.

> "All are but parts of one stupendous whole,
> Whose body Nature is and God the soul,"[1]

The passive principle is matter devoid of qualities, while the active principle is immanent Reason or God. Natural beauty or finality in Nature point to the existence of a principle of thought in the universe, God, Who, in His Providence, has arranged everything for the good of man. Moreover, since the highest phenomenon of nature, man, is possessed of consciousness, we cannot suppose that the whole world is devoid of consciousness, for the whole cannot be less perfect than the part. God, therefore, is the Consciousness of the world. Nevertheless God, like the substrate on which He works, is material. "(Zeno) *Nullo modo arbitrabatur quidquam effici posse ab ea (natura) quae expers esset corporis—nec vero aut quod efficeret aut quod efficeretur, posse esse non corpus.*"[2] ὄντα γὰρ μόνα τὰ σώματα καλοῦσιν.[3] Like Heraclitus the Stoics make Fire to be the stuff of all things. God is the active Fire (πῦρ τεχνικόν), which is immanent in the universe (πνεῦμα διῆκον δι' ὅλου τοῦ κόσμου), but He is at the same time the primal Source from which the crasser elements, that make the corporeal world, come forth. These crasser elements proceed from God and are at length resolved into Him again, so that all that exists is either the primal Fire—God in Himself—or God in His different states. When the world is in existence God stands to it as soul to body, being the soul of the world. He is not something entirely different from the stuff of the world, His Body, but is a finer stuff, the moving and forming principle—the crasser stuff, of which the world is formed, being itself motionless and unformed, though capable of receiving all sorts of movement and form.

[1] Pope, *Essay on Man*, I, 267. [2] Cic., *Acad. Post.*, 1, 11, 39.
[3] Plut., *De Comm. Notit.*, 1073 E.

"*Zenoni et reliquis fere Stoicis aether videtur summus deus, mente praeditus, qua omnia reguntur.*"[1]

God therefore, ὁ Λόγος, is the Active Principle which contains within itself the active forms of all the things that are to be, these forms being the λόγοι σπερματικοί. These active forms—but material—are as it were "seeds," through the activity of which individual things come into being as the world develops; or rather they are seeds which unfold themselves in the forms of individual things. (The conception of λόγοι σπρερματικοί is found in Neo-Platonism and in St. Augustine, under the name of *rationes seminales*.) In the actual development of the world part of the fiery vapour, of which God consists, is transformed into air and from air is formed water. From part of the water comes earth, while a second part remains water and a third part is transformed into air, which through rarefaction becomes the elementary fire. Thus does the "body" of God come into being.

Now Heraclitus, as we have seen, most probably never taught the doctrine of the universal conflagration, in which the whole world returns to the primeval fire, from which it was born. The Stoics, however, certainly added this doctrine of the ἐκπύρωσις, according to which God forms the world and then takes it back into Himself through a universal conflagration, so that there is an unending series of world-constructions and world-destructions. Moreover, each new world resembles its predecessor in all particulars, every individual man, for example, occurring in each successive world and performing the identical actions that he performed in his previous existence. (Cf. Nietzsche's idea of the "Eternal Recurrence.") Consistently with this belief the Stoics denied human freedom, or rather liberty for them meant doing consciously, with assent, what one will do in any case. (We are reminded somewhat of Spinoza.) This reign of necessity the Stoics expressed under the concept of Fate ('Ειμαρμένη), but Fate is not something different from God and universal reason, nor is it different from Providence (Πρόνοια) which orders all things for the best. Fate and Providence are but different aspects of God. But this cosmological determinism is modified by their insistence on interior freedom, in the sense that a man can alter his judgment on events and his attitude towards events, seeing them and welcoming them as the expression of "God's Will." In this sense man is free.

[1] Cic., *Acad. Prior.*, 2, 41, 126.

Since the Stoics held that God orders all things for the best, they had to explain the evil in the world or at least to bring it into harmony with their "optimism." Chrysippus especially undertook the perennial difficulty of formulating a theodicy, taking as his fundamental tenet the theory that the imperfection of individuals subserves the perfection of the whole. It would follow that there is really no evil when things are looked at *sub specie aeternitatis*. (If we are reminded here of Spinoza, we are reminded also of Leibniz, not only by Stoic optimism, but also by their doctrine that no two individual phenomena of Nature are completely alike.) Chrysippus, in his fourth book on Providence, argues that goods could not have existed without evils, on the ground that of a pair of contraries neither can exist without the other, so that if you take away the one, you take away both.[1] There is certainly a great deal of truth in this contention. For instance, the existence of a sensible creature capable of pleasure implies also the capacity for feeling pain—unless, of course, God determines otherwise; but we are now speaking of the natural state of affairs and not of preternatural Divine ordinances. Moreover, pain, though spoken of as an evil, would seem to be—in a certain aspect—a good. For example, given the possibility of our teeth decaying, toothache would seem to be a definite good or benefit. The privation of right order in the teeth is certainly an evil, but—given the possibility of decay—we should be worse off if toothache were impossible, since it serves as a danger-signal, warning us that it is time that we had our teeth examined by a dentist. Similarly, if we never felt hungry—a pain—we might ruin our health by insufficient nourishment. Chrysippus saw this clearly and argued that it is good for man to have his head of delicate construction, though the very fact of its delicate construction involves at the same time the possibility of danger from a comparatively slight blow.

But though physical evil is not so great a difficulty, what of moral evil? According to the Stoics no act is evil and reprehensible *in itself*: it is the intention, the moral condition of the agent from whom the act proceeds, that makes the act evil: the act as a physical entity is indifferent. (If this were taken to mean that a good intention justifies any act, then such an act is in the moral order and will be either good or bad—though if the agent performs a bad act with a sincerely good intention in a state of inculpable

[1] Apud Gellium, *Noctes Atticae*, 6, 1.

ignorance of the fact that the act is contrary to right reason, the action is only *materialiter* evil and the agent is not guilty of formal sin.[1] However, if the act be considered merely in itself, as a positive entity, apart from its character as a human act, then Chrysippus is right in saying that the act as such is not evil —in fact, it is good. That it cannot of itself be evil, can easily be shown by an example. The physical action, the positive element, is precisely the same when a man is murderously shot as when he is shot in battle during a just war: it is not the positive element in the murder, the action considered merely abstractly, that is the *moral* evil. Moral evil, considered precisely as such, cannot be a positive entity, since this would reflect on the goodness of the Creator, the Source of all being. Moral evil consists essentially in a privation of right order in the human will, which, in the human bad act, is out of harmony with right reason.) Now, if a man can have a right intention, he can also have a wrong intention; hence, in the moral sphere, no less than in the physical sphere, contraries involve one another. How, asked Chrysippus, can courage be understood apart from cowardice or justice apart from injustice? Just as the capacity of feeling pleasure implies the capacity of feeling pain, so the capacity of being just implies the capacity of being unjust.

In so far as Chrysippus simply meant that the capacity for virtue implies *de facto* the capacity for vice, he was enunciating a truth, since for man in his present state in this world, with his limited apprehension of the *Summum Bonum*, freedom to be virtuous implies also freedom to commit sin, so that, if the possession of moral freedom is a good thing for man and if it is better to be able to choose virtue freely (even though this implies the possibility of vice) than to have no freedom at all, no valid argument against Divine Providence can be drawn from the possibility, or even the existence, of moral evil in the world. But in so far as Chrysippus implies that the presence of virtue in the universe necessarily implies the presence of its contrary, on the ground that opposites always involve one another, he is implying what is false, since human moral freedom, while involving the *possibility* of vice in this life, does not necessarily involve its

[1] An act, i.e. a human act, one proceeding from the free will of the human agent, is *materialiter* (or *objectively*) good or evil, in so far as it is objectively in conformity with, or not in conformity with, right reason, with the objective Natural Law. The agent's conscious intention cannot alter the objective or material character of a human act, even though, in the case of an objectively evil act, it may excuse him from formal moral fault.

actuality. (The apology for moral evil, as also for physical evil, which consists in saying that the good is thrown into higher relief through the presence of the bad, might, if pressed, imply the same false view. Given this present order of the world, it is certainly better that man should be free, and so *able* to sin, than that he should be without freedom; but it is better that man should use his freedom to choose virtuous actions, and the best condition of the world would be that all men should always do what is right, however much the presence of vice may set the good in high relief.)

Chrysippus was not so happy when he speculated whether external misfortunes might not be due to oversight on the part of Providence, as when trifling accidents occur in a large household that is, in general, well administered, through neglect of some kind;[1] but he rightly saw that those physical evils that befall the good may be turned into a blessing, both through the individual (through his interior attitude towards them) or for mankind at large (e.g. by stimulating medical investigation and progress). Further, it is interesting to notice, that Chrysippus gives an argument which recurs later in, e.g. Neo-Platonism, St. Augustine, Berkeley and Leibniz, to the effect that evil in the universe throws the good into greater relief, just as the contrast of light and shadow is pleasing in a picture or, to use an actual example employed by Chrysippus, as "Comedies have in them ludicrous verses which, though bad in themselves, nevertheless lend a certain grace to the whole play."[2]

In inorganic objects the Universal Reason or πνεῦμα operates as a ἕξις or principle of cohesion, and this holds good also for plants—which have no soul—though in them the ἕξις has the power of movement and has risen to the rank of φύσις. In animals there is soul (ψυχή), which shows itself in the powers of φαντασία and ὁρμή, and in human beings there is reason. The soul of man is therefore the noblest of souls: indeed it is part of the divine Fire which descended into men at their creation and is then passed on at generation, for, like all else, it is material. τὸ ἡγεμονικόν the dominant part of the soul, has its seat in the heart according to Chrysippus, apparently on the ground that the voice, which is the expression of thought, proceeds from the heart. (Some other Stoics placed τὸ ἡγεμονικόν in the head.) Personal immortality was

[1] Plut., *De Stoic. Repugn.*, 1051 c.
[2] Plut., *De Comm. Notit.*, 1065 d; Marcus Aurel., *To Himself*, VI, 42.

scarcely possible in the Stoic system, and the Stoics admitted that all souls return to the primeval Fire at the conflagration. The only dispute was on the subject of what souls persist after death until the conflagration; and while Cleanthes considered that this held good for all human souls, Chrysippus admitted it only in regard to the souls of the wise.

In a monistic system such as that of the Stoics we would hardly expect to find any attitude of personal devotion towards the Divine Principle; but in point of fact such a tendency is indubitably visible. This tendency is particularly observable in the celebrated hymn to Zeus by Cleanthes:

O God most glorious, called by many a name,
Nature's great King, through endless years the same;
Omnipotence, who by thy just decree
Controllest all, hail, Zeus, for unto thee
Behoves thy creatures in all lands to call.
We are thy children, we alone, of all
On earth's broad ways that wander to and fro,
Bearing thy image wheresoe'er we go.
Wherefore with songs of praise thy power I will forth show.
Lo! yonder heaven, that round the earth is wheeled,
Follows thy guidance, still to thee doth yield
Glad homage; thine unconquerable hand
Such flaming minister, the levin-brand,
Wieldeth, a sword two-edged, whose deathless might
Pulsates through all that Nature brings to light;
Vehicle of the universal Word, that flows
Through all, and in the light celestial glows
Of stars both great and small. O King of Kings
Through ceaseless ages, God, whose purpose brings
To birth, whate'er on land or in the sea
Is wrought, or in high heaven's immensity;
Save what the sinner works infatuate.
Nay, but thou knowest to make the crooked straight:
Chaos to thee is order: in thine eyes
The unloved is lovely, who did'st harmonise
Things evil with things good, that there should be
One Word through all things everlastingly.
One Word—whose voice alas! the wicked spurn;
Insatiate for the good their spirits yearn:
Yet seeing see not, neither hearing hear
God's universal law, which those revere,
By reason guided, happiness who win.
The rest, unreasoning, diverse shapes of sin
Self-prompted follow: for an idle name
Vainly they wrestle in the lists of fame:

Others inordinately Riches woo,
Or dissolute, the joys of flesh pursue.
Now here, now there they wander, fruitless still,
For ever seeking good and finding ill.
Zeus the all-beautiful, whom darkness shrouds,
Whose lightning lightens in the thunder clouds;
Thy children save from error's deadly sway:
Turn thou the darkness from their souls away:
Vouchsafe that unto knowledge they attain;
For thou by knowledge art made strong to reign
O'er all, and all things rulest righteously.
So by thee honoured, we will honour thee,
Praising thy works continuously with songs,
As mortals should; nor higher meed belongs
E'en to the gods, than justly to adore
The universal law for evermore.[1]

But this attitude of personal devotion towards the Supreme Principle on the part of some of the Stoics does not mean that they rejected the popular religion; on the contrary, they took it under their protection. Zeno did indeed declare that prayers and sacrifices are of no avail, but polytheism was nevertheless justified by the Stoics on the ground that the one Principle or Zeus manifests itself in phenomena, e.g. the heavenly bodies, so that divine reverence is due to these manifestations—a reverence which is also to be extended to deified man or "heroes." Moreover, Stoicism found a place for divination and oracles. This fact need really cause no great surprise, if we reflect that the Stoics maintained a deterministic doctrine and held that all the parts and events of the universe are mutually interconnected.

IV. *The Stoic Ethic*

The importance of the ethical part of philosophy for the Stoics may be exemplified by the description of philosophy given by Seneca. Seneca belongs, of course, to the later Stoa, yet the emphasis laid by him on philosophy as the science of conduct was common to the early Stoa as well. *Philosophia nihil aliud est quam recta vivendi ratio vel honeste vivendi scientia vel ars rectae vitae agendae. non errabimus, si dixerimus philosophiam esse legem bene honesteque vivendi, et qui dixerit illam regulam vitae, suum illi nomen reddidit.*[2] Philosophy, therefore, is primarily concerned with conduct. Now the end of life, happiness, εὐδαιμονία, consists

[1] Trans. by Dr. James Adam, quoted in Hicks' *Stoic and Epicurean*, pp. 14–16 (Longmans, 1910).
[2] Seneca, Frag. 17.

in Virtue (in the Stoic sense of the term), i.e. in the natural life or life according to nature (ὁμολογουμένως τῇ φύσει ζῆν), the agreement of human action with the law of nature, or of the human will with the divine Will. Hence the famous Stoic maxim, "Live according to nature." For man to conform himself to the laws of the universe in the wide sense, and for man to conform his conduct to his own essential nature, reason, is the same thing, since the universe is governed by the law of nature. While earlier Stoics thought of "Nature," the Φύσις which man should follow, rather as the nature of the universe, later Stoics—from Chrysippus—tended to conceive nature from a more anthropological point of view.

The Stoic conception of life according to nature differs therefore from the old Cynic conception, as exemplified in the conduct and teaching of Diogenes. For the Cynics "nature" meant rather the primitive and instinctive, and so life according to nature implied a deliberate flouting of the conventions and traditions of civilised society, a flouting that externalised itself in conduct that was eccentric and not infrequently indecent. For the Stoics on the other hand, life according to nature meant life according to the principle that is active in nature, λόγος, the principle shared in by the human soul. The ethical end, therefore, according to the Stoics, consists essentially in submission to the divinely appointed order of the world, and Plutarch informs us that it was a general principle of Chrysippus to begin all ethical inquiries with a consideration of the order and arrangement of the universe.[1]

The fundamental instinct implanted in the animal by nature is the instinct of self-preservation, which means for the Stoics pretty well what we would call self-perfection or self-development. Now, man is endowed with reason, the faculty which gives him his superiority over the brute: therefore for man "life in accordance with nature is rightly understood to mean life in accordance with reason. Hence Zeno's definition of the end is to live in conformity with nature, which means to live a life of virtue, since it is to virtue that nature leads. On the other hand, a virtuous life is a life which conforms to our experience of the course of nature, our human natures being but parts of universal nature. Thus the end is a life which follows nature, whereby is meant not only our own nature, but the nature of the universe, a life wherein we do nothing that is forbidden by the universal, i.e. by right reason, which pervades all things and is identical with Zeus, the

[1] Plut., *De Stoic. Repugn.*, c. 9 (1035 a 1–f 22).

guide and governor of the universe."[1] Diogenes Laërtius' account of the ethical teaching of the Stoics thus declares that virtue is a life in accordance with nature, while a life in conformity with nature is, i.e. for man, life in accordance with right reason. (As has been pointed out by others, this does not tell us very much, since the statements that it is reasonable to live in accordance with nature and natural to live in accordance with reason do not give much help to determining the content of virtue.)

Since the Stoics held that everything necessarily obeys the laws of nature, the objection was bound to be raised: "What is the good in telling man to obey the laws of nature, if he cannot help doing so in any case?" The Stoics answered that man is rational and so, though he will follow the laws of nature in any case, he has the privilege of knowing these laws and of assenting to them consciously. Hence there is a purpose in moral exhortation: man is free to change his interior attitude. (This involves, of course, a modification of the deterministic position, to say the least of it—but then no determinists are or can be really consistent, and the Stoics are no exception to the rule.) The consequence is that, strictly speaking, no action is in itself right or wrong, for determinism leaves no place for voluntary action and moral responsibility, while in a monistic system evil is really only evil when seen from some particular standpoint—*sub specie aeternitatis* all is right and good. The Stoics seem to have accepted—theoretically at least—the notion that no actions are wrong in themselves, as when Zeno admitted that not even cannibalism, incest or homosexuality are wrong in themselves.[2] Zeno did not, of course, mean to commend such actions: he meant that the physical act is indifferent, moral evil pertaining to the human will and intention.[3] Cleanthes declared that the human being necessarily follows the path of Destiny: "—if, to evil prone, my will rebelled, I needs must follow still."[4] And the same thought occurs in the celebrated dictum of Seneca, *Ducunt volentem fata, nolentem trahunt.*[5] However, the determinism of the Stoics was greatly modified in practice, since the doctrine that the wise man is he who *consciously* follows the path of Destiny (a doctrine brought out in the dictum of Seneca just quoted), when coupled with their exhortatory ethic,

[1] Diog. Laërt., 7, 86 ff.
[2] Von Arnim, *Stoic. Vet. Frag.*, Vol. I, pp. 59–60. (Pearson, pp. 210 ff.)
[3] Cf. Origen, *c. Cels*, 4, 45 (*P.G.*, 11, 1101).
[4] Frag. 91. (Pearson, *The Fragments of Zeno and Cleanthes*, 1891.)
[5] Seneca, *Ep.*, 107, 11.

implies liberty to a certain extent, as we have already remarked—a man is free to change his inner attitude and to adopt one of submission and resignation rather than of rebellion. Moreover, they admitted a scale of values, as we shall see, and it is at least tacitly implied that the wise man is free to choose the higher values and eschew the lower. But no deterministic system can be consistent in practice, a fact which need cause no surprise, since freedom is an actuality of which we are conscious, and even if it be theoretically denied, it creeps in again through the back door.

According to the Stoics virtue alone is a good in the full sense of the word: everything which is neither virtue nor vice is also neither good nor evil but indifferent (ἀδιάφορον). "Virtue is a disposition conformable to reason, desirable in and for itself and not because of any hope or fear or any external motive."[1] It was in accord with this view of the self-sufficiency and self-desirability of virtue that the Platonic myths concerning rewards and punishments in the next life were ridiculed by Chrysippus. (We may compare therewith the doctrine of Kant.) However, in regard to this middle realm of the indifferent the Stoics admitted that some things are preferable (προηγμένα) and others to be rejected (ἀποπροηγμένα), while others again are indifferent in a narrower sense. This was a concession to practice, perhaps at the expense of theory, but it was doubtless demanded by the Stoic doctrine, that virtue consists in conformity to nature. Hence among the morally indifferent things the Stoics introduced a division into (i) those things which are in accordance with nature and to which a value may therefore be ascribed (τὰ προηγμένα); (ii) those things which are contrary to nature and so valueless (τὰ ἀποπροηγμένα); and (iii) those things which possess neither value nor "disvalue" (τὰ ἀπαξία). In this way they constructed a scale of values. Pleasure is a result or accompaniment of activity and may never be made into an end. On this all the Stoics were agreed, though they did not all go so far as Cleanthes, who held that pleasure is not according to nature.

The Cardinal Virtues are Moral Insight (φρόνησις), Courage, Self-control or Temperance, and Justice. These virtues stand or fall together, in the sense that he who possesses one possesses all. Zeno found the common source of all virtues in φρόνησις, while for Cleanthes it was self-mastery, φρόνησις being replaced by ἐγκρατεία.

[1] Diog. Laërt., 7, 89.

In spite of differences, however, the Stoics in general adhered to the principle that the Virtues are indissolubly connected as expressions of one and the same character, so that the presence of one virtue implies the presence of all. Conversely, they thought that when one vice is present, all the vices must be present. Character, then, is the chief point stressed and truly virtuous conduct—which is fulfilment of duty (τὸ καθῆκον, a term apparently invented by Zeno, but denoting rather what is suitable than duty in our sense) in the right spirit—is performed only by the wise man. The wise man is without passions, and in respect of his interior worth he takes second place to none, not even to Zeus. Moreover, he is lord over his own life, and may commit suicide.

If all the virtues are so bound up with one another that he who possesses the one must possess the others, it is an easy step to supposing that there are no degrees in virtue. Either a man is virtuous, i.e. completely virtuous, or he is not virtuous at all. And this would seem to have been the position of the early Stoics. Thus, according to Chrysippus, a man who has *almost* completed the path of moral progress is not yet virtuous, has not yet that virtue which is true happiness. A consequence of this doctrine is that very few attain to virtue and then only late in life. "Man walks in wickedness all his life, or, at any rate, for the greater part of it. If he ever attains to virtue, it is late and at the very sunset of his days."[1] But while this strict moral idealism is characteristic of the earlier Stoicism, later Stoics emphasised much more the conception of progress, devoting their attention to encouraging man to begin and continue in the path of virtue. Admitting that no individual actually corresponds to the ideal of the wise man, they divided mankind into fools and those who are progressing towards virtue or wisdom.

Characteristic of the Stoic ethic is their doctrine in regard to the passions and affections. These—pleasure (ἡδονή), sorrow or depression (λύπη), desire (ἐπιθυμία) and fear (φόβος) are irrational and unnatural; and so it is not so much a question of moderating and regulating them as of getting rid of them and inducing a state of Apathy. At least when the passions or affections become habits (νόσοι ψυχῆς) they have to be eliminated. Hence the Stoic ethic is in practice largely a fight against the "affections," an endeavour to attain to a state of moral freedom and sovereignty. (The Stoics tended, however, to moderate somewhat this extreme

[1] Von Arnim, I, 529, p. 119 (i.e. Sext. Empir., *Adv. Math.*, 9, 90, of Cleanthes).

position, and we find some admitting rational emotions—εὐπάθειαι—in the wise man.) A quotation from Seneca well illustrates the Stoic attitude in regard to self-conquest.

> "*Quid praecipuum in rebus humanis est? non classibus maria complesse nec in rubri maris litore signa fixisse nec deficiente ad iniurias terra errasse in oceano ignota quaerentem, sed animo omnia vidisse et, qua maior nulla victoria est, vitia domuisse. Innumerabiles sunt, qui populos, qui urbes habuerunt in potestate, paucissimi qui se. quid est praecipuum? erigere animum supra minas et promissa fortunae, nihil dignam illam habere putare, quod speres: quid enim habet dignum, quod concupiscas? qui a divinorum conversatione, quotiens ad humana recideris, non aliter caligabis, quam quorum oculi in densam umbram ex claro sole redierunt. quid est praecipuum? posse laeto animo tolerare adversa. quidquid acciderit, sic ferre, quasi volueris tibi accidere. debuisses enim velle, si scires omnia ex decreto dei fieri: flere, queri, gemere desciscere est.quid est praecipuum? in primis labris animam habere. haec res efficit non e iure Quirium liberum, sed e iure naturae. liber enim est, qui servitutem effugit. haec est assidua et ineluctabilis et per diem et per noctem aequaliter premens. sine intervallo, sine commeatu. sibi servire gravissima est servitus: quam discutere facile est, si desieris multa te posceris, si desieris tibi referre mercedem, si ante oculos et naturam tuam et aetatem posueris, licet prima sit, ac tibi ipsi dixeris: quid insanio? quid anhelo? quid sudo? Quid terram, quid forum verso? nec multo opus est, nec diu.*"[1]

This side of the Stoic ethic—namely the endeavour to acquire complete independence of all externals—represents its Cynic heritage; but it has another side, whereby it passes beyond Cynicism and that is its Cosmopolitanism. Every man is naturally a social being, and to live in society is a dictate of reason. But reason is the common essential nature of all men: hence there is but one Law for all men and one Fatherland. The division of mankind into warring States is absurd: the wise man is a citizen, not of this or that particular State, but of the World. From this foundation it follows that all men have a claim to our goodwill, even slaves having their rights and even enemies having a right to our mercy and forgiveness. Now, this transcendence of narrow

[1] Seneca, *Nat. Quaest.*, III, Praef., 10–17.

social limits was obviously favoured by the monism of the Stoic system, but an ethical basis for the Stoic Cosmopolitanism was found in the fundamental instinct or tendency of self-preservation or self-love (οἰκείωσις). In the first place, of course, this instinctive tendency to self-preservation shows itself in the form of self-love, i.e. the individual's self-love. But it extends beyond self-love in the narrow sense to embrace all that belongs to the individual, family, friends, fellow-citizens and, finally, the whole of humanity. It is naturally stronger in regard to what stands closer to the individual, and grows weaker in proportion as the object is more remote, so that the individual's task, from the ethical viewpoint, is to raise the οἰκείωσις to the same pitch of intensity in regard to the remote objects as it manifests in regard to the nearer objects. In other words, the ethical ideal is attained when we love all men as we love ourselves or when our self-love embraces all that is connected with the self, including humanity at large, with an equal intensity.

CHAPTER XXXVII

EPICUREANISM

1. THE founder of the Epicurean School, Epicurus, was born at Samos in 342/1 B.C. At Samos he listened to Pamphilus, a Platonist,[1] and then at Teos to Nausiphanes, a follower of Democritus, who exercised considerable influence upon him, in spite of Epicurus' later contentions.[2] When eighteen, Epicurus came to Athens for his military service, and then seems to have given himself to study at Colophon. In 310 he taught at Mitylene—though he afterwards transferred to Lampsacus—and in 307/6 he moved to Athens and there opened his School.[3] This School was instituted in Epicurus' own garden, and we learn from Diogenes Laërtius that the philosopher in his will bequeathed the house and garden to his disciples. From the situation of the School the Epicureans got the name of οἱ ἀπὸ τῶν κήπων. Almost divine honours were paid to Epicurus even in his lifetime, and this cult of the founder is no doubt responsible for the fact that philosophic orthodoxy was maintained among the Epicureans more than in any other School. The chief doctrines were given the pupils to learn by heart.[4]

Epicurus was a voluminous writer (according to Diog. Laërt. he wrote about 300 works), but most of his writings are lost. However, Diogenes Laërtius has given us three didactic letters, of which the letters to Herodotus and Menoeceus are considered authentic while that to Pythocles is considered to be an extract from Epicurus' writing made by a pupil. Fragments have also been preserved of his chief work, Περὶ Φύσεως, from the library of the Epicurean Piso (thought to be L. Piso, Consul in 58 B.C.).

Epicurus was succeeded as Scholarch by Hermarchus of Mitylene, who was in turn succeeded by Polystratus. An immediate disciple of Epicurus, together with Hermarchus and Polyaenus, was Metrodorus of Lampsacus. Cicero heard Phaedrus (Scholarch at Athens about 78–70) at Rome about 90 B.C But the best-known disciple of the School is the Latin poet, T. Lucretius Carus (91–51 B.C.), who expressed the Epicurean philosophy in

[1] Diog. Laërt., 10, 14. [2] Cic., *De Nat. D.*, I, 26, 73; Diog. Laërt., 10, 8. [3] Diog. Laërt., 10, 2. [4] Diog. Laërt., 10, 12.

his poem *De Rerum Natura*, having as his chief aim the liberation of men from the fear of the gods and of death and the leading of them to peace of soul.

II. *The Canonic*

Epicurus was not interested in dialectic or logic as such, and the only part of logic to which he paid any attention was that dealing with the criterion of truth. That is to say, he was interested in dialectic only in so far as it directly subserved Physics. But Physics again interested him only in so far as it subserved Ethics. Epicurus therefore concentrated on Ethics even more than did the Stoics, depreciating all purely scientific pursuits and declaring mathematics useless, since it has no connection with the conduct of life. (Metrodorus declared that "It need not trouble any one, if he had never read a line of Homer and did not know whether Hector was a Trojan or a Greek.")[1] One of Epicurus' reasons for objecting to mathematics was that it is not substantiated by sense-knowledge, since in the real world the geometer's points, lines and surfaces are nowhere to be found. Now, sense-knowledge is the fundamental basis of all knowledge. "If you fight against all your sensations, you will have no standard to which to refer and thus no means of judging even those sensations which you pronounce false."[2] Lucretius asks what can be accounted of higher certainty than sense. Reason, by which we judge of sense-data, is itself wholly founded on the senses, and if the senses are untrue, then all reason as well is rendered false.[3] Moreover, the Epicureans pointed out that in astronomical questions, for instance, we cannot attain certainty, as we can argue for this position just as well as for that position, e.g. "For the heavenly phenomena may depend for their production on many different causes."[4] (It must be remembered that the Greeks lacked our modern scientific appliances, and that their opinions on scientific subjects were, very largely, of the nature of guesses, unsubstantiated by exact observation.)

Epicurus' Logic or Canonic deals with the norms or canons of knowledge and the criteria of truth. The fundamental criterion of truth is Perception (ἡ αἴσθησις), in which we attain what is clear (ἡ ἐνάργεια). Perception takes place when images (εἴδωλα)

[1] Frag. 24. (Metrodori Epicurei Fragmenta, A. Körte, 1890.) But cf. Sext. Emp., *Adv. Math.*, 1, 49.

[2] Diog. Laërt., 10, 146.

[3] Cf. *De Rerum Nat.*, IV, 478–99.

[4] Diog. Laërt., 10, 86.

of objects penetrate the sense-organs (cf. Democritus and Empedocles), and is always true. It is to be noted that the Epicureans included under perception imaginative representations (φανταστικαὶ ἐπιβολαὶ τῆς διανοίας), *all* perception taking place through the reception of εἴδωλα. When these images stream continuously from the same object and enter by the sense-organs, we have perception in the narrower sense: when, however, individual images enter through the pores of the body they become, as it were, mixed up and imaginative pictures arise, e.g. of a centaur. In either case we have "perception," and, as both sorts of images arise from objective causes, both types of perception are true. How then does error arise? Only through *judgment*. If, for instance, we judge that an image corresponds exactly to an external object, when in point of fact it does not so correspond, we are in error. (The difficulty, of course, is to know when the image corresponds to an external object and when it does not, and when it corresponds perfectly or imperfectly; and on this point the Epicureans give us no help.)

The first criterion is therefore Perception. A second criterion is afforded by Concepts (προλήψεις). The concept, according to the Epicureans, is simply a memory image (μνήμη τοῦ πολλάκις ἔξωθεν φανέντος).[1] After we have had perception of an object, e.g. of a man, the memory image or general image of man arises when we hear the word "man." These προλήψεις are always true, and it is only when we proceed to form opinions or judgments that the question of truth or falsity arises. If the opinion or judgment (ὑπόληψις) has reference to the future, then it must be confirmed by experience, while if it has reference to hidden and unperceived causes (e.g. the atoms) it must at least not contradict experience.

There is yet a third criterion, namely feelings or πάθη, which are criteria for conduct. Thus the feeling of pleasure is the criterion of what we should choose, while the feeling of pain shows us what we should avoid. Hence Epicurus could say that "the criteria of truth are the senses, and the preconceptions, and the passions."[2]

III. *The Physics*

Epicurus' choice of a physical theory was determined by a practical end, that of freeing man from the fear of the gods and of the afterworld and so giving them peace of soul. While not

[1] Diog. Laërt., 10, 33. [2] Diog. Laërt., 10, 31.

denying the existence of the gods he wished to show that they do not interfere in human affairs and that man need not therefore occupy himself with propitiation and petition and "superstition" in general. Moreover, by rejecting immortality he hoped to free man from fear of death—for what reason is there to fear death when it is mere extinction, absence of all consciousness and feeling, when there is no judgment and when no punishment awaits one in the afterworld? "Death is nothing to us; for that which is dissolved is devoid of sensation, and that which is devoid of sensation is nothing to us."[1] Moved by these considerations Epicurus chose the system of Democritus (which he adopted with but slight modifications), since this system seemed best calculated to serve his end. Did it not explain all phenomena by the mechanical motions of atoms, thus rendering any recourse to divine intervention superfluous and did it not afford an easy handle for the rejection of immortality—the soul, as well as the body, being composed of atoms? This practical aim of the Epicurean Physics appears in a marked manner in Lucretius' *De Rerum Natura*, clothed in the splendid language and imagery of the poet.

Nothing proceeds from nothing, nothing passes into nothingness, declared Epicurus, re-echoing the thought of the old Cosmologists. "And, first of all, we must admit that nothing can come out of that which does not exist; for, were the fact otherwise, everything would be produced from everything and there would be no need of any seed. And if that which disappeared were so absolutely destroyed as to become non-existent, then everything would soon perish, as the things with which they would be dissolved would have no existence."[2] We may compare the lines of Lucretius, *Nunc age, res quoniam docui non posse creari de nilo neque item genitas ad nil revocari.*[3] The bodies of our experience are composed of pre-existing material entities—atoms—and their perishing is but a resolution into the entities of which they are composed. The ultimate constituents of the universe are therefore atoms, Atoms and the Void. "Now the universal whole is a body; for our senses bear us witness in every case that bodies have a real existence; and the evidence of the senses, as I have said before, ought to be the rule of our reasonings about everything which is not directly perceived. Otherwise, if that which we call the vacuum, or space, or intangible nature, had not a real

[1] Diog. Laërt., 10, 139. [2] Diog. Laërt., 10, 38–9. [3] *De Rerum Nat.*, I, 265–6.

existence, there would be nothing in which the bodies could be contained, or across which they could move, as we see that they really do move. Let us add to this reflection that one cannot conceive, either in virtue of perception, or of any analogy founded on perception, any general quality peculiar to all beings which is not either an attribute, or an accident of the body, or of the vacuum."[1] These atoms vary in size, form and weight (the Epicureans certainly attributed weight to the atoms, whatever the earlier atomists may have done) and are indivisible and infinite in number. In the beginning they rained down through the void or empty space, though Lucretius compares their motion to that of motes in a sunbeam, and it may be that the Epicureans did not think of the atoms as ever in actuality raining down in parallel straight lines—a conception which would make the "collision" very much of a *deus ex machina*.

In order to account for the origin of the world, Epicurus had to allow for a collision of atoms: moreover he wished at the same time to afford some explanation of human freedom (which the School maintained). He postulated, therefore, a spontaneous oblique movement or declination from the straight line of descent on the part of individual atoms. Thus occurred the first collision of atoms, and from the collision and the entanglements consequent on the deviation the rotary movements were set up which led to the formation of innumerable worlds, separated from one another by empty spaces (the μετακόσμια or *intermundia*). The human soul is also composed of atoms, smooth and round, but in distinction to the animals it possesses a rational part which is seated in the breast, as is shown by the emotions of fear and joy. The irrational part, the principle of life, is spread throughout the whole body. At death the atoms of the soul are separated, and there can be no more perception: death is the privation of perception (στέρησις αἰσθήσεως).

The world is, therefore, due to mechanical causes and there is no need to postulate teleology. On the contrary, the Epicureans entirely rejected the anthropocentric teleology of the Stoics and would have nothing to do with the Stoic theodicy. The evil with which human life is afflicted is irreconcilable with any idea of divine guidance in the universe. The gods dwell in the *intermundia*, beautiful and happy and without thought of human affairs, eating and drinking and speaking Greek!

[1] Diog. Laërt., 10, 39–40.

Apparet divinum numen sedesque quietae
Quas neque concutiunt venti nec nubila nimbis
Aspergunt neque nix acri concreta pruina
Cana cadens violat semperque innubilus aether
Integit, et largo diffuso lumine rident.[1]

The gods are anthropomorphically conceived, for they too are composed of atoms—even if of the finest atoms and possessing only ethereal or quasi-bodies—and are divided sexually: they are like to mankind in appearance and breathe and eat as we do. Epicurus not only needed the gods in order to present them as an embodiment of his ethical ideal of calm tranquillity, but he also considered that the universality of belief in the gods can only be explained on the hypothesis of their objective existence. εἴδωλα come to us from the gods, especially in sleep, but perception presents us only with the existence and anthropomorphic character of the gods: knowledge of their happy condition is attained by reason or λόγος. Men may honour the gods for their excellence and may even take part in the customary ceremonial worship, but all fear of them is out of place and also all attempts to win their favour by sacrifices. True piety consists in right thought.

nec pietas ullast velatum saepe videri
vertier ad lapidem atque omnis accedere ad aras
nec procumbere humi prostratum et pandere palmas
ante deum delubra nec aras sanguine multo
spargere quadrupedum nec votis nectere vota,
sed mage pacata posse omnia mente tueri.'[2]

The wise man, therefore, does not fear death—for death is mere extinction—nor the gods—for they are unconcerned with human affairs and exact no retribution. We may recall the celebrated lines of Virgil:

felix qui potuit rerum cognoscere causas:
atque metus omnes et inexorabile fatum
subiecit pedibus strepitumque Acherontis avari.[3]

IV. *The Epicurean Ethic*

Like the Cyrenaics Epicurus made *pleasure* the end of life. Every being strives after pleasure, and it is in pleasure that happiness consists. ". . . we affirm that pleasure is the beginning and

[1] *De Rerum Nat.*, III, 18–22. [2] *De Rerum Nat.*, V, 1198–1203.
[3] *Georgics*, II, 490–2.

end of living happily; for we have recognised this as the first good, being connate with us; and it is with reference to it that we begin every choice and avoidance; and to this we come as if we judged of all good by passion as the standard . . ."[1] The question then arises what Epicurus understands by pleasure, when he makes it the end of life. Two facts are to be noted: first, that Epicurus meant, not the pleasures of the moment, individual sensations, but the pleasure which endures throughout a lifetime; and secondly, that pleasure for Epicurus consisted rather in the absence of pain than in positive satisfaction. This pleasure is to be found pre-eminently in serenity of soul (ἡ τῆς ψυχῆς ἀταραξία). With this serenity of soul Epicurus conjoined also health of body, but the emphasis is rather on intellectual pleasure, for, while very severe bodily pains are of short duration, less severe pains may be overcome or rendered endurable by intellectual pleasures. ". . . a correct theory . . . can refer all choice and avoidance to the health of the body and the freedom from disquietude of the soul." ". . . at times we pass over many pleasures when any difficulty is likely to ensue from them; and we think many pains better than pleasures when a greater pleasure follows them, if we endure the pain for a time."[2] When Epicurus speaks of choice among pleasures and rejects certain pleasures, it is to the permanence of pleasure that he is looking, and to the presence or absence of subsequent pain, for there is really no room in his ethic for a discrimination between pleasures that is based on a difference of moral value. (Though we may well discern a differentiation of pleasures on grounds of moral value creeping in unawares—as it is bound to do in any hedonistic ethic, unless the hedonist is prepared to admit that the "basest" pleasures are on the same level as the more refined pleasures. And what serious moral philosopher has ever been prepared to admit that, without introducing qualifications that suggest another criterion beside pleasure?) "Every pleasure is therefore a good on account of its own nature, but it does not follow that every pleasure is worthy of being chosen; just as every pain is an evil, and yet every pain must not be avoided." "When, therefore, we say that pleasure is a chief good, we are not speaking of the pleasures of the debauched man, or those which lie in sensual enjoyment, as some think who are ignorant, and who do not entertain our opinions, or else interpret them perversely; but we mean the freedom of the body from pain

[1] Diog. Laërt., 10, 129.

[2] Diog. Laërt., 10, 128 and 129.

and of the soul from confusion. For it is not continued drinkings and revels . . . that make life pleasant, but sober contemplations, which examine into the reasons for all choice and avoidance, and which put to flight the vain opinions from which the greater part of the confusion arises which troubles the soul."[1] "No pleasure is intrinsically bad: but the efficient causes of some pleasures bring with them a great many perturbations of pleasure."[2]

In practice we have to consider whether any individual pleasure may not be productive of greater pain and any individual pain may not be productive of greater pleasure. For instance, an individual pleasure might be very intense for the moment but might lead to ill-health or to enslavement to a habit; in which case it would be productive of greater pain. Conversely, a pain might be intense for the moment—as in an operation—and yet be productive of a greater good, health. Therefore, although every pain, abstractly considered, is an evil, and every pleasure is a good, we must in practice look to the future and endeavour to attain the maximum of durable pleasure—in Epicurus' opinion, health of body and tranquillity of soul. Epicurean hedonism would not then result in libertinism and excess, but in a calm and tranquil life; for a man is unhappy either from fear or from unlimited and vain desires, and if he but bridle these he may secure for himself the blessings of reason. The wise man will not multiply his needs, since that is to multiply sources of pain: he will rather reduce his needs to a minimum. (The Epicureans even went so far as to say that the wise man can be perfectly happy even when undergoing bodily torture. Thus Epicurus declared that, "Though he is being tortured on the rack, the wise man is still happy."[3] An extreme statement of this position is found in the saying: "If the wise man is being burned, if he is being tortured—nay, within the very bull of Phalaris, he will say: 'How delightful this is! How little I care for it'!"[4]) Hence the Epicurean ethic leads to a moderate asceticism, self-control and independence. "To accustom one's self, therefore, to simple and inexpensive habits is a great ingredient in the perfecting of health, and makes a man free from hesitation with respect to the necessary uses of life."[5]

Virtue is a condition of ἀταραξία or tranquillity of soul, though

[1] Diog. Laërt., 10, 129 and 131–2. [2] Diog. Laërt., 10, 141. [3] Diog. Laërt., 10, 118. [4] Cic., *Tusc.*, 2, 7, 17. [5] Diog. Laërt., 10, 131.

of course its value is estimated by Epicurus according to its power of producing pleasure. Virtues such as simplicity, moderation, temperance, cheerfulness, are much more conducive to pleasure and happiness than are unbridled luxury, feverish ambition and so on. "It is not possible to live pleasantly without living prudently, and honourably, and justly; nor to live prudently, and honourably, and justly, without living pleasantly. But he to whom it does not happen to live prudently, honourably, and justly, cannot possibly live pleasantly." "The just man is the freest of all men from disquietude; but the unjust man is a perpetual prey to it." "Injustice is not intrinsically bad; it has this character only because there is joined with it a fear of not escaping those who are appointed to punish actions marked with that character." "When, without any fresh circumstances arising, a thing which has been declared just in practice does not agree with the impressions of reason, that is a proof that the thing was not really just. In the same way, when in consequence of new circumstances, a thing which has been pronounced just does not any longer appear to agree with utility, the thing which was just, inasmuch as it was useful to the social relations and intercourse of mankind, ceases to be just at the moment when it ceases to be useful."[1] Moreover, in spite of the fact that the ethic of the Epicureans is fundamentally selfish or egocentric, in that it is based on the individual's pleasure, it was not in practice so selfish as it might sound. Thus the Epicureans thought that it is really pleasanter to do a kindness than to receive one, and the founder himself was commended for his contented and kind character. "He who desires to live tranquilly without having anything to fear from other men, ought to make himself friends; those whom he cannot make friends of, he should, at least, avoid rendering enemies; and if that is not in his power, he should, as far as possible, avoid all intercourse with them, and keep them aloof, as far as it is for his interest to do so." "The happiest men are they who have arrived at the point of having nothing to fear from those who surround them. Such men live with one another most agreeably, having the firmest grounds of confidence in one another, enjoying the advantages of friendship in all their fullness, and not lamenting, as a pitiable circumstance, the premature death of their friends."[2] It is probably true to say that Epicurus' practical moral judgment was sounder than the theoretical

[1] Diog. Laërt., 10; Maxims, 5, 17, 37, 42. [2] Diog. Laërt., 10, 154.

foundations of his ethic, an ethic which could obviously give little account of moral obligation.

Owing to the fact that man should not pursue heedlessly the first pleasure that offers itself, there is need of an art of calculation or mensuration in the conduct of life. We must therefore practise συμμέτρησις, and it is in the right mensuration of pleasures and pains, in the ability to take into account and balance one against another present or future happiness and unhappiness, that the essence of insight or φρόνησις, the highest virtue, consists. If a man is to live a truly happy, pleasurable and contented life, he must possess this insight, he must be φρόνιμος. "Now, the beginning and the greatest good of all these things is prudence, on which account prudence is something more valuable than even philosophy, inasmuch as all the other virtues spring from it, teaching us that it is not possible to live pleasantly unless one also lives prudently, and honourably, and justly; and that one cannot live prudently, and honourably, and justly, without living pleasantly; for the virtues are connate with living agreeably, and living agreeably is inseparable from the virtues."[1] When a man is φρόνιμος, he is virtuous, for the virtuous man is not so much the person who is actually enjoying pleasure at any given moment as the man who knows how to conduct himself in the search for pleasure. Once virtue has been thus defined, it is obvious that it is an absolutely necessary condition for lasting happiness.

Epicurus laid great stress on *Friendship*. "Of all the things which wisdom provides for the happiness of the whole life, by far the most important is the acquisition of friendship."[2] This may seem strange in a fundamentally egoistic ethic, but the emphasis on friendship is itself based on egoistic considerations, namely that without friendship a man cannot live a secure and tranquil life, while on the other hand friendship gives pleasure. Friendship rests, therefore, on an egoistic basis, the thought of personal advantage. This egoism was, however, modified through the Epicurean doctrine that an unselfish affection arises in the course of the friendship and that in a friendship a wise man loves the friend as he does himself. Nevertheless it remains true that the social theory of the Epicureans is egoistic in character, a fact that comes out clearly in their teaching that the wise man will not mix himself up in politics, as this disturbs tranquillity of soul. There are, however, two exceptions: the first, that of the man

[1] Diog. Laërt., 10, 132. [2] Diog. Laërt., 10, 148.

who needs to take part in politics in order to ensure his own personal security, the second, that of a man who has such an urge towards a political career that ἀταραξία would be quite impossible for him, were he to remain in retirement.

Pleasure and personal advantage are again decisive for the Epicurean theory of law. It is pleasanter to live in a society where law reigns and "rights" are respected than in a condition of *bellum omnium contra omnes.* The latter condition would be by no means favourable to tranquillity of soul or to ἀταραξία.

The Epicureans, as we have seen, went back to the School of Leucippus and Democritus for their Physics, as the Stoa went back to the Cosmology of Heraclitus. The Epicurean ethics, on the other hand, are more or less in agreement with that of the Cyrenaics. Both Aristippus and Epicurus make pleasure the end of life, and in both Schools attention is paid to the future, to calculation, to the "measuring" of pleasures and pains. There are, however, differences between the Epicureans and the Cyrenaics. For while the latter—in general, that is to say—considered *positive* pleasure (the smooth movement or λεία κίνησις) to be the end, the Epicureans stressed more the negative side, calm and tranquillity, ἡ καταστηματικὴ ἡδονή. Again, while the Cyrenaics considered bodily suffering worse than mental suffering, the Epicureans accounted mental suffering worse than bodily suffering, on the ground that the body suffers only from present evil whereas the soul can suffer also from the recollection of past evil and the expectation or fear of future evil. All the came it can be truly said that Cyrenaicism was absorbed in Epicureanism. Did not Epicurus agree with the Cyrenaic Hegesias in laying the emphasis on absence of suffering and with Anniceris in recommending to the wise the cultivation of friendship?

The Epicurean philosophy is, therefore, not a philosophy of heroes, nor has it the moral grandeur of the Stoic creed. Yet it is neither so selfish nor so "immoral" as its fundamental tenet might at first sight imply, and its attraction for certain types of men is easily understandable. It is certainly not a heroic creed or philosophy; but it was not meant by its author to be an incentive to base living, whatever its tenets might lead to in popular application to practice.

Note on Cynicism in the First Period of the Hellenistic Epoch

Cynicism in this period tended to lose its serious character of emphasis on independence, suppression of desire and physical endurance, and to give itself rather to mockery of convention and tradition and prevailing beliefs and modes of behaviour. Not of course that this tendency was absent from the earlier Cynicism —we have only to think of Diogenes—but it showed itself in this period through the new literary genre of the satire or σπουδογέλοιον. In the first half of the third century B.C., *Bion of Borysthenes*, influenced by Cyrenaicism (he had listened to the Cyrenaic Theodorus at Athens), propagated the so-called "hedonistic Cynicism" in his "diatribes," dwelling on the happiness and pleasurable character of the simple Cynic life. *Teles*, who taught at Megara about 240 B.C., followed Bion in the composition of such "diatribes"—popular and anecdotal pieces—dealing with appearance and reality, poverty and riches, cynical "apathy," etc.

Menippus of Gadara (about 250 B.C.) created the Satire, in which he combined poetry with prose, criticised under various forms—e.g. journeys to Hades, letters to the gods—natural philosophy and specialist learning, and mocked at the idolatrous honour paid to Epicurus by his followers. He was imitated by Varro, Seneca in his *Apocolocyntosis*, and Lucian.

Cercides of Megalopolis, composer of meliambs, displayed the same satyric tone, declaring, for example, that he would leave to the μετεωροσκόποι the solution of the ticklish question, why Cronus showed himself a father to some people and a stepfather to others.

CHAPTER XXXVIII

THE OLDER SCEPTICS, THE MIDDLE AND NEW ACADEMIES

1. *The Older Sceptics*

JUST as in the Stoa and in the Garden of Epicurus theory was subordinated to practice, so in the School of Pyrrho, the founder of Scepticism, though there is of course this big difference, that whereas the Stoics and Epicureans looked to science or positive knowledge as a means to peace of soul, the Sceptics sought to attain the same end by the disavowal of knowledge, i.e. by scepticism, the opposite of science.

Pyrrho of Elis (*c.* 360–*c.* 270), who is said to have accompanied Alexander on his march to India,[1] was apparently influenced by the Democritean theory of the sense-qualities, the relativism of the Sophists and the Cyrenaic epistemology. He taught that the human reason cannot penetrate to the inner substance of things (things are ἀκατάληπτα in our regard):[2] we can only know how things appear to us. The same things appear differently to different people, and we cannot know which is right: to any assertion we could oppose the contradictory assertion with equally good grounds (ἰσοθένεια τῶν λόγων). We cannot, therefore, be certain of anything and the wise man will withhold his judgment (ἐπέχειν). Rather than say, "This is so," we should say, "So it appears to me" or "It may be so."

The same scepticism and consequent suspension of judgment is extended to the practical sphere. Nothing is in itself ugly or beautiful, right or wrong, or at least we cannot be sure of it: all external things in our lives are indifferent and the wise man will aim simply at tranquillity of soul and endeavour to preserve his soul in that condition. It is true that even the wise man cannot avoid acting and taking part in practical life, but he will follow in practice probable opinion, custom and law, conscious that absolute truth is unattainable.

Diogenes Laërtius informs us that Pyrrho expressed his philosophical views only by word of mouth,[3] but his views are known through those of his pupil *Timon of Phlius* (*c.* 320–230 B.C.), who

[1] Diog. Laërt., 9, 61. [2] Diog. Laërt., Proem., 16.
[3] Diog. Laërt., Proem., 16; 9, 102.

is called by Sextus Empiricus ὁ προφήτης τῶν Πύρρωνος λόγων.[1] Timon composed Σίλλοι or mocking verses, in which he parodied Homer and Hesiod and made fun of the Greek philosophers, with the exception of Xenophanes and Pyrrho himself. According to Timon we can trust neither sense-perception nor reason. We must accordingly suspend all judgment, not allowing ourselves to be caught in any theoretical assertion, and then we shall attain to true ἀταραξία or tranquillity of soul.

(Cicero apparently did not know of Pyrrho as a Sceptic, but considered him rather as a moralist who preached and practised indifference towards external things. It may be, then, that Pyrrho did not personally develop the Sceptic position. But as he left no writings, we can hardly attain certainty on this point.)

II. *The Middle Academy*

Plato had held that the objects of sense-perception are not the objects of true knowledge, but he was very far from being a Sceptic, the whole point of his Dialectic being the attainment of true and certain knowledge of the eternal and abiding. A sceptical current of thought manifests itself, however, in what is known as the Second or Middle Academy, a scepticism directed principally against the Stoic dogmatism but also expressed in universal terms. Thus *Arcesilaus* (315/14–241/40), the founder of the Middle Academy, is reputed to have said that he was certain of nothing—not even of the fact that he was certain of nothing,[2] thus going further than Socrates, who knew that he knew nothing. He practised therefore a similar suspension of judgment or ἐποχή to that of the Pyrrhonists.[3] While trying to support his position by the example and practice of Socrates, Arcesilaus made the Stoic epistemology a special object of attack. No representation is given that might not be false: none of our sense-perceptions or presentations possess the guarantee of their own objective validity, for we may feel an equally intense subjective certainty even when the presentation is objectively false. We can therefore never be certain.

III. *The New Academy*

1. The founder of the Third or New Academy was *Carneades of Cyrene* (214/12–129/8 B.C.), who accompanied the Stoic

[1] *Adv. Math.*, I, 53. [2] Cic., *Acad. Post* I, 12, 45. [3] Cic., *de Orat.*, 3, 18, 67.

Diogenes on the embassy to Rome in 156/5. Following the scepticism of Arcesilaus, Carneades taught that knowledge is impossible and that there is no criterion of truth. Against the Stoics he maintained that there is no sense-presentation by the side of which we could not place a false presentation that is indistinguishable from the true, appealing to the influence upon us of presentations in e.g. dreams, presentations which are, however, unreal, and to the facts of hallucination and delusion. Impressions of sense are, therefore, not infallible, and the Stoics cannot look to reason as a remedy, since they themselves admit that concepts are founded on experience.[1]

We are unable to prove anything, since any proof rests on assumptions which must themselves be proved. But this latter proof will itself rest on assumptions, and so on indefinitely. All dogmatic philosophy is accordingly out of the question: for either side in a question equally good—or equally bad—reasons can be adduced. Carneades attacked the Stoic theology, trying to show that their proofs for God's existence are not conclusive and that their doctrine as to God's Nature contained antinomies.[2] For example, the Stoics appealed to the *consensus gentium* as an argument for the divine existence. Now, if they can prove this *consensus gentium*, then they have proved a universal *belief* in the divine existence, but that does not prove that there *are* gods. And on what grounds do the Stoics assert that the Universe is wise and rational? It must first be proved to be *animate*, and this they have not proved. If they argue that there must be a universal Reason, from which man's reason proceeds, they have first to prove that the human mind cannot be the spontaneous product of nature. Again, the argument from design is not conclusive. If the universe is a designed product, then there must be a Designer; but the whole point at issue is, whether the universe is a designed product or not. Might it not be the undesigned product of natural forces?

The Stoic God is animate and so must be possessed of feeling. But if he can feel and receive impressions, then he can suffer from impressions and is ultimately liable to disintegration. Moreover, if God is rational and perfect, as the Stoics suppose Him to be, He cannot be "virtuous," as the Stoics also suppose Him to be. How, for example, can God be brave or courageous? What dangers

[1] Cf. Sext. Emp., *Adv. Math.*, 7, 159 and 166 ff.; Civ., *Acad. Prior.*, 2, 30, 98 ff.
[2] Cf. Sext. Emp., *Adv. Math.*, 9, 13 ff.; Cic., *De Nat. D.*, 3, 17, 44; 3, 29 ff.

or pains or labours affect Him, in respect of which He can show courage?

The Stoics maintain a doctrine of Divine Providence. But if this be so, how can they explain the presence of e.g. poisonous snakes? The Stoics say that God's Providence is manifested in His gift of reason to man. Now, the great majority of men use this reason to degrade themselves, so that to such men the possession of reason is an injury and not a benefit. If God really exercised Providence over all men, He should have made all men good and given all *right* reason. Moreover, it is useless for Chrysippus to speak of "neglect" on the part of God—i.e. in regard to "little" matters. In the first place what Providence has neglected to provide for, is not a little matter: in the second place, the neglect could not be intentional in God (for intentional neglect is a fault even in an earthly ruler); while in the third place unintentional neglect is inconceivable in respect of the Infinite Reason.

These and other criticisms of Carneades are directed against the Stoic doctrines, and so they are, in part, of but academic interest. By maintaining a materialistic doctrine of God the Stoics involved themselves in insurmountable difficulties, for if God were material He could disintegrate, and if He were the Soul of the world—possessed of a body—He could feel pleasure and pain. Criticisms against such a conception of the Deity can have for us no more than academic interest. Moreover, we would not dream of ascribing virtues to God in the anthropomorphic manner that the line of criticism adopted by Carneades presupposes. Nor would we undertake to prove in philosophy that everything is created for the good of man. Yet some of the difficulties raised by Carneades are of lasting interest, and an attempt must be made to meet them in every Theodicy, e.g. the presence of physical suffering and of moral evil in the world. I have already made some remarks on this subject when treating of the Stoic theodicy, and I hope to show later on, how other philosophers, mediaeval and modern, tried to answer these questions; but it must always be remembered that, even if the human reason is unable to answer fully and with complete satisfaction all the difficulties that can be raised against a position, that does not compel us to abandon that position, if it rests on valid argument.

Carneades saw that complete suspension of judgment is

impossible, and so he elaborated a theory of Probability (πιθανότης). Probability has various grades and is both necessary and sufficient for action. He showed, for example, how we may approximate to the truth—even if we can never attain certainty—by the accumulation of reasons for accepting some position. If I merely saw the shape of someone I knew, it might be an hallucination, but if I hear the person speak, if I touch him, if he eats, I may for all practical purposes accept the presentation as true. It enjoys a very high degree of probability, especially if it is also intrinsically probable that the person should be in that place at that time. If a man leaves his wife in England and goes to India on business, he might well doubt the objective validity of the presentation, if he seems to see his wife on the quay when he disembarks at Bombay. But if, on returning to England, he finds his wife waiting for him on the landing-stage, the validity of the presentation bears its own inherent probability.

2. The Academy returned to dogmatism under *Antiochus* of Ascalon (d. *c.* 68 B.C.), who apparently started as an agnostic but later came to abandon this position,[1] and whose lectures were heard by Cicero in the winter of 79/8. He pointed out the contradiction involved in asserting that nothing is knowable or that all is doubtful; for, in asserting that all is doubtful, I am at any rate asserting my knowledge that all is doubtful. His own criterion of truth he apparently found in the agreement of eminent philosophers and endeavoured to show that the Academic, Peripatetic and Stoic systems were in essential agreement with each other. In fact he openly taught Stoic doctrines, shamelessly asserting that Zeno had borrowed them from the old Academy. He thus tried to deprive the Sceptics of one of their principal arguments, namely, the contradiction between the various philosophic systems. He shows himself at the same time to be an Eclectic.

This eclectic tendency comes out in his moral teaching. For, while holding with the Stoics that virtue is sufficient for happiness, he also taught with Aristotle that for happiness in its highest degree external goods and health of the body are also necessary. In spite of the fact, then, that Cicero declares him to have been more of a Stoic than an Academician,[2] Antiochus was undoubtedly an Eclectic.

3. A Roman Eclectic was *M. Terentius Varro* (116–27 B.C.),

[1] Cic., *Acad. Prior.*, 2, 22, 69; Numenius cited by Euseb., *Prep. Evang.*, 614, 9, 2 (*P.G.* 21, 1216–17); Aug., *contra Acad.*, 2, 6, 15; 3, 18, 41.

[2] Cic., *Acad. Prior.*, 2, 43, 132.

scholar and philosopher. The only true theology in Varro's opinion is that which recognises *one* God, Who is the Soul of the world, which He governs according to reason. The mythical theology of the poets is to be rejected on the ground that it attributed unworthy characteristics and actions to the gods, while the physical theologies of the natural philosophers contradict one another. We must not, however, neglect the official cult of the State, since this has a practical and popular value. Varro even suggested that the popular religion was the work of earlier statesmen, and that if the work had to be done over again, it might be done better in the light of philosophy.[1]

Varro seems to have been greatly influenced by Poseidonius. From the latter he accepted many theories concerning the origin and development of culture, geography, hydrology, etc., and by his exposition of these theories he influenced later Romans such as Vitruvius and Pliny. Varro's tendency to Pythagorean "number-mysticism" also derives from the thought of Poseidonius and thereby he influenced later writers like Gellius, Macrobius and Martianus Capella. Cynic influence is visible in Varro's *Saturae Menippeae*, of which we possess only fragments. Therein he opposed Cynic simplicity to the luxury of the rich, whose gluttony he subjected to mockery, and he made fun of the philosophers' squabbles.

4. The most celebrated of all Roman eclectics is *M. Tullius Cicero*, the great orator (Jan. 3rd 106–Dec. 7, 43 B.C.). In his youth Cicero was a pupil of Phaedrus the Epicurean, Philon the Academician, Diodotus the Stoic, Antiochus of Ascalon, and Zeno the Epicurean. In Rhodes he listened to the teaching of Poseidonius the Stoic. To the philosophic studies of his youth at Athens and Rhodes there succeeded years spent in public life and official activity, but in the last three years of his life Cicero returned to philosophy. The majority of his philosophic writings date from these later years (e.g. the *Paradoxa*, the *Consolatio*, the *Hortensius*, the *Academica*, the *De Finibus*, the *Tusculana*, the *De Natura Deorum*, the *De Senectute*, the *De Divinatione*, the *De Fato*, the *De Amicitia*, the *De Virtutibus*). The *De Republica* (54 B.C. seq.) and the *De Legibus* (*c.* 52 seq.) are earlier compositions. The writings of Cicero are scarcely to be called original in content, as Cicero himself openly admits—"ἀπόγραφα *sunt, minore labore fiunt, verba tantum affero, quibus abundo*."[2] He had,

[1] *De Civit. Dei*, 6, 4.

[2] *Ad. Att.*, 12, 52, 3.

however, the gift of presenting the doctrine of the Greeks to Roman readers in a clear style.

While Cicero was unable to effect a scientific refutation of Scepticism (he was inclined to the latter, owing to the conflict of opposing philosophical Schools and doctrines), he found a refuge in the intuitions of the moral consciousness, which are immediate and certain. Realising the danger of Scepticism for morality, he sought to place the moral judgment beyond its corroding influence and speaks of *notiones innatae, natura nobis insitae.* These moral concepts proceed therefore from our nature, and they are confirmed by general agreement—*consensus gentium.*

In his ethical doctrine Cicero was inclined to agree with the Stoics that virtue is sufficient for happiness, but he could not bring himself to reject altogether the Peripatetic teaching, which attributed value to external goods as well, though he seems to have hesitated somewhat in his opinion on this matter.[1] He agreed with the Stoics that the wise man should be without πάθη[2] and combated the Peripatetic teaching that virtue is a mean between opposite πάθη. (But it is to be noted that Cicero's notion of πάθος or *perturbatio* is that of *aversa a recta ratione contra naturam animi commotio.*[3]) For Cicero again, as for the Stoics, practical, and not speculative, virtue is the higher.[4]

In the sphere of natural philosophy Cicero was inclined to scepticism, though he by no means despised this province of human thought.[5] He was particularly interested in the proof of God's existence from nature and rejected the doctrine of atheistic atomism. "*Hoc* (i.e. the formation of the world from the chance collision of atoms) *qui existimat fieri potuisse non intelligo cur non idem putet, si innumerabiles unius et viginti formae litterarum vel aureae vel qualesilibet aliquo coiciantur, posse ex iis in terram excussis annales Enni ut deinceps legi possint, effici.*"[6]

Cicero considered that the popular religion should be preserved in the interests of the community at large, while at the same time it should be purified from gross superstition and the practice of attributing immorality to the gods (e.g. the story of the rape of Ganymede).[7] Especially should we preserve belief in Providence and the immortality of the soul.[8]

[1] *De Fin.*, 5, 32, 95; *De Off.*, 3, 3, 11; cf. *De Fin.*, 5, 26, 77 ff, and *Tusc.*, 5, 13, 39 ff.

[2] *Tusc.*, 4, 18, 41 ff.

[3] *Tusc.*, 4, 6, 11; 4, 21, 47.

[4] *De Off.*, 1, 44, 158.

[5] *Acad. Prior.*, 2, 41, 127.

[6] *De Nat. D.*, 2, 37, 93.

[7] *Tusc.*, 1, 26, 65; 4, 33, 71.

[8] *Tusc.*, 1, 12, 26 ff.; 1, 49, 117 ff.

Cicero stressed the ideal of human fellowship (cf. the Stoa), and appealed to the ninth letter of Plato. "*—ut profectus a caritate domesticorum ac suorum serpat longius et se implicet primum civium, deinde omnium mortalium societate atque, ut ad Archytam scripsit Plato, non sibi se solum natum meminerit sed patriae, sed suis, ut perexigua pars ipsi relinquatur.*"[1]

[1] *De Fin.*, 2, 14, 45.

CHAPTER XXXIX

THE MIDDLE STOA

In the second and third centuries before Christ the Stoic philosophers show a marked tendency to Eclecticism, admitting Platonic and Aristotelian elements into the School and departing from orthodox Stoicism. They were impelled to this course, not only by the attacks levelled against the Stoic dogmatism by the Academicians, but also by their contact with the Roman world, which was much more interested in the practical application of philosophic doctrines than in speculation. The dominant names of the Middle Stoa are those of Panaetius and Poseidonius.

1. *Panaetius of Rhodes* (*c.* 185–110/9 B.C.) lived for some time in Rome, where he interested the younger Scipio and Laelius in Greek philosophy and greatly influenced the Roman historian Q. Mucius Scaevola and the Greek historian Polybius. Cicero made use of his works, especially in the first two books of the *De Officiis.*[1] In 129 B.C. he succeeded Antipater of Tarsus as Scholarch at Athens.

While Panaetius modified certain Stoic doctrines on the one hand, he did not hesitate on the other hand to jettison altogether some of the cargo of Stoic orthodoxy. Thus he modified Stoic "puritanism" by allowing that the end of life in the case of ordinary men is simply the rational perfection of their individual nature. Stoicism thus became rather less "idealistic" in the hands of Panaetius, especially as he seems to have denied the existence of the truly wise man, the old Stoic ideal, and to have set the proficient (προκόπτων) to all intents and purposes in the first place. Moreover, he attached more value to external goods than did the early Stoa and rejected the ideal of "Apathy."

While thus modifying the Stoic ethic Panaetius cast overboard the Stoic theory of divination (which the early Stoics maintained on a philosophical basis of determinism), rejected astrology and jettisoned the doctrines of the world-conflagration and of the relative "immortality" of the soul.[2] He had little sympathy with popular theology.[3] In his political teaching he appears to have been influenced by Plato and Aristotle, though he advocated a

[1] *Ad. Att.*, 16, 11, 4. [2] Cic., *Tusc.*, 1, 32, 79. [3] Cic., *De Div.*, 1, 3, 6.

wider ideal, in accordance with Stoic doctrine, than that of the two Greek philosophers.

It was apparently from Panaetius that Scaevola got his threefold division of theology (cf. Varro). He distinguished (i) the theology of the poets, which is anthropomorphic and false, (ii) the theology of the philosophers, which is rational and true, but unfitted for popular use, and (iii) the theology of the statesmen, which maintains the traditional cult and is indispensable for public education.[1]

2. The greatest of the disciples of Panaetius was *Poseidonius of Apamaea* (*c.* 135–51 B.C.). At first a pupil of Panaetius at Athens, Poseidonius then made extensive journeys, to Egypt, for example, and to Spain, after which he opened a School at Rhodes in 97 B.C. It was here that Cicero came to hear him in 78 B.C., and he was twice visited by Pompey. His works have disappeared and it is only recently, through the critical analysis of the literature that was indebted to his influence, that some idea has been obtained—even if not in all points a very clear idea—of the greatness of Poseidonius. Historian and geographer, rationalist and mystic, he bound together various philosophic currents in a framework of Stoic monism, tried to support his speculative doctrines by a wealth of empirical knowledge, and infused into the whole the warmth of religious inspiration. Indeed Zeller does not hesitate to call him "the most universal mind that Greece had seen since the time of Aristotle."[2] Proclus (*in Eukleiden*) mentions Poseidonius and his School seven times in connection with the philosophy of mathematics, e.g. on parallels, on the distinction between theorems and problems, and on existence theorems.

Stoic monism is fundamental to the philosophy of Poseidonius, and he tries to display the articulated unity of Nature in detail. The phenomenon of the tide's ebb and flow, as caused by the moon, revealed to him the "sympathy" that prevails between all parts of the cosmic system. The world is a hierarchy of grades of being, from inorganic entities, as in the mineral kingdom, through plants and animals up to man, and so to the superorganic sphere of the Divine, the whole being bound together in one great system and every detail being arranged by Divine Providence. This universal harmony and structural ordering of the universe postulates Absolute Reason, God, at the summit of

[1] *St. Aug., De Civit. Dei*, 4, 27. [2] *Outlines*, p. 249.

the hierarchy and as the all-pervading Rational Activity.[1] The world is permeated by a vital force (ζωτικὴ δύναμις) which proceeds from the sun, and God Himself is represented by Poseidonius, following in the footsteps of the orthodox Stoicism, as a rational, fiery breath. Moreover, in contradistinction to his teacher Panaetius, Poseidonius reaffirmed the Stoic doctrine of the conflagration or ἐκπύρωσις, a doctrine which emphasises the monistic character of the universe.

But, though his philosophy was monistic, Poseidonius admitted a dualism, apparently under the influence of Platonism. There are two divisions of the Cosmos, the supralunar world and the infralunar world. While the latter world is earthly and perishable, the former is heavenly and "imperishable" and sustains the lower world through the forces which it imparts. These two worlds are, however, bound together in man, who is the bond (δεσμός) between them.[2] Composed of body and spirit, he stands on the borderline between the perishable and the imperishable or the earthly and the heavenly; and as man is the ontological bond, so is knowledge of man the epistemological bond, binding together in itself all knowledge, knowledge of the heavenly and knowledge of the earthly. Moreover, just as man from the *corporeal* viewpoint is the *highest* grade, so, conversely, from the *spiritual* viewpoint he is the *lowest* grade. In other words, between man and the Supreme Godhead there exist "demons" or higher spiritual beings, who form an intermediate gradation between man and God. The hierarchical character of the universe is thus uninterrupted, though the dualism remains. This dualism is emphasised in the psychology of Poseidonius, for, although with the older Stoics he makes the soul a fiery πνεῦμα—and so material like the body—he then proceeds to emphasise the dualism of soul and body in a manner reminiscent of Plato. Thus the body is a hindrance to the soul, impeding the free development of its knowledge.[3] Further than that, Poseidonius readopted the Platonic theory of the preexistence of the soul, which naturally underlined the dualism, and also admitted—against Panaetius—the immortality of the soul. This immortality, however, could be no more than a relative immortality (i.e. relative to the body) in the philosophy of Poseidonius, since he had reaffirmed the Stoic world-conflagration. His teaching on "immortality" thus followed that of the older Stoics.

[1] Cic., *De Nat. D.*, 2, 33 ff. [2] Cf. *Plat. Tim.*, 31 b c.
[3] Cic., *De Div.*, 1, 49, 110; 1, 57, 129–30.

In spite of this dualism in his psychology of man Poseidonius' influenced by Plato and Aristotle, emphasised the gradation-aspect in his general psychology. Thus the plants, which in the earlier Stoic view possess only φύσις and not ψυχή, enjoy τὸ ἐπιθυμητικόν, and also the θρεπτική and αὐξητικὴ δύναμεις, while the animals possess in addition τὸ θυμοειδές, ἡ αἴσθησις, τὸ ὀρεκτικόν, and τὸ κινητικὸν κατὰ τόπον. Man, higher than the animals, possesses τὸ λογιστικόν and so the capacity of λόγος, νοῦς and διάνοια.

Thus, although Poseidonius admits the Platonic dualism, he subordinates it to an ultimate monism, influenced by the Heraclitean theory of opposition in harmony or unity in difference. In this attempt at a synthesis of dualism and monism he marks a stage on the way to Neo-Platonism.

In contrast to Panaetius, Poseidonius reaffirmed the Stoic theory of divination. Because of the universal harmony of the Cosmos and the reign of Fate the future can be divined in the present: moreover, the Providence of God would not have withheld from men the means of divining future events.[1] In states like sleep and ecstasy the soul, free from the body's hindrance, may see the underlying connection of events and divine the future. We have already mentioned that Poseidonius admitted the existence of "demons": he believed too that man can enter into communication with them.

Poseidonius propounded a theory of history or of cultural development. In the primitive golden age the wise, i.e. the philosophers, ruled (corresponding in mankind to the natural leadership of the strongest beast in the herd within the animal kingdom), and it was they who made those inventions which raised man from his primitive way of life to more refined conditions of material civilisation. Thus the wise discovered metals and founded the art of making tools, etc.[2] In the moral sphere the primitive stage of innocence was followed by decadence, and the prevalence of violence necessitated the institution of laws. The philosophers accordingly, leaving to others the elaboration of technical appliances, set themselves to the task of raising the moral condition of mankind, first of all through practical and political activity and later by a self-dedication to the life of speculation or θεωρία. Yet all these activities, from the lowest to the highest, were but different grades of one and the same wisdom or σοφία.

[1] Cic., *De Div.*, 1, 49, 110; 1, 55, 125.
[2] Cf. Seneca, *Epist.*, 90; Lucr., *De Rerum Nat.*, V

Poseidonius also interested himself in ethnographical questions, stressing the influence of climate and natural conditions on the character and way of life of a people, his travels affording him material for observation on this matter. In addition, his empirical bent led him to extend his activity over a wide field in the domain of the special sciences, e.g. in mathematics, astronomy, history and literature. But his outstanding characteristic is his ability for reducing all this wealth of empirical knowledge to the unity of a philosophical system, discovering everywhere connections, interactions and harmonies, trying to penetrate and exhibit the rational structure of the universe and the rational development of history.

Note on the Peripatetic School in the Hellenistic-Roman Period

1. *Strato of Lampsacus*, ὁ φυσικός, succeeded Theophrastus as head of the Peripatetic School at Athens and occupied that position from about 287–269 B.C. His philosophic teaching betrays the influence of Democritus, which impelled him towards a monistic view of the universe. The world consists of particles, between which there is empty space. These particles, however, are endlessly divisible, and appear to possess qualities, since Strato assumes ultimate characteristics or qualities, namely the Warm and the Cold. The world was formed by natural necessity or the laws of nature, and can be ascribed to God only so far as God is to be identified with the unconscious forces of Nature itself. Thus, although Strato does not follow Democritus in matters of detail, the inspiration of his materialistic monism and his denial of the Aristotelian dualism must be attributed to the influence of the Democritean philosophy. This transformation of the Peripatetic system in the hands of Strato is consonant with the latter's special interest in physical science—it was this that won him the title of ὁ φυσικός. He appears to have influenced the medicine, astronomy and mechanics of the Alexandrian period.

In Strato's eyes all psychical activities, such as thought and feeling, are reducible to *motion*, and they are activities of the one rational soul, which is situated between the eyebrows. We can have as objects of our thought only that which has been the cause of a previous sense-impression,[1] and, conversely, every perception involves intellectual activity.[2] This might seem at first sight to be but a repetition of Aristotelian epistemology, but Strato seems

[1] Simplic., *Phys.*, 965, 16 a. [2] Plut., *de sol. animal.*, 3 (961 a).

to have meant it in a sense which involves the denial of a rational principle in man, essentially distinct from the animal soul. His denial of immortality was, therefore, a logical conclusion, for, if all thinking is essentially dependent on sense, there can be no question of a principle of thought surviving independently of the body.

2. Under Strato's successors—Lycon of Troas, Ariston of Chios, Critolaus of Phaselis, Diodorus of Tyre and Erymneus—the Peripatetic School does not seem to have made any real contribution to philosophy. Moreover, an eclectic tendency made itself visible in the School. Thus although Critolaus defended Aristotle's doctrine of the eternity of the world against the Stoics, he accepted the Stoics' reduction of God and the human soul to matter (Aether) and adopted the Cynic attitude in regard to pleasure.

3. With *Andronicus of Rhodes* the School took a new turn. Andronicus was the tenth Scholarch at Athens (i.e. excluding Aristotle himself) and occupied the post from about 70 B.C. to 50 B.C. He published the "pedagogical" works of Aristotle, investigated their authenticity, and commented on many of the works, giving special attention to logic. The line of commentators culminated in *Alexander of Aphrodisias*, who lectured on the Peripatetic philosophy at Athens between A.D. 198 and 211. Alexander was the most celebrated of the commentators of Aristotle, but he did not hesitate to depart from the latter's teaching. For instance, he adopted a nominalist position in regard to universals and denied anthropocentric teleology. Moreover, he identified the νοῦς ποιητικὸς with τὸ πρῶτον αἴτιον. Man possesses at birth only the νοῦς φυσικός or ὑλικός and later acquires the νοῦς ἐπίκτητος under the influence of the νοῦς ποιητικός. A consequence of this is the denial of the human soul's immortality. While in denying the immortality of the human soul Alexander is probably at one with Aristotle, it must be admitted that the denial follows much more obviously from Alexander's teaching than it does from the somewhat ambiguous remarks of Aristotle.

4. Alexander's eloquent defence of the study of logic in his commentary on the *Prior Analytics* is worthy of mention. He there declares that logic is not less deserving of our attention and study owing to the fact that it is an instrument of philosophy rather than an actual part of philosophy. For if man's greatest good is to become like to God, and if this likeness is attained through contemplation and knowledge of truth, and the knowledge

of truth through demonstration, then we should hold demonstration in the greatest honour and esteem, and so syllogistic reasoning also, inasmuch as demonstration is a form of syllogistic reasoning.[1] Together with this scholarly tendency grew the tendency to eclecticism. Thus the famous physician *Galen* (A.D. 129 to about A.D. 199) and *Aristocles* of Messana (*c.* A.D. 180) inclined to Stoicism with their doctrine of the immanent and active Nous, that pervades all nature.

5. The Peripatetics of the latest period can indeed hardly be called Peripatetics—certainly not without qualification: to all intents and purposes the School was absorbed in Neo-Platonism, the last great effort of Greek philosophy, and the late Peripatetics either inclined to eclecticism or contented themselves with commenting on the works of Aristotle. Thus Anatolius of Alexandria, who became bishop of Laodicea about A.D. 268 and may be identical with the Anatolius who was the teacher of Iamblichus,[2] combined, in his treatise on the numbers one to ten, consideration of the real properties of numbers with Pythagorean "number-mysticism."

Themistius (*c.* A.D. 320–*c.* 390), who taught at Constantinople and other places in the East and never became a Christian, affirmed indeed that he had chosen Aristotle as his guide to wisdom, and either paraphrased or commented on some of Aristotle's works, but was in fact much influenced by Platonism. With the later Platonism he defined philosophy as ὁμοίωσις θεοῦ κατὰ τὸ δυνατὸν ἀνθρώπῳ. (Cf. Plat. *Theaet.* 176 b.)

[1] *C.A.G.*, 11/1, 4; 30 and 6 : 8. [2] Eunap., *Vit. Soph.*, II.

CHAPTER XL

THE LATER STOA

In the early Roman Empire the chief characteristic of the Stoa is its insistence on the practical and moral principles of the School, which take on a religious colouring, being bound up with the doctrine of man's kinship with God and his duty of love towards his fellow-men. The noble morality of the Stoa is strikingly displayed in the teaching of the great Stoics of the period, Seneca, Epictetus and the Emperor Marcus Aurelius. At the same time a certain tendency to eclecticism is visible in the Stoa as in other Schools. Nor was the contemporary scientific interest absent from the Stoa: we may think, for example, of the geographer Strabo. We are fortunate in possessing an extensive Stoic literature from this period, which enables us to form a clear idea of the teaching of the School and the characteristics of its great personalities. Thus we are well provided in regard to Seneca's writings and we have four of the eight books in which Flavius Arrianus reported the lectures of Epictetus, while the Meditations of Marcus Aurelius show us the Stoic philosopher on the Roman throne.

1. *L. Annaeus Seneca* of Córdoba was tutor and minister to the Emperor Nero, and it was in obedience to the latter's command that the philosopher opened his veins in A.D. 65.

As we would expect of a Roman, Seneca emphasises the practical side of philosophy, ethics, and—within the sphere of ethics—is more concerned with the practice of virtue than with theoretical investigations into its nature. He does not seek intellectual knowledge for its own sake, but pursues philosophy as a means to the acquirement of virtue. Philosophy is necessary, but it is to be pursued with a practical end in view. *Non delectent, verba nostra, sed prosint—non quaerit aeger medicum eloquentem.*[1] His words on this topic not infrequently recall those of Thomas à Kempis, e.g. *plus scire quam sit satis, intemperantiae genus est.*[2] To spend one's time in the so-called liberal studies without having a practical end in view is waste of time—*unum studium vere liberale est quod liberum facit.*[3] and he calls on Lucilius to abandon

[1] *Ep.*, 75, 5 [2] *Ep.*, 88, 36. [3] *Ep.*, 88, 2.

the literary game of reducing sublime themes to grammatical and dialectical jugglery.[1] Seneca is interested to a certain extent in physical theories, but he insists that it is the conquest of the passions that is the really important point and which makes man equal to God,[2] and he often uses physical subjects simply as an opportunity for moralising conclusions, as when he makes use of the earthquakes in Campania (A.D. 63) to furnish matter for a moral discourse.[3] However, he certainly praises the study of Nature (under the influence of Poseidonius) and even declares that knowledge of Nature is to be sought for its own sake,[4] but even here the practical and human interest is visible.

Seneca adheres theoretically to the old Stoic materialism,[5] but in practice he certainly tends to regard God as transcending matter. This tendency to metaphysical dualism was a natural consequence or accompaniment of his marked tendency to psychological dualism. True, he affirms the materiality of the soul, but he proceeds to speak in Platonic strain of the conflict between soul and body, between the aspirations of the higher man and the doctrines of the flesh. *Nam corpus hoc animi pondus ac poena est, premente illo urgetur, in vinculis est.*[6] True virtue and true worth rest within: external goods do not confer true happiness but are transitory gifts of Fortune in which it would be foolish to place our trust. *Brevissima ad divitias per contemptum divitiarum via est.*[7] Seneca, as courtier of Caligula and Claudius and the wealthy tutor and minister of the young Nero, has been accused of practical inconsistency and hypocrisy, but it must be remembered that his very experience of the contrast between great wealth and splendour on the one hand and the constant fear of death on the other would very much help a man of his temperament to realise the ephemeral character of wealth, position and power. Moreover, he had unrivalled opportunities of observing human degradation, lust and debauchery at close quarters. Some ancient writers accumulated gossip about Seneca's private life, calculated to show that he did not live up to his own principles.[8] But, even if, allowing for the exaggeration and gossip of opponents, he did not pass through life without falls from his moral ideal—as is indeed only too likely in a man of his position

[1] *Ep.*, 71, 6. [2] *Ep.*, 73, 13. [3] *Nat. Q.*, 6, 32. [4] *Nat. Q.*, 6, 4.

[5] *Ep.*, 66, 12; 117, 2; 57, 8.

[6] *Ep.*, 120, 14; 65, 16. Cf. *Dies iste, quem tamquam extremum reformidas, aeterni natalis est. Ep.*, 102, 26.

[7] *Ep.*, 62, 3. [8] Cf. Dion Cassius, 61, 10.

and connections, attached to a depraved Court[1]—that does not mean that he was insincere in his teaching and preaching. His knowledge of the force of temptation and of the degradation to which avarice, ambition and lust could lead—to a certain extent perhaps from personal experience, but far more from his observation of others—lent power and force to his pen and to his moral exhortation. In spite of all rhetoric Seneca knew what he was talking about.

Although theoretically adhering to the traditional Stoic determinism, Seneca maintained that, as rational, every man has the power to take the path of virtue if he will only *will* to do so. *Satis natura dedit roboris si illo utamur.*[2] Moreover, God will help those who strive to help themselves. *Non sunt di fastidiosi: adscendentibus manum porrigunt*, and *O te miserum si contemnis hunc testem.*[3] The man who does help himself, conquer his passions and lead a life in accordance with right reason, is better off than our ancestors of the Golden Age, for, if they were innocent, they were innocent from ignorance and absence of temptation. *Non fuere sapientes—ignorantia rerum innocentes erant.*[4]

Since he aimed at encouraging men to set their feet upon the path of virtue and to continue therein in spite of temptation and fall, Seneca was naturally forced to temper the strict moral idealism of the earlier Stoics. He knew too much about the moral struggle to suppose that man can become virtuous by sudden conversion. And so we find him distinguishing three classes of *proficientes.* (i) Those who have abandoned some of their sins, but not all; (ii) those who have formed the resolution to renounce evil passions in general, even if still liable to occasional relapse; (iii) those who have got beyond possibility of relapse, but still lack confidence in themselves and the consciousness of their own wisdom. They *approximate*, therefore, to wisdom and perfect virtue.[5] Moreover, Seneca admits that external goods, e.g. wealth, may be used for good ends. The wise man will be the master of his wealth and not its slave. He gives practical counsel as to how to secure moral progress, e.g. by the use of the daily self-examination, which he himself practised.[6] It is useless to retire into solitude, if you do not attempt at the same time to change yourself: change of place does not necessarily mean change of

[1] Does he not himself admit, *Non de me loquor, qui multum ab homine tolerabili nedum a perfecto absum? Ep.* 57, 3.

[2] *Ep.*, 116, 7. [3] *Ep.*, 73, 15; 43, 5. [4] *Ep.*, 90, 46. [5] *Ep.*, 75, 8.

[6] *De Ira*, 3, 36, 3.

heart, and wherever you go, you will still have to struggle with yourself. It is easy to understand, how the legend of Seneca's correspondence with St. Paul could grow up, when we read such phrases as *Nos quoque evincamus omnia, quorum praemium non corona nec palma est.*[1]

Seneca lays emphasis on the Stoic doctrine of the relationship that exists among all human beings, and instead of the self-sufficiency of the wise man—a self-sufficiency tinged with contempt for others—he calls on us to help our fellow-men and to forgive those who have injured us. *Alteri vivas oportet, si vis tibi vivere.*[2] He stresses the necessity of active benevolence. "Nature bids me to be of use to men whether they are slave or free, freedmen or free born. Wherever there is a human being there is room for benevolence."[3] "See that you are beloved by all while you live and regretted when you die."

Yet punishment of evil-doers is necessary. *Bonis nocet qui malis parcet.*[4] The most effective punishment, however, for the purpose of reformation is the mildest. Punishment should not be inflicted out of rage or the desire of revenge (cf. *De Ira* and *De Clementia*).

2. *Epictetus of Hierapolis* (c. A.D. 50–138) was at first a slave belonging to a member of Nero's bodyguard, and, when he became a freedman, continued to live in Rome until the expulsion of the philosophers by the Emperor Domitian (A.D. 89 or 93). He then founded a School at Nicopolis in Epirus and probably continued at its head until his death. It was at Nicopolis that his lectures were attended by Flavius Arrianus, who composed eight books of Διατριβαί on the basis of the lectures. Of these eight books we possess four. Arrian also published a small catechism or handbook of his master's doctrines, the Ἐγχειρίδιον.

Epictetus insists that all men have the capacity for virtue and that God has given to all men the means of becoming happy, of becoming men of steadfast character and self-control. "What then is a man's nature? To bite, to kick, to throw into prison, and to behead? No, but to do good, to co-operate with others, to wish them well."[5] All men have the sufficient initial moral intuitions on which they can build up the moral life. "Observe whom you yourself praise when you praise without partiality? Do you praise the just or the unjust, the moderate or the immoderate, the temperate or the intemperate?"[6] "There are

[1] *Ep.*, 78, 16, 4. [2] *Ep.*, 48, 2. [3] *De Vita Beata*, 24, 3. [4] Fr. 114. [5] *Disc.*, 4, 1, 22. [6] *Disc.*, 3, 1, 8.

certain things which men who are not altogether perverted see by the common notions which all possess."[1]

Yet, though all men possess sufficient basis for the building-up of the moral life, philosophic instruction is necessary for all, in order that they may be able to apply their primary conceptions (προλήψεις) of good and evil to particular circumstances. "Primary conceptions are common to all men,"[2] but a conflict or difficulty may arise in the application of these primary conceptions to particular facts. It is this which explains the diversity of ethical notions, in the sense of applied notions, among different peoples and between various individuals.[3] Education is, therefore, necessary and, inasmuch as the right application of principles depends on reasoning and reasoning on logic, a knowledge of logic is not to be despised. The important thing, however, is not that a man should possess a knowledge of formal dialectic, but that he should be able to apply his principles to practice and, above all, that he should actually carry them into practice in his conduct. There are two factors in which education chiefly consists: (i) in learning to apply the natural primary conceptions to particular circumstances in accordance with "nature", and (ii) in learning to distinguish between things in our power and things not in our power.[4] Epictetus, in common with the Stoic School in general, makes a great deal of this latter distinction. To acquire honours and wealth, to enjoy continual health, to avoid physical maltreatment or the disfavour of the Emperor, to ward off death or disaster from himself or his friends and relatives, all this does not depend solely on the efforts of any individual man: he must be careful, then, not to set his heart on any of these things, but to accept all that happens to himself or his relatives and friends as Fate, as the will of God: he must accept all events of this kind without rebellion or discontent, as being the expression of the Divine Will. What, then, is in man's power? His judgments on events and his will: these he can control, and his self-education consists in attaining true judgment and a right will. "The essence of good and evil lies in an attitude of the will,"[5] and this will lies within a man's power, for "the will may conquer itself, but nothing else can conquer it."[6] That which is really necessary for man is, therefore, to *will* virtue, to *will* victory over sin. "Be well assured that nothing is more tractable than the human soul. You must exercise your will and the thing is done, it is set right;

[1] *Disc.*, 3, 6, 8. [2] *Disc.*, 1, 22. [3] *Ibid.* [4] *Ibid.* [5] *Disc.*, 1, 29. [6] *Ibid.*

as on the other hand relax your vigilance and all is lost, for from within comes ruin and from within comes help."[1] Sins differ from the material standpoint, but from the moral standpoint they are equal in that they all involve a perverted will. To overcome and set right this perverted will is within the power of all. "Now will you not help yourself? And how much easier is this help? There is no need to kill or imprison any man or to treat him with contumely or to go into the law-courts. You must just talk to yourself. You will be most easily persuaded; no one has more power to persuade you than you yourself."[2]

As practical means to moral progress Epictetus advises the daily examination of conscience (the faithful use of which leads to the substitution of good habits for bad ones), avoidance of bad companions and occasions of sin, constant self-vigilance, etc. We must not be discouraged by falls but must persevere, setting before our eyes some ideal of virtue, e.g. Socrates or Zeno. Again, ". . . remember that Another looks from above on what is happening and that you must please Him rather than this man."[3] In the course of moral progress he distinguishes three stages:

(i) A man is taught to order his *desires* in accordance with right reason, freeing himself from morbid emotions and attaining to tranquillity of soul.

(ii) A man is trained to action, to performance of his duty (τὸ καθῆκον), coming to act as a true son, brother, citizen, etc.

(iii) The third stage relates to judgment and assent, and "its aim is to make the other two secure, so that even in sleep, intoxication, or hypochondria we may not let any presentation pass untested."[4] An unerring moral judgment is produced.

Duties towards oneself must begin with cleanliness of the body. "I indeed would rather that a young man, when first moved to philosophy, should come to me with his hair carefully trimmed, than with it dirty and rough."[5] That is to say, if a man has a feeling for natural cleanliness and beauty there is more hope of elevating him to the perception of moral beauty. Epictetus inculcates temperance, modesty, and chastity, censuring, for example, the adulterer. Simplicity is to be cultivated, though there is no harm in pursuing wealth, if this is done for good ends. "If I can acquire money, and also keep myself modest and faithful and magnanimous, point out the way and I will acquire it. But

[1] *Disc.*, 4, 9, 16. [2] *Disc.*, 4, 9, 13. [3] *Disc.*, 1, 30.
[4] *Disc.*, 3, 2; cf. 1, ch. 18 (end). [5] *Disc.*, 4, 11, 25.

if you ask me to lose the things which are good and my own, in order that you may gain the things which are not good, see how unfair and silly you are."[1] (This to people who urge a friend to acquire money that they also may have some.) Like all the Stoics, Epictetus lauded veracity and loyalty.

True piety is to be encouraged. "Of religion towards the Gods, know that the chief element is to have right opinions concerning them, as existing and governing the whole in fair order and justice, and then to set thyself to obey them, and to yield to them in each event, and submit to it willingly, as accomplished under the highest counsels."[2] Atheism and denial of Divine Providence, both general and particular, are condemned. "Concerning the Gods, there are some who say that a Divine Being does not exist; and others, that it exists indeed, but is idle and uncaring, and hath no forethought for anything; and a third class say that there is such a Being, and he taketh forethought also, but only in respect of great and heavenly things, but of nothing that is on the earth; and a fourth class, that he taketh thought of things both in heaven and earth, but only in general, and not of each thing severally. And there is a fifth class, whereof are Odysseus and Socrates, who say, 'Nor can I move without thy knowledge.' "[3]

Marriage and the family are in accordance with right reason, though the "missionary" may remain celibate in order to be free for his work.[4] The child must always obey the father, unless the latter commands something immoral. Patriotism and active sharing in public life are encouraged—somewhat inconsistently —but war is condemned and the ruler should win the allegiance of his subjects by his example and by his self-sacrificing care for them.

Yet cosmopolitanism and the love of humanity transcend narrow patriotism. All men have God for their Father and are brothers by nature. "Will you not remember who you are and whom you rule? That they are kinsmen, that they are brethren by nature, that they are the offspring of Zeus?"[5] To all men we owe love and should not return evil for evil. "To suppose that we shall be easily despised by others unless in every possible way we do injury to those who first show us hostility, is the work of very ignoble and foolish men, for this implies that inability to

[1] *Ench.*, 24. [2] *Ench.*, 31. [3] *Disc.*, 1, 12. [4] Cf. *Disc.*, 3, 22; 3, 26, 67. [5] *Disc.*, 1, 13.

do injury is the reason why we are thought contemptible, whereas the really contemptible man is not he who cannot do injury but he who cannot do benefit."[1] Epictetus does not, however, reject punishment any more than the other Stoics. They insist that violation of law must be punished, but that this punishment must proceed from mature deliberation and not from hasty anger, and that it should be tempered with mercy, calculated to be, not merely a deterrent, but also a remedy for the offender.

In *Disc.* 3, 22, Epictetus devotes a chapter to Cynicism, in which the Cynic philosopher appears as the preacher of the truth concerning good and evil, as the ambassador of God. Without sharing the Cynic contempt for science, Epictetus seems to have admired the Cynic's indifference towards external goods. This is all the more natural in that for Epictetus happiness depends on that which alone is in our power and independent of external conditions —namely, our will, our ideas concerning things, and the use that we make of our ideas. If we seek our happiness in goods which do not depend entirely on ourselves for attainment or continued possession, we invite unhappiness: we must practise abstinence therefore—ἀνέχου καὶ ἀπέχου—and seek our happiness within.

(Dr. Praechter tells of the Director of a Swiss sanatorium, who was accustomed to hand to his neurasthenic and psychasthenic patients a copy of the Enchiridion in a German translation, and who found it to be a valuable aid in effecting a cure.[2])

3. *Marcus Aurelius*, Roman Emperor from A.D. 161 to 180, composed his Meditations (in the Greek language) in twelve books in aphoristic form. For Epictetus he had a lively admiration,[3] and he was at one with Epictetus and Seneca in giving a religious colouring to his philosophy. With Marcus Aurelius, too, we find stress laid on Divine Providence and a wise ordering of the universe, the close relationship between man and God, the duty of love towards one's fellow-men. Thus the Emperor teaches compassion for human infirmity. "When any one does you a wrong, set yourself at once to consider what was the point of view, good or bad, that led him wrong. As soon as you perceive it you will be sorry for him, not surprised or angry. For your own view of good is either the same as his or something like in kind, and you will make allowance. Or, supposing your own view of good and bad has altered, you will find charity for his mistake

[1] Stob., *Flor.*, 20, 61.
[2] Ueberweg-Praechter, p. 498, Note.
[3] *Med.*, 1, 7.

comes easier."[1] "It is man's special gift to love even those who fall into blunders; this takes effect the moment we realise that men are our brothers, that sin is ignorance and unintentional, that in a little while we shall both be dead, that, above all, no injury is done us; our inner self is not made worse than it was before."[2] Active benevolence is stressed. "Does the eye demand a recompense for seeing, or the feet for walking? Just as this is the end for which they exist, and just as they find their reward in realising the law of their being, so, too, man is made for kindness, and whenever he does an act of kindness or otherwise helps forward the common good, he thereby fulfils the law of his being and comes by his own."[3] "Love mankind, follow God."[4]

Marcus Aurelius shows a decided tendency to break through the Stoic materialism. He adheres indeed to the Stoic monism, as in the following passage: "All harmonises with me which is in harmony with thee, O universe. Nothing for me is too early nor too late which is in due season for thee. For thee are all things, in thee are all things, to thee all things return. The poet says, Dear City of Cecrops; and wilt not thou say, Dear City of Zeus?"[5] Moreover, the Emperor was punctiliously observant of the forms of polytheistic worship, a fact which will partly explain the persecution of Christians during his reign, since he clearly looked upon the fulfilment of the requirements of State-worship as implied in good citizenship. But although Marcus Aurelius adheres to the Stoic monism, he tends to transcend materialism by his division of man into three parts—σῶμα, ψυχή and νοῦς, ψυχή being material but νοῦς being expressly distinguished from all four elements, and so—logically speaking at least—from matter. The human νοῦς or τὸ νοερόν comes from the νοερόν of the Universe, it is an ἀπόσπασμα of God,[6] it is τὸ ἡγεμονικόν.[7] The influence of Platonism is clear, but it is possible that the Emperor, who had Claudius Severus, a Peripatetic, as one of his teachers,[8] was influenced also by the doctrine of Aristotle.

The νοῦς is the δαίμων which God has given to every man to be his guide, and this δαίμων is an emanation of the Divinity. It follows, then, that whoever disobeys the commands of the δαίμων which are the commands of reason, acts not only irrationally but also impiously. Immorality is thus impiety.[9] "Live with the gods, And he lives with the gods whoever presents to them his

[1] *Med.*, 7, 26. [2] *Med.*, 7, 22. [3] *Med.*, 9, 42. [4] *Med.*, 7, 31. [5] *Med.*, 4, 23.
[6] *Med.*, 5, 27. [7] *Med.*, 12, 1. [8] Capitol, *Vit. M. Ant.*, 3, 3.
[9] *Med.*, 2, 13: 11, 20: 9, 1.

soul accepting their dispensations and busied about the will of God, even that particle of Zeus which Zeus gives to every man for his controller and governor—to wit, his mind and reason."[1] Man has it in his power to avoid wickedness. "As for those things which are truly evil, as vice and wickedness, such things they (the gods) have put in a man's own power, that he might avoid them if he would."[2]

Marcus Aurelius, after the Stoic tradition, admits only limited immortality. Although he stresses, as Seneca did, the dualism between soul and body and depicts death as a liberation,[3] he allows not only the possibility of the soul's "reabsorption" at the world-conflagration, but also the possibility that the soul is reabsorbed in the Cosmic Reason in virtue of the constant change in nature—a theme dwelt upon by the Emperor, who compares the flow of phenomena to a river.[4] In any case the soul enjoys but a limited persistence after death.[5]

[1] *Med.*, 5, 27. [2] *Med.*, 2, 11. [3] *Med.*, 9, 3; 11, 3. [4] *Med.*, 4, 14; 4, 43; 5, 23. [5] *Med.*, 4, 21.

CHAPTER XLI

CYNICS, ECLECTICS, SCEPTICS

1. *Cynics*

THE moral corruption in the Roman Empire not unnaturally prompted a revival of Cynicism, and the writing of letters under the names of ancient Cynics seems to have been calculated to forward this revival. Thus we have 51 letters under the name of Diogenes and 36 under that of Crates.

Roman Stoics of the type of Seneca addressed themselves mainly to members of the highest classes in society, to men who belonged to that circle which was naturally drawn into court-life, to men, above all, who possessed some hankering after virtue and tranquillity of soul, but who were at the same time bewildered by the luxurious and sensation-loving life of the aristocracy, who felt the power of the flesh and the attractions of sin and yet were also weary of self-indulgence and ready to grasp and hold the helping hand that might be held out to them. But beside the aristocracy and the men of wealth there were the masses, who may have benefited to a certain extent by the humanitarian ideals propagated among their masters by the Stoics, but who were not directly touched by men like Seneca. To meet the spiritual and moral needs of the masses there grew up a different type of "apostle," that of the Cynic preacher or missionary. These men led the life of itinerant preachers, poor and self-denying, aiming at the "conversion" of the masses who came to listen to them—as when the celebrated Apollonius of Tyana (who belongs rather to the story of Neo-Pythagoreanism), mystic and reported miracle-worker, preached a rivalry of public spirit to the inhabitants of Smyrna, who were torn apart by faction, or discoursed on virtue to the crowd gathered at Olympia to witness the games and races[1]—as when Musonius (who, in spite of his affinity with Cynicism, actually belonged to the Stoic School and was the teacher of Epictetus), harangued the troops of Vespasian and Vitellius on the blessings of peace and the horrors of civil war at the risk of his own life[2] or denounced impiety and demanded virtue from men and women alike. They were often men of undaunted courage, as may be seen from the example of Musonius, just

[1] Philostr., *Apoll. Tyan.*, 4, 8; 4, 31.

[2] Tac., *Hist.*, 3, 81

described, or from Demetrius' defiance of Nero: "You threaten me with death, but nature threatens you."[1] Demetrius, praised by Seneca in his writings, consoled the last hours of Thrasea by discoursing on the soul and its destiny.[2]

Lucian criticises the Cynic preachers unmercifully, particularly for their bad manners, their lack of culture, their coarseness and buffoonery, their vulgarity and obscenity. Lucian was a foe to all enthusiasm, and religious fervour and "mystic" exaltation were repugnant to him, so that he often doubtless does an injustice to the Cynics owing to his lack of sympathy and understanding; but it must be remembered that Lucian was not alone in his criticism, for Martial, Petronius, Seneca, Epictetus, Dion Chrysostom and others are agreed in condemning abuses which were undoubtedly real. Some of the Cynics were certainly impostors and buffoons who brought the name of philosophy into contempt, as Dion Chrysostom states plainly.[3] Moreover, some of them betrayed a repulsive egoism and lack of good taste and proper respect, as when that same Demetrius, who had denounced Nero, took it upon himself to insult the Emperor Vespasian—who was no Nero—or as when Peregrinus attacked the Emperor Antoninus Pius.[4] (Vespasian took no notice of Demetrius, while Peregrinus was merely told by the Prefect to leave the city. The Cynic who publicly attacked Titus in the theatre for his intercourse with Berenice was scourged, however, while Heros, who repeated the performance, was beheaded.[5]) Lucian is inclined to put the worst interpretation on the conduct of the Cynics. Thus, when Peregrinus—called Proteus—who had become a Christian in Palestine, but who had subsequently joined the ranks of the Cynics, publicly burnt himself to death at Olympia in order to give an example of contempt for death, to imitate the Cynic patron Heracles and to unite himself with the divine element, Lucian assumes that his action was due simply to a love of notoriety—κενοδοξία.[6] The motive of vainglory may very well have entered in, but it may not have been the sole motive operative with Peregrinus.

Nevertheless, in spite of extravagance and in spite of the existence of impostors and buffoons, Cynicism cannot be condemned root and branch. *Demonax* (c. A.D. 50–150) was universally honoured at Athens for his goodness,[7] and when the Athenians proposed to institute gladiatorial shows in the city he advised

[1] Epict., *Disc.*, 1, 25. [2] Tac., *Ann.*, 16, 34. [3] e.g. *Or.*, 32, 9.
[4] Suet., *Vesp.*, 13; Dion Cass., 66, 13; Luc., *De morte Peregr.*, c. 18.
[5] Cf. Dio. Cass., 66, 15. [6] *De Morte Peregr.*, 4; 20 ff. [7] Cf. *Demonax* (Lucian).

them first of all to demolish the altar of Pity. Though simple and frugal in his ways he seems to have avoided ostentatious singularity. Brought before the Athenian courts on a charge of impiety, since he declined to offer sacrifice and refused to seek initiation into the Eleusinian Mysteries, he replied that God has no need of sacrifices, while, as for the Mysteries, if they contained a revelation of good tidings to man, he would have to publish it, whereas, if they were of no value, he would feel bound to warn the people against them.[1] *Oenomaus* of Gadara dismissed the pagan anthropomorphic fables concerning the gods and fiercely attacked the revival of belief in divination and oracles. The oracles, he said, were mere deception, while in any case man is possessed of free will and man alone is responsible for his actions. Julian the Apostate, champion of paganism, was aroused to indignation by the very memory of such a man as Oenomaus, who had attacked the pagan oracles.[2]

A celebrated and honourable Cynic preacher was *Dion Chrysostom*, who was born about A.D. 40 and lived, at any rate, well into the reign of the Emperor Trajan. He came of an aristocratic family of Prusa (Bithynia) and was at first a rhetorician and Sophist. Condemned to banishment from Bithynia and Italy in A.D. 82 during the reign of the Emperor Domitian, he led a wandering life of poverty. During the period of exile he underwent a sort of "conversion" and became an itinerant Cynic preacher with a mission to the submerged masses of the Empire. Dion retained his rhetorical manner and liked, in his Orations, to clothe the moral truths he expressed in an attractive and elegant form; but though true to the rhetorical tradition, he insisted in his preaching on living in conformity with the Divine Will, on the moral ideal, on the practice of true virtue and on the insufficiency of purely material civilisation. In the Ἐυβοϊκός he depicts the life of the poor countryman as being more natural, freer and happier than that of the rich town-dweller; but he occupies himself also with the question, how the poor in the cities can most satisfactorily live their lives without hankering after luxury or involving themselves in what is harmful to soul or body. He warned the people of Tarsus that they had a wrong sense of values. Happiness is to be found, not in stately buildings, wealth and delicate living, but in temperance, justice and true piety. The great materialistic civilisations of the past—Assyria, for

[1] *Demonax*, 11.

[2] Julian, *Or.*, 7, 209.

example—have perished, while the great Empire of Alexander is gone and Pella is a heap of bricks.[1] He harangues the people of Alexandria on their vices and lust for sensation, on their lack of dignity and their trivial interests.[2]

Dion's social interests led him towards Stoicism and he made use of the Stoic doctrines of world-harmony and of cosmopolitanism. As God rules over the world, so should the Monarch rule over the State, and as the world is a harmony of many phenomena, so should individual States be preserved, but in such a way that they live in peace and harmony and free intercourse with one another. Besides the influence of Stoicism Dion seems to have undergone the influence of Poseidonius, taking from him, the division of a threefold theology, that of the philosophers, that of the poets and that of the official or State cult. He became, after the end of his period of banishment under Domitian, a favourite of Trajan, who used to invite the philosopher to his table and take him as a companion in his carriage, though he did not pretend to understand Dion's rhetoric. τὶ μὲν λέγεις, οὐκ οἶδα. φιλῶ δε σε ὡς ἐμαυτόν.[3] It was before the court of Trajan that Dion delivered some of his orations, contrasting the ideal monarch with the tyrant. The true monarch is the shepherd of his people, appointed by God for the good of his subjects. He must be a truly religious[4] and virtuous man, the father of his people, a hard worker, hostile to flatterers.

For Dion Chrysostom the idea of God is innate and universal among all men, brought into full consciousness by the contemplation of the design and providence in the universe. Yet God is hidden from us, and we are like little children stretching out their hands for father or mother.[5] Yet though God in Himself is veiled from us, we naturally try to imagine Him as best we can, and this is best accomplished by the poets. Artists, too, attempt the same task, though more inadequately, for no sculptor or painter can portray the Nature of God. All the same, in portraying God in human form they do not do wrong, since it is only natural to have recourse to the highest being of which we have direct experience as an image of the Divine.

Later we find evidence of a Christianised Cynicism, e.g. in the person of Maximus of Alexandria, who came to Constantinople

[1] *Or.* 33. [2] *Or.* 32. [3] Philostr., *Vit. Soph.*, 1, 7. [4] Cf. *Or.* 1–4.

[5] *Or.* 12, 61. ὥσπερ νήπιοι παῖδες πατρὸς ἢ μητρὸς ἀπεσπασμένοι δεινὸν ἵμερον ἔχοντες καὶ πόθον ὀρέγουσι χεῖρας . . .

in A.D. 379 or 380 and formed an intimate friendship with St. Gregory Nazianzen, though he afterwards had himself consecrated bishop behind St. Gregory's back. Maximus imitated the ways of the Stoics, though there does not seem to have been much consistency in his behaviour.[1]

II. *Eclectics*

A professedly Eclectic School was founded by *Potamon* of Alexandria in the time of the Emperor Augustus. According to Diogenes Laërtius the School was named Ἐκλεκτικὴ αἵρεσις[2] and it seems to have combined Stoic and Peripatetic elements, though Potamon also wrote a commentary on Plato's *Republic*.

Eclectic tendencies were also shown by the School of *Q. Sextius* (b. *c.* 70 B.C.). They adopted Stoic and Cynic principles, with which they combined Pythagorean and Platonico-Aristotelian elements. Thus Sextius adopted the Pythagorean customs of self-examination and abstinence from flesh-meat, while his disciple Sotion of Alexandria took over from the Pythagoreans the theory of metempsychosis. The School does not appear to have been of any great consequence, though Seneca was a disciple of Sotion.[3]

III. *Sceptics*

Although the Academy before the time of Antiochus of Ascalon had shown, as we have seen, a marked sceptical tendency, it was to the School of Pyrrho that the revived Scepticism looked as its ancestor rather than to the Academy. Thus the founder of the revived School, Aenesidemus of Knossos, wrote eight books Πυρρωνείων λόγων. The members of the School attempted to show the relative character of all judgments and opinions, embodying their arguments for this position in what they called Τρόποι. However, though they naturally opposed philosophic dogmatism, they did not fail to recognise the claims of practical life, and stated norms according to which man should act in practice. This was not alien to the spirit of Pyrrho who, in spite of his scepticism, declared that custom, tradition, State law, afforded a norm for practical life.

Aenesidemus of Knossos (who taught at Alexandria and probably composed his work round about 43 B.C.) gave ten Τρόποι or arguments for the sceptical position.[4] They were:

[1] Greg., *Adv. Maxim.*, *P.G.*, 37, 1339 ff.
[2] Diog. Laërt., *Proem.*, 21.
[3] Sen., *Ep.*, 108, 17.
[4] Sext. Emp., *Pyrr. Hyp.*, 1, 36 ff.

(1) Difference between types of living beings imply different—and so relative—"ideas" of same object.
(2) Differences between individual men imply the same.
(3) The different structure and presentation of our various senses (e.g. there is an eastern fruit that smells unpleasant but tastes delicious).
(4) The difference between our various states, e.g. waking or sleeping, youth or age. For example, a current of air may seem a pleasant breeze to a young man, while to an old man it is a detestable draught.
(5) Differences of perspective, e.g. the stick immersed in water appears bent, the square tower appears round from a distance.
(6) The objects of perception are never presented in their purity, but a medium is always involved, such as air. Hence the mixing or ἐπιμιξία. For example, grass appears green at noon, golden in the evening light. A lady's dress looks different in sunlight to what it looks in electric light.
(7) Differences in perception due to differences of quality, e.g. one grain of sand appears rough, while if sand is allowed to slip through the fingers it appears smooth and soft.
(8) Relativity in general, ὁ ἀπὸ τοῦ πρός τι.
(9) Difference in impression due to frequency or infrequency of perception, e.g. the comet, seldom seen, makes more impression than the sun.
(10) Different ways of life, moral codes, laws, myths, philosophic systems, etc. (cf. Sophists).

These ten Τρόποι of Aenesidemus were reduced to five by Agrippa.[1]

(1) The variation of views concerning the same objects.
(2) The infinite process involved in proving anything (i.e. the proof rests on assumptions that require to be proved, and so on indefinitely).
(3) The relativity involved in the fact that objects appear differently to people according to the temperament, etc., of the percipient and according to their relation with other objects.
(4) The arbitrary character of dogmatic assumptions, assumed as starting-points, in order to escape the *regressus in infinitum*.

[1] Sext. Emp., *Pyrr. Hyp.*, 1, 164 ff.

(5) The vicious circle or the necessity of assuming in the proof of anything the very conclusion that has to be proved.

Other Sceptics meanwhile reduced the Τρόποι to two:[1]

(1) Nothing can be rendered certain through itself. Witness the variety of opinions, between which no choice can be made with certainty.
(2) Nothing can be rendered certain through anything else, since the attempt to do so involves either the *regressus in infinitum* or the vicious circle.

(It is clear that these arguments for relativism have, for the most part at least, to do with perception. But perception does not err, since perception does not judge, and error lies in the false judgment. Moreover, it is in the power of reason to prevent error by avoiding precipitate judgment, by considering the matter more closely, by suspending judgment in certain cases, etc.)

Sextus Empiricus (*c*. A.D. 250), who is our main source for the details of Sceptic doctrine, argued against the possibility of proving any conclusion syllogistically.[2] The major premiss—for instance, "All men are mortal"—can be proved only by a complete induction. But the complete induction involves a knowledge of the conclusion—"Socrates is a mortal." For we cannot say, that *all* men are mortal unless we already know that Socrates is mortal. The Syllogism is, therefore, an instance of a vicious circle. (We may note that this objection against the syllogism, which was revived by John Stuart Mill in the nineteenth century, would only be valid if the Aristotelian doctrine of the specific essence were rejected in favour of Nominalism. It is in virtue of our perception of the essence or universal nature of man that we are entitled to assert that all men are mortal and not because we lay claim to any perfect and complete enumeration of particulars through actual observation, which in the case in point would be out of the question. The major premiss is founded, therefore, on the nature of man, and does not require explicit knowledge of the conclusion of the syllogism. The conclusion is contained *implicitly* in the major premiss, and the syllogistic process renders this implicit knowledge clear and explicit. The nominalist standpoint demands, of course, a new logic, and this Mill attempted to supply.) The Sceptics also argued against the validity of the notion of Cause, but they do not seem to have anticipated the

[1] Sext. Emp., *Pyrr. Hyp.*, 1, 178 ff. [2] Sext. Emp., *Pyrr. Hyp.*, 2, 193 ff.

epistemological difficulties raised by David Hume.[1] Cause is essentially *relative*, but the relative is not objective but is attributed extrinsically by the mind. Again, the cause must be either simultaneous with the effect or prior or posterior. It cannot be simultaneous, since then B might just as well be called the cause of A as A of B. Nor could the cause be prior to the effect, since then it would first exist without relation to its effect, and cause is essentially relative to the effect. Nor could the cause be posterior to the effect—for obvious reasons.

The Sceptics also attempted to prove the existence of antinomies in theology. For instance, God must be either infinite or finite.[2] Not the former, for He would then be unmoved and so without life or soul: not the latter, as He would then be less perfect than the Whole, whereas God is *ex hypothesi* perfect. (This is an argument against the Stoics for whom God is material: it does not affect those for whom God is Infinite Spirit. Infinite Spirit cannot move, but is living, or rather is Infinite Life.) Again, the Stoic doctrine of Providence is necessarily involved in a dilemma. There is much evil and suffering in the world. Now, either God has the will and power to stop this evil and suffering or He has not. The latter supposition is incompatible with the notion of God (though J. S. Mill arrived at the strange notion of a finite God, with Whom we co-operate). He has, therefore, the will and power to stop the evil and suffering in the world. But this He obviously does not do. It follows that there is at least no *universal* Providence on the part of God. But we can give no explanation why Divine Providence should extend to this being and not to that. We are forced, therefore, to conclude that there is *no* Providence at all.[3]

In regard to practical life the Sceptics taught that we should follow the presentations of perception and thought, satisfy our natural instincts, adhere to law and tradition, and pursue science. We can never indeed attain to certainty in science, but we can go on *seeking*.[4]

[1] Sext. Emp., *Adv. Matn.*, 9, 207 ff. Cf. 8, 453 ff.
[2] Sext. Emp., *Adv. Math.*, 9, 148 ff. [3] Sext. Emp., *Pyrr. Hyp.*, 3, 9 ff.
[4] Sext. Emp., *Pyrr. Hyp.*, 1, 3; 1, 226; *Adv. Math.*, 7, 435 ff.

CHAPTER XLII

NEO-PYTHAGOREANISM

THE old Pythagorean School seems to have become extinct in the fourth century B.C.: if it did continue, we have certainly no evidence of effective and vigorous life. But in the first century B.C. the School came to life again under the form of what is known as Neo-Pythagoreanism. It was related to the old School, not only by reverence for the Founder, but also by a certain interest in scientific pursuits and, above all, by its religious colouring. Much of the old Pythagorean asceticism was adopted by the new School, which naturally adhered to the soul-body dualism—a salient feature, as we have seen, of the Platonic philosophy—and to this it added mystical elements, which answered the contemporary demand for a purer and more personal religion. Direct intuition of the Deity was claimed, and revelation—so much so that the philosopher is sometimes depicted as prophet and wonder-worker, e.g. Apollonius of Tyana.[1] The new School was very far, however, from being a mere reproduction of the former Pythagorean system, for it followed the current tendency to Eclecticism, and we find the Neo-Pythagoreans drawing widely on the Platonic, Aristotelian and Stoic philosophies. These borrowed elements were not fused together into one synthesis, common to all the members of the School, for the various members constructed their different syntheses, in one of which Stoic themes might predominate, in another themes from the Platonic philosophy. Neo-Pythagoreanism is of some historical importance, however, not only because it stands in close relation to the religious life of the time (it seems to have originated in Alexandria, the meeting-point of Hellenistic philosophy, special science and Oriental religion), but also because it marks a step on the way to Neo-Platonism. Thus Numenius taught the doctrine of the Divine Hierarchy—the first god, the πρῶτος θεός, being the οὐσίας ἀρχή or πατήρ, the second god being the Demiurge and the third god being the World, τὸ ποίημα.

Sextus Empiricus tells us of various tendencies within Neo-Pythagoreanism. Thus in one form of Neo-Pythagoreanism

[1] See Note on Apoll. Tyana, pp. 449–50.

everything is derived from the monad or point (ἐξ ἑνὸς σημείου). The point generates the line in its flow, while from lines are generated surfaces, and from surfaces three-dimensional bodies. Here we have a monistic system, though obviously influenced by older mathematical conceptions. In another form of Neo-Pythagoreanism, although everything is derived ultimately from the point or μονάς, the greatest emphasis is laid on the dualism of the μονάς, and the ἀόριστος δυάς. All "unities" participate in the μονάς and all dualities in the ἀόριστος δυάς.[1] There is nothing particularly original in these forms of Neo-Pythagoreanism, but the notion of "emanation" is clearly present, which was to play a leading rôle in Neo-Platonism.

One of the motives that prompted the Neo-Platonic theory of emanation and the assertion of beings intermediary between the corporeal world and the supreme God was the desire of maintaining God's purity free from all contact with the things of sense. God's utter transcendence, His position "beyond being," is brought into sharp relief. Now, this theme of the transcendence of God is already discernible in Neo-Pythagoreanism. It may have been influenced by the Judaeo-Alexandrian philosophy and by Oriental tradition, though we may discern its latent germs within the thought of Plato himself. The noted wonder-worker Apollonius of Tyana (who flourished about the end of the first century A.D.), whose "life" was written by Philostratus, distinguished the first god from the other gods. To this first god men should not offer any material sacrifice, since all material things are tainted with impurity. We should sacrifice to the other gods, but not to the first god, to whom we should offer none but the service of our reason, without outward speech or offering.

An interesting figure is that of *Nicomachus of Gerasa* (in Arabia), who lived about A.D. 140, and was author of an ἀριθμητικὴ εἰσαγωγή. In his system the Ideas existed before the formation of the world (Plato), and the Ideas are numbers (Plato again). But the Number-Ideas did not exist in a transcendental world of their own: rather were they Ideas in the Divine Mind, and so patterns or archetypes according to which the things of this world were formed (cf. Philo the Jew, Middle Platonism and Neo-Platonism). The transposition of the Ideas into the Mind of God had, therefore, taken place before the rise of Neo-Platonism, from which it passed over into the Christian tradition.

[1] *Adv. Math.*, 10, 281 ff.

A similar transposition is to be observed in the philosophy of *Numenius of Apamea* (Syria), who lived in the second half of the second century A.D. and seems to have been well acquainted with the Jewish philosophy of Alexandria. According to Clement he spoke of Plato as Μωϋσῆς ἀττικίζων.[1] In Numenius' philosophy the πρῶτος θεός is the Principle of Being (οὐσίας ἀρχή) and the βασιλεύς.[2] He is also the activity of Pure Thought (νοῦς), and has no direct share in the formation of the world. Moreover, He is the Good. Numenius thus seems to have identified the Platonic Form of the Good with the Aristotelian God or νόησις νοήσεως. The second god is the Demiurge (*Timaeus*), who is good by participation in the being of the First God and who, as γενέσεως ἀρχή, forms the world. He does this by working on matter and forming it on the pattern of the archetypal Ideas. The world itself, the production of the Demiurge, is the third god. These three gods are also characterised by Numenius as πατήρ, ποιητής and ποίημα respectively, or as πάππος, ἔγγονος and ἀπόγονος.[3]

Dualism is very apparent in the psychology of Numenius, since he postulates two souls in man, a rational soul and an irrational soul, and declares the entry of the soul into the body as something evil, as a "fall." He seems also to have taught the existence of a good and a bad world-soul.[4]

The philosophy of Numenius was thus a syncretism or harmonisation of elements taken from preceding thinkers, a philosophy which laid great emphasis on the divine transcendence and which, in general, asserted a sharp antithesis between "higher" and "lower," both in reality as a whole and in human nature in particular.

In connection with Neo-Pythagoreanism stand the so-called *Hermetic Literature* and the *Chaldaic Oracles*. The former is the name given to a type of "mystical" literature that arose in the first century A.D. and that may, or may not, owe a debt to previous Egyptian writings. The Greeks found in Hermes the Egyptian god Thoth, and their appellation "Hermes Trismegistos" is derived from the Egyptian "Great Thoth." But whatever be the truth concerning the supposed influence of Egyptian tradition on the Hermetic literature, the latter owes its main contents to earlier Greek philosophy, and seems to have been indebted particularly to Poseidonius. The fundamental notion expressed in this

[1] Clem. Alex., *Strom.*, 1, 22, 148. (*P.G.*, 8, 895.) [2] Cf. Plato, *Ep.*, 2.
[3] Procl. *in Tim.*, I, 303, 27 ff. [4] Chalcid., *in Tim.*, c. 295.

literature is that of *salvation through knowledge of God*—γνῶσις—a notion that played a great part in "Gnosticism." A similar doctrine of salvation formed the content of the Chaldaic Oracles, a poem that was composed about A.D. 200, and which, like the Hermetic literature, combines Orphic-Pythagorean, Platonic and Stoic elements.

In its close relation to the religious interest and needs of the time, and in the work of preparing the ground for Neo-Platonism, Neo-Pythagoreanism resembles Middle Platonism, to which we must now turn.

Note on Apollonius of Tyana

The rhetorician Philostratus undertook the composition of the life of Apollonius at the request of Julia Domna, second wife of Septimius Severus. The book was composed about A.D. 200. The story given by Philostratus about the Memoirs of Apollonius by his disciple Damis, an Assyrian, which are said to have been given to Julia Domna by a relative of Damis, is probably a literary fiction.[1] In any case the motive of Philostratus seems to have been that of representing Apollonius as a wise man, as a true servant of the gods and a miracle-worker, instead of the magician or conjurer depicted by Moeragenes in his *Memorabilia* of Apollonius.[2] There are indications that Philostratus knew and utilised the Gospels, Acts of the Apostles and Lives of the Saints, but it remains uncertain how far it was his conscious intention to substitute the ideal of a "Hellenistic Christ" for the Christian Christ: resemblances have been greatly exaggerated. If the intention of Philostratus remains obscure, so does the foundation of truth at the base of his narrative: it is practically impossible to say exactly what sort of a man the historic Apollonius actually was.

The work of Philostratus had a great success and led to a cult of Apollonius. Thus Caracalla raised a shrine to the wonder-worker,[3] while Alexander Severus included him in his *Lararium* along with his Penates, Abraham, Orpheus and Christ.[4] Aurelian spared the city of Tyana, which he had vowed to destroy, out of respect for the birthplace of Apollonius.[5] Eunapius honours him in his Lives of the Sophists,[6] while Ammianus Marcellinus,

[1] Cf. Ed. Meyer, *Hermes*, 197, pp. 371 ff.
[2] Orig., *Contra Celsum*, 6, 41 (*P.G.*, 11, 1357).
[3] Dion Cass., 77, 18.
[4] Lamprid., *Alex.*, 29.
[5] Lamprid., *Aurel.*, 24.
[6] Ed. Boissonade, p. 500, Didot.

companion of the Emperor Julian, cites him along with Plotinus as one of the privileged mortals who were visited by the *familiares genii.*[1]

Whatever the intention of Philostratus himself may have been, it is certain that the pagan apologists made use of the figure of Apollonius in their fight against Christianity. Thus Hierocles, Governor of Lower Egypt under Diocletian and a ferocious enemy of Christianity, tried to lessen the importance of the miracles of Christ by citing the "miracles" of Apollonius and tried to show the superiority of pagan wisdom in that they refrained from elevating Apollonius to the rank of God because of these miracles.[2] Porphyry also made use of Apollonius, citing his miracles and opposing his bold defiance of Domitian to the humiliations of Christ in His Passion.[3] St. Augustine bears testimony to this sort of apologetic exploitation of Apollonius on the part of the pagans.[4]

Towards the end of the fourth century Virius Nicomachus Flavianus, a pagan, translated Philostratus' book into Latin, and it was repolished by the grammarian Tascius Victorinus. It seems to have excited some interest in Christian circles, since Sidonius Apollinaris revised it also and speaks of Apollonius with great deference.[5]

[1] *Rerum gest.*, 21, 14, 5.
[2] Lact., *Div. Inst.*, V, 3; *P.L.* 6, 556 ff.
[3] St. Jerome, in Ps. 81 (*P.L.* 26, 1130).
[4] Cf. *Ep.*, 136, I; 102, 32; 138, 18.
[5] *Ep.*, 8, 3; ed. Mohr, p. 173.

CHAPTER XLIII
MIDDLE PLATONISM

WE have already seen how the Middle and New Academies inclined to scepticism, and how, when the Academy returned to dogmatism under Antiochus of Ascalon, the latter maintained the theory of the fundamental unity of the Platonic and Peripatetic philosophies. It is, therefore, not surprising to find Eclecticism as one of the leading characteristics of Middle Platonism. Platonists did not possess the lectures of Plato, but the more popular dialogues, and this fact made it more difficult for any rigid orthodoxy to assert itself: it was not as though the founder had left a systematised and carefully-articulated philosophic deposit, which could be passed on as the norm and canon of Platonism. There is no reason, then, to be astonished that Middle Platonism took over the Peripatetic logic, for example, since the Peripatetics had a more carefully-elaborated logical foundation than the Platonists possessed.

Platonism, no less than Neo-Pythagoreanism, felt the influence of contemporary religious interests and demands and the result was that Platonism borrowed from Neo-Pythagoreanism or developed germs latent in itself under the influence of the latter School. Hence we find in Middle Platonism the same insistence on the divine transcendence that we have already observed in Neo-Pythagoreanism, together with the theory of intermediary beings and a belief in mysticism.

On the other hand—and here again Middle Platonism was in line with the contemporary tendencies—much attention was devoted to the work of studying and commenting on the Platonic dialogues.[1] The result of this was a more intense reverence for the person and actual *dicta* of the founder and, consequently, a tendency to stress the differences between Platonism and the other philosophical systems. Thus we find writings directed against the Peripatetics and the Stoics. These two movements, the one towards philosophic "orthodoxy" and the other towards eclecticism, were obviously in conflict, and the consequence is

[1] The tetralogic arrangement of the Platonic Dialogues was attached to the name of Thrasyllus, the court-astronomer of Tiberius, who joined the Platonic School.

that Middle Platonism does not present the character of a unitary whole: different thinkers amalgamated the various elements in different ways. Middle Platonism is accordingly *Middle* Platonism; that is to say, it bears the mark of a transition-stage: it is only in Neo-Platonism that anything like a real synthesis and fusion of the various currents and tendencies can be found. Neo-Platonism is thus like the sea, to which the various contributing rivers are flowing and in which their waters are at length mingled.

1. The eclectic tendency of Middle Platonism and the orthodox tendency of the same School may be observed together in the thought of *Eudorus of Alexandria* (about 25 B.C.). In accordance with the *Theaetetus* (176 b) Eudorus affirmed that the end of philosophy is ὁμοίωσις θεῷ κατὰ τὸ δυνατόν. In this conception of the end of philosophy Socrates, Plato and Pythagoras are in agreement, said Eudorus. This shows the eclectic side of Eudorus' thought and, in particular, the influence of Neo-Pythagoreanism, in accordance with which he distinguished a threefold One or ἕν. The first is the supreme Godhead and is the ultimate source of being, and from Him proceeds the second ἕν (also called μονάς,, together with the ἀόριστος δυάς, the second ἕν being τεταγμένο), περιττόν, φῶς, etc., the ἀόριστος δυάς being ἄτακτον, ἄρτιον, σκότονς etc. But though Eudorus obviously felt the influence of Neo-Pythagoreanism and to this extent was eclectic, we learn that he composed a work against the Aristotelian κατηγορίαι, thus showing the "orthodox" as over against the eclectic tendency.

2. A prominent figure of Middle Platonism is the author of the celebrated lives of Greek and Roman worthies, *Plutarch of Chaeronea*. This distinguished man was born about A.D. 45 and was educated at Athens, where he was stimulated to mathematical studies by the Platonist Ammonius. He often visited Rome and was on terms of friendship with important personages in the imperial city. According to Suidas[1] the Emperor Trajan gave him the consular dignity and told the officials of Achaea to ask for Plutarch's approval for all their measures. Plutarch also became Archon Eponymos of his native city and was for some years priest to the Delphic Apollo. Besides the *Lives* and the *Moralia* Plutarch wrote commentaries on Plato (e.g. Πλατωνικὰ ζητήματα), books against the Stoics and the Epicureans (e.g. Περὶ Στοικῶν ἐναντιωμάτων and Ὅτι οὐδὲ ζῆν ἔστιν ἡδέως κατ' Ἐπίκουρον), works

[1] Suid., Πλούταρχος.

on psychology and astronomy, on ethics and on politics. To these must be added compositions on family life, on pedagogy and on religion (e.g. Περὶ τῶν ὑπὸ τοῦ θείου βραδέως τιμωρουμένων and Περὶ δεισιδαιμονίας). A number of works that pass under his name are not by Plutarch (e.g. the *Placita* and the Περὶ εἱμαρμένης).

Plutarch's thought was decidedly eclectic in character, for he was influenced not only by Plato but also by the Peripatetics, the Stoics and especially the Neo-Pythagoreans. Moreover, while on the one hand the scepticism of the Middle and New Academies led him to adopt a somewhat distrustful attitude towards theoretical speculation and a strong opposition to superstition (the latter due more, perhaps, to his desire for a purer conception of the Deity), he combined therewith a belief in prophecy and "revelation" and "enthusiasm." He speaks of an immediate intuition or contact with the Transcendental, which doubtless helped to prepare the way for the Plotinian doctrine of ecstasy.[1]

Plutarch aimed at a purer conception of God. "While we are here below, encumbered by bodily affections, we can have no intercourse with God save as in philosophic thought we may faintly touch Him, as in a dream. But when our souls are released, and have passed into the region of the pure, invisible, and changeless, this God will be the guide and king of those who depend on Him and gaze with insatiable longing on the beauty which may not be spoken of by the lips of man."[2] This desire for a purer conception of God led him to deny God's authorship of evil. Some other cause had to be found for the evil in the world, and this Plutarch found in the World-Soul. This is postulated as the cause of evil and imperfection in the world and is set over against God as the pure Good, so that a dualism is asserted of two principles, the good and the bad. The evil principle, however, seems to have become the divine World-Soul at creation by participating in, or being filled with, reason, which is an emanation from the Godhead. The World-Soul is therefore not destitute of reason and harmony, but on the other hand it continues to act as the evil principle and thus the dualism is maintained.

Since God, freed from all responsibility for evil, is elevated far above the world, it is but natural that Plutarch should introduce intermediary beings below God. Thus he accepted the star-gods and followed Xenocrates and Poseidonius in postulating a number

[1] *De Is. et Osir.*, 77.   [2] *De Is. et Osir.*, 78.

of "Demons" who form the connecting link between God and man. Some of these are more akin to God, others are tainted by the evil of the lower world.[1] Extravagant rites, barbarous and obscene sacrifices are really offered to the evil demons. The good demons are the instruments of Providence (on which Plutarch lays great stress). Plutarch, as I have already mentioned, professed himself a foe to superstition and condemned myths that were unworthy of God (like Poseidonius, he distinguished a threefold theology); but that did not prevent him from showing considerable sympathy for the popular religion. Thus according to him the various religions of mankind all worship the same God under different names, and he makes use of allegorical interpretation, in order to justify popular beliefs. For instance, in his *De Iside et Osiride* he tries to show that Osiris represents the good principle and Tryphon the bad principle, while Isis represents matter, which is not evil in Plutarch's view but, though neutral in itself, has a natural tendency and love for the Good.

Plutarch's psychology gives evidence of mythological and fantastic notions of the origin of the soul and its relation with the Demons, into which it is unnecessary to enter. One may, however, point out the dualism asserted between ψυχή and νοῦς, that is superimposed upon the soul-body dualism. Just as ψυχή is better and more divine than the body, so is νοῦς better and more divine than ψυχή, the latter being subject to passions, the former being the "Demon" in man and the element which should rule. Immortality is affirmed by Plutarch and he depicts the happiness of the after-life, when the soul not only attains to a knowledge of the truth but also enjoys once more the company of relatives and friends.[2] In his ethic the philosopher was clearly influenced by the Peripatetic tradition, since he emphasises the need of attaining the happy mean between ὑπερβολή and ἔλλειψις, excess and defect. To get rid of the affections is neither possible nor desirable; we should aim rather at moderation and the golden mean. Plutarch, however, follows the Stoics in permitting suicide, and he was influenced too by their Cosmopolitanism, especially when seen under the light of his experience of the Roman Empire. The ruler represents God.

The world was created in time, for this is necessitated by the principle of the soul's priority over the body and of God's priority

[1] *De Is. et Osir.*, 26. [2] *Non p. suav.*, 28 ff.; *De ser. num. vind.*, 18.

in regard to the world.[1] There are five elements (adding aether) and five worlds.[2]

3. *Albinus* (A.D. second century), a disciple of Gaius the Middle Platonist, distinguished the πρῶτος θεός, νοῦς and ψυχή. The πρῶτος θεός is unmoved (Aristotle) but is not mover, and he would appear to be identical with the ὑπερουράνιος θεός. The first god does not operate immediately—since he is unmoved but not mover—but operates through the Νοῦς or World-Intellect.[3] Between God and the world are the star-gods and others, οἱ γεννητοὶ θεοί. The Platonic Ideas are made eternal ideas of God and are patterns or exemplary causes of things: the Aristotelian εἴδη are subordinated to them as copies.[4] The conception of God as unmoved and as not acting through efficient causality is, of course, Aristotelian in origin, though elements in the conception of God are developments of Platonic doctrine, e.g. the transposition of the Ideas into Ideas of God, a doctrine which we have already met in Neo-Pythagoreanism. Albinus also makes use of the gradual elevation to God through the various degrees of beauty, an ascent suggested by Plato's *Symposium*, while the conception of the World-Soul is obviously to be connected with the *Timaeus*.[5] In this fusion of Platonic and Aristotelian elements Albinus, like Numenius the Neo-Pythagorean, helped to prepare the way for Neo-Platonism. His distinction of πρῶτος θεός, νοῦς and ψυχή was also a direct step on the way to the Neo-Platonic distinction of τὸ ἕν, νοῦς and ψυχή. (In his psychology and ethics Albinus combined Platonic, Aristotelian and Stoic elements, e.g. identifying the Stoic ἡγεμονικόν with the Platonic λογιστικόν, introducing the Aristotelian παθητικόν over against the λογιστικόν, distinguishing with Plato τὸ θυμικόν (Plat. θυμοειδές) and τὸ ἐπιθυμητικόν, making use of the Stoic οἰκείωσις, declaring the end of ethics to be the Platonic end of ὁμοίωσις θεῷ κατὰ τὸ δυνατόν, following the Stoics in making φρόνησις the first of the cardinal virtues and Plato in making δικαιοσύνη the general virtue, opposing the Stoic "Apathy" in favour of the Platonic- Aristotelian "Metriopathy." An eclectic indeed!)

4. Among other Middle Platonists we may mention *Apuleius* (b. *c.* A.D. 125), *Atticus* (*c.* A.D. 176), *Celsus* and *Maximus of Tyre* (*c.* A.D. 180). Atticus represented the more orthodox Platonic tradition in contrast to the eclectic tendency, as we have observed

[1] *De anim. procr.*, 4 ff.
[2] *De def. orac.*, 32 ff., 37; cf. Plat., *Tim.*, 31 a b, 34 b, 55 cd, where Plato opts for one world.
[3] *Didaskalikos*, 164, 21 ff. [4] *Didask.*, 163–4. [5] *Didask.*, 169, 26 ff.

it in Albinus. Thus he attacked Aristotle for neglecting Divine Providence, teaching the eternity of the world, and for denying immortality or not expressing it clearly. But he seems to have been influenced by Stoic doctrine, as he emphasises the Divine Immanence and stresses the all-sufficiency of virtue, in contrast to the Peripatetic doctrine that corporeal and external goods are necessary for happiness. He naturally maintained the Platonic Ideas, but, characteristically of his time, made them thoughts or ideas of God. In addition he identified the Demiurge of the *Timaeus* with the Form of the Good, and he attributed to matter an evil soul as its principle.

Celsus is best known to us as a determined opponent of Christianity: we are acquainted with the content of his Ἀληθὴς λόγος (written about A.D. 179) through Origen's reply to it. He emphasised God's utter transcendence and would not allow that the corporeal is the work of God. To bridge the gulf between God and the world he admitted "Demons," angels and heroes. God's Providence has the universe as its object and is not, as the Christians believe, anthropocentric.

A similar emphasis on the Divine Transcendence, together with the admission of inferior gods and demons, as also the referring of evil to matter, is found in the case of Maximus of Tyre (*c.* A.D. 180). Maximus speaks of the vision of the transcendent God. "Thou shalt see Him fully only when He calls thee, in age or death, but meantime glimpses of the Beauty which eye hath not seen nor can tongue speak of, may be won, if the veils and wrappings which hide His splendour be torn away. But do not thou profane Him by offering vain prayers for earthly things which belong to the world of chance or which may be obtained by human effort, things for which the worthy need not pray, and which the unworthy will not obtain. The only prayer which is answered is the prayer for goodness, peace, and hope in death."[1] The angels are servants of God and helpers of men; "thrice ten thousand are they upon the fruitful earth, immortal, ministers of Zeus."[2]

[1] *Diss.*, 17, 11: 11, 2 and 7. [2] *Diss.*, 14, 8.

CHAPTER XLIV

JEWISH-HELLENISTIC PHILOSOPHY

It was at Alexandria particularly that the influence of Greek speculation on the Jewish mind became most apparent, although traces of such influence may be seen in Palestine itself, as in the doctrine of the sect of the Essenes (mentioned by Josephus for the first time in his picture of the period of Jonathan the Hasmonaean, about 160 B.C.),[1] which shows Orphic-Pythagorean traits. For example, the Essenes maintained a clear dualism of soul and body, with which they coupled a belief, not only in the soul's survival after death but also in its pre-existence before birth. Blood-offerings and the consumption of flesh and wine were banned, and great importance was attached to the belief in angels or intermediary beings. Moreover it is a significant feature—even if not to be overstressed—that when Antiochus Epiphanes attempted a forcible Hellenisation of the Palestinian Jews, he was able to rely on a certain amount of support among the Jews themselves, though he encountered a determined opposition on the part of the more orthodox, who resolutely adhered to the tradition of their fathers and were naturally irreconcilable enemies of the moral abuses that they considered accompaniments of Hellenism. However, Alexandria, that great cosmopolitan city set on the confines of East and West, became the real centre of the Jewish-Hellenistic philosophy, which culminated in the thought of Philo. Away from their native home the Jews were naturally more prone to accept Greek influence, and this showed itself largely in an attempt to reconcile Greek philosophy with Jewish theology, an attempt that led on the one hand to the selection of those elements in Greek speculation that harmonised best with Jewish religion and on the other hand to the practice of allegorising the Jewish Scriptures and interpreting them in such a way that they would harmonise with Greek thought. Thus we even find Jews asserting that the great Greek philosophers were indebted to the Scriptures for their leading ideas. This notion is of course void of historical foundation as it concerns Plato, for instance, but it is symptomatic

[1] *Ant. Jud.*, 13, 5, 9.

of the syncretistic tendencies of the Hellenised Jews of the Empire.[1]

The chief figure of the Jewish-Hellenistic philosophy is *Philo of Alexandria*, who was born about 25 B.C. and died some time after A.D. 40, the year in which he was at Rome as ambassador of the Alexandrian Jews to the Emperor Gaius. We possess a large number of his works, though some have perished.[2]

Filled with admiration for the Greek philosophers Philo maintained that the same truth is to be found in both the Greek philosophy and Jewish Scriptures and tradition. While believing that the philosophers had made use of the Sacred Scriptures, he at the same time did not hesitate to interpret the Scriptures allegorically when he deemed it necessary. Thus in his work Ὅτι ἄτρεπτον τὸ θεῖον he shows that God cannot properly be said to move, since He is in no way corporeal. We must accordingly recognise two senses in the anthropomorphic passages of the Scriptures, a higher and non-anthropomorphic sense and a lower or anthropomorphic sense, which is suited to ordinary people. It might be supposed that this work of allegorisation and of discerning "higher" meanings would, if pushed far enough, lead to a denial of the necessity of observing literally the ceremonial precepts of the Law, at least for those who are capable of discerning the higher sense. But this Philo would not allow. Soul is above body, yet body is part of man; and though the allegorical sense is higher than the literal, we are not entitled to disregard the literal sense—rather should we pay heed to both letter and spirit. His intention was therefore not that of destroying or superseding Jewish orthodoxy but rather that of reconciling it with philosophy, while at the same time preserving the observance of the Law intact.[3]

God is personal, as the Jewish theology teaches, but He is at the same time Pure Being (τὸ ὄντως ὄν), absolutely simple (φύσις ἁπλῆ), free and self-sufficient.[4] He does not occupy space or place but rather contains all things within Himself.[5] Yet He is absolutely transcendent, transcending even the Idea of the Good and

[1] Consideration of the question, What influence was exercised by Greek speculation on Jewish Apocryphal writings and even on certain books of the O.T. itself, is here omitted.

[2] Cf. Euseb., *Hist. Eccles.*, 2, 18. References to the works of Philo are given according to the edition of Leopold Cohen and Paul Wendland, Berlin (Vol. 6, Cohen and Reiter).

[3] Cf. *De migrat. Abrah.*, 16, 92.

[4] Cf. *De post. Caini*, 48, 167; *Leg. alleg.*, 2, 1, 2 f.; *De Mutat nom.*, 4, 27.

[5] *De conf. ling.*, 27, 136; *De somniis*, I, 11; 63.

the Idea of Beauty (αὐτὸ τὸ ἀγαθὸν καὶ αὐτὸ τὸ καλόν).[1] Man attains to God, not through scientific understanding (λόγων ἀποδείξει)—"In order to comprehend God we must first become God, which is impossible"[2]—but in immediate intuition (ἐνάργειᾳ).[3] God is thus ineffable Being, Who is above thought and can be attained only through ecstasy or intuition. We see how Philo was influenced by the contemporary tendency to exalt the Divine Transcendence—though we must not forget that the transcendence of the Divine Being was clearly maintained in Jewish scriptural theology, even if not expressed in philosophic terminology.

This insistence on the Divine Transcendence and on God's elevation above everything material not unnaturally led, as later on, for example, in Albinus the Middle Platonist and Numenius the Neo-Pythagorean, to the conception of intermediary beings, in order to bridge the gulf between God Himself and the material cosmos. The highest of these intermediary beings is the Logos or Nous. The Logos is spoken of as the first-born of God, being πρεσβύτατος καὶ γενικώτατος τῶν ὅσα γέγονε.[4] The Logos is for Philo definitely inferior to God and is to be placed in the rank of ὅσα γέγονε, which includes many other beings besides the Logos, even if the latter has the primacy. The Philonic conception of the Logos is therefore not identical with the dogma of the Logos as maintained in Christian theology, even if it influenced early Christian thinkers. Sometimes indeed the Logos seems to be conceived as an aspect of God, but even in this case there would still be a clear distinction between the Philonic and the Christian idea of the Logos. It has been well said, that Philo wavered between "Monarchianism" and "Arianism" but never asserted "Athanasianism"—provided, of course, that it is understood that in the Philonic doctrine of the Logos there is no reference to an historic Man. The Platonic Ideas are placed in the Logos, so that the Logos is the Τόπος or place in which the ideal world (ὁ ἐκ τῶν ἰδεῶν κόσμος) is situated.[5] In this conception Philo is at one with Neo-Pythagoreanism, which placed the Ideas in Nous. (Numenius was influenced by the Philonic philosophy.) Generally speaking Philo speaks simply of the Logos, though he distinguishes two aspects or functions of Logos, ὁ λόγος ἐνδιάθετος and ὁ λόγος προφορικός, the first consisting in the immaterial world of the

[1] *De opif. mundi.*, 2, 8. [2] Frag. a 654. [3] *De post. Caini*, 48, 167.
[4] *Leg. alleg.*, 3, 61, 175. [5] *De opif. mundi.*, 4, 17 ff.

Ideas, the second in the visible things of this world, in so far as they are copies of the immaterial Ideas.[1] This division of the Logos corresponds to the vision in man between the λόγος ἐνδιάθετος or faculty of reason itself and the λόγος προφορικός or spoken word, which proceeds from the λόγος ἐνδιάθετος as the stream from its source. An example of Philo's allegorising is to be found in the fact that he discovers a symbol of this twofold Logos in the double breastplate of the High Priest. The Logos is God's instrument in the formation of the world, and Philo found a reference to this in the words of the Pentateuch, καὶ ἐποίησεν ὁ θεὸς τὸν ἄνθρωπον κατ εἰκόνα θεοῦ.[2]

It is to be noted that, when the Old Testament mentions the angel of God in describing the theophanies, Philo identifies the angel with the Logos, just as, when several angels are mentioned, he identifies them with the Powers (see below). This Logos is an incorporeal substance, the immaterial Word or Voice of God; but, in so far as it is conceived as really distinct from God, it is conceived as subordinate to God, as God's instrument. Philo utilised, not only the conception of the Divine Wisdom, as found in the Sapiential Books, but also Platonic exemplarism (the Logos is the image, the shadow, of God and is itself the exemplar of creation) and Stoic themes (the Logos is the immanent, yet at the same time, transcendent, principle of law in the world and organising bond of creatures); but the general conception seems to be that of a descending scale of being. In other words, the Philonic Logos, so far as it is really distinct from the ultimate Godhead, Yahweh, is a subordinate and intermediary being, through which God expresses Himself and acts: it is not the consubstantial Word of the Father, the Second Person of the Blessed Trinity. The Philonic philosophy, in respect to the Logos, is more akin to Neo-Platonism than to Christian Trinitarianism.[3]

Besides the Logos there are other Powers (δύναμεις) or intermediary beings subordinate to God, such as ἡ ποιητική and ἡ βασσλική or κύριος (sometimes named ἀγαθότης and ἐξουσία), ἡ προνοητική, ἡ νομοθητική, etc. But just as Philo seems to have wavered between conceiving the Logos as an aspect of God and conceiving it as an independent being, so he wavered between conceiving the other Powers as attributes or powers of God,

[1] *Quod Deus sit immut.*, 7, 34; cf. *De vita Mos.*, 2 (3), 13, 127.
[2] *De opif. mundi.*, 6, 25.
[3] On this subject, cf. Jules Lebreton, S.J., *Histoire du Dogme de la Trinité.* (Beauchesne, 1910.)

corresponding to the Ideas (i.e. as operative functions of the Ideas) and conceiving them as relatively independent beings. They all appear to be comprehended in the Logos, but this does not help much in settling the question as to their personality or lack of it. If the Logos is conceived as an aspect of God, then the Powers will be qualities or ideas of God, while if the Logos is conceived as a relatively independent being, subordinate to God, then the Powers may be minor subordinate beings or forces; but it does not appear that Philo ever came to a settled or clear decision on the matter. Dr. Praechter can thus say, that "Philo wavers between two conceptions, the 'Analoga' of which recur in the Christian Church as Monarchianism and Arianism; but a doctrine analogous to that of Athanasius is wholly foreign to him and would contradict both his religious and his philosophic consciousness."[1] Moreover, it does not require much thought to recognise that the Philonic philosophy could never admit the Christian doctrine of the Incarnation—at least if Philonism were to remain self-consistent—since it lays such stress on the Divine Transcendence that direct "contact" with matter is excluded. It is indeed perfectly true that Christianity itself insists on the Divine Transcendence and that the Incarnation is a mystery; but on the other hand the spirit of the Christian attitude towards matter is not that of the Philonic or Neo-Platonic philosophies.

Influenced by Platonism, Philo maintains a sharp dualism of soul and body or of the rational and sensual elements in man, and insists on the necessity of man's liberating himself from the power of the sensual.[2] Virtue is the only true good, and in regard to the passions apathy is to be aimed at. But though Philo was influenced by Stoic and Cynic ethical teaching, he emphasised trust in God rather than trust in oneself. Virtue then is to be pursued and man's task is to attain the greatest possible likeness to God.[3] This is an interior task and so public life is discouraged because of its distracting influence, while science is to be pursued only so far as it is an aid to the soul's inner life. In this development there are stages, for above conceptual knowledge of God is to be ranked heavenly wisdom or the immediate intuition of the ineffable Godhead. The passive state of ecstasy thus becomes the highest stage of the soul's life on earth, as it was later to be in the Neo-Platonic philosophy.[4]

[1] Ueb.-P., p. 577.
[2] E.g. *De somn.*, 123, 149.
[3] *De opif. mundi.*, 50, 144; *De human.*, 23, 168.
[4] Cf. *Quis rer. div. her.*, 14, 68 ff.; *De gigant.*, II, 52 f.

While Philo's influence on early Christian thought has doubtless been exaggerated,[1] it will be recognised that Philonism helped to prepare the way for Neo-Platonism through its insistence on the utter Transcendence of God, the existence of intermediary beings, and the soul's ascent to God culminating in ecstasy.

[1] It is probable, however, that Origen's habit of allegorising is due in large measure to Philo.

CHAPTER XLV
PLOTINIAN NEO-PLATONISM

1. *Life of Plotinus*

THE birthplace of Plotinus is uncertain, since it is given as Lycon by Eunapius and as Lycopolis by Suidas.[1] In any case he was born in Egypt about A.D. 203 or 204 (Porphyry gives 205/6). Plotinus, we are told by Porphyry, attended the lectures of various professors at Alexandria in turn, but did not find what he was looking for until he came upon Ammonius Saccas, when he was about twenty-eight. He remained a pupil of Ammonius until the year 242 when he joined the Persian expedition of the Emperor Gordian, in order to make the acquaintance of Persian philosophy. However, the expedition came to grief when Gordian was assassinated in Mesopotamia, and Plotinus made his way to Rome where he arrived in his fortieth year. At Rome he opened a school and soon came to enjoy the favour of the highest officials, even of the Emperor Gallienus and his wife. Plotinus conceived the notion of founding a city, Platonopolis, in the Campagna, which was to be the concrete realisation of Plato's Republic, and he seems to have obtained the Emperor's consent to the project; but for some reason or other the Emperor withdrew his consent after a while and so the plan fell through.

When Plotinus was about sixty years old he received as a pupil the celebrated Porphyry, who afterwards wrote the life of the Master whom he so greatly admired. It was Porphyry who attempted to arrange the writings of Plotinus in systematic form, dividing them into six books, each of which contained nine chapters. Hence the name *Enneads*, which is applied to the works of Plotinus. Although the philosopher is said to have had a pleasant and eloquent oral style, his written composition was somewhat difficult and the difficulty was not lessened by the fact that his weak eyesight prevented him from correcting the manuscript. Porphyry had therefore no easy task to start with, and as he made a point of preserving the style of the writer, Plotinus' treatises have always been a source of difficulty to later editors.

At Rome, Plotinus was frequently approached for help and

[1] Eunap., *Vit. Soph.*, 6; Porph., *Isag.*, 12b; Suid., *Plot.*

advice, and so exercised the office of a sort of "spiritual director." Moreover he took into his house orphaned children and acted as their guardian—an example of his kindness and amiability. He made many friends and no enemies, and though his personal life was ascetic, he was gentle and affectionate in character. We are told that he was somewhat diffident and nervous, a fact that tended to show itself in his lectures. He led a deep spiritual life and Porphyry relates that his Master experienced ecstatic union with God four times in the six years in which he was his disciple.[1] Plotinus did not enjoy strong health, and his infirmities had a fatal termination in A.D. 269/70, when he died at a country-house in the Campagna. Porphyry was at that time in Sicily, whither he had gone on Plotinus' advice, in order to recover from a state of melancholy and depression into which he had fallen; but a friend of Plotinus, the physician Eustochius, arrived from Puteoli in time to hear the philosopher's last words: "I was waiting for you, before that which is divine in me departs to unite itself with the Divine in the universe."

Although Plotinus attacked the Gnostics, he is silent about Christianity, which he must have known to some extent. But though he never became a Christian, he was a resolute witness to spiritual and moral ideals, not only in his writings but also in his own life, and it was the spiritual idealism of his philosophy that enabled it to exercise such an influence on the great Latin doctor, St. Augustine of Hippo.

II. *Doctrine of Plotinus*

God is absolutely transcendent: He is the One, beyond all thought and all being, ineffable and incomprehensible, οὗ μὴ λόγος, μηδὲ ἐπιστήμη, ὃ δὴ καὶ ἐπέκεινα λέγεται εἶναι οὐσίας.[2] Neither essence nor being nor life can be predicated of the One, not of course that it is less than any of these things but because it is *more*, τὸ ὑπὲρ πάντα ταῦτα εἶναι.[3] The One cannot be identical with the sum of individual things, for it is these individual things which require a Source or Principle, and this Principle must be distinct from them and logically prior to them. (We might say that, however much you increase the number of contingent things, you cannot thus arrive at a Necessary Being.)

[1] Ἔτυχε δὲ τετράκις που, ὅτε συνήμην αὐτῷ, τοῦ σκόπου, ἐνεργείᾳ ἀρρήτῳ, καὶ οὐ δυνάμει. *Plotini Vita*, 23, 138

[2] *Enn.*, 5 4, 1 (516 b–c).

[3] *Enn.*, 3, 8, 9 (352 b).

Moreover, if the One were identical with each individual thing taken separately, then each thing would be identical with every other and the distinction of things, which is an obvious fact, would be illusion. "Thus the One cannot be any existing thing, but is prior to all existents."[1] The One of Plotinus is not, therefore, the One of Parmenides, a monistic principle, but is the One, whose transcendence we have seen emphasised in Neo-Pythagoreanism and Middle Platonism. Indeed, just as Albinus had set the πρῶτος θεός above νοῦς and distinguished the ὑπερουράνιος θεός from the ἐπουράνιος θεός, and as Numenius had set the πρῶτος θεός above the Demiurge, and as Philo had set God above the world-forming Powers, so Plotinus sets the ultimate Deity, the One or πρῶτος θεός,, beyond being, ἐπέκεινα τῆς οὐσίας.[2] This does not mean, however, that the One is nothing or non-existent; rather does it mean that the One transcends all being of which we have experience. The concept of being is drawn from the objects of our experience, but the One transcends all those objects and consequently transcends also the concept that is founded on those objects.

Since God is one, without any multiplicity or division, there can be in the One no duality of substance and accident, and Plotinus is accordingly unwilling to ascribe to God any positive attributes. We should not say that the One is "thus" or "not thus," for if we say this we thereby delimit it and make it a particular thing, whereas in reality, it is beyond all things which can be delimited by such predication, ἄλλο τοίνυν παρὰ ἅπαντα τὸ οὕτως.[3] Nevertheless, Goodness may be attributed to the One, provided that it is not attributed as an inhering quality. God is accordingly *The Good* rather than "good."[4] Moreover, we can legitimately ascribe to the One neither thought nor will nor activity. Not thought, since thought implies a distinction between the thinker and the object of his thought;[5] not will, since this also implies distinction: not activity, for then there would be a distinction between the agent and the object on which he acts. God is the One, beyond all distinctions whatsoever: He cannot even distinguish Himself from Himself, and so is beyond self-consciousness. Plotinus allows, as we have seen, the predicates of unity and goodness to be ascribed to God (in the sense that God is the

[1] *Enn.*, 3, 8, 8 (351 d). [2] Cf. *Rep.*, 509 b 9. [3] *Enn.*, 6, 8, 9 (743 e).

[4] *Enn.*, 6, 7, 38.

[5] *Enn.*, 3, 8, 8. Εἰ οὖν τοῦτο νοῦν ἐγγένησεν, ἁπλούστερον νοῦ δεῖ αὐτὸ εἶναι (351 c).

One and the Good); yet he stresses the fact that even these predicates are inadequate and can be applied to God only analogously. For unity expresses the denial of plurality and goodness expresses an effect on something else. All we can say is that the One is—though, indeed, God is beyond being, One, indivisible, unchanging, eternal, without past or future, a constant self-identity.

On this view of God, the ultimate Principle, how can Plotinus account for the multiplicity of finite things? God cannot limit Himself to finite things, as though they were part of Him; nor can He create the world by a free act of His Will, since creation is an activity and we are not justified in ascribing activity to God and so impairing His unchangeability. Plotinus, therefore, had recourse to the metaphor of emanation. But although he makes use of metaphorical terms like ῥεῖν and ἀπορρεῖν, Plotinus expressly rejects the notion that God becomes in any way less through the process of emanation: He remains untouched, undiminished, unmoved. A free creative act would imply that God issues forth from His state of tranquil self-containedness, and this Plotinus would not admit: he maintained, then, that the world issues from God or proceeds from God by necessity, there being a principle of necessity that the less perfect should issue from the more perfect. It is a principle that every nature should make that which is immediately subordinate to it (τὸ μετ' αὐτὴν ποιεῖν), unfolding itself, as a seed unfolds itself, the procession being from an undivided source or principle to a goal in the universe of sense. The prior Principle, however, remains always in its own place (μένοντος μὲν ἀεὶ τοῦ προτέρου ἐν τῇ οἰκείᾳ ἕδρᾳ), the consequent being engendered out of an ineffable power (ἐκ δυνάμεως ἀφάτου) which is in the prior Principles, it being unfitting that this power should be stayed in its operation by any jealousy or selfishness.[1] (Plotinus also uses the metaphors περίλαμψις, ἔλλαμψις; likening the One to the sun, which illuminates, itself undiminished. He also employs the comparison of the mirror, since the object which is mirrored is reduplicated, yet without itself undergoing any change or any loss.)

We have, therefore, to be careful, if we wish to make the

[1] *Enn.*, 4, 8, 6 (474 b–c). The assertion that the prior Principle is not stayed by jealousy is an echo of Plato's words in the *Timaeus*. Plotinus' comparison of the One or the Good with the sun is a development of the comparison already given by Plato in the *Republic*. The view of God as the uncreated Light and of creatures as participated lights, hierarchically ordered according to their degree of luminosity, which we find in some Christian philosophers comes from Neo-Platonism.

statement that the process of emanation in Plotinus is pantheistic in character. It is quite true that for Plotinus the world proceeds from God *secundum necessitatem naturae* and that he rejects free creation *ex nihilo*; but it should also be remembered that for him the prior Principle remains "in its own place," undiminished and unimpaired, always transcending the subordinate being. The truth of the matter would seem to be that, while rejecting free creation out of nothing on the ground that this would involve change in God, Plotinus equally rejects a fully pantheistic self-canalisation of the Deity in individual creatures, a self-diremption of God. In other words he tries to steer a middle course between theistic creation on the one hand and a fully pantheistic or monistic theory on the other hand. We may well think that (since an ultimate dualism does not enter into the question) no such compromise is possible; but that is no reason for calling Plotinus a pantheist without due qualification.

The first emanation from the One is Thought or Mind, Νοῦς, which is intuition or immediate apprehension, having a twofold object, (*a*) the One, (*b*) itself. In Nous exist the Ideas, not only of classes but also of individuals,[1] though the whole multitude of Ideas is contained indivisibly in Nous. (τὴν δὲ ἐν τῶ νοητῷ ἀπειρίαν, οὐ δεῖ δεδιέναι . πᾶσα γὰρ ἐν ἀμερεῖ, καὶ οἷον προείσιν, ὅταν ἐνεργῇ.) Nous is identified with the Demiurge of the Platonic *Timaeus*, and Plotinus uses the phrase πατὴρ τοῦ αἰτίου of the One, identifying the αἴτιον with the Nous and the Demiurge. That Nous is itself ὁ κόσμος νοητός[2] is a point insisted on by Plotinus against Longinus, who had made the Ideas to be apart from Nous, appealing to the *Timaeus* of Plato, where the Ideas are depicted as being distinct from the Demiurge. (Porphyry held the same opinion as Longinus, until Plotinus persuaded him to change it.) It is in Nous, therefore, that multiplicity first appears, since the One is above all multiplicity, above even the distinction of νοεῖν and νοητόν; yet the distinction in Nous is not to be understood absolutely, for it is one and the same Nous that is both τὸ νοοῦν and τὸ νούμενον. The Demiurge of Plato and the νόησις νοήσεως of Aristotle thus come together in the Plotinian Nous. Nous is eternal and beyond time, its state of blessedness being not an acquired state but an eternal possession. Nous

[1] *Enn.*, 5, 7, 1 ff.

[2] *Enn.*, 5, 9, 9. ἀναγκαῖον καὶ ἐν νῷ τὸ ἀρχέτυπον πᾶν εἶναι, καὶ κόσμον νοητὸν τοῦτον τὸν νοῦν εἶναι, ὃν φησὶν ὁ Πλάτων, ἐν τῷ ὅ ἐστι ζῷον.

enjoys, therefore, that eternity which time does but mimic.[1] In the case of Soul its objects are successive, now Socrates, now a horse, now some other thing; but Nous knows all things together, having neither past nor future but seeing all in an eternal present.

From Nous, which is Beauty, proceeds Soul, corresponding to the World-Soul of the *Timaeus*. This World-Soul is incorporeal and indivisible, but it forms the connecting-link between the super-sensual world and the sensual world, and so looks not only upwards to the Nous but also downwards towards the world of nature. Whereas Plato, however, had posited only one World-Soul, Plotinus posited two, a higher and a lower, the former standing nearer to Nous and being in no immediate contact with the material world, the latter (γέννημα ψυχῆς προτέρας) being the real soul of the phenomenal world. This second soul Plotinus termed nature or φύσις.[2] Moreover, although the phenomenal world owes all the reality it possesses to its participation in the Ideas, which are in Nous, these Ideas do not operate in the sensible world and have no direct connection with it, so that Plotinus posited reflections of the Ideas in the World-Soul, calling them λόγοι σπερματικοί and saying that they are comprised within the λόγος—an obvious adoption of Stoic doctrine. In order to fit in this conception with his distinction of two World-Souls, he further distinguished πρῶτοι λόγοι, comprised within the higher Soul, from the derivate λόγοι, comprised within the lower Soul.[3]

Individual human souls proceed from the World-Soul, and, like the World-Soul, they are subdivided into two elements (in accordance with the Pythagorean-Platonic tripartition Plotinus admits also a third and mediating element), a higher element which belongs to the sphere of Nous (cf. the Aristotelian Nous) and a lower element, which is directly connected with the body. The soul pre-existed before its union with the body, which is represented as a fall, and survives the death of the body, though apparently without memory of the period of earthly existence. (Transmigration is also admitted.) But although Plotinus speaks of individual souls as bound together in the unity of the World-Soul,[4] he is not prepared to deny personal immortality: the soul is real and nothing that is real will perish. Can we suppose that Socrates, who existed as Socrates on this earth, will cease to be

[1] *Enn.*, 5, 1, 4. ὁ ὄντως αἰὼν ὃ μιμεῖται χρόνος περιθέων ψυχὴν (485 b).
[2] *Enn.*, 3, 8, 3. ἡ λεγομένη φύσις ψυχὴ οὖσα γέννημα ψυχῆς προτέρας (345 e).
[3] *Enn.*, 4, 3, 10; 5, 9, 3; 5, 9, 9; 2, 3, 17.
[4] *Enn.*, 3, 5, 4. οὐκ ἀποτετμημένη, ἐμπεριεχομένη δὲ, ὡς εἶναι πάσας μίαν.

Socrates, just because he has reached the best of all abodes? In the after-life, therefore, each individual soul will persist, each remaining one, yet all being one together.[1]

Below the sphere of Soul is that of the material world. In accord with his conception of the emanative process as radiation of light, Plotinus pictures light as proceeding from the centre and passing outwards, growing gradually dimmer, until it shades off into that total darkness which is matter-in-itself, conceived as the privation of light, as στέρησις.[2] Matter, then, proceeds from the One (ultimately), in the sense that it becomes a factor in creation only through the process of emanation from the One; but in itself, at its lowest limit, it forms the lowest stage of the universe and is the antithesis to the One. In so far as it is illumined by form and enters into the composition of material objects (Aristotle's ὕλη) it cannot be said to be complete darkness; but in so far as it stands over against the intelligible and represents the ἀνάγκη of the *Timaeus*, it is unilluminated, darkness. Plotinus thus combined Platonic with Aristotelian themes, for though he adopted the Platonic conception of matter as ἀνάγκη, as the antithesis to the intelligible, as the privation of light, he also adopted the Aristotelian conception of matter as the substrate of form, as an integral component of material objects. The transmutation of one element into another shows that there must be some substrate of bodies, which is distinct from the bodies themselves.[3] If we consider bodies and make complete abstraction of form, then the residuum is what we mean by matter.[4] Matter is thus partially illuminated by its information and does not exist separately in the concrete as complete darkness, the principle of not-being. Moreover, just as the phenomenal world in general has its pattern in the intelligible, so does matter in nature correspond to a νοητὴ ὕλη.[5]

In addition to this fusion of Platonic and Aristotelian cosmological themes Plotinus asserts the Orphic and Neo-Pythagorean view of matter as the principle of evil. At its lowest grade, as devoid of quality, as unilluminated privation, it is evil itself (not, however, having evil as an inhering quality any more than the Good has goodness as an inhering quality), and so stands over against the Good as its radical antithesis. (The evil of matter does

[1] *Enn.*, 4, 3, 5 (375 c–f).
[2] *Enn.*, 2, 4; 3, 67; 6, 3, 7
[3] *Enn.*, 2, 4, 6 (162 c–e).
[4] *Enn.*, 1, 8, 9 (79 a b)
[5] *Enn.*, 2, 4, 4–5; 3, 5, 6 (ὕλην δεῖ νοητὴν ὑποθέσθαι, 296 e).

not, of course, pertain to the νοητὴ ὕλη.) Plotinus thus comes perilously near to asserting a dualism which would be opposed to the real character of his system, though it must be remembered that matter itself is privation and not a positive principle. In any case we might suppose that Plotinus would be led logically to depreciate the visible universe, though in point of fact he does not do so. It is true that a certain tendency to depreciate the visible universe does show itself in his psychological and ethical teaching; but this is offset, so far as his cosmology is concerned, by his insistence on the unity and harmony of the cosmos. Plotinus opposed the Gnostic contempt for the world and praised the latter as the work of the Demiurge and the World-Soul: it is an eternal and unified creature, bound together in a harmony of parts, governed by Divine Providence. He expressly says that we must not allow that the universe is an evil creation, in spite of all the vexatious things that are in it. It is the image of the intelligible, but it is too much to demand that it should be the precise counterpart of the intelligible. What cosmos, he asks, could be better than the one we know, with the exception of the intelligible cosmos?[1] The material world is the exteriorisation of the intelligible, and the sensible and the intelligible are bound together for ever, the former reproducing the latter according to the measure of its capacity.[2] This universal harmony and cosmic unity form the rational basis for prophecy and for the magical influencing of superhuman powers. (Besides the star-gods Plotinus admitted other "gods" and "demons," which are invisible to man.)

In his psychology Plotinus assigns three parts to the individual soul. The highest of these (corresponding to the Nous of Aristotle) is uncontaminated by matter and remains rooted in the intelligible world,[3] but in so far as the soul enters into real union with the body, to form the compositum (τὸ κοινόν), it is contaminated by matter, and so there follows the necessity of an ethical ascent, with the θεῷ ὁμοιωθῆναι as the proximate goal and union with the One as the ultimate goal. In this ascent the ethical element (πρᾶξις) is subservient to the theoretical or intellectual element (θεωρία), as in Aristotle. The first stage of the ascent, undertaken under the impulse of Eros (cf. Plato's *Symposium*) consists in κάθαρσις, the process of purification by which man frees himself from the dominion of the body and the senses

[1] *Enn.*, 2, 9, 4 (202 d–e). [2] *Enn.*, 4, 8, 6 (474 d–e). [3] *Enn.*, 4, 8, 8 (476 a–d).

and rises to the practice of the πολιτικαὶ ἀρεταί, by which Plotinus means the four cardinal virtues. (The highest of these is Φρόνησις.[1]) Secondly the soul must rise above sense-perception, turning towards Nous and occupying herself with philosophy and science.[2] A higher stage, however, carries the soul beyond discursive thought to union with Nous which Plotinus characterises as πρώτως καλός. In this union the soul retains her self-consciousness. But all these stages are but a preparation for the final stage, that of mystical union with God or the One (Who transcends beauty) in an ecstasy characterised by the absence of all duality. In thought *of* God or *about* God the Subject is separated from the Object; but in ecstatic union there is no such separation. "There shall a man see, as seeing may be in Heaven, both God and himself: himself made radiant, filled with the intelligible light, or rather grown one with that light in its purity, without burden or any heaviness, transfigured to godhead, nay, being in essence God. For that hour he is enkindled; but when once more he is become heavy, it is as though the fire were quenched." "That sight is hard to put into words. For how should a man bring back report of the Divine, as of a thing distinct, when in the seeing he knew it not distinct but one with his own consciousness?"[3] (Needless to say, the ascent to God is not meant to imply that God is spatially present "out there." In meditation on God it is not necessary to cast one's thought outwards, as though God were present in any one place in such a way that He leaves other places destitute of Himself.[4] On the contrary, God is everywhere present. He is "outside" no one but is present to all, even if they know it not.[5]) This ecstatic union is, however, of brief duration so far as this life is concerned: we look for its complete and permanent possession in the future state, when we are freed from the hindrance of the body. "He will lapse again from the vision: but let him again awaken the virtue which is in him, again know himself made perfect in splendour; and he shall again be lightened of his burden, ascending through virtue to the Intelligence, and thence through wisdom to the Supreme. This is the life of gods and of the godlike and happy among men; a quittance from things alien and earthly, a life beyond earthly pleasure, a flight of the alone to the Alone."[6]

[1] *Enn.*, 1, 2, 1.
[2] *Enn.*, 1, 3, 4.
[3] *Enn.*, 6, 9, 9 (768 f–769 a); 6, 9, 10 (769 d). (Professor Dodds' translation.)
[4] *Enn.*, 6, 9, 7 (765 c).
[5] *Enn.*, 6, 9, 7 (766 a).
[6] *Enn.*, 6, 9, 11 (771 b). (Professor Dodds' translation.)

In the system of Plotinus, then, the Orphic-Platonic-Pythagorean strain of "otherworldliness," intellectual ascent, salvation through assimilation to and knowledge of God, reach their most complete and systematic expression. Philosophy now includes, not only logic, cosmology, psychology, metaphysics and ethics, but also the theory of religion and mysticism: in fact, since the highest type of knowledge is the mystical knowledge of God and since Plotinus, who most probably based his theory of mysticism on his own experience as well as on past speculation, evidently regards mystical experience as the supreme attainment of the true philosopher, we may say that in Plotinian Neo-Platonism philosophy tends to pass into religion—at least it points beyond itself: speculation does not set itself up as the ultimate goal to be achieved. This made it possible for Neo-Platonism to act as a rival to Christianity, though on the other hand its complicated philosophic system and its "anhistorical" spirit prevented it from proving the rival that it might have been: it lacked the popular appeal exercised by the mystery religions, for instance. Neo-Platonism was really the intellectualist reply to the contemporary yearning for personal salvation, those spiritual aspirations of the individual, which are so marked a feature of the period. "Truly the words of counsel 'Let us flee to our own fatherland,'[1] might be uttered with a deep meaning. The Fatherland to us is that place from whence we came; and in that place is the Father."[2] Christianity, rooted in history, combining popular appeal with a growing speculative background, insistence on the Beyond with a sense of a mission to be accomplished in the Here, mystical communion with ethical probity, asceticism with a consecration of the natural, would have a far wider and deeper appeal than the transcendental philosophy of the Neo-Platonists or the fashionable devotions of the mystery cults. Yet, from the point of view of Christianity itself, Neo-Platonism had an important function to fulfil, that of contributing to the intellectual statement of the Revealed Religion, and so the convinced Christian cannot but look with sympathy, and a certain reverence, on the figure of Plotinus, to whom the greatest of the Latin Fathers (and so the Universal Church) owed no inconsiderable debt.

III. *School of Plotinus*

The tendency to increase the intermediary beings between

[1] *Iliad*, 2, 140. [2] *Enn.*, 1, 6, 8 (56 g). (Professor Dodds' translation.)

God and corporeal objects is already observable in Plotinus' disciple *Amelius*, who distinguished three hypostases in Nous, namely τὸν ὄντα, τὸν ἔχοντα, and τὸν ὁρωντα.[1] A more important philosopher, however, was *Porphyry of Tyre* (A.D. 232/3—after 301), who joined Plotinus in Rome in 262/3. Porphyry's life of his master I have already mentioned: in addition to this he wrote a great number of other works and on a great variety of subjects, his most celebrated book being his *Isagoge* or introduction to the *Categories* of Aristotle. This was translated into Latin (e.g. by Boethius), Syrian, Arabic and Armenian and exercised great influence, not only in Antiquity but on into the Middle Ages, being itself made the subject of many commentaries. The work treats of 'Αι πέντε φωναί—genus (γένος), species (εἶδος), difference (διαφορά), property (ἴδιον) and accident (συμβεβηκός). Porphyry composed many other commentaries both on Plato (e.g. on the *Timaeus*) and on Aristotle (mainly on his logical works), and tried to show—in his Περὶ τοῦ μίαν εἶναι τὴν Πλάτωνος 'Αριστοτέλους αἵρεσιν—that the Platonic and Aristotelian philosophies are in essential agreement.

Porphyry set himself to propound the doctrine of Plotinus in a clear and comprehensible manner, but he laid more stress on the practical and religious sides than even Plotinus had done. The end of philosophy is salvation (ἡ τῆς ψυχῆς σωτερία), and the soul must purify itself by turning its attention from what is lower to what is higher, a purification to be accomplished by asceticism and knowledge of God. The lowest stage of virtue consists in the practice of the πολιτικαὶ ἀρεταί, which are essentially "metriopathic" virtues, i.e. consisting in the reduction of the affections of the soul to the golden mean under the dominion of reason, and concerning man's intercourse with his fellow men. Above these virtues stand the cathartic or purifying virtues, which aim rather at "Apathy." This is realised in the πρὸς θεὸν ὁμοίωσις. In the third stage of virtue the soul turns towards Nous (for Porphyry evil does not lie in the body as such but rather in the soul's conversion to inferior objects of desire),[2] while the highest stage of virtue, that of the παραδειγματικαὶ ἀρεταί, belongs to the νοῦς as such. The four cardinal virtues recur at each stage, but of course at different degrees of elevation. In order to facilitate the soul's ascent Porphyry stresses the need for ascetic practices, such as abstinence from flesh-meat, celibacy, abstinence from theatrical

[1] Procl., *in Plat. Tim.*, I, 306, 1 ff. [2] *Ad Marcellam*, 29.

performances, etc. Positive religion occupies an important place in his philosophy. While issuing a warning against the misuse of divination and other such superstitions (which he, however, accepted and permitted in themselves, since he believed in demonology), Porphyry at the same time lent his support to the popular and traditional religion, making the pagan myths allegorical representations of philosophic truth. He insisted on the importance of works, affirming that God does not prize the wise man's words, but his deeds.[1] The truly pious man is not for ever at prayer and sacrifice, but practises his piety in works: God does not accept a man for his reputation or for the empty formulae he employs, but for a life in accordance with his professions.[2]

During his residence in Sicily Porphyry composed fifteen books against the Christians. These polemical works were burnt in the year A.D. 448 under the Emperors Valentinian III and Theodosius II, and only fragments have come down to us: we have to rely largely on the writings of Christians for testimony as to the line of attack adopted by Porphyry. (Answers were composed by, among others, Methodius and Eusebius of Caesarea.) St. Augustine says that if Porphyry had ever had a true love of wisdom and had known Jesus Christ ". . . *nec ab eius saluberrima humilitate resiluisses.*"[3] This phrase would not seem to be conclusive evidence that Porphyry was ever actually a Christian or even a catechumen, for the Saint gives no further evidence that he looked on Porphyry as an apostate, though it is true that the historian Socrates affirms that Porphyry abandoned Christianity (τὸν χριστιανισμὸν ἀπέλειτε) and attributed the apostasy to the philosopher's indignation at being assaulted by some Christians at Caesarea in Palestine.[4] It seems that we cannot attain absolute certainty on the question whether or not Porphyry ever was a Christian: he is not quoted as saying himself that he ever adhered to the Christian religion. Porphyry wanted to prevent the conversion of cultured people to Christianity, and he endeavoured to show that the Christian religion was illogical, ignoble, involved in contradictions, etc. He made a special point of attacking the Bible and the Christian exegesis, and it is interesting to observe his anticipation of Higher Criticism, e.g. by denying the authenticity of the book of Daniel and declaring the prophecies therein

[1] *Ad Marc.*, 16.
[2] *Ad Marc.*, 17.
[3] *De Civit. Dei.*, 10, 28. (P. knew Origen while a youth. Euseb., *Hist. Ecc.*, 6, 19, 5.)
[4] *Hist. Eccl.*, 3, 23, (*P.G.*, 67, 445).

contained to be *vaticinia ex eventu*, denying that the Pentateuch was by Moses, pointing out apparent inconsistencies and contradictions in the Gospels, etc. The Divinity of Christ was a particular point of attack, and he brought many arguments against the Divinity of Christ and the doctrines of Christ.[1]

[1] "Obscurity, incoherence, illogicality, lying, abuse of confidence and stupidity, Porphyry saw scarcely anything else in Christianity, to judge by the *membra disiecta* of his work." (Pierre de Labriolle, *La Réaction Païenne*, p. 286, 1934.)

CHAPTER XLVI

OTHER NEO-PLATONIC SCHOOLS

1. *The Syrian School*

THE chief figure of the Syrian School of Neo-Platonism is Iamblichus (d. *c.* A.D. 330), a pupil of Porphyry. Iamblichus carried much further the Neo-Platonic tendency to multiply the members of the hierarchy of beings, which he combined with an insistence on the importance of theurgy and occultism in general.

1. The tendency to multiply the members of the hierarchy of being was present in Neo-Platonism from the very beginning, as a consequence of the desire to emphasise the transcendence of the Supreme Godhead and remove God from all contact with the world of sense. But while Plotinus had restrained this tendency within reasonable bounds, Iamblichus gave it wings. Thus above the One of Plotinus he asserted yet another One, which exceeds all qualifications whatsoever and stands beyond the good.[1] This One, which transcends all predicates or indeed any statements on our part—except that of unity—is therefore superior to the One of Plotinus, which is identical with the Good. From the One proceeds the world of ideas or intelligible objects—ὁ κόσμος νοητός—and from this again the world of intellectual beings—ὁ κόσμος νοερός[2]—consisting of Νοῦς, an intermediary hypostasis and the Demiurge, though Iamblichus seems not to have been content with this complication, but to have distinguished further the members of the κόσμος νοερός.[3] Below the κόσμος νοερός is the Super-terrestrial Soul, and from this Soul proceeds two others. As for the gods of the popular religion and the "heroes," these—together with a host of angels and demons—belong to the world, and Iamblichus tried to arrange them according to numbers. But while endeavouring to establish this fantastic scheme by means of the speculative reason, Iamblichus insisted on the immediate and innate character of our knowledge of the gods, which is given us together with our innate psychical impulse towards the Good.

2. The religious interest of Iamblichus is apparent in his

[1] ἡ πάντῃ ἄρρητος ἀρχή Damasc., *Dubit.*, 43. [2] Procl., *in Tim.*, 1308, 21 d.
[3] Procl., *in Tim.*, 1308, 21 ff. d. Damasc., *Dubit.*, 54.

ethical doctrine. Accepting Porphyry's distinction of the political, cathartic and paradigmatic virtues he then proceeds to introduce, between the two last, the *theoretical* virtues, by which the soul contemplates Nous as its object and views the procession of the orders from the final Principle. By the paradigmatic virtues the soul identifies herself with Nous, the place of ideas and παραδείγμα of all things. Finally, above these four types of virtue stand the *priestly* virtues, in the exercise of which the soul is ecstatically united to the One. (These virtues are therefore also called ἑνιαῖαι). As we must look to divine revelation in order to ascertain the means of entering upon union with God, the priest is superior to the philosopher. Purification from the sensual, theurgy, miracles, divination, play an important part in the system of Iamblichus.

II. *The School of Pergamon*

The Pergamene School was founded by *Aedesius*, a pupil of Iamblichus, and is characterised mainly by its interest in theurgy and in the restoration of polytheism. Thus while *Maximus*, one of the Emperor Julian's tutors, gave particular attention to theurgy, Sallustius wrote a work *On the gods and the world* as propaganda for polytheism, while the rhetorician Libonius, another of Julian's tutors, wrote against Christianity, as did also *Eunapius* of Sardes. *Julian* (322–363) was brought up as a Christian but became a pagan. In his short reign (361–363), Julian showed himself to be a fanatical opponent of Christianity and adherent of polytheism, combining this with Neo-Platonic doctrines, for which he relied largely on Iamblichus. He interpreted, for example, the worship of the sun according to the Neo-Platonic philosophy, by making the sun the intermediary between the intelligible and the sensible realms.[1]

III. *The Athenian School*

In the Athenian School of Neo-Platonism there flourished a lively interest in the writings of Aristotle, as well of course as in those of Plato, an interest that showed itself in the commentary on the *De Anima* composed by Plutarch of Athens, the son of Nestorius and Athenian Scholarch (d. A.D. 431/2) and in the commentaries on the *Metaphysics* by Syrianus (d. *c*. 430), the successor of Plutarch in the headship of the School at Athens.

[1] Julian, *Or.*, 4.

But Syrianus was no believer in the agreement of Plato and Aristotle: on the contrary not only did he account the study of the philosophy of Aristotle merely a preparation for the study of Plato, but—in his commentary on the *Metaphysics*—he defended the Platonic ideal theory against Aristotle's attacks, clearly recognising the difference between the two philosophers on this point. Yet that did not prevent him from trying to show the agreement between Plato, the Pythagoreans, the Orphics and the "Chaldaic" literature. He was succeeded by *Domninus*, a Syrian of Jewish origin, who wrote on mathematics.

Much more important, however, than any of these men is the celebrated *Proclus* (410–485), who was born at Constantinople and was Athenian Scholarch for many years. He was a man of untiring diligence, and though much of his work has perished, we still possess his commentaries on the *Timaeus*, *Republic*, *Parmenides*, *Alcibiades I* and *Cratylus*, in addition to his works Στοιχείωσις Θεολογική, 'Είς τὴν Πλάτωνος Θεολογίαν and the *De decem dubitationibus circa providentiam*, the *De providentia et fato et eo quod in nobis* and the *De malorum subsistentia*—the last three works being preserved in the Latin translation of William of Moerbeke. Possessed of a wide knowledge concerning the philosophies of Plato and Aristotle and of his Neo-Platonic predecessors, Proclus combined with this knowledge a great interest in and enthusiasm for all sorts of religious beliefs, superstitions and practices, even believing that he received revelations and was the reincarnation of the Neo-Pythagorean Nicomachus. He had, therefore, an immense wealth of information and learning at his disposal, and he attempted to combine all these elements in one carefully articulated system, a task rendered all the easier by his dialectical ability. This has won for him the reputation of being the greatest Scholastic of Antiquity, in that he brought his dialectical ability and genius for subtle systematisation to bear on the doctrines that he had received from others.[1]

The main *motif* of Proclus' dialectical systematisation is that of triadic development. This principle was certainly used by Iamblichus, but Proclus employed it with considerable dialectical subtlety and made it the dominant principle in the procession of beings from the One, i.e. in the emanation of the orders of being from the highest 'Αρχή down to the most inferior stage. The

[1] In his commentary on Euclid I Proclus gives much valuable information concerning Platonic, Aristotelian, Neo-Platonic and other positions in mathematical philosophy (ed. Friedlein, Leipzig, 1873).

effect, or being that proceeds, is partly similar to the cause or source of emanation and partly dissimilar. In so far as the being that proceeds is similar to its origin, it is regarded as being in some degree identical with its principle, for it is only in virtue of the self-communication of the latter that the procession takes place. On the other hand, since there *is* a procession, there must be something in the proceeding being that is not identical with, but different from, the principle. We have, therefore, at once two moments of development, the first being that of remaining in the principle (μονή), in virtue of partial identity, the second being that of difference, in virtue of external procession (πρόοδος). In every being that proceeds, however, there is a natural tendency towards the Good, and, in virtue of the strictly hierarchical character of the development of beings, this natural tendency towards the Good means a turning-back towards the immediate source of emanation on the part of the being that emanates or proceeds. Proclus thus distinguishes three moments of development, (i) μονή or remaining in the principle; (ii) πρόοδος or proceeding out of the principle, and (iii) ἐπιστροφή or turning-back towards the principle. This triadic development, or development in three moments dominates the whole series of emanations.[1]

The original principle of the whole process of development is the primary one, τὸ αὐτὸ ἕν.[2] Beings must have a cause, and cause is not the same as effect. Yet we cannot admit a *regressus ad infinitum*. There must be, therefore, a First Cause, whence the multiplicity of beings proceed "as branches from a root," some being nearer to the First Cause, others more remote. Moreover, there can be only one such First Cause, for the existence of a multiplicity is always secondary to unity.[3] This must exist since we are logically compelled to refer all multiplicity back to unity, all effects to an ultimate Cause and all participated good to an Absolute Good; yet as a matter of fact the primary Principle transcends the predicates of Unity, Cause and Good, just as it transcends Being. It follows that we are really not entitled to predicate anything positively of the ultimate Principle: we can only say what it is *not*, realising that it stands above all discursive thought and positive predication, ineffable and incomprehensible.

From the primary One proceed the Units or ἑνάδες, which are nevertheless looked on as super-essential and incomprehensible

[1] *Instit. Theol.*. 30 ff.; *Theol. Plat.*, 2, 4; 3, 14; 4, 1.
[2] *Instit. Theol.*, 4, 6; *Theol. Plat.*, 2, 4.
[3] *Instit. Theol.*, 11.

gods, the source of providence, and of which goodness is to be predicated. From the Henads proceeds the sphere of Nous, which subdivides into the spheres of the νοητοί, the νοητοί καὶ νοεροί and the νοεροί (cf. Iamblichus), the spheres corresponding respectively to the concepts of Being, Life and Thought.[1] Not content with these divisions Proclus introduces further subdivisions in each of the three spheres of Nous, the first two being sub-divided into three triads, the third into seven hebdomads, and so on.

Below the general sphere of Nous is the sphere of the Soul, which is the intermediary between the supersensible and the sensible worlds, mirroring the former as a copy (εἰκονικῶς) and serving as a pattern for the latter (παραδειγματικῶς). This sphere of soul is subdivided into three sub-spheres, that of divine souls, that of "demonic" souls, and that of ψυχαί or human souls. Each sub-sphere is again sub-divided. The Greek gods appear in the sphere of divine souls, but the same name is found in different groups according to the different aspect or function of the god in question. For instance, Proclus seems to have posited a threefold Zeus. The sphere of demonic souls, which serves as a bridge between gods and men, is subdivided into angels, demons and heroes.

The world, a living creature, is formed and guided by the divine souls. It cannot be evil—nor can matter itself be evil—since we cannot refer evil to the divine. Rather is evil to be thought of as imperfection, which is inseparable from the lower strata of the hierarchy of being.[2]

In this process of emanation the productive cause, Proclus insists, remains itself unaltered. It brings into actuality the subordinate sphere of being, but it does so without movement or loss, preserving its own essence, "neither transmuted into its consequents nor suffering any diminution." The product, therefore, does not arise through the self-diremption of the producer, nor by its transformation. In this way Proclus tries, like Plotinus, to steer a middle course between *creatio ex nihilo* on the one hand and true monism or pantheism on the other hand, for, while the productive being is neither altered nor diminished through the production of the subordinate being, it nevertheless furnishes the subordinate being out of its own being.[3]

[1] *Theol. Plat.*, 3, 14; 4, 1.
[2] *Theol. Plat.*, 1, 17; in *Remp.*, I, 37, 27 ff.
[3] *Instit. Theol.*, 27.

On the principle that like can only be attained by like, Proclus attributed to the human soul a faculty above thought, by which it can attain the One.[1] This is the unitary faculty, which attains the ultimate Principle in ecstasy. Like Porphyry, Iamblichus, Syrianus and others, Proclus also attributed to the soul an ethereal body composed of light, which is midway between the material and the immaterial and is imperishable. It is with the eyes of this ethereal body that the soul can perceive theophanies. The soul ascends through the different grades of virtue (as in Iamblichus) to ecstatic union with the primary One. Proclus distinguishes three general stages in the soul's ascent, Eros, Truth and Faith. Truth leads the soul beyond love of the beautiful and fills it with knowledge of true reality, while Faith consists in the mystical silence before the Incomprehensible and Ineffable.

Proclus was succeeded in the headship of the School by *Marinus*, a native of Samaria. Marinus distinguished himself in mathematics and through his sober and restrained interpretation of Plato. For instance, in his commentary on the *Parmenides* he insisted that the One and so on denote *ideas* and not gods. However, that did not prevent him from following the contemporary fashion of attributing great importance to religious superstitions, and at the summit of the scale of virtues he placed the θεουργικαὶ ἀρεταί. Marinus was succeeded as Scholarch by Isidorus.

The last of the Athenian Scholarchs was Damascius (Sch. from *c.* A.D. 520), whom Marinus had instructed in mathematics. Having been forced to the conclusion that the human reason cannot understand the relation of the One to the proceeding beings, Damascius seems to have considered that human speculation cannot really attain the truth. All the words we employ in this connection, "cause" and "effect," "processions," etc., are but analogies and do not properly represent the actuality.[2] Since on the other hand he was not prepared to abandon speculation, he gave full rein to theosophy, "Mysticism" and superstition.

A well-known disciple of Damascius is *Simplicius*, who wrote valuable commentaries on the *Categories*, *Physics*, *De Caelo* and *De Anima* of Aristotle. That on the *Physics* is particularly valuable because of the fragments of the pre-Socratics therein contained.

In the year 529 the Emperor Justinian forbade the teaching of

[1] *In Alcib.*, III; *de Prov.*, 24.
[2] *Dubit.*, 38, I 79, 20 ff.; 41, I 83, 26 ff.; 42 I 85, 8 ff.; 107 I 278, 24 f.

philosophy at Athens, and Damascius, together with Simplicius and five other members of the Neo-Platonic School, went to Persia, where they were received by king Chosroes. In 533, however, they returned to Athens, apparently disappointed with the cultural state of Persia. It does not appear that there were any more pagan Neo-Platonists surviving shortly after the middle of the century.

IV. *The Alexandrian School*

1. The Alexandrian School of Neo-Platonism was a centre for investigation in the department of the special sciences and for the labour of commenting on the works of Plato and Aristotle. Thus *Hypatia* (best known for her murder in A.D. 415 by a fanatical mob of Christians) wrote on mathematics and astronomy and is said to have lectured on Plato and Aristotle, while *Asclepiodotus* of Alexandria (second half of A.D. fifth century), who later resided at Aphrodisias in Caria, studied science and medicine, mathematics and music. *Ammonius, Ioannes Philoponus, Olympiodorus* and others commented on works of Plato and Aristotle. In the commentaries of the School special attention was paid to the logical works of Aristotle, and in general it may be said of these commentaries that they show moderation and a desire on the part of their authors to give the natural interpretation of the works on which they are commenting. Metaphysical and religious interests tend to retreat from the foreground, the multiplication of intermediary beings, so characteristic of Iamblichus and Proclus, being abandoned and little attention being paid to the doctrine of ecstasy. Even the pious and somewhat mystically inclined Asclepiodotus, who was a pupil of Proclus, avoided the latter's complicated and highly speculative metaphysic.

2. Characteristic of Alexandrian Neo-Platonism is its relation to Christianity and the thinkers of the celebrated Catechetical School. The result of the abandonment of the speculative extravagancies of Iamblichus and Proclus was that the Neo-Platonic School at Alexandria gradually lost its specifically pagan character and became rather a "neutral" philosophical institute: logic and science were obviously subjects on which Christians and pagans could meet on more or less common ground. It was this growing association of the School with Christianity which made possible the continuation of Hellenic thought at Constantinople. (Stephanus of Alexandria migrated to Constantinople and there

expounded Plato and Aristotle in the university in the first half of the seventh century, during the reign of the Emperor Heraclius, i.e. a century after Justinian had closed the School at Athens.) An instance of the close relation between Neo-Platonists and Christians at Alexandria is the life of Hypatia's disciple, Synesius of Cyrene, who became bishop of Ptolemais in A.D. 411. Another striking instance is the conversion of Ioannes Philoponus to Christianity. As a convert he wrote a book against Proclus' conception of the eternity of the world and supported his own view by an appeal to Plato's *Timaeus* which he interpreted as teaching creation in time. Philoponus also held the view that Plato drew his wisdom from the Pentateuch. One may mention also *Nemesius*, bishop of Emesa in Phoenicia, who was influenced by the Alexandrian School.

3. But if Neo-Platonism exercised a profound influence on Christian thinkers at Alexandria, it is also true that Christian thinkers were not without influence on non-Christian philosophers. This can be seen in the case of *Hierocles of Alexandria*, who lectured at Alexandria from about A.D. 420. Hierocles shows affinity with Middle Platonism rather than with his Neo-Platonist predecessors, for, neglecting the Plotinian hierarchy of beings which had been so exaggerated by Iamblichus and Proclus, he admits only one super-terrestrial being, the Demiurge. But what is particularly striking is that Hierocles asserts *voluntary creation out of nothing* by the Demiurge.[1] He rejects indeed creation in time, but that does not militate against the very great probability of Christian influence, especially as Fate or 'Αιμαρμένη denotes for Hierocles, not mechanical determinism, but the apportioning of certain effects to man's free actions. Thus petitionary prayer and providential 'Αιμαρμένη are not mutually exclusive,[2] and the doctrine of Necessity or Fate is brought more into harmony with the Christian insistence on human freedom on the one hand and Divine Providence on the other.

v. *Neo-Platonists of the Latin West*

One would scarcely be justified in speaking of a "School" of Neo-Platonism in the Latin West. However, there is a characteristic common to those thinkers who are usually classed as "Neo-Platonists of the Latin West" and that is, that the speculative side of Neo-Platonism is no longer in evidence while the learned

[1] Phot., 460 b 23 ff.; 461 b 6 ff. [2] Phot., 465 a 16 ff.

side is very much to the fore. By their translation of Greek works into Latin and by their commentaries on Platonic and Aristotelian writings, as well as on writings of Latin philosophers, they helped to spread the study of philosophy in the Roman world and at the same time constructed a bridge whereby Ancient Philosophy passed to the Middle Ages. Thus in the first half of the fourth century A.D. *Chalcidius* (who probably was or became a Christian) made a Latin translation of Plato's *Timaeus* and wrote a Latin commentary on it—apparently in dependence on Poseidonius' commentary (with the possible use of intermediate writings). This translation and its commentary were much used in the Middle Ages.[1] In the same century *Marius Victorinus* (who became a Christian when of advanced years) translated into Latin Aristotle's *Categories* and *De Interpretatione*, Porphyry's *Isagoge* and some Neo-Platonist works. He also wrote commentaries on Cicero's *Topics* and *De Inventione* and composed original works *De Definitionibus* and *De Syllogismis Hypotheticis*. As a Christian he also composed some theological works, of which a great part are still extant. (St. Augustine was influenced by Marius Victorinus.) One may also mention *Vettius Agonius Praetextatus* (d. 384), who translated Themistius' paraphrase of Aristotle's *Analytics*, and *Macrobius* (he seems to have become a Christian in later years), who wrote the *Saturnalia* and also a commentary on Cicero's *Somnium Scipionis* about A.D. 400. In this commentary the Neo-Platonist theories of emanation appear and it seems that Macrobius made use of Porphyry's commentary on the *Timaeus*, which itself made use of that of Poseidonius.[2] Fairly early in the fifth century *Martianus Capella* composed his (still extant) *De Nuptiis Mercurii et Philologiae*, which was much read in the Middle Ages. (For instance, it was commented on by Remigius of Auxerre.) This work, which is a kind of Encyclopaedia, treats of each of the seven liberal arts, books three to nine being each devoted to one of the arts. This was of importance for the Middle Ages, which made the seven liberal arts the basis of education as the *Trivium* and *Quadrivium*.

[1] As this work contains extracts from other dialogues of Plato, as well as extracts and texts and opinions from other Greek philosophers, it came about that up to the twelfth century A.D. Chalcidius was regarded as one of the chief sources for a knowledge of Greek philosophy.

[2] As Macrobius introduces into his Commentary ideas on number-symbolism, emanation, the Plotinian gradation of virtues, and even polytheism, the work is "really a syncretic product of Neo-Platonist paganism." (Maurice De Wulf, *Hist. Med. Phil.*, I, p. 79. Trans. E. Messenger, Ph.D., Longmans, 3rd Eng. edit., 1935.)

More important, however, than any of the afore-mentioned writers is the Christian *Boethius* (*c.* A.D. 480–524/5), who studied at Athens, held high office under Theodoric, king of the Ostrogoths, and was finally executed on a charge of treason after a term of imprisonment, during which he composed the famous *De Consolatione Philosophiae*. As it is more convenient to treat of the philosophy of Boethius by way of introduction to Mediaeval Philosophy, I shall content myself here with mentioning some of his works.

Although it was the aim of Boethius to translate into Latin, and to furnish with commentaries, all the works of Aristotle (*De Interpret.* I, 2), he did not succeed in carrying his project to completion. He did, however, translate into Latin the *Categories*, the *De Interpretatione*, the *Topics*, both *Analytics* and the *Sophistical Arguments*. It may be that Boethius translated other works of Aristotle besides the *Organon*, in accordance with his original plan; but this is uncertain. He translated Porphyry's *Isagoge*, and the dispute concerning universals which so agitated the early Middle Ages took its *point de départ* in remarks of Porphyry and Boethius.

Besides furnishing the *Isagoge* (in the translation of Marius Victorinus) with a double commentary, Boethius also commented on the *Categories*, the *De Interpretatione*, the *Topics*, the *Analytics* and *Sophistical Arguments* (probably) and on Cicero's *Topics*. In addition to these commentaries he composed original treatises, the *Introductio ad categoricos syllogismos*, *De categoricis syllogismis*, *De hypotheticis syllogismis*, *De divisione*, *De topicis differentiis*, *De Consolatione Philosophiae*, *De Institutione arithmetica*, etc. In the last period of his life several theological opuscula came from his pen.

On account of this extensive labour expended on translation and commenting, Boethius may be called the principal mediator between Antiquity and the Middle Ages, "the last Roman and the first Scholastic," as he has been called. "Down to the end of the twelfth century he was the principal channel by which Aristotelianism was transmitted to the West."[1]

[1] M. De Wulf, *Hist. Med. Phil.*, I, p. 109

CHAPTER XLVII

CONCLUDING REVIEW

When we look back at the philosophy of Greece and of the Greco-Roman world, as we watch its naïve beginnings on the shore of Asia Minor, as we see the intellectual power and comprehensive mind of a Heraclitus or a Parmenides struggling with a crippling poverty of philosophic language, as we trace the development of two of the greatest philosophies the world has ever seen, the philosophies of Plato and of Aristotle, as we see the broadening influence of the Stoic School and witness the evolution of the final creative effort of ancient thought, the system of Plotinian Neo-Platonism, we cannot but acknowledge that we have before us one of the supreme achievements of the human race. If we gaze with admiration at the Greek temples of Sicily, at the Gothic cathedrals of the Middle Ages, at the work of a Fra Angelico or a Michelangelo, a Rubens or a Velasquez, if we treasure the writings of a Homer or a Dante, a Shakespeare or a Goethe, we should pay the tribute of a like admiration to what is great in the realm of pure thought and count it as one of the greatest treasures of our European heritage. Mental effort and perseverance are no doubt required in order to penetrate the riches of Greek thought, but any effort that is expended in the attempt to understand and appreciate the philosophy of those two men of genius, Plato and Aristotle, is amply rewarded: it can no more be wasted than the effort we expend to appreciate at its full value the music of Beethoven or Mozart or the beauty of the cathedral at Chartres Greek drama, Greek architecture, Greek sculpture, are imperishable memorials of the Greek genius and culture, of the glory of Hellas; but that glory would be incomplete without Greek philosophy and we cannot appreciate fully the culture of the Greeks unless we know something of Greek philosophy. It may be of help towards the appreciation of that philosophy if, in these concluding remarks, I make a few suggestions (some of them already touched upon) concerning different ways in which we may regard Greek philosophy as a whole.

1. I have already mentioned, particularly in connection with the Pre-Socratic philosophers, the problem of the One and the

Many; but the theme of the relation between the One and the Many and of the character of both may be discerned running through the whole of Greek philosophy, just as it runs indeed through the whole of philosophy, owing to the fact that while the Many are given in experience, the philosopher strives to see the Many with a synoptic vision, to arrive, so far as is possible, at a comprehensive view of Reality, i.e. to see the Many in the light of the One or in some sense to reduce the Many to the One. This attempt at a synoptic vision is very clear in the case of the pre-Socratic cosmologists and there is no need to dwell on this point again, beyond recalling to mind that their attempt to reconcile the Many of experience with the One demanded by thought was pursued predominantly on the material plane; the Many are material and the One also, the Unity-in-difference is material, water or the indeterminate or air or fire. Sometimes the aspect of Unity is predominant, as in the Eleatic system, sometimes the Many are triumphant, as in the atomistic philosophy of Leucippus and Democritus; but mind, partly no doubt owing to poverty of language, hardly rises above the material plane, though in Pythagoreanism we see, for example, a much clearer distinction between soul and body, while with Anaxagoras the concept of Nous tends to liberation from materialism.

So far as we can speak of the Sophists as occupying themselves at all with this problem, it is rather the aspect of multiplicity that is stressed (the multiplicity of ways of life, of ethical judgments, of opinions), while with Socrates the aspect of unity is stressed, inasmuch as the basic unity of true judgments of value is set in clear light; but it is Plato who really develops the complexity and richness of the problem. The fleeting multiplicity of phenomena, the data of experience, is seen against the background of the unitary realities of the exemplary Ideas, apprehended by the human mind in the concept, and this assertion of the Ideal realm of reality forces the philosopher to consider the problem of the One and the Many not only in the logical sphere, but also in the ontological sphere of immaterial being. The result is that the immaterial unities (themselves a multiplicity) are viewed in function of the One, the synthesising reality of the transcendental sphere and the ultimate Exemplar. Moreover, although the particulars of sense-experience, the Many of the older Cosmologists, are "dismissed," precisely in regard to their particularity considered as impenetrable by conceptual thought, into the infinite or indeterminate, the whole material world is regarded as ordered and informed by Mind or Soul. On the other hand a "chorismos" is left between exemplary Reality and the fleeting particulars, while—apparently at least—no satisfactory answer is given as to the precise relation between the Exemplary and Efficient Causes, so that, although Plato brings the complexity of the problem into greater relief and definitely transcends the pre-Socratic materialism, he fails to give any adequate solution to the problem and leaves us with a dualism, the sphere of Reality on the one hand and the sphere of semi-reality or Becoming on the other hand. Not even his assertion of the immaterial, which sets him above both Parmenides and Heraclitus, can suffice to explain the relation of Being and Becoming or of the One and the Many.

With Aristotle we find a greater realisation of the wealth and richness of the material world and he attempts, through his doctrine of immanent substantial form, to effect some synthesis of the realities of the One and the Many, the multiplicity of members within a species being united in the possession of a similar specific form, though there is no numerical identity. Again, the doctrine of hylomorphism enabled Aristotle to assert a real unifying principle in the terrestrial world, while at the same time he avoided any over-emphasis of unity, such as would conflict with the evident multiplicity given in experience: he thus provided a principle of stability and a principle of change and so did justice to both Being and Becoming. Moreover, Aristotle's Unmoved Mover, the ultimate Final Cause of the universe, served in some degree as a unifying and harmonising Principle, drawing the multiplicity of phenomena into an intelligible unity. On the other hand, however, Aristotle's dissatisfaction with the Ideal Theory of Plato and his perception of its weaknesses led him into an unfortunate rejection of the Platonic Exemplarism as a whole, while his insistence on final causality to the apparent exclusion of cosmic efficient causality meant the assertion of an ultimate dualism between God and an *independent* world.

In post-Aristotelian philosophy it is perhaps not fanciful to see in Stoicism an over-stressing of the One, resulting in cosmic pantheism (which has its noble reflection in ethical cosmopolitanism), and in Epicureanism an over-assertion of the Many, appearing in a cosmology built on an atomistic basis and in a (theoretically at least) egoistic ethic. In Neo-Pythagoreanism and Middle

Platonism we see that growing syncretism of Pythagorean, Platonic, Aristotelian and Stoic elements which culminated in the Neo-Platonic system. In that system the only possible way of settling the problem of the One and the Many is apprehended, namely that the Many must issue in some way from the One, the dualism between God and an independent world being avoided on the one hand and monism being avoided on the other hand, so that justice could be done to the reality of the One and the Many, to the supreme reality of the One and the dependent reality of the Many. But, while the Neo-Platonists rejected cosmic monism through their doctrine of the hierarchy of being and rejected any self-diremption of the transcendent One and while they admitted a "manifold Many" and did not attempt to dismiss the cosmos and the subordinate degrees of Being as illusory, they failed to see the unsatisfactory character of their attempt to steer a middle way between a true creation and monism and that their theory of "emanation," given their denial of creation out of nothing on the one hand and their denial of the self-diremption of God on the other hand, could possess no intelligible significance, but remained a mere metaphor. It was left for Christian philosophy to assert the true solution of *creatio ex nihilo sui et subiecti*.

2. Under a slightly different aspect we might regard Greek philosophy in its totality as an attempt to discover the ultimate cause or causes of the world. The pre-Socratics in general, as Aristotle observes, were concerned with the material cause, the *Urstoff* of the world, that which remains permanent beneath the constant changes. Plato, however, gave special emphasis to the Exemplary Cause, ideal and supra-material Reality, while he also asserted the Efficient operative Cause, Mind and Soul, developing the first steps of the pre-Socratic Anaxagoras. Nor did he, in spite of what Aristotle says, neglect final causality, since the exemplary causes are also final causes: they are not only Ideas, but also Ideals. God acts in the world with a view to an end, as is clearly stated in the *Timaeus*. But Plato seems to have left a dichotomy between the Exemplary Cause and the Efficient Cause (at least this is suggested by what he actually says and we have not sufficient warrant to state categorically that he brought the two ultimate Causes together), while in the terrestrial world he does not give that clear place to the immanent formal cause that Aristotle supplied. Yet while Aristotle developed a clear theory concerning the immanent formal and material causes in the

terrestrial world, his system is sadly deficient in relation to the ultimate Efficient and Exemplary Causes. The Aristotelian God works as ultimate Final Cause, but, since the philosopher did not see how God's changelessness and self-sufficiency could be reconciled with the exercise of efficient causality, he neglected to provide an ultimate Efficient Cause. He thought, no doubt, that the exercise of final causality by the Unmoved Mover was also all the ultimate efficient causality that was requisite; but this meant that for Aristotle the world was not only eternal, but also ontologically independent of God: the Unmoved Mover could scarcely be regarded as drawing the world into existence through the unconscious exercise of final causality.

A synthesis of Plato and Aristotle was, therefore, necessary, and in Neo-Platonism (as also, to a greater or less extent, in the intermediate philosophies leading up to it) the God of Aristotle and the Exemplary and Efficient Causes of Plato were brought more or less together, even if not in a thoroughly satisfactory manner. In Christian philosophy on the other hand the ultimate Efficient, Exemplary and Final Causes are explicitly identified in the one spiritual God, supreme Being and Reality and the Source of all created and dependent being.

3. Again, we might look on Greek philosophy as a whole from the humanistic viewpoint, according to the position attributed to man in the individual systems. The pre-Socratic cosmology, as I pointed out earlier, was particularly concerned with the Object, the material cosmos and man was regarded as an item in that cosmos, his soul being, for example, a contraction of the primal Fire (Heraclitus) or composed of a particular type of atoms (Leucippus). On the other hand, the doctrine of transmigration of souls, as found for instance in the Pythagorean philosophy and in the teaching of Empedocles, implied that there was in man a principle superior to matter, an idea which bore splendid fruit in the philosophy of Plato.

With the Sophists and with Socrates we find a swing-over, due to various causes, from the Object to the Subject, from the material cosmos as such to man. But it is in the Platonic philosophy that the first real attempt is made to combine both realities in a comprehensive synthesis. Man appears as the knowing and willing subject, the being who realises, or should realise, true values in his individual life and in the life of society, the being endowed with an immortal soul; and human knowledge, human nature, human conduct and human society, are made the subject of profound and penetrating analyses and considerations. On the other hand man appears as a being set between two worlds, the full immaterial world of Reality above him and the merely material limit below him: he thus appears, in his dual character of embodied spirit, as what Poseidonius, the outstanding thinker of the Middle Stoa, was later to term the δεσμός or bond between the two worlds of the immaterial and the material.

In Aristotle's philosophy man is again a midway being. as it were, for neither Plato nor Aristotle considered man to be the highest being: the founder of the Lyceum, no less than the founder of the Academy, was convinced that above men there is unchanging Being and that contemplation of unchanging Being is the exercise of man's highest faculty. Again, Aristotle, no less than Plato, gave profound consideration to human psychology, human conduct and human society. Yet of Aristotle's philosophy we may perhaps say that it was at once more and also less human than that of Plato: more human in that, for example, he knits together soul and body more closely than does Plato and so produces a more "realistic" epistemology, attributes a greater value to human aesthetic experience and artistic production, and is more "commonsense" in his treatment of political society, less human in that his identification of the active intellect in all man (according to what seems the more probable interpretation of the *De Anima*) would result in denial of personal immortality. Moreover, there is nothing in Aristotle to suggest that man can ever become united to God in any real sense.

Yet, although it is true that Plato and Aristotle attribute an important position to the study of man and his conduct, as individual and as a member of society, it is also true that both of them (notwithstanding Aristotle's trend towards empirical science) are great metaphysicians and speculative philosophers and of neither of them could we say that he fixes his attention exclusively in man. In the Hellenistic and Roman periods, however, man comes to occupy more and more the centre of the picture: cosmological speculation tends to flag and is unoriginal in character, while in Epicureanism and the developed Stoa the philosopher is concerned above all with human conduct. This preoccupation with man produces the noble doctrine of the later Stoa, of Seneca, Marcus Aurelius and—most strikingly perhaps —of Epictetus, in which all men, as rational beings, appear as brethren, children of "Zeus." But if it is man's moral conduct that is most insisted on in the Stoic School, it is man's religious capacity, need and yearning that come to occupy a prominent position in the Schools and thinkers that are influenced by the Platonic tradition: a doctrine of "salvation," of knowledge of God and assimilation to God, culminates in the Plotinian doctrine of ecstatic union with the One. If Epicureanism and Stoicism (the latter with some qualification perhaps) concern themselves with man on what we might call the horizontal level, Neo-Platonism concerns itself rather with the vertical, with man's ascent to God.

4. Epistemology or the theory of knowledge is generally regarded as a branch of philosophy, the study of which is peculiar to our modern era, and for some modern thinkers it has constituted practically the whole of philosophy. There is, of course, a good deal of truth in the assertion that it was modern philosophy that first made epistemology a really serious and critical study, but it is not a completely true statement, if asserted without qualification. Leaving out of account the philosophy of the Middle Ages, which also dealt with epistemological themes, it can scarcely be denied that the great thinkers of Antiquity concerned themselves to some extent with epistemological questions, even if it was not recognised as a separate branch of philosophy or accorded that critical importance which has generally been attributed to it in modern times, since the time of Immanuel Kant at least. Without attempting to give anything like a complete survey of the development of epistemology in ancient philosophy, I will suggest one or two points which may help to throw into relief the fact that important epistemological problems at least raised their heads above the ground in the ancient world, even if they did not emerge into full light of day and receive that close attention which they deserve.

The pre-Socratic philosophers were, in the main, "dogmatists," in the sense that they assumed that man can know reality objectively. It is true that the Eleatic philosophy made a distinction between the way of truth and the way of belief or opinion or appearance; but the Eleatics themselves did not realise the importance of the problems involved in their philosophy. They adopted a monistic position on rationalistic grounds and, since this position conflicted with the data of sense-experience, cavalierly denied the objective reality of phenomena: they did not question their general philosophical position or the power of the human mind to transcend phenomena, but rather assumed this power. Nor did they realise apparently that, by rejecting the objective reality of appearance, they were undermining their metaphysic. In general, therefore, the thinkers of the Eleatic School cannot be termed exceptions to the generally uncritical attitude of the pre-Socratics, in spite of the dialectical ability of a man like Zeno.

The Sophists did indeed assert relativism to a greater or less extent, and the assertion of relativism involved an implicit epistemology. If Protagoras' dictum that man is the measure of all things is to be taken in a broad sense, it is tantamount to an assertion, not only of the independence of man in the ethical sphere, as a creator of moral values, but also of the inability of man to attain metaphysical truth. Did not Protagoras adopt a sceptical attitude in regard to theology and did not the Sophists in general regard cosmological speculation as little more than waste of time? Now, if the Sophists had gone on to institute a critique of human knowledge and had attempted to show why human knowledge is necessarily confined to phenomena, they would have been epistemologists; but in point of fact their interests were, for the most part, other than philosophical and their relativistic theories do not seem to have been based on any profound consideration either of the nature of the subject or of that of the object. The epistemology involved in their general position remained, therefore, implicit and was not elaborated into an explicit theory of knowledge. *We*, of course, can discern the germs of epistemological theories or problems, not only in Sophism but also in pre-Socratic philosophy; but that is not to say that either the Sophists or the pre-Socratic cosmologists had a reflective realisation of these problems.

When we turn to Plato and Aristotle, however, we find explicit theories of knowledge. Plato had a clear notion what he meant by knowledge and sharply distinguished the nature of true knowledge from the nature of opinion and of imagination, he possessed a clear reflective knowledge of the relativistic and variable elements in sense-perception and he discussed the question, how error of judgment takes place and in what it consists. His whole theory of the ascending degrees of knowledge and the corresponding objects of knowledge entitles him without a doubt to rank as an epistemologist. The same is true of Aristotle, who asserted a theory of abstraction, of the function of the image, of the active and passive principle in cognition, of the distinction between sense-perception and conceptual thought, of the different functions of reason. Of course, if we wished to restrict the scope of epistemology to consideration of the question, "*Can* we attain knowledge?", then the Aristotelian epistemology would belong rather to psychology, since it purports to answer the question, "*How* do we come to know?", rather than the question, "*Can* we know?"; but if we are willing to extend the scope of epistemology to cover the nature of the process of coming to know, then we must certainly reckon Aristotle an epistemologist. He may have treated the questions he raises in his psychology and we might to-day include most of them under the heading of psychology, but, labels apart, it remains an undoubted fact that Aristotle had a theory of knowledge.

On the other hand, though both Plato and Aristotle elaborated theories of knowledge, there is no use in pretending that they were not "dogmatists." Plato, as I have said, had a clear idea of what he meant by knowledge; but that such knowledge was possible for man, he assumed. If he accepted from Heraclitus his insistence on the changing character of the material world and from the Sophists the relativity of sense-perception, he accepted also from the Eleatics and the Pythagoreans the rationalistic assumption that the human mind can transcend phenomena and from Socrates the starting-point of his metaphysics of essence. Moreover, it was essential for Plato's ethical and political aims that the possibility of knowing the unchanging values and exemplary essences should be admitted: he never really questioned this possibility nor did he ever seriously raise the question of a purely subjective *a priori* element in human cognition: he attributed the *a priori* element (which he admitted) to "reminiscence," i.e. to previous objective knowledge. Nor did Aristotle ever raise the "critical problem": he assumed that the human mind can transcend phenomena and attain to a certain knowledge of unchanging and necessary objects, the objects of theoretic contemplation. Plato was an untiring dialectician, Aristotle was always ready to consider fresh problems and was careful in the statement of his own theories, even if not in that of other people's theories; but of neither the one nor the other can we say that he was the Kant or the anti-Kantian of the ancient world, for Kant's problem was not considered by them. Nor is this really surprising, since both men were dominated by the problem of Being (whereas in modern philosophy so many thinkers have started from *Consciousness*), so that their theories of knowledge were elaborated in function of their metaphysics and general philosophic positions rather than as a necessary *prolegomenon* to any metaphysic.

In the post-Aristotelian philosophy, if we except the Sceptics, we find in general the same "dogmatic" attitude, though it is also true that considerable attention was devoted to the question of the criteria of truth, e.g. by the Stoics and Epicureans. In other words, thinkers were alive to the difficulty that arises through the variability of sense-perception and attempted to meet this difficulty; in fact they had to meet it, in order to be able to erect their several philosophical structures. They were much more critical than the pre-Socratics; but that does not mean that they were critical philosophers in the Kantian sense, for they confined themselves more or less to a particular problem and tried to differentiate between, e.g. objective sense-perception, imagination and hallucination. In the New Academy, however, a radical scepticism showed itself, as when Carneades taught that there is no criterion of truth and that knowledge is impossible, on the ground that no sense-presentation is certainly true and that conceptual reasoning, since it is founded on sense-experience, is no more reliable than the latter, and the later Sceptics elaborated a systematic criticism of dogmatism and argued the relative character of both sensation and judgment, so that they were determined anti-metaphysicians. Dogmatism indeed won the final victory in ancient philosophy; but in view of the attacks of the Sceptics it cannot be said that ancient philosophy was altogether uncritical or that epistemology had no place in the consideration of Greek philosophers. This is the point I want to make: I am not concerned to admit that the attacks on metaphysics were justified, for I believe that they can be answered. I only wish to point out that not all Greek philosophers were naïve "dogmatists" and that, even if this can be legitimately asserted of the pre-Socratics, it would be a far too sweeping assertion in regard to Greek philosophers in general.

5. Closely allied with epistemology is psychology, and it may be as well to make a few remarks on the development of psychology in ancient philosophy. It is the Pythagorean School which stands out among the pre-Socratics as possessing a definite concept of the soul as a permanent principle, persisting in its individuality,

even after death. The philosophy of Heraclitus recognised, of course, a part of man which is more akin to the ultimate Principle of the universe than the body, and Anaxagoras asserted that Nous is present in man; but the latter did not succeed in transcending, *verbally* at least, the materialism of the pre-Socratic system, while for Heraclitus the rational element in man was but a purer manifestation of the fiery Principle. The Pythagorean psychology, however, by its distinction between soul and body at least implied a distinction between the spiritual and corporeal. Indeed, the doctrine of metempsychosis over-emphasised the distinction between soul and body, since it involved the conclusion that the soul stands in no intrinsic relation to any particular body. Moreover, acceptance of metempsychosis involves the acceptance of the theory that memory and reflective consciousness of continued self-identity are not essential to individual persistence. (If Aristotle held that there is a separate active intellect in each man and that the active intellect persists in its individuality, his notion that memory perishes with death may have been due not only to his own psychology and physiology, but to relics of the Pythagorean doctrine and its implication.) As to the Pythagorean theory of the tripartite nature of the soul, this was doubtless ultimately due to empirical observation of man's rational and emotional functions and of the conflict between reason and passion.

The Pythagorean conception of the soul exercised a very considerable influence on the thought of Plato. Rejecting epiphenomenalism, he made the soul the principle of life and movement in man, a principle that does not depend essentially on the body for the exercise of its highest intellectual functions, a principle that comes from "without" and survives the death of the body. Tripartite in nature, the soul has various functions or "parts," the hierarchy of which was fitted by Plato into his general metaphysical position. The lower parts or functions depend essentially on the body, but the rational soul belongs to the sphere of abiding Reality: in its proper dialectical and intuitive processes its activity is on a higher plane than that of phenomena and demonstrates the "divine" or immortal character of the soul. But Plato was not primarily interested in the soul from the strictly psychological aspect, still less from the point of view of the biologist: he was interested first and foremost in the soul as apprehending values and as realising values, in its ethical aspect. Hence the tremendous importance that he attached to education and culture of the soul.

If he sharpened, as he did, the antithesis between soul and body and spoke of the soul as inhabiting the body, as being lodged in the body like a captain in a ship, destined to rule the body, it was mainly his ethical interest that led him to do so. It is true that he attempted to prove the soul's pre-existence, intrinsic independence of the body and immortality, with epistemological arguments, arguing, e.g. from the *a priori* element in human knowledge; but all the time he was under the sway of ethical, and to a certain extent religious interests, and at the close of his life we find him still insisting that the soul is man's dearest possession and tendance of the soul man's highest task and duty. This is what we might call the characteristic side of Plato's psychology, for, though he certainly attributed a biological function to the soul, i.e. as source of movement and vital principle, he placed the emphasis on ethical and metaphysical aspects to such a degree that it may well be doubted if his treatment of these aspects really squares with his treatment of the soul in its biological function.

Aristotle began with the Platonic conception of the soul and the Platonic metaphysico-ethical picture of the soul and features of this conception are salient features of his psychology as represented in the pedagogical works. Thus, according to Aristotle, the highest part of man's soul, the active intellect, comes from without and survives death, while insistence on education and on moral culture is prominent in the philosophy of Aristotle as in that of Plato. Nevertheless, one can hardly avoid the impression that this aspect of his doctrine of the soul is not the really characteristic aspect of the Aristotelian psychology. However much he may have insisted on education and however prominent his intellectualist attitude may be in the picture of the ideal life for man as given in the *Ethics*, it would seem true to say that Aristotle's characteristic contribution to psychology is to be found rather in his treatment of the soul in its biological aspects. The sharp antithesis drawn by Plato between soul and body tends to retreat into the background, to give place to the conception of the soul as the immanent form of the body, as wedded to this particular body. The active intellect (whether monistically conceived or not) survives death, but the soul in its generality, including the passive intellect and including the functions of memory, etc., depends on the bodily organism and perishes at death. Where does it come from, this soul of man (excluding the active intellect)? It does not come from "without," it is not "made" by any Demiurge: is it perhaps a function of the body, little more than an epiphenomenon? Aristotle gave an extensive empirical treatment of such psychical functions as memory, imagination, dreams, sensations, and it would appear that his realisation of the dependence of so many of these functions on physiological factors and conditions was leading him towards an epiphenomenalist view of the soul, even if he never explicitly repudiated the totality of his Platonic inheritance or realised the tension between what he had retained of the Platonic psychology and that view of the soul to which his own researches and bent of mind were leading him.

The most important contribution of post-Aristotelian philosophy to psychology in a broad sense was perhaps the emphasis it laid on the religious aspect of the human soul: this is true at least of Neo-Platonism and of the Schools that led up to Neo-Platonism, though not, of course, of all post-Aristotelian Schools. The thinkers of the movement which culminated in Neo-Platonism working from the viewpoint of the Platonic tradition, set in clear relief man's kinship to the Divine, the soul's transcendental orientation and destiny. In other words, it was the characteristically Platonic attitude that triumphed in ancient philosophy rather than the characteristically Aristotelian attitude. As for the Stoics and Epicureans, the former could not achieve a really unified psychology owing to the simple fact that their dogmatic materialism demanded one psychology and their ethic another. Moreover, they did not investigate the nature and function of the psyche for their own sake and endeavour to establish a rational psychology on sure empirical foundations; but, adopting and adapting a pre-Socratic cosmology and centering their attention on ethical conduct, fitted a rationalist psychology, as best they could, to a hybrid system. Nevertheless, the tendency of Stoic doctrine and the effect of its influence was certainly to increase the direction of interest to the ethical and religious aspects of the soul rather than to its biological aspects. The Epicureans denied the immortality of the soul and asserted its atomic character; but they did so in the interest of their own ethic and not, of course, because they had discovered that the soul is in reality composed of atoms, though it must be admitted that the Epicurean psychology fits in better with their banal ethic than the Stoic psychology with the Stoic idealist ethic. Both Stoic psychology and Stoic ethic were constantly striving, as it were, to break the bonds of the traditional materialistic monism in which they were bound, and the Stoics could no more explain rational thought in terms of their system than the Epicureans could explain thought in terms of the motion of atoms. The Epicureans may have anticipated to some extent the psychology of Hobbes or of thinkers of the French Enlightenment, but neither in the ancient world nor in eighteenth-century France, nor even in the twentieth century, can the psychical be satisfactorily explained in terms of the corporeal, the rational in terms of irrational, the conscious in terms of the unconscious. On the other hand, if the psychical cannot be reduced to the corporeal, no more can the corporeal be reduced to the psychical: the two remain distinct, though in man, the bond between the purely spiritual and the purely material spheres, the two elements are intimately related. Plato laid the emphasis on the fact of distinction, Aristotle on that of the intimate relationship: both factors need to be borne in mind if one would avoid occasionalism or modern idealism on the one hand and epiphenomenalism on the other hand.

6. A few remarks on the development of ethics in ancient philosophy, particularly in regard to the relationship between ethical norms and a transcendental foundation of morality. I am quite aware that the question of the relation between ethics and metaphysics is hotly debated, and I do not propose to discuss the problem on its own merits: I wish to do no more than indicate what I consider one of the main trends in Greek ethical thought.

We have to distinguish between moral philosophy as such and the unsystematised moral judgments of mankind. Moral judgments had been made by Greeks long before the Sophists, Socrates, Plato, Aristotle, the Stoics, etc., reflected on them, and the fact that the ordinary moral judgments of man formed the material for their reflection meant that the theories of the philosophers mirrored to a greater or less extent the ordinary moral consciousness of the time. These moral judgments, however, are in turn dependent, in part at least, on education, social tradition and environment, are moulded by the community, so that it is only natural that they should differ somewhat from community to community, nation to nation. Now, in face of this difference two ways of reaction at any rate lie open to the philosopher.

(i) Perceiving that a given community holds fast to its own traditional code and considers it the only one, the "natural" one, while on the other hand not all communities have exactly the same code, he may react by drawing the conclusion that morals are relative, that though one code may be more useful, more expedient, than another, there exists no absolute code of morals. This was the line taken by the Sophists.

(ii) The philosopher may attribute a good deal of the observed differences to *error* and assert a sure standard and norm of morality. This was the way taken by Plato and Aristotle. In fact the ethical intellectualism, particularly characteristic of Socrates, though also of Plato to a less extent, bears witness to the fact that they ascribed differences in moral judgment to mistake, to error. Thus to the man who thinks, or professes to think, that the natural and proper procedure is to injure one's enemies or to pursue a career of unabashed egoism, Plato attempts to show that he is quite mistaken in his notion. He may at times appeal to self-interest, even if only in *argumentum ad hominem*; but, whatever he appeals to in order to prove his view, Plato was certainly no relativist in ethics: he believed in abiding standards, objectively true and universally valid.

Now, if we look at the moral philosophies of Plato and Aristotle, this fact is apparent, that in either case the standard of conduct is measured by their conception of human nature. The ideal was regarded by Plato as something fixed, eternal and transcendent, not subject to relativity and variation. The different faculties of man are faculties of activity according to certain habits or virtues, and of each virtue there is an ideal pattern, comprised in the all-embracing ideal, the Ideal of the Good. There is an ideal of man and ideals of man's virtues, and it is man's moral function to conform himself to those ideals. When he does so, when his nature is harmoniously developed and perfected according to the ideal, he is a "just" or good man, he is a true example of a man and has attained true well-being. Moreover, for Plato God is constantly operative in the world, striving to realise the ideal in the concrete and actual world. God Himself never departs from the ideal, but always has the ideal, the best, in view: He is the Reason, Divine Providence, operative in the cosmos. God is also the source of the human reason and is depicted symbolically in the *Timaeus* as forming the human reason Himself, so that man's rational soul is akin to the Divine and has as its task the same task as the Deity, the realisation of the ideal, of value, in the world. Man is thus by nature a co-operator with God: in that consists his vocation, to work towards the realisation of the ideal, of value, in his personal life and in that of society or the State. It is God Who sets the standard, not man, says Plato against Protagoras, and man's end is the greatest possible likeness to God. Plato says little of moral obligation, it is true, but he evidently considered, even if without a fully reflective consciousness of the fact, that man is under an obligation to act as truly befits a man. The ethical intellectualism which he inherited from Socrates, was doubtless a hindrance in the way of a clear realisation of moral obligation and responsibility; but do not the myths of the future life, of reward and punishment, clearly imply some realisation of moral obligation? Plato certainly gave a transcendental foundation to the *content* of the moral law and, though the same cannot be said in regard to the *form* of the moral law, the categorical imperative, he does seem to have had a dim awareness of the fact that a moral law, if its morally binding and universally valid character is to be substantiated, must be given a transcendental foundation, not only in regard to its content, but also in regard to its form.

When we turn to Aristotle, we find a very fine analysis of the good life, of the moral and intellectual virtues, which were analysed by Aristotle much more completely and systematically than by Plato; but the transcendental values of Plato have been swept away or been replaced by the immanent form. It is true that Aristotle calls on man to think divine things, to imitate, as far as he can, God's contemplation of the highest object, so that in a sense there is, even for Aristotle, an eternal pattern of human life; but the theoretic life is inaccessible to most men, while on the other hand Aristotle affords no ground for a man thinking that he is called upon to co-operate with the Divine, since the God of the *Metaphysics* at least does not operate consciously and efficiently in the world. Aristotle never really synthesised satisfactorily the life of the moral virtues and the theoretic life, and the moral law for Aristotle is, it would seem, devoid of any real transcendental foundation, in regard to both content and form. What could he say to anyone who questioned the obligation of living in the manner proposed in the *Ethics*? He could appeal to aesthetic standards, to good form, to "fairness," and he could reply that to act otherwise is to miss the goal of happiness, which all necessarily seek, with the consequence that one would be acting irrationally; but he left no place for an appeal to a specifically moral obligation with a firm foundation in absolute Reality.

Later Greek philosophers, if we except, e.g. the Epicureans, seem to have seen the necessity of founding a standard morality on an absolute basis. The Stoics insist on duty, on the Divine Will, on the life of reason which is life in accordance with nature, since man's rational nature proceeds from God, the all-pervasive Reason, and returns to Him. Their pantheism certainly involved them in ethical difficulties; but, none the less, they viewed morality as ultimately the expression of the Divine in man and in human life. As God is one, as human nature is constant, there can be but one morality. It would be an anachronism to read into their expression for "duty" all the meaning that the term has acquired in modern times; but at least they had some conception of duty and of moral obligation, even if the clear statement of this conception was hampered by the determinism consequent on their pantheism. In the Neo-Platonic system or systems ethics proper was subordinated to insistence on the religious aspect of human life and man's ascent to God; but the practice of the moral life was regarded as an integral part of that ascent and, in practising it, man conforms himself to transcendentally-grounded standards. Moreover, the fact that those Romans who aspired to a moral life and attached importance to moral values, saw the necessity of purifying the idea of God and of emphasising Divine Providence serves to illustrate the practical benefit of founding ethics ultimately on metaphysics and so serves as an empirical confirmation of the theoretical assertion of that foundation.

7. The mention of ethics and of an ascription to morality of a transcendental foundation naturally leads one on to a brief consideration of Greek philosophy viewed as a preparatory intellectual instrument for Christianity, as a *preparatio evangelica*. Only a few suggestions can be made, however: any adequate treatment of the subject would require more space than I can devote to it in this concluding chapter. (Consideration of the doctrines actually borrowed directly or indirectly by Christian philosophy from Greek thinkers is best reserved for the next volume, that dealing with mediaeval philosophy.)

In the philosophy of Heraclitus we find the beginnings of the doctrine of an immanent Reason operative in the world, though the Logos is conceived on the material plane, as identical with the primal Fire (a conception that was elaborated in later times by the Stoics), while Anaxagoras contributes the theory of Nous as the primary moving Principle. But in both cases there is but a hint of the developments that were to come later, and it is not until Plato that we find anything like a natural theology. But, if among the pre-Socratics we find little more than hints of the doctrine of (what we would call) God, as First Efficient Cause (Anaxagoras) and as Providence or immanent Reason (Heraclitus), we find in Pythagoreanism a somewhat clearer enunciation of the distinction between soul and body, the superiority of soul to body and the necessity of tending the former and preserving it from contamination. However, in regard to pre-Socratic philosophy as a whole, it is the search for the ultimate nature of the world and its conception of the world as a law-ordered world, rather than any specific doctrines (with the exception perhaps of the Orphic-Pythagorean psychology), which entitles it to be regarded in any sense as a remote *preparatio evangelica*, a preparation of the pagan mind for the reception of the revealed religion. For it is the conception of a law-ordered world that naturally leads on to the conception of a Lawgiver and Orderer. Before this further step could be taken, however, it was necessary to arrive at a clear distinction between soul and body, the immaterial and the material, and for the apprehension of this distinction the Orphics and Pythagoreans paved the way, though it was really Plato who extended the Pythagorean anthropological distinction between the transcendental and the phenomenal, the immaterial and the material.

It would be difficult to exaggerate the importance of Plato in the intellectual *preparatio evangelica* of the pagan world. By his doctrine of exemplarism, his theory of the transcendental Exemplary Cause, by his doctrine of Reason or Mind operative in the world and forming the world for the best, he obviously remotely paved the way for the ultimate acceptance of the one Transcendent-Immanent God. Again, by his doctrine of the immortal and rational soul of man, of retribution, of moral purification, he made easier the intellectual acceptance of Christian psychology and asceticism, while his insistence on absolute moral standards in accordance with the teaching of his great Master, Socrates, and the hints he drops as to the assimilation with God were a remote preparation for the acceptance of the Christian ethic. Nor must we forget that in the *Laws* Plato gave reasons why we should admit the existence of Mind operative in the universe, thus foreshadowing the later natural theologies. But it is rather the total attitude fostered by the Platonic philosophy—I refer to the belief in transcendental Reality, eternal values, immortality, righteousness, Providence, etc., and the characteristic mental and emotional attitude that is logically fostered by such belief—rather than any specific arguments which helped to lead up to the acceptance of Christianity. It is true that the doctrine of the Transcendental, as developed in Middle and Neo-Platonism, was used *against* Christianity, under the plea that the dogma of the Incarnation is incompatible with the transcendent character of God: but the transcendent character of God is an integral doctrine of Christianity and it can scarcely be denied that the Platonic ascent above pre-Socratic materialism was a predisposing factor towards the acceptance of a religion which insists on the supreme reality of the transcendental and on the abiding character of spiritual values. Early Christian thinkers certainly recognised in Platonism a certain kinship, even if more or less remote, with their own *Weltanschauung* and, though Aristotle was later to become the philosopher *par excellence* of Scholasticism, Augustinianism stands rather in the line of the Platonic tradition. Moreover, Platonic-Augustinian elements are very far from being entirely absent in the philosophy of that very Scholastic who adopted—and adapted—Aristotelianism, St. Thomas Aquinas. Thus, if Platonism helped in some degree to prepare the way for Christianity, even if largely through succeeding Schools that developed the Platonic tradition, Christianity may also be said to have borrowed some of its philosophic "outfit" from Platonism.

By mediaeval philosophers of the Augustinian tradition, such as St. Bonaventure (one of whose main objections against Aristotle was that he rejected exemplarism), Aristotelianism tended to be regarded as inimical to the Christian religion, largely because he became known to the West principally through the Arabian commentators. (Thus Averroes interpreted Aristotle—probably rightly—as denying, for example, the *personal* immortality of the human soul.) But though it is true, for instance, that the conception of God in the *Metaphysics* as entirely self-engrossed and caring nought for the world and man, is not that of Christianity, it must surely be admitted that the natural theology of Aristotle was a preparation for the acceptance of Christianity. God appears as transcendent, immaterial Thought, the absolute Final Cause, and when the Platonic Ideas came later to be placed in the Mind of God and a certain syncretism of Platonism and Aristotelianism took place, the ultimate Efficient, Exemplary and Final Causes tending to coalesce, a conception of reality was provided that made it easier than it might otherwise have been to accept Christianity from the intellectual standpoint.

Of the post-Aristotelian philosophy much might be said in the present connection; I can but select a few points for mention. Stoicism, with its doctrine of the immanent Logos and its "providential" operation in the world, with its noble ethic, was an important factor in the world in which Christianity was implanted and grew. It is quite true that the Stoic philosophy remained theoretically materialist and more or less determinist; but, from the practical viewpoint, the insistence on man's kinship with God, on purification of the soul by self-control and moral education, on submission to the "Divine Will," together with the broadening influence of its cosmopolitanism, served as a preparation in some minds for the acceptance of the universal religion which, while transcending the materialism of the Stoics, insisted on the brotherhood of men as children of God and introduced a dynamic influence which was wanting in the Stoic system. Moreover, in so far as ethical Stoicism was an answer to the contemporary need for moral guidance and direction as to the right course to be pursued by the individual, swamped in the great cosmopolitan Empire, this need was far better met by the Christian doctrine, which could appeal to the uneducated and simple in a way that Stoicism could hardly do and which held out the prospect of complete happiness in the future life as the term of moral endeavour in a way that Stoicism, by its very system, was debarred from doing.

Besides the strictly ethical needs of man there were also his religious capacity and need to be satisfied. While the State cult was unable to meet this need, the mystery-religions and even philosophy (in a far less popular form, e.g. in Neo-Platonism) catered for its satisfaction. By attempting to cater for man's deeper spiritual aspirations they at the same time tended to develop and intensify those aspirations, with the result that Christianity fell on an already prepared ground. Christianity, with its doctrine of salvation, its sacramental system, its dogmas, its doctrine of incorporation with Christ through membership of the Church and of the final vision of God, its offer of supernatural life, was *the* "mystery-religion"; but it had the inestimable advantage over all pagan mystery-religions that it was an *historical* religion, based on the Life, Death and Resurrection of the God-Man, Jesus Christ, Who lived and suffered in Palestine in a certain historical period: it was based on historical fact, not on myth. As to the doctrine of "salvation" as found in philosophical Schools and the doctrine of ecstatic union with God as developed in Neo-Platonism, this was far too intellectualist in character to admit of its having a popular appeal. Through the Sacraments and the reception of the supernatural life Christianity offered to *all* men, educated and uneducated alike, union with God, imperfect in this life, perfect in the next, and so, even from the purely natural viewpoint, was obviously destined to exercise a far wider influence than philosophy as such could ever exercise, even a philosophy that was strongly tinctured with religious elements. Moreover, the Neo-Platonic philosophy was unhistorical, in the sense that a doctrine like that of the Incarnation was alien to its spirit, and an historical religion is bound to have a wider popular appeal than a metaphysical philosophy. Nevertheless, in spite of the shocked and scandalised attitude that some early Christian writers adopted (very naturally) in regard to the mystery-religions, particularly that of Mithras, with its quasi-sacramental rites, both the more or less popular mystery-religions and intellectualist Neo-Platonism served the purpose of preparing men's minds for the acceptance of Christianity. They may have tended to set themselves up as rivals to Christianity and they may have kept some individuals from embracing Christianity who would otherwise have done so; but that does not mean that they could not and did not serve as a way to Christianity. Porphyry attacked Christianity, but was not St. Augustine brought to Christianity by way of Plotinus? Neo-Platonism was the last breath, the last flower, of ancient pagan philosophy; but in the thought of St. Augustine it became the first stage of Christian philosophy. Christianity was not, of course, in any sense the outcome of ancient philosophy, nor can it be called a philosophic system, for it is the revealed religion and its historical antecedents are to be found in Judaism; but when Christians began to philosophise, they found ready at hand a rich material, a store of dialectical instruments and metaphysical concepts and terms, and those who believe that divine Providence is operative in history will hardly suppose that the provision of that material and its elaboration through the centuries was simply and solely an accident.

APPENDIX I

SOME ABBREVIATIONS USED IN THIS VOLUME

AËTIUS. Collectio placitorum (philosophorum).
ALBINUS. Didask. (Didaskalikos).
AMMIANUS MARCELLINUS. Rerum gest. (Rerum gestarum libri 18).
AUGUSTINE. Contra Acad. (Contra Academicos).
C.D. (De Civitate Dei).
BURNET. E.G.P. (Early Greek Philosophy).
G.P., I. (Greek Philosophy. Part I, Thales to Plato).
CAPITOLINUS, JULIUS.. Vit. M. Ant. (Vita Marci Antonini Pii).
CHALCIDIUS. In Tim. (Commentary on Plato's *Timaeus*).
CICERO. Acad. Prior. (Academica Priora).
Acad. Post. (Academica Posteriora).
Ad Att. (Letters to Atticus).
De Div. (De Divinatione).
De Fin. (De Finibus).
De Nat. D. (De Natura Deorum).
De Off. (De Officiis).
De Orat. (De Oratore).
De Senect. (De Senectute).
Somn. Scip. (Somnium Scipionis).
Tusc. (Tusculanae Disputationes).
CLEMENS ALEXANDRINUS. Protrep. (Protrepticus).
Strom. (Stromata).
DAMASCIUS. Dubit. (Dubitationes et solutiones de primis principiis).
DIOGENES LAËRTIUS. Lives of the Philosophers.
EPICTETUS. Disc. (Discourses).
Ench. (Enchiridion).
EUDEMUS. Phys. (*Physics*, of which only fragments remain).
EUNAPIUS. Vit. Soph. (Lives of the Sophists).
EUSEBIUS. Hist. Eccl. (Historia Ecclesiastica).
Prep. Evan. (Preparatio Evangelica).
GELLIUS, AULUS. Noct. Att. (Noctes Atticae).
GREGORY OF NAZIANZEN. adv. Max. (adversus Maximum).
HIPPOLYTUS. Ref. (Refutationis omnium haeresium libri X).
JOSEPHUS. Ant. Jud. (Jewish Antiquities).
LACTANTIUS. Div. Inst. (Institutiones divinae).
LAMPRIDIUS. Alex. (Life of Alexander Severus).
Aurel. (Life of Aurelian).
LUCIAN. De morte Peregr. (De morte Peregrini).

MARCUS AURELIUS. Med. (Meditations or To Himself).
MAXIMUS OF TYRE. Diss. (Dissertationes).
ORIGEN. *c.* Cels. (Contra Celsum).
P.G. Patrologia Graeca (ed. Migne).
P.L. Patrologia Latina (ed. Migne).
PHILO. De conf. ling. (De confusione linguarum).
De gigant. (De gigantibus).
De human. (De humanitate).
De migrat. Abrah. (De migratione Abrahami).
De mutat. nom. (De mutatione nominum).
De opif. mundi (De opificio mundi).
De post. Caini (De posteritate Caini).
De somn. (De somniis).
De vita Mos. (De vita Moysis).
Leg. alleg. (Legum allegoriarum libri).
Quis rer. div. her. (Quis rerum divinarum heres sit).
Quod Deus sit immut. (Quod Deus sit immutabilis).
PHOTIUS. Bibliotheca (about A.D. 857).
PLUTARCH. Cat. Mai. (Cato Maior).
De anim. proc. (De animae procreatione in Timaeo).
De comm. notit. (De communibus notitiis adversus Stoicos).
De def. orac. (De defectu oraculorum).
De gloria Athen. (Bellone an pace clariores fuerint Athenienses).
De Is. et Osir. (De Iside et Osiride).
De prim. frig. (De primo frigido).
De ser. num. vind. (De sera numinis vindicta).
De sol. animal. (De sollertia animalium).
De Stoic repug. (De repugnantiis Stoicis).
Non p. suav. (Ne suaviter quidem vivi posse secundum Epicurum).
PSEUDO-PLUTARCH. Strom. (Fragments of the stromateis conserved in Eusebius' *Preparatio Evangelica*).
PORPHYRY. Isag. (Isagoge, i.e. introd. to Aristotle's *Categories*).
PROCLUS. De Prov. (De providentia et fato et eo quod in nobis).
In Alcib. (Commentary on *Alcibiades* I of "Plato").
In Remp. (Commentary on *Republic* of Plato).
In Parmen. (Commentary on *Parmenides* of Plato).
In Tim. (Commentary on *Timaeus* of Plato).
Instit. Theol. (Institutio Theologica).
Theol. Plat. (In Platonis Theologiam).
SENECA. Nat. Quaest. (Naturalium Quaestionum libri VII).
SEXTUS EMPIRICUS. adv. math. (Adversus mathematicos).
Pyrr. Hyp. (Pyrrhonenses Hypotyposes).

SIMPLICIUS. In Arist. Categ. (Commentary on Aristotle's *Categories*).
Phys. (Commentary on Aristotle's *Physics*).

—STACE, W. T. Crit. Hist. (A Critical History of Greek Philosophy).

STOBAEUS. Flor. (Florilegium).

TACITUS. Ann. (Annales).
Hist. (Historiae).

THEOPHRASTUS. Phys. Opin. (Physicorum Opiniones).

XENOPHON. Cyneg. (Cynegeticus).
Mem. (Memorabilia).

APPENDIX II

A NOTE ON SOURCES

Since on the one hand some philosophers did not write at all, while on the other hand the works of many philosophers who did write have been lost, we have to rely in very many cases on the testimony of later writers for information as to the course of Greek philosophy.

The chief source of knowledge in the ancient world concerning the pre-Socratic philosophy was the work of Theophrastus entitled *Physicorum Opiniones*, a work which, unfortunately, we possess only in fragmentary form. Theophrastus' work became the source of various other compilations, epitomes or "doxographies," in some of which the opinions of the philosophers were arranged according to theme, while in others the opinions were set forth under the names of the respective philosophers. Of the former type were the *Vetusta Placita*, written by an unknown disciple of Poseidonius in the first half of the first century A.D. We do not possess this work, but that it existed and that it was based on Theophrastus' work, has been shown by Diels. The *Vetusta Placita* in turn formed the main source of the so-called *Aëtii Placita* or Συναγωγὴ τῶν Ἀρεσκόντων (about A.D. 100). Aetiüs' work in turn served as a basis for the *Placita philosophorum* of the Pseudo-Plutarch (compiled about A.D. 150) and the doxographical extracts given by John Stobaeus (A.D. fifth century) in the first book of his *Eclogae*. These two last works are the most important doxographical compilations which we possess, and it has become evident that the main ultimate source for both was the work of Theophrastus, which was also ultimately the chief, though not the only, source for the first book of Hippolytus' *Refutation of all heresies* (in which the subject-matter is arranged under the names of the respective philosophers concerned), and for the fragments, falsely attributed to Plutarch, which are quoted in the *Preparatio Evangelica* of Eusebius.

Further information on the opinions of Greek philosophers is provided by such works as the *Noctes Atticae* of Aulus Gellius (about A.D. 150), the writings of philosophers like Plutarch, Cicero and Sextus Empiricus, and the works of the Christian Fathers and early Christian writers. (Care must be exercised, however, in the use of such historical sources, since, for example, Cicero drew his knowledge of early Greek philosophers from intermediate sources, while Sextus Empiricus was mainly concerned to support his own sceptical position by drawing attention to the contradictory opinions of the dogmatic philosophers. In regard to Aristotle's testimony as to the opinions of his predecessors we must not forget that Aristotle tended to look on earlier philosophies simply from the viewpoint of his own system and to see in them preparatory work for his own achievement. His attitude on this matter was doubtless largely justified, but it does mean that he was not always concerned to give what we should consider a purely objective and scientific account of the course of philosophic thought.) The commentaries composed by authors of Antiquity on the works of eminent philosophers are also of considerable importance, for instance, the commentary by Simplicius on the Physics of *Aristotle.*

In regard to the lives of the philosophers the most important work which we possess is that of Diogenes Laërtius (A.D. third century). This work is a compilation of material taken from various sources and is of very unequal merit, much of the biographical material being anecdotal, legendary and valueless in character, "tall stories" and different, sometimes contradictory, accounts of an event being included by the author, accounts which he had collected from previous writers and compilers. On the other hand it would be a great mistake to allow the unscientific character of the work to obscure its importance and very real value. The indices of the works of the philosophers are important, and we are indebted to Diogenes for a considerable amount of valuable information on the opinions and lives of the Greek philosophers. In assessing the historical value of Diogenes' statements it is obviously necessary to know (as far as this is possible) the particular source to which he was indebted on any given occasion, and no little painstaking and fruitful labour has been expended by scholars, in order to attain this knowledge.

For the chronology of the Greek philosophers the chief source is the *Chronica* of Apollodorus, who based the first part of his chronicle on the *Chronographia* of Eratosthenes of Cyrene (third century before Christ), but added a supplement, carrying it down to about the year 110 B.C. Apollodorus had not, of course, exact material at his disposal, and he had recourse to the arbitrary method of linking up some event of importance which was supposed to have occurred during the period of a philosopher's life, with the philosopher's prime or ἀκμή (taken as the fortieth year) and then reckoning backward to the date of the philosopher's birth. Similarly, it was taken as a general rule that a disciple was forty years younger than his master. Accuracy, therefore, was not to be expected.

(On the general subject of sources see e.g. Ueberweg-Praechter, *Die Philosophie des Altertums*, pp. 10–26 (Apollodorus' Chronicle is given on pp. 667–71), A. Fairbanks, *The First Philosophers of Greece*, pp. 263–88, L. Robin, *Greek Thought and the Origins of the Scientific Spirit*, pp. 7–16, and the *Stellenregister* to Diels' *Fragmente der Vorsokratiker*.

APPENDIX III

A FEW BOOKS

1. *General Histories of Greek Philosophy*

ADAMSON, R. (ed. Sorley and Hardie). The Development of Greek Philosophy. London, 1908.

ARMSTRONG, A. H. An Introduction to Ancient Philosophy. Methuen, 1947.

BENN, A. W. The Greek Philosophers. London, 1914.

BRÉHIER, E. Histoire de la philosophie. Tome I. Paris, 1943.

BURNET, J. Greek Philosophy, Part I. Thales to Plato. Macmillan. (This scholarly work is indispensable to the student).

ERDMANN, J. E. A History of Philosophy, vol. I. Swan Sonnenschein, 1910. (Erdmann was an eminent historian of the Hegelian School.)

GOMPERZ, TH. Greek Thinkers, 4 vols. (Trs. L. Magnus.) John Murray.

ROBIN, L. La pensée grecque et les origines de l'esprit scientifique. Paris, 1923.

Greek Thought and the Origins of the Scientific Spirit. London, 1928.

RUGGIERO, G. DE. La filosofia greca. 2 vols. Bari, 1917. (Professor de Ruggiero writes from the viewpoint of an Italian Neo-Hegelian.)

STACE, W. T. A Critical History of Greek Philosophy. Macmillan, 1920.

STENZEL, J. Metaphysik des Altertums. Berlin, Oldenbourg, 1929. (Particularly valuable for the treatment of Plato.)

STOCKL, A. A Handbook of the History of Philosophy. Part I. Pre-Scholastic Philosophy. Trs. by T. A. Finlay, S.J. Dublin, 1887.

UEBERWEG-PRAECHTER. Die Philosophie des Altertums. Berlin, Mittler, 1926.

WERNER, C. La philosophie grecque. Paris, Payot, 1938.

ZELLER, E. Outlines of the History of Greek Philosophy. Kegan Paul, 1931. (Revised by W. Nestle, translated by L. R. Palmer.)

2. *Pre-Socratic Philosophy*

The best collection of the fragments of the Pre-Socratics is to be found in Hermann Diels' *Vorsokratiker*, fifth edition. Berlin, 1934–5.

BURNET, J. Early Greek Philosophy. Black, 3rd edition, 1920; 4th edition, 1930. (This extremely useful work includes very many fragments.)

COVOTTI, A. I Presocratici. Naples, 1934.

FAIRBANKS, A. The First Philosophers of Greece. London, 1898.

FREEMAN, K. Companion to the Pre-Socratic Philosophers. Blackwell, 1949 (2nd edition).

JAEGER, WERNER. The Theology of the Early Greek Philosophers. Oxford, 1947.

ZELLER, E. A History of Greek Philosophy from the earliest period to the time of Socrates. Trs. S. F. Alleyne. 2 vols. Longmans, 1881.

3. *Plato*

The Works of Plato are published, under the editorship of J. Burnet, in the *Oxford Classical Texts.* A well-known translation, in five volumes, is that by B. Jowett, O.U.P., 3rd edition, 1892. There are also more literal translations.

ARCHER-HIND, R. D. The Timaeus of Plato. Macmillan, 1888.

CORNFORD, F. M. Plato's Theory of Knowledge. Kegan Paul, 1935. (A translation of the *Theaetetus* and *Sophist*, with commentary.)
Plato's Cosmology. Kegan Paul, 1937. (A translation of the *Timaeus*, with running commentary.)
Plato and Parmenides. Kegan Paul, 1939. (Translation of the *Parmenides*, with commentary and discussion.)
The Republic of Plato. Translated with Introduction and Notes. O.U.P.

DEMOS, R. The Philosophy of Plato. Scribners, 1939.

DIÈS, AUGUSTE. Autour de Platon. Beauchesne, 1927.
Platon. Flammarion, 1930.

FIELD, G. C. Plato and his Contemporaries. Methuen, 1930.
The Philosophy of Plato. Oxford, 1949.

GROTE, C. Plato and the other Companions of Socrates. John Murray, 2nd edition, 1867.

HARDIE, W. F. R. A Study in Plato. O.U.P., 1936.

HARTMANN, N. Platons Logik des Seins. Giessen, 1909.

LODGE, R. C. Plato's Theory of Ethics. Kegan Paul, 1928.

LUTOSLAWSKI, W. The Origin and Growth of Plato's Logic. London, 1905.

MILHAUD, G. Les philosophes-géomètres de la Grèce. 2nd edition, Paris, 1934.

NATORP, P. Platons Ideenlehre. Leipzig, 1903.

NETTLESHIP, R. L. Lectures on the Republic of Plato. Macmillan, 1898.

RITTER, C. The Essence of Plato's Philosophy. George Allen & Unwin, 1933. (Translated by Adam Alles.)
Platon, sein Leben, seine Schriften, seine Lehre. 2 vols. Munich, 1910 and 1923.

ROBIN, L. La théorie Platonicienne des idées et des nombres. Paris, 1933.
Platon. Paris, 1936.
La physique de Platon. Paris, 1919.

SHOREY, P. The Unity of Plato's Thought. Chicago, 1903.

STENZEL, J.. Plato's Method of Dialectic. O.U.P., 1940. (Translated by D. G. Allan.)
Zahl und Gestalt bei Platon und Aristoteles. 2nd edition. Leipzig, 1933.
Platon der Erzieher. 1928.
Studien zur Entwicklung der Platonischen Dialektik. Breslau, 1917.

STEWART, J. A. The Myths of Plato. O.U.P., 1905.
Plato's Doctrine of Ideas. O.U P., 1909.

TAYLOR, A. E. Plato, the Man and his Work. Methuen, 1926. (No student of Plato should be unacquainted with this masterly work.)
A Commentary on Plato's Timaeus. O.U.P., 1928.
Article on Plato in Encyc. Brit., 14th edition.
Platonism and its Influence. U.S.A. 1924 (Eng. Harrap).

WILAMOWITZ-MOELLENDORF, U. VON. Platon. 2 vols. Berlin, 1919.

ZELLER, E. Plato and the Older Academy. Longmans, 1876. (Translated by S. F. Alleyne and A. Goodwin.)

4. *Aristotle*

The Oxford translation of the works of Aristotle is published in eleven volumes, under the editorship of J. A. Smith and W. D. Ross.

BARKER, E. The Political Thought of Plato and Aristotle. Methuen, 1906.
Article on Aristotle in the Encyc. Brit., 14th edition.

CASE, T. Article on Aristotle in the Encyc. Brit., 11th edition.

GROTE, G. Aristotle. London, 1883.

JAEGER, WERNER. Aristotle. Fundamentals of the History of his Development. O.U.P., 1934. (Translated by R. Robinson.)

LE BLOND, J. M. Logique et Méthode chez Aristote. Paris, Vrin, 1939

MAIER, H. Die Syllogistik des Aristoteles. Tübingen, 1896. New edition, 1936.

MURE, G. R. G. Aristotle. Benn, 1932.

PIAT, C. Aristote. Paris, 1912.

ROBIN, L. Aristote. Paris, 1944.

ROSS, SIR W. D. Aristotle. Methuen, 2nd edition, 1930.
(A survey of Aristotle's thought by a great Aristotelian scholar.)
Aristotle's Metaphysics. 2 vols. O.U.P., 1924.
Aristotle's Physics. O.U.P., 1936.
(These two commentaries are invaluable.)

TAYLOR, A. E. Aristotle. Nelson, 1943.

ZELLER, E. Aristotle and the earlier Peripatetics. 2 vols. Longmans, 1897.

5. *Post-Aristotelian Philosophy*

ARMSTRONG, A. P. The Architecture of the Intelligible Universe in the Philosophy of Plotinus. Cambridge, 1940.
(A very careful study of the origins and nature of Plotinian Neo-Platonism.)

ARNOLD, E. V. Roman Stoicism. 1911.

BAILEY, C. The Greek Atomists and Epicurus. O.U.P.

BEVAN, E. E. Stoics and Sceptics. O.U.P., 1913.
Hellenistic Popular Philosophy. Cambridge, 1923.

BIGG, C. Neoplatonism. S.P.C.K., 1895.

BRÉHIER, E. Philon d'Alexandrie. Paris, 1908.
La philosophie de Plotin. Paris, 1928.

CAPES, W. W. Stoicism. S.P.C.K., 1880.

DILL, SIR S. Roman Society from Nero to Marcus Aurelius. Macmillan, 1905.

DODDS, E. R. Select Passages illustrating Neoplatonism. S.P.C.K., 1923.

FULLER, B. A. G. The Problem of Evil in Plotinus. Cambridge, 1912.

HENRY, PAUL (S.J.). Plotin et l'Occident. Louvain, 1934.
Vers la reconstitution de l'enseignement oral de Plotin. Bulletin de l'Academie royale de Belgique, 1937.

HICKS, R. D. Stoic and Epicurean. Longmans, 1910.

INGE, W. R. The Philosophy of Plotinus. 2 vols. 3rd edition. Longmans, 1928.

KRAKOWSKI, E. Plotin et le Paganisme Religieux. Paris, Denoël et Steele, 1933.

LEBRETON, J. (S.J.). Histoire du Dogme de la Trinité. Beauchesne, 1910.

MARCUS AURELIUS. The Meditations of the Emperor Marcus Aurelius Edited with Translation and Commentary by A. S. L. Farquharson. 2 vols., O.U.P. 1944.

PLOTINUS. The *Enneads* have been translated into English, in five vols. by S. MacKenna and B. S. Page. 1917–30.

PROCLUS. The Elements of Theology. O.U.P.
(A Revised Text with Translation, Introduction and Commentary by E. R. Dodds.)

REINHARDT, K. Poseidonios. Munich, 1921.

ROBIN, L. Pyrrhon et le Scepticisme Grec. Paris, 1944.

TAYLOR, T. Select Works of Plotinus (ed. G. R. S. Mead). G. Bell & Sons, 1929.

WHITTAKER, T. The Neo-Platonists. 2nd edition, Cambridge, 1901.

WITT, R. E. Albinus and the History of Middle Platonism. Cambridge,

ZELLER, E. The Stoics, Epicureans and Sceptics. Longmans, 1870.
(Translated by O. J. Reichel.)
A History of Eclecticism in Greek Philosophy. Longmans, 1883.
(Translated by S. F. Alleyne.)

INDEX

(A small *n* after a number indicates that the reference is to a footnote on the page in question.)

Volume II
AUGUSTINE TO SCOTUS

CONTENTS

PART II

THE CAROLINGIAN RENAISSANCE

PART III

THE TENTH, ELEVENTH AND TWELFTH CENTURIES

PART IV

ISLAMIC AND JEWISH PHILOSOPHY: TRANSLATIONS

PART V

THE THIRTEENTH CENTURY

APPENDICES

MEDIAEVAL PHILOSOPHY

CHAPTER I

INTRODUCTION

1. In this second volume of my history of philosophy I had originally hoped to give an account of the development of philosophy throughout the whole period of the Middle Ages, understanding by mediaeval philosophy the philosophic thought and systems which were elaborated between the Carolingian renaissance in the last part of the eighth century A.D. (John Scotus Eriugena, the first outstanding mediaeval philosopher was born about 810) and the end of the fourteenth century. Reflection has convinced me, however, of the advisability of devoting two volumes to mediaeval philosophy. As my first volume[1] ended with an account of neo-Platonism and contained no treatment of the philosophic ideas to be found in the early Christian writers, I considered it desirable to say something of these ideas in the present volume. It is true that men like St. Gregory of Nyssa and St. Augustine belonged to the period of the Roman Empire, that their philosophic affiliations were with Platonism, understood in the widest sense, and that they cannot be termed mediaevals; but the fact remains that they were Christian thinkers and exercised a great influence on the Middle Ages. One could hardly understand St. Anselm or St. Bonaventure without knowing something of St. Augustine, nor could one understand the thought of John Scotus Eriugena without knowing something of the thought of St. Gregory of Nyssa and of the Pseudo-Dionysius. There is scarcely any need, then, to apologise for beginning a history of mediaeval philosophy with a consideration of thinkers who belong, so far as chronology is concerned, to the period of the Roman Empire.

The present volume, then, begins with the early Christian period and carries the history of mediaeval philosophy up to the end of the thirteenth century, including Duns Scotus (about 1265–1308). In my third volume I propose to treat of the philosophy of the fourteenth century, laying special emphasis on Ockhamism. In

[1] *A History of Philosophy*, Vol. I, Greece and Rome, London, 1946.

that volume I shall also include a treatment of the philosophies of the Renaissance, of the fifteenth and sixteenth centuries, and of the 'Silver Age' of Scholastic thought, even though Francis Suarez did not die until the year 1617, twenty-one years after the birth of Descartes. This arrangement may appear to be an arbitrary one, and to some extent it is. But it is extremely doubtful if it is possible to make any hard and fast dividing line between mediaeval and modern philosophy, and a good case could be made out for including Descartes with the later Scholastics, contrary to tradition as this would be. I do not propose, however, to adopt this course, and if I include in the next volume, the third, some philosophers who might seem to belong properly to the 'modern period', my reason is largely one of convenience, to clear the decks, so that in the fourth volume I may develop in a systematic manner the interconnection between the leading philosophical systems from Francis Bacon in England and Descartes in France up to and including Kant. Nevertheless, whatever method of division be adopted, one has to remember that the compartments into which one divides the history of philosophic thought are not watertight, that transitions are gradual, not abrupt, that there is overlapping and interconnection, that succeeding systems are not cut off from one another with a hatchet.

2. There was a time when mediaeval philosophy was considered as unworthy of serious study, when it was taken for granted that the philosophy of the Middle Ages was so subservient to theology that it was practically indistinguishable therefrom and that, in so far as it was distinguishable, it amounted to little more than a barren logic-chopping and word-play. In other words, it was taken for granted that European philosophy contained two main periods, the ancient period, which to all intents and purposes meant the philosophies of Plato and Aristotle, and the modern period, when the speculative reason once more began to enjoy freedom after the dark night of the Middle Ages when ecclesiastical authority reigned supreme and the human reason, chained by heavy fetters, was compelled to confine itself to the useless and fanciful study of theology, until a thinker like Descartes at length broke the chains and gave reason its freedom. In the ancient period and the modern period philosophy may be considered a free man, whereas in the mediaeval period it was a slave.

Apart from the fact that mediaeval philosophy naturally shared in the disesteem with which the Middle Ages in general were commonly regarded, one factor which was partly responsible for the attitude adopted towards mediaeval thinkers was doubtless the language used concerning Scholasticism by men like Francis Bacon and René Descartes. Just as Aristotelians are prone to evaluate Platonism in terms of Aristotle's criticism, so admirers of the movement apparently initiated by Bacon and Descartes were prone to look on mediaeval philosophy through their eyes, unaware of the fact that much of what Francis Bacon, for instance, has to say against the Scholastics could not legitimately be applied to the great figures of mediaeval thought, however applicable it may have been to later and 'decadent' Scholastics, who worshipped the letter at the expense of the spirit. Looking on mediaeval philosophy from the very start in this light historians could perhaps scarcely be expected to seek a closer and first-hand acquaintance with it: they condemned it unseen and unheard, without knowledge either of the rich variety of mediaeval thought or of its profundity: to them it was all of a piece, an arid playing with words and a slavish dependence on theologians. Moreover, insufficiently critical, they failed to realise the fact that, if mediaeval philosophers were influenced by an external factor, theology, modern philosophers were also influenced by external factors, even if by other external factors than theology. It would have seemed to most of these historians a nonsensical proposition were one to suggest to them that Duns Scotus, for example, had a claim to be considered as a great British philosopher, at least as great as John Locke, while in their praise of the acumen of David Hume they were unaware that certain thinkers of the late Middle Ages had already anticipated a great deal of the criticism which used to be considered the peculiar contribution to philosophy of the eminent Scotsman.

I shall cite one example, the treatment accorded to mediaeval philosophy and philosophers by a man who was himself a great philosopher, Georg Wilhelm Friedrich Hegel. It is an interesting example, since Hegel's dialectical idea of the history of philosophy obviously demanded that mediaeval philosophy should be portrayed as making an essential contribution to the development of philosophic thought, while Hegel personally was no mere vulgar antagonist of mediaeval philosophy. Now, Hegel does indeed admit that mediaeval philosophy performed one useful function, that of expressing in philosophic terms the 'absolute content' of Christianity, but he insists that it is only formalistic repetition of the content of faith, in which God is represented as something 'external', and if one remembers that for Hegel faith is the mode of religious consciousness and is definitely inferior to the philosophic or speculative standpoint, the standpoint of pure reason, it is clear that in his eyes mediaeval philosophy can be philosophy only in name. Accordingly he declares that Scholastic philosophy is really theology. By this Hegel does not mean that God is not the object of philosophy as well as of theology: he means that mediaeval philosophy considered the same object as is considered by philosophy proper but that it treated that object according to the categories of theology instead of substituting for the external connections of theology (for example, the relation of the world to God as external effect to free creative Cause) the systematic, scientific, rational and necessary categories and connections of philosophy. Mediaeval philosophy was thus philosophy according to content, but theology according to form, and in Hegel's eyes the history of mediaeval philosophy is a monotonous one, in which men have tried in vain to discern any distinct stages of real progress and development of thought.

In so far as Hegel's view of mediaeval philosophy is dependent on his own particular system, on his view of the relation of religion to philosophy, of faith to reason, of immediacy to mediacy, I cannot discuss it in this volume; but I wish to point out how Hegel's treatment of mediaeval philosophy is accompanied by a very real ignorance of the course of its history. It would be possible no doubt for an Hegelian to have a real knowledge of the development of mediaeval philosophy and yet to adopt, precisely because he was an Hegelian, Hegel's general standpoint in regard to it; but there can be no shadow of doubt, even allowing for the fact that the philosopher did not himself edit and publish his lectures on the history of philosophy, that Hegel did not possess the real knowledge in question. How could one, for instance, attribute a real knowledge of mediaeval philosophy to a writer who includes Roger Bacon under the heading 'Mystics' and simply remarks 'Roger Bacon treated more especially of physics, but remained without influence. He invented gunpowder, mirrors, telescopes, and died in 1297'? The fact of the matter is that Hegel relied on authors like Tennemann and Brucker for his information concerning mediaeval philosophy, whereas the first valuable studies on mediaeval philosophy do not antedate the middle of the nineteenth century.

In adducing the instance of Hegel I am not, of course, concerned to blame the philosopher: I am rather trying to throw into relief the great change that has taken place in our knowledge of mediaeval philosophy through the work of modern scholars since about 1880. Whereas one can easily understand and pardon the misrepresentations of which a man like Hegel was unconsciously guilty, one would have little patience with similar misrepresentations to-day, after the work of scholars like Baeumker, Ehrle, Grabmann, De Wulf, Pelster, Geyer, Mandonnet, Pelzer, etc. After the light that has been thrown on mediaeval philosophy by the publication of texts and the critical editing of already published works, after the splendid volumes brought out by the Franciscan Fathers of Quaracchi, after the publications of so many numbers of the *Beiträge* series, after the production of histories like that of Maurice De Wulf, after the lucid studies of Étienne Gilson, after the patient work done by the Mediaeval Academy of America, it should no longer be possible to think that mediaeval philosophers were 'all of a piece', that mediaeval philosophy lacked richness and variety, that mediaeval thinkers were uniformly men of low stature and of mean attainments. Moreover, writers like Gilson have helped us to realise the continuity between mediaeval and modern philosophy. Gilson has shown how Cartesianism was more dependent on mediaeval thought than was formerly supposed. A good deal still remains to be done in the way of edition and interpretation of texts (one needs only to mention William of Ockham's Commentary on the *Sentences*), but it has now become possible to see the currents and development, the pattern and texture, the high lights and low lights of mediaeval philosophy with a synoptic eye.

3. But even if mediaeval philosophy was in fact richer and more varied than has been sometimes supposed, is it not true to say that it stood in such a close relation to theology that it is practically indistinguishable therefrom? Is it not, for example, a fact that the great majority of mediaeval philosophers were priests and theologians, pursuing philosophic studies in the spirit of a theologian or even an apologist?

In the first place it is necessary to point out that the relation of theology to philosophy was itself an important theme of mediaeval thought and that different thinkers adopted different attitudes in regard to this question. Starting with the endeavour to understand the data of revelation, so far as this is possible to human reason, early mediaevals, in accordance with the maxim *Credo, ut intelligam*, applied rational dialectic to the mysteries of faith in an attempt to understand them. In this way they laid the foundations of Scholastic theology, since the application of reason to theological data, in the sense of the data of revelation, is and remains theology: it does not become philosophy. Some thinkers indeed, in their enthusiastic desire to penetrate mysteries by reason to the utmost degree possible, appear at first sight to be rationalists, to be what one might call Hegelians before Hegel. Yet it is really an anachronism to regard such men as 'rationalists' in the modern sense, since when St. Anselm, for example, or Richard of St. Victor, attempted to prove the mystery of the Blessed Trinity by 'necessary reasons' they had no intention of acquiescing in any reduction of the dogma or of impairing the integrity of divine revelation. (To this subject I shall return in the course of the work.) So far they were certainly acting as theologians, but such men, who did not make, it is true, any very clear delimitation of the spheres of philosophy and theology, certainly pursued philosophical themes and developed philosophical arguments. For instance, even if St. Anselm is primarily important as one of the founders of Scholastic theology, he also contributed to the growth of Scholastic philosophy, for example, by his rational proofs of God's existence. It would be inadequate to dub Abelard a philosopher and St. Anselm a theologian without qualification. In any case in the thirteenth century we find a clear distinction made by St. Thomas Aquinas between theology, which takes as its premisses the data of revelation, and philosophy (including, of course, what we call 'natural theology'), which is the work of the human reason unaided positively by revelation. It is true that in the same century St. Bonaventure was a conscious and determined upholder of what one might call the integralist, Augustinian view; but, though the Franciscan Doctor may have believed that a purely philosophical knowledge of God is vitiated by its very incompleteness, he was perfectly well aware that there are philosophical truths which are ascertainable by reason alone. The difference between him and St. Thomas has been stated thus.[1] St. Thomas held that it would be possible, *in principle*, to excogitate a satisfactory philosophical system, which, in respect of knowledge of God for instance, would be incomplete but not false,

[1] This bald statement, however, though sponsored by M. Gilson, requires a certain modification. See pp. 245–9.

whereas St. Bonaventure maintained that this very incompleteness or inadequacy has the character of a falsification, so that, though a true natural philosophy would be possible without the light of faith, a true metaphysic would not be possible. If a philosopher, thought St. Bonaventure, proves by reason and maintains the unity of God, without at the same time knowing that God is Three Persons in One Nature, he is attributing to God a unity which is not the divine Unity.

In the second place, St. Thomas was perfectly serious when he gave philosophy its 'charter'. To a superficial observer it might appear that when St. Thomas asserted a clear distinction between dogmatic theology and philosophy, he was merely asserting a formalistic distinction, which had no influence on his thought and which he did not take seriously in practice; but such a view would be far from the truth, as can be seen by one example. St. Thomas believed that revelation teaches the creation of the world in time, the world's non-eternity; but he maintained and argued stoutly that the philosopher as such can prove neither that the world was created from eternity nor that it was created in time, although he can show that it depends on God as Creator. In holding to this point of view he was at variance with, for example, St. Bonaventure, and the fact that he maintained the point of view in question shows clearly that he seriously accepted in practice his theoretical delimitation of the provinces of philosophy and dogmatic theology.

In the third place, if it were really true to say that mediaeval philosophy was no more than theology, we should expect to find that thinkers who accepted the same faith would accept the same philosophy or that the differences between them would be confined to differences in the way in which they applied dialectic to the data of revelation. In point of fact, however, this is very far from being the case. St. Bonaventure, St. Thomas Aquinas, and Duns Scotus, Giles of Rome, and, one may pretty safely say, William of Ockham accepted the same faith, but their philosophical ideas were by no means the same on all points. Whether or not their philosophies were equally compatible with the exigencies of theology is, of course, another question (William of Ockham's philosophy could scarcely be considered as altogether compatible with these exigencies); but that question is irrelevant to the point at issue, since, whether they were all compatible with orthodox theology or not, these philosophies existed and were not the same.

The historian can trace the lines of development and divergence in mediaeval philosophy, and, if he can do this, there must clearly be such a thing as mediaeval philosophy: without existence it could not have a history.

We shall have to consider different views on the relation between philosophy and theology in the course of this work, and I do not want to dwell any more on the matter at present; but it may be as well to admit from the very start that, owing to the common background of the Christian faith, the world presented itself for interpretation to the mediaeval thinker more or less in a common light. Whether a thinker held or denied a clear distinction between the provinces of theology and philosophy, in either case he looked on the world as a Christian and could hardly avoid doing so. In his philosophic arguments he might prescind from Christian revelation, but the Christian outlook and faith were none the less there at the back of his mind. Yet that does not mean that his philosophic arguments were not philosophic arguments or that his rational proofs were not rational proofs: one would have to take each argument or proof on its own merits or demerits and not dismiss them as concealed theology on the ground that the writer was a Christian.

4. Having argued that there really was such a thing as mediaeval philosophy or at any rate that there could be such a thing, even if the great majority of mediaeval philosophers were Christians and most of them theologians into the bargain, I want finally to say something about the aim of this book (and of the succeeding volume) and the way in which it treats its subject.

I certainly do not intend to attempt the task of narrating all the known opinions of all known mediaeval philosophers. In other words, the second and third volumes of my history are not designed to constitute an encyclopaedia of mediaeval philosophy. On the other hand, it is not my intention to give simply a sketch or series of impressions of mediaeval philosophy. I have endeavoured to give an intelligible and coherent account of the development of mediaeval philosophy and of the phases through which it passed, omitting many names altogether and choosing out for consideration those thinkers who are of special importance and interest for the content of their thought or who represent and illustrate some particular type of philosophy or stage of development. To certain of these thinkers I have devoted a considerable amount of space, discussing their opinions at some length. This fact may possibly tend to obscure the general lines of connection and development, but, as I have said, it was not my intention to provide simply a sketch of mediaeval philosophy, and it is probably only through a somewhat detailed treatment of the leading philosophical systems that one can bring out the rich variety of mediaeval thought. To place in clear relief the main lines of connection and development and at the same time to develop at some length the ideas of selected philosophers is certainly not an easy task, and it would be foolish to suppose that my inclusions and omissions or proportional allotment of space will be acceptable to everybody: to miss the trees for the wood or the wood for the trees is easy enough, but to see both clearly at the same time is not so easy. However, I consider it a task worth attempting, and while I have not hesitated to consider at some length the philosophies of St. Bonaventure, St. Thomas, Duns Scotus and Ockham, I have tried to make intelligible the general development of mediaeval philosophy from its early struggles, through its splendid maturity, to its eventual decline.

If one speaks of a 'decline', it may be objected that one is speaking as philosopher and not as historian. True enough, but if one is to discern an intelligible pattern in mediaeval philosophy, one must have a principle of selection and to that extent at least one must be a philosopher. The word 'decline' has indeed a valuational colouring and flavour, so that to use such a word may seem to constitute an overstepping of the legitimate territory of the historian. Possibly it is, in a sense; but what historian of philosophy was or is *merely* an historian in the narrowest meaning of the term? No Hegelian, no Marxist, no Positivist, no Kantian writes history without a philosophic viewpoint, and is the Thomist alone to be condemned for a practice which is really necessary, unless the history of philosophy is to be rendered unintelligible by being made a mere string of opinions?

By 'decline', then, I mean decline, since I frankly regard mediaeval philosophy as falling into three main phases. First comes the preparatory phase, up to and including the twelfth century, then comes the period of constructive synthesis, the thirteenth century, and finally, in the fourteenth century, the period of destructive criticism, undermining and decline. Yet from another point of view I should not hesitate to admit that the last phase was an inevitable phase and, in the long run, may be of benefit, as stimulating Scholastic philosophers to develop and establish their principles more firmly in face of criticism and, moreover, to utilise all that subsequent philosophy may have to offer of positive value. From one point of view the Sophistic phase in ancient philosophy (using the term 'Sophist' in more or less the Platonic sense) constituted a decline, since it was characterised by, among other things, a flagging of constructive thought; but it was none the less an inevitable phase in Greek philosophy, and, in the long run, may be regarded as having produced results of positive value. No one at least who values the thought of Plato and Aristotle can regard the activity and criticism of the Sophists as an unmitigated disaster for philosophy.

The general plan of this volume and of its successor is thus the exhibition of the main phases and lines of development in mediaeval philosophy. First of all I treat briefly of the Patristic period, going on to speak of those Christian thinkers who had a real influence on the Middle Ages: Boethius, the Pseudo-Dionysius and, above all, St. Augustine of Hippo. After this more or less introductory part of the volume I proceed to the preparatory phase of mediaeval thought proper, the Carolingian renaissance, the establishment of the Schools, the controversy concerning universal concepts and the growing use of dialectic, the positive work of St. Anselm in the eleventh century, the schools of the twelfth century, particularly those of Chartres and St. Victor. It is then necessary to say something of Arabian and Jewish philosophy, not so much for its own sake, since I am primarily concerned with the philosophy of mediaeval Christendom, as for the fact that the Arabs and Jews constituted an important channel whereby the Aristotelian system in its fullness became known to the Christian West. The second phase is that of the great syntheses of the thirteenth century, the philosophies of St. Bonaventure, St. Thomas Aquinas and Duns Scotus in particular. The succeeding phase, that of the fourteenth century, contains the new directions and the destructive criticism of the Ockhamist School in a wide sense. Finally, I have given a treatment of the thought which belongs to the period of transition between mediaeval and modern philosophy. The way will then be clear to start a consideration of what is generally called 'modern philosophy' in the fourth volume of this history.

In conclusion it may be as well to mention two points. The first is that I do not conceive it to be the task of the historian of philosophy to substitute his own ideas or those of recent or contemporary philosophers for the ideas of past thinkers, as though the thinkers in question did not know what they meant. When Plato stated the doctrine of reminiscence, he was not asserting neo-Kantianism, and though St. Augustine anticipated Descartes by saying *Si fallor, sum*, it would be a great mistake to try to force his philosophy into the Cartesian mould. On the other hand, some problems which have been raised by modern philosophers were also raised in the Middle Ages, even if in a different setting, and it is legitimate to draw attention to similarity of question or answer. Again, it is not illegitimate to ask if a given mediaeval philosopher could, out of the resources of his own system, meet this or that difficulty which a later philosopher has raised. Therefore, although I have tried to avoid the multiplication of references to modern philosophy, I have on occasion permitted myself to make comparisons with later philosophies and to discuss the ability of a mediaeval system of philosophy to meet a difficulty which is likely to occur to a student of modern thought. But I have strictly rationed my indulgence in such comparisons and discussions, not only out of considerations of space but also out of regard for historical propriety.

The second point to be mentioned is this. Largely owing to the influence of Marxism there is a certain demand that an historian of philosophy should draw attention to the social and political background of his period and throw light on the influence of social and political factors on philosophic development and thought. But apart from the fact that to keep one's history within a reasonable compass one must concentrate on philosophy itself and not on social and political events and developments, it is ridiculous to suppose that all philosophies or all parts of any given philosophy are equally influenced by the social and political *milieu*. To understand a philosopher's political thought it is obviously desirable to have some knowledge of the actual political background, but in order to discuss St. Thomas's doctrine on the relation of essence to existence or Scotus's theory of the univocal character of the concept of being, there is no need at all to introduce references to the political or economic background. Moreover, philosophy is influenced by other factors as well as politics and economics. Plato was influenced by the advance of Greek mathematics; mediaeval philosophy, though distinguishable from theology, was certainly influenced by it; consideration of the development of physics is relevant to Descartes's view of the material world; biology was not without influence on Bergson, and so on. I regard it, therefore, as a great mistake to dwell so exclusively on economics and political development, and to explain the advance of other sciences ultimately by economic history, that one implies the truth of the Marxist theory of philosophy. Apart, then, from the fact that considerations of space have not permitted me to say much of the political, social and economic background of mediaeval philosophy, I have deliberately disregarded the unjustifiable demand that one should interpret the 'ideological superstructure' in terms of the economic situation. This book is a history of a certain period of mediaeval philosophy: it is not a political history nor a history of mediaeval economics.

PART I
PRE-MEDIAEVAL INFLUENCES

CHAPTER II
THE PATRISTIC PERIOD

Christianity and Greek philosophy—Greek Apologists (Aristides, St. Justin Martyr, Tatian, Athenagoras, Theophilus)—Gnosticism and writers against Gnosticism (St. Irenaeus, Hippolytus)—Latin Apologists (Minucius Felix, Tertullian, Arnobius, Lactantius)—Catechetical School of Alexandria (Clement, Origen)—Greek Fathers (St. Basil, Eusebius, St. Gregory of Nyssa)—Latin Fathers (St. Ambrose)—St. John Damascene—Summary.

1. CHRISTIANITY came into the world as a revealed religion: it was given to the world by Christ as a doctrine of redemption and salvation and love, not as an abstract and theoretical system, and He sent His Apostles to preach, not to occupy professors' chairs. Christianity was 'the Way', a road to God to be trodden in practice, not one more philosophical system added to the systems and schools of antiquity. The Apostles and their successors were bent on converting the world, not on excogitating a philosophical system. Moreover, so far as their message was directed to the Jews, the Apostles had to meet theological rather than philosophical attacks, while, in regard to the non-Jews, we are not told, apart from the account of St. Paul's famous sermon at Athens, of their being confronted with, or of their approaching, Greek philosophers in the academic sense.

However, as Christianity made fast its roots and grew, it aroused the suspicion and hostility, not merely of the Jews and the political authorities, but also of pagan intellectuals and writers. Some of the attacks levelled against Christianity were due simply to ignorance, credulous suspicion, fear of what was unknown, misrepresentation; but other attacks were delivered on the theoretical plane, on philosophical grounds, and these attacks had to be met. This meant that philosophical as well as theological arguments had to be used. There are, then, philosophical elements in the writings of early Christian apologists and Fathers; but it would obviously be idle to look for a philosophical system, since the interest of these writers was primarily theological, to defend the Faith. Yet, as Christianity became more firmly established and better known and as it became possible for Christian scholars to develop thought and learning, the philosophical element tended to become more strongly marked, especially when there was question of meeting the attacks of pagan professional philosophers.

The influence of apologetic on the growth of Christian philosophy was clearly due primarily to a cause external to Christianity, namely hostile attack; but there was also another reason for this growth which was internal, independent of attacks from outside. The more intellectual Christians naturally felt the desire to penetrate, as far as it was open to them to do so, the data of revelation and also to form a comprehensive view of the world and human life in the light of faith. This last reason operated in a systematic way perhaps later than the first and, so far as the Fathers are concerned, reached the zenith of its influence in the thought of St. Augustine; but the first reason, the desire to penetrate the dogmas of the Faith (an anticipation of the *Credo, ut intelligam* attitude), was operative in some way from the beginning. Partly through a simple desire to understand and appreciate, partly through the need of further clearer definition of dogma in face of heresy, the original data of revelation were rendered more explicit, 'developed', in the sense of the implicit being made explicit. From the beginning, for instance, Christians accepted the fact that Christ was both God and Man, but it was only in the course of time that the implications of this fact were made clear and were enshrined in theological definitions, for example, that the perfect human Nature of Christ implied His possession of a human will. Now, these definitions were of course theological, and the advance from the implicit to the explicit was an advance in theological science; but in the process of argument and definition concepts and categories were employed which were borrowed from philosophy. Moreover, as the Christians had no philosophy of their own to start with (i.e. in the academic sense of philosophy), they very naturally turned to the prevailing philosophy, which was derived from Platonism but was strongly impregnated with other elements. As a rough generalisation, therefore, one may say that the philosophic ideas of the early Christian writers were Platonic or neo-Platonic in character (with an admixture of Stoicism) and that the Platonic tradition continued for long to dominate Christian thought from the philosophic viewpoint. In saying this, however, one must remember that the Christian writers did not make any clear distinction between theology and philosophy: they aimed rather at presenting the Christian wisdom or 'philosophy' in a very wide sense, which was primarily theological, though it contained philosophical elements in the strict sense. The task of the historian of philosophy is to isolate these philosophic elements: he cannot reasonably be expected to present an adequate picture of early Christian thought, for the very good reason that he is not, *ex hypothesi*, an historian of dogmatic theology or of exegesis.

Since on the one hand pagan philosophers were inclined to attack the Church and her doctrine, while on the other hand Christian apologists and theologians were inclined to borrow the weapons of their adversaries when they thought that these weapons could serve their purpose, it is only to be expected that the Christian writers should show a divergence of attitude in regard to ancient philosophy, according as they chose to regard it as a foe and rival of Christianity or as a useful arsenal and store-house or even as a providential preparation for Christianity. Thus while in Tertullian's eyes pagan philosophy was little more than the foolishness of this world, Clement of Alexandria regarded philosophy as a gift of God, a means of educating the pagan world for Christ, as the Jews' means of education had been the Law. He thought indeed, as Justin thought before him, that Plato had borrowed his wisdom from Moses and the Prophets (a Philonic contention); but just as Philo had tried to reconcile Greek philosophy with the Old Testament, so Clement tried to reconcile Greek philosophy with the Christian religion. In the end, of course, it was the attitude of Clement, not that of Tertullian, which triumphed, since St. Augustine made abundant use of neo-Platonic ideas when presenting the Christian *Weltanschauung*.

2. As the first group of those Christian writers whose works contain philosophic elements one can count the early apologists who were particularly concerned to defend the Christian faith against pagan attack (or rather to show to the Imperial authorities that Christianity had a right to exist), men like Aristides, Justin, Melito, Tatian, Athenagoras and Theophilus of Antioch. In a brief sketch of Patristic philosophy, a sketch which is admittedly only included by way of preparation for the main theme of the book, one can treat neither of all the apologists nor of any one of them fully: my intention is rather to indicate the sort of philosophical elements which their works contain.

(i) *Marcianus Aristides*, styled a 'philosopher of Athens', wrote an Apology, which is to be dated about A.D. 140 and is addressed to the Emperor Antoninus Pius.[1] A good deal of this work is devoted to an attack on the pagan deities of Greece and Egypt, with some animadversions on the morals of the Greeks; but at the beginning Aristides declares that 'amazed at the arrangement of the world', and understanding that 'the world and all that is therein are moved by the impulse of another', and seeing that 'that which moveth is more powerful than that which is moved', he concludes that the Mover of the world 'is God of all, who made all for the sake of man'. Aristides thus gives in a very compendious form arguments drawn from the design and order in the world and from the fact of motion, and identifies the designer and mover with the Christian God, of whom he proceeds to predicate the attributes of eternity, perfection, incomprehensibility, wisdom, goodness. We have here, then, a very rudimentary natural theology presented, not for purely philosophic reasons, but in defence of the Christian religion.

(ii) A much more explicit attitude towards philosophy is to be found in the writings of *Flavius Justinus* (St. Justin Martyr), who was born at Neapolis (Nablus) of pagan parents about A.D. 100, became a Christian, and was martyred at Rome about 164. In his Dialogue with Trypho he declares that philosophy is a most precious gift of God, designed to lead man to God, though its true nature and its unity have not been recognised by most people, as is clear from the existence of so many philosophical schools.[2] As to himself, he went first for instruction to a Stoic, but, finding the Stoic doctrine of God unsatisfactory, betook himself to a Peripatetic, whose company he soon forsook, as he turned out to be a grasping fellow.[3] From the Peripatetic he went, with zeal still unabated, to a Pythagorean of repute, but his own lack of acquaintance with music, geometry and astronomy unfitted him for philosophy in his prospective teacher's eyes, and as he did not wish to spend a lot of time in acquiring knowledge of these sciences, he turned to the Platonists and was so delighted with the doctrine of the immaterial Ideas that he began to expect a clear vision of God, which, says Justin, is the aim of Plato's philosophy.[4] Shortly afterwards, however, he fell in with a Christian, who showed him the insufficiency of pagan philosophy, even of that of

[1] Quotations from the edition published in *Texts and Studies*, Vol. I.
[2] 2, 1. [3] 2, 3. [4] 2, 4–6.

Plato.[1] Justin is thus an example of the cultured convert from paganism, who, feeling his conversion as the term of a process, could not adopt a merely negative and hostile attitude to Greek philosophy.

Justin's words concerning Platonism in the *Dialogue* show clearly enough the esteem in which he held the Platonic philosophy. He prized its doctrine of the immaterial world and of the being beyond essence, which he identified with God, though he became convinced that the sure and safe and certain knowledge of God, the true 'philosophy', is to be attained only through the acceptance of revelation. In his two *Apologies* he makes frequent use of Platonic terms, as when he speaks of God as the 'Demiurge'.[2] I am not suggesting that when Justin makes use of Platonic or neo-Platonic words and phrases he is understanding the words in precisely the Platonic sense: the use of them is rather the effect of his philosophic training and of the sympathy which he retained for Platonism. Thus he does not hesitate on occasion to point out analogies between Christian and Platonic doctrine, in regard, for example, to reward and punishment after death,[3] and his admiration for Socrates is evident. When Socrates, in the power of *logos*, or as its instrument, tried to lead men away from falsehood into truth, evil men put him to death as an impious atheist: so Christians, who follow and obey the incarnate Logos itself and who denounce the false gods, are termed atheists.[4] In other words, just as the work of Socrates, which was a service of truth, was a preparation for the complete work of Christ, so the condemnation of Socrates was, as it were, a rehearsal or anticipation of the condemnation of Christ and His followers. Again, the actions of men are not determined, as the Stoics thought, but they act rightly or wrongly according to their free choice, while it is owing to the activity of the evil demons that Socrates and those like him are persecuted, while Epicurus and those like him are held in honour.[5]

Justin thus made no clear distinction between theology and philosophy in the strict sense: there is one wisdom, one 'philosophy', which is revealed fully in and through Christ, but for which the best elements in pagan philosophy, especially Platonism, were a preparation. In so far as the pagan philosophers divined the truth, they did so only in the power of *logos*: Christ, however, is the Logos itself, incarnate. This view of Greek philosophy and

[1] 3, 1 ff. [2] E.g. *Apol.*, I, 8, 2. [3] *Ibid.*, I, 8, 4.
[4] *Ibid.*, I, 5, 3 ff. [5] *Ibid.*, II, 6 (7), 3.

of its relation to Christianity was of considerable influence on later writers.

(iii) According to Irenaeus,[1] *Tatian* was a pupil of Justin. He was of Syrian nationality, was educated in Greek literature and philosophy, and became a Christian. There is no real reason for doubting the truth of the statement that Tatian was in some sense a pupil of Justin Martyr, but it is quite clear from his *Address to the Greeks* that he did not share Justin's sympathy for Greek philosophy in its more spiritual aspects. Tatian declares that we know God from His works; he has a doctrine of the Logos, distinguishes soul (ψυχή) from spirit (πνεῦμα), teaches creation in time and insists on free-will; but all these points he could have got from the Scriptures and Christian teaching: he had little use for Greek learning and Greek thought, though he can hardly have escaped its influence altogether. He was in fact inclined to excessive rigorism, and we learn from St. Irenaeus and St. Jerome[2] that after Justin's martyrdom Tatian fell away from the Church into Valentinian Gnosticism, subsequently founding the sect of the Encratites, denouncing not only the drinking of wine and the use of ornaments by women but even marriage as such, which he said was defilement and fornication.[3]

Tatian certainly recognised the human mind's ability to prove God's existence from creatures and he made use of philosophical notions and categories in the development of theology, as when he maintains that the Word, proceeding from the simple essence of God, does not 'fall into the void', as human words do, but remains in its subsistence and is the divine instrument of creation. He thus uses the analogy of the formation of human thought and speech to illustrate the procession of the Word, and, while holding to the doctrine of creation, he uses language reminiscent of the *Timaeus* in respect of the Demiurge. But, if he made use of terms and ideas taken from pagan philosophy, he did not do so in any spirit of sympathy, but rather with the notion that the Greek philosophers had taken from the Scriptures whatever truth they possessed and that whatever they added thereto was nothing but falsity and perversion. The Stoics, for instance, perverted the doctrine of providence by the diabolic theory of fatalistic determinism. It is indeed something of an historical irony that a writer who betrayed so pronounced an hostility towards Greek thought

[1] *Against the Heresies*, I, 28. [2] E.g. *Adv. Jovin.*, 1, 3; *Comm. in Amos.*
[3] Iren., *Against the Heresies*, I, 28.

and who drew so sharp a distinction between pagan 'sophistry' and Christian wisdom should himself end in heresy.

(iv) A more tactful approach to the Greeks, and one in harmony with that of Justin Martyr, was the approach of *Athenagoras*, who addressed to the Emperors Marcus Aurelius and Commodus, 'conquerors of Armenia and Sarmatia, and above all philosophers', a *Plea for the Christians* (πρεσβεία περὶ χριστιανῶν) about the year A.D. 177. In this book the author is concerned to defend the Christians against the three accusations of atheism, cannibalistic feasts and incest, and in answering the first accusation he gives a reasoned defence of the Christian belief in one eternal and spiritual God. First of all he cites various Greek philosophers themselves, for instance Philolaus, Plato, Aristotle and the Stoics. He quotes Plato in the *Timaeus* to the effect that it is difficult to find the Maker and Father of the universe and impossible, even when He is found, to declare Him to all, and asks why Christians, believing in one God, should be called atheists, when Plato is not so called because of his doctrine of the Demiurge. The poets and philosophers, moved by a divine impulse, have striven to find God and men pay heed to their conclusions: how foolish it would be, then, to refuse to listen to the very Spirit of God, speaking through the mouths of the Prophets.

Athenagoras then goes on to show that there cannot be a multitude of material gods, that God, who forms matter, must transcend matter (though he scarcely succeeds in conceiving God without relation to space), that the Cause of perishable things must be imperishable and spiritual, and he appeals especially to the testimony of Plato. He thus adopts the same attitude as that of Justin Martyr. There is one true 'philosophy' or wisdom, which is attained adequately only through the Christian revelation, though Greek philosophers divined something of the truth. In other words, their very respect for the Greek thinkers and poets should lead thoughtful men like Marcus Aurelius to appreciate and esteem, even if not to embrace, Christianity. His primary purpose is theological and apologetic, but he utilises philosophic arguments and themes in his pursuit of that purpose. For instance, in his attempt to prove the reasonable character of the doctrine of the resurrection of the body, he makes clear his conviction, as against the Platonic view, that the body belongs to the integral man, that man is not simply a soul using a body.[1]

[1] *On the Resurrection.*

(v) A similar appeal to the intelligent pagan was made by *Theophilus of Antioch* in his *Ad Autolycum*, written about A.D. 180. After emphasising the fact that moral purity is necessary for anyone who would know God, he proceeds to speak of the divine attributes, God's incomprehensibility, power, wisdom, eternity, immutability. As the soul of man, itself invisible, is perceived through the movements of the body, so God, Himself invisible, is known through His providence and works. He is not always accurate in his account of the opinions of Greek philosophers, but he clearly had some esteem for Plato, whom he considered 'the most respectable philosopher among them',[1] though Plato erred in not teaching creation out of nothing (which Theophilus clearly affirms) and in his doctrine concerning marriage (which Theophilus does not give correctly).

3. The foregoing Apologists, who wrote in Greek, were mainly concerned with answering pagan attacks on Christianity. We can now consider briefly the great opponent of Gnosticism, St. Irenaeus, to whom we add, for the sake of convenience, Hippolytus. Both men wrote in Greek and both combated the Gnosticism which flourished in the second century A.D., though Hippolytus's work has a wider interest, containing, as it does, many references to Greek philosophy and philosophers.

Of Gnosticism suffice it to say here that, in general, it was a monstrous conflation of Scriptural and Christian, Greek and Oriental elements, which, professing to substitute knowledge (*gnosis*) for faith, offered a doctrine of God, creation, the origin of evil, salvation, to those who liked to look upon themselves as superior persons in comparison with the ordinary run of Christians. There was a Jewish Gnosticism before the 'Christian' form, and the latter itself can be looked on as a Christian heresy only in so far as the Gnostics borrowed certain specifically Christian themes: the Oriental and Hellenic elements are far too conspicuous for it to be possible to call Gnosticism a Christian heresy in the ordinary sense, although it was a real danger in the second century and seduced those Christians who were attracted by the bizarre theosophical speculations which the Gnostics offered as 'knowledge'. As a matter of fact, there were a number of Gnostic systems, such as those of Cerinthus, Marcion, the Ophites, Basilides, Valentinus. We know that Marcion was a Christian who suffered excommunication; but the Ophites were probably of Jewish-Alexandrian

[1] *Ad Autol.*, 3. 6.

origin, while in regard to famous Gnostics like Basilides and Valentinus (second century) we do not know that they were ever Christians.

Characteristic of Gnosticism in general was a dualism between God and matter, which, though not absolute, approached that of the later Manichaean system. The resulting gulf between God and matter was filled up by the Gnostics with a series of emanations or intermediary beings in which Christ found a place. The complement of the process of emanation was the return to God by way of salvation.

In the system of Marcion, as one would expect, the Christian element was to the fore. The God of the Old Testament, the Demiurge, is inferior to the God of the New Testament, who remained unknown until He revealed Himself in Jesus Christ. In the systems of Basilides and Valentinus, however, the Christian element is less important: Christ is depicted as an inferior being (an Eon) in a fantastic hierarchy of divine and semi-divine emanations, and His mission is simply that of transmitting to man the salvific knowledge or *gnosis*. As matter is evil, it cannot be the work of the Supreme God, but it is due to the 'great Archon', who was worshipped by the Jews and who gave himself out as the one Supreme God. The Gnostic systems were thus not dualistic in the full Manichaean sense, since the Demiurge, identified with the God of the Old Testament, was not made an independent and original principle of evil (the neo-Platonic element was too prominent to admit of absolute dualism), and their main common characteristic was not so much the tendency to dualism as the insistence on *gnosis* as the means of salvation. The adoption of Christian elements was largely due to the desire to absorb Christianity, to substitute *gnosis* for faith. To enter further upon the differentiating features of the various Gnostic systems and to detail the series of emanations would be a tiresome and profitless task: it is enough to point out that the general framework was a mixture of Oriental and Greek (e.g. neo-Pythagorean and neo-Platonic) themes, with a varying dosage of Christian elements, taken both from Christianity proper and from apocryphal and spurious documents. To us to-day it is difficult to understand how Gnosticism could ever have been a danger to the Church or an attraction to any sane mind; but we have to remember that it arose at a time when a welter of philosophical schools and mystery-religions was seeking to cater for the spiritual needs of men. Moreover, esoteric and theosophical systems, surrounded with the pseudo-glamour of 'eastern wisdom', have not entirely lost their attraction for some minds even in much more recent times.

(i) *St. Irenaeus* (born about A.D. 137 or 140), writing against the Gnostics in his *Adversus Haereses*, affirms that there is one God, who made all things, Creator of heaven and earth. He appeals, for example, to the argument from design and to that from universal consent, observing that the very heathen have learnt from creation itself, by the use of reason, the existence of God as Creator.[1] God created the world freely, and not by necessity.[2] Moreover, He created the world out of nothing and not out of previously existing matter, as the Gnostics pretend relying on 'Anaxagoras, Empedocles and Plato'.[3] But, though the human mind can come to know God through reason and revelation, it cannot comprehend God, whose essence transcends the human intelligence: to pretend to know the ineffable mysteries of God and to go beyond humble faith and love, as the Gnostics do, is mere conceit and pride. The doctrine of reincarnation is false, while the revealed moral law does not abrogate, but fulfils and extends, the natural law. In fine, 'the teaching of the Apostles is the true *gnosis*'.[4]

According to Irenaeus the Gnostics borrowed most of their notions from Greek philosophers. Thus he accuses them of borrowing their morals from Epicurus and the Cynics, their doctrine of reincarnation from Plato. In this tendency to attach Gnostic theories to Greek philosophies Irenaeus was closely followed by

(ii) *Hippolytus* (died probably about A.D. 236), who was a disciple of Irenaeus, according to Photius,[5] and certainly utilised his teaching and writing. In the *Proemium* to his *Philosophumena* (now generally attributed to Hippolytus) he declares his intention, only imperfectly fulfilled, of exposing the plagiarism of the Gnostics by showing how their various opinions were taken from Greek philosophers, though they were made worse by the Gnostics, and, in order to do this more easily, he first recounts the opinions of the philosophers, relying for his information mainly, if not entirely, on the doxography of Theophrastus. The information, however, is not always accurate. His main accusation against the Greeks is that they glorified the parts of the creation with dainty phrases, but were ignorant of the Creator of all things, who made them freely out of nothing according to His wisdom and foreknowledge.

[1] 2, 9, 1. [2] 2, 1, 1; 2, 5, 3. [3] 2, 14, 4. [4] 4, 33, 8. [5] *Bibl.* cod. 121.

4. The foregoing authors wrote in Greek; but there was also a group of Latin Apologists, Minucius Felix, Tertullian, Arnobius and Lactantius, of whom the most important is Tertullian.

(i) It is uncertain whether *Minucius Felix* wrote before or after Tertullian, but in any case his attitude towards Greek philosophy, as shown in his *Octavius*, was more favourable than Tertullian's. Arguing that God's existence can be known with certainty from the order of nature and the design involved in the organism, particularly in the human body, and that the unity of God can be inferred from the unity of the cosmic order, he affirmed that Greek philosophers, too, recognised these truths. Thus Aristotle recognised one Godhead and the Stoics had a doctrine of divine providence, while Plato speaks in almost Christian terms when he talks in the *Timaeus* of the Maker and Father of the universe.

(ii) *Tertullian*, however, speaks in a rather different way of Greek philosophy. Born about A.D. 160 of pagan parents and educated as a jurist (he practised in Rome), he became a Christian, only to fall into the Montanist heresy, a form of rigorous and excessive Puritanism. He was the first outstanding Christian Latin writer, and in his works his contempt for paganism and pagan learning is made clear and explicit. What have the philosopher and the Christian in common, the disciple of Greece, the friend of error, and the pupil of heaven, the foe of error and friend of truth?[1] Even Socrates' wisdom did not amount to much, since no one can really know God apart from Christ, nor Christ apart from the Holy Spirit. Moreover, Socrates was, self-confessedly, guided by a demon![2] As to Plato, he said that it was hard to find the Maker and Father of the universe, whereas the simplest Christian has already found Him.[3] Moreover, the Greek philosophers are the patriarchs of the heretics,[4] inasmuch as Valentinus borrowed from the Platonists, Marcion from the Stoics, while the philosophers themselves borrowed ideas from the Old Testament and then distorted them and claimed them as their own.[5]

However, in spite of the antithesis he makes between Christian wisdom and Greek philosophy, Tertullian himself developed philosophical themes and was influenced by the Stoics. He affirms that the existence of God is known with certainty from His works,[6] and also that from the uncreatedness of God we can argue to His perfection (*Imperfectum non potest esse, nisi quod factum est*);[7] but he

[1] *Apol.*, 46. [2] *De Anima*, 1. [3] *Apol.*, 46. [4] *De Anima*, 3.
[5] *Apol.*, 47. [6] *De Resurrect.*, 2–3. [7] *Herm.*, 28.

makes the astounding statement that everything, including God, is corporeal, bodily. 'Everything which exists is a bodily existence *sui generis*. Nothing lacks bodily existence but that which is non-existent':[1] 'for who will deny that God is a body, although "God is a Spirit"? For Spirit has a bodily substance of its own kind, in its own form.'[2] Many writers have concluded from these statements that Tertullian maintained a materialistic doctrine and held God to be really a material being, just as the Stoics considered God to be material: some, however, have suggested that by 'body' Tertullian often meant simply substance and that when he attributes materiality to God, he is really simply attributing substantiality to God. On this explanation, when Tertullian says that God is a *corpus sui generis*, that He is *corpus* and yet *spiritus*, he would mean that God is a spiritual substance: his language would be at fault, while his thought would be acceptable. One is certainly not entitled to exclude this explanation as impossible, but it is true that Tertullian, speaking of the human soul, says that it must be a bodily substance since it can suffer.[3] However, he speaks ambiguously even on the nature of the soul, and in his *Apology*[4] he gives as a reason for the resurrection of the bodies of the wicked that 'the soul is not capable of suffering without the solid substance, that is, the flesh'. It is probably best to say, then, that, while Tertullian's language often implies materialism of a rather crass sort, his meaning *may* not have been that which his language would often imply. When he teaches that the soul of the infant is derived from the father's seed like a kind of sprout (*surculus, tradux*),[5] he would seem to be teaching a clearly materialistic doctrine; but this 'traducianism' was adopted partly for a theological reason, to explain the transmission of original sin, and some later writers who inclined to the same view, did so for the same theological reason, without apparently realising the materialistic implications of the doctrine. This does not show, of course, that Tertullian was *not* a materialist; but it should at least lead one to hesitate before forming the conviction that his general meaning always coincided with the words he used. His assertion of the freedom of the will and of the natural immortality of the soul will scarcely fit in, from the logical viewpoint, with sheer materialism; but that again would not justify one in flatly denying that he was

[1] *De Carne Christi*, 11. [2] *Adv. Prax.*, 7. [3] *De Anima*, 7; cf. 8.
[4] 48. [5] Cf. *De Anima*, 19.

a materialist, since he may have held a materialistic theory without realising the fact that some of the attributes he ascribed to the soul were incompatible with a fully materialist position.

One of the great services rendered by Tertullian to Christian thought was his development of theological and, to some extent, of philosophical terminology in the Latin language. Thus the technical use of the word *persona* is found for the first time in his writings: the divine Persons are distinct as *Personae*, but they are not different, divided, *substantiae*.[1] In his doctrine of the Word[2] he appeals explicitly to the Stoics, to Zeno and Cleanthes.[3] However, of Tertullian's theological developments and of his orthodoxy or unorthodoxy it is not our concern to speak.

(iii) In his *Adversus Gentes* (about 303) *Arnobius* makes some curious observations concerning the soul. Thus, although he affirms creationism, as against the Platonic doctrine of pre-existence, he makes the creating agent a being inferior to God, and he also asserts the *gratuitous* character of the soul's immortality, denying a natural immortality. One motive was evidently that of using the gratuitous character of immortality as an argument for becoming a Christian and leading a moral life. Again, while combating the Platonic theory of reminiscence, he asserts the experiential origin of all our ideas with one exception, the idea of God. He depicts a child brought up in solitude, silence and ignorance throughout his youth and declares that, as a result, he would know nothing: he would certainly not have any knowledge by 'reminiscence'. Plato's proof for his doctrine in the *Meno* is not cogent.[4]

(iv) The origin of the soul by God's direct creation, in opposition to any form of traducianism, was clearly affirmed by *Lactantius* (about 250 to about 325) in his *De opificio Dei*.[5]

5. Gnosticism, as combated by St. Irenaeus and Hippolytus, was, so far as it can reasonably be connected with Christianity, an heretical speculative system, or, more accurately, set of systems, which, in addition to Oriental and Christian elements, incorporated elements of Hellenic thought. One of its effects, therefore, was to arouse a determined opposition to Hellenic philosophy on the part of those Christian writers who exaggerated the connections between Gnosticism and Greek philosophy, which they considered to be the seed-ground of heresy; but another effect was to contribute to the effort to construct a non-heretical 'gnosis', a Christian

[1] *Adv. Prax.*, 12. [2] *Sermo, Ratio.* [3] *Apol.*, 21. [4] 2, 20 ff. [5] 19.

theologico-philosophical system. This effort was characteristic of the Catechetical School at Alexandria, of which the two most famous names are Clement and Origen.

(i) *Titus Flavius Clemens* (*Clement of Alexandria*) was born about 150, perhaps at Athens, came to Alexandria in 202 or 203 and died there about 219. Animated by the attitude which was later summed up in the formula, *Credo, ut intelligam,* he sought to develop the systematic presentation of the Christian wisdom in a true, as opposed to a false *gnosis.* In the process he followed the spirit of Justin Martyr's treatment of the Greek philosophers, looking on their work rather as a preparation for Christianity, an education of the Hellenic world for the revealed religion, than as a folly and delusion. The divine Logos has always illumined souls; but whereas the Jews were enlightened by Moses and the Prophets, the Greeks had their wise men, their philosophers, so that philosophy was to the Greeks what the Law was to the Hebrews.[1] It is true that Clement thought, following Justin again, that the Greeks borrowed from the Old Testament and distorted, from vainglorious motives, what they borrowed; but he was also firmly convinced that the light of the Logos enabled the Greek philosophers to attain many truths, and that philosophy is in reality simply that body of truths which are not the prerogative of any one Greek School but are found, in different measure and degree, in different Schools, though Plato was indeed the greatest of all the philosophers.[2]

But not only was philosophy a preparation for Christianity: it is also an aid in understanding Christianity. Indeed, the person who merely believes and makes no effort to understand is like a child in comparison with a man: blind faith, passive acceptance, is not the ideal, though science, speculation, reasoning, cannot be true if they do not harmonise with revelation. In other words, Clement of Alexandria, as the first Christian man of learning, wanted to see Christianity in its relation to philosophy and to use the speculative reason in the systematisation and development of theology. Incidentally it is interesting to note that he rejects any real *positive* knowledge of God: we know in truth only what God is not, for example, that He is not a genus, not a species, that He is beyond anything of which we have had experience or which we can conceive. We are justified in predicating perfections of God, but at the same time we must remember that all names we apply

[1] *Strom.*, 1, 5. [2] *Paedagogus*, 3, 11.

to God are inadequate—and so, in another sense, inapplicable. In dependence, then, on some remarks of Plato in the *Republic* concerning the Good and in dependence on Philo Clement asserted the *via negativa*, so dear to the mystics, which reached its classical expression in the writings of the Pseudo-Dionysius.

(ii) *Origen*, foremost member of the Catechetical School at Alexandria, was born in A.D. 185 or 186. He studied the works of Greek philosophers and is said to have attended the lectures of Ammonius Saccas, teacher of Plotinus. He had to abandon the headship of the Alexandrian School because of a synodical process (231 and 232) directed against certain features of his doctrine and also against his ordination (he had, it was said, been ordained priest in Palestine in spite of his act of self-mutilation), and subsequently founded a school at Caesarea in Palestine, where St. Gregory Thaumaturge was one of his pupils. He died in 254 or 255, his death being the consequence of the torture he had had to endure in the persecution of Decius.

Origen was the most prolific and learned of all Christian writers before the Council of Nicaea, and there is no doubt that he had every intention of being and remaining an orthodox Christian; but his desire to reconcile the Platonic philosophy with Christianity and his enthusiasm for the allegorical interpretation of the Scriptures led him into some heterodox opinions. Thus, under the influence of Platonism or rather of neo-Platonism, he held that God, who is purely spiritual, the μονάς or ἑνάς[1] and who transcends truth and reason, essence and being (in his book against the pagan philosopher Celsus[2] he says, following the mind of Plato, that God is ἐπέκεινα νοῦ καὶ οὐσίας), created the world from eternity and by a necessity of His Nature. God, who is goodness, could never have been 'inactive', since goodness always tends to self-communication, self-diffusion. Moreover, if God had created the world in time, if there was ever a 'time' when the world was not, God's immutability would be impaired, which is an impossibility.[3] Both these reasons are conceived in dependence on neo-Platonism. God is indeed the creator of matter and is thus Creator in the strict and Christian sense,[4] but there is an infinity of worlds, one succeeding the other and all different from one another.[5] As evil is privation, and not something positive, God cannot be accused of being the author of evil.[6] The Logos or Word is the exemplar

[1] *De principiis*, 1, 1, 6. [2] 7, 38. [3] *De principiis*, 1, 2, 10; 3, 4, 3.
[4] *Ibid.*, 2, 1, 4. [5] *Ibid.*, 3, 5, 3; 2, 3, 4–5. [6] *In Joann.*, 2, 7.

of creation, the ἰδέα ἰδεῶν,[1] and by the Logos all things are created, the Logos acting as mediator of God and creatures.[2] The final procession within the Godhead is the Holy Spirit, and immediately below the Holy Spirit are the created spirits, who, through the power of the Holy Spirit, are lifted up to become sons of God, in union with the Son, and are finally participants in the divine life of the Father.[3]

Souls were created by God exactly like to one another in quality, but sin in a state of pre-existence led to their being clothed with bodies, and the qualitative difference between souls is thus due to their behaviour before their entry into this world. They enjoy freedom of will on earth, but their acts depend not merely on their free choice but also on the grace of God, which is apportioned according to their conduct in the pre-embodied state. Nevertheless, all souls, and even the devil and demons, too, will at length, through purificatory suffering, arrive at union with God. This is the doctrine of the restoration of all things (ἐπανόρθωσις, ἀποκατάστασις πάντων) whereby all things will return to their ultimate principle and God will be all in all.[4] This involves, of course, a denial of the orthodox doctrine of hell.

From even the little which has been said concerning Origen's thought it should be clear that he attempted a fusion of Christian doctrine with Platonic and neo-Platonic philosophy. The Son and the Holy Ghost in the Blessed Trinity, though within the Godhead, are spoken of in a manner which indicates the influence of the emanationism of Philonic and neo-Platonic thought. The theory of the Logos as 'Idea of ideas' and that of eternal and necessary creation come from the same source, while the theory of pre-existence is Platonic. Of course, the philosophical ideas which Origen adopted were incorporated by him in a Christian setting and framework, so that he may rightly be considered the first great synthetic thinker of Christianity, but although he attached them to Scriptural passages freely interpreted, his enthusiasm for Greek thought led him sometimes into heterodoxy.

6. The Greek Fathers of the fourth and fifth centuries were occupied mainly with theological questions. Thus *St. Athanasius*, who died in 373, was the great foe of Arianism; *St. Gregory Nazianzen*, who died in 390 and was known as the Theologian, is particularly remarkable for his work on Trinitarian and Christological

[1] *Contra Celsum*, 6, 64. [2] *De principiis*, 2, 6, 1. [3] *Ibid.*, 6, 1–3.
[4] Cf. *ibid.*, 3, 6, 1 ff.; 1, 6, 3.

theology; *St. John Chrysostom* (died 406) is celebrated as one of the greatest orators of the Church and for his work on the Scriptures. In treating of dogmas like those of the Blessed Trinity and the Hypostatic Union the Fathers naturally made use of philosophical terms and expressions; but their application of reasoning in theology does not make them philosophers in the strict sense and we must pass them over here. One may point out, however, that *St. Basil* (died 379) studied in the University of Athens, together with St. Gregory Nazianzen, and that in his *Ad Adolescentes* he recommends a study of the Greek poets, orators, historians and philosophers, though a selection should be made from their writings which would exclude immoral passages: Greek literature and learning are a potent instrument of education, but moral education is more important than literary and philosophic formation. (St. Basil himself in his descriptions of animals apparently depended almost entirely on the relevant works of Aristotle.)

But, though we cannot consider here the theological speculations of the Greek Fathers, something must be said of two eminent figures of the period, the historian Eusebius and St. Gregory of Nyssa.

(i) *Eusebius of Caesarea* was born in Palestine about 265, became Bishop of Caesarea, his birthplace, in 313, and died there in 339 or 340. Best known as a great Church historian, he is also of importance for his Christian apologetic, and under this heading comes his attitude towards Greek philosophy, since, in general, he regarded Greek philosophy, especially Platonism, as a preparation of the heathen world for Christianity, though he was fully alive to the errors of Greek philosophers and to the contradictions between the many philosophical Schools. Yet, though he speaks sharply on occasion, his general attitude is sympathetic and appreciative, an attitude which comes out most clearly in his *Praeparatio evangelica* in fifteen books. It is greatly to be regretted that we have not got the twenty-five books of the work which Eusebius wrote in answer to Porphyry's attack on Christianity, as his reply to the eminent neo-Platonist and pupil of Plotinus would doubtless throw much light on his philosophical ideas; but the *Praeparatio evangelica* is sufficient to show, not only that Eusebius shared the general outlook of Justin Martyr, Clement of Alexandria and Origen, but also that he had read widely in the literature of the Greeks. He was in fact an extremely learned man, and his work is one of the sources for our knowledge of the philosophy of those thinkers whose works have perished.

One would probably only expect, given the attitude of his predecessors, to find Eusebius especially appreciative of Plato: in fact he devotes to Platonism three books (11–13) of the *Praeparatio*. Clement had spoken of Plato as Moses writing in Greek, and Eusebius, agreeing with Clement, considered that Plato and Moses were in agreement,[1] that Plato may be called a prophet of the economy of salvation.[2] Like Clement and Origen, and like Philo also, Eusebius thought that Plato had borrowed the truths he exposes from the Old Testament;[3] but at the same time he is willing to admit the possibility of Plato having discovered the truth for himself or of his having been enlightened by God.[4] In any case, not only does Plato agree with the sacred literature of the Hebrews in his idea of God, but he also suggests, in his Letters, the idea of the Blessed Trinity. On this point Eusebius is, of course, interpreting Plato in a neo-Platonic sense and is referring to the three principles of the One or Good, the *Nous* or Mind, and the World-Soul.[5] The Ideas are the ideas of God, of the Logos, the exemplar patterns of creation, and the picture of creation in the *Timaeus* is similar to that contained in Genesis.[6] Again, Plato agrees with the Scriptures in his doctrine of immortality,[7] while the moral teaching of the *Phaedrus* reminds Eusebius of St. Paul.[8] Even Plato's political ideal found its realisation in the Jewish theocracy.[9]

Nevertheless, it remains true that Plato did not affirm these truths without an admixture of error.[10] His doctrine of God and of creation is contaminated by his doctrine of emanation and by his acceptance of the eternity of matter, his doctrine of the soul and of immortality by his theory of pre-existence and of reincarnation, and so on. Thus Plato, even if he was a 'prophet', was no more than a prophet: he did not himself enter into the promised land of truth, though he approached near to it: it is Christianity alone which is the true philosophy. Moreover, Plato's philosophy was highly intellectualist, caviar for the multitude, whereas Christianity is for all, so that men and women, rich and poor, learned and unlearned, can be 'philosophers'.

To discuss Eusebius's interpretation of Plato would be out of place here: it is sufficient to note that he, in common with most

[1] 11, 28. [2] 13,13. [3] 10, 1; 10, 8; 10, 14. [4] 11, 8. [5] 11, 16; 11, 20.
[6] 11, 23; 11, 29; 11, 31. [7] 11, 27. [8] 12, 27. [9] 13, 12; 12, 16. [10] 13, 19.

other Christian Greek writers, gives the palm to Plato among Hellenic thinkers, and that, in common with all the early Christian writers, he makes no real distinction between theology in a strict sense and philosophy in a strict sense. There is one wisdom, which is found adequately and completely only in Christianity: Greek thinkers attained to true philosophy or wisdom in so far as they anticipated Christianity. Among those who anticipated the true philosophy Plato is the most outstanding; but even he stood only on the threshold of truth. Naturally the notion that Plato and other Hellenic thinkers borrowed from the Old Testament, although itself partly a consequence of their understanding of 'philosophy', helped also to confirm Christian writers like Eusebius in their very wide interpretation of 'philosophy', as including not only the result of human speculation but also the data of revelation. In fact, in spite of his very favourable judgement on Plato, the logical conclusion from Eusebius's and others' conviction that the Greek philosophers borrowed from the Old Testament would inevitably be that human speculation unaided by direct illumination from God is not of any great avail in the attainment of truth. For what are the errors with which even Plato contaminated the truth but the result of human speculation? If you say that the truth contained in Greek philosophy came from the Old Testament, that is to say, from revelation, you can hardly avoid the conclusion that the errors in Greek philosophy came from human speculation, with a consequently unfavourable judgement as to the power of that speculation. This attitude was very common among the Fathers and, in the Middle Ages, it was to be clearly expressed by St. Bonaventure in the thirteenth century, though it was not to be the view that ultimately prevailed in Scholasticism, the view of St. Thomas Aquinas and of Duns Scotus.

(ii) One of the most learned of the Greek Fathers and one of the most interesting from the philosophic standpoint was the brother of St. Basil, *St. Gregory of Nyssa,* who was born in Caesarea (in Cappadocia, not Palestine) about A.D. 335 and, after having been a teacher of rhetoric, became Bishop of Nyssa, dying about the year 395.

Gregory of Nyssa realised clearly that the data of revelation are accepted on faith and are not the result of a logical process of reasoning, that the mysteries of faith are not philosophical and scientific conclusions: if they were, then supernatural faith, as exercised by Christians, and Hellenic philosophising would be indistinguishable. On the other hand, the Faith has a rational basis, in that, logically speaking, the acceptance of mysteries on authority presupposes the ascertainability by natural reasoning of certain preliminary truths, especially the existence of God, which are capable of philosophic demonstration. Accordingly, though the superiority of faith must be maintained, it is only right to invoke the aid of philosophy. Ethics, natural philosophy, logic, mathematics, are not only ornaments in the temple of truth but may also contribute to the life of wisdom and virtue: they are, therefore, not to be despised or rejected,[1] though divine revelation must be accepted as a touchstone and criterion of truth since human reasoning must be judged by the word of God, not the word of God by human reasoning.[2] Again, it is right to employ human speculation and human reasoning in regard to dogma; but the conclusions will not be valid unless they agree with the Scriptures.[3]

The cosmic order proves the existence of God, and from the necessary perfection of God we can argue to His unity, that there is one God. Gregory went on to attempt to give reasons for the Trinity of Persons in the one Godhead.[4] For instance, God must have a Logos, a word, a reason. He cannot be less than man, who also has a reason, a word. But the divine Logos cannot be something of fleeting duration: it must be eternal, just as it must be living. The internal word in man is a fleeting accident, but in God there can be no such thing: the Logos is one in Nature with the Father, for there is but one God, the distinction between the Logos and the Father, the Word and the Speaker, being a distinction of relation. To enter into Gregory's Trinitarian doctrine as such is not our concern here; but the fact that he tries, in some sense, to 'prove' the doctrine is of interest, since it afforded a precedent for the later attempts of St. Anselm and Richard of St. Victor to deduce the Trinity, to prove it *rationibus necessariis*.

Obviously, however, St. Gregory's intention, like that of St. Anselm, was to render the mystery more intelligible by the application of dialectic, not to 'rationalise' the mystery in the sense of departing from dogmatic orthodoxy. Similarly, his theory that the word 'man' is primarily applicable to the universal and only secondarily to the individual man was an attempt to render the

[1] *De Vita Moysis*; *P.G.*, 44, 336 DG, 360 BC.
[2] Cf. *De anima et resurrectione*; *P.G.*, 46, 49 C.
[3] Cf. *Contra Eunom.*; *P.G.*, 45, 341 B.
[4] Cf. *Oratio Catechetica*; *P.G.*, 45.

mystery more intelligible, the application of the illustration being this, that the word 'God' refers primarily to the divine essence, which is one, and only secondarily to the divine Persons, who are Three, so that the Christian cannot be rightly accused of tritheism. But, though the illustration was introduced to defeat the charge of tritheism and make the mystery more intelligible, it was an unfortunate illustration, since it implied a hyperrealist view of universals.

St. Gregory's 'Platonism' in regard to universals comes out clearly in his *De hominis opificio*, where he distinguishes the heavenly man, the ideal man, the universal, from the earthly man, the object of experience. The former, the ideal man or rather ideal human being, exists only in the divine idea and is without sexual determination, being neither male nor female: the latter, the human being of experience, is an expression of the ideal and is sexually determined, the ideal being, as it were, 'splintered' or partially expressed in many single individuals. Thus, according to Gregory, individual creatures proceed by creation, not by emanation, from the ideal in the divine Logos. This theory clearly goes back to neo-Platonism and to Philonism, and it was adopted by the first outstanding philosopher of the Middle Ages, John Scotus Eriugena, who was much influenced by the writings of St. Gregory of Nyssa. It must be remembered, however, that Gregory never meant to imply that there was ever an historic ideal man, sexually undetermined; God's idea of man will be realised only eschatologically, when (according to St. Paul's words as interpreted by Gregory) there will be neither male nor female, since in heaven there will be no marriage.

God created the world out of an abundance of goodness and love, in order that there might be creatures who could participate in the divine goodness; but though God is goodness and created the world out of goodness, He did not create the world from necessity, but freely. A share in this freedom God has given to man, and God respects this freedom, permitting man to choose evil if he so wills. Evil is the result of man's free choice, God is not responsible. It is true that God foresaw evil and that He permits it, but in spite of this foreknowledge He created man, for He knew also that He would in the end bring all men to Himself. Gregory thus accepted the Origenist theory of the 'restoration of all things': every human being, even Satan and the fallen angels, will at length turn to God, at least through the purifying sufferings of the hereafter. In a sense, then, every human being will at length return to the Ideal and be therein contained, though Gregory certainly accepted individual immortality. This notion of the return of all things to God, to the Principle from whom they sprang, and of the attainment of a state in which God is 'all in all', was also borrowed by John Scotus Eriugena from St. Gregory, and in interpreting the somewhat ambiguous language of John Scotus one should at least bear in mind the thought of St. Gregory, even while admitting the possibility of John Scotus having attached a different meaning to similar words.

But, though St. Gregory of Nyssa shared Origen's theory of the restoration of all things, he did not share Origen's acceptance of the Platonic notion of pre-existence, and in the *De hominis opificio*[1] he says that the author of the *De Principiis* was led astray by Hellenic theories. The soul, which is not confined to any one portion of the body, is 'a created essence (οὐσία γεννητή), a living essence, intellectual, with an organic and sensitive body, an essence that has the power of giving life and perceiving sensible objects, so long as the bodily instruments endure'.[2] As simple and uncompounded (ἁπλῆν καὶ ἀσύνθετον), the soul has the power of surviving the body,[3] with which, however, it will in the end be reunited. The soul is thus spiritual and incorporeal; but how is it different from body, for body, i.e. a concrete material object, is composed, according to Gregory, of qualities which in themselves are incorporeal? In the *De hominis opificio*[4] he says that the union of qualities like colour, solidity, quantity, weight, results in body, whereas their dissolution spells the perishing of the body. In the preceding chapter he has proposed a dilemma: either material things proceed from God, in which case God, as their Source, would contain matter in Himself, would be material, or, if God is not material, then material things do not proceed from Him and matter is eternal. Gregory, however, rejects both the materiality of God and dualism, and the natural conclusion of this would be that the qualities of which bodily things are composed are not material. It is true that, while asserting creation *ex nihilo*, Gregory asserts that we cannot comprehend how God creates the qualities out of nothing; but it is reasonable to suppose that in his eyes the qualities which form body are not themselves bodies: in fact they could not be, since there is no concrete body at all except in and through their *union*. Presumably he was influenced

[1] *P.G.*, 44, 229 ff. [2] *De anima et res.*; *P.G.* 46, 29. [3] *Ibid.*, 44. [4] Ch. 24.

by Plato's doctrine of the qualities in the *Timaeus*. How, then, are they not spiritual? And, if they are spiritual, how does soul differ essentially from body? The reply would doubtless be that, though the qualities unite to *form* body and cannot, considered in abstraction, be called 'bodies', yet they have an essential relation to matter, since it is their function to form matter. An analogous difficulty recurs in regard to the Aristotelian-Thomistic doctrine of matter and form. Prime matter is not in itself body, but it is one of the principles of body: how, then, considered in *itself*, does it differ from the immaterial and spiritual? Thomistic philosophers answer that prime matter never *exists* by itself alone and that it has an exigency for quantity, an essential ordination to concrete body, and presumably Gregory of Nyssa would have to say something of the same sort in regard to his primary qualities. In passing, one may note that similar difficulties might be raised in regard to certain modern theories concerning the constitution of matter. Plato, one might reasonably suppose, would welcome these theories, were he alive to-day, and it is not improbable that St. Gregory of Nyssa would follow suit.

From what has been said it is clear that Gregory of Nyssa was much influenced by Platonism, neo-Platonism, and the writings of Philo (he speaks, for example, of the ὁμοίωσις Θεῷ as being the purpose of man, of the 'flight of the alone to the Alone', of justice-in-itself, of *eros* and the ascent to the ideal Beauty); but it must be emphasised that, although Gregory undeniably employed Plotinian themes and expressions, as also to a less extent those of Philo, he did not by any means always understand them in a Plotinian or Philonic sense. On the contrary, he utilised expressions of Plotinus or Plato to expose and state Christian doctrines. For example, the 'likeness to God' is the work of grace, a development under the activity of God, with man's free co-operation, of the image or εἰκών of God implanted in the soul at baptism. Again, justice-in-itself is not an abstract virtue nor even an idea in *Nous*; it is the Logos indwelling in the soul, the effect of this inhabitation being the participated virtue. This Logos, moreover, is not the *Nous* of Plotinus, nor is it the Logos of Philo: it is the Second Person of the Blessed Trinity, and between God and creatures there is no intermediary procession of subordinate hypostases.

Finally, it is noteworthy that St. Gregory of Nyssa was the first real founder of systematic mystical theology. Here again he utilised Plotinian and Philonic themes, but he employed them in a Christian sense and within a Christocentric framework of thought. Naturally speaking man's mind is fitted to know sensible objects, and contemplating these objects the mind can come to know something of God and His attributes (symbolic theology, which is partly equivalent to natural theology in the modern sense). On the other hand, though man by nature has as his proper object of knowledge sensible things, these things are not fully real, they are mirage and illusion except as symbols or manifestations of immaterial reality, that reality towards which man is spiritually drawn. The consequent tension in the soul leads to a state of ἀνελπιστία or 'despair', which is the birth of mysticism, since the soul, drawn by God, leaves its natural object of knowledge, without, however, being able to see the God to whom it is drawn by love: it enters into the darkness, what the mediaeval treatise calls the Cloud of Unknowing. (To this stage corresponds the negative theology, which so influenced the Pseudo-Dionysius.) In the soul's advance there are, as it were, two movements, that of the indwelling of the Triune God and that of the soul's reaching out beyond itself, culminating in 'ecstasy'. Origen had interpreted the Philonic ecstasy intellectually, as any other form of 'ecstasy' was then suspect, owing to Montanist extravagances; but Gregory set ecstasy at the summit of the soul's endeavour, interpreting it first and foremost as ecstatic *love*.

The 'darkness' which envelops God is due primarily to the utter transcendence of the divine essence, and Gregory drew the conclusion that even in heaven the soul is always pressing forward, drawn by love, to penetrate further into God. A static condition would mean either satiety or death: spiritual life demands constant progress and the nature of the divine transcendence involves the same progress, since the human mind can never comprehend God. In a sense, then, the 'divine darkness' *always* persists, and it is true to say that Gregory gave to this knowledge in darkness a priority over intellectual knowledge, not because he despised the human intellect but because he realised the transcendence of God.

St. Gregory's scheme of the soul's ascent certainly bears some resemblance to that of Plotinus; but at the same time it is thoroughly Christocentric. The advance of the soul is the work of the Divine Logos, Christ. Moreover, his ideal is not that of a solitary union with God, but rather of a realisation of the *Pleroma* of Christ: the advance of one soul brings grace and blessing to others and the indwelling of God in the individual affects the whole Body. His mysticism is also thoroughly sacramental in character: the εἰκών is restored by Baptism, union with God is fostered by the Eucharist. In fine, the writings of St. Gregory of Nyssa are the source from which not only the Pseudo-Dionysius and mystics down to St. John of the Cross drew, directly or indirectly, much of their inspiration; but they are also the fountain-head of those Christian philosophical systems which trace out the soul's advance through different stages of knowledge and love up to the mystical life and the Beatific Vision. If a purely spiritual writer like St. John of the Cross stands in the line that goes back to Gregory, so does the mystical philosopher St. Bonaventure.

7. Of the Latin Fathers the greatest, without a shadow of doubt, is St. Augustine of Hippo; but, because of the importance of his thought for the Middle Ages, I shall consider his philosophy separately and rather more at length. In this section it is sufficient to mention very briefly *St. Ambrose* (about 333 to 397), Bishop of Milan.

St. Ambrose shared the typically Roman attitude towards philosophy, i.e. an interest in practical and ethical matters, coupled with little facility or taste for metaphysical speculation. In his dogmatic and Scriptural work he depended mainly on the Greek Fathers; but in ethics he was influenced by Cicero, and in his *De officiis ministrorum*, composed about 391 and addressed to the clergy of Milan, he provided a Christian counterpart to the *De officiis* of the great Roman orator. In his book the Saint follows Cicero closely in his divisions and treatment of the virtues, but the whole treatment is naturally infused with the Christian ethos, and the Stoic ideal of happiness, found in the possession of virtue, is complemented by the final ideal of eternal happiness in God. It is not that St. Ambrose makes any particularly new contributions to Christian ethic: the importance of his work lies rather in its influence on succeeding thought, in the use made of it by later writers on ethics.

8. The Greek Fathers, as has been seen, were mainly influenced by the Platonic tradition; but one of the factors which helped to prepare the way for the favourable reception eventually accorded to Aristotelianism in the Latin West was the work of the last of the Greek Fathers, St. John Damascene.

St. John Damascene, who died probably at the end of the year

A.D. 749, was not only a resolute opponent of the 'Iconoclasts' but also a great systematiser in the field of theology, so that he can be looked on as the Scholastic of the Orient. He explicitly says that he does not intend to give new and personal opinions, but to preserve and hand on the thoughts of holy and learned men, so that it would be useless to seek in his writings for novelty of content; yet in his systematic and ordered presentation of the ideas of his predecessors a certain originality may be ascribed to him. His chief work is the *Fount of Wisdom*, in the first part of which he gives a sketch of the Aristotelian logic and ontology, though he draws on other writers besides Aristotle, e.g. Porphyry. In this first part, the *Dialectica*, he makes clear his opinion that philosophy and profane science are the instruments or handmaids of theology, adopting the view of Clement of Alexandria and the two Gregories, a view which goes back to Philo the Alexandrian Jew and was often repeated in the Middle Ages.[1] In the second part of his great work he gives a history of heresies, using material supplied by former writers, and in the third part, the *De Fide Orthodoxa*, he gives, in four books, an orderly treatment of orthodox Patristic theology. This third part was translated into Latin by Burgundius of Pisa in 1151 and was used by, among others, Peter Lombard, St. Albert the Great and St. Thomas Aquinas. In the East, St. John Damascene enjoys almost as much esteem as St. Thomas Aquinas in the West.

9. From even the brief survey given above it is evident that one would look in vain for a systematic philosophical synthesis in the works of any of the Greek Fathers or indeed in any of the Latin Fathers save Augustine. The Greek Fathers, making no very clear distinction between the provinces of philosophy and theology, regarded Christianity as the one true wisdom or 'philosophy'. Hellenic philosophy they tended to regard as a propaedeutic to Christianity, so that their main interest in treating of it was to point out the anticipation of Christian truth which they saw therein contained and the aberrations from truth which were also clear to them. The former they frequently attributed to borrowing from the Old Testament, the latter to the weakness of human speculation and to the perverse desire of originality, the vainglory, of the philosophers themselves. When they adopted ideas from Hellenic philosophy they generally accepted them because they thought that they would help in the exposition and presentation

[1] *P.G.*, 94, 532 AB.

of the Christian wisdom, not in order to incorporate them in a philosophic system in the strict sense.

Nevertheless, there are, as we have seen, philosophic elements in the writings of the Fathers. For instance, they make use of rational arguments for God's existence, particularly the argument from order and design; they speculate about the origin and nature of the soul; St. Gregory of Nyssa even had some ideas which fall under the heading of philosophy of nature or cosmology. Still, since their arguments, the arguments for God's existence, for example, are not really worked out in any developed, systematic and strict manner, it may appear out of place to have considered them at all. I think, however, that this would be a mistake, as even a brief treatment of Patristic thought is sufficient to bring out one point which may tend to be forgotten by those who know little of Christian philosophic thought. Owing to the fact that St. Thomas Aquinas, who has in recent times been accorded a peculiar status among Catholic philosophers, adopted a great deal of the Aristotelian system, and owing to the fact that early thinkers of the 'modern era', e.g. Descartes and Francis Bacon, fulminate against Scholastic Aristotelianism, it is sometimes taken for granted that Christian philosophy, or at least Catholic philosophy, means Aristotelianism and nothing else. Yet, leaving out of account for the present later centuries, a survey of Patristic thought is sufficient to show that Plato, and not Aristotle, was the Greek thinker who won the greatest esteem from the Fathers of the Church. This may have been due in great part to the fact that neo-Platonism was the dominant and vigorous contemporary philosophy and to the fact that the Fathers not only saw Plato more or less in the light of neo-Platonic interpretation and development but also knew comparatively little about Aristotle, in most cases at least; but it also remains true that, whatever may have been the cause or causes, the Fathers tended to see in Plato a forerunner of Christianity and that the philosophic elements they adopted were adopted, for the most part, from the Platonic tradition. If one adds to this the further consideration that Patristic thought, especially that of Augustine, profoundly influenced, not only the early Middle Ages, not only such eminent thinkers as St. Anselm and St. Bonaventure, but even St. Thomas Aquinas himself, it will be seen that, from the historical viewpoint at least, some knowledge of Patristic thought is both desirable and valuable.

CHAPTER III

ST. AUGUSTINE—I

Life and writings—St. Augustine and Philosophy.

1. In Latin Christendom the name of Augustine stands out as that of the greatest of the Fathers both from a literary and from a theological standpoint, a name that dominated Western thought until the thirteenth century and which can never lose its lustre, notwithstanding the Aristotelianism of St. Thomas Aquinas and his School, especially as this Aristotelianism was very far from disregarding and still further from belittling the great African Doctor. Indeed, in order to understand the currents of thought in the Middle Ages, a knowledge of Augustinianism is essential. In the present work the thought of Augustine cannot be treated with the fullness which it merits, but treated it must be, even if summarily.

Born at Tagaste in the Province of Numidia on November 13th, A.D. 354, Augustine came of a pagan father, Patricius, and a Christian mother, St. Monica. His mother brought up her child as a Christian, but Augustine's baptism was deferred, in accordance with a common, if undesirable, custom of the time.[1] The child learnt the rudiments of Latin and arithmetic from a schoolmaster of Tagaste, but play, at which he wished always to be the winner, was more attractive to him than study, and Greek, which he began after a time, he hated, though he was attracted by the Homeric poems considered as a story. That Augustine knew practically no Greek is untrue; but he never learned to read the language with ease.

In about A.D. 365 Augustine went to the town of Madaura, where he laid the foundation of his knowledge of Latin literature and grammar. Madaura was still largely a pagan place, and the effect of the general atmosphere and of his study of the Latin classics was evidently to detach the boy from the faith of his mother, a detachment which his year of idleness at Tagaste (369–70) did nothing to mitigate. In 370, the year in which his father died after having become a Catholic, Augustine began the study of rhetoric at Carthage, the largest city he had yet seen. The

[1] *Conf.*, 1, 11, 17.

licentious ways of the great port and centre of government, the sight of the obscene rites connected with cults imported from the East, combined with the fact that Augustine, the southerner, was already a man, with passions alive and vehement, led to his practical break with the moral ideals of Christianity and before long he took a mistress, with whom he lived for over ten years and by whom he had a son in his second year at Carthage. In spite, however, of his irregular life Augustine was a very successful student of rhetoric and by no means neglected his studies.

It was soon after reading the *Hortensius* of Cicero, which turned the youth's mind to the search for truth, that Augustine accepted the teaching of the Manichaeans,[1] which seemed to offer him a rational presentation of truth, in distinction from the barbaric ideas and illogical doctrines of Christianity. Thus Christians maintained that God created the whole world and that God is good: how, then, could they explain the existence of evil and suffering? The Manichaeans, however, maintained a dualistic theory, according to which there are two ultimate principles, a good principle, that of light, God or Ormuzd, and an evil principle, that of darkness, Ahriman. These principles are both eternal and their strife is eternal, a strife reflected in the world which is the production of the two principles in mutual conflict. In man the soul, composed of light, is the work of the good principle, while the body, composed of grosser matter, is the work of the evil principle. This system commended itself in Augustine's eyes because it seemed to explain the problem of evil and because of its fundamental materialism, for he could not yet conceive how there could be an immaterial reality, imperceptible to the senses. Conscious of his own passions and sensual desires, he felt that he could now attribute them to an evil cause outside himself. Moreover, although the Manichaeans condemned sexual intercourse and the eating of flesh-meat and prescribed ascetic practices such as fasting, these practices obliged only the elect, not the 'hearers', to which level Augustine belonged.

Augustine, now detached from Christianity both morally and intellectually, returned to Tagaste in 374 and there taught grammar and Latin literature for a year, after which he opened a school of rhetoric at Carthage in the autumn of 374. He lived with his mistress and their child, Adeodatus, and it was during this period that he won a prize for poetry (a dramatic piece, not now extant)

[1] Manichaeanism, founded by Manes or Mani in the third century, originated in Persia and was a mixture of Persian and Christian elements.

and published his first prose work, *De pulchro et apto*. The sojourn at Carthage lasted until 383 and it was shortly before Augustine's departure for Rome that an event of some importance occurred. Augustine had been troubled by difficulties and problems which the Manichaeans could not answer; for example, the problem of the source of certitude in human thought, the reason why the two principles were in eternal conflict, etc. It happened that a noted Manichaean bishop, Faustus by name, came to Carthage, and Augustine resolved to seek from him a satisfactory solution of his difficulties; but, though he found Faustus agreeable and friendly, he did not find in his words the intellectual satisfaction which he sought. It was, therefore, with his faith in Manichaeism already somewhat shaken that he set out for Rome. He made the journey partly because the students at Carthage were ill-mannered and difficult to control, whereas he had heard good reports of the students' behaviour at Rome, partly because he hoped for greater success in his career in the imperial metropolis. Arrived at Rome, Augustine opened a school in rhetoric, but, though the students were well behaved in class, they had the inconvenient habit of changing their school just before the payment of fees was due. He accordingly sought for and obtained a position at Milan as municipal professor of rhetoric in 384; but he did not leave Rome without having lost most of his belief in Manichaeanism and having been consequently attracted towards Academic scepticism, though he retained a nominal adherence to Manichaeanism and still accepted some of the Manichaean positions, for example their materialism.

At Milan, Augustine came to think a little better of Christianity owing to the sermons on the Scriptures delivered by St. Ambrose, Bishop of Milan; but though he was ready to become a catechumen again, he was not yet convinced of the truth of Christianity. Moreover, his passions were still too strong for him. His mother wished him to marry a certain girl, hoping that marriage would help to reform his life; but, being unable to wait the necessary time for the girl in question, he took another mistress in place of the mother of Adeodatus, from whom he had parted in sorrow in view of the proposed marriage. At this time Augustine read certain 'Platonic' treatises in the Latin translation of Victorinus, these treatises being most probably the *Enneads* of Plotinus. The effect of neo-Platonism was to free him from the shackles of materialism and to facilitate his acceptance of the idea of immaterial reality. In addition, the Plotinian conception of evil as privation rather than as something positive showed him how the problem of evil could be met without having to have recourse to the dualism of the Manichaeans. In other words, the function of neo-Platonism at this period was to render it possible for Augustine to see the reasonableness of Christianity, and he began to read the New Testament again, particularly the writings of St. Paul. If neo-Platonism suggested to him the idea of the contemplation of spiritual things, of wisdom in the intellectual sense, the New Testament showed him that it was also necessary to lead a life in accordance with wisdom.

These impressions were confirmed by his meeting with two men, Simplicianus and Pontitianus. The former, an old priest, gave Augustine an account of the conversion of Victorinus, the neo-Platonist, to Christianity, with the result that the young man 'burned with the desire to do likewise',[1] while the latter spoke of the life of St. Anthony of Egypt, which made Augustine disgusted with his own moral state.[2] There followed that intense moral struggle, which culminated in the famous scene enacted in the garden of his house, when Augustine hearing a child's voice over a wall crying repeatedly the refrain *Tolle lege! Tolle lege!* opened the New Testament at random and lighted on the words of St. Paul in the Epistle to the Romans,[3] which sealed his moral conversion.[4] It is perfectly clear that the conversion which then took place was a moral conversion, a conversion of will, a conversion which followed the intellectual conversion. His reading of neo-Platonic works was an instrument in the intellectual conversion of Augustine, while his moral conversion, from the human viewpoint, was prepared by the sermons of Ambrose and the words of Simplicianus and Pontitianus, and confirmed and sealed by the New Testament. The agony of his second or moral conversion was intensified by the fact that he already knew what he ought to do, though on the other hand he felt himself without the power to accomplish it: to the words of St. Paul, however, which he read in the garden, he gave, under the impulse of grace, a 'real assent' and his life was changed. This conversion occurred in the summer of 386.

A lung ailment from which he was suffering gave Augustine the excuse he wanted to retire from his professorship and at Cassiciacum, through reading and reflection and discussions with friends, he endeavoured to obtain a better understanding of the Christian religion, using as an instrument concepts and themes taken from

[1] *Conf.*, 8, 5, 10. [2] *Ibid.*, 8, 7, 16. [3] *Rom.*, 13, 13–14. [4] *Conf.* 8, 8–12.

neo-Platonic philosophy, his idea of Christianity being still very incomplete and tinctured, more than it was to be later, by neo-Platonism. From this period of retirement date his works *Contra Academicos*, *De Beata Vita* and *De Ordine*. Returning to Milan Augustine wrote the *De Immortalitate Animae* (the *Soliloquia* were also written about this time) and began the *De Musica*. On Holy Saturday of 387 Augustine was baptised by St. Ambrose, soon after which event he set out to return to Africa. His mother, who had come over to Italy, died at Ostia, while they were waiting for a boat. (It was at Ostia that there occurred the celebrated scene described in the *Confessions*.[1]) Augustine delayed his return to Africa and while residing at Rome wrote the *De libero arbitrio*, the *De Quantitate Animae* and the *De moribus ecclesiae Catholicae et de moribus Manichaeorum*. In the autumn of 388 he set sail for Africa.

Back at Tagaste, Augustine established a small monastic community. From this period (388–91) date his *De Genesi contra Manichaeos*, *De Magistro* and *De Vera Religione*, while he completed the *De Musica*. It is probable that he also polished up or completed the *De moribus*, mentioned above. At Cassiciacum Augustine had resolved never to marry, but he did not apparently intend to seek ordination, for it was contrary to his own wishes that the Bishop of Hippo ordained him priest in 391, when he was on a visit to that seaport town, about a hundred and fifty miles due west of Carthage. The bishop desired Augustine's help, and the latter settled down at Hippo and established a monastery. Engaged in controversy with the Manichaeans he composed the *De utilitate credendi*, the *De duabus animabus*, the *Disputatio contra Fortunatum*, the *De Fide et Symbolo*, a lecture on the Creed delivered before a synod of African bishops, and, against the Donatists, the *Psalmus contra partem Donati*. He started a literal commentary on *Genesis*, but, as its name implies (*De Genesi ad litteram liber imperfectus*), left it unfinished. The *De diversis quaestionibus* (389–96), the *Contra Adimantum Manichaeum*, *De sermone Domini in monte*, the *De Mendacio* and *De Continentia*, as well as various Commentaries (on *Romans* and *Galatians*) also date from the early period of Augustine's priestly life.

In the year 395–6 Augustine was consecrated auxiliary Bishop of Hippo, setting up another monastic establishment within his residence very shortly after his consecration. When Valerius,

[1] 9, 10, 23–6.

Bishop of Hippo, died in 396, within a year of Augustine's consecration, he became ruling Bishop of Hippo in Valerius's place, and remained in that post until his death. This meant that he had to face the task of governing a diocese in which the Donatist schism was well entrenched instead of being able to devote himself to a life of quiet prayer and study. However, whatever his personal inclinations, Augustine threw himself into the anti-Donatist struggle with ardour, preaching, disputing, publishing anti-Donatist controversy. Nevertheless, in spite of this activity, he found time for composing such works as the *De diversis quaestionibus ad Simplicianum* (397), part of the *De Doctrina Christiana* (the fourth book being added in 426), part of the *Confessions* (the whole work being published by 400), and the *Annotationes in Job*. Augustine also exchanged controversial letters with the great scholar St. Jerome, on Scriptural matters.

In the year 400 St. Augustine started on one of his greatest treatises, the fifteen books *De Trinitate*, which were completed in 417, and in 401 began the twelve books of the *De Genesi ad litteram*, completed in 415. In the same year (400) appeared the *De catechizandis rudibus*, the *De Consensu Evangelistarum*, the *De Opera Monachorum*, the *Contra Faustum Manichaeum* (thirty-three books), the first book of the *Contra litteras Petiliani* (Donatist Bishop of Cirta), the second book dating from 401–2 and the third from 402–3. These were followed by other anti-Donatist works, such as the *Contra Cresconium grammaticum partis Donati* (402), though various publications have not been preserved, and several writings against the Manichaeans. In addition to this controversial activity Augustine was constantly preaching and writing letters: thus the letter to Dioscorus,[1] in which, in answer to certain questions about Cicero, Augustine develops his views on pagan philosophy, still showing a strong predilection for neo-Platonism, dates from 410.

Imperial edicts were issued in the course of time against the Donatists, and about the year 411, after the conference that then took place, Augustine was able to turn his attention to another set of opponents, the Pelagians. Pelagius, who exaggerated the rôle of human volition in man's salvation and minimised that of grace, denying original sin, visited Carthage in 410 accompanied by Coelestius. In 411, after Pelagius had left for the East, Coelestius was excommunicated by a Council at Carthage. Pelagius

[1] *Epist.*, 118.

had tried to use texts from Augustine's *De libero arbitrio* in support of his own heresy, but the bishop made his position quite clear in his *De peccatorum meritis et remissione, et de baptismo parvulorum, ad Marcellinum*, following it up in the same year (412) by the *De spiritu et littera*, and later by the *De fide et operibus* (413), the *De natura et gratia contra Pelagium* (415) and the *De perfectione iustitiae hominis* (415). However, not content with his anti-Pelagian polemic, Augustine began, in 413, the twenty-two books of the *De Civitate Dei* (completed in 426), one of his greatest and most famous works, written against the background of the barbarian invasion of the Empire, and prepared many of his *Enarrationes in Psalmos*. In addition he published (415) the *Ad Orosium, contra Priscillianistas et Origenistas*, a book against the heresy started by the Spanish bishop, Priscillian, and in the course of further anti-Pelagian polemic the *De Gestis Pelagii* (417) and the *De Gratia Christi et peccato originali* (418). As if all this were not enough, Augustine finished the *De Trinitate*, and wrote his *In Joannis Evangelium* (416–17) and *In Epistolas Joannis ad Parthos* (416), not to speak of numerous letters and sermons.

In 418 Pelagianism was condemned, first by a Council of African bishops, then by the Emperor Honorius, and finally by Pope Zosimus, but the controversy was not yet over, and when Augustine was accused by Julian, heretical Bishop of Eclanum, of having invented the concept of original sin, the Saint replied in the work *De nuptiis et concupiscentia* (419–20), while in 420 he addressed two books, *Contra duas epistolas Pelagianorum ad Bonifatium Papam*, to the Pope, and followed them up by his *Contra Iulianum haeresis Pelagianae defensorem* (six books) in 421. The *De anima et eius origine* (419), the *Contra mendacium ad Consentium* (420), the *Contra adversarium Legis et Prophetarum* (420), the *Enchiridion ad Laurentium, De fide, spe, caritate* (421), the *De cura pro mortuis gerenda, ad Paulinum Nolanum* (420–1), also date from this period.

In 426 Augustine, feeling that he would not live very much longer, provided for the future of his diocese by nominating his successor, the priest Eraclius, the nomination being acclaimed by the people; but the Saint's literary activity was by no means over, and in 426–7 he published the *De gratia et libero arbitrio ad Valentinum*, the *De correptione et gratia* and the two books of *Retractiones*, which contain a critical survey of his works and are of great value for establishing their chronology. All this time the situation of the Empire was going from bad to worse, and in 429

Genseric led the Vandals from Spain into Africa; but Augustine continued writing. In 427 he published the *Speculum de Scriptura Sacra*, a selection of texts from the Bible, and in 428 his *De haeresibus ad Quodvultdeum*, followed by the *De praedestinatione sanctorum ad Prosperum* and the *De dono perseverantiae ad Prosperum* in 428–9. In addition, Augustine began the *Opus imperfectum contra Julianum* in 429, a refutation of an anti-Augustinian treatise by the Pelagian Julian which had been written some time previously but had come into the Saint's hands only in 428; but he did not live to finish the work (hence its name). Augustine also came into contact with Arianism, and in 428 appeared his *Collatio cum Maximino Arianorum episcopo* and his *Contra Maximinum haereticum*.

In the late spring or early summer of 430 the Vandals laid siege to Hippo, and it was during the siege that Augustine died on August 28th, 430, as he was reciting the Penitential Psalms. Possidius remarks that he left no will, since, as one of God's paupers, he had nothing to leave. The Vandals subsequently burnt the city, though the cathedral and the library of Augustine were left intact. Possidius wrote the Life of Augustine, which is to be found in the Latin Patrology. 'Those who read what he (Augustine) has written on divine things can profit much; but I think that they would profit more were they able to hear and see him preaching in the church, and especially those who were privileged to enjoy intimate conversation with him.'[1]

2. It may perhaps seem strange that I have spoken of St. Augustine's theological controversies and listed a large number of theological treatises; but a sketch of his life and activity will suffice to make it plain that, with a few exceptions, Augustine did not compose purely philosophical works in our sense. In a book like this, one does not, of course, intend to treat of Augustine's purely theological doctrine, but, in order to elicit his philosophical teaching one has to have frequent recourse to what are primarily theological treatises. Thus, in order to obtain light on Augustine's theory of knowledge, it is necessary to consult the relevant texts of the *De Trinitate*, while the *De Genesi ad litteram* expounds the theory of *rationes seminales* and the *Confessions* contain a treatment of time. This mingling of theological and philosophical themes may appear odd and unmethodical to us to-day, used as we are to a clear distinction between the provinces of dogmatic

[1] *Vita S. Aug.*, 31.

theology and philosophy; but one must remember that Augustine, in common with other Fathers and early Christian writers, made no such clear distinction. It is not that Augustine failed to recognise, still less that he denied, the intellect's power of attaining truth without revelation; it is rather that he regarded the Christian wisdom as one whole, that he tried to penetrate by his understanding the Christian faith and to see the world and human life in the light of the Christian wisdom. He knew quite well that rational arguments can be adduced for God's existence, for example, but it was not so much the mere intellectual assent to God's existence that interested him as the real assent, the positive adhesion of the will to God, and he knew that in the concrete such an adhesion to God requires divine grace. In short, Augustine did not play two parts, the part of the theologian and the part of the philosopher who considers the 'natural man'; he thought rather of man as he is in the concrete, fallen and redeemed mankind, man who is able indeed to attain truth but who is constantly solicited by God's grace and who requires grace in order to appropriate the truth that saves. If there was question of convincing someone that God exists, Augustine would see the proof as a stage or as an instrument in the total process of the man's conversion and salvation: he would recognise the proof as *in itself* rational, but he would be acutely conscious, not only of the moral preparation necessary to give a real and living assent to the proof, but also of the fact that, according to God's intention for man in the concrete, recognition of God's existence is not enough, but should lead on, under the impulse of grace, to supernatural faith in God's revelation and to a life in accordance with Christ's teaching. Reason has its part to play in bringing a man to faith, and, once a man has the faith, reason has its part to play in penetrating the data of faith; but it is the total relation of the soul to God which primarily interests Augustine. Reason, as we have seen, had its part to play in the intellectual stage of his own conversion and reason had its part to play after his conversion: generalising his own experience, then, he would consider the fullness of wisdom to consist in a penetration of what is believed, though in the approach to wisdom reason helps to prepare a man for faith. 'The medicine for the soul, which is effected by the divine providence and ineffable beneficence, is perfectly beautiful in degree and distinction. For it is divided between Authority and Reason. Authority demands of us faith, and prepares man for reason. Reason leads to perception and cognition, although authority also does not leave reason wholly out of sight, when the question of who may be believed is being considered.'[1]

This attitude was characteristic of the Augustinian tradition. St. Anselm's aim is expressed in his words *Credo ut intelligam*, while St. Bonaventure, in the thirteenth century, explicitly rejected the sharp delimitation of the spheres of theology and philosophy. The Thomist distinction between the sciences of dogmatic theology and philosophy, with the accompanying distinction of the modes of procedure to be employed in the two sciences, no doubt evolved inevitably out of the earlier attitude, though, quite apart from that consideration, it obviously enjoys this very great advantage that it corresponds to an actual and real distinction between revelation and the data of the 'unaided' reason, between the supernatural and natural spheres. It is at once a safeguard of the doctrine of the supernatural and also of the powers of man in the natural order. Yet the Augustinian attitude on the other hand enjoys this advantage, that it contemplates always man *as he is*, man in the concrete, for *de facto* man has only one final end, a supernatural end, and, as far as actual existence is concerned, there is but man fallen and redeemed: there never has been, is not, and never will be a purely 'natural man' without a supernatural vocation and end. If Thomism, without of course neglecting the fact that man in the concrete has but a supernatural end, places emphasis on the distinction between the supernatural and the natural, between faith and reason, Augustinianism, without in the least neglecting the gratuitous character of supernatural faith and grace, always envisages man in the concrete and is primarily interested in his actual relation to God.

This being so, it is only natural that we should have to unravel Augustine's 'purely philosophical' ideas from the total fabric of his thought. To do this is, of course, to survey Augustinianism more or less from a Thomist viewpoint, but that does not mean that it is an illegitimate approach: it means that one is asking what ideas of Augustine are philosophical in the academic understanding of the term. It does indeed mean tearing his ideas from their full context, but in a history of philosophy, which presupposes a certain idea of what philosophy is, one can do nothing else. It must, however, be admitted that a concentration of this sort on Augustine's philosophical ideas, using the word in the Thomist

[1] *De vera relig.*, 24, 45.

sense, tends to give a rather poor idea of the Saint's intellectual achievement, at least to one who is trained in the academic and objective atmosphere of Thomism, since he never elaborated a philosophical system as such, nor did he develop, define and substantiate his philosophical ideas in the manner to which a Thomist is accustomed. The result is that it is not infrequently difficult to say precisely what Augustine meant by this or that idea or statement, how precisely he understood it: there is often an aura of vagueness, allusion, lack of definition about his ideas which leaves one dissatisfied, perplexed and curious. The rigid type of Thomist would, I suppose, maintain that Augustine's philosophy contains nothing of value which was not much better said by St. Thomas, more clearly delineated and defined; but the fact remains that the Augustinian tradition is not dead even to-day, and it may be that the very incompleteness and lack of systematisation in Augustine's thought, its very 'suggestiveness', is a positive help towards the longevity of his tradition, for the 'Augustinian' is not faced by a complete system to be accepted, rejected or mutilated: he is faced by an approach, an inspiration, certain basic ideas which are capable of considerable development, so that he can remain perfectly faithful to the Augustinian spirit even though he departs from what the historic Augustine actually said.

CHAPTER IV

ST. AUGUSTINE—II: KNOWLEDGE

Knowledge with a view to beatitude—Against scepticism—Experiential knowledge—Nature of sensation—Divine ideas—Illumination and Abstraction.

1. To start with the 'epistemology' of St. Augustine is perhaps to give the impression that Augustine was concerned with elaborating a theory of knowledge for its own sake or as a methodological propaedeutic to metaphysics. This would be a wrong impression, however, since Augustine never sat down, as it were, to develop a theory of knowledge and then, on the basis of a realist theory of knowledge, to construct a systematic metaphysic. If Spinoza, according to his own words,[1] aimed at developing the philosophy of God or Substance because it is only contemplation of an infinite and eternal Object which can fully satisfy mind and heart and bring happiness to the soul, far more could an analogous statement be made of Augustine, who emphasised the fact that knowledge of the truth is to be sought, not for purely academic purposes, but as bringing true happiness, true beatitude. Man feels his insufficiency, he reaches out to an object greater than himself, an object which can bring peace and happiness, and knowledge of that object is an essential condition of its attainment; but he sees knowledge in function of an end, beatitude. Only the wise man can be happy and wisdom postulates knowledge of the truth; but there is no question in Augustine's thought of speculation as an end in itself. When the young man Licentius, in the *Contra Academicos*, maintains that wisdom consists in seeking for the truth and declares, like Lessing, that happiness is to be found rather in the pursuit of truth than in the actual attainment and possession of truth, Augustine retorts that it is absurd to predicate wisdom of a man who has no knowledge of truth. In the *De Beata Vita*[2] he says that no one is happy who does not possess what he strives to possess, so that the man who is seeking for truth but has not yet found it, cannot be said to be truly happy. Augustine himself sought for truth because he felt a need for it, and looking back on his development in the light of attainment, he interpreted this as

[1] *De Intellectus Emendatione.* [2] 2, 10 and 14; 4, 27ff.

a search for Christ and Christian wisdom, as the attraction of the divine beauty, and this experience he universalised. This universalisation of his own experience, however, does not mean that his ideas were purely subjective: his psychological introspection enabled him to lay bare the dynamism of the human soul.

Yet to say that Augustine was not an 'intellectualist' in an academic sense and that his philosophy is eudaemonistic is not to say that he was not acutely conscious of the problem of certitude. It would, however, be a mistake to think that Augustine was preoccupied with the question, '*Can* we attain certainty?' As we shall see shortly, he did answer this question, but the question that occupied his attention in the mature period of his thought was rather this, '*How* is it that we can attain certainty?' That we do attain certainty being assumed as a datum, the problem remains: 'How does the finite, changing human mind attain certain knowledge of eternal truths, truths which rule and govern the mind and so transcend it?' After the breakdown of his faith in Manichaeism, Augustine was tempted to relapse into Academic scepticism: his victory over this temptation he expressed in the *Contra Academicos*, where he shows that we indubitably do attain certainty of some facts at least. This granted, his reading of 'Platonic works' suggested to him the problem, how it is that we are able not only to know with certainty eternal and necessary truths, but also to know them as eternal and necessary truths. Plato explained this fact by the theory of reminiscence; how was Augustine to explain it? The discussion of the problem no doubt interested him in itself, for its own sake; but he also saw in what he considered to be the right answer a clear proof of God's existence and operation. The knowledge of eternal truth should thus bring the soul, by reflection on that knowledge, to knowledge of God Himself and God's activity.

2. As I have already said, in the *Contra Academicos* Augustine is primarily concerned to show that wisdom pertains to happiness, and knowledge of truth to wisdom; but he also makes it clear that even the Sceptics are certain of some truths, for example, that of two disjunctive propositions one is true and the other false. 'I am certain that there is either one world or more than one world, and, if more than one, then that there is either a finite or an infinite number of worlds.' Similarly I know that the world either has no beginning or end or has a beginning but no end or had no beginning but will have an end or has both a beginning and an end. In other

words, I am at least certain of the principle of contradiction.[1] Again, even if I am sometimes deceived in thinking that appearance and reality always correspond, I am at least certain of my subjective impression. 'I have no complaint to make of the senses, for it is unjust to demand of them more than they can give: whatever the eyes can see they see truly. Then is that true which they see in the case of the oar in the water? Quite true. For, granted the cause why it appears in that way (i.e. bent), if the oar, when plunged into the water, appeared straight, I should rather accuse my eyes of playing me false. For they would not see what, granted the circumstances, they ought to see. . . . But I am deceived, if I give my assent, someone will say. Then don't give assent to more than the fact of appearance, and you won't be deceived. For I do not see how the sceptic can refute the man who says, "I know that this object seems white to me, I know that this sound gives me pleasure, I know this smell is pleasant to me, I know that this tastes sweet to me, I know that this feels cold to my touch." '[2] St. Augustine refers in the above passage to the Epicureans and it is clear that what he means is that the senses as such never lie or deceive us, even if we may deceive ourselves in judging that things exist objectively in the same way that they appear. The mere appearance of the bent oar is not deception, for there would be something wrong with my eyes were it to appear straight. If I go on to judge that the oar is really bent in itself, I am wrong, but as long as I simply say, 'It appears to me bent', I am speaking the truth and I know that I am speaking the truth. Similarly, if I come out of a hot room and put my hand in tepid water, it may seem to me cold, but as long as I merely say, 'This water *seems* cold to me', I am saying something the truth of which I am certain of, and no sceptic can refute me.

Again, everyone who doubts knows that he is doubting, so that he is certain of this truth at least, namely the fact that he doubts. Thus every one who doubts whether there is such a thing as truth, knows at least one truth, so that his very capacity to doubt should convince him that there is such a thing as truth.[3] We are certain, too, of mathematical truths. When anyone says that seven and three make ten, he does not say that they ought to make ten, but knows that they do make ten.[4]

[1] *C. Acad.*, 3, 10, 23.
[2] *Ibid.*, 3, 11, 26.
[3] *De vera relig.*, 39, 73.
[4] *De lib. arbit.*, 12, 34.

3. But what of real existences? Are we certain of the existence of any real object or are we confined to certain knowledge of abstract principles and mathematical truths? Augustine answers that a man is at least certain of his existence. Even supposing that he doubts of the existence of other created objects or of God, the very fact of his doubt shows that he exists, for he could not doubt, did he not exist. Nor is it of any use to suggest that one might be deceived into thinking that one exists, for 'if you did not exist, you could not be deceived in anything.'[1] In this way St. Augustine anticipates Descartes: *Si fallor, sum.*

With existence Augustine couples life and understanding. In the *De libero arbitrio*[2] he points out that it is clear to a man that he exists, and that this fact would not and could not be clear, unless he were alive. Moreover, it is clear to him that he understands both the fact of his existence and the fact that he is living. Accordingly he is certain of three things, that he exists, that he lives and that he understands. Similarly, in the *De Trinitate*,[3] he observes that it is useless for the sceptic to insinuate that the man is asleep and sees these things in his dreams, for the man is affirming not that he is awake but that he lives: 'whether he be asleep or awake he lives.' Even if he were mad, he would still be alive. Again, a man is certainly conscious of what he wills. If someone says that he wills to be happy, it is mere impudence to suggest to him that he is deceived. Sceptical philosophers may babble about the bodily senses and the way in which they deceive us, but they cannot invalidate that certain knowledge which the mind has by itself, without the intervention of the sense.[4] 'We exist and we know that we exist and we love that fact and our knowledge of it; in these three things which I have enumerated no fear of deception disturbs us; for we do not attain them by any bodily sense, as we do external objects.'[5]

Augustine thus claims certainty for what we know by inner experience, by self-consciousness: what does he think of our knowledge of external objects, the things we know by the senses? Have we certainty in their regard? That we can deceive ourselves in our judgements concerning the objects of the senses Augustine was well aware, and some of his remarks show that he was conscious of the relativity of sense-impressions, in the sense that a judgement as to hot or cold, for example, depends to a certain extent on the condition of the sense-organs: moreover, he did not

[1] *De lib. arbit.*, 2, 3, 7. [2] 2, 3, 7. [3] 15, 12, 21. [4] *Ibid.* [5] *De Civit. Dei*, 11, 26.

consider that the objects apprehensible by the senses constitute the proper object of the human intellect. Being chiefly interested in the soul's orientation to God, corporeal objects appeared to him as a starting-point in the mind's ascent to God, though even in this respect the soul itself is a more adequate starting-point: we should return within ourselves, where truth abides, and use the soul, the image of God, as a stepping-stone to Him.[1] Nevertheless, even if corporeal things, the objects of the senses, are essentially mutable and are far less adequate manifestations of God than is the soul, even if it is through concentration on the things of sense that the most harmful errors arise, we are dependent on the senses for a great deal of our knowledge and Augustine had no intention of maintaining a purely sceptical attitude in regard to the objects of the senses. It is one thing to admit the possibility of error in sense-knowledge and quite another to refuse any credence at all to the senses. Thus, after saying that philosophers may speak against the senses but cannot refute the consciousness of self-existence, Augustine goes on at once to say, 'far be it from us to doubt the truth of what we have learned by the bodily senses; since by them we have learned to know the heaven and the earth.' We learn much on the testimony of others, and the fact that we are sometimes deceived is no warrant for disbelieving all testimony: so the fact that we are sometimes deceived in regard to the objects of our senses is no warrant for complete scepticism. 'We must acknowledge that not only our own senses, but those of other persons too, have added very much to our knowledge.'[2] For practical life it is necessary to give credence to the senses,[3] and the man who thinks that we should never believe the senses falls into a worse error than any error he may fall into through believing them. Augustine thus says that we 'believe' the senses, that we give credence to them, as we give credence to the testimony of others, but he often uses the word 'believe' in opposition to direct inner knowledge, without meaning to imply that such 'belief' is void of adequate motive. Thus when someone tells me a fact about his own mental state, for example, that he understands or wishes this or that, I 'believe': when he says something that is true of the human mind itself, not simply of his own mind in particular, 'I recognise and give my assent, for I know by self-consciousness and introspection that what he says is true.'[4] In

[1] Cf. *De vera relig.*, 39, 72; *Serm.*, 330, 3; *Retract.*, 1, 8, 3; etc.
[2] *De Trinit.*, 15, 12, 21. [3] *Conf.*, 6, 5, 7. [4] *De Trinit.*, 9, 6, 9.

fine, Augustine may have anticipated Descartes by his '*Si fallor, sum*', but he was not occupied with the question whether the external world really exists or not. That it exists, he felt no doubt, though he saw clearly enough that we sometimes make erroneous judgements about it and that testimony is not always reliable, whether it be testimony of our own senses or of other people. As he was especially interested in the knowledge of eternal truths and in the relation of that knowledge to God, it would hardly occur to him to devote very much time to a consideration of our knowledge of the mutable things of sense. The fact of the matter is that his 'Platonism', coupled with his spiritual interest and outlook, led him to look on corporeal objects as not being the proper object of knowledge, owing to their mutability and to the fact that our knowledge of them is dependent on bodily organs of sense which are no more always in the same state than the objects themselves. If we have not got 'true knowledge' of sense-objects, that is due, not merely to any deficiency in the subject but also to a radical deficiency in the object. In other words, Augustine's attitude to sense-knowledge is much more Platonic than Cartesian.[1]

4. The lowest level of knowledge is, therefore, that of sense-knowledge, dependent on sensation, sensation being regarded by Augustine, in accordance with his Platonic psychology, as an act of the soul using the organs of sense as its instruments. *Sentire non est corporis sed animae per corpus.* The soul animates the whole body, but when it increases or intensifies its activity in a particular part, i.e. in a particular sense-organ, it exercises the power of sensation.[2] From this theory it would seem to follow that any deficiency in sense-knowledge must proceed from the mutability both of the instrument of sensation, the sense-organ, and of the object of sensation, and this is indeed what Augustine thought. The rational soul of man exercises true knowledge and attains true certainty when it contemplates eternal truths in and through itself: when it turns towards the material world and uses corporeal instruments it cannot attain true knowledge. Augustine assumed, with Plato, that the objects of true knowledge are unchanging, from which it necessarily follows that knowledge of changing objects is not true knowledge. It is a type of knowledge or grade of knowledge which is indispensable for practical life; but

[1] Scotus repeated St. Augustine's suggestion that the status of sense-knowledge may be connected with original sin.

[2] Cf. *De Musica*, 6–5, 9, 10; *De Trinit.*, 11, 2, 2–5.

the man who concentrates on the sphere of the mutable thereby neglects the sphere of the immutable, which is the correlative object of the human soul in regard to knowledge in the full sense.

Sensation in the strict sense is common, of course, to men and brutes; but men can have and do have a rational knowledge of corporeal things. In the *De Trinitate*[1] St. Augustine points out that the beasts are able to sense corporeal things and remember them and to seek after what is helpful, avoiding what is harmful, but that they cannot commit things to memory deliberately nor recall them at will nor perform any other operation which involves the use of reason; so that, in regard to knowledge of sense-objects, human knowledge is essentially superior to that of the brute. Moreover, man is able to make rational judgements concerning corporeal things and to perceive them as approximations to eternal standards. For instance, if a man judges that one object is more beautiful than another, his comparative judgement (granted the objective character of the beautiful) implies a reference to an eternal standard of beauty, while a judgement that this or that line is more or less straight, that this figure is a well-drawn circle, implies a reference to ideal straightness and the perfect geometrical circle. In other words, such comparative judgements involve a reference to 'ideas' (not to be understood as purely subjective). 'It is the part of the higher reason to judge of these corporeal things according to incorporeal and eternal considerations, which, if they were not above the human mind, would certainly not be immutable. And yet, unless something of our own were subjoined to them, we should not be able to employ them as standards by which to judge of corporeal things. . . . But that faculty of our own which is thus concerned with the treatment of corporeal and temporal things, is indeed rational, in that it is not common to us and the beasts, but is drawn, as it were, out of the rational substance of our mind, by which we depend upon and adhere to the intelligible and immutable truth and which is deputed to handle and direct the inferior things.'[2]

What St. Augustine means is this. The lowest level of knowledge, so far as it can be called knowledge, is sensation, which is common to men and brutes; and the highest level of knowledge, peculiar to man, is the contemplation of eternal things (wisdom) by the mind alone, without the intervention of sensation; but between these two levels is a kind of half-way house, in which

[1] 12, 2, 2. [2] *Ibid.*

mind judges of corporeal objects according to eternal and incorporeal standards. This level of knowledge is a rational level, so that it is peculiar to man and is not shared by brutes; but it involves the use of the senses and concerns sensible objects, so that it is a lower level than that of direct contemplation of eternal and incorporeal objects. Moreover, this lower use of reason is directed towards action, whereas wisdom is contemplative not practical. 'The action by which we make good use of temporal things differs from the contemplation of eternal things, and the former is classed as knowledge, the latter as wisdom. . . . In this distinction it must be understood that wisdom pertains to contemplation, knowledge to action.'[1] The ideal is that contemplative wisdom should increase, but at the same time our reason has to be partly directed to the good use of mutable and corporeal things, 'without which this life does not go on', provided that in our attention to temporal things we make it subserve the attainment of eternal things, 'passing lightly over the former, but cleaving to the latter'.[2]

This outlook is markedly Platonic in character. There is the same depreciation of sense-objects in comparison with eternal and immaterial realities, the same almost grudging admission of practical knowledge as a necessity of life, the same insistence on 'theoretic' contemplation, the same insistence on increasing purification of soul and liberation from the slavery of the senses to accompany the epistemological ascent. Yet it would be a mistake to see in Augustine's attitude a mere adoption of Platonism and nothing more. Platonic and neo-Platonic themes are certainly utilised, but Augustine's interest is always first and foremost that of the attainment of man's supernatural end, beatitude, in the possession and vision of God, and in spite of the intellectualist way of speaking which he sometimes uses and which he adopted from the Platonic tradition, in the total scheme of his thought the primacy is always given to love: *Pondus meum, amor meus*.[3] It is true that even this has its analogy in Platonism, but it must be remembered that for Augustine the goal is the attainment, not of an impersonal Good but of a personal God. The truth of the matter is that he found in Platonism doctrines which he considered admirably adapted for the exposition of a fundamentally Christian philosophy of life.

5. The objects of sense, corporeal things, are inferior to the human intellect, which judges of them in relation to a standard in

[1] *De Trinit.*, 12, 14, 22. [2] *Ibid.*, 12, 13, 21. [3] *Conf.*, 13, 9, 10.

reference to which they fall short; but there are other objects of knowledge which are above the human mind, in the sense that they are discovered by the mind, which necessarily assents to them and does not think of amending them or judging that they should be otherwise than they are. For example, I see some work of art and I judge it to be more or less beautiful, a judgement which implies not only the existence of a standard of beauty, an objective standard, but also my knowledge of the standard, for how could I judge that this arch or that picture is imperfect, deficient in beauty, unless I had some knowledge of the standard of beauty, of beauty itself, the idea of beauty? How could my supposedly objective judgement be justified unless there were an objective standard, not mutable and imperfect, like beautiful *things*, but immutable, constant, perfect and eternal?[1] Again, the geometer considers perfect circles and lines, and judges of the approximate circles and lines according to that perfect standard. Circular things are temporal and pass away, but the nature of circularity in itself, the idea of the circle, its essence, does not change. Again, we may add seven apples and three apples and make ten apples, and the apples which we count are sensible and mutable objects, are temporal and pass away; but the numbers seven and three considered in themselves and apart from things are discerned by the arithmetician to make ten by addition, a truth which he discovers to be necessary and eternal, not dependent on the sensible world or on the human mind.[2] These eternal truths are common to all. Whereas sensations are private, in the sense that, e.g., what seems cold to one man does not necessarily seem cold to another, mathematical truths are common to all and the individual mind has to accept them and recognise their possession of an absolute truth and validity which is independent of its own reactions.

Augustine's attitude in this matter is obviously Platonic. The standards of goodness and beauty, for example, correspond to Plato's first principles or ἀρχαί the exemplary ideas, while the ideal geometrical figures correspond to Plato's mathematical objects, τὰ μαθηματικά the objects of διάνοια. The same question which could be raised in regard to the Platonic theory recurs again, therefore, in regard to the Augustinian theory, namely, 'Where are these ideas?' (Of course, one must remember, in regard to

[1] Cf. *De Trinit.*, 9, 6, 9–11.
[2] Cf. *ibid.*, 12, 14, 22–3; 12, 15, 24; *De lib. arbit.*, 2, 13, 35; 2, 8, 20–4.

both thinkers, that the 'ideas' in question are not subjective ideas but objective essences, and that the query 'where?' does not refer to locality, since the 'ideas' are *ex hypothesi* immaterial, but rather to what one might call ontological situation or status.) Neo-Platonists, seeing the difficulty in accepting a sphere of impersonal immaterial essences, i.e. the condition *apparently* at least assigned to the essences in Plato's published works, interpreted the Platonic ideas as thoughts of God and 'placed' them in *Nous*, the divine mind, which emanates from the One as the first proceeding hypostasis. (Compare Philo's theory of the ideas as contained within the Logos.) We may say that Augustine accepted this position, if we allow for the fact that he did not accept the emanation theory of neo-Platonism. The exemplar ideas and eternal truths are in God. 'The ideas are certain archetypal forms or stable and immutable essences of things, which have not themselves been formed but, existing eternally and without change, are contained in the divine intelligence.'[1] This theory must be accepted if one wishes to avoid having to say that God created the world unintelligently.[2]

6. A difficulty, however, immediately arises. If the human mind beholds the exemplar ideas and eternal truths, and if these ideas and truths are in the mind of God, does it not follow that the human mind beholds the essence of God, since the divine mind, with all that it contains, is ontologically identical with the divine essence? Some writers have believed that Augustine actually meant this. Among philosophers, Malebranche claimed the support of Augustine for his theory that the mind beholds the eternal ideas in God, and he tried to escape from the seemingly logical conclusion that in this case the human mind beholds the essence of God, by saying that the mind sees, not the divine essence as it is in itself (the supernatural vision of the blessed) but the divine essence as participable *ad extra*, as exemplar of creation. The ontologists too claim the support of Augustine for their theory of the soul's immediate intuition of God.

Now, it is impossible to deny that some texts of Augustine taken by themselves favour such an interpretation. But, granting that Augustine seems on occasion to teach ontologism, it seems clear to me that, if one takes into account the totality of his thought, such an interpretation is inadmissible. I should certainly not be so bold as to suggest that Augustine was never inconsistent, but what I do believe is that the ontologistic interpretation of

[1] *De Ideis*, 2. [2] Cf. *Retract.*, 1, 3, 2.

Augustine fits in so badly with his spiritual doctrine that, if there are other texts which favour a non-ontologistic interpretation (and there are such texts), one should attribute a secondary position and a subordinate value to the apparently ontologistic texts. Augustine was perfectly well aware that a man may discern eternal and necessary truths, mathematical principles, for example, without being a good man at all: such a man may not see these truths in their ultimate Ground, but he undoubtedly discerns the truths. Now, how can Augustine possibly have supposed that such a man beholds the essence of God, when in his spiritual doctrine he insists so much on the need of moral purification in order to draw near to God and is well aware that the vision of God is reserved to the saved in the next life? Again, a man who is spiritually and morally far from God can quite well appreciate the fact that Canterbury Cathedral is more beautiful than a Nissen hut, just as St. Augustine himself could discern degrees of sensible beauty before his conversion. In a famous passage of the *Confessions* he exclaims: 'Too late am I come to love Thee, O thou Beauty, so ancient and withal so new; too late am I come to love Thee . . . in a deformed manner I cast myself upon the things of Thy creation, which yet Thou hadst made fair.'[1] Similarly, in the *De quantitate animae*[2] he clearly affirms that the contemplation of Beauty comes at the end of the soul's ascent. In view of this teaching, then, it seems to me inconceivable that Augustine thought that the soul, in apprehending eternal and necessary truths, actually apprehends the very content of the divine mind. The passages which appear to show that he did so think can be explained as due to his adoption of Platonic or neo-Platonic expressions which do not, literally taken, fit in with the general direction of his thought. It does not seem possible to state exactly how Augustine conceived of the status of the eternal truths as apprehended by the human mind (the ontological side of the question he probably never worked out); but, rather than accept a purely neo-Platonic or an ontologistic interpretation, it seems to me preferable to suppose that the eternal truths and ideas, as they are in God, perform an ideogenetic function; that it is rather that the 'light' which comes from God to the human mind enables the mind to see the characteristics of changelessness and necessity in the eternal truths.

One may add, however, a further consideration against an ontologistic interpretation of Augustine. The Saint utilised the

[1] *Conf.*, 10, 27, 38.
[2] 35, 79.

apprehension of eternal and necessary truths as a proof for the existence of God, arguing that these truths require an immutable and eternal Ground. Without going any further into this argument at the moment it is worth pointing out that, if the argument is to have any sense, it clearly presupposes the possibility of the mind's perceiving these truths without at the same time perceiving God, perhaps while doubting or even denying God's existence. If Augustine is prepared to say to a man, 'You doubt or deny God's existence, but you must admit that you recognise absolute truths, and I shall prove to you that the recognition of such truths implies God's existence,' he can scarcely have supposed that the doubter or atheist had any vision of God or of the actual contents of the divine mind. This consideration seems to me to rule out the ontologistic interpretation. But before pursuing this subject any further it is necessary to say something of Augustine's theory of illumination, as this may make it easier to understand his position, though it must be admitted that the interpretation of this theory is itself somewhat uncertain.

7. We cannot, says Augustine, perceive the immutable truth of things unless they are illuminated as by a sun.[1] This divine light, which illumines the mind, comes from God, who is the 'intelligible light', in whom and by whom and through whom all those things which are luminous to the intellect become luminous.[2] In this doctrine of light, common to the Augustinian School, Augustine makes use of a neo-Platonic theme which goes back to Plato's comparison of the Idea of the Good with the sun,[3] the Idea of the Good irradiating the subordinate intelligible objects or Ideas. For Plotinus the One or God is the sun, the transcendent light. The use of the light-metaphor, however, does not by itself tell us very clearly what Augustine meant. Happily we have to help us such texts as the passage of the *De Trinitate*[4] where the Saint says that the nature of the mind is such that, 'when directed to intelligible things in the natural order, according to the disposition of the Creator, it sees them in a certain incorporeal light which is *sui generis*, just as the corporeal eye sees adjacent objects in the corporeal light'. These words seem to show that the illumination in question is a spiritual illumination which performs the same function for the objects of the mind as the sun's light performs for the objects of the eye: in other words, as the sunlight makes corporeal things visible to the eye, so the divine illumination makes

[1] *Solil.*, 1, 8, 15. [2] *Ibid.*, 1, 1, 3. [3] *Rep.*, 514–18. [4] 12, 15, 24.

the eternal truths visible to the mind. From this it would appear to follow that it is not the illumination itself which is seen by the mind, nor the intelligible Sun, God, but that the characteristics of necessity and eternity in the necessary and eternal truths are made visible to the mind by the activity of God. This is certainly not an ontologistic theory.

But why did St. Augustine postulate such an illumination; why did he think it necessary? Because the human mind is changeable and temporal, so that what is unchangeable and eternal transcends it and seems to be beyond its capacity. 'When the human mind knows and loves itself, it does not know and love anything immutable,'[1] and if truth 'were equal to our minds, it also would be mutable', for our minds see the truth, now more now less, and by this very fact show themselves to be mutable. In fact, truth is neither inferior nor equal to our minds, but 'superior and more excellent'.[2] We need, therefore, a divine illumination, in order to enable us to apprehend what transcends our minds, 'for no creature, howsoever rational and intellectual, is lighted of itself, but is lighted by participation of eternal Truth'.[3] 'God hath created man's mind rational and intellectual, whereby he may take in His light . . . and He so enlighteneth it of Himself, that not only those things which are displayed by the truth, but even truth itself may be perceived by the mind's eye.'[4] This light shines upon the truths and renders visible to the mutable and temporal human mind their characteristics of changelessness and eternity.

That the divine illumination is something imparted and *sui generis* is explicitly stated by St. Augustine, as we have seen. It hardly seems possible, therefore, to reduce the illumination-theory to nothing more than a statement of the truth that God conserves and creates the human intellect and that the natural light of the intellect is a participated light. Thomists, who wish to show St. Augustine the same reverence that St. Thomas showed him, are naturally reluctant to admit a radical difference of opinion between the two great theologians and philosophers and are inclined to interpret St. Augustine in a way that would attenuate the difference between his thought and that of St. Thomas; but St. Augustine most emphatically did not mean by 'light' the intellect itself or its activity, even with the ordinary concurrence of God, since it is precisely because of the deficiencies of the human

[1] *De Trinit.*, 9, 6, 9.
[2] *De lib. arbit.*, 2, 13, 35.
[3] *In. Ps.* 119; *Serm.*, 23, 1.
[4] *In Ps.* 118; *Serm.*, 18, 4.

intellect that he postulated the existence and activity of the divine illumination. To say that St. Augustine was wrong in postulating a special divine illumination and that St. Thomas was right in denying the necessity of such an illumination is an understandable attitude; but it seems to be carrying conciliation too far, if one attempts to maintain that both thinkers were saying the same thing, even if one affirms that St. Thomas was saying clearly and unambiguously what St. Augustine had said obscurely and with the aid of metaphor.

I have already indicated that I accept the interpretation of Augustine's thought, according to which the function of the divine illumination is to render visible to the mind the element of necessity in the eternal truths, and that I reject the ontologistic interpretation in any form. This rejection obviously involves the rejection of the view that according to Augustine the mind beholds directly the idea of beauty, for example, as it is in God; but I am also unwilling to accept the view that according to Augustine God actually infuses the idea of beauty or any other normative idea (i.e. in reference to which we make comparative judgements of degree, such as that this object is more beautiful than that, this action juster than that, etc.) ready-made into the mind. This extreme ideogenetic view would make the function of divine illumination that of a kind of separate active intellect: in fact, God would Himself be an ontologically separate active intellect which infuses ideas into the human mind without any part being played by the human sensibility or intellect other than the mind's purely passive rôle. (This reference to an active intellect is not, of course, meant to imply that Augustine thought or spoke in terms of the Aristotelian psychology.) It does not seem to me that such an interpretation, although doubtless much can be said for it,[1] is altogether satisfactory. According to St. Augustine, the activity of the divine illumination in regard to the mind is analogous to the function of the sun's light in regard to vision, and though the sunlight renders corporeal objects visible, Augustine certainly did not think of it as creating images of the objects in the human subject. Again, although the divine illumination takes the place in Augustine's thought of reminiscence in the Platonic philosophy, so that the illumination would seem to fulfil some ideogenetic function, it must be remembered that Augustine's problem is one

[1] See, for example, the article on Augustine by Portalié in the *Dictionnaire de théologie catholique*.

concerning *certitude*, not one concerning the content of our concepts or ideas: it concerns far more the form of the certain judgement and the form of the normative idea than the actual content of the judgement or the idea. In the *De Trinitate*[1] Augustine remarks that the mind 'gathers the knowledge of corporeal things through the senses of the body', and, so far as he deals at all with the formation of the concept, he would seem to consider that the human mind discerns the intelligible in the sensible, performing what is in some way at least equivalent to abstraction. But when it comes to discerning that a corporeal thing is, for example, more or less beautiful, to judging the object according to a changeless standard, the mind judges under the light of the regulative action of the eternal Idea, which is not itself visible to the mind. Beauty itself illuminates the mind's activity in such a way that it can discern the greater or less approximation of the object to the standard, though the mind does not behold Beauty itself directly. It is in this sense that the illumination of Augustine supplies the function of Plato's reminiscence. Again, though Augustine does not clearly indicate *how we obtain* the notions of seven and three and ten, the function of illumination is not to infuse the notions of these numbers but so to illuminate the judgement that seven and three make ten that we discern the necessity and eternity of the judgement. From a passage already referred to,[2] as from other passages,[3] it seems to follow that, while we obtain the concept of corporeal objects, a horse, for example, in dependence on the senses, and of an immaterial object like the soul through self-consciousness and interpretation, our certain judgements concerning these objects are made in the light of 'illumination' under the regulative action of the eternal Ideas. If the illumination has an ideogenetic function, as I believe it to have in Augustine's view, then this function has reference not to the content of the concept, as if it infused that content, but to the quality of our judgement concerning the concept or to our discernment of a character in the object, its relation to the norm or standard, which is not contained in the bare notion of the thing. If this is so, then the difference between St. Augustine and St. Thomas does not so much consist in their respective attitudes towards abstraction (since, whether Augustine explicitly says so or not, his view, as interpreted above, would at least *demand* abstraction in some form) as in the fact that Augustine

[1] 9, 3, 3. [2] *Ibid.*
[3] *Solil.*, 1, 8, 15; *In Joann. Evang.*, 35, 8, 3; *De Trinit.*, 9, 15, 24; etc.

thought it necessary to postulate a special illuminative action of God, beyond His creative and conserving activity, in the mind's realisation of eternal and necessary truths, whereas St. Thomas did not.

On this view of illumination one can understand how it was that St. Augustine regarded the qualities of necessity and unchangeability in the eternal truths as constituting a proof of God's existence, whereas it would be inexplicable on the ontologistic interpretation, since, if the mind perceives God or the divine ideas directly, it can need no proof of God's existence. That Augustine did not explain in detail how the content of the concept is formed, may be regrettable, but it is none the less understandable, since, though interested in psychological observation, he was interested therein, not from an academic motive, but rather from spiritual and religious motives: it was the soul's relation to God which concerned him primarily and, while the necessity and unchangeability of the eternal truths (as contrasted with the contingency and changeability of the human mind) and the doctrine of illumination helped to set this relation in a clear light and to stimulate the soul in its Godward direction, an investigation concerning the formation of the concept as such would not have had such a clear relation to the *Noverim me, noverim Te*.

To sum up. St. Augustine asks himself the question, How is it that we attain knowledge of truths which are necessary, immutable and eternal? That we do attain such knowledge is clear to him from experience. We cannot gain such knowledge simply from sense-experience, since corporeal objects are contingent, changeable and temporal. Nor can we produce the truths from our minds, which are also contingent and changeable. Moreover, such truths rule and dominate our minds, impose themselves upon our minds, and they would not do this if they depended on us. It follows that we are enabled to perceive such truths under the action of the Being who alone is necessary, changeless and eternal, God. God is like a sun which illumines our minds or a master who teaches us. At this point the difficulty in interpretation begins. The present writer inclines to the interpretation that, while the content of our concepts of corporeal objects is derived from sense-experience and reflection thereon, the regulative influence of the divine ideas (which means the influence of God) enables man to see the relation of created things to eternal supersensible realities, of which there is no direct vision in this life, and that God's light enables the mind to discern the elements of necessity, immutability and eternity in that relation between concepts which is expressed in the necessary judgement. Owing, however, to St. Augustine's use of metaphor and to the fact that he was not primarily interested in giving a systematic and carefully defined 'scholastic' account of the process of knowledge, it does not seem possible to obtain a definitive interpretation of his thought which would adequately explain all the statements he made.

CHAPTER V

ST. AUGUSTINE—III: GOD

Proof of God from eternal truths—Proofs from creatures and from universal consent—The various proofs as stages in one process—Attributes of God—Exemplarism.

1. It is probably true to say that the central and favourite proof of God's existence given by St. Augustine is that from thought, i.e. a proof from within. The starting-point of this proof is the mind's apprehension of necessary and changeless truths, of a truth 'which thou canst not call thine, or mine, or any man's, but which is present to all and gives itself to all alike.'[1] This truth is superior to the mind, inasmuch as the mind has to bow before it and accept it: the mind did not constitute it, nor can it amend it: the mind recognises that this truth transcends it and rules its thought rather than the other way round. If it were inferior to the mind, the mind could change it or amend it, while if it were equal to the mind, of the same character, it would itself be changeable, as the mind is changeable. The mind varies in its apprehension of truth, apprehending it now more clearly now less clearly, whereas truth remains ever the same. 'Hence if truth is neither inferior nor equal to our minds, nothing remains but that it should be superior and more excellent.'[2]

But the eternal truths must be founded on being, reflecting the Ground of all truth. Just as human imaginations reflect the imperfection and changeable character of the human mind in which they are grounded, and as the impressions of sense reflect the corporeal objects in which they are grounded, so the eternal truths reveal their Ground, Truth itself, reflecting the necessity and immutability of God. This refers to all essential standards. If we judge of an action that it is more or less just, for example, we judge of it according to an essential and invariable standard, essence or 'idea': human actions in the concrete may vary, but the standard remains the same. It is in the light of the eternal and perfect standard that we judge of concrete acts, and this standard must be grounded in the eternal and all-perfect Being. If there is an intelligible sphere of absolute truths, this cannot be conceived

[1] *De lib. arbit.*, 2, 12, 33.
[2] *Ibid.*

without a Ground of truth, 'the Truth, in whom, and by whom, and through whom those things are true which are true in every respect'.[1]

This argument to God as the Ground of eternal and necessary truth was not only accepted by the 'Augustinian School', but reappears in the thought of several eminent philosophers, like Leibniz.

2. St. Augustine does indeed prove the existence of God from the external, corporeal world; but his words on the subject are rather of the nature of hints or reminders or summary statements than developed proofs in the academic sense: he was not so much concerned to prove to the atheist that God exists as to show how all creation proclaims the God whom the soul can experience in itself, the living God. It was the dynamic attitude of the soul towards God which interested him, not the construction of dialectical arguments with a purely theoretical conclusion. To acknowledge with a purely intellectual assent that a supreme Being exists is one thing; to bring that truth home to oneself is something more. The soul seeks happiness and many are inclined to seek it outside themselves: St. Augustine tries to show that creation cannot give the soul the perfect happiness it seeks, but points upwards to the living God who must be sought within. This basically religious and spiritual attitude must be borne in mind, if one is to avoid first looking on Augustine's proofs as dialectical proofs in a theoretic sense and then belittling them as inadequate and trifling statements of what St. Thomas was to express much better. The purposes of the two men were not precisely the same.

Thus when Augustine, commenting on Psalm 73, remarks, 'How do I know that thou art alive, whose soul I see not? How do I know? Thou wilt answer, Because I speak, because I walk, because I work. Fool! by the operations of the body I know thee to be living, canst thou not by the works of creation know the Creator?' he is indeed stating the proof of God's existence from His effects; but he is not setting out to develop the proof for its own sake, as it were: he brings it in by way of commentary in the course of his Scriptural exegesis. Similarly, when he asserts in the *De Civitate Dei*[2] that 'the very order, disposition, beauty, change and motion of the world and of all visible things silently proclaim that it could only have been made by God, the ineffably and invisibly great and the ineffably and invisibly beautiful', he is

[1] *Solil.*, 1, 1, 3. [2] 11, 4, 2.

rather reminding Christians of a fact than attempting to give a systematic proof of God's existence. Again, when Augustine, commenting on Genesis,[1] states that 'the power of the Creator and His omnipotent and all-swaying strength is for each and every creature the cause of its continued existence, and if this strength were at any time to cease from directing the things which have been created, at one and the same time both their species would cease to be and their whole nature would perish . . . ', he is stating the fact and necessity of divine conservation, reminding his readers of an acknowledged fact, rather than proving it philosophically.

Augustine gives, again in very brief form, what is known as the argument from universal consent. 'Such', he says, 'is the power of true Godhead that it cannot be altogether and utterly hidden from the rational creature, once it makes use of its reason. For, with the exception of a few in whom nature is excessively depraved, the whole human race confesses God to be the author of the world.'[2] Even if a man thinks that a plurality of gods exists, he still attempts to conceive 'the one God of gods' as 'something than which nothing more excellent or more sublime exists. . . . All concur in believing God to be that which excels in dignity all other objects.'[3] No doubt St. Anselm was influenced by these words of Augustine when he took as the universal idea of God in the 'ontological argument' 'that than which no greater can be conceived'.

3. Professor Gilson, in his *Introduction à l'étude de Saint Augustin*,[4] remarks that in the thought of St. Augustine there is really one long proof of God's existence, a proof which consists of various stages.[5] Thus from the stage of initial doubt and its refutation through the *Si fallor, sum*, which is a kind of methodical preliminary to the search for truth, assuring the mind of the attainability of truth, the soul proceeds to consider the world of sense. In this world, however, it does not discover the truth which it seeks and so it turns inwards, where, after considering its own fallibility and changeableness, it discovers immutable truth which transcends the soul and does not depend on the soul. It is thus led to the apprehension of God as the Ground of all truth.

The picture of Augustine's total proof of the existence of God

[1] *De Gen. ad litt.*, 4, 22, 22.
[2] *In Joann. Evang.*, 106, 4.
[3] *De doct. Christ.*, 1, 7, 7.
[4] Ch. 2.
[5] Cf. also G. Grunwald: *Geschichte der Gottesbeweise im Mittelalter*, in *Beiträge*, 6, 3, p. 6.

given by M. Gilson is doubtless representative of the Saint's mind and it has the great advantage not only of bringing into prominence the proof from thought, from the eternal truths, but also of linking up the 'proof' with the soul's search for God as the source of happiness, as objective beatitude, in such a way that the proof does not remain a mere academic and theoretic string or chain of syllogisms. This picture is confirmed by a passage such as that contained in Augustine's two hundred and forty-first sermon,[1] where the Saint depicts the human soul questioning the things of sense and hearing them confess that the beauty of the visible world, of mutable things, is the creation and reflection of immutable Beauty, after which the soul proceeds inwards, discovers itself and realises the superiority of soul to body. 'Men saw these two things, pondered them, investigated both of them, and found that each is mutable in man.' The mind, therefore, finding both body and soul to be mutable goes in search of what is immutable. 'And thus they arrived at a knowledge of God the Creator by means of the things which He created.' St. Augustine, then, in no way denies what we call a 'natural' or 'rational' knowledge of God ; but this rational knowledge of God is viewed in close connection with the soul's search for beatifying Truth and is seen as itself a kind of self-revelation of God to the soul, a revelation which is completed in the full revelation through Christ and confirmed in the Christian life of prayer. Augustine would thus make no sharp dichotomy between the spheres of natural and revealed theology, not because he failed to see the distinction between reason and faith, but rather because he viewed the soul's cognition of God in close connection with its spiritual search for God as the one Object and Source of beatitude. When Harnack reproaches Augustine with not having made clear the relation of faith to science,[2] he fails to realise that the Saint is primarily concerned with the spiritual experience of God and that in his eyes faith and reason each have their part to play in an experience which is an organic unity.

4. Augustine insists that the world of creatures reflects and manifests God, even if it does so in a very inadequate manner, and that 'if any thing worthy of praise is noticed in the nature of things, whether it be judged worthy of slight praise or of great, it must be applied to the most excellent and ineffable praise of

[1] *Serm.*, 241, 2, 2 and 3, 3.
[2] *Lehrbuch der Dogmengeschichte*, 3rd edit., t. 3, p. 119.

the Creator.' Creatures tend indeed to not-being, but as long as they are, they possess some form, and this is a reflection of the Form which can neither decline nor pass away.[1] Thus the order and unity of Nature proclaims the unity of the Creator,[2] just as the goodness of creatures, their positive reality, reveals the goodness of God[3] and the order and stability of the universe manifest the wisdom of God.[4] On the other hand, God, as the self-existent, eternal and immutable Being, is infinite, and, as infinite, incomprehensible. God is His own Perfection, is 'simple', so that His wisdom and knowledge, His goodness and power, are His own essence, which is without accidents.[5] God, therefore, transcends space in virtue of His spirituality and infinity and simplicity, as He transcends time in virtue of His eternity: 'God is Himself in no interval nor extension of place, but in His immutable and pre-eminent might is both interior to everything because all things are in Him and exterior to everything because He is above all things. So too He is in no interval nor extension of time, but in His immutable eternity is older than all things because He is before all things and younger than all things because the same He is after all things.'[6]

5. From all eternity God knew all things which He was to make: He does not know them because He has made them, but rather the other way round: God first knew the things of creation though they came into being only in time. The species of created things have their ideas or *rationes* in God, and God from all eternity saw in Himself, as possible reflections of Himself, the things which He could create and would create. He knew them before creation as they are in Him, as Exemplar, but He made them as they exist, i.e. as external and finite reflections of His divine essence.[7] God did nothing without knowledge, He foresaw all that He would make, but His knowledge is not distinct acts of knowledge, but 'one eternal, immutable and ineffable vision'.[8] It is in virtue of this eternal act of knowledge, of vision, to which nothing is past or future, that God sees, 'foresees', even the free acts of men, knowing 'beforehand', for example, 'what we should ask of Him and when, and to whom He would listen or not listen, and on what subjects'.[9] An adequate discussion of this last point, which would

[1] *De lib. arbit.*, 2, 17, 46. [2] *Ibid.*, 3, 23, 70. [3] *De Trinit.*, 11, 5, 8.
[4] *De Civit. Dei*, 11, 28.
[5] *De Trinit.*, 5, 2, 3; 5, 11, 12; 6, 4, 6; 6, 10, 11; 15, 43, 22; *In Joann. Evang.*, 99, 4; etc.
[6] *De Gen. ad litt.*, 8, 26, 48. [7] Cf. *ibid.*, 5, 15, 33; *Ad Orosium*, 8, 9.
[8] *De Trinit.*, 15, 7, 13. [9] *Ibid.*, 15, 13, 22.

necessitate consideration of the Augustinian theory of grace, cannot be attempted here.

Contemplating His own essence from eternity God sees in Himself all possible limited essences, the finite reflections of His infinite perfection, so that the essences or *rationes* of things are present in the divine mind from all eternity as the divine ideas, though, in view of Augustine's teaching on the divine simplicity previously mentioned, this should not be taken to mean that there are 'accidents' in God, ideas which are ontologically distinct from His essence. In the *Confessions*[1] the Saint exclaims that the eternal 'reasons' of created things remain unchangeably in God, and in the *De Ideis*[2] he explains that the divine ideas are 'certain archetypal forms or stable and unchangeable reasons of things, which were not themselves formed but are contained in the divine mind eternally and are always the same. They neither arise nor pass away, but whatever arises and passes away is formed according to them.' The corollary of this is that creatures have ontological truth in so far as they embody or exemplify the model in the divine mind, and that God Himself is the standard of truth. This exemplarist doctrine was, of course, influenced by neo-Platonic theory, according to which the Platonic exemplary ideas are contained in *Nous*, though for Augustine the ideas are contained in the Word, who is not a subordinate hypostasis, like the neo-Platonic *Nous*, but the second Person of the Blessed Trinity, consubstantial with the Father.[3] From Augustine the doctrine of exemplarism passed to the Middle Ages. It may be thought of as characteristic of the Augustinian School; but it must be remembered that St. Thomas Aquinas did not deny it, though he was careful to state it in such a way as not to imply that there are ontologically separate ideas in God, a doctrine which would impair the divine simplicity, for in God there is no real distinction save that between the three divine Persons.[4] Still, though Aquinas was in this respect a follower of Augustine, it was St. Bonaventure who most insisted in the thirteenth century on the doctrine of exemplarism and on the presence of the divine Ideas in the Word of God, an insistence which contributed to his hostile attitude to Aristotle the metaphysician, who threw overboard the ideas of Plato.

[1] 1, 6, 9. [2] 2. [3] *De Trinit.*, 4, 1, 3.
[4] Cf. e.g. *Summa Theol.*, Ia, 15, 2 and 3.

CHAPTER VI

ST. AUGUSTINE—IV: THE WORLD

*Free creation out of nothing—Matter—*Rationes seminales*—Numbers—Soul and body—Immortality—Origin of soul.*

ONE would hardly expect, once given the general attitude and complexion of Augustine's thought, to find the Saint showing very much interest in the material world for its own sake: his thought centred round the soul's relation to God; but his general philosophy involved a theory of the corporeal world, a theory consisting of elements taken from former thinkers and set in a Christian framework. It would be a mistake, however, to think that Augustine drew purely mechanically on previous thinkers for his theories: he emphasised those lines which seemed to him best calculated to underline nature's relation to and dependence on God.

1. A doctrine which was not developed by pagan thinkers, but which was held by Augustine in common with other Christian writers, was that of the creation of the world out of nothing by God's free act. In the Plotinian emanation-theory the world is depicted as proceeding in some way from God without God becoming in any way diminished or altered thereby, but for Plotinus God does not act freely (since such activity would, he thought, postulate change in God) but rather *necessitate naturae*, the Good necessarily diffusing itself. The doctrine of free creation out of nothing is not to be found in neo-Platonism, if we except one or two pagan thinkers who had most probably been influenced by Christian teaching. Augustine may have thought that Plato had taught creation out of nothing in time, but it is improbable, in spite of Aristotle's interpretation of the *Timaeus*, that Plato really meant to imply this. However, whatever Augustine may have thought about Plato's views on the matter, he himself clearly states the doctrine of free creation out of nothing and it is essential to his insistence on the utter supremacy of God and the world's entire dependence on Him. All things owe their being to God.[1]

2. But suppose that things were made out of some formless matter? Would not this formless matter be independent of God? First of all, says Augustine, are you speaking of a matter which is

[1] *De lib. arbit.*, 3, 15, 42.

absolutely formless or of a matter which is formless only in comparison with completely formed? If the former, then you are speaking of what is equivalent to nothingness. 'That out of which God has created all things is what possesses neither species nor form; and this is nothing other than nothing.' If, however, you are speaking of the latter, of matter which has no completed form, but which has inchoate form, in the sense of possessing the capacity to receive form, then such matter is not altogether nothing indeed, but, as something, it has what being it has only from God. 'Wherefore, even if the universe was created out of some formless matter, this very matter was created from something which was wholly nothing.'[1] In the *Confessions*[2] Augustine identifies this matter with the mutability of bodies (which is equivalent to saying that it is the potential element) and observes that if he could call it 'nothing' or assert that it does not exist, he would do so; but if it is the capacity of receiving forms, it cannot be called absolutely nothing. Again, he remarks in the *De vera religione*[3] that not only the possession of form but even the capacity to receive form is a good, and what is a good cannot be absolute nothing. Yet this matter, which is not absolutely nothing, is itself the creation of God, not preceding formed things in time but concreated with form,[4] and he identified the 'unformed matter which God made out of nothing' with the heaven and earth mentioned in the first verse of the first chapter of Genesis as the primary creation of God.[5] In other words, St. Augustine is stating in rudimentary form the Scholastic doctrine that God created out of nothing not absolutely formless 'prime matter', apart from all form, but form and matter together, though, if we choose to think of Augustine's statements as a rudimentary expression of the more elaborate Scholastic doctrine, we should also remember that the Saint is not so concerned with developing a philosophical doctrine for its own sake as with emphasising the essential dependence of all creatures on God and the perishable nature of all corporeal creatures, even when once constituted in existence. They have their being from God, but their being is bound up with their mutability.

3. A theory which was dear to Augustine himself and to his followers, though it was rejected by St. Thomas, and which was calculated to exalt the divine agency at the expense of the causal

[1] Cf. *De vera relig.*, 18, 35–6. [2] 12, 6, 6. [3] *Loc. cit.*
[4] *De Gen. ad litt.*, 1, 15, 29. [5] *De Gen. contra Manich.*, 1, 17, 11.

activity of creatures, was that of the *rationes seminales* or 'seminal reasons', the germs of those things which were to develop in the course of time. Thus even man, as regards his body at least, to leave the origin of the soul out of account for the moment, was created in the *rationes seminales*, 'invisibly, potentially, causally, in the way that things are made which are to be but have not yet been made'.[1] The *rationes seminales* are germs of things or invisible powers or potentialities, created by God in the beginning in the humid element and developing into the objects of various species by their temporal unfolding. The idea of these germinal potentialities was to be found, and doubtless was found by Augustine, in the philosophy of Plotinus and ultimately it goes back to the *rationes seminales* or λόγοι σπερματικοί of Stoicism, but it is an idea of rather vague content. Indeed, St. Augustine never supposed that they were the object of experience, that they could be seen or touched: they are invisible, having inchoate form or a potentiality to the development of form according to the divine plan. The seminal reasons are not purely passive, but tend to self-development, though the absence of the requisite conditions and circumstances and of other external agencies may hinder or prevent their development.[2] St. Bonaventure, who maintained the theory of St. Augustine on this point, compared the *ratio seminalis* to the rosebud, which is not yet actually the rose but will develop into the rose, given the presence of the necessary positive agencies and the absence of negative or preventive agencies.

That St. Augustine asserted a rather vague theory regarding objects which are not the term of direct experience will appear less surprising if one considers *why* he asserted it. The assertion was the result of an exegetic, not a scientific problem, and the problem arose in this way. According to the book of Ecclesiasticus[3] 'He that liveth for ever created all things together', while on the other hand according to the book of Genesis the fishes and birds, for instance, appeared only on the fifth 'day' of creation, while the cattle and beasts of the earth appeared only on the sixth 'day'. (Augustine did not interpret 'day' as our day of twenty-four hours, since the sun was made only on the fourth 'day'.) How then can these two statements be reconciled, that God created all things together and that some things were made after others, that is to say, that *not* all things were created together? St. Augustine's

[1] *De Gen. ad litt.*, 6, 5, 8. [2] *De Trinit.*, 3, 8, 13. [3] 18, 1.

way of solving the problem was to say that God did indeed create all things together in the beginning, but that He did not create them all in the same condition: many things, all plants, fishes, birds, animals, and man himself, He created invisibly, latently, potentially, in germ, in their *rationes seminales.* In this way God created in the beginning all the vegetation of the earth before it was actually growing on the earth,[1] and even man himself. He would thus solve the apparent contradiction between Ecclesiasticus and Genesis by making a distinction. If you are speaking of actual formal completion, then Ecclesiasticus is not referring to this, whereas Genesis is: if you are including germinal or seminal creation, then this is what Ecclesiasticus refers to.

Why did not Augustine content himself with 'seeds' in the ordinary sense, the visible seeds of plants, the grain and so on? Because in the book of Genesis it is implied that the earth brought forth the green herb *before* its seed,[2] and the same thing is implied in regard to the other living things which reproduce their kind. He found himself compelled, therefore, to have recourse to a different kind of seed. For example, God created in the beginning the *ratio seminalis* of wheat, which, according to God's plan and activity, unfolded itself at the appointed time as actual wheat, which then contained seed in the ordinary sense.[3] Moreover, God did not create all seeds or all eggs in act at the beginning, so that they too require a *ratio seminalis.* Each species, then, with all its future developments and particular members, was created at the beginning in the appropriate seminal reason.

From what has been said it should be clear that the Saint was not considering primarily a scientific problem but rather an exegetic problem, so that it is really beside the point to adduce him either as a protagonist or as an opponent of evolution in the Lamarckian or Darwinian sense.

4. St. Augustine made use of the Platonic number-theme, which goes back to Pythagoreanism. Naturally his treatment of number sometimes appears to us as fanciful and even fantastic, as when he speaks of perfect and imperfect numbers or interprets references to numbers in the Scriptures; but, speaking generally, he looks on number as the principle of order and form, of beauty and perfection, of proportion and law. Thus the Ideas are the eternal numbers, while bodies are temporal numbers, which unfold themselves in

[1] *De Gen. ad litt.,* 5, 4, 7–9. [2] Gen. 1. 11.
[3] *De Gen. ad litt.,* 5, 4, 9.

time. Bodies indeed can be considered as numbers in various ways, as being wholes consisting of a number of ordered and related parts, as unfolding themselves in successive stages (the plant, for example, germinates, breaks into leaf, produces flower and fruit, seminates), or as consisting of a number of parts well disposed in space; in other words, as exemplifying intrinsic number, local or spatial number, and temporal number. The 'seminal reasons' are hidden numbers, whereas bodies are manifest numbers. Again, just as mathematical number begins from one and ends in a number which is itself an integer, so the hierarchy of beings begins with the supreme One, God, which brings into existence and is reflected in more or less perfect unities. This comparison or parallel between mathematical number and metaphysical number was derived, of course, from Plotinus, and in general Augustine's treatment of number adds nothing of substance to the treatment already accorded it in the Pythagorean-Platonic tradition.

5. The peak of the material creation is man, who consists of body and immortal soul. Augustine is quite clear about the fact that man does consist of soul and body, as when he says that 'a soul in possession of a body does not constitute two persons but one man'.[1] Why is it necessary to mention such an obvious point? Because Augustine speaks of the soul as a substance in its own right (*substantia quaedam rationis particeps, regendo corpori accomodata*)[2] and even defines man as 'a rational soul using a mortal and earthly body'.[3] This Platonic attitude towards the soul has its repercussions, as we have already seen, in Augustine's doctrine of sensation, which he represents as an activity of the soul using the body as an instrument, rather than as an activity of the total psycho-physical organism: it is, in fact, a temporary increase of intensity in the action by which the soul animates a certain part of the body. The soul, being superior to the body, cannot be acted on by the body, but it perceives the changes in the body due to an external stimulus.

6. The human soul is an immaterial principle, though, like the souls of brutes, it animates the body. A man may say or even think that his soul is composed of air, for example, but he can never know that it is composed of air. On the other hand he knows very well that he is intelligent, that he thinks, and he has no reason to suppose that air can think.[4] Moreover, the soul's

[1] *In Joann. Evang.*, 19, 5, 15. [2] *De quant. animae*, 13, 21.
[3] *De moribus eccl.*, 1, 27, 52; *In Joann. Evang.*, 19, 5, 15.
[4] *De Gen. ad litt.*, 7, 21, 28; *De Trinit.*, 10, 10, 14.

immateriality and its substantiality assure it of immortality. On this point Augustine uses arguments which go back to Plato.[1] For example, Augustine utilises the argument of the *Phaedo* that, as the soul is the principle of life and as two contraries are incompatible, the soul cannot die. Apart from the fact that this argument is not very convincing in any case, it could not be acceptable to Augustine without modification, since it would seem to imply that the soul exists of itself or is a part of God. He adapted the argument, therefore, by saying that the soul participates in Life, holding its being and essence from a Principle which admits of no contrary, and by arguing that, as the being which the soul receives from this Principle (which admits no contrary) is precisely *life*, it cannot die. The argument, however, might clearly be taken to imply that the animal soul is immortal also, since it too is a principle of life, and so would prove too much. It must, then, be taken in conjunction with another argument, also derived from Plato, to the effect that the soul apprehends indestructible truth, which shows that it is itself indestructible. In the *De quantitate animae*[2] Augustine distinguishes the souls of beasts, which possess the power of sensation but not that of reasoning and knowing, from human souls, which possess both, so that this argument applies only to human souls. Plato had argued that the human soul, as capable of apprehending the Ideas, which are eternal and indestructible, shows itself to be akin to them, to be 'divine', that is to say, indestructible and eternal, and Augustine, without affirming pre-existence, proves the immortality of the soul in an analogous manner. In addition, he argues from the desire of beatitude, the desire for perfect happiness, and this became a favourite argument among Augustinians, with St. Bonaventure, for example.

7. Augustine clearly held that the soul is created by God,[3] but does not seem to have made up his mind as to the precise time and mode of its origin. He seems to have toyed with some form of the Platonic pre-existence theory while refusing to allow that the soul was put into the body as a punishment for faults committed in a pre-earthly condition, but the chief question for him was whether God creates each individual soul separately or created all other souls in Adam's, so that the soul is 'handed on' by the parents (Traducianism). This second opinion would appear logically to

[1] Cf. *Solil.*, 2, 19, 33; *Ep.*, 3, 4; *De Immortal. An.*, ch. 1–6.

[2] 28, 54 ff.

[3] *De anima et eius origine*, 1, 4, 4.

involve a materialistic view of the soul, whereas in fact Augustine certainly did not hold any such view and insisted that the soul is not present in the body by local diffusion;[1] but it was for theological, not philosophical, reasons that he inclined towards traducianism, as he thought that in this way original sin could be explained as a transmitted stain on the soul. If original sin is looked on as something positive and not as in itself a privation, there is indeed a difficulty, even if not an insuperable difficulty, in affirming individual creation by God of each single human soul, but even apart from that it does not alter the fact that traducianism is inconsistent with a clear affirmation of the soul's spiritual and immaterial character.

[1] *Ep.*, 156.

CHAPTER VII

ST. AUGUSTINE—V: MORAL THEORY

Happiness and God—Freedom and Obligation—Need of grace—Evil—the two Cities.

1. ST. AUGUSTINE'S ethic has this in common with what one might call the typical Greek ethic, that it is eudaemonistic in character, that it proposes an end for human conduct, namely happiness; but this happiness is to be found only in God. 'The Epicurean who places man's supreme good in the body, places his hope in himself,'[1] but 'the rational creature . . . has been so made that it cannot itself be the good by which it is made happy':[2] the human being is mutable and insufficient to itself, it can find its happiness only in the possession of what is more than itself, in the possession of an immutable object. Not even virtue itself can be the end: 'it is not the virtue of thy soul that maketh thee happy, but He who hath given thee the virtue, who hath inspired thee to will, and hath given thee the power to do.'[3] It is not the ideal of the Epicurean that can bring happiness to man, nor even that of the Stoic, but God Himself: 'the striving after God is, therefore, the desire of beatitude, the attainment of God is beatitude itself.'[4] That the human being strives after beatitude or happiness, and that beatitude means the attainment of an object, Augustine knew well from his own experience, even if he found confirmation of this fact in philosophy; that this object is God, he learnt also from his personal experience, even if he had been helped to realise the fact by the philosophy of Plotinus. But when he said that happiness is to be found in the attainment and possession of the eternal and immutable Object, God, he was thinking, not of a purely philosophic and theoretic contemplation of God, but of a loving union with and possession of God, and indeed of the supernatural union with God held up to the Christian as the term of his grace-aided endeavour: one cannot well separate out in Augustine's thought a natural and a supernatural ethic, since he deals with man in the concrete, and man in the concrete has a supernatural vocation: he regarded the neo-Platonists as discerning something of that which

[1] *Serm.*, 150, 7, 8.
[2] *Ep.*, 140, 23, 56.
[3] *Serm.*, 150, 8, 9.
[4] *De moribus eccl.*, 1, 11, 18.

was revealed by Christ, neo-Platonism as an inadequate and partial realisation of the truth.

The ethic of Augustine is, then, primarily an ethic of love: it is by the will that man reaches out towards God and finally takes possession of and enjoys Him. 'When therefore the will, which is the intermediate good, cleaves to the immutable good . . . , man finds therein the blessed life';[1] 'for if God is man's supreme good . . . it clearly follows, since to seek the supreme good is to live well, that to live well is nothing else but to love God with all the heart, with all the soul, with all the mind.'[2] Indeed, after quoting the words of Christ, as recorded by St. Matthew,[3] 'Thou shalt love the Lord thy God with thy whole heart, and with thy whole soul, and with thy whole mind' and 'thou shalt love thy neighbour as thyself', Augustine asserts that 'Natural philosophy is here, since all the causes of all natural things are in God the Creator', and that, 'Ethics are here, since a good and honest life is not formed otherwise than by loving as they should be loved those things which we ought to love, namely, God and our neighbour.'[4] Augustine's ethic thus centres round the dynamism of the will, which is a dynamism of love (*pondus meum, amor meus*),[5] though the attainment of beatitude, 'participation in the immutable good', is not possible for man unless he be aided by grace, unless he receives 'the gratuitous mercy of the Creator'.[6]

2. The will, however, is free, and the free will is subject to moral obligation. The Greek philosophers had a conception of happiness as the end of conduct, and one cannot say that they had no idea of obligation; but owing to his clearer notion of God and of divine creation Augustine was able to give to moral obligation a firmer metaphysical basis than the Greeks had been able to give it.

The necessary basis of obligation is freedom. The will is free to turn away from the immutable Good and to attach itself to mutable goods, taking as its object either the goods of the soul, without reference to God, or the goods of the body. The will necessarily seeks happiness, satisfaction, and *de facto* this happiness can be found only in God, the immutable Good, but man has not the vision of God in this life, he can turn his attention to and cling to mutable goods in place of God, and 'this turning away and this turning to are not forced but voluntary actions'.[7]

[1] *De lib. arbit.*, 2, 19, 52. [2] *De moribus eccl.*, 1, 25, 46. [3] 22. 37–9.
[4] *Ep.*, 137, 5, 17. [5] *Conf.*, 13, 9, 10. [6] *Ep.*, 140, 21, 14.
[7] *De lib. arbit.*, 2, 19, 35.

The human will is, then, free to turn to God or away from God, but at the same time the human mind must recognise the truth, not only that what it seeks, happiness, can be found only in the possession of the immutable Good, God, but also that the direction of the will to that good is implanted by God and willed by God, who is the Creator. By turning away from God the will runs counter to the divine law, which is expressed in human nature, made by God for Himself. All men are conscious to some extent of moral standards and laws: 'even the ungodly . . . rightly blame and rightly praise many things in the conduct of men.' How are they enabled to do so, save by seeing the rules according to which men ought to live, even if they do not personally obey these laws in their own conduct? Where do they see these rules? Not in their own minds, since their minds are mutable, whereas the 'rules of justice' are immutable; not in their characters, since they are *ex hypothesi* unjust. They see the moral rules, says Augustine, using his customary, if obscure, manner of speaking, 'in the book of that light which is called Truth'. The eternal laws of morality are impressed in the heart of man, 'as the impression of a ring passes into the wax, yet does not leave the ring'. There are indeed some men who are more or less blind to the law, but even they are 'sometimes touched by the splendour of the omnipresent truth'.[1] Thus, just as the human mind perceives eternal theoretic truths in the light of God, so it perceives, in the same light, practical truths or principles which should direct the free will. Man is by his nature, his nature considered in the concrete, set towards God; but he can fulfil the dynamism of that nature only by observing the moral laws which reflect the eternal law of God, and which are not arbitrary rules but follow from the Nature of God and the relationship of man to God. The laws are not arbitrary caprices of God, but their observance is willed by God, for He would not have created man without willing that man should be what He meant him to be. The will is free, but it is at the same time subject to moral obligations, and to love God is a duty.

3. The relationship of man to God, however, is the relationship of a finite creature to the infinite Being, and the result is that the gulf cannot be bridged without the divine aid, without grace: grace is necessary even to begin to will to love God. 'When man tries to live justly by his own strength without the help of the liberating grace of God, he is then conquered by sins; but in free will he has

[1] *De Trinit.*, 14, 15, 21.

it in his power to believe in the Liberator and to receive grace.'[1] 'The law was therefore given that grace might be sought; grace was given that the law might be fulfilled.'[2] 'Our will is by the law shown to be weak, that grace may heal its infirmity.'[3] 'The law of teaching and commanding that which cannot be fulfilled without grace demonstrates to man his weakness, in order that the weakness thus proved may resort to the Saviour, by whose healing the will may be able to do what in its feebleness it found impossible.'[4]

It would be out of place here to enter on the question of Augustine's doctrine of grace and its relation to the free will, which is in any case a difficult question; but it is necessary to grasp the fact that when Augustine makes the love of God the essence of the moral law, he is referring to that union of the will with God which requires the elevation effected by grace. This is only natural, once given the fact that he is considering and treating man in the concrete, man endowed with a supernatural vocation, and it means that he supplements and completes the wisdom of philosophy with the wisdom of the Scriptures. One can, for purposes of schematism, try to separate Augustine the philosopher and Augustine the theologian; but in his own eyes the true philosopher is a man who surveys reality in the concrete, as it is, and it cannot be seen as it is without taking into account the economy of redemption and of grace.

4. If moral perfection consists in loving God, in directing the will to God and bringing all other powers, e.g. the senses, into harmony with this direction, evil will consist in turning the will away from God. But what is evil in itself, moral evil? Is it something positive? It cannot, first of all, be something positive in the sense of something created by God: the cause of moral evil is not the Creator but the created will. The cause of good things is the divine goodness, whereas the cause of evil is the created will which turns away from the immutable Good:[5] evil is a turning-away of the created will from the immutable and infinite Good.[6] But evil cannot strictly be termed a 'thing', since this word implies a positive reality, and if moral evil were a positive reality, it would have to be ascribed to the Creator, unless one were willing to attribute to the creature the power of positive creation out of nothing. Evil, then, is 'that which falls away from essence and tends to non-being. . . . It tends to make that which is cease to be.'[7]

[1] *Expos. quarumdam prop. ex epist. ad Rom.*, 44. [2] *De spir. et litt.*, 19, 34. [3] *Ibid.*, 9, 15. [4] *Ep.*, 145, 3, 4. [5] *Enchirid.*, 23. [6] *De lib. arbit.*, 1, 16, 35. [7] *De moribus eccl.*, 2, 2, 2.

Everything in which there is order and measure is to be ascribed to God, but in the will which turns away from God there is disorder. The will itself is good, but the absence of right order, or rather the privation of right order, for which the human agent is responsible, is evil. Moral evil is thus a privation of right order in the created will.

This doctrine of evil as a privation was the doctrine of Plotinus, and in it Augustine found the answer to the Manichees. For if evil is a privation and not a positive thing, one is no longer faced with the choice of either ascribing moral evil to the good Creator or of inventing an ultimate evil principle responsible for evil. This doctrine was adopted by the Scholastics generally from Augustine and finds adherents among several modern philosophers of note, Leibniz, for example.

5. If the principle of morality is love of God and the essence of evil is a falling-away from God, it follows that the human race can be divided into two great camps, that of those who love God and prefer God to self and that of those who prefer self to God: it is by the character of their wills, by the character of their dominant love, that men are ultimately marked. Augustine sees the history of the human race as the history of the dialectic of these two principles, the one in forming the City of Jerusalem, the other the City of Babylon. 'Let each one question himself as to what he loveth; and he shall find of which (city) he is a citizen.'[1] 'There are two kinds of love; . . . These two kinds of love distinguish the two cities established in the human race . . . in the so to speak commingling of which the ages are passed.'[2] 'You have heard and know that there are two cities, for the present mingled together in body, but in heart separated.'[3]

To the Christian history is necessarily of profound importance. It was in history that man fell, in history that he was redeemed: it is in history, progressively, that the Body of Christ on earth grows and develops and that God's plan is unfolded. To the Christian, history apart from the data of revelation is shorn of its significance: it is small wonder, then, that Augustine looked on history from the Christian standpoint and that his outlook was primarily spiritual and moral. If we speak of a philosophy of history in Augustine's thought, the word 'philosophy' must be understood in a wide sense as Christian wisdom. The knowledge of the facts of history may be mainly a natural knowledge, for

[1] *In Ps.*, 64, 2. [2] *De Gen. ad litt.*, 11, 15, 20. [3] *In Ps.*, 136, 1.

example, knowledge of the existence and development of the Assyrian and Babylonian empires; but the principles by which the facts are interpreted and given meaning and judged are not taken from the facts themselves. The temporal and passing is judged in the light of the eternal. That Augustine's tendency to concentrate on the aspect of Assyria under which it appeared to him as an embodiment of the City of Babylon (in the moral sense) would not commend itself to the modern historian is understandable enough; but Augustine was not concerned to play the part of an historian in the ordinary sense, but rather to give the 'philosophy' of history as he envisaged it, and the 'philosophy' of history, as he understood it, is the discernment of the spiritual and moral significance of historical phenomena and events. Indeed, so far as there can be a philosophy of history at all, the Christian at least will agree with Augustine that only a Christian philosophy of history can ever approach adequacy: to the non-Christian the position of the Jewish people, for example, is radically different from the position it occupies in the eyes of the Christian. If it were objected, as it obviously could be, that this involves a theological interpretation of history, a reading of history in the light of dogma, the objection would not cause Augustine any difficulty, since he never pretended to make that radical dichotomy between theology and philosophy which is implied in the objection.

CHAPTER VIII

ST. AUGUSTINE—VI: THE STATE

The State and the City of Babylon not identical—The pagan State does not embody true justice—Church superior to State.

1. As I have already remarked, Augustine saw in history, as he saw in the individual, the struggle between two principles of conduct, two loves, on the one hand the love of God and submission to His law, on the other hand love of self, of pleasure, of the world. It was only natural, then, that as he saw the embodiment of the heavenly city, Jerusalem, in the Catholic Church, so he should see in the State, particularly in the pagan State, the embodiment of the City of Babylon, and the result of Augustine's attitude in this matter is that one is tempted to assume that for him the City of God can be identified with the Church as a visible society and the City of Babylon with the State as such. Does he not ask, 'Without justice what are kingdoms but great bands of robbers? What is a band of robbers but a little kingdom?' And does he not approve the pirate's reply to Alexander the Great, 'Because I do it with a little ship, I am called a robber, and you, because you do it with a great fleet, are called an emperor'?[1] Assyria and pagan Rome were founded, increased and maintained by injustice, violence, rapine, oppression: is not this to affirm that the State and the City of Babylon are one and the same thing?

Undeniably Augustine thought that the most adequate historical embodiments of the City of Babylon are to be found in the pagan empires of Assyria and Rome, just as he certainly thought that the City of Jerusalem, the City of God, is manifested in the Church. None the less, the ideas of the heavenly and earthly cities are moral and spiritual ideas, the contents of which are not exactly coterminous with any actual organisation. For instance, a man may be a Christian and belong to the Church; but if the principle of his conduct is self-love and not the love of God, he belongs spiritually and morally to the City of Babylon. Again, if an official of the State is governed in his conduct by the love of God, if he pursues justice and charity, he belongs spiritually and morally to the City of Jerusalem. 'We see now a citizen of Jerusalem, a citizen of the

[1] *De Civit. Dei*, 4, 4.

kingdom of heaven, holding some office upon earth; as, for example, wearing the purple, serving as magistrate, as aedile, as proconsul, as emperor, directing the earthly republic, but he hath his heart above if he is a Christian, if he is of the faithful. . . . Let us not therefore despair of the citizens of the kingdom of heaven, when we see them engaged in the affairs of Babylon, doing something terrestrial in a terrestrial republic; nor again let us forthwith congratulate all men whom we see engaged in celestial matters, for even the sons of the pestilence sit sometimes in the seat of Moses. . . . But there will come a time of winnowing when they will be separated, the one from the other, with the greatest care. . . .'[1] Even if, then, the City of Babylon in the moral and spiritual sense tends to be identified with the State, particularly the pagan State, and the City of Jerusalem tends to be identified with the Church as a visible organisation, the identification is not complete: one cannot legitimately conclude that because a man is, for example, a Church official, he is necessarily a citizen of the spiritual City of Jerusalem, for as far as his spiritual and moral condition is concerned he may belong to the City of Babylon. Moreover, if the State were necessarily coincident with the City of Babylon, no Christian could legitimately hold office in the State, or even be a citizen, if he could help it, and St. Augustine certainly did not subscribe to any such opinion.

2. But if the State and the City of Babylon cannot simply be identified, St. Augustine certainly did not think that the State as such is founded on justice or that true justice is realised in any actual State, not at any rate in any pagan State. That there is some justice even in a pagan State is sufficiently obvious, but true justice demands that that worship should be paid to God which He requires, and pagan Rome did not pay that worship, indeed in Christian times she did her best to prevent its being paid. On the other hand pagan Rome was obviously a State. How, then, is the conclusion to be avoided that true justice must not be included within the definition of the State? For, if it is, one would be reduced to the impossible position of denying that pagan Rome was a State. Augustine accordingly defines a society as a 'multitude of rational creatures associated in a common agreement as to the things which it loves'.[2] If the things which it loves are good, it will be a good society, while, if the things which it loves are bad, it will be a bad society; but nothing is said in the definition of a

[1] *In Ps.*, 51, 6. [2] *De Civit. Dei*, 19, 24.

people as to whether the objects of its love are good or bad, with the result that the definition will apply even to the pagan State.

This does not mean, of course, that in Augustine's eyes the State exists in a non-moral sphere: on the contrary, the same moral law holds good for States as for individuals. The point he wants to make is that the State will not embody true justice, will not be a really moral State, unless it is a Christian State: it is Christianity which makes men good citizens. The State itself, as an instrument of force, has its roots in the consequences of original sin and, given the fact of original sin and its consequences, is a necessary institution; but a just State is out of the question unless it is a Christian State. 'No State is more perfectly established and preserved than on the foundations, and by the bond, of faith and of firm concord, when the highest and truest good, namely God, is loved by all and men love each other in Him without dissimulation because they love one another for His sake.'[1] The State, in other words, is informed by love of this world, when it is left to itself; but it can be informed by higher principles, principles which it must derive from Christianity.

3. From this there follow two consequences of importance. (1) The Christian Church will try to inform civil society with its own celestial principles of conduct: it has a mission to act as the leaven of the earth. Augustine's conception of the Christian Church and her mission was essentially a dynamic and a social conception: the Church must permeate the State by her principles. (2) The Church is thus the only really perfect society and is definitely superior to the State, for, if the State must take her principles from the Church, the State cannot be above the Church nor even on a level with the Church. In maintaining this view St. Augustine stands at the head of the mediaeval exaltation of the Church *vis-à-vis* the State, and he was only consistent in invoking the help of the State against the Donatists, since, on his view, the Church is a superior society to which Christ has subjected the kingdoms of the world, and which has the right to make use of the powers of the world.[2] But if Augustine's view of the relation of Church to State was the one which became characteristic of western Christendom and not of Byzantium, it does not follow that his view necessarily tended to undermine the significance of civic and social life. As Christopher Dawson has pointed out,[3]

[1] *Ep.*, 137, 5, 18.
[2] Cf. *ibid.*, 105, 5, 6; 35, 3.
[3] *A Monument to St. Augustine*, pp. 76–7.

although Augustine deprived the State of its aura of divinity, he at the same time insisted on the value of the free human personality and of moral responsibility, even against the State, so that in this way he 'made possible the ideal of a social order resting upon the free personality and a common effort towards moral ends'.

CHAPTER IX
THE PSEUDO-DIONYSIUS

Writings and author—Affirmative way—Negative way—Neo-Platonic interpretation of Trinity—Ambiguous teaching on creation—Problem of evil—Orthodoxy or unorthodoxy?

1. DURING the Middle Ages the writings which were then ascribed to St. Paul's Athenian convert, Dionysius the Areopagite, enjoyed high esteem, not only among mystics and authors of works on mystical theology, but also among professional theologians and philosophers, such as St. Albert the Great and St. Thomas Aquinas. The reverence and respect paid to these writings were, of course, in great part due to the mistaken notion as to their authorship, a mistake which originated in the author's use of a pseudonym. 'Dionysius the Presbyter, to his fellow-presbyter Timothy.'[1] In 533 the Patriarch of Antioch, Severus, appealed to the writings of Dionysius, in support of his Monophysite doctrine, a fact which can be safely taken to mean that the writings were already regarded as possessed of authority. But, even if Severus appealed to the works in question in support of heretical doctrine, their ascription to St. Dionysius would free them from any suspicion as to their orthodoxy. In the Eastern Church they were widely circulated, being commented on by Maximus the Confessor in the seventh century and appealed to by the great Eastern Doctor, St. John Damascene, in the eighth century, though Hypatius of Ephesus attacked their authenticity.

In the West, Pope Martin I appealed to the writings as authentic at the first Lateran Council in 649, and about the year 858 John Scotus Eriugena, at the request of Charles the Bald, made a translation from the Greek text which had been presented to Louis the Fair in 827 by the Emperor Michael Balbus. John Scotus, besides translating the writings of the Pseudo-Dionysius, also commented on them, thus furnishing the first of a series of commentaries in Western Christendom. For example, Hugh of St. Victor (d. 1141) commented on the *Celestial Hierarchy*, using Eriugena's translation, while Robert Grosseteste (d. 1253) and Albert the Great (d. 1280) also commented on the writings.

[1] *Exordium* to the *Divine Names*.

St. Thomas Aquinas composed a commentary on the *Divine Names* about 1261. All these authors, as also, for example, Denis the Carthusian, accepted the authenticity of the writings; but in time it was bound to become clear that they embodied important elements taken from developed neo-Platonism and that they constituted in fact an attempt to reconcile neo-Platonism and Christianity, so that they would have to be attributed to an author of a much later date than the historic Dionysius the Areopagite. However, the question of the authenticity of the writings is not the same as the question of their orthodoxy from the Christian standpoint, and though in the seventeenth century, when critics began to attack the authenticity of the writings, their orthodoxy was also assailed, a recognition of their unauthentic character did not necessarily involve an admission of their incompatibility with Christian doctrine, though it was obviously no longer possible to maintain their orthodoxy on the *a priori* ground that they were composed by a personal disciple of St. Paul. Personally I consider that the writings are orthodox in regard to the rejection of monism; but that on the question of the Blessed Trinity it is highly questionable at least if they can be reconciled with orthodox Christian dogma. Whatever the intentions of the author may have been, his words, besides being obscure, as Aquinas admitted, are scarcely compatible, as they stand, with the Trinitarian teaching of Augustine and Thomas Aquinas. It may be objected that insufficient attention is paid to the dogma of the Incarnation, which is essential to Christianity, but the author clearly maintains this doctrine, and in any case to say little about one particular doctrine, even a central one, is not the same as to deny it. Taking the relevant passages of the Pseudo-Dionysius in the large, it does not seem possible to reject them as definitely unorthodox on this point, unless one is prepared also to reject as unorthodox, for example, the mystical doctrine of St. John of the Cross, who is a Doctor of the Church.

But though no one now supposes that the writings are actually the work of Dionysius the Areopagite, it has not proved possible to discover the real author. Most probably they were composed at the end of the fifth century, as they apparently embody ideas of the neo-Platonist Proclus (418–85), and it has been conjectured that the Hierotheus who figures therein was the Syrian mystic Stephen Bar Sadaili. If the writings of the Pseudo-Dionysius actually depend to any degree on the philosophy of Proclus, they cannot well have been composed before the closing decades of the fifth century, while as they were appealed to at the Council of 533, they can hardly have been composed much after 500. The ascription of about 500 as the date of their composition is, therefore, doubtless correct, while the supposition that they originated in Syria is reasonable. The author was a theologian, without doubt an ecclesiastic also; but he cannot have been Severus himself, as one or two writers have rashly supposed. In any case, though it would be interesting to know with certainty who the author was, it is probably unlikely that anything more than conjecture will ever be possible, and the chief interest of the writings is due, not to the personality of the author, but to the content and influence of the writings, these writings being the *Divine Names* (*De divinis Nominibus*), the *Mystical Theology* (*De mystica Theologia*), the *Celestial Hierarchy* (*De coelesti Hierarchia*) and the *Ecclesiastical Hierarchy* (*De ecclesiastica Hierarchia*), as well as ten letters. The works are printed in Migne's *Patrologia Graeca*, volumes 3–4; but a critical edition of the text has been begun.

2. There are two ways of approaching God, who is the centre of all speculation, a positive way (καταφατική) and a negative way (ἀποφατική). In the former way or method the mind begins 'with the most universal statements, and then through intermediate terms (proceeds) to particular titles',[1] thus beginning with 'the highest category'.[2] In the *Divine Names* the Pseudo-Dionysius pursues this affirmative method, showing how names such as Goodness, Life, Wisdom, Power, are applicable to God in a transcendental manner and how they apply to creatures only in virtue of their derivation from God and their varying degrees of participation in those qualities which are found in God not as inhering qualities but in substantial unity. Thus he begins with the idea or name of goodness, which is the most universal name, inasmuch as all things, existent or possible, share in goodness to some degree, but which at the same time expresses the Nature of God: 'None is good save one, that is, God.'[3] God, as the Good, is the overflowing source of creation and its final goal, and 'from the Good comes the light which is an image of Goodness, so that the Good is described by the name of "Light", being the archetype of that which is revealed in the image'.[4] Here the neo-Platonic light-motive is brought in, and the Pseudo-Dionysius's dependence

[1] *Myst. Theol.*, 2.
[2] *Ibid.*, 3.
[3] *Div. Names*, 2, 1; St. Matt. 19. 17.
[4] *Div. Names*, 4, 4.

on neo-Platonism is particularly manifest in his language when he goes on to speak of the Good as Beauty, as the 'super-essential beautiful', and uses the phrases of Plato's *Symposium*, which reappear in the *Enneads* of Plotinus. Again, when in chapter 13 of the *Divine Names*[1] the Pseudo-Dionysius speaks of 'One' as 'the most important title of all', he is clearly writing in dependence on the Plotinian doctrine of the ultimate Principle as the One.

In brief, then, the affirmative method means ascribing to God the perfections found in creatures, that is, the perfections which are compatible with the spiritual Nature of God, though not existing in Him in the same manner as they exist in creatures, since in God they exist without imperfection and, in the case of the names which are ascribed to the Divine Nature, without real differentiation. That we start, in the affirmative way, with the highest categories, is, says the author,[2] due to the fact that we should start with what is most akin to God, and it is truer to affirm that He is life and goodness than that He is air or stone. The names 'Life' and 'Goodness' refer to something which is actually in God, but He is air or stone only in a metaphorical sense or in the sense that He is the cause of these things. Yet the Pseudo-Dionysius is careful to insist that, even if certain names describe God better than others, they are very far from representing an adequate knowledge and conception of God on our part, and he expresses this conviction by speaking of God as the super-essential Essence, the super-essential Beautiful, and so on. He is not simply repeating phrases from the Platonic tradition, but he is expressing the truth that the objective reference or content of these names as actually found in God infinitely transcends the content of the names as experienced by us. For example, if we ascribe intelligence to God, we do not mean to ascribe to Him human intelligence, the only intelligence of which we have immediate experience and from which we draw the name: we mean that God is *more*, infinitely more, than what we experience as intelligence, and this fact is best expressed by speaking of God as super-Intelligence or as the super-essential Intelligence.

3. The affirmative way was mainly pursued by the Pseudo-Dionysius in the *Divine Names* and in his (lost) *Symbolical Theology* and *Outlines of Divinity*, whereas the negative way, that of the exclusion from God of the imperfections of creatures, is characteristic of the *Mystical Theology*. The distinction of the two

[1] 13, 1. [2] *Myst. Theol.*, 3.

ways was dependent on Proclus, and as developed by the Pseudo-Dionysius it passed into Christian philosophy and theology, being accepted by St. Thomas Aquinas, for example; but the palm is given by the Pseudo-Dionysius to the negative way in preference to the affirmative way. In this way the mind begins by denying of God those things which are farthest removed from Him, e.g. 'drunkenness or fury,'[1] and proceeds upwards progressively denying of God the attributes and qualities of creatures, until it reaches 'the super-essential Darkness'.[2] As God is utterly transcendent, we praise Him best 'by denying or removing all things that are—just as men who, carving a statue out of marble, remove all the impediments that hinder the clear perception of the latent image and by this mere removal display the hidden statue itself in its hidden beauty'.[3] The human being is inclined to form anthropomorphic conceptions of the Deity, and it is necessary to strip away these human, all-too-human conceptions by the *via remotionis*; but the Pseudo-Dionysius does not mean that from this process there results a clear view of what God is in Himself: the comparison of the statue must not mislead us. When the mind has stripped away from its idea of God the human modes of thought and inadequate conceptions of the Deity, it enters upon the 'Darkness of Unknowing',[4] wherein it 'renounces all the apprehension of the understanding and is wrapped in that which is wholly intangible and invisible . . . united . . . to Him that is wholly unknowable';[5] this is the province of mysticism. The 'Darkness of Unknowing' is not due, however, to the unintelligibility of the Object considered in itself, but to the finiteness of the human mind, which is blinded by excess of light. This doctrine is doubtless partly influenced by neo-Platonism, but it is also to be found in the writings of Christian mystical theologians, notably St. Gregory of Nyssa, whose writings in turn, though influenced, as far as language and presentation are concerned, by neo-Platonic treatises, were also the expression of personal experience.

4. The neo-Platonic influence on the Pseudo-Dionysius comes out very strongly in his doctrine of the Blessed Trinity, for he seems to be animated by the desire to find a One behind the differentiation of Persons. He certainly allows that the differentiation of Persons is an eternal differentiation and that the Father,

[1] *Myst. Theol.*, 3. [2] *Ibid.*, 2. [3] *Ibid.*

[4] The author of the mediaeval mystical treatise, *The Cloud of Unknowing*, doubtless wrote in immediate or mediate dependence on the writings of the Pseudo-Dionysius. [5] *Myst. Theol.*, 1.

for example, is not the Son, and the Son not the Father, but so far as one can achieve an accurate interpretation of what he says, it appears that, in his opinion, the differentiation of Persons exists on the plane of manifestation. The manifestation in question is an eternal manifestation, and the differentiation an eternal differentiation within God, to be distinguished from the external manifestation of God in differentiated creatures; but God in Himself, beyond the plane of manifestation, is undifferentiated Unity. One can, of course, attempt to justify the language of the Pseudo-Dionysius by reference to the Nature of God which, according to orthodox Trinitarianism, is one and undivided and with which each of the divine Persons is substantially identical; but it would seem most probable, not to say certain, that the author was influenced, not only by Plotinus's doctrine of the One, but also by Proclus's doctrine of the primary Principle which transcends the attributes of Unity, Goodness, Being. The super-essential Unity would seem to represent Proclus's first Principle, and the distinction of three Persons in unity of Nature would seem to represent the neo-Platonic conception of emanation, being a stage, if an eternal stage, in the self-manifestation or revelation of the ultimate Godhead or Absolute. When we speak of the all-transcendent Godhead as a Unity and a Trinity, it is not a Unity or a Trinity such as can be known by us . . . (though) 'we apply the titles of "Trinity" and "Unity" to that which is beyond all titles, expressing under the form of Being that which is beyond being. . . . (The transcendent Godhead) hath no name, nor can it be grasped by the reason. . . . Even the title of "Goodness" we do not ascribe to it because we think such a name suitable. . . .'[1] (The Godhead) 'is not unity or goodness, nor a Spirit, not Sonship nor Fatherhood, . . . nor does it belong to the category of non-existence or to that of existence.'[2]

It is true that such phrases could be defended, as regards the intention of the author if not as regards his actual words, by pointing out that it is correct to say that the term 'Father', for instance, belongs to the first Person as Person and not to the Son, though the divine substance exists in numerical identity and without intrinsic real differentiation in each of the three divine Persons, and also by allowing that the term 'Father', as applied to the first Person, though the best term available in human language for the purpose, is borrowed from a human relationship,

[1] *Div. Names*, 13, 3. [2] *Myst. Theol.*, 5.

and applied to God in an analogical sense, so that the content of the idea of 'Father' in our minds is not adequate to the reality in God. Moreover, the Pseudo-Dionysius certainly speaks of 'a differentiation in the super-essential doctrine of God', referring to the Trinity of Persons and the names applicable to each Person in particular,[1] and explicitly denies that he is 'introducing a confusion of all distinctions in the Deity',[2] affirming that, while names such as 'Super-vital' or 'Super-wise' belong to 'the entire Godhead', the 'differentiated names', the names of 'Father', 'Son' and 'Spirit', 'cannot be interchanged, nor are they held in common'.[3] Again, though there is a 'mutual abiding and indwelling' of the divine Persons 'in an utterly undifferentiated and transcendent Unity', this is 'without any confusion'.[4] Nevertheless, though much of what the Pseudo-Dionysius has to say on the subject of the Blessed Trinity can be interpreted and defended from the standpoint of theological orthodoxy, it is hardly possible not to discern a strong tendency to go behind, as it were, the distinction of Persons to a super-transcendent undifferentiated Unity. Probably the truth of the matter is that the Pseudo-Dionysius, though an orthodox Trinitarian in intention, was so much influenced by the neo-Platonic philosophy that a tension between the two elements underlies his attempt to reconcile them and makes itself apparent in his statements.

5. In regard to the relation of the world to God, the Pseudo-Dionysius speaks of the 'emanation' (πρόοδος) of God into the universe of things;[5] but he tries to combine the neo-Platonic emanation theory with the Christian doctrine of creation and is no pantheist. For example, since God bestows existence on all things that are, He is said to become manifold through bringing forth existent things from Himself; yet at the same time God remains One even in the act of 'self-multiplication' and without differentiation even in the process of emanation.[6] Proclus had insisted that the prior Principle does not become less through the process of emanation and the Pseudo-Dionysius repeats his teaching on this matter; but the influence of neo-Platonism does seem to have meant that he did not clearly realise the relation of creation to the divine will or the freedom of the act of creation, for he is inclined to speak as though creation were a natural and even a spontaneous effect of the divine goodness, even though

[1] *Div. Names*, 2, 5. [2] *Ibid.*, 2. [3] *Ibid.*, 3. [4] *Ibid.*, 4.
[5] *Ibid.*, 5, 1. [6] *Ibid.*, 2, 11.

God is distinct from the world. God exists indivisibly and without multiplication of Himself in all individual, separate and multiple things, and, though they participate in the goodness which springs from Him and though they may in a certain sense be thought of as an 'extension' of God, God Himself is not involved in their multiplication: the world, in short, is an outflowing of the divine goodness, but it is not God Himself. On this point of God's transcendence as well as on that of His immanence the Pseudo-Dionysius is clear; but his fondness for depicting the world as the outflowing of the over-brimming Goodness of God, as well as for drawing a kind of parallel between the internal divine Processions and the external procession in creation, lead him to speak as though creation were a spontaneous activity of God, as if God created by a necessity of nature.

That God is the transcendent Cause of all things, the Pseudo-Dionysius affirms several times, explaining in addition that God created the world through the exemplary or archetypal Ideas, the 'preordinations' (προορισμοί) which exist in Him:[1] in addition, God is the final Cause of all things, drawing all things to Himself as the Good.[2] He is, therefore, 'the Beginning and the End of all things',[3] 'the Beginning as their Cause, the End as their Final Purpose'.[4] There is, then, an outgoing from God and a return to God, a process of multiplication and a process of intercommunion and return. This idea became basic in the philosophy of the 'Areopagite's' translator, John Scotus Eriugena.

6. As the Pseudo-Dionysius insisted so much on the divine goodness, it was incumbent on him to give some attention to the existence and the consequent problem of evil, and this he gave in the *Divine Names*,[5] relying, partly at least, on Proclus's *De subsistentia mali*. In the first place he insists that, although evil would have to be referred to God as its Cause, were it something positive, it is in fact not something positive at all: precisely as evil it has no being. If it is objected that evil must be positive, since it is productive, sometimes even of good, and since debauchery, for example, which is the opposite of temperance, is something evil and positive, he answers that nothing is productive precisely as evil, but only in so far as it is good, or through the action of good: evil as such tends only to destroy and debase. That evil has no positive being of itself is clear from the fact that

[1] *Div. Names*, 5, 8. [2] *Ibid.*, 4, 4 ff. [3] *Ibid.*, 4, 35. [4] *Ibid.*, 5, 10. [5] 4, 18 ff.

good and being are synonymous: everything which has being proceeds from the Good and, as being, is good. Does this mean, then, that evil and non-existence are precisely the same? The Pseudo-Dionysius certainly tends to speak as if that were the case, but his real meaning is given in his statement that 'all creatures in so far as they have being are good and come from the Good, and in so far as they are deprived of the Good, neither are they good nor have they being'.[1] In other words, evil is a deprivation or privation: it consists, not simply in non-being or in the absence of being, but rather in the absence of a good that ought to be present. The sinner, for instance, is good in so far as he has being, life, existence, will; the evil consists in the deprivation of a good that ought to be there and actually is not, in the wrong relation of his will to the rule of morality, in the absence of this or that virtue, etc.

It follows that no creature, considered as an existent being, can be evil. Even the devils are good in so far as they exist, for they hold their existence from the Good, and that existence continues to be good: they are evil, not in virtue of their existence, their natural constitution, but 'only through a lack of angelic virtues':[2] 'they are called evil through the deprivation and the loss whereby they have lapsed from their proper virtues.' The same is true of bad human beings, who are called evil in virtue of 'the deficiency of good qualities and activities and in virtue of the failure and fall therefrom due to their own weakness'. 'Hence evil inheres not in the devils or in us as evil, but only as a deficiency and lack of the perfection of our proper virtues.'[3]

Physical, non-moral evil is treated in a similar manner. 'No natural force is evil: the evil of nature lies in a thing's inability to fulfil its natural functions.'[4] Again, 'ugliness and disease are a deficiency in form and a want of order', and this is not wholly evil, 'being rather a lesser good'.[5] Nor can matter as such be evil, since 'matter too has a share in order, beauty and form':[6] matter cannot be evil in itself, since it is produced by the Good and since it is necessary to Nature. There is no need to have recourse to two ultimate Principles, good and evil respectively. 'In fine, good comes from the one universal Cause; evil from many partial deficiencies.'[7]

If it be said that some people desire evil, so that evil, as the

[1] *Div. Names*, 4, 20. [2] *Ibid.*, 23. [3] *Ibid.*, 24. [4] *Ibid.*, 26.
[5] *Ibid.*, 27. [6] *Ibid.*, 28. [7] *Ibid.*, 30.

object of desire, must be something positive, the Pseudo-Dionysius answers that all acts have the good as their object, but that they may be mistaken, since the agent may err as to what is the proper good or object of desire. In the case of sin the sinner has the power to know the true good and the right, so that his 'mistake' is morally attributable to him.[1] Moreover, the objection that Providence should lead men into virtue even against their will is foolish, for 'it is not worthy of Providence to violate nature': Providence provides for free choice and respects it.[2]

7. In conclusion one may remark that, although Ferdinand Christian Baur[3] would seem to have gone too far in saying that the Pseudo-Dionysius reduced the Christian doctrine of the Trinity to a mere formal use of the Christian terms void of the Christian content and that his system will not allow of a special Incarnation, it must be admitted that there was a tension in his thought between the neo-Platonic philosophy which he adopted and the Christian dogmas, in which, we have no real reason to deny, he believed. The Pseudo-Dionysius meant to harmonise the two elements, to express Christian theology and Christian mysticism in a neo-Platonic philosophical framework and scheme; but it can scarcely be gainsaid that, when a clash occurred, the neo-Platonic elements tended to prevail. A specific and peculiar Incarnation was one of the major points in Christianity that pagan neo-Platonists, such as Porphyry, objected to, and though, as I have said, we cannot be justified in asserting that the Pseudo-Dionysius denied the Incarnation, his acceptance of it does not well adapt itself to his philosophical system, nor does it play much part in his extant writings. One may well doubt whether his writings would have exercised the influence they did on Christian mediaeval thinkers, had the latter not taken the author's pseudonym at its face value.

[1] *Div. Names*, 4, 35. [2] *Ibid.*, 33.
[3] In his *Christliche Lehre von der Dreieinigkeit und Menschwerdung Gottes*, Vol. 2, p. 42.

CHAPTER X

BOETHIUS, CASSIODORUS, ISIDORE

Boethius's transmission of Aristotelian ideas—Natural theology—Influence on Middle Ages—Cassiodorus on the seven liberal arts and the spirituality of the soul—Isidore's Etymologies *and* Sentences.

1. If one of the channels whereby the philosophy of the ancient world was passed on to the Middle Ages was the writings of the Pseudo-Dionysius, another channel, and in some respects a complementary one, was constituted by the writings of Boethius (*c.* A.D. 480–524/5), a Christian who, after studying at Athens and subsequently holding high magisterial office under the king of the Ostrogoths, Theodoric, was finally executed on a charge of high treason. I use the word 'complementary' since, while the Pseudo-Dionysius helped to impregnate early mediaeval philosophy, especially that of John Scotus Eriugena, with elements drawn from neo-Platonic speculation, Boethius transmitted to the early mediaevals a knowledge of at least the logic of Aristotle. His works I have listed in my volume on Greek and Roman philosophy,[1] and I shall not repeat them here; suffice it to recall that he translated into Latin the *Organon* of Aristotle and commented thereon, besides commenting on the *Isagoge* of Porphyry and composing original treatises on logic. In addition he wrote several theological opuscula and while in prison his celebrated *De Consolatione Philosophiae.*

It is uncertain whether or not Boethius translated, in accordance with his original plan, other works of Aristotle besides the *Organon*; but in his extant works mention is made of several salient Aristotelian doctrines. The earlier mediaeval thinkers were predominantly concerned with the discussion of the problem of universals, taking as their starting-point certain texts of Porphyry and Boethius, and they took little notice of the Aristotelian metaphysical doctrines to be found in Boethius's writings. The first great speculative thinker of the Middle Ages, John Scotus Eriugena, was more indebted to the Pseudo-Dionysius and other writers dependent on neo-Platonism than to any Aristotelian influence,

[1] p. 485.

and it was not until the Aristotelian *corpus* had become available to the West at the close of the twelfth and the beginning of the thirteenth centuries that a synthesis on Aristotelian lines was attempted. But that does not alter the fact that Aristotelian doctrines of importance were incorporated in the writings of Boethius. For instance, in his theological work against Eutyches[1] Boethius speaks clearly of 'matter', the common substrate of bodies, which is the basis for, and renders possible, substantial change in bodies, corporeal substances, while its absence in incorporeal substances renders impossible the change of one immaterial substance into another or the change of a corporeal substance into an incorporeal substance or *vice versa*. The discussion is carried on in a theological setting and with a theological purpose, for Boethius wishes to show that in Christ the divine Nature and the human Nature are distinct and both real, against Eutyches who held that 'the union with Godhead involved the disappearance of the human nature';[2] but within that theological setting a philosophical discussion is included and the categories employed are Aristotelian in character. Similarly, in the *De Trinitate,*[3] Boethius speaks of the correlative principle to matter, namely form. For instance, earth is not earth by reason of unqualified matter, but because it is a distinctive form. (For 'unqualified matter' Boethius uses the Greek phrase ἄποια ὕλη, taking it doubtless from Alexander of Aphrodisias.[4] On the other hand, God, the Divine Substance, is Form without matter and cannot be a substrate. As pure Form, He is one.

Again, in the *De Trinitate,*[5] Boethius gives the ten Categories or *Praedicamenta* and goes on to explain that when we call God 'substance', we do not mean that He is substance in the same sense in which a created thing is substance: He is 'a substance that is super-substantial'. Similarly, if we predicate a quality of God, such as 'just' or 'great', we do not mean that He has an inhering quality, for 'with Him to be just and to be God are one and the same', and while 'man is merely great, God is greatness'. In the *Contra Eutychen*[6] occurs Boethius's famous definition of person, *naturae rationalis individua substantia*, which was accepted by St. Thomas and became classical in the Schools.

2. In his doctrine of the Blessed Trinity, Boethius relied largely on St. Augustine; but in the *De Consolatione Philosophiae* he

[1] *Contra Eutychen*, 6. [2] *Ibid.*, 5. [3] 2.
[4] Cf. the latter's *De Anima*, 17, 17, and his *De anima ibri mantissa*, 124, 7.
[5] 4. [6] 3.

developed in outline a natural theology on Aristotelian lines, thus implicitly distinguishing between natural theology, the highest part of philosophy, and dogmatic theology which, in distinction from the former, accepts its premisses from revelation. In the third book[1] he at least mentions the rational argument for the existence of God as unmoved Mover, while in the fifth book[2] he treats of the apparent difficulty in reconciling human freedom with the divine foreknowledge. 'If God beholdeth all things and cannot be deceived, that must of necessity follow which His providence foreseeth to be to come. Wherefore, if from eternity He doth foreknow not only the deeds of men, but also their counsels and wills, there can be no free-will.'[3] To answer that it is not that future events will take place because God knows them, but rather that God knows them because they will take place is not a very satisfactory answer, since it implies that temporal events and the temporal acts of creatures are the cause of the eternal foreknowledge of God. Rather should we say that God does not, strictly speaking, 'foresee' anything: God is eternal, eternity being defined in a famous phrase as *interminabilis vitae tota simul et perfecta possessio*,[4] and His knowledge is the knowledge of what is eternally present to Him, of a never-fading instant, not a foreknowledge of things which are future to God. Now, knowledge of a present event does not impose necessity on the event, so that God's knowledge of man's free acts, which from the human viewpoint are future, though from the divine viewpoint they are present, does not make those acts determined and necessary (in the sense of not-free). The eternity of God's vision, 'which is always present, concurs with the future quality of an action'.

Boethius drew not merely on Aristotle, but also on Porphyry and other neo-Platonic writers, as well as on Cicero, for example, and it may be that the division of philosophy or speculative science into Physics, Mathematics and Theology was taken directly from the *Isagoge* of Porphyry; but it must be remembered that Porphyry himself was indebted to Aristotle. In any case, in view of the predominantly neo-Platonic character of foregoing Christian philosophy, the Aristotelian element in the thought of Boethius is more remarkable and significant than the specifically neo-Platonic elements. It is true that he speaks of the divine Goodness and its overflowing in a manner reminiscent of neo-Platonism (in the *De Consol. Phil.*[5] he says that 'the substance of God consisteth in

[1] 12. [2] 2ff. [3] 5, 3. [4] 5, 6. [5] 3, 9.

nothing else but in goodness') and that he sometimes uses such terms as *defluere* in connection with the procession of creatures from God;[1] but he is quite clear about the distinction between God and the world and about the Christian doctrine of creation. Thus he expressly affirms that God, 'without any change, by the exercise of a will known only to Himself, determined of Himself to form the world and brought it into being when it was absolutely nothing, not producing it from His own substance',[2] denying that the divine substance *in externa dilabatur*[3] or that 'all things which are, are God'.[4]

3. Boethius, then, was of very considerable importance, for he transmitted to the earlier Middle Ages a great part of the knowledge of Aristotle then available. In addition, his application of philosophical categories to theology helped towards the development of theological science, while his use of and definition of philosophical terms was of service to both theology and philosophy. Lastly we may mention the influence exercised by his composition of commentaries, for this type of writing became a favourite method of composition among the mediaevals. Even if not particularly remarkable as an original and independent philosopher, Boethius is yet of major significance as a transmitter and as a philosopher who attempted to express Christian doctrine in terms drawn, not simply from the neo-Platonists, but also from the philosopher whose thought was to become a predominant influence in the greatest philosophical synthesis of the Middle Ages.

4. *Cassiodorus* (*c.* 477–*c.* 565/70) was a pupil of Boethius and, like his master, worked for a time in the service of Theodoric, King of the Ostrogoths. In his *De artibus ac disciplinis liberalium litterarum* (which is the second book of his *Institutiones*) he treated of the seven liberal arts, i.e. the three *scientiae sermocinales* (Grammar, Dialectic and Rhetoric) and the four *scientiae reales* (Arithmetic, Geometry, Music and Astronomy). He did not aim at novelty or originality of thought, but rather at giving a synopsis of the learning he had culled from other writers,[5] and his book on the arts, like that of Martianus Capella, was much used as a text-book in the early Middle Ages. In his *De anima* Cassiodorus drew on St. Augustine and on Claudianus Mamertus (died *c.* 474) in proving the spirituality of the human soul. While the soul cannot be a part of God, since it is changeable and capable of

[1] Cf. *Lib. de hebdom.*, 173. [2] *De Fide Catholica.* [3] *De Consol. Phil.*, 3, 12.
[4] *Quomodo Substantiae.* I do not, of course mean to imply that there is any doctrine of creation in Aristotle. [5] *De anima*, 12.

evil, it is not material and cannot be material, since it can have what is spiritual as the object of its knowledge, and only that which is itself spiritual can know the spiritual. As spiritual, the soul is wholly in the whole body and wholly in each part, being indivisible and unextended; but it operates in a given part of the body, e.g. a sense-organ, now with greater, now with less intensity.[1]

5. Cassiodorus, then, was much more a 'transmitter' than an original thinker, and the same can be said of *Isidore* (died *c.* 636), who became Archbishop of Seville in the Visigothic kingdom and whose encyclopaedia, the *Originum seu Etymologiarum libri XX*, was very popular in the early Middle Ages, being included in every monastic library of note. In this work Isidore deals with the seven liberal arts, as also with a great number of scientific or quasi-scientific facts and theories on subjects from Scripture and jurisprudence and medicine to architecture, agriculture, war, navigation, and so on. He shows his conviction about the divine origin of sovereignty and the paramount authority of morality, law and justice in civil society, even in regard to the conduct and acts of the monarch. In addition to his *Etymologies* Isidore's *Libri tres sententiarum*, a collection of theological and moral theses taken from St. Augustine and St. Gregory the Great, was also widely used. His treatise on numbers, *Liber Numerorum*, which treats of the numbers occurring in the Sacred Scriptures, is often fanciful in the extreme in the mystical meanings which it attaches to numbers.

[1] *De anima*, 4.

PART II

THE CAROLINGIAN RENAISSANCE

CHAPTER XI

THE CAROLINGIAN RENAISSANCE

Charlemagne—Alcuin and the Palatine School—Other schools, curriculum, libraries—Rhabanus Maurus.

1. IN A.D. 771 the death of Carloman left Charles (Charlemagne) sole ruler of the Frankish dominions, and his subsequent destruction of the Lombard kingdom and his general policy made him, by the close of the century, the paramount sovereign in Western Christendom. His coronation as emperor by the Pope on December 25th, 800, symbolised the success of his imperial policy and the culmination of Frankish power. The Frankish Empire was later to break up and the imperial crown was to pass to Germany, but for the moment Charlemagne was undisputed master in Western Christendom and was enabled to set on foot the work of reorganisation and reform which had become a crying need under the Merovingian dynasty. The emperor was by no means simply a soldier nor even simply soldier and political organiser combined: he had also at heart the work of raising the cultural level of his subjects by the extension and improvement of education. For this purpose he needed scholars and educational leaders, and since these were not easily obtainable in the Frankish kingdom itself, he had to introduce them from abroad. Already in the fifth century the old culture of Romanised Gaul was fast on the wane and in the sixth and seventh centuries it was at a very low point indeed; what schools there were, were teaching only reading, writing and some rudimentary knowledge of Latin, besides, of course, giving religious instruction. It was to remedy this lamentable state of learning and education that Charlemagne made use of foreign scholars like Peter of Pisa and Paul the Deacon, who were both Italians. The former appears to have been already advanced in age when he taught Latin at the Palace School of Charlemagne, while the latter (Paul Warnefrid, the Deacon), who had come to France in 782, in an attempt to obtain the freedom of his brother,

a prisoner of war, taught Greek from 782 to 786, when he retired to Monte Cassino, where he composed his *History of the Lombards.* Another Italian teacher at the Palatine School was Paulinus of Aquileia, who taught from about 777 to 787.

In addition to the group of Italian grammarians one may mention two Spaniards who came to France as refugees: Agobard, who became Archbishop of Lyons in 816, and Theodulf, who became Bishop of Orleans and died in 821. The latter was familiar with the Latin classics and was himself a Latin poet. Incidentally the oldest known mediaeval manuscript of Quintilian comes from Theodulf's private library. From the point of view of practical importance in the educational work of Charlemagne, however, the Italians and the Spaniards are overshadowed by the celebrated English scholar, Alcuin of York.

2. *Alcuin* (*c.* 730–804) received his early education at York. Learning had been making progress in England since the year 669, when Theodore of Tarsus, a Greek monk, arrived in the country as Archbishop of Canterbury and, together with Abbot Hadrian, developed the school of Canterbury and enriched its library. This work was carried on by men like Benedict Biscop, who founded the monasteries of Wearmouth (674) and Jarrow (682), and Aldhelm, who, after studying under Theodore and Hadrian, organised the monastery of Malmesbury in Wiltshire, of which he became abbot. A more important figure in Anglo-Saxon scholarship was, however, that of the great exegete and historian Bede (674–735), a priest and monk of Jarrow. It was due to the labours of Bede's friend and pupil Egbert, who became Archbishop of York shortly before Bede's death, that the school of York became the leading cultural and educational centre of England and noted for the richness of its library.

At York Alcuin was more particularly under the care of Aelbert, in company with whom he travelled to Rome, meeting Charles on the way, and when Aelbert succeeded Egbert as Archbishop of York in 767, the chief work in the school devolved on Alcuin. However, in 781, Alcuin was sent by Aelbert to Rome, and in Parma he met Charles for the second time, the king utilising the meeting to urge the English scholar to enter his service. After receiving the permission of his own king and his archbishop, Alcuin accepted the invitation and in 782 took over the direction of the Palatine School, which he maintained (save for a short visit to England in 786 and a longer one from 790 to

793) until 796, when he accepted the abbacy of St. Martin at Tours, where he spent the last years of his life.

Probably about the year 777 Charlemagne wrote a letter to Baugulf, Abbot of Fulda,[1] in which he exhorts the abbot and community to zeal for learning, and this is merely one of the examples of his constant solicitude in the cause of education. The school which is, however, particularly associated with the name of Charlemagne is the so-called Palace or Palatine School, which though not a new creation of the emperor, owed its development to him. Before its development under Charlemagne the school would seem to have existed for the purpose of training the royal princes and children of the higher nobility in the knightly way of life; but the emperor laid emphasis on intellectual training and, as a result of his reform, the pupils appear to have been drawn from a wider circle than the court. French writers have commonly claimed that the Palatine School was the origin of the University of Paris; but it must be remembered that the emperor's court was at Aachen or Aix-la-Chapelle, and not at Paris, though it would seem to have been later removed to Paris by Charles the Bald (d. 877). However, as the University of Paris eventually grew up out of an amalgamation of the Parisian schools, it may be said that the Palatine School was in some sense a remote ancestor of the University, even if the connection was somewhat loose.

Charlemagne's main instrument in the organisation of the Palatine School was Alcuin, from whose writings we can form some idea of the curriculum. Alcuin was certainly not an original thinker, and his educational works, written in dialogue form, rely for the most part on former authors. For example, the *De Rhetorica* makes use of Cicero, with additions from other authors, while in other treatises Alcuin draws on Donatus, Priscian, Cassiodorus, Boethius, Isidore, Bede. But, though Alcuin was unoriginal and mediocre as a writer and can hardly be held to merit the title of philosopher, he seems to have been eminent and successful as a teacher, and some of the best-known figures of the Carolingian renaissance, e.g. Rhabanus Maurus, were his pupils. When he retired to the abbey of St. Martin at Tours, he continued this work of teaching, as is clear from a celebrated letter to the emperor, in which Alcuin describes how he serves to some youths

[1] If, however, Baugulf became abbot only in 788, the letter cannot be dated before that year.

the honey of the Holy Scriptures, while others he tries to intoxicate with the wine of ancient literature: some are nourished on the apples of grammatical studies, while to others he displays the order of the shining orbs which adorn the azure heavens. (Charlemagne had a considerable personal interest in astronomy and the two men corresponded on this subject.)

At Tours Alcuin enriched the library with copies of manuscripts which he brought from York, the best library in western Europe. He also devoted his attention to improving the method of copying manuscripts. In a letter of 799[1] he speaks of his daily battle with the 'rusticity' of Tours, from which one may conclude that the path of reform was not always an easy one. It is certain that Alcuin also gave attention to the accurate copying and amending of the manuscripts of the Scriptures, since he speaks explicitly of this in letters to Charlemagne in 800[2] and 801;[3] but it is not certain exactly what part he took in producing the revision of the Vulgate which was ordered by the emperor, known as the 'Alcuinian revision'. However, in view of the important position occupied by the scholar in the implementation of the emperor's reforms, it would seem only reasonable to suppose that he took a leading part in this important work, which helped to arrest the progress of manuscript corruption.

3. As regards the development of other schools (i.e. other than the Palatine School and that of Tours), one may mention the schools attached to the monasteries of St. Gall, Corbie and Fulda. In the monasteries education was provided not only for those pupils who were destined to become members of the religious order, but also for other pupils, though it appears that two separate schools were maintained, the *schola claustri* for the former class of pupil, the *schola exterior* for the latter. Thus at St. Gall the *schola claustri* was within the precincts of the monastery, while the *schola exterior* was among the outer buildings. A capitulary of Louis the Pious (817) ordained that the monasteries should only possess schools for the 'oblates'; but it seems that not much notice was taken of this ordinance.

If one sets the Palatine School in a class by itself, the other schools fall, then, into two main classes, the episcopal or capitular schools and the monastic schools. As for the curriculum this consisted, apart from the study of theology and exegesis, especially in the case of those pupils who were preparing for the priesthood

[1] *Ep.*, 4, 172. [2] *Ibid.*, 195. [3] *Ibid.*, 205.

or the religious life, in the study of the *Trivium* (grammar, rhetoric and dialectic) and the *Quadrivium* (arithmetic, geometry, astronomy and music), comprising the seven liberal arts. There was, however, little fresh or original work done on these subjects. Thus grammar, which included literature, would be studied in the writings of Priscian and Donatus, and in the text-books of Alcuin, for example, though some commentaries were composed on the works of the ancient grammarians, by Smaragdus, for instance, on Donatus, and a few undistinguished grammatical works were written, such as the *Ars grammaticae* of Clemens Scotus, who began teaching at the Palatine School in the later years of Charlemagne. Logic too was studied in the handbooks of Alcuin or, if something more was required, in the works of the authors on whom Alcuin relied, e.g. Boethius. In geometry and astronomy little work was done in the ninth century, though the theory of music was advanced by the *Musica enchiriadis*, attributed to Hoger the Abbot of Werden (d. 902). Libraries, e.g. the library of St. Gall, received a considerable increase in the ninth century and they included, besides the theological and religious works which composed the bulk of the items listed, legal and grammatical works, as well as a certain number of classical authors; but it is clear that, as far as philosophy is concerned, logic or dialectic (which, according to Aristotle, is a propaedeutic to philosophy, not a branch of philosophy itself) was the only subject studied. There was only one real speculative philosopher in the ninth century, and that was John Scotus Eriugena. Charlemagne's renaissance aimed at a dissemination of existing learning and what it accomplished was indeed remarkable enough; but it did not lead to original thought and speculation, except in the one instance of John Scotus's system. If the Carolingian empire and civilisation had survived and continued to flourish, a period of original work would doubtless have eventuated at length; but actually it was destined to be submerged in the new Dark Ages and there would be need of another renaissance before the mediaeval period of positive, constructive and original work could be realised.

4. Because of his importance for education in Germany one must mention, in connection with the Carolingian renaissance, the name of Rhabanus Maurus, who was born about 776 and who, after having been a pupil of Alcuin, taught at the monastery of Fulda, where he became abbot in 822. In 847 he was appointed Archbishop of Mainz and continued in that post until his death

in 856. Rhabanus concerned himself with the education of the clergy, and for this purpose he composed his work *De Institutione Clericorum* in three books. In addition to a treatment of the ecclesiastical grades, the liturgy, the training of the preacher and so on, this work also deals with the seven liberal arts, but Rhabanus showed no more originality in this work than in his *De rerum naturis*, an encyclopaedia which was derived very largely from that of Isidore. In general the author depended almost entirely on former writers like Isidore, Bede and Augustine. In regard to exegesis he favoured mystical and allegorical interpretations. In other words, the *Praeceptor Germaniae* was a faithful product of the Carolingian renaissance, a scholar with a real enthusiasm for learning and a lively zeal for the intellectual formation of the clergy, but markedly unoriginal in thought.

CHAPTER XII

JOHN SCOTUS ERIUGENA—I

Life and works

ONE of the most remarkable phenomena of the ninth century is the philosophical system of John Scotus Eriugena, which stands out like a lofty rock in the midst of a plain. We have seen that there was a lively educational activity in the course of the century and, considering the standard, materials and opportunities of the time, a growing interest in learning and scholarship; but there was little original speculation. This is a fact which need cause no surprise in regard to a period of conservation and dissemination; but it is all the more remarkable that an isolated case of original speculation on the grand scale should suddenly occur, without warning and indeed without any immediate continuation. If John Scotus had confined himself to speculation on one or two particular points, we might not have been so surprised, but in point of fact he produced a system, the first great system of the Middle Ages. It may, of course, be said that he relied largely on the former speculations of St. Gregory of Nyssa, for instance, and particularly on the work of the Pseudo-Dionysius, and this is quite true; but one can scarcely avoid the impression, when reading his *De Divisione Naturae*, that one is watching a vigorous, profound and original mind struggling with the categories and modes of thought and ideas which former writers had bequeathed to him as the material on which and with which he had to work, moulding them into a system and impregnating the whole with an atmosphere, a colour and a tone peculiar to himself. It is indeed interesting, if not altogether profitable, to wonder on what lines the thought of John Scotus would have evolved, had he lived at a later and richer period of philosophical development: as it is, one is confronted with a mind of great power, hampered by the limitations of his time and by the poverty of the material at his disposal. Moreover, while it is, of course, a mistake to interpret the system of John Scotus in terms of a much later philosophy, itself conditioned by the previous development of thought and the historical circumstances of the time, for example, the Hegelian system, one is not thereby debarred from endeavouring to discern the peculiar characteristics of John's thought, which, to a certain extent, altered the meaning of the ideas and categories he borrowed from previous writers.

Of the life of John Scotus we do not know very much. He was born in Ireland about 810 and studied in an Irish monastery. 'Eriugena' means 'belonging to the people of Erin', while the term 'Scotus' need not be taken as indicating any near connection with Scotland, since in the ninth century Ireland was known as *Scotia Maior* and the Irish as *Scoti*. It was doubtless in an Irish monastery that he acquired his knowledge of the Greek language. In the ninth century the study of Greek was, speaking generally, peculiar to the Irish monasteries. Bede, it is true, attained to a working knowledge of the language, but neither Alcuin nor Rhabanus Maurus knew any Greek worth speaking of. The former used Greek phrases in his commentaries but, though he must have known at least the Greek alphabet, these *Graeca* were taken over from the writings of other authors, and, in general, it has been shown that the occurrence of Greek phrases in a manuscript points to Irish authorship or to some association with or influence from an Irish writer. The attention given to Greek at St. Gall, for instance, was due originally to Irish monks. However, even if the presence of *Graeca* in a manuscript indicates an Irish influence, direct or indirect, and even if the study of Greek in the ninth century was characteristic of the Irish monasteries, it would be extremely rash to conclude that all Irish writers who used Greek phrases, still less that all Irish monks, studied and knew Greek in any real sense. The use of a Greek phrase is, by itself, no more a proof of a real knowledge of the Greek language than the use of a phrase like *fait accompli* is, by itself, a proof of a real knowledge of French, and the number of even Irish monks who knew much more than the rudiments of Greek was doubtless small. John Scotus Eriugena at any rate was among their number, as is shown clearly by the fact that he was able, when in France, to translate from the Greek writings of St. Gregory of Nyssa and the works of the Pseudo-Dionysius, and even attempted the composition of Greek verse. It would be absurd to take John's knowledge of the language as typical of the century or even as typical of Irish monasteries: the truth of the matter is that he was, for the ninth century, an outstanding Greek scholar.

Sometime in the forties John Scotus crossed over to France. In any case he was at the court of Charles the Bald by 850 and occupied a prominent position in the Palatine School. There is no sure evidence that he was ever ordained priest; but, whether layman or not, he was induced by Hincmar, Bishop of Rheims, to intervene in a theological dispute concerning predestination and the result was his work *De praedestinatione* which pleased neither side and brought its author under suspicion of heresy. John thereupon turned his attention to philosophy and in 858 he undertook, at the request of Charles the Bald, the translation of the works of the Pseudo-Dionysius from Greek into Latin. These works had been presented to Louis the Fair in 827 by the Emperor Michael Balbus, but they had never been adequately translated. John, then, undertook not only to translate them, but also to comment on them, and in fact he published commentaries on the Pseudo-Dionysius's writings, except on the *Mystical Theology*, though Pope Nicholas I made it a subject of complaint that the publication had taken place without any reference to him. John Scotus also published translations of the *Ambigua* of Maximus the Confessor and the *De Hominis Opificio* of St. Gregory of Nyssa, and it appears that later he commented on St. John's Gospel and on Boethius's *De Consolatione Philosophiae* and theological *opuscula*.

The work for which John Scotus is celebrated, however, is the *De Divisione Naturae*, which he composed probably between 862 and 866. This work consists of five books and is written in dialogue form, a form of composition which was popular at the time and which was much used by Alcuin and others. It is not a very easy work to interpret, since the author's attempt to express Christian teaching and the philosophical doctrine of Augustine on lines suggested by the Pseudo-Dionysius and the neo-Platonic philosophy leaves room for dispute whether John Scotus was an orthodox Christian or very nearly, if not quite, a pantheist. Those scholars who maintain his orthodox intentions can point to such statements as that 'the authority of the Sacred Scriptures must be followed in all things',[1] while those who maintain that he regarded philosophy as superior to theology and anticipated the Hegelian rationalism can point, for example, to the statement[2] that 'every authority' (e.g. that of the Fathers) 'which is not confirmed by true reason seems to be weak, whereas true reason does not need to be supported by any authority'. However, one cannot profitably discuss the question of interpretation until the

[1] *De Div. Nat.*, 1, 64. [2] *Ibid.*, 1, 69.

doctrine of the *De Divisione Naturae* has first been exposed, though it is as well to indicate beforehand the fact that there is a dispute about its correct interpretation.

John Scotus seems not to have outlived Charles the Bald, who died in 877. There are indeed various stories about his later life which are given by chroniclers, e.g. that he became Abbot of Athelney and was murdered by the monks, but there seems to be little evidence for the truth of such stories, and probably they are either legends or are due to a confusion with some other John.

CHAPTER XIII

JOHN SCOTUS ERIUGENA—II

Nature—God and creation—Knowledge of God by affirmative and negative ways; inapplicability of categories to God—How, then, can God be said to have made the world?—Divine Ideas in the Word—Creatures as participations and theophanies; creatures are in God—Man's nature—Return of all things to God—Eternal punishment in light of cosmic return—Interpretation of John Scotus's system.

1. AT the beginning of the first book of the *De Divisione Naturae* John Scotus explains through the lips of the Master, in a dialogue which takes place between a *Magister* and a *Discipulus*, what he means by 'Nature', namely the totality of the things that are and the things that are not, and he gives various ways of making this general division. For example, things which are perceived by the senses or are penetrable by the intellect are the things that are, while the objects that transcend the power of the intellect are the things that are not. Again, things which lie hid in their *semina*, which are not actualised, 'are not', while the things which have developed out of their seeds 'are'. Or again, the objects which are objects of reason alone may be said to be the things which are, while the objects which are material, subject to space and time and to dissolution, may be called the things which are not. Human nature, too, considered as alienated from God by sin may be said 'not to be', whereas when it is reconciled with God by grace, it begins to be.

The term 'Nature', then, means for John Scotus Eriugena, not only the natural world, but also God and the supernatural sphere: it denotes all Reality.[1] When, therefore, he asserts[2] that nature is divided into four species, namely Nature which creates and is not created, Nature which is created and creates, Nature which is created and does not create, and Nature which neither creates nor is created, thus apparently making God and creatures species of Nature, it might well seem that he is asserting a monistic doctrine, and indeed, if these words be taken in their literal significance, we should have to conclude that he was. Nevertheless at the beginning of Book 2, in a long and somewhat complicated period, he

[1] Cf. 3, 1. [2] 1, 1.

makes it clear that it is not his intention to assert that creatures are actually a part of God or that God is a genus of which creatures are a species, although he retains the fourfold division of 'Nature' and says that God and creatures may be looked at as forming together a *universitas*, a 'universe' or totality. The conclusion is warranted that John Scotus did not intend to assert a doctrine of pantheistic monism or to deny the distinction between God and creatures, though his philosophic explanation or rationalisation of the egress of creatures from God and their return to God may, taken by itself, imply pantheism and a denial of the distinction.

2. 'Nature which creates and is not created' is, of course, God Himself, who is the cause of all things but is Himself without cause. He is the beginning or first principle, since all creatures proceed from Him, the 'middle' (*medium*); since it is in Him and through Him that creatures subsist and move; and the end or final cause, since He is the term of the creature's movement of self-development and perfection.[1] He is the first cause, which brought creatures into existence from a state of non-existence, out of nothing (*de nihilo*).[2] This doctrine of God is in accordance with Christian theology and contains a clear enunciation of the divine transcendence and self-existence; but John Scotus goes on to say that God may be said to be created in creatures, to be made in the things which He makes, to begin to be in the things which begin to be. It would, however, be an anachronism to suppose that he is asserting an evolutionary pantheism, and maintaining that nature, in the ordinary sense, is God-in-His-otherness, for he proceeds to explain[3] that when he says that God is made in creatures, he means that God 'appears' or manifests Himself in creatures, that creatures are a theophany. Some of the illustrations he uses are indeed somewhat unfortunate from the orthodox standpoint, as when he says that, just as the human intellect, when it proceeds into actuality in the sense of actually thinking, may be said to be made in its thoughts, so God may be said to be made in the creatures which proceed from Him, an illustration which would seem to imply that creatures are an actualisation of God; but, whatever illustrations John Scotus may use and however much he is influenced by the philosophical tradition which derived from neo-Platonism, it seems clear that his intention at least was to conserve the real distinction between God and creatures and

[1] 1, 11. [2] 1, 12. [3] *Ibid.*

that God, in relation to creation, is *Natura quae creat et non creatur*. On the truth of this formula he is emphatic.

3. In attaining to some knowledge of the *Natura quae creat et non creatur* one can use the affirmative (καταφατική) and negative (ἀποφατική) ways. When using the negative method one denies that the divine essence or substance is any of those things, 'which are', i.e. which can be understood by us: when using the affirmative method one predicates of God those things 'which are', in the sense that the cause is manifested in the effect.[1] This twofold method of theology was borrowed by John Scotus from the Pseudo-Dionysius, as he himself plainly affirms,[2] and it was from the same writer that he took the idea that God should not be called, e.g. Truth or Wisdom or Essence, but rather super-Truth, super-Wisdom and super-Essence, since no names borrowed from creatures can be applied to God in their strict and proper sense: they are applied to God *metaphorice* or *translative*. Moreover, in a succeeding passage[3] John Scotus indulges in a most ingenious piece of dialectic in order to show that the use of the affirmative method does not contradict the doctrine of the ineffable and incomprehensible character of the Godhead and that the negative method is the fundamental one. For example, by the affirmative method we say that God is Wisdom, while by the negative way we say that God is not wisdom, and this appears at first sight to be a contradiction; but in reality, when we say that God is Wisdom, we are using the word 'wisdom' in a 'metaphorical' sense (an 'analogical' sense, the Scholastic would say), while when we say that God is not wisdom, we are using the word in its proper and primary sense (i.e. in the sense of human wisdom, the only wisdom of which we have direct experience). The contradiction is, therefore, not real, but only verbal, and it is reconciled by calling God super-Wisdom. Now, as far as words go, to predicate super-Wisdom of God would seem to be an act of mind pursuing the affirmative way, but if we examine the matter more closely we shall see that, although the phrase belongs formally and verbally to the *via affirmativa*, the mind has no content, no idea, corresponding to the word 'super', so that in reality the phrase belongs to the *via negativa*, and the addition of the word 'super' to the word 'wisdom' is equivalent to a negation. Verbally there is no negation in the predicate 'super-Wisdom', but in regard to the mind's content there is a negation. The *via negativa* is thus

[1] 1, 13. [2] 1, 14. [3] *Ibid.*

fundamental, and as we do not pretend to define *what* the 'super' is in itself, the ineffability and incomprehensibility of the Godhead is unimpaired. Of course, if we say that the use of the word 'super' is *simply and solely* equivalent to a negation, the obvious objection arises (and would be raised by a Logical Positivist) that there is no meaning in our minds when we use the phrase, that the phrase is non-significant. John Scotus, however, though he does not discuss this real difficulty, provides one answer when he indicates that when we say that God is, for example, super-Wisdom, we mean that He is *more than* wisdom. If this is so, then the addition of 'super' cannot be simply equivalent to a negation, since we can say that 'a stone is not wise' and we certainly mean something different when we say 'God is not wise' and 'a stone is not wise': we mean that if 'wise' be taken to refer to human wisdom, then God is not wise, in the sense that He is *more* than human wisdom, whereas a stone is not wise, in the sense that the stone is *less* than wise. This thought would seem to be indicated by John Scotus's concluding example. '(God) is essence', an affirmation; 'He is not essence', a negation; 'He is super-essential', an affirmation and negation at the same time.[1] The thesis and the antithesis are thus reconciled dialectically in the synthesis.

If, then, God cannot be properly termed wise, for this term is not predicated of purely material things, much less can we predicate of Him any of the ten categories of Aristotle, which are found in purely material objects. For example, quantity can certainly not be predicated of God, as quantity implies dimensions, and God has no dimensions and does not occupy space.[2] Properly speaking, God is not even substance or οὐσία, for He is infinitely more than substance, though He can be called substance *translative*, inasmuch as He is the creator of all substances. The categories are founded on and apply to created things and are strictly inapplicable to God: nor is the predicate 'God' a genus or a species or an accident. Thus God transcends the *praedicamenta* and the *praedicabilia*, and on this matter John Scotus is clearly no monist but he emphasises the divine transcendence in the way that the Pseudo-Dionysius had done. The theology of the Blessed Trinity certainly teaches us that relation is found in God, but it does not follow that the relations in God fall under the category of relation. The word is used *metaphorice* or *translative* and, as applied to the divine Persons, it is not used in its proper and intelligible sense: the

[1] I, 14. [2] I, 15.

divine 'relations' are more than relations. In fine, though we can learn from creatures *that* God is, we cannot learn *what* He is. We learn that He is more than substance, more than wisdom and so on; but what that more is, what substance or wisdom mean as applied to God, we cannot know, for He transcends every intellect, whether of angels or of men.

4. But though the doctrine of the inapplicability of the categories to God would seem to place the transcendence of God and the clear distinction between Him and creatures beyond all doubt, consideration of the categories of *facere* and *pati* seems to lead John Scotus to a very different conclusion. In a most ingenious discussion[1] he shows, what is obvious enough, that *pati* cannot be predicated of God and at the same time argues that both *facere* and *pati* involve motion. Is it possible to attribute motion to God? No, it is not. Then neither can making be attributed to God. But, how in this case, are we to explain the Scriptural doctrine that God made all things? In the first place, we cannot suppose that God existed before He made the world, for, if that were so, God would not only be in time but also His making would be an accident accruing to Him, and both suppositions are impossible. God's making, therefore, must be co-eternal with Himself. In the second place, even if the making is eternal and identical with God, and not an accident of God, we cannot attribute motion to God, and motion is involved in the category of making. What does it mean, then, to say that God made all things? 'When we hear that God makes all things, we should understand nothing else but that God is in all things, i.e. is the essence of all things. For He alone truly is, and everything which is truly said to be in those things which are, is God alone.'[2] Such a statement would seem to come very near, to put it mildly, to pantheism, to the doctrine of Spinoza, and it is small wonder that John Scotus prefaces his discussion with some remarks on the relation of reason to authority[3] in which he says that reason is prior to authority and that true authority is simply 'the truth found by the power of reason and handed on in writing by the Fathers for the use of posterity'. The conclusion is that the words, expressions and statements of Scripture, however suited for the uneducated, have to be rationally interpreted by those capable of doing so. In other words, John Scotus does not think of himself as unorthodox or intend to be unorthodox, but his philosophic interpretation of Scripture

[1] I, 70–2. [2] I, 72. [3] I, 69.

sometimes seems equivalent to its rationalisation and to the setting of reason above authority and faith. However, this point of view should not be overstressed. For example, in spite of the pantheistic passage quoted he goes on to reaffirm creation out of nothing, and it is clear that when he refuses to say that God makes or made the world, he is not intending to deny creation but rather to deny of God making in the only sense in which we understand making, namely as an accident, as falling under a particular category. God's existence and essence and His act of making are ontologically one and the same,[1] and all the predicates we apply to God really signify the one incomprehensible super-Essence.[2]

The truth of the matter seems to be that John Scotus, while maintaining the distinction between God and creatures, wishes at the same time to maintain the conception of God as the one all-comprehensive Reality, at least when God is regarded *altiori theoria*. Thus he points out[3] that the first and fourth divisions of Nature (*Natura quae creat et non creatur* and *Natura quae nec creat nec creatur*) are verified only in God, as first efficient cause and final cause, while the second and third divisions (*Natura quae et creatur et creat* and *Natura quae creatur et non creat*) are verified in creatures alone; but he goes on to say[4] that inasmuch as every creature is a participation of Him who alone exists of Himself, all Nature may be reduced to the one Principle, and Creator and creature may be regarded as one.

5. The second main division of Nature (*Natura quae et creatur et creat*) refers to the 'primordial causes', called by the Greeks πρωτότυπα, ἰδέαι, etc.[5] These primordial causes or *praedestinationes* are the exemplary causes of created species and exist in the Word of God: they are in fact the divine ideas, the prototypes of all created essences. How, then, can they be said to be 'created'? John Scotus means that the eternal generation of the Word or Son involves the eternal constitution of the archetypal ideas or exemplary causes in the Word. The generation of the Word is not a temporal but an eternal process, and so is the constitution of the *praedestinationes*: the priority of the Word, considered abstractly, to the archetypes is a logical and not a temporal priority. The emergence of these archetypes is thus part of the eternal procession of the Word by 'generation', and it is in this sense only that they are said to be created.[6] However, the logical priority of the Word to the archetypes and the dependence of the archetypes on the

[1] 1, 77. [2] 1, 75. [3] 2, 2. [4] *Ibid.* [5] *Ibid.* [6] 2, 20.

Word mean that, although there never was a time when the Word was without the archetypes, they are not *omnino coaeternae* (*causae*) with the Word.[1]

In what sense, then, can the primordial causes be said to create? If one were to press statements such as this, that the πρωτότυπον is diffused (*diffunditur*) through all things giving them essence, or again that it penetrates all the things which it has made,[2] one would naturally incline to a pantheistic interpretation; yet John Scotus repeats[3] that the Holy Trinity 'made out of nothing all things that it made', which would imply that the prototypes are causes only in the sense of exemplary causes. Nothing is created except that which was eternally pre-ordained, and these eternal *praeordinationes* or θεῖα θηλήματα are the prototypes. All creatures 'participate' in the archetypes, e.g. human wisdom in the Wisdom-in-itself.[4] He drew copiously on the Pseudo-Dionysius and Maximus for his doctrine and it would seem that he intended to reconcile his philosophic speculation with orthodox Christian theology; but his language rather gives the impression that he is straining at the leash and that his thought, in spite of his orthodox intentions, tends towards a form of philosophic pantheism. That his intentions were orthodox seems clear enough from the frequent *cautelae* he gives.

Is there actually and ontologically a plurality of *praedestinationes* in the Word? John Scotus answers in the negative.[5] Numbers proceed from the *monas* or unit, and in their procession they are multiplied and receive an order; but, considered in their origin, in the monad, they do not form a plurality but are undivided from one another. So the primordial causes, as existing in the Word, are one and not really distinct, though in their effects, which are an ordered plurality, they are multiple. The monad does not become less or undergo change through the derivation of numbers, nor does the primordial cause undergo change or diminution through the derivation of its effects, even though, from another point of view, they are contained within it. On this point John Scotus adheres to the neo-Platonic standpoint, according to which the principle undergoes no change or diminution through the emanation of the effect, and it seems that his philosophy suffers from the same tension that is observable in neo-Platonism, i.e. between a theory of emanation and a refusal to allow that emanation or procession impairs the integrity of the principle.

[1] 2, 21. [2] 2, 27. [3] 2, 24, col. 580. [4] 2, 36. [5] Cf. 3, 1.

6. *Natura quae creatur et non creat* consists of creatures, exterior to God, forming the world of nature in the narrow sense, which was made by God out of nothing. John Scotus calls these creatures 'participations', and asserts that they participate in the primordial causes, as the latter participate immediately in God.[1] The primordial causes, therefore, look upwards towards the ultimate Principle and downwards towards their multiple effects, a doctrine which obviously smacks of the neo-Platonic emanation theory. 'Participation' means, however, derivation from, and, interpreting the Greek μετοχή or μετουσία as meaning μεταέχουσα or μεταουσία (*post-essentia* or *secunda essentia*), he says that participation is nothing else than the derivation of a second essence from a higher essence.[2] Just as the water rises in a fountain and is poured out into the river-bed, so the divine goodness, essence, life, etc., which are in the Fount of all things, flow out first of all into the primordial causes and cause them to be, and then proceed through the primordial causes into their effects.[3] This is clearly an emanation metaphor, and John Scotus concludes that God is everything which truly is, since He makes all things and is made in all things, 'as Saint Dionysius the Areopagite says'.[4] The divine goodness is progressively diffused through the universe of creation, in such a way that it 'makes all things, and is made in all things, and is all things'.[5] This sounds as if it were a purely pantheistic doctrine of the emanation type; but John Scotus equally maintains that the divine goodness created all things out of nothing, and he explains that *ex nihilo* does not imply the pre-existence of any material, whether formed or unformed, which could be called *nihil*: rather does *nihil* mean the negation and absence of all essence or substance, and indeed of all things which have been created. The Creator did not make the world *ex aliquo*, but rather *de omnino nihilo*.[6] Here again, then, John Scotus tries to combine the Christian doctrine of creation and of the relation of creatures to God with the neo-Platonic philosophy of emanation, and it is this attempt at combination which is the reason for diversity of interpretation, according as one regards the one or other element in his thought as the more fundamental.

This tension became even clearer from the following consideration. Creatures constitute, not only a 'participation' of the divine goodness, but also the divine self-manifestation or theophany. All objects of intellection or sensation are 'the appearance of the

[1] 3, 3. [2] *Ibid.* [3] 3, 4. [4] *Ibid.* [5] *Ibid.* [6] 3, 5.

non-appearing, the manifestation of the hidden, the affirmation of the negated (a reference to the *via negativa*), the comprehension of the incomprehensible, the speaking of the ineffable, the approach of the unapproachable, the understanding of the unintelligible, the body of the incorporeal, the essence of the super-essential, the form of the formless', etc.[1] Just as the human mind, itself invisible, becomes visible or manifest in words and writing and gestures, so the invisible and incomprehensible God reveals Himself in nature, which is, therefore, a true theophany. Now, if creation is a theophany, a revelation of the divine goodness, which is itself incomprehensible, invisible and hidden, does not this suggest a new interpretation of the *nihilum* from which creation proceeds? Accordingly John Scotus explains in a later passage[2] that *nihilum* means 'the ineffable and incomprehensible and inaccessible brightness of the divine goodness', for what is incomprehensible may, *per excellentiam*, be called 'nothing', so that when God begins to appear in His theophanies, He may be said to proceed *ex nihilo in aliquid*. The divine goodness considered in itself may be said to be *omnino nihil*, though in creation it comes to be, 'since it is the essence of the whole universe'. It would indeed be an anachronism to ascribe to John Scotus a doctrine of Absolutism and to conclude that he meant that God, considered in Himself apart from the 'theophanies', is a logical abstraction; but it does seem that two distinct lines of thought are present in his teaching about creation, namely the Christian doctrine of free creation 'in time' and the neo-Platonic doctrine of a necessary diffusion of the divine goodness by way of 'emanation'. Probably he intended to maintain the Christian doctrine, but at the same time considered that he was giving a legitimate philosophic explanation of it. Such an attitude would, of course, be facilitated by the fact that there was at the time no clear distinction between theology and philosophy and their respective spheres, with the result that a thinker could, without being what we would nowadays call a rationalist, accept a revealed dogma like the Trinity, and then proceed in all good faith to 'explain' or deduce it in such a way that the explanation practically changed the dogma into something else. If we want to call John Scotus an Hegelian before Hegel, we must remember that it is extremely unlikely that he realised what he was doing.

The precise relation of the created nature to God in the philosophy of John Scotus is not an easy matter to determine. That

[1] 3, 4. [2] 3, 19.

the world is eternal in one sense, namely in its *rationes*, in the primordial causes, in God's will to create, occasions no difficulty, and if the author, when he maintains that the world is both eternal and created, meant simply that as foreseen and willed by God it is eternal, while as made it is temporal and outside God, there would be no cause for surprise; but he maintains that the world is not outside God and that it is both eternal and created *within* God.[1] As regards the first point, that the world is not *extra Deum*, one must understand it in terms of the theory of participation and 'assumption' (*est igitur participatio divinae essentiae assumptio*).[2] As creatures are derived from God and owe all the reality they possess to God, apart from God they are nothing, so that in this sense it can be said that there is nothing outside God: if the divine activity were withdrawn, creatures would cease to be. But we must go further.[3] God saw from eternity all that He willed to create. Now, if He saw creatures from all eternity, He also made them from all eternity, since vision and operation are one in God. Moreover, as He saw creatures in Himself, He made them in Himself. We must conclude, therefore, that God and creatures are not distinct, but one and the same (*unum et id ipsum*), the creature subsisting in God and God being created in the creature 'in a wonderful and ineffable manner'. God, then, 'contains and comprehends the nature of all sensible things in Himself, not in the sense that He contains within Himself anything beside Himself, but in the sense that He is substantially all that He contains, the substance of all visible things being created in Him'.[4] It is at this point that John Scotus gives his interpretation of the 'nothing' out of which creatures proceed as the divine goodness,[5] and he concludes that God is everything, that from the super-essentiality of His nature (*in qua dicitur non esse*) He is created by Himself in the primordial causes and then in the effects of the primordial causes, in the theophanies.[6] Finally, at the term of the natural order, God draws all things back into Himself, into the divine Nature from which they proceeded, thus being first and final Cause, *omnia in omnibus*.

The objection may be raised that first of all John Scotus says that God is *Natura quae creat et non creatur* and then goes on to identify with God the *Natura quae creatur et non creat*: how can the two positions be reconciled? If we regard the divine Nature as

[1] See the long discussion in 3, 5 ff. [2] 3, 9. [3] 3, 17.
[4] 3, 18 [5] 3, 19. [6] 3, 10.

it is in itself, we see that it is without cause, ἄναρχος and ἀναίτιος,[1] but at the same time it is the cause of all creatures: it is, then, rightly to be called 'Nature which creates and is not created'. From another point of view, looking on God as final Cause, as *term* of the rhythm of the cosmic process, He may be called 'Nature which neither creates nor is created'. On the other hand, considered as issuing out from the hidden depths of His nature and beginning 'to appear', He appears first of all in the primordial causes or *rationes aeternae*. These are identical with the Word, which contains them, so that, in 'creating' the primordial causes or principles of essences, God appears to Himself, becomes self-conscious, and creates Himself, i.e. as generating the Word and the *rationes* contained in the Word. God is thus 'Nature which both creates and is created'. In the second stage of the divine procession or theophany God comes to be in the effects of the primordial causes, and so is 'Nature which is created', while, since these effects have a term and include together all created effects, so that there are no further effects, He is also 'Nature which does not create'.[2]

7. John Scotus's allegorical explanation of the Biblical account of the six days of creation,[3] which he explains in terms of his own philosophy, brings him, in the fourth book, to his doctrine of man. We can say of man that he is an animal, while we can also say that he is not an animal,[4] since while he shares with the animals the functions of nutrition, sensation, etc., he has also the faculty of reason, which is peculiar to him and which elevates him above all the animals. Yet there are not two souls in man, an animal soul and a rational soul: there is a rational soul which is simple and is wholly present in every part of the body, performing its various functions. John Scotus is therefore willing to accept the definition of man as *animal rationale*, understanding by *animal* the genus and by *rationale* the specific difference. On the other hand the human soul is made in the image of God, is like to God, and this likeness to God expresses the true substance and essence of man. As it exists in any actual man it is an effect: as it exists in God it is a primordial cause, though these are but two ways of looking at the same thing.[5] From this point of view man can be defined as *Notio quaedam intellectualis in mente divina aeternaliter facta.*[6] *That* this substance of man, the likeness to God or participation in God, exists, can be known by the human mind, just as the human mind

[1] 3, 23. [2] *Ibid.* [3] 3, 24 ff. [4] 4, 5. [5] 4, 7. [6] *Ibid.*

can know *that* God exists, but *what* its substance is the human mind cannot know, just as it cannot know *what* God is. While, then, from one point of view man is definable, from another point of view he is undefinable, since the mind or reason of man is made in the image of God and the image, like God Himself, exceeds our power of understanding. In this discussion of the definition of man we can discern Aristotelian elements and also neo-Platonic and Christian elements, which give rise to different attitudes and views on the matter.

John Scotus emphasises the fact that man is the microcosm of creation, since he sums up in himself the material world and the spiritual world, sharing with the plants the powers of growth and nutrition, with the animals the powers of sensation and emotional reaction, with the angels the power of understanding: he is in fact what Poseidonius called the bond or δέσμος, the link between the material and spiritual, the visible and invisible creation. From this point of view one can say that every genus of animal is in man rather than that man is in the genus animal.[1]

8. The fourth stage of the process of Nature is that of *Natura quae nec creat nec creatur*, namely of God as the term and end of all things, God all in all. This stage is that of the return to God, the corresponding movement to the procession from God, for there is a rhythm in the life of Nature and, as the world of creatures proceeded forth from the primordial causes, so will it return into those causes. 'For the end of the whole movement is its beginning, since it is terminated by no other end than by its principle, from which its movement begins and to which it constantly desires to return, that it may attain rest therein. And this is to be understood not only of the parts of the sensible world, but also of the whole world. Its end is its beginning, which it desires, and on finding which it will cease to be, not by the perishing of its substance, but by its return to the ideas (*rationes*), from which it proceeds.'[2] The process is thus a cosmic process and affects all creation, though mutable and unspiritualised matter which John Scotus, following St. Gregory of Nyssa, represented as a complex of accidents and as appearance,[3] will perish.

Besides the cosmical process of creation as a whole, there is the specifically Christian theme (though John Scotus not infrequently does a little 'rationalising') of the return of man to God. Fallen man is led back to God by the incarnate Logos, who has assumed

[1] 4, 8. [2] 5, 3. [3] 1, 34.

human nature and redeemed all men in that human nature, and John Scotus emphasises the solidarity of mankind both in Adam's fall and in Christ's resurrection. Christ brings mankind back to God, though not all are united to God in the same degree, for, though He redeemed all human nature, 'some He restores to the former state of human nature, while others He deifies beyond human nature', yet in no one except Himself is human nature substantially united with the Godhead.[1] John Scotus thus affirms the unique character of the Incarnation and of the relation of Christ's human nature to the Deity, though, when he gives the stages of the return of human nature to God, another—and less orthodox—point of view seems to show itself. These stages are:[2] (1) the dissolution of the human body into the four elements of the sensible world; (2) the resurrection of the body; (3) the change of body into spirit; (4) the return of human nature in its totality into the eternal and unchangeable primordial causes; and (5) the return of nature and the primordial causes to God. 'For God will be all in all, where nothing will exist but God alone.' Yet if at first sight this latter viewpoint seems quite inconsistent with orthodox theology and especially with the unique position of Christ, John Scotus clearly did not mean to assert a real pantheistic absorption in God, since he goes on to state that he does not mean to imply a perishing of individual substance but its elevation. He uses the illustration of the iron made white-hot in the fire and observes that, though the iron may be said to be transmuted into fire, the substance of the iron remains. Thus when, for example, he says that the human body is changed into spirit, what he refers to is the glorification or 'spiritualisation' of the human body, not to a kind of transubstantiation. Moreover, it must be remembered that John Scotus expressly states that he is basing his teaching on the doctrine of St. Gregory of Nyssa and his commentator Maximus, and his teaching must accordingly be understood in the light of that statement. Lest it be thought, he says, that he is entirely neglecting the Latins in favour of the Greeks, he adds the testimony of St. Ambrose. Though the heavens and the earth will perish and pass away (their perishing being interpreted as a *reditus in causas*, which means the cessation of the generated material world), that does not mean that the individual souls of men, in their *reditus in causas*, will cease to exist: their *deificatio* no more means their substantial absorption in God than the

[1] 5, 25. [2] 5, 8.

permeation of the air by light means its destruction or transubstantiation. John Scotus is quite clear on that point.

The fact is that in the case of the cosmic 'return', as elsewhere, John Scotus tries to combine the teaching of the Scriptures and the Fathers with philosophical speculation of the neo-Platonic tradition or rather to express the Christian *Weltanschauung* in terms of such speculation. As the Christian wisdom is looked at as a totality, no clear distinction being made between revealed theology and philosophy, the application of John's speculative method necessarily means a *de facto* rationalisation on occasion, however orthodox his intentions may have been. For instance, though he insists on the fact that the return to God does not spell the annihilation or the complete absorption of the individual human being and though he expresses himself perfectly clearly on this point, yet his attitude towards matter as the term of the descending divine procession leads him to say[1] that before the Fall human beings were not sexually differentiated and that after the resurrection they will return to this state (in support of which views he appeals to St. Paul, St. Gregory and Maximus). Man, had he not fallen, would have been sexually undifferentiated and in the primordial cause human nature is sexually undifferentiated: the *reditus in causam* involves, therefore, a return to the state of human nature *in causa* and a liberation from the state consequent on the Fall. The *reditus in causam,* however, is a stage in the cosmic process of Nature, so that John Scotus has to maintain that the resurrection of the body takes place by nature, *natura et non per gratiam,*[2] though he appeals for support in this to St. Gregory of Nyssa, Maximus and St. Epiphanius. On the other hand, it is certain, theologically at least, that something is attributable to grace, and John Scotus accordingly attributes the *deificatio*, which is not attained by all human beings, to the free gift and disposition of God, to grace. This is an example of his attempt to combine revelation with the exigencies of his speculative system, an attempt for which, of course, he undoubtedly received support from the writings of earlier Christian authors. On the one hand John Scotus, owing to his Christian intentions, must attribute the resurrection in at least one aspect to God's free grace operating through Christ, while on the other hand, his philosophical doctrine of the return of all things to God means that he must make the resurrection in some degree a natural and

[1] 5, 20. [2] 5, 23.

necessary process, not only because human nature itself has to return into its cause, but because all creation has to return into its cause and endure eternally, and this it does effectively as being contained in man, the microcosm.[1]

9. But if there is to take place a cosmic return to God in and through human nature, so that God, as St. Paul says, will be 'all in all', how is it possible to maintain the theologically orthodox doctrine of the eternal punishment of the damned? The Scriptures teach that the fallen angels and human beings who are finally impenitent will be eternally punished, while on the other hand reason teaches that evil cannot be without end, since God will be all in all and evil is diametrically opposed to God, who is goodness.[2] How can one reconcile these two positions without rejecting either authority or reason? John Scotus's answer[3] is ingenious and affords a good example of his 'rationalisation'. Nothing that God has made can be evil: the substances or natures, therefore, of the devils and evil men must be good. On this point he quotes the Pseudo-Dionysius. The demons and evil men will never, then, suffer annihilation. All that God has made will return to God and all 'nature' will be contained in God, human nature included, so that it is impossible that human nature should undergo eternal punishment. What, then, of the punishments described in the Scriptures? In the first place they cannot be corporeal or material in character, while in the second place they can only affect what God has not made and what, in this sense, is outside 'nature'. Now, God did not make the perverse will of demons or evil men, and it is this which will be punished. But, if all things are to return to God and God will be all in all, how can punishment be contained in God? Moreover, if the malice has disappeared and all impiety, what is there left to punish? The punishment must consist in the eternal prevention by God of the will's tendency to fix itself on the images, conserved in the memory, of the objects desired on earth. God, then, will be all in all, and all evil will have perished, but the wicked will be eternally punished. It is obvious, however, that from the viewpoint of orthodox theology 'wicked' and 'punished' must be placed in inverted commas, since John Scotus has rationalised the Scriptural teaching in order to satisfy the exigencies of his philosophical system.[4] All human nature, all men without exception, will rise with spiritualised bodies and the full possession of natural goods, though only the elect will enjoy 'deification'.[5]

[1] 5, 25. [2] 5, 26–7. [3] 5, 27–8. [4] 5, 29–36. [5] 5, 36.

The conclusion is, then, that the divine nature is the end and term of all things, which will return into their *rationes aeternae* and there abide, 'ceasing to be called by the name of creature', for God will be all in all, 'and every creature will be cast into the shade, i.e. changed into God, as the stars at the rising of the sun'.[1]

10. Although the *De Divisione Naturae* did not have the effect that its outstanding quality as a systematic metaphysic deserved, it was utilised by a succession of mediaeval writers from Remigius of Auxerre to Amalric of Bene, including Berengarius, Anselm of Laon, William of Malmesbury, who praised the work, though he disapproved of John Scotus's predilection for Greek authors, and Honorius of Autun, while the Pseudo-Avicenna borrowed from the work in his *De Intelligentiis*, written in the middle or later part of the twelfth century. However, the fact that the Albigensians appealed to the book, while Amalric of Bene (end of twelfth century) used the doctrine of John Scotus in a pantheistic sense, led to its condemnation in 1225 by Pope Honorius III, who ordered that the work should be burnt, though the order was by no means always fulfilled. This condemnation of the *De Divisione Naturae* and the interpretation which led to the condemnation naturally raises the question, whether John Scotus was or was not a pantheist.

That John Scotus was in intention orthodox has already been given as my opinion; but there are several points that might be mentioned by way of summary argument in support of this statement. First of all, he draws copiously on the writings and ideas of authors whom he certainly regarded as orthodox and with whose ideas he felt his own thought to be in harmony. For example, he makes extensive use of St. Gregory of Nyssa, of the Pseudo-Dionysius (whom he regarded as St. Dionysius the Areopagite), and, not to appear to neglect the Latins, quotes St. Augustine and St. Ambrose in favour of his views. Moreover, John Scotus considered his speculation to be founded on the Scriptures themselves. For instance, the theory of the fourth stage of Nature, *Deus omnia in omnibus*, has its foundation in the words of St. Paul:[2] 'And when all things shall be subdued unto him, then the Son also himself shall be subject unto him that put all things under him, that God may be all in all,' while the doctrine of the body 'becoming spirit' at the resurrection is based on the Pauline statement that the body is sown in corruption and raised in incorruption,

[1] 3, 23. [2] 1 Cor., 15. 28.

that the risen body is a 'spiritual' body. Again, John Scotus draws from the first chapter of St. John's Gospel the conception of the Logos by whom all things were made, in his account of creation, while the theme of *deificatio* was common in the writings of the Fathers.

But, even if John Scotus wrote as though his system had a foundation in Scripture and Tradition, might it not be that he was consciously rationalising the text of Scripture, that he had, to put it crudely, 'his tongue in his cheek'? Does he not say[1] that authority proceeds from true reason and reason in no way from authority; that every authority which is not approved by true reason seems to be weak; that true reason does not need the confirmation of any authority and that authority is nothing else but the truth found by the power of reason and handed on by the Fathers in their writings for the use of posterity; and does not this indicate that he set no store by authority? It seems to me that, to judge by the context, when John Scotus speaks about 'authority' here, he is not referring to the words of Scripture but to the teaching of the Fathers and to the interpretation they had put on the words of the Scriptures. Of course, although it is true that authority must rest on reason, in the sense that the authority must have good credentials, the statement of John Scotus to the effect that authority is nothing else than the truth found by reason and handed on by the Fathers is, as it stands, unacceptable from the theological standpoint (I mean, if compared with the orthodox doctrine of Tradition); but what John Scotus apparently *means* is, not that the doctrine of the Trinity, for example, is simply a truth found by reason and not revealed, but that the attempted 'explanation' or development of the dogma by this or that Father is simply the result of the Father's rational effort and is not final. He does not mean to suggest that the bare dogma, as found in Scripture and preserved by, for example, St. Augustine, can legitimately be questioned, but rather that the intellectual development of the dogma given by St. Augustine, though worthy of respect, is the work of reason and cannot be placed on the same level as the dogma itself. His position is, therefore, this. If St. Paul says that God will be *omnia in omnibus*, this is a revealed truth, but when it comes to deciding what St. Paul meant by this statement and how precisely it is to be understood, reason is the final court of appeal. I am not trying to suggest that this attitude

[1] 1, 69.

is theologically acceptable: my point is rather that, whether his actual view is acceptable or not, John Scotus is not questioning a dogma as such or claiming a right to deny it, but is claiming the right to interpret it, and that his 'rationalisation' consists in this. He has not got his tongue in his cheek when he appeals to Scripture, for he sincerely believed that the data of revelation have to be interpreted rationally and, as we would say, philosophically. This is partly due to the fact that he makes no clear-cut distinction between theology and philosophy. His system presupposes the 'Christian wisdom' (including truths discoverable by reason alone, e.g. God's existence, and truths which are revealed, but not discoverable by reason alone, e.g. the Trinity of Persons in the Godhead) and is a speculative attempt to exhibit the Christian wisdom as an organic and interconnected whole, without making any clear distinction between the spheres of philosophy and revelation, and this attempt inevitably involves some rationalisation. I repeat that I am not trying to defend John Scotus's rationalisation, but to explain his attitude, and my thesis is that it is a mistake to interpret his 'rationalisation' as if it post-dated the clear division of philosophy and theology: his attitude is not essentially different from that of later mediaeval theologians who attempted to prove the Trinity *rationibus necessariis*. If John Scotus had consciously been a 'philosopher' in the narrow sense and nothing more, we would have had to call him a rationalist in the modern sense; but he was both theologian and philosopher in combination (in confusion, if one prefers), and his rationalisation was, *psychologically*, quite compatible with a belief in revelation. Therefore, when he says[1] that he does not want to seem to resist the Apostle or the testimony *summae ac sanctae auctoritatis*, he is quite sincere. Indeed his true attitude is admirably indicated by his statement[2] that 'it is not for us to judge the opinions of the holy Fathers, but to accept them with piety and reverence, though we are not prohibited from choosing (among their opinions) that which appears to reason to agree better with the divine words'. John Scotus accepts, for instance, the doctrine of eternal punishment, because it is revealed, and he accepts it sincerely; but he does not consider that this prevents him from attempting to explain the doctrine in such a way that it will fit in with the rest of his system, a system which he regards as fundamentally based on revelation.

[1] 1, 7. [2] 2, 16.

The discussion may seem to have strayed from the point at issue; but this is not so in reality. For instance, revelation, Christian dogma, teaches clearly that the world was made by God from nothing and that creatures are not God. Now John Scotus' general system demands that creatures should return to God and that God should be all in all. Regarding both truths as founded on divine teaching, John Scotus has to reconcile them rationally, in such a way that the *reditus in Deum* does not lead to the conclusion to which it might seem to lead, namely pantheistic absorption, and that the presentation of the distinction between God and creatures does not contradict the Pauline statement that God will be all in all. The process of reconciliation may involve him in what the Thomist theologians would call 'rationalisation', but his *cautelae*, e.g. that creatures return to God and 'become' God, not *ita ut non sint* but '*ut melius sint*', are not sops thrown to the theologians with the writer's tongue in his cheek, but they are sincere expressions of John Scotus' desire to preserve Christian teaching or what he regards, rightly or wrongly, as Christian teaching.

That a tension develops between the Christian and neo-Platonic elements in John Scotus' thought has already been pointed out, but it is as well to emphasise it again, as it has a bearing on the question of his 'rationalism'. In accordance with the neo-Platonic tradition inherited through the Pseudo-Dionysius, John Scotus maintained[1] that God in Himself, *Natura quae creat et non creatur*, is impenetrable to Himself, unknown to Himself, as being infinite and super-essential, and that He becomes luminous to Himself only in His theophanies. This is, of course, an echo of the neo-Platonic doctrine that the One, the ultimate Godhead, is beyond thought, beyond self-consciousness, since thought and self-consciousness involve a duality of subject and object. Now, that God in Himself is incomprehensible to the created mind is certainly a Christian tenet, but that He is not self-luminous is not the teaching of Christianity. John Scotus, therefore, has to reconcile the two positions somehow, if he wishes to retain them both, and he attempts to do so by making the first 'theophany' the emergence of the Logos containing the primordial causes, so that in and through the Logos God becomes (though not temporally) self-conscious, appearing to Himself. The Logos thus corresponds to the neo-Platonic *Nous*, and a rationalisation arises out of the

[1] E.g. 3, 23.

desire to preserve both the Christian doctrine and the principles of what John Scotus regards as true philosophy. The desire to preserve Christian doctrine is sincere enough, but a tension between the two elements is inevitable. If one takes a particular set of isolated statements of John Scotus one would have to say that he was either a pantheist or a theist. For example, the statement that the distinction between the second and third stages of Nature is due only to the forms of human reasoning[1] is in itself clearly pantheistic, while the statement that the substantial distinction between God and creatures is always preserved is clearly theistic. It might seem that we should opt for one or the other set in an unqualified manner, and it is this attitude which has given rise to the notion that John Scotus was a conscious pantheist who made verbal concessions to orthodoxy with his tongue in his cheek. But if one realises that he was a sincere Christian, who yet attempted to reconcile Christian teaching with a predominantly neo-Platonic philosophy or rather to express the Christian wisdom in the only framework of thought which was then at hand, which happened to be predominantly neo-Platonic, one should also be able to realise that, in spite of the tension involved and the tendency to rationalise Christian dogma, as far as the subjective standpoint of the philosopher was concerned a satisfactory reconciliation was effected. This does not, of course, alter the fact that not a few statements, if taken in isolation, affirm a pantheistic doctrine and that other statements are irreconcilable with orthodox theological teaching on such points as eternal punishment, and it was in view of such statements that the *De Divisione Naturae* was subsequently condemned by ecclesiastical authority. However, whether orthodox or not, the work bears testimony to a powerful and acute mind, the mind of a speculative philosopher who stands head and shoulders above any other thinker of his day.

[1] 2, 2.

PART III

THE TENTH, ELEVENTH AND TWELFTH CENTURIES

CHAPTER XIV

THE PROBLEM OF UNIVERSALS

Situation following death of Charlemagne—Origin of discussion in texts of Porphyry and Boethius—Importance of the problem—Exaggerated realism—Roscelin's 'nominalism'—St. Peter Damian's attitude to dialectic—William of Champeaux—Abelard—Gilbert de la Porrée and John of Salisbury—Hugh of St. Victor—St. Thomas Aquinas.

1. ONE might have expected that the revival of letters and learning under Charlemagne would lead to a gradual and progressive development of philosophy and (the retention of what was already possessed having been provided for) that thinkers would be able to extend knowledge and pursue a more speculative path, especially as western Europe had been already supplied with an example of philosophical speculation and systematising by John Scotus Eriugena. In point of fact, however, this was not the case, since historical factors outside the sphere of philosophy plunged the empire of Charlemagne into a new Dark Age, the Dark Ages of the tenth century, and belied the promise of the Carolingian renaissance.

Cultural progress depended to some extent on the maintenance of the tendency to centralisation which had been apparent during the reign of Charlemagne; but after his death the empire was divided and the division of the empire among the descendants of Charlemagne was accompanied by the growth of feudalism, that is, by decentralisation. As nobles could be rewarded practically only through gifts of land, they tended, through the acquisition of land, to become more and more independent of the monarchy: their interests diverged or conflicted. Churchmen of the higher grades became feudal lords, monastic life was degraded (for example, through the common practice of the appointment of lay-abbots), bishoprics were used as means of honouring or rewarding servants of the king. The Papacy, which might have attempted to check and to remedy the worsening conditions in France, was itself at a very low ebb of spiritual and moral prestige, and, since education and learning were mainly in the hands of monks and ecclesiastics, the inevitable result of the break-up of the empire of Charlemagne was the decay of scholarship and educational activity. Reform did not begin until the establishment of Cluny in 910, and the influence of the Cluniac reform made itself felt only gradually, of course. St. Dunstan, who had been in the Cluniac monastery of Ghent, introduced the ideals of Cluny into England.

In addition to the internal factors which prevented the fruit of the Carolingian renaissance coming to maturity (such as the political disintegration which led in the tenth century to the transference of the imperial crown from France to Germany, the decay of monastic and ecclesiastical life, and the degradation of the Papacy), there were also operative such external factors as the attacks of the Norsemen in the ninth and tenth centuries, who destroyed centres of wealth and culture and checked the development of civilisation, as also the attacks of the Saracens and the Mongols. Internal decay, combined with external dangers and attacks, rendered cultural progress impossible. To conserve, or to attempt to do so, was the only practicable course: progress in scholarship and philosophy lay again in the future. Such interest in philosophy as existed, centred largely round dialectical questions, and particularly round the problem of universals, the starting-point for the discussion being supplied by certain texts of Porphyry and Boethius.

2. Boethius, in his commentary on the *Isagoge* of Porphyry,[1] quotes Porphyry as remarking that at present he refuses to state whether genera and species are subsistent entities or whether they consist in concepts alone; if subsisting, whether they are material or immaterial and, further, whether they are separate from sensible objects or not, on the ground that such exalted matters cannot be treated in an introduction. Boethius himself, however, goes on to treat of the matter, first of all remarking on the difficulty of the question and the need of care in considering it and then pointing out that there are two ways in which an idea may be so formed that its content is not found in extramental objects precisely as it exists in the idea. For example, one may join together arbitrarily man and horse, to form the idea of a centaur, joining together objects which nature does not suffer to be joined together, and such arbitrarily constructed ideas are

[1] *P.L.*, 64, col. 82–6.

'false'. On the other hand, if we form the idea of a line, i.e. a mere line as considered by the geometer, then, although it is true that no mere line exists by itself in extramental reality, the idea is not 'false', since bodies involve lines and all we have done is to isolate the line and consider it in abstraction. Composition (as in the composition of horse and man to form the centaur) produces a false idea, whereas abstraction produces an idea which is true, even though the thing conceived does not exist extramentally in a state of abstraction or separation.

Now, the ideas of genera and species are ideas of the latter type, formed by abstraction. The likeness of humanity is abstracted from individual men, and this likeness, considered by the mind, is the idea of the species, while the idea of the genus is formed by considering the likeness of diverse species. Consequently, 'genera and species are in individuals, but, as thought, are universals'. They 'subsist in sensible things, but are understood without bodies'. Extramentally there is only one subject for both genus and species, i.e. the individual, but that no more prevents their being considered separately than the fact that it is the same line which is both convex and concave prevents our having different ideas of the convex and concave and defining them differently.

Boethius thus afforded the material for an Aristotelian solution of the problem, though he goes on to say that he has not thought it proper to decide between Plato and Aristotle, but that he has been following out the opinions of Aristotle since his book is concerned with the *Categories* of which Aristotle was the author. But, though Boethius afforded material for a solution of the problem of universals on the lines of moderate realism and though his quotations from Porphyry and his comments on them started the discussion of the problem in the early Middle Ages, the first solution of the mediaevals was not on the lines suggested by Boethius but was a rather *simpliste* form of extreme realism.

3. The thoughtless might suppose that in occupying themselves with this problem the early mediaevals were canvassing a useless topic or indulging in a profitless dialectic juggling; but a short reflection should be sufficient to show the importance of the problem, at least if its implications are considered.

Although what we see and touch are particular things, when we think these things we cannot help using general ideas and words, as when we say, 'This particular object which I see is a tree, an elm to be precise.' Such a judgement affirms of a particular object that it is of a certain kind, that it belongs to the genus tree and the species elm; but it is clear that there may be many other objects besides the actual one perceived to which the same terms may be applied, which may be covered by the same ideas. In other words, objects outside the mind are individual, whereas concepts are general, universal in character, in the sense that they apply indifferently to a multitude of individuals. But, if extra-mental objects are particular and human concepts universal, it is clearly of importance to discover the relation holding between them. If the fact that subsistent objects are individual and concepts general means that universal concepts have no foundation in extramental reality, if the universality of concepts means that they are mere ideas, then a rift between thought and objects is created and our knowledge, so far as it is expressed in universal concepts and judgements, is of doubtful validity at the very least. The scientist expresses his knowledge in abstract and universal terms (for example, he does not make a statement about this particular electron, but about electrons in general), and if these terms have no foundation in extramental reality, his science is an arbitrary construction, which has no relation to reality. In so far indeed as human judgements are of a universal character or involve universal concepts, as in the statement that this rose is red, the problem would extend to human knowledge in general, and if the question as to the existence of an extramental foundation of a universal concept is answered in the negative, scepticism would result.

The problem may be raised in various ways, and, historically speaking, it has taken various forms at various times. It may be raised in this form, for instance. 'What, if anything, in extra-mental reality corresponds to the universal concepts in the mind?' This may be called the ontological approach, and it was under this form that the early mediaevals discussed the matter. Or one may ask *how* our universal concepts are formed. This is the psychological approach and the emphasis is different from that in the first approach, though the two lines of approach are closely connected and one can scarcely treat the ontological question without answering in some way the psychological question as well. Then again, if one supposes a conceptualist solution, that universal concepts are simply conceptual constructions, one may ask how it is that scientific knowledge, which for all *practical* purposes is a fact, is *possible*. But, however the problem be raised and whatever form it takes, it is of fundamental importance. Perhaps one of the factors which may give the impression that the mediaevals were discussing a comparatively unimportant question is this, that they practically confined their attention to genera and species in the category of substance. Not that the problem, even in this restricted form, is unimportant, but if the problem is raised in regard to the other categories as well, its implications in regard to at least the greater part of human knowledge becomes more evident. It becomes clear that the problem is ultimately the epistemological problem of the relation of thought to reality.

4. The first solution to the problem given by the mediaevals was that known as 'Exaggerated Realism'. That it was chronologically the first solution is borne out by the fact that the opponents of this view were for some time known as the *moderni*, while Abelard, for instance, refers to it as the *antiqua doctrina*. According to this view, our generic and specific concepts correspond to a reality existing extramentally in objects, a subsistent reality in which individuals share. Thus the concept Man or Humanity reflects a reality, humanity or the substance of human nature, which exists extramentally in the same way as it is thought, that is, as a unitary substance in which all men share. If for Plato the concept Man reflects the ideal of human nature subsisting apart from and 'outside' individual men, an ideal which individual men embody or 'imitate' to a greater or less extent, the mediaeval realist believed that the concept reflects a unitary substance existing extramentally, in which men participate or of which they are accidental modifications. Such a view is, of course, extremely naïve, and indicates a complete misunderstanding of Boethius's treatment of the question, since it supposes that unless the object reflected by the concept exists extramentally in exactly the same way that it exists intramentally, the concept is purely subjective. In other words, it supposes that the only way of saving the objectivity of our knowledge is to maintain a naïve and exact correspondence between thought and things.

Realism is already implied in the teaching of e.g. *Fredegisius* who succeeded Alcuin as Abbot of St. Martin's Abbey at Tours and maintained that every name or term supposes a corresponding positive reality (e.g. Darkness or Nothing). It is also implied in the teaching of *John Scotus Eriugena*. We find a statement of the doctrine in the teaching of *Remigius of Auxerre* (*c.* 841–908), who held that the species is a *partitio substantialis* of the genus and that the species, e.g. Man, is the substantial unity of many individuals (*Homo est multorum hominum substantialis unitas*). A statement of this kind, if understood as meaning that the plurality of individual men have a common substance which is numerically one, has as its natural consequence the conclusion that individual men differ only accidentally from one another, and *Odo of Tournai* (d. 1113) of the Cathedral School of Tournai (who is also called Odo of Cambrai, from the fact that he became Bishop of Cambrai) did not hesitate to draw this conclusion, maintaining that when a child comes into being God produces a new property of an already existing substance, not a new substance. Logically this ultra-realism should result in sheer monism. For example, we have the concepts of substance and of being, and, on the principles of ultra-realism, it would follow that all objects to which we apply the term substance are modifications of one substance and, more comprehensively, that all beings are modifications of one Being. It is probable that this attitude weighed with John Scotus Eriugena, in so far as the latter can justly be called a monist.

As Professor Gilson and others have pointed out, those who maintained ultra-realism in the early Middle Ages were philosophising as logicians, in the sense that they assumed that the logical and real orders are exactly parallel and that because the meaning of, for example, 'man' in the statements 'Plato is a man' and 'Aristotle is a man' is the same, there is a substantial identity in the real order between Plato and Aristotle. But it would, I think, be a mistake to suppose that the ultra-realists were influenced simply by logical considerations: they were influenced also by theological considerations. This is clear in the case of Odo of Tournai, who used ultra-realism in order to explain the transmission of original sin. If one understands by original sin a positive infection of the human soul, one is at once faced by an apparent dilemma: either one has to say that God creates out of nothing a new human substance each time a child comes into being, with the consequence that God is responsible for the infection, or one has to deny that God creates the individual soul. What Odo of Tournai maintained was a form of traducianism, i.e. that the human nature or substance of Adam, infected by original sin, is handed on at generation and that what God creates is simply a new property of an already existing substance.

It is not always easy to assess the precise significance to be attached to the words of the early mediaevals, as we cannot always tell with certainty if a writer fully recognised the implications of his words or if he was making an emphatic point in controversy, perhaps as an *argumentum ad hominem*, without consciously wishing his statement to be understood according to its literal meaning. Thus when Roscelin said that the three Persons of the Blessed Trinity might well be called three gods, if usage permitted, on the ground that every existing being is an individual, *St. Anselm* (1033–1109) asked how he who does not understand how a multitude of men are specifically one man, can understand how several Persons, each of whom is perfect God, are one God.[1] On the strength of this statement St. Anselm has been called an ultra- or exaggerated realist, and indeed the natural interpretation of the statement, in the light of the theological dogma involved, is that, just as there is but one Substance or Nature in the Godhead, so there is but one substance or nature (i.e. numerically one) in all men. Yet it might be that St. Anselm was arguing *ad hominem* and that his question, as intended, amounts to asking how a man who does not realise the specific unity of men (supposing, rightly or wrongly, that Roscelin denied *all* reality to the universal) can possibly grasp the far greater union of the divine Persons in the one Nature, a Nature which is *numerically* one. St. Anselm may have been an ultra-realist, but the second interpretation of his question is supported by the fact that he obviously understood Roscelin to hold that universals have no reality but are mere *flatus vocis* and by the fact that in the *Dialogus de Grammatico*[2] he distinguished between primary and secondary substances, mentioning Aristotle by name.

5. If the implied principle of the ultra-realists was the exact correspondence of thought and extramental reality, the principle of the adversaries of ultra-realism was that only individuals exist. Thus *Eric* (Heiricus) *of Auxerre* (841–76) observed that if anyone tries to maintain that white or black exist absolutely and without a substance in which they adhere, he will be unable to point to any corresponding reality but will have to refer to a white man or a black horse. General names have no general or universal objects corresponding to them; their only objects are individuals. How, then, do universal concepts arise and what is their function and their relation to reality? Neither the understanding nor the memory can grasp all individuals, and so the mind gathers together (*coarctat*) the multitude of individuals and forms the idea

[1] *De fide Trin.*, 2. [2] 10.

of the species, e.g. man, horse, lion. But the species of animals or plants are themselves too many to be comprehended by the mind at once, and it gathers the species together to form the genus. There are, however, many genera and the mind takes a further step in the process of *coarctatio*, forming the still wider and more extensive concept of *usia* (οὐσία). Now, at first sight this seems to be a nominalist position and to remind one of the shorthand note theory of J. S. Mill; but, in the absence of more extensive evidence, it would be rash to affirm that this actually was Eric's consciously held view. Probably he merely meant to affirm emphatically that only individuals exist, that is, to deny ultra-realism, and at the same time to give attention to the psychological explanation of our universal concepts. We have not sufficient evidence to warrant an affirmation that he denied any real foundation to the universal concept.

A similar difficulty of interpretation arises in regard to the teaching of *Roscelin* (*c.* 1050–1120), who, after studying at Soissons and Rheims, taught at Compiègne, his birthplace, Loches, Besançon and Tours. His writings have been lost, except for a letter to Abelard, and we have to rely on the testimony of other writers like St. Anselm, Abelard and John of Salisbury. These writers make it perfectly clear indeed that Roscelin was an opponent of ultra-realism and that he maintained that only individuals exist, but his positive teaching is not so clear. According to St. Anselm,[1] Roscelin held that the universal is a mere word (*flatus vocis*) and accordingly he is numbered by St. Anselm among the contemporary heretics in dialectic. Anselm goes on to remark that these people think that colour is nothing else but body and the wisdom of man nothing else but the soul, and the chief fault of the 'dialectical heretics' he finds in the fact that their reason is so bound up with their imagination that they cannot free themselves from images and contemplate abstract and purely intelligible objects.[2] Now, that Roscelin said that universals are words, general words, we cannot call in question, since St. Anselm's testimony is quite clear; but it is difficult to assess precisely what he meant by this. If we interpret St. Anselm as more or less an Aristotelian, i.e. as no ultra-realist, then we should have to say that he understood Roscelin's teaching as involving a denial of any kind of objectivity to the universal; whereas if we interpret Anselm as an ultra-realist we can then suppose that Roscelin was

[1] *De fide Trin.*, 2; *P.L.* 158, 265A.
[2] *De fide Trin.*, 2; *P.L.* 158, 265B.

merely denying ultra-realism in a very emphatic way. It is, of course, undeniable that the statement that the universal is a mere *flatus vocis* is, taken literally, a denial not only of ultra-realism and moderate realism but even of conceptualism and the presence of universal concepts in the mind; but we have not sufficient evidence to say what Roscelin held about the concept as such, if indeed he gave any attention to the matter: it might be that, in his determination to deny ultra-realism, the formal subsistence of universals, he simply opposed the *universale in voce* to the subsistent universal, meaning that only individuals exist and that the universal does not, as such, exist extramentally, but without meaning to say anything about the *universale in mente*, which he may have taken for granted or never have thought about. Thus it is clear from some remarks of Abelard in his letter on Roscelin to the Bishop of Paris[1] and in his *De divisione et definitione* that, according to Roscelin, a part is a mere word, in the sense that when we say that a whole substance consists of parts, the idea of a whole consisting of parts is a 'mere word', since the objective reality is a plurality of individual things or substances; but it would be rash to conclude from this that Roscelin, if called upon to define his position, would have been prepared to maintain that we have no *idea* of a whole consisting of parts. May he not have meant simply that our idea of a whole consisting of parts is purely subjective and that the only objective reality is a multiplicity of individual substances? (Similarly he appears to have denied the logical unity of the syllogism and to have dissolved it into separate propositions.) According to Abelard, Roscelin's assertion that the ideas of whole and part are mere words is on a par with his assertion that species are mere words; and if the above interpretation is tenable in regard to the whole-part relation, we could apply it also to his doctrine of genera and species and say that his identification of them with words is an affirmation of their subjectivity rather than a denial that there is such a thing as a general idea.

One has, of course, no axe to grind in interpreting Roscelin. He may indeed have been a nominalist in a naïve and complete sense, and I am certainly not prepared to say that he was not a nominalist pure and simple. John of Salisbury seems to have understood him in this sense, for he says that 'some have the idea that the words themselves are the genera and species, although this view was long

[1] *P.L.*, 178, 358B.

ago rejected and has disappeared with its author',[1] an observation which must refer to Roscelin, since the same author says in his *Metalogicus*[2] that the view which identifies species and genera with words practically disappeared with Roscelin. But though Roscelin may have been a pure nominalist and though the fragmentary testimony as to his teaching, if taken literally, certainly supports this interpretation, still it does not seem possible to assert without doubt that he paid any attention to the question whether we have *ideas* of genera or species or not, still less that he denied it, even if his actual words imply this. All we are entitled to say with certainty is that, whether nominalist or conceptualist, Roscelin was an avowed anti-realist.

6. It has been remarked earlier that Roscelin proposed a form of 'Tritheism' which excited the enmity of St. Anselm and which led to his being condemned and having to retract his theory at a Council at Soissons in 1092. It was the fact of such incursions into theology on the part of the dialecticians which was largely responsible for the hostility shown towards them by men like St. Peter Damian. The peripatetic dialecticians or sophists, laymen who came from Italy and travelled from one centre of study to another, men like Anselmus Peripateticus of Parma, who attempted to ridicule the principle of contradiction, naturally put dialectic in a rather poor light through their verbal sophistry and jugglery; but as long as they restricted themselves to verbal disputes, they were probably little more than an irritating nuisance: it was when they applied their dialectic to theology and fell into heresy, that they aroused the enmity of theologians. Thus *Berengarius of Tours* (*c.* 1000–88), maintaining that accidents cannot exist without their supporting substance, denied the doctrine of Transubstantiation. Berengarius was a monk and not a *Peripateticus*, but his spirit of disregard of authority seems to have been characteristic of a group of dialecticians in the eleventh century, and it was mainly this sort of attitude which led St. Peter Damian to pronounce dialectics a superfluity or Otloh of St. Emmeran (*c.* 1010–70) to say that certain dialecticians put more faith in Boethius than in the Scriptures.

St. Peter Damian (1007–72) had little sympathy with the liberal arts (they are useless, he said) or with dialectics, since they are not concerned with God or the salvation of the soul, though, as theologian and writer, the Saint had naturally to make use of

[1] *Polycraticus*, 7, 12; *P.L.*, 199, 665A. [2] 2, 17; *P.L.*, 199, 874C.

dialectic himself. He was, however, convinced that dialectic is a very inferior pursuit and that its use in theology is purely subsidiary and subordinate, not merely because dogmas are revealed truths but also in the sense that even the ultimate principles of reason may fail to apply in theology. For instance, God, according to St. Peter Damian, is not only arbiter of moral values and the moral law (he would have had some sympathy with Kierkegaard's reflections on Abraham), but can also bring it about that an historical event should be 'undone', should not have occurred, and if this seems to go counter to the principle of contradiction, then so much the worse for the principle of contradiction: it merely shows the inferiority of logic in comparison with theology. In short, the place of dialectic is that of a handmaid, *velut ancilla dominae.*[1]

The 'handmaid' idea was also employed by *Gerard of Czanad* (d. 1046), a Venetian who became Bishop of Czanad in Hungary. Gerard emphasised the superiority of the wisdom of the Apostles over that of Aristotle and Plato and declared that dialectic should be the *ancilla theologiae.* It is indeed often supposed that this is the Thomist view of the province of philosophy, but, given St. Thomas's delineation of the separate provinces of theology and philosophy, the handmaid idea does not fit in with his professed doctrine on the nature of philosophy: it was rather (as M. De Wulf remarks) the idea of a 'restricted group of theologians', men who had no use for the newfangled science. However, they could not avoid using dialectic themselves, and *Archbishop Lanfranc* (who was born about the year 1010 and died as Archbishop of Canterbury in 1089) was only talking common sense when he observed that it is not dialectic itself, but the abuse of it, which should be condemned.

7. The opposition of a saint and a rigorist theologian to dialectic is also one of the motifs in the life of Abelard, whose controversy with William of Champeaux forms the next stage in the story of the discussion on universals, though it affected only Abelard's life, not the ultimate triumph of his fight against ultra-realism.

William of Champeaux (1070–1120), after studying at Paris and Laon, studied under Roscelin at Compiègne. He adopted, however, the very opposite theory to that of Roscelin, and the doctrine he taught at the Cathedral School of Paris was that of ultra-realism. According to Abelard, who attended William's lectures at Paris

[1] *De div. omnip.; P.L.*, 145, 63.

and from whom we have to derive our knowledge of William's teaching, the latter maintained the theory that the same essential nature is wholly present at the same time in each of the individual members of the species in question, with the inevitable logical consequence that the individual members of a species differ from one another, not substantially but only accidentally.[1] If this is so, says Abelard,[2] there is the same substance in Plato in one place and in Socrates in another place, being made Plato through one set of accidents and Socrates through another set of accidents. Such a doctrine is, of course, the form of ultra-realism current in the early Middle Ages, and Abelard had no difficulty in showing the absurd consequences it involved. For example, if the human species is substantially, and therefore wholly, present in both Socrates and Plato at the same time, then Socrates must be Plato and he must be present in two places at once.[3] Furthermore, such a doctrine leads ultimately to pantheism, since God is substance and all substances will be identical with the divine substance.

Under pressure of criticism of this kind William of Champeaux changed his theory, abandoning the identity-theory for the indifference-theory and saying that two members of the same species are the same thing, not essentially (*essentialiter*), but indifferently (*indifferenter*). We have this information from Abelard,[4] who evidently treated the new theory as a mere subterfuge, as though William were now saying that Socrates and Plato are not the same, but yet are not different. However, fragments from William's *Sententiae*[5] makes his position clear. He there says that the two words 'One' and 'same' can be understood in two ways, *secundum indifferentiam et secundum identitatem eiusdem prorsus essentiae*, and goes on to explain that Peter and Paul are 'indifferently' men or possess humanity *secundum indifferentiam* in that, as Peter is rational, so is Paul, and as Peter is mortal, so is Paul, etc., whereas their humanity is not the same (he means that their essence or nature is not numerically the same) but like (*similis*), since they are two men. He adds that this mode of unity does not apply to the divine Nature, referring, of course, to the fact that the divine Nature is identical in each of the three divine Persons. This fragment, then, in spite of somewhat obscure language, is clearly opposed to ultra-realism. When William says that Peter and Paul are one and the same in humanity *secundum indifferentiam*

[1] *Hist. calam.*, 2; *P.L.*, 178, 119AB. [2] *Dialectica*, edit. Geyer, p. 10.
[3] *De generibus et speciebus;* Cousin, *Ouvrages inédits d'Abélard*, p. 153.
[4] *Hist. calam.*, 2; *P.L.*, 178, 119B. [5] Edit. Lefèvre, p. 24.

he means that their essences are alike and that this likeness is the foundation of the universal concept of man, which applies 'indifferently' to Peter or Paul or any other man. Whatever Abelard may have thought about this modified theory or under whatever interpretation he may have attacked it, it would seem to be in reality a denial of ultra-realism and not much different from Abelard's own view.

It should be mentioned that the above is somewhat of a simplification, in that the exact course of events in the dispute between Abelard and William is not clear. For instance, although it is certain that William, after being defeated by Abelard, retired to the Abbey of St. Victor and taught there, becoming subsequently Bishop of Châlons-sur-Marne, it is not certain at what point in the controversy he retired. It would seem probable that he changed his theory while teaching at Paris and then, under fresh criticism from Abelard, whether justified or not, retired from the fray to St. Victor, where he continued teaching and may have laid the foundation for the mystical tradition of the abbey; but, according to M. De Wulf, he retired to St. Victor and there taught the new form of his theory, the indifference-theory. It has also been held that William held three theories: (i) the identity-theory of ultra-realism; (ii) the indifference-theory, which was attacked by Abelard as indistinguishable from the first theory; and (iii) an anti-realist theory, in which case he would presumably have retired to St. Victor after teaching the first and second theories. This may be correct, and possibly it is supported by Abelard's interpretation and criticism of the indifference-theory; but it is questionable if Abelard's interpretation was anything more than polemical and I am inclined to agree with De Wulf that the indifference-theory involved a denial of the identity-theory, i.e. that it was not a mere verbal subterfuge. In any case the question is not one of much importance, since all are agreed that William of Champeaux eventually abandoned the ultra-realism with which he had begun.

8. The man who worsted William of Champeaux in debate, *Abelard* (1079–1142), was born at Le Pallet, Palet or Palais near Nantes, deriving thence his name of *Peripateticus Palatinus*, and studied dialectic under Roscelin and William, after which he opened a school of his own, first at Melun, then at Corbeil and subsequently at Paris, where he conducted the dispute with his former master. Later he turned his attention to theology, studied under Anselm of Laon and started teaching theology himself at

Paris in 1113. As a result of the episode with Héloise Abelard had to withdraw to the abbey of St. Denis. In 1121 his book *De Unitate et Trinitate divina* was condemned at Soissons and he then founded the school of Le Paraclet near Nogent-sur-Seine, only to abandon the school in 1125, in order to become Abbot of St. Gildas in Brittany, though he left the monastery in 1129. From 1136 to 1149 at any rate, he was teaching at Ste. Geneviève at Paris, where John of Salisbury was one of his pupils. However, St. Bernard accused him of heresy and in 1141 he was condemned at the Council of Sens. His appeal to Pope Innocent II led to his further condemnation and an injunction against lecturing, after which he retired to Cluny and remained there until his death.

Abelard was, it is clear, a man of combative disposition and unsparing of his adversaries: he ridiculed his masters in philosophy and theology, William of Champeaux and Anselm of Laon. He was also, though somewhat sentimental, egoistic and difficult to get on with: it is significant that he left both the abbey of St. Denis and that of St. Gildas because he was unable to live in peace with the other monks. He was, however, a man of great ability, an outstanding dialectician, far superior in this respect to William of Champeaux; he was no mediocrity who could be ignored, and we know that his brilliance and dialectical dexterity, also no doubt his attacks on other teachers, won him great audiences. His incursions into theology, however, especially in the case of a brilliant man of great reputation, made him seem a dangerous thinker in the eyes of those who had little natural sympathy for dialectic and intellectual cleverness, and Abelard was pursued by the unremitting hostility of St. Bernard in particular, who appears to have looked on the philosopher as an agent of Satan; he certainly did everything he could to secure Abelard's condemnation. Among other charges he accused Abelard of holding an heretical doctrine of the Blessed Trinity, a charge the truth of which Abelard stoutly denied. Probably the philosopher was no rationalist in the usual sense, so far as intentions were concerned (he did not mean to deny revelation or explain away mystery); but at the same time, in his application of dialectic to theology he does seem to have offended against theological orthodoxy, in fact if not in intention. On the other hand it was the very application of dialectic to theology which made theological progress possible and facilitated the Scholastic systematisation of theology in the thirteenth century.

Abelard had no difficulty, as we have seen, in showing the absurdities to which William of Champeaux's ultra-realism logically led; but it was incumbent on him to produce a more satisfactory theory himself. Accepting Aristotle's definition of the universal, as given by Boethius (*quod in pluribus natum est praedicari, singulare vero quod non*), he went on to state that it is not a thing which is predicated but a name, and he concludes that 'it remains to ascribe universality of this sort to words alone'.[1] This sounds like the purely nominalistic view traditionally ascribed to Roscelin (under whom Abelard had studied), but the fact that he was willing to speak of universal and particular words shows that we cannot immediately conclude that Abelard denied any reality corresponding to the universal word, for he certainly did not deny that there is reality corresponding to the particular words, the reality in this case being the individual. Moreover, Abelard proceeded (in the *Logica nostrorum petitioni sociorum*) to distinguish *vox* and *sermo* and to say, not that *Universale est vox*, but that *Universale est sermo*. Why did he make this distinction? Because *vox* signifies the word as a physical entity (*flatus vocis*), a thing, and no thing can be predicated of another thing, whereas *sermo* signifies the word according to its relation to the logical content and it is this which is predicated.

What then is the logical content, what is the *intellectus universalis* or universal idea, which is expressed by the *nomen universale*? By universal ideas the mind 'conceives a common and confused image of many things . . . When I hear *man* a certain figure arises in my mind which is so related to individual men that it is common to all and proper to none.' Such language suggests indeed that, according to Abelard, there are really no universal concepts at all, but only confused images, generic or specific according to the degree of confusion and indistinctness; but he goes on to say that universal concepts are formed by abstraction and that through these concepts we conceive what is *in* the object, though we do not conceive it *as* it is in the object. 'For, when I consider this man only in the nature of substance or of body, and not also of animal or of man or of grammarian, obviously I understand nothing except what is in that nature, but I do not consider all that it has.' He then explains that when he said that our idea of man is 'confused', he meant that by means of abstraction the nature is set free, as it were, from all individuality and is

[1] *Ingredientibus*, edit. Geyer, 16.

considered in such a way that it bears no special relation to any particular individual but can be predicated of all individual men. In fine, *that which* is conceived in specific and generic ideas is in things (the idea is not void of objective reference), but it is not in them, i.e. in individual things, *as* it is conceived. Ultra-realism, in other words, is false; but that does not mean that universals are purely subjective constructions, still less that they are mere words. When Abelard says that the universal is a *nomen* or *sermo*, what he means is that the logical unity of the universal concept affects only the predicate, that it is a *nomen* and not a *res* or individual thing. If we wish, with John of Salisbury, to call Abelard a 'nominalist', we must recognise at the same time that his 'nominalism' is simply a denial of ultra-realism and an assertion of the distinction between the logical and real orders, without involving any denial of the objective foundation of the universal concept. The Abelardian doctrine is an adumbration, in spite of some ambiguous language, of the developed theory of 'moderate realism'.

In his *Theologia Christiana* and *Theologia* Abelard follows St. Augustine, Macrobius and Priscian in placing in the mind of God *formae exemplares* or divine ideas, generic and specific, which are identical with God Himself, and he commends Plato on this point, understanding him in a neo-Platonic sense, as having placed the Ideas in the divine mind, *quam Graeci Noyn appellant*.

9. Abelard's treatment of the problem of universals was really decisive, in the sense that it gave a death-blow to ultra-realism by showing how one could deny the latter doctrine without at the same time being obliged to deny all objectivity to genera and species, and, though the School of Chartres in the twelfth century (in contradistinction to the School of St. Victor) inclined to ultra-realism, two of the most notable figures connected with Chartres, namely Gilbert de la Porrée and John of Salisbury, broke with the old tradition.

(i) *Gilbert de la Porrée* or *Gilbertus Porretanus* was born at Poitiers in 1076, became a pupil of Bernard of Chartres and himself taught at Chartres for more than twelve years. Later he taught at Paris, though he became Bishop of Poitiers in 1142. He died in 1154.

On the subject of each man having his own humanity or human nature Gilbert de la Porrée was firm;[1] but he had a peculiar view

[1] *In Boeth. de dual. nat.; P.L.*, 64, 1378.

as to the inner constitution of the individual. In the individual we must distinguish the individualised essence or substance, in which the accidents of the thing inhere, and the *formae substantiales* or *formae nativae.*[1] These native forms are common in the sense that they are alike in objects of the same species or genus, as the case may be, and they have their exemplars in God. When the mind contemplates the native forms in things, it can abstract them from the matter in which they are embodied or rendered concrete and consider them alone in abstraction: it is then attending to genus or species, which are *subsistentiae*, but not substantially existing objects.[2] For example, the genus is simply the collection (*collectio*) of *subsistentiae* obtained by comparing things which, though differing in species, are alike.[3] He means that the idea of the species is obtained by comparing the similar essential determinations or forms of similar individual objects and gathering them together into one idea, while the idea of the genus is obtained by comparing objects which differ specifically but which yet have some essential determinations or forms in common, as horse and dog have animality in common. The form, as John of Salisbury remarks apropos of Gilbert's doctrine,[4] is sensible in the sensible objects, but is conceived by the mind apart from sense, that is, immaterially, and while individual in each individual, it is yet common, or alike, in all the members of a species or genus.

His doctrines of abstraction and of comparison make it clear that Gilbert was a moderate realist and not an ultra-realist, but his curious idea of the distinction between the individual essence or substance and the common essence ('common' meaning alike in a plurality of individuals) landed him in difficulties when he came to apply it to the doctrine of the Blessed Trinity and distinguished as different things *Deus* and *Divinitas*, *Pater* and *Paternitas*, just as he would distinguish Socrates from humanity, that is, from the humanity of Socrates. He was accused of impairing the unity of God and teaching heresy, St. Bernard being one of his attackers. Condemned at the Council of Rheims in 1148, he retracted the offending propositions.

(ii) *John of Salisbury* (*c.* 1115–80) went to Paris in 1136 and there attended the lectures of, among others, Abelard, Gilbert de la Porrée. Adam Parvipontanus (Smallbridge) and Robert Pulleyn. He became secretary to the Archbishop of Canterbury, first to

[1] *In Boeth. de Trinit.*; *P.L.*, 64, 1393. Cf. John of Salisbury, *Metalog.*, 2, 17; *P.L.*, 64, 875–6.

[2] *P.L.*, 64, 1267. [3] *Ibid.*, 64, 1389. [4] *Ibid.*, 64, 875–6.

Archbishop Theobald and then to St. Thomas à Becket, being subsequently appointed Bishop of Chartres in 1176.

In discussing the problem of universals, says John, the world has grown old: more time has been taken up in this pursuit than was required by the Caesars for conquering and governing the world.[1] But anyone who looks for genera and species outside the things of sense is wasting his time:[2] ultra-realism is untrue and contradicts the teaching of Aristotle,[3] for whom John had a predilection in dialectical matters, remarking, apropos of the *Topics*, that it is of more use than almost all the books of dialectic which the moderns are accustomed to expound in the schools.[4] Genera and species are not things, but are rather the forms of things which the mind, comparing the likeness of things, abstracts and unifies in the universal concepts.[5] Universal concepts or genera and species abstractly considered are mental constructions (*figurata rationis*), since they do not exist as universals in extramental reality; but the construction in question is one of comparison of things and abstraction from things, so that universal concepts are not void of objective foundation and reference.[6]

10. It has been already mentioned that the School of St. Victor inclined to moderate realism. Thus *Hugh of St. Victor* (1096–1141) adopted more or less the position of Abelard and maintained a clear doctrine of abstraction, which he applied to mathematics and to physics. It is the province of mathematics to attend to *actus confusos inconfuse*,[7] abstracting, in the sense of attending to in isolation, the line or the plane surface, for example, although neither lines nor surfaces exist apart from bodies. In physics, too, the physicist considers in abstraction the properties of the four elements, although in concrete reality they are found only in varying combinations. Similarly the dialectician considers the forms of things in isolation or abstraction, in a unified concept, though in actual reality the forms of sensible things exist neither in isolation from matter nor as universals.

11. The foundations of the Thomist doctrine of moderate realism had thus been laid before the thirteenth century, and indeed we may say that it was Abelard who really killed ultra-realism. When St. Thomas declares that universals are not subsistent things but exist only in singular things,[8] he is re-echoing what Abelard and John of Salisbury had said before him. Humanity,

[1] *Polycrat.*, 7, 12. [2] *Metal.*, 2, 20. [3] *Ibid.* [4] *Ibid.*, 3, 10.
[5] *Ibid.*, 2, 20. [6] *Ibid.*, 3, 3. [7] *Didasc.*, 2, 18; *P.L.*, 176, 785.
[8] *Contra Gent.*, 1, 65.

for instance, human nature, has existence only in this or that man, and the universality which attaches to humanity in the concept is a result of abstraction, and so is in a sense a subjective contribution.[1] But this does not involve the falsity of the universal concept. If we were to abstract the specific form of a thing and at the same time think that it actually existed in a state of abstraction, our idea would indeed be false, for a false judgement concerning the thing itself would be involved; but, though in the universal concept the mind conceives something in a manner different to its mode of concrete existence, our judgement about the thing itself is not erroneous; it is simply that the form, which exists in the thing in an individualised state, is abstracted, i.e. is made the object of the exclusive attention of the mind by an immaterial activity. The objective foundation of the universal specific concept is thus the objective and individual essence of the thing, which essence is by the activity of the mind set free from individualising factors, that is, according to St. Thomas, matter, and considered in abstraction. For example, the mind abstracts from the individual man the essence of humanity which is alike, but not numerically the same in the members of the human species, while the foundation of the universal generic concept is an essential determination which several species have in common, as the species of man, horse, dog, etc., have 'animality' in common.

St. Thomas thus denied both forms of ultra-realism, that of Plato and that of the early mediaevals; but, no more than Abelard was he willing to reject Platonism lock, stock and barrel, that is to say, Platonism as developed by St. Augustine. The ideas, exemplar ideas, exist in the divine mind, though not ontologically distinct from God nor really a plurality, and, as far as this truth is concerned, the Platonic theory is justified.[2] St. Thomas thus admits (i) the *universale ante rem*, while insisting that it is not a subsistent thing, either apart from things (Plato) or in things (early mediaeval ultra-realists), for it is God considered as perceiving His Essence as imitable *ad extra* in a certain type of creature; (ii) the *universale in re*, which is the concrete individual essence alike in the members of the species; and (iii) the *universale post rem*, which is the abstract universal concept.[3] Needless to say, the term *universale in re*, used in the *Commentary on the Sentences*, is to be interpreted in the light of St. Thomas's general doctrine.

[1] *S.T.*, Ia, 85, 1, ad 1; Ia, 85, 2, ad 2.
[2] *Contra Gent.*, 3, 24.
[3] *In Sent.*, 2; *Dist.* 3, 2 ad 1.

i.e. as the *foundation* of the universal concept, the foundation being the concrete essence or *quidditas rei.*[1]

In the later Middle Ages the problem of universals was to be taken up afresh and a different solution was to be given by William of Ockham and his followers; but the principle that only individuals exist as subsistent things had come to stay: the new current in the fourteenth century was set not towards realism but away from it. The history of this movement I shall consider in the next volume.

[1] The distinction between *universale ante rem, in re* and *post rem* had been made by Avicenna.

CHAPTER XV

ST. ANSELM OF CANTERBURY

St. Anselm as philosopher—Proofs of God's existence in the Monologium—*The proof of God's existence in the* Proslogium—*Idea of truth and other Augustinian elements in St. Anselm's thought.*

1. ST. ANSELM was born at Aosta in Piedmont in 1033. After preliminary studies in Burgundy, at Avranches and afterwards at Bec he entered the Benedictine Order and later became Prior of Bec (1063), and subsequently abbot (1078). In 1093 he became Archbishop of Canterbury in succession to his former teacher, friend and religious superior Lanfranc, and in that post he died (1109).

In general the thought of St. Anselm is rightly said to belong to the Augustinian tradition. Like the great African Doctor, he devoted his chief intellectual effort to the understanding of the doctrine of the Christian faith and the statement of his attitude which is contained in the *Proslogium*[1] bears the unmistakable stamp of the Augustinian spirit. 'I do not attempt, O Lord, to penetrate Thy profundity, for I deem my intellect in no way sufficient thereunto, but I desire to understand in some degree Thy truth, which my heart believes and loves. For I do not seek to understand, in order that I may believe; but I believe, that I may understand. For I believe this too, that unless I believed, I should not understand.' This *Credo, ut intelligam* attitude is common to both Augustine and Anselm, and Anselm is in full accord with Augustine when he remarks in the *Cur Deus Homo*[2] that it is negligence if we make no attempt to understand what we believe. In practice, of course, this means for Anselm an application of dialectic or reasoning to the dogmas of faith, not in order to strip them of mystery but in order to penetrate them, develop them and discern their implications, so far as this is possible to the human mind, and the results of this process, for instance his book on the Incarnation and Redemption (*Cur Deus Homo*), make Anselm of importance in the history of theological development and speculation.

Now, the application of dialectic to the data of theology remains

[1] *P.L.*, 158, 227. [2] *Ibid.*, 158, 362.

theology, and St. Anselm would scarcely earn a place in the history of philosophy through his theological speculation and developments, except indeed as the application of philosophical categories to revealed dogmas necessarily involves some treatment and development of those philosophical categories. In point of fact, however, the use of the *Credo, ut intelligam* motto was not confined by Anselm, any more than by Augustine, to the understanding of those truths exclusively which have been revealed and not discovered dialectically, but was extended to truths like the existence of God, which are indeed believed but which can be reached by human reasoning. Besides, then, his work as dogmatic theologian there is also his work as natural theologian or metaphysician to be considered, and on this count alone St. Anselm deserves a place in the history of philosophy, since he contributed to the development of that branch of philosophy which is known as natural theology. Whether his arguments for the existence of God are considered valid or invalid, the fact that he elaborated these arguments systematically is of importance and gives his work a title to serious consideration by the historian of philosophy.

St. Anselm, like St. Augustine, made no clear distinction between the provinces of theology and philosophy, and his implied attitude of mind may be illustrated as follows. The Christian should try to understand and to apprehend rationally all that he believes, so far as this is possible to the human mind. Now, we believe in God's existence and in the doctrine of the Blessed Trinity. We should, therefore, apply our understanding to the understanding of both truths. From the point of view of one who, like the Thomist, makes a clear distinction between philosophy and dogmatic theology the application of reasoning to the first truth, God's existence, will fall within the province of philosophy, while the application of reasoning to the second truth, the Trinity, will fall within the province of theology, and the Thomist will hold that the first truth is demonstrable by human reasoning, while the second truth is not demonstrable by human reasoning, even though the human mind is able to make true statements about the mystery, once revealed, and to refute the objections against it which human reasoning may raise. But, if one puts oneself in the position of St. Anselm, that is, in a state of mind anterior to the clear distinction between philosophy and theology, it is easy to see how the fact that the first truth is demonstrable, coupled with the desire to understand all that we believe, the attempt to satisfy this desire being regarded as a duty, naturally leads to an attempt to demonstrate the second truth as well, and in point of fact St. Anselm speaks of demonstrating the Trinity of Persons by 'necessary reasons'[1] and of showing in the same way that it is impossible for a man to be saved without Christ.[2] If one wishes to call this 'rationalism', as has been done, one should first of all be quite clear as to what one means by rationalism. If by rationalism one means an attitude of mind which denies revelation and faith, St. Anselm was certainly no rationalist, since he accepted the primacy of faith and the fact of authority and only then went on to attempt to understand the data of faith. If, however, one is going to extend the term 'rationalism' to cover the attitude of mind which leads to the attempt to prove mysteries, not because the mysteries are not accepted by faith or would be rejected if one could not prove them, but because one desires to understand all that one believes, without having first clearly defined the ways in which different truths are accessible to us, then one might, of course, call the thought of St. Anselm 'rationalism' or an approximation to rationalism. But it would show an entire misunderstanding of Anselm's attitude, were one to suppose that he was prepared to reject the doctrine of the Trinity, for example, if he was unable to find *rationes necessariae* for it: he believed the doctrine first of all, and only then did he attempt to understand it. The dispute about Anselm's rationalism or non-rationalism is quite beside the point, unless one first grasps quite clearly the fact that he had no intention of impairing the integrity of the Christian faith: if we insist on interpreting St. Anselm as though he lived after St. Thomas and had clearly distinguished the separate provinces of theology and philosophy, we shall only be guilty of an anachronism and of a misinterpretation.

2. In the *Monologium*[3] St. Anselm develops the proof of God's existence from the degrees of perfection which are found in creatures. In the first chapter he applies the argument to goodness, and in the second chapter to 'greatness', meaning, as he tells us, not quantitative greatness, but a quality like wisdom, the more of which a subject possesses, the better, for greater quantitative size does not prove qualitative superiority. Such qualities are found in varying degrees in the objects of experience, so that the argument proceeds from the empirical observation of degrees of,

[1] *De fide Trin.*, 4; *P.L.*, 158, 272. [2] *Cur Deus Homo*; *P.L.*, 158, 361.
[3] *P.L.*, 158.

for example, goodness, and is therefore an *a posteriori* argument. But judgement about different degrees of perfection (St. Anselm assumes, of course, that the judgement is objectively grounded) implies a reference to a standard of perfection, while the fact that things participate objectively in goodness in different degrees shows that the standard is itself objective, that there is, for example, an absolute goodness in which all good things participate, to which they approximate more or less nearly, as the case may be.

This type of argument is Platonic in character (though Aristotle also argued, in his Platonic phase, that where there is a better, there must be a best) and it reappears in the *Via quarta* of St. Thomas Aquinas. It is, as I have said, an *a posteriori* argument: it does not proceed from the idea of absolute goodness to the existence of absolute goodness but from observed degrees of goodness to the existence of absolute goodness and from degrees of wisdom to the existence of absolute wisdom, the absolute goodness and wisdom being then identified as God. The developed form of the argument would necessitate, of course, a demonstration both of the objectivity of the judgement concerning the differing degrees of goodness and also of the principle on which St. Anselm rests the argument, the principle, namely that if objects possess goodness in a limited degree, they must have their goodness from absolute goodness itself, which is good *per se* and not *per aliud*. It is also to be noted that the argument can be applied only to those perfections which do not *of themselves* involve limitation and finiteness: it could not be applied to quantitative size, for instance. (Whether the argument is valid and demonstrative or not, it is scarcely the province of the historian to decide.)

In the third chapter of the *Monologium* St. Anselm applies the same sort of argument to being. Whatever exists, exists either through something or through nothing. The latter supposition is absurd; so whatever exists, must exist through something. This means that all existing things exist either through one another or through themselves or through one cause of existence. But that X should exist through Y, and Y through X, is unthinkable: the choice lies between a plurality of uncaused causes or one such cause. So far indeed the argument is a simple argument from causality, but St. Anselm goes on to introduce a Platonic element when he argues that if there is a plurality of existent things which have being of themselves, i.e. are self-dependent and uncaused, there is a form of being-of-itself in which all participate, and at this point the argument becomes similar to the argument already outlined, the implication being that, when several beings possess the same form, there must be a unitary being external to them which *is* that form. There can, therefore, be but one self-existent or ultimate Being, and this must be the best and highest and greatest of all that is.

In chapters seven and eight St. Anselm considers the relation between the caused and the Cause and argues that all finite objects are made out of nothing, *ex nihilo*, not out of a preceding matter nor out of the Cause as matter. He explains carefully that to say that a thing is made *ex nihilo* is not to say that it is made out of nothing as its material: it means that something is created *non ex aliquo*, that, whereas before it had no existence outside the divine mind, it now has existence. This may seem obvious enough, but it has sometimes been maintained that to say that a creature is made *ex nihilo* is either to make nothing something or to lay oneself open to the observation that *ex nihilo nihil fit*, whereas St. Anselm makes it clear that *ex nihilo* does not mean *ex nihilo tamquam materia* but simply *non ex aliquo*.

As to the attributes of the *Ens a Se*, we can predicate of it only those qualities, to possess which is *absolutely* better than not to possess them.[1] For example, to be gold is better for gold than to be lead, but it would not be better for a man to be made of gold. To be corporeal is better than to be nothing at all, but it would not be better for a spirit to be corporeal rather than incorporeal. To be gold is better than not to be gold only *relatively*, and to be corporeal rather than non-corporeal is better only *relatively*. But it is *absolutely* better to be wise than not to be wise, living than non-living, just than not-just. We must, then, predicate wisdom, life, justice, of the supreme Being, but we cannot predicate corporeity or gold of the supreme Being. Moreover, as the supreme Being does not possess His attributes through participation, but through His own essence, He *is* Wisdom, Justice, Life, etc.,[2] and furthermore, since the supreme Being cannot be composed of elements (which would then be logically anterior, so that He would not be the supreme Being), these attributes are identical with the divine essence, which is simple.[3] Again, God must necessarily transcend space in virtue of His simplicity and spirituality, and time, in virtue of His eternity.[4] He is wholly present in everything but not locally or *determinate*, and all things

[1] Ch. 15. [2] Ch. 16. [3] Ch. 17. [4] Ch. 20–4.

are present to His eternity, which is not to be conceived as endless time but as *interminabilis vita simul perfecte tota existens.*[1] We may call Him substance, if we refer to the divine essence, but not if we refer to the category of substance, since He is incapable of change or of sustaining accidents.[2] In fine, if we apply to Him any name that we also apply to creatures, *valde procul dubio intelligenda est diversa significatio.*

St. Anselm proceeds, in the *Monologium*, to give reasons for the Trinity of Persons in one Nature, without giving any clear indication that he is conscious of leaving the province of one science to enter that of another, and into this subject, interesting as it may be to the theologian, we cannot follow him. Enough has been said, however, to show that St. Anselm made a real contribution to natural theology. The Platonic element is conspicuous and, apart from remarks here and there, there is no considered treatment of analogy; but he gives *a posteriori* arguments for God's existence which are of a much more systematic character than those of St. Augustine and he also deals carefully with the divine attributes, God's immutability, eternity, etc. It is clear, then, how erroneous it is to associate his name with the 'Ontological Argument' in such a way as to imply that St. Anselm's only contribution to the development of philosophy was an argument the validity of which is at least questionable. His work may have not exercised any very considerable influence on contemporary thinkers and those who immediately followed him, because of their preoccupation with other matters (dialectical problems, reconciling the opinions of the Fathers, and so on), but looked at in the light of the general development of philosophy in the Middle Ages he must be acknowledged as one of the main contributors to Scholastic philosophy and theology, on account both of his natural theology and of his application of dialectic to dogma.

3. In the *Proslogium* St. Anselm develops the so-called 'ontological argument', which proceeds from the idea of God to God as a reality, as existent. He tells us that the requests of his brethren and consideration of the complex and various arguments of the *Monologium* led him to inquire whether he could not find an argument which would be sufficient, by itself alone, to prove all that we believe concerning the Divine Substance, so that one argument would fulfil the function of the many complementary arguments of his former *opusculum*. At length he thought that he

[1] Ch. 24. [2] Ch. 26.

had discovered such an argument, which for convenience sake may be put into syllogistic form, though St. Anselm himself develops it under the form of an address to God.

God is that than which no greater can be thought:
But that than which no greater can be thought must exist, not only mentally, in idea, but also extramentally:
Therefore God exists, not only in idea, mentally, but also extramentally.
The *Major Premiss* simply gives the idea of God, the idea which a man has of God, even if he denies His existence.
The *Minor Premiss* is clear, since if that than which no greater can be thought existed only in the mind, it would not be that than which no greater can be thought. A greater could be thought, i.e. a being that existed in extramental reality as well as in idea.

This proof starts from the idea of God as that than which no greater can be conceived, i.e. as absolutely perfect: that is what is *meant* by God.

Now, if such a being had only ideal reality, existed only in our subjective idea, we could still conceive a greater being, namely a being which did not exist simply in our idea but in objective reality. It follows, then, that the idea of God as absolute perfection is necessarily the idea of an existent Being, and St. Anselm argues that in this case no one can at the same time have the idea of God and yet deny His existence. If a man thought of God as, for instance, a superman, he would be quite right to deny 'God's' existence in that sense, but he would not really be denying the objectivity of the idea of God. If, however, a man had the right idea of God, conceived the meaning of the term 'God', he could indeed deny His existence with his lips, but if he realises what the denial involves (i.e. saying that the Being which must exist of its essence, the necessary Being, does not exist) and yet asserts the denial, he is guilty of a plain contradiction: it is only the fool, the *insipiens*, who has said *in his heart*, 'there is no God.' The absolutely perfect Being is a Being the essence of which is to exist or which necessarily involves existence, since otherwise a more perfect being could be conceived; it is the necessary Being; and a necessary being which did not exist would be a contradiction in terms.

St. Anselm wanted his argument to be a demonstration of all that we believe concerning the divine Nature, and, since the argument concerns the absolutely perfect Being, the attributes of God are contained implicitly in the conclusion of the argument. We have only to ask ourselves what is implied by the idea of a Being than which no greater can be thought, in order to see that God must be omnipotent, omniscient, supremely just and so on. Moreover, when deducing these attributes in the *Proslogium*, St. Anselm gives some attention to the clarification of the notions in question. For example, God cannot lie: is not this a sign of lack of omnipotence? No, he answers, to be able to lie should be called impotence rather than power, imperfection rather than perfection. If God could act in a manner inconsistent with His essence, that would be a lack of power on His part. Of course, it might be objected that this *presupposes* that we already know what God's essence is or involves, whereas what God's essence is, is precisely the point to be shown; but St. Anselm would presumably reply that he has already established that God is all-perfect and so that He is both omnipotent and truthful: it is merely a question of showing what the omnipotence of perfection really means and of exposing the falsity of a wrong idea of omnipotence.

The argument given by St. Anselm in the *Proslogium* was attacked by the monk Gaunilo in his *Liber pro Insipiente adversus Anselmi in Proslogio ratiocinationem*, wherein he observed that the idea we have of a thing is no guarantee of its extramental existence and that St. Anselm was guilty of an illicit transition from the logical to the real order. We might as well say that the most beautiful islands which are possible must exist somewhere, because we can conceive them. The Saint, in his *Liber Apologeticus contra Gaunilonem respondentem pro Insipiente*, denied the parity, and denied it with justice, since, if the idea of God is the idea of an all-perfect Being and if absolute perfection involves existence, this idea is the idea of an existent, and necessarily existent Being, whereas the idea of even the most beautiful islands is not the idea of something which must exist: even in the purely logical order the two ideas are not on a par. If God is possible, i.e. if the idea of the all-perfect and necessary Being contains no contradiction, God must exist, since it would be absurd to speak of a *merely possible necessary Being* (it is a contradiction in terms), whereas there is no contradiction in speaking of merely possible beautiful islands. The main objection to St. Anselm's proof, which was raised against Descartes and which Leibniz tried to answer, is that we do not know *a priori* that the idea of God, the idea of infinite and absolute Perfection, is the idea of a *possible* Being. *We* may not see any contradiction in the idea, but, say the objectors, this 'negative' possibility is not the same as 'positive' possibility; it does not show that there really is no contradiction in the idea. That there is no contradiction in the idea is clear only when we have shown *a posteriori* that God exists.

The argument of the *Proslogium* aroused little immediate interest; but in the thirteenth century it was employed by St. Bonaventure, with a less logical and more psychological emphasis, while it was rejected by St. Thomas. Duns Scotus used it as an incidental aid. In the 'modern' era it has had a distinguished, if chequered career. Descartes adopted and adapted it, Leibniz defended it in a careful and ingenious manner, Kant attacked it. In the Schools it is generally rejected, though some individual thinkers have maintained its validity.

4. Among the Augustinian characteristics of St. Anselm's philosophy one may mention his theory of truth. When he is treating of truth in the judgement,[1] he follows the Aristotelian view in making it consist in this, that the judgement or proposition states what actually exists or denies what does not exist, the thing signified being the cause of the truth, the truth itself residing in the judgement (correspondence-theory); but when, after treating of truth (rectitude) in the will,[2] he goes on to speak of the truth of being or essence[3] and makes the truth of things to consist in being what they 'ought' to be, that is, in their embodiment of or correspondence to their idea in God, the supreme Truth and standard of truth, and when he concludes from the eternal truth of the judgement to the eternity of the cause of truth, God,[4] he is treading in the footsteps of Augustine. God, therefore, is the eternal and subsistent Truth, which is cause of the ontological truth of all creatures. The eternal truth is only cause and the truth of the judgement is only effect, while the ontological truth of things is at once effect (of eternal Truth) and cause (of truth in the judgement). This Augustinian conception of ontological truth, with the exemplarism it presupposes, was retained by St. Thomas in the thirteenth century, though he laid far more emphasis, of course, on the truth of the judgement. Thus, whereas St. Thomas's characteristic definition of truth is *adaequatio rei et intellectus*, that of St. Anselm is *rectitudo sola mente perceptibilis*.[5]

In his general way of speaking of the relation of soul to body and in the absence of a theory of hylomorphic composition of the

[1] *Dialogus de Veritate*, 2; *P.L.*, 158. [2] *Dial.*, 4. [3] *Ibid.*, 7 ff.
[4] *Ibid.*, 10. [5] *Ibid.*, 11.

two, Anselm follows the Platonic-Augustinian tradition, though, like Augustine himself, he was perfectly well aware that soul and body form one man, and he affirms the fact. Again, his words in the *Proslogium*[1] on the divine light recall the illumination-theory of Augustine: *Quanta namque est lux illa, de qua micat omne verum, quod rationali menti lucet.*

In general perhaps one might say that though the philosophy of Anselm stands in the line of the Augustinian tradition, it is more systematically elaborated than the corresponding elements of Augustine's thought, his natural theology, that is, and that in the methodic application of dialectic it shows the mark of a later age.

[1] Ch. 14.

CHAPTER XVI
THE SCHOOL OF CHARTRES

*Universalism of Paris, and systematisation of sciences in twelfth century—Regionalism, humanism—Platonism of Chartres—Hylomorphism at Chartres—*Prima facie *pantheism—John of Salisbury's political theory.*

1. ONE of the greatest contributions made by the Middle Ages to the development of European civilisation was the university system, and the greatest of all mediaeval universities was unquestionably that of Paris. This great centre of theological and philosophical studies did not receive its definitive charter as a University in the formal sense until early in the thirteenth century; but one may speak, in an untechnical sense, of the Parisian schools as already forming a 'university' in the twelfth century. Indeed in some respects the twelfth century was more dominated by French learning than was the thirteenth century, since it was in the thirteenth century that other universities, such as Oxford, came into prominence and began to display a spirit of their own. This is true of northern Europe at least: as to the South, the University of Bologna, for instance, received its first charter in 1158, from Frederick I. But, though France was the great centre of intellectual activity in the twelfth century, a fact which led to the oft-quoted saying that 'Italy has the Papacy, Germany the Empire, and France has Knowledge', this does not mean, of course, that intellectual activity was pursued simply by Frenchmen: European culture was international, and the intellectual supremacy of France meant that students, scholars and professors came in large numbers to the French schools. From England came men like Adam Smallbridge and Alexander Neckham, twelfth-century dialecticians, Adelard of Bath and Robert Pulleyn, Richard of St. Victor (d. 1173) and John of Salisbury; from Germany, Hugh of St. Victor (d. 1141), theologian, philosopher and mystic; from Italy, Peter Lombard (*c.* 1100–60), author of the celebrated *Sentences*, which were made the subject of so many commentaries during the Middle Ages, by St. Thomas Aquinas and Duns Scotus, for example. Thus the University of Paris may be said to have represented the international character of mediaeval European

culture, as the Papacy represented the international, or rather supra-national, character of mediaeval religion, though the two were, of course, closely bound together, as the one religion gave a common intellectual outlook and the language of learning, the Latin tongue, was the language of the Church. These two unities, the religious and the cultural, so closely bound together, were what one might call effective and real unities, whereas the political unity of the Holy Roman Empire was rather theoretical than effective, for, though the absolute monarchies were a development of the future, nationalism was already beginning to increase, even if its growth was checked by feudalism, by the local character of mediaeval political and economic institutions and by the common language and intellectual outlook.

This growing and expanding university life naturally found an intellectual and academic expression in the attempt to classify and systematise the science, knowledge and speculation of the time, an attempt which shows itself already in the twelfth century. We may give two examples, the systematisations of Hugh of St. Victor and of Peter Lombard. The former, in his *Didascalion,*[1] more or less follows the Aristotelian classification. Thus Logic is a propaedeutic or preamble to science proper and deals with concepts, not with things. It is divided into Grammar and into the *Ratio Disserendi*, which in turn subdivides into *Demonstratio, Pars Probabilis* and *Pars Sophistica* (Dialectic, Rhetoric and Sophistic). Science, to which Logic is a preamble and for which it is a necessary instrument, is divided under the main headings of Theoretical Science, Practical Science and 'Mechanics'. Theoretical Science comprises Theology, Mathematics (Arithmetic, dealing with the numerical aspect of things; Music, dealing with proportion; Geometry, concerned with the extension of things; Astronomy, concerned with the movement of things), and Physics (which has as its subject-matter the inner nature or inner qualities of things, and thus penetrates farther than Mathematics). Practical Science is subdivided into Ethics, 'Economics' and Politics, while Mechanics comprises the seven 'illiberal arts' or *scientiae adulterinae*, since the craftsman borrows his form from nature. These 'illiberal arts' are Wool-making, etc., Armoury and Carpentry, Navigation or Commerce, which, according to Hugh, 'reconciles peoples, quiets wars, strengthens peace, and makes private goods to be for the common use of all', Agriculture, Hunting (including cookery),

[1] *P.L.*, 176

Medicine and Theatricals. It is clear that Hugh's classification depended, not only on Aristotle, through Boethius, but also on the encyclopaedic work of writers like Isidore of Seville.

Peter Lombard, who was educated at the School of St. Victor, taught at the Cathedral School of Paris, and ultimately became bishop of that city between 1150 and 1152, composed his *Libri Quattuor Sententiarum*, a work which, although unoriginal in respect of content, exercised a tremendous influence, in that it stimulated other writers to the work of systematic and comprehensive exposition of dogma and became itself the subject of compendia and many commentaries, up to the end of the sixteenth century. The *Sentences* of the Lombard are admittedly a text-book[1] and were designed to gather the opinions or *sententiae* of the Fathers on theological doctrines, the first book being devoted to God, the second to creatures, the third to the Incarnation and Redemption and to the virtues, the fourth to the seven Sacraments and to the last things. The greatest number of quotations and the bulk of the doctrine are taken from St. Augustine, though other Latin Fathers are quoted, and even St. John Damascene makes an appearance, though it has been shown that the Lombard had seen only a small part of Burgundius of Pisa's Latin translation of the *Fons Scientiae*. Obviously enough the *Sentences* are predominantly a theological work, but the Lombard speaks of those things which are understood by the natural reason and can be so understood before they are believed, i.e. by faith:[2] such are the existence of God, the creation of the world by God and the immortality of the soul.

2. We have seen that the developing and expanding intellectual life of the twelfth century showed itself in the growing predominance of the 'university' of Paris and in the first attempts at classification and systematisation of knowledge; but the position of Paris did not mean that regional schools were not flourishing. Indeed, vigour of local life and interests was a complementary feature in the mediaeval period to the international character of religious and intellectual life. For example, though some of the scholars who came to Paris to study remained there to teach, others returned to their own lands or provinces or became attached to local educational institutions. Indeed there was a tendency to specialisation, Bologna, for instance, being noted for its school of law and Montpellier for medicine, while mystical theology

[1] Cf. the Prologue. [2] 3, 24, 3.

was a prominent feature of the School of St. Victor, outside Paris.

One of the most flourishing and interesting of the local schools of the twelfth century was that of Chartres, in which certain Aristotelian doctrines, to be noted presently, began to come into prominence, associated, however, with a very strong admixture of Platonism. This school was also associated with humanistic studies. Thus *Theodoric of Chartres* (Thierry), who, after being in charge of the school in 1121, taught at Paris, only to return to Chartres in 1141, where he became chancellor in succession to Gilbert de la Porrée, was described by John of Salisbury, himself a humanist, as *artium studiosissimus investigator*. His *Heptateuchon* was concerned with the seven liberal arts and he vigorously combated the anti-humanists, the 'Cornificians', who decried study and literary form. Similarly *William of Conches* (*c.* 1080–1154), who studied under Bernard of Chartres, taught at Paris and became tutor to Henry Plantagenet, attacked the Cornificians and himself paid attention to grammatical studies, thereby drawing from John of Salisbury the assertion that he was the most gifted grammarian after Bernard of Chartres.[1] But it was *John of Salisbury* (1115/20–1180) who was the most gifted of the humanist philosophers associated with Chartres. Though not educated at Chartres, he became, as we have seen earlier, Bishop of Chartres in 1176. A champion of the liberal arts and acquainted with the Latin classics, with Cicero in particular, he had a detestation for barbarity in style, dubbing those persons who opposed style and rhetoric on principle 'Cornificians'. Careful of his own literary style, he represents what was best in twelfth-century philosophic humanism, as St. Bernard, though not perhaps with full intention, represents humanism by his hymns and spiritual writings. In the next century, the thirteenth, one would certainly not go to the works of the philosophers as such for Latinity, most of them being far more concerned with content than with form.

3. The School of Chartres, though its *floreat* fell in the twelfth century, had a long history, having been founded in 990 by *Fulbert*, a pupil of *Gerbert of Aurillac*. (The latter was a very distinguished figure of the tenth century, humanist and scholar, who taught at Rheims and Paris, paid several visits to the court of the German Emperor, became in turn Abbot of Bobbio, Archbishop of Rheims and Archbishop of Ravenna, and ascended the

[1] *Metal.*, 1, 5.

papal throne as Sylvester II, dying in 1003.) Founded in the tenth century, the School of Chartres preserved, even in the twelfth century, a certain conservative spirit and flavour, which shewed itself in its Platonist tradition, especially in its devotion to the *Timaeus* of Plato and also to the more Platonically inclined writings of Boethius. Thus *Bernard of Chartres*, who was head of the school from 1114 to 1119 and chancellor from 1119 to 1124, maintained that matter existed in a chaotic state before its information, before order was brought out of disorder. Called by John of Salisbury the 'most perfect among the Platonists of our time',[1] Bernard also represented Nature as an organism and maintained the Platonic theory of the World-Soul. In this he was followed by *Bernard of Tours* (*Silvestris*), who was chancellor at Chartres about 1156 and composed a poem *De mundi universitate*, using Chalcidius's commentary on the *Timaeus* and depicting the World-Soul as animating Nature and forming natural beings out of the chaos of prime matter according to the Ideas existing in God or *Nous*. William of Conches went even further by identifying the World-Soul with the Holy Spirit, a doctrine which led to his being attacked by William of St. Theodoric. Retracting, he explained that he was a Christian and not a member of the Academy.

In conjunction with these speculations in the spirit of the *Timaeus* one may mention the inclination of the School of Chartres to ultra-realism, though, as we have seen, two of the most outstanding figures associated with Chartres, Gilbert de la Porrée and John of Salisbury, were not ultra-realists. Thus *Clarembald of Arras*, a pupil of Theodoric of Chartres, who became Provost of Arras in 1152 and Archdeacon of Arras in 1160, maintained, in his Commentary on the *De Trinitate* of Boethius, as against Gilbert de la Porrée, that there is but one and the same humanity in all men and that individual men differ only *propter accidentium varietatem*.[2]

4. In spite, however, of their fondness for the *Timaeus* of Plato, the members of the School of Chartres showed also an esteem for Aristotle. Not only did they follow Aristotle in logic, but they also introduced his hylomorphic theory: indeed it was at Chartres that this theory made its first appearance in the twelfth century. Thus, according to Bernard of Chartres, natural objects are constituted by form and matter. These forms he called *formae nativae* and he represented them as copies of the Ideas in God. This information we have from John of Salisbury, who tells us that Bernard and his

[1] *Metal.*, 4, 35.

[2] Ed. W. Janssen, p. 42.

disciples tried to mediate between or reconcile Plato and Aristotle.[1] For Bernard of Tours too the forms of things are copies of the Ideas in God, as we have already seen, while Clarembald of Arras represented matter as being always in a state of flux and as being the mutability or *vertibilitas* of things, the form being the perfection and integrity of the thing.[2] He thus interpreted the matter of Aristotle in the light of Plato's teaching about the mutability and evanescent character of material things. William of Conches indeed struck out on a line of his own by maintaining the atomic theory of Democritus;[3] but in general we may say that the members of the School of Chartres adopted the hylomorphic theory of Aristotle, though they interpreted it in the light of the *Timaeus*.[4]

5. The doctrine that natural objects are composed of matter and form, the form being a copy of the exemplar, the Idea in God, clearly makes a distinction between God and creatures and is non-pantheistic in character; but certain members of this School used terminology which, if taken literally and without qualification, would naturally be understood to imply pantheism. Thus Theodoric of Chartres, who was the younger brother of Bernard, maintained that 'all forms are one form; the divine form is all forms' and that the divinity is the *forma essendi* of each thing, while creation is depicted as the production of the many out of the one.[5] Again, Clarembald of Arras argued that God is the *forma essendi* of things and that, since the *forma essendi* must be present wherever a thing is, God is always and everywhere essentially present.[6] But, though these texts, taken literally and in isolation, are pantheistic or monistic in character, it does not appear that either Theodoric of Chartres or Clarembald of Arras meant to teach a monistic doctrine. For instance, immediately after saying that the divine form is all forms Theodoric observes that, though the divine form is all forms by the fact that it is the perfection and integrity of all things, one may not conclude that the divine form is humanity. It would seem that Theodoric's doctrine must be understood in the light of exemplarism, since he says expressly that the divine form cannot be embodied, and cannot, therefore, be the actual concrete form of man or horse or stone. Similarly, Clarembald of Arras's general doctrine of exemplarism and his

[1] *Metal.*, 2, 17. [2] Ed. W. Janssen, pp. 44 and 63. [3] *P.L.*, 90, 1132.

[4] Gilbert de la Porrée draws attention to the hylomorphic theory when commenting on Boethius's *Contra Eutychen* or *Liber de duabus Naturis et una Persona Christi*; *P.L.*, 64, 1367.

[5] *De sex dierum operibus*, ed. W. Janssen, pp. 16, 21, 108, 109.

[6] Ed. W. Janssen, p. 59.

insistence that the forms of material things are copies, *imagines*, is incompatible with full pantheism. The phrases which seem to teach a doctrine of emanation are borrowed from Boethius, and it is probable that they no more express a literal understanding of emanation in Theodoric or Clarembald than they do in Boethius: in a sense they are stock phrases, canonised, as it were, by their antiquity, and they should not be pressed unduly.

6. Although John of Salisbury was not educated at Chartres, it is convenient to say something here of his philosophy of the State, as given in his *Polycraticus*. The quarrels between the Holy See and the Empire and the investiture controversies had naturally led to those writers who took part in the disputes having to express some view, even if only by the way, on the function of the State and its ruler. One or two writers went beyond mere asides, as it were, and gave a rude sketch of political theory. Thus *Manegold of Lautenbach* (eleventh century) even referred the power of the ruler to a pact with the people[1] and declared[2] that if the king forsakes rule by law and becomes a tyrant, he is to be considered to have broken the pact to which he owes his power and may be deposed by the people. Such ideas concerning the reign of law and justice as essential to the State and concerning the natural law, of which the civil law should be an expression, were based on texts of Cicero, the Stoics and the Roman jurists, and they reappear in the thought of John of Salisbury, who also made use of St. Augustine's *De Civitate Dei* and the *De Officiis* of St. Ambrose.

Although John of Salisbury did not put forward any compact theory after the fashion of Manegold of Lautenbach, he was insistent that the prince is not above law and declared that whatever the whitewashers of rulers might trumpet abroad to the contrary, he would never allow that the prince is free from all restrictions and all law. But what did he mean when he said that the prince is subject to law? Partly at least he had in mind (and this was indeed his main consideration) the natural law, in accordance with the Stoic doctrine that there is a natural law, to which all positive law does, or ought to, approximate. The prince, then, is not free to enact positive laws which go counter to, or are irreconcilable with, both the natural law and that *aequitas* which is *rerum convenientia, tribuens unicuique quod suum est.* The positive law defines and applies natural law and natural justice, and the attitude of the ruler on this matter shows whether he is prince

[1] *Liber ad Gebehardum*, 30 and 47. [2] *Ibid.*, 47.

or tyrant. If his enactments define, apply or supplement natural law and natural justice, he is a prince; if they infringe natural law and natural justice, he is a tyrant, acting according to caprice and not fulfilling the function of his office.

Did John of Salisbury understand anything else by law, when he maintained that the prince is subject to the law? Did he maintain that the prince is in any way subject to defined law? It was certainly the common opinion that the prince was subject in some way to the customs of the land and the enactments of his ancestors, to the local systems of law or tradition which had grown up in the course of time, and, although John of Salisbury's political writing shows little concern with feudalism, since he relied so largely on writers of the Roman period, it is only reasonable to suppose that he shared the common outlook on this matter. His actual judgements on the power and office of the prince express the common outlook, though his formal approach to the subject is through the medium of Roman law, and he would certainly not have envisaged the application in an absolutist sense to the feudal monarch of the Roman Jurist's maxim, *Quod principi placuit legis habet vigorem*.

Now, since John of Salisbury praised Roman law and regarded it as one of the great civilising factors of Europe, he was faced with the necessity of interpreting the maxim quoted above, without at the same time sacrificing his convictions about the restricted power of the prince. First of all, how did Ulpian himself understand his maxim? He was a lawyer and it was his aim to justify, to explain the legality of the Emperor's enactments and *constitutiones*. According to Republican lawyers the law governed the magistrate, but it was obvious that in the time of the Empire the Emperor was himself one of the sources of positive law, and the lawyers had to explain the legality of this position. Ulpian accordingly said that, though the Emperor's legislative authority is derived from the Roman people, the people, by the *lex regia*, transfers to him and vests in him all its own power and authority, so that, once invested with his authority, the will of the Emperor has the force of law. In other words, Ulpian was simply explaining the legality of the Roman Emperor's enactments: he was not concerned to establish a political theory by maintaining that the Emperor was entitled to disregard all natural justice and the principles of morality. When John of Salisbury observed, with express reference to Ulpian's dictum, that when the prince is said to be free from the law, this is not to be understood in the sense that he may do what is unjust, but in the sense that he ought to follow equity or natural justice out of a real love of justice and not from fear of punishment, which does not apply to him, he was expressing the general tradition of feudal lawyers and at the same time was not contradicting Ulpian's maxim. When in the late Middle Ages some political theorists detached Ulpian's maxim from the person of the Emperor, and transferring it to the national monarch interpreted it in an absolutist sense, they were forsaking the general mediaeval outlook and were at the same time changing the legal maxim of Ulpian into an abstract statement of absolutist political theory.

In conclusion it may be remarked that John of Salisbury accepted the supremacy of the ecclesiastical power (*Hunc ergo gladium de manu Ecclesiae accipit princeps*),[1] while he carried his distinction between prince and tyrant to its logical conclusion by admitting tyrannicide as legitimate. Indeed, since the tyrant is opposed to the common good, tyrannicide may sometimes be obligatory,[2] though he made the curious stipulation that poison should not be employed for this purpose.

[1] *Polycrat.*, 4, 3. [2] *Ibid.*, 8, 10.

CHAPTER XVII

THE SCHOOL OF ST. VICTOR

Hugh of St. Victor; proofs of God's existence, faith, mysticism—Richard of St. Victor; proofs of God's existence—Godfrey of St. Victor and Walter of St. Victor.

THE Abbey of St. Victor outside the walls of Paris belonged to the Augustinian Canons. We have seen that William of Champeaux was associated with the abbey, retiring there after being worsted by Abelard, but the school is of note principally owing to the work of two men, one a German, Hugh of St. Victor, the other a Scotsman, Richard of St. Victor.

1. *Hugh of St. Victor* was born in Saxony in 1096 of noble parentage, and made his early studies in the monastery of Hamersleben near Halberstadt. After taking the habit he went to Paris in 1115 to continue his studies in the Abbey of St. Victor. In 1125 he started lecturing and from 1133 until his death in 1141 he was in charge of the school. One of the foremost theologians, dogmatic and mystical, of his time, he was yet no enemy to the cultivation of the arts, considering not only that the study of the arts, if rightly pursued, conduces to progress in theology, but also that all knowledge is of utility. 'Learn everything; you will see afterwards that nothing is superfluous.'[1] His chief work, from the philosophical viewpoint, is the *Didascalion* in seven books, in which he treats of the liberal arts (three books), theology (three books) and religious meditation (one book), but his writings on the theology of the Sacraments are also important to the theologian. He also compared exegetic and mystical works and a commentary on the *Celestial Hierarchy* of the Pseudo-Dionysius, using the Latin translation of John Scotus Eriugena.

Of Hugh's classification and systematisation of the sciences mention has already been made, in connection with the systematising tendency already discernible in the twelfth century and due partly to the application of dialectic in theology, as also of his theory of abstraction, in connection with the discussion on universals.[2] These two points bring out the Aristotelian aspects of his thought, whereas his psychology is distinctly Augustinian in

[1] *P.L.*, 176, 800C. [2] See p. 153.

character. 'No one is really wise who does not see that he exists; and yet, if a man begins truly to consider what he is, he sees that he is none of all those things which are either seen in him or can be seen. For that in us which is capable of reasoning, although it is, so to speak, infused into and mingled with the flesh, is yet distinguishable by reason from the substance of the flesh and is seen to be different therefrom.'[1] In other words, consciousness and introspection bear witness, not only to the existence of the soul, but also to its spirituality and immateriality. Moreover, the soul is of itself a person, having, as a rational spirit, personality of itself and through itself, the body forming an element in human personality only in virtue of its union with the rational spirit.[2] The mode of union is one of 'apposition' rather than of composition.[3]

Hugh contributed to the systematic advance of natural theology by giving *a posteriori* arguments both from internal and external experience. As regards the first line of proof, it rests upon the experiential fact of self-consciousness, the consciousness of a self which is 'seen' in a purely rational way and cannot be material. Regarding self-consciousness as necessary to the existence of a rational being, Hugh maintains that, as the soul has not always been conscious of its existence, there was a time when it did not exist. But it could not have given itself existence: it must, then, owe its existence to another being, and this being must be a necessary and self-existent being, God.[4] This proof is somewhat compressed, involving the premisses that the cause of a rational principle must itself be rational and that an infinite regress is impossible. Its 'interiority' certainly reminds one of Augustine, but it is not Augustine's proof from the soul's knowledge of eternal truths, nor does it presuppose religious, still less mystical, experience since it rests on the natural experience of the soul's self-consciousness, and it is this reliance on experience which characterises Hugh's proofs of God's existence.

The second proof, that from external experience,[5] rests on the experienced fact of change. Things are constantly coming into being and passing away, and the totality, which is composed of such changing things, must itself have had a beginning. It requires, therefore, a Cause. Nothing which lacks stability, which ceases to be, can have come into being without a Cause external to itself. The idea of such a proof is contained in the *De Fide Orthodoxa* of

[1] *P.L.*, 176, 825A. [2] *Ibid.*, 176, 409. [3] *Ibid.*
[4] *De Sacramentis*, 3, 7; *P.L.*, 176, 219.
[5] *De Sacramentis*, 3, 10; *P.L.*, 176, 219, and *Sent.* 1, 3; *P.L.*, 176, 45.

St. John Damascene;[1] but Hugh of St. Victor attempts to supply the deficiencies in St. John Damascene's procedure.

In addition to the proof from change Hugh gives a teleological proof in several parts.[2] In the world of animals we see that the senses and appetites find their satisfaction in objects: in the world in general we see a great variety of movements (the reference is to local motion), which, however, are ordered in harmony. Again, growth is a fact of experience, and growth, since it means the addition of something new, cannot be accomplished solely by the thing which grows. Hugh concludes that these three considerations exclude chance and postulate a Providence which is responsible for growth and guides all things according to law.[3] The proof is clearly somewhat unconvincing in the form given, but it is based on facts of experience, as the starting-point, and this is characteristic of Hugh's proofs in general. Hugh adopted the theory of William of Conches concerning the atomic structure of matter. These atoms are simple bodies, which are capable of increase and growth.[4]

Hugh was thus quite clear about the possibility of a natural knowledge of God's existence, but he was equally insistent on the necessity of faith. This faith is necessary, not only because the *oculus contemplationis*, whereby the soul apprehends God within herself *et ea quae in Deo erant*, has been completely darkened by sin, but also because mysteries which exceed the power of the human reason are proposed to man's beliefs. These mysteries are *supra rationem*, in that revelation and faith are required to apprehend them, but they are *secundum rationem*, not *contra rationem*: in themselves they are reasonable and can be the object of knowledge, but they cannot be the object of knowledge in the strict sense in this life, as man's mind is too weak, especially in its sin-darkened state. Knowledge, then, considered in itself, stands higher than faith, which is a certitude of the mind concerning absent things, superior to opinion but inferior to science or knowledge, since those who comprehend the object as immediately present (the *scientes*) are superior to those who believe on authority. We may say, therefore, that Hugh of St. Victor made a clear distinction between faith and knowledge and that, though he recognised the superiority of the latter, he did not thereby impugn the necessity of the former. His doctrine of the superiority of knowledge to faith is by no means equivalent to the Hegelian

[1] 1, 3; *P.G.*, 94, 796A. [2] *P.L.*, 176, 826.
[3] Cf. *De Fide Orthodoxa*, 1, 3; *P.G.*, 94, 795B.
[4] *De Sacramentis*, 1, 6, 37; *P.L.*, 176, 286.

doctrine, since Hugh certainly did not consider that knowledge can, naturally at least, be substituted for faith in this life.

But, though the *oculus contemplationis* has been darkened by sin, the mind, under the supernatural influence of grace, can ascend by degrees to contemplation of God in Himself. Thus supernatural mysticism crowns the ascent of knowledge in this life as the beatific vision of God crowns it in heaven. To enter upon a discussion of Hugh's mystical teaching would scarcely be in place here; but it is worth pointing out that the mystical tradition of St. Victor was not simply a spiritual luxury; their mystical theology formed an integral part of their theologico-philosophical synthesis. In philosophy God's existence is proved by the natural use of reason, while in theology the mind learns about the Nature of God and applies dialectic to the data of revelation accepted on faith. But philosophical knowledge and theological (dialectical) knowledge are knowledge about God: higher still is the experience of God, the direct knowledge of God, which is attained in mystical experience, a loving knowledge or a knowing love of God. On the other hand, mystical knowledge is not full vision, and God's presence to the soul in mystical experience blinds by excess of light, so that above both knowledge about God by faith and direct mystical knowledge of God there stands the beatific vision of heaven.

2. *Richard of St. Victor* was born in Scotland but went to Paris early in life and entered the Abbey of St. Victor, where he became sub-prior about 1157 and prior in 1162. He died in 1173. The abbey passed through a difficult period during these years, as the abbot, an Englishman named Ervisius, wasted its goods and ruined its discipline, behaving in such an independent manner that Pope Alexander III called him 'another Caesar'. With some difficulty he was induced to resign in 1172, a year before the death of Richard. However, even if his abbot was a somewhat independent and high-handed individual, the prior, we are told by the abbey necrology, left behind him the memory of a good example, a holy life and beautiful writings.

Richard is an important figure in mediaeval theology, his chief work being the *De Trinitate* in six books, but he was also a philosopher, as well as being a mystical theologian who published two works on contemplation, the *Beniamin minor*, on the preparation of the soul for contemplation, and the *Beniamin maior*, on the grace of contemplation. In other words, he was a worthy successor of Hugh of St. Victor, and like him he insisted on the necessity of using the reason in the pursuit and investigation of truth. 'I have frequently read that there is only one God, that He is eternal, uncreated, immense, omnipotent and Lord of all: . . . I have read concerning my God that He is one and three, one in Substance, three in Persons: all this I have read; but I do not remember that I have read how all these things are proved.'[1] Again, 'In all these matters authorities abound, but not arguments; in all these matters *experimenta desunt*, proofs are becoming rare; so I think that I shall have done something, if I am able to help the minds of the studious a little, even if I cannot satisfy them.'

The general attitude of St. Anselm is evident in the above quotations: *Credo, ut intelligam*. The data of the Christian religion presupposed, Richard of St. Victor sets out to understand them and to prove them. Just as St. Anselm had declared his intention of trying to prove the Blessed Trinity by 'necessary reasons', so Richard declares at the beginning of his *De Trinitate*[2] that it will be his intention in that work, so far as God grants, to adduce not only probable, but also necessary reasons for the things which we believe. He points out that there must be necessary reasons for what necessarily exists; so that, as God is necessarily Three in One, there must be a necessary reason for this fact. Of course, it by no means follows from the fact that God is necessarily Triune (God is the necessary Being) that we can discern this necessity, and Richard admits indeed that we cannot fully comprehend the mysteries of Faith, particularly that of the Blessed Trinity,[3] but that does not prevent his attempting to show that a plurality of Persons in the Godhead necessarily follows from the fact that God is Love and to demonstrate the trinity of Persons in one Nature.

Richard's speculation on the Trinity had a considerable influence on later Scholastic theology; but from the philosophical viewpoint his proofs for the existence of God are of greater import. Such proofs, he insists, must rest on experience: 'We ought to begin from that class of things, of which we can have no manner of doubt, and by means of those things which we know by experience to conclude rationally what we must think concerning the objects which transcend experience.'[4] These objects of experience are contingent objects, things which begin to be and can cease to

[1] *De Trinit.*, 1, 5; *P.L.*, 196, 893BC. [2] *P.L.*, 196, 892C. [3] *Ibid.*, 196, 72A.
[4] *Ibid.*, 196, 894.

be. Such things we can come to know only through experience, since what comes into being and can perish cannot be necessary, so that its existence cannot be demonstrated *a priori*, but can be known only by experience.[1]

The starting-point of the argument is thus provided by the contingent objects of experience; but, in order that our reasoning on this basis may be successful, it is necessary to start from a clearly solid and, as it were, immovable foundation of truth;[2] that is, the argument needs a sure and certain principle on which it may rest. This principle is that every thing which exists or can exist has being either of itself or from another than itself, and that every thing which exists or can exist either has being from eternity or begins to be in time. This application of the principle of contradiction allows us to form a division of being. Any existent thing must be either (i) from eternity and from itself, and so self-existent, or (ii) neither from eternity nor from itself, or (iii) from eternity, but not from itself, or (iv) not from eternity but yet from itself. This logical division into four admits immediately of a reduction to a threefold division, since a thing which is not from eternity but is *a se*, is impossible, for a thing which began to be obviously cannot either have given itself being or be a necessary existent.[3] A beginning in time and aseity are thus incompatible, and it remains to refer back to the things of experience and apply the general principle. The things of experience, as we observe them in the human, animal and vegetable kingdoms, and in nature in general, are perishable and contingent: they begin to be. If, then, they begin to be, they are not from eternity. But what is not from eternity cannot be from itself, as already said. Therefore it must be from another. But ultimately there must exist a being which exists of itself, i.e. necessarily, since, if there is no such being, there would be no sufficient reason for the existence of anything: nothing would exist, whereas in point of fact something does exist, as we know by experience. If it be objected that there must indeed be an *ens a se* but that this may very well be the world itself, Richard would retort that he has already excluded this possibility by pointing out that we experience the contingent character of the things of which the world is composed.

If in this first proof Richard's procedure shows a marked change from that of St. Anselm, in his next proof he adopts a familiar

[1] *P.L.*, 196, 892. [2] *Ibid.*, 196, 893. [3] Cf. *ibid.*, 196, 893.

Anselmian position.[1] It is a fact of experience that there are different and varying degrees of goodness or perfection, the rational, for example, being higher than the irrational. From this experiential fact Richard proceeds to argue that there must be a highest, than which there is no greater or better. As the rational is superior to the irrational, this supreme substance must be intellectual, and as the higher cannot receive what it possesses from the lower, from the subordinate, it must have its being and existence from itself. This necessarily means that it is eternal. Something must be eternal and *a se*, as has been already shown, since otherwise nothing would exist, and experience teaches us that something does exist, and, if the higher cannot receive what it possesses from the lower, it must be the highest, the supreme Substance, which is the eternal and necessary Being.

In the third place Richard attempts to prove the existence of God from the idea of possibility.[2] In the whole universe nothing can exist, unless it has the possibility of being (the potentiality or power to be) from itself or receives it from another. A thing which lacks the possibility of being, which is completely impossible, is nothing at all, and in order that anything should exist, it must receive the ability to exist (*posse esse*) from the ground of possibility. (That the objects in the universe cannot receive their possibility from themselves, cannot be self-grounded, Richard here takes for granted: in his first proof he has already shown the incompatibility of aseity and temporality or beginning to be.) This ground of possibility, then, which is the source of the possibility and the existence of all things, must be self-dependent, ultimate. Every essence, every power, every wisdom, must depend on this Ground, so that the latter must itself be the supreme Essence as the ground of all essences, the supreme Power as source of all power, and supreme Wisdom as source of all wisdom, since it is impossible that a source should confer a gift greater than itself. But there can be no wisdom apart from a rational substance in which it is immanent: so there must be a rational and supreme Substance, in which supreme wisdom is immanent. The Ground of all possibility is, therefore, the supreme Substance.

These arguments are, of course, exercises of the rational, discursive intelligence, of the *oculus rationis*, superior to the *oculus imaginationis*, which views the corporeal world, but inferior to the

[1] *De Trinit.*, 1, 11; *P.L.*, 196, 895–6.

[2] *De Trinit.*, 1, 12; *P.L.*, 196, 896.

oculus intelligentiae, by which God is contemplated in Himself.[1] On the inferior level the objects of sense are viewed immediately as present; on the middle level the mind thinks discursively about things not immediately visible, arguing, for example, from effect to cause or *vice versa*; on the superior level the mind views an invisible object, God, as immediately present.[2] The level of contemplation is thus, as it were, the spiritual analogue of sense-perception, being like to it in immediacy and concreteness in contrast with discursive thought, though it differs in that it is a purely spiritual activity, directed to a purely spiritual object. Richard's division of the six stages of knowledge, from the perception of God's beauty in the beauty of creation to the *mentis alienatio*, under the action of grace, influenced St. Bonaventure in the composition of his *Itinerarium mentis in Deum*.

3. Godfrey of St. Victor (d. 1194) wrote a *Fons Philosophiae*, in which he classifies the sciences and treats of such philosophers and transmitters as Plato, Aristotle, Boethius and Macrobius, devoting a special chapter to the problem of universals and the professed solutions of the problem. *Walter of St. Victor* (died after 1180) was the author of the celebrated diatribe *Contra Quattuor Labyrinthos Franciae*, Abelard, Peter Lombard, Peter of Poitiers and Gilbert de la Porrée, the representatives of dialectical theology, who, according to Walter, were puffed up with the spirit of Aristotle, treated with Scholastic levity of the ineffable things of the Blessed Trinity and the Incarnation, vomited out many heresies and bristled with errors. In other words, Walter of St. Victor was a reactionary who does not represent the genuine spirit of St. Victor, of Hugh the German and Richard the Scotsman, with its reasoned combination of philosophy, dialectical theology and mysticism. In any case the hands of the clock could not be put back, for dialectical theology had come to stay and in the following century it attained its triumph in the great systematic syntheses.

[1] *De gratia contemplationis*, 1, 3, 7; *P.L.*, 196, 66CD, 72C.
[2] *De gratia contemplationis*, 1, 3, 9; *P.L.*, 196, 110D.

CHAPTER XVIII

DUALISTS AND PANTHEISTS

Albigensians and Cathari—Amalric of Bene—David of Dinant.

1. In the thirteenth century St. Dominic preached against the Albigensians. This sect, as well as that of the Cathari, was already widespread in southern France and in Italy during the twelfth century. The principal tenet of these sects was a dualism of the Manichaean type, which came into western Europe by way of Byzantium. There exist two ultimate Principles, the one good and the other bad, of which the former caused the soul, the latter the body and matter in general. From this hypothesis they drew the conclusion that the body is evil and has to be overcome by asceticism and also that it is wrong to marry and propagate the human race. It may seem strange that a sect whose members held such doctrines should flourish; but it must be remembered that it was considered sufficient if the comparatively few *perfecti* led this ascetic existence, while their less exalted followers could safely lead a more ordinary life, if they received the blessing of one of the 'perfect' before death. It must also be remembered, when one is considering the attention which the Albigensians and Cathari received from the ecclesiastical and civil powers, that the condemnation of procreation and of marriage as evil leads naturally to the conclusion that concubinage and marriage are on much the same footing. Moreover, the Cathari denied the legitimacy of oaths and of all war. It was, then, only natural that the sects were looked on as constituting a danger to Christian civilisation. The sect of the Waldenses, which still exists, goes back to the Catharist movement and was originally a sect of dualists, though it was absorbed by the Reformation and adopted anti-Romanism and anti-sacerdotalism as its chief tenets.[1]

2. *Amalric of Bene* was born near Chartres and died as a professor of theology at Paris about 1206/7. St. Thomas Aquinas[2] observes that 'others said that God is the formal principle of all things, and this is said to have been the opinion of the Amalricians', while Martin of Poland says of Amalric that he held God to be the

[1] The sources for our knowledge of the doctrine of the Albigensians are not rich, and the history of the movement is somewhat obscure.

[2] *S.T.*, Ia, 3, 8, *in corpore.*

essence of all creatures and the existence of all creatures. Apparently he interpreted in a pantheistic sense the teaching of John Scotus Eriugena, as well as the phrases used by Theodoric of Chartres and Clarembald of Arras, even going so far as to say that the Persons of the Trinity are creatures, that all three became incarnate and that every single man is as much God as was Christ. From this doctrine some of his followers seem to have drawn the conclusion that sin is an unreal concept, on the ground that, if every man is divine, there can be no question of his sinning. Whether Amalric consciously upheld real pantheism or not, he was in any case accused of heresy and had to retract, his doctrines being condemned in 1210, after his death, along with those of John Scotus Eriugena.

3. If for Amalric of Bene God is the form of all things, for *David of Dinant* He was identified with prime matter, in the sense of the potentiality of all things. Very little is known of the life of David of Dinant, or of the sources from which he derived his doctrines, or of the doctrines themselves, since his writings, condemned in 1210 and forbidden at Paris in 1215, have perished. St. Albert the Great[1] ascribes to him a *De tomis, hoc est de divisionibus*, while the documents of the Council of Paris (1210) ascribe to him a *Quaterni* or *Quaternuli*, though Geyer, for example, supposes that these two titles refer to the same work, which consisted of a number of sections or paragraphs (*quaterni*). In any case we have to rely for our knowledge of his doctrine on quotations and reports by St. Albert the Great, St. Thomas and Nicholas of Cusa.

In the *Summa Theologica*[2] St. Thomas states that David of Dinant 'very foolishly affirmed that God is prime matter'. Elsewhere[3] he says that David divided things into three classes: bodies, souls and eternal substances, bodies being constituted of *Hyle*, souls of *Nous* or mind, and the eternal substances of God. These three constituent sources are the three indivisibles, and the three indivisibles are one and the same. Thus all bodies would be modes of one indivisible being, *Hyle*, and all souls would be modes of one indivisible being, *Nous*; but these two indivisible beings are one, and were identified by David with God, who is the one Substance. 'It is manifest (according to David) that there is only one substance not only of all bodies, but also of all souls, and that this substance is nothing else but God himself. . . . It is clear, then, that God is

[1] *S.T.*, Ia, 4, 20, 2, *quaest. incidens.*

[2] Ia, 3, 8, *in corpore.*

[3] 2 *Sent.*, 17, 1, 1.

the substance of all bodies and all souls, and that God and *Hyle* and *Mens* are one substance.'[1]

David of Dinant tried to prove this position dialectically. For two kinds of substances to differ from one another they must differ in virtue of a difference, and the presence of a difference implies the presence of a common element. Now, if matter differed from mind, there would have to be a *differentia* in prime matter, i.e. a form and a matter, and in this case we should go on to infinity.[2] St. Thomas puts the argument this way.[3] When things in no way differ from one another, they are the same. Now, whatever things differ from one another, differ in virtue of *differentiae*, and in this case they must be composite. But God and prime matter are altogether simple, not composite things. Therefore they cannot differ in any way from one another, and must consequently be the same. To this argument St. Thomas replies that composite things such as, for example, man and horse, do indeed differ from one another in virtue of *differentiae*, but that simple things do not: simple things should be said, strictly speaking, to be diverse (*diversa esse*), not to be different (*differre*). In other words he accuses David of playing with terms, of choosing, to express the diversity of God and matter, a term which implies composition in God and matter.

Why did St. Albert and St. Thomas think it worth while giving such attention to a pantheistic system, the theoretical support of which was more or less a dialectical quibble? Probably the reason was not so much that David of Dinant exercised an extensive influence as that they feared that the heresy of David might compromise Aristotle. The sources from which David drew his theories constitute a disputed point, but it is generally agreed that he drew on the exposition of ancient materialism given in the *Physics* and *Metaphysics*, and it is clear that he utilises the Aristotelian ideas of prime matter and form. In 1210 the same Council of Paris which condemned David's writings forbad also the public and private teaching of the natural philosophy of Aristotle in the University. Most probably, then, St. Thomas wished to show that David of Dinant's monism by no means followed from the teaching of Aristotle; and in his reply to the objection already cited he expressly refers to the *Metaphysics*.

[1] S. Alb. M., *S.T.*, IIa, t. 12, q. 72, membr. 4, a. 2, n. 4.
[2] *Ibid.*, Ia, t. 4, q. 20, membr. 2; *In Metaph.*, t. 4, c. 7.
[3] *S.T.*, Ia, 3, 8, ob. 3.

PART IV

ISLAMIC AND JEWISH PHILOSOPHY: TRANSLATIONS

CHAPTER XIX

ISLAMIC PHILOSOPHY

Reasons for discussing Islamic philosophy—Origins of Islamic philosophy—Alfarabi—Avicenna—Averroes—Dante and the Arabian philosophers.

1. To come upon a chapter on the philosophy of the Arabs in a work devoted to mediaeval thought, in the sense of the thought of mediaeval Christendom, might astonish a reader who was making his first acquaintance with the philosophy of the Middle Ages; but the influence, positive and negative, of Islamic philosophy on that of Christendom is now a matter of common knowledge among historians, and one can scarcely avoid saying something on the subject. The Arabian philosophy was one of the principal channels whereby the complete Aristotle was introduced to the West; but the great philosophers of mediaeval Islam, men like Avicenna and Averroes, were more than mere transmitters or even commentators; they changed and developed the philosophy of Aristotle, more or less according to the spirit of neo-Platonism, and several of them interpreted Aristotle on important points in a sense which, whether exegetically correct or not, was incompatible with the Christian theology and faith.[1] Aristotle, therefore, when he appeared to mediaeval Christian thinkers in the shape given him by Averroes, for example, naturally appeared as an enemy of Christian wisdom, Christian philosophy in the wide sense. This fact explains to a large extent the opposition offered to Aristotelianism in the thirteenth century by many upholders of the Christian tradition who looked on the pagan philosopher as the foe of Augustine, Anselm and the great philosophers of Christianity. The opposition varied in degree, from a rather crude dislike and fear of novelty, to the reasoned opposition of a thinker like St. Bonaventure; but it becomes easier to understand the opposition

[1] It is true, however, that some Islamic philosophers, like Avicenna, facilitated through their writings a Christian interpretation of Aristotle.

if one remembers that a Moslem philosopher such as Averroes claimed to give the right interpretation of Aristotle and that this interpretation was, on important questions, at variance with Christian belief. It explains too the attention paid to the Islamic philosophers by those (particularly, of course, St. Thomas Aquinas) who saw in the Aristotelian system not only a valuable instrument for the dialectical expression of Christian theology but also the true philosophy, for such thinkers had to show that Aristotelianism did not necessarily involve the interpretation given to it by the Moslems: they had to dissociate themselves from Averroes and to distinguish their Aristotelianism from his.

In order, then, fully to understand the polemics of St. Thomas Aquinas and others, it is necessary to know something of mediaeval Islamic philosophy; but it is also necessary for a connected reason, namely that there arose in Paris a School of philosophers who claimed to represent integral Aristotelianism, the chief figure of this School being the celebrated opponent of St. Thomas, Siger of Brabant. These 'integral' Aristotelians, the genuine Aristotelians as they thought themselves to be, meant by genuine Aristotelianism the system of Aristotle as interpreted by Averroes, the Commentator *par excellence.* In order, therefore, to understand this school and an important phase of the controversies at Paris, it is obviously necessary to be acquainted with the place of Averroes in the history of philosophy and with his doctrine.

But, though some treatment of mediaeval Islamic philosophy must be given, it does not come within the scope of this book to discuss the Islamic philosophy for its own sake. It has indeed its own peculiar interest (for example, its relations to Islamic theology, their attempted reconciliation and the tension between them, as well as the relation of Islamic thought to mysticism in the Islamic world, and of Islamic philosophy to Islamic culture in general, have their own intrinsic interest), but the reader must expect here no more than a brief sketch of Islamic philosophy in the mediaeval period, a treatment of it less for its own sake than in function of its influence on the thought of mediaeval Christendom. This perhaps rather one-sided treatment is not designed to belittle the achievements of Moslem philosophers, nor does it involve a denial of the intrinsic interest of Islamic philosophy for its own sake: it is simply dictated by the general purpose and scope of this book, as well as, of course, by considerations of space.

2. If Islamic philosophy was connected with the philosophy of

Christendom in the way just mentioned, it was also connected with Christianity in its origins, owing to the fact that it was Christian Syrians who first translated Aristotle and other ancient philosophers into Arabic. The first stage consisted of the translation of Greek works into Syriac at the school of Edessa in Mesopotamia, which was founded by St. Ephrem of Nisibis in 363 and was closed by the Emperor Zeno in 489 because of the Nestorianism which prevailed there. At Edessa some of the works of Aristotle, principally the logical works, as well as Porphyry's *Isagoge*, were translated into Syriac, and this work was continued in Persia, at Nisibis and Gandisapora, whither the scholars betook themselves on the closure of the school. Thus works of Aristotle and Plato were translated into Persian. In the sixth century works of Aristotle and Porphyry and the writings of the Pseudo-Dionysius were translated into Syriac at the Monophysite schools of Syria.

The second stage consisted in the translation of the Syriac translations into Arabic. Even before the time of Mohammed (569–632) there had been a number of Nestorian Christians who worked among the Arabs, mainly as physicians, and when the 'Abbāsid dynasty replaced that of the Ommaiades in 750, Syrian scholars were invited to the Arab court at Baghdad. Medical works were translated first of all; but after a time philosophical works were also translated, and in 832 a school of translators was established at Baghdad, an institution which produced Arabic versions of Aristotle, Alexander of Aphrodisias, Themistius, Porphyry and Ammonius. Plato's *Republic* and *Laws* were also translated, as well as (in the first half of the ninth century) the so-called *Theology of Aristotle*, which consisted of a compilation of the *Enneads* (4–6) of Plotinus, erroneously attributed to Aristotle. To this must be added the fact that the *Liber de Causis*, really the *Institutio Theologica* of Proclus, was also attributed to Aristotle. These false attributions, as well as the translation into Arabic of neo-Platonic commentators on Aristotle, helped to popularise among the Arabs a neo-Platonic interpretation of the Aristotelian system, though other influences, as well as Aristotle and the neo-Platonists, contributed to the formation of Islamic philosophy, e.g. the Islamic religion itself and the influence of Oriental religious thought, such as that of Persia.

3. The Moslem philosophers may be divided into two groups, the eastern group and the western group. In this section I shall treat briefly of three thinkers belonging to the eastern group.

(i) *Alfarabi*, who belonged to the school of Baghdad and died about 950, is a good example of a thinker upon whom the influences mentioned above made themselves felt. Thus he helped to introduce the Islamic cultured world to the logic of Aristotle, while by his classification of the departments of philosophy and theology he made philosophy self-conscious, as it were, marking it off from theology. Logic is a propaedeutic and preparation for philosophy proper, which Alfarabi divided into physics, comprising the particular sciences (psychology being included and the theory of knowledge being treated of in psychology) and metaphysics (physics and metaphysics being the two branches of theoretical philosophy) and ethics or practical philosophy. His scheme for theology included as sections (1) omnipotence and justice of God; (2) the unity and other attributes of God; (3) the doctrine of sanctions in the next life; (4) and (5) the individual's rights and the social relations of the Moslem. By making philosophy a separate province, then, Alfarabi did not mean to supplant or undermine the Islamic theology: rather did he place schematisation and logical form at the service of theology.

In addition, Alfarabi utilised Aristotelian arguments in proving the existence of God. Thus, on the supposition that the things of the world are passively moved, an idea which fitted in well with Islamic theology, he argued that they must receive their movement from a first Mover, God. Again, the things of this world are contingent, they do not exist of necessity: their essence does not involve their existence, as is shown by the fact that they come into being and pass away. From this it follows that they have received their existence, and ultimately one must admit a Being which exists essentially, necessarily, and is the Cause of the existence of all contingent beings.

On the other hand, when it comes to the general system of Alfarabi, the neo-Platonic influence is manifest. Thus the theme of emanation is employed to show how from the ultimate Deity or One there proceed the Intelligence and the World-Soul, from the thoughts or ideas of which proceeds the Cosmos, from the higher or outer spheres to the lower or inner spheres. Bodies are composed of matter and form. The intelligence of man is illuminated by the cosmic intelligence, which is the active intellect of man (the νοῦς ἐπίκτητος of Alexander of Aphrodisias). Moreover, the illumination of the human intellect is the explanation of the fact that our concepts 'fit' things, since the Ideas in God are at once the exemplar and source of the concepts in the human mind and of the forms in things.

This doctrine of illumination is connected, not only with neo-Platonism, but also with Oriental mysticism. Alfarabi himself became attached to the mystical school or sect of the Sufis, and his philosophy had a religious orientation. The highest task of man is to know God, and, just as the general process of the universe is a flowing out from God and a return to God, so should man, who proceeds from God in the emanative process and who is enlightened by God, strive after the return to and likeness with God.

(ii) The greatest Moslem philosopher of the eastern group is without a doubt *Avicenna* or *Ibn Sīnā* (980–1037), the real creator of a Scholastic system in the Islamic world.[1] A Persian by birth, born near Bokhara, he received his education in the Arab tongue, and most of his works, which were extremely numerous, were written in Arabic. A precocious boy, he learnt in succession the Koran, Arabic literature, geometry, jurisprudence, logic. Outstripping his instructors, he studied by himself theology, physics, mathematics and medicine, and at sixteen years of age he was already practising as a doctor. He then devoted a year and a half to the study of philosophy and logic, but it was only when he chanced upon a commentary by Alfarabi that he was able to understand to his satisfaction the *Metaphysics* of Aristotle, which he had read, he tells us, forty times without being able to understand it. The rest of his life was a busy and adventurous one, as he acted as Vizir to several Sultans and practised medicine, experiencing in his travels the ups and downs of life and the favour and disfavour of princes, but being always the philosopher, pursuing his studies and writings wherever he was, even in prison and on horseback. He died at Hamadan at the age of fifty-seven, after performing his ablutions, repenting of his sins, distributing abundant alms and freeing his slaves. His principal philosophical work is the *Aš-Šifā*, known in the Middle Ages as the *Sufficientiae*, which comprised logic, physics (including the natural sciences), mathematics, psychology and metaphysics. The *Najāt* was a collection of texts, taken from the first work and arranged in a different order.

Avicenna's division of philosophy in the wide sense into logic,

[1] The name Avicenna, by which Ibn Sîna was known to the mediaeval world, comes from the Hebrew version, Aven Sina.

the propaedeutic to philosophy, speculative philosophy (physics, mathematics and theology) and practical philosophy (ethics, economics and politics) offers no remarkable features, save that theology is divided into first theology (equivalent to ontology and natural theology) and second theology (involving Islamic themes), and this marks off Islamic theology from the Greek. But his metaphysic, in spite of its borrowing both from Aristotle and from neo-Platonism, shows features of its own, which make it plain that, however much he borrowed from former philosophers, Avicenna had thought out his system carefully and independently and had welded it into a system of a peculiar stamp. For instance, although he is at one with Aristotle in assigning the study of being as being to metaphysics, Avicenna employs an un-Aristotelian illustration to show that the mind necessarily apprehends the idea of being, though it is acquired normally through experience. Imagine a man suddenly created, who cannot see or hear, who is floating in space and whose members are so disposed that they cannot touch one another. On the supposition that he cannot exercise the senses and acquire the notion of being through sight or touch, will he thereby be unable to form the notion? No, because he will be conscious of and affirm his own existence, so that, even if he cannot acquire the notion of being through external experience, he will at least acquire it through self-consciousness.[1]

In Avicenna's eyes the notion of necessity is also a primary notion, for to him all beings are necessary. It is necessary, however, to distinguish two kinds of necessity. A particular object in the world is not necessary of itself: its essence does not involve existence necessarily, as is shown by the fact that it comes into being and passes away; but it is necessary in the sense that its existence is determined by the necessary action of an external cause. Accordingly a contingent being means, for Avicenna, a being the existence of which is due, not to the essence of the being itself, but to the necessary action of an external cause. Such beings are indeed caused and so 'contingent', but none the less the action of the cause is determined.

This leads him on to argue that the chain of causes cannot be infinite, since then there would be no reason for the existence of anything, but that there must be a first cause which is itself uncaused. This uncaused Being, the necessary Being, cannot receive its essence from another, nor can its existence form part

[1] *Šifā*, 1, 281 and 363.

of its essence, since composition of parts would involve an anterior uniting cause: essence and existence must therefore be identical in the necessary Being. This ultimate Being is necessary of itself, whereas 'contingent' beings are not necessary of themselves but necessary through another, so that the concept 'being', as applied to necessary and contingent being, has not the same sense. They are not, then, species of one genus; but rather does Being belong *par excellence*, properly and primarily, to the necessary Being and is predicated of contingent being only secondarily and analogically.

Closely allied with the distinction between the possible and the necessary is the distinction between potentiality and act. Potentiality, as Aristotle said, is the principle of change into another as other, and this principle may exist either in the agent (active potency) or in the patient (passive potency). Moreover, there are degrees of potency and act, ranging between the lower limit, pure potentiality, prime matter, and the upper limit, pure act, the necessary Being, though Avicenna does not use the phrase 'Pure Act' *quoad verbum*. From this position Avicenna proceeds to show that God is Truth, Goodness, Love and Life. For example, the Being which is always in act, without potentiality or privation, must be absolute Goodness, and since the divine attributes are ontologically indistinguishable, the divine Goodness must be identical with absolute Love.

As God is absolute Goodness, He necessarily tends to diffuse His goodness, to radiate it, and this means that He creates necessarily. As God is the necessary Being, all His attributes must be necessary: He is, therefore, necessarily Creator. This in turn involves the conclusion that creation is from eternity, for, if God is necessarily Creator and God is eternal, creation must be eternal. Moreover, if God creates by the necessity of His Nature, it follows also that there is no free choice in creation, that God could not create otherwise or create other things than He actually creates. But God can produce immediately only by a being like Himself: it is impossible for God to create material things directly. The logically first being to proceed from God is, therefore, the first Intelligence. This Intelligence is created, in the sense that it proceeds from God: it receives, then, its existence, and in this way duality begins. Whereas in the One there is no duality, in the primary Intelligence there is a duality of essence and existence, in that existence is received, while there is also a duality of knowledge, in that the primary Intelligence knows the One or God as necessary and itself as 'possible'. In this way Avicenna deduces the ten Intelligences which exhibit a growing multiplicity and so bridges the gap between the unity of God and the multiplicity of creation. The tenth Intelligence is the 'giver of forms', which are received in prime matter, pure potentiality (or rather potentiality 'deprived of' form, and so, in a sense, 'evil'), and so rendered capable of multiplication within the species. The separate Intelligences can differ from one another only specifically, in virtue of their greater or less proximity to the One and the decreasing simplicity in the process of emanation; but, as matter is the principle of individuation, the same specific form can be multiplied in a plurality of individual concrete objects, though prime matter has first to be taken out of its state of indetermination and disposed for the reception of specific form, first through the *forma corporeitatis* and then through the action of external causes which predispose matter for the reception of one particular specific form.

The tenth Intelligence has another function to perform besides that of *Dator formarum*, for it also exercises the function of the active intellect in man. In his analysis of abstraction Avicenna will not credit the human intellect as such with the final act of abstraction, the apprehension of the universal in a state of pure intelligibility, as this would mean that the intellect passes from a state of potentiality to act entirely by its own power, whereas no agent can proceed from passive potency to act except under the influence of an agent external to itself but like itself. He distinguished, therefore, the active and passive intellects, but made the active intellect a separate and unitary intelligence which illumines the human intellect or confers on it its intellectual and abstract grasp of essences (the essence or universal *post rem*, to be distinguished from the essence *ante rem* and *in re*).

Avicenna's idea of necessary creation and his denial that the One has direct knowledge of the multiplicity of concrete objects set him at variance with the theology of the Koran; but he tried, so far as he could, to reconcile his Aristotelian-neo-Platonist system with orthodox Islam. For example, he did not deny the immortality of the human soul, in spite of his doctrine concerning the separateness of the active intellect, and he maintained a doctrine of sanctions in the after life, though he interpreted this in an intellectualist manner, reward consisting in the knowledge of purely intelligible objects, punishment in the deprivation of such knowledge.[1] Again, though his analysis and explanation of creation and the relation of the world to God necessarily involved a theory of emanation and, in this respect, tended towards pantheism, he tried to safeguard himself from pantheism by affirming the distinction between essence and existence in all beings which proceed, immediately or mediately, from God. Possibly the Islamic doctrine of the divine omnipotence, when interpreted 'speculatively', tends to pantheism, and it may well be that some fundamental principles of Avicenna's system would favour pantheism; but he was certainly no pantheist by intention.

When portions of the writings of Avicenna were translated into Latin in the twelfth century, the Christian world found itself faced for the first time with a closely knit system which was bound to exercise a strong attraction on certain minds. Thus *Gundissalinus* (d. 1151) translated into Latin the Spanish translation made by Joannes Hispanus (Avendeath) and utilised the thought of Avicenna in his *De Anima*, following the Avicennian psychology (and citing the latter's allegory of the 'flying man'), though he left Avicenna for Augustine by making the active intellect, as source of illumination, identical with God. Moreover, in his *De Processione Mundi* he attempted to reconcile the cosmogony of Avicenna with Christian doctrine, though his example in this matter was not followed. Before the entire *Metaphysics* of Aristotle became available, uncertainty reigned as to which doctrines were to be attributed to Avicenna and which to Aristotle. Thus Roger Bacon thought that Avicenna must have followed Aristotle throughout, though he (Bacon) had not got books M and N of the *Metaphysics* and so could not check the truth or untruth of this supposition. The result was that *William of Auvergne* (died *c.* 1249), the first vigorous opponent of Avicenna, attributed the cosmogony of Avicenna to Aristotle himself. This cosmogony, said William, was erroneous, in that it admitted intermediaries in the process of creation, thus allowing to creatures a divine power, denied the divine freedom, asserted the eternity of the world, made matter the principle of individuation and regarded the separate active

[1] It should be noted that it was the Averroistic doctrine of the unicity of the passive or possible intellect which *necessarily* involved the denial of personal immortality. The doctrine of the unicity of the active intellect does not necessarily involve such a denial, whether the active intellect is identified with a subordinate Intelligence or with God in His function as illuminator. As for Aristotle, he may not have believed in personal immortality himself, but the rejection of personal immortality does not *necessarily* follow from his doctrine of the active intellect, whereas it does follow from the doctrine of Averroes. On this point the positions of Avicenna and Averroes must be clearly distinguished.

intellect as the efficient cause of human souls. None the less William himself followed Avicenna by introducing into Latin Scholasticism the distinction between essence and existence. Moreover, denying Avicenna's doctrine of the active intellect, he pretty well identified it with God. Other thinkers, such as Alexander of Hales, John of la Rochelle and St. Albert, while denying the doctrine of a separate active intellect, made use of Avicenna's theory of abstraction and of the necessity of illumination, whereas Roger Bacon and Roger Marston found Avicenna's error to consist only in not identifying the separate and illuminating active intellect with God. Without going any further into the question of Avicenna's influence, which would require a distinct monograph, one can say that he influenced Latin Scholasticism in regard to at least three themes, that of knowledge and illumination, that of the relation of essence and existence, and that of matter as the principle of individuation.[1] Criticism of Avicenna by a Latin Scholastic does not mean, of course, that the Scholastic learnt nothing from Avicenna. For instance, St. Thomas found it necessary to criticise the Moslem philosopher's treatment of possibility,[2] but that does not mean that St. Thomas did not develop his own position partly through a consideration of Avicenna's doctrine, even if it is difficult to assess the precise degree of influence exercised by the latter's writings on the greatest of the Scholastics. Scotus, however, was much more influenced by Avicenna than was St. Thomas, though he certainly could not be called with propriety a disciple of Avicenna.

(iii) *Algazel* (1058–1111), who lectured for a time at Baghdad, opposed the views of Alfarabi and Avicenna from the viewpoint of Mohammedan orthodoxy. In his *Maqāsid* or *Intentiones Philosophorum* he summed up the views of these two philosophers, and this exposition, translated into Latin by Gundissalinus, gave the impression, when taken by itself, that Algazel agreed with the opinions expressed. Thus William of Auvergne coupled together as objects of attack the 'followers of Aristotle', Alfarabi, Algazel and Avicenna, being unaware of the fact that Algazel had proceeded to criticise the systems of the philosophers in his *Destructio philosophorum*,[3] which tried to show how the philosophers contradicted themselves. This book elicited later from Averroes a

[1] On Avicenna's influence, cf. Roland-Gosselin, commentary on the *De ente et essentia*, pp. 59 and 150.
[2] Cf. *De Pot.*, 5, 3; *Contra Gent.*, 2, 30.
[3] More properly *Incoherentia philosophorum*.

Destructio destructionis philosophorum. In his *Revivification of the Religious Sciences* he gave his positive views, defending the orthodox doctrine of the creation of the world in time and out of nothing against Avicenna's ideas of emanation and of the eternity of the world. He defended also the doctrine of God's universal causality, making the connection between cause and effect to depend on the divine power, not on any causal activity on the part of creatures. The philosopher sees consequence or constant conjunction and concludes to the relation of cause and effect, whereas in truth the following of one event on another is simply due to the power and action of God. In other words he maintained an occasionalistic doctrine.

Algazel was very far from being simply a philosopher who wished to counteract the unorthodox tendencies of his Hellenising predecessors: he was also an eminent Sufi, a mystic and spiritual writer. Leaving his work at Baghdad he retired into Syria, where he lived a life of asceticism and contemplation. Sometimes indeed he emerged from his retirement and in any case he had disciples: he even founded a kind of theological college and a school of Sufism at his place of retirement, Tūs; but the major interest of his life was the revival of religion, in the sense of mysticism. Drawing not only on previous Islamic sources, but utilising neo-Platonic ideas, and even ideas from Judaism and Christianity, he built up a system of spirituality which was personalist, i.e. non-pantheistic, in character. Some of Algazel's expressions would seem at first sight to imply or involve pantheism, but his neo-Platonism was put at the service of religious mysticism rather than of speculation. It is not that he tends to identify the world with God, but rather that his fusion of the Islamic doctrines of predestination and divine omni-causality with strongly emphasised religious mysticism leads him into a kind of panentheism. The Semitic monotheism, when seen in the light of neo-Platonism and fused with mysticism, could lead him probably in no other direction. In the field of purely philosophical speculation he shows a somewhat sceptical attitude, and he represents the protest of religious mysticism against rationalism as well as that of Islamic theology against Aristotelian philosophy.

4. The background of the Moslem philosophers of the West was provided by the brilliant Islamic civilisation which grew up in Spain in the tenth century and which, at that period, was so greatly superior to what western Christendom had to offer. The

first philosopher of the western group was *Ibn Masarrah* (d. 931), who adopted ideas from the Pseudo-Empedocles, while *Avempace* or *Ibn Bājja* (d. 1138) and *Abubacer* or *Ibn Tufail* (d. 1185) represented mystical tendencies; but the greatest figure of this group is undoubtedly Averroes, who occupies that prominent position in the western group which Avicenna represents in the eastern group.

Averroes or *Ibn Rušd* (the *Commentator* of the Latin Scholastics) was born at Córdoba in 1126, the son of a judge. After studying theology, jurisprudence, medicine, mathematics and philosophy, he occupied judicial posts, first at Seville and afterwards at Córdoba, becoming physician to the Caliph in 1182. Subsequently he fell into disfavour with the Caliph al-Mansūr and was banished from court. He later crossed to Morocco, dying there in 1198.

Being convinced that the genius of Aristotle was the final culmination of the human intellect, Averroes naturally devoted a great deal of energy to the composition of commentaries. These fall into three classes: (i) the lesser or 'middle' commentaries, in which Averroes gives the content of Aristotle's doctrine, adding his own explanations and developments in such a way that it is not always easy to distinguish what comes from Aristotle and what from Averroes; (ii) the greater commentaries, in which Averroes gives first a portion of the actual text of Aristotle and then adds his own commentary; and (iii) the little commentaries (paraphrases or compendia), in which he gives the conclusions arrived at by Aristotle, omitting proofs and historical references, and which were designed for students unable to go to the sources or larger commentaries. (Apparently he composed the middle commentaries and the compendia before the greater commentaries.) The entire *Organon* of Aristotle, in the lesser commentary and in the compendium, is extant, as also Latin translations of all three classes of commentary for the *Posterior Analytics*, the *Physics*, the *De Caelo*, the *De Anima* and the *Metaphysics*. In addition to these and other commentaries in Latin translations the Christian Scholastics possessed Averroes's answer to Algazel (i.e. the *Destructio destructionis philosophorum*), several logical works, a letter on the connection between the abstract intelligence and man, a work on the beatitude of the soul, etc.

The metaphysical scale reaches from pure matter as the lowest limit to pure Act, God, as the highest limit, between these limits being the objects composed of potency and act, which form *Natura naturata.* (The phrases of the Latin translation, *Natura naturans* and *Natura naturata*, reappear eventually in the system of Spinoza.) Prime matter, as equivalent to non-being, as pure potentiality and the absence of all determination, cannot be the term of the creative act: it is, therefore, co-eternal with God. God, however, draws or educes the forms of material things from the potency of pure matter, and creates the Intelligences, ten in number, connected extrinsically with the spheres, so that the Avicennian emanation-theory is avoided and real pantheism is excluded. The order of the creation or generation of things is, however, determined.

Nevertheless, even if Averroes's rejection of emanation makes him in a sense more orthodox than Avicenna, he did not follow Avicenna in accepting personal immortality. Averroes did indeed follow Themistius and other commentators in holding that the *intellectus materialis* is the same substance as the *intellectus agens* and that both survive death, but he followed Alexander of Aphrodisias in holding that this substance is a separate and unitary Intelligence. (It is the Intelligence of the moon, the lowest sphere.) The individual passive intellect in the individual man becomes, under the action of the active intellect, the 'acquired intellect', which is absorbed by the active intellect in such a way that, although it survives bodily death, it does so not as a personal, individual existent, but as a moment in the universal and common intelligence of the human species. There is, therefore, immortality, but there is no personal immortality. This view was earnestly combated by St. Thomas Aquinas and other Scholastics, though it was maintained by the Latin Averroists as a philosophical truth.

More interesting, however, than Averroes's particular philosophical doctrine is his notion of the general relation of philosophy to theology. Holding, as he did, that Aristotle was the completer of human science,[1] the model of human perfection and the author of a system which is the supreme truth, interpreting Aristotle as holding the unicity of the active intellect and accepting the doctrine of the eternity of matter, Averroes had necessarily to attempt a reconciliation of his philosophical ideas with orthodox Islamic theology, especially as those were not wanting who were ready to accuse him of heresy because of his devotion to a pagan thinker. He accordingly attempted this reconciliation by means of the so-called 'double truth' theory. This does not mean that,

[1] *De Anima*, 3, 2.

according to Averroes, a proposition can be true in philosophy and false in theology or *vice versa*: his theory is that one and the same truth is understood clearly in philosophy and expressed allegorically in theology. The scientific formulation of truth is achieved only in philosophy, but the same truth is expressed in theology, only in a different manner. The picture-teaching of the Koran expresses the truth in a manner intelligible to the ordinary man, to the unlettered, whereas the philosopher strips away the allegorical husk and attains the truth 'unvarnished', free from the trappings of *Vorstellung*. Averroes's idea of the relation of philosophy to theology resembles somewhat that of Hegel, and it would be unacceptable, and was unacceptable, to the orthodox Islamic theologian; but it was not the absurd idea that one proposition can be true in philosophy and the diametrically opposite proposition true in theology. What Averroes did was to make theology subordinate to philosophy, to make the latter the judge of the former, so that it belongs to the philosopher to decide what theological doctrines need to be allegorically interpreted and in what way they should be interpreted. This view was accepted by the Latin Averroists, and it was this view, moreover, which drew upon Averroes, and upon philosophy generally, the hostility of the Islamic theologians. In regard to statements attributed to Averroes which taken literally imply that one proposition, for example, that the active intellect is numerically single, is true in philosophy and false in theology, it has been suggested that this was simply a sarcastic way of saying that the theological doctrine is nonsense. When Averroes says that some proposition is true in the fideistic theology of the conservatives, who rejected philosophy, he means that it is 'true' in the School of the enemies of science, i.e. that it is simply false. He had no use for the traditionalists as the traditionalists had no use for him, and his attitude in this matter led to the prohibition in Islamic Spain of the study of Greek philosophy and to the burning of philosophic works.

5. Of the influence of Averroes in Latin Christendom I shall speak later; but it may be of interest to add a word here on the attitude of Dante (1265–1321) towards the Arabian philosophers.[1] The question of Dante's attitude to the Arab philosophers arose when scholars began to ask themselves seriously and without prejudice why Dante, who in the *Divina Commedia* places Mohammed in hell, not only placed Averroes and Avicenna in

[1] For some further remarks on this subject see pp. 439–40.

Limbo, but also placed the Latin Averroist Siger of Brabant in heaven and even went so far as to put his eulogium into the mouth of St. Thomas Aquinas, who was a doughty opponent of Siger. Obviously Dante was treating these men as philosophers, and it was because of this fact that he placed the two Islamic thinkers as high in the scale as he could: as they were not Christians, he did not consider that he could release them from *Inferno* altogether, and so he placed them in Limbo. Siger on the other hand was a Christian, and so Dante placed him in heaven. That he made St. Thomas speak his praises and that he put him on the left of St. Thomas, while St. Albert the Great was on Aquinas's right, is explicable if we remember that the Thomist system presupposes a philosophy which is built up by natural reason alone and that to build up a philosophy by reason alone was precisely what Siger of Brabant professed to do: it is not necessary to suppose that Dante approved all Siger's notions, but he takes him as the symbol of 'pure philosophy'.

However, why did Dante single out Avicenna, Averroes and Siger of Brabant? Was it simply because they were philosophers or did Dante owe something himself to the Moslems? It has been shown by Bruno Nardi,[1] and the theme has been resumed by Asín Palacios,[2] that Dante owed to the systems of Alfarabi, Avicenna, Algazel and Averroes important points in his philosophy, for example, the light-doctrine of God, the theory of the Intelligences, the influence of the celestial spheres, the idea that only the intellectual part of the soul is directly and properly created, the need of illumination for intellection, etc. Some of these ideas were found in the Augustinian tradition, it is true; but it has been shown that Dante, far from being a Thomist pure and simple, owed a considerable debt to the Moslems and to Averroes in particular. This will explain why he singles out for special treatment the most eminent of the Islamic philosophers, and why he places in heaven the greatest of the Latin Averroists.

[1] *Intorno al tomismo di Dante e alla quistione di Sigieri* (*Giornale Dantesco*, XXII, 5).

[2] *Islam and the Divine Comedy* (abridged Engl. Transl., London, 1926).

CHAPTER XX

JEWISH PHILOSOPHY

The Cabala—Avicebron—Maimonides.

1. PHILOSOPHY among the Jews really owes its origin to intercourse with other nations and cultures. Thus in the first volume of this history I have already treated of Philo, the Alexandrian Jew (*c.* 25 B.C.–*c.* A.D. 40), who attempted a reconciliation of the Jewish Scriptural theology and Greek philosophy, producing a system in which elements of the Platonic tradition (the theory of Ideas), of Stoicism (doctrine of the Logos) and of Oriental thought (intermediary beings) were combined. In the philosophy of Philo the transcendence of God was strongly emphasised, and this insistence on the divine transcendence was characteristic of the doctrine of the *Cabala*, as modified by Greek, particularly by Platonic, theories. The *Cabala* consisted of two works, the *Jezîrah* (creation), which was probably composed after the middle of the ninth century A.D., and the *Sohar* (brightness), which was built up from the beginning of the thirteenth century and committed to writing by a Spanish Jew about the year 1300. Additions and commentaries were subsequently made. The Cabalistic philosophy shows the influence of neo-Platonism in its doctrine of emanation and intermediary beings between God and the world, and one of the channels by which neo-Platonism influenced the construction of the emanationist philosophy of the *Sohar* was the thought of the Spanish Jew who was known to the Latin Scholastics as Avicebron.

2. *Salomon Ibn Gabirol* or *Avicebron* (so called by the Latin Scholastics, who thought that he was an Arab) was born at Malaga about 1021, was educated at Saragossa and died in 1069/70. He was naturally influenced by the Arabian philosophy and his chief work, the *Fons Vitae*, was originally composed in Arabic. The Arabic original is, however, no longer extant, though we possess the work in the Latin translation of Joannes Hispanus (Avendeath) and Dominicus Gundissalinus. The work consists of five books and had a considerable influence on the Christian Scholastics.

The neo-Platonic influence shows itself in the emanationist scheme of Avicebron's philosophy. The summit of the hierarchy of being and the source of all limited being is, of course, God, who is one and unknowable by the discursive reason, apprehensible only in the intuition of ecstasy. To this Avicebron added a peculiar doctrine concerning the divine will by which are created, or from which emanate, all lesser beings. The divine will, like God Himself, transcends the composition of matter and form and can be apprehended only in mystical experience; but the exact relation of the divine will to God is not easy to determine. The distinction drawn between the divine essence and the divine will would appear to make of the latter a distinct hypostasis, though on the other hand the divine will is depicted as being God Himself as active *ad extra*, as God in His appearance. In any case there is a substitution of Will for Logos. From God, *via* the divine will, whether God under one aspect or a distinct hypostasis, proceeds the cosmic spirit or World-Soul, which is inferior to God and is composed of matter and form, *materia universalis* and *forma universalis*. From the World-Soul in turn proceed pure spirits and corporeal things.

The interesting point about Avicebron's system is, however, not his emanationist scheme, but rather his doctrine of universal hylomorphic composition in all beings inferior to God, a doctrine which was derived, at least indirectly, from Plotinus and which influenced one tradition of Christian Scholasticism. Just as from the World-Soul proceed the individual forms, so from the World-Soul proceed also spiritual matter, which is present in the Intelligence and in the rational soul, and corporeal matter. Matter, then, which does not *of itself* involve corporeality, is the principle of limitation and finiteness in all creatures: it is the hylomorphic composition in creatures which marks them off from God, for in God there is no composition. This doctrine of universal hylomorphic composition in creatures was maintained by St. Bonaventure, for example, the great Franciscan contemporary of St. Thomas Aquinas. Moreover, there is a plurality of forms in every being which possesses in itself a plurality of grades of perfection, as the human being, for example, the microcosm, possesses the perfections of corporeality, vegetative life, sensitive life and intellectual life. Every corporeal being possesses the *forma corporeitatis*, but it has further to be given its determinate place in the hierarchy of being, and this is accomplished by the reception of the form or forms by which it becomes, e.g. living thing, animal, dog. It has been maintained that the doctrine of Avicebron was the real origin of the Augustinian School's theory of the plurality of forms, but, even granting this, it must also be remembered that the doctrine fitted well into the scheme of the Augustinians' philosophy, since Augustine had himself taught that the function of the lower forms is to lead on to the higher forms and that this is true also of these forms as represented in human knowledge, i.e. that contemplation of the lower stages of being should lead the mind to higher stages.

3. The most interesting of the Jewish mediaeval philosophers is, however, *Moses Maimonides*, who was born at Córdoba in 1135 and died in Cairo in 1204, having had to abandon Moorish Spain, which was no longer favourable to philosophers. In his *Guide of the Doubting* he attempted to give to theology its rational basis in philosophy, which for him meant the philosophy of Aristotle, whom he reverenced as the greatest example of human intellectual power apart from the Prophets. We must hold fast to what is given us in sense-perception and what can be strictly demonstrated by the intellect: if statements contained in the Old Testament plainly contradict what is plainly established by reason, then such statements must be interpreted allegorically. This view, however, did not mean that Maimonides discarded the teaching of theology whenever Aristotle held something different to that which the Scripture taught. For example, theology teaches the creation of the world in time out of nothing, and this means both that God must be the author of matter as well as of form and that the world cannot be eternal. If the eternity of the world could be demonstrated by reason in such a way that the opposite was clearly seen to be an impossibility, then we should have to interpret the Scriptural teaching accordingly; but, as a matter of fact, the Scriptural teaching is clear and the philosophical arguments adduced to prove the eternity of the world are inconclusive: we must, then, reject Aristotle's teaching on this point. Plato came nearer to the truth than Aristotle, but even he accepted an uncreated matter. The creation out of nothing of both matter and form is also necessary, according to Maimonides, if the fact of miracles, plainly taught in the Old Testament, is to be allowed, since, if God is able to suspend the operation of natural laws, He must be the absolute Sovereign of nature and He would not be that unless He were Creator in the full sense of the word. To the fanatics Maimonides's allegorical interpretation of some of the Scriptural pictures of God seemed to be a selling of the Holy Scripture to the Greeks, and some Jews in France even went so far as to try to enlist the aid of the Inquisition against this

'heresy'; but in point of fact he was merely saying that there can be a fountain of certain truth besides theology. In other words, he gave a charter to philosophy, and he thus influenced the growth of philosophical interest among the Jews in Spain, even if his chief influence lay in the province of theology. That he was no blind worshipper of Aristotle has been shown already. Aristotle, thought Maimonides, went wrong in teaching the eternity of the world, and even if philosophy cannot demonstrate creation in time, it can at least show that the arguments brought up in favour of the Aristotelian position are inconclusive and unsound.

Relying partly on the natural theology of Alfarabi and Avicenna, Maimonides proved the existence of God in various ways, arguing from creatures to God as first Mover, as necessary Being and as first Cause. These arguments he supported from statements of Aristotle in the *Physics* and *Metaphysics*. But if Maimonides anticipated most of the types of proof given later by St. Thomas, he was more insistent than the latter on the inapplicability of positive predicates to God. God is pure Act, without matter and without potency, infinitely removed from creatures, and, in regard to 'qualities', we can say what God is *not*, rather than what He is. He is one and transcendent (between God and the world there is a hierarchy of Intelligences or pure spirits), but we cannot form any adequate positive idea of God. St. Thomas, of course, would admit this, but Maimonides was rather more insistent on the *via negativa*. We can, however, ascribe to God activities, the activities of creation and providence, for example, provided that we realise that the difference of names does not correspond to any difference in God Himself and that God Himself is unchangeable. Unlike Avicebron, Maimonides admitted a special providence on God's part in regard to particular creatures, though this is true only of men, so far as the material world is concerned. The active intellect is the tenth Intelligence (the Intelligences are without 'matter'), but the passive intellects of the just are immortal. Immortality, then, he admitted only in a limited extension, for the just; but he maintained the freedom of the will, whereby men become just, and he denied the determining influence of the celestial bodies and spheres in regard to human conduct. In fine, Moses Maimonides made a better business of reconciling Greek philosophy with Jewish orthodoxy than Avicebron had made of it, and it is noteworthy that the influence of the Aristotelian system is more in evidence in the former's philosophy than in the latter's.

CHAPTER XXI

THE TRANSLATIONS

The translated works—Translations from Greek and from Arabic —Effects of translations and opposition to Aristotelianism.

1. BEFORE the twelfth century part of the *Organon* of Aristotle (the *Categories* and the *De Interpretatione*) had been available to mediaeval philosophers in the Latin version by Boethius (*Logica vetus*), but the entire *Organon* became available fairly early in the twelfth century. Thus about 1128 James of Venice translated the *Analytics*, the *Topics* and the *Sophistical Arguments* from Greek into Latin, the newly translated books of the *Organon* being known as the *Logica nova*. It appears that portions at least of other books of the *Organon* besides the *Categories* and the *De Interpretatione* had survived into the twelfth century in the translation of Boethius; but in any case a complete translation of the *Organon* into Latin had been effected by the middle of the century. It is to be noted that the translation by James of Spain was made from the Greek, as was also the translation of the fourth book of the *Meteorologica* made by Henricus Aristippus before 1162. Henricus Aristippus was Archdeacon of Catania in Sicily, an island which was an important centre in the work of translation. Thus it was in twelfth-century Sicily that Ptolemy's μεγάλη σύνταξις and the *Optics*, some of the works of Euclid and Proclus's *Elementatio physica* were translated from Greek into Latin.

Sicily was one centre of the work of translation; Spain was another, the most famous school of translators being that of Toledo. Thus under Archbishop Raymond (1126–51) Joannes Hispanus (Avendeath) translated from the Arabic into Latin (*via* Spanish) the Logic of Avicenna, while Dominicus Gundissalinus translated (with help from other scholars) the *Metaphysics* of Avicenna, parts of his *Physics*, his *De Sufficientia*, *De Caelo et Mundo* and *De Mundo*, the *Metaphysics* of Algazel and the *De Scientiis* of Alfarabi. Dominicus Gundissalinus and John of Spain also translated from Arabic into Latin the *Fons Vitae* of Avicebron.

A distinguished member of this group of scholars was Gerard of Cremona, who took up work at Toledo in 1134 and died in 1187. He translated from Arabic into Latin Aristotle's *Posterior Analytics* (together with the commentary of Themistius), *Physics*, *De Caelo et Mundo*, *De Generatione et Corruptione*, *Meteorologica* (first three books); Alkindi's *De Intellectu*, *De Somno et Visione*, *De quinque Essentiis*; the *Liber de Causis* and some other works.

The Toledo school of translators was still of importance in the thirteenth century. Thus Michael Scot (Michael Scottus, died *c*. 1235) translated at Toledo the *De Caelo et Mundo*, the *De Anima*, the zoological writings and also (probably) the *Physics of Aristotle*, as well as Averroes's commentaries on the *De Caelo et Mundo* and the *De Anima*, Avicenna's compendium of the *De Animalibus*, while Herman the German, who died in 1272, as Bishop of Astorga, translated Averroes's 'middle commentary' on the *Nicomachean Ethics* and also his compendium of the same work and his commentaries on the *Rhetoric* and the *Poetics*.

2. It will be seen from what has already been said that it is a mistake to imagine that the Latin Scholastics were entirely dependent on translations from Arabic or even that translation from the Arabic always preceded translation from the Greek. Thus Henricus Aristippus's translation of the fourth book of the *Meteorologica* from the Greek preceded Gerard of Cremona's translation of the first three books of the same work from the Arabic. Moreover, some of the *Metaphysics* had been translated from the Greek before the Arabic translation was made. The translation from the Greek,[1] which did not comprise simply the first three books and a small part of book four, as was formerly supposed, was in use at Paris by 1210 and was known as the *Metaphysica vetus*, in distinction from the translation from the Arabic, which was made by Gerard of Cremona or Michael Scot and was known (in the first half of the thirteenth century) as the *Metaphysica nova*. Books K, M, N, as well as smaller passages, were missing in this translation. In the second half of the century the title *Metaphysica nova* or *Translatio nova* was given to the translation from the Greek by William of Moerbeke (after 1260), upon which translation St. Thomas based his commentary. It has also been shown that there was a *translatio media* from the Greek, on which St. Albert the Great based his commentary and which was known to St. Thomas.

As regards the ethical writings of Aristotle, a translation of Books 2 and 3 of the *Nicomachean Ethics* was available by the end of the twelfth century. This translation had been made from the Greek (possibly it was the work of Boethius himself) and was

[1] St. Thomas's *Translatio Boethii*.

known as the *Ethica vetus*, while a later translation (of Book 1) was known as the *Ethica nova*. A full translation, generally ascribed to Robert Grosseteste (d. 1253), was then made from the Greek, the first three books being a recension of the *Ethica vetus* and the *Ethica nova*. The *Magna Moralia* were translated by Bartholomew of Messina in the reign of King Manfred (1258–66); but only the seventh book of the *Eudemian Ethics* was known in the thirteenth century.

The *De Anima* was translated from the Greek before 1215, the translation from the Arabic by Michael Scot being somewhat later. William of Moerbeke produced a further version from the Greek or a corrected edition of the first translation from the Greek. Similarly there was a translation of the *Physics* from the Greek before the two translations from the Arabic by Gerard of Cremona and Michael Scot, while a translation of the *De Generatione et Corruptione* from the Greek preceded the translation from the Arabic by Gerard of Cremona. The *Politics* were translated from the Greek about 1260 by William of Moerbeke (there was no translation from the Arabic), who probably also translated the *Economics* about 1267. This eminent man, who was born about 1215 and died in 1286, as Archbishop of Corinth, not only translated Aristotle's works from the Greek and re-edited earlier translations (thus enabling his friend, St. Thomas Aquinas, to write his commentaries), but also translated from the Greek some commentaries by Alexander of Aphrodisias, Simplicius, Joannes Philoponus and Themistius, as also some works of Proclus and the latter's exposition of the *Timaeus* of Plato.[1] His translation of Proclus's *Elementatio theologica* brought to St. Thomas the realisation that the *Liber de Causis* was not the work of Aristotle, as it was previously supposed to be, but was based on the work of Proclus. It was also William of Moerbeke who translated the *Rhetoric* of Aristotle. As to the *Poetics*, the mediaevals possessed only Herman the German's translation of Averroes's commentary.[2]

As modern investigation has shown that translations from the Greek generally preceded translations from the Arabic, and that, even when the original translation from the Greek was incomplete, the Arabic-Latin version soon had to give place to a new and

[1] The *Timaeus* of Plato was known to the West, thanks to Cicero and Chalcidius, but it was not until the twelfth century that the *Meno* and *Phaedo* were translated (by Henricus Aristippus).

[2] How far St. Thomas actually used William's translation has been much discussed.

better translation from the Greek, it can no longer be said that the mediaevals had no real knowledge of Aristotle, but only a caricature of his doctrine, a picture distorted by the hand of Arabian philosophers. What can, however, be said is that they were not always able to distinguish what was to be ascribed to Aristotle from what was not to be ascribed to Aristotle. A great step forward was taken when St. Thomas came to realise that the *Liber de Causis* was not the work of Aristotle. He was already quite conscious of the fact that Averroes's commentaries were not to be taken as the unquestionable interpretation of Aristotle's philosophy, but even he seems to have thought, at least for a time, that the Pseudo-Dionysius was not far from being a follower of Aristotle. The fact of the matter is, not that the mediaevals had no reliable texts of Aristotle, but that they were deficient in historical knowledge: they did not, for example, adequately realise the relation of Aristotle to Plato or of neo-Platonism to Plato and Aristotle. That St. Thomas was an able commentator on Aristotle can be denied only by those unacquainted with his commentaries; but it would be foolish to claim even for St. Thomas a knowledge of the history and development of Greek philosophy such as is open to the modern scholar. He made good use of the information available to him; but that information was rather limited.

3. The translation of works of Aristotle and his commentators, as well as of the Arabian thinkers, provided the Latin Scholastics with a great wealth of intellectual material. In particular they were provided with the knowledge of philosophical systems which were methodologically independent of theology and which were presented as the human mind's reflection on the universe. The systems of Aristotle, of Avicenna, of Averroes, opened up a wide vista of the scope of the human reason and it was clear to the mediaevals that the truth attained in them must have been independent of Christian revelation, since it had been attained by a Greek philosopher and his Greek and Islamic commentators. In this way the new translations helped to clarify in the minds of the mediaevals the relation between philosophy and theology and contributed very largely to the delimitation of the provinces of the two sciences. It is, of course, true that Aristotle's system not unnaturally took the limelight in preference to those of his commentators, and his philosophy tended to appear in the eyes of those Latins who were favourably impressed as the *ne plus ultra* of human intellectual endeavour, since it constituted the

most sustained and extensive effort of the human mind with which they were acquainted; but they were quite well aware that it was the work of reason, not a set of revealed dogmas. To us, looking back from a long way off, it may seem that some of the mediaevals exaggerated the genius of Aristotle (we also know that they did not realise the existence of different strata or periods in Aristotle's thought), but we should put ourselves for a moment in their place and try to imagine the impression which would be made on a mediaeval philosopher by the sight of what in any case is one of the supreme achievements of the human mind, a system which, in regard to both completeness and close reasoning, was unparalleled in the thought of the early Middle Ages.

However, the system of Aristotle did not meet with universal welcome and approbation, though it could not be ignored. Largely because the *Liber de Causis* (until St. Thomas discovered the truth), the so-called *Theologia Aristotelis* (extracts from the *Enneads* of Plotinus) and the *De secretis secretorum* (composed by an Arab philosopher in the eleventh or beginning of the twelfth century) were wrongly attributed to Aristotle, the latter's philosophy tended to appear in a false light. Moreover, the attribution of these books to Aristotle naturally made it appear that the Arab commentators were justified in their neo-Platonic interpretation. Hence it came about that in 1210 the Provincial Council of Paris, meeting under the presidency of Peter of Corbeil, Archbishop of Sens, forbad the public or private teaching of Aristotle's 'natural philosophy' or of the commentaries on them. This prohibition was imposed under pain of excommunication and applied to the University of Paris. In all probability 'natural philosophy' included the metaphysics of Aristotle, since when the statutes of the university were sanctioned by Robert de Courçon, Papal Legate, in 1215 Aristotle's works on metaphysics and natural philosophy, as well as compendia of these works and the doctrines of David of Dinant, Amalric of Bene and Maurice of Spain (probably Averroes, the Moor or *Maurus*) were prohibited, though the study of Aristotle's logic was ordered. The study of the *Ethics* was not forbidden.

The reason for the prohibition was, as already indicated, largely due to the ascription to Aristotle of works which were not by him. Amalric of Bene, whose writings were included in the prohibition of 1215, maintained doctrines which were at variance with Christian teaching and which would naturally appear to find some support in the philosophy of Aristotle, if the latter were interpreted in the light of all the books attributed to him, while David of Dinant, the other heretical philosopher whose writings were prohibited, had actually appealed to the *Metaphysics*, which had been translated into Latin from the Greek version brought from Byzantium before 1210. To these considerations must be added the undoubted fact that Aristotle maintained the eternity of the world. It was, therefore, not unnatural that the Aristotelian system, especially when coupled with the philosophies of David of Dinant, Amalric of Bene and Averroes, should appear as a danger to orthodoxy in the eyes of the traditionalists. The logic of Aristotle had long been in use, even if the full *Organon* had come into circulation only comparatively recently, but the complete metaphysical and cosmological teaching of Aristotle was a novelty, a novelty rendered all the more dangerous through association with heretical philosophies.

However, in 1231 Pope Gregory IX, while maintaining the prohibition, appointed a commission of theologians, William of Auxerre, Stephen of Provins and Simon of Authie, to correct the prohibited books of Aristotle, and as this measure obviously implied that the books were not fundamentally unsound, the prohibition tended to be neglected. It was extended to Toulouse in 1245 by Innocent IV, but by that date it was no longer possible to check the spread of Aristotelianism and from 1255 all the known works of Aristotle were officially lectured on in the University of Paris. The Holy See made no move against the university, though in 1263 Urban IV renewed the prohibition of 1210, probably out of a fear of Averroism, the renewed prohibition remaining a dead letter. The Pope must have known perfectly well that William of Moerbeke was translating the prohibited works of Aristotle at his own court, and the prohibition of 1263 must have been designed as a check to Averroism, not as a seriously meant attempt to put an end to all study of the Aristotelian philosophy. In any case the prohibition was of no effect, and finally in 1366 the Legates of Urban V required from all candidates for the Licentiate of Arts at Paris a knowledge of all the known works of Aristotle. It had by then long been clear to the mediaevals that a work like the *Liber de Causis* was not Aristotelian and that the philosophy of Aristotle was not, except, of course, in the eyes of the Latin Averroists, bound up with the interpretation given it by Averroes but could be harmonised with the Christian faith. Indeed the dogmas of faith themselves had by then been expressed by theologians in terms taken from the Aristotelian system.

This brief summary of the official attitude to Aristotle on the part of ecclesiastical and academic authority shows that Aristotelianism triumphed in the end. This does not mean, however, that all mediaeval philosophers of the thirteenth and fourteenth centuries extended an equal welcome to Aristotle or that they all understood him in the same way: the vigour and variety of mediaeval thought will be made clear in succeeding chapters. There is truth in the statement that the shadow of Aristotle hung over and dominated the philosophic thought of the Middle Ages, but it is not the whole truth, and we would have a very inadequate idea of mediaeval philosophy in the thirteenth and fourteenth centuries if we imagined that it was inspired and characterised by a slavish acceptance of every word of the great Greek philosopher.

PART V
THE THIRTEENTH CENTURY

CHAPTER XXII
INTRODUCTION

The University of Paris—Universities closed and privileged corporations—Curriculum—Religious Orders at Paris—Currents of thought in the thirteenth century.

1. THE leading philosophers and theologians of the thirteenth century were all associated, at some period, with the University of Paris, which arose out of the body of professors and students attached to the Cathedral School of Notre Dame and the other schools of Paris, the statutes of the university being sanctioned by Robert de Courçon, Papal Legate, in 1215. Alexander of Hales, St. Bonaventure, St. Albert the Great, St. Thomas Aquinas, Matthew of Aquasparta, Roger Marston, Richard of Middleton, Roger Bacon, Giles of Rome, Siger of Brabant, Henry of Ghent, Raymond Lull, Duns Scotus (d. 1308), all either studied or taught (or both) at Paris. Other centres of higher education were, however, growing in importance and acquiring a tradition of their own. Thus with the University of Oxford were associated the names of men like Robert Grosseteste, Roger Bacon and Duns Scotus, and whereas Paris was the scene of the triumph of Aristotelianism, the name of Oxford recalls a characteristic mingling of the Augustinian tradition with 'empiricism', as in the philosophy of Roger Bacon. Yet in spite of the importance of Oxford, Bologna and, at times, the Papal Court, the University of Paris was easily the most important centre of higher studies in the Christendom of the thirteenth century. Scholars might come to Paris for their studies and then return to Oxford or Bologna to teach, thus carrying with them the spirit and ideals of the great university, and even those scholars who never themselves set foot in Paris were subject to Parisian influence. Robert of Grosseteste, for instance, who possibly never studied at Paris, was certainly influenced by professors of Paris.

The international character of the University of Paris, with its consequent importance in the intellectual expression and defence of Christianity, naturally made the maintenance of religious orthodoxy within its precincts one of the interests of the Holy See. Thus the Averroistic controversy must be seen in the light of the university's international standing: it represented in itself the intellectual culture of the Middle Ages, as far as philosophy and theology were concerned, and the spread within its walls of a system of thought which was irreconcilable with Christianity could not be a matter of indifference to Rome. On the other hand it would be a mistake to suppose that there was any rigid imposition of one particular tradition. St. Thomas Aquinas met with difficulties, it is true, in his acceptance and propagation of Aristotelianism; but such difficulties did not last, and even if the philosophy of Aristotle came in the end to dominate the intellectual life of the university, in the thirteenth and fourteenth centuries there was still plenty of room for different philosophical outlooks.

2. The universities, to be constituted as such, had to receive a formal charter, either from pope or emperor (the University of Naples received its charter from Frederick II) or, later, from kings. These charters conferred considerable privileges on professors and students, privileges which were jealously guarded. The two most important privileges were those of internal jurisdiction (which still survives at Oxford, for example) and of power to give the degree, which carried with it licence to teach. The students were exempt from military service, except in special circumstances, and the university was generally exempt from a great deal of taxation, particularly local taxation. In northern Europe the professors controlled the university, the rector being elected, whereas the universities of southern Europe were often distinctly democratic in their governmental arrangements, but in either case the university was a largely independent and closed corporation, which maintained its privileges against Church and State. In this respect the universities of Oxford and Cambridge represent more faithfully the mediaeval tradition and practice than do those continental universities where rectors and professors are appointed by the State.

3. In mediaeval times, and the same is true of a much later period as well, students entered the university at a much earlier age than they do at present. Thus boys of thirteen or fourteen might begin attending the university, and if one remembers this fact, the number of years required in order to obtain the doctorate

will not appear so surprising. The course in arts lasted some four and a half to six years, according to the university (though at Oxford some seven years were required), and for a time at least the student had to qualify in the faculty of arts before he could proceed to theology. In the theological course he had to spend four years in attending lectures on the Bible and then two more years in attending lectures on the *Sentences*, after which, if by then twenty-six years of age, he became a Baccalaureate and lectured for the two following years on two books of the Bible. He could then lecture on the *Sentences* and finally, after several years spent in study and disputations, he could take the doctorate and teach theology, the minimum age for this being thirty-four. For teaching the arts the minimum age required was twenty. At Paris the tendency was to increase the number of years required for obtaining the doctorate, though at Oxford the arts course was longer and the theological course shorter than at Paris.

Those students who took the doctorate and left the university were known as *magistri non regentes*, whereas those who remained to teach were known as *magistri regentes*; but, however many students there may have been who fell into the first class, it is clear that the long university course was designed to produce professors and teachers by career.

As for the curriculum, the general practice in the university of the thirteenth century was to lecture or listen to lectures on certain texts. Thus, apart from the writings of the grammarians like Priscian and Donatus and certain other classical texts, the writings of Aristotle came to dominate the arts school altogether in the course of time, and it is significant that 'Latin Averroism' was represented principally by professors in that faculty. In theology the Bible and the *Sentences* of Peter Lombard dominated the scene, and the professor gave his own views by way of commentary. Besides the lectures there was another essential feature of the curriculum, namely the disputation, which took the form either of an 'ordinary' disputation (*disputatio ordinaria*) or the 'general' disputation (*de quolibet*). The *disputationes de quolibet*, in which a choice was made from a great variety of topics, were held at solemn feasts, and after the disputation in the strict sense, that is, between a defendant or *respondens* and the objectors, *opponentes*, the professor summed up the whole matter, arguments, objections and replies, and finished by giving his considered solution (*determinatio*) of the point at issue, in which he began with the words,

Respondeo dicendum. The final result, arranged by the professor, was then published as a *Quodlibet.* (St. Thomas left some eleven or twelve *Quodlibets.*) The *disputatio ordinaria* was also followed by a *determinatio* and was published as a *quaestio disputata.* There were other forms of disputation as well; but these two, the *disputatio ordinaria* and the *disputatio de quolibet*, were the most important. They were designed to increase the student's understanding of a particular theme, and his power of argument and of refuting objections. In fact, generally speaking, mediaeval university education aimed rather at imparting a certain body of knowledge and dexterity in dealing with it than at increasing factual knowledge as in a modern research institute. Of course, scholars certainly aimed at increasing knowledge speculatively; but the increase of scientific knowledge, for example, had little place in mediaeval education, though in the fourteenth century science made some progress at Paris and at Vienna.

4. Of considerable importance in the life of Paris and Oxford were the religious Orders, particularly the two mendicant Orders founded in the thirteenth century, the Dominicans and the Franciscans. The former Order established itself in Paris in 1217, the latter a few years later, and both Orders then proceeded to claim chairs of theology in the university, i.e. they claimed that their chairs of theology should be incorporated in the university and that their professors and students should enjoy the university privileges. There was considerable opposition to this claim from the teaching body of the university; but in 1229 the Dominicans received one chair and in 1231 a second, in the same year that the Franciscans obtained their first chair (they did not receive a second). Roland of Cremona and John of St. Giles were the first Dominican professors, Alexander of Hales the first Franciscan professor. In 1248 the General Chapter of the Dominican Order decreed the erection of *studia generalia* (houses of study for the whole Order, distinct from the houses of study of particular provinces) at Cologne, Bologna, Montpellier and Oxford, while the Franciscans meanwhile erected *studia generalia* at Oxford and Toulouse. In 1260 the Augustinians opened a house at Paris, the first official doctor being Giles of Rome, while the Carmelites opened houses at Oxford in 1253 and at Paris in 1259. Other Orders also followed suit.

The religious Orders, particularly the Dominicans and Franciscans, accomplished a great work in the intellectual field and produced men of outstanding eminence (we have only to think of St. Albert the Great and St. Thomas Aquinas in the Dominican, of Alexander of Hales and St. Bonaventure in the Franciscan Order); but they had to put up with a good deal of opposition, doubtless inspired in part by jealousy. Not only did their opponents demand that no religious Order should occupy more than one chair at one time, but they even set about attacking the religious state itself. Thus in 1255 William of St. Amour published a pamphlet, *De periculis novissimorum temporum*, which drew from St. Thomas's pen the *Contra impugnantes Dei cultum*. William of St. Amour's pamphlet was condemned and in 1257 the seculars were forbidden to publish writings against the regulars; but in spite of this prohibition Gerard of Abbeville restarted the opposition with his *Contra adversarium perfectionis christianae*. St. Bonaventure and St. Thomas, however much they might disagree on matters philosophical, were united in a determination to defend the religious Orders, and both published replies to Gerard's work, and these in their turn evoked a counterblast from Nicholas of Lisieux, writing on behalf of the seculars. The quarrel between regulars and seculars broke out again on various later occasions, but, as far as the main point was concerned, the incorporation into the university of the regular chairs, judgement had been given in favour of the regulars and it was not revoked. One result followed, however, which is worthy of mention, and that is the founding of the College of the Sorbonne in 1253 by Robert de Sorbon, chaplain to Louis IX, for the education of students in theology, secular students being admitted. If I call the founding of the College of the Sorbonne and similar colleges a 'result' of the controversy between seculars and regulars, all I mean is that such colleges were founded partly perhaps to counterbalance the influence and position of the regulars and certainly in order to extend to a wider field the benefits of the type of education and training provided by the religious.

5. In the thirteenth century one can distinguish various currents of thought which tended eventually, in the religious Orders, to become more or less fixed in traditional schools. First of all there is the Augustinian current of thought, conservative in character and generally reserved in its attitude towards Aristotelianism, its attitude varying from marked hostility to partial acceptance. This current is characteristic of the Franciscan thinkers (and indeed of the first Dominicans), represented by Grosseteste, Alexander of

Hales and St. Bonaventure. Secondly there is the Aristotelian current of thought, which became characteristic of the Dominicans, represented by St. Albert the Great (in part) and (fully) by St. Thomas Aquinas. Thirdly there are the Averroists, represented by Siger of Brabant. Fourthly one has to take into consideration the independent and eclectic thinkers like Giles of Rome and Henry of Ghent. Fifthly, at the turn of the century, there is the great figure of Duns Scotus who revised the Franciscan tradition in the light of Aristotelianism and who, rather than St. Bonaventure, became the accepted Doctor of his order. I cannot enter in detail into the thought of all the philosophers of the thirteenth century; but I shall endeavour to put in clear relief their salient characteristics, show the variety of thought within a more or less common framework and indicate the formation and development of the different traditions.

CHAPTER XXIII
WILLIAM OF AUVERGNE

Reasons for treating of William of Auvergne—God and creatures; essence and existence—Creation by God directly and in time—Proofs of God's existence—Hylomorphism—The soul—Knowledge—William of Auvergne a transition-thinker.

1. WILLIAM OF AUVERGNE (or William of Paris), author of a *De Trinitate* or *De primo principio* (*c.* 1225), a *De Anima* (1230), a *De universo creaturarum* (*c.* 1231) and other smaller treatises, was Bishop of Paris from 1228 to 1249, the year in which he died. He is not, it is true, one of the best-known thinkers of the Middle Ages; but he claims our attention as a philosopher and theologian who was Bishop of Paris at the time when Gregory IX appointed the commission of theologians to amend the works of Aristotle and thus tacitly modified the Church's attitude towards the pagan philosopher. Indeed William of Auvergne represents the attitude adopted by Gregory IX when he (William) says in his *De Anima* that although Aristotle often contradicts the truth and so must be rejected, his teaching should be accepted when it conforms to the truth, that is, when it is compatible with Christian doctrine. In his fundamental line of thought William continues the tradition of Augustine, Boethius and Anselm, but he knew not only the works of Aristotle, but also the writings of the Arabian and Jewish philosophers and he did not hesitate to utilise their ideas extensively. In general, therefore, one may say that in William of Auvergne we see an intelligent and open-minded adherent of the old tradition who was willing to utilise the new currents of thought but who was perfectly conscious of the points in which the Arabians and Aristotle himself were at variance with Christian doctrine. He is, then, an embodiment of the meeting of the twelfth and thirteenth centuries and has a title to be considered when one is treating of the earlier thinkers of the latter century. Moreover, he was a secular priest who occupied the episcopal see of Paris at the time when the mendicant Orders obtained their first chairs, and on this count too there is justification for discussing his philosophical ideas before proceeding to deal with the thinkers of the Franciscan and Dominican Orders. Nor is he himself a

negligible figure: on the contrary, his thought is vigorous, original and systematic.

2. From Avicenna, William of Auvergne adopted the distinction between essence and existence and made it the explanation of the creature's finitude and dependence. *Esse*, existence, does not belong to the *ratio* or essence of any object save that one object (God) in which it is identical with the essence; of all other objects existence is predicated only 'accidentally', i.e. it belongs to them by participation (*per participationem*). If we consider any finite object, we realise that there is a distinction between its *ratio* or essential nature and its existence, it is not necessary that it should exist; but if we consider the necessary Being, we realise that its essence cannot be conceived without existence. In fine, 'in everything (other than God) *ens* is one thing, *esse* or *entitas* another'.[1] This means that God alone is pure existence, existence being His essence, whereas objects do not exist essentially, because they must, but because their existence is acquired, received. The relation, then, of objects other than God to God must be one of creature to Creator, from which it follows that the theory of emanation is false:[2] God is absolutely simple. Things did not pre-exist in God as parts of God, as they would have had to do if they flowed from God as the waters from a fountain, but only in the *formae exemplares*, which are identical with God. God sees Himself as the exemplary cause of all creatures.[3]

3. If William of Auvergne rejects the neo-Platonist-Arabian theory of emanation, he rejects also the notion of creation by way of intermediaries. The hierarchy of Intelligences posited by Aristotle and his followers has no foundation in reality:[4] God created the world directly. From this it follows that He exercises providence in regard to individual things and William appeals at length to the instinctive activities of the brutes as an illustration of the operation of divine providence.[5] Again, the Aristotelian doctrine of the eternity of the world is rejected. Whatsoever people may say and however much they may try to excuse Aristotle, it is a certain fact that he held that the world is eternal and that it did not begin to be, and Avicenna followed him in this opinion.[6] Accordingly William not only gives the reasons why Aristotle and Avicenna held this opinion, but he even tries to put them in the best light by improving on their arguments, after

[1] Cf. *De Universo*, 1, 3, 26; 2, 2, 8; *De Trinitate*, 1 and 2.
[2] *De Universo*, 1, 1, 17.
[3] *Ibid.*, 1, 1, 17.
[4] *Ibid.*, 1, 1, 24 ff.
[5] *Ibid.*, 1, 3, 2–3.
[6] *Ibid.*, 1, 2, 8.

which he refutes the arguments. For example, the idea that if God preceded the creation of the world, an infinite duration would have to be passed through before creation, and the idea that there would be empty time before creation both rest on a confusion of time with eternity. The idea of infinite duration elapsing before creation would have significance only if eternity were the same as time, i.e. if it were not eternity, if God were in time; and the idea of empty time before creation is also meaningless, since before creation there can be no time. We have to speak of God preceding creation, of existing before the world, it is true, but at the same time we must remember that such phrases are borrowed from temporal duration and that when applied to what is eternal, they are used in an analogical, not in a univocal sense.

However, as William of Auvergne remarks,[1] it is not sufficient to contradict one's opponents and to show the insufficiency of their arguments unless one goes on to prove one's own position positively. He, therefore, gives various arguments for the creation of the world in time, some of which appear again in St. Bonaventure and are declared inconclusive by St. Thomas. For example, William argues, taking the words out of his adversary's mouth, as it were, that if the world had been eternally in existence, an infinite time would have been passed through before the present moment. But it is impossible to pass through an infinite time. Therefore the world cannot have existed from eternity. Therefore it was created in time, that is, a first moment of time is assignable. Again, supposing that the revolutions of Saturn stand to the revolutions of the sun in a proportion of one to thirty, the sun will have made thirty times as many revolutions since creation as Saturn. But if the world exists from eternity, both Saturn and the sun will have made an infinite number of revolutions. Now, how can an infinity be thirty times greater than another infinity?

From what has been already said it is clear that William of Auvergne did not simply deny the neo-Platonic conception of emanation and the Aristotelian idea of an eternal world, while maintaining the Augustinian doctrine of direct and free creation by God in time. On the contrary, he vigorously and exactly detailed and refuted the arguments of his opponents and elaborated systematic proofs of his own thesis. That he was able to do this was largely due to the fact that he was acquainted at first hand with the writings of Aristotle and the Arabians and did not

[1] *De Universo*, 1, 2, 11.

hesitate to utilise not only the Aristotelian logic and the Aristotelian categories but also the ideas of Aristotle, Avicenna and others, when they were acceptable. His utilisation of Avicenna's distinction between essence and existence, for instance, has been already mentioned, and indeed he was the first mediaeval Scholastic to make this distinction an explicit and fundamental point in his philosophy. To this distinction, which enabled him to develop clearly the relation of creature to Creator, William added the doctrine of analogy. Apropos of the statement that finite things possess *esse* 'by participation', he observes that the reader is not to be upset or troubled by the fact that the same word or concept is applied to both God and creatures, since it is not applied in the same sense (*univoce*) or equally: it is applied primarily to God, who *is esse*, and only secondarily to creatures who *have esse*, who participate, that is, in existence in virtue of receiving it through God's creative act. Health, he comments, is predicated of man, of urine, of medicine and of food, but it is not predicated in the same sense or in the same way.[1] The illustration of health is somewhat hackneyed, but it shows that William of Auvergne had apprehended the doctrine of analogy, which is essential to a theistic philosophy.

4. In regard to proofs of God's existence it is a curious fact that William of Auvergne made little use of the proofs used by Aristotle or even by Maimonides. The Aristotelian proof of God as first unmoved mover is not given, and although William certainly looks on God as the first efficient cause, his characteristic proof is one that recalls at least the line of argument adopted by St. Anselm, even though Anselm's argument is not reproduced. The argument in question is from the being which exists by participation to the being which exists essentially, *per essentiam*. This immediately suggests the proof from contingency, which appears in the Arabian and Jewish philosophy, but William prefers to argue from the one concept to the other. For example, the concept *esse adunatum* has as its correlative concept *esse non causatum, esse causatum* involves *esse non causatum, esse secundarium, esse primum*, and so on.[2] William speaks of the *analogia oppositorum* and points out how the one concept or word necessarily involves its correlative concept or word, so that Grunwald[3] can say that William prefers a purely logical or even grammatical mode of proof, in that from one word

[1] *De Trinit.*, 7. [2] *Ibid.*, 6.
[3] *Gesch. der Gottesbeweise im Mittelalter; Beiträge*, 6, 3, p. 92.

he concludes to another word which is contained in or presupposed by the first word. That the argument does tend to give this impression is true, and, if it were a purely verbal argument, it would be open to the retort that the words, or concepts, *esse participatum* or *esse causatum* certainly involve the words, or concepts, *esse per essentiam* or *esse non causatum*, but this is no proof that *esse per essentiam* or *esse non causatum* actually exists, unless it has first been shown that there is an *esse participatum* or an *esse causatum*. Otherwise the proof would be no more a demonstration of God's existence than is St. Anselm's *a priori* argument. However, although William does not sufficiently develop the experiential character of the proof in regard to its starting-point, his argument is by no means purely verbal, since he shows that the object which comes into being cannot be self-dependent or self-caused. *Esse indigentiae* demands *esse sufficientiae* as the reason for its existence, just as *esse potentiale* requires being in act to bring it into a state of actuality. The whole universe requires necessary Being as its cause and reason. In other words, though one may often get the impression that William is simply analysing concepts and hypostasising them, he gives a proof which is not merely logical or verbal but also metaphysical.

5. William of Auvergne accepted the Aristotelian doctrine of hylomorphic composition, but he refused to admit Avicebron's notion that the Intelligences or angels are hylomorphically composed.[1] It is clear that Aristotle did not think that the rational soul contains *materia prima*, since he clearly asserts that it is an immaterial form, and the account of prime matter given by Averroes, according to which prime matter is the potentiality of sensible substance and sensible substance the final act of prime matter, clearly implies the same, that is, that prime matter is the matter of sensible substance only. Moreover, what could be the use of prime matter in the angels, what function could it serve? Matter in itself is something dead; it cannot contribute in any way to intellectual and spiritual operations or even receive them. As he had already utilised the distinction between essence and existence to explain the finitude of creatures and their radical difference from God, William did not require universal hylomorphic composition for this purpose, and as he considered that to postulate the presence of prime matter in the angels would hinder rather than facilitate the explanation of their purely spiritual

[1] *De Universo*, 2, 2, 8.

operations, he restricted prime matter to the sensible world, as St. Thomas did after him.

6. In his psychology, as set forth in the *De Anima*, William of Auvergne combines Aristotelian and Augustinian themes. Thus he expressly adopts the Aristotelian definition of the soul as *perfectio corporis physici organici potentia vitam habentis*,[1] though he warns the reader that he is not quoting Aristotle as an unquestionable authority, but proposes to show the truth of the definition. That he has a soul should be clear to every man, since he is conscious that he understands and judges;[2] but the soul is not the whole of man's nature. If it were, then a human soul joined to an aerial body, for example, would still be a man, whereas in point of fact it would not be. Aristotle, then, was correct in saying that the soul is to the body, as form is to matter.[3] However, that does not prevent him from saying that the soul is a substance on the ground that it must be either substance or accident and cannot be an accident, and he uses the Augustinian comparison of the soul with a harpist, the body being the harp. It might appear that in man there are three souls, one being the principle of life (vegetative soul), the second being the principle of sensation (animal or sensitive soul) and the third being the principle of intellection (rational soul); but a little reflection will show that this cannot be so. If there was an animal soul in man, distinct from the rational or human soul, then humanity, human nature, would not involve animality, whereas in point of fact a man is an animal because he is man, animality belonging to human nature.[4] There is, then, one soul in man, which exercises various functions. It is created and infused by God alone, neither generated by the parents nor educed from the potentiality of matter,[5] and it is, moreover, immortal, as William proceeds to show by arguments, some of which are of Platonic origin. For example, if the malice of an evil soul does not injure or destroy its *esse*, how can bodily death destroy it?[6] Again, since the body receives life from the soul and the soul's power is such that it vivifies a body which, considered in itself, is dead, that is, lacking life, the fact that the body ceases to live cannot destroy the vital power inherent in the soul.[7] Further, the soul can communicate with *substantiae separatae* and is thus like to them, immortal; but as the human soul is indivisible and one, it

[1] *De Anima*, 1, 1. [2] *Ibid.*, 1, 3. [3] *Ibid.*, 1, 2.
[4] *Ibid.*, 4, 1–3. [5] *Ibid.*, 5, 1 ff. [6] *Ibid.*, 6, 1.
[7] *Ibid.*, 6, 7.

follows that the whole human soul is immortal, not simply a rational part.[1]

But though he accepts the Peripatetic doctrine of the soul as form of the body (one must make the reservation that he sometimes uses Platonic-Augustinian expressions in regard to the soul's union with the body), William of Auvergne follows St. Augustine in refusing to recognise a real distinction between the soul and its faculties.[2] Only a substance can understand or will, an accident could not do so. Therefore it is the soul itself which understands or wills, though it exercises itself in regard to different objects, or to the same objects, in different ways, now by apprehending them, now by desiring them. From this it would naturally follow that the Aristotelian distinction between the active and the passive intellects must be rejected, and indeed William of Auvergne rejects the doctrines of the active intellect and of the *species intelligibilis* altogether. The followers of Aristotle and of his commentators swallow the theory of the active intellect without any real reflection, whereas not only are the arguments adduced to prove the theory insufficient, but also very good arguments can be adduced to prove the contrary, the argument from the simplicity of the soul, for example. The active intellect is, then, to be rejected as a useless fiction.[3] *A fortiori*, of course, William rejects the Arabian idea of a *separate* active intellect, an idea which, following Averroes, he ascribed (and probably rightly) to Aristotle himself.

7. In regard to the active intellect, then, William of Auvergne parts company with Aristotle and the Arabians in favour of Augustine, and the Augustinian influence is observable also in his theory of knowledge. Like Augustine he emphasises the soul's knowledge of itself, its direct self-consciousness, and, again like Augustine, he minimises the importance of the senses. It is true that man is inclined to concentrate on bodily things, the objects of the senses; that is why a man may neglect the data of self-consciousness and even be so foolish as to deny the very existence of the immaterial soul. It is also true that for sense-perception the senses are necessary, obviously enough, and that corporeal objects produce a physical impression on the organs of sense. But the intelligible forms, abstract and universal, by which we know the objects of the corporeal world, cannot arise either from the objects themselves or from the phantasms of such objects, since both the

[1] *De Anima*, 6, 8. [2] *Ibid.* [3] *Ibid.*, 7, 3.

objects and the images are particular. How, then, are our abstract and universal ideas of sensible objects produced? They are produced by the understanding itself, which is not purely passive, but active, *effectrix earum* (*scientiarum quae a parte sensibilium ei advenire videntur*) *apud semetipsam et in semetipsa.*[1] This activity is an activity of the soul itself, though it is exercised on the occasion of sense-impressions.

What guarantee is there, then, of the objective character of abstract and universal ideas? The guarantee is the fact that the intellect is not merely active but also passive, though it is in regard to God that it is passive, not in regard to the things of sense. God impresses on the intellect not only the first principles, but also our abstract ideas of the sensible world. In the *De Anima*[2] William teaches explicitly that it is not only the first principles (*regulae primae et per se notae*) and the laws of morality (*regulae honestatis*) which are known in this way, but also the intelligible forms of sensible objects. The human soul occupies a position on the bounds of two worlds (*velut in horizonte duorum mundorum naturaliter esse constitutam et ordinatam*), the one being the world of sensible objects, to which it is joined by the body, the other being, not Plato's universal Ideas or Aristotle's separate Intelligence, but God Himself, *creator ipse,* who is the *exemplar*, the *speculum*, the *liber vivus*, so present to the human intellect that the latter reads off, as it were, in God (*absque ullo alio medio*) the principles and rules and intelligible forms. In this way William of Auvergne makes the active intellect of Aristotle and the Arabians to be God Himself, combining this theory with the Augustinian theory of illumination, interpreted ideogenetically.

8. It may cause surprise that a special chapter has been dedicated to a man whose name is not among the most famous of mediaeval thinkers; but William of Auvergne is of interest not only as a vigorous and systematic philosopher, but also as an illustration of the way in which the metaphysical, cosmological and psychological ideas of Aristotle and the Arabians could affect an open-minded man who stood, generally speaking, in the line of the older tradition. William of Auvergne was quite ready to accept ideas from the Aristotelians; he adopted Aristotle's definition of the soul, for instance, and utilised Avicenna's distinction between essence and existence; but he was first and foremost a Christian philosopher and, apart from any personal predilection

[1] *De Anima*, 5, 6.

[2] 7, 6.

for Augustine, he was not the type of man to adopt Aristotelian or supposedly Aristotelian doctrines when these seemed to him to be incompatible with the Christian faith. Thus the Aristotelian doctrine of the eternity of the world, the neo-Platonic-Arabian notions of emanation and of 'creation' by intermediaries, the theory of a separate, unitary and infra-divine active intellect, he unhesitatingly rejected. It would, however, be a mistake to suppose that he rejected these ideas as incompatible with Christianity and left it at that, for he was clearly satisfied in his own mind that the arguments for the offending positions were inconclusive and insufficient, while the arguments for his own tenets were conclusive. In other words, he was a philosopher and wrote as a philosopher, even though in his works we find theological and philosophical themes treated together in the same book, a feature common to most other mediaeval thinkers.

One may say, then, that William of Auvergne was a transition-thinker. He helped, through his intimate acquaintance with the writings of Aristotle and of the Arabian and Jewish philosophers, and through his limited acceptance of their theories, to pave the way for the completer Aristotelianism of St. Albert and St. Thomas, while, on the other hand, his clear rejection of some leading notions of Aristotle and his followers paved the way for the explicitly anti-Aristotelian attitude of an Augustinian like St. Bonaventure. He is, as I have said earlier, the embodiment of the meeting of the twelfth and thirteenth centuries: he is, one might say, the twelfth century meeting the thirteenth century sympathetically, yet by no means with uncritical admiration or acceptance.

But though we are entitled to regard William of Auvergne as a transition-thinker in respect of the rising influence and growing acceptance of Aristotelianism, i.e. as a stage in the development of thought from the older Augustinianism to the Christian Aristotelianism of St. Thomas, we are also entitled to look upon his philosophy as a stage in the development of Augustinianism itself. St. Anselm had made comparatively little use of Aristotelianism, of which he had but a very restricted knowledge; but later Augustinians were forced to take account of Aristotle, and we find Duns Scotus in the thirteenth century attempting the construction of a synthesis in which Augustinianism would be expounded and defended with the help of Aristotle. Of course, whether one should regard these thinkers as Augustinians who modified and enriched Augustinianism under the influence of Aristotle or as incomplete

Aristotelians, is disputable, and one's estimate of William's philosophy will differ, according as one adopts the one or the other point of view, but unless one is determined to view mediaeval philosophy simply in function of Thomism, one should be prepared to admit that William of Auvergne could be regarded as preparing the way for Duns Scotus just as well as preparing the way for St. Thomas. Probably both judgements are true, though from different viewpoints. In a sense any pre-Thomistic mediaeval philosopher who made some use of Aristotle was preparing the way for a more complete adoption of Aristotelianism, and there can be no difficulty in admitting it; yet it is also legitimate to ask whether Aristotelian elements were employed in the service of the Augustinian tradition, so that the resulting philosophy was one in which characteristic Augustinian themes predominated, or whether they were employed in the construction of a philosophy which was definitely orientated towards Aristotelianism as a system. If one asks this question, there can be little doubt about the answer so far as William of Auvergne is concerned; so that M. Gilson can affirm that 'the complex Augustinian of the thirteenth century is almost completely represented by the doctrine of William of Auvergne' and that while nothing could stop the invasion of the Schools by Aristotle, 'the influence of William certainly did much to retard and limit its progress'.[1]

[1] *La Philosophie au Moyen Age*, third edition, 1944, pp. 423–4.

CHAPTER XXIV

ROBERT GROSSETESTE AND ALEXANDER OF HALES

(a) Robert Grosseteste's life and writings—Doctrine of light—God and creatures—Doctrine of truth and of illumination.
(b) Alexander of Hales's attitude to philosophy—Proofs of God's existence—The divine attributes—Composition in creatures—Soul, intellect, will—Spirit of Alexander's philosophy.

WHEN one is treating of mediaeval philosophy, it is not easy to decide in what way one will group the various thinkers. Thus one might very well treat Oxford and Paris separately. At Oxford the general tendency in metaphysics and psychology was conservative, Augustinian, while at the same time an interest was developed in empirical studies, and the combination of these two factors would afford some reason for tracing the course of philosophy at Oxford from Robert Grosseteste to Roger Bacon in a continuous line; while as regards Paris the Augustinianism of Alexander of Hales and St. Bonaventure on the one hand and the Aristotelianism of St. Albert and St. Thomas on the other hand, together with the relation between the two Schools, might make it desirable to treat them in close proximity. However, such a method has its disadvantages. For example, Roger Bacon died (*c.* 1292) long after Alexander of Hales (1245), in regard to whose writings he made some slighting remarks, and also after St. Albert the Great (1280), towards whom he seems to have felt a special hostility, so that it would seem desirable to consider Roger Bacon after considering these two thinkers. One might, even then, leave over Robert Grosseteste for consideration with Roger Bacon, but the fact remains that Grosseteste died (1253) well before the Oxford condemnation of series of theses, among which figured some of those maintained by St. Thomas (1277 and 1284), whereas Roger Bacon was alive at the time of the condemnations and criticised that of 1277, in so far as he felt that it concerned him personally. While admitting, then, that there would be a great deal to say in favour of another mode of grouping, in which more attention would be paid to spiritual affinities than to chronology, I decided to treat first of Robert Grosseteste at Oxford and Alexander of Hales at Paris, then of Alexander's disciple St. Bonaventure, the greatest representative of the Augustinian tradition in the thirteenth century, then of the Aristotelianism of St. Albert and St. Thomas and of the ensuing controversies, and only afterwards to consider Roger Bacon, in spite of his spiritual affinity with Grosseteste.

(*a*) ROBERT GROSSETESTE

1. Robert Grosseteste was born in Suffolk about 1170 and became Chancellor of Oxford University about 1221. From 1229 to 1232 he was Archdeacon of Leicester and in 1235 he became Bishop of Lincoln, a post which he occupied until his death in 1253. Besides translations (it has already been mentioned that he probably translated the *Ethics* directly from the Greek), Robert Grosseteste composed commentaries on the *Posterior Analytics*, the *Sophistical Arguments*, the *Physics*, though the 'commentary' on the *Physics* was rather a compendium than a commentary, and on the writings of the Pseudo-Dionysius. The statement by Roger Bacon to the effect that Grosseteste *neglexit omnino libros Aristotelis et vias eorum*[1] cannot, therefore, be taken as meaning that he was ignorant of the writings of Aristotle, but must be understood in the sense that, though acquainted with the thought of Aristotle, Grosseteste approached philosophical problems in a different manner. Bacon's further words make this clear, as he says that Grosseteste was dependent on other authors than Aristotle and that he also relied on his own experience.

Of original works Robert Grosseteste published books: *De unica forma omnium*, *De Intelligentiis*, *De statu causarum*, *De potentia et actu*, *De veritate*, *De veritate propositionis*, *De scientia Dei*, *De ordine emanandi causatorum a Deo* and *De libero arbitrio*, the authenticity of the *De Anima* not being certain. In works such as those just named it is quite clear that Grosseteste stood in the Augustinian tradition, although he knew the philosophy of Aristotle and utilised some of his themes. But with his Augustinianism he combined an interest in empirical science which influenced Roger Bacon and excited his admiration, so that Bacon was led to say of his master that he knew the sciences better than other men[2] and was able to explain causes by the aid of mathematics.[3] Thus Grosseteste wrote *De utilitate artium*, *De generatione sonorum*, *De sphaera*, *De computo*, *De generatione stellarum*, *De cometis*, *De impressione aeris*, *De luce*, *De lineis, angulis et figuris*, *De natura locorum*, *De iride*, *De colore*, *De calore solis*, *De differentiis localibus*,

[1] *Compendium studii*, ed. Brewer, p. 469.
[2] *Ibid.*, p. 472.
[3] *Opus Maius*, ed. Bridges, 1, 108.

De impressionibus elementorum, De motu corporali, De motu supercaelestium, De finitate motus et temporis and *Quod homo sit minor mundus*.

2. The philosophy of Robert Grosseteste centres round the idea of light, so dear to the mind of the Augustinian. In the *De luce*[1] Grosseteste remarks that the first corporeal form, which some call corporeity, is in his judgement light. Light unites with matter, that is, with Aristotelian prime matter, to form a simple substance without dimensions. Why does Grosseteste make light the first corporeal form? Because it is the nature of light to diffuse itself and he uses this property of light to explain how a substance composed of non-dimensional form and non-dimensional matter acquires tridimensionality. If we suppose that the function of light is to multiply itself and to diffuse itself and so to be responsible for actual extension, we must conclude that light *is* the first corporeal form, since it would not be possible for the first corporeal form to produce extension through a secondary or consequent form. Moreover, light is the noblest of all forms and bears the greatest resemblance to the separate intelligences, so that on this title also it is the first corporeal form.

Light (*lux*) diffuses itself in all directions, 'spherically', forming the outermost sphere, the firmament, at the farthest point of its diffusion, and this sphere consists simply of light and prime matter. From every part of the firmament light (*lumen*) is diffused towards the centre of the sphere, this light (the light of experience) being *corpus spirituale, sive mavis dicere spiritus corporalis*.[2] This diffusion takes place by means of a self-multiplication and generation of light, so that at intervals, so to speak, there arises a new sphere, until the nine celestial and concentric spheres are complete, the innermost being the sphere of the moon. This sphere in turn produces light, but the rarefaction or diffusion is less as the light approaches the centre, and the four infra-lunar spheres, of fire, air, water and earth are produced. There are, then, thirteen spheres in all in the sensible world, the nine celestial spheres, which are incorruptible and changeless, and the four infra-celestial spheres, which are corruptible and capable of change.

The degree of light possessed by each kind of body determines its place in the corporeal hierarchy, light being the *species et perfectio corporum omnium*.[3] Grosseteste also explains colour in terms of light, declaring that it is *lux incorporata perspicuo*.[4] An

[1] Ed. Baur, p. 51. [2] P. 55. [3] P. 56. [4] *De colore*, p. 78.

abundance of light *in perspicuo puro* is whiteness, while *lux pauca in perspicuo impuro nigredo est*, and he explains in this sense the statement of Aristotle[1] and Averroes that blackness is a privation. Light again is the principle of motion, motion being nothing else but the *vis multiplicativa lucis.*[2]

3. So far light has been considered as something corporeal, as a component of the corporeal; but Grosseteste extends the conception of light to embrace the spiritual world as well. Thus God is pure Light, the eternal Light (not in the corporeal sense, of course), and the angels are also incorporeal lights, participating in the eternal Light. God is also the 'Form of all things', but Grosseteste is careful to explain that God is not the form of all things as entering into their substance, uniting with their matter, but as their exemplary form.[3] God precedes all creatures, but 'precedes' must be understood as meaning that God is eternal, the creature temporal: if it is understood as meaning that there is a common duration in which both God and creatures exist, the statement will be incorrect, since the Creator and the creature do not share any common measure.[4] We naturally *imagine* a time in which God existed before creation, just as we naturally imagine space outside the universe; but reliance on the imagination in such matters is a source of error.

4. In the *De veritate propositionis*[5] Grosseteste says that *veritas sermonis vel opinionis est adaequatio sermonis vel opinionis et rei*, but he concentrates more on 'ontological truth', on the Augustinian view of truth. He is willing to accept the Aristotelian view of the truth of enunciation as *adaequatio sermonis et rei* or *adaequatio rei ad intellectum*, but truth really means the conformity of things to the eternal Word *quo dicuntur* and consists in their conformity to the divine Word.[6] A thing is true, in so far as it is what it ought to be, and it is what it ought to be when it is conformed to the Word, that is, to its exemplar. This conformity can be perceived only by the mind, so that truth may also be defined with St. Anselm as *rectitudo sola mente perceptibilis.*[7]

From this it follows that no created truth can be perceived except in the light of the supreme Truth, God. Augustine bore witness to the fact that a created truth is visible only in so far as the light of its *ratio eterna* is present to the mind.[8] How is it, then,

[1] *Physics*, 201 a 6; *Metaph.*, 1065 b 11. [2] *De motu corporali et luce*, p. 92.
[3] *De unica forma omnium*, p. 109.
[4] *De ordine emanandi causatorum a Deo*, p. 149. [5] P. 144.
[6] *De veritate*, pp. 134–5. [7] *Ibid.*, p. 135. [8] *Ibid.*, p. 137.

that the wicked and impure can attain truth? They cannot be supposed to see God, who is seen only by the pure of heart. The answer is that the mind does not perceive the Word or the *ratio eterna* directly, but perceives truth in the light of the Word. Just as the bodily eye sees corporeal objects in the light of the sun without looking directly at the sun or even perhaps adverting to it at all, so the mind perceives truth in the light of the divine illumination without thereby perceiving God, the *Veritas summa*, directly or even without necessarily realising at all that it is only in the divine light that it sees truth.[1] Thus Grosseteste follows the Augustinian doctrine of divine illumination, but explicitly rejects any interpretation of the doctrine which would involve a vision of God.

Into Grosseteste's views on mathematics, perspective, etc., I cannot enter: enough has been said to show how Grosseteste's philosophy was built upon Augustinian lines by a man who yet knew and was willing to utilise Aristotelian ideas.

(*b*) ALEXANDER OF HALES

5. There was within the Franciscan Order a party of zealots who adopted a hostile attitude towards learning and other accommodations to the needs of life, which they regarded as treason to the simple idealism of the Seraphic Father; but these 'Spirituals' were frowned upon by the Holy See, and in point of fact the Franciscan Order produced a long line of distinguished theologians and philosophers, the first eminent figure being that of the Englishman, Alexander of Hales, who was born in Gloucestershire between 1170 and 1180, entered the Franciscan Order about 1231 and died in 1245. He was the first Franciscan professor of theology at Paris and occupied the chair until within a few years of his death, having as his successor John of la Rochelle.

It is difficult to ascertain exactly what contributions to philosophy are to be ascribed to Alexander of Hales in person, since the *Summa theologica* which passes under his name, and which drew caustic comments from Roger Bacon, comprises elements, particularly in the latter portion, taken from the writings of other thinkers and seems to have attained its final form some ten years or more after Alexander's death.[2] In any case, however, the work represents a stage in the development of western philosophy and

[1] *De veritate*, p. 138.

[2] References below are to the *Summa theologica* in the Quaracchi edition, according to volume and section.

a tendency in that development. It represents a stage, since the Aristotelian philosophy as a whole is clearly known and utilised: it represents a tendency, since the attitude adopted towards Aristotle is critical, in the sense that Alexander not only attacks certain doctrines of Aristotle and the Aristotelians but also considers that the pagan philosophers were unable to formulate a satisfactory 'philosophy', in the wide sense, owing to the fact that they did not possess the Christian revelation: a man on a hill can see more even of the valley than the man at the foot of the hill can see. He followed, therefore, his Christian predecessors (the Fathers, especially St. Augustine, Boethius, the Pseudo-Dionysius, St. Anselm, the Victorines) rather than Aristotle.

6. The doctrine of the Blessed Trinity cannot be attained by man's unaided reason, owing to the weakness of the human intellect,[1] but God's existence can be known by all men, whether they are good or bad.[2] Distinguishing God's existence (*quia est*) from His nature (*quid est*) Alexander teaches that all can know God's existence by means of creatures, recognising God as efficient and final cause.[3] Moreover, though the natural light of reason is insufficient to attain to a knowledge of the divine nature as it is in itself, that does not mean that all knowledge of God's nature is barred to the natural intellect, since it can come to know something of God, for example, His power and wisdom, by considering His operation in creatures, a degree of knowledge open to those who are not in a state of grace.[4] This type of knowledge is not univocal but analogical.[5] For example, goodness is predicated of God and of creatures, but while it is predicated of God *per naturam*, as being identical with His nature and as the self-existent source of all goodness, it is predicated of creatures *per participationem*, inasmuch as creatures depend on God, are God's effects, and receive a limited degree of goodness from Him.

In proving God's existence Alexander makes use of a variety of arguments. Thus he uses Richard of St. Victor's proof from contingency, St. John Damascene's argument from causality and Hugh of St. Victor's argument from the soul's knowledge that it had a beginning; but he also employs St. Augustine's and St. Anselm's proof from the eternity of truth and accepts the latter's proof from the idea of the Perfect, as given in the *Proslogium*.[6] In addition he maintains that it is impossible to be ignorant of God's

[1] 1, no. 10. [2] 1, no. 15. [3] 1, no. 21. [4] 1, no. 15.
[5] 1, no. 21. [6] 1, no. 25.

existence.[1] This is a startling proposition, but it is necessary to bear in mind certain distinctions. For instance, we must distinguish habitual knowledge and actual knowledge (*cognitio habitu, cognitio actu*). The former, says Alexander, is a habit naturally impressed on the intellect, enabling the intellect to know God, and would seem to be little more than implicit knowledge, if 'implicit knowledge' can be called knowledge at all. St. Albert the Great comments, rather sarcastically, that this distinction is a *solutio mirabilis*.[2] Actual knowledge itself must also be distinguished, since it may comprise the soul's recognition that it is not *a se* or it may mean a concentration on creatures. In so far as actual knowledge of the first sort is concerned, the soul cannot fail to know God's existence, though it would appear that the actual recognition of God may even here be 'implicit', but in so far as the soul is turned away from God by sin and error and rivets its attention on creatures, it may fail to realise God's existence. In this latter case, however, a further distinction must be introduced between knowledge of God *in ratione communi* and knowledge of God *in ratione propria*. For example, the man who places his happiness in riches or sensual pleasures knows God in a sense, since God is Beatitude, but he does not have a true notion of God, *in ratione propria*. Similarly the idolater recognises God *in communi*, for example, as 'Something', but not as He really is, *in ratione propria*. Such distinctions may indeed appear somewhat far-fetched, but Alexander is taking into account such facts as St. Paul's[3] saying that the heathen know God but have not glorified Him as God or St. John Damascene's declaration that the knowledge of God is naturally impressed on the mind.[4] The view that the human mind cannot be without any knowledge of God is characteristic of the Augustinian School; but, in view of the fact that idolaters and, at least, professed atheists exist, any writer who wishes to maintain such a view is bound to introduce the distinction between implicit and explicit knowledge or between knowledge of God *in ratione communi* and knowledge of God *in ratione propria*.

7. Alexander treats of the divine attributes of immutability, simplicity, infinity, incomprehensibility, immensity, eternity, unity, truth, goodness, power and wisdom, giving objections, his own reply to the general question and answers to the objections.

[1] 1, no. 26. [2] *S.T.*, p.1., tr. 4, q. 19.
[3] Romans 1. [4] *De fide orthod.*, 1, cc. 1 and 3; *P.G.*, 94, 790 and 794.

Appeals to former writers and quotations from authorities like Augustine and Anselm are frequent, nor is the doctrine developed in a particularly original fashion, but the arrangement is systematic and careful, and a considerable amount of general philosophical reflection is included. For instance, when treating of the unity of the divine nature, Alexander begins by considering unity in general, defining *unitas* as *indivisio entis* and *unum* as *ens indivisum in se, divisum autem ab aliis*,[1] and goes on to consider the relation of unity to being, truth and goodness.[2] As regards the divine knowledge, Alexander maintains, following Augustine and Anselm, that God knows all things in and through Himself. The exemplar or eternal 'ideas' of creatures are in God, though, considered in themselves, they do not form a plurality but are identical with the one divine essence, so that it is by knowing Himself that God knows all things. How, then, does He know evil and sin? Only as defect, i.e. a defect from goodness. If light, says Alexander, following the Pseudo-Dionysius, were gifted with the power of knowing, it would know that this or that object was unreceptive of its action: it would not know darkness in itself without any relation to light. This involves, of course, the view that evil is nothing positive but rather a privation,[3] for, if evil were something positive, it would be necessary either to maintain dualism or to say that evil has an exemplar in God.

In treating of the divine will Alexander raises the question whether or not God can order actions which are against the natural law. The immediate origin of the question is a problem of Scriptural exegesis; how, for example, to explain God's order to the Israelites to despoil the Egyptians, but the question has, of course, a much wider significance. God, he answers, cannot order an action which would be formally contrary to the natural law, since this would be to contradict Himself; He cannot, for instance, will that man should have any other end but God, since God is essentially the final end. Nor could God order the Israelites to steal in the proper sense of the word, as implying an act directed against God Himself, a sin. God can, however, deprive the Egyptians of their property and so order the Israelites to take it. He can also order the Israelites to take something that belongs to another, since this affects only the *ordo ad creaturam*, but cannot order them to take it *ex cupiditate*, since this affects the *ordo ad Deum* and would involve self-contradiction on God's part.[4]

[1] 1, no. 72. [2] 1, no. 73. [3] Cf. 1, nos. 123ff. [4] 1, no. 276.

Similarly, God could order the prophet Osee to have intercourse with a woman who was not his wife, in so far as this act involved the *ordo ad creaturam*, but He could not order Osee to do this *ex libidine*, since this would involve the *ordo ad Deum*. Alexander's distinctions on this matter are somewhat obscure and not always satisfactory, but it is in any case clear that he did not believe that the moral law depends on God's arbitrary *fiat*, as Ockham was later to maintain.

8. God is the immediate Creator of the world, in regard both to matter and form, and the non-eternity of the world can be proved.[1] Thus Alexander rejects the Aristotelian notion of the eternity of the world, but he accepts the doctrine of hylomorphic composition. This composition is found in every creature, since 'matter' equals potentiality, but a more fundamental composition, also found in every creature, is that between the *quo est* and the *quod est*.[2] It may appear that this is the distinction between essence and existence, but it seems rather that the *quod est* refers to the concrete being, a man, for instance, and the *quo est* to the abstract essence, humanity, for example. In any case the distinction is a 'rational' distinction, since we can predicate the *quo est* of the *quod est*, in a certain sense at least, as when we say that this being is a man. There is no real distinction between a man and his humanity; yet the humanity is received. In God there is no dependence, no reception, and so no composition between the *quod est* (*Deus*) and the *quo est* (*Deitas*).

9. In accordance with his general spirit of reliance on tradition, Alexander of Hales gives and defends seven definitions or descriptions of the human soul.[3] For example, the soul may be defined as *Deiforme spiraculum vitae*,[4] or as *substantia quaedam rationis particeps, regendo corpori accommodata*[5] or as *substantia spiritualis a Deo creata, propria sui corporis vivificatrix.*[6] Other definitions are taken from St. Augustine, St. John Damascene and Seneca. The soul, insists Alexander, is not a substance simply in the sense that it is a substantial form, but it is an *ens in se*, a substance *simpliciter*, composed of 'intellectual' matter and form. If in this respect he follows the Platonic-Augustinian tradition, even suggesting that the soul must be a substance since it stands to the body as the sailor to the ship, he also insists that the soul vivifies the body.

[1] 2, no. 67. [2] 2, nos. 59–61. [3] 2, no. 321.
[4] Cf. *De sp. et an.*, c. 42, (placed among works of Augustine; P. L. 40, 811) and St. Aug., *De Gen. ad litt.*, 7 cc. 1–3.
[5] St. Aug., *De quant. an.*, c. 13, n. 22. [6] Cassiodorus, *De Anima*, c. 2.

An angel is also *spiraculum vitae*, but an angel is not *spiraculum vitae corporis*, whereas the soul is the principle of the body's life.

Each human soul is created by God out of nothing.[1] The human soul is not an emanation of God, part of the divine substance,[2] nor is it propagated in the manner postulated by the traducianists. Original sin can be explained without recourse to a traducianist theory.[3] The soul is united with the body after the manner of the union of form with matter (*ad modum formae cum materia*),[4] but this must be interpreted in an Augustinian sense, since the rational soul is joined to its body *ut motor mobili et ut perfectio formalis suo perfectibili*.[5] The soul has the three powers of the *vis vegetativa*, the *vis sensitiva* and the *vis intellectiva*, and though these powers are not to be called parts of the soul, in the strict sense of the word 'part',[6] they are yet distinct from one another and from the essence of the soul. Alexander, therefore, explains Augustine's assertion of the identity of the soul and its powers by saying that this identity is to be referred to the substance, not to the essence of the soul.[7] The soul cannot subsist without its powers nor are the powers intelligible apart from the soul, but just as *esse* and *operari* are not identical, so are *essentia* and *potentia* not identical.

The active and passive intellects are *duae differentiae* of the rational soul, the former referring to the spiritual form of the soul, the latter to its spiritual matter, and the active intellect is not separate from the soul but belongs to it.[8] But together with the Aristotelian classification of the rational powers of the soul Alexander gives also the classifications of St. Augustine and St. John Damascene and attempts to reconcile them. For example, 'intellect' in the Aristotelian philosophy refers to our power of acquiring knowledge of intelligible forms by means of abstraction,[9] and it corresponds, therefore, to the Augustinian *ratio*, not to the Augustinian *intellectus* or *intelligentia*, which has to do with spiritual objects. Intellect in the Aristotelian sense has to do with embodied forms and abstracts them from the *phantasmata*, but intellect in the Augustinian sense has to do with non-embodied, spiritual forms, and when there is question of knowing those forms which are superior to the human soul, the intellect is powerless unless it is illuminated by God.[10] Alexander provides no clear

[1] 2, nos. 329 and 322. [2] 2, no. 322. [3] 2, no. 327. [4] 2, no. 347. [5] 2, no. 345. [6] 2, no. 351. [7] 2, no. 349. [8] 2, no. 372. [9] 2, no. 368. [10] 2, no. 372.

explanation of what this illumination precisely is, but he at least makes it clear that he accepts the Aristotelian doctrine of abstraction in regard to the corporeal world, though in regard to the spiritual world the doctrine of Aristotle has to be supplemented by that of Augustine. One may also remark that Alexander was quite right in seeing in the Peripatetic classification a psychological analysis and in the Augustinian classification a division according to the objects of knowledge.

Alexander gives three definitions of free will, that of St. Anselm (*potestas servandi rectitudinem propter se*), that of St. Augustine (*facultas rationis et voluntatis, qua bonum eligitur gratia assistente et malum eadem desistente*) and that of St. Bernard (*consensus ob voluntatis inamissibilem libertatem et rationis indeclinabile iudicium*) and attempts to reconcile them.[1] *Liberum arbitrium* is common to God and the soul, but it is predicated neither universally nor equivocally, but analogically, primarily of God, secondarily of the creature.[2] In man it is one faculty or function of reason and will in union, and it is in this sense only that it may be termed distinct from reason and will: it is not in reality a separate power of the soul. Moreover, inasmuch as it is bound up with the possession of reason and will, it is inseparable from the soul, that is, as far as natural liberty is concerned. Following St. Bernard, Alexander distinguishes *libertas arbitrii* and *libertas consilii et complaciti* and declares that, while the latter may be lost, the former cannot.

10. Alexander of Hales is of interest, since his main work is a sustained effort of systematic thought, being a Scholastic presentation of the Christian theology and philosophy. In regard to form it belongs to the mediaeval period of the *Summas*, sharing in the merits and defects of that type of compilation, in their succinctness and orderly arrangement as in their aridity and absence of developments which, from our point of view, might be desirable. As regards content, on the one hand Alexander's *Summa* stands in close connection with the past, as the author is determined to be faithful to tradition and very frequently quotes Augustine or Anselm, Bernard or John Damascene, instead of developing his own arguments. This does not mean that he appeals simply to authority, in the sense of merely citing famous names, since he often quotes the arguments of his predecessors; but it does mean that the developed arguments which would have been desirable even at the time he wrote, are absent. However, his work is, of

[1] Cf. 2, nos. 393–6. [2] 2, no. 402.

course, a *Summa*, and a *Summa* is admittedly a summary. On the other hand the work shows a knowledge of Aristotle, though he is not often explicitly mentioned, and it makes some use of the Peripatetic doctrine. There is always present, however, the desire to harmonise the elements taken from Aristotle with the teaching of Augustine and Anselm, and the general tendency is towards a contrast between the God-enlightened Christian thinkers on the one hand and the Philosophers on the other hand. It is not that Alexander gives the impression of being a polemical writer nor that he confuses philosophy and theology,[1] but he is chiefly concerned with the knowledge of God and of Christ. To say that, is simply to say that he was faithful to the tradition of the Augustinian School.

[1] Cf. I, no. 2.

CHAPTER XXV

ST. BONAVENTURE—I

Life and works—Spirit—Theology and philosophy—Attitude to Aristotelianism.

1. ST. BONAVENTURE, Giovanni Fidanza, was born at Bagnorea in Tuscany in the year 1221. Healed of a sickness while a child, through his mother's invocation of St. Francis of Assisi, he entered the Franciscan Order at a date which cannot be exactly determined. It may have been shortly before or after 1240, but in any case Bonaventure must have become a Franciscan in time to study under Alexander of Hales at Paris before the latter's death in 1245. The teaching of Alexander evidently made a great impression on his pupil, for in his *Praelocutio prooemio in secundum librum Sententiarum praemissa* Bonaventure declares that just as in the first book of the *Sentences* he has adhered to the common opinions of the masters, and especially to those of 'our master and father of happy memory Brother Alexander', so in the following books he will not stray from their footsteps.[1] In other words Bonaventure imbibed the Franciscan, i.e. the Augustinian, tradition, and he was determined to keep to it. It might perhaps be thought that this determination indicated simply a pious conservatism and that Bonaventure was ignorant of or at least ignored and adopted no definite and positive attitude towards the new philosophical tendencies at Paris; but the Commentary on the *Sentences* dates from 1250–1 (he started lecturing in 1248, on St. Luke's Gospel) and at that date Bonaventure cannot have made his studies at Paris and yet have been ignorant of the Aristotelian philosophy. Moreover, we shall see later that he adopted a very definite attitude towards that philosophy, an attitude which was not simply the fruit of ignorance but proceeded from reflection and reasoned conviction.

St. Bonaventure was involved in the same difficulties between regulars and seculars in which St. Thomas Aquinas was involved, and in 1255 he was excluded from the university, that is, he was refused recognition as a doctor and professor of the university

[1] Alexander appears again as 'our father and master' in 2 *Sent.*, 23, 2, 3; II, p. 547.

staff. He may have been readmitted in 1256, but in any case he was accepted, along with Aquinas, in October 1257, as a result of Papal intervention. He was then a professor of theology at the university, as far as acceptance was concerned, and would doubtless have proceeded to exercise that office had he not been elected Minister General of his Order on February 2nd, 1257. The fulfilment of the normal functions of his office would by itself have prevented his living the settled life of a university professor, but in addition there were differences of opinion at the time within the Order itself in regard to its spirit, practice and function, and Bonaventure was faced with the difficult task of maintaining or restoring peace. However, in 1259 he wrote the *Itinerarium mentis in Deum*, in 1261 his two lives of St. Francis, in 1267 or 1268 the *Collationes de decem praeceptis* (Lenten sermons), the *De decem donis Spiritus sancti* (about 1270), the *Collationes in Hexaëmeron* in 1273. The *Breviloquium* was written before 1257. The Commentaries on the Scriptures, short mystical treatises, sermons, and letters on points connected with the Franciscan Order make up his other writings at various periods of his life.

Although in 1265 Bonaventure had succeeded in inducing the Pope to rescind his appointment to the Archbishopric of York, he was appointed Bishop of Albano and Cardinal in 1273. In 1274 he was present at the Council of Lyons, where he preached on the reunion of the Eastern Church with Rome, but on the conclusion of the Council he died (July 15th, 1274) and was buried at Lyons in the presence of Pope Gregory X.

2. St. Bonaventure was not only himself a man of learning, but he also encouraged the development of studies within the Franciscan Order, and this may appear strange in the case of a Franciscan saint, when it can hardly be said that the founder had envisaged his friars devoting themselves to erudition. But it is, of course, perfectly clear to us, as it was to Bonaventure, that an order consisting largely of priests, with a vocation which involved preaching, could not possibly fulfil its vocation unless its members, at least those who were destined for the priesthood, studied the Scriptures and theology. But it was impossible to study Scholastic theology without acquiring a knowledge of philosophy, so that philosophical and theological studies were both necessary. And once this general principle was admitted, as admitted it must be, it was hardly practicable to set a limit to the degree of study. If the students were to be trained in philosophy and theology, they

had to have professors and the professors had not only to be competent themselves but to educate their successors. Moreover, if apostolic work might involve contact with learned men, perhaps also with heretics, one could not set on *a priori* grounds a limit to the study which might be advisable.

One might indeed multiply such practical considerations, which justified the development of studies within the Franciscan Order; but, as far as Bonaventure is concerned, there is an equally important consideration to be mentioned. St. Bonaventure was perfectly faithful to the spirit of St. Francis in regarding union with God as the most important aim in life; but he saw very well that this would scarcely be attained without knowledge of God and the things of God, or at least that such knowledge, so far from being a hindrance to union with God, should predispose the soul to closer union. After all, it was the study of the Scriptures and of theology which he recommended and himself pursued, not the study of questions which had no connection with God, and this was one of the reasons why he disliked and mistrusted the metaphysical philosophy of Aristotle, which had no place for personal communion with the Godhead and no place for Christ. There is, as M. Gilson has pointed out, a certain parallel between the life of St. Francis and the teaching of St. Bonaventure. For just as the former's personal life culminated in mystical communion with God, so the latter's teaching culminated in his mystical doctrine, and just as Francis had approached God through Christ and had seen, *concretely*, all things in the light of the divine Word, so Bonaventure insisted that the Christian philosopher must see the world in its relation to the creative Word. Christ, as he expressly says, is the *medium* or Centre of all sciences, and so he could not accept the Aristotelian metaphysic, which, so far from knowing anything of Christ, had rejected even the exemplarism of Plato.

In the end the Franciscan Order accepted Duns Scotus as its doctor *par excellence*; but though it was doubtless right in so doing and though Scotus was undoubtedly a man of genius, a thinker of great speculative and analytic ability, one may perhaps say that it was St. Bonaventure who stood nearer in thought, as in time, to the spirit of the Seraphic Father. Indeed, it is not without reason that he was accorded the title of the Seraphic Doctor.

3. St. Bonaventure's view of the purpose and value of study, determined as much by his own inclinations and spiritual tendencies as by his intellectual training under Alexander of Hales and

his membership of the Franciscan Order, naturally placed him in the Augustinian tradition. St. Augustine's thought centred round God and the soul's relation to God, and, since the man who is related to God is the concrete and actual man of history, who has fallen from grace and who has been redeemed by grace, Augustine dealt with man in the concrete and not with the 'natural man', not, that is, with man considered apart from his supernatural vocation and in abstraction from the operation of supernatural grace. This meant that St. Augustine could make no very rigid distinction between philosophy and theology, even though he distinguished between the natural light of reason and supernatural faith. There is, of course, adequate justification for treating in philosophy of man in 'the state of nature', since the order of grace is super-natural and one can distinguish between the order of grace and the order of nature; but the point I want to make is simply this, that if one is principally interested in the soul's advance to God, as Augustine and Bonaventure were, then one's thought will centre round man in the concrete, and man in the concrete is man with a supernatural vocation. Man considered in the 'state of nature', is a legitimate abstraction; but this legitimate abstraction will not appeal to one whose thought centres round the actual historical order. It is largely a question of approach and method. Neither Augustine nor Bonaventure would deny the distinction between the natural and the supernatural, but since they were both primarily interested in the actual historical man, who, be it repeated, is man with a supernatural vocation, they naturally tended to mingle theological and philosophical themes in one Christian wisdom rather than to make a rigid, methodological distinction between philosophy and theology.

It may be objected that in this case St. Bonaventure is simply a theologian and not a philosopher at all; but one can give a similar answer in the case of Bonaventure as in that of Augustine. If one were to define a philosopher as one who pursues the study of Being or the ultimate causes, or whatever other object one is pleased to assign to the philosopher, without any reference to revelation and prescinding *completely* from dogmatic theology, the Christian dispensation and the supernatural order, then of course neither Augustine nor Bonaventure could be termed a philosopher; but if one is willing to admit into the ranks of the philosophers all those who pursue what are generally recognised as philosophical themes, then both men must be reckoned philosophers. Bonaventure may sometimes treat, for instance, of the stages of the soul's ascent from knowledge of God through creatures to immediate and interior experience of God and he may speak of the stages without any clear demarcation of what is proper to theology and what is proper to philosophy; but that does not alter the fact that in treating of knowledge of God through creatures, he develops proofs of God's existence and that these proofs are reasoned arguments and so can be termed philosophical arguments. Again, Bonaventure's interest in the material world may be principally an interest in that world as the manifestation of God and he may delight to see therein *vestigia* of the Triune God, but that does not alter the fact that he holds certain opinions about the nature of the world and its constitution which are cosmological, philosophical, in character. It is true that to isolate Bonaventure's philosophical doctrines is in a sense to impair the integrity of his system; but there are philosophical doctrines in his system and this fact entitles him to a place in the history of philosophy. Moreover, as I shall mention shortly, he adopted a very definite attitude towards philosophy in general and the Aristotelian system in particular, and on this count alone he merits a place in the history of philosophy. One could hardly exclude Kierkegaard from the history of philosophy, although his attitude towards philosophy, in his understanding of the term, was hostile, for he philosophised about philosophy: still less can one exclude Bonaventure whose attitude was less hostile than that of Kierkegaard and who represents a particular standpoint in regard to philosophy, the standpoint of those who maintain not only that there is such a thing as Christian philosophy, but also that every independent philosophy is bound to be deficient and even partly erroneous as philosophy. Whether this standpoint is right or wrong, justified or unjustified, it deserves consideration in a history of philosophy.

Bonaventure was, then, of the Augustinian tradition; but it must be remembered that a great deal of water had flowed under the bridge since the time of Augustine. Since that time Scholasticism had developed, thought had been systematised, the Aristotelian metaphysic had been fully made known to the western Christian world. Bonaventure commented on the *Sentences* of Peter Lombard and he was acquainted with the thought of Aristotle: we would only expect, then, to find in his writings not only far more elements of Scholasticism and of the Scholastic method than in Augustine but also an adoption of not a few

Aristotelian ideas, for Bonaventure by no means rejected Aristotle lock, stock and barrel: on the contrary he respected him as a natural philosopher, even if he had no high opinion of his metaphysics, of his theology at least. Thus from the point of view of the thirteenth century the Bonaventurian system was a modern Augustinianism, an Augustinianism developed through the centuries and re-thought in relation to Aristotelianism.

4. What then was Bonaventure's view of the general relation of philosophy to theology and what was his view of Aristotelianism? The two questions can be taken together, since the answer to the first determines the answer to the second.

As has already been remarked, Augustine distinguished faith and reason, and Bonaventure naturally followed him, quoting Augustine's words to the effect that what we believe we owe to authority, what we understand to reason.[1] It follows from this, one might think, that philosophy and theology are two separate sciences and that an independent philosophy of a satisfactory character is, at least theoretically, possible. Indeed Bonaventure actually makes an explicit and clear distinction between dogmatic theology and philosophy. For example, in the *Breviloquium*[2] he says that theology begins with God, the supreme Cause, with whom philosophy ends. In other words, theology takes its data from revelation and proceeds from God Himself to His effects, whereas philosophy starts with the visible effects and argues to God as cause. Again, in the *De Reductione Artium ad Theologiam*[3] he divides 'natural philosophy' into physics, mathematics and metaphysics, while in the *In Hexaëmeron*[4] he divides philosophy into physics, logic and ethics.

In view of the above, how can it be maintained that St. Bonaventure did not admit of any rigid distinction between philosophy and theology? The answer is that he admitted a methodological distinction between the sciences and also a distinction of subject-matter, but insisted that no satisfactory metaphysic or philosophical system can be worked out unless the philosopher is guided by the light of faith and philosophises in the light of faith. For instance, he was well aware that a philosopher can arrive at the existence of God without the aid of revelation. Even if he had not been convinced of this by his own reason and by the testimony of the Scriptures, the philosophy of Aristotle would have been

[1] Aug., *De utilitate credendi*, 11, 25; Bonav., *Breviloq.*, 1, 1, 4.
[2] 1, 1. [3] 4. [4] 4, 2.

sufficient to persuade him of the fact. But he was not content to say that the knowledge of God so attained is incomplete and stands in need of the completion provided by revelation: he went further and stated that such purely rational knowledge is, and must be, in important points erroneous. This point he proved empirically. For example, 'the most noble Plotinus of the sect of Plato and Tully of the academic sect', in spite of the fact that their views on God and the soul were preferable to those of Aristotle, fell into error since they were unaware of the supernatural end of man, of the true resurrection of the body and of eternal felicity.[1] They could not know these things without the light of faith, and they fell into error precisely because they had not got the light of faith. Similarly, a mere metaphysician may come to the knowledge of the supreme Cause, but if he is a mere metaphysician he will stop there, and if he stops there he is in error, since he thinks of God otherwise than He is, not knowing that God is both one and three. 'Philosophical science is the way to other sciences; but he who wishes to stop there, falls into darkness.'[2] In other words, Bonaventure is not denying the power of the philosopher to attain truth, but he maintains that the man who is satisfied with philosophy, who is a mere philosopher, necessarily falls into error. It is one thing if a man comes by reason to know that there exists one God and then goes on to recognise, in the light of faith, that this unity is a unity of Nature in Trinity of Persons, and quite another thing if a man stops short at the unity of God. In the latter case the man affirms the unity of Nature to the exclusion of the Trinity of Persons, and to do this is to fall into error. If it is objected that it is not necessary to exclude the Trinity, since a philosopher may prescind from revelation altogether, so that his philosophical knowledge, though incomplete, remains valid and true, Bonaventure would doubtless answer that if the man is simply a philosopher and rests in philosophy, he will be convinced that God is one in Nature and not three in Persons. In order to make due allowance for the completion, he must already possess the light of faith. The light of faith does not supply the rational arguments for God's existence (there is such a thing as philosophy), but it ensures that the philosophy remains 'open' and that it does not close in on itself in such a way that error results.

Bonaventure's view of Aristotelianism follows easily enough from these premisses. That Aristotle was eminent as a natural

[1] *In Hexaëm.*, 7, 3 ff. [2] *De Donis*, 3, 12.

philosopher, that is, in regard to sensible objects, Bonaventure admits: what he will not admit is that Aristotle was a true metaphysician, that is, that the metaphysics of Aristotle are satisfactory. Some people, seeing that Aristotle was so eminent in other sciences, have imagined that he must also have attained truth in metaphysics; but this does not follow, since the light of faith is necessary in order to form a satisfactory metaphysical system. Moreover, Aristotle was so competent in other sciences precisely because his mind and interests were of such a kind that he was not inclined to form a philosophy which should point beyond itself. Thus he refused to find the principle of the world outside the world: he rejected the ideas of Plato[1] and made the world eternal.[2] From his denial of the Platonic theory of ideas there followed not only the denial of creationism, but also the denial of God's knowledge of particulars, and of divine foreknowledge and providence.[3] Again, the doctrine of the unicity of the intellect is at least attributed to Aristotle by Averroes, and from this there follows the denial of individual beatitude or punishment after death.[4] In short, though all pagan philosophers have fallen into error, Aristotle was more involved in error than Plato or Plotinus.

Possibly one may obtain a clearer view of Bonaventure's notion of the relation of philosophy to theology if one bears in mind the attitude of the Catholic philosopher in practice. The latter works out arguments for the existence of God, for example, but he does not make himself an atheist for the time being nor does he deny his faith in the dogma of the Trinity: he philosophises in the light of what he already believes and he will not conclude to a unity in God of such a kind that it will exclude the Trinity of Persons. On the other hand his arguments for God's existence are rational arguments: in them he makes no reference to dogma, and the value of the proofs as such rests on their philosophical merits or demerits. The philosopher pursues his arguments, psychologically speaking, in the light of the faith which he already possesses and which he does not discard during his philosophical studies, and his faith helps him to ask the right questions and to avoid untrue conclusions, though he does not make any formal use of the faith in his philosophic arguments. The Thomist would, of course, say that the faith is to the philosopher an extrinsic norm, that the philosopher prescinds from his faith, even though he does not deny it,

[1] *In Hexaëm.*, 6, 2. [2] *Ibid.*, 4. [3] *Ibid.*, 2–3. [4] *Ibid.*, 4.

and that a pagan could, theoretically at least, reach the same conclusions in philosophy. St. Bonaventure, however, would reply that, even though the philosopher may make no formal use of dogma in this or that metaphysical argument, he certainly philosophises in the light of faith and that this is something positive: the action of faith is a positive influence on the mind of the philosopher and without it he will inevitably fall into error. One cannot exactly say that St. Bonaventure believed only in a total Christian wisdom comprising indifferently philosophical and theological truths, since he admitted a classification of the sciences in which philosophy figures; but, this latter point once admitted, one can say that his ideal was the ideal of a Christian wisdom in which the light of the Word is shed not only on theological but also on philosophical truths, and without which those truths would not be attained.

I have argued that since St. Bonaventure certainly treated of philosophical questions, he has a claim to be included in a history of philosophy, and I do not see how this contention can be seriously disputed; but it remains true that he was a theologian, that he wrote as a theologian and that he did not really consider philosophical questions and problems for their own sake. St. Thomas Aquinas was also primarily a theologian, and he wrote primarily as a theologian; but he did consider philosophical problems at length and even composed some philosophical works, which St. Bonaventure did not do. The Commentary on the *Sentences* was not what we would to-day call a philosophical work. It seems, therefore, to constitute something of an exaggeration when M. Gilson maintains, in his magnificent study of St. Bonaventure's philosophical thought, that there is a Bonaventurian philosophical system, the spirit and content of which can be sharply defined. We have seen that St. Bonaventure recognised philosophy as a definite science, separate from theology; but as far as he himself is concerned, he might be called a philosopher *per accidens*. In a sense the same is true, of course, of any mediaeval thinker who was primarily a theologian, even of St. Thomas; but it is most relevant in the case of a thinker who was chiefly concerned with the soul's approach to God. Moreover, M. Gilson probably tends to exaggerate St. Bonaventure's hostility to pagan philosophy and to Aristotle in particular. I have indeed admitted that St. Bonaventure attacked the Aristotelian metaphysic (this is a fact which cannot be denied) and that he considered that any philosopher who is merely a philosopher will inevitably fall into error; but it is desirable in this connection to call to mind the fact that St. Thomas himself insisted on the moral necessity of revelation. On that point St. Bonaventure and St. Thomas were in agreement. They both rejected pagan philosophy where it was incompatible with Christianity, though they differed as to what precise points were to be rejected and how far one could go in following Aristotle.

However, though I think that M. Gilson's genius for capturing the peculiar spirit of the individual thinker and for setting it in clear relief leads him to exaggerate the systematic aspect of St. Bonaventure's philosophy and to find a greater opposition between the views of Bonaventure and Thomas in regard to the pagan philosophers than probably exists in actual fact, I cannot subscribe to the judgement of M. Fernand Van Steenberghen[1] that 'the philosophy of St. Bonaventure is an eclectic and neo-platonising Aristotelianism, put at the service of an Augustinian theology'. That Bonaventure made considerable use of Aristotelianism is perfectly true; but the inspiration of his philosophy is, in my opinion, what for want of a better word we call 'Augustinian'. As I remarked in regard to William of Auvergne, it depends to a large extent on one's point of view whether one calls those Augustinian theologians who adopted selected Aristotelian doctrines in philosophy incomplete Aristotelians or modified Augustinians; but in the case of a man whose whole interest centred round the soul's ascent to God, who laid such stress on the illuminative action of God and who, as M. Van Steenberghen himself states when criticising M. Gilson, never worked out a philosophy for its own sake, it seems to me that 'Augustinian' is the only fit word for describing his thought, if for no better reason than the principle that *maior pars trahit minorem* and that the spirit must take precedence of the letter.

[1] *Aristote en Occident*, p. 147.

CHAPTER XXVI

ST. BONAVENTURE—II: GOD'S EXISTENCE

*Spirit of Bonaventure's proofs of God's existence—Proofs from sensible world—*A priori *knowledge of God—The Anselmian argument—Argument from truth.*

1. We have seen that St. Bonaventure, like St. Augustine, was principally interested in the soul's relation to God. This interest had an effect on his treatment of the proofs for God's existence; he was chiefly concerned to exhibit the proofs as stages in the soul's ascent to God or rather to treat them in function of the soul's ascent to God. It must be realised that the God to whom the proofs conclude is not, then, simply an abstract principle of intelligibility, but is rather the God of the Christian consciousness, the God to whom men pray. I do not, of course, mean to suggest that there is, ontologically, any discrepancy or any irreconcilable tension between the God of the 'philosophers' and the God of experience; but since Bonaventure is primarily interested in God as Object of worship and prayer and as goal of the human soul, he tends to make the proofs so many acts of drawing attention to the self-manifestation of God, whether in the material world or within the soul itself. Indeed, as one would expect, he lays more emphasis on proofs from within than on proofs from the material world, from without. He certainly does prove God's existence from the external sensible world (St. Augustine had done this) and he shows how from the knowledge of finite, imperfect, composite, moving and contingent beings man can rise to the apprehension of the infinite, perfect, simple, unchanging and necessary Being; but the proofs are not systematically elaborated, the reason for this being, not any inability on Bonaventure's part to develop the proofs dialectically, but rather his conviction that the existence of God is so evident to the soul through reflection on itself that extra-mental creation serves mainly to remind us of it. His attitude is that of the Psalmist, when he says: *Coeli enarrant gloriam Dei, et opera manuum eius annuntiat firmamentum.* Thus it is quite true that the imperfection of finite and contingent things demands and proves the existence of absolute perfection, God; but, asks St. Bonaventure in a truly Platonic manner, 'how could the intellect

know that this being is defective and incomplete, if it had no knowledge of Being without any defect?'[1] In other words, the idea of imperfection presupposes the idea of perfection, so that the idea of perfection or the perfect cannot be obtained simply by way of negation and abstraction, and consideration of creatures in their finiteness and imperfection and dependence serves simply to remind the soul or to bring the soul to a clearer awareness of what is in some sense already evident to it, already known to it.

2. St. Bonaventure does not deny for a moment that God's existence can be proved from creatures: on the contrary he affirms it. In the Commentary on the *Sentences*[2] he declares that God can be known through creatures as Cause through effect, and he goes on to say that this mode of cognition is natural to man inasmuch as for us sensible things are the means by which we arrive at the knowledge of '*intelligibilia*', that is, objects transcending sense. The Blessed Trinity cannot be proved in the same way, however, by the natural light of reason, since we cannot conclude to the Trinity of Persons either by denying certain properties or limitations of creatures or by the positive way of attributing to God certain qualities of creatures.[3] St. Bonaventure thus teaches clearly enough the possibility of a natural and 'philosophic' knowledge of God, and his remark on the psychological naturalness of this approach to God through sensible objects is Aristotelian in character. Again, in the *In Hexaëmeron*[4] he argues that if there exists being which is produced, there must be a first Being, since there must be a cause: if there is being *ab alio*, there must be Being *a se*: if there is a composite being, there must be simple Being: if there is changeable being, there must be unchanged Being, *quia mobile reducitur ad immobile*. The last statement is obviously a reference to the Aristotelian proof of the existence of the unmoved mover, though Bonaventure mentions Aristotle only to say that he argued on these lines to the eternity of the world and that on this point the Philosopher was wrong.

Similarly in the *De Mysterio Trinitatis*[5] Bonaventure gives a series of brief arguments to show how clearly creatures proclaim the existence of God. For instance, if there is *ens ab alio*, there must exist *ens non ab alio*, because nothing can bring itself out of a state of non-being into a state of being, and finally there must be a first Being which is self-existent. Again, if there is *ens*

[1] *Itin.*, 3, 3.
[2] 1, 3, 2: *Utrum, Deus sit cognoscibilis per creaturas.*
[3] 1 *Sent.*, 3, 4.
[4] 5, 29.
[5] 1, 1, 10-20.

possibile, Being which can exist and can not exist, there must be *ens necessarium*, being which has no possibility of non-existence, since this is necessary in order to explain the eduction of possible being into a state of existence; and if there is *ens in potentia*, there must be *ens in actu*, since no potency is reducible to act save through the agency of what is itself in act; and ultimately there must be *actus purus*, a Being which is pure Act, without any potentiality, God. Again, if there is *ens mutabile*, there must be *ens immutabile* because, as the Philosopher proves, motion has as its principle an unmoved being and exists for the sake of unmoved being, which is its final cause.

It might indeed appear from such passages, where Bonaventure employs Aristotelian arguments, that the statements to the effect that Bonaventure regarded the witness of creatures to God's existence in function of the soul's ascent to God and that he regarded the existence of God as a self-evident truth, cannot stand. But he makes it quite clear in various places[1] that he regards the sensible world as the mirror of God and sense-knowledge or knowledge obtained through sense and reflection on sensible objects as, formally, the first step in the stages of the soul's spiritual ascent, the highest stage of which in this life is the experimental knowledge of God by means of the *apex mentis* or *synderesis scintilla* (on this point he shows himself faithful to the tradition of Augustine and the Victorines), while in the very article of the *De Mysterio Trinitatis* where he gives the proofs cited he affirms emphatically that God's existence is indubitably a truth naturally implanted in the human mind (*quod Deum esse sit menti humanae indubitabile, tanquam sibi naturaliter insertum*). He goes on to declare that, in addition to what he has already said on this matter, there is a second way of showing that the existence of God is an indubitable truth. This second way consists in showing that what every creature proclaims is an indubitable truth, and it is at this point that he gives his succession of proofs or rather of indications that every creature really does proclaim God's existence. Subsequently he adds that there is a third way of showing that God's existence cannot be doubted and proceeds to give his version of St. Anselm's proof in the *Proslogium*. There can, then, be no doubt at all that Bonaventure affirmed that God's existence is self-evident and cannot be doubted: the question is rather what exactly he meant by this, and we will consider this in the next section.

[1] For example, in the *Itinerarium mentis in Deum*, c. 1.

3. In the first place St. Bonaventure did not suppose that everyone has an explicit and clear knowledge of God, still less that he has such a knowledge from birth or from the first use of reason. He was well aware of the existence of idolaters and of the *insipiens*, the fool who said in his heart that there is no God. The existence of idolaters does not, of course, cause much difficulty since idolaters and pagans do not so much deny the existence of God as possess a wrong idea of God; but what of the *insipiens*? The latter sees, for example, that the impious are not always punished in this world or at least that they sometimes appear to be better off in this world than many good people, and he concludes from this that there is no divine Providence, no divine Ruler of the world.[1] Moreover, he explicitly affirms,[2] in answer to the objection that it is useless to prove the existence of that which is self-evident, of that concerning which no one doubts, that though the existence of God is indubitable so far as objective evidence is concerned, it can be doubted *propter defectum considerationis ex parte nostra* because of want of due consideration and reflection on our part. Does not this look as if Bonaventure is saying no more than that objectively speaking, the existence of God is indubitable (i.e. the evidence, when considered, is indubitable and conclusive), but that subjectively speaking it may be doubted (i.e. because this or that human being does not give sufficient attention to the objective evidence); and if this is what he means when he says that God's existence is indubitable and self-evident, how does his position differ from that of St. Thomas?

The answer seems to be this. Although St. Bonaventure did not postulate an explicit and clear idea of God in every human being, still less any immediate vision or experience of God, he certainly postulated a dim awareness of God in every human being, an implicit knowledge which cannot be fully denied and which can become an explicit and clear awareness through interior reflection alone, even if it may sometimes need to be supported by reflection on the sensible world. The universal knowledge of God is, therefore, implicit, not explicit; but it is implicit in the sense that it can at least be rendered explicit through interior reflection alone. St. Thomas admitted an implicit knowledge of God, but by this he meant that the mind has the power of attaining to the knowledge of God's existence through reflection on the things of sense and by arguing from effect to cause, whereas St. Bonaventure meant

[1] *De Mysterio Trinitatis*, 1, 1, *conclusio*. [2] *Ibid.*, 12.

something more by implicit knowledge, that is, virtual knowledge of God, a dim awareness which can be rendered explicit without recourse to the sensible world.

Application of this view to Bonaventure's concrete instances may make the understanding of it easier. For instance, every human being has a natural desire for happiness (*appetitus beatitudinis*). But happiness consists in the possession of the supreme Good, which is God. Therefore every human being desires God. But there can be no desire without some knowledge of the object (*sine aliquali notitia*). Therefore the knowledge that God or the supreme Good exists is naturally implanted in the soul.[1] Similarly, the rational soul has a natural knowledge of itself, because it is present to itself and is knowable by itself. But God is most present to the soul and is knowable. Therefore a knowledge of its God is implanted in the soul. If it be objected that while the soul is an object proportionate to its own power of knowing, God is not, the reply can be made that, if that were true, the soul could never come to the knowledge of God, which is obviously false.[2]

According to the above line of argument, then, the human will is naturally orientated towards the supreme Good, which is God, and not only is this orientation of the will inexplicable unless the supreme Good, God, really exists, but it also postulates an *a priori* knowledge of God.[3] This knowledge is not necessarily explicit or clear, since if it were there could be no atheists, but it is implicit and vague. If it is objected that an implicit and vague knowledge of this kind is not knowledge at all, it may be answered that an unprejudiced man who reflects on the orientation of his will towards happiness can come to realise that the direction of his will implies the existence of an adequate object and that this object, the complete Good, must exist and is what we call God. He will realise not only that in seeking happiness he is seeking God, but that this search implies an inkling, as it were, of God, since there can be no search for what is *entirely* unknown. Therefore, by reflecting on itself, on its own dependence and on its own desires for wisdom, peace or felicity, the soul can recognise God's existence and even God's presence, God's activity within it: it is not necessary for it to seek without, it has only to follow Augustine's

[1] *De Mysterio Trinitatis*, 1, 1, 7. [2] *Ibid.*, 10.

[3] When speaking here of a 'natural' orientation of the will, I do not mean to use the term in a strictly theological sense, but rather in the sense that the will of man in the concrete is directed to the attainment of God, prescinding altogether from the question whether or not there is a *desiderium naturale videndi Deum*.

advice and enter within itself, when it will see that it was never without some inkling, some dim awareness, a 'virtual' knowledge of God. To seek for happiness (and every human being must seek for happiness) and to deny God's existence is really to be guilty of a contradiction, to deny with the lips what one affirms with the will and, in the case of wisdom at least, with the intellect. Whether this line of argument is valid or not, I do not propose to discuss here. It is obviously open to the objection, cogent or otherwise, that if there were no God, then the desire for happiness might be *frustra* or might have some other cause than the existence of God. But it is at least clear that St. Bonaventure did not postulate an innate idea of God in the crude form under which Locke later attacked innate ideas. Again, when St. Bonaventure declares that the soul knows God as most present to it, he is not affirming ontologism or saying that the soul sees God immediately: he means that the soul, recognising its dependence, recognises, if it reflects, that it is the image of God: it sees God in His image. As it necessarily knows itself, is conscious of itself, it necessarily knows God in at least an implicit manner. By contemplating itself it can make this implicit awareness explicit, without reference to the external world. Whether the absence of reference to the external world is more than formal, in the sense that the external world is not explicitly mentioned, is perhaps disputable.

4. We have seen that for St. Bonaventure the very arguments from the external world presuppose some awareness of God, for he asks how the mind can know that sensible things are defective and imperfect if it has no previous awareness of perfection, in comparison with which it recognises the imperfections of creatures. This point of view must be borne in mind when considering his statement of St. Anselm's proof, which he adopted from the *Proslogium*.

In the Commentary on the *Sentences*[1] St. Bonaventure resumes the Anselmian argument. God is that than which no greater can be thought. But that which cannot be thought not to exist is greater than that which can be thought not to exist. Therefore, since God is that than which no greater can be thought, God cannot be thought not to exist. In the *De Mysterio Trinitatis*[2] he quotes and states the argument at somewhat greater length and points out[3] that doubt may arise if someone has an erroneous notion of God and does not realise that He is that than which no

[1] 1, 8, 1, 2. [2] 1, 1, 21–4. [3] *Ibid.*, *conclusio.*

greater can be thought. Once the mind realises what the idea of God is, then it must also realise not only that the existence of God cannot be doubted, but also that His non-existence cannot even be thought. As regards Gaunilo's objection about the best of all possible islands St. Bonaventure answers[1] that there is no parity, for while there is no contradiction involved in the concept of a Being than which no greater can be thought the idea of an island than which no better can be thought is a contradiction in terms (*oppositio in adiecto*), since 'island' denotes an imperfect being whereas 'than which no better can be thought' denotes a perfect being.

This method of argument may appear to be purely dialectical, but, as already mentioned, Bonaventure did not regard the idea of the perfect as obtained simply through a negation of the imperfection of creatures, but as something presupposed by our recognition of the imperfection of creatures, at least in the sense that man's desire of the perfect implies a previous awareness. In accordance with the Platonic-Augustinian tradition Bonaventure presupposed, then, a virtual innate idea of the perfect, which can be nothing else but God's imprint on the soul, not in the sense that the soul is perfect but in the sense that the soul receives the idea of the perfect or forms the idea of the perfect in the light of God, through the divine illumination. The idea is not something negative, the realisation of which in concrete existence can be denied, for the presence of the idea itself necessarily implies God's existence. On this point we may note the resemblance at least between St. Bonaventure's doctrine and that of Descartes.[2]

5. St. Augustine's favourite argument for the existence of God had been that from truth and the existence of eternal truths: St. Bonaventure utilised this argument as well. For example, every affirmative proposition affirms something as true; but the affirmation of any truth affirms also the cause of all truth.[3] Even if someone says that a man is an ass, this statement, whether correct or not, affirms the existence of the primal truth, and even if a man declares that there is no truth, he affirms this negation as true and so implies the existence of the foundation and cause of truth.[4] No truth can be seen save through the first truth, and the truth

[1] *De Mysterio Trinitatis*, 1, 1, 6.

[2] Cf. E. Gilson's Commentary on the *Discours de la Méthode*, concerning the idea of the perfect.

[3] 1 *Sent.*, 8, 1, 2, *conclusio*.

[4] *Ibid.*, 5 and 7. Cf. *De Mysterio Trinitatis*, 1, 1, 26.

through which every other truth is seen, is an indubitable truth: therefore, since the first Truth is God, God's existence is indubitable.[1]

But here again St. Bonaventure is not pursuing a merely verbal and dialectical argument. In a passage of the *In Hexaëmeron*,[2] where he points out that the man who says there is no truth contradicts himself, since he affirms it as true that there is no truth, he remarks that the light of the soul is truth, which so enlightens the soul that it cannot deny truth's existence without contradicting itself, and in the *Itinerarium mentis in Deum*[3] he maintains that the mind can apprehend eternal truths and draw certain and necessary conclusions only in the divine light. The intellect can apprehend no truth with certainty save under the guidance of Truth itself. To deny God's existence, then, is not simply to be guilty of a dialectical contradiction; it is also to deny the existence of the Source of that light which is necessary for the mind's attainment of certitude, the light *quae illuminat omnem hominem venientem in hunc mundum*: it is to deny the Source in the name of that which proceeds from the Source.

[1] *De Mysterio Trinitatis*, 1, 1, 25. [2] 4, 1. [3] 3, 2ff.

CHAPTER XXVII

ST. BONAVENTURE—III
RELATION OF CREATURES TO GOD

Exemplarism—The divine knowledge—Impossibility of creation from eternity—Errors which follow from denial of exemplarism and creation—Likeness of creatures to God, analogy—Is this world the best possible world?

1. WE have seen that the lines of proof adopted by St. Bonaventure lead, not to the transcendent and self-enclosed unmoved Mover of Aristotle (though he does not hesitate to utilise the Philosopher's thought and to cite him when he considers it apposite), but to the God, at once transcendent and immanent, who is the Good which draws the will, the Truth which is not only foundation of all particular truths but also the Light which through its radiation within the soul makes the apprehension of certain truth possible, the Original which is mirrored in the human soul and in nature, and the Perfect which is responsible for the idea of the perfect within the human soul. In this way the arguments for God's existence stand in close relation to the spiritual life of the soul, revealing to it the God whom it has always sought, if only in a semi-conscious fashion, and the God who has always operated within it. The further knowledge of God which is given by revelation crowns the philosophic knowledge and opens up to the soul higher levels of spiritual life and the possibility of a closer union with God. Philosophy and theology are thus integrated together, the former leading on to the latter, the latter shedding light on the deeper meaning of the former.

A similar integration of philosophy and theology is seen in Bonaventure's doctrine of exemplarism, which in his eyes was a matter of the greatest importance. In the *In Hexaëmeron*[1] he makes exemplarism the central point of metaphysics. The metaphysician, he says, proceeds from the consideration of created, particular substance to the uncreated and universal substance (not in the pantheistic sense, of course), and so, in so far as he deals in general with the originating Principle of all things, he is akin to the natural philosopher who also considers the origins of

[1] 1, 13.

things, while in so far as he considers God as final end he shares his subject-matter to some degree with the moral philosopher, who also considers the supreme Good as the last end, giving his attention to happiness in the practical or speculative order. But in so far as the metaphysician considers God, the supreme Being, as exemplary cause of all things, he shares his subject-matter with no one else (*cum nullo communicat et verus est metaphysicus*). The metaphysician, however, if he will attain the truth concerning exemplarism, cannot stop at the mere fact that God is the exemplary Cause of all things, for the *medium* of creation, the express image of the Father and the exemplar of all creatures, is the divine Word. Precisely as a philosopher he cannot come to a certain knowledge of the Word, it is true;[1] but then if he is content to be a mere philosopher, he will fall into error: he must, enlightened by faith, proceed beyond mere philosophy and realise that the divine Word is the exemplary Cause of all things. The purely philosophic doctrine of exemplarism thus prepares the way for the theology of the Word and, conversely, the theology of the Word sheds light on the truth attained by philosophy, and in this sense Christ is the *medium* not only of theology, but also of philosophy.

An obvious conclusion in regard to Aristotle follows from this position. Plato had maintained a doctrine of archetypal ideas or essences and, whatever Plato himself may or may not have thought, the neo-Platonists at least 'located' these ideas in the divine mind, so that St. Augustine was enabled to praise Plato and Plotinus on this account; but Aristotle rejected the ideas of Plato and attacked his theory with bitterness (*in principio Metaphysicae et in fine et in multis aliis locis exsecratur ideas Platonis*).[2] In the *Ethics* too he attacks the doctrine, though the reasons he gives are worthless (*nihil valent rationes suae*).[3] Why did he attack Plato? Because he was simply a natural philosopher, interested in the things of the world for their own sake, and gifted with the *sermo scientiae* but not with the *sermo sapientiae*. In refusing to despise the sensible world and in refusing to restrict certainty to knowledge of the transcendent Aristotle was right as against Plato, who, in his enthusiasm for the *via sapientiae*, destroyed the *via scientiae*, and he rightly censured Plato on this point, but he himself went to the opposite extreme and destroyed the *sermo sapientiae*.[4] Indeed, by denying the doctrine of exemplarism,

[1] *In Hexaëm.*, 1, 13. [2] *Ibid.*, 6, 2. [3] *Ibid.* [4] *Serm.*, 18.

Aristotle necessarily involved himself also in a denial of divine creation and divine providence, so that his error was worse than that of Plato. Now, exemplarism, on which Plato insisted, is, as we have seen, the key to and centre of metaphysics, so that Aristotle, by rejecting exemplarism, excluded himself from the rank of metaphysicians, in Bonaventure's understanding of the term.

But we have to go beyond Plato and learn from Augustine, to whom was given both the *sermo sapientiae* and the *sermo scientiae*,[1] for Augustine knew that the ideas are contained in the divine Word, that the Word is the archetype of creation. The Father knows Himself perfectly and this act of knowledge is the image and expression of Himself: it is His Word, His *similitudo expressiva*.[2] As proceeding from the Father the Word is divine, the divine Son (*filius* denotes the *similitudo hypostatica*, the *similitudo connaturalis*),[3] and as representing the Father, as *Imago*, as *similitudo expressa*, the Word expresses also, represents, all that the Father can effect (*quidquid Pater potest*).[4] If anyone could know the Word, he would know all knowable objects (*si igitur intelligis Verbum, intelligis omnia scibilia*).[5] In the Son or Word the Father expressed all that He could make (i.e. all possible beings are ideally or archetypally represented in the Word) and all that He would make.[6] The 'ideas' of all creatures, therefore, possible and actual, are contained in the Word, and these ideas extend not only to universals (*genera* and *species*), but also to singular or individual things.[7] They are infinite in number, as representing all possibles, as representing the infinite power of God.[8] But when it is said that there is an infinity of ideas in the Word, it is not meant that the ideas are really distinct in God, for there is no distinction in God save the distinctions of Persons: considered as existent in God, they are not distinct from the divine Essence or from one another (*ideae sunt unum secundum rem*).[9] It follows that, not being distinct from one another, they cannot form a real hierarchy.[10] However, although the ideas are ontologically one and there is no real distinction between them, there is a distinction of reason, so that they are *plures secundum rationem intelligendi*.[11] The foundation of the distinction cannot be any real distinction in the divine Essence, since not only are the ideas ontologically identical with the simple divine Essence, but also there is no real relation on the part of God to creatures, for He is in no way

[1] *Serm.*, 4, 19. [2] *Breviloq.*, 1, 3. [3] *Ibid.* [4] *In Hexaëm.*, 3, 4.
[5] *Ibid.* [6] *Ibid.*, 1, 13. [7] 1 *Sent.*, 35, *art. unicus*, 4. [8] *Ibid.*, 5.
[9] *Ibid.*, 2. [10] *Ibid.*, 6. [11] *Ibid.*, 3.

dependent on creatures, though there is a real relation on the part of creatures to God and God and creatures are not the same, so that from the point of view of the things signified or connoted the ideas are distinct *secundum rationem intelligendi*. In God the ideas are one, but from our point of view they stand midway, as it were, between God the knower and the thing known, the distinction between them being, not a distinction in what they are (i.e. not a real distinction) but a distinction in what they connote, and the foundation of the distinction being the real multiplicity of the things connoted (i.e. creatures), not any real distinction in the divine Essence or in the divine knowledge.

Plato was working towards this theory of ideas, but as he lacked the light of faith, he could not ascend to the true doctrine but necessarily stopped short: in order to possess the true doctrine of ideas, it is necessary to have knowledge of the Word. Moreover, just as creatures were produced through the medium of the Word and could not have been produced save through the Word, so they cannot be truly known save in the light of their relation to the Word. Aristotle may have been, indeed was, an eminent natural philosopher, but he could not know truly even the selected objects of his studies, since he did not see them in their relation to the Word, as reflections of the divine Image.

2. God, then, in knowing Himself knows also all ways in which His divine essence can be mirrored externally. He knows all the finite good things which will be realised in time, and this knowledge Bonaventure calls the *cognitio approbationis*, the knowledge of those things to which His *beneplacitum voluntatis* extends. He knows too, not only all the good things which have been, are and will be in the course of time, but also all the evil things, and this knowledge Bonaventure calls the *cognitio visionis*. Needless to say St. Bonaventure does not mean to imply that evil has its exemplary idea in God: evil is rather the privation in the creature of that which it ought to have according to its idea in God. God knows too all possible things, and this knowledge Bonaventure terms *cognitio intelligentiae*. Its objects, the possibles, are infinite in number, whereas the objects of the two former types of knowledge are finite.[1] The three types of knowledge are, however, not accidents in God, distinct from one another: considered ontologically, as in God, they are one act of knowledge, identical with the divine essence.

[1] Cf. 1 *Sent.*, 39, 1, 2 and 3; *De Scientia Christi*, 1.

God's act of knowledge is infinite and eternal, so that all things are present to Him, even future events: there is no succession in the divine knowledge, and if we speak of God's 'foreknowledge' we must understand the futurity as concerning the objects themselves (in the sense that they succeed one another in time and are known by God to succeed one another in time), not as concerning the divine knowledge itself. God knows all things by one eternal act and there is no temporal succession in that act, no before and after; but God knows eternally, through that one act, things as succeeding one another in time. Bonaventure therefore makes a distinction in regard to the statement that God knows all things *praesenter*, pointing out that this *praesentialitas* must be understood in reference to God (*a parte cognoscentis*), not in reference to the objects known (*a parte cognitorum*). If it were understood in the latter sense, the implication would be that all things are present to one another, which is false, for they are not all present to one another, though they are all present to God.[1] Imagine, he says,[2] an eye fixed and motionless on a wall and observing the successive movements of all persons and things down below with a single act of vision. The eye is not changed, nor its act of vision, but the things under the wall are changed. This illustration, remarks Bonaventure, is really in no way like what it illustrates, for the divine knowledge cannot be pictured in this way; but it may help towards an understanding of what is meant.

3. If there were no divine ideas, if God had no knowledge of Himself and of what He can effect and will effect, there could be no creation, since creation demands knowledge on the Creator's part, knowledge and will. It is not a matter for surprise, then, that Aristotle, who rejected the ideas, rejected also creation and taught the eternity of the world, a world uncreated by God. At least he is judged to have held this by all the Greek Doctors, like Gregory of Nyssa, Gregory Nazianzen, Damascene and Basil, and by all the Arabian commentators, while you will never find Aristotle himself saying that the world had a beginning: indeed he censures Plato, the only Greek philosopher who seems to have declared that time had a beginning.[3] St. Bonaventure need not have spoken so cautiously, since Aristotle certainly did not believe in a divine creation of the world out of nothing.

St. Thomas saw no incompatibility, from the philosophical standpoint, between the idea of creation on the one hand and of

[1] Cf. 1 *Sent.*, 39, 2, 3, *conclusio*. [2] *Ibid.*, 2, *conclusio*. [3] *In Hexaëm.*, 6, 4.

the world's eternity on the other, so that for him the world might have had no beginning in time and yet have been created, that is, God might have created the world from eternity; but St. Bonaventure considered that the eternity of the world is impossible and that God could not have created it from eternity: if it is created, then time necessarily had a beginning. It follows that to deny that time had a beginning is to deny that the world was created, and to prove that eternal motion or time without a beginning is impossible is to prove that the world was created. St. Bonaventure, therefore, regarded the Aristotelian idea of the world's eternity as *necessarily* bound up with a denial of creation, and this opinion, which Aquinas did not share, sharpened his opposition to Aristotle. Both Bonaventure and Aquinas naturally accepted the *fact* of the world having had a beginning in time, since this is taught by theology; but they differed on the question of the abstract possibility of creation from eternity, and Bonaventure's conviction of its impossibility naturally made him resolutely hostile to Aristotle, since the latter's assertion of it as a fact, and not merely as a possibility, necessarily seemed to him an assertion of the independence of the world in relation to God, an assertion which he thought was primarily due to the Philosopher's rejection of exemplarism.

For what reasons did Bonaventure hold eternal motion or time without a beginning to be impossible? His arguments are more or less those which St. Thomas treats as objections to his own position. I give some examples.

(i) If the world had existed from eternity, it would follow that it is possible to add to the infinite. For instance, there would have been already an infinite number of solar revolutions, yet every day another revolution is added. But it is impossible to add to the infinite. Therefore the world cannot have always existed.[1]

St. Thomas answers[2] that if time is supposed eternal, it is infinite *ex parte ante*, but not *ex parte post*, and there is no cogent objection to an addition being made to the infinity at the end at which it is finite, that is, terminates in the present. To this St. Bonaventure retorts that, if one considers simply the past, then one would have to admit an infinite number of lunar revolutions. But there are twelve lunar revolutions to one solar revolution. Therefore we are faced with two infinite numbers, of which the one is twelve times greater than the other, and this is an impossibility.

[1] 2 *Sent.*, 1, 1, 1, 2, 1.

[2] *Contra Gent.*, 2, 38.

(ii) It is impossible to pass through an infinite series, so that if time were eternal, that is, had no beginning, the world would never have arrived at the present day. But it is clear that it has.[1] To this St. Thomas answers[2] that every passing through or *transitus* requires a beginning term and a final term. But if time is of infinite duration, there was no first term and consequently no *transitus*, so that the objection cannot arise. St. Bonaventure retorts, however, that there is either a revolution of the sun which is infinitely distant, in the past, from to-day's revolution or there is not. If there is not, then the distance is finite and the series must have had a beginning. If there is, then what of the revolution immediately following that which is infinitely distant from to-day's? Is this revolution also infinitely distant from to-day's or not? If not, then the hypothetically infinitely distant revolution cannot be infinitely distant either, since the interval between the 'first' and second revolution is finite. If it is, then what of the third and fourth revolutions, and so on? Are they also infinitely distant from to-day's revolution? If they are, then to-day's revolution is no less distant from them than from the first. In this case there is no succession and they are all synchronous, which is absurd.

(iii) It is impossible for there to be in existence at the same time an infinity of concrete objects. But, if the world existed from eternity, there would be in existence now an infinity of rational souls. Therefore the world cannot have existed from eternity.[3]

To this Aquinas answers[4] that some say that human souls do not exist after the death of the body, while others maintain that only a (common) intellect remains: others again hold a doctrine of reincarnation, while certain writers maintain that an infinite number in act is possible in the case of things which are not ordered (*in his quae ordinem non habent*). St. Thomas naturally held none of the first three positions himself; as to the fourth position his own final attitude seems to be doubtful, so that Bonaventure was able to remark rather caustically that the theory of reincarnation is an error in philosophy and is contrary to the psychology of Aristotle, while the doctrine that a common intellect alone survives is an even worse error. As to the possibility of an infinite number in act he believed that it was an erroneous notion, on the ground that an infinite multitude could not be ordered and

[1] 2 *Sent.*, 1, 1, 1, 2, 3.
[2] 2 *Sent.*, 1, 1, 1, 2, 5.
[3] *Contra Gent.*, 2, 38: *S.T.*, Ia, 46, 2, ad 6.
[4] *Contra Gent.*, 2, 38.

so could not be subject to divine providence, whereas in fact all that God has created is subject to His providence.

Bonaventure was thus convinced that it can be philosophically proved, as against Aristotle, that the world had a beginning and that the idea of creation from eternity involves a 'manifest contradiction', since, if the world was created from nothing, it has being after not-being (*esse post non-esse*)[1] and so cannot possibly have existed from eternity. St. Thomas answers that those who assert creation from eternity do not say that the world was made *post nihilum*, but that it was made out of nothing, the opposite of which is 'out of something'. The idea of time, that is to say, is in no way implicated. In Bonaventure's eyes it is bad enough to say that the world is eternal and is uncreated (that is an error which can be philosophically disproved), but to say that it was created eternally out of nothing is to be guilty of a glaring contradiction, 'so contrary to reason that I should not have believed that any philosopher, of however little understanding, could have asserted it'.[2]

4. If the doctrine of exemplarism is denied, and if God did not create the world, it is only natural to conclude that God knows only Himself, that He moves only as final Cause, as object of desire and love (*ut desideratum et amatum*) and that He knows no particular thing outside Himself.[3] In this case God can exercise no providence, not having in Himself the *rationes rerum*, the ideas of things, by which He may know them.[4] The doctrine of St. Bonaventure is, of course, that God knows things other than Himself, but that He knows them in and through Himself, through the exemplary ideas. If he did not hold this, he would have to say that the divine knowledge receives a complement or perfection from things outside of God, depends in some way on creatures. In reality it is God who is completely independent: creatures are dependent on Him and cannot confer on His Being any perfection.[5] But if God is wrapped up in Himself, in the sense of having no knowledge of creatures and exercising no providence, it follows that the changes or movements of the world proceed either from chance, which is impossible, or from necessity, as the Arabian philosophers held, the heavenly bodies determining the movements of things in this world. But if this be so, then all doctrine of reward or punishment in this life disappears, and in point of

[1] 2 *Sent.*, 1, 1, 1, 2, 6. [2] *Ibid.*, *conclusio.* [3] *In Hexaëm.*, 6, 2.
[4] *Ibid.*, 3. [5] Cf. 1 *Sent.*, 39, 1, 1, *conclusio.*

fact you will never find Aristotle speaking of a beatitude after the present life.[1] All these erroneous conclusions follow, then, from a denial of exemplarism, and it is more than ever clear that exemplarism is the key to a true metaphysic and that without it a philosopher will inevitably fall into errors if he discusses metaphysical themes.

5. From the doctrine of exemplarism it follows that there is some resemblance between creatures and God; but we have to distinguish various kinds of resemblance (*similitudo*) in order to attain to a correct idea of the relation of creatures to God, in order to avoid pantheism on the one hand and an independent world on the other hand. In the Commentary on the *Sentences*[2] Bonaventure says that *similitudo* may mean the agreement of two things in a third (and this he calls *similitudo secundum univocationem*), or it may mean the likeness of one thing to another without any agreement in a third thing being implied, and it is in this sense that the creature is said to be a likeness of God. In the same *conclusio* (*ad* 2) he distinguishes *similitudo univocationis sive participationis* and *similitudo imitationis, et expressionis*, going on to remark that the former does not hold good of the relation between creatures and God, because there is no common term (*quia nihil est commune*, because there is nothing common to God and the creature, that is). What he means is that God and the creature do not participate in Being, for example, *univocally* (precisely in the same sense), for if they did, the creature would be God and pantheism would result. The creature is, however, an imitation of God, of the idea of it in God, and God expresses the idea externally in the finite creature. Therefore, when Bonaventure rejects *similitudo participationis*, we must understand participation as referring here to participation in something common to both God and creatures in a univocal sense, in a *tertium commune* as he puts it.

It may be objected that if there is nothing common between God and creatures, there can be no likeness; but the community which St. Bonaventure wishes to exclude is *univocal* community, to which he opposes *analogy*. The likeness of the creature to God or of God to the creature (*exemplaris ad exemplatum*) is one kind of analogy, the other being that of *proportionalitas* (*habitudo duorum ad duo*), which exists between sets of things belonging to different genera, though in the case of the relation between creatures and

[1] *In Hexaëm.*, 6, 3. [2] 1, 35, *art. un.*, 1, *conclusio.*

God it is only the creature which is a member of a generic class. Thus a teacher is to his school what a pilot is to his ship, since both direct.[1] In the latter place Bonaventure distinguishes proportion in a wide sense, which includes proportionality, from proportion in a strict sense, which exists between members of the same class, arithmetical numbers, for example. Proportion in this strict sense cannot, of course, exist between God and creatures.

But though Bonaventure speaks of analogy of proportionality, the analogies to which he gives most attention are those of likeness, for he loved ever to find expressions, manifestations, images and *vestigia* of God in the world of creatures. Thus in the Commentary on the *Sentences*,[2] after excluding *similitudo per convenientiam omnimodam in natura*, which holds good between the three divine Persons, each of whom is identical with the divine Nature, and *similitudo per participationem alicuius naturae universalis*, which holds good between man and ass, in virtue of their common sharing in the *genus* animal, he admits proportionality, *similitudo secundum proportionalitatem* (giving here the example of the pilot and the charioteer in relation to the objects they direct) and *similitudo per convenientiam ordinis* (*sicut exemplatum assimilatur exemplari*), and proceeds to discuss these latter types of analogy, both of which, as already mentioned, hold good between the creature and God.

Every creature, says Bonaventure, is a *vestigium* of God, and the two types of analogy (that of the *exemplatum* to the *exemplar* and that of proportionality) apply to every creature, the first inasmuch as every creature is the effect of God and is conformed to God through the divine idea, the second inasmuch as the creature also produces an effect, although not in the same way as God produces His effect (*sicut enim Deus producit suum effectum, sic et agens creatum, licet non omnino*—for the creature is not the total cause of its effect). But though every creature is a *vestigium Dei*, this general conformity of the creature to God is comparatively remote (*magis de longinquo*): there is another type of likeness which is closer (*de proximo*) and more express and which applies only to certain creatures. All creatures are ordered to God, but only rational creatures are directed immediately (*immediate*) to God, the irrational creatures being directed to God mediately (*mediante creatura rationali*). The rational creature alone can know God, can

[1] Cf. 1 *Sent.*, 3, 1, *art. un.*, 2, 3 and 1 *ibid.*, 48, 1, 1, *conclusio.*
[2] 2 *Sent.*, 16, 1, 1, *conclusio.*

praise God and serve God consciously, and so has a greater conformity to God, a greater *convenientia ordinis* than the irrational creature. Now, the greater the *convenientia ordinis*, the greater and closer and more express is the resemblance or *similitudo*. This closer resemblance is called by Bonaventure *imago*. Every creature is, then, a *vestigium Dei*, but only the rational creature is an *imago Dei*, for it resembles God in the possession of spiritual powers through which it can become ever more and more conformed to God.

A similar difference between the rational creature and the irrational creature can be observed if we consider the analogy of proportionality. We can say, if we make the due allowances and reservations, that as God is to the creature, as Cause, that is, to His effect, so is the creature to its effect, and this holds good of all creatures in so far as they are active agents: but the effect considered is *extrinsic* to the agent, whereas in the case of rational creatures, and of them alone, there is an *intrinsic* proportion. In God there is a unity of Nature in a Trinity of Persons, and in man there is a unity of essence with a trinity of powers which are ordered to one another, the relation between them resembling in some way the relations in God (*quasi consimili modo se habentium, sicut se habent personae in divinis*). Bonaventure does not mean that we can prove the doctrine of the Trinity by the natural light of reason from a consideration of human nature, for he denies the possibility of any strict philosophical proof of the mystery, but rather that, guided by the light of faith, we can find an analogy to the Trinity in human rational nature. As the divine Nature is to the three divine Persons, so (*quasi consimili modo*) is the human nature or essence to its three powers. This is an 'express' resemblance of proportion and on this count, too, man is to be called the image of God. The word 'express' means that the Blessed Trinity has expressed itself, manifested itself to some degree in the constitution of human nature, and it is clear that for Bonaventure the analogy of resemblance (i.e. *exemplati ad exemplar*) is more fundamental than the analogy of proportionality, the latter being really treated in function of the former and having no concrete value or meaning apart from it.

In this way Bonaventure is enabled to order the hierarchy of being according to the closeness or remoteness of the likeness of the creature to God. The world of purely sensible things is the *vestigium* or *umbra Dei*, though here too he finds analogies of the

Trinity; it is the *liber scriptus forinsecus*. When considered by the natural philosopher who is nothing else but a natural philosopher it is simply *natura*: such a man cannot read the book of nature, which is to him no *vestigium Dei* but something considered for its own sake and without reference to God.[1] The rational creation stands above the purely sensible creation and is *imago Dei*, God's image in a special sense. But the phrase 'image of God' is itself of wide application, for it covers not only the natural substance of men and angels, but also that supernatural likeness which is the result of the possession of grace. The soul in grace is the image of God in a higher sense than is the purely natural essence of man, and the soul in heaven, enjoying the beatific vision, is God's image in a yet deeper sense. Thus there are many grades of analogy, of likeness to God, and every grade must be seen in the light of the Word, who is the consubstantial image of the Father and the Exemplar of all creation, reflected in creatures according to various degrees of 'expression'. We may note not only the constant integration of theology and philosophy, but also the fact that the various degrees of likeness stand in close relation to the intellectual and spiritual life of man. The ascent to God on the part of the individual involves a turning from the *umbra* or pure *vestigium*, contemplated by the senses, from the *liber scriptus forinsecus*, to the interior reflection of God, the *imago Dei*, the *liber scriptus intrinsecus*, in obedience to the command of Augustine to go within oneself, and so ultimately to the contemplation of God in Himself, the *exemplatum*. The fact that St. Bonaventure does not treat theology and philosophy in watertight compartments of their own enables him to link up his vision of the universe with the ascetical and mystical life and so to deserve the name of a specifically Christian thinker.

6. Is this world, which reflects so admirably the Divine Creator, the best of all possible worlds? We must first of all distinguish two questions. Could God make a better world than this world? Could God have made this world better than it is? Bonaventure answers to the first question that God could have made a better world than this one, by creating nobler essences, and that this cannot be denied without thereby limiting the divine power. As to the second question, it all depends on what you mean by 'world' and by 'better'. If you refer to the substances which go to make up the world, are you asking if God could make these

[1] *In Hexaëm.*, 12, 15.

substances better in the sense of making them nobler essences or substances, that is, of a higher kind, or are you asking if God could make these substances accidentally better, that is, while remaining within their own class? If the former, then the answer is that God could indeed change the substances into nobler ones, but it would not be the same world and God would not be making *this* world better. If the latter, then God could make this world better. To take an example. If God changed a man into an angel, the man would no longer be a man and God would not be making the man better; but God could make a man better by increasing his intellectual power or his moral qualities.[1] Again, while God could make *this* man or *this* horse a better man or horse, we must make another distinction if it is asked whether or not God could make man as such better, in the sense of placing him in better conditions. Absolutely speaking He could; but if one takes into consideration the purpose for which He has placed man in these conditions or allowed him to be in these conditions it may very well be that He could not make man better. For instance, if God brought it about that all men served Him well, He would be making man better, from the abstract viewpoint; but if you consider the purpose for which God has permitted man to serve Him well or ill, He would not be making man better by practically overriding his free will. Finally, if anyone asks why, if God could have made or could make the world better, He has not done so or does not do so, no answer can be given save this, that He so willed and that He Himself knows the reason (*solutio non potest dari nisi haec, quia voluit, et rationem ipse novit*).[2]

[1] 1 *Sent.*, 44, 1, 1, *conclusio*. [2] *Ibid.*, *ad* 4.

CHAPTER XXVIII

ST. BONAVENTURE—IV: THE MATERIAL CREATION

*Hylomorphic composition in all creatures—Individuation—Light—Plurality of forms—*Rationes seminales.

1. St. Bonaventure accepted from his master, Alexander of Hales, the doctrine of the hylomorphic composition of all creatures, the doctrine, that is, that all creatures are composed of matter and form. By 'matter' he naturally meant in this connection the principle of potentiality in the widest sense, not 'matter' in the sense in which matter is opposed to spirit. 'Matter *considered in itself* is neither spiritual nor corporeal', and so in itself it is indifferent to the reception either of a spiritual or of a corporeal form; but as matter never exists on its own, apart from a definite form, and as, once united with a corporeal or a spiritual form, it always remains corporeal or spiritual as the case may be, it follows that the matter actually present in a corporeal substance is different in kind from that in a spiritual substance.[1] 'Matter' may be regarded in more than one way. If one considers it from the point of view of 'privation' (*per privationem*), abstracting from all forms, whether substantial or accidental, one must admit that it is essentially the same in all creatures, 'for if either kind of matter is separated from all forms and all accidents, no difference at all will be seen.' But if matter is looked at 'analogically' (*secundum analogiam*), that is, as potentiality, as a foundation for form, one must make a distinction. In so far as matter is looked on as providing a foundation for form in regard simply to being (*in ratione entis*), it is essentially the same in both spiritual and material creatures, since both spiritual and material creatures exist and subsist, and one can consider their existence by itself, without going on to consider the precise way in which they exist or the kind of things they are. This is the way in which the metaphysician considers matter, and so in the eyes of the metaphysician matter is similar in the spiritual and in the material creation. If, however, matter is simply looked on in its relation to motion in the wide sense, understood, that is, as change, then it is not the same in creatures which cannot undergo substantial

[1] 2 *Sent.*, 3, 1, 1, 2, *conclusio ad* 3.

change or receive corporeal forms and in creatures which can undergo substantial change and receive corporeal forms, though it can be considered as *analogically* similar, inasmuch as angels are susceptible of, for example, divine influence. It is the natural philosopher or *physicus* who considers matter in this light.

Without going into the further distinctions made by Bonaventure and without attempting a judgement on his doctrine, one can say, then, that his teaching on the hylomorphic composition of all creatures is this, that matter is the principle of potentiality as such. Both spiritual creatures and material creatures are dependent beings, not self-existent beings, so that if one considers potentiality in abstraction from all form, looking on it as a co-principle of being, one can say with the metaphysician that it is essentially the same in both. If, however, one considers it as actually existent, as standing in relation to a concrete form, spiritual or material, it is not the same in both. The natural philosopher considers bodies and is concerned with matter, not its abstract essence but as existent in a particular type of being, as standing in a concrete relation to a certain kind of form, material form; and matter considered in this light is not to be found in spiritual beings. One might, of course, object that if matter as concretely existing, as united with form, is of different kinds and remains different, there must be something in the matter itself which makes it of different kinds so that its similarity in the spiritual and material created orders cannot be more than analogical; but Bonaventure admits that matter never actually exists apart from form and only states that if it is considered, as it can be considered, in abstraction from all form, as mere potentiality, then it can justly be said to be essentially the same. If the angels have an element of possibility, of potency in them, as they have, they must possess matter, for matter, considered in itself, is simply possibility or potency. It is only in the Being who is pure Act, without any potency or possibility, that there is no matter.

2. Is matter the principle of individuation? Some thinkers, says St. Bonaventure,[1] have held this, relying on the words of Aristotle, but it is very difficult to see how that which is common to all can be the principal cause of distinction, of individuality. On the other hand, to say that form is the principle of individuation and to postulate an individual form, following on that of the species, is to go to the opposite extreme and forget that every created form

[1] 2 *Sent.*, 3, 1, 2, 3, *conclusio.*

is capable of having another like it. It is better to hold that individuation arises from the actual union of matter and form, which appropriate one another, as it were, through their union. Seals are made by different impressions in wax, and without the wax there would be no plurality of seals, but without the different impressions the wax would not become many. Similarly, matter is necessary if there is to be distinction and multiplicity, number, but form is also necessary, for distinction and multiplication presuppose the constitution of a substance through the elements composing it. That an individual substance is something definite, of a definite kind, it owes to the form; that it is *this* something, it owes principally to matter, by which the form acquires position in place and time. Individuation denotes principally something substantial, a substance composed of matter and form, but it also denotes something which can be considered an accident, namely number. Individuality (*discretio individualis*) denotes two things: individuation, which arises from the union of the two principles, matter and form, and secondly distinction from other things, which is the origin of number; but the former, individuation, is the more fundamental.

Personality (*discretio personalis*) arises when the form united with matter is a rational form, and it thus adds to individuality the dignity of rational nature, which holds the highest place among created natures and is not in potency to a higher substantial form. But there is something more needed to constitute personality, namely that within the *suppositum* there should be no other nature of a greater eminence and dignity, that within the *suppositum* rational nature should possess *actualem eminentiam*. (In Christ the human nature, though perfect and complete, does not possess *actualem eminentiam* and so is not a person.) 'We must say, then, that just as individuality arises from the existence of a natural form in matter, so personality arises from the existence of a noble and supereminent nature in the substance.'[1]

As St. Bonaventure attributes matter, that is, a spiritual matter, to the angels, he is able to admit a plurality of individual angels within the same species without being compelled like St. Thomas to postulate as many angelic species as there are angels. The Scriptures show us some angels as exercising similar functions and this argues similarity of being, while the 'love of charity' also demands the multiplicity of angels within the same species.[2]

[1] 2 *Sent.*, 3, 1, 2, 2, *conclusio*. [2] *Ibid.*, 3, 1, 2, 1.

3. In the corporeal creation there is one substantial form which all bodies possess, and that is the form of light.[1] Light was created on the first day, three days before the production of the sun, and it is corporeal in Bonaventure's opinion, although St. Augustine interpreted it as meaning the angelic creation. It is not, properly speaking, a body but the form of a body, the first substantial form, common to all bodies and the principle of their activity, and the different kinds of body form a graded hierarchy according as they participate more or less in the form of light. Thus the 'empyrean' stands at one end of the scale, while the earth stands at the other, the lower end. In this way the light-theme, so dear to the Augustinian School and going back to Plotinus and to Plato's comparison of the Idea of the Good with the sun, finds a prominent place in the philosophy of St. Bonaventure.

4. Obviously if Bonaventure holds that light is a substantial form, possessed by all bodies, he must also hold that there can be a plurality of substantial forms in one substance. For him there was no difficulty in holding this, since he looked on form as that which prepares the body for the reception of other and higher perfections. While for St. Thomas substantial form was limitative and definitive, so that there could not be more than one substantial form in a body, for St. Bonaventure form looked forward and upward, so to speak, not so much rounding off the body and confining it as preparing it for fresh possibilities and perfections. In the *In Hexaëmeron*[2] he went so far as to say that it is mad (*insanum*) to say that the final form is added to prime matter without there being something which is a disposition for it or in potency to it, without there being any intermediate form, and he loved to trace a parallel between the order of grace and that of nature. Just as the gift of knowledge disposes for the gift of wisdom and is not itself annulled by the gift of wisdom, and as the gifts do not annul the theological virtues, so one form predisposes for a higher form and the latter, when received, does not expel the former but crowns it.

5. It is only to be expected that St. Bonaventure, who avowedly walked in the path of the Augustinian tradition, would accept the doctrine of *rationes seminales*, especially as this doctrine lays emphasis on the work of the Creator and diminishes the independence of the natural agent, though it was no more a 'scientific' doctrine in the modern sense of the word with St. Bonaventure

[1] Cf. 2 *Sent.*, 13. [2] 4, 10.

than it was with St. Augustine: for both men it was required by true Scriptural exegesis or rather by a philosophy which took account of the data of revelation, with the added reason in the case of Bonaventure that it was held by his great predecessor, the Christian philosopher *par excellence,* who was endowed with both the *sermo sapientiae* and the *sermo scientiae.* 'I believe that this position should be held, not only because reason inclines us to it, but also because the authority of Augustine, in his literal commentary on Genesis, confirms it.'[1]

Bonaventure thus maintained a certain *latitatio formarum* of things in matter; but he refused to accept the view that the forms of things which appear in time were originally in matter in an *actual* state, like a picture covered with a cloth, so that the particular agent only uncovers them, like the man who takes away the cloth from the picture and lets the painting appear. On this view contrary forms, which exclude one another, would have been together at the same time in the same subject, which is impossible. Nor will he accept the view that God is the only efficient cause in the eduction of forms, for this would mean that God creates all forms in the way in which He creates the rational human soul and that the secondary agent really does nothing at all, whereas it is clear that its activity really does contribute something to the effect. The second of these two views would reduce or do away altogether with the activity of the created agent, while the first would reduce it to a minimum, and Bonaventure is unwilling to accept either of them. He prefers the view 'which seems to have been that of Aristotle, and which is now commonly held by the doctors of philosophy and theology' that 'almost all the natural forms, corporeal forms at least, such as the forms of the elements and the forms of mixtures, are contained in the potency of matter and are reduced to act (*educuntur in actum*) through the action of a particular agent.' But this may be understood in two ways. It may mean that matter has both the potency to receive the form and the inclination to co-operate in the production of the form and that the form to be produced is in the particular agent as in its effective and original principle, so that the eduction of the form takes place by the multiplication of the form of the agent, as one burning candle may light a multitude of candles, or it may mean that matter contains the form to be educed not only as that in which and, to a certain extent, by which the form is produced, but

[1] 2 *Sent.*, 7, 2, 2, 1, *resp.*

also as that from which it is produced, though in the sense that it is concreated with matter and in matter, not as an actual, but as a virtual form. On the first hypothesis the forms are not indeed said to be created by the agent, since they do not come out of nothing, though all the same a new essence would seem to be produced in some way, whereas on the second hypothesis no new essence or quiddity is produced, but the form which existed in potency, virtually, is reduced to act, is given a new *dispositio*. The second hypothesis, therefore, attributes less to the created agent than does the first, since the created agent simply brings it about that what formerly existed in one way now exists in another way, whereas on the first hypothesis the created agent would produce something positively new, even if not by way of creation out of nothing. If a gardener tends the rose-tree so that the rose-buds can blossom into roses he does something, it is true, but less than he would do, were he to produce a rose-tree from some other form of tree. Bonaventure, then, anxious to avoid attributing even the semblance of creative powers to a created agent, chooses the hypothesis which attributes less to the work of the created agent and more to the work of the Creator.

The forms which are educed were, therefore, originally in matter in a virtual state. These virtual forms are the *rationes seminales*. A *ratio seminalis* is an active power, existing in matter, the active power being the essence of the form to be educed, standing to the latter in the relation of *esse incompletum* to *esse completum* or of *esse in potentia* to *esse in actu*.[1] Matter is thus a *seminarium* or seed-bed in which God created in a virtual state corporeal forms which would be successively educed therefrom. This applies not only to the forms of inorganic things, but also to the souls of brutes and vegetables. Needless to say, Bonaventure is aware that the activity of particular agents is necessary for the birth of an animal, but he will not admit the traducianist theory, according to which the soul of a new animal is produced by 'multiplication' of the soul of the parent, yet without any diminution on the latter's part, as this theory implies that a created form can produce a similar form out of nothing.[2] What happens is that the parent animals act upon what they have themselves received, the seminal principle, the seminal principle being an active power or potency containing the new soul in germ, though the activity of the parents is necessary in order that the virtual should become actual. Bonaventure thus

[1] 2 *Sent.*, 18, 1, 3, *resp.* [2] *Ibid.*, 2, 15, 1, 1, *resp.*

steers a middle course between attributing too little or nothing to the created agent and attributing what seemed to him too much, his general principle being that while God produces things out of nothing, a created agent can only produce something which already existed in potency, by which he means in a virtual state.[1] It is, however, useless to look for an exact description and explanation of the concrete working of his theory of *rationes seminales*, since it is founded partly on authority and partly on *a priori* philosophic reasoning, not on empirical observation or scientific experiment.

[1] Cf. 2 *Sent.*, 7, 2, 2, 2, *resp.*

CHAPTER XXIX

ST. BONAVENTURE—V: THE HUMAN SOUL

Unity of human soul—Relation of soul to body—Immortality of the human soul—Falsity of Averroistic monopsychism—Knowledge of sensible objects and of first logical principles—Knowledge of spiritual realities—Illumination—The soul's ascent to God—Bonaventure as philosopher of the Christian life.

1. We have seen that, according to St. Bonaventure, the souls of animals are produced *seminaliter*; but this does not, of course, apply to the human soul, which is produced immediately by God, created by Him out of nothing. The human soul is the image of God, called to union with God, and on this count (*propter dignitatem*) its production was fittingly reserved by God to Himself. This reasoning involves theology, but Bonaventure also argues that since the human soul is immortal, incorruptible, its production can be effected only by that Principle which has life and perpetuity of itself. The immortality of the human soul implies a 'matter' in the soul which is incapable of being an element in substantial change; but the activity of created agents is confined to working on transmutable matter and the production of a substance with unchangeable matter transcends the power of such agents. It follows that the traducianist view must be rejected, even if Augustine inclined to it on occasion because he thought that thereby he could explain the transmission of original sin.[1]

What is it that God creates? It is the entire human soul, not the rational faculty alone. There is one soul in man, endowed with rational and sensitive faculties, and it is this soul which God creates. The body was contained *seminaliter* in the body of Adam, the first man, and it is transmitted by means of the seed, but this does not mean that the body has a sensitive soul, educed from the potency of matter and distinct from the created and infused rational soul. The seed contains, it is true, not only the superfluity of the father's nourishment, but also something of his *humiditas radicalis*, so that there is in the embryo, before the infusion of the soul, an active disposition towards the act of sensation, a kind of inchoate sensibility; but this disposition is a

[1] *2 Sent.*, 18, 2, 3, *resp.*

disposition to accomplishing the act of sensation through the power of the soul, once it has been infused: at the complete animation of the embryo by the infusion of the soul this inchoate sensibility ceases or rather it is subsumed under the activity of the soul, which is the principle of sensation as well as of intellection. In other words, St. Bonaventure is careful to maintain the continuity of life and the reality of parentage while avoiding any splitting of the human soul into two.[1]

2. The human soul is the form of the body: St. Bonaventure uses the Aristotelian doctrine against those who hold that the souls of all men are one substance. 'The rational soul is the act and entelechy of the human body: therefore since human bodies are distinct, the rational souls which perfect those bodies will also be distinct':[2] the soul is an existent, living, intelligent form, endowed with liberty.[3] It is present wholly in every part of the body, according to the judgement of St. Augustine, which Bonaventure approves as preferable to the theory that the soul is primarily present in a determinate part of the body, the heart for instance. 'Because it is the form of the whole body, it is present in the whole body; because it is simple, it is not present partly here and partly there; because it is the sufficient moving principle (*motor sufficiens*) of the body, it has no particular situation, is not present at one point or in a determinate part.'[4]

But though Bonaventure accepts the Aristotelian definition of the soul as the form of the body, his general tendency is Platonic and Augustinian in character, inasmuch as he insists that the human soul is a spiritual substance, composed of spiritual form and spiritual matter. It is not enough to say that there is in the soul composition of *ex quo est* and *quod est*, since the soul can act and be acted upon, move and be moved, and this argues the presence of 'matter', the principle of passivity and mutability, though this matter transcends extension and corruptibility, being spiritual and not corporeal matter.[5] This doctrine may seem to contradict the admitted simplicity of the human soul, but Bonaventure points out[6] that 'simplicity' has various meanings and degrees. Thus 'simplicity' may refer to absence of quantitative parts, and this the soul enjoys, being simple in comparison with corporeal things; or it may refer to absence of constitutive parts, and this the soul does not enjoy. The main point, however,

[1] Cf. 2 *Sent.*, 30, 3, 1 and 31, 1, 1.
[2] *Ibid.*, 18, 2, 1, *contra* 1.
[3] *Breviloq.*, 2, 9.
[4] 1 *Sent.*, 8, 2, *art. un.*, 3, *resp.*
[5] 2 *Sent.*, 17, 1, 2, *resp.*
[6] *Ibid.*, *ad* 5.

is that the soul, though form of the body and moving principle of the body, is also much more than this, and can subsist by itself, being *hoc aliquid*, though as a *hoc aliquid* which is partly passive and mutable it must have in it spiritual matter. The doctrine of the hylomorphic composition of the human soul is thus calculated to ensure its dignity and its power of subsistence apart from the body.

If the soul is composed of form and spiritual matter, it follows that it is individuated by its own principles.[1] If this is so, however, why is it united with the body, for it is an individual spiritual substance in its own right? The answer is that the soul, even though a spiritual substance, is so constituted that it not only can inform a body but also has a natural inclination to do so. Conversely, the body, though also composed of matter and form, has an *appetitus* for being informed by the soul. The union of the two is thus for the perfection of each and is not to the detriment of either soul or body.[2] The soul does not exist simply, or even primarily, to move the body[3] but to enjoy God; yet it exercises its powers and potentialities fully only in informing the body and it will one day, at the resurrection, be reunited with the body. Aristotle was ignorant of this, and it is not to be wondered at that he was ignorant of it, for 'a philosopher necessarily falls into some error, unless he is aided by the light of faith'.[4]

3. The doctrine of the hylomorphic composition of the human soul naturally facilitates the proof of its immortality, since Bonaventure does not link the soul so closely to the body as does the Aristotelian doctrine; but his favourite proof is the one drawn from the consideration of the ultimate purpose of the soul (*ex consideratione finis*). The soul seeks for perfect happiness (a fact which no one doubts, 'unless his reason is entirely perverted'). But no one can be perfectly happy if he is afraid of losing what he possesses: on the contrary, it is this very fear which makes him miserable. Therefore, as the soul has a natural desire for perfect happiness, it must be naturally immortal. This proof presupposes the existence of God, of course, and the possibility of attaining perfect happiness, as also the existence of a natural desire for human happiness; but it was Bonaventure's favourite proof because of its spiritual character, because of its connection with

[1] 2 *Sent.*, 18, 2, 1, *ad* 1.
[2] Cf., *ibid.* 17, 1, 2, *ad* 6.
[3] *Ibid.*, 18, 2, 1, *ad* 6.
[4] *Ibid.*

the movement of the soul towards God: it is for him the *ratio principalis*, the principle argument.[1]

In a rather similar way he argues[2] from consideration of the formal cause, from the nature of the soul as the image of God. Because the soul has been made for the attainment of happiness, which consists in the possession of the supreme Good, God, it must be capable of possessing God (*capax Dei*) and so must be made in His image and likeness. But it would not be made in the likeness of God if it were mortal. Therefore it must be immortal. Again (arguing *ex parte materiae*), Bonaventure declares that the form of the rational soul is of such dignity that it makes the soul like to God, with the result that the matter which is united to this form (i.e. the spiritual matter) finds its satisfaction and completion in union with this form alone, so that it must be likewise immortal.

Bonaventure gives other arguments, such as that from the necessity of sanctions in an after life[3] and from the impossibility of God's bringing the good to frustration. In the latter proof he argues that it would be against divine justice for that which has been well done to tend towards evil and frustration. Now, according to all moral teaching a man ought to die rather than commit injustice. But if the soul were mortal, then its adhesion to justice, lauded by all moral philosophers, would come to nothing, and this is contrary to divine justice. More Aristotelian in character are the arguments drawn from the soul's power of reflection on itself and from its intellectual activity, which has no intrinsic dependence on the body, to prove its superiority to corporeal matter and its incorruptibility.[4] But though these Aristotelian proofs are probably more acceptable to us, as presupposing less and as involving no theology, in Bonaventure's eyes it was the proofs borrowed from Augustine or dependent on his line of thought which were more telling, especially that from the desire of beatitude. The Augustinian proof from the soul's apprehension of and assimilation to abiding truth is given by Bonaventure,[5] but it does not appear as a *potissimus modus* of proving the soul's immortality. This qualification is reserved for the proofs drawn from the desire for beatitude.

If it were objected against Bonaventure that this form of proof presupposes the desire for union with God, for beatitude in the full sense, and that this desire is elicited only under the action of grace

[1] 2 *Sent.*, 19, 1, 1, *resp.* [2] *Ibid.* [3] *Ibid.*, *sed contra* 3, 4.
[4] *Ibid.*, 7 ff.; cf. *De Anima*, Bk. 3. [5] 2 *Sent.*, 11.

and so belongs to the supernatural order and not to the order of nature, which is the object of the philosopher's study, the Saint would doubtless answer that he had not the slightest intention of denying the work of grace or its supernatural character, but that, on the other hand, the true philosopher considers the world and human life as they are and that one of the data is precisely the desire for complete happiness. Even though the desire may imply the operation of grace, it is a datum of experience and so can be taken into account by the philosopher. If the philosopher cannot explain it without recourse to theology, that is only another proof of Bonaventure's principle that no philosophy can be satisfactory unless it is illumined by the light of faith. In other words, whereas the 'Thomist' systematically eliminates from the data of experience all he knows to be supernatural and then, as philosopher, considers the resulting 'nature', the Bonaventurian philosopher starts from nature in the sense of the given. It is perfectly true that grace is not something 'given' in the sense of visible or apprehensible with certainty by unaided reason, but some of its effects are given in experience and these the philosopher will take into account, though he cannot explain them without reference to theology. The Thomist approach and the Bonaventurian approach are therefore different and one cannot force them into the same mould without thereby distorting one or the other.

4. All that has been said on the human soul implies the individuality of the soul, but Bonaventure was quite aware of the Averroistic interpretation of Aristotle and argued explicitly against it. Averroes maintained that both the active and passive intellects survive death, and, whatever Aristotle himself may have taught, his commentator, Averroes, certainly held that these intellects are not individual to each man, are not parts or faculties of individual men, but rather unitary substances, cosmic intelligences. Such a position, however, is not only heretical and contrary to the Christian religion, but also against reason and experience.[1] It is against reason since it is clear that the intellectual soul is a perfection of man as man, and men differ from one another, are individual persons, as men and not merely as animals, which would be the case if the rational soul were numerically one in all men. It is against experience, since it is a matter of experience that different men have different thoughts. And it is no good saying that this difference of thoughts comes simply from the diversity of *species*

[1] 2 *Sent.*, 18, 2, 1, *resp.*

in the imaginations of different men, that is, that it is only the perishable imagination, fed by the senses, which is different in different individuals, since men differ in ideas, for example, of the virtues, which are not founded on sense-perception and which are not abstracted from imaginative *species*. Nor, from the point of view of Bonaventure, is it a good argument to say that the intellectual soul is independent of the body and cannot therefore be individuated by it, for the soul is not individuated by the body but by the union of its two constitutive principles, spiritual matter and spiritual form.

5. In regard to the content of the soul's knowledge of sensible objects, this is dependent on sense-perception, and St. Bonaventure agrees with Aristotle that the soul does not of itself have either knowledge or species of sensible objects: the human intellect is created in a state of 'nudity' and is dependent on the senses and imagination.[1] The sensible object acts upon the sense organ and produces therein a sensible species, which in turn acts upon the faculty of sensation, and then perception takes place. It will be noted that St. Bonaventure, in admitting a passive element in sensation, departs from the teaching of St. Augustine; but at the same time he holds that the faculty of sensation or sensitive power of the soul judges the content of sensation, for example, that this is white, the passive reception of the species being attributed primarily to the organ, the activity of the judgement to the faculty.[2] This judgement is not, of course, a reflective judgement, it is rather a spontaneous awareness; but it is possible because the faculty of sensation is the sensitive faculty of a rational soul, for it is the soul which communicates to the body the act of sensation.[3] The separate sensations, for example, of colour and touch, are unified by the 'common sense' and preserved in the imagination, which is not the same as 'memory' if the latter is taken as meaning *recordatio* or recalling at will.[4] Finally the active and passive intellects, working in co-operation, abstract the species from the imagination. The active and passive intellects are not two powers, one of which can work without the other, but are two 'differences' of the same intellectual faculty of the soul. We can indeed say that the active intellect abstracts and the passive intellect receives, but Bonaventure qualifies this statement by affirming that the

[1] 2 *Sent.*, 3, 2, 2, 1, *resp.* and *ad* 4. [2] *Ibid.*, 8, 1, 3, 2, *ad* 7.
[3] *Ibid.*, 25, 2, *art. un.*, 6, *resp.*
[4] *Ibid.*, 7, 2, 1, 2, *resp.*, where Bonaventure distinguishes memory as habit, *retentio speciei*, from the act of remembering or *recordatio*.

passive intellect has the power of abstracting the species and judging it, though *only* with the help of the active intellect, while the active intellect is dependent for its activity of knowing on the information of the passive intellect by the species. There is, in fact, only one complete act of intellection and the active and passive intellects co-operate inseparably in that act.[1]

Clearly, then, apart from various 'Augustinianisms', such as the refusal to make a real distinction between the faculties of the soul, Bonaventure's view of the way in which we acquire our knowledge of sensible objects approximates more or less closely to the Aristotelian theory. He admits that the soul, in regard to knowledge of such objects, is originally a *tabula rasa*,[2] and he has no place for innate ideas. Moreover, this rejection of innate ideas applies also to our knowledge of first principles. Some people have said that these principles are innate in the active intellect, though acquired as far as the possible intellect is concerned; but such a theory agrees neither with the words of Aristotle nor with the truth. For if these principles were innate in the active intellect, why could it not communicate them to the possible intellect without the help of the senses, and why does it not know these principles from the very beginning? A modified version of innatism is that the principles are innate in their most general form while the conclusions or particular applications are acquired, but it would be difficult on such a view to show why a child does not know the first principles in their general form. Moreover, even this modified innatism contradicts both Aristotle and Augustine. Bonaventure doubtless considered that a theory which united against it both Aristotle and Augustine could not possibly be true. It remains then to say that the principles are innate only in the sense that the intellect is endowed with a natural light which enables it to apprehend the principles in their universality when it has acquired knowledge of the relevant species or ideas. For example, no one knows what a whole is or a part until he has acquired the species or idea in dependence on sense-perception; but once he has acquired the idea, the light of the intellect enables him to apprehend the principle that the whole is greater than the part.[3] On this matter, therefore, St. Bonaventure is at one with St. Thomas.

6. But though we have no innate knowledge of sensible objects or of their essences or of the first principles, logical or mathematical,

[1] 2 *Sent.*, 24, 1, 2, 4. [2] *Ibid.*, *resp.* [3] *Ibid.*, 39, 1, 2, *resp.*

it does not follow that our knowledge of purely spiritual realities is acquired through sense-perception. 'God is not known by means of a likeness drawn from sense',[1] but rather by the soul's reflection on itself. It has no intuitive vision of God, of the divine Essence, in this life, but it is made in the image of God and is orientated towards God in desire and will, so that reflection on its own nature and on the direction of the will enables the soul to form the idea of God without recourse to the external sensible world. In this sense the idea of God is 'innate', though not in the sense that every man has from the beginning a clear, explicit and accurate knowledge of God. The direction of the will, its desire for complete happiness, is the effect of the divine action itself, and reflection on this desire manifests to the soul the existence of the Object of the desire, which indeed it already knows in a kind of vague awareness, though not necessarily in an explicit idea. 'The knowledge of this truth (God's existence) is innate in the rational mind, inasmuch as the mind is an image of God, by reason of which it has a natural appetite and knowledge and memory of Him in whose image it has been made and towards whom it naturally tends, that it may find its beatitude in Him.'[2] The knowledge of God is of various kinds: God has a comprehensive knowledge of Himself, the Blessed know Him clearly (*clare et perspicue*), we know Him partly and in a hidden way (*ex parte et in aenigmate*), this last knowledge being contained implicitly in or implied by the knowledge which each soul has that it did not always exist and must have had a beginning.[3]

The knowledge of the virtues too must be 'innate' in the sense that it is not derived from sense-perception. An unjust man can know what justice is; but obviously he cannot know justice through its presence in his soul, since he does not possess it, nor can he know it through abstraction from sensible species, since it is not an object of sense and has no likeness in the world of sense. He cannot know it by its effects, since he would not recognise the effects of justice unless he previously knew what justice is, just as one cannot recognise the effects of a man's activity as the effects of a man's activity unless one previously knows what a man is.[4] There must, therefore, be some *a priori* or innate knowledge of the virtues. In what sense is it innate? There is no innate idea (*species innata*) in the sense of a clear idea or intellectual likeness of the

[1] 2 *Sent.*, 39, 1, 2, *resp.*

[2] *De Myst. Trinit.*, 1, 1, *resp.*

[3] *Ibid.*, 1, 2, *ad* 14.

[4] *De Scientia Christi*, 4, 23.

virtue in the mind from its beginning; but there is present in the soul a natural light by which it can recognise truth and rectitude, and there is present also an affection or inclination of the will. The soul knows, therefore, what rectitude is and what an affection or inclination of the will is, and in this way it recognises what *rectitudo affectionis* is. As this is charity, it knows what charity is, even though it does not actually possess the virtue of charity.[1]

Thus the knowledge of the virtues is innate in much the same sense as knowledge of God is innate, not as an innate explicit species or idea, but in the sense that the soul has in itself all the material needed to form the explicit idea, without its being necessary for it to have recourse to the sensible world. The innate idea of Bonaventure is a virtually innate idea. Of course, there is one big difference between our knowledge of the virtues and our knowledge of God, for while we can never apprehend the essence of God in this life, it is possible to apprehend the essence of the virtues. However, the ways in which we arrive at the knowledge of the virtues and of God are similar, and we can say that the soul possesses an innate knowledge of the principles necessary to its conduct. It knows by self-reflection what God is, what fear is and what love is, and so it knows what it is to fear and to love God.[2] If anyone quotes in opposition the Philosopher's dictum *nihil est in intellectu, quod prius non fuerit in sensu*, the answer is that the dictum must be understood as having reference only to our knowledge of sensible objects or to the acquisition of ideas which are capable of being formed by abstraction from sensible species.[3]

7. But though Bonaventure will not admit that the first principles relating to the world about us or indeed even the first principles of conduct are explicit in the mind from the beginning or infused into it from outside apart from any activity on the part of the mind itself, it does not follow that he is prepared to dispense with the Augustinian doctrine of illumination; on the contrary, he regards it as one of the cardinal truths of metaphysics.

Truth is the *adaequatio rei et intellectus*,[4] involving the object known and the knowing intellect. In order that truth in this sense, truth apprehended, may exist, conditions are required on the part of both subject and object, immutability on the part of the latter and infallibility on the part of the former.[5] But if Bonaventure is prepared to echo in this way the words of the

[1] 1 *Sent.*, 17, 1, *art. un.*, 4, *resp.* [2] 2 *Sent.*, 39, 1, 2, *resp.* [3] *Ibid.*
[4] 1 *Sent.*, *resp.*, *ad* 1, 2, 3; cf. *Breviloq.*, 6, 8. [5] *De Scientia Christi*, 4, *resp.*

Theaetetus, demanding these two conditions in order that *cognitio certitudinalis*, certain knowledge, may exist, he is necessarily faced by problems similar to those with which Plato and Augustine were faced, since no created object is strictly immutable and all sensible objects are perishable, while the human mind is not *of itself* infallible in regard to any class of object. It must, therefore, receive help from outside, and naturally Bonaventure had recourse to the Augustinian theory of illumination, which commended itself to him, not only because St. Augustine had held it but also because it emphasised both the dependence of the human intellect on God and the interior activity of God in the human soul. For him it was both an epistemological truth and a religious truth, something that could be established as a necessary conclusion from a study of the nature and requirements of certainty and also something upon which one could profitably meditate in the religious sense. Indeed for him the intellectual life and the spiritual life cannot properly be separated.

The human mind, then, is subject to change, doubt, error, while the phenomena which we experience and know are also changeable. On the other hand it is an indubitable fact that the human mind does possess certainties and knows that it does so and that we apprehend unchanging essences and principles. It is only God, however, who is unchanging, and this means that the human mind is aided by God and that the object of its certain knowledge is seen in some way as rooted in God, as existing in the *rationibus aeternis* or divine ideas. But we do not apprehend these divine ideas directly, in themselves, and Bonaventure points out with Augustine that to follow the Platonic doctrine is to open the door to scepticism, since if the only certain knowledge attainable is direct knowledge of the eternal archetypes or exemplars and if we have no direct knowledge of these archetypes, the necessary conclusion is that true certainty is unattainable by the human mind.[1] On the other hand it is not sufficient to say that the *ratio aeterna* influences the mind in this sense only, that the knowing mind attains not the eternal principle itself but only its influence, as a *habitus mentis*, for the latter would be itself created and subject to the same conditions as the mind of which it is a disposition.[2] The *rationes aeternae*, then, must have a direct regulative action on the human mind, though remaining themselves unseen. It is they which move the mind and rule the mind in its certain judgements,

[1] *De Scientia Christi*, 4, *resp*. [2] *Ibid.*

enabling it to apprehend the certain and eternal truths in the speculative and moral orders and to make certain and true judgements even concerning sensible objects: it is their action (which is the divine illumination) which enables the mind to apprehend the unchanging and stable essences in the fleeting and changing objects of experience. This does not mean that Bonaventure contradicts the approval he has given to Aristotle's doctrine about our knowledge of the sensible world, but it does mean that he considers it insufficient. Without sense-perception we would never indeed know sensible objects and it is quite true that the intellect abstracts, but the divine illumination, the direct action of the *ratio aeterna*, is necessary in order that the mind should see in the object the reflection of the unchanging *ratio* and be able to make an infallible judgement concerning it. Sense-perception is required in order that our ideas of sensible objects should arise, but the stability and necessity of our judgements concerning them are due to the action of the *rationes aeternae*, since neither are the sensible objects of our experience unchanging nor are the minds which know them infallible of themselves. The dim (*obtenebratae*) species of our minds, affected by the obscurity of *phantasmata*, are thus illumined in order that the mind should know. 'For if to have real knowledge means to know that a thing cannot possibly be otherwise, it is necessary that He alone should cause us to know, who knows the truth and has the truth in Himself.'[1] Thus it is through the *ratio aeterna* that the mind judges all those things which we know by the senses.[2]

In the *Itinerarium Mentis in Deum*[3] St. Bonaventure describes how the exterior sensible objects produce a likeness of themselves (*similitudo*) first in the medium and then through the medium on the organ of sense, and so on the interior sense. The particular sense, or the faculty of sensation acting through the particular sense, judges that this object is white or black or whatever it is, and the interior sense that it is pleasing, beautiful, or the reverse. The intellectual faculty, turning itself towards the species, asks why the object represented is beautiful and judges that it is beautiful because it possesses certain characteristics. But this judgement implies a reference to an idea of beauty which is stable and unchanging, not bound to place or time. This is where the divine illumination comes in, namely to explain the judgement in its unchanging and supertemporal aspect by reference to the

[1] *In Hexaëm.*, 12, 5. [2] *Itin. Mentis in Deum*, 2, 9. [3] 2, 4–6.

directing and regulating *ratio aeterna*, not to supersede or annul the work of the senses or the activity of abstraction. All sensible objects which are known enter the mind through the three psychical operations of *apprehensio*, *oblectatio* and *diiudicatio*, but the latter operation, to be true and certain, must be a judgement made in the light of the *rationes aeternae*.

Now, as we have seen earlier, the *rationes aeternae* are ontologically identified and are in fact identical with the Word of God. It follows then that it is the Word which illuminates the human mind, that Word which enlightens every man who comes into the world. 'Christ is the interior teacher and no truth is known except through Him, not by His speaking as we speak, but by His enlightening us interiorly. . . . He is intimately present to every soul and by His most clear ideas He shines upon the dark ideas of our minds.'[1] We have no vision of the Word of God and though the light is so intimately within us, it is invisible, *inaccessibilis*: we can only reason to its presence from observation of its effects.[2] Thus Bonaventure's doctrine of illumination and his interpretation of Augustine do not involve ontologism. His doctrine completes his seemingly Aristotelian affirmation of abstraction and his denial of the properly innate character of even the first principles, giving to his teaching a peculiar and non-Aristotelian, an Augustinian flavour and colour. We abstract, yes, but we could not seize the intelligible and stable merely through abstraction, we need also the divine illumination: we can attain knowledge of moral principles by interior reflection, yes, but we could not apprehend their unchanging and necessary character without the regulative and guiding action of the divine light. Aristotle failed to see this, he failed to see that as we cannot know creatures fully unless we see them as *exemplata* of the divine *exemplar*, so we cannot form certain judgements about them without the light of the divine Word, of the *Ratio Aeterna*. Exemplarism and illumination are closely connected, the true metaphysician recognises them both: Aristotle recognised neither.

8. There are only four faculties of the soul, the vegetative and sensitive powers, the intellect and the will; but Bonaventure distinguishes various 'aspects' of the soul and, in particular, of the intellect or mind according to the objects to which its attention is directed and according to the way in which it is directed. It would, then, be a mistake to suppose that he meant that *ratio*,

[1] *In Hexaëm.*, 12, 5.

[2] *Ibid.*, 12, 11.

intellectus, *intelligentia* and *apex mentis* or *synderesis scintilla*[1] are all different faculties of the soul:. they denote rather different functions of the rational soul in its upward ascent from sensible creatures to God Himself. In the Commentary on the *Sentences*[2] he says expressly that the division of the reason into lower and higher (*ratio inferior* and *ratio superior*) is not a division into different faculties: it is a division into *officia* and *dispositiones*, which is something more than a division into aspects (*aspectus*). The lower reason is reason turned towards sense-objects, the higher reason is reason turned towards intelligible objects, and the term 'lower' and 'higher' thus refer to different functions or *officia* of the same faculty; but there is this further point to be added, that the reason as directed to intelligibles is strengthened and invigorated, whereas, directed to sensibles, it is in a manner weakened and drawn down, so that although there is only one *ratio*, the distinction between higher and lower reason corresponds not only to different functions, but also to different dispositions of the one reason.

The stages of the upward ascent of the mind scarcely need much elaboration, as they are more connected with ascetical and mystical theology than with philosophy in our sense; but since they are connected with philosophy in Bonaventure's understanding of the term, it is as well to touch very briefly on them, as they illustrate his tendency to integrate philosophy and theology as closely as possible. Walking in the footsteps of Augustine and the Victorines Bonaventure traces the ascending stages of the soul's life, stages which correspond to different potentialities in the soul and lead him from the sphere of nature into that of grace. Starting from the soul's sensitive powers (*sensualitas*) he shows how the soul may see in sensible objects the *vestigia Dei*, as it contemplates sensible things first as God's effects, then as things wherein God is present, and he accompanies it, with Augustine, as it retires within itself and contemplates its natural constitution and powers as the image of God. The intelligence is then shown contemplating God in the soul's faculties renewed and elevated by grace, being enabled to do so by the Word of God. In this stage, however, the soul still contemplates God in His image, which is the soul itself, even if elevated by grace, and it can proceed yet further, to the contemplation of God *supra nos*, first as Being, then as the Good. Being is good, and the contemplation of God as Being, the perfection of being, leads to the realisation of Being as the Good, as

[1] *Itin. Mentis in Deum*, 1, 6.

[2] *2 Sent.*, 24, 1, 2, 2, *resp.*

diffusivum sui, and so to the contemplation of the Blessed Trinity. Further than this the intellect cannot go: beyond lies the luminous darkness of mystical contemplation and ecstasy, the *apex affectus* outstripping the mind. The will, however, is a faculty of the one human soul and, though issuing from the substance of the soul, it is not a distinct accident, so that to say that the affection of the will outruns the intellect is simply to say that the soul is united to God by love so closely that the light infused into it blinds it. There can be but one higher stage, reserved for the next life, and that is the vision of God in heaven.

9. It will be remembered that the three cardinal points of metaphysics for Bonaventure are creation, exemplarism and illumination. His metaphysical system is thus a unity in that the doctrine of creation reveals the world as proceeding from God, created out of nothing and wholly dependent on Him, while the doctrine of exemplarism reveals the world of creatures as standing to God in the relation of imitation to model, of *exemplatum* to *exemplar*, while the doctrine of illumination traces the stages of the soul's return to God by way of contemplation of sensible creatures, of itself and finally of Perfect Being. The divine action is always emphasised. Creation out of nothing can be proved, as also God's presence and activity in creatures and especially in the soul itself: God's action enters into the apprehension of every certain truth, and even though for the establishment of the higher stages of the soul's ascent the data of theology are required, there is in a sense a continuity of divine action in increasing intensity. God acts in every man's mind when he attains truth, but at this stage the activity of God is not all-sufficient, man is also active through the use of his natural powers: in the higher stages God's action progressively increases until in ecstasy God takes possession of the soul and man's intellectual activity is superseded.

Bonaventure may thus be termed the philosopher of the Christian life, who makes use of both reason and faith in order to produce his synthesis. This integration of reason and faith, philosophy and theology, is emphasised by the place he accords to Christ, the Word of God. Just as creation and exemplarism cannot be properly understood apart from the realisation that it is through the Word of God that all things are created and that it is the Word of God, the consubstantial image of the Father, whom all creatures mirror, so illumination in its various stages cannot be properly understood apart from the realisation that it is the Word of God who illumines every man, the Word of God who is the door through which the soul enters into God above itself, the Word of God who, through the Holy Spirit whom He has sent, inflames the soul and leads it beyond the limitations of its clear ideas into the ecstatic union. Finally it is the Word of God who shows us the Father and opens to us the beatific vision of heaven. Christ in fact is the *medium omnium scientiarum*,[1] of metaphysics as of theology, for though the metaphysician as such cannot attain to knowledge of the Word through the use of the natural reason, he can form no true and certain judgements without the illumination of the Word, even if he is quite unaware of this, and in addition his science is incomplete and vitiated by its incompleteness unless it is crowned by theology.

[1] *In Hexaëm.*, I, 11.

CHAPTER XXX

ST. ALBERT THE GREAT

Life and intellectual activity—Philosophy and theology—God—Creation—The soul—Reputation and importance of St. Albert.

1. ALBERT THE GREAT was born in 1206 at Lauingen in Swabia, but left Germany in order to study the arts at Padua, where he entered the Dominican Order in 1223. After having lectured in theology at Cologne and other places he received the doctorate at Paris in 1245, having Thomas Aquinas among his pupils from 1245 to 1248. In the latter year he returned to Cologne accompanied by Thomas, in order to establish the Dominican house of studies there. His purely intellectual work was interrupted, however, by administrative tasks which were laid upon him. Thus from 1254 until 1257 he was Provincial of the German Province and from 1260 until 1262 Bishop of Ratisbon. Visits to Rome and the preaching of a Crusade in Bohemia also occupied his time, but he seems to have adopted Cologne as his general place of residence. It was from Cologne that he set out for Paris in 1277, to defend the opinions of Thomas Aquinas (died 1274), and it was at Cologne that he died on November 15th, 1280.

It is clear enough from his writings and activities that Albert the Great was a man of wide intellectual interests and sympathies, and it is hardly to be expected that a man of his type would ignore the rise of Aristotelianism in the Parisian Faculty of Arts, especially as he was well aware of the stir and trouble caused by the new tendencies. As a man of open mind and ready intellectual sympathy he was not one to adopt an uncompromisingly hostile attitude to the new movement, though, on the other hand, he was not without strong sympathy for the neo-Platonist and Augustinian tradition. Therefore, while he adopted Aristotelian elements and incorporated them into his philosophy, he retained much of the Augustinian and non-Aristotelian tradition, and his philosophy bears the character of a transitional stage on the way to that fuller incorporation of Aristotelianism which was achieved by his great pupil, St. Thomas Aquinas. Moreover, being primarily a theologian, Albert could not but be sensible of the important points on which Aristotle's thought clashes with Christian doctrine, and that uncritical acceptance of Aristotle which became fashionable in a section of the Faculty of Arts was impossible for him. It is indeed no matter for surprise that though he composed paraphrases on many of the logical, physical (for example, on the *Physics* and *De Caelo et Mundo*), metaphysical and ethical works (*Nicomachean Ethics* and *Politics*) of Aristotle, he did not hesitate to point out errors committed by the Philosopher and published a *De unitate intellectus* against Averroes. His declared intention in composing the paraphrases was to make Aristotle intelligible to the Latins, and he professed to give simply an objective account of Aristotle's opinions; but in any case he could not criticise Aristotle without showing something of his own ideas, even if his commentaries are for the most part impersonal paraphrases and explanations of the Philosopher's works.

It has not been found possible to determine with any degree of accuracy the dates of Albert's writings or even the order in which he published them, but it seems that the publication of his Commentary on the *Sentences* of Peter Lombard and the *Summa de Creaturis* antedate the publication of his paraphrases of Aristotle's works. He also published Commentaries on the books of the Pseudo-Dionysius. The *De unitate intellectus* appears to have been composed after 1270, and the *Summa theologiae*, which may be a compilation due to other hands, remained unfinished.

One cannot pass over in silence a remarkable side of Albert's interest and activity, his interest in the physical sciences. In an enlightened manner he insisted on the necessity of observation and experiment in these matters, and in his *De vegetalibus* and *De animalibus* he gives the results of his own observations as well as ideas of earlier writers. Apropos of his description of trees and plants he remarks that what he has set down is the result of his own experience or has been borrowed from authors whom he knows to have confirmed their ideas by observation, for in such matters experience alone can give certainty.[1] His speculations are often very sensible, as when, in opposition to the idea that the earth south of the equator is uninhabitable, he affirms that the reverse is probably true, though the cold at the poles may be so excessive as to prevent habitation. If, however, there are animals living there, we must suppose that they have coats thick enough to protect them against the climate and these coats are probably white in colour. In any case it is unreasonable to suppose that

[1] *Liber* 6, *de Veget. et Plantis*, Tract. 1, c. 1.

people living on the lower part of the earth would fall off, since the term 'lower' is only relative to us.[1] Naturally Albert relies very much on the opinions, observations and guesses of his predecessors; but he frequently appeals to his own observation, to what he has personally noticed of the habits of migrating birds, or of the nature of plants, for example, and he shows a robust common sense, as when he makes it plain that *a priori* arguments for the uninhabitable character of the 'torrid zone' cannot outweigh the evident fact that parts of lands which we know to be inhabited lie in that zone. Again, when speaking of the lunar halo or 'rainbow',[2] he remarks that according to Aristotle this phenomenon occurs only twice in fifty years, whereas he and others have observed it twice in one year, so that Aristotle must have been speaking from hearsay and not from experience. In any case, whatever value the particular conclusions drawn by St. Albert have, it is the spirit of curiosity and the reliance on observation and experiment which is remarkable and helps to distinguish him from so many Scholastics of a later period. Incidentally this spirit of inquiry and wide interests brings him near, in this respect, to Aristotle, since the Philosopher himself was well aware of the value of empirical research in scientific matters, however much later disciples may have received all his dicta as unquestionable and lacked his inquiring spirit and many-sided interests.

2. St. Albert the Great is quite clear as to the distinction between theology and philosophy, and so between the theology which takes as its foundation the data of revelation and the theology which is the work of the unaided natural reason and belongs to metaphysical philosophy. Thus metaphysics or first theology treats of God as the first Being (*secundum quod substat proprietatibus entis primi*), while theology treats of God as known by faith (*secundum quod substat attributis quae per fidem attribuuntur*). Again, the philosopher works under the influence of the general light of reason given to all men, by which light he sees the first principles, while the theologian works by the supernatural light of faith, through which he receives the revealed dogmas.[3] St. Albert has, therefore, little sympathy for those who deny or belittle philosophy, since not only does he make use of dialectic in theological reasoning, but he also recognises philosophy itself as an independent science. Against those who assert that it is wrong

[1] Cf. *De Natura Locorum*, Tract. 1, cc. 6, 7, 8, 12.
[2] *Liber* 3, *Meteorum*, Tract. 4, c. 11. [3] 1 *Summa Theol.*, 1, 4, *ad* 2 *et* 3.

to introduce philosophic reasoning into theology, he admits that such reasoning cannot be primary, since a dogma is proved *tamquam ex priori*, that is, a dogma is shown by the theologian to have been revealed and is not a conclusion from philosophic argument; but he goes on to say that philosophic arguments can be of real utility in a secondary capacity, when dealing with objections brought by hostile philosophers, and speaks of the ignorant people who want to attack in every way the employment of philosophy and who are like 'brute animals blaspheming against that of which they are ignorant'.[1] Even in the Order of Preachers there was opposition to philosophy and the study of such 'profane' science, and one of the greatest services rendered by St. Albert was to promote the study and use of philosophy in his own Order.

3. The doctrine of St. Albert is not a homogeneous system, but rather a mixture of Aristotelian and neo-Platonic elements. For instance, he appeals to Aristotle when giving a proof for God's existence from motion,[2] and he argues that an infinite chain of *principia* is impossible and contradictory, since there would in reality be no *principium*. The *primum principium* or first principle must, by the very fact that it is the first principle, have its existence from itself and not from another: its existence (*esse*) must be its substance and essence.[3] It is the necessary Being, without any admixture of contingence or of potency, and Albert shows also that it is intelligent, living, omnipotent, free, and so on, in such a way that it is its own intelligence; that in God's knowledge of Himself there is no distinction between subject and object; that His will is not something distinct from His essence. Finally he carefully distinguishes God, the first Principle, from the world by observing that none of the names which we ascribe to God can be predicated of Him in their primary sense. If, for example, He is called substance, this is not because He falls within the category of substance, but because He is above all substances and the whole category of substance. Similarly, the term 'being' primarily refers to the general abstract idea of being, which cannot be predicated of God.[4] In fine, it is truer to say of God that we know what He is not rather than what He is.[5] One may say, then, that in the philosophy of St. Albert God is depicted, in dependence on Aristotle, as first unmoved Mover, as pure Act and as the self-

[1] *Comm. in Epist.* 9 *B. Dion. Areop.*, 7, 2.
[2] *Lib.* I, *de causis et proc. universitatis*, I, 7. [3] *Ibid.*, I, 8. [4] *Ibid.*, 3, 6.
[5] *Comm. in Epist.* 9 *B. Dion. Areop.*, I.

knowing Intellect, but emphasis is laid, in dependence on the writings of the Pseudo-Dionysius, on the fact that God transcends all our concepts and all the names we predicate of Him.

4. This combination of Aristotle and the Pseudo-Dionysius safeguards the divine transcendence and is the foundation for a doctrine of analogy; but when it comes to describing the creation of the world Albert interprets Aristotle according to the doctrine of the *Peripatetici*, that is to say, according to what are in reality neo-Platonic interpretations. Thus he uses the words *fluxus* and *emanatio* (*fluxus est emanatio formae a primo fonte, qui omnium formarum est fons et origo*)[1] and maintains that the first principle, *intellectus universaliter agens*, is the source whence flows the second intelligence, the latter the source whence flows the third intelligence, and so on. From each subordinate intelligence is derived its own proper sphere, until eventually the earth comes into being. This general scheme (Albert gives several particular schemes, culled from the 'ancients') might seem to impair the divine transcendence and immutability, as also the creative activity of God; but St. Albert does not, of course, think of God as becoming less through the process of emanation or as undergoing any change, while he also insists that a subordinate cause works only in dependence on, with the help of, the higher cause, so that the whole process must ultimately be referred to God. This process is variously represented as a graded diffusion of goodness or as a graded diffusion of light. However, it is clear that in this picture of creation St. Albert is inspired far more by the *Liber de causis*, the neo-Platonists and the neo-Platonising Aristotelians than by the historic Aristotle, while on the other hand he does not appear to have realised that the neo-Platonic notion of emanation, though not strictly pantheistic, since God remains distinct from all other beings, is yet not fully in tune with the Christian doctrine of free creation out of nothing. I do not mean to suggest for a moment that St. Albert intended to substitute the neo-Platonic emanation process for the Christian doctrine: rather did he try to express the latter in terms of the former, without apparently realising the difficulties involved in such an attempt.

St. Albert departs from the Augustinian-Franciscan tradition by holding that reason cannot demonstrate with certainty the world's creation in time, that is, that the world was not created from eternity,[2] and also by denying that angels and the human soul are

[1] *Lib.* 1, *de causis et proc. universitatis*, 4, 1. [2] *In Phys.*, 8, 1, 13.

composed of matter and form, in this evidently thinking of matter as related to quantity; but on the other hand he accepts the doctrine of the *rationes seminales* and that of light as the *forma corporeitatis*. Moreover, besides adopting doctrines sometimes from Aristotelianism and sometimes from Augustinianism or neo-Platonism, St. Albert adopts phrases from the one tradition while interpreting them in the sense of the other, as when he speaks of seeing essences in the divine light, while meaning that the human reason and its operation is a reflection of the divine light, an effect thereof, but not that a special illuminating activity of God is required over and above the creation and conservation of the intellect. In general he follows the Aristotelian theory of abstraction. Again, Albert by no means always makes his meaning clear, so that it remains doubtful whether or not he considered that the distinction between essence and existence is real or conceptual. As he denied the presence of matter in the angels, while affirming that they are composed of 'essential parts', it would indeed seem reasonable to suppose that he maintained the theory of the real distinction, and he speaks in this sense on occasion; but at other times he speaks as if he held the Averroist theory of a conceptual distinction. We are left in difficulty as to the interpretation of his thought on this and other points owing to his habit of giving various different theories without any definite indication of which solution to the problem he himself adopted. It is not always clear how far he is simply reporting the opinions of others and how far he is committing himself to the affirmation of the opinions in question. It is impossible, then, to speak of a completed 'system' of Albert the Great: his thought is really a stage in the adoption of the Aristotelian philosophy as an intellectual instrument for the expression of the Christian outlook. The process of adopting and adapting the Aristotelian philosophy was carried much further by St. Albert's great pupil, Thomas Aquinas; but it would be a mistake to exaggerate the Aristotelianism even of the latter. Both men remained to a great extent in the tradition of Augustine, though both men, St. Albert in an incomplete, St. Thomas in a more complete fashion, interpreted Augustine according to the categories of Aristotle.

5. St. Albert was convinced that the immortality of the soul can be demonstrated by reason. Thus in his book on the nature and origin of the soul[1] he gives a number of proofs, arguing, for

[1] *Liber de natura et origine animae*, 2, 6; cf. also *De Anima*, 3.

example, that the soul transcends matter in its intellectual operations, having the principle of such operations in itself, and so cannot depend on the body *secundum esse et essentiam*. But he will not allow that the arguments for the unicity of the active intellect in all men are valid, arguments which, if probative, would deny personal immortality. He treats of this matter not only in the *De Anima*, but also in his special work on the subject, the *Libellus de unitate intellectus contra Averroem*. After remarking that the question is very difficult and that only trained philosophers, accustomed to metaphysical thinking, should take part in the dispute,[1] he goes on to expose thirty arguments which the Averroists bring forward or can bring forward to support their contention and observes that they are very difficult to answer. However, he proceeds to give thirty-six arguments against the Averroists, outlines his opinion on the rational soul and then answers in turn[2] the thirty arguments of the Averroists. The rational soul is the form of man, so that it must be multiplied in individual men: but what is multiplied numerically must also be multiplied substantially. If it can be proved, then, as it can be proved, that the rational soul is immortal, it follows that the multiplicity of rational souls survive death. Again, *esse* is the act of the final form of each thing (*formae ultimae*), and the final or ultimate form of man is the rational soul. Now, either individual men have their own separate *esse* or they have not. If you say that they do not possess their own individual *esse*, you must be prepared to admit that they are not individual men, which is patently false, while if you admit that each man has his own individual *esse*, then he must also have his own individual rational soul.

6. St. Albert the Great enjoyed a high reputation, even during his own lifetime, and Roger Bacon, who was far from being an enthusiastic admirer of his work, tells us that 'just as Aristotle, Avicenna and Averroes are quoted (*allegantur*) in the Schools, so is he'. Roger Bacon means that St. Albert was cited by name, which was contrary to the custom then in vogue of not mentioning living writers by name and which gives witness to the esteem he had won for himself. This reputation was doubtless due in large part to the Saint's erudition and to his many-sided interests, as theologian, philosopher, man of science and commentator. He had a wide knowledge of Jewish and Arabian philosophy and frequently

[1] C. 3. [2] C. 7.

quotes the opinions of other writers, so that, in spite of his frequent indefiniteness of thought and expression and his mistakes in historical matters, his writings give the impression of a man of extensive knowledge who had read very widely and was interested in many lines of thought. His disciple, Ulric of Strasbourg, a Dominican, who developed the neo-Platonic side of St. Albert's thought, called him 'the wonder and miracle of our time';[1] but, apart from his devotion to experimental science, St. Albert's thought is of interest to us primarily because of its influence on St. Thomas Aquinas, who, unlike Ulric of Strasbourg and John of Fribourg, developed the Aristotelian aspect of that thought. The master, who outlived his pupil, was devoted to the latter's memory, and we are told that when St. Albert, as an old man, used to think of Thomas at the commemoration of the dead in the Canon of the Mass, he would shed tears as he thought of the death of him who had been the flower and glory of the world.

St. Albert's reputation as a man of learning and wide-ranging interests was justly merited; but his chief merit, as several historians have noticed, was that he saw what a treasure for the Christian West was contained in the system of Aristotle and in the writings of the Arabian philosophers. Looking back on the thirteenth century from a much later date, one is inclined to contemplate the invasion and growing dominance of Aristotelianism in the light of the arid Scholastic Aristotelianism of a later period, which sacrificed the spirit to the letter and entirely misunderstood the inquiring mind of the great Greek philosopher, his interest in science and the tentative nature of many of his conclusions; but to regard the thirteenth century in this light is to be guilty of an anachronism, for the attitude of the decadent Aristotelians of a later period was not the attitude of St. Albert. The Christian West possessed nothing of its own in the way of pure philosophy or of natural science which could compare with the philosophy of Aristotle and the Arabians. St. Albert realised this fact clearly; he saw that a definite attitude must be adopted towards Aristotelianism, that it could not simply be disregarded, and he was rightly convinced that it would be wasteful and even disastrous to attempt to disregard it. He saw too, of course, that on some points Aristotle and the Arabians held doctrines which were incompatible with dogma; but at the same time he realised that this was no reason for rejecting in its entirety what one had

[1] *Summa de bono*, 4, 3, 9.

to reject in part. He endeavoured to make Aristotelianism intelligible to the Latins and to show them its value, while pointing out its errors. That he accepted this or that point, rejected this or that theory, is not so important as the fact that he realised the general significance and value of Aristotelianism, and it is surely not necessary to be a rigid Aristotelian oneself in order to be able to appreciate his merits in this respect. It is a mistake so to stress St. Albert's independence, in regard to some of Aristotle's scientific observations, for example, that one loses sight of the great service he did in drawing attention to Aristotle and displaying something of the wealth of Aristotelianism. The passage of years certainly brought a certain unfortunate ossification in the Aristotelian tradition; but the blame for that cannot be laid at the door of St. Albert the Great. If one tries to imagine what mediaeval philosophy would have been without Aristotle, if one thinks away the Thomistic synthesis and the philosophy of Scotus, if one strips the philosophy of St. Bonaventure of all Aristotelian elements, one will hardly look on the invasion of Aristotelianism as an historical misfortune.

CHAPTER XXXI

ST. THOMAS AQUINAS—I

Life—Works—Mode of exposing St. Thomas's philosophy—The spirit of St. Thomas's philosophy.

1. THOMAS AQUINAS was born in the castle of Roccasecca, not far from Naples, at the end of 1224 or beginning of 1225, his father being the Count of Aquino. At the age of five years he was placed by his parents in the Benedictine Abbey of Monte Cassino as an oblate, and it was there that the future Saint and Doctor made his first studies, remaining in the monastery from 1230 to 1239, when the Emperor Frederick II expelled the monks. The boy returned to his family for a few months and then went to the University of Naples in the autumn of the same year, being then fourteen years old. In the city there was a convent of Dominican friars, and Thomas, attracted by their life, entered the Order in the course of the year 1244. This step was by no means acceptable to his family, who no doubt wished the boy to enter the abbey of Monte Cassino, as a step to ecclesiastical preferment, and it may have partly been due to this family opposition that the Dominican General resolved to take Thomas with him to Bologna, where he was himself going for a General Chapter, and then to send him on to the University of Paris. However, Thomas was kidnapped by his brothers on the way and was kept a prisoner at Aquino for about a year. His determination to remain true to his Order was proof against this trial, and he was able to make his way to Paris in the autumn of 1245.

Thomas was probably at Paris from 1245 until the summer of 1248, when he accompanied St. Albert the Great to Cologne, where the latter was to found a house of studies (*studium generale*) for the Dominican Order, remaining there until 1252. During this period, first at Paris, then at Cologne, Thomas was in close contact with Albert the Great, who realised the potentialities of his pupil, and while it is obvious that his taste for learning and study must in any case have been greatly stimulated by intimate contact with a professor of such erudition and such intellectual curiosity, we can hardly suppose that St. Albert's attempt to utilise what was valuable in Aristotelianism was without direct influence on his pupil's mind. Even if St. Thomas did not at this early date in his career conceive the idea of completing what his master had begun, he must at least have been profoundly influenced by the latter's open-mindedness. Thomas did not possess the all-embracing curiosity of his master (or one might say perhaps that he had a better sense of mental economy), but he certainly possessed greater powers of systematisation, and it was only to be expected that the meeting of the erudition and open-mindedness of the older man with the speculative power and synthesising ability of the younger would result in splendid fruit. It was St. Thomas who was to achieve the expression of the Christian ideology in Aristotelian terms, and who was to utilise Aristotelianism as an instrument of theological and philosophical analysis and synthesis; but his sojourn at Paris and Cologne in company with St. Albert was undoubtedly a factor of prime importance in his intellectual development. Whether or not we choose to regard St. Albert's system as incomplete Thomism is really irrelevant: the main fact is that St. Albert (*mutatis mutandis*) was Thomas's Socrates.

In 1252 St. Thomas returned from Cologne to Paris and continued his course of studies, lecturing on the Scriptures as *Baccalaureus Biblicus* (1252–4) and on the *Sentences* of Peter Lombard as *Baccalaureus Sententiarius* (1254–6), at the conclusion of which period he received his Licentiate, the licence or permission to teach in the faculty of theology. In the course of the same year he became *Magister* and lectured as Dominican professor until 1259. Of the controversy which arose concerning the Dominican and Franciscan chairs in the university mention has already been made. In 1259 he left Paris for Italy and taught theology at the *studium curiae* attached to the Papal court until 1268. Thus he was at Anagni with Alexander IV (1259–61), at Orvieto with Urban IV (1261–4), at Santa Sabina in Rome (1265–7), and at Viterbo with Clement IV (1267–8). It was at the court of Urban IV that he met the famous translator, William of Moerbeke, and it was Urban who commissioned Thomas to compose the Office for the feast of Corpus Christi.

In 1268 Thomas returned to Paris and taught there until 1272, engaging in controversy with the Averroists, as also with those who renewed the attack on the religious Orders. In 1272 he was sent to Naples in order to erect a Dominican *studium generale*, and he continued his professorial activity there until 1274, when Pope Gregory X summoned him to Lyons to take part in the

Council. The journey was begun but never completed, as St. Thomas died on the way on March 7th, 1274, at the Cistercian monastery of Fossanuova, between Naples and Rome. He was forty-nine years of age at the time of his death, having behind him a life devoted to study and teaching. It had not been a life of much external activity or excitement, if we except the early incident of his imprisonment, the more or less frequent journeys and the controversies in which the Saint was involved; but it was a life devoted to the pursuit and defence of truth, a life also permeated and motivated by a deep spirituality. In some ways Thomas Aquinas was rather like the professor of legend (there are several stories concerning his fits of abstraction, or rather concentration, which made him oblivious to his surroundings), but he was a great deal more than a professor or theologian, for he was a Saint, and even if his devotion and love are not allowed to manifest themselves in the pages of his academic works, the ecstasies and mystical union with God of his later years bear witness to the fact that the truths of which he wrote were the realities by which he lived.

2. St. Thomas's Commentary on the *Sentences* of Peter Lombard dates probably from 1254 to 1256, the *De principiis naturae* from 1255, the *De ente et essentia* from 1256 and the *De Veritate* from between 1256 and 1259. It may be that the *Quaestiones quodlibetales* 7, 8, 9, 10 and 11 were also composed before 1259, i.e. before Thomas left Paris for Italy. The *In Boethium de Hebdomadibus* and the *In Boethium de Trinitate* are also to be assigned to this period. While in Italy St. Thomas wrote the *Summa contra Gentiles*, the *De Potentia*, the *Contra errores Graecorum*, the *De emptione et venditione* and the *De regimine principum*. To this period belong also a number of the Commentaries on Aristotle: for example, those on the *Physics* (probably), the *Metaphysics*, the *Nicomachean Ethics*, the *De Anima*, the *Politics* (probably). On his return to Paris, where he became engaged in controversy with the Averroists, St. Thomas wrote the *De aeternitate mundi contra murmurantes* and the *De unitate intellectus contra Averroistas*, the *De Malo* (probably), the *De spiritualibus creaturis*, the *De anima* (i.e. the *Quaestio disputata*), the *De unione Verbi incarnati*, as well as the *Quaestiones quodlibetales* 1 to 6 and the commentaries on the *De causis*, the *Meteorologica*[1] and the *Perihermeneias*, also

[1] The supplement to the Commentary on the *Meteorologica* seems to have been completed by an anonymous writer, drawing on Peter of Auvergne.

belong to this period, while during his stay at Naples St. Thomas wrote the *De mixtione elementorum*, the *De motu cordis*, the *De virtutibus*, and the commentaries on Aristotle's *De Caelo* and *De generatione et corruptione*. As to the *Summa Theologica*, this was composed between 1265 (at the earliest) and 1273, the *Pars prima* being written in Paris, the *Prima secundae* and *Secunda secundae* in Italy, and the *Tertia pars* in Paris between 1272 and 1273. The *Supplementum*, made up from previous writings of St. Thomas, was added by Reginald of Piperno, St. Thomas's secretary from the year 1261. One must add that Peter of Auvergne completed the commentary on the *De Caelo* and that on the *Politics* (from Book 3, *lectio* 7), while Ptolemy of Lucca was responsible for part of the *De regimine principum*, St. Thomas having written only the first book and the first four chapters of the second book. The *Compendium theologiae*, an unfinished work, was a product of the later years of St. Thomas's life, but it is not certain if it was written before or after his return to Paris in 1268.

A number of works have been attributed to St. Thomas which were definitely not written by him, while the authenticity of certain other small works is doubtful, for example, the *De natura verbi intellectus*. The chronology which has been given above is not universally agreed upon, Mgr. Martin Grabmann and Père Mandonnet, for instance, ascribing certain works to different years. On this subject the relevant works mentioned in the Bibliography can be consulted.

3. To attempt to give a satisfactory outline of the 'philosophical system' of the greatest of the Schoolmen is to attempt a task of considerable magnitude. It does not indeed appear to me an acute question whether one should attempt a systematic or a genetic exposition, since the literary period of St. Thomas's life comprises but twenty years and though there were modifications and some development of opinion in that period, there was no such considerable development as in the case of Plato and still less was there any such succession of phases or periods as in the case of Schelling.[1] To treat the thought of Plato genetically might well be considered desirable (though actually, for purposes of convenience and clarity, I adopted a predominantly systematic form of exposition in my first volume) and to treat the thought of Schelling genetically is essential; but there is no real reason against

[1] Recent research, however, tends to show that there was more development in St. Thomas's thought than is sometimes supposed.

presenting the system of St. Thomas systematically: on the contrary, there is every reason why one should present it systematically.

The difficulty lies rather in answering the question, what precise form the systematic exposition should take and what emphasis and interpretation one should give to the component parts of its content. St. Thomas was a theologian and although he distinguished the sciences of revealed theology and philosophy, he did not himself elaborate a systematic exposition of philosophy by itself (there is theology even in the *Summa contra Gentiles*), so that the method of exposition is not already decided upon by the Saint himself.

Against this it may be objected that St. Thomas certainly did fix the starting-point for an exposition of his philosophy, and M. Gilson, in his outstanding work on St. Thomas,[1] argues that the right way of exposing the Thomistic philosophy is to expose it according to the order of the Thomistic theology. St. Thomas was a theologian and his philosophy must be regarded in the light of its relation to his theology. Not only is it true to say that the loss of a theological work like the *Summa Theologica* would be a major disaster in regard to our knowledge of St. Thomas's philosophy, whereas the loss of the Commentaries on Aristotle, though deplorable, would be of less importance; but also St. Thomas's conception of the content of philosophy or of the object which the philosopher (i.e. theologian-philosopher) considers, was that of *le révélable*, that which could have been revealed but has not been revealed and that which has been revealed but need not have been revealed, in the sense that it can be ascertained by the human reason, for example, the fact that God is wise. As M. Gilson rightly remarks, the problem for St. Thomas was not how to introduce philosophy into theology without corrupting the essence and nature of *philosophy*, but how to introduce philosophy without corrupting the essence and nature of *theology*. Theology treats of the revealed, and revelation must remain intact; but some truths are taught in theology which can be ascertained without revelation (God's existence, for example), while there are other truths which have not been revealed but which might have been revealed and which are of importance for a total view of God's creation. St. Thomas's philosophy should thus be regarded in the light of its relation to theology, and it is a mistake to collect

[1] *Le Thomisme*, 5th edition, Paris, 1944.

the philosophical items from St. Thomas's works, including his theological works, and construct a system out of them according to one's own idea of what a philosophical system should be, even though St. Thomas would very likely have refused to recognise such a system as corresponding with his actual intentions. To reconstruct the Thomistic system in such a way is legitimate enough for a philosopher, but it is the part of the historian to stick to St. Thomas's own method.

M. Gilson argues his point with his customary lucidity and cogency, and it seems to me that his point must, in general, be admitted. To begin an historical exposition of St. Thomas's philosophy by a theory of knowledge, for example, especially if the theory of knowledge were separated from psychology or the doctrine of the soul, would scarcely represent St. Thomas's own procedure, though it would be legitimate in an exposition of 'Thomism' which did not pretend to be primarily historical. On the other hand, St. Thomas certainly wrote some philosophical works before he composed the *Summa Theologica*, and the proofs of the existence of God in the latter work obviously presuppose a good many philosophical ideas. Moreover, as those philosophical ideas are not mere ideas, but are, on the principles of St. Thomas's own philosophy, abstracted from experience of the concrete, there seems to me ample justification for starting with the concrete sensible world of experience and considering some of St. Thomas's theories about it before going on to consider his natural theology. And this is the procedure which I have actually adopted.

Another point. St. Thomas was an extremely clear writer; but none the less there have been and are divergences of interpretation in regard to certain of his doctrines. To discuss fully the *pros* and *cons* of different interpretations is, however, not possible in a general history of philosophy: one can do little more than give the interpretation which commends itself in one's own eyes. At the same time, as far as the present writer is concerned, he is not prepared to state that on points where a difference of interpretation has arisen, he can give what is the indubitably correct interpretation. After all, concerning which great philosopher's system is there complete and universal agreement of interpretation? Plato, Aristotle, Descartes, Leibniz, Kant, Hegel? In the case of some philosophers, especially in the case of those who have expressed their thought clearly and carefully, like St. Thomas, there is a pretty generally accepted interpretation as to the main body of the system; but it is doubtful if the consent ever is or ever will be absolute and universal. A philosopher may write clearly and yet not express his final thought on all problems which arise in connection with his system, especially as some of those problems may not have occurred to him: it would be absurd to expect of any philosopher that he should have answered all questions, settled all problems, even that he should have rounded off and sealed his system in such a way that there could be no possible ground for divergence of interpretation. The present writer has the greatest respect and reverence for the genius of St. Thomas Aquinas, but he does not see that anything is to be gained by confusing the finite mind of the Saint with Absolute Mind or by claiming for his system what its author himself would certainly never have dreamed of claiming.

4. The philosophy of St. Thomas is essentially realist and concrete. St. Thomas certainly adopts the Aristotelian statement that first philosophy or metaphysic studies being as being; but it is perfectly clear that the task he sets himself is the explanation of existent being, so far as this is attainable by the human mind. In other words, he does not presuppose a notion from which reality is to be deduced; but he starts from the existent world and inquires what its being is, how it exists, what is the condition of its existence. Moreover, his thought concentrates on the supreme Existence, on the Being which does not merely possess existence, but is Its own existence, which is the very plenitude of existence, *ipsum esse subsistens*: his thought remains ever in contact with the concrete, the existent, both with that which has existence as something derived, something received, and with that which does not receive existence but is existence. In this sense it is true to say that Thomism is an 'existential philosophy', though it is very misleading, in my opinion, to call St. Thomas an 'existentialist', since the *Existenz* of the existentialists is not the same thing as St. Thomas's *esse*; nor is St. Thomas's method of approach to the problem of existence the same as that of the philosophers who are now called existentialists.

It has been maintained that St. Thomas, by bringing *esse* to the forefront of the philosophic stage, advanced beyond the philosophies of essence, particularly beyond Plato and the philosophies of Platonic inspiration. There is certainly truth in this contention: although Plato did not disregard the question of existence, the salient characteristic of his philosophy is the explanation of the world in terms of essence rather than of existence, while even for Aristotle, God, although pure Act, is primarily Thought, or Idea, the Platonic Good rendered 'personal'. Moreover, although Aristotle endeavoured to explain form and order in the world and the intelligible process of development, he did not explain the existence of the world; apparently he thought that no explanation was needed. In neo-Platonism again, though the derivation of the world is accounted for, the general scheme of emanation is primarily that of an emanation of essences, though existence is certainly not left out of account: God is primarily the One or the Good, not *ipsum esse subsistens*, not the *I am who am*. But one should remember that creation out of nothing was not an idea at which any Greek philosopher arrived without dependence on Judaism or Christianity and that without this idea the derivation of the world tends to be explained as a necessary derivation of essences. Those Christian philosophers who depended on and utilised neo-Platonic terminology spoke of the world as flowing from or emanating from God, and even St. Thomas used such phrases on occasion; but an orthodox Christian philosopher, whatever his terminology, regards the world as created freely by God, as receiving *esse* from *ipsum esse subsistens*. When St. Thomas insisted on the fact that God is subsistent existence, that His essence is not primarily goodness or thought but existence, he was but rendering explicit the implications of the Jewish and Christian view of the world's relation to God. I do not mean to imply that the idea of creation cannot be attained by reason; but the fact remains that it was not attained by the Greek philosophers and could hardly be attained by them, given their idea of God.

Of St. Thomas's general relation to Aristotle I shall speak later; but it may be as well to point out now one great effect which Aristotelianism had on St. Thomas's philosophical outlook and procedure. One might expect that St. Thomas, being a Christian, a theologian, a friar, would emphasise the soul's relation to God and would begin with what some modern philosophers call 'subjectivity', that he would place the interior life in the foreground even of his philosophy, as St. Bonaventure did. In point of fact, however, one of the chief characteristics of St. Thomas's philosophy is its 'objectivity' rather than its 'subjectivity'. The immediate object of the human intellect is the essence of the material thing, and St. Thomas builds up his philosophy by reflection on sense-experience. In the proofs which he gives of God's existence the process of argument is always from the sensible world to God. No doubt certain of the proofs could be applied to the soul itself as a starting-point and be developed in a different way; but in actual fact this was not the way of St. Thomas, and the proof which he calls the *via manifestior* is the one which is most dependent on Aristotle's own arguments. This Aristotelian 'objectivity' of St. Thomas may appear disconcerting to those for whom 'truth is subjectivity'; but at the same time it is a great source of strength, since it means that his arguments can be considered in themselves, apart from St. Thomas's own life, on their own merits or demerits, and that observations about 'wishful thinking' are largely irrelevant, the relevant question being the objective cogency of the arguments themselves. Another result is that St. Thomas's philosophy appears 'modern' in a sense in which the philosophy of St. Bonaventure can hardly do. The latter tends to appear as essentially bound up with the general mediaeval outlook and with the Christian spiritual life and tradition, so that it seems to be on a different plane from the 'profane' philosophies of modern times, whereas the Thomistic philosophy can be divorced from Christian spirituality and, to a large extent, from the mediaeval outlook and background, and can enter into direct competition with more recent systems. A Thomistic revival has taken place, as everybody knows; but it is a little difficult to imagine a Bonaventurian revival, unless one were at the same time to change the conception of philosophy, and in this case the modern philosopher and the Bonaventurian would scarcely speak the same language.

Nevertheless, St. Thomas was a Christian philosopher. As already mentioned, St. Thomas follows Aristotle in speaking of metaphysics as the science of being as being; but the fact that his thought centres round the concrete and the fact that he was a Christian theologian led him to emphasise also the view that 'first philosophy is wholly directed to the knowledge of God as the last end' and that 'the knowledge of God is the ultimate end of every human cognition and operation'.[1] But actually man was created for a profounder and more intimate knowledge of God than he can attain by the exercise of his natural reason in this life, and so revelation was morally necessary in order that his mind might be raised to something higher than his reason can attain to in this life and that he should desire and zealously strive towards

[1] *Contra Gent.*, 3, 25.

something 'which exceeds the whole state of this life.'[1] Metaphysics has its own object, therefore, and a certain autonomy of its own, but it points upwards and needs to be crowned by theology: otherwise man will not realise the end for which he was created and will not desire and strive towards that end. Moreover, as the primary object of metaphysics, God, exceeds the apprehension of the metaphysician and of the natural reason in general, and as the full knowledge or vision of God is not attainable in this life, the conceptual knowledge of God is crowned in this life by mysticism. Mystical theology does not enter the province of philosophy, and St. Thomas's philosophy can be considered without reference to it; but one should not forget that for St. Thomas philosophical knowledge is neither sufficient nor final.

[1] *Contra Gent.*, 1, 5.

CHAPTER XXXII

ST. THOMAS AQUINAS—II

PHILOSOPHY AND THEOLOGY

Distinction between philosophy and theology—Moral necessity of revelation—Incompatibility of faith and science in the same mind concerning the same object—Natural end and supernatural end—St. Thomas and St. Bonaventure—St. Thomas as 'innovator'.

1. THAT St. Thomas made a formal and explicit distinction between dogmatic theology and philosophy is an undoubted and an indubitable fact. Philosophy and the other human sciences rely simply and solely on the natural light of reason: the philosopher uses principles which are known by the human reason (with God's natural concurrence, of course, but without the supernatural light of faith), and he argues to conclusions which are the fruit of human reasoning. The theologian, on the other hand, although he certainly uses his reason, accepts his principles on authority, on faith; he receives them as revealed. The introduction of dialectic into theology, the practice of starting from a revealed premiss or from revealed premisses and arguing rationally to a conclusion, leads to the development of Scholastic theology, but it does not turn theology into philosophy, since the principles, the data, are accepted as revealed. For instance, the theologian may attempt with the aid of categories and forms of reasoning borrowed from philosophy to understand a little better the mystery of the Trinity; but he does not thereby cease to act as a theologian, since all the time he accepts the dogma of the Trinity of Persons in one Nature on the authority of God revealing: it is for him a datum or principle, a revealed premiss accepted on faith, not the conclusion of a philosophical argument. Again, while the philosopher starts from the world of experience and argues by reason to God in so far as He can be known by means of creatures, the theologian starts with God as He has revealed Himself, and the natural method in theology is to pass from God in Himself to creatures rather than to ascend from creatures to God, as the philosopher does and must do.

It follows that the principal difference between theology and philosophy lies in the fact that the theologian receives his principles as revealed and considers the objects with which he deals as revealed or as deducible from what is revealed, whereas the philosopher apprehends his principles by reason alone and considers the objects with which he deals, not as revealed but as apprehensible and apprehended by the natural light of reason. In other words, the fundamental difference between theology and philosophy does not lie in a difference of objects concretely considered. Some truths are proper to theology, since they cannot be known by reason and are known only by revelation, the mystery of the Trinity, for example, while other truths are proper to philosophy alone in the sense that they have not been revealed; but there are some truths which are common to both theology and philosophy, since they have been revealed, though at the same time they can be established by reason. It is the existence of these common truths which makes it impossible to say that theology and philosophy differ primarily because each science considers different truths: in some instances they consider the same truths, though they consider them in a different manner, the theologian considering them as revealed, the philosopher as conclusions of a process of human reasoning. For example, the philosopher argues to God as Creator, while the theologian also treats of God as Creator; but for the philosopher the knowledge of God as Creator comes as the conclusion of a purely rational argument, while the theologian accepts the fact that God is Creator from revelation, so that it is for him a premiss rather than a conclusion, a premiss which is not hypothetically assumed but revealed. In technical language it is not *primarily* a difference of truths considered 'materially', or according to their content, which constitutes the difference between a truth of theology and a truth of philosophy, but rather a difference of truths considered 'formally'. That is to say, the same truth may be enunciated by both the theologian and the philosopher; but it is arrived at and considered by the theologian in a different way from that in which it is arrived at and considered by the philosopher. *Diversa ratio cognoscibilis diversitatem scientiarum inducit. . . .* 'There is, therefore, no reason why another science should not treat of the very same objects, as known by the light of divine revelation, which the philosophical sciences treat of according as they are knowable by the light of natural reason. Hence the theology which belongs to sacred doctrine differs generically from that theology which is a part of philosophy.'[1] Between dogmatic theology and natural theology there is a certain overlapping; but the sciences differ generically from one another.

2. According to St. Thomas, almost the whole of philosophy is directed to the knowledge of God, at least in the sense that a good deal of philosophical study is presupposed and required by natural theology, that part of metaphysics which treats of God. Natural theology, he says, is the last part of philosophy to be learnt.[2] Incidentally, this statement does not support the view that one should start the exposition of the Thomist philosophy with natural theology; but in any case the point I now want to make is that St. Thomas, seeing that natural theology, if it is to be properly grasped, requires much previous study and reflection, insists that revelation is morally necessary, given the fact that God is man's end. Moreover, not only does natural theology require more reflection and study and ability than most men are in a position to devote to it, but also, even when the truth is discovered, history shows that it is often contaminated by error. Pagan philosophers have certainly discovered God's existence; but error was often involved in their speculations, the philosopher either not realising properly the unity of God or denying divine providence or failing to see that God is Creator. If it were a question simply of astronomy or natural science, errors would not matter so much, since man can perfectly well attain his end even if he holds erroneous opinions concerning astronomical or scientific matters; but God is Himself man's end, and knowledge of God is essential in order that man should direct himself rightly towards that end, so that truth concerning God is of great importance and error concerning God is disastrous. Granted, then, that God is man's end, we can see that it is morally necessary that the discovery of truths so important for life should not be left simply to the unaided powers of those men who have the ability, the zeal and the leisure to discover them, but that these truths should also be revealed.[3]

3. At once the question arises whether the same man can at the same time believe (accept on authority by faith) and know (as a result of rational demonstration) the same truth. If God's existence, for instance, has been demonstrated by a philosopher, can he at the same time believe it by faith? In the *De Veritate*[4]

[1] *S.T.*, Ia, 1, 1, *ad* 2.
[2] *Contra Gent.*, 1, 4.
[3] Cf. *S.T.*, Ia, 1, 1; *Contra Gent.*, 1, 4.
[4] 14, 9.

St. Thomas answers roundly that it is impossible for there to be faith and knowledge concerning the same object, that the same truths should be both known scientifically (philosophically) and at the same time believed (by faith) by the same man. On this supposition it would seem that a man who has proved the unity of God cannot believe that same truth by faith. In order, then, that it should not appear that this man is failing to give assent to articles of faith, St. Thomas finds himself compelled to say that such truths as the unity of God are not properly speaking articles of faith, but rather *praeambula ad articulos.*[1] He adds, however, that nothing prevents such truths being the object of belief to a man who cannot understand or has no time to consider the philosophical demonstration,[2] and he maintains his opinion that it was proper and fitting for such truths to be proposed for belief.[3] The question whether a man who understands the demonstration but who is not attending to it or considering it at the moment, can exercise faith in regard to the unity of God he does not explicitly answer. As to the opening phrase of the Creed (*Credo in unum Deum*, I believe in one God), which might seem to imply that faith in the unity of God is demanded of all, he would, on his premisses, have to say that the unity of God is here not to be understood by itself but together with what follows, that is, as a unity of Nature in a Trinity of Persons.

To go into this question further and to discuss with what sort of faith the uneducated believe the truths which are known (demonstratively) by the philosopher, would be inappropriate here, not only because it is a theological question, but also because it is a question which St. Thomas does not explicitly discuss: the main point in mentioning the matter at all is to illustrate the fact that St. Thomas makes a real distinction between philosophy on the one hand and theology on the other. Incidentally, if we speak of a 'philosopher', it must not be understood as excluding the theologian: most of the Scholastics were both theologians and philosophers, and St. Thomas distinguishes the sciences rather than the men. That St. Thomas took this distinction seriously can also be seen from the position he adopted towards the question of the eternity of the world (to which I shall return later). He considered that it can be demonstrated that the world was created, but he did not think that reason can demonstrate that the world

[1] *S.T.*, Ia, 2, 2, *ad* 1; *De Verit.*, 14, 9, *ad* 9.
[2] *S.T.*, Ia, 2, 2, *ad* 1.
[3] *Contra Gent.*, 1, 4.

was not created from eternity, although it can refute the proofs adduced to show that it *was* created from eternity. On the other hand we know by revelation that the world was not created from eternity but had a beginning in time. In other words, the theologian knows through revelation that the world was not created from eternity, but the philosopher cannot prove this—or rather no argument which has been brought forward to prove it is conclusive. This distinction obviously presupposes or implies a real distinction between the two sciences of philosophy and theology.

4. It is sometimes said that St. Thomas differs from St. Augustine in that while the latter considers man simply in the concrete, as man called to a supernatural end, St. Thomas distinguishes two ends, a supernatural end, the consideration of which he assigns to the theologian, and a natural end, the consideration of which he assigns to the philosopher. Now, that St. Thomas distinguishes the two ends is quite true. In the *De Veritate*[1] he says that the final good as considered by the philosopher is different from the final good as considered by the theologian, since the philosopher considers the final good (*bonum ultimum*) which is proportionate to human powers, whereas the theologian considers as the final good that which transcends the power of nature, namely life eternal, by which he means, of course, not simply survival but the vision of God. This distinction is of great importance and it has its repercussion both in morals, where it is the foundation of the distinction between the natural and the supernatural virtues, and in politics, where it is the foundation of the distinction between the ends of the Church and the State and determines the relations which should exist between the two societies; but it is not a distinction between two ends which correspond to two mutually exclusive orders, the one supernatural, the other that of 'pure nature': it is a distinction between two orders of knowledge and activity in the same concrete human being. The concrete human being was created by God for a supernatural end, for perfect happiness, which is attainable only in the next life through the vision of God and which is, moreover, unattainable by man by his own unaided natural power; but man can attain an imperfect happiness in this life by the exercise of his natural powers, through coming to a philosophic knowledge of God through creatures and through the attainment and exercise of the natural

[1] 14, 3.

virtues.[1] Obviously these ends are not exclusive, since man can attain the imperfect felicity in which his natural end consists without thereby putting himself outside the way to his supernatural end; the natural end, imperfect beatitude, is proportionate to human nature and human powers, but inasmuch as man has been created for a supernatural final end, the natural end cannot satisfy him, as St. Thomas argues in the *Contra Gentiles*[2]; it is imperfect and points beyond itself.

How does this affect the question of the relation between theology and philosophy? In this way. Man has one final end, supernatural beatitude, but the existence of this end, which transcends the powers of mere human nature, even though man was created to attain it and given the power to do so by grace, cannot be known by natural reason and so cannot be divined by the philosopher: its consideration is restricted to the theologian. On the other hand, man can attain through the exercise of his natural powers to an imperfect and limited natural happiness in this life, and the existence of this end and the means to attain it are discoverable by the philosopher, who can prove the existence of God from creatures, attain some analogical knowledge of God, define the natural virtues and the means of attaining them. Thus the philosopher may be said to consider the end of man in so far as this end is discoverable by human reason, i.e. only imperfectly and incompletely. But both theologian and philosopher are considering man in the concrete: the difference is that the philosopher, while able to view and consider human nature as such, cannot discover all there is in man, cannot discover his supernatural vocation; he can only go part of the way in discovering man's destiny, precisely because man was created for an end which transcends the powers of his nature. It is, therefore, not true to say that for St. Thomas the philosopher considers man in a hypothetical state of pure nature, that is, man as he would have been, had he never been called to a supernatural end: he considers man in the concrete, but he cannot know all there is to be known about that man in the concrete. When St. Thomas raises the question whether God could have created man *in puris naturalibus*[3] he is asking simply if God could have created man (who even in this hypothesis was created for a supernatural end) without

[1] Cf. *In Boethium de Trinitate*, 6, 4, 5; *In 1 Sent., prol.*, 1, 1; *De Veritate*, 14, 2; *S.T.*, Ia, IIae, 5, 5.
[2] 3, 27ff.
[3] *In 2 Sent.*, 29, 1, 2; *ibid.*, 29, 2, 3; *S.T.*, Ia, 95, 1, 4; *Quodlibet*, 1, 8.

sanctifying grace, that is to say, if God could have first created man without the means of attaining his end and then afterwards have given it; he is not asking if God could have given man a purely natural ultimate end, as later writers interpreted him as saying. Whatever, then, the merit of the idea of the state of pure nature considered in itself may be (this is a point I do not propose to discuss), it does not play a part in St. Thomas's conception of philosophy. Consequently he does not differ from St. Augustine so much as has been sometimes asserted, though he defined the spheres of the two sciences of philosophy and theology more clearly than Augustine had defined them: what he did was to express Augustinianism in terms of the Aristotelian philosophy, a fact which compelled him to utilise the notion of natural end, though he interpreted it in such a way that he cannot be said to have adopted a starting-point in philosophy totally different from that of Augustine.

Actually the idea of the state of pure nature seems to have been introduced into Thomism by Cajetan. Suarez, who himself adopted the idea, remarks that 'Cajetan and the more modern theologians have considered a third state, which they have called purely natural, a state which can be thought of as possible, although it has not in fact existed'.[1] Dominicus Soto[2] says that it is a perversion of the mind of St. Thomas, while Toletus[3] observes that there exist in us a natural desire and a natural appetite for the vision of God, though this opinion, which is that of Scotus and seems to be that of St. Thomas, is contrary to that of Cajetan.

5. St. Thomas certainly believed that it is *theoretically* possible for the philosopher to work out a true metaphysical system without recourse to revelation. Such a system would be necessarily imperfect, inadequate and incomplete, because the metaphysician is primarily concerned with the Truth itself, with God who is the principle of all truth, and he is unable by purely human rational investigation to discover all that knowledge of Truth itself, of God, which is necessary for man if he is to attain his final end. The mere philosopher can say nothing about the supernatural end of man or the supernatural means of attaining that end, and as the knowledge of these things is required for man's salvation, the insufficiency of philosophical knowledge is apparent. On the other

[1] *De Gratia, Prolegom.*, 4, c. 1, n. 2. [2] *In 4 Sent.*, 49, 2, 1; p. 903, 1613 edit.
[3] *In Summam Sancti Thomae*, Ia, 1, 1, t. 1, pp. 17–19, 1869 edit.

hand, incompleteness and inadequacy do not necessarily mean falsity. The truth that God is one is not vitiated by the very fact that nothing is said or known of the Trinity of Persons; the further truth completes the first, but the first truth is not false, even taken by itself. If the philosopher states that God is one and simply says nothing about the Trinity, because the idea of the Trinity has never entered his head; or if he knows of the doctrine of the Trinity and does not himself believe it, but simply contents himself with saying that God is one; or even if he expresses the view that the Trinity, which he understands wrongly, is incompatible with the divine unity; it still remains true that the statement that God is one in Nature is a correct statement. Of course, if the philosopher states positively that God is one Person, he is stating what is false; but if he simply says that God is one and that God is personal, without going on to state that God is one Person, he is stating the truth. It may be unlikely that a philosopher would stop short at saying that God is personal, but it is at least theoretically possible. Unless one is prepared to condemn the human intellect as such or at any rate to debar it from the discovery of a true metaphysic, one must admit that the establishment of a satisfactory metaphysic is abstractly possible, even for the pagan philosopher. St. Thomas was very far from following St. Bonaventure in excluding Aristotle from the ranks of the metaphysicians: on the contrary, the latter was in Thomas's eyes the philosopher *par excellence*, the very embodiment of the intellectual power of the human mind acting without divine faith, and he attempted, wherever possible, to interpret Aristotle in the most 'charitable' sense, that is, in the sense which was most compatible with Christian revelation.

If one emphasises simply this aspect of St. Thomas's attitude towards philosophy, it would seem that a Thomist could not legitimately adopt a consistently hostile and polemical attitude towards modern philosophy. If one adopts the Bonaventurian position and maintains that a metaphysician cannot attain truth unless he philosophises in the light of faith (though without, of course, basing his philosophical proofs on theological premisses), one would only expect that a philosopher who rejected the supernatural or who confined religion within the bounds of reason alone, should go sadly astray; but if one is prepared to admit the possibility of even a pagan philosopher elaborating a more or less satisfactory metaphysic, it is unreasonable to suppose that in several centuries of intensive human thought, no truth has come to light. It would seem that a Thomist should expect to find fresh intellectual illumination in the pages of the modern philosophers and that he should approach them with an initial sympathy and expectancy rather than with an *a priori* suspicion, reserve and even hostility.

On the other hand, though St. Thomas's attitude towards the pagan philosophers, and towards Aristotle in particular, differed from that of St. Bonaventure, it is not right to exaggerate their difference of outlook. As has already been mentioned, St. Thomas gives reasons why it is fitting that even those truths about God which can be discovered by reason should be proposed for men's belief. Some of the reasons he gives are not indeed relevant to the particular point I am discussing. For example, it is perfectly true that many people are so occupied with earning their daily bread that they have not the time to give to metaphysical reflection, even when they have the capacity for such reflection, so that it is desirable that those metaphysical truths which are of importance for them in their lives should be proposed for their belief: otherwise they will never know them at all,[1] just as most of us would have neither the time nor the energy to discover America for ourselves, did we not already accept the fact that it exists on the testimony of others; but it does not necessarily follow that those who have the time and ability for metaphysical reflection will probably draw wrong conclusions, except in so far as metaphysical thinking is difficult and requires prolonged attention and concentration, whereas 'certain people', as St. Thomas remarks, are lazy. However, there is this further point to be borne in mind,[2] that on account of the weakness of our intellect in judging and on account of the intrusion of the imagination falsity is generally (*plerumque*) mixed with truth in the human mind's conclusions. Among the conclusions which are truly demonstrated there is sometimes (*aliquando*) included a false conclusion which has not been demonstrated but is asserted on the strength of a probable or sophistical reasoning passing under the name of demonstration. The practical result will be that even certain and sure conclusions will not be whole-heartedly accepted by many people, particularly when they see philosophers teaching different doctrines while they themselves are unable to distinguish a doctrine which has been truly demonstrated from one which rests on a merely probable or sophistical

[1] *Contra Gent.*, I, 4. [2] *Ibid.*

argument. Similarly, in the *Summa Theologica*, St. Thomas observes that the truth about God is arrived at by the human reason only by a few men and after a long time and 'with the admixture of many errors'.[1] When the Saint says that it is desirable that even those truths about God which are rationally demonstrable should be proposed as objects of belief, to be accepted on authority, he emphasises indeed the practical requirements of the many rather than the speculative insufficiency of metaphysics as such, but he does admit that error is frequently mixed with the truth, either because of over-hastiness in jumping to conclusions or because of the influence of passion and emotion or of imagination. Possibly he did not himself apply this idea with perfect consistency in regard to Aristotle and was too ready to interpret Aristotle in the sense which was most compatible with Christian doctrine, but the fact remains that he acknowledges theoretically the weakness of the human intellect in its present condition, though not its radical perversion. Accordingly, though he differs from St. Bonaventure in that he admits the abstract possibility, and indeed, in Aristotle's case, the concrete fact, of a 'satisfactory' metaphysic being elaborated by a pagan philosopher and also refuses to allow that its incompleteness vitiates a metaphysical system, he also admits it is likely that any independent metaphysical system will contain error.

Perhaps it is not fanciful to suggest that the two men's abstract opinions were largely settled by their attitude towards Aristotle. It might, of course, be retorted that this is to put the cart before the horse, but it will appear more reasonable if one considers the actual circumstances in which they lived and wrote. For the first time Latin Christendom was becoming acquainted with a great philosophical system which owed nothing to Christianity and which was represented by its fervent adherents, such as Averroes, as being the last word in human wisdom. The greatness of Aristotle, the depth and comprehensiveness of his system, was a factor which could not be ignored by any Christian philosopher of the thirteenth century; but it could be met and treated in more than one way. On the one hand, as expounded by Averroes, Aristotelianism conflicted on several very important points with Christian doctrine, and it was possible to adopt a hostile and unreceptive attitude towards the Aristotelian metaphysic on this count. If, however, one adopted this course, as St. Bonaventure

[1] *S.T.*, Ia, 1, 1, *in corpore*.

did, one had to say either that Aristotle's system affirmed philosophical truth but that what was true in philosophy might not be true in theology, since God could override the demands of natural logic, or else that Aristotle went wrong in his metaphysics. St. Bonaventure adopted the second course. But why, in Bonaventure's view, did Aristotle go wrong, the greatest systematiser of the ancient world? Obviously because any independent philosophy is bound to go wrong on important points simply because it is independent: it is only in the light of the Christian faith that one can elaborate anything like a complete and satisfactory philosophical system, since it is only in the light of the Christian faith that the philosopher will be enabled to leave his philosophy open to revelation: if he has not that light, he will round it off and complete it, and if he rounds it off and completes it, it will be thereby vitiated in part at least, especially in regard to those parts, the most important parts, which deal with God and the end of man. On the other hand, if one saw in the Aristotelian system a magnificent instrument for the expression of truth and for the welding together of the divine truths of theology and philosophy, one would have to admit the power of the pagan philosopher to attain metaphysical truth, though in view of the interpretation of Aristotle given by Averroes and others one would have also to allow for and explain the possibility of error even on the part of the Philosopher. This was the course adopted by St. Thomas.

6. When one looks back on the thirteenth century from a much later date, one does not always recognise the fact that St. Thomas was an innovator, that his adoption of Aristotelianism was bold and 'modern'. St. Thomas was faced with a system of growing influence and importance, which seemed in many respects to be incompatible with Christian tradition, but which naturally captivated the minds of many students and masters, particularly in the faculty of arts at Paris, precisely because of its majesty, apparent coherence and comprehensiveness. That Aquinas boldly grasped the bull by the horns and utilised Aristotelianism in the building up of his own system was very far from being an obscurantist action: it was, on the contrary, extremely 'modern' and was of the greatest importance for the future of Scholastic philosophy and indeed for the history of philosophy in general. That some Scholastics in the later Middle Ages and at the time of the Renaissance brought Aristotelianism into discredit by their obscurantist adherence to all the Philosopher's *dicta*, even on scientific

matters, does not concern St. Thomas: the plain fact is that they were not faithful to the spirit of St. Thomas. The Saint rendered, on any count, an incomparable service to Christian thought by utilising the instrument which presented itself, and he naturally interpreted Aristotle in the most favourable sense from the Christian standpoint, since it was essential to show, if he was to succeed in his undertaking, that Aristotle and Averroes did not stand or fall together. Moreover, it is not true to say that St. Thomas had no sense of accurate interpretation: one may not agree with all his interpretations of Aristotle, but there can be no doubt that, given the circumstances of the time and the paucity of relevant historical information at his disposal, he was one of the most conscientious and the finest commentators of Aristotle who have ever existed.

In conclusion, however, it must be emphasised that though St. Thomas adopted Aristotelianism as an instrument for the expression of his system, he was no blind worshipper of the Philosopher, who discarded Augustine in favour of the pagan thinker. In theology he naturally treads in the footsteps of Augustine, though his adoption of the Aristotelian philosophy as an instrument enabled him to systematise, define and argue logically from theological doctrines in a manner which was foreign to the attitude of Augustine: in philosophy, while there is a great deal which comes straight from Aristotle, he often interprets Aristotle in a manner consonant with Augustine or expresses Augustine in Aristotelian categories, though it might be truer to say that he does both at once. For instance, when treating of divine knowledge and providence, he interprets the Aristotelian doctrine of God in a sense which at least does not exclude God's knowledge of the world, and in treating of the divine ideas he observes that Aristotle censured Plato for making the ideas independent both of concrete things and of an intellect, with the tacit implication that Aristotle would not have censured Plato, had the latter placed the ideas in the mind of God. This is, of course, to interpret Aristotle *in meliorem partem* from the theological standpoint, and although the interpretation tends to bring Aristotle and Augustine closer together, it most probably does not represent Aristotle's actual theory of the divine knowledge. However, of St. Thomas's relation to Aristotle I shall speak later.

CHAPTER XXXIII

ST. THOMAS AQUINAS—III
PRINCIPLES OF CREATED BEING

Reasons for starting with corporeal being—Hylomorphism—Rejection of rationes seminales*—Rejection of plurality of substantial forms—Restriction of hylomorphic composition to corporeal substances—Potentiality and act—Essence and existence.*

1. IN the *Summa Theologica*, which, as its name indicates, is a theological synopsis, the first philosophical problem of which St. Thomas treats is that of the existence of God, after which he proceeds to consider the Nature of God and then the divine Persons, passing subsequently to creation. Similarly, in the *Summa contra Gentiles*, which more nearly resembles a philosophical treatise (though it cannot be called simply a philosophical treatise, since it also treats of such purely dogmatic themes as the Trinity and the Incarnation), St. Thomas also starts with the existence of God. It might seem, then, that it would be natural to begin the exposition of St. Thomas's philosophy with his proofs of God's existence; but apart from the fact (mentioned in an earlier chapter) that St. Thomas himself says that the part of philosophy which treats of God comes after the other branches of philosophy, the proofs themselves presuppose some fundamental concepts and principles, and St. Thomas had composed the *De ente et essentia*, for example, before he wrote either of the *Summae*. It would not in any case be natural, then, to start immediately with the proofs of God's existence, and M. Gilson himself, who insists that the natural way of expounding St. Thomas's philosophy is to expound it according to the order adopted by the Saint in the *Summae*, actually begins by considering certain basic ideas and principles. On the other hand, one can scarcely discuss the whole general metaphysic of St. Thomas and all those ideas which are explicitly or implicitly presupposed by his natural theology: it is necessary to restrict the basis of one's discussion.

To a modern reader, familiar with the course and problems of modern philosophy, it might seem natural to begin with a discussion of St. Thomas's theory of knowledge and to raise the question whether or not the Saint provides an epistemological justification of the possibility of metaphysical knowledge. But although St. Thomas certainly had a 'theory of knowledge' he did not live after Kant, and the problem of knowledge did not occupy that position in his philosophy which it has come to occupy in later times. It seems to me that the natural starting-point for an exposition of the Thomist philosophy is the consideration of corporeal substances. After all, St. Thomas expressly teaches that the immediate and proper object of the human intellect in this life is the essence of material things. The fundamental notions and principles which are presupposed by St. Thomas's natural theology are not, according to him, innate, but are apprehended through reflection on and abstraction from our experience of concrete objects, and it seems, therefore, only reasonable to develop those fundamental notions and principles first of all through a consideration of material substances. St. Thomas's proofs of God's existence are *a posteriori*; they proceed from creatures to God, and it is the creature's nature, the lack of self-sufficiency on the part of the immediate objects of experience, which reveals the existence of God. Moreover, we can, by the natural light of reason, attain only that knowledge of God which can be attained by reflection on creatures and their relation to Him. On this count too it would seem only 'natural' to begin the exposition of the Thomist philosophy with a consideration of those concrete objects of experience by reflection on which we arrive at those fundamental principles which lead us on to develop the proofs of God's existence.

2. In regard to corporeal substances St. Thomas adopts from the very outset the common-sense standpoint, according to which there are a multiplicity of substances. The human mind comes to know in dependence on sense-experience, and the first concrete objects the mind knows are material objects into relation with which it enters through the senses. Reflection on these objects, however, at once leads the mind to form a distinction, or rather to discover a distinction, in the objects themselves. If I look out of my window in the spring I see the beech-tree with its young and tender green leaves, while in the autumn I see that the leaves have changed colour, though the same beech-tree stands out there in the park. The beech is substantially the same, a beech-tree, in spring and autumn, but the colour of its leaves is not the same: the colour changes without the beech-tree changing substantially. Similarly, if I go to the plantation, one year I see the larches as small trees, newly planted; later on I see them as bigger trees: their

size has changed but they are still larches. The cows in the field I see now in this place, now in that, now in one posture, now in another, standing up or lying down, now doing one thing, now another, eating the grass or chewing the cud or sleeping, now undergoing one thing, now another, being milked or being rained on or being driven along, but all the time they are the same cows. Reflection thus leads the mind to distinguish between substance and accident, and between the different kinds of accident, and St. Thomas accepts from Aristotle the doctrine of the ten categories, substance and the nine categories of accident.

So far reflection has led us only to the idea of accidental change and the notion of the categories: but further reflection will introduce the mind to a profounder level of the constitution of material being. When the cow eats grass, the grass no longer remains what it was in the field, but becomes something else through assimilation, while on the other hand it does not simply cease to be, but something remains in the process of change. The change is substantial, since the grass itself is changed, not merely its colour or size, and the analysis of substantial change leads the mind to discern two elements, one element which is common to the grass and to the flesh which the grass becomes, another element which confers on that something its determination, its substantial character, making it to be first grass, then cow-flesh. Moreover, ultimately we can conceive any material substance changing into any other, not necessarily directly or immediately, of course, but at least indirectly and mediately, after a series of changes. We come thus to the conception on the one hand of an underlying substrate of change which, *when considered in itself*, cannot be called by the name of any definite substance, and on the other hand of a determining or characterising element. The first element is 'prime matter', the indeterminate substrate of substantial change, the second element is the substantial form, which makes the substance what it is, places it in its specific class and so determines it as grass, cow, oxygen, hydrogen, or whatever it may be. Every material substance is composed in this way of matter and form.

St. Thomas thus accepts the Aristotelian doctrine of the hylomorphic composition of material substances, defining prime matter as pure potentiality and substantial form as the first act of a physical body, 'first act' meaning the principle which places the body in its specific class and determines its essence. Prime matter is in potentiality to all forms which can be the forms of bodies, but considered in itself it is without any form, pure potentiality: it is, as Aristotle said, *nec quid nec quantum nec quale nec aliud quidquam eorum quibus determinatur ens.*[1] For this reason, however, it cannot exist by itself, for to speak of a being actually existing without act or form would be contradictory: it did not, then, precede form temporally, but was created together with form.[2] St. Thomas is thus quite clear on the fact that only concrete substances, individual compositions of matter and form, actually exist in the material world. But though he is at one with Aristotle in denying the separate existence of universals (though we shall see presently that a reservation must be made in regard to this statement), he also follows Aristotle in asserting that the form needs to be individuated. The form is the universal element, being that which places an object in its class, in its species, making it to be horse or elm or iron: it needs, then, to be individuated, in order that it should become the form of this particular substance. What is the principle of individuation? It can only be matter. But matter is of itself pure potentiality: it has not those determinations which are necessary in order that it should individuate form. The accidental characteristics of quantity and so on are logically posterior to the hylomorphic composition of the substance. St. Thomas was, therefore, compelled to say that the principle of individuation is *materia signata quantitate*, in the sense of matter having an exigency for the quantitative determination which it receives from union with form. This is a difficult notion to understand, since although matter, and not form, is the foundation of quantitative multiplication, matter considered in itself is without quantitative determination: the notion is in fact a relic of the Platonic element in Aristotle's thought. Aristotle rejected and attacked the Platonic theory of forms, but his Platonic training influenced him to the extent of his being led to say that form, being of itself universal, requires individuation, and St. Thomas followed him in this. Of course, St. Thomas did not think of forms first existing separately and then being individuated, for the forms of sensible objects do not exist in a state of temporal priority to the composite substances; but the idea of individuation is certainly due originally to the Platonic way of thinking and speaking of forms: Aristotle substituted the notion of the immanent substantial form for that of the 'transcendent' exemplar form, but it would

[1] *In 7 Metaph., lectio* 2.

[2] *S.T.*, Ia, 66, 1, *in corpore.*

not become an historian to turn a blind eye to the Platonic legacy in Aristotle's thought and consequently in that of St. Thomas.

3. As a logical consequence of the doctrine that prime matter as such is pure potentiality, St. Thomas rejected the Augustinian theory of *rationes seminales*:[1] to admit this theory would be to attribute act in some way to what is in itself without act.[2] Non-spiritual forms are educed out of the potentiality of matter under the action of the efficient agent, but they are not previously in prime matter as inchoate forms. The agent does not, of course, work on prime matter as such, since this latter cannot exist by itself; but he or it so modifies or changes the dispositions of a given corporeal substance that it develops an exigency for a new form, which is educed out of the potentiality of matter. Change thus presupposes, for Aquinas as for Aristotle, a 'privation' or an exigency for a new form which the substance has not yet got but 'demands' to have in virtue of the modifications produced in it by the agent. Water, for example, is in a state of potentiality to becoming steam, but it will not become steam until it has been heated to a certain point by an external agent, at which point it develops an exigency for the form of steam, which does not come from outside, but is educed out of the potentiality of matter.

4. Just as St. Thomas rejected the older theory of *rationes seminales*, so he rejected the theory of the plurality of substantial forms in the composite substance, affirming the unicity of the substantial form in each substance. In his Commentary on the *Sentences* St. Thomas seems indeed to accept the *forma corporeitatis* as the first substantial form in the corporeal substance;[3] but even if he accepted it at first, he certainly rejected it afterwards. In the *Contra Gentiles*[4] he argues that if the first form constituted the substance as substance, the subsequent forms would arise in something which was already *hoc aliquid in actu*, something actually subsisting, and so could be no more than accidental forms. Similarly he argues against the theory of Avicebron[5] by pointing out that only the first form can be the substantial form, since it would confer the character of substance, with the result that other

[1] *In 2 Sent.*, 18, 1, 2.

[2] St. Thomas certainly employed the name, *rationes seminales*, but he meant thereby primarily the active forces of concrete objects, e.g. the active power which controls the generation of living things and restricts it to the same species, not the doctrine that there are inchoate forms in prime matter. This last theory he either rejected or said that it did not fit in with the teaching of St. Augustine (cf. *loc. cit.*, *S.T.*, Ia, 115, 2; *De Veritate*, 5, 9, *ad* 8 and *ad* 9).

[3] Cf. *In 1 Sent.*, 8, 5, 2; 2 *Sent.*, 3, 1, 1.

[4] 4, 81.

[5] *Quodlibet*, 11, 5, 5, *in corpore*.

subsequent forms, arising in an already constituted substance, would be accidental. (The necessary implication is, of course, that the substantial form directly informs prime matter.) This view aroused much opposition, being stigmatised as a dangerous innovation, as we shall see later when dealing with the controversies in which St. Thomas's Aristotelianism involved him.

5. The hylomorphic composition which obtains in material substances was restricted by St. Thomas to the corporeal world: he would not extend it, as St. Bonaventure did, to the incorporeal creation, to angels. That angels exist, St. Thomas considered to be rationally provable, quite apart from revelation, for their existence is demanded by the hierarchic character of the scale of being. We can discern the ascending orders or ranks of forms from the forms of inorganic substances, through vegetative forms, the irrational sensitive forms of animals, the rational soul of man, to the infinite and pure Act, God; but there is a gap in the hierarchy. The rational soul of man is created, finite and embodied, while God is uncreated, infinite and pure spirit: it is only reasonable, then, to suppose that between the human soul and God there are finite and created spiritual forms which are without body. At the summit of the scale is the absolute simplicity of God: at the summit of the corporeal world is the human being, partly spiritual and partly corporeal: there must, therefore, exist between God and man beings which are wholly spiritual and yet which do not possess the absolute simplicity of the Godhead.[1]

This line of argument was not new: it had been employed in Greek philosophy, by Poseidonius, for example. St. Thomas was also influenced by the Aristotelian doctrine of separate Intelligences connected with the motion of the spheres, this astronomical view reappearing in the philosophy of Avicenna, with which St. Thomas was familiar; but the argument which weighed most with him was that drawn from the exigencies of the hierarchy of being. As he distinguished the different grades of forms in general, so he distinguished the different 'choirs' of angels, according to the object of their knowledge. Those who apprehend most clearly the goodness of God in itself and are inflamed with love thereat are the Seraphim, the highest 'choir', while those who are concerned with the providence of God in regard to particular creatures, for example, in regard to particular men, are the angels in the narrower sense of the word, the lowest choir. The choir which is

[1] Cf. *De spirit. creat.*, 1, 5.

concerned with, *inter alia*, the movement of the heavenly bodies (which are universal causes affecting this world) is that of the Virtues. Thus St. Thomas did not postulate the existence of angels primarily in order to account for the movement of the spheres.

Angels exist therefore; but it remains to be asked if they are hylomorphically composed. St. Thomas affirmed that they are not so composed. He argued that the angels must be purely immaterial, since they are intelligences which have as their correlative object immaterial objects, and also that their very place in the hierarchy of being demands their complete immateriality.[1] Moreover, as St. Thomas places in matter an exigency for quantity (which possibly does not altogether square with its character of pure potentiality), he could not in any case attribute hylomorphic composition to the angels. St. Bonaventure, for example, had argued that angels must be hylomorphically composed, since otherwise they would be pure act and God alone is pure act; but St. Thomas countered this argument by affirming that the distinction between essence and existence in the angels is sufficient to safeguard their contingency and their radical distinction from God.[2] To this distinction I shall return shortly.

A consequence of the denial of the hylomorphic composition of the angels is the denial of the multiplicity of angels within one species, since matter is the principle of individuation and there is no matter in the angels. Each angel is pure form: each angel, then, must exhaust the capacity of its species and be its own species. The choirs of angels are not, then, so many species of angels; they consist of angelic hierarchies distinguished not specifically but according to function. There are as many species as there are angels. It is of interest to remember that Aristotle, when asserting in the *Metaphysics* a plurality of movers, of separated intelligences, raised the question how this could be possible if matter is the principle of individuation, though he did not answer the question. While St. Bonaventure, admitting the hylomorphic composition of angels, could and did admit their multiplicity within the species, St. Thomas, holding on the one hand that matter is the principle of individuation and denying its presence in the angels on the other hand, was forced to deny their multiplicity within the species. For St. Thomas, then, the intelligences really became separate universals, though not, of course, in the

[1] *S.T.*, Ia, 50, 2; *De spirit. creat.*, 1, 1.

[2] *De spirit. creat.*, 1, 1; *S.T.*, Ia, 50, 2, *ad* 3; *Contra Gent.*, 2, 30; *Quodlibet*, 9, 4, 1.

sense of hypostatised concepts. It was one of the discoveries of Aristotle that a separate form must be intelligent, though he failed to see the historic connection between his theory of separate intelligences and the Platonic theory of separate forms.

6. The establishment of the hylomorphic composition of material substances reveals at once the essential mutability of those substances. Change is not, of course, a haphazard affair, but proceeds according to a certain rhythm (one cannot assume that a given substance can become immediately any other substance one likes, while change is also guided and influenced by the general causes, such as the heavenly bodies); yet substantial change cannot take place except in bodies, and it is only matter, the substrate of change, which makes it possible. On the principle which St. Thomas adopted from Aristotle that what is changed or moved is changed or moved 'by another', *ab alio*, one might argue at once from the changes in the corporeal world to the existence of an unmoved mover, with the aid of the principle that an infinite regress in the order of dependence is impossible; but before going on to prove the existence of God from nature, one must first penetrate more deeply into the constitution of finite being.

Hylomorphic composition is confined by St. Thomas to the corporeal world; but there is a more fundamental distinction, of which the distinction between form and matter is but one example. Prime matter, as we have seen, is pure potentiality, while form is act, so that the distinction between matter and form is a distinction between potency and act, but this latter distinction is of wider application than the former. In the angels there is no matter, but there is none the less potentiality. (St. Bonaventure argued that because matter is potentiality, therefore it can be in angels. He was thus forced to admit the *forma corporeitatis*, in order to distinguish corporeal matter from matter in the general sense. St. Thomas, on the other hand, as he made matter pure potentiality and yet denied its presence in the angels, was forced to attribute to matter an exigency for quantity, which comes to it through form. Obviously there are difficulties in both views.) The angels can change by performing acts of intellect and will, even though they cannot change substantially: there is, therefore, some potentiality in the angels. The distinction between potentiality and act runs, therefore, through the whole of creation, whereas the distinction between form and matter is found only in the corporeal creation. Thus, on the principle that the reduction of potentiality to act requires a principle which is itself act, we should be in a position to argue from the fundamental distinction which obtains in all creation to the existence of pure Act, God; but first of all we must consider the basis of potentiality in the angels. In passing, one can notice that the distinction of potency and act is discussed by Aristotle in the *Metaphysics*.

7. We have seen that hylomorphic composition was restricted by St. Thomas to corporeal substance; but there is a profounder composition which affects every finite being. Finite being is being because it exists, because it has existence: the substance is that which is or has being, and 'existence is that in virtue of which a substance is called a being'.[1] The essence of a corporeal being is the substance composed of matter and form, while the essence of an immaterial finite being is form alone; but that by which a material substance or an immaterial substance is a real being (*ens*) is existence (*esse*), existence standing to the essence as act to potentiality. Composition of act and potentiality is found, therefore, in every finite being and not simply in corporeal being. No finite being exists necessarily; it has or possesses existence which is distinct from essence as act is distinct from potentiality. The form determines or completes in the sphere of essence, but that which actualises the essence is existence. 'In intellectual substances which are not composed of matter and form (in them the form is a subsistent substance), the form is that which is; but existence is the act by which the form is; and on that account there is in them only one composition of act and potentiality, namely composition of substance and existence. . . . In substances composed of matter and form, however, there is a double composition of act and potentiality, the first a composition in the substance itself, which is composed of matter and form, the second a composition of the substance itself, which is already composite, with existence. This second composition can also be called a composition of the *quod est* and *esse*, or of the *quod est* and the *quo est*.'[2] Existence, then, is neither matter nor form; it is neither an essence nor part of an essence; it is the act by which the essence is or has being. '*Esse* denotes a certain act; for a thing is not said to be (*esse*) by the fact that it is in potentiality, but by the fact that it is in act.'[3] As neither matter nor form, it can be neither a substantial nor an accidental form; it does not belong to the sphere of essence, but is that by which forms are.

[1] *Contra Gent.*, 2, 54. [2] *Ibid.* [3] *Ibid.*, 1, 22.

Controversy has raged in the Schools round the question whether St. Thomas considered the distinction between essence and existence to be a real distinction or a conceptual distinction. Obviously the answer to this question depends largely on the meaning attached to the phrase 'real distinction'. If by real distinction were meant a distinction between two things which could be separated from one another, then certainly St. Thomas did not hold that there is a real distinction between essence and existence, which are not two separable physical objects. Giles of Rome practically held this view, making the distinction a physical distinction; but for St. Thomas the distinction was metaphysical, essence and existence being the two constitutive metaphysical principles of every finite being. If, however, by real distinction is meant a distinction which is independent of the mind, which is objective, it seems to me not only that St. Thomas maintained such a distinction as obtaining between essence and existence, but that it is essential to his system and that he attached great importance to it. St. Thomas speaks of *esse* as *adveniens extra*, in the sense that it comes from God, the cause of existence; it is act, distinct from the potentiality which it actualises. In God alone, insists St. Thomas, are essence and existence identical: God exists necessarily because His essence is existence: all other things receive or 'participate in' existence, and that which receives must be distinct from that which is received.[1] The fact that St. Thomas argues that that whose existence is other than its essence must have received its existence from another, and that it is true of God alone that His existence is not different from or other than His essence, seems to me to make it perfectly clear that he regarded the distinction between essence and existence as objective and independent of the mind. The 'third way' of proving the existence of God appears to presuppose the real distinction between essence and existence in finite things.

Existence determines essence in the sense that it is act and through it the essence has being; but on the other hand existence, as act, is determined by essence, as potentiality, to be the existence of this or that kind of essence.[2] Yet we must not imagine that essence existed before receiving existence (which would be a contradiction in terms) or that there is a kind of neutral existence which is not the existence of any thing in particular until it is united with essence: the two principles are not two physical things

[1] Cf. *S.T.*, Ia, 3, 4; *Contra Gent.*, 1, 22. [2] *De Potentia*, 7, 2, *ad* 9.

united together, but they are two constitutive principles which are concreated as principles of a particular being. There is no essence without existence and no existence without essence; the two are created together, and if its existence ceases, the concrete essence ceases to be. Existence, then, is not something accidental to the finite being: it is that by which the finite being is a being. If we rely on the imagination, we shall think of essence and existence as two things, two beings; but a great deal of the difficulty in understanding St. Thomas's doctrine on the subject comes from employing the imagination and supposing that if he maintained the real distinction, he must have understood it in the exaggerated and misleading fashion of Giles of Rome.

The Moslem philosophers had already discussed the relation of existence to essence. Alfarabi, for example, had observed that analysis of the essence of a finite object will not reveal its existence. If it did, then it would be sufficient to know what human nature is, in order to know that man exists, which is not the case. Essence and existence are, therefore, distinct, and Alfarabi drew the somewhat unfortunate conclusion that existence is an accident of the essence. Avicenna followed Alfarabi in this matter. Although St. Thomas certainly did not regard existence as an 'accident', in the *De ente et essentia*[1] he follows Alfarabi and Avicenna in their way of approaching the distinction. Every thing which does not belong to the concept of the essence comes to it from without (*adveniens extra*) and forms a composition with it. No essence can be conceived without that which forms part of the essence; but every finite essence can be conceived without existence being included in the essence. I can conceive 'man' or 'phoenix' and yet not know if they exist in nature. It would, however, be a mistake to interpret St. Thomas as though he maintained that the essence, prior to the reception of existence, was something on its own, so to speak, with a diminutive existence proper to itself: it exists only through existence, and created existence is always the existence of this or that kind of essence. Created existence and essence arise together, and although the two constitutive principles are objectively distinct, existence is the more fundamental. Since created existence is the act of a potentiality, the latter has no actuality apart from existence, which is 'among all things the most perfect' and 'the perfection of all perfections'.[2]

St. Thomas thus discovers in the heart of all finite being a

[1] C. 4. [2] *De Potentia*, 7, 2, *ad* 9.

certain instability, a contingency or non-necessity, which immediately points to the existence of a Being which is the source of finite existence, the author of the composition between essence and existence, and which cannot be itself composed of essence and existence but must have existence as its very essence, existing necessarily. It would indeed be absurd and most unjust to accuse Francis Suarez (1548–1617) and other Scholastics who denied the 'real distinction' of denying the contingent character of finite being (Suarez denied a real distinction between essence and existence and maintained that the finite object is limited because *ab alio*); but I do not personally feel any doubt that St. Thomas himself maintained the doctrine of the real distinction, provided that the real distinction is not interpreted as Giles of Rome interpreted it. For St. Thomas, existence is not a state of the essence, but rather that which places the essence in a state of actuality.

It may be objected that I have evaded the real point at issue, namely the precise way in which the distinction between essence and existence is objective and independent of the mind. But St. Thomas did not state his doctrine in such a manner that no controversy about its meaning is possible. Nevertheless it seems clear to me that St. Thomas held that the distinction between essence and existence is an objective distinction between two metaphysical principles which constitute the whole being of the created finite thing, one of these principles, namely existence, standing to the other, namely essence, as act to potency. And I do not see how St. Thomas could have attributed that importance to the distinction which he did attribute to it, unless he thought that it was a 'real' distinction.

CHAPTER XXXIV

ST. THOMAS AQUINAS—IV: PROOFS OF GOD'S EXISTENCE

Need of proof—St. Anselm's argument—Possibility of proof—The first three proofs—The fourth proof—The proof from finality—The 'third way' fundamental.

1. BEFORE actually developing his proofs of God's existence St. Thomas tried to show that the provision of such proofs is not a useless superfluity, since the idea of God's existence is not, properly speaking, an innate idea nor is 'God exists' a proposition the opposite of which is inconceivable and cannot be thought. To us indeed, living in a world where atheism is common, where powerful and influential philosophies eliminate or explain away the notion of God, where multitudes of men and women are educated without any belief in God, it seems only natural to think that God's existence requires proof. Kierkegaard and those philosophers and theologians who follow him may have rejected natural theology in the ordinary sense; but normally speaking we should not dream of asserting that God's existence is what St. Thomas calls a *per se notum*. St. Thomas, however, did not live in a world where theoretic atheism was common, and he felt himself compelled to deal not only with statements of certain early Christian writers which seemed to imply that knowledge of God is innate in man, but also with the famous argument of St. Anselm which purports to show that the non-existence of God is inconceivable. Thus in the *Summa Theologica*[1] he devotes an article to answering the question *utrum Deum esse sit per se notum*, and two chapters in the *Summa contra Gentiles*[2] to the consideration *de opinione dicentium quod Deum esse demonstrari non potest, quum sit per se notum*.

St. John Damascene[3] asserts that the knowledge of God's existence is naturally innate in man; but St. Thomas explains that this natural knowledge of God is confused and vague and needs elucidation to be made explicit. Man has a natural desire of happiness (*beatitudo*), and a natural desire supposes a natural knowledge; but although true happiness is to be found only in God, it does not follow that every man has a natural knowledge

[1] Ia, 2, 1. [2] 1, 10–11. [3] *De fide orthodoxa*, 1, 3.

of God as such: he has a vague idea of happiness since he desires it, but he may think that happiness consists in sensual pleasure or in the possession of wealth, and further reflection is required before he can realise that happiness is to be found only in God. In other words, even if the natural desire for happiness may form the basis for a proof of God's existence, a proof is none the less required. Again, in a sense it is *per se notum* that there is truth, since a man who asserts that there is no truth inevitably asserts that it is true that there is no truth, but it does not follow that the man knows that there is a primal or first Truth, a Source of truth, God: further reflection is necessary if he is to realise this. Once again, although it is true that without God we can know nothing, it does not follow that in knowing anything we have an actual knowledge of God, since God's influence, which enables us to know anything, is not the object of direct intuition but is known only by reflection.[1]

In general, says St. Thomas, we must make a distinction between what is *per se notum secundum se* and what is *per se notum quoad nos*. A proposition is said to be *per se nota secundum se* when the predicate is included in the subject, as in the proposition that man is an animal, since man is precisely a rational animal. The proposition that God exists is thus a proposition *per se nota secundum se*, since God's essence is His existence and one cannot know God's nature, what God is, without knowing God's existence, that He is; but a man has no *a priori* knowledge of God's nature and only arrives at knowledge of the fact that God's essence is His existence after he has come to know God's existence, so that even though the proposition that God exists is *per se nota secundum se*, it is not *per se nota quoad nos*.

2. In regard to the 'ontological' or *a priori* proof of God's existence given by St. Anselm, St. Thomas answers first of all that not everyone understands by God 'that than which no greater can be thought'. Possibly this observation, though doubtless true, is not altogether relevant, except in so far as St. Anselm considered that everyone understands by 'God' that Being whose existence

[1] It may appear that St. Thomas's attitude in regard to 'innate' knowledge of God does not differ substantially from that of St. Bonaventure. In a sense this is true, since neither of them admitted an explicit innate idea of God; but St. Bonaventure thought that there is a kind of initial implicit awareness of God, or at least that the idea of God can be rendered explicit by interior reflection alone, whereas the proofs actually given by St. Thomas all proceed by way of the external world. Even if we press the 'Aristotelian' aspect of Bonaventure's epistemology, it remains true that there is a difference of emphasis and approach in the natural theology of the two philosophers.

he intended to prove, namely the supremely perfect Being. It must not be forgotten that Anselm reckoned his argument to be an argument or proof, not the statement of an immediate intuition of God. He then argues, both in the *Summa contra Gentiles* and in the *Summa Theologica*, that the argument of St. Anselm involves an illicit process or transition from the ideal to the real order. Granted that God is conceived as the Being than which no greater can be thought, it does not follow necessarily that such a Being exists, apart from its being conceived, that is, outside the mind. This, however, is not an adequate argument, when taken by itself at least, to disprove the Anselmian reasoning, since it neglects the peculiar character of God, of the Being than which no greater can be thought. Such a Being is its own existence and if it is possible for such a Being to exist, it must exist. The Being than which no greater can be thought is the Being which exists necessarily, it is the necessary Being, and it would be absurd to speak of a merely possible necessary Being. But St. Thomas adds, as we have seen, that the intellect has no *a priori* knowledge of God's nature. In other words, owing to the weakness of the human intellect we cannot discern *a priori* the positive possibility of the supremely perfect Being, the Being the essence of which is existence, and we come to a knowledge of the fact that such a Being exists not through an analysis or consideration of the idea of such a Being, but through arguments from its effects, *a posteriori*.

3. If God's existence cannot be proved *a priori*, through the idea of God, through His essence, it remains that it must be proved *a posteriori*, through an examination of God's effects. It may be objected that this is impossible since the effects of God are finite while God is infinite, so that there is no proportion between the effects and the Cause and the conclusion of the reasoning process will contain infinitely more than the premisses. The reasoning starts with sensible objects and should, therefore, end with a sensible object, whereas in the proofs of God's existence it proceeds to an Object infinitely transcending all sensible objects.

St. Thomas does not deal with this objection at any length, and it would be an absurd anachronism to expect him to discuss and answer the Kantian Critique of metaphysics in advance; but he points out that though from a consideration of effects which are disproportionate to the cause we cannot obtain a perfect knowledge of the cause, we can come to know that the cause exists. We can argue from an effect to the existence of a cause, and if the effect is of such a kind that it can proceed only from a certain kind of cause, we can legitimately argue to the existence of a cause of that kind. (The use of the word 'effect' must not be taken as begging the question, as a *petitio principii*: St. Thomas argues from certain facts concerning the world and argues that these facts require a sufficient ontological explanation. It is true, of course, that he presupposes that the principle of causality is not purely subjective or applicable only within the sphere of 'phenomena' in the Kantian sense; but he is perfectly well aware that it has to be shown that sensible objects are effects, in the sense that they do not contain in themselves their own sufficient ontological explanation.)

A modern Thomist, wishing to expound and defend the natural theology of the Saint in the light of post-mediaeval philosophic thought, would rightly be expected to say something in justification of the speculative reason, of metaphysics. Even if he considered that the onus of proof falls primarily on the opponent of metaphysics, he could not neglect the fact that the legitimacy and even the significance of metaphysical arguments and conclusions have been challenged, and he would be bound to meet this challenge. I cannot see, however, how an historian of mediaeval philosophy in general can justly be expected to treat St. Thomas as though he were a contemporary and fully aware not only of the Kantian criticism of the speculative reason, but also of the attitude towards metaphysics adopted by the logical positivists. Nevertheless, it is true that the Thomist theory of knowledge itself provides, apparently at least, a strong objection against natural theology. According to St. Thomas the proper object of the human intellect is the *quidditas* or essence of the material object: the intellect starts from the sensible objects, knows in dependence on the phantasm and is proportioned, in virtue of its embodied state, to sensible objects. St. Thomas did not admit innate ideas nor did he have recourse to any intuitive knowledge of God, and if one applies strictly the Aristotelian principle that there is nothing in the intellect which was not before in the senses (*Nihil in intellectu quod non prius fuerit in sensu*), it might well appear that the human intellect is confined to knowledge of corporeal objects and cannot, owing to its nature or at least its present state, transcend them. As this objection arises out of the doctrine of Thomas himself, it is relevant to inquire if the Saint attempted to meet it and, if so, how he met it. With the Thomist theory of human knowledge I shall deal later;[1] but I shall give immediately a brief statement of what appears to be St. Thomas's position on this point without development or references.

Objects, whether spiritual or corporeal, are knowable only in so far as they partake of being, are in act, and the intellect as such is the faculty of apprehending being. Considered simply in itself, therefore, the intellect has as its object all being; the primary object of intellect is being. The fact, however, that a particular kind of intellect, the human intellect, is embodied and is dependent on sense for its operation, means that it must start from the things of sense and that, naturally speaking, it can come to know an object which transcends the things of sense (consideration of self-knowledge is here omitted) only in so far as sensible objects bear a relation to that object and manifest it. Owing to the fact that the human intellect is embodied its natural and proper object, proportionate to its present state, is the corporeal object; but this does not destroy the primary orientation of the intellect to being in general, and if corporeal objects bear a discernible relation to an object which transcends them, the intellect can know that such an object exists. Moreover, in so far as material objects reveal the character of the Transcendent, the intellect can attain some knowledge of its nature; but such a knowledge cannot be adequate or perfect, since sense-objects cannot reveal adequately or perfectly the nature of the Transcendent. Of our natural knowledge of God's nature I shall speak later:[2] let it suffice to point out here that when St. Thomas says that the corporeal object is the natural object of the human intellect, he means that the human intellect in its present state is orientated towards the essence of the corporeal object, but that just as the embodied condition of the human intellect does not destroy its primary character as intellect, so its orientation, in virtue of its embodied state, towards the corporeal object does not destroy its primary orientation towards being in general. It can therefore attain to some natural knowledge of God, in so far as corporeal objects are related to Him and reveal Him; but this knowledge is necessarily imperfect and inadequate and cannot be intuitive in character.

4. The first of the five proofs of God's existence given by St. Thomas is that from motion, which is found in Aristotle[3] and was utilised by Maimonides and St. Albert. We know through sense-perception that some things in the world are moved, that motion

[1] See Ch. XXXVIII. [2] See Ch. XXXV. [3] *Metaph.*, Bk. 12; *Physics*, Bk. 8.

is a fact. Motion is here understood in the wide Aristotelian sense of reduction of potency to act, and St. Thomas, following Aristotle, argues that a thing cannot be reduced from potency to act except by something which is already in act. In this sense 'every thing which is moved is moved by another'. If that other is itself moved, it must be moved by yet another agent. As an infinite series is impossible, we come in the end to an unmoved mover, a first mover, 'and all understand that this is God'.[1] This argument St. Thomas calls the *manifestior via*.[2] In the *Summa contra Gentiles*[3] he develops it at considerable length.

The second proof, which is suggested by the second book of Aristotle's *Metaphysics*[4] and which was used by Avicenna, Alan of Lille and St. Albert, also starts from the sensible world, but this time from the order or series of efficient causes. Nothing can be the cause of itself, for in order to be this, it would have to exist before itself. On the other hand, it is impossible to proceed to infinity in the series of efficient causes: therefore there must be a first efficient cause, 'which all men call God'.

The third proof, which Maimonides took over from Avicenna and developed, starts from the fact that some beings come into existence and perish, which shows that they can not be and can be, that they are contingent and not necessary, since if they were necessary they would always have existed and would neither come into being nor pass away. St. Thomas then argues that there must exist a necessary being, which is the reason why contingent beings come into existence. If there were no necessary being, nothing at all would exist.

There are several remarks which must be made, though very briefly, concerning these three proofs. First of all, when St. Thomas says that an infinite series is impossible (and this principle is utilised in all three proofs), he is not thinking of a series stretching back in time, of a 'horizontal' series, so to speak. He is not saying, for example, that because the child owes its life to its parents and its parents owe their lives to their parents and so on, there must have been an original pair, who had no parents but were directly created by God. St. Thomas did not believe that it can be proved philosophically that the world was not created from eternity: he admits the abstract possibility of the world's creation from eternity and this cannot be admitted without the possibility of a beginningless series being admitted at the same time. What he

[1] *S.T.*, Ia, 2, 3, *in corpore*. [2] *Ibid.* [3] I, 13. [4] C. 2.

denies is the possibility of an infinite series in the order of actually depending causes, of an infinite 'vertical' series. Suppose that the world had actually been created from eternity. There would be an infinite horizontal or historic series, but the whole series would consist of contingent beings, for the fact of its being without beginning does not make it necessary. The whole series, therefore, must depend on something outside the series. But if you ascend upwards, without ever coming to a stop, you have no explanation of the existence of the series: one must conclude with the existence of a being which is not itself dependent.

Secondly, consideration of the foregoing remarks will show that the so-called mathematical infinite series has nothing to do with the Thomist proofs. It is not the possibility of an infinite series as such which St. Thomas denies, but the possibility of an infinite series in the ontological order of dependence. In other words, he denies that the movement and contingency of the experienced world can be without any ultimate and adequate ontological explanation.

Thirdly, it might seem to be rather cavalier behaviour on St. Thomas's part to assume that the unmoved mover or the first cause or the necessary being is what we call God. Obviously if anything exists at all, there must be a necessary Being: thought must arrive at this conclusion, unless metaphysics is rejected altogether; but it is not so obvious that the necessary being must be the personal Being whom we call God. That a purely philosophical argument does not bring us to the full revealed notion of God needs no elaboration; but, even apart from the full notion of God as revealed by Christ and preached by the Church, does a purely philosophical argument give us a personal Being at all? Did St. Thomas's belief in God lead him perhaps to find more in the conclusion of the argument than was actually there? Because he was looking for arguments to prove the existence of the God in whom he believed, was he not perhaps over-hasty in identifying the first mover, the first cause and the necessary being with the God of Christianity and religious experience, the personal Being to whom man can pray? I think that we must admit that the actual phrases which St. Thomas appends to the proofs given in the *Summa Theologica* (*et hoc omnes intelligunt Deum, causam efficientem primam quam omnes Deum nominant, quod omnes dicunt Deum*) constitute, if considered in isolation, an over-hasty conclusion; but, apart from the fact that the *Summa Theologica* is a summary (and mainly) theological text-book, these phrases should not be taken in isolation. For example, the actual summary proof of the existence of a necessary being contains no explicit argument to show whether that being is material or immaterial, so that the observation at the end of the proof that this being is called by everyone God might seem to be without sufficient warrant; but in the first article of the next question St. Thomas asks if God is material, a body, and argues that He is not. The phrases in the question should, therefore, be understood as expressions of the fact that God is recognised by all who believe in Him to be the first Cause and necessary Being, not as an unjustifiable suppression of further argument. In any case the proofs are given by St. Thomas simply in outline: it is not as though he had in mind the composition of a treatise against professed atheists. If he had to deal with Marxists, he would doubtless treat the proofs in a different, or at least in a more elaborate and developed manner: as it is, his main interest is to give a proof of the *praeambula fidei*. Even in the *Summa contra Gentiles* the Saint was not dealing primarily with atheists, but rather with the Mohammedans, who had a firm belief in God.

5. The fourth proof is suggested by some observations in Aristotle's *Metaphysics*[1] and is found substantially in St. Augustine and St. Anselm. It starts from the degrees of perfection, of goodness, truth, etc., in the things of this world, which permit of one making such comparative judgements as 'this is more beautiful than that', 'this is better than that'. Assuming that such judgements have an objective foundation, St. Thomas argues that the degrees of perfection necessarily imply the existence of a best, a most true, etc., which will be also the supreme being (*maxime ens*).

So far the argument leads only to a relatively best. If one can establish that there actually are degrees of truth, goodness and being, a hierarchy of being, then there must be one being or several beings which are comparatively or relatively supreme. But this is not enough to prove the existence of God, and St. Thomas proceeds to argue that what is supreme in goodness, for example, must be the cause of goodness in all things. Further, inasmuch as goodness, truth and being are convertible, there must be a supreme Being which is the cause of being, goodness, truth, and so of all perfection in every other being; *et hoc dicimus Deum*.

[1] 2, 1; 4, 4.

As the term of the argument is a Being which transcends all sensible objects, the perfections in question can obviously be only those perfections which are capable of subsisting by themselves, pure perfections, which do not involve any necessary relation to extension or quantity. The argument is Platonic in origin and presupposes the idea of participation. Contingent beings do not possess their being of themselves, nor their goodness or ontological truth; they receive their perfections, share them. The ultimate cause of perfection must itself be perfect: it cannot receive its perfection from another, but must be its own perfection: it is self-existing being and perfection. The argument consists, then, in the application of principles already used in the foregoing proofs to pure perfections: it is not really a departure from the general spirit of the other proofs, in spite of its Platonic descent. One of the main difficulties about it, however, is, as already indicated, to show that there actually are objective degrees of being and perfection before one has shown that there actually exists a Being which is absolute and self-existing Perfection.

6. The fifth way is the teleological proof, for which Kant had a considerable respect on account of its antiquity, clarity and persuasiveness, though, in accordance with the principles of the *Kritik der reinen Vernunft*, he refused to recognise its demonstrative character.

St. Thomas argues that we behold inorganic objects operating for an end, and as this happens always or very frequently, it cannot proceed from chance, but must be the result of intention. But inorganic objects are without knowledge: they cannot, then, tend towards an end unless they are directed by someone who is intelligent and possessed of knowledge, as 'the arrow is directed by the archer'. Therefore there exists an intelligent Being, by whom all natural things are directed to an end; *et hoc dicimus Deum*. In the *Summa contra Gentiles* the Saint states the argument in a slightly different manner, arguing that when many things with different and even contrary qualities co-operate towards the realisation of one order, this must proceed from an intelligent Cause or Providence; *et hoc dicimus Deum*. If the proof as given in the *Summa Theologica* emphasises the internal finality of the inorganic object, that given in the *Summa contra Gentiles* emphasises rather the co-operation of many objects in the realisation of the one world order or harmony. By itself the proof leads to a Designer or Governor or Architect of the universe, as Kant observed; further reasoning is required in order to show that this Architect is not only a 'Demiurge', but also Creator.

7. The proofs have been stated in more or less the same bold and succinct way in which St. Thomas states them. With the exception of the first proof, which is elaborated at some length in the *Summa contra Gentiles*, the proofs are given only in very bare outline, both in the *Summa Theologica* and in the *Summa contra Gentiles*. No mention has been made, however, of Aquinas's (to our view) somewhat unfortunate physical illustrations, as when he says that fire is the cause of all hot things, since these illustrations are really irrelevant to the validity or invalidity of the proofs as such. The modern disciple of St. Thomas naturally has not only to develop the proofs in far greater detail and to consider difficulties and objections which could hardly have occurred to St. Thomas, but also to justify the very principles on which the general line of proof rests. Thus, in regard to the fifth proof given by St. Thomas, the modern Thomist must take some account of recent theories which profess to render intelligible the genesis of the order and finality in the universe without recourse to the hypothesis of any spiritual agent distinct from the universe, while in regard to all the proofs he has not only, in face of the Kantian Critique, to justify the line of argument on which they rest, but he has to show, as against the logical positivists, that the word 'God' has some significance. It is not, however, the task of the historian to develop the proofs as they would have to be developed to-day, nor is it his task to justify those proofs. The way in which St. Thomas states the proofs may perhaps cause some dissatisfaction in the reader; but it must be remembered that the Saint was primarily a theologian and that, as already mentioned, he was concerned not so much to give an exhaustive treatment of the proofs as to prove in a summary fashion the *praeambula fidei*. He, therefore, makes use of traditional proofs, which either had or seemed to have some support in Aristotle and which had been employed by some of his predecessors.

St. Thomas gives five proofs, and among these five proofs he gives a certain preference to the first, to the extent at least of calling it the *via manifestior*. However, whatever we may think of this assertion, the fundamental proof is really the third proof or 'way', that from contingency. In the first proof the argument from contingency is applied to the special fact of motion or change, in the second proof to the order of causality or causal production, in the fourth proof to degrees of perfection and in the fifth proof to finality, to the co-operation of inorganic objects in the attainment of cosmic order. The argument from contingency itself is based on the fact that everything must have its sufficient reason, the reason why it exists. Change or motion must have its sufficient reason in an unmoved mover, the series of secondary causes and effects in an uncaused cause, limited perfection in absolute perfection, and finality and order in nature in an Intelligence or Designer. The 'interiority' of the proofs of God's existence as given by St. Augustine or St. Bonaventure is absent from the five ways of St. Thomas; but one could, of course, apply the general principles to the self, if one so wished. As they stand, the five proofs of St. Thomas may be said to be an explicitation of the words of the *Book of Wisdom*[1] and of St. Paul in *Romans*[2] that God can be known from His works, as transcending His works.

[1] Ch. 13. [2] Ch. 1.

CHAPTER XXXV

ST. THOMAS AQUINAS—V: GOD'S NATURE

The negative way—The affirmative way—Analogy—Types of analogy—A difficulty—The divine ideas—No real distinction between the divine attributes—God as existence itself.

1. ONCE it has been established that the necessary Being exists, it would seem only natural to proceed to the investigation of God's nature. It is very unsatisfactory simply to know that a necessary Being exists, unless at the same time we can know what sort of a Being the necessary Being is. But a difficulty at once arises. We have in this life no intuition of the divine essence; we are dependent for our knowledge on sense-perception, and the ideas which we form are derived from our experience of creatures. Language too is formed to express these ideas and so refers primarily to our experience and would seem to have objective reference only within the sphere of our experience. How, then, can we come to know a Being which transcends sense-experience? How can we form ideas which express in any way the nature of a Being which transcends the range of our experience, the world of creatures? How can the words of any human language be at all applicable to the Divine Being?

St. Thomas was well aware of this difficulty, and indeed the whole tradition of Christian philosophy, which had undergone the influence of the writings of the Pseudo-Dionysius, himself dependent on neo-Platonism, would have helped, if help had been needed, to prevent him indulging in any over-confidence in the power of the human reason to penetrate the divine essence. Rationalism of the Hegelian type was quite foreign to his mind, and we find him saying that we cannot come to know of God *quid sit*, what He is (His essence), but only *an sit* or *quod sit*, that He is (His existence). This statement, if taken alone, would seem to involve complete agnosticism as regards the divine nature, but this is not St. Thomas's meaning, and the statement must be interpreted according to his general doctrine and his explanation of it. Thus in the *Summa contra Gentiles*[1] he says that 'the divine substance exceeds by its immensity every form which our intellect

[1] I, 14.

attains; and so we cannot apprehend it by knowing what it is, but we have some notion of it by coming to know what it is not.' For example, we come to know something of God by recognising that He is not, and cannot be, a corporeal substance: by denying of Him corporeality we form some notion of His nature, since we know that He is not body, though this does not give us of itself a positive idea of what the divine substance is in itself, and the more predicates we can deny of God in this way, the more we approximate to a knowledge of Him.

This is the famous *via remotionis* or *via negativa*, so dear to the Pseudo-Dionysius and other Christian writers who had been strongly influenced by neo-Platonism; but St. Thomas adds a very useful observation concerning the negative way.[1] In the case of a created substance, he says, which we can define, we first of all assign it to its genus by which we know in general what it is, and then we add the difference by which it is distinguished from other things; but in the case of God we cannot assign Him to a genus, since He transcends all genera, and so we cannot distinguish Him from other beings by positive differences (*per affirmativas differentias*). Nevertheless, though we cannot approach to a clear idea of God's nature in the same way in which we can attain a clear idea of human nature, that is, by a succession of positive or affirmative differentiations, such as living, sensitive or animal, rational, we can attain some notion of His nature by the negative way, by a succession of negative differentiations. For example, if we say that God is not an accident, we distinguish Him from all accidents; if we say that He is not corporeal, we distinguish Him from some substances; and thus we can proceed until we obtain an idea of God which belongs to Him alone (*propria consideratio*) and which suffices to distinguish Him from all other beings.

It must, however, be borne in mind that when predicates are denied of God, they are not denied of Him because He lacks any perfection expressed in that predicate, but because He infinitely exceeds that limited perfection in richness. Our natural knowledge has its beginning in sense and extends as far as it can be led by the help of sensible objects.[2] As sensible objects are creatures of God, we can come to know that God exists, but we cannot attain by means of them any adequate knowledge of God, since they are effects which are not fully proportionate to the divine power. But we can come to know about Him what is necessarily true of Him

[1] *Contra Gent.*, I, 14.

[2] *S.T.*, Ia, 12, 12, *in corpore*.

precisely as cause of all sensible objects. As their cause, He transcends them and is not and cannot be a sensible object Himself: we can, then, deny of Him any predicates which are bound up with corporeality or which are inconsistent with His being the first Cause and necessary Being. But *haec non removentur ab eo propter ejus defectum, sed quia superexcedit.*[1] If we say, therefore, that God is not corporeal, we do not mean that God is less than body, that He *lacks* the perfection involved in being body, but rather that He is *more than* body, that He possesses none of the imperfections necessarily involved in being a corporeal substance.

Arguing by means of the negative way St. Thomas shows that God cannot be corporeal, for example, since the unmoved Mover and the necessary Being must be pure Act, whereas every corporeal substance is in potentiality. Again, there cannot be any composition in God, either of matter and form or of substance and accident or of essence and existence. If there were composition of essence and existence, for instance, God would owe His existence to another being, which is impossible, since God is the first Cause. There cannot in fine be any composition in God, as this would be incompatible with His being as first Cause, necessary Being, pure Act. We express this absence of composition by the positive word 'simplicity', but the idea of the divine simplicity is attained by removing from God all the forms of composition which are found in creatures, so that 'simplicity' here means absence of composition. We cannot form an adequate idea of the divine simplicity as it is in itself, since it transcends our experience: we know, however, that it is at the opposite pole, so to speak, from simplicity or comparative simplicity in creatures. In creatures we experience the more complex substance is the higher, as a man is higher than an oyster; but God's simplicity means that He possesses the fullness of His being and perfection in one undivided and eternal act.

Similarly, God is infinite and perfect, since His *esse* is not something received and limited, but is self-existent; He is immutable, since the necessary Being is necessarily all that it is and cannot be changed; He is eternal, since time requires motion and in the immutable Being there can be no motion. He is one, since He is simple and infinite. Strictly speaking, however, says St. Thomas, God is not eternal, but is eternity, since He is His own subsistent *esse* in one undivided act. To go through all the various attributes of God which can be known by the negative way is unnecessary:

[1] *S.T.*, Ia, 12, 12, *in corpore.*

it is sufficient to have given some examples to show how, after proving that God exists as unmoved Mover, first Cause, and necessary Being, St. Thomas then proceeds to remove from God, to deny of God, all those predicates of creatures which are incompatible with God's character as unmoved Mover, first Cause and necessary Being. There cannot be in God corporeality, composition, limitation, imperfection, temporality, etc.

2. Predicates or names such as 'immutable' and 'infinite' suggest by their very form their association with the negative way, immutable being equivalent to not-mutable and infinite to not-finite; but there are other predicates applied to God which suggest no such association, such as good, wise, etc. Moreover, while a negative predicate, says St. Thomas,[1] refers directly not to the divine substance, but to the 'removal' of something from the divine substance, that is, the denial of some predicate's applicability to God, there are positive predicates or names which are predicated of the divine substance affirmatively. For example, the predicate 'non-corporeal' denies corporeality of God, removes it from Him, whereas the predicate good or wise is predicated affirmatively and directly of the divine substance. There is, then, an affirmative or positive way, in addition to the negative way. But what is its justification if these perfections, goodness, wisdom, etc., are experienced by us as they are in creatures, and if the words we use to express these perfections express the ideas we derive from creatures? Are we not applying to God ideas and words which have no application save within the realm of experience? Are we not faced with the following dilemma? Either we are predicating of God predicates which apply only to creatures, in which case our statements about God are false, or we have emptied the predicates of their reference to creatures, in which case they are without content, since they are derived from our experience of creatures and express that experience?

First of all, St. Thomas insists that when affirmative predicates are predicated of God, they are predicated positively of the divine nature or substance. He will not allow the opinion of those who, like Maimonides, make all predicates of God equivalent to negative predicates, nor the opinion of those who say that 'God is good' or 'God is living' means simply 'God is the cause of all goodness' or 'God is the cause of life'. When we say that God is living or God is life, we do not mean merely that God is not non-living: the

[1] *S.T.*, Ia, 13, 2, *in corpore*.

statement that God is living has a degree of affirmation about it that is wanting to the statement that God is not a body. Nor does the man who states that God is living mean only that God is the cause of life, of all living things: he means to say something positive about God Himself. Again, if the statement that God is living meant no more than that God is the cause of all living things, we might just as well say that God is body, since He is the cause of all bodies. Yet we do not say that God is body, whereas we do say that God is living, and this shows that the statement that God is living means more than that God is the cause of life, and that a positive affirmation is being made concerning the divine substance.

On the other hand, none of the positive ideas by means of which we conceive the nature of God represent God perfectly. Our ideas of God represent God only in so far as our intellects can know Him; but we know Him by means of sensible objects in so far as these objects represent or mirror God, so that inasmuch as creatures represent God or mirror Him only imperfectly, our ideas, derived from our experience of the natural world, can themselves represent God only imperfectly. When we say that God is good or living, we mean that He contains, or rather is the perfection of, goodness or life, but in a manner which exceeds and excludes all the imperfections and limitations of creatures. As regards *what is predicated* (goodness, for example), the affirmative predicate which we predicate of God signifies a perfection without any defect; but as regards the *manner of predicating it* every such predicate involves a defect, for by the word (*nomen*) we express something in the way it is conceived by the intellect. It follows, then, that predicates of this kind may, as the Pseudo-Dionysius observed, be both affirmed and denied of God; affirmed *propter nominis rationem*, denied *propter significandi modum*. For example, if we make the statement that God is wisdom, this affirmative statement is true in regard to the perfection as such; but if we meant that God is wisdom in precisely that sense in which we experience wisdom, it would be false. God is wise, but He is wisdom in a sense transcending our experience; He does not possess wisdom as an inhering quality or form. In other words, we affirm of God the essence of wisdom or goodness or life in a 'supereminent' way, and we deny of God the imperfections attendant on human wisdom, wisdom as we experience it.[1] When, therefore, we say that God is good, the

[1] *Contra Gent.*, 1, 30.

meaning is not that God is the cause of goodness or that God is not evil, but that what we call goodness in creatures pre-exists in God *secundum modum altiorem.* From this it does not follow that goodness belongs to God inasmuch as He causes goodness, but rather that because He is good, He diffuses goodness into things, according to the saying of Augustine, 'because He is good, we exist'.[1]

3. The upshot of the foregoing considerations is, therefore, that we cannot in this life know the divine essence as it is in itself, but only as it is represented in creatures, so that the names we apply to God signify the perfections manifested in creatures. From this fact several important conclusions must be drawn, the first being this, that the names we apply to God and to creatures are not to be understood in an univocal sense. For example, when we say that a man is wise and that God is wise, the predicate 'wise' is not to be understood in an univocal sense, that is, in precisely the same sense. Our concept of wisdom is drawn from creatures, and if we applied precisely this concept to God, we should be saying something false about God, since God is not, and cannot be, wise in precisely the same sense in which a man is wise. On the other hand, the names we apply to God are not purely equivocal, that is to say, they are not entirely and completely different in meaning from the meaning they bear when applied to creatures. If they were purely equivocal, we should have to conclude that we can gain no knowledge of God from creatures. If wisdom as predicated of man and wisdom as predicated of God signified something completely different, the term 'wise' as applied to God would have no content, no significance, since our knowledge of wisdom is drawn from creatures and is not based on direct experience of the divine wisdom. Of course, it might be objected that, though it is true that if the terms predicated of God were used in an equivocal sense, we should know nothing of God from creatures, it does not follow that we can know anything about God from creatures; but St. Thomas's insistence that we can know something of God from creatures is based on the fact that creatures, as effects of God, must manifest God, though they can do this only imperfectly.

Yet if the concepts derived from our experience of creatures and then applied to God are used neither in an univocal nor in an equivocal sense, in what sense are they used? Is there any half-way house? St. Thomas replies that they are used in an analogical

[1] *S.T.*, Ia, 13, 2.

sense. When an attribute is predicated analogically of two different beings, this means that it is predicated according to the relation they have to some third thing or according to the relation the one has to the other. As an example of the first type of analogical predication St. Thomas gives his favourite example, health.[1] An animal is said to be healthy because it is the subject of health, possesses health, while medicine is said to be healthy as being the cause of health, and a complexion is said to be healthy as being the sign of health. The word 'healthy' is predicated in different senses of the animal in general, the medicine and the complexion, according to the different relations they bear to health; but it is not predicated in a purely equivocal sense, for all three bear some real relation to health. Medicine is not healthy in the same sense that animal is healthy, for the term 'healthy' is not employed univocally, but the senses in which it is used are not equivocal or purely metaphorical, as when we speak of a smiling meadow. But this, says St. Thomas, is not the way in which we predicate attributes of God and creatures, for God and creatures have no relation to any third object: we predicate attributes of God and creatures, in so far as the creature has a real relation to God. When, for example, we predicate being of God and creatures, we attribute being first and foremost to God, as self-existing being, secondarily to creatures, as dependent on God. We cannot predicate being univocally of God and creatures, since they do not possess being in the same way, nor do we predicate being in a purely equivocal sense, since creatures have being, though their being is not like the divine being but is dependent, participated being.

As regards what is meant by the words we apply to God and creatures, it is attributed primarily to God and only secondarily to creatures. Being, as we have seen, belongs essentially to God, whereas it does not belong essentially to creatures but only in dependence on God: it is being, but it is a different kind of being from the divine being, since it is received, derived, dependent, finite. Nevertheless, though the thing signified is attributed primarily to God, the name is predicated primarily of creatures. The reason is tnat we know creatures before we know God, so that since our knowledge of wisdom, for example, is derived from creatures and the word primarily denotes the concept derived from our experience of creatures, the idea of wisdom and the word

[1] *Contra Gent.*, 1, 34; *S.T.*, Ia, 13, 5.

are predicated primarily of creatures and analogically of God, even though in actual fact wisdom itself, the thing signified, belongs primarily to God.

4. Analogical predication is founded on resemblance. In the *De Veritate*[1] St. Thomas distinguishes resemblance of proportion (*convenientia proportionis*) and resemblance of proportionality (*convenientia proportionalitatis*). Between the number 8 and the number 4 there is a resemblance of proportion, while between the proportions of 6 to 3 and of 4 to 2 there is a resemblance of proportionality, that is, a resemblance or similarity of two proportions to one another. Now, analogical predication in a general sense may be made according to both types of resemblance. The predication of being in regard to created substance and accident, each of which has a relation to the other, is an example of analogical predication according to proportion, while the predication of vision in regard to both ocular and intellectual vision is an example of analogical predication according to proportionality. What corporeal vision is to the eye, that intellectual apprehension or vision is to the mind. There is a certain similarity between the relation of the eye to its vision and the relation of mind to its intellectual apprehension, a similarity which enables us to speak of 'vision' in both cases. We apply the word 'vision' in the two cases neither univocally nor purely equivocally, but analogically.

Now, it is impossible to predicate anything analogically of God and creatures in the same way that it is possible to predicate being of substance and accident, for God and creatures have no mutual real relationship: creatures have a real relation to God, but God has no real relation to creatures. Nor is God included in the definition of any creature in the way that substance is included in the definition of accident. It does not follow, however, that there can be no analogy of proportion between God and creatures. Though God is not related to creatures by a real relation, creatures have a real relation to God, and we are able to apply the same term to God and creatures in virtue of that relation. There are perfections which are not bound up with matter and which do not necessarily imply any defect or imperfection in the being of which they are predicated. Being, wisdom and goodness are examples of such perfections. Obviously we gain knowledge of being or goodness or wisdom from creatures; but it does not follow

[1] 2, 11, *in corpore*.

that these perfections exist primarily in creatures and only secondarily in God, or that they are predicated primarily of creatures and only secondarily of God. On the contrary, goodness, for instance, exists primarily in God, who is the infinite goodness and the cause of all creaturely goodness, and it is predicated primarily of God and only secondarily of creatures, even though creaturely goodness is what we first come to know. Analogy of proportion is possible, then, in virtue of the creature's relation and likeness to God. To this point I shall return shortly.

It has been argued that St. Thomas came to abandon analogy of proportionality in favour of the analogy of proportion (in the acceptable sense); but this does not seem to me likely. In the Commentary on the *Sentences*[1] he gives both types of analogy, and even if in later works, like the *De Potentia*, the *Summa contra Gentiles* and the *Summa Theologica*, he seems to emphasise analogy of proportion, that does not seem to me to indicate that he ever abandoned analogy of proportionality. This type of analogical predication may be used in two ways, symbolically or properly. We can speak of God as 'the Sun', meaning that what the sun is to the bodily eye, that God is to the soul; but we are then speaking symbolically, since the word 'sun' refers to a material thing and can be predicated of a spiritual being only in a symbolic sense. We can say, however, that there is a certain similarity between God's relation to His intellectual activity and man's relation to his intellectual activity, and in this case we are not speaking merely symbolically, since intellectual activity as such is a pure perfection.

The foundation of all analogy, then, that which makes analogical predication possible, is the likeness of creatures to God. We do not predicate wisdom of God merely because God is the cause of all wise things, for in that case we might just as well call God a stone, as being the cause of all stones; but we call Him wise because creatures, God's effects, manifest God, are like to Him, and because a pure perfection like wisdom can be formally predicated of Him. But what is this likeness? In the first place it is only a one-way likeness, that is, the creature is like to God, but we cannot properly say that God is like the creature. God is the absolute standard, as it were. In the second place creatures are only imperfectly like God; they cannot bear a perfect resemblance to Him. This means that the creature is *at the same time* both like and unlike God. It is like God in so far as it is an imitation of Him; it is unlike God in

[1] *In* 4 *Sent.*, 49, 2, 1, *ad* 6.

so far as its resemblance to Him is imperfect and deficient. Analogical predication, therefore, lies between univocal and equivocal predication. In analogical predication the predicate is applied to God and creatures neither in precisely the same sense nor in totally different senses; it is applied at the same time in similar and dissimilar senses.[1] This notion of simultaneous similarity and difference is fundamental in analogy. The notion may, it is true, occasion considerable difficulties from the logical standpoint; but it would be inappropriate to discuss here the objections of modern positivists to analogy.

St. Thomas distinguishes, then, *analogy of proportion* (*analogia secundum convenientiam proportionis*) and *analogy of proportionality* (*analogia secundum convenientiam proportionalitatis*). As we have seen, he does not admit in regard to God and creatures that analogy of proportion which is applicable to substance and accident in respect of being; by analogy of proportion in natural theology he means that analogy in which a predicate is applied primarily to one analogue, namely God, and secondarily and imperfectly to the other analogue, namely the creature, in virtue of the creature's real relation and likeness to God. The perfection attributed to the analogues is really present in both of them, but it is not present in the same way, and the one predicate is used at the same time in senses which are neither completely different nor completely similar. Terminology has changed since the time of St. Thomas, and this kind of analogy is now called analogy of attribution. Analogy of proportionality, the resemblance of proportions, is sometimes called analogy of proportion, in distinction from the analogy of attribution; but not all Scholastics and commentators on St. Thomas employ the terms in precisely the same way.

Some Scholastics have maintained that being, for example, is predicable of God and creatures only by analogy of proportionality and not by analogy of attribution. Without, however, wishing to enter on a discussion of the value of analogy of proportionality as such, I do not see how we could know that God has any perfection save by way of the analogy of attribution. All analogical predication rests on the real relation and likeness of creatures to God, and it seems to me that the analogy of proportionality presupposes analogy of proportion or attribution and that the latter is the more fundamental of the two kinds of analogy.

5. If one reads what St. Thomas has to say of analogy, it may

[1] Cf. *S.T.*, Ia, 13, 5, *in corpore*.

appear that he is simply examining the way in which we speak about God, the verbal and conceptual implications of our statements, and that he is not actually establishing anything about our real knowledge of God. But it is a fundamental principle with St. Thomas that the perfections of creatures must be found in the Creator in a super-eminent manner, in a manner compatible with the infinity and spirituality of God. For example, if God has created intellectual beings, God must be possessed of intellect; we cannot suppose that He is less than intellectual. Moreover, a spiritual being must be an intellectual form, as Aristotle says, and the infinite spiritual being must be possessed of infinite intelligence. On the other hand, God's intelligence cannot be a faculty distinct from His essence or nature, since God is pure Act and not a composite being, nor can God know things successively, since He is changeless and incapable of accidental determination. He knows future events in virtue of His eternity, by which all things are present to Him.[1] God must possess the perfection of intellectuality, but we cannot form any adequate concept of what the divine intelligence is, since we have no experience of it: our knowledge of the divine intelligence is imperfect and inadequate, but it is not false; it is analogical knowledge. It would be false only if we were unaware of its imperfection and actually meant to ascribe to God finite intelligence as such: we cannot help thinking and speaking of the divine intelligence in terms of human concepts and language, since there are no others available to us, but at the same time we are aware that our concepts and language are imperfect. We cannot, for instance, help speaking as though God 'foresaw' future events, but we are aware that for God there is not past or future. Similarly we must ascribe to God the perfection of free will in respect of other objects than Himself, but God's free will cannot involve changeableness: He willed freely to create the world in time, but He willed it freely from all eternity, in virtue of the one act of will which is identical with His essence. Of the divine free will we can, therefore, form no adequate conception; but the relation of creatures to God shows us that God must possess free will and we can realise some of the things which the divine free will cannot mean; yet the positive reality of the divine free will exceeds our comprehension, precisely because we are creatures and not God. Only God can comprehend Himself.

It can scarcely be denied, however, that a grave difficulty arises

[1] Cf. *S.T.*, Ia, 14, 13.

in connection with the doctrine of analogy. If our idea of intelligence, for example, is derived from human intelligence, it obviously cannot, as such, be applied to God, and St. Thomas insists that no predicate which is applied to God and creatures is applied univocally. On the other hand, unless we were willing to acquiesce in agnosticism, we could not allow that such predicates are used in a purely equivocal sense. What, then, is the positive content of our concept of the divine intelligence? If St. Thomas adhered simply to the *via negativa* the difficulty would not arise: he would be saying simply that God is not not-intelligent or that He is super-intelligent, admitting that we have no positive idea of what the divine intelligence is. But St. Thomas does not stick simply to the *via negativa*: he admits the *via affirmativa*. Our idea of divine intelligence has, therefore, a positive content; but what can that positive content be? Is the reply that a positive content is obtained by denying the limitations of human intelligence, its finiteness, discursive character, potentiality and so on? In this case, however, we either attain a positive concept of the divine intelligence as such or we attain a concept of the 'essence' of intelligence, apart from finitude or infinity, which would seem to be univocal in respect of God and creatures. It might even appear that the negations either cancel out the content altogether or make it into an idea of the essence of intelligence which would be univocal in respect of divine and human intelligence. It was for this reason that Duns Scotus later insisted that we can form univocal concepts applicable to both God and creatures, though there is no univocity in the real order in respect of God and creatures. It is sometimes said that analogical concepts are partly the same as and partly different from univocal concepts; but the same difficulty recurs. The element of 'sameness' will be an univocal element, while the element of 'difference' will either be negative or it will have no content, since we have no immediate experience of God from which the idea can be derived. But further consideration of this point is best reserved for our treatment of St. Thomas's doctrine of knowledge.[1]

6. Mention of the divine intelligence naturally leads one on to raise the question what St. Thomas thought of the doctrine of the divine ideas. In the first place he establishes that there must be ideas in the divine mind, *necesse est ponere in mente divina ideas*,[2] since God has created things not by chance, but intelligently,

[1] Cf. Ch. XXXVIII, sect. 4.

[2] *S.T.*, Ia, 15, 1.

according to the exemplary idea He conceived in His mind. He remarks that Plato erred in asserting the existence of ideas which were not in any intellect, and he observes that Aristotle blamed Plato on this account. As a matter of fact, Aristotle, who did not believe in any free creation by God, did not blame Plato for making the ideas independent of the divine mind, but for maintaining their subsistence apart from the human mind, if one is considering their subjective reality, and apart from things, if one is considering their objective reality as forms. In asserting the existence of ideas in the divine mind St. Thomas is therefore following in the wake of the tradition which began with Plato, was developed in Middle Platonism and neo-Platonism and lived on, in a Christian setting, in the philosophy of Augustine and those who followed him.

One of the reasons why the neo-Platonists placed the ideas in the *Nous*, the second hypostasis or first emanating divine being, and not in the One or supreme Godhead was that the presence of a multiplicity of ideas in God would, they thought, impair the divine unity. How did St. Thomas meet this difficulty, when the only real distinction he could admit in God was the distinction between the three divine Persons in the Trinity (and with this distinction he was not, of course, concerned as philosopher)? His answer is that from one point of view we must say that there is a plurality of ideas in God, as Augustine said, since God knows each individual thing to be created, but that from another point of view there cannot be a plurality of ideas in God, since this would contradict the divine simplicity. What he means is this. If by idea one refers to the content of the idea, then one must admit a plurality of ideas in God, since God knows many objects; but if by idea one means the subjective mental determination, the species, then one cannot admit a plurality of ideas in God, since God's intellect is identical with His undivided essence and cannot receive determinations or any sort of composition. God knows His divine essence not only as it is in itself, but also as imitable outside itself in a plurality of creatures. This act of knowledge, as it exists in God, is one and undivided and is identical with His essence; but since God not only knows His essence as imitable in a multiplicity of creatures, but also knows that in knowing His essence He knows a multiplicity of creatures, we can and must speak of a plurality of ideas in God, for 'idea' signifies, not the divine essence as it is in itself, but the divine essence as the exemplar of this or that object. And it is the exemplar of many objects. In other words, the truth or falsity of our statements in regard to God must be estimated in terms of human language. To deny a plurality of ideas in God without qualification would be to deny that God knows a plurality of objects; but the truth that God knows His essence as imitable by a plurality of creatures must not be stated in such a way as to imply that there is a multiplicity of real species or really distinct modifications in the divine intellect.[1]

This discussion of the divine ideas is of some interest because it shows that St. Thomas is by no means simply an Aristotelian, but that in this respect at least he adheres to the Platonic-Augustinian tradition. Indeed, although he sees clearly that he has to provide against any impairing of the divine simplicity, he is not content with saying that God by one act of His intellect, one 'idea', knows His essence as imitable in a plurality of creatures, but he asserts that there is a plurality of ideas in God. He certainly gives his reasons for doing so, but one has the impression that one unstated reason was his reverence for Augustine and Augustine's mode of speaking. However, it is true that a distinction must be made. When we to-day use the term 'idea' we naturally refer to the subjective idea or mental modification, and in this sense St. Thomas does not admit in God a plurality of ideas really distinct from one another; but St. Thomas was primarily thinking of 'idea' in the sense of exemplary form, and since the divine essence as known by the divine intellect is known as imitable in a plurality of creatures, as the exemplar of many objects, he felt himself entitled to speak of a plurality of *rationes* in God, though he had to insist that this plurality consists simply in God's knowledge of His essence in respect of the multiplicity of creatures and not in a real distinction in God.

7. We have spoken of the divine intelligence and the divine will, the divine goodness, unity, simplicity and so on. Are these attributes of God really distinct from one another? And if they are not distinct from one another, what is our justification for speaking of them as though they were distinct? The attributes of God are not really distinct from one another, since God is simple: they are identical with the divine essence. The divine intelligence is not really distinct from the divine essence, nor is the divine will: the divine justice and the divine mercy are identical as they exist in God. Nevertheless, apart from the fact that the structure of

[1] Cf. *S.T.*, Ia, 15, 1–3; *Contra Gent.*, I, 53–4.

our language compels us to speak in terms of subject and predicate, we apprehend the divine perfection piecemeal, as it were. We attain our natural knowledge of God only by considerations of creatures, God's effects, and since the perfections of creatures, the manifestations or reflections of God in creatures are different, we use different names to signify those different perfections. But if we could comprehend the divine essence as it is in itself and if we could give it its proper name, we should use one alone.[1] We cannot, however, comprehend the divine essence, and we know it only by means of diverse concepts: we have, therefore, to employ diverse words to express the divine essence, though we know at the same time that the actual reality corresponding to all those names is one simple reality. If it is objected that to conceive an object otherwise than it is is to conceive it falsely, the answer is that we do not conceive the object to exist otherwise than it actually exists, for we know that God is actually a simple Being, but we conceive in a composite manner the object which we know to be non-composite. This means simply that our intelligences are finite and discursive and that they cannot apprehend God save by means of His different reflections in creatures. Our knowledge of God is thus inadequate and imperfect, but it is not false.[2] There is indeed a certain foundation in God for our composite and distinct concepts, this foundation, however, not being any real distinction in God between the divine attributes but simply His infinite perfection which, precisely because of its infinite richness, cannot be apprehended by the human mind in one concept.

8. According to St. Thomas[3] the most appropriate name of God is the name He gave to Moses at the burning bush,[4] *Qui est*, He who is. In God there is no distinction between essence and existence; He does not receive His existence, but is His existence; His essence is to exist. In no creature, however, is the distinction between essence and existence absent. Every creature is good and every creature is true; but no creature is its own existence: it is not the essence of any creature to exist. Existence itself *ipsum esse*, is the essence of God, and the name which is derived from that essence is most appropriate to God. God is goodness, for example, and His goodness is identical with His essence, but goodness, in our human experience, follows on and accompanies *esse*; though not really distinct, it is conceived as secondary; but

[1] *Contra Gent.*, I, 31.
[2] Cf. *S.T.*, Ia, 13, 12, *in corpore* and *ad* 3.
[3] *S.T.*, Ia, 13, 11; *Contra Gent.*, I, 22.
[4] Exodus 3. 14.

to say that God is *ipsum esse* is to give, as it were, His inner nature. Every other name is in some way inadequate. If we say, for example, that God is infinite Justice, we say what is true, but as our intelligences necessarily distinguish Justice and Mercy, even though we know that they are identical in God, the statement that God is infinite Justice is an inadequate expression of the divine essence. The names we employ in speaking of God are derived from our experience of determinate forms and express primarily those forms; but the name *He who is* signifies not a determinate form, but 'the infinite ocean of substance'.

CHAPTER XXXVI

ST. THOMAS AQUINAS—VI: CREATION

Creation out of nothing—God alone can create—God created freely—The motive of creation—Impossibility of creation from eternity has not been demonstrated—Could God create an actually infinite multitude?—Divine omnipotence—The problem of evil.

1. SINCE God is the first Cause of the world, since finite beings are contingent beings owing their existence to the necessary Being, finite beings must proceed from God through creation. Moreover, this creation must be creation out of nothing. If creatures were made out of a pre-existent material, this material would be either God Himself or something other than God. But God cannot be the material of creation, since He is simple, spiritual, unchangeable; nor can there be any thing independent of the first Cause: there can be but one necessary Being. God, therefore, is absolutely prior, and if He cannot change, cannot exteriorise Himself in creation, He must have created the world out of nothing, *ex nihilo*. This phrase must not be taken to imply that nothing, *nihil*, is a material out of which God made the world: when it is said that God created the world out of nothing, it is meant either that first there was nothing and then there was something or the phrase *ex nihilo* must be understood as equivalent to *non ex aliquo*, not out of something. The objection that out of nothing comes nothing is, therefore, irrelevant, since nothing is looked on neither as efficient cause nor as material cause; in creation God is the efficient Cause and there is no material cause whatsoever.[1] Creation is thus not a movement or change in the proper sense, and since it is not a movement, there is no succession in the act of creation.

Creation, considered in the term of the act of creation, that is, in the creature, is a real relation to God as the principle of the creature's being. Every creature, by the very fact that it is created, has a real relation to God as Creator. But one cannot argue the other way round, that God has a real relation to the creature. Such a relation in God would either be identical with the divine substance or it would be an accident in God; but the divine substance cannot be necessarily related to creatures, since

[1] On the sense of *creatio ex nihilo*, cf. *De Potentia*, 3, 1, *ad* 7; *S.T.*, Ia, 45, 1, *ad* 3.

in that case God would depend in some way on creatures for His very existence, while on the other hand God, as absolutely simple, cannot receive or possess accidents.[1] The statement that God as Creator has no real relation to creatures certainly sounds rather strange at first hearing, as it might seem to follow that God has no care for His creatures; but it is a strictly logical conclusion from St. Thomas's metaphysic and doctrine of the divine Nature. That God is related to creatures by His very substance St. Thomas could not possibly admit, since in that case not only would creation necessarily be eternal, and we know from revelation that it is not eternal, but God could not exist apart from creatures: God and creatures would form a Totality and it would be impossible to explain the generation and perishing of individual creatures. On the other hand, if one is speaking of relation as falling within one of the nine categories of accidents, such a relation also is inadmissible in God. The acquisition of such an accident would allow of creation in time, it is true; but such an acquisition on the part of God is impossible if God is pure act, without potentiality. It was, therefore, impossible for St. Thomas to admit that God as Creator has a real relation to creatures; he had to say that the relation is a mental relation of reason alone (*relatio rationis*), attributed to God by the human intellect. The attribution is, however, legitimate, since God is Creator and we cannot express this fact in human language without speaking as though God were related to creatures: the important point is that, when we speak of creatures as related to God and of God as related to creatures, we should remember that it is creatures which depend on God and not God on creatures, and that consequently the real relation between them, which is a relation of dependence, is found in creatures alone.

2. The power of creation is a prerogative of God alone and cannot be communicated to any creature.[2] The reason why some philosophers, Avicenna, for example, introduced intermediary beings was because they thought of God as creating by a necessity of nature, so that there must be intermediary stages between the absolute simplicity of the supreme Godhead and the multiplicity of creatures; but God does not create by a necessity of nature and there is no reason why He should not create directly a multiplicity of creatures. Peter Lombard thought that the power of creation is communicable by God to a creature in such a way

[1] *Contra Gent.*, 2, 11–13; *S.T.*, Ia, 45, 3; *De Potentia*, 3, 3.
[2] Cf. *De Potentia*, 3, 4.

that the latter could act as an instrument, not by its own power; but this is impossible, since if the creature is to contribute in any way to creation, its own power and activity will be involved, and this power, being finite like the creature itself, cannot accomplish an act which demands infinite power, the act of bridging the infinite gulf between not-being and being.

3. But if God does not create by a necessity of nature, how does He create? An intellectual being, in whom there is, so to speak, no element of unconsciousness, but who is perfectly self-luminous and 'self-possessed', cannot act in any other way than according to wisdom, with full knowledge. To put the matter crudely, God must act for a motive, in view of a purpose, a good. But God's nature is not only infinite intelligence, but also infinite will, and that will is free. God loves Himself necessarily, since He is Himself the infinite good, but objects distinct from Himself are not necessary to Him, since, as infinite perfection, He is self-sufficient: His will is free in their regard. Therefore, although we know that God's intellect and will are not really distinct from His essence, we are bound to say that God chose freely an object or end conceived by Him as good. The language employed is certainly anthropomorphic, but we have only human language at our disposal, and we cannot express the truth that God created the world freely without making it clear that the act of will by which God created was neither a blind act nor a necessary act, but an act which followed, to speak in human fashion, the apprehension of a good, apprehended as a good though not as a good necessary to God.

4. What was the motive for which God acted in creation? As infinite perfection God cannot have created in order to acquire anything for Himself: He created, not in order to obtain, but to give, to diffuse His goodness (*intendit solum communicare suam perfectionem quae est ejus bonitas*).[1] When it is said, then, that God created the world for His own glory the statement must not be taken to mean that God needed something which He had not already got; still less that He wanted to obtain, if one may so speak without irreverence, a chorus of admirers; but rather that God's will cannot depend on anything apart from God, that He Himself as the infinite good must be the end of His infinite act of will, and that in the case of the act of creation the end is His own goodness as communicable to beings outside Himself. The divine goodness is represented in all creatures, though rational creatures

[1] *S.T.*, Ia, 44, 4.

have God as their end in a manner peculiar to themselves, since they are able to know and to love God: all creatures glorify God by representing and participating in His goodness, while rational creatures are capable of consciously appreciating and loving the divine goodness. God's glory, the manifestation of His goodness, is thus not something separate from the good of creatures, for creatures attain their end, do the best for themselves, by manifesting the divine goodness.[1]

5. That God created the world freely, does not of itself show that He created it in time, that time had a beginning. As God is eternal, He might have created the world from eternity. That this had been shown to be an impossible supposition St. Thomas refused to allow. He believed that it can be philosophically proved that the world was created out of nothing, but he maintained that none of the philosophical proofs adduced to prove that this creation took place in time, that there is, ideally, a first assignable moment of time, were conclusive, differing on this point from St. Albert. On the other hand, St. Thomas maintained, against the Averroists, that it cannot be shown philosophically that the world cannot have begun in time, that creation in time is an impossibility. In other words, though well aware that the world was actually created in time and not from eternity, St. Thomas was convinced that this fact is known only through revelation, and that the philosopher cannot settle the question whether the world was created in time or from eternity. Thus he maintained, against the *murmurantes*, the possibility (as far as we can see) of creation from eternity. In practice this meant that he showed, or at least was satisfied that he could show, that the type of argument brought forward by St. Bonaventure to prove the impossibility of creation from eternity was inconclusive. It is, however, unnecessary to mention St. Thomas's replies again, since these, or some of them at least, have already been given when we were considering the philosophy of St. Bonaventure.[2] Let it suffice to recall the fact that St. Thomas saw no contradiction in the notion of a series without a beginning. In his eyes the question whether it would be possible for the world to have passed through infinite time does not arise, since there is strictly no passing through an infinite series if there is no first term in the series. Moreover, for St. Thomas a series can be infinite *ex parte ante* and finite *ex parte post*, and it can be added to at the end at which it is finite. In general, there

[1] Cf. *S.T.*, Ia, 65, 2.

[2] pp. 262–5.

is no contradiction between being brought into existence and existing from eternity: if God is eternal, God could have created from eternity.

On the other hand, St. Thomas rejects the arguments adduced to show that the world must have been created from eternity. 'We must hold firmly, as the Catholic faith teaches, that the world has not always existed. And this position cannot be overcome by any physical demonstration.'[1] It may be argued, for example, that as God is the Cause of the world and as God is eternal, the world, God's effect, must also be eternal. As God cannot change, as He contains no element of potentiality and cannot receive new determinations or modifications, the creative act, God's free act of creation, must be eternal. The effect of this act must, therefore, also be eternal. St. Thomas has to agree, of course, that the creative act as such, that is, God's act of will, is eternal, since it is identical with God's essence; but he argues that what follows from this is simply that God willed freely from eternity to create the world, not that the world came into existence from eternity. If we consider the matter merely as philosophers, if, that is, we prescind from our knowledge, gained from revelation, that God actually created the world in time, all we can say is that God may have willed freely from eternity that the world should come into existence in time or that God may have willed freely from eternity that the world should come into existence from eternity: we are not entitled to conclude that God *must* have willed from eternity that the world should exist from eternity. In other words, God's creative act is certainly eternal, but the external effect of that act will follow in the way willed by God, and if God willed that the external effect should have *esse post non-esse* it will not have *esse ab aeterno*, even though the creative act, considered precisely as an act in God, is eternal.[2]

6. One of the reasons adduced by St. Bonaventure to show that the world must have been created in time and could not have been created from eternity was that, if it had been created from eternity, there would be in existence now an infinite number of immortal human souls and that an infinite actual multitude is an impossibility. What did St. Thomas maintain concerning God's power to create an infinite multitude? The question arises in connection with a multitude *extra genus quantitatis*, since St. Thomas followed

[1] *De Potentia*, 3, 17.

[2] On this subject see *Contra Gent.*, 2, 31–7; *S.T.*, Ia, 46, 1; *De Potentia*, 3, 17; *De aeternitate mundi contra murmurantes*.

Aristotle in rejecting the possibility of an infinite quantity. In the *De Veritate*[1] the Saint remarks that the only valid reason for saying that God could not create an actual infinite multitude would be an essential repugnance or contradiction in the notion of such an infinity, but he defers any decision on the matter. In the *Summa Theologica*[2] he affirms categorically that there cannot be an actual infinite multitude, since every created multitude must be of a certain number, whereas an infinite multitude would not be of a certain number. But in the *De aeternitate mundi contra Murmurantes*, when dealing with the objection against the possibility of the world's creation from eternity that there would then be in existence an infinite number of immortal human souls, he replies that God might have made the world without men, or that He could have made the world from eternity but have made man only when He did make him, while on the other hand 'it has not yet been demonstrated that God cannot make an infinity in act'. It may be that the last remark indicates a change of mind on St. Thomas's part or a hesitancy concerning the validity of his own previous demonstration; but he does not explicitly recall what he said in the *Summa Theologica*, and the remark might be no more than an *argumentum ad hominem*, '*you* have not yet demonstrated that an existing infinite multitude is impossible'. In any case, in view of the statement in the *Summa Theologica* and in view of the proximity in time of the *De aeternitate mundi* to the first part of the *Summa Theologica*, it would seem rash to conclude to more than a possible hesitancy on St. Thomas's part as to the impossibility of an infinite multitude in act.

7. The mention of God being able or unable to create an actually infinite multitude naturally raises the wider question of the sense in which the divine omnipotence is to be understood. If omnipotence means the ability to do all things, how can God be omnipotent if He cannot make it come about that a man should be a horse or that what has happened should not have happened? In answer St. Thomas observes first of all that the divine attribute of omnipotence means that God can do all that is possible. But 'all that is possible' must not be understood, he goes on to say, as equivalent to 'all that is possible to God', for in this case when we say that God is omnipotent we should mean that God is able to do all that He is able to do a statement which would tell us nothing. How, then, are we to understand the phrase 'all that is possible'? That

[1] 2, 10. [2] Ia, 7, 4; 1, 46, *ad* 8.

is possible which has no intrinsic repugnance to being, in other words, that the existence of which would not involve a contradiction. That which involves a contradiction in its very notion is neither actual nor possible, but not-being. For example, that a man, while remaining a man, should also be a horse, involves a contradiction: man is rational, a horse irrational, and rational and irrational are contradictories. We can certainly speak of a human horse or an equine man, but the phrases do not indicate a thing, whether actual or possible; they are mere verbiage, signifying nothing conceivable. To say, therefore, that God's omnipotence means that God can do all that is possible does not indicate a limit to God's power, for power has meaning only in regard to the possible. Whatever has or can have being is the object of divine omnipotence, but that which is intrinsically contradictory is not an object at all. 'So it is better to say that what involves contradiction cannot be done rather than that God cannot do it.'[1]

It must not, however, be imagined that there is a principle of contradiction which stands behind God and to which God is subject as the Greek gods were subject to *Moira* or Destiny. God is supreme Being, *ipsum esse subsistens*, and His will to create is a will to create His own similitude, something, that is, which can participate in being. That which involves a contradiction is at the utmost remove from Being; it neither has nor ever can have any likeness to God, any being. If God could will what is self-contradictory He could depart from His own nature, could love that which bears no resemblance whatsoever to Himself, that which is nothing at all, that which is utterly unthinkable. But if God could act in this way, He would not be God. It is not that God is subject to the principle of contradiction, but rather that the principle of contradiction is founded on the nature of God. To suppose, then, with St. Peter Damian (or with Leo Chestov) that God is superior to the principle of contradiction, in the sense that God can do what is self-contradictory, is to suppose that God can act in a manner inconsistent with and contrary to His own nature, and this is an absurd supposition.[2]

But this does not mean that God can do only what He actually does. It is certainly true that since God actually wills the order of things which He has created and which actually exists, He cannot will another order, since the divine will cannot change, as

[1] Cf. *S.T.*, Ia, 25, 3–4; *De Potentia*, 1, 7. [2] Cf. *Contra Gent.*, 1, 84.

our finite wills can change; but the question is not concerning the divine power *ex suppositione*, on the supposition that God has already chosen, but concerning the absolute divine power, i.e. whether God was restricted to willing the actual order He has willed or whether He could have willed another order. The answer is that God did not will this present order of things necessarily, and the reason is that the end of creation is the divine goodness which so exceeds any created order that there is not and cannot be any link of necessity between a given order and the end of creation. The divine goodness and the created order are incommensurable, and there cannot be any one created order, any one universe, which is necessary to a divine goodness that is infinite and incapable of any addition. If any created order were proportionate to the divine goodness, to the end, then the divine wisdom would be determined to choose that particular order; but since the divine goodness is infinite and creation necessarily finite, no created order can be proportionate in the full sense to the divine goodness.[1]

From the above is made apparent the answer to the questions whether God could make better things than He has made or could make the things which He has made better than they are.[2] In one sense God must always act in the best possible manner, since God's act is identical with His essence and with infinite goodness; but we cannot conclude from this that the extrinsic object of God's act, creatures, must be the best possible and that God is bound, on account of His goodness, to produce the best possible universe if He produces one at all. As God's power is infinite, there can always be a better universe than the one God actually produces, and why He has chosen to produce a particular order of creation is His secret. St. Thomas says, therefore, that absolutely speaking God could make something better than any given thing. But if the question is raised in regard to the existent universe, a distinction must be drawn. God could not make a given thing better than it actually is in regard to its substance or essence, since that would be to make another thing. For example, rational life is in itself a higher perfection than merely sensitive life; but if God were to make a horse rational it would no longer be a horse and in that case God could not be said to make the horse better. Similarly, if God changed the order of the universe, it would not

[1] Cf. *S.T.*, Ia, 19, 3; 1, 25, 5; *Contra Gent.*, 2, 26–7; *De Potentia*, 1, 5.
[2] *S.T.*, Ia, 25, 6.

be the same universe. On the other hand, God could make a thing accidentally better; He could, for example, increase a man's bodily health or, in the supernatural order, his grace.

It is plain, then, that St. Thomas would not agree with the Leibnizian 'optimism' or maintain that this is the best of all possible worlds. In view of the divine omnipotence the phrase 'the best of all possible worlds' does not seem to have much meaning: it has meaning only if one supposes from the start that God creates from a necessity of His nature, from which it would follow, since God is goodness itself, that the world which proceeds from Him necessarily must be the best possible. But if God creates not from a necessity of nature, but according to His nature, according to intelligence and will, that is, freely, and if God is omnipotent, it must always be possible for God to create a better world. Why, then, did He create this particular world? That is a question to which we cannot give any adequate answer, though we can certainly attempt to answer the question why God created a world in which suffering and evil are present: that is to say, we can attempt to answer the problem of evil, provided that we remember that we cannot expect to attain any comprehensive solution of the problem in this life, owing to the finitude and imperfection of our intelligences and the fact that we cannot fathom the divine counsel and plans.

8. In willing this universe God did not will the evils contained in it. God necessarily loves His own essence, which is infinite goodness, and He freely wills creation as a communication of His goodness; He cannot love what is opposed to goodness, namely evil. But did not God, to speak in human language, foresee the evils in the world; and if He foresaw the evils in the world and yet willed the world, did He not will the evils in the world? If evil were a positive entity, something created, then it would have to be ascribed to God as Creator, since there is no ultimate principle of evil, as the Manichaeans thought; but evil is not a positive entity; it is, as St. Augustine taught, following Plotinus, a *privation*. It is not *aliquid*, a positive thing, and God cannot have created it, since it is not creatable, but it only exists as a privation in what itself, as being, is good. Moreover, evil as such cannot be willed even by a human will, for the object of the will is necessarily the good or what appears as such. The adulterer, says St. Thomas, does not will the evil, the sin, precisely as such; he wills the sensible pleasure of an act which involves evil. It might be objected that

some people have indulged in diabolic wickedness, have committed acts precisely because they were an offence against God; but even in this case it is some apparent good, complete independence, for example, which is the object of the will: the evil defiance of God appears as a good and is willed *sub specie boni*. No will, therefore, can desire evil precisely as such, and God, in creating a world the evils of which He 'foresaw', must be said, not to have willed the evils but to have willed the world which, as such, is good and to have willed to permit the evils which He foresaw.

It must not, however, be imagined that by maintaining the doctrine that evil as such is a privation St. Thomas means to imply that evil is unreal, in the sense of being an illusion. This would be to misunderstand his position completely. Evil is not a being, *entitas*, in the sense that it falls under any of the ten categories of being, but in reply to the question whether evil exists or not, the answer must be in the affirmative. This certainly sounds paradoxical, but St. Thomas means that evil exists as a privation in the good, not in its own right as a positive entity. For example, lack of ability to see is not a privation in a stone, for it does not pertain to a stone to see, and 'blindness' in a stone is the mere absence of a power which would be incompatible with the nature of the stone; but blindness in a man is a privation, the absence of something which belongs to the fullness of man's nature. This blindness is not, however, a positive entity, it is a privation of sight; yet the privation exists, is real, it is by no means an unreal illusion. It has no meaning or existence apart from the being in which it exists, but as existing in that being the privation is real enough. Similarly, evil cannot of and by itself cause anything, but it exists and can be a cause through the good being in which it exists. For example, the difformity in the will of a fallen angel cannot by itself be a cause, but it is a real privation and can be a cause by means of the positive being in which it exists. Indeed, the more powerful the being in which it exists, the greater are its effects.[1]

God did not, then, create evil as a positive entity, but must He not be said to have willed evil in some sense, since He created a world in which He foresaw that evil would exist? It is necessary to consider separately physical evil and moral evil (*malum culpae*). Physical evil was certainly permitted by God and it can in a sense be even said to have been willed by God. God did not will it for

[1] Cf. *S.T.*, Ia, 48, 1–3.

its own sake, of course, *per se*, but He willed a universe, a natural order, which involved at least the possibility of physical defect and suffering. By willing the creation of sensitive nature God willed that capacity for feeling pain as well as pleasure which is, naturally speaking, inseparable from human nature. He did not will suffering as such, but He willed that nature (a good) which is accompanied by the capacity for suffering. Moreover, the perfection of the universe requires, says St. Thomas, that there should be, besides incorruptible beings, corruptible beings, and if there are corruptible beings, corruption, death, will take place according to the natural order. God, then, did not will corruption (needless to say, the word is not being used in the moral sense) for its own sake, but He can be said to have caused it *per accidens*, in that He willed to create and created a universe the order of which demanded the capacity for defect and corruption on the part of some beings. Again, the preservation of the order of justice demands that moral evil should meet with punishment (*malum poenae*), and God may be said to will and cause that punishment not for its own sake, but so that the order of justice may be preserved.

In treating of physical evil, therefore, St. Thomas tends to treat God as an artist and the universe as a work of art. The perfection of that work of art requires a variety of beings, among which will be found beings which are mortal and capable of suffering, so that God may be said to have willed physical evil not *per se* but *per accidens*, for the sake of a good, the good of the whole universe. But when it is a question of the moral order, the order of freedom, and of considering human beings precisely as free agents, his attitude is different. Freedom is a good and without it human beings could not give God that love of which He is worthy, could not merit and so on: freedom makes man more like to God than he would be, were he not free. On the other hand, man's liberty, when he has not got the vision of God, involves the power of choosing against God and the moral law, of sinning. God did not will moral disorder or sin in any sense, but He permitted it. Why? For the sake of a greater good, that man might be free and that he might love and serve God of his own free choice. The physical perfection of the universe required the presence of some beings who could and would die, so that God, as we have seen, can be said to have willed death *per accidens*; but though the perfection of the universe required that man should be free, it did not require that he should misuse his freedom, should sin, and God cannot be said to have willed moral evil either *per se* or *per accidens*. Nevertheless, it was impossible for there to be a human being in the natural order who should be free and at the same time incapable of sinning, so that it is true to say that God permitted a moral evil, though He permitted it only for the sake of a greater good.

There would, of course, be a great deal more to say on this subject, were one to introduce considerations drawn from theology, and any purely philosophical consideration of the problem is necessarily far less satisfactory than a treatment in which both theological and philosophical truths are utilised. The doctrines of the Fall and the Redemption, for instance, throw a light on the problem of evil which cannot be shed by purely philosophical reasoning. However, arguments based on revelation and dogmatic theology must be omitted here. St. Thomas's philosophical answer to the problem of evil in its relation to God can be summed up in the two statements, first that God did not will moral evil in any sense whatever but only permitted it for a greater good than could be attained by preventing it, that is, by not making man free, and secondly that though God did not will physical evil for its own sake, He may be said to have willed certain physical evils *per accidens*, for the perfection of the universe. I say 'certain *physical evils*', since St. Thomas does not mean to imply that God can be said to have willed all physical evils, even *per accidens*. Corruptibility or death pertains to a certain kind of being, but many physical evils and sufferings are not bound up with the perfection or good of the universe at all, but are the result of moral evil on man's part: they are not 'inevitable'. Such physical evils God only permitted.[1]

[1] On the subject of evil and its relation to God see, for example, *S.T.*, Ia, 19, 9; Ia, 48–9; *Contra Gent.*, 3, 4–5; *De Malo*, questions 1–3; *De Potentia*, 1, 6.

CHAPTER XXXVII

ST. THOMAS AQUINAS—VII: PSYCHOLOGY

One substantial form in man—The powers of the soul—The interior senses—Free will—The noblest faculty—Immortality—The active and passive intellects are not numerically the same in all men.

1. We have already seen[1] that St. Thomas maintained the Aristotelian doctrine of hylomorphism and that, departing from the views of his predecessors, he defended the unicity of the substantial form in the substance. It may be that at first St. Thomas accepted the existence of a *forma corporeitatis* as the first substantial form in a material substance;[2] but in any case he soon opposed this opinion and held that the specific substantial form informs prime matter immediately and not by the medium of any other substantial form. This doctrine he applied to man, maintaining that there is but one substantial form in the human *compositum.* This one substantial form is the rational soul, which informs matter directly: there is no *forma corporeitatis*, still less are there vegetative and sensitive substantial forms. The human being is a unity, and this unity would be impaired, were we to suppose a plurality of substantial forms. The name 'man' applies neither to the soul alone nor to the body alone, but to soul and body together, to the composite substance.

St. Thomas, then, follows Aristotle in stressing the unity of the human substance. It is the one soul in man which confers on him all his determinations as man, his corporeity (by informing prime matter), his vegetative, sensitive and intellectual operations. In a plant there is present only the vegetative principle or soul, conferring life and the powers of growth and reproduction; in the brute there is present only the sensitive soul which acts as the principle not only of vegetative life, but also of sensitive life; in man there is present only the rational principle or soul, which is not only the principle of the operations peculiar to itself, but also of the vegetative and sensitive functions. When death comes and the soul is separated from the body, the body disintegrates: it is not merely that rational functions cease, for the sensitive and

[1] Ch. XXXIII.

[2] Cf. *In* 1 *Sent.*, 8, 5, 2; *In* 2 *Sent.*, 3, 1, 1.

vegetative functions also cease: the one principle of all these operations no longer informs the matter which it previously informed and instead of the unified human substance there results a multiplicity of substances, the new substantial forms being educed from the potentiality of matter.

Clearly, therefore, the Platonic idea of the relation of soul to body was unacceptable to St. Thomas. It is the one individual man who perceives not only that he reasons and understands, but also that he feels, and exercises sensation. But one cannot have sensation without a body, so that the body, and not the soul only, must belong to man.[1] A man is generated when the rational soul is infused and a man dies when the rational soul departs from the body: there is no other substantial form in man than the rational soul and this soul exercises the functions of inferior forms, itself performing in the case of man what the vegetative soul does in the case of plants and the sensitive soul in the case of irrational animals.[2] It follows from this that the union of soul with body cannot be something unnatural: it cannot be a punishment to the soul for sin in a preceding state, as Origen thought. The human soul has the power of sensation, for example, but it cannot exercise this function without a body; it has the power of intellection, but it has no innate ideas and has to form its ideas in dependence on sense-experience, for which it needs a body; the soul, then, is united to a body because it needs it, because it is naturally the form of a body. The union of soul and body is not to the detriment, but to the good of the soul, *propter animam*. Matter exists for the form and not the other way about, and the soul is united to the body in order that it (the soul) may act according to its nature.[3]

2. But though St. Thomas emphasised the unity of man, the close union between soul and body, he held that there is a real distinction between the soul and its faculties, and between the faculties themselves. In God alone are the power of acting and the act itself identical with the substance, since in God alone is there no potentiality: in the human soul there are faculties or powers of acting which are in potentiality to their acts and which are to be distinguished according to their respective acts and objects.[4] Some of these powers or faculties belong to the soul as such and are not intrinsically dependent on a bodily organ, while

[1] *S.T.*, Ia, 76, 1. [2] *Ibid.*, Ia, 76, 4. [3] Cf. *ibid.*, Ia, 76, 5; Ia, 89, 1.
[4] *Ibid.*, Ia, 77, 1–3; *De Anima*, 1, *lectio* 2.

others belong to the *compositum* and cannot be exercised without the body: the former, therefore, remain in the soul even when it is separated from the body, whereas the latter remain in the separated soul only potentially or virtually (*virtute*), in the sense that the soul still has the remote power to exercise the faculties, but only if it were reunited with the body: in its separated state it cannot use them. For instance, the rational or intellectual faculty is not intrinsically dependent on the body, though in the state of union with the body there is a certain dependence in regard to the material of knowledge (in a sense to be explained later); but the power of sensation can obviously not be exercised without the body. On the other hand it cannot be exercised by the body without the soul. Its 'subject', therefore, is neither soul alone nor body alone but the human *compositum*. Sensation cannot be attributed simply to the soul using a body (as St. Augustine thought); body and soul play their respective parts in producing the act of sensation, and the power of sensation belongs to both in union rather to either of them separately.

In the powers or faculties there is a certain hierarchy. The vegetative faculty, comprising the powers of nutrition, growth and reproduction, has as its object simply the body united to the soul or living by means of the soul. The sensitive faculty (comprising the exterior senses, of sight, hearing, smell, taste, touch, and the interior senses of *sensus communis*, *phantasia* or imagination, *vis aestimativa* and *vis memorativa* or memory) has as its object, not simply the body of the sentient subject but rather every sensible body. The rational faculty (comprising the active and passive intellects) has as its object, not only sensible bodies but being in general. The higher the power, therefore, the wider and more comprehensive its object. The first general faculty is concerned with the subject's own body; but the other two faculties, the sensitive and intellectual, are also concerned with objects extrinsic to the subject itself, and a consideration of this fact shows us that there are other powers in addition to those already mentioned. If we consider the aptitude of the external object to be received in the subject through cognition, we find there are two kinds of faculty, sensitive and intellective, the former of which is more restricted in scope than the latter; but if we consider the inclination and tendency of the soul towards the external object, we find that there are two other powers, that of locomotion, by which the subject attains the object through its own motion, and that of appetition, by which the object is desired as an end or *finis*. The power of locomotion belongs to the level of sensitive life; but the power of appetition is twofold, comprising desire on the sensitive level, the sensitive appetite, and desire on the intellectual level, volition. On the vegetative level of life, therefore, we find the three powers of nutrition, growth and reproduction, on the sensitive level the five exterior senses, the four interior senses, the power of locomotion and the sensitive appetite, on the rational level of life the active intellect, the passive intellect and the will. In man they are all present.

These powers and faculties proceed from the essence of the soul as from their principle, but they are really distinguished from one another. They have different formal objects (sight, for example, has colour as its object), their activities are different, and so they are really distinct powers (*operatio sequitur esse*). But real distinctions must not be multiplied without a sufficient reason. For instance, one of the interior senses is the *vis memorativa* or sensitive memory, by means of which the animal remembers friend or foe, what has given it pleasure and what has injured it, and according to St. Thomas the memory of the past as past belongs to the sensitive memory, since the past as past refers to particulars and it is the sensitive memory which is concerned with particulars. If, however, we mean by memory the conservation of ideas or concepts, it is necessary to refer this to the intellect, and we can speak of the intellectual memory; but the intellectual memory is not a power really distinct from the intellect itself, more precisely the passive intellect: it is the intellect itself regarded under one of its aspects or functions. Again, the act of apprehending a truth, of resting in the apprehension of the truth, does not proceed from a power or faculty different from the faculty by which we reason discursively: *intellectus* and *ratio* are not distinct faculties, for it is the same mind which apprehends truth and reasons from that truth to another truth. Nor is the 'higher reason' (*ratio superior*) concerned with eternal things, a faculty different from the *ratio inferior*, by which we attain rational knowledge of temporal things. The two are one and the same faculty, though the faculty receives different names according to the objects of its different acts, as Augustine said. The same applies to the speculative and practical intellects, which are but one faculty.

3. It may be as well to say a few more words on the subject of the 'interior senses', which are common to animal as well as

human beings. St. Thomas observes[1] that Avicenna in his book *On the Soul* postulated five interior senses, but that in reality there are only four. What does St. Thomas mean by 'senses' in this connection? Obviously not senses in our use of the term, since when we use the word senses, we refer to the five exterior senses. Why, then, does he call them senses? To indicate that they are operations belonging to the level of sensitive life and that they do not involve reason. There must, for example, be an instinctive operation by which the bird 'judges' that the twigs it sees will be useful for building a nest: it cannot see the utility simply by vision, which is directed to colour, while on the other hand it does not reason or judge in the proper sense: it has, therefore, an 'interior sense' by which it apprehends the utility of the twigs.

First of all, there must be an interior sense by which the data of the special exterior senses are distinguished and collated. The eye sees colour, the ear hears sounds, but though the sense of sight distinguishes one colour from another, it cannot distinguish colour from sound, since it cannot hear; and for the same reason it cannot refer the sound to the coloured object seen, for example, when a man is talking to his dog. This function of distinction and collation is performed by the general sense or *sensus communis*. Secondly, the animal is able to conserve the forms apprehended by sense, and this function is performed by the imagination (*phantasia* or *imaginatio*), which is 'a certain treasury of the forms received through the senses'. Thirdly, the animal is able to apprehend things which it cannot perceive through the senses, for example, that something is useful to it, that someone or something is friendly or unfriendly, and this task is performed by the *vis aestimativa*, while, lastly, the *vis memorativa* conserves such apprehensions. As regards sensible forms, there is, says St. Thomas, no difference between men and animals, since they are affected by exterior sensible objects in the same way; but in regard to apprehensions of things which are not directly perceived by the exterior senses, there is a difference between men and animals. The latter perceive such things as utility and inutility, friendliness and hostility by a natural instinct, whereas man compares particular things. What in animals, therefore, he calls the *vis aestimativa naturalis*, St. Thomas calls *vis cogitativa* in the case of human beings. Something more than mere instinct is involved.

4. Besides the five exterior senses, the four interior senses, the

[1] *S.T.*, Ia, 78, 4.

power of locomotion, the sensitive appetite and the rational cognitive faculties (to which I shall return in the next chapter, when treating of St. Thomas's theory of knowledge), man has also will (*voluntas*). The will differs from the sensitive appetite, since it desires the good as such or the good in general (*bonum sub communi ratione boni*), whereas the sensitive appetite does not desire good in general, but the particular objects of desire presented by the senses. Moreover, the will is of its very nature orientated towards good in general, and it necessarily desires the good in general. This necessity is not, however, a necessity of coercion, a necessity which bears upon the will with violence; it proceeds from the will itself, which of its very nature desires the last end or happiness (*beatitudo*). The will, since it is an appetitive faculty, cannot be understood apart from its natural object of desire, its natural *finis*, and this object, says St. Thomas, following Aristotle, is beatitude, happiness, the good in general. We necessarily desire to be happy, we cannot help desiring it; but the necessity in question is not a necessity imposed from without by violence (*necessitas coactionis*) but a necessity of nature (*necessitas naturalis*) proceeding from the nature of the will.

Yet although man necessarily desires happiness, this does not mean that he is not free in regard to his particular choices. There are some particular goods which are not necessary to happiness, and a man is free to will them or not. Moreover, even though true happiness is to be found only in the possession of God, only in the attainment of the infinite Good, that does not mean that every man must have a conscious desire of God or that he must necessarily will those means which will bring him to God. In this life the intellect has not got that clear vision of God as the infinite good and only source of happiness which would be needed to determine the will: man necessarily desires happiness, but the connection between happiness and God is not so steadfastly clear to him that he is unable to will something other than God. In a sense, of course, he is always willing God, because he necessarily wills happiness and, *de facto*, happiness is to be found only in the attainment of God, the infinite Good; but owing to his lack of clear vision of God as the infinite Good, objects may appear to him as necessarily related to his happiness which are not so related, and he can place his happiness in something other than God. Whatever he wills, he wills as a good, real or apparent (he necessarily wills *sub ratione boni*), but he does not necessarily will the actual infinite Good. In an interpretative sense he may be said to be always willing God; but as far as conscious choice is concerned, he may will something other than God, even to the exclusion of God. If he shuts his eyes to the truth and turns his attention to sensual pleasures, for example, placing his happiness in them, he is morally guilty; but that does not alter the fact that the incompatibility between indulgence in inordinate sensual pleasure and the attainment of true happiness is not so compellingly self-evident to him that he cannot take indulgence in inordinate pleasure of sense as his end. One can take a parallel example from the activity of the intellect. If a man knows what the terms mean, it is impossible for him not to assent to the first principles in the intellectual order, for example, the principle of identity, but when a chain of reasoning is involved, as in a metaphysical proof of God's existence, he may refuse his assent, not because the argument is insufficient, but because he does not wish to assent and turns away his intellect from perceiving or dwelling on the necessary connection of the conclusion with the premisses. Similarly, a man necessarily wills *sub ratione boni*, he necessarily desires happiness; but he can turn his attention away from the necessary connection between happiness and God and allow something other than God to appear to him as the source of true happiness.

Free will (*liberum arbitrium*) is not a power or faculty different from the will; but there is a mental distinction between them, since the term 'will signifies the faculty as principle of all our volition, whether necessary (in regard to the end, happiness) or free (in regard to the choice of means to the end), whereas 'free will' signifies the same faculty as principle of our free choice of means to the end. As already mentioned, St. Thomas maintained that though man necessarily wills the end, happiness, he has no compelling vision of the connection between particular means and this end, and therefore he is free in regard to the choice of these means, being necessitated neither from without nor from within. That man is free follows from the fact that he is rational. A sheep 'judges' by a natural instinct that the wolf is to be avoided, but man judges that some good is to be attained or some evil to be avoided by a free act of his intelligence.[1] The reason, unlike instinct, is not determined in its judgement concerning particular choices. Choice concerns the means to the final end (happiness), and it is possible for a man to consider any particular object from

[1] *S.T.*, Ia, 83, 1.

more than one point of view: he may consider it under its aspect as a good and judge that it should be chosen or he may consider it under its aspect as evil, that is, as lacking some good, and judge that it should be avoided.[1] *Liberum arbitrium* is thus the power by which a man is able to judge freely.[2] It might seem, then, that freedom belongs to the intellect and not to will; but St. Thomas observes[3] that when it is said that *liberum arbitrium* is the power by which a man is able to judge freely, the reference is not to any kind of judgement but to the decisive judgement of choice which puts an end to the deliberation which arises from the fact that a man can consider a possible object of choice from different points of view. For example, if there is a question of my going for a walk or not going for a walk, I can regard the walk as a good, as healthy exercise, or as evil, as taking up time which should be given to writing a letter for the afternoon post. The decisive judgement which says that I will go for a walk (or not, as the case may be) is made under the influence of the will. *Liberum arbitrium*, therefore, is the will, but it designates the will not absolutely, but in its relation to the reason. Judgement as such belongs to the reason, but freedom of judgement belongs immediately to the will. Still, it is true that St. Thomas's account of freedom is intellectualist in character.

5. This intellectualism is apparent in his answer to the question whether the intellect or the will is the nobler faculty. St. Thomas answers that, absolutely speaking, the intellect is the nobler faculty, since the intellect through cognition possesses the object, contains it in itself through mental assimilation, whereas the will tends towards the object as external, and it is more perfect to possess the perfection of the object in oneself than to tend towards it as existing outside oneself. In regard to corporeal objects, therefore, knowledge of them is more perfect and nobler than volition in respect to them, since by knowledge we possess the forms of these objects in ourselves, and these forms exist in a nobler way in the rational soul than they do in the corporeal objects. Similarly, the essence of the beatific vision consists in the act of knowledge by which we possess God. On the other hand, although possession of the object by the intellect is in itself more perfect than tending towards the object by volition, the will may be nobler than the intellect in certain respects, *secundum quid*, because of accidental reasons. For example, in this life our knowledge

[1] *S.T.*, Ia, IIae, 13, 6. [2] *De Veritate*, 24, 4 and 6. [3] *Ibid.*, 24, 6.

of God is imperfect and analogical, we know God only indirectly, whereas the will tends to God directly: love of God is, therefore, more perfect than knowledge of God. In the case of objects which are less noble than the soul, corporeal objects, we can have immediate knowledge, and such knowledge is more perfect than volition; but in the case of God, an object which transcends the human soul, we have only mediate knowledge in this life, and our love of God is more perfect than our knowledge of God. In the beatific vision in heaven, however, when the soul sees the essence of God immediately, the intrinsic superiority of intellect to will reasserts itself, as it were. In this way St. Thomas, while adopting the intellectualist attitude of Aristotle, interprets it in a Christian setting.[1]

6. We have seen that St. Thomas rejected the Platonic-Augustinian view of the relation of soul to body and adopted the Aristotelian view of the soul as form of the body, emphasising the closeness of the union between the two. There is no *forma corporeitatis*, there is but one substantial form in man, the rational soul, which directly informs prime matter and is the cause of all human activities on the vegetative, sensitive and intellectual levels: sensation is an act not of the soul using a body, but of the *compositum*; we have no innate ideas, but the mind is dependent on sense-experience for its knowledge. The question arises, therefore, whether the closeness of the union between soul and body has not been so emphasised that the possible subsistence of the human soul apart from the body must be ruled out. In other words, is not the Aristotelian doctrine of the relation of soul to body incompatible with personal immortality? If one starts with the Platonic theory of the soul, immortality is assured, but the union of soul and body is rendered difficult to understand; whereas if one starts with the Aristotelian theory of the soul, it might seem that one has to sacrifice immortality, that the soul is so closely bound to the body that it cannot subsist apart from the body.

The soul is indeed the form of the body and, according to St. Thomas, it always retains its aptitude to inform a body, precisely because it is naturally the form of the body; but it is none the less a rational soul and its powers are not exhausted in informing the body. When actually dealing with the immortality of the soul St. Thomas argues that the soul is incorruptible because it is a subsistent form. A thing which corrupts is corrupted either by

[1] *De Veritate*, 22, 11; cf. *S.T.*, Ia, 82, 3.

itself (*per se*) or accidentally (*per accidens*), that is, through the corruption of something else on which it depends for existence. The soul of the brute is dependent on the body for all its operations and corrupts when the body corrupts (*corruptio per accidens*): the rational soul, however, being a subsistent form, cannot be affected by the corruption of the body on which it does not intrinsically depend.[1] If this were all St. Thomas had to say by way of proving immortality, he would obviously be guilty of a gross *petitio principii*, since it is presupposed that the human soul is a *forma subsistens*, and this is precisely the point which has to be proved. St. Thomas argues, however, that the rational soul must be spiritual and a subsistent form, because it is capable of knowing the natures of all bodies. If it were material, it would be determined to a specified object, as the organ of vision is determined to the perception of colour. Again, if it depended intrinsically on a bodily organ, it would be confined to the knowledge of some particular kind of bodily object, which is not the case,[2] while if it were itself a body, material, it could not reflect on itself.[3] For these and other reasons the human soul, which is a rational soul, must be immaterial, i.e. spiritual, from which it follows that it is incorruptible or naturally immortal. Physically speaking, it could, of course, be annihilated by the God who created it; but its immortality follows from its nature and is not simply gratuitous, save in the sense that its very existence, like the existence of any other creature, is gratuitous.

St. Thomas argues also from the desire of persistence in being. There is a natural desire for immortality and a natural desire, as implanted by God, cannot be in vain.[4] 'It is impossible for a natural appetite to be in vain. But man has a natural appetite for perpetual persistence in being. This is clear from the fact that existence (*esse*) is desired by all things, but a man has an intellectual apprehension of *esse* as such, and not only of *esse* here and now as the brutes have. Man therefore attains immortality as regards his soul, by which he apprehends *esse* as such and without temporal limit.'[5] Man, as distinct from the irrational animal, can conceive perpetual existence, divorced from the present moment, and to this apprehension there corresponds a natural desire for immortality. As this desire must have been implanted by the Author of Nature, it cannot be in vain (*frustra* or *inane*). Against

[1] *S.T.*, Ia, 75, 6; *Contra Gent.*, 2, 79. [2] *S.T.*, Ia, 75, 2. [3] *Contra Gent.*, 2, 49.
[4] *S.T.*, Ia, 75, 6. [5] *Contra Gent.*, 2, 79.

this Duns Scotus later argued that, as far as a natural desire (*desiderium naturale*) is concerned, man and brute are on a level in that both naturally shun death, while in regard to an elicited or conscious desire we have first to show that its fulfilment is possible before we can argue that it must be fulfilled.[1] One might reply that the possibility of the fulfilment of the desire is shown by proving that the soul is not intrinsically dependent on the body but is spiritual. This would be to admit that the argument from the spirituality of the soul is fundamental.

In view of St. Thomas's epistemology, of his insistence on the origin of human ideas in sense-experience and on the rôle of the phantasm in the formation of such ideas, it might appear that he contradicts himself when he says that the human mind is not intrinsically dependent on the body, and it might also appear that the soul in a state of separation would be incapable of intellectual activity. In regard to the first point, however, he maintains that the mind needs the body for its activity not as an organ of mental activity, for this is an activity of the mind alone, but because of the natural object of the human mind in this life, when conjoined to a body. In other words, the mind is not intrinsically dependent on the body for its subsistence. Can it, then, exercise its activity in a state of separation from the body? Yes, for its mode of cognition follows the state in which it is. When united to the body, the rational soul does not come to know things save *convertendo se ad phantasmata*; but when it is in a state of separation it is no longer unable to know itself and other souls perfectly and directly, the angels imperfectly. It might seem indeed that in this case it is better for the soul to be in a state of separation from the body than united to it, since spirits are nobler objects of knowledge than corporeal things; but St. Thomas cannot admit this, since he has insisted that it is natural for the soul to be united to the body and that their union is for the good of the soul. He does not hesitate, then, to draw the conclusion that the state of separation is *praeter naturam* and that the soul's mode of cognition in the state of separation is also *praeter naturam*.[2]

7. When St. Thomas proves the immortality of the soul, he is naturally referring to personal immortality. Against the Averroists he argues that the intellect is not a substance distinct from the human soul and common to all men, but that it is multiplied 'according to the multiplication of bodies'.[3] It is impossible to

[1] *Opus Oxon.*, 4, 43, 2, nos. 29ff. [2] *S.T.*, Ia, 89, 1 ff. [3] *Ibid.*, Ia, 76, 2.

explain the diversity of ideas and intellectual operations in different men on the supposition that all men have but one intellect. It is not only sensations and phantasms which differ from man to man but their intellectual lives and activities as well. It is as absurd to suppose that they have one intellect as it would be to suppose that they have one vision.

It is important to realise that it is not the opinion of Avicenna concerning the unicity and separate character of the *active* intellect which necessarily does away with personal immortality (some mediaeval philosophers who certainly maintained personal immortality identified the active intellect with God or God's activity in the soul), but rather the opinion of Averroes concerning the unicity and separate character of the *passive* as well as of the active intellect. That Averroes was the chief enemy on this point St. Thomas makes quite clear at the beginning of his *De unitate intellectus contra Averroistas*. If the Averroistic theory is accepted 'it follows that after death nothing remains of men's souls but one intellect; and in this way the bestowal of rewards and punishments is done away with.' This is not to say, of course, that St. Thomas accepted the theory of the unicity of the active intellect: he argues against it in the *Summa contra Gentiles*, for example,[1] as also in the *Summa Theologica*.[2] One of his arguments is to the effect that if the active intellect were one in all men, then its functioning would be independent of the individual's control and would be constant, whereas in point of fact we can pursue intellectual activity at will and abandon it at will. Incidentally, St. Thomas interprets the notoriously obscure passage in Aristotle's *De Anima*[3] as teaching the individual character of the active intellect in individual men. It is impossible to say with certainty that the Thomist interpretation of Aristotle is wrong, though I incline to this opinion; but the rightness or wrongness of his interpretation of Aristotle obviously does not affect the question of the truth or falsity of his own idea of the active intellect.[4]

Against the unicity of the passive intellect St. Thomas argues in the *De unitate intellectus contra Averroistas* and in the *Summa contra Gentiles*.[5] His arguments presuppose for the most part the Aristotelian psychology and epistemology; but the presupposition is only to be expected, not only because St. Thomas accepted the Aristotelian doctrine as he understood and interpreted it, but also

[1] 2, 76. [2] Ia, 79, 4–5. [3] 3, 5; 430 a. 17ff.

[4] On Aristotle, see *Summa contra Gentiles*, 2, 78, and the Commentary on the *De Anima*, 3, *lectio* 10. [5] 2, 73–5.

because the Averroists were Aristotelians. To say, then, that St. Thomas presupposed the Aristotelian psychology and epistemology is simply to say that he tried to show the Averroists that their notion of the unitary and separate character of the passive intellect was inconsistent with their own principles. If the soul is the form of the body, how could the passive intellect be one in all men? One principle could not be the form of a plurality of substances. Again, if the passive intellect were a separate principle, it would be eternal; it should, then, contain all the *species intelligibiles* which have ever been received, and every man should be able to understand all those things which have ever been understood by men, which is manifestly not the case. Furthermore, if the active intellect were separate and eternal, it would be functioning from eternity and the passive intellect, also supposed to be separate and eternal, would be receiving from eternity; but this would render the senses and imagination unnecessary for intellectual operations, whereas experience shows that they are indispensable. And how could one explain the different intellectual capacities of different men? Men's differences in this respect certainly depend to some extent on their different infra-intellectual capacities.

It may be somewhat difficult for us to-day to understand the excitement produced by the Averroistic theory and the interest it aroused; but it was obviously incompatible with the Christian doctrines of immortality and of sanctions in the next life, and even if St. Thomas shows a desire to dissociate Aristotle from Averroes, the moral and religious consequences of the Averroistic doctrine were more important to him than Averroes's attempt to father his doctrine on the Greek philosopher. Against the Averroists Augustinians and Aristotelians made common cause. One might compare the reaction provoked by modern metaphysical and psychological systems which appear to endanger the human personality. On this point absolute idealism, for instance, aroused opposition on the part of philosophers who were otherwise sharply divided among themselves.

CHAPTER XXXVIII

ST. THOMAS AQUINAS—VIII: KNOWLEDGE

'Theory of knowledge' in St. Thomas—The process of knowledge; knowledge of the universal and of the particular—The soul's knowledge of itself—The possibility of metaphysics.

1. To look for an epistemology in St. Thomas, in the sense of a justification of knowledge, a proof or attempted proof of the objectivity of knowledge in face of subjective idealism of one kind or another, would be to look in vain. That everyone, even the self-styled sceptic, is convinced that knowledge of some sort is attainable was as clear to St. Thomas as it was to St. Augustine, and so far as there is a problem of knowledge for St. Thomas it is rather how to safeguard and justify metaphysics in face of the Aristotelian psychology than to justify the objectivity of our knowledge of the extramental world in face of a subjective idealism which had not yet arisen or to show the legitimacy of metaphysics in face of a Kantian criticism which still lay far in the future. This is not to say, of course, that the Thomist principles cannot be developed in such a way as to afford answers to subjective idealism and Kantianism; but one should not be guilty of the anachronism of making the historic Thomas answer questions with which he was not actually faced. Indeed, to treat St. Thomas's theory of knowledge separately from his psychological doctrine is itself something of an anachronism, yet I think it is capable of being justified, since it is out of the psychology that a problem of knowledge arises, and one can, for the sake of convenience at least, treat this problem separately. For the purpose of making this problem clear it is necessary first of all to give a brief sketch of the way in which we attain our natural ideas and knowledge, according to Aquinas.

2. Corporeal objects act upon the organs of sense, and sensation is an act of the *compositum*, of soul and body, not of the soul alone using a body, as Augustine thought. The senses are naturally determined to the apprehension of particulars, they cannot apprehend universals. Brutes have sensation, but they have no grasp of general ideas. The phantasm or image, which arises in the imagination and which represents the particular material object

perceived by the senses, is itself particular, the phantasm of a particular object or objects. Human intellectual cognition, however, is of the universal: the human being in his intellectual operations apprehends the form of the material object in abstraction; he apprehends a universal. Through sensation we can apprehend only particular men or trees, for example, and the interior images or phantasms of men or trees are always particular. Even if we have a composite image of man, not representing any one actual man distinctly but representing many confusedly, it is still particular, since the images or parts of the images of particular actual men coalesce to form an image which may be 'generic' in respect of actual particular men but which is itself none the less particular, the image of a particular imagined man. The mind, however, can and does conceive the general idea of man as such, which includes all men in its extension. An image of man certainly will not apply to all men, but the intellectual idea of man, even though conceived in dependence on the sensitive apprehension of particular men, applies to all men. The image of a man must be either of a man who has or of a man who has not some hair on his head. If the former, it does not in that respect represent bald men; if the latter, it does not in that respect represent men who are not bald; but if we form the concept of man as a rational animal, this idea covers all men, whether they are bald or not, white or black, tall or short, because it is the idea of the essence of man.

How, then, is the transition from sensitive and particular knowledge to intellectual cognition effected? Although sensation is an activity of soul and body together, the rational and spiritual soul cannot be affected directly by a material thing or by the phantasm: there is need, therefore, of an activity on the part of the soul, since the concept cannot be formed simply passively. This activity is the activity of the active intellect which 'illumines' the phantasm and abstracts from it the universal or 'intelligible species'. St. Thomas thus speaks of illumination, but he does not use the word in the full Augustinian sense (not at least according to what is probably the true interpretation of Augustine's meaning); he means that the active intellect by its natural power and without any special illumination from God renders visible the intelligible aspect of the phantasm, reveals the formal and potentially universal element contained implicitly in the phantasm. The active intellect then abstracts the universal element by itself, producing in the passive intellect the *species impressa.* The reaction of the passive intellect to this determination by the active intellect is the *verbum mentis* (*species expressa*), the universal concept in the full sense. The function of the active intellect is purely active, to abstract the universal element from the particular elements of the phantasm, to cause in the passive intellect the *species impressa.* The intellect of man contains no innate ideas but is in potentiality to the reception of concepts: it has, therefore, to be reduced to act, and this reduction to act must be effected by a principle itself in act. As this active principle has no ready-made ideas of itself to supply, it must draw its materials from what is provided by the senses, and this means that it must abstract the intelligible element from the phantasm. To abstract means to isolate intellectually the universal apart from the particularising notes. Thus the active intellect abstracts the universal essence of man from a particular phantasm by leaving out all particular notes which confine it to a particular man or particular men. As the active intellect is purely active, it cannot impress the universal on itself; it impresses it on the potential element of the human intellect, on the passive intellect, and the reaction to this impression is the concept in the full sense, the *verbum mentis.*

It is important to realise, however, that the abstract concept is not the object of cognition, but the means of cognition. If the concept, the modification of the intellect, were itself the object of knowledge, then our knowledge would be a knowledge of ideas, not of things existing extramentally, and the judgements of science would concern not things outside the mind but concepts within the mind. In actual fact, however, the concept is the likeness of the object produced in the mind and is thus the means by which the mind knows the object: in St. Thomas's language it is *id quo intelligitur*, not *id quod intelligitur.*[1] Of course, the mind has the power of reflecting on its own modifications and so can turn the concept into an object; but it is only secondarily an object of knowledge, primarily it is the instrument of knowledge. By saying this St. Thomas avoids putting himself in a position which would be that of subjective idealism and which would land him in the difficulties attending that form of idealism. The theory he actually contrasts with his own is the theory of Plato; but that does not alter the fact that by adopting the attitude he did he escaped a snare from which it is practically impossible to extricate oneself.

[1] *S.T.*, Ia, 5, 2.

As he held that the intellect knows directly the essence, the universal, St. Thomas drew the logical conclusion that the human mind does not know directly singular material things. The emphasis is, of course, on 'mind' and 'know', since it cannot be denied that the human being apprehends particular material objects sensitively: the object of sense is precisely the sensible particular. The intellect, however, comes to know by abstracting the intelligible species from the individualising matter, and in this case it can have direct knowledge of universals only. Nevertheless, even after abstracting the intelligible species, the intellect exercises its activity of knowing only through a 'conversion', a turning of attention to the phantasms in which it apprehends the universals, and in this way it has a reflexive or indirect knowledge of the particular things represented by the phantasms. Thus the sensitive apprehension of Socrates enables the mind to abstract the universal 'man'; but the abstract idea is a means of knowledge, an instrument of knowledge to the intellect only in so far as the latter adverts to the phantasm, and so it is able to form the judgement that Socrates is a man. It is thus not true to say that the intellect, according to St. Thomas, has no knowledge of corporeal particulars: what he held was that the mind has only an indirect knowledge of such particulars, the direct object of knowledge being the universal.[1] But this should not be taken to imply that the primary object of intellectual cognition is the abstract idea as such: the mind apprehends the formal element, the potentially universal element in Socrates, for example, and abstracts this from the individualising matter. In technical language its primary object of knowledge is the direct universal, the universal apprehended in the particular: it is only secondarily that it apprehends the universal precisely as universal, the reflexive universal.

Two explanatory remarks should be added. St. Thomas explains that when he says that the mind abstracts the universal from the corporeal particular by abstracting it from the individualising matter, he means that when the mind abstracts the idea of man, for example, it abstracts it from *this* flesh and *these* bones, that is, from the particular individualising matter, not from matter in general, 'intelligible matter' (i.e. substance as subject to quantity). Corporeality enters into the idea of man as such, though particular matter does not enter into the universal idea of man.[2] Secondly, St. Thomas does not mean to imply that it is the particular thing

[1] *S.T.*, Ia, 86, 1. [2] *Ibid.*, Ia, 85, 1.

as such which cannot be the direct object of intellectual cognition, but rather the particular sensible or corporeal object. In other words, the particular corporeal object is debarred from being the direct object of intellectual cognition not precisely because it is particular but because it is material and the mind knows only by abstracting from matter as principle of individuation, that is, from this or that matter.[1]

3. According to St. Thomas, then, the human mind is originally in potentiality to knowledge; but it has no innate ideas. The only sense in which ideas are innate is that the mind has a natural capacity for abstracting and forming ideas: as far as actual ideas go, the mind is originally a *tabula rasa*. Moreover, the source of the mind's knowledge is sense-perception, since the soul, the form of the body, has as its natural object of knowledge the essences of material objects. The rational soul knows itself only by means of its acts, apprehending itself, not directly in its essence but in the act by which it abstracts intelligible species from sensible objects.[2] The soul's knowledge of itself is not, therefore, an exception to the general rule that all our knowledge begins with sense-perception and is dependent on sense-perception. This fact St. Thomas expresses by saying that the intellect, when united to a body in the present life, cannot come to know anything *nisi convertendo se ad phantasmata*.[3] The human mind does not think without the presence of a phantasm, as is clear from introspection, and it is dependent on the phantasm, as is shown by the fact that a disordered power of imagination (as in mad people) hinders knowledge; and the reason for this is that the cognitive power is proportioned to its natural object.[4] In brief, the human soul, as Aristotle said, understands nothing without a phantasm, and we can say, *nihil in intellectu quod prius non fuerit in sensu*.

4. From this it obviously follows that the human mind cannot in this life attain a direct knowledge of immaterial substances, which are not and cannot be the object of the senses.[5] But the problem also arises whether there can be metaphysical knowledge at all on these premisses, whether the human mind can rise above the things of sense and attain any knowledge of God, for example, since God cannot be an object of sense. If our intellects are dependent on the phantasm, how can they know those objects of which there are no phantasms, which do not act on the senses?[6]

[1] *S.T.*, Ia, 86, 1, *ad* 3. [2] *Ibid.*, Ia, 87, 1. [3] *Ibid.*, Ia, 84, 7.
[4] *Ibid.*, Ia, 84, 7. [5] *Ibid.*, Ia, 88, 1. [6] *Ibid.*, Ia, 84, 7, *ad* 3.

On the principle, *nihil in intellectu quod prius non fuerit in sensu*, how can we attain knowledge of God when we cannot say *quod Deus prius fuerit in sensu*? In other words, once given the Thomist psychology and epistemology, it would appear that the Thomist natural theology is inevitably invalidated: we cannot transcend the objects of sense and are debarred from any knowledge of spiritual objects.

In order to understand St. Thomas's reply to this serious objection, it is necessary to recall his doctrine of intellect as such. The senses are necessarily determined to one particular kind of object, but the intellect, being immaterial, is the faculty of apprehending being. Intellect as such is directed towards all being. The object of the intellect is the intelligible: nothing is intelligible except in so far as it is in act, partakes of being, and all that is in act is intelligible in so far as it is in act, i.e. partakes of being. If we consider the human intellect precisely as intellect, we must admit, then, that its primary object is being. *Intellectus respicit suum obiectum secundum communem rationem entis; eo quod intellectus possibilis est quo est omnia fieri.*[1] *Primo autem in conceptione intellectus cadit ens; quia secundum hoc unumquodque cognoscibile est, inquantum est actu . . . Unde ens est proprium obiectum intellectus.*[2] The first movement of the intellect is thus towards being, not towards sensible being in particular, and the intellect can know the essence of a material thing only in so far as it is being: it is only in the second place that a particular kind of intellect, the human intellect, is directed towards a particular kind of being. Owing to its embodied state and the necessity of the *conversio ad phantasma* the human intellect has, in its embodied state, the sensible object as the natural and 'proper' object of its apprehension, but it does not lose its orientation towards being in general. As *human* intellect it must start from sense, from material beings, but as human *intellect* it can proceed beyond sense, not being confined to material essences, though it can do this only in so far as the immaterial objects are manifested in and through the sensible world, in so far as the material things have a relation to immaterial objects. As embodied intellect, as a *tabula rasa*, the natural object of which is the material essence, the intellect does not and cannot by its own power apprehend God directly; but sensible objects, as finite and contingent, reveal their relation to God, so that the intellect can know that God exists. Moreover,

[1] *S.T.*, Ia, 79, 7. [2] *Ibid.*, Ia, 5, 2.

sensible objects, as the effects of God, manifest God to some extent, so that the intellect can come to know something of God's nature, though this knowledge cannot (naturally) be more than analogical. The necessity of the *conversio ad phantasma* means that we cannot know God directly, but we can know Him in so far as sensible objects manifest His existence and enable us to attain an analogical, indirect and imperfect knowledge of His nature: we can know God *ut causam, et per excessum, et per remotionem.*[1]

A presupposition of this position is the activity of the human intellect. If the human intellect were merely passive, if the *conversio ad phantasma* meant that ideas were caused simply passively, there could obviously be no natural knowledge of God, since sensible objects are not God and of God and other immaterial beings *non sunt phantasmata.* It is the active power of the intellect which enables it to read off, as it were, the relation to immaterial being in sensible being. Sensible cognition is not the total and perfect cause of our intellectual cognition, but is rather the *materia causae* of intellectual cognition: the phantasm is made actually intelligible by the active intellect through its abstractive operation. Inasmuch, then, as sensitive cognition is not the total cause of intellectual cognition, 'it is nothing to be astonished at if intellectual cognition extends farther than sensitive cognition'.[2] The human intellect, as united to a body, has as its natural object the essences of material things, but by means of these essences it can ascend to 'some sort of knowledge of invisible things'. These immaterial objects we can know only *per remotionem,* by denying of them the characteristics peculiar to sensible objects, or analogically; but we could not know them at all, were it not for the active power of the intellect.[3]

A further difficulty, already mentioned, remains. How can there be any positive content to our idea of God, or indeed of any spiritual object? If we say, for example, that God is personal, we obviously do not mean to ascribe to God human personality. If, however, we simply mean that God is not less than what we know as personal, is there any positive content to our idea of divine personality? Is 'not-less-than-personal' a positive idea? If we state it in affirmative terms, 'more-than-personal', has it a positive content? If it has not, then we are confined to the *via negativa* and can know God only *per remotionem.* But St. Thomas does not

[1] *S.T.*, Ia, 84, 7 *ad* 3.
[2] *Ibid.*, Ia, 84, 6, *in corpore* and *ad* 3.
[3] Cf. *ibid.*, Ia, 84, 7, *in corpore* and *ad* 3.

adhere simply to the *via negativa*: he utilises also the *via affirmativa*, maintaining that we can know God *per excessum*. Now, if when we ascribe wisdom, for instance, to God, we say that we are ascribing wisdom *modo eminentiori*, it is difficult to see what the content of our idea of divine wisdom actually is. It must be based on human wisdom, which is the only wisdom we experience naturally and directly; and yet it cannot be precisely human wisdom. But if it is human wisdom without the limitations and forms of human wisdom, what positive content does the idea possess, when we have no experience of wisdom without limitations? It would seem that if one is determined to maintain that the idea has a positive content, one must say either that the idea of human wisdom plus a negation of its limitations is a positive idea or, with Scotus, that we can attain an idea of the essence of wisdom, so to speak, which can be predicated univocally of God and man. The latter theory, though helpful in some ways, is not altogether satisfactory, since neither St. Thomas nor Scotus would hold that wisdom or any other perfection is realised univocally in God and creatures. As to the first answer, it may seem at first hearing to constitute an evasion of the difficulty; but reflection will show that to say that God is wise, meaning that God is more than wise (in the human sense), is not at all the same thing as saying that God is not wise (in the human sense). A stone is not wise (in the human sense), neither is it more than wise: it is less than wise. It is true that if we use the word 'wise' as signifying precisely the wisdom we experience, namely human wisdom, we can say with truth not only that the stone is not wise, but also that God is not wise; but the meaning of the two statements is not the same, and if the meaning is not the same, there must be a positive content in the statement that God is not wise (i.e. that God is more than wise in the specifically human sense). The statement, therefore, that God is wise ('wise' meaning infinitely more than wise in the human sense) has a positive content. To demand that the content of analogical ideas should be perfectly clear and expressible, so that they could be understood perfectly in terms of human experience, would be to misunderstand altogether the nature of analogy. St. Thomas was no rationalist, though he allowed that we can attain to *aliqualis cognitio Dei*. The infinity of the object, God, means that the finite human mind can attain no adequate and perfect idea of God's nature; but it does not mean that it cannot attain an imperfect and inadequate notion of God's nature. To know that

God understands is to know something positive about God, since it tells us at the very least that God is not irrational like a stone or a plant, even though to know what the divine understanding is in itself exceeds our power of comprehension.

To return to the example of personality. The assertion that God is personal depends on the argument that the necessary Being and first Cause cannot be less perfect than what proceeds from it and depends on it. On the other hand, the Aristotelian-Thomist psychology and epistemology prevent one from saying that an argument of this kind will afford any adequate idea of what the divine personality is in itself. If one claimed that one had such an idea, it would be derived from experience and it would inevitably represent the data of experience. In practice this would mean that one would affirm that God is *a* Person, and the consequence would be a contradiction between revelation and philosophy. If, however, one realises that one can by philosophical argument alone attain no adequate idea of the divine personality, one will realise that all one is entitled to say from the philosophical viewpoint is that God is personal, not that God is *a* Person. When revelation informs us that God is three Persons in one Nature, our knowledge of God is extended, but no contradiction between theology and philosophy is involved. Moreover, when we say that God is personal, we really mean that He is not less than what we experience as personality, in the sense that the perfection of personality must be in Him in the only manner in which it can be in an infinite Being. If it is objected that this is to beg the question, since the question is precisely whether personality and infinity are compatible, one can reply that the proofs of God's personality and of His infinity are independent, so that we know that personality and infinity must be compatible, even though we have no direct experience of the divine personality or of the divine infinity. That there is a positive content of some sort to our idea of divine personality is shown by the fact that the meaning in the statement 'God is super-personal' (i.e. more than that which we directly experience as personality) is different from the meaning in the statement 'God is not personal' (i.e. in any sense, just as a stone is not personal). If we had reason to believe that God were not personal in the sense in which a stone is not personal, we should see the uselessness of worship and prayer; but the statement that God is personal suggests immediately that worship and prayer are in place, even though we have no adequate idea of what the divine personality is in itself. Of an infinite Being we can have but a finite and analogical natural knowledge, precisely because we ourselves are finite; but a finite and imperfect knowledge is not the same thing as no knowledge at all.

CHAPTER XXXIX

ST. THOMAS AQUINAS—IX: MORAL THEORY

Eudaemonism—The vision of God—Good and bad—The virtues —The natural law—The eternal law and the foundation of morality in God—Natural virtues recognised by St. Thomas which were not recognised by Aristotle; the virtue of religion.

To treat the moral theory of St. Thomas in detail would be impracticable here, but a discussion of some important points may help to show its relation to the Aristotelian ethic.

1. In the *Nicomachean Ethics* Aristotle argues that every agent acts for an end and that the human agent acts for happiness, with a view to the acquisition of happiness. Happiness, he says, must consist in an activity, primarily in the activity which perfects the highest faculty in man directed to the highest and noblest objects. He comes to the conclusion, therefore, that human happiness consists primarily in *theoria*, in contemplation of the highest objects, chiefly in the contemplation of the unmoved Mover, God, though he held that the enjoyment of other goods, such as friendship and, in moderation, external goods, is necessary to perfect happiness.[1] Aristotle's ethic was thus eudaemonistic in character, teleological, and markedly intellectualist, since it is clear that for him contemplation meant philosophical contemplation: he was not referring to a religious phenomenon, such as the ecstasy of Plotinus. Moreover, the end (*telos*) of moral activity is an end to be acquired in this life: as far as the ethics of Aristotle are concerned there is no hint of any vision of God in the next life, and it is indeed questionable whether he believed in personal immortality at all. Aristotle's truly happy man is the philosopher, not the saint.

Now, St. Thomas adopted a similar eudaemonological and teleological standpoint, and his theory of the end of human conduct is in some respects intellectualist; but a change of emphasis soon becomes visible which marks a very considerable difference between his ethical theory and that of Aristotle. The only acts of man which fall properly within the moral sphere are free acts, acts which proceed from man precisely as man, as a rational and free

[1] For a fuller treatment of the Aristotelian ethic, see the first volume of this history, pp. 332–50.

being. These human acts (*actiones humanae*, as distinguished from *actiones hominis*) proceed from man's will, and the object of the will is the good (*bonum*). It is the prerogative of man to act for an end which he has apprehended, and every human act is performed for an apprehended end; but the particular end or good, for the attainment of which a particular human act is performed, does not and cannot fully perfect and satisfy the human will, which is set towards the universal good and can find its satisfaction only in the attainment of the universal good. What is the universal good in the concrete? It cannot consist in riches, for example, for riches are simply a means to an end, whereas the universal good is necessarily the final end and cannot be itself a means to a further end. It cannot consist in sensible pleasure, since this perfects only the body, not the whole man; nor can it consist in power, which does not perfect the whole man or satisfy the will completely and which, moreover, can be abused, whereas it is inconceivable that the ultimate and universal good can be abused or employed for an unworthy or evil purpose. It cannot consist even in consideration of the speculative sciences, since philosophic speculation certainly does not satisfy completely the human intellect and will. Our natural knowledge is drawn from sense-experience; yet man aspires to a knowledge of the ultimate cause as it is in itself, and this cannot be acquired by metaphysics. Aristotle may have said that the good of man consists in the consideration of the speculative sciences, but he was speaking of imperfect happiness, such as is attainable in this life. Perfect happiness, the ultimate end, is not to be found in any created thing, but only in God, who is Himself the supreme and infinite Good. God is the universal good in the concrete, and though He is the end of all things, of both rational and irrational creatures, it is only rational creatures who can attain this final good by way of knowledge and love: it is only rational creatures who can attain the vision of God in which alone perfect happiness lies. In this life man can know that God exists and he can attain an imperfect and analogical notion of God's nature, but it is only in the next life that he can know God as He is in Himself and no other end can fully satisfy man.[1]

Aristotle, says St. Thomas, was speaking of imperfect happiness such as is attainable in this life; but Aristotle, as I have already mentioned, says nothing in the *Ethics* of any other happiness. His

[1] On the foregoing, see particularly *S.T.*, Ia, IIae, questions 1–3.

ethic was an ethic of human conduct in this life, whereas St. Thomas has not proceeded far before he has brought in consideration of the perfect happiness attainable only in the next life, this happiness consisting principally in the vision of God, though it also includes, of course, satisfaction of the will, while other goods, such as the society of friends, contribute to the *bene esse* of beatitude, though no good save God is *necessary* for happiness.[1] At once, therefore, St. Thomas's moral theory is seen to move on a different plane from that of Aristotle, since however much St. Thomas may use Aristotle's language, the introduction of the next life and of the vision of God into moral theory is foreign to the thought of Aristotle.[2] What Aristotle calls happiness, St. Thomas calls imperfect happiness or temporal happiness or happiness as attainable in this life, and this imperfect happiness he regards as ordered to perfect happiness, which is attainable only in the next life and consists principally in the vision of God.

2. St. Thomas's statement that the perfect happiness of man consists in the vision of God raises a very difficult problem for any interpreter of the Saint's moral theory, a problem which is of much greater importance than might at first appear. The ordinary way of presenting the Thomist ethic has been to assimilate it to the ethic of Aristotle so far as is consistent with St. Thomas's position as a Christian, and to say that St. Thomas as moral philosopher considers man 'in the natural order' without reference to his supernatural end. When he speaks of beatitude as a moral philosopher he would, therefore, be speaking of natural beatitude, that attainment of the supreme Good, God, which is open to man in the natural order, without supernatural grace being necessary. His difference from Aristotle would lie in the fact that he, unlike the latter, introduces consideration of the next life, concerning which Aristotle is silent. Beatitude would consist principally in the natural knowledge and love of God attainable in this life (imperfect natural beatitude) and in the next life (perfect natural beatitude). Those actions would be good which lead to or are compatible with the attainment of such beatitude, while those actions would be bad which are incompatible with the attainment of such beatitude. The fact that St. Thomas speaks of the attainment of the vision of the divine essence (which is man's supernatural end and is unattainable without supernatural grace) when

[1] See *S.T.*, Ia, IIae, 4.

[2] This is true of St. Thomas's moral teaching in the *Summae*. I do not mean to imply that St. Thomas rejected the possibility of a purely philosophical ethic.

we would expect him to continue speaking as a moral philosopher would, then, be due to the fact that he makes in practice no very methodical separation between the rôles of philosopher and theologian and speaks sometimes as the one, sometimes as the other, without any clear indication of the change. Alternatively one would have to explain away references to the vision of God as meaning not the supernatural vision of the divine essence, but merely the knowledge of God which would be attainable by man in the next life, had man no supernatural end. In some such way one would make of St. Thomas a moral philosopher who completed the Aristotelian ethic by introducing consideration of the next life.

Unfortunately for upholders of this interpretation not only does St. Thomas seem to refer to the vision of God in the proper sense, but he even speaks of a 'natural desire' for the vision of God. 'Ultimate and perfect beatitude can consist only in the vision of the divine essence.' This, say some commentators, does not refer to the vision of God as supreme good, as He is in Himself, but only to the vision of God as first cause. But how could St. Thomas speak of knowledge of God as first cause as though such knowledge were or could be a vision of the divine essence? By the natural light of reason we can know that God is first cause, but St. Thomas states that 'for perfect beatitude it is required that the intellect should arrive at the very essence of the first cause'.[1] Again, 'Ultimate beatitude consists in the vision of the divine essence, which is the very essence of goodness.'[2] For the attainment of that vision there is in man a natural desire, as man naturally desires to know the essence, the nature of the first cause.[3] Whether or not St. Thomas was right in saying this, it is to me inconceivable that he meant to refer only to what Cajetan calls a *potentia obedientialis*: what can a 'natural desire' be, if it is not something positive? On the other hand, it is out of the question to suppose that St. Thomas meant to deny the supernatural and gratuitous character of the beatific vision of God. Some commentators (Suarez, for example) have got rid of the difficulty by saying that St. Thomas meant to affirm the presence in man of a *conditional* natural desire, that is, conditional on God's elevating man to the supernatural order and giving him the means to attain the supernatural end. This is a reasonable position, no doubt; but is it necessary to suppose that by a natural desire St. Thomas meant more than a desire to know the nature of the first cause, a desire

[1] *S.T.*, Ia, IIae, 3, 8. [2] *Ibid.*, 4, 4. [3] *Ibid.*, 3, 8.

which *in the concrete*, that is, given man's elevation to the supernatural order and his being destined for a supernatural end, means a desire for the vision of God? In other words, I suggest that St. Thomas is considering man in the concrete and that when he says that there is in man a 'natural desire' to know God's essence, and so to attain the vision of God, he means that man's natural desire to know as much as possible of the ultimate cause is, in the concrete and actual order, a desire to see God. Just as the will is naturally set towards the universal good and this movement of the will can reach satisfaction and quiescence only in the possession of God, so the intellect is made for truth and can be satisfied only by the vision of the absolute Truth.

It may be objected that this implies either that man has a natural desire for the beatific vision (using the word natural as opposed to supernatural), and in this case it is difficult to safeguard the gratuity of the supernatural order, or that by 'natural' St. Thomas means simply natural in the sense in which we frequently use the word, as opposed to 'unnatural' rather than supernatural, which is to interpret him in an arbitrary and unjustifiable fashion. But what I am suggesting is that St. Thomas is speaking pretty well as St. Augustine might speak, that he is considering man in the concrete, as called to a supernatural end, and that when he says that man has a natural desire to know the essence of God, he does not mean to imply that man in a hypothetical state of nature would have had such a natural desire, whether absolute or conditional, of seeing God, but simply that the term of the natural movement of the human intellect towards truth is *de facto* the vision of God, not because the human intellect can of itself see God, whether in this life or the next, but because *de facto* the only end of man is a supernatural end. I do not think that St. Thomas is considering the hypothetical state of nature at all, when he speaks of the *desiderium naturale*, and if this is so, it obviously means that his moral theory is not and cannot be a purely philosophical theory. His moral theory is partly theological and partly philosophical: he utilises the Aristotelian ethic but fits it into a Christian setting. After all, Aristotle was himself considering man in the concrete, as far as he knew what man in the concrete actually is, and St. Thomas, who knew much better than Aristotle what man in the concrete actually is, was fully justified in utilising the thought of Aristotle when he believed it to be correct and found it compatible with his Christian standpoint.

It is perfectly true that St. Thomas speaks of imperfect beatitude, of man's temporal good, and so on; but that does not mean that he is considering man in a hypothetical state of pure nature. If St. Thomas says that the Church is instituted to help man to attain his supernatural good, and the State to help man to attain his temporal good, it would be absurd to conclude that in considering man in relation to the State he is considering man in a purely hypothetical condition: he is considering actual man in certain aspects and functions. It is not that St. Thomas ignores the fact that the attainment of man's true end exceeds man's unaided powers, but that in his moral theory he considers man as set towards, as called to that end. When answering the question if beatitude, once attained, can be lost, he answers that the imperfect beatitude of this life can be lost, but that the perfect beatitude of the next life cannot be lost, since it is impossible for anyone who has once seen the divine essence to desire not to see it.[1] This shows clearly enough that he is speaking of supernatural beatitude. In the reply to the second objection he says that the will is ordered to the last end by a natural necessity;[2] but this does not mean either that the last end in question is purely natural or, if it is supernatural, that God *could not* have created man without directing him to this end. The will necessarily desires happiness, beatitude, and *de facto* this beatitude can be found only in the vision of God: we can say, therefore, that the concrete human being necessarily desires the vision of God.

It seems to me that this interpretation is confirmed by the doctrine of the *Summa contra Gentiles*. First of all[3] St. Thomas argues that the end of every intellectual substance is to know God. All creatures are ordered to God as to their last end,[4] and rational creatures are ordered to God principally and peculiarly by way of their highest faculty, the intellect. But though the end and happiness of man must consist principally in the knowledge of God, the knowledge in question is not that knowledge which is obtained philosophically, by demonstration. By demonstration we come to know rather what God is not than what He is, and man cannot be happy unless he knows God as He is.[5] Nor can human happiness consist in the knowledge of God which is obtained through faith, even though by faith we are able to know more about God than we can learn through philosophical demonstration. The 'natural desire' is satisfied by the attainment of the

[1] *S.T.*, Ia, IIae, 5, 4. [2] *Ibid.* [3] 3, 25. [4] 3, 18. [5] 3, 39.

final end, complete happiness, but 'knowledge by faith does not satisfy the desire, but rather inflames it, since everyone desires to see what he believes'.[1] Man's final end and happiness must consist, therefore, in the vision of God as He is in Himself, in the vision of the divine essence, a vision which is promised us in the Scriptures and by which man will see God 'face to face'.[2] It is only necessary to read St. Thomas in order to see that he is talking of the vision of the divine essence properly speaking. On the other hand, it is only necessary to read St. Thomas in order to see that he is perfectly aware that 'no created substance can by its natural power come to see God in His essence'[3] and that to attain this vision supernatural elevation and aid are required.[4]

What, then, of the 'natural desire'? Does not St. Thomas explicitly say that 'since it is impossible for a natural desire to be in vain (*inane*), and since this would be the case if it were not possible to arrive at the knowledge of the divine substance, which all minds naturally desire, it is necessary to say that it is possible for the substance of God to be seen by the intellect',[5] even though this vision cannot be attained in this life?[6] If there is really a 'natural desire' for the vision of God, is not the gratuitous character of supernatural beatitude endangered? In the first place it may be pointed out once again that St. Thomas explicitly states that man cannot attain to the vision of God by his own efforts: its attainment is made possible only through the grace of God, as he clearly affirms.[7] But there certainly is a difficulty in seeing how the grace of God, which alone makes possible the attainment of the final end, is not in some sense due to man, if there is a 'natural desire' for the vision of God and if it is impossible for a natural desire to be in vain. To come to a definitive conclusion as to what St. Thomas precisely understood by *desiderium naturale* in this connection may not be possible; but it seems legitimate to suppose that he was regarding the natural desire of the intellect to know absolute Truth in the light of the actual and concrete order. Man's intellect has a natural orientation towards happiness, which must consist primarily in the knowledge of the absolute Truth; but man in the concrete actual order has been destined for a supernatural end and cannot be satisfied with anything less. Regarding the natural desire in the light of the facts known by revelation, one can say, then, that man has a 'natural desire' for the vision of God.

[1] 3, 40. [2] 3, 51. [3] 3, 52. [4] 3, 52–4. [5] 3, 51.
[6] 3, 47–8. [7] 3, 52.

In the *De Veritate*[1] St. Thomas says that man, according to his nature, has a natural appetite for *aliqua contemplatio divinorum*, such as it is possible for a man to obtain by the power of nature, and that the inclination of his desire towards the supernatural and gratuitous end (the vision of God) is the work of grace. In this place, then, St. Thomas does not admit a 'natural desire' in the strict sense for the vision of God, and it seems to me only reasonable to suppose that when in the *Summa Theologica* and the *Summa contra Gentiles* he speaks of a natural desire for the vision of God, he is not speaking strictly as a *philosopher*,[2] but as a theologian and philosopher combined, that is, presupposing the supernatural order and interpreting the data of experience in the light of that presupposition. In any case what has been said should be sufficient to show the difference between Aristotle's and St. Thomas's views of the end of man.[3]

3. The will, therefore, desires happiness, beatitude, as its end, and human acts are good or bad in so far as they are or are not means to the attainment of that end. Happiness must, of course, be understood in relation to man as such, to man as a rational being: the end is that good which perfects man as a rational being, not indeed as a disembodied intellect, for man is not a disembodied intellect, but in the sense that the perfecting of his sensitive and vegetative tendencies must be accomplished in subordination to his primary tendency, which is rational: the end is that which perfects man as such, and man as such is a rational being, not a mere animal. Every individual human act, that is to say, every deliberate act, is either in accordance with the order of reason (its immediate end being in harmony with the final end) or out of accordance with the order of reason (its immediate end being incompatible with the final end), so that every human act is either good or bad. An indeliberate act, such as the reflex act of brushing away a fly, may be 'indifferent'; but no human, deliberate act, can be indifferent, neither good nor bad.[4]

4. St. Thomas follows Aristotle in treating the moral and intellectual virtues as habits, as good qualities or habits of the mind, by which a man lives rightly.[5] The virtuous habit is formed by good acts and facilitates the performance of subsequent acts for

[1] 27, 2.
[2] Cf. *De Veritate, loc. cit.*, and cf. also *De Malo*, 5, 1, 15.
[3] On the question of the 'natural desire' for the vision of God, cf. the summary and discussion of the opinions by A. Motte in the *Bulletin Thomiste*, 1931 (nos. 651–76) and 1934 (nos. 573–90).
[4] *S.T.*, Ia, IIae, 18, 9.
[5] *Ibid.*, Ia, IIae, 55 ff.

the same end. It is possible to have the intellectual virtues with the exception of prudence without the moral virtues, and it is possible to have the moral virtues without the intellectual virtues, with the exception of prudence and of understanding.[1] Moral virtue consists in a mean (*in medio consistit*). The object of moral virtue is to secure or facilitate conformity to the rule of reason in the appetitive part of the soul; but conformity implies the avoidance of the extremes of excess and defect, it means that the appetite or passion is reduced to the rule of reason. Of course, if one is considering simply conformity to reason, virtue is an extreme and all difformity with the rule of reason, whether by excess or defect, constitutes the other extreme (to say that virtue consists in a mean is not to say that it consists in mediocrity); but if one considers moral virtue in regard to the matter with which it is concerned, the passion or appetite in question, it is then seen to consist in a mean. The adoption of this theory of Aristotle might seem to make it difficult to defend virginity or voluntary poverty, for example, but St. Thomas points out that complete chastity, for instance, is virtuous only when it is in conformity with reason enlightened by God. If it is observed in accordance with God's will or invitation and for man's supernatural end, it is in accord with the rule of reason and so is, in St. Thomas's use of the word, a mean: if, however, it were observed out of superstition or vainglory, it would be an excess. In general, a virtue may be looked at as an extreme in relation to one circumstance, as a mean in regard to another.[2] In other words, the fundamental factor in virtuous action is conformity to the rule of reason, directing man's acts to his final end.

5. The rule and measure of human acts is the reason, for it belongs to the reason to direct a man's activity towards his end.[3] It is reason, therefore, which gives orders, which imposes obligation. But this does not mean that the reason is the arbitrary source of obligation or that it can impose whatever obligations it likes. The primary object of the practical reason is the good, which has the nature of an end, and the practical reason, recognising the good as the end of human conduct, enunciates its first principle, *Bonum est faciendum et prosequendum, et malum vitandum*, good is to be done and pursued, and evil avoided.[4] But the good for man is that which befits his nature, that to which he has a natural

[1] *S.T.*, Ia, IIae, 58, 4–5.
[2] *Ibid.*, Ia, IIae, 64, 1.
[3] *Ibid.*, Ia, IIae, 90, 1.
[4] *Ibid.*, Ia, IIae, 94, 2.

inclination as a rational being. Thus man, in common with all other substances, has a natural inclination to the preservation of his being, and reason, reflecting on this inclination, orders that the means necessary to the preservation of life are to be taken. Conversely, suicide is to be avoided. Again, man, in common with other animals, has a natural inclination to the propagation of the species and the bringing up of children, while as a rational being he has a natural inclination to seek out the truth, especially concerning God. Reason, therefore, orders that the species is to be propagated and children educated, and that truth is to be sought, especially that truth which is necessary to the attainment of man's end. Obligation, therefore, is imposed by reason, but it is founded immediately on human nature itself; the moral law is rational and natural, in the sense of not being arbitrary or capricious: it is a natural law, *lex naturalis*, which has its basis in human nature itself, though it is enunciated and dictated by reason.

As the natural law is founded in human nature as such, in that nature which is the same in all men, it has regard primarily to those things which are necessary to human nature. There is an obligation, for example, to preserve one's life, but that does not mean that every man has to preserve his life in exactly the same way: a man must eat, but it does not follow that he is under an obligation to eat this or that, this much or that much. In other words, acts may be good and according to nature without being obligatory. Moreover, though reason sees that no man can preserve his life without eating and that no man can order his life rightly without knowledge of God, it also sees that the precept of propagating the species falls not on the individual, but on the multitude, and that it is fulfilled, even though not all individuals actually fulfil it. (This would be St. Thomas's answer to the objection that virginity is contrary to the natural law.)[1]

From the fact that the natural law is founded on human nature itself it follows that it cannot be changed, since human nature remains fundamentally the same, and that it is the same for all. It can be 'added to', in the sense that precepts useful for human life can be promulgated by divine law and by human law, even though these precepts do not fall directly under the natural law; but it cannot be changed, if by change is meant subtraction from the law.[2]

[1] Cf. *S.T.*, IIa, IIae, 152, 2.

[2] *Ibid.*, Ia, IIae, 94, 5.

The primary precepts of the natural law (e.g. life is to be preserved) are entirely unchangeable, since their fulfilment is absolutely necessary for the good of man, while the proximate conclusions from the primary precepts are also unchangeable, though St. Thomas admits that they may be changed in a few particular cases on account of special reasons. But St. Thomas is not thinking here of what we call 'hard cases': he is thinking rather of cases like that of the Israelites who made off with the goods of the Egyptians. His meaning is that in this case God, acting as supreme lord and owner of all things rather than as legislator, transferred the ownership of the goods in question from the Egyptians to the Israelites, so that the Israelites did not really commit theft. Thus St. Thomas's admission of the changeability of the secondary precepts of the natural law in particular cases refers rather to what the Scholastics call a *mutatio materiae* than to a change in the precept itself: it is rather that the circumstances of the act are so changed that it no longer falls under the prohibition than that the prohibition itself is changed.

Moreover, precisely because the natural law is founded on human nature itself, men cannot be ignorant of it in regard to the most general principles, though it is true that they may fail on account of the influence of some passion to apply a principle to a particular case. As regards the secondary precepts men may be ignorant of these through prejudice or passion, and that is all the more reason why the natural law should be confirmed by positive divine law.[1]

6. Obligation, as we have seen, is the binding of the free will to perform that act which is necessary for the attainment of the last end, an end which is not hypothetical (an end which may or may not be desired) but absolute, in the sense that the will cannot help desiring it, the good which must be interpreted in terms of human nature. So far the ethic of St. Thomas follows closely that of Aristotle. Is there nothing further? Is the natural law, promulgated by reason, without any transcendental foundation? Aristotle's eudaemonological ethic fitted in, of course, with his general finalistic outlook; but it was not grounded in God and could not be, since the Aristotelian God was not Creator nor did He exercise providence: He was final cause, but not first efficient cause or supreme exemplary cause. In St. Thomas's case, however, it would be extremely strange were ethics to be left without demonstrable

[1] *S.T.*, Ia, IIae, 95, 6; 99, 2, *ad* 2.

connection with metaphysics, and in fact we find that connection insisted on.

On the supposition that God created and rules the world (the proof of this does not pertain to ethics), it follows that the divine wisdom must be conceived as ordering man's actions towards his end. God, to speak somewhat anthropomorphically, has an exemplar idea of man and of the acts which fulfil man's nature and which are required for the attainment of man's end, and the divine wisdom as directing man's acts to the attainment of that end constitutes the eternal law. As God is eternal and His idea of man eternal, the promulgation of the law is eternal *ex parte Dei*, though it is not eternal *ex parte creaturae*.[1] This eternal law, existing in God, is the origin and fount of the natural law, which is a participation of the eternal law. The natural law is expressed passively in man's natural inclinations, while it is promulgated by the light of reason reflecting on those inclinations, so that inasmuch as every man naturally possesses the inclinations to the end of man and possesses also the light of reason, the eternal law is sufficiently promulgated for every man. The natural law is the totality of the universal dictates of right reason concerning that good of nature which is to be pursued and that evil of man's nature which is to be shunned, and man's reason could, at least in theory, arrive by its own light at a knowledge of these dictates or precepts. Nevertheless, since, as we have seen, the influence of passion and of inclinations which are not in accordance with right reason may lead men astray and since not all men have the time or ability or patience to discover the whole natural law for themselves, it was morally necessary that the natural law should be positively expressed by God, as was done by the revelation of the Decalogue to Moses. It must also be added that man has *de facto* a supernatural end, and in order that he should be able to attain this supernatural end, it was necessary that God should reveal the supernatural law, over and above the natural law. 'Since man is destined to the end of eternal beatitude, which exceeds the capacity of the human natural faculty, it was necessary that besides the natural law and human law he should also be directed to his end by a divinely given law.'[2]

It is very important to realise clearly that the foundation of the natural law in the eternal law, the metaphysical foundation of the natural law, does not mean that the natural law is capricious

[1] *S.T.*, Ia, IIae, 9, 1; 93, 1 ff. [2] *Ibid.*, Ia, IIae, 91, 4.

or arbitrary; that it could be otherwise than it is: the eternal law does not depend primarily on the divine will but on the divine reason, considering the exemplar idea of human nature. Given human nature, the natural law could not be otherwise than it is. On the other hand, we must not imagine that God is subject to the moral law, as something apart from Himself. God knows His divine essence as imitable in a multiplicity of finite ways, one of those ways being human nature, and in that human nature He discerns the law of its being and wills it: He wills it because He loves Himself, the supreme Good, and because He cannot be inconsistent with Himself. The moral law is thus ultimately founded on the divine essence itself and so cannot change: God wills it certainly, but it does not depend on any arbitrary act of the divine will. Hence to say that the moral law does not depend primarily on the divine will is not at all equivalent to saying that there is a moral law which in some mysterious way stands behind God and rules God: God is Himself the supreme Value and the source and measure of all value: values depend on Him, but in the sense that they are participations or finite reflections of God, not in the sense that God arbitrarily confers on them their character as values. St. Thomas's doctrine of the metaphysical foundation, the theistic foundation, of the moral law in no way threatens its rational or necessary character: ultimately the moral law is what it is because God is what He is, since human nature, the law of whose being is expressed in the natural law, itself depends on God.

7. Finally one can point out that St. Thomas's realisation of God as Creator and supreme Lord led him, in company, of course, with other Scholastics, to recognise natural values which Aristotle did not envisage and could not envisage once given his view of God. To take one example, that of the virtue of religion (*religio*). Religion is the virtue by which men pay to God the worship and reverence which they owe Him as 'first Principle of the creation and government of things'. It is superior to the other moral virtues, inasmuch as it is more closely concerned with God, the last end.[1] It is subordinate to the virtue of justice (as a *virtus annexa*), inasmuch as through the virtue of religion a man pays to God his debt of worship and honour, a debt which is owing in justice.[2] Religion is thus grounded in man's relationship to God, as creature to Creator, as subject to Lord. As Aristotle did not

[1] On the virtue of religion, cf. *S.T.*, IIa, IIae, 81, 1–8.
[2] *S.T.*, Ia, IIae, 80, *articulus unicus*.

look upon God as Creator nor as exercising conscious government and providence, but regarded Him as the final Cause alone, wrapped up in Himself and drawing the world unconsciously, he could not envisage a personal relationship between man and the unmoved Mover, though he expected, of course, that man would recognise and in a sense honour the unmoved Mover, as the noblest object of philosophic contemplation. St. Thomas, however, with his clear idea of God as Creator and as provident Governor of the universe, could and did envisage as man's primary duty the expression in act of the relationship which is bound up with his very being. The virtuous man of Aristotle is, in a sense, the most independent man, whereas the virtuous man of St. Thomas is, in a sense, the most dependent man, that is, the man who realises truly and fully expresses his relation of dependence on God.

CHAPTER XL

ST. THOMAS AQUINAS—X: POLITICAL THEORY

St. Thomas and Aristotle—The natural origin of human society and government—Human society and political authority willed by God—Church and State—Individual and State—Law—Sovereignty—Constitutions—St. Thomas's political theory an integral part of his total system.

1. St. Thomas's ethical theory or theory of the moral life was based philosophically on the moral theory of Aristotle, though St. Thomas supplied it with a theological basis which was lacking in Aristotle's theory. In addition, the Thomist theory is complicated by the fact that St. Thomas believed, as a Christian, that man has *de facto* only one end, a supernatural end, so that a purely philosophical ethic was bound to be in his eyes an insufficient guide to practice: he could not simply adopt Aristotelianism lock, stock and barrel. The same is true of his political theory, in which he adopted the general framework of Aristotle's treatment, but had at the same time to leave the political theory 'open'. Aristotle certainly supposed that the State satisfied or ideally could satisfy all the needs of man;[1] but St. Thomas could not hold this, since he believed that man's end is a supernatural end and that it is the Church and not the State which caters for the attainment of that end. This meant that a problem which was not, and could not be, treated by Aristotle had to be considered by St. Thomas, as by other mediaeval writers on political theory, the problem of the relations of Church and State. In other words, though St. Thomas borrowed largely from Aristotle in regard to the subject-matter and method of treatment of political theory, he considered the matter in the light of the Christian mediaeval outlook and modified or supplemented his Aristotelianism in accordance with the exigencies of his Christian faith. The Marxist may like to point to the influence of mediaeval economic, social and political conditions on St. Thomas's theory, but the important difference between Aristotle and St. Thomas is not that the former lived in a Greek City-state and the latter in the feudal epoch; it is rather that for the former the natural end of man is self-sufficient and is attained

[1] This at least was the view which Aristotle took over and which he can hardly be said to have repudiated expressly, though it is true that the individualistic ideal of theoretic contemplation tended to break through the ideal of the City-state's self-sufficiency.

through life in the State, whereas for the latter the end of man is supernatural and is fully attainable only in the next life. Whether the amalgamation of Aristotelianism with the Christian view of man and his end constitutes a fully consistent and coherent synthesis or a somewhat fragile partnership, is a further question; what is insisted on at the moment is that it is a mistake to place a greater emphasis on the influence of mediaeval conditions on St. Thomas than on the influence of the Christian religion as such, which did not grow up in the Middle Ages and is not confined to the Middle Ages. The precise form taken by the problem of the relations of Church and State must of course be seen in the light of mediaeval conditions; but ultimately the problem arises from the confrontation of two different conceptions of man and his destiny; its precise formulation at any given time or by one thinker is incidental.

2. The State is for St. Thomas, as for Aristotle, a natural institution, founded on the nature of man. At the beginning of the *De regimine principum*[1] he argues that every creature has its own end, and that whereas some creatures attain their end necessarily or instinctively, man has to be guided to its attainment by his reason. But man is not an isolated individual who can attain his end simply as an individual by using his own individual reason; he is by nature a social or political being, born to live in community with his fellows. Indeed, man needs society more than other animals do. For whereas nature has provided the animals with clothing, means of defence, etc., she has left man unprovided, in a condition where he has to provide for himself by the use of his reason, and this he can do only through co-operation with other men. Division of labour is necessary, by which one man should devote himself to medicine, another to agriculture, and so on. But the most evident sign of the social nature of man is his faculty of expressing his ideas to other men through the medium of language. Other animals can express their feelings only through very general signs, but man can express his concepts completely (*totaliter*). This shows that man is naturally fitted for society more than any other gregarious animal, more even than the ants and the bees.

Society, therefore, is natural to man; but if society is natural, so also is government. Just as the bodies of men and animals disintegrate when the controlling and unifying principle (the soul) has left them, so would human society tend to disintegrate owing

[1] 1, 1.

to the number of human beings and their natural preoccupation with self, unless there was someone to take thought for the common good and direct the activities of individuals with a view to the common good. Wherever there is a multitude of creatures with a common good to be attained there must be some common ruling power. In the body there is a principal member, the head or the heart; the body is ruled by the soul, and in the soul the irascible and concupiscible parts are directed by the reason; in the universe at large inferior bodies are ruled by the superior, according to the disposition of divine providence. What is true, then, of the universe at large, and of man as an individual, must be true also of human society.

3. If human society and government are natural, are prefigured in human nature, it follows that they have a divine justification and authority, since human nature has been created by God. In creating man God willed human society and political government, and one is not entitled to say that the State is simply the result of sin. If no one did wrong, then obviously some activities and institutions of the State would be unnecessary; but even in the state of innocence, if it had persisted, there would have to have been an authority to care for the common good. 'Man is by nature a social animal. Hence in the state of innocence men would have lived in society. But a common social life of many individuals could not exist, unless there were someone in control, to attend to the common good.'[1] Moreover, there would have been some inequality of gifts even in the state of innocence, and if one man had been supereminent in knowledge and righteousness, it would not have been proper that he should have no opportunity to exercise his outstanding talents for the common good by direction of common activities.

4. By declaring the State a natural institution St. Thomas gave it, in a sense, a utilitarian foundation, but his utilitarianism is Aristotelian; he certainly did not consider the State simply the creation of enlightened egoism. He recognised the force of egoism, of course, and its centrifugal tendency in regard to society; but he also recognised the social tendency and impulse in man, and it is this social tendency which enables society to endure in spite of the tendency to egoism. As Hobbes regarded egoism as the only fundamental impulse, he had to find the practical principle of cohesion in force, once society had been founded by the prudential

[1] *S.T.*, Ia, 96, 4.

dictates of enlightened egoism; but in point of fact neither force nor enlightened egoism would be sufficient to make society endure, if man had no social tendency implanted by nature. In other words, the Christianised Aristotelianism of St. Thomas enabled him to avoid both the notion that the State is the result of original sin, a notion to which St. Augustine seems to have tended, and the notion that the State is simply the creation of egoism: it is prefigured in human nature, and since human nature is God's creation, it is willed by God. From this there follows the important consequence that the State is an institution in its own right, with an end of its own and a sphere of its own. St. Thomas could not, then, adopt an extremist position in regard to the problem of the relations between Church and State: he could not, if he was to be logical, turn the Church into a super-State and the State into a kind of dependency of the Church. The State is a 'perfect society' (*communitas perfecta*), that is, it has at its disposal all the means necessary for the attainment of its end, the *bonum commune* or common good of the citizens.[1] The attainment of the common good postulates first of all peace within the State, among the citizens, secondly the unified direction of the activities of the citizens *ad bene agendum*, thirdly the adequate provision for the needs of life; and the government of the State is instituted to secure these necessary conditions of the common good. It is also necessary for the common good that hindrances to the good life, such as danger from foreign enemies and the disintegrating effects of crime within the State, should be averted, and the monarch has at his disposal the means necessary to avert these hindrances, namely armed force and the judiciary system.[2] The end of the Church, a supernatural end, is higher than that of the State, so that the Church is a society superior to the State, which must subordinate itself to the Church in matters bearing upon the supernatural life; but that does not alter the fact that the State is a 'perfect society', autonomous within its own sphere. In terms of later theology, then, St. Thomas must be reckoned as an upholder of the *indirect power* of the Church over the State. When Dante in his *De Monarchia* recognises the two spheres of Church and State, he is at one with St. Thomas, as far at least as the Aristotelian aspect of the latter's political theory is concerned.[3]

[1] Cf. *S.T.*, Ia, IIae, 90, 2.

[2] Cf. *De regimine principum*, 1, 15.

[3] Dante was actually more concerned to uphold the authority of the Emperor against that of the Pope and was somewhat behind the times in his imperial dreams; but he carefully adhered to the two spheres theory.

However, the attempted synthesis between the Aristotelian idea of the State and the Christian idea of the Church was somewhat precarious. In the *De regimine principum*[1] St. Thomas declares that the end of society is the good life and that the good life is a life according to virtue, so that a virtuous life is the end of human society. He then goes on to observe that the *final* end of man is not to live virtuously, but by living virtuously to attain to the enjoyment of God, and that the attainment of this end exceeds the powers of human nature. 'Because man does not attain the end of enjoyment of God by human power, but by divine power, according to the words of the Apostle "the grace of God, life eternal",[2] to lead man to this end will pertain not to human but to divine rule': the leading of man to his final end is entrusted to Christ and His Church, so that under the new Covenant of Christ kings must be subject to priests. St. Thomas certainly recognises that the king has in his hands the direction of human and earthly matters, and he cannot be rightly interpreted as meaning to deny that the State has its own sphere; but he insists that it pertains to the king to procure the good life of his subjects with a view to the attainment of eternal beatitude: 'he should order those things which lead to heavenly beatitude and prohibit, as far as possible, their contraries.'[3] The point is that St. Thomas does not say that man has, as it were, two final ends, a temporal end which is catered for by the State and a supernatural, eternal end which is catered for by the Church: he says that man has one final end, a supernatural end, and that the business of the monarch, in his direction of earthly affairs, is to facilitate the attainment of that end.[4] The power of the Church over the State is not a *potestas directa*, since it is the business of the State, not the Church, to care for economic concerns and the preservation of peace; but the State must care for these concerns with an eye on the supernatural end of man. In other words, the State may be a 'perfect society', but the elevation of man to the supernatural order means that the State is very much a handmaid of the Church. This point of view is based not so much on mediaeval practice as on the Christian faith, and it is, needless to say, not the view of Aristotle who knew nothing of man's eternal and supernatural end. That there is a certain synthesis between the Aristotelian political theory and the demands of the Christian faith in the thought of St. Thomas,

[1] 1, 14. [2] Romans 6. 23. [3] *De regimine principum*, 1, 15.
[4] St. Thomas is, of course, addressing a Christian prince.

I should not attempt to deny; but I do think that the synthesis is, as I have already suggested, somewhat precarious. If the Aristotelian elements were pressed, the result would be a theoretical separation of Church and State of a kind which would be quite foreign to the thought of St. Thomas. In fact, his view of the relation of Church and State is not unlike his view of the relation between Faith and Reason. The latter has its own sphere, but philosophy is none the less inferior to theology: similarly, the State has its own sphere, but it is none the less, to all intents and purposes, the handmaid of the Church. Conversely, if one adheres to the historic Aristotle so closely as to make philosophy absolutely autonomous in its own sphere, one will naturally, in political theory, tend to make the State absolutely autonomous within its own sphere: this is what the Averroists did, but St. Thomas was most emphatically not an Averroist. One may say, then, that St. Thomas's political theory does represent to some extent the actual situation, in which the nation-State was becoming self-conscious but in which the authority of the Church had not yet been expressly repudiated. St. Thomas's Aristotelianism allowed him to make the State a perfect society, but his Christianity, his conviction that man has but one ultimate end, effectually prevented him from making the State an absolutely autonomous society.

5. A similar ambiguity shows itself in St. Thomas's doctrine of the relation of the individual to the State. In the *Summa Theologica*[1] he remarks that since the part is ordered to the whole as what is imperfect to what is perfect, and since the individual is a part of the perfect society, it is necessary that law should properly be concerned with the common happiness. It is true that he is trying to show simply that law is concerned primarily with the common good rather than with the good of the individual, but he does speak as though the individual citizen were subordinated to the whole of which he forms a part. The same principle, that the part exists for the whole, is applied by St. Thomas in more than one place to the individual's relation to the community. For example,[2] he argues that it is right for the public authority to deprive an individual citizen of life for the graver crimes on the ground that the individual is ordered to the community, of which he forms a part, as to an end. And it is really an application of this principle when he insists in the Commentary on the *Ethics*[3] that

[1] Ia, IIae, 90, 2. [2] *S.T.*, IIa, IIae, 65, 1. [3] 3 *Ethic.*, *lect.* 4.

courage is shown by giving one's life for the best things, as is the case when a man dies in defence of his country.

If this principle, that the part is ordered to the whole, which represents St. Thomas's Aristotelianism, were pressed, it would seem that he subordinates the individual to the State to a remarkable degree; but St. Thomas also insists that he who seeks the common good of the multitude seeks his own good as well, since one's own good cannot be attained unless the common good is attained, though it is true that in the *corpus* of the article in question he remarks that right reason judges that the common good is better than the good of the individual.[1] But the principle should not be over-emphasised, since St. Thomas was a Christian theologian and philosopher as well as an admirer of Aristotle, and he was well aware, as we have already seen, that man's final end is outside the sphere of the State: man is not simply a member of the State, indeed the most important thing about him is his supernatural vocation. There can, then, be no question of 'totalitarianism' in St. Thomas, though it is obvious that his Aristotelianism would make it impossible for him to accept such a theory of the State as that of Herbert Spencer: the State has a positive function and a moral function. The human being is a person, with a value of his own; he is not simply an 'individual'.

6. That totalitarianism is foreign to St. Thomas's thought is shown clearly by his theory of law and of the origin and nature of sovereignty. There are four kinds of law: the eternal law, the natural law, the divine positive law and human positive law. The divine positive law is the law of God as positively revealed, imperfectly to the Jews, perfectly through Christ,[2] while the law of the State is human positive law. Now, the function of the human legislator is primarily to apply the natural law[3] and to support the law by sanctions.[4] For example, murder is forbidden by the natural law, but reason shows the desirability of positive enactments whereby murder is clearly defined and whereby sanctions are added, since the natural law does not of itself clearly define murder in detail or provide immediate sanctions. The legislator's primary function is, therefore, that of defining or making explicit the natural law, of applying it to particular cases and of making it effective. It follows that human positive law is derived from the natural law, and that every human law is a true law only in

[1] *S.T.*, IIa, IIae, 47, 10, *in corpore* and *ad* 2.
[2] *Ibid.*, Ia, IIae, 91, 5.
[3] *Ibid.*, 3.
[4] *Ibid.*, 95, 1.

so far as it is derived from the natural law. 'But if it disagrees with the natural law in something, it will not be a law, but the perversion of law.'[1] The ruler is not entitled to promulgate laws which go counter to or are incompatible with the natural law (or, of course, the divine law): he has his legislative power ultimately from God, since all authority comes from God, and he is responsible for his use of that power: he is himself subject to the natural law and is not entitled to transgress it himself or to order his subjects to do anything incompatible with it. Just human laws bind in conscience in virtue of the eternal law from which they are ultimately derived; but unjust laws do not bind in conscience. Now, a law may be unjust because it is contrary to the common good or because it is enacted simply for the selfish and private ends of the legislator, thus imposing an unjustifiable burden on the subjects, or because it imposes burdens on the subjects in an unjustifiably unequal manner, and such laws, being more acts of violence than laws, do not bind in conscience, unless perhaps on occasion their non-observance would produce a greater evil. As for laws which are contrary to the divine law, it is never licit to obey them, since we ought to obey God rather than men.[2]

7. It will be seen, then, that the legislator's power is very far from being absolute in the thought of St. Thomas; and the same is clear from a consideration of his theory of sovereignty and government. That St. Thomas held that political sovereignty comes from God is admitted by all, and it seems probable that he maintained the view that sovereignty is given by God to the people as a whole, by whom it is delegated to the actual ruler or rulers; but this latter point does not seem to me to be quite so certain as some writers have made out, since texts can be alleged to show that he held otherwise. Yet it is undeniable that he speaks of the ruler as representing the people[3] and that he states roundly[4] that the ruler possesses legislative power only in so far as he stands in place (*gerit personam*) of the people,[5] and such statements may reasonably be taken to imply that he did hold that sovereignty comes to the ruler from God *via* the people, though at the same time it must be admitted that St. Thomas scarcely discusses the question in a formal and explicit manner. In any case, however, the ruler possesses his sovereignty only for the good of the whole

[1] *S.T.*, Ia, IIae, 95, 2. [2] Cf. *ibid.*, Ia, IIae, 96, 4. [3] Cf. *ibid.*, Ia, IIae, 90, 3.
[4] Though apparently referring to elected government.
[5] *S.T.*, Ia, IIae, 97, 3, *ad* 3.

people, not for his private good, and if he abuses his power, he becomes a tyrant. Assassination of a tyrant was condemned by St. Thomas and he speaks at some length of the evils which may attend rebellions against a tyrant. For example, the tyrant may become more tyrannical, if the rebellion fails, while if it is successful, it may simply result in the substitution of one tyranny for another. But deposition of a tyrant is legitimate, especially if the people have the right of providing themselves with a king. (Presumably St. Thomas is referring to an elective monarchy.) In such a case the people do no wrong in deposing the tyrant, even if they had subjected themselves to him without any time limit, for he has deserved deposition by not keeping faith with his subjects.[1] Nevertheless, in view of the evils which may attend rebellion, it is far preferable to make provision beforehand to prevent a monarchy turning into a tyranny than to have to put up with or to rebel against tyranny once established. If feasible, no one should be made ruler if he is likely to turn himself into a tyrant; but in any case the power of the monarch should be so tempered that his rule cannot easily be turned into a tyranny. The best constitution will in fact be a 'mixed' constitution, in which some place is given to aristocracy and also to democracy, in the sense that the election .of certain magistrates should be in the hands of the people.[2]

8. In regard to classification of forms of government St. Thomas follows Aristotle. There are three good types of government (law-abiding democracy, aristocracy and monarchy) and three bad forms of government (demagogic and irresponsible democracy, oligarchy and tyranny), tyranny being the worst of the bad forms and monarchy the best of the good forms. Monarchy gives stricter unity and is more conducive to peace than other forms: moreover, it is more 'natural', bearing an analogy to the rule of reason over the other functions of the soul and of the heart over the other members of the body. Moreover, the bees have their monarch, and God rules over all creation.[3] But the ideal of the best man as monarch is not easily attainable, and in practice the best constitution, as we have seen, is a mixed constitution, in which the power of the monarch is tempered by that of magistrates elected by the people. In other words and in modern terms St. Thomas favours limited or constitutional monarchy, though

[1] *De regimine principum*, I, 6.
[2] *S.T.*, Ia, IIae, 105, I.
[3] *De regimine principum*, I, 2.

he does not regard any particular form of decent government as divinely ordained: it is not the precise form of government which is of importance, but the promotion of the public good, and if in practice the form of government is an important consideration, it is its relation to the public good which makes it of importance. St. Thomas's political theory, therefore, is flexible in character, not rigid and doctrinaire, and while he rejects absolutism, he also implicitly rejects the *laissez-faire* theory. The ruler's task is to promote the public good, and this he will not do unless he promotes the economic well-being of the citizens. In fine, St. Thomas's political theory is characterised by moderation, balance and common sense.

9. In conclusion one may point out that St. Thomas's political theory is an integral part of his total philosophical system, not just something added on. God is supreme Lord and Governor of the universe, but He is not the only cause, even though He is the first Cause and the final Cause; He directs rational creatures to their end in a rational manner through acts the fitness and rightness of which are shown by reason. The right of any creature to direct another, whether it be the right of the father of the family over the members of the family or of the sovereign over his subjects, is founded on reason and must be exercised according to reason: as all power and authority is derived from God and is given for a special purpose, no rational creature is entitled to exercise unlimited, capricious or arbitrary authority over another rational creature. Law is defined, then, as 'an ordinance of reason for the common good, made by him who has care of the community, and promulgated'.[1] The sovereign occupies a natural place in the total hierarchy of the universe, and his authority must be exercised as part of the general scheme by which the universe is directed. Any idea of the sovereign being completely independent and irresponsible would thus be essentially alien to St. Thomas's philosophy. The sovereign has his duties and the subjects have their duties: 'legal justice', which should exist both in the sovereign and in his subjects, directs the acts of all the virtues to the common good;[2] but these duties are to be seen in the light of the relationship of means to end which obtains in all creation. As man is a social being, there is need for political society, in order that his nature may be fulfilled; but man's vocation to live in political society must itself be seen in the light of the final end

[1] *S.T.*, Ia, IIae, 90, 4. [2] *Ibid.*, IIa, IIae, 58, 6.

for which man was created. Between the supernatural end of man and the natural end of man there must be due harmony and the due subordination of the latter to the former; so that man must prefer the attainment of the final end to anything else, and if the sovereign orders him to act in a manner incompatible with the attainment of the final end, he must disobey the sovereign. Any idea of the complete and total subordination of the individual to the State would be necessarily abhorrent to St. Thomas, not because he was an extreme 'Papalist' in political affairs (he was not), but because of his total theological-philosophical system, in which order, proportion and subordination of the lower to the higher reign, though without the enslavement or moral annihilation of the lower. In the whole scheme of creation and providence man has his place: abuses and practical exaggerations cannot alter the ideal order and hierarchy which are ultimately based on God Himself. Forms of government may alter; but man himself has a fixed and abiding essence or nature, and on that nature the necessity and moral justification of the State are grounded. The State is neither God nor Antichrist: it is one of the means by which God directs the rational embodied creation to its end.

Note on St. Thomas's aesthetic theory.

One cannot say that there is a formal discussion of aesthetic theory in the philosophy of St. Thomas, and what he does have to say on the matter is mostly borrowed from other writers, so that though his remarks may be taken as the starting-point of an aesthetic theory, it would be a mistake to develop an aesthetic theory on the basis of his remarks and then attribute that theory to him, as if he had himself developed it. Nevertheless, it may be as well to point out that when he remarks that *pulchra dicuntur quae visa placent*[1], he does not mean to deny the objectivity of beauty. The beautiful consists, he says, in proper proportion and belongs to the formal cause: it is the object of the cognitive power, whereas the good is the object of desire.[2] For beauty three elements are required, integrity or perfection, proper proportion and clarity:[3] the form shines out, as it were, through colour, etc., and is the object of disinterested (non-appetitive) apprehension. St. Thomas recognises, therefore, the objectivity of beauty and the fact that aesthetic appreciation or experience is something *sui generis*, that it cannot be identified simply with intellectual cognition and that it cannot be reduced to apprehension of the good.

[1] *S.T.*, Ia, 5, 4, *ad* 1. [2] *Ibid.* [3] *Ibid.*, Ia, 39, 8.

CHAPTER XLI

ST. THOMAS AND ARISTOTLE: CONTROVERSIES

St. Thomas's utilisation of Aristotle—Non-Aristotelian elements in Thomism—Latent tensions in the Thomist synthesis—Opposition to Thomist 'novelties'.

1. ALTHOUGH St. Albert had gone some way in the utilisation of the Aristotelian philosophy, it was left to St. Thomas to attempt the full reconciliation of the Aristotelian system with Christian theology. The desirability of attempting this reconciliation was clear, since to reject the Aristotelian system would mean rejecting the most powerful and comprehensive intellectual synthesis known to the mediaeval world. Moreover, St. Thomas, with his genius for systematisation, saw clearly the use that could be made of the principles of the Aristotelian philosophy in achieving a systematic theological and philosophical synthesis. But when I say that St. Thomas saw the 'usefulness' of Aristotelianism, I do not mean to imply that his approach was pragmatic. He regarded the Aristotelian principles as true and, because true, as useful; he did not regard them as 'true' because they were useful. It would be absurd, of course, to suggest that the Thomist philosophy is simply Aristotelianism, since he makes use of other writers like St. Augustine and the Pseudo-Dionysius, as also of his mediaeval predecessors and of Jewish (Maimonides in particular) and Arabian philosophers; but none the less the Thomist synthesis is unified by the application of fundamental Aristotelian principles. A great deal of St. Thomas's philosophy is indeed the doctrine of Aristotle, but it is the doctrine of Aristotle re-thought by a powerful mind, not slavishly adopted. If St. Thomas adopted Aristotelianism, he adopted it primarily because he thought it true, not simply because Aristotle was a great name or because an 'unbaptised' Aristotle might constitute a grave danger to orthodoxy: a man of St. Thomas's serious mind, devoted to truth, would certainly not have adopted the system of a pagan philosopher, had he not considered it to be in the main a true system, especially when some of the ideas he put forward ran contrary to tradition and created some scandal and lively opposition. Yet his conviction as to the truth of the philosophy which he adopted did not lead

St. Thomas to adopt mechanically an ill-digested system: he gave a great deal of thought and attention to Aristotelianism, as can be seen from his commentaries on Aristotle's works, and his own works bear evidence of the care with which he must have considered the implications of the principles he adopted and their relation to Christian truth. If I suggest presently that the synthesis of Christianity and Aristotelianism in St. Thomas's thought was in some respects rather precarious, I do not mean to take back what I have just said and to imply that the Saint adopted Aristotelianism purely mechanically, though I think it is true that he did not fully realise the latent tension, in regard to certain points, between his Christian faith and his Aristotelianism. If this is really the case, however, it need cause no surprise; St. Thomas was a great theologian and philosopher, but he was not infinite mind, and a much smaller intellect can look back and discern possibly weak points in the system of a great mind, without the latter's greatness being thereby impugned.

Of St. Thomas's utilisation of Aristotelian themes for the purpose of systematisation one can afford space for only one or two examples. One of the fundamental ideas in the Aristotelian philosophy is that of act and potency or potentiality. St. Thomas, like Aristotle before him, saw the interplay, the correlation of act and potency in the accidental and substantial changes of the material world and in the movements (in the broad Aristotelian sense) of all creatures. Adopting the Aristotelian principle that nothing is reduced from potentiality to act, save by the agency of that which is itself in act, he followed Aristotle in arguing from the observed fact of movement, of change, to the existence of the unmoved Mover. But St. Thomas saw deeper than Aristotle: he saw that in every finite thing there is a duality of principles, of essence and existence, that the essence is in potency its existence, that it does not exist necessarily, and so he was enabled to argue not merely to the Aristotelian unmoved Mover, but to the necessary Being, God the Creator. He was able, moreover, to discern the essence of God as existence, not simply as self-thinking thought but as *ipsum esse subsistens*, and thus while following in the footsteps of Aristotle he was able to go beyond Aristotle. Not distinguishing clearly essence and existence in finite being, Aristotle could not arrive at the idea of Existence itself as the essence of God, from whom all limited existence comes.

Again, a fundamental idea in the Aristotelian philosophy is that of finality; indeed, this idea is in one sense more fundamental than that of act and potency, since all reduction from potentiality to act takes place in view of the attainment of an end, and potency exists only for the realisation of an end. That St. Thomas uses the idea of finality in his cosmological, psychological, ethical and political doctrines is a point which needs no labouring; but one may point out the help it was to him in explaining creation. God, who acts according to wisdom, created the world for an end, but that end can be none other than God Himself: He created the world, therefore, in order to manifest His own perfection, by communicating it to creatures by participation, by diffusing His own goodness. Creatures exist *propter Deum*, for God, who is their ultimate end, though He is not the ultimate end of all creatures in the same way; it is only rational creatures who can possess God by knowledge and love. Creatures have, of course, their proximate ends, the perfecting of their natures, but this perfecting of creatures' natures is subordinate to the final end of all creation, the glory of God, the manifestation of His divine perfection, which is manifested precisely by the perfecting of creatures, so that the glory of God and the good of creatures are by no means antithetical ideas. In this way St. Thomas was able to utilise the Aristotelian doctrine of finality in a Christian setting or rather in a way which would harmonise with the Christian religion.

Among the individual ideas borrowed by St. Thomas from Aristotle or thought out in dependence on the philosophy of Aristotle one may mention the following. The soul is the form of the body, individualised by the matter it informs; it is not a complete substance in its own right, but soul and body together make up a complete substance, a man. This stressing of the close union of soul and body, with the rejection of the Platonic theory on this point, makes it much easier to explain why the soul should be united to the body (the soul is by nature the form of the body), but it suggests that, granted the immortality of the soul, the resurrection of the body is demanded by the soul.[1] As for the doctrine of matter as the principle of individuation, which has as its consequence the doctrine that angelic beings, because devoid of matter, cannot be multiplied within the same species, this

[1] The answer can only be that it is *conveniens*, but not a strict debt, since it cannot be realised by natural means. We would then seem to be faced by the dilemma, that either the soul after death would, apart from God's intervention, remain in an 'unnatural' condition or that the doctrine of the soul's union with the body must be revised.

doctrine excited the hostility of critics of Thomism, as we shall see presently. The same can be said of the doctrine that there is only one substantial form in any substance, a doctrine which, when applied to the human substance, means the rejection of any *forma corporeitatis*.

The adoption of Aristotelian psychology naturally went hand in hand with the adoption of Aristotelian epistemology and with insistence on the fact that human knowledge is derived from sense-experience and reflection thereon. This meant the rejection of innate ideas, even in a virtual form, and the rejection of the theory of divine illumination or rather the interpretation of divine illumination as equivalent to the natural light of the intellect with the ordinary and natural concurrence of God. This doctrine raises difficulties, as we have seen earlier on, in regard to man's analogical knowledge of God.

But though St. Thomas did not hesitate to adopt an Aristotelian position even when this led him into conflict with traditional theories, he did so only when he considered that the Aristotelian positions were true in themselves and were thus compatible with Christian revelation. When it was a question of positions which were clearly incompatible with the Christian doctrine, he rejected them, or maintained that the Averroistic interpretation of Aristotle on such points was not the true interpretation or at least was not rendered necessary by Aristotle's actual words. For example, commenting on Aristotle's description of God as self-thinking Thought, St. Thomas observes that it does not follow that things other than God are unknown to Him, for by knowing Himself He knows all other things.[1] Probably, however, the historic Aristotle did not think of the unmoved Mover as knowing the world or as exercising any providence: He is the cause of movement as final, not as efficient, cause. Similarly, as already mentioned, when commenting on the very obscure words of Aristotle in the *De Anima* concerning the active intellect and its persistence after death, St. Thomas interprets the passage *in meliorem partem* and not in the Averroistic sense: it is not necessary to conclude that for Aristotle the intellect is one in all men and that there is no personal immortality. St. Thomas was anxious to rescue Aristotle from the toils of Averroes and to show that his philosophy did not necessarily involve the denial of divine providence or of personal immortality, and in this he succeeded, even if his interpretation of

[1] *In 12 Metaph.*, *lect.* 11.

what Aristotle actually thought on these matters is probably not the correct one.

2. St. Thomas's Aristotelianism is so obvious that one sometimes tends to forget the non-Aristotelian elements in his thought, though such elements certainly exist. For example, the God of Aristotle's *Metaphysics*, though final cause, is not efficient cause; the world is eternal and was not created by God. Moreover, Aristotle envisaged the possibility at least of a multiplicity of unmoved movers corresponding to the different spheres, the relation of which to one another and to the highest unmoved mover he left in obscurity.[1] The God of St. Thomas's natural theology on the other hand is first efficient cause and Creator, as well as final cause: He is not simply wrapped in splendid isolation, the object of *eros*, but He acts *ad extra*, creating, preserving, concurring, exercising providence. St. Thomas made a certain concession to Aristotle perhaps in allowing that the possibility of creation from eternity had not been disproved; but even if the world could have had no beginning in time, its creation, its utter dependence on God, can none the less be proved. All that St. Thomas admits is that the idea of *creatio ab aeterno* has not been shown to be self-contradictory, not that creation cannot be demonstrated. It may be said that St. Thomas's position in natural theology constituted a supplement to or a completion of Aristotle's position and that it cannot be said to be non-Aristotelian; but it must be remembered that for St. Thomas God creates according to intelligence and will and that He is efficient cause, Creator, as exemplary cause: that is to say, He creates the world as a finite imitation of His divine essence, which He knows as imitable *ad extra* in a multiplicity of ways. In other words, St. Thomas utilises the position of St. Augustine in regard to the divine ideas, a position which, philosophically speaking, was derived from neo-Platonism, which in turn was a development of the Platonic philosophy and tradition. Aristotle rejected the exemplary ideas of Plato, as he rejected the Platonic Demiurge; both of these notions, however, are present in the thought of St. Augustine, transmuted and rendered philosophically consistent, coupled also with the doctrine of *creatio ex nihilo*, at which the Greeks did not arrive; and St. Thomas's acceptance of these notions links him on this point with Augustine, and so with Plato through Plotinus, rather than with Aristotle.

[1] Cf. the first volume of this history, pp. 315–16.

Again, St. Thomas's Christian faith frequently impinges on or has some effect on his philosophy. For instance, convinced that man has a supernatural final end, and a supernatural final end alone, he was bound to envisage the term of man's intellectual ascent as the knowledge of God as He is in Himself, not as the knowledge of the metaphysician and astronomer; he was bound to place the final goal of man in the next life, not in this, thus transmuting the Aristotelian conception of beatitude; he was bound to recognise the insufficiency of the State for fulfilling the needs of the whole man; he was bound to acknowledge the subordination of State to Church in point of value and dignity; he was bound, not only to allow for divine sanctions in the moral life of man, but also to link up ethics with natural theology, and indeed to admit the insufficiency of the natural moral life in regard to the attainment of beatitude, since the latter is supernatural in character and cannot be attained by purely human means. Instances of this impinging of theology on philosophy could no doubt be multiplied; but what I want to draw attention to now is the latent tension on some points between St. Thomas's Christianity and his Aristotelianism.

3. If one looks on the philosophy of Aristotle as a complete system, a certain tension is bound to be present when one attempts to combine it with a supernatural religion. For the Aristotelian philosopher it is the universal and the totality which really matters, not the individual as such: the viewpoint is what one might call that of the physicist, and partly that of the artist. Individuals exist for the good of the species: it is the species which persists through the succession of individuals; the individual human being attains his beatitude in this life or he does not attain it at all: the universe is not a setting for man, subordinate to man, but man is an item in, a part of, the universe; to contemplate the heavenly bodies is really more worth while than to contemplate man. For the Christian on the other hand the individual human being has a supernatural vocation and his vocation is not an earthly vocation, nor is his final beatitude attainable in this life or by his own natural efforts; the individual stands in a personal relation to God, and however much one may stress the corporate aspect of Christianity, it remains true that each human person is ultimately of more value than the whole material universe, which exists for the sake of man, though both man and the material universe exist ultimately for God. One can, it is true, legitimately adopt a point

of view from which man is regarded as a member of the universe, since he is a member of the universe, rooted in the material universe through his body, and if one adopts, as St. Thomas adopted, the Aristotelian psychology, the doctrine of the soul as by nature the form of the body, individualised by the body and dependent on the body for its knowledge, one emphasises the more man's place as a member of the cosmos. It is from this point of view, for instance, that one is led to regard physical defects and physical suffering, the death and corruption of the individual, as contributing to the good and harmony of the universe, as the shadows that throw into relief the lights of the total picture. It is from this point of view too that St. Thomas speaks of the part as existing for the whole, the member for the whole body, using an analogy taken from the organism. There is, as has been admitted, truth in this point of view, and it has been strenuously defended as a corrective to false individualism and to anthropocentricism: the created universe exists for the glory of God, and man is a part of the universe. No doubt; but there is another point of view as well. Man exists for the glory of God and the material universe exists for man; it is not quantity, but quality which is truly significant; man is small from the point of view of quantity, but qualitatively all the heavenly bodies together pale into insignificance beside one human person; moreover, 'man', existing for the glory of God, is not simply the species man, but a society of immortal persons, each of whom has a supernatural vocation. To contemplate man is more worth while than to contemplate the stars; human history is more important than astronomy; the sufferings of human beings cannot be explained simply 'artistically'. I am not suggesting that the two viewpoints cannot be combined, as St. Thomas attempted to combine them; but I do suggest that their combination involves a certain tension and that this tension is present in the Thomist synthesis.

Since, historically speaking, Aristotelianism was a 'closed' system, in the sense that Aristotle did not and could not envisage the supernatural order, and since it was a production of reason unaided by revelation, it naturally brought home to the mediaevals the potentialities of the natural reason: it was the greatest intellectual achievement they knew. This meant that any theologian who accepted and utilised the Aristotelian philosophy as St. Thomas did was compelled to recognise the theoretical autonomy of philosophy, even though he also recognised theology as an extrinsic norm and criterion. As long as it was a question of theologians, the balance between theology and philosophy was, of course, preserved; but when it was a question of thinkers who were not primarily theologians, the charter granted to philosophy tended to become a declaration of independence. Looking back from the present day and bearing in mind human inclinations, characters, temperaments and intellectual bents, we can see that the acceptance of a great system of philosophy known to have been thought out without the aid of revelation was almost certain sooner or later to lead to philosophy going her own way independently of theology. In this sense (and the judgement is an historical, not a valuational judgement) the synthesis achieved by St. Thomas was intrinsically precarious. The arrival of the full Aristotle on the scene almost certainly meant in the long run the emergence of an independent philosophy, which would first of all stand on its own feet while trying to keep the peace with theology, sometimes sincerely, sometimes perhaps insincerely, and then in the end would try to supplant theology, to absorb the content of theology into itself. At the beginning of the Christian era we find the theologians utilising this or that element of Greek philosophy to help them in their statement of the data of revelation and this process continued during the stages of mediaeval Scholastic development; but the appearance of a fully-fledged system of philosophy, though an inestimable boon in the creation of the Thomist synthesis, could hardly be anything else but a challenge in the long run. It is not the purpose of the present writer to dispute the utility of the Aristotelian philosophy in the creation of a Christian theological and philosophical synthesis or in any way to belittle the achievement of St. Thomas Aquinas, but rather to point out that when philosophic thought had become more or less full-grown and had won a certain autonomy, it was not to be expected that it should for ever be content to sit at home like the elder son in the parable of the prodigal. St. Thomas's baptism of philosophy in the person of Aristotle could not, historically speaking, arrest the development of philosophy, and in that sense his synthesis contained a latent tension.

4. To turn finally, but of necessity briefly, to the opposition caused by the Thomist adoption of Aristotle. This opposition must be looked at against the background of the alarm caused by Averroism, i.e. the Averroistic interpretation of Aristotle, which we shall consider in the next chapter. The Averroists were

accused, and certainly not without justice, of preferring the authority of a pagan philosopher to that of St. Augustine and the *Sancti* in general, and of impairing the integrity of revelation; and St. Thomas was regarded by some zealous traditionalists as selling the pass to the enemy. They accordingly did their best to involve Thomism in the condemnations levelled against Averroism. The whole episode reminds us that St. Thomas in his own day was an innovator, that he struck out on new paths: it is useful to remember this at a time when Thomism stands for tradition, for theological soundness and security. Some of the points on which St. Thomas was most bitterly attacked by the hot-heads may not appear particularly startling to us to-day; but the reasons why they were attacked were largely theological in character, so that it is clear that Thomist Aristotelianism was once regarded as 'dangerous' and that the man who now stands before us as the pillar of orthodoxy was once regarded, by hot-heads at least, as a sower of novelties. Nor was the attack confined to people outside his own religious Order; he had to bear the hostility even of Dominicans, and it was only by degrees that Thomism became the official philosophy of the Dominican Order.

One of the principal points attacked was St. Thomas's theory of the unicity of the substantial form. It was combated at a debate in Paris, before the bishop, about 1270, Dominicans and Franciscans, especially the Franciscan Peckham, accusing St. Thomas of maintaining an opinion which was contrary to the teaching of the saints, particularly Augustine and Anselm. Peckham and the Dominican Robert Kilwardby maintained this point of view vigorously in their letters, the chief ground of complaint being that the Thomist doctrine was unable to explain how the dead body of Christ was the same as the living body, since according to St. Thomas there is only one substantial form in the human substance and this form, the soul, is withdrawn at death, other forms being educed out of the potentiality of matter. St. Thomas certainly held that the dead body of a man is not precisely the same as the living body, but is the same only *secundum quid*,[1] and Peckham and his friends regarded this theory as fatal to the veneration of the bodies and relics of the saints. St. Thomas, however, maintained that the dead body of Christ remained united to the Divinity, so that it was, even in the tomb, united to the Word of God and worthy of adoration. The doctrine of the

[1] *S.T.*, IIIa, 50, 5.

passivity of matter and that of the simplicity of the angels were also among the novel opinions to which exception was taken.

On March 7th, 1277, Stephen Tempier, Bishop of Paris, condemned two hundred and nineteen propositions, threatening with excommunication anyone who should uphold them. This condemnation was levelled chiefly against the Averroists, particularly Siger of Brabant and Boethius of Dacia, but a number of propositions were common to Siger of Brabant and St. Thomas so that Thomism was affected by the bishop's act. Thus the theories of the necessary unicity of the world, of matter as the principle of individuation, of the individualisation of angels and their relation to the universe were condemned, though that of the unicity of substantial form does not appear in the condemnation and seems never to have been formally condemned at Paris, apart from being censured in Scholastic debates and disputations.

The Parisian condemnation was followed, on March 18th, 1277, by a condemnation at Oxford, inspired by Robert Kilwardby, O.P., Archbishop of Canterbury, in which figured, among other propositions, those of the unicity of the substantial form and the passivity of matter. Kilwardby remarked in a letter that he forbad the propositions as dangerous, without condemning them as heretical, and indeed he does not seem to have been over-sanguine as to the probable results of his prohibition since he offered an indulgence of forty days to anyone who would abstain from propounding the offending ideas. Kilwardby's condemnation was repeated by his successor in the Archbishopric of Canterbury, the Franciscan Peckham, on October 29th, 1284, though by that time Thomism had been officially approved in the Dominican Order. However, Peckham again prohibited the novel propositions on April 30th, 1286, declaring them to be heretical.

Meanwhile Thomism had been growing in popularity among the Dominicans as was indeed only to be expected in the case of such a splendid achievement by one of their number. In the year 1278 the Dominican Chapter at Milan and in 1279 the Chapter of Paris took steps to counteract the hostile attitude which was evident among the Oxford Dominicans, the Paris Chapter forbidding the condemnation of Thomism, though not enjoining its acceptance. In 1286 another Chapter of Paris declared that professors who showed hostility to Thomism should be relieved of their office, though it was not until the fourteenth century that its acceptance was made obligatory on members of the Order. The growing popularity of Thomism in the last two decades of the thirteenth century, however, naturally led to the publication by Dominican authors of replies to the attacks levelled against it. Thus the *Correctorium Fratris Thomas*, published by William de la Mare, a Franciscan, called forth a series of Corrections of the Correction, such as the *Apologeticum veritatis super corruptorium* (as they called the *Correctorium*), published by Rambert of Bologna near the end of the century, to which the Franciscans replied in their turn. In 1279 the latter, in their General Chapter at Assisi, prohibited the acceptance of the propositions condemned at Paris in 1277, while in 1282 the General Chapter of Strasbourg ordered that those who utilised Thomas's *Summa Theologica* should not do so without consulting William de la Mare's *Correctorium*. However, the attacks of Franciscans and others naturally diminished after the canonisation of St. Thomas on July 18th, 1323, and in 1325 the then Bishop of Paris withdrew the Parisian censures. At Oxford there does not seem to have been any formal withdrawal of this kind, but Peckham's successors did not confirm or repeat his censures and the battle gradually came to an end. Early in the fourteenth century Thomas of Sutton speaks of Aquinas as being, according to the testimony of all, the Common Doctor (*in ore omnium communis doctor dicitur*).

Thomism naturally established itself in the estimation of Christian thinkers owing to its completeness, its lucidity and its depth: it was a closely reasoned synthesis of theology and philosophy which drew on the past and incorporated it into itself, while at the same time it utilised the greatest purely philosophical system of the ancient world. But though the suspicion and hostility which Thomism, or certain aspects of it, at first aroused were destined to die a natural death in face of the undeniable merits of the system, it must not be supposed that Thomism ever acquired in the Middle Ages that official position in the intellectual life of the Church which it has occupied since the Encyclical *Aeterni Patris* of Pope Leo XIII. The *Sentences* of Peter Lombard, for example, continued to be commented upon for very many years, while at the time of the Reformation there existed Chairs in the universities for the exposition of the doctrines not only of St. Thomas and Duns Scotus and Giles of Rome, but also of Nominalists like William of Ockham and Gabriel Biel. Variety was in fact the rule, and though Thomism became at an early date the official system of the Dominican Order, many centuries elapsed before it became in any real sense the official system of the Church. (I do not mean to imply that even after *Aeterni Patris* Thomism, in the sense in which it is distinguished from Scotism, for example, is imposed on all religious Orders and ecclesiastical institutes of higher studies; but Thomism is certainly proposed as a norm from which the Catholic philosopher should dissent only when inspired by reasons which seem to him compelling, and then without disrespect. The singular position now accorded to Thomism must be looked at in the light of the historical circumstances of recent times, in order to be understood; these circumstances were not those obtaining in the Middle Ages.)

CHAPTER XLII

LATIN AVERROISM: SIGER OF BRABANT

Tenets of the 'Latin Averroists'—Siger of Brabant—Dante and Siger of Brabant—Opposition to Averroism; condemnations.

1. THE term 'Latin Averroism' has become so common that it is difficult not to make use of it, but it must be recognised that the movement characterised by this name was one of integral or radical Aristotelianism: Aristotle was the real patron of the movement, not Averroes, though the latter was certainly looked on as the commentator *par excellence* and was followed in his monopsychistic interpretation of Aristotle. The doctrine that the passive intellect, no less than the active intellect, is one and the same in all men and that this unitary intellect alone survives at death, so that individual personal immortality is excluded, was understood in the thirteenth century as being the characteristic tenet of the radical Aristotelians, and as this doctrine was supported by the Averroistic interpretation of Aristotle its upholders came to be known as the Averroists. I do not see how exception can really be taken to the use of this term, provided that it is clearly realised that the 'Averroists' regarded themselves as Aristotelians rather than as Averroists. They seem to have belonged to the faculty of arts of Paris and to have pushed their adherence to Aristotle as interpreted by Averroes so far that they taught doctrines in philosophy which were incompatible with Christian dogma. The salient point in their doctrine, and the one which attracted most attention, was the theory that there is only one rational soul in all men. Adopting Averroes's interpretation of Aristotle's obscure and ambiguous teaching on this matter, they maintained that not only the active intellect, but also the passive intellect is one and the same in all men. The logical consequence of this position is the denial of personal immortality and of sanctions in the next life. Another of their heterodox doctrines, and one which incidentally was an undoubtedly Aristotelian doctrine, was that of the eternity of the world. On this point it is important to note the difference between the Averroists and St. Thomas. Whereas for St. Thomas the eternity of the (created) world has not been proved impossible, though it certainly has not

been proved true (and we know from revelation that as a matter of fact the world was not created from eternity), the Averroists held that the eternity of the world, the eternity of change and movement, can be philosophically demonstrated. Again, it appears that some of them, following Aristotle, denied divine providence and followed Averroes in maintaining determinism. It can, therefore, be understood without difficulty why the theologians attacked the Averroists, either, like St. Bonaventure, attacking Aristotle himself or, like St. Thomas, arguing not only that the peculiar Averroistic positions were intrinsically false, but also that they did not represent the real thought, or at least the clear teaching, of Aristotle.

The Averroists or radical Aristotelians were thus forced to reconcile their philosophical doctrines with theological dogmas, unless they were prepared (and they were not prepared) simply to deny the latter. In other words, they had to provide some theory of the relation of reason to faith which would permit them to assert with Aristotle that there is only one rational soul in all men and at the same time to assert with the Church that every man has his own individual rational soul. It is sometimes said that in order to effect this conciliation they had recourse to the theory of the double truth, maintaining that a thing can be true in philosophy or according to reason and yet that its opposite can be true in theology or according to faith; and indeed Siger of Brabant speaks in this way, implying that certain propositions of Aristotle and Averroes are irrefutable, though the opposite propositions are true according to faith. Thus it can be rationally proved that there is but one intellectual soul in all men, though faith makes us certain that there is one intellectual soul to each human body. Looked at from the logical standpoint this position would lead to the rejection of either theology or philosophy, faith or reason; but the Averroists seem to have meant that in the natural order, with which the philosopher deals, the intellectual soul would have been one in all men, but that God has miraculously multiplied the intellectual soul. The philosopher uses his natural reason, and his natural reason tells him that the intellectual soul is one in all men, while the theologian, who treats of the supernatural order and expounds the divine revelation, assures us that God has miraculously multiplied what by nature could not be multiplied. It is in this sense that what is true in philosophy is false in theology and *vice versa*. This mode of self-defence naturally did not appeal to the theologians, who were quite unprepared to admit that God intervened to perform miraculously what was rationally impossible. Nor had they much sympathy with the alternative method of self-defence adopted by the Averroists, namely the contention that they were simply reporting the teaching of Aristotle. According to a contemporary sermon, perhaps by St. Bonaventure, 'there are some students of philosophy who say certain things which are not true according to faith; and when they are told that something is contrary to faith, they reply that Aristotle says it, but that they themselves do not assert it and are only reporting Aristotle's words'. This defence was treated as a mere subterfuge by the theologians, and justifiably, in view of the Averroists' attitude towards Aristotle.

2. The foremost of the Averroists or radical Aristotelians was *Siger of Brabant*, who was born about the year 1235 and became a teacher in the faculty of arts at Paris. In 1270 he was condemned for his Averroistic doctrines, and it appears that he not only defended himself by saying that he was simply reporting Aristotle and did not intend to assert what was incompatible with the Faith, but also somewhat modified his position. It has been suggested that he was converted from Averroism by the writings of St. Thomas, but there is no certain evidence that he definitely abandoned his Averroism. If he did so, it would be difficult to explain why he was involved in the condemnation of 1277 and why in that year the Inquisitor of France, Simon du Val, ordered him to appear before his court. In any case the question of the changes in Siger's opinions cannot be settled with certainty until the chronology of his works has been settled. The works which have been discovered include the *De anima intellectiva*, *De aeternitate mundi*, *De necessitate et contingentia causarum*, *Compendium de generatione et corruptione*, some *Quaestiones naturales*, some *Quaestiones morales*, some *Quaestiones logicales*, *Quaestiones in Metaphysicam*, *Quaestiones in Physicam*, *Quaestiones in libros tres de Anima*, six *Impossibilia*, and fragments of the *De intellectu* and the *Liber de felicitate*. It appears that the *De intellectu* was a reply to St. Thomas's *De unitate intellectus contra Averroistas* and that in his reply Siger maintained that the active intellect is God, and that man's beatitude on earth consists in union with the active intellect. Whether Siger was still a monopsychist at this time or not, depends, however, on what he thought about the unicity or multiplication of the passive intellect: it cannot be concluded

without more ado from the identification of the active intellect with God that he was still a monopsychist in the Averroistic sense. If Siger appealed from the Inquisition to Rome, it may be that he felt he had been unjustly accused of heterodoxy. He died at Orvieto about 1282, being assassinated by his mad secretary.

To mention Siger of Brabant simply in connection with the Averroistic controversy is to give a partial view of his thought, since it was a system that he expounded, and not simply isolated points in regard to which he followed Averroes. His system, however, though professedly a system of true Aristotelianism, differed very much in important respects from the philosophy of the historic Aristotle, and this was bound to be so if he followed Averroes. For example, while Aristotle looked on God as the first mover in the sense of ultimate final cause, not in the sense of first efficient cause, Siger followed Averroes in making God the first creative cause. God operates mediately, however, through intermediate causes, the successively emanating intelligences, and in this respect Siger followed Avicenna rather than Averroes, so that, as M. Van Steenberghen has noted, Siger's philosophy cannot, with strict accuracy, be called radical Averroism. Nor for the matter of that can it accurately be termed radical Aristotelianism, if one is thinking of the historic Aristotle, though it is a convenient enough term if one is thinking of Siger's intentions. On the question of the eternity of creation Siger follows 'Aristotle', but rather because the Arabian philosophers followed 'Aristotle' on this point than because of what Aristotle himself said on the matter, since the latter did not envisage creation at all. Similarly, Siger's notion that all terrestrial events are determined by the movements of the heavenly bodies smacks of the Islamic philosophy. Again, while the idea that no species can have had a beginning, so that there can have been no first man, is Aristotelian in origin, the idea of the eternal recurrence or cyclic process of determined events is not found in Aristotle.

As regards the salient Averroistic theses of monopsychism and the eternity of the world, Siger seems to have retracted his heterodox opinions. Commenting on the *De Anima*, for example, he not only admits that the monopsychism of Averroes is not true, but proceeds to admit the weight of the objections brought against it by St. Thomas and others. Thus he allows that it is impossible for two different individual acts in two different human beings to proceed simultaneously from an intellectual faculty or principle which is numerically one. Similarly, in his Questions on the *Physics*, he concedes that motion is not eternal and that it had a beginning, although this beginning cannot be rationally demonstrated. However, as has already been noted, it is difficult to ascertain with certainty whether this apparent change of front involved a real change of opinion or whether it was a prudential course adopted in view of the condemnation of 1270.

3. The fact that Dante not only places Siger of Brabant in Paradise, but even puts his praises on the lips of St. Thomas, his adversary, is difficult to explain. Mandonnet, believing on the one hand that Siger of Brabant was a real Averroist and on the other hand that Dante was an anti-Averroist, was forced to suggest that Dante was probably unacquainted with Siger's doctrines. But, as M. Gilson has pointed out, Dante also places in Paradise and attaches to St. Bonaventure the Abbot Joachim of Flores, whose doctrines were rejected by both St. Bonaventure and St. Thomas, and it is extremely unlikely that Dante was unaware of what he was doing in the case of either Joachim or Siger. M. Gilson himself has suggested that Siger of Brabant, as he appears in the *Divine Comedy*, is not so much the actual historical Siger of Brabant as a symbol. St. Thomas symbolises speculative theology, St. Bernard mystical theology, and while Aristotle represents philosophy in limbo Siger, being a Christian, represents it in Paradise. When, therefore, Dante makes St. Thomas praise Siger of Brabant, he is not intending to make the historic Thomas praise the historic Siger, but rather to make speculative theology pay her compliments to philosophy. (M. Gilson explains in an analogous manner St. Bonaventure's praise of Joachim in the *Divine Comedy*.)

M. Gilson's explanation of the problem seems to me to be reasonable. There are, however, other possibilities. Bruno Nardi argued (and he was followed by Miguel Asín) that the explanation of the problem lies in the fact that Dante was not a pure Thomist, but that he incorporated doctrines not only from other Scholastic sources, but also from the Moslem philosophers, notably Averroes, whom he particularly admired. As Dante could not place Avicenna and Averroes in Paradise, he consigned them to limbo, whereas Mohammed he placed in hell proper; but as Siger was a Christian he placed him in Paradise. Dante would thus have acted with deliberation, showing his appreciation of Siger's devotion to Islamic philosophy.

Even if what Bruno Nardi says of Dante's philosophical sources is true, it seems to me that his explanation could well be combined with that of M. Gilson. If Dante admired the Moslem philosophers and was influenced by them, it would explain why he placed Siger in Paradise; but would it explain why he placed Siger's praises on the lips of St. Thomas? If Dante knew that Siger was an Averroist, he certainly knew also that St. Thomas was an anti-Averroist. May it not have been that Dante made St. Thomas the symbol of speculative theology, as Gilson suggests, and Siger, the Averroist, he made the symbol of philosophy, precisely because Siger was a member of the faculty of arts and not a theologian? In that case, as M. Gilson says, St. Thomas's praise of Siger would simply represent theology's tribute to philosophy.

The question has been complicated by M. Van Steenberghen's contention that Siger of Brabant abandoned Averroism inasmuch as it conflicted with theology and approximated to St. Thomas's position. If this is true, and if Dante were aware of the fact that Siger changed his opinions, the difficulty of explaining how St. Thomas could be made to praise Siger would obviously be greatly lessened. In other words, in order to obtain an adequate explanation of the fact why the poet not only placed Siger in heaven, but also made his adversary, St. Thomas, speak his praises, one would have to obtain first an adequate and accurate idea not only of Dante's philosophical sympathies, but also of the evolution of Siger's opinions.[1]

4. We have seen that the philosophy of St. Thomas aroused considerable opposition on the part of other Scholastic philosophers; but even if an attempt was made to implicate St. Thomas in the condemnation of Averroistic Aristotelianism, it remains true that the controversy over such Thomist doctrines as the unicity of the substantial form was a domestic controversy which can be distinguished from the Averroistic controversy proper in which the theologians in general, including St. Thomas, were united in a common front against the heterodox philosophers. Thus the Franciscans, from Alexander of Hales and St. Bonaventure to Duns Scotus, were at one with Dominicans like St. Albert and St. Thomas, Augustinians like Giles of Rome and secular clergy like Henry of Ghent, in opposing what they regarded as a dangerous movement. From the philosophic standpoint the most important

[1] Cf. P. Mandonnet: *Siger de Brabant*, second edit., 1911; B. Nardi: *Sigieri di Brabante nella Divina Commedia* and *le fonti della filosofia di Dante*, 1912; F. Van Steenberghen: *Les œuvres et la doctrine de Siger de Brabant*, 1938; E. Gilson: *Dante et la philosophie*, 1939 (English translation, 1948).

feature of their opposition was, of course, their critical refutation of the offending theories, and in this respect one may mention St. Albert's *De unitate intellectus contra Averroem* (1256), St. Thomas's *De unitate intellectus contra Averroistas* (1270), Giles of Rome's *De purificatione intellectus possibilis contra Averroem* and his *Errores Philosophorum* (which lists the errors of Aristotle and the Moslem philosophers, but does not treat of Siger of Brabant), and Raymund Lull's *Liber contra errores Boetii et Segerii* (1298), *Liber reprobationis aliquorum errorum Averrois, Disputatio Raymundi et Averroistae* and *Sermones contra Averroistas.*

The theologians were not, however, content with writing and speaking against the Averroists; they also endeavoured to secure their official condemnation by ecclesiastical authority. This was only natural, as can be seen from considering the clash on important points between Averroistic philosophy and the Faith, and also from considering the theoretical and possible practical consequences of such theories as those of monopsychism and determinism. Accordingly, in 1270 the Bishop of Paris, Stephen Tempier, condemned the doctrines of monopsychism, denial of personal immortality, determinism, eternity of the world and denial of divine providence. In spite of this condemnation, however, the Averroists continued to teach in secret ('in corners and before boys', as St. Thomas puts it), although in 1272 the professors of the faculty of arts were forbidden to treat of theological matters, and in 1276 secret teaching in the university was prohibited. This led to a further condemnation on March 7th, 1277, when the Bishop of Paris condemned 219 propositions and excommunicated anyone who should persist in maintaining them. The condemnation was aimed principally at the teaching of Siger of Brabant and Boethius of Dacia, and it involved the 'double truth' subterfuge. Boethius of Dacia, who was a contemporary of Siger of Brabant, upheld the intellectualist idea of beatitude expounded by Aristotle, maintaining that only philosophers can attain true happiness, while non-philosophers sin against the natural order. The condemned propositions, that 'there is no more excellent state than to devote oneself to philosophy' and that 'the wise men of the world are the philosophers alone', seem to have been taken from or to have summarised the teaching of Boethius, who, as professor of the faculty of arts, omitted all mention of the supernatural order and treated the Aristotelian conception of beatitude as adequate, at least from the standpoint of reason.

CHAPTER XLIII

FRANCISCAN THINKERS

Roger Bacon, life and works—Philosophy of Roger Bacon—Matthew of Aquasparta—Peter John Olivi—Roger Marston—Richard of Middleton—Raymond Lull.

1. ONE of the most interesting of mediaeval thinkers is *Roger Bacon* (*c.* 1212 to after 1292), called the *Doctor Mirabilis.* He would be of interest, were it only for his interest in and respect for experimental science and the application of mathematics in science; but what makes him considerably more interesting is that his scientific interests are combined with a lively interest in philosophy proper, and that both these interests were combined with a typically Franciscan emphasis on mysticism. Traditional elements were thus fused with a scientific outlook which was really foreign to the mentality of the majority of contemporary theologians and philosophers.[1] Moreover, Roger Bacon, impulsive, somewhat intolerant and hot-headed, convinced of the truth and value of his own opinions and of the obscurantism of many of the leading thinkers of his time, particularly those of Paris, is interesting not only as philosopher, but also as a man. He was something of a stormy petrel in his Order, but he is at the same time one of the glories of that Order and one of the leading figures of British philosophy. If a comparison were instituted between Roger Bacon and Francis Bacon (1561–1626), the comparison would by no means be to the unqualified advantage of the latter. As Professor Adamson remarked, 'it is more than probable that in all fairness, when we speak of the Baconian reform of science, we should refer to the forgotten monk of the thirteenth century rather than to the brilliant and famous Chancellor of the seventeenth',[2] while Bridges observes that though Francis Bacon was 'immeasurably superior as a writer, Roger Bacon had the sounder estimate and the firmer grasp of that combination of deductive with inductive matters which marks the scientific discoverer'.[3]

Born at Ilchester, Roger Bacon studied at Oxford under Adam Marsh and Robert Grosseteste. For the latter Bacon had the

[1] I refer, of course, to experimental science.
[2] *Roger Bacon: The Philosophy of Science in the Middle Ages,* p. 7.
[3] J. H. Bridges: Introduction to *Opus Maius,* pp. xci–xcii.

liveliest admiration, remarking that he knew mathematics and perspective, and that he could have known everything; Grosseteste also knew enough of languages to understand the wise men of antiquity.[1] From Oxford, Bacon went to Paris, where he apparently taught for a few years. For the Parisian professors he had little respect. Thus of Alexander of Hales's *Summa* he remarks that it weighed more than a horse, though he contests its authenticity,[2] while he blames the theologians for their incursions into philosophy, for their ignorance of the sciences, and for the unmerited deference they paid to Alexander of Hales and Albert the Great.[3] Ignorance of the sciences and of languages were his chief charges against contemporary thinkers, though he also found fault with the veneration given to the *Sentences* of Peter Lombard, which, he says, was preferred to the Bible itself, and with faulty Scriptural exegesis. In other words, his criticism (which was often unfair, as in regard to St. Albert) shows the twofold character of his thought, a devotion to science coupled with a traditional or conservative attitude in respect to theology and metaphysics. As regards Aristotle, Bacon was an admirer of the Philosopher, but he detested what he regarded as bad and misleading Latin translations of his works and declared that he would have them all burnt, if it lay in his power to do so.[4]

But though Bacon had little use for the great figures of the University of Paris and contrasted the Parisian thinkers unfavourably with his fellow countrymen, he met at Paris one man at least who had a lasting influence on his thought, Peter of Maricourt, a Picard and author of an *Epistola de magnete* and a *Nova compositio Astrolabii particularis*.[5] According to Roger Bacon[6] he was the one man who could safely be praised for his achievements in scientific research. 'For the last three years he has been working at the production of a mirror which shall produce combustion at a distance; a problem which the Latins have neither solved nor attempted, though books have been written upon the subject.' Peter evidently stimulated Roger Bacon's leaning to experimental science and won his respect by putting his questions to Nature herself instead of attempting to answer them *a priori* and without recourse to experiment.

About the year 1250 Bacon entered the Franciscan Order and

[1] *Opus Tertium*, c. 25.
[2] *Opus Minus*, edit. J. S. Brewer, p. 326.
[3] *Ibid.*, p. 322 ff.
[4] *Compendium philosophiae*, p. 469.
[5] Peter's name of *Peregrinus* seems to be due to the fact that he went on a crusade.
[6] *Opus Tertium*, c. 13.

taught at Oxford until 1257, when he had to abandon public teaching, having incurred the suspicion or hostility of his superiors. He was still permitted to write, however, though not to publish his works. In June 1266 Pope Clement IV, a friend of Bacon, told the latter to send him his works; but the Pope died shortly afterwards and it is not known with certainty if the manuscripts ever reached Rome and, if they did, what reception was accorded them. In any case Bacon got into trouble in 1277 by writing the *Speculum astronomiae* in order to defend his ideas on astrology and to criticise Stephen Tempier's condemnation of astrology. The Franciscan General of the time, Jerome of Ascoli, had Bacon brought before a Chapter in Paris under suspicion of teaching novelties, and this resulted in Bacon's imprisonment in 1278. He seems to have remained in prison until 1292, and it was in this year or not long afterwards that he died, being buried at Oxford in the Franciscan Church.

Bacon's chief work was the *Opus Maius*, which may have been completed and sent to the Pope. The *Opus Minus* and the *Opus Tertium* are more or less summaries of material incorporated in the *Opus Maius*, though they contain additional matter as well. It is in the *Opus Minus* that Bacon treats of the seven sins of theology, for example. A number of other works, such as the *Quaestiones supra libros octo Physicorum Aristotelis* and the *Quaestiones supra libros Primae Philosophiae*, have been published in the fourteen volumes of the *Opera hactenus inedita Rogeri Baconi* of which sixteen fascicules have so far appeared. Some of these works seem to have been written as parts of a projected *Scriptum Principale*. Bacon also wrote a *Compendium Philosophiae*, a *Compendium studii Philosophiae* and a *Compendium studii Theologiae*.

2. In the first part of the *Opus Maius* Bacon enumerates four principal causes of human ignorance and failure to attain truth: subjection to unworthy authority, the influence of habit, popular prejudice, and making a show of apparent wisdom to cover one's own ignorance. The first three causes of error were recognised by men like Aristotle, Seneca, Averroes; but the fourth is the most dangerous, as it makes a man conceal his own ignorance by holding up as true wisdom the result of worshipping untrustworthy authority, of habit and of popular prejudice. For example, because Aristotle said something, it is considered true; but Avicenna may have corrected Aristotle on the point, and Averroes may have corrected Avicenna. Again, because the Fathers did not pursue scientific studies, it is taken for granted that such studies are

valueless; but the circumstances of that time were quite different, and what was an excuse for them is not necessarily an excuse for us. Men do not realise the value of studying mathematics and languages, and so they belittle these studies out of prejudice.

In the second part Bacon emphasises the dominating character of theology among the sciences: all truth is contained in the Scriptures. But for the elucidation of the Scriptures we need the help of canon law and of philosophy. Philosophy and the use of reason in general cannot be condemned, since reason is of God. God is the active intellect (so Bacon interpreted St. Augustine, appealing also to Aristotle and Avicenna), and He enlightens the individual human mind, concurring with it in its activity. Philosophy has as its purpose to lead man to the knowledge and service of God; it culminates in moral philosophy. The speculative and moral sciences of the pagans were certainly inadequate and find their completion only in Christian theology and the Christian ethic; but it is not right to condemn or to neglect any particle of truth. As a matter of fact, says Bacon, philosophy was not a pagan invention, but was revealed to the Patriarchs. Subsequently the revelation was obscured through human depravity, but the pagan philosophers helped to rediscover it, or part of it. The greatest of these philosophers was Aristotle, and Avicenna is his principal expounder. As for Averroes, he was a man of real wisdom who improved in many points on what his predecessors had said, though his own theories also stand in need of correction. In fine, we should use pagan philosophy in an intelligent manner, without ignorant rejection and condemnation on the one hand or slavish adherence to any particular thinker on the other. It is our business to carry on and perfect the work of our predecessors, remembering that though it is the function of truth to lead man to God, we should not regard as valueless studies which have at first sight no immediate relation to theology: all truth of whatever kind leads ultimately to God.

The third part Bacon devotes to the subject of language, emphasising the practical importance of the scientific study of languages. Without a real knowledge of Hebrew and Greek the Scriptures cannot be properly interpreted and translated, nor can manuscripts be corrected when faulty; and good translations of Greek and Arabian philosophers are also needed. But for purposes of translation something more than a smattering of a language is necessary, if slavish translations are to be avoided.

In the fourth part Bacon discusses mathematics, the 'door and key' of other sciences. Mathematics were studied by the Patriarchs and came to the knowledge of the Greeks by way of the Chaldeans and Egyptians; but among the Latins they have fallen into neglect. Yet mathematical science is *quasi innata*, or at least it is learnt more easily and immediately and with less dependence on experience than other sciences, so that it may be said to be presupposed by other sciences. Logic and grammar are dependent to a certain extent on mathematics, while it is obvious that without mathematics no advance can be made in astronomy, and they are useful even for theology: mathematical astronomy can, for instance, demonstrate the comparative insignificance of the earth as compared with the heavens, not to speak of the facts that mathematics are useful for solving the chronological problems in the Scriptures and that they show the inadequacy of the Julian Calendar, a matter to which the Pope would do well to attend. Bacon proceeds to speak about light, its propagation, reflection and refraction; about eclipses, tides, the spherical shape of the earth, the unicity of the universe, and so on; and then passes to geography and astrology. Astrology is regarded with suspicion as it is thought to involve determinism; but this suspicion is unjust. The influence and movements of the heavenly bodies affect terrestrial and human events and produce even natural dispositions in human beings, but they do not destroy free will: it is only prudent to gain all the knowledge we can and use it for a good end. Bacon approves Aristotle's advice to Alexander concerning the treatment to be meted out to certain tribes of perverse ways: change their climate, that is, change their place of abode and thus change their morals.

Optics form the subject of the fifth part, in which Bacon treats of the structure of the eye, the principles of vision and the conditions of vision, reflection, refraction, and finally the practical application of the science of optics. Mirrors, he suggests, might be erected in elevated spots in order that the layout and movements of an enemy's camp might be observed, while by the use of refraction we could make small things appear great and distant objects appear near. There is no evidence to show that Bacon actually invented the telescope; but he conceived the possibility of such a thing.

In the sixth part Bacon considers experimental science. Reasoning may guide the mind to a right conclusion, but it is only confirmation by experience which removes doubt. That is one reason why diagrams and figures are employed in geometry. Many beliefs are refuted by experience. Experience, however, is of two kinds. In one kind of experience we employ our bodily senses, aided by instruments and by the evidence of trustworthy witnesses, while the other kind is experience of spiritual things and needs grace. This latter type of experience advances through various stages to the mystical states of rapture. The former type of experience can be used to prolong life (by improving the science of medicine, and discovering antidotes to poisons), to invent explosive substances, to transmute baser metals into gold and to refine gold itself, and so to disabuse the heathen of their false magical beliefs.

Finally, in the seventh part of the *Opus Maius*, Bacon treats of moral philosophy, which stands on a higher level than philology, or mathematics and experimental science. These sciences are related to action of various kinds, whereas moral philosophy is related to the actions by which we become good or bad, and it instructs man about his relations with God, his fellow men and himself. It is thus closely related to theology and shares in the latter's dignity. Supposing the 'principles of metaphysics', which include Christian revelation, Bacon treats of civic morality and then, more at length, of personal morality, making use of the writings of Greek, Roman and Moslem philosophers, particularly of Seneca, the Roman Stoic. In conclusion he treats of the grounds for accepting the Christian religion. Revelation is necessary and the Christian accepts the Faith on authority; but in dealing with non-Christians we cannot appeal simply to authority, but must have recourse to reason. Thus philosophy can prove the existence of God, His unity and infinity, while the credibility of the sacred writers is established by their personal sanctity, their wisdom, the evidence of miracles, their firm steadfastness under persecution, the uniformity of their faith, and their victory in spite of their humble origin and temporal condition. Bacon ends with the doctrine of man's incorporation with Christ and his participation through Christ in the divine life. *Et quid potest homo plus petere in hac vita?* And what more can a man seek in this life?

From what has been said, the twofold character of Bacon's philosophy is clear. His emphasis on the relation of philosophy to theology, on the former's function of leading man to God, and on the practical or moral aspect of philosophy, the place he attributes in his philosophy to inner knowledge of God and spiritual things, culminating in rapture, the close relation he establishes between theology and philosophy, his doctrine of God as the illuminating active intellect,[1] his adoption of the theories of 'seminal reasons' (for the development of which matter has a kind of active appetite), of the universal hylomorphic composition of creatures, and of the plurality of forms (from the form of corporeity up to the *forma individualis*), all mark him as an adherent, to a large extent, of the Augustinian tradition. In spite of his respect for Aristotle he not infrequently misinterprets him and even ascribes to him doctrines which he certainly never held. Thus he discerns elements of the Christian revelation in the philosophy of Aristotle which were actually not there; and though he refers to St. Thomas he does not seem to have been influenced by the Thomist positions or to have been particularly interested in them. On the other hand, the breadth of his interests and the vigour of his insistence on experimental science in general, on the development of astronomy by the aid of mathematics, and on the practical applications of science mark him out as a herald of the future. By temperament he was somewhat self-assured, inclined to impatience and to sometimes unjust criticism and condemnation; but he laid his finger on many weak points in contemporary science as also in contemporary moral and ecclesiastical life. For his scientific theories he depended very much on other thinkers, as was only natural; but he was quick to see the possibility of their development and application, and, as has already been remarked, he had a firmer grasp of scientific method, of the combination of deduction and induction, than was possessed by Francis Bacon, the Chancellor of England, whose insistence on experiment and observation and the practical applications of knowledge has sometimes been depicted as if without parallel or anticipation among philosophers of an earlier period.

3. An Augustinian of a different type was *Matthew of Aquasparta* (*c.* 1240–1302), who studied at Paris, taught at Bologna and Rome, and became General of the Franciscan Order in 1287, being created a cardinal in 1288. The author of, among other works, a Commentary on the *Sentences*, *Quaestiones disputatae* and *Quaestiones quodlibetales*, Matthew adhered in general to the position of St. Bonaventure, regarding St. Augustine as the great fount of wisdom. Thus, while he admitted that man's ideas of corporeal objects are formed only in dependence on sense-experience, he

[1] Obviously this doctrine is not Averroistic. The latter's monopsychism Bacon condemned as error and heresy.

refused to admit that corporeal objects can affect more than the body: it is the soul itself which is responsible for sensation as such, as St. Augustine had held, though, of course, sensation requires that a sense-organ should be affected by a sensible object. Again, it is the active intellect which transforms the *species sensibilis* and produces the idea in the passive intellect. Matthew appeals explicitly to St. Augustine on this matter.[1] Yet the soul's activity alone is not sufficient to explain knowledge: the divine illumination is required. What is this divine illumination? It is really God's immediate concurrence with the operation of the human intellect, a concurrence by the aid of which the intellect is moved to know the object. God moves us to know the object of which we receive the *species sensibilis*, this movement being the divine illumination. The object is related to its eternal exemplar foundation, the *ratio aeterna* or divine idea, and it is the divine light which enables us to discern this relation, the *rationes aeternae* exercising a regulative effect on the intellect. But we do not discern the divine light or concurrence, nor are the eternal ideas objects directly perceived; we know them rather as principles which move the intellect to know the created essence, *ut obiectum movens et in aliud ducens*, not as *obiectum in se ducens*.[2] There is, then, no difficulty in seeing how the divine light operates in all men, good or bad, since there is no question of a vision of the divine ideas and of the divine essence as such, in themselves. God co-operates in all the activities of creatures; but the human mind is made in the image of God in a special manner and God's concurrence with the mind's activity is rightly termed illumination.

In the same *De cognitione* to which reference has already been made, Matthew mentions the Thomist doctrine that the intellect knows the singular thing *per quandam reflexionem*, by a certain act of reflection[3] and rejects it. It is difficult to understand this position, he says, for the knowledge of the singular thing *per reflexionem ad phantasma* means that the intellect knows the singular thing either in the phantasm or directly in itself. The latter supposition is ruled out by the Thomist view, while on the other hand the phantasm is not actually intelligible (*intelligibile actu*), but the *species intelligibilis* has to be abstracted. In opposition to the Thomist view Matthew asserts that the intellect knows singular things in themselves and directly, by means of *species singulares*. It is sense intuition which apprehends the object as existing and

[1] *Q. Disp. de cognitione*, p. 291 and p. 280. [2] *Ibid.*, p. 254. [3] p. 307.

intellectual intuition which apprehends the individual quiddity or essence; but unless the mind had first of all an intuition of the singular thing, it could not abstract the universal notion. The *species universalis* thus presupposes the *species singularis*. Of course, the singular thing is not intelligible if by intelligible you mean deductively demonstrable, since it is contingent and passing; but if by intelligible you mean what can be apprehended by the intellect, then in this case it must be allowed that the singular thing is intelligible.[1] Otherwise it is not possible to explain satisfactorily the abstraction and real foundation of the universal idea.

Another theory of St. Thomas which Matthew rejects is the theory that the soul while united to the body has no direct intuition of itself and its dispositions and powers, but knows indirectly that it itself and its dispositions exist, through its perception of the act by which it knows objects through *species* abstracted from phantasms. This theory of the soul's purely indirect knowledge of itself Matthew rejects, as being contrary to the teaching of St. Augustine and also to what reason demands. It is unreasonable to suppose that the soul is so immersed in the body that it can apprehend nothing without an image or phantasm and that it can apprehend itself and its dispositions only indirectly. 'It seems altogether absurd to suppose the intellect so blind that it does not see itself, when it is by the intellect that the soul knows all things.'[2] His own theory Matthew states with considerable care. As regards the *beginning* of knowledge 'I say without any doubt that the soul can intuit neither itself nor the habits which are in it, nor can the first act of knowledge be directed to itself or the things which are in it.'[3] The soul needs a stimulus from the bodily senses for the beginning of knowledge, and then by reflecting on its own perceived act of knowing it comes to know its powers and itself as existent. But afterwards the soul turns in on itself, as it were (*quadam spirituali conversione in semetipsam revocata est*),[4] and then it can have a direct intuition of itself and its habits, these being no longer simply the non-intuited conclusions of a process of reasoning, but the direct object of a mental vision. In order that this intellectual vision should take place, four conditions are required, just as for sensitive vision, namely a visible object which is present as visible, a properly disposed power of vision, mutual proportion, and illumination. All these conditions are or can be fulfilled. The soul is an intellectually visible object and it is present

[1] *De cognitione*, p. 311. [2] *Ibid.*, p. 328. [3] *Ibid.*, p. 329. [4] *Ibid.*, p. 329.

to the intellect; the intellect is an immaterial power and is not intrinsically dependent on a sense-organ; both the intellect and the soul itself are intellectual finite objects, and nothing is so proportioned to the soul as the soul itself; lastly the divine illumination is always present.[1]

Matthew of Aquasparta thus adhered closely, though reasonably and with moderation, to the Augustinian tradition, and it is only to be expected that he would maintain the theories of the *rationes seminales* and the *forma corporeitatis*. In addition he upheld the Bonaventurian doctrine of the universal hylomorphic composition of creatures, rejecting the real distinction of essence and existence as an adequate explanation of their finitude and contingence.

4. A much less faithful Augustinian was *Peter John Olivi* (*c.* 1248–98), a prominent figure among the Franciscan 'spirituals'. Thus while he clung to the theory of the hylomorphic composition of all creatures and the multiplicability of angels in the same species, as also to the doctrine of plurality of forms, he not only denied the existence of *rationes seminales*, but even maintained that this denial was in accordance with the doctrine of St. Augustine. An anticipation of Scotus's *distinctio formalis a parte rei*, intermediate between a real distinction and a conceptual distinction, is to be found in his philosophy; and it exists between the divine attributes, for instance, as Scotus also thought. Olivi is also remarkable for having adopted the *impetus* theory of Joannes Philoponus, i.e. the theory that when a projectile is set in motion, the mover or thrower confers an impetus or *impulsus* on the projectile which carries the projectile on even when it is no longer in contact with the mover, though it may be overcome by the resistance of the air and other opposing forces. But consideration of this theory, which meant the abandonment of the Aristotelian theory of 'unnatural' motion, is best reserved for the next volume, in connection with those thinkers who drew some novel conclusions from the doctrine and paved the way for a new conception of the corporeal world. Further consideration of the *distinctio formalis a parte rei* will be reserved for the treatment of the Scotist system. My real reason for mentioning Olivi here is to allude briefly to his theory of the soul and its relation to the body. This theory, or part of it, was condemned at the Council of Vienne in 1311, and the matter is worth mentioning since certain

[1] The doctrines of the soul's intuition of itself and of the intellectual knowledge of the singular thing appear also in the teaching of the Franciscan *Vital du Four* (d. 1327).

writers in the past have claimed that the Council meant to condemn what they certainly did not mean to condemn.

According to Olivi, there are three constitutive 'parts' in the human soul, the vegetative principle or form, the sensitive principle or form, and the intellectual principle or form. These three forms together constitute the one human soul, the rational soul, as constitutive parts of the whole soul. There was no particular novelty in maintaining a doctrine of plurality of forms; but Olivi drew from his theory the peculiar conclusion that the three formal parts are united by the spiritual matter of the soul in such a way that the higher form influences and moves the lower forms only through the mediation of the spiritual matter. He concluded further that while the vegetative and sensitive parts inform the body, the intellectual part does not of itself inform the body, though it moves the others parts as its instruments and subjects. He maintained that the rooting of all three parts in the spiritual matter of the soul safeguarded the unity of man and the substantial union of soul and body; but at the same time he refused to allow that the intellectual part of the soul informs the body directly. This last point aroused opposition among the Franciscans themselves. One of the reasons of their opposition was that if it were true that the intellectual form did not inform the body directly but only mediately, through the sensitive form, it would follow that Christ was not, as Man, composed of a rational soul and a body, as the Faith teaches.[1] The end of the matter was that in 1311 the Council of Vienne condemned as heretical the proposition that the rational or intellectual soul does not inform the body directly (*per se*) and essentially (*essentialiter*). The Council did not, however, condemn the doctrine of the plurality of forms and affirm the Thomist view, as some later writers have tried to maintain. The Fathers of the Council, or the majority of them at least, themselves held the doctrine of the plurality of forms. The Council simply wished to preserve the unity of man by affirming that the intellectual soul informs the body directly. This is shown clearly by the reference to Christology. The human nature of Christ consists of a passible human body and a rational human soul which informs the body, the two together forming human nature. The Council did not concern itself with the question of the *forma corporeitatis* or with the question whether there

[1] In support of Olivi's thesis the reason was given that if the intellectual form informed the body directly, it would either give its own immortality to the body or lose its own immortality through informing the body.

are or are not various 'parts' in the human soul: what it says is simply that the rational soul informs the body directly and so is a principle integral to man: it was the separation between the intellectual soul and the human body which it condemned, not the doctrine of the plurality of forms. It is, therefore, quite erroneous to state that the Council of Vienne declared that the human soul informs prime matter directly and that the Thomist theory is imposed by the Church.

5. If Peter John Olivi was an independent thinker who departed on some points from the Augustinian tradition and prepared the way for later stages in Franciscan thought, *Roger Marston* (d. 1303), who was for a time Minister of the English Franciscan province, was a whole-hearted Augustinian. He embraced all the characteristic 'Augustinian' theories, such as the intellectual apprehension of the singular thing, the pre-eminence of will over intellect, universal hylomorphic composition in creatures, plurality of forms, and he criticised St. Thomas for admitting the apparent possibility of creation from eternity and for throwing overboard the *rationes seminales*. Indeed, this resolute English conservative found even Matthew of Aquasparta too accommodating and firmly rejected any attempt to water down what he regarded as the genuine doctrine of St. Augustine and St. Anselm. We should prefer the 'saints' to those 'infernal men', the pagan philosophers.

In his *De Anima* Roger Marston gives an uncompromising interpretation of St. Augustine's teaching on the divine illumination. The active intellect may indeed be called a part of the soul if by active intellect is meant a natural disposition in the soul for the knowledge of truth (*sicut perspicuitas naturalis in oculo*); but if by active intellect is meant the act of illumination, we must say that it is a separate substance, God Himself.[1] The active intellect is the uncreated or eternal light which impresses on the mind, as a seal on the wax, a certain active impression which leaves a passive impression that is the formal principle in the knowledge of unchanging truths.[2] It is not the concepts or terms of the judgement which are provided by the eternal light, God; but the eternal truth.[3] For example, the eternal light does not infuse into the mind the concept of the whole and the concept of the part, but it is the radiation of the eternal light which enables the mind to apprehend infallibly the relation between the terms, the eternal truth that the whole is greater than the part. The eternal ideas

[1] *De Anima*, p. 259. [2] *Ibid.*, p. 263. [3] *Ibid.*, p. 262.

are thus the ultimate foundation of the certain and infallible judgement (*rationes aeternae aliqualiter attinguntur*). The explanation of the fact that the human race agrees about the fundamental truths is to be found in the common illumination of all minds by the one divine light, and Roger Marston refuses to allow that this divine light consists simply in the creation of the human intellect as a finite imitation of the divine intellect. Those who deny that the active intellect is the primal and uncreated light are people who are 'drunk with the nectar of philosophy' and who pervert the meaning of St. Augustine and the *Sancti*.[1] If St. Augustine had not intended to say any more than these people make him say, then his arguments would be without point and would beg the question, since if the human intellect was assumed to be the source of its own light, one could not argue to the existence of an uncreated light, as St. Augustine certainly does.[2]

6. Another English Franciscan of note was *Richard of Middleton*, who studied at Oxford and Paris. He went to Paris in 1278, and after taking his degree he occupied one of the Franciscan chairs of theology until 1286, when he became tutor to St. Louis of Toulouse, the son of Charles II of Sicily. The date of his death is uncertain, but it must have occurred about the turn of the century. He composed the customary Commentary on the *Sentences* of Peter Lombard and was responsible for *Quaestiones Disputatae* and *Quodlibets*.

In some points Richard of Middleton followed the general Franciscan tradition, maintaining, for example, the impossibility of creation from eternity, since this would involve a created infinite, universal hylomorphic composition in creatures, the plurality of forms and the primacy of the will. On other points, however, he approximated to the Thomist position, and in this matter he represents the new movement among Franciscan thinkers towards a modified Augustinianism, the greatest exponent of which was Duns Scotus. Thus Richard insists not only that all valid demonstrations of God's existence are *a posteriori*, but also that our intellectual knowledge of spiritual as well as of corporeal beings is abstracted from sense-experience and that it is unnecessary to postulate any special illumination or to identify the active intellect with God. On the other hand, the mind apprehends the singular, though it does so by means of the same concept by which it apprehends the universal.

[1] *De Anima*, p. 273. [2] *Ibid*., p. 256.

In addition, Richard maintained some more or less original ideas. One of the less happy of these ideas was the notion that what the mind directly attains is not the individual existent thing itself, but its *esse repraesentatum*. He also invented a *principium pure possibile*, in order to explain how new forms can appear under the action of a created agent. It might appear at first that this is nothing else but prime matter; but matter, which differs in kind in spiritual and corporeal beings and so is not homogeneous, has some actuality of its own in Richard's eyes, whereas the *principium pure possibile* has no actuality of its own, is concreated with matter and cannot exist separately. If matter is understood as the primary foundation of natural change, as that which is common to corrupted and generated bodies and receives form, then it is really distinct from the purely potential principle, which is transmuted into the form itself. The purely potential principle may then be called the potentiality of matter (*potentia materiae*), if the potentiality of matter is understood as meaning the principle out of which the created agent educes the form and which is transmuted into the form educed; but in this case the *potentia materiae* is really distinct from matter itself. Conversely, if by *potentia materiae* is meant matter's power to receive form, it is the same as matter itself; but in this case it is really distinct from the *principium pure possibile.*[1] In other words, the power to receive form is not the same as the power to become form. Besides prime matter as the subject of change, which has some actuality of its own and which receives form, Richard postulates, then, a kind of receptacle of forms, a purely potential principle which is transmuted into those forms which are received in matter. He considered that this theory constituted an improvement on the theory of *rationes seminales*, and he tried to interpret St. Augustine as teaching the existence, not of active forces (which would amount to a *latitatio formarum*), but of a purely potential principle which becomes forms. In virtue of this positive potentiality forms may be said to be created from the beginning in potency, but this must not be taken to imply the presence of 'seeds'. The principle in question is in matter, and Richard calls it the more intimate part of matter and the passive potentiality of matter; but, as we have seen, it is not identical with matter as subject of change and recipient of form.[2] It is not, therefore, something altogether separate from matter, but it is distinct from matter in the ordinary

[1] *In 2 Sent.*, 12, 1, 10.

[2] *Ibid.*, 12, 1, 1.

sense. This may appear to involve an approximation to the Thomist view of prime matter, and to a certain extent this seems to be true; but Richard refused to abandon the traditional view of matter as having some actuality of its own, and so he had to distinguish matter as element in the composite thing from the potential principle which becomes forms under the action of the created agent.

In addition to being composed of matter and form every creature is also composed of essence and existence. But existence is not something really distinct from the essence, to which it comes as an accident. On the other hand, existence is not merely conceptually distinct from essence, since it does add something to essence. What does it add? A twofold relation: a *relatio rationis* to itself, inasmuch as existence confers on essence the dignity of being an hypostasis or substance, and a real relation to the Creator.[1] On this matter Richard of Middleton accepted the position of Henry of Ghent.

At the end of his work *Richard de Middleton*[2] Père E. Hocedez, S.J., remarks: *Richard finit une époque.* The last representative of the Seraphic School, he attempted a synthesis (*prudemment nouvelle*) in which the main positions of Bonaventure, deepened and perfected, should be integrated with what he considered best in Aristotelianism and in the theology of St. Thomas. That Richard of Middleton incorporated ideas from outside the Augustinian tradition is clear enough; but I cannot agree with Père Hocedez that this movement of thought 'had no morrow' and that Scotus directed Franciscan philosophy 'in new ways which were soon to end in nominalism'. Rather did Richard's philosophy form a stage on the way to Scotism, which opened the door wider to Aristotelianism, but was certainly not nominalistic or favourable to nominalism.

7. One of the most interesting of the Franciscan philosophers is *Raymond Lull* (1232/35–1315). Born in Majorca, Raymond Lull was for a time at the court of King James II; but about 1265 he underwent a religious conversion and abandoned his family in order to devote himself to what he considered his great task in life, to fight against Islam and to help in the rooting out of Averroism. With this end in view he devoted nine years to the study of Arabic and philosophy, the first fruit of the period of study being his *Ars Magna*, followed by the *Liber principiorum*

[1] *In 2 Sent.*, 3, 1, 1; *Quodlibet*, 1, 8. [2] Paris, 1925.

philosophiae. He joined the Third Order of St. Francis and travelled to Africa to convert the Moors; he taught at Paris and combated Averroism; he wrote logic, philosophy, theology and poetry, writing in his native Catalan and in Arabic, as well as in Latin. Finally he was martyred in Tunisia in 1315. Besides the two above-mentioned works one may mention the *Ars demonstrativa*, the *Ars brevis*, the *Ars generalis ultima*, and the anti-Averroistic works such as the *Liber contra errores Boetii et Segerii* (i.e. against Boethius of Dacia and Siger of Brabant), the *De naturali modo intelligendi*, the *Liber reprobationis aliquorum errorum Averrois*, the *Disputatio Raymundi et Averroistae* and the *Sermones contra Averroistas*. But this forms but a selection of the astonishing literary output of a man who was apostle and traveller, poet and mystic.

The apostolic interests of Raymond Lull were by no means irrelevant to his philosophy; they were partly responsible for the general attitude he adopted towards philosophy, whose ancillary relation to theology he stressed. He was quite aware of the distinction between faith and reason, and he compared faith to oil which continues to rest unmixed on the water, even if the water is increased; but his interest in the conversion of the Moslems naturally led to an insistence, not only on philosophy's subordinate relation to theology, but also on reason's ability to make acceptable the dogmas of the Faith. It is in the light of this general attitude that we must understand his proposal to 'prove' the articles of faith by 'necessary reasons'. He no more proposed to rationalise (in the modern sense) the Christian mysteries than did St. Anselm or Richard of St. Victor, when they spoke of 'necessary reasons' for the Trinity, and he expressly declares that faith treats of objects which the human reason cannot understand; but he wished to show the Moslems that Christian beliefs are not contrary to reason and that reason can meet the objections adduced against them. Moreover, believing that the accusation brought against the Averroists that they held a 'double truth' theory was justified and that the theory in question was contradictory and absurd, he was concerned to show that there is no need to have recourse to any such radical separation of theology and philosophy, but that theological dogmas harmonise with reason and cannot be impugned by reason. In regard to the peculiar theories of the Averroists themselves, he argued that these are contrary both to faith and reason. Monopsychism, for instance, contradicts the testimony of consciousness: we are conscious that our acts of thought and will are our own.

If one looked merely at the familiar 'Augustinian' theories maintained by Lull, such as the impossibility of creation from eternity, universal hylomorphic composition of creatures, plurality of forms, the primacy of will over intellect, and so on, there would not appear to be any particularly interesting feature in his philosophy; but we find such a feature in his *Ars combinatoria*. Raymond Lull supposes first of all that there are certain general principles or categories, which are self-evident and which are common to all sciences, in the sense that without them there can be neither philosophy nor any other science. The most important of these are the nine absolute predicates, goodness, greatness, eternity, power, wisdom, will, virtue, truth, glory. (These predicates express attributes of God.) There are nine other concepts which express relations (between creatures): difference, agreement, contrariety, beginning, middle, end, majority, equality, minority. In addition, there are sets of fundamental questions, such as how, when, where, etc., of virtues and of vices. Lull cannot have attached any particular importance to the number nine, which appears in the *Ars generalis*, as elsewhere he gives other numbers of divine attributes or absolute predicates; for example, in the *Liber de voluntate infinita et ordinata* he gives twelve, while in the *De possibili et impossibili* he gives twenty: the main point is that there are certain fundamental ideas which are essential to philosophy and science.

These fundamental ideas being presupposed, Raymond Lull speaks as though through their combination one could discover the principles of the particular sciences and even discover new truths, and in order that the work of combination might be facilitated, he had recourse to symbolism, the fundamental concepts being symbolised by letters, and to mechanical means of tabulating and grouping. For example, God was represented by the letter A, and, in the later writings, nine *principia*, also symbolised by letters representing the divine attributes, surround Him. These principles could be combined in a hundred and twenty ways through the use of figures and concentric circles. It is not to be wondered at, therefore, that some writers have seen in Lull's scheme an anticipation of Leibniz's dream of the *caracteristica universalis* and *Ars combinatoria*, of an algebraic symbolism, the use of which would permit the deduction from fundamental concepts not only of already ascertained truths, but even of new truths. As already mentioned, Lull does seem to imply such an aim on occasion, and if this had been his real object, he would obviously have to be considered as separating himself from the Scholastic tradition; but in point of fact he expressly asserts[1] that his aim was to facilitate the use of the memory. Moreover, we must remember his apostolic interests, which suggest that his scheme was designed for purposes of exposition and explanation rather than of deduction in the strict sense. The fact that Leibniz was influenced by Lull proves nothing as to the latter's intentions, of course. According to Dr. Otto Keicher, O.F.M.,[2] it is the *principia* which form the essence not only of the *Ars generalis*, but of the whole system of Raymond Lull; but though it is obvious enough that what Lull regarded as fundamental concepts formed in a sense the basis of his system, it does not seem that one can reduce his 'art' to the establishment of certain principles or categories: the philosopher himself regarded it as something more than that. Of course, if one stresses the expository, didactic aspect of the art, it is scarcely necessary to debate what are the essential and unessential elements in it; but if one chooses to regard it as an anticipation of Leibniz, then it would be relevant to make a distinction between Lull's schematism and mechanical technique on the one hand and on the other hand the general notion of deducing the principles of the sciences from a combination of fundamental concepts, since Lull might have anticipated Leibniz in regard to the latter's general principle, even though his 'logical algebra' was radically deficient. This is more or less the view of Dr. Bernhard Geyer,[3] and I believe it to be correct. That Lull pursues his deduction in reliance on three main principles;[4] to hold as true everything which affirms the greatest harmony between God and created being, to attribute to God that which is the most perfect, and to assume that God has made whatever truly appears to be the better, is no argument against this interpretation: it doubtless shows the spiritual kinship between Lull and the Augustinian tradition, but it also reminds one of important points in the system of Leibniz some centuries later.

[1] *Compendium artis demonstrativae*, prol.

[2] *Beiträge*, 7, 4–5, p. 19.

[3] Ueberweg-Geyer, *Die patristische und scholastische Philosophie*, p. 460.

[4] Cf. Article, 'Lulle' by Père E. Longpré in *Dictionnaire de théologie catholique*, vol. 9.

CHAPTER XLIV

GILES OF ROME AND HENRY OF GHENT

(*a*) Giles of Rome. *Life and works—The independence of Giles as a thinker—Essence and existence—Form and matter; soul and body—Political theory.*
(*b*) Henry of Ghent. *Life and works—Eclecticism, illustrated by doctrines of illumination and innatism—Idea of metaphysics—Essence and existence—Proofs of God's existence—General spirit and significance of Henry's philosophy.*

(*a*) *Giles of Rome*

1. Giles (Aegidius) of Rome was born in 1247 or a little earlier and entered the Order of the Hermits of St. Augustine about 1260. He made his studies at Paris and seems to have attended the lectures of St. Thomas Aquinas from 1269 to 1272. It appears that he composed the *Errores Philosophorum* about 1270, in which he enumerates the errors of Aristotle, Averroes, Avicenna, Algazel, Alkindi and Maimonides. The Commentaries on the *De generatione et corruptione*, the *De Anima*, the *Physics*, the *Metaphysics* and the logical treatises of Aristotle, the Commentary on the first book of the *Sentences* and the works entitled *Theoremata de Corpore Christi* and *De plurificatione intellectus possibilis* were apparently also written before 1277. In that year occurred the famous condemnation by Stephen Tempier, Bishop of Paris (March 7th); but between Christmas 1277 and Easter 1278 Giles wrote the *De gradibus formarum*, in which he came out strongly against the doctrine of plurality of forms. For this and similar offences Giles was called upon to make a retractation; but he refused and was excluded from the University of Paris before he had completed his theological studies. In his period of absence from Paris he wrote the *Theoremata de esse et essentia* and his Commentary on the second and third books of the *Sentences*.

In 1285 Giles returned to Paris and was permitted to receive the licentiate in theology, though he had to make a public retractation first. He then taught theology at Paris, until he was elected General of the Order in 1292. In 1295 he was appointed Archbishop of Bourges. The works he wrote after his return to Paris in 1285 include *Quaestiones disputatae de esse et essentia*, *Quaestiones Quodlibetales*, a Commentary on the *Liber de Causis*, exegetical works such as the *In Hexaëmeron* and political treatises like the *De regimine principum* and the *De potestate ecclesiastica*. Giles died at Avignon in 1316.

2. Giles of Rome has sometimes been represented as a 'Thomist'; but though he found himself in agreement with St. Thomas on some points, as against the Franciscans, he can scarcely be called a disciple of St. Thomas: he was an independent thinker, and his independence shows itself even in matters where he might at first sight appear to be following St. Thomas. For instance, though he certainly maintained a real distinction between essence and existence, he equally certainly went beyond what St. Thomas taught on this question. Moreover, though he rejected the plurality of forms in 1277, going so far as to declare that this doctrine was contrary to the Catholic faith,[1] it has been shown that this had not always been his view. In the Commentary on the *De Anima*[2] he spoke hesitantly and doubtfully on the unicity of the substantial form in man, and the same is true in regard to the *Theoremata de Corpore Christi*,[3] while in the *Errores Philosophorum* he had stated that the doctrine of the unicity of the substantial form in man is false.[4] It is clear, then, that he began with the 'Augustinian' or Franciscan view, and that he advanced to the opposite theory only gradually.[5] No doubt he was influenced by St. Thomas in the matter, but it does not look as though he simply accepted Thomas's doctrine without question. He did not hesitate to criticise Thomist positions or to deviate from them when he wished to; and when he agreed with them, it is evident that he agreed as a result of personal thought and reflection, not because he was or had been a disciple of St. Thomas. The legend of Giles of Rome as a 'Thomist' was really a conclusion from the fact that he listened to lectures by St. Thomas for a period; but attendance at a professor's lectures is not a sure guarantee of discipleship.

3. Giles of Rome was considerably influenced by the neo-Platonist theory of participation. Existence (*esse*) flows from God and is a participation of the divine existence. It is received by essence and is really distinct from essence. That it is received by essence can be empirically established as regards corporeal things, since they have a beginning of existence and are not always joined to existence, a fact which shows that they are in potentiality to existence, and that existence is really distinct from the essence

[1] *De gradibus formarum*, f. 211 v. [2] 1, 12, 16. [3] Prop. 47, f. 36 v. [4] 1, 11.
[5] On the question of the dating and authenticity of the *Errores Philosophorum* see the edition by J. Koch, listed in the bibliography.

of the sensible thing. Indeed, if existence were not really distinct from essence in all created things, creatures would not be creatures: they would exist in virtue of their own essence and would thus be independent of God's creative activity. The real distinction is, therefore, an essential safeguard of the doctrine of creation. Needless to say, the statement that created existence is a participation of the divine existence was not meant to imply pantheism. It was precisely the created character of finite things, of the participations, which Giles wanted to uphold. By essence Giles meant, in the case of material things, the composite of form and matter. The composite or corporeal essence possesses a mode of being (*modus essendi*) which is derived from the union of form and matter (in the case of immaterial creatures the mode of being comes from the form alone); but it does not of itself possess existence in the proper sense (*esse simpliciter*), which is received. The attribution of a *modus essendi* to the essence would seem to make of the latter a thing, and this aspect of the theory is accentuated by Giles's explicit teaching that essence and existence are not only really distinct, but also separable. In fact, he does not hesitate to speak of them as separable things.

This exaggerated version of the theory of the real distinction led to a lively controversy between Giles of Rome and Henry of Ghent, who attacked Giles's doctrine in his first *Quodlibet* (1276). The *Quaestiones disputatae de esse et essentia* contained Giles's answer to Henry; but the latter returned to the attack in his tenth *Quodlibet* (1286), to which Giles retorted in his twelfth *Quaestio disputata*, maintaining therein that unless existence and essence were really distinct, in the sense in which he taught the real distinction, annihilation of a creature would be impossible. He continued to hold, therefore, that his real distinction is absolutely necessary, in order to safeguard the creature's total dependence on God. The fact that he taught a real distinction between essence and existence links him with St. Thomas; but St. Thomas certainly did not teach that essence and existence are two separable things: this was an original, if somewhat strange contribution of Giles himself.

4. Giles of Rome was inclined, as his theory of essence and existence shows, to suppose that wherever the mind detects a real distinction there is separability. Thus the mind abstracts the universal from the individual (abstraction being the work of the passive intellect, when the active intellect has illumined the passive

intellect and the phantasm) by apprehending the form of the object without the matter. Therefore, form and matter are really distinct and separable. Now, matter, which is found only in corporeal things, is the principle of individuation, and it follows that if matter and all the individual conditions which follow from it could be removed, the individuals of any given species would be one. Perhaps this is a legitimate conclusion from the doctrine of matter as the principle of individuation; but in any case the tendency to ultra-realism is obvious, and Giles's inclination to equate 'really distinct from' with 'separable from' is partly responsible.

Again, form (soul) and body are really distinct and separable. There is nothing novel in this idea, of course; but Giles suggested that the body may remain a body, that is, numerically the same body, after separation from the form, since before actual separation it was separable, and actual separation does not change its numerical identity.[1] Body in this sense would mean extended and organised matter. Incidentally, this theory afforded him a simple explanation of the way in which Christ's body was numerically identical before and after Christ's death on the Cross. He neither had to have recourse to the doctrine of a *forma corporeitatis* (in which he did not believe) nor was he compelled to refer the numerical identity of Christ's body in the sepulchre with His body before death simply to its union with the Divinity. Moreover, one of the reasons why Giles of Rome attacked the doctrine of plurality of forms as incompatible with theological orthodoxy was that, in his opinion, it endangered the doctrine of Christ's death. If there are several forms in man and only one of them, which is peculiar to man and is not found in other animals, is separated at death, then Christ could not be said to have undergone bodily death. The theological reason was not his only reason by any means for attacking the plurality of forms; he believed, for instance, that different forms are contrary and cannot be found together in the same substance.

5. The *De ecclesiastica potestate* is of interest not merely intrinsically, as treating of the relation between Church and State, but also because it was one of the works which were utilised by Pope Boniface VIII in the composition of his famous Bull, *Unam*

[1] It might appear that on Giles's theory the soul (i.e. the form) in a state of separation from the body would not be individual; but it must be remembered that for him, as for St. Thomas, it was individuated by union with matter and retained its individuality.

Sanctam (November 18th, 1302). In his *De regimine principum*, written for the prince who was to become Philip the Fair of France, Giles wrote in dependence on Aristotle and St. Thomas; but in the *De potestate ecclesiastica* he propounded a doctrine of papal absolutism and sovereignty and of the Pope's jurisdiction even in temporal matters which was aimed especially against the pretensions of monarchs and which was most acceptable to Boniface VIII. In this work he relied much more on the attitude shown by St. Augustine towards the State than on the political thought of St. Thomas, and what St. Augustine had said with the pagan empires principally in mind was applied by Giles to contemporary kingdoms, the doctrine of Papal supremacy being added.[1] There are indeed two powers, two swords, that of the Pope and that of the king; but temporal power is subject to the spiritual. 'If the earthly power goes wrong, it will be judged by the spiritual power as by its superior; but if the spiritual power, and especially the power of the supreme pontiff, acts wrongly, it can be judged by God alone.'[2] When Philip IV of France accused Boniface VIII of asserting, in the *Unam Sanctam*, that the Holy See has direct power over kings even in temporal matters, the Pope replied that that had not been his intention: he did not mean to usurp the power of kings, but to make it clear that kings, like any other members of the Church, were subject to the Church *ratione peccati*. It would appear, however, that Giles of Rome, who spoke, of course, simply as a private theologian, went much further in this matter than Boniface VIII. He admits that there are two swords and two powers and that the one power is vested in the monarch, the other in the Church, and especially in the Papacy; but he goes on to say that although priests and especially the supreme pontiff ought not under the new law, that is, in the Christian dispensation, to wield the material sword as well as the spiritual sword; this is not because the Church does not possess the material sword, but rather because it possesses the material sword, *non ad usum, sed ad nutum*. In other words, just as Christ possessed all power, spiritual and temporal, but did not actually use His temporal power, so the Church possesses power in temporal matters, though it is not expedient for her to exercise this power immediately and continually. Just as the body is ordered to the soul and should be subject to the soul, so the temporal power is ordered to the

[1] I do not mean to imply that Augustine rejected the pre-eminence of the Roman See; but it would be absurd to say that he maintained the doctrine of Papal jurisdiction in temporal affairs.

[2] I, 5.

spiritual power and should be subject to it, even in temporal matters. The Church has, then, supreme jurisdiction even in temporal matters; and the logical consequence is that kings are little more than lieutenants of the Church.[1] 'All temporal things are placed under the dominion and power of the Church and especially of the supreme pontiff.'[2] This theory was followed by James of Viterbo in his *De regimine Christiano* before September 1302.

In 1287 the signal honour was paid to Giles of Rome of being made the Doctor of his Order during his own lifetime, not only in regard to what he had already written, but also in regard to what he should write in the future.

(*b*) *Henry of Ghent*

6. Henry of Ghent was born at Tournai or at Ghent at a date which cannot be determined. (His family came originally from Ghent in any case; but it was not a noble family, as legend had it.) By 1267 he was a Canon of Tournai, and in 1276 he became Archdeacon of Bruges. In 1279 he was made principal Archdeacon of Tournai. His archidiaconal duties do not seem to have been very exacting, as he taught at Paris, first in the faculty of arts and later (from 1276) in that of theology. In 1277 he was a member of the commission of theologians which assisted Stephen Tempier, Bishop of Paris. His works include a *Summa Theologica*, fifteen *Quodlibets*, *Quaestiones super Metaphysicam Aristotelis* (1–6), *Syncathegorematum Liber* and a *Commentum in Librum de Causis*; but it does not appear that the last three works can be attributed to him with certainty, and the same can be said of the Commentary on the *Physics* of Aristotle. It is, therefore, the *Summa Theologica* and the *Quodlibets* which constitute the sure source for our knowledge of Henry's teaching. He died on June 29th, 1293. He was never a member of the Servite Order, as was once maintained.

7. Henry of Ghent was an eclectic thinker and can be called neither an Augustinian nor an Aristotelian. This eclecticism may be illustrated by his theory of knowledge. If one read a proposition such as *omnis cognitio nostra a sensu ortum habet*,[3] one might suppose that Henry was a decided Aristotelian, with little sympathy for Augustinianism, and especially if one read the proposition in conjunction with his statement that man can know that which is true in the creature without any special divine illumination, but simply through his natural powers aided by God's ordinary

[1] Cf. 1, 8–9. [2] 2, 4. [3] *Summa*, 3, 3, 4; 3, 4, 4.

concurrence.[1] But this is only one aspect of his thought. The knowledge of creatures which we can attain through sense-experience is but a superficial knowledge, and though we can without illumination know what is true in the creature, we cannot without illumination know its truth. The reason why knowledge based simply on sense-experience is superficial, is this. The *species intelligibilis* contains no more than was contained in the *species sensibilis*: by the latter we apprehend the object in its singularity and by the former we apprehend the object in its universal aspect; but neither the one nor the other gives us the intelligible essence of the object in its relation to the divine ideas, and without the apprehension of the intelligible essence we cannot form a certain judgement concerning the object. The 'truth' (*Veritas*) of the object consists in its relation to the unchanging truth, and in order to apprehend this relation we need the divine illumination.[2] Thus when Henry of Ghent says that our knowledge comes from sense, he restricts the extension of 'knowledge': 'it is one thing to know concerning a creature that which is true in it, and it is another thing to know its truth.' The 'truth' of a thing is conceived by him in an Augustinian manner, and to apprehend it illumination is necessary. He may have made comparatively little use of the illumination theory and watered down Augustinianism to a certain extent, but the Augustinian element was certainly present in his thought: the natural operations of sense and intellect explain what one might call man's normal knowledge, which is a comparatively superficial knowledge of objects, but they do not and cannot explain the whole range of possible human knowledge.

A similar eclectic tendency can be seen in his doctrine of innatism. He rejected the Platonic doctrine of innatism and reminiscence and he rejected the theory of Avicenna that in this life ideas are impressed by the *Dator formarum*; but he did not accept the doctrine of Aristotle (as commonly interpreted) that all our ideas are formed by reflection on the data of sense-experience. Henry made his own the statement of Avicenna that the ideas of being, thing, and necessity are of such a kind that they are imprinted immediately on the soul by an impression which owes nothing to anterior and better-known ideas.[3] On the other hand, the primary ideas, of which the most important and the ultimate is that of being, are not innate in the strict sense, but are conceived

[1] *Summa*, 1, 2, 11 and 13. [2] *Ibid.*, 1, 2, 26.
[3] Avicenna, *Metaphysics*, 1, 2, 1; Henry, *Summa*, 1, 12, 9; 3, 1, 7.

together with experience of sense-objects, even if they are not derived from that experience.[1] The mind seems to draw these ideas out of itself or rather to form them from within on the occasion of sense-experience.[2] As the idea of being embraces both uncreated and created being,[3] the idea of God may be called innate in a certain sense; but this does not mean that man has from birth an actual idea of God, the origin of which is quite independent of experience: the idea is only virtually innate, in the sense that a man forms it from the idea of being, which is itself presupposed by experience of concrete objects but does not arise in clear consciousness, is not actually formed, until experience is enjoyed. As metaphysics really consist in an investigation of the idea of being and in the realisation of the relation between the intelligible essences of created being and uncreated being, one would expect that the necessity of illumination would be emphasised; but Henry frequently describes the genesis of ideas and of knowledge without any reference to a special illumination, possibly under the influence of Aristotle and of Avicenna. His tendency to eclecticism seems to have led to a certain carelessness in regard to consistency.

8. While the natural philosopher or *physicus* starts with the singular object and then forms by abstraction the universal notion of the sensible object, the metaphysician starts with the idea of being (or *res* or *aliquid*) and proceeds to discover the intelligible essences virtually contained in that idea.[4] There is a certain overlapping, of course, between the provinces of physics and metaphysics, since, for example, when the metaphysician says that man is a rational animal, he apprehends the same object as the physicist, who says that man is a body and a soul; but the starting-point and the mode of approach of the metaphysician is different from that of the physicist. The metaphysician, proceeding from the more universal to the less universal, from genus to species, defines the intelligible essence of man, whereas the physicist starts from the individual man and by abstraction apprehends and states the physical components of all men.

Being or *res* in the widest sense comprises *res secundum opinionem* (such as a golden mountain) which have only mental being, and *res secundum veritatem*, which have an actual or possible extramental existence,[5] and it is being in the second sense which

[1] Cf. *Summa*, 1, 11, 6; 1, 5, 5.
[2] Cf. *ibid.*, 1, 11, 18.
[3] For the qualification which makes this statement not strictly true, see section 10.
[4] *Quodlibet*, 4, 4, 143.
[5] *Ibid.*, 7, 1, 389.

is *ens metaphysicum*, the object of metaphysics. Just as *ens* in the widest sense is divided analogically, so is *ens metaphysicum* divided analogically into that which is *ipsum esse*, God, and that *cui convenit esse*, creatures. Being is thus not a genus or predicament. Again, being in the last sense, *aliquid cui convenit vel natum est convenire esse*, comprises and is divided analogically into substances, to which it pertains to exist in themselves (*esse in se*) and accidents, to which it pertains to exist in another (*esse in alio*), that is, in a substance. It is quite true that for Aristotle too metaphysics was the science of being as being; but for Aristotle the idea of being was not the starting-point, the analysis of which leads to the discovery of the analogical divisions of being: Henry of Ghent was inspired in this matter by the thought of Avicenna, whose philosophy was also influential in the building of the Scotist system. According to both Henry of Ghent and Scotus the metaphysician studies the idea of being, and metaphysics move primarily on the conceptual level.

It might appear that on this view not only is it difficult to effect a passage from the essential level to the existential level, but also that there would be confusion between the *res secundum opinionem* and the *res secundum veritatem*. However, Henry maintained that essences which are actualised or which are objectively possible have and can be discerned as having a certain reality of their own, an *esse essentiae*, the possession of which distinguishes them from pure *entia rationis*. The theory of *esse essentiae*, which Henry took from Avicenna, must not be understood, however, to imply a kind of inchoate existence, as though the essence had an extramental existence of a rudimentary sort; Henry accused Giles of Rome of maintaining a theory of this kind: it means that the essence exists actually in thought, that it is definable, that it is an intelligible essence.[1] Its intelligibility, its intrinsic possibility, distinguishes it from the *res secundum opinionem*, from the notion, for example, of a being half man and half goat, which is a contradictory notion. As to the relation between the essential level and the existential level, it is evident enough that we can know the existence of the singular only through experience of the singular (there is no question in Henry's philosophy of any deduction of singulars), while the intelligible essence, which is universal in character, is not deduced from the notion of being so much as 'arranged' under the notion of being. As we have seen, the natural philosopher detects

[1] Cf. *Quodlibet*, 3, 2, 80.

in man his physical components, body and soul; but man is defined by the metaphysician as a rational animal, in terms of genus and species, in terms of his intelligible essence. This intelligible essence is thus arranged under the notion of being and its (analogical) 'contractions', as a particular kind of substance; but that man actually exists is known only by experience. On the other hand, the intelligible essence is a reflection (an *exemplatum* or *ideatum*) of the Idea in God, the exemplar or absolute essence, and God knows singular things through essence considered as multipliable in numerically different substances or *supposita*: there are no ideas of singular things as such in God, but the latter are known by Him in and through the specific essence.[1] From this it would seem to follow either that singular things are contained in the universal idea in some way and are, theoretically at least, deducible from it or that one must relinquish any prospect of rendering singular things intelligible.[2] Henry would not allow that individuality adds any real element to the specific essence:[3] individual things differ from one another simply in virtue of the fact that they exist actually and extramentally. If, then, the individuation cannot be explained in terms of a real added element, it must be explained in terms of a negation, a double negation, that of internal or intrinsic division and that of identity with any other being. Scotus attacked this view on the ground that the principle of individuation cannot be a negation and that the negation must presuppose something positive; but, of course, Henry did presuppose something positive, namely existence.[4]

The above may seem a confusing and perhaps somewhat irrelevant account of varied items of Henry's doctrine, but it is meant to bring out a fundamental difficulty in his system. In so far as metaphysics are a study of the idea of being and of intelligible essences and in so far as individuals are considered as intelligible only as contained in the essence, Henry's metaphysic is of a Platonic type, whereas his theory of individuation looks forward to the Ockhamist view that there is no need to seek for any principle of individuation, since a thing is individual by the very fact that it exists. If the first point of view demands an explanation of objects in terms of essence, the second demands an explanation in terms of existence, of creation and making; and

[1] Scotus attacked this theory of Henry of Ghent.
[2] Cf. *Quodlibet*, 2, 1, 46.
[3] *Ibid.*, 8, 57f.
[4] For Henry's doctrine of the double negation, cf. *Quodlibet*, 5, 8, 245ff.

Henry juxtaposes the two points of view without achieving any adequate reconciliation.

9. We have seen that Henry of Ghent endowed the intelligible essence with an *esse essentiae*, as distinguished from the *esse existentiae*. What is the nature of the distinction in question? In the first place Henry rejected the theory of Giles of Rome, who transported the distinction on to the physical plane and made it a distinction between two separable things, essence and existence. Against this view Henry argued in his first (9), tenth (7) and eleventh (3) *Quodlibets*. If existence were distinct from essence in the sense postulated by Giles of Rome, existence would itself be an essence and would require another existence in order to exist; so that an infinite process would be involved. Moreover, what would existence, really distinct from essence, be? Substance or accident? One could maintain neither answer. Furthermore, Henry rejected the real distinction understood as a metaphysical distinction: the essence of an existent object is in no way indifferent to existence or non-existence; in the concrete order a thing either is or it is not. Existence is not a constitutive element or principle of a thing, of such a kind that the thing would be a synthesis of essence and existence; any synthesis there may be, that is, by way of addition of existence to essence, is the work of the mind.[1] On the other hand, the content of the concept of essence is not identical with the content of the concept of existence: the idea of an existent essence contains more, to our view, than the mere idea of essence as such. The distinction, therefore, though not a real distinction, is not a purely logical distinction, but an 'intentional' distinction, expressing different *intentiones* concerning the same simple thing.[2]

But if the actualised essence contains more than the essence conceived as possible and if the real distinction between essence and existence is not to be reintroduced, what can this 'more' be? According to Henry of Ghent, it consists in a relation, the relation of effect to Cause, of creature to Creator. It is one and the same thing for a creature to exist and to depend on God:[3] to be an effect of God and to have *esse existentiae ab ipso* are the same, namely a *respectus* or relation to God. The essence considered merely as possible is an *exemplatum* and depends on the divine knowledge, whereas the actualised or existent essence depends on

[1] Cf. *Quodlibet*, 3, 9, 100; *Summa*, 21, 4, 10.
[2] Cf. *Summa*, 21, 4, 7ff.; 27, 1, 25; 28, 4, 7.
[3] *Quodlibet*, 10, 7, 153.

the divine creative power,[1] so that the notion of the latter contains more than the notion of the former; but though the relation of the actualised essence to God is a real relation of dependence, it is not distinct from the essence in the concrete order with a real distinction. From the metaphysical point of view, then, God alone can be thought without relation to any other being; the creature, apart from the twofold relationship to God (as *exemplatum* to Exemplar and as effect to Cause), is nothing. Through the first relationship *by itself* the essence does not exist 'outside' God; by the second relationship it exists as an actualised essence; but apart from that relationship it has no *esse existentiae*, since the *esse existentiae* and the *respectus ad Deum* are the same.

10. Henry of Ghent admitted the *a posteriori* proofs of God's existence; but he regarded them as physical in character (his ideas of physics or natural philosophy and of metaphysics could lead to no other conclusion) and as inferior to the *a priori* proof. The physical proofs can lead us to the recognition of a pre-eminent Being, but they cannot reveal to us the essence of that Being: as far as these proofs are concerned, the existence of God is an existence of fact, which is not revealed as also an existence of right. The metaphysical proof, however, makes us see God's existence as necessarily contained in, or rather identical with His essence.[2] Similarly, it is only the metaphysical proof which can firmly establish the unicity of God, by showing that the divine essence has an intrinsic repugnance to any multiplication.[3]

The *a priori* idea of God, that of the supreme conceivable simple Perfection, which cannot not exist, was assumed by Henry of Ghent as one of the primary notions, namely Being, thing or essence, and Necessity. One might expect that he would attempt to deduce the notions of necessary Being and contingent being from an original univocal concept of being; but in point of fact he refused to admit the univocal character of the concept of being. Our realisation of what necessary Being is and our realisation of what contingent being is grow *pari passu*: we cannot have an imperfect knowledge of the latter without an imperfect knowledge of the former, nor a perfect knowledge of the latter without a perfect knowledge of the former.[4] There is no one univocal concept of being common to God and creatures: there are two concepts, that of necessary Being and that of contingent being, and our

[1] *Summa*, 21, 4, 10.
[2] Cf. *ibid.*, 24, 6, 7; 22, 4; 22, 5.
[3] *Ibid.*, 22, 3; 25, 2–3.
[4] *Ibid.*, 24, 8, 6; 7, 7.

concept of being must be one or the other. We can, however, confuse the two. There are two sorts of indetermination, negative indetermination and privative indetermination. A being is negatively indeterminate when it excludes all possibility of determination in the sense of finitude, and God alone is indeterminate in this sense, while a being is privatively indeterminate when it can or must be determined but is not yet determined or is considered in abstraction from its determinations.[1] Thus if one considers being in abstraction from its determinations, one is considering *created* being, which must in the concrete be either substance or accident but which can be considered in abstraction from these determinations, and this concept of the *privative indeterminatum* does not comprise God, the *negative indeterminatum.* But the mind can easily confuse the two concepts and conceive them as one, although they are in reality two. In saying this and in excluding any univocal concept of being common to God and creatures Henry of Ghent wished to avoid the Avicennian idea of necessary creation, which would seem to follow if one could deduce from an original univocal concept of being both necessary and created being; but he came perilously near to teaching, and he was accused by Scotus of so teaching, that the two concepts of being are equivocal. It is perfectly true that Henry expounded a doctrine of analogy and asserted that 'being' is not used purely equivocally of God and creatures;[2] but he insisted so much that the concept of being is either the concept of God or the concept of creatures and that there is no positive community between them, but only negative, (without there being any positive foundation whatsoever for the negation, i.e. the 'indetermination') that there would seem to be considerable justification for Scotus's accusation.[3] Scotus objected that on Henry's view every argument from creatures to God must be fallacious, and it would indeed appear that if that aspect of Henry's thought to which Scotus objected is emphasised, the only way of safeguarding man's philosophical knowledge of God would be to recognise the existence of an *a priori* idea of God, not derived from experience of creatures.

11. Henry of Ghent was, it has been said, an eclectic, and of this eclecticism some examples have been given. While he combated the theory of the real distinction put forward by Giles of Rome (and even that of St. Thomas, though Giles was the

[1] Cf. *Summa*, 21, 2, 14.
[2] Cf. *ibid.*, 21, 2, 6 and 8.
[3] Cf. *ibid.*, 21, 2, 17; 21, 2, *ad* 3.

particular object of attack), while he refused to allow the possibility of creation from eternity, and while he rejected the Thomist theory of individuation, he also rejected the doctrine of universal hylomorphism in creatures and opposed the doctrine of plurality of forms so far as material beings other than man were concerned. In the first *Quodlibet* Henry adopted the Thomist theory of the unicity of the substantial form in man, but in the second *Quodlibet* he changed his opinion and admitted the *forma corporeitatis* in man. On the other hand, while he postulated special illumination of a restricted type and while he maintained the superiority of the free will to the intellect, he borrowed a good deal from Aristotle, was strongly influenced by the philosophy of Avicenna and, in his doctrine of individuation, bears more resemblance to the thinkers of the Ockhamist movement than to his predecessors. Yet to call a philosopher an 'eclectic' without qualification implies that he achieved no synthesis and that his philosophy is a collection of juxtaposed opinions borrowed from various sources. In the case of Henry of Ghent, to picture him in this light would be to commit an injustice. He was certainly not always consistent, nor do his opinions and tendencies of thought always harmonise well with one another; but he belonged definitely to the Platonic tradition in Christian thought and his borrowings from Aristotle and Aristotelian thinkers do not really affect this fact; St. Bonaventure himself had utilised Aristotle, but he was none the less an Augustinian. The main tendency of Henry as metaphysician was to construct a metaphysic of the intelligible, a metaphysic of essences rather than of the concrete, and this marks him off as a philosopher of the Platonic tradition.

But if Henry belonged to the Platonic tradition, he was also a Christian philosopher. Thus he maintained clearly the doctrine of free creation out of nothing. He did not attempt to deduce created existence from the idea of being, and in his desire to avoid making creation necessary he rejected the univocity of the concept of being as a starting-point for metaphysical deduction. Plato himself, of course, never attempted an 'idealist' deduction of this type; but Henry, unlike Plato or any other pagan Greek philosopher, had a clear idea of creation and he stressed the dependence of all created things on God, maintaining that they were nothing apart from their relationship to Him. This prominent Christian element in his thought sets him in the Augustinian tradition, from which he drew his doctrines of illumination and of virtually innate ideas, of ideas which can be formed from within. On the other hand, while he tried to avoid what he considered to be the faults of the philosophy of Avicenna, his metaphysic was strongly influenced by the Moslem philosopher's thought, so that M. Gilson has been able to speak in this connection of an *augustinisme avicennisant.* Apart from the fact that Henry brings together God in His function as illuminator (St. Augustine) with the separate active intellect of Avicenna (a *rapprochement* which was not peculiar to Henry), his doctrine of mitigated innatism naturally inclined him to a metaphysic of intelligible essences rather than to a metaphysic of the concrete, and, like Avicenna, he attributed a certain reality or objectivity, though not independent of God, to essences considered as possible, essences which follow necessarily from the divine intellect and so are, in themselves at least, deducible. But when it was a question of existence, of the concrete existent world of creation, he had to part company with Avicenna. The latter, regarding the divine will as subject to the same necessity as the divine intellect, made the emergence of existences parallel to the emergence of essences, the subordinate Intelligences being responsible for prolonging the activity of the first Cause and bringing about the transition from the universal to the particular; but Henry of Ghent, as a Christian thinker, could not hold this: he had to admit free creation and also creation in time. He saw quite well that the sensible and concrete cannot be rendered fully intelligible, if to render fully intelligible means to explain in terms of essence, and therefore he made a sharp distinction between metaphysics and physics, each of the sciences having its own starting-point and mode of procedure.

In spite, however, of the Platonic and Avicennian tendencies in his thought, Henry of Ghent helped in a certain sense to prepare the way for nominalism. Insistence on illumination easily leads to a certain scepticism concerning the mind's power of achieving a metaphysical system based on experience, while Henry's tendency to simplification when dealing with the created world (for example, by the denial of any real distinction between essence and existence and by his theory of individuation, which involves the rejection of realism) may, if considered by itself, be regarded as heralding the simplifying tendencies and the conceptualism of the fourteenth century. Of course, this is but one aspect of his philosophy and it is not the most important and characteristic, but it is a real aspect none the less. Ockham criticised Henry of

Ghent's thought under its other aspects; but that does not mean that Henry's thought was without influence on the movement of which Ockham was the chief figure. Henry has been called an 'intermediary' figure, intermediary between the thirteenth and fourteenth centuries, and this can hardly be denied; but before Ockhamism arose, Duns Scotus, who so frequently criticised Henry, as Henry had criticised Giles of Rome, was to attempt to develop and justify a synthesis of Augustinianism and Aristotelianism, thus endeavouring, in spite of his polemics against Henry of Ghent, to accomplish satisfactorily what Henry had not accomplished satisfactorily.

CHAPTER XLV

SCOTUS—I

Life—Works—Spirit of Scotus's philosophy.

1. JOHN DUNS SCOTUS, *Doctor Subtilis*, was born in Scotland, at Maxton in the county of Roxburgh, his family name, Duns, being originally taken from a place in the county of Berwick. That he was a Scotsman can be now taken as certain, not simply from the fact that by his time Scotsmen and Irishmen were no longer called indiscriminately *Scoti*, but also as having been proved by the discovery of a series of documents, the authority of which can scarcely be called in question. But if the country of his birth is certain, the date is not so certain, though it is probable that he was born in 1265 or 1266, and that he entered the Order of Friars Minor in 1278, taking the habit in 1280 and being ordained priest in 1291. The traditional date of his death is November 8th, 1308. He died at Cologne and was buried in the Franciscan Church in that city.

The dates of Scotus's academic career are by no means certain; but it appears that he studied at Paris under Gonsalvus of Spain from 1293 to 1296, after a brief sojourn at Oxford. According to the traditional view Scotus then went to Oxford, where he commented on the *Sentences* and produced the *Opus Oxoniense* or Oxford Commentary on the *Sentences*. The fact that in the fourth book of the *Opus Oxoniense* Scotus quotes a bull of Benedict XI, of January 31st, 1304, is no certain argument against the traditional view, as Scotus certainly retouched and made later additions to the work.[1] In 1302 Scotus returned to Paris and commented there on the *Sentences*; but in 1303 he was banished from Paris, as he had supported the Papal party against King Philip the Fair. Where he spent the time of banishment is not quite clear: Oxford, Cologne and Bologna have all been suggested. In any case he taught at Oxford in the academic year 1303–4, returning to Paris in 1304 and receiving the doctorate in theology in 1305. It is possible that he returned to Oxford again for a short while, but he was certainly at Paris, engaged in commenting on the *Sentences*,

[1] Scotus is said to have taught at Cambridge also, either before or after his teaching at Oxford.

when he was sent to Cologne in the summer of 1307. At Cologne he resumed his work of teaching; but in 1308, as already mentioned, he died, when about forty-two or forty-three years of age.

2. The uncertainty concerning the exact course of Scotus's life is to be regretted; but far more to be regretted is the uncertainty concerning the authentic character of some works attributed to him in the edition of Luke Wadding. Happily, however, the general authenticity of the two great commentaries on the *Sentences* is not in question, though neither the *Opus Oxoniense* nor the *Reportata Parisiensia* in their traditional form can be ascribed in their totality to Scotus. As to the *Opus Oxoniense*, the original text as Scotus left it (the *Ordinatio*, of which no manuscript has yet been discovered) was added to by disciples who wished to complete the work of the master by presenting a complete exposition of his thought, though in some subsequent codices the scribes attempted to note the additions which had been made. A similar situation presents itself in regard to the *Reportata Parisiensia*, since in their case too the desire to give a complete account of Scotus's teaching led the master's disciples to assemble together partial accounts from various sources, without, however, making any serious attempt to discover the respective authority and value of the different parts of the mosaic. The task of the Commission appointed to superintend the production of the critical edition of Scotus's works is, then, no easy one; but although the Oxford and Paris Commentaries represent basically the thought of Scotus, no secure and final picture of that thought can be given until the critical edition of the Commentaries appears, more especially until the original *Ordinatio* or *Liber Scoti* is published, free from accretions.

The authentic character of the *De primo principio* is not in question, though the arguments adduced by Father Ciganotto to show that it was Scotus's last work, written at Cologne, do not appear to be decisive. The *Quaestiones Quodlibetales* are also authentic,[1] as are also the forty-six *Collationes* (Wadding knew of only forty, but C. Balic discovered another six) and the first nine books of the *Quaestiones subtilissimae super libros Metaphysicorum Aristotelis*. As to the *De Anima*, the question of its authenticity has been a matter for dispute. Pelster maintained that it was authentic, while Longpré tried to show that it was unauthentic,

[1] P. Glorieux: *La littérature quodlibétique*, t. 2 (Bibliothèque thomiste, 21), Paris, 1935.

though his arguments were declared insufficient by Fleig. It is now generally accepted as authentic, even by Longpré. On the other hand, the *Grammatica speculativa* is to be attributed to Thomas of Erfurt, while the *De rerum principio* is also unauthentic, being probably, in part at least, a plagiarism from the *Quaestiones Quodlibetales* of Godfrey of Fontaines. Also unauthentic are the *Metaphysica textualis* (probably to be attributed to Antoine André), the *Conclusiones metaphysicae* and the commentaries on Aristotle's *Physics* and *Meteorology*.

To determine with certainty which are and which are not authentic works of Scotus is obviously a matter of importance. Some doctrines which appear in the *De rerum principio*, for example, do not appear in the certainly authentic works, so that if one were to accept the authenticity of the *De rerum principio* (as already mentioned, it is now rejected), one would have to assume that Scotus first taught a doctrine which he later abandoned, since it would clearly be out of the question to assume that his thought contained patent contradictions. To assert a change of opinion on some comparatively minor doctrine when no such change actually took place might not perhaps be a mistake of great importance, even if it resulted in an inaccurate account of Scotus's doctrinal development; but the question of authenticity or unauthenticity is of much greater importance where the *Theoremata* are concerned. In this work the author states that it cannot be proved that there is only one ultimate Principle or that God is infinite or that He is intelligent, and so on, such statements being, at first sight at least, in clear contradiction with the teaching of the certainly authentic works of Scotus. If, then, one were to accept the *Theoremata* as authentic, one would either have to assume an astonishing *volte-face* on Scotus's part or one would have to attempt a difficult task of interpretation and conciliation.

The first attack on the authenticity of the *Theoremata* was that of Father de Basly in the year 1918, and this attack was continued by Father Longpré. The latter argued that no manuscript had yet been discovered which explicitly attributed the work to Scotus, that the teaching contained in the work is contrary to that contained in Scotus's certainly authentic works, that Ockham and Thomas of Sutton, who attacked Scotus's natural theology, never quote the work as his, that the doctrine of the *Theoremata* is nominalistic in character and must be attributed to the Ockhamist School, and that John of Reading, who knew Scotus, quotes from the authentic works when he is dealing with the question whether God's existence can be proved or not by the natural light of reason, but does not mention the *Theoremata*. These arguments appeared to be convincing and were generally accepted as settling the question, until Father Balic brought forward other arguments to contest Longpré's view. Noting that Longpré's arguments were, for the most part, based on internal evidence, Balic tried to show not only that the arguments drawn from internal evidence were unconvincing, but also that there were good arguments drawn from external evidence to prove that the *Theoremata* were really the work of Scotus. Thus four codices explicitly attribute the work to Scotus, while in the fourth chapter of the *De primo principio* occur the words *In sequenti, scilicet in Theorematibus, ponentur credibilia*. The phrase *scilicet in Theorematibus* cannot have been added by Wadding, since it is found in some codices. In addition, the *Theoremata* are given as the work of Scotus by, among others, Joannes Canonicus, a fourteenth-century Scotist. Baudry then tried to show that even if some of the theories contained in the *Theoremata* betray a nominalistic spirit, the fundamental doctrines of the work are not of Ockhamist origin, and Gilson (in the *Archives d'histoire doctrinale et littéraire du moyen âge*, 1937–8) attempted to prove that the first sixteen *Theoremata* do not stand in contradiction with the certainly authentic works of Scotus. According to Gilson, Scotus speaks in the *Theoremata* (supposing that the work is really by him) as a philosopher showing what the unaided human reason can achieve, while in the *Opus Oxoniense*, which is a theological work, he shows what can be achieved by metaphysics aided by theology. Even if the conclusions arrived at in the *Theoremata* seem to approximate to those of Ockham, the spirit is different, since Scotus believed that the theologian can give metaphysical and demonstrative arguments for God's existence and attributes, whereas Ockham denied this and had recourse to faith alone. In the latest edition (1944) of his work, *La philosophie au moyen âge*, Gilson leaves the question of the authenticity or unauthenticity of the *Theoremata* an open question; but he maintains that if the *Theoremata* are the work of Scotus, there is no difficulty in reconciling the doctrine they contain with the doctrine of the *Opus Oxoniense*. The pure philosopher treats of being in a universal sense and can never get beyond a first mover who is first in the chain of causes but who is nevertheless in the chain; he cannot arrive at the conception of God which can be attained by the philosopher who is also a theologian.

I feel rather doubtful of the validity of M. Gilson's contention. In the Oxford Commentary Scotus states that many essential attributes of God can be known by the metaphysician,[1] and in both commentaries he asserts that man can attain a natural knowledge of God, although he cannot *ex puris naturalibus* come to know such truths as that of the Trinity.[2] I find it hard to suppose that when Scotus said that man can come to know truths about God *ex puris naturalibus*, he was thinking of a metaphysician who is also a theologian. Nor do I see that Scotus meant to confine the pure philosopher's knowledge of God to knowledge of Him as first Mover: he says clearly that the metaphysician can proceed further than the *physicus*.[3] Moreover, it seems to me extremely odd, supposing that the *Theoremata* are Scotus's work, that Scotus should prove in the *De primo principio* that God or the first Principle is, for example, intelligent, and that then in the *Theoremata* he should declare that this truth is a *credibile* and cannot be proved. He certainly restricted somewhat the scope of the natural reason in regard to God (he did not think that God's omnipotence is capable of strict proof by the natural reason); but it would seem from the *Commentaries*, from the *De primo principio* and from the *Collationes* that Scotus undoubtedly considered a natural theology to be possible, irrespective of the question whether the philosopher is also a theologian or not.[4] Of course, if it were ever proved conclusively by external evidence that the *Theoremata* are the authentic work of Scotus, one would have to have recourse to some such theory as that of M. Gilson in order to explain the apparently flat contradiction between the *Theoremata* and the other works of Scotus; but meanwhile it seems to me to be pressing conciliation too far to suggest that there is no contradiction, and I propose in my exposition of Scotus's natural theology to disregard the *Theoremata*. But, while disregarding the *Theoremata*, I admit, as just mentioned, that in the event of the work's authenticity being satisfactorily proved, one would be

[1] *Ox.*, Prol., 4, no. 32.

[2] *Ibid.*, 1, 3, 1; *Rep.*, 1, 3, 1; *Rep.*, Prol., 3, nos. 1 and 4. [3] *Rep.*, Prol., 3, 1.

[4] Minges, accepting the *Theoremata*, tries to show that in that work Scotus understands demonstration in the strictest Aristotelian sense, as *demonstratio ex causis*. If that could be proved, there would, of course, be no contradiction between the *Theoremata* and the certainly authentic works of Scotus. Longpré, however, argues against this interpretation of the author's meaning. Cf. Minges, Vol. 2, pp. 29–30; Longpré, p. 109 (cf. Bibliography).

compelled to say with Gilson that in that work Scotus is considering simply the power of the natural philosopher (the *physicus*) in regard to the attainment of natural knowledge of God. My point is, however, that until the authenticity of the *Theoremata* is proved, there does not seem to be any adequate or compelling reason for affirming that the metaphysician of the certainly authentic works is necessarily a metaphysician who possesses the background of faith. I shall, therefore, treat the *Theoremata* for practical purposes as unauthentic, without, however, pretending to settle the question definitively or to add any further grounds than those already alleged by other writers for rejecting the work as spurious.

The problem of the *Theoremata* has been discussed at some length in order to show the difficulty there is in interpreting accurately the mind of Scotus. Even if one maintains that the doctrines of the *Theoremata* and of the *Opus Oxoniense* are not at variance, but can be reconciled, the very reconciliation results in a picture of Scotus's philosophy which would hardly be that suggested by a first acquaintance with the *Opus Oxoniense*. Still, even if the authenticity of the *Theoremata* has not been demonstrated and even if it would appear preferable to reject it, convenience of exposition is no sure criterion of authenticity or unauthenticity, and one cannot, in view of recent attempts to rehabilitate the work, exclude the possibility that it may at some future date be shown to be certainly authentic, even though internal evidence may suggest the contrary.

3. Various general interpretations of Scotus's philosophy have been given, ranging from the interpretation of Scotus as a revolutionary, as a direct precursor of Ockham and of Luther, to the attempt to soften down the sharp differences between Scotism and Thomism and to interpret Scotus as a continuator of the work of St. Thomas. The first interpretation, that of Landry, can be dismissed, in its extreme form at least, as extravagant and insufficiently grounded, while on the other hand it is impossible to deny that Scotism does differ from Thomism. But is Scotus to be regarded as a continuator of the Franciscan tradition who at the same time adopted a great deal from Aristotle and from non-Franciscan mediaeval predecessors, or is he to be regarded as a thinker who carried on the Aristotelian tradition of St. Thomas but at the same time corrected St. Thomas in the light of what he himself considered to be the truth, or is he simply to be

regarded as an independent thinker who at the same time depended, as all philosophers must, on preceding thinkers in regard to the problems raised and discussed? The question is not an easy one to answer, and any attempt to answer it definitively must be postponed until the production of the critical edition of Scotus's works; but it would seem that there is truth in each of the foregoing suggestions. Scotus was, indeed, a Franciscan Doctor, and even if he discarded a number of doctrines which were generally held in common by former Franciscan thinkers, he certainly regarded himself as faithful to the Franciscan tradition. Again, although Scotus certainly criticised St. Thomas's views on important points, he can also be regarded as continuing the work of synthesis to which St. Thomas had devoted himself. Finally, Scotus certainly was an independent thinker; but at the same time he built on already existing foundations. But although Scotism did not involve a complete break with the past, it is only reasonable to lay stress on its comparatively original and independent aspects and thus draw attention to the difference between Scotism and other systems.

In some aspects of his thought Scotus did indeed carry on the Augustinian-Franciscan tradition: in his doctrine of the superiority of will to intellect, for example, as also in his admission of plurality of forms and in his utilisation of the Anselmian argument for God's existence. Moreover, it has been shown that Scotus did not invent the *distinctio formalis a parte rei*, but that it had been employed by some preceding Franciscan thinkers. Nevertheless, Scotus often gave a peculiar stamp or emphasis to the elements he adopted from tradition. Thus in his treatment of the relation of will to intellect he emphasised freedom rather than love, though he held, it is true, to the superiority of love to knowledge, a superiority which is closely connected with his theory that the supreme practical principle is that God should be loved above all things. Again, though he utilised the Anselmian argument, the so-called 'ontological argument', he did not accept it as a conclusive proof of God's existence but maintained, not only that it must be 'coloured' before it can be usefully employed, but also that even then it is not a demonstrative proof of God's existence, since the only demonstrative arguments are *a posteriori*.

But if Scotus in some respects carried on the Augustinian-Franciscan tradition, in other respects he departed from that tradition. It is not quite clear whether he did or did not teach the hylomorphic composition of angels; but he expressly rejected as unnecessary the theories of *rationes seminales* and of a special illumination of the human intellect, while he saw no contradiction, as St. Bonaventure had seen, in the idea of creation from eternity, even though he speaks more hesitantly than St. Thomas on this matter. In Scotism, then, the influence of Aristotelianism had penetrated further than it had in the philosophy of St. Bonaventure, and one must mention in particular the influence of Avicenna. For example, Scotus insists that the object of the metaphysician is being as being, and in his insistence on this point, as in his treatment of the problem of God, he seems to have been influenced by the Islamic philosopher, whose name occurs not infrequently in the pages of Scotus's works. It is true that Aristotle himself had declared that metaphysics, or rather first philosophy, is the science of being as being; but the Aristotelian metaphysic centres in practice round the doctrine of the four causes, whereas Scotus treats at length of the idea and nature of being, and the impulse thereto seems to have been partly derived from Avicenna. Scotus's discussion of universals, for instance, was also not without a debt to Avicenna.

Yet even if Scotus owed much more to Aristotle and his commentators than did St. Bonaventure, and even if he appeals to the authority of Aristotle in support of this or that theory, he was far from being a mere follower of 'the Philosopher', whom he does not hesitate to criticise. But, apart from individual pieces of criticism, Scotus's philosophical inspiration, so to speak, was different from that of Aristotle. In his eyes the conception of God as first Mover was a very inadequate conception, as it does not pass beyond the physical world and attain the transcendent, infinite Being on which all finite beings essentially depend. Again, it follows from Scotus's ethical doctrine that the Aristotelian ethic must be insufficient, as the notion of obligation, depending on the divine will, does not appear therein. It may be said, of course, that any Christian philosopher would find Aristotle deficient on such matters, and that St. Thomas was compelled to supplement Aristotle with Augustine; but the point is that Scotus did not go out of his way to 'explain' Aristotle or to 'reconcile' his opinions with what he himself considered to be the truth. In so far, for example, as there is a moral philosophy in the strict sense in Scotism, its dependence on or borrowing from Aristotelianism is far from being conspicuous.

Scotus's attitude to St. Thomas has been depicted in recent years in a rather different light to that in which it was formerly sometimes depicted: there has been, and not unnaturally, a tendency to minimise his divergences from Thomism. It has been pointed out, for example, that in his polemics he often has other thinkers in mind, Henry of Ghent, for example. This is quite true, of course; but the fact remains that he frequently criticises Thomist positions, giving St. Thomas's arguments and refuting them. But whatever the justice or injustice of this or that individual criticism may be, Scotus certainly did not criticise for the sake of criticism. If he insisted, for example, on some intellectual intuition of the singular object and if he emphasised the reality of the 'common nature', without however, falling into the exaggerated realism of early mediaeval philosophers, he did so, not simply in order to differ from St. Thomas, but in order to safeguard, as he believed, the objectivity of knowledge. Similarly, if he insisted on the univocal character of the concept of being, he did so because he considered his own doctrine to be absolutely necessary if agnosticism were to be avoided, that is, in order to safeguard the objective character of natural theology. If he made extensive use of the *distinctio formalis a parte rei*, this was not simply in order to display his subtlety, though he certainly was a subtle and sometimes a tortuous thinker and dialectician, but because he considered that such use was necessitated by the facts and by the objective reference of our concepts. In so far, then, as Scotus can be looked on as a successor of St. Thomas or as a continuator of Thomism, one must recognise that he endeavoured to correct what he regarded, rightly or wrongly, as dangerous deficiencies and tendencies in the Thomist philosophy.

It is well to bear in mind Scotus's concern for the theoretical safeguarding of the objectivity of human knowledge and of natural theology in particular, since the realisation of this concern acts as a counterbalance to the tendency to look on him as predominantly a destructive critic. It is true that Scotus was somewhat rigorous in his idea of what constitutes a proof, and he would not allow that the proofs adduced for the soul's immortality, for example, were conclusive, demonstrative; but all the same his philosophy remains one of the great mediaeval syntheses, an effort of constructive and positive thought. Moreover, it had a religious inspiration, as one can see from the invocations of God which sometimes appear in his writings and which one cannot simply dismiss as literary convention.

Nevertheless, if one looks on Scotism in its position as a stage in the development of mediaeval thought, it would be idle to deny that *de facto* it helped to stimulate the critical movement of the fourteenth century. When Scotus asserted that certain of the divine attributes cannot be proved by natural reason and when he denied the demonstrative character of the arguments adduced for the immortality of the human soul, he did not intend to undermine positive philosophy; but, looking at the matter from the purely historical viewpoint, his criticism obviously helped to prepare the way for the much more radical criticism of Ockham. That the latter regarded Scotism with hostility is not really relevant to the point at issue. Similarly, though it is quite untrue that Scotus made the whole moral law to depend on the arbitrary choice of the divine will, it can hardly be denied that the elements of voluntarism in his philosophy helped to prepare the way for the authoritarianism of Ockham. For example, his doctrine of moral obligation and his assertion that the secondary precepts of the decalogue do not belong, in the strict sense, to the natural law and are subject to divine dispensation in particular cases. I am not suggesting that Ockhamism is the legitimate child of Scotism, but simply that after the attainment of the supreme mediaeval synthesis of Thomism the work of the critical intellect or of the critical function of philosophy was only to be expected, and that the restricted and moderate use of criticism by Scotus prepared the way, as a matter of fact, for the radical and destructive criticism which is characteristic of Ockhamism. An historical judgement of this type does not necessarily mean that Scotus's criticism was not justified and the radical criticism of later thinkers unjustified: that is a matter for the philosopher to decide, not the historian. Of course, if the *Theoremata* were ever proved to be authentic, that would but serve to emphasise the critical aspect of Scotism.

In fine, then, the philosophy of Scotus looks backward as well as forward. As a positive and constructive system it belongs to the thirteenth century, the century which witnessed the philosophies of St. Bonaventure and, above all, of St. Thomas; but in its critical aspects and in its voluntaristic elements, associated though the latter are with the Augustinian-Franciscan tradition, it looks forward to the fourteenth century. A triumph of dialectical skill and of careful and patient thought the philosophy of Scotus is the work of a man who was, though impregnated with tradition, a powerful, vigorous and original thinker, a man who really belonged to the closing epoch of 'dogmatic philosophy' but who at the same time heralded the new movement.

CHAPTER XLVI

SCOTUS—II: KNOWLEDGE

The primary object of the human intellect—Why the intellect depends on the phantasm—The soul's inability to intuit itself in this life—Intellectual apprehension of the individual thing—Is theology a science?—Our knowledge is based on sense-experience, and no special illumination is required for intellectual activity—Intuitive and abstractive knowledge—Induction.

1. THE primary natural object of our intellect is being as being, from which it follows that every being, every thing which is intelligible, falls within the scope of the intellect.[1] Scotus gives, among other proofs, one taken from Avicenna to the effect that if being were not the primary object of the intellect, being could be described or explained in terms of something more ultimate, which is impossible. But if being as being is the natural object of the intellect and if being is taken to include every intelligible object, does it not follow that infinite Being, God, is a natural object of the human intellect? In a sense the answer must be in the affirmative, since being includes infinite being and finite being, but it does not follow that man has an immediate natural knowledge of God, since man's intellect in its present state is directed immediately to sensible things. But, says Scotus, if we are speaking of the primary object of the intellect, it is only reasonable to assign as its primary object that which is the primary object of intellect as such, not that which is the primary object of the intellect in this or that particular case. We do not say, for example, that the primary object of vision is that which the eye can see in candlelight; but we assign as its primary object that which is its object simply as a power or faculty.[2] Therefore, even if man in his present state (*homo viator*) comes first of all to know creatures, this does not mean that the primary adequate object of his intellect is not being as being. It may be added that this doctrine does not mean that the human intellect has a natural power of knowing the divine essence in itself or the divine Persons in the Trinity, since the general (and univocal) concept of being does not include *this particular essence as particular*, while creatures are not such perfect imitations of God that they reveal the divine

[1] *Ox.*, Prol., q. 1. [2] *Ibid.*, 1, 3, 3, no. 24.

essence as it is in itself.[1] The divine essence as such moves (*movet*) naturally, is the natural object of the divine intellect only; it can be known by the human intellect only through God's free choice and activity, not through the human intellect's natural power.

But if Scotus in assigning being as being as the primary adequate object of the human intellect certainly did not confuse supernatural and natural knowledge, he equally certainly meant to reject St. Thomas's view, or what he regarded as such, of the primary object of the human mind. St. Thomas[2] maintained that the natural object of the human intellect is the essence of the material thing, which essence becomes intelligible to the intellect when it is abstracted from the individualising matter. It is natural to the angelic intellect to know natures which do not exist in matter; but the human intellect cannot do this in its present state, when united to the body. And to be united to the body is the natural state of the human intellect; to be separated from the body is *praeter naturam*. So St. Thomas argues that, inasmuch as the natural object of the human intellect is the form of the material thing and inasmuch as we know this kind of form by abstracting it from the 'phantasm', the human intellect necessarily depends on the 'phantasm', and so on sense-experience, for its knowledge.[3] Scotus[4] interprets St. Thomas as teaching that the quiddity or essence, known by way of abstraction from the phantasm, is the primary object of the human intellect considered not simply as being in a certain state, that is, in the present life, but in its nature as a power or faculty of a certain kind, and he replies that this opinion is untenable by a theologian, i.e. by a man who accepts the next life and the doctrine of eternal happiness. In heaven the soul knows immaterial things directly. Now, the intellect remains the same power in heaven as it was on earth. Therefore, if it can know immaterial things in heaven, we cannot say that its primary object is the essence of the material thing: its primary object, if we consider the intellect as a power, must embrace both immaterial and material things, even if in this life it cannot know immaterial things directly. Its restriction in this life to a certain type of object must be secondary, not primary. If it is answered that in heaven the intellect is elevated, so that it can know immaterial objects directly, Scotus replies that this knowledge either exceeds the power of the intellect or it does not.

[1] *Ox.*, 3, 2, 16, cf. *Quodlibet* 14: *Utrum anima suae naturali perfectioni relicta possit cognoscere Trinitatem personarum in Divinis.*

[2] *S.T.*, Ia, 12. 4. [3] Cf. *ibid.*, Ia, 85, 1. [4] *Ox.*, 1, 3, 3, nos. 1 ff.

If the latter is the case, then the primary object of the intellect considered *ex natura potentiae* cannot be the quiddity of the material thing, whereas, if the former is the case, then the intellect in heaven becomes another power, which St. Thomas certainly does not intend to teach.

Scotus also argues that if St. Thomas's view were correct, metaphysical science would be impossible for our intellects, since metaphysics are the science of being as being. If the primary object of the human intellect were the essence of the material thing, it could no more know being as being than the power of vision could extend further than its natural object, colour and light.[1] If the Thomist view were true, metaphysics would either be impossible, if understood in its proper sense, or it would not transcend physics. In fine, 'it does not seem fitting to confine the intellect, considered as a power, to the sensible thing, so that it transcends the senses only through its mode of cognition', that is, not through its object as well.

Since Scotus also maintains[2] that there is in the human intellect a natural desire to know 'the cause' distinctly and that a natural desire cannot be in vain, and since he concludes that the primary object of the intellect cannot, therefore, be material things, which are the effect of the immaterial cause, it might appear that he is contradicting his assertion that we cannot have a natural knowledge of the divine essence; but it must be remembered that he does not deny that the human intellect in its present state is limited in range, though he insists that the object of a power in a certain condition must not be confused with the object of the power considered in itself. Moreover, he did not consider that an analysis of being as being can yield knowledge of the divine essence as it is in itself, for even if being is the primary and adequate object of the human intellect, it does not follow that we form our idea of being by any other way than abstraction. In general, we may say that Scotus accepted the Aristotelian account of abstraction, though he considered that the active and passive intellects are not two distinct powers, but are two aspects or functions of one power.[3]

2. As to the reason why the human intellect in its present state, in this life, depends on the phantasm, Scotus declares that it is due to the order established by divine wisdom, either as a penalty for original sin or with a view to the harmonious operation of our

[1] *Ox.*, 1, 3, 3, nos. 1 ff. [2] *Ibid.*, 1, 3, 3, no. 3. [3] *De Anima*, 13.

various powers (*propter naturalem concordiam potentiarum animae in operando*), sense and imagination apprehending the individual thing, the intellect apprehending the universal essence of that thing, or else on account of our infirmity (*ex infirmitate*). The intellect in its present condition, he repeats, is moved immediately only by what is imaginable or sensible, and the reason for this may be punitive justice (*forte propter peccatum, sicut videtur Augustinus dicere*) or it may be a natural cause, inasmuch as the order or harmony of powers may require it so far as this present state is concerned. 'Nature' in this connection means, therefore, nature in a particular state or condition, not nature absolutely considered: on this point Scotus insists.[1] This is not a very satisfactory or a very clear or decided explanation; but what Scotus is quite clear about is that the intellect, absolutely considered, is the faculty of being as being, and he decisively rejects what he regards as the Thomist doctrine. Whether Scotus is fair in his interpretation of St. Thomas is another matter. Sometimes St. Thomas states explicitly that the proper object of the intellect is being.[2]

However, it is true that St. Thomas insists on the natural character of the necessity of the *conversio ad phantasma*,[3] arguing that if this necessity were simply the result of union with a body and not natural to the soul itself, it would follow that the union of soul and body takes place for the good of the body, not of the soul, since the soul would be hampered in its natural operations through its union with the body. Emphasising this aspect of the Thomist doctrine, Scotus concluded that Thomism is unable, logically speaking, to justify the possibility of metaphysical science.

3. Scotus's view on the primary object of the human intellect naturally had its effect on his treatment of the disputed question concerning the soul's knowledge of itself. According to St. Thomas Aquinas, the soul in its present state, which is its natural state, comes to know by means of ideas abstracted from sensible objects, and from this he concludes that the soul has no immediate knowledge of its own essence, but that it comes to know itself only indirectly, by reflecting on the acts by which it abstracts ideas and knows objects in those ideas.[4] Scotus, however, maintained that though the soul actually lacks an immediate intuition of itself in this life, it is a natural object of intellection to itself and

[1] Cf. *Ox.*, 1, 3, 3, no. 24; 2, 3, 8, no. 13.
[2] As in *S.T.*, Ia, 5, 2, for instance.
[3] *S.T.*, Ia, 89, 1.
[4] Cf. *ibid.*, Ia, 87, 1.

would actually intuit itself, 'were it not hindered'.[1] He then proceeds to suggest the causes of this hindrance which have already been mentioned. The difference between Scotus and St. Thomas concerns, then, the explanation of a fact rather than the fact itself. Both agree that the soul is actually without an immediate intuition of itself in this life; but, whereas St. Thomas explains this fact in terms of the nature of the human soul, attacking the Platonist view of the relation of soul to body, Scotus explains it, not in terms of the soul's nature, absolutely considered, but in terms of a hindrance, even suggesting that this hindrance may be due to sin and quoting St. Augustine in support of this suggestion. St. Thomas's attitude follows from his adoption of the Aristotelian psychology, whereas Scotus's position can be associated with the Augustinian tradition. On this matter one should regard Scotus not as an innovator or revolutionary or a destructive critic of Thomism, but rather as an upholder of the Augustinian-Franciscan tradition.

4. We have seen that Scotus considered his doctrine concerning the primary object of the intellect to be essential for the maintenance and justification of metaphysics: he also considered his doctrine of the intellectual apprehension of the individual thing as essential to the maintenance of the objectivity of human knowledge. According to St. Thomas[2] the intellect cannot know individual material things directly, since the intellect comes to know only by abstracting the universal from matter, the principle of individuation. He admits, however, that the mind has an indirect knowledge of individual things, since it cannot actually know the abstracted universal except through the 'conversion to the phantasm'. The imagination always plays its part, and the image is an image of the individual thing; but the primary and direct object of intellectual knowledge is the universal.

Scotus refused to accept this Thomist doctrine. The vehement repudiation of the doctrine wherein it is declared false and even heretical (on the ground that the Apostles believed that a certain visible, palpable, individual human being was God) comes from an unauthentic work, the *De rerum principio*; but the authentic works of Scotus make the latter's position perfectly clear. He accepted in general the Aristotelian account of abstraction; but he insists that the intellect has a confused primary intuition of the singular thing. His principle is that the higher power knows

[1] *Ox.*, 2, 3, 8, no. 13. [2] *S.T.*, Ia, 86, 1.

what the lower power apprehends, though the higher power knows the object in a more perfect manner than the lower power does, so that the intellect, which co-operates in perception, knows intuitively the singular thing apprehended by the senses. The intellect knows true contingent propositions and reasons from them; and such propositions concern individual things known intuitively as existing. Therefore, although abstract and scientific knowledge concerns universals, as Aristotle rightly taught, we must also recognise an intellectual knowledge of the singular thing as existent.[1] As already mentioned, the very vehement repudiation of the Thomist position, which is ascribed to Scotus by Father Parthenius Minges, for example,[2] comes from the unauthentic *De rerum principio*, and certain remarks which are found in the authentic works might lead one to suppose that Scotus's position on the question of the intellectual knowledge of the singular thing is exactly parallel to his position in regard to the soul's intuition of itself. He insists that the singular thing is intelligible in itself and that the human intellect has at least the remote capability of understanding it; but he seems to imply, or even to state explicitly, that in its present condition it is unable to do so. 'The singular thing is intelligible in itself, as far as the thing itself is concerned; but if it is not intelligible to some intellect, to ours, for example, this is not due to unintelligibility on the part of the singular thing itself.'[3] Again, 'it is not an imperfection to know the singular thing', but 'if you say that our intellect does not understand the singular thing, I reply that this is an imperfection (which obtains) in its present state'.[4] However, Scotus seems to mean that while we have no clear knowledge of the singular thing as singular, a deficiency which is due, not to the singular thing's lack of intelligibility, but to the imperfection of our intellectual operations in this life, we none the less have a primary, though confused, intellectual intuition of the singular thing as existent. This seems to be the view expressed in the *Quodlibet*[5] where Scotus argues that if it is said that we have an intellectual knowledge of the universal and sense-experience of the singular, this is not to be understood in the sense that the two powers are equal and disparate, so that the intellect would not know the singular at all, but in the sense that the lower power is subordinate to the higher and that though the higher power can operate in a way that

[1] *Ox.*, 4, 45, 3, no. 17.
[2] *J. Duns Scoti Doctrina Philosophica et Theologica*, p. 247.
[3] *Ox.*, 2, 3, 6, no. 16. [4] *Ibid.*, 2, 3, 9, no. 9. [5] 13, 8–10.

the lower cannot, the opposite cannot be assumed as true. From the fact that sense cannot know the universal it does not follow that the intellect cannot know the singular. The intellect can have an intuitive knowledge of the singular as existent, even if its knowledge of the essence is knowledge of the universal.

If we are willing to accept the *De Anima* as authentic, Scotus's opinion is placed beyond doubt. In that work[1] Scotus rejects the Thomist doctrine on our knowledge of the singular, and also the Thomist doctrine of the principle of individuation, on which the first doctrine rests, and argues that the singular thing is (i) intelligible in itself; (ii) intelligible by us even in our present state; (iii) not intelligible by us in our present state so far as clear knowledge is concerned. The singular thing is intelligible in itself, since what is not intelligible in itself could not be known by any intellect, whereas the singular thing is certainly known by the divine and angelic intellects. It is intelligible by us even in our present state, as is shown by the process of induction and by the fact that we can love the individual thing, love presupposing knowledge. It is not, however, intelligible by us in our present state in a complete and clear manner (*sub propria ratione*). If two material things were deprived of all difference of accidents (of place, colour, shape, etc.), neither sense nor intellect could distinguish them from one another, even though their 'singularities' (Scotus's *haecceitas*) remained, and this shows that we have, in our present state, no clear and complete knowledge of the singularity of a thing. We can say, therefore, that the object of sense is the individual thing and the object of intellect the universal, if we mean that the intellect is not moved by singularity as such and does not know it clearly and completely in its present state; but we are not entitled to say that the intellect has no intuition of the individual thing as existent. If we say this, we destroy the objectivity of knowledge. 'It is impossible to abstract universals from the singular without previous knowledge of the singular; for in this case the intellect would abstract without knowing from what it was abstracting.'[2] It is clear that Scotus rejected the Thomist doctrine not merely because he rejected the Thomist idea of individuation, nor even merely because a process like induction seemed to him to prove the Thomist doctrine false; but also because he was convinced that the Thomist doctrine endangered the objectivity of that scientific and universal knowledge

[1] 22. [2] *De Anima*, 22, 3.

on which the Thomists laid such stress. Scotus did not mean to reject (he makes this quite clear) the Aristotelian doctrine that human science is of the universal; but he considered it essential to supplement that doctrine by accepting our intellectual intuition of the singular thing as existent, and he considered that this supplementation was necessitated by the facts. Concern for the safeguarding of the objectivity of human knowledge shows itself also in Scotus's handling of the problem of universals; but consideration of this problem is best left for the chapter on metaphysics, where it can be treated in connection with the problem of individuation.

5. From one point of view it would not be unreasonable to maintain, as has been maintained, that Scotus's ideal of science was mathematical science. If science is understood in the sense in which Aristotle uses the word in the first book of the *Posterior Analytics*, that is, as involving necessity of the object, as well as evidence and certainty, we cannot say that theology, as concerned with the Incarnation and with God's relations with man in general, is a science, since the Incarnation is not a necessary or a deducible event.[1] On the other hand, if we consider theology as concerned with its primary object, with God as He is in Himself, it treats of necessary truths like the Trinity of Persons, and is a science; but we must add that it is a science in itself and not for us, since the truths in question, though certain, are not self-evident to us. If someone were unable to understand the arguments of the geometers, but accepted their conclusions on their word, geometry would be for him an object of belief, not a science, even though it would still be a science in itself.[2] Theology considered as concerned with God in Himself, is thus a science in itself, though not for us, since, in spite of the necessity of the object, the data are accepted on faith. Theology as concerned with God's external operations, however, treats of 'contingent', that is, non-necessary events, and so is not a science in that sense. Scotus is clearly taking geometrical science as the model of science in the strict sense.

It should be added, however, that when Scotus denies that theology is a science in the senses above indicated, he does not intend to disparage theology or to cast doubts upon its certainty. He expressly says that if one understands 'science', not in the strictest sense, but as understood by Aristotle in the sixth book of the *Ethics*, namely as contrasted with opinion and conjecture,

[1] *Ox.*, Prol., 3, no. 28. [2] *Ibid.*, Prol., 2 lat., no. 4.

it is a science, since it is certain and true, though it is more properly to be termed 'wisdom'.[1] Moreover, theology is not subordinate to metaphysics, since, although its object is in some degree comprised in the object of metaphysics, for God as knowable by the natural light of reason is comprised in the object of metaphysics, it does not receive its principles from metaphysics, nor are the truths of dogmatic theology demonstrable by means of the principles of being as such. The principles of dogmatic theology are accepted on faith, on authority; they are not demonstrated by natural reason nor are they demonstrable by the metaphysician. On the other hand, metaphysics are not, in the strict sense, a subordinate science to theology, since the metaphysician does not borrow his principles from the theologian.[2]

Theology, according to Scotus, is a practical science; but he explains very carefully and at length what he means by this.[3] 'Even necessary theology', that is, theological knowledge of necessary truths concerning God in Himself, is logically prior to the elicited act of will by which we choose God, and the first principles of salutary conduct are taken from it. Scotus discusses the views of Henry of Ghent and others, rejecting them in favour of his own view. He thus parts company with St. Thomas, who says[4] that theology is a speculative science, just as he parts company with St. Thomas when the latter declares that theology is a science.[5] Scotus, as one would expect in view of his doctrine of the priority of will over intellect, emphasises the aspect of theology under which it is a norm of salutary conduct for man.

The foregoing considerations may seem to be irrelevant, referring, as they do, to dogmatic theology; but if one understands Scotus's position in regard to dogmatic theology, one can see how unjust and false are some of the accusations which have been brought against him. If one said simply that whereas St. Thomas considered theology to be a science, a speculative science, Scotus declared that theology is not a science and that, in so far as it can be called a science, it is a practical science, one might conclude that theological doctrines were, for Scotus, postulates having only practical or pragmatic value; and in point of fact, Scotus has actually been compared with Kant. But if one considers Scotus's meaning, such an interpretation is obviously unjust and false. For example, Scotus does not deny that theology is a science as

[1] *Ox.*, Prol., 3, no. 28. [2] *Ibid.*, Prol., 3, no. 29. [3] *Ibid.*, Prol. 4.
[4] *S.T.*, Ia, 1, 4. [5] *Ibid.*, Ia, 1, 2.

far as certainty is concerned; he simply says that if you define science in the sense in which geometry is a science, then theology cannot be called a science. With this position St. Thomas would agree. Theology, he says, is a science, because its principles are derived from those of a higher science, proper to God and the blessed, so that they are absolutely certain; it is not a science in the same sense in which geometry and arithmetic are sciences, since its principles are not self-evident to the natural light of reason.[1] Again, Scotus says that theology is for us a practical science, mainly because revelation is given as a norm for salutary conduct, that we may attain our last end, whereas for St. Thomas[2] theology is primarily a speculative science, though not exclusively, because it deals more with divine things than with human acts. In other words, the main difference between them on this matter is one of emphasis: it is a difference which one would expect in view of St. Thomas's general emphasis on intellect and theoretic contemplation and Scotus's general emphasis on will and love, and it has to be seen in the light of the Aristotelian and Franciscan traditions rather than in the light of Kantianism and Pragmatism. If anyone wishes to make out that Scotus was a Kantian before Kant, he will find no solid reasons to support his contention in Scotus's doctrine concerning dogmatic theology.

6. Although Scotus insists, as we have seen, that the primary object of the intellect is being in general and not simply material essences, his Aristotelianism leads him also to emphasise the fact that our actual knowledge originates with sensation. There are no innate ideas, therefore. In the *Quaestiones subtilissimae super libros Metaphysicorum*[3] he affirms that the intellect does not, in virtue of its own constitution, possess any natural knowledge, either in simple or in complex notions, 'because all our knowledge arises from sensation'. This applies even to the knowledge of the first principles. 'For first the sense is moved by some simple, and not complex object, and through the movement of the sense the intellect is moved and apprehends simple objects: this is the intellect's first act. Secondly, after the apprehension of simple objects there follows another act, that of bringing together simple objects, and after this composition the intellect is able to assent to the truth of the complex, if it is a first principle.' Natural knowledge of the first principles means no more than that when the simple terms have been understood and combined, the intellect

[1] *S.T.*, Ia, 1, 2. [2] *Ibid.*, Ia, 1, 4. [3] 2, 1, no. 2.

immediately assents, in virtue of its own natural light, to the truth of the principle; 'but the knowledge of the terms is acquired from sensible objects'. What Scotus means is this. We obtain the notions of 'whole' and 'part', for example, through sense-experience; but when the intellect brings together the terms, it sees immediately the truth of the proposition that the whole is greater than the part. The knowledge of what a whole is and what a part is comes from sense-experience; but the natural light of the intellect enables it to see immediately the truth of the complex object, the first principle. In answer to Averroes's objection that in this case all men would assent to the first principles, whereas in point of fact the Christians do not assent to the principle that 'out of nothing nothing is made', Scotus replies that he is speaking of first principles in the strict sense, such as the principle of contradiction and the principle that the whole is greater than its part, not of principles which some people think to be or which may be conclusions from the first principles. In the Paris Commentary, however,[1] he insists that the intellect cannot err in regard to those principles and conclusions which it sees to follow clearly from the first principles. In the same place he speaks of the intellect as a *tabula nuda*, which has no innate principles or ideas.

Scotus also rejects the doctrine that a special illumination of the intellect is necessary in order that it should apprehend certain truth. Thus he gives the arguments of Henry of Ghent on behalf of the illumination theory[2] and proceeds to criticise them, objecting that Henry's arguments seem to result in the conclusion that all certain and natural knowledge is impossible.[3] For example, if it were true that no certainty can be obtained concerning a continually changing object (and sensible objects are constantly changing, according to Henry), illumination would not help in any way, for we do not attain certainty when we know an object otherwise than it actually is. In any case, Scotus adds, the doctrine that sensible objects are continually changing is the doctrine of Heraclitus and is false. Similarly, if the changing character of the soul and its ideas are an obstacle to certainty, illumination will not remedy the defect. In fine, Henry's opinion would lead to scepticism.

Scotus thus defends the activity and natural power of the human intellect, and a similar preoccupation shows itself in his rejection of St. Thomas's doctrine that the soul, when separated from the

[1] 2, 23, no. 3. [2] *Ox.*, 1, 3, 4, nos. 2–4. [3] *Ibid.*, 1, 3, 4, no. 5.

body, cannot acquire new ideas from things themselves.[1] He gives the opinion of St. Thomas in more or less the same words that the latter uses in his Commentary on the *Sentences*[2] and argues that it belongs to the nature of the soul to know, to abstract, to will, so that, since the soul is also of such a nature that it can exist in separation from the body, we may legitimately conclude that it can acquire fresh knowledge by natural means in this state of separation. The opinion of St. Thomas, Scotus says, degrades the human soul. Scotus's own opinion is, of course, connected with his view that the soul's dependence on the senses in this life is *pro statu isto, forte ex peccato*. It is also connected with his rejection of the doctrine that the soul is purely passive and that the phantasm causes the idea. The soul in the state of separation from the body is, therefore, not cut off from the acquisition of new knowledge, nor is it even confined to intuition: it can exercise the power of abstraction too.

7. Scotus distinguishes intuitive and abstractive knowledge. Intuitive knowledge is knowledge of an object as present in its actual existence and it is against the nature of intuitive knowledge that it should be knowledge of an object which is not actually existent and present.[3] However, Scotus makes a distinction between perfect intuitive knowledge, which is immediate knowledge of an object as present, and imperfect intuitive knowledge, which is knowledge of an existent object as existing in the future, as anticipated, or as existing in the past, as remembered.[4] Abstractive knowledge on the other hand is knowledge of the essence of an object considered in abstraction from its existence or non-existence.[5] The difference between intuitive and abstractive knowledge is not, then, that the former is knowledge of an existent object, the latter of a non-existent object, but rather that the former is knowledge of an object as existent and actually present, that is, in intuition properly speaking, whereas the latter is knowledge of the essence of an object considered in abstraction from existence, whether the object actually exists or not. 'There can be abstractive knowledge of a non-existent object as well as of an existent object, but there can be intuitive knowledge only of an existent object as existent.'[6] We should have to add the words 'and present', for 'it is against the nature of intuitive knowledge that it should be of something which is not actually

[1] *Ox.*, 4, 45, 2.
[2] 4, 50, 1, 1; and cf. *S.T.*, Ia, 89, 1-4.
[3] *Ox.*, 1, 2, 7, no. 42; 2, 9, 2, no. 29.
[4] *Ibid.*, 3, 14, 3, no. 6.
[5] *Ibid.*, 2, 3, 9, no. 6.
[6] *Quodlibet*, 7, no. 8.

existent and present'.[1] Accordingly Scotus says that though the blessed could see him in God, that is, in the beatific vision, as existing and writing, this knowledge would not be intuitive knowledge, since 'I am not actually present in God, whom the blessed behold in heaven'.[2] Scotus's doctrine of abstractive knowledge, the knowledge of essences in abstraction from existence and non-existence, has led to the comparison of this aspect of his thought with the method of the modern Phenomenological School.

8. Scotus was sufficiently permeated by the spirit of the Aristotelian logic to lay stress on deduction and to have a rigorous idea of demonstrative proof; but he made some interesting remarks on induction. We cannot have experience of all instances of a particular type of natural event; but experience of a number of instances may be sufficient to show the scientist that the event in question proceeds from a natural cause and will always follow that cause. 'Whatever happens in most cases (that is, in the cases we have been able to observe) does not proceed from a free cause, but is the natural effect of the cause.' This proposition is recognised as true by the intellect, which sees that a free cause will not produce the same effect: if the cause could produce another effect, we should observe it doing so. If an effect is frequently produced by the same cause (Scotus means if the same effect is produced by the same cause, so far as our experience goes), the cause cannot be a free cause in that respect, nor can it be a 'casual' cause, but it must be the natural cause of that effect. Sometimes we have experience of the effect and are able to reduce the effect to a self-evident causal relation, in which case we can proceed to deduce the effect and so obtain a still more certain knowledge than we had through experience, while on other occasions we may have experience of the cause in such a way that we cannot demonstrate the necessary connection between cause and effect, but only that the effect proceeds from the cause as a natural cause.[3]

[1] *Ox.*, 2, 9, 2, no. 29. [2] *Ibid.*, 4, 14, 3, no. 6. [3] *Ibid.*, 1, 3, 4, no. 9.

CHAPTER XLVII

SCOTUS—III: METAPHYSICS

*Being and its transcendental attributes—The univocal concept of being—The formal objective distinction—Essence and existence—Universals—Hylomorphism—*Rationes seminales *rejected, plurality of forms retained—Individuation.*

1. METAPHYSICS is the science of being as being. The concept of being is the simplest of all concepts, and it is irreducible to other more ultimate concepts: being, therefore, cannot be defined.[1] We can conceive being distinctly by itself, for in its widest signification it simply means that which includes no contradiction, that which is not intrinsically impossible; but every other concept, every concept of a distinct kind of being, includes the concept of being.[2] Being in its widest sense thus includes that which has extramental being and that which has intramental being,[3] and it transcends all genera.[4]

There are various *passiones entis* (categories of being one might call them, provided that the word 'category' is not understood in the Aristotelian sense), the *passiones convertibiles* and the *passiones disiunctae.* The former are those categories of being which are designated by one name, which do not go in distinct pairs, and are convertible with being. For example, *one, true, good,* are *passiones convertibiles.* Every being is one, true, and good by the very fact that it is being, and there is no real distinction between these *passiones convertibiles* or between them and being, but there is a formal distinction, since they denote different aspects of being.[5] The *passiones disiunctae,* on the other hand, are not simply convertible with being if one takes them singly, though they are convertible if one takes them in pairs. For example, not every being is necessary and not every being is contingent; but every being is either necessary or contingent. Similarly, not every being is simply act and not every being is potency; but every being must be either act or potency or act in one respect and potency in another. Scotus speaks of the *passiones disiunctae* as transcendent,[6] since although no *passio disiuncta* comprises all being or is simply

[1] *Quodlibet,* 7, no. 14; 1, 39, no. 13.
[2] *Ox.,* 1, 3, 2, no. 24.
[3] *Quodlibet,* 3, no. 2.
[4] *Ox.,* 2, 1, 4, no. 26.
[5] *Ibid.,* 1, 3, 3, no. 7; 2, 16, no. 17.
[6] *Ibid.,* 1, 8, 3, no. 19.

convertible with the notion of being, it does not place an object in any definite genus or category, in the Aristotelian sense. The fact that a being is contingent, for example, does not tell one whether it is substance or accident.

As Scotus held that the concept of being is univocal, in the sense shortly to be discussed, it might appear that he tried to deduce the actuality of the *passiones disiunctae*; but this was not his intention. We can never deduce from the notion of being that contingent being exists, nor can we show that contingent being exists if necessary being exists, though we can show that if contingent being exists, necessary being exists and that if finite being exists, infinite being exists. In other words, we cannot deduce the existence of the less perfect *passio disiuncta* from the more perfect, though we can proceed the other way round. That contingent being actually exists is known only by experience.[1]

2. We have seen that in Scotus's opinion it is necessary to maintain that the primary object of the intellect is being in general, if one wishes to safeguard the possibility of metaphysics. By saying this I do not mean to suggest that Scotus's doctrine of the primary object of the intellect was motivated simply by pragmatic considerations. Rather did he hold that the intellect as such is the faculty of apprehending being in general, and, holding this, he then pointed out what appeared to him to be the unfortunate conclusion which followed from the Thomist position. Similarly, Scotus maintained that unless there is a concept of being which is univocal in respect of God and creatures, no metaphysical knowledge of God is possible; but he did not assert this doctrine of the univocal character of the concept of being for a purely utilitarian reason; he was convinced that there is actually a univocal concept of this kind, and then pointed out that unless its existence is admitted, one cannot safeguard the possibility of any metaphysical knowledge of God. Our concepts are formed in dependence on sense-perception and represent immediately material quiddities or essences. But no concept of a material quiddity as such is applicable to God, for God is not included among material things. Therefore, unless we can form a concept which is not restricted to the material quiddity as such, but is common to infinite being and to finite being, to immaterial and to material being, we can never attain a true knowledge of God by means of concepts which are proper to Him. If Henry of Ghent's doctrine of the equivocal

[1] *Ox.*, 1, 39, no. 13.

character of the concept of being as applied to God and to creatures were true, it would follow that the human mind was restricted (in this life at least) to the knowledge of creatures alone; agnosticism would thus be the consequence of Henry's theory.[1] If I have mentioned this aspect of the question first, I have done so not in order to imply that Scotus was motivated simply by utilitarian or pragmatic considerations, but rather in order to show that the question was not a purely academic one in Scotus's eyes.

What did Scotus mean by the univocal concept of being? In the Oxford Commentary[2] he says: *et ne fiat contentio de nomine univocationis, conceptum univocum dico, qui ita est unus, quod ejus unitas sufficit ad contradictionem, affirmando et negando ipsum de eodem. Sufficit etiam pro medio syllogistico, ut extrema unita in medio sic uno, sine fallacia aequivocationis, concludantur inter se unum.* Scotus's first point is, therefore, that a univocal concept means for him a concept the unity of which is sufficient to involve a contradiction if one affirms and denies the idea of the same subject at the same time. If one were to say 'the dog (i.e. the animal) is running' and at the same time 'the dog (meaning the star or the dog-fish) is not running', there would be no real contradiction, since 'running' and 'not running' are not affirmed of the same subject: the contradiction is purely verbal. Similarly, if one were to say 'the unicorn is' (meaning that the unicorn has an intramental existence) and 'the unicorn is not' (meaning that the unicorn has no extramental existence in nature), there would be no real contradiction. Scotus, however, is referring to a word the meaning of which is sufficiently the same to bring about a real contradiction if one were to affirm and deny it of the same subject at the same time. For instance, if one said that the unicorn is and that the unicorn is not, understanding 'is' in both judgements as referring to extramental existence, there would be a real contradiction. Similarly, if one said that God is and that God is not, referring in both cases to real existence, there would be a contradiction. What does Scotus mean by *sufficit*? In the judgements 'God is' and 'God is not' it is sufficient for the production of a contradiction that 'is' should mean opposed to nothingness or not-being. A contradiction is involved in saying both that God is opposed to nothingness and that God is not opposed to nothingness. It must be remembered that Scotus is maintaining the

[1] *Ox.*, 1, 8, 3, nos. 4 ff. This represents Scotus' interpretation of Henry's doctrine.
[2] 1, 3, 2, no. 5.

existence of a univocal concept of being which is applicable to God and creatures, so that one can say that God is and the creature is, using the word 'is' in the same sense. He is perfectly well aware, of course, that God and the creature are actually opposed to nothingness in different ways, and he does not mean to deny this; but his point is that if you mean by 'is' simply the opposite of nothingness or not-being, then you can use the word 'being' of God and creatures in the same sense, prescinding from the concrete ways in which they are opposed to nothingness. Accordingly he says *sufficit ad contradictionem* so as not to imply that God and the creatures are opposed to nothingness in the same way. But though they are opposed to nothingness in different ways, they are none the less both opposed to nothingness, and if one forms a concept of being denoting sheer opposition to nothingness, a concept which involves contradiction if affirmed and denied of the same subject at the same time, this concept can be predicated univocally of God and creatures.

As to the remark about the syllogism, Scotus says that a univocal concept, as he understands it, is a concept which, when employed as middle term in a syllogism, has a meaning 'sufficiently' the same in both premisses to prevent the fallacy of equivocation being committed. To take a crude example, if one argued 'every ram is an animal, this object (meaning an instrument for pumping water) is a ram, therefore this object is an animal', the syllogism would involve the fallacy of equivocation and would not be valid. Now take the following argument. If there is wisdom in some creatures, there must be wisdom in God; but there is wisdom in some creatures; therefore there is wisdom in God. If the term 'wisdom' is used equivocally, in completely different senses, in regard to God and in regard to creatures, the argument would be fallacious: if the argument is to be valid, the idea of wisdom as applied to God and to creatures must be sufficiently the same for equivocation to be avoided. Scotus is attacking Henry of Ghent, according to whose opinion the predicates we apply to God and creatures are equivocal, though the two meanings so resemble one another that one word can be used for both. Scotus objects that to admit the truth of Henry's opinion would be to admit that every argument from creatures to God employs the fallacy of equivocation and is fallacious. The univocity which Scotus asserts is not restricted, then, to the concept of being. 'Whatsoever things are common to God and the creature are such as belong to being as indifferent to finite and finite.'[1] If one considers being in abstraction from the distinction between infinite and finite being, that is, as signifying mere opposition to nothing, one has a univocal concept of being, and the transcendental attributes of being, the *passiones convertibiles*, can also give rise to univocal concepts. If one can form a univocal concept of being, one can also form univocal concepts of *one, true, good.*[2] What, then, of wisdom? Goodness is a *passio convertibilis*, inasmuch as every being is good by the mere fact that it is a being; but not every being is wise. Scotus answers[3] that the *passiones disiunctae*, such as *necessary* or *possible, act* or *potency*, are transcendent in the sense that neither member determines its subject as belonging to any special genus, and that wisdom and suchlike attributes can also be called transcendent, that is, as transcending the division of being into genera.

Scotus lays a strong emphasis on this doctrine of univocity. Every metaphysical investigation concerning God involves the consideration of some attribute and the removal from our idea of it of the imperfection which attaches to that attribute as found in creatures. In this way we attain an idea of the essence of *ratio formalis* of the attribute, and then we can predicate it of God in a supremely perfect sense. Scotus takes the example of wisdom, intellect and will.[4] First we remove from the idea of wisdom, for example, the imperfections of finite wisdom and attain to a concept of the *ratio formalis* of wisdom, what wisdom is in itself. Then we attribute wisdom to God in the most perfect manner (*perfectissime*). 'Therefore every investigation concerning God supposes that the intellect has the same univocal concept, which it receives from creatures.'[5] If it is denied that we can thus form an idea of the *ratio formalis* of wisdom, and so on, the conclusion would follow that we could arrive at no knowledge of God. On the one hand our knowledge is founded on our experience of creatures, while on the other hand we cannot predicate of God any attribute precisely as it is found in creatures. Therefore, unless we can attain a common middle term with a univocal meaning, no argument from creatures to God is possible or valid. That we can form a univocal concept of being, without reference to infinite or finite, uncreated or created, Scotus regarded as a fact of experience.[6]

[1] *Ox.*, 1, 8, 3, no. 18. [2] *Ibid.*, 1, 8, 3, no. 19. [3] *Ibid.*
[4] *Ibid.*, 1, 3, 2, no. 10. [5] *Ibid.* [6] Cf. *ibid.*, 1, 3, 2, no. 6.

Scotus agrees with Henry of Ghent that God is not in a genus, but he will not agree with his denial of the univocal character of the concept of being. 'I hold my middle opinion, that it is compatible with the simplicity of God that there should be some concept common to Him and to the creature, but this common concept is not a generically common concept.'[1] Now, Henry of Ghent, in Scotus's view, maintained that the concept of being as applied to God and to creatures is equivocal, and it is easily understandable that Scotus rejects this opinion. But what was his attitude towards St. Thomas's doctrine of analogy? In the first place Scotus asserts firmly that God and the creature are completely different in the real order, *sunt primo diversa in realitate, quia in nulla realitate conveniunt.*[2] Hence to accuse Scotus of Spinozism is clearly absurd. In the second place Scotus does not reject the analogy of attribution, since he admits that being belongs primarily and principally to God and teaches that creatures are to God as *mensurata ad mensuram, vel excessa ad excedens*,[3] while in the *De Anima*[4] he says that *omnia entia habent attributionem ad ens primum, quod est Deus.* In the third place, however, he insists that analogy itself presupposes a univocal concept, since we could not compare creatures with God as *mensurata ad mensuram, vel excessa ad excedens*, unless there was a concept common to both.[5] God is knowable by man in this life only by means of concepts drawn from creatures, and unless these concepts were common to God and creatures, we should never be able to compare creatures with God as the imperfect with the perfect: there would be no bridge between creatures and God. Even those masters who deny univocity with their lips, really presuppose it.[6] If there were no univocal concepts, we should have only a negative knowledge of God, which is not the case. We may say that God is not a stone, but we can also say that a chimaera is not a stone, so that in saying that God is not a stone we know no more of God than we do of a chimaera.[7] Further, knowledge that something is an effect of God is not sufficient by itself to give us our knowledge of God. A stone is an effect of God; but we do not say that God is a stone, because He is the cause of the stone, whereas we do say that He is wise, and this presupposes a univocal concept of wisdom which is transcendent (in Scotus's sense). In fine, Scotus's teaching is that although all creatures have an essential relation of dependence

[1] *Ox.*, I, 8, 3, no. 16. [2] *Ibid.*, I, 8, 3, no. 11. [3] *Ibid.*, I, 8, 3, no. 12.
[4] 21, no. 14. [5] *Ox.*, I, 8, 3, no. 12. [6] *Rep.*, I, 3, I, no. 7.
[7] *Ox.*, I, 3, 2; I, 8, 3, no. 9.

to God, this fact would not be sufficient to afford us any positive knowledge of God, since we possess no natural intuition of God, unless we could form univocal concepts common to God and creatures. Therefore he says that 'all beings have an attribution to the first being, which is God . . .; yet in spite of this fact there can be abstracted from all of them one common concept which is expressed by this word *being*, and is one logically speaking, although it is not (one) naturally and metaphysically speaking', that is, speaking either as a natural philosopher or as a metaphysician.[1]

This last remark gives rise to the question whether or not Scotus considered the univocity of the concepts of being to be really restricted to the logical order. Some writers affirm that he did. The passage from the *De Anima* which has just been quoted seems to state it positively, and Scotus's observation, quoted above, that God and creatures *sunt primo diversa in realitate, quia in nulla realitate conveniunt*, would seem to teach the same. But if the univocal concept of being were restricted to the logical order in such a way that it was an *ens rationis*, how would it help to ensure objective knowledge of God? Moreover, in the Oxford Commentary[2] Scotus considers the objection to his theory that matter has an *esse* of its own. The objection is that in the case of analogues a thing or attribute is present really only in the primary analogue: in the other it is not present really, except by way of a relation to the primary analogue. Health is present really in the animal, whereas it is present in urine only *per attributionem ad illud*. *Esse* comes from the form: therefore it is not present really in matter, but only through its relation to the form. In answer to this objection Scotus says that the example given is valueless, since there are a hundred examples to the contrary, and then remarks, 'for there is no greater analogy than that of the creature to God *in ratione essendi*, and yet *esse*, existence, belongs primarily and principally to God in such a way that it yet belongs really and univocally to the creature; and similarly with goodness and wisdom and the like'.[3] Here he uses the words 'really and univocally' (*realiter et univoce*) together. If the doctrine of univocity is meant to ensure an objective knowledge of God from creatures, it would seem to be essential to that doctrine that the univocal concept should not be an *ens rationis* merely, but that it should have a real foundation or counterpart in extramental reality. On

[1] *De Anima*, 21, no. 14. [2] 2, 12, 2, no. 2. [3] *Ox.*, 2, 12, 2, no. 8.

the other hand, Scotus is insistent that God is not in a genus and that God and creatures are in the real order *primo diversa*. How can the two sets of statements be reconciled?

The concept of being is abstracted from creatures, and it is the concept of being without any determination; it is logically prior to the division of being into infinite and finite being. But in actual fact every being must be either infinite or finite: it must be opposed to nothingness either as infinite being or as finite being: there is no actually existent being which is neither infinite nor finite. In this sense the univocal concept of being, as logically prior to the division of being into infinite and finite, possesses a unity which belongs to the logical order. The natural philosopher obviously does not consider being in this sense, nor does the metaphysician in so far as he is concerned with actually existent being and with possible being, since the concept of a being which would be neither infinite nor finite would not be the concept of a possible being. On the other hand, even though every actual being is either finite or infinite, every being is really opposed to nothingness, though in different ways, so that there is a real foundation for the univocal concept of being. As *intentio prima* the concept of being is founded on reality, for otherwise it could not be abstracted, and has objective reference, while as *intentio secunda* it is an *ens rationis*; but the concept of being as such, whether considered as *intentio prima* or *intentio secunda*, does not express something which has a formal existence outside the mind. It is, therefore, a logical concept. The logician 'considers second intentions as applied to first intentions', says Scotus when speaking of universals,[1] and what is univocal for the logician is equivocal[2] for the philosopher who is studying real things. One can say, then, that the univocal concept of being is an *ens rationis*. On the other hand, the univocal concept of being has a real foundation in actuality. The case is not without parallel to that of the universal. No doubt, Scotus did not consider adequately all the possible objections against his theory; but the truth of the matter seems to be that he was so intent on refuting the doctrine of Henry of Ghent, which he considered to endanger or render impossible any objective knowledge of God in this life, that he did not give his full attention to all the complexities of the problem and to the difficulties which

[1] *Ox.*, 2, 3, 1, no. 7.

[2] For Scotus 'equivocal' means, of distinct or different meanings. The scientist, for instance, considers actual bodies, which differ, but one can form a common concept of body in general.

might be raised against his own theory. It must be remembered, however, that Scotus postulated a formal distinction between the attributes of being and between the attributes and being. 'Being contains many attributes which are not different things from being itself, as Aristotle proves in the beginning of the fourth book of the *Metaphysics*, but which are distinguished formally and quidditatively, that is, by a formal, objectively grounded distinction, from one another, and also from being, by a real and quidditative formality, I say.'[1] In this case the univocal concept of being cannot be a mere *ens rationis*, in the sense of a purely subjective construction. There is no separate or separable thing, existing extramentally, which corresponds to the univocal concept of being; but there is an objective foundation for the concept none the less. One can say, then, that the univocal concept of being is not purely logical, provided that one does not mean to imply that there is any *thing* in extramental reality which corresponds to the concept.

3. I have treated the doctrine of univocity at some length, not only because the doctrine is one of the characteristics of Scotism, but also because Scotus attached very considerable importance to the doctrine, as a safeguard of natural theology. I turn now to a brief consideration of another characteristic doctrine of Scotus, that of the *distinctio formalis a parte rei*, the objective formal distinction, which plays an important rôle in the Scotist system and one use of which has just been mentioned.

The doctrine of the formal distinction was not an invention of Scotus: one finds it in the philosophy of Olivi, for example, and it has been ascribed to St. Bonaventure himself. In any case it became a common doctrine among the Franciscan thinkers, and what Scotus did was to take over the doctrine from his predecessors and make extensive use of it. In brief, the doctrine is that there is a distinction which is less than the real distinction and more objective than a virtual distinction. A real distinction obtains between two things which are physically separable, at least by divine power. It is obvious enough that there is a real distinction between a man's two hands, since these are distinct things; but there is also a real distinction between the form and matter of any material object. A purely mental distinction signifies a distinction made by the mind when there is no corresponding objective distinction in the thing itself. The distinction between a thing and its definition, for example, between 'man'

[1] *Ox.*, 2, 16, *quaestio unica*, no. 17.

and 'rational animal', is purely mental. A formal distinction obtains when the mind distinguishes in an object two or more *formalitates* which are objectively distinct, but which are inseparable from one another, even by divine power. For instance, Scotus asserted a formal distinction between the divine attributes. Mercy and justice are formally distinct, though the divine justice and the divine mercy are inseparable, since, in spite of the formal distinction between them, each is really identical with the divine essence.

An example from psychology may make Scotus's meaning clearer. There is only one soul in man, and there cannot be a real distinction between the sensitive soul and the intellectual or rational soul in man: it is in virtue of the one vital principle that a man thinks and exercises sensation. Not even God can separate a man's rational soul from his sensitive soul, for it would no longer be a human soul. On the other hand, sensation is not thought: rational activity can exist without sensitive activity, as in the angels, and sensitive activity can exist without rational activity, as in the case of the purely sensitive soul of the brute. In man, then, the sensitive and rational principles are formally distinct, with a distinction which is objective, that is, independent of the mind's distinguishing activity; but they are not really distinct *things*; they are distinct *formalitates* of one thing, the human soul.

Why did Scotus assert the existence of this formal distinction, and why was he not content to call it a *distinctio rationis cum fundamento in re*? The ultimate reason was, of course, that he thought the distinction to be not only warranted, but also demanded by the nature of knowledge and the nature of the object of knowledge. Knowledge is the apprehension of being, and if the mind is forced, so to speak, to recognise distinctions in the object, that is, if it does not simply construct actively a distinction in the object, but finds the recognition of a distinction imposed upon it, the distinction cannot be simply a mental distinction, and the foundation of the distinction in the mind must be an objective distinction in the object. On the other hand, there are cases when the foundation of the distinction cannot be the existence of distinct separable factors in the object. It is necessary, then, to find room for a distinction which is less than a real distinction, such as obtains between soul and body in man, but which at the same time is founded on an objective distinction in the object, a distinction which can be only between different, but not separable formalities of one and the same object. Such a distinction will maintain the objectivity of knowledge, without, however, impairing the unity of the object. It may be objected, of course, that the formal distinction as applied by Scotus does, in some cases at least, impair the requisite unity of the object and that it surrenders too much to 'realism'; but it would appear that Scotus considered the distinction to be necessary if the objectivity of knowledge is to be maintained.

4. One of the questions in which Scotus applies his formal distinction is the question of the distinction which obtains between essence and existence in the creature.[1] He refuses to admit a real distinction between essence and existence: 'it is simply false, that existence (*esse*) is something different from essence'.[2] Similarly, 'the proposition is false, that just as existence stands to essence, so operation (*operari*) stands to potency, for existence is really the same as the essence and does not proceed from the essence, whereas act or operation proceeds from potency and is not really the same as potency'.[3] The assertion, *simpliciter falsum est, quod esse sit aliud ab essentia*, would indeed appear to be directed against such statements of St. Thomas as *Ergo oportet quod omnis talis res, cuius esse est aliud a natura sua, habeat esse ab alio*;[4] but, given Scotus's conception of a real distinction, his denial of a real distinction between essence and existence in creatures is more relevant to the doctrine of Giles of Rome, for whom essence and existence were physically separable, than to that of St. Thomas Aquinas.

But when Scotus discusses the relation of essence and existence, his polemic is directed not so much against St. Thomas or even Giles of Rome as against Henry of Ghent. Henry did not maintain a real distinction between essence and existence in creatures, but he distinguished *esse essentiae* and *esse existentiae*, the former being the state of the essence as known by God, the latter being its state after creation, creation adding no positive element to the essence, but only a relation to God. Henry had asserted this doctrine of the *esse essentiae* in order to account for the fact of science, in the sense of knowledge of timeless truths about essences, irrespective of the actual existence of such objects, but Scotus argued that Henry's doctrine destroyed the Christian idea of creation. For example, creation is production out of

[1] It must be admitted that Scotus confines himself to denying the real distinction and does not explicitly apply the formal objective distinction to the relation of essence and existence in the creature; but the doctrine of Scotists on this point seems to me to be a reasonable interpretation of Scotus's meaning.

[2] *Ox.*, 4, 13, 1, no. 38. [3] *Ibid.*, 2, 16, no. 10. [4] *De ente et essentia*, 5.

nothing; but if a stone formerly, before its creation, had *esse verum reale*, then when it is produced by the efficient cause, it is not produced from nothing.[1] Moreover, as the essence is known eternally by God, it would follow from this notion that the essence before actual existence already possesses *esse reale* and that creation is eternal: one would thus have to admit other necessary beings besides God. Only that which actually exists has *esse reale*; possible existence (*esse possibile*) is only *esse secundum quid*.[2] The essence as known may be said to possess *esse diminutum*; but this existence (*esse*) of an essence in the divine mind before its actual production is simply *esse cognitum*. Scotus and St. Thomas are at one on this point, that creation means the production of the whole object out of nothing and that the essence before creation did not possess any *esse* of its own, though Scotus differed from St. Thomas in his view of the relationship which obtains between the essence and the existence in the created object, since he rejected a real distinction, though, as already remarked, this rejection was actually a rejection of the real distinction maintained by Giles of Rome rather than of that taught by St. Thomas.

5. The formal objective distinction was also employed by Scotus in his discussion of universals. In regard to universals Scotus was certainly not an exaggerated realist, and Suarez's assertion[3] that Scotus taught that the common nature is numerically the same in all individuals of the species, misrepresents Scotus's position, at least if taken out of its setting and out of relation to Suarez's own doctrine. Scotus states unambiguously that 'the universal in act does not exist except in the intellect' and that there is no actually existing universal which is predicable of another object than that in which it exists.[4] The common nature is not numerically the same in Socrates and in Plato; it cannot be compared to the divine essence, which is numerically the same in the three divine Persons.[5] Nevertheless, there is a unity which is less than numerical (*unitas minor quam numeralis*). Though the physical nature of an object is inseparable from the object's *haecceitas* (the object's 'thisness' or principle of individuation, which we shall consider shortly) and though it cannot exist in any other object, there is a formal objective distinction between the human nature and the 'Socratesness' or *haecceitas* in Socrates, but not a real distinction, so that the human nature can be considered simply as

[1] *Ox.*, 1, 36, no. 3.
[2] *Ibid.*, 1, 30, 2, no. 15.
[3] *Disputationes Metaphysicae*, 6, 1, no. 2.
[4] *Rep.*, 2, 12, 5, no. 12.
[5] *Ibid.*, 2, 12, 5, no. 13.

such, without reference to individuality or to universality. Appealing to Avicenna,[1] Scotus observes that horseness is simply horseness (*equinitas est tantum equinitas*) and that of itself it has neither *esse singulare* nor *esse universale.*[2] In other words, there exists between the *haecceitas* and the nature in a concrete object a *distinctio formalis a parte rei*, and it is necessary to suppose such a distinction, since otherwise, that is, if the nature were *of itself* individual, if it were, for example, of itself the nature of Socrates, there would be no objective foundation, no valid ground for our universal statements. The abstraction of the logical universal presupposes a distinction in the object between the nature and the *haecceitas.*

It is, however, important to remember that this distinction is not a real distinction, not, that is, a distinction between two separable entities. Form and matter are separable; but the nature and the *haecceitas* are not separable. Not even the divine power can separate physically the 'Socratesness' of Socrates and the human nature of Socrates. Therefore, even though Scotus's assertion of the formal objective distinction is indeed a concession in one sense to realism, it does not imply that the human nature of Socrates is objectively and numerically identical with the human nature of Plato. Scotus is concerned, not to support exaggerated realism, but rather to account for the objective reference of our universal judgements. Whether or not one agrees with his theory is, of course, another matter; but in any case to accuse him of falling into the early mediaeval form of exaggerated realism is to misunderstand and misrepresent his position. Scotus is willing to say with Averroes,[3] *Intellectus est qui facit universalitatem in rebus*; but he insists that this proposition must not be understood as excluding the *unitas realis minor unitate numerali* which exists prior to the mind's operation, since this exclusion would make it impossible to explain why 'the intellect is moved to abstract one specific concept from Socrates and Plato rather than from Socrates and a stone'.[4] It is the objective reference of science which interests Scotus.

J. Kraus[5] has maintained that Duns Scotus distinguishes three universals. First, there is the physical universal, which is the specific nature existing really in individual objects; secondly, there is the metaphysical universal, which is the common nature, not

[1] In *Metaphysics*, 5, 1. [2] *Ibid.*, 5, 11. [3] *De Anima*, 1, 8. [4] *Rep.*, 2, 12, 5, no. 13.
[5] *Die Lehre des J. Duns Skotus von der natura communis*, Fribourg, 1927.

as it actually exists in the concrete thing, but with the characteristics which it acquires through abstraction by the active intellect, namely positive indetermination or predicability of many individuals *in potentia proxima*; and thirdly, there is the logical universal, the universal in the strict sense, which is the metaphysical universal conceived reflexly in its predicability and analysed into its constitutive notes. But this threefold distinction must not be understood as implying that the physical universal is separable or really distinct from the individuality of the object in which it exists. The concrete object consists of the nature and the *haecceitas*, and between them there is, not a real distinction but a *distinctio formalis a parte rei*. Scotus's mention of the relation of matter to successive forms[1] should not mislead us, since for Scotus there is a real distinction between matter and form, and the same matter can exist under successive forms, though it cannot exist simultaneously under different ultimately determining forms. The physical universal, however, though indifferent, as considered *in itself*, to this or that *haecceitas*, cannot exist in itself extramentally and is physically inseparable from its *haecceitas*.

6. That Scotus taught the doctrine of hylomorphism is clear enough;[2] but it is not so clear whether or not he accepted the Bonaventurian attribution of hylomorphic composition to angels. If the *De rerum principio* were authentic, there could be no doubt as to Scotus's acceptance of the Bonaventurian view, but the *De rerum principio* is not the work of Scotus, and in his authentic writings the latter nowhere expressly states the Bonaventurian doctrine. Thus Father Parthenius Minges, O.F.M., who draws on the *De rerum principio* in his *Joannis Duns Scoti Doctrina philosophica et theologica*, has to admit that 'in the Commentaries on the *Sentences*, the *Quaestiones quodlibetales* and the *Questions on the Metaphysics of Aristotle* Scotus does not expressly state this doctrine, but only more or less touches on, insinuates or supposes it'.[3] It seems to me that Scotus's treatment of matter in the Commentaries can be said to 'suppose' the doctrine of the hylomorphic composition of rational soul and of angels only if one is determined on other grounds to assume that he held this doctrine, if, for example, one is determined to accept the *De rerum principio* as Scotus's work; but it is true that in the *De Anima*[4] he remarks that 'probably it can be said that in the soul there is matter'. However, Scotus is here engaged in showing that the presence of

[1] *Loc. cit.* [2] Cf. *Ox.*, 2, 12, 1. [3] p. 46. [4] 15, no. 3ff.

matter in the soul can be deduced with probability from the premisses of Aristotle and St. Thomas, even though St. Thomas did not hold the doctrine. For example, he argues that if matter is the principle of individuation, as St. Thomas (but not Scotus) held, then there must be matter in the rational soul. It is useless to say that the soul, when separated from the body, is distinguished from other souls by its relation to the body, first because the soul does not exist for the sake of the body, secondly because the relation or inclination to the body, which no longer exists, would be no more than a *relatio rationis*, and thirdly because the inclination or relation supposes a foundation, i.e. *this* soul, so that the thisness could not be due to the relation. Thus Scotus in the *De Anima* is trying to show that if one maintains with St. Thomas that matter is the principle of individuation, one ought to assert the presence of matter in the rational soul, in order to explain the individuality of the rational soul after death; he does not state that this conclusion represents his own opinion. It may be that it does represent Scotus's own opinion and that he wished to show that the Thomist ought, on his own premisses, to share that opinion; but one is hardly in a position to state positively that Scotus without a doubt maintained the Bonaventurian doctrine, and if one were prepared to reject the authenticity of the *De Anima*, there would seem to be no very cogent reason for stating that Scotus even probably maintained the doctrine.

But whatever Scotus's opinion on universal hylomorphism may have been, he certainly held that matter, really distinct from form, is an entity in its own right and that it is *potentia subjectiva* and not simply *potentia objectiva*, that is, that it is something existing, not something which is merely possible.[1] Moreover, matter is an *ens absolutum*, in the sense that it could exist by itself without form, at least through the divine power.[2] An entity which is distinct from and prior to another entity can exist apart from that other entity without any contradiction being involved. That matter is distinct from form is proved by the fact that together with form it makes a real composite being, while that it is prior to form, logically prior at least, is proved by the fact that it receives form and that what receives form must be logically prior to form.[3] Similarly, since God creates matter immediately, He could conserve it immediately, that is, without any secondary conserving agency. Again, form does not belong to the essence of

[1] *Ox.*, 2, 12, 1, no. 10. [2] Cf. *ibid.*, 2, 12, 2; *Rep.* 2, 12, 2. [3] *Ox.*, *loc. cit.*, no. 3.

matter nor does the *esse* which form confers on matter belong to the matter itself, since it is removed in substantial change.[1] In other words, the reality of substantial change postulates the reality of matter. In answer to the Thomist objection that it is contradictory to speak of matter as a real entity, that is, as actually existing without form, since to say that matter actually exists on its own account and to say that it has a form is one and the same, Scotus answers that act and form are not necessarily convertible terms. Of course, if act is taken to mean act which is received and which actuates and distinguishes, then matter, which is receptive, is not act; but if act and potency are understood in a wider sense, every thing which is *extra causam suam* is in act, even privations, and in this sense matter is in act, though it is not form.[2]

7. Scotus rejects the theory of *rationes seminales*, on the ground that the theory is not needed in order to avoid the conclusion that the created efficient agent creates and annihilates in the changes it brings about, and that there is no other cogent reason for accepting it.[3] But though he rejects the theory of *rationes seminales*, he retains that of plurality of forms. Against the assertion of the Thomists that there is no need to postulate a form of corporeity, since *sine necessitate non est ponenda pluralitas*, Scotus replies that in this case there is a need, *hic enim est necessitas ponendi plura*, and he goes on to argue that although the body, when the soul has departed, is continually tending to dissolution, it remains a body, for a time at least, and must possess that form which makes a body a body.[4] Moreover, the Body of Christ in the tomb must have possessed a form of corporeity. From the fact that a human body naturally tends to dissolution when the soul has departed it does not follow that the body, in a state of separation from the soul, has no proper form of its own; it follows only that it has not got a *perfect* subsistence of its own, and the reason of this is that the form of corporeity is an imperfect form which disposes the body for a higher form, the soul.

But though Scotus affirms the existence of a form of corporeity in the human body, and, of course, in every organic body, which is transmitted by the parents at the same time that God infuses the rational soul and which is really distinct from the rational soul,

[1] *Rep.*, 2, 12, 2, no. 5.

[2] *Ox.*, 2, 12, 2, no. 7. The distinction of prime matter into *materia primo prima*, *materia secundo prima* and *materia tertio prima* is found only in the unauthentic *De rerum principio*.

[3] *Rep.*, 2, 18, 1.

[4] *Ox.*, 4, 11, 3, nos. 54ff.

from which it can be separated, it should not be imagined that he breaks up the human soul into three really distinct forms or even parts, the vegetative, sensitive and intellective principles; and he rejects the theories which appear to him to impair the unity of the soul. The rational soul of man comprises these three powers *unitive*, 'although they are formally distinct'.[1] It would be false to suggest that Scotus taught the existence of three souls in man or that he maintained that the vegetative and sensitive powers are distinct from the rational power in the same way in which the form of corporeity is distinct. Whereas the distinction between the form of corporeity and the human soul is a real distinction, that between the powers within the soul itself is a formal distinction, which obtains between inseparable *formalitates* of one object, not between separable entities or forms.

8. It is necessary to say something about Scotus's somewhat obscure doctrine of individuation, the obscurity lying rather on the positive than on the negative side of the doctrine.

Scotus criticises and rejects St. Thomas's theory that prime matter is the principle of individuation. Prime matter cannot be the primary reason of distinction and diversity since it is of itself indistinct and indeterminate.[2] Moreover, if matter is the principle of individuation, it follows that in the case of substantial change the two substances, that corrupted and that generated, are precisely the same substance, since the matter is the same, even though the forms are different. St. Thomas's theory seems to imply that quantity is actually the principle of individuation; but quantity is an accident and a substance cannot be individuated by an accident. Incidentally, Scotus tries to show that Aristotle is wrongly cited as an authority for the Thomist view of individuation.

The principle of individuation is thus not prime matter, nor can it be the nature as such, since it is precisely with the individuation of the nature that we are concerned. What is it, then? It is an *entitas individualis*. 'This entity is neither matter nor form nor the composite thing, in so far as any of these is a nature; but it is the ultimate reality of the being which is matter or form or a composite thing.'[3] The *entitas singularis* and the *entitas naturae*, whether the latter is matter or form or a *compositum*, are formally distinct; but they are not, and cannot be, two things. They are not separable things; nor does the *entitas singularis* stand to the

[1] *Ox.*, 2, 16, no. 17. [2] *Ibid.*, 2, 3, 5, no. 1. [3] *Ibid.*, 2, 3, 6, no. 15.

entitas naturae as specific difference to genus.[1] The word *haecceitas* is not used for the principle of individuation in the Oxford Commentary, though it is so used in the *Reportata Parisiensia*[2] and in the *Quaestiones in libros Metaphysicorum.*[3]

It is not so easy to understand exactly what this *haecceitas* or *entitas singularis vel individualis* or *ultima realitas entis* actually is. It is, as we have seen, neither matter nor form nor the composite thing; but it is a positive entity, the final reality of matter, form and the composite thing. A human being, for instance, is *this* composite being, composed of *this* matter and *this* form. The *haecceitas* does not confer any further qualitative determination; but it seals the being as *this* being. Scotus's view certainly cannot be equated with the theory that every nature is of itself individual, since this he expressly denies, though in view of the fact that Scotus, while postulating a formal distinction between *haecceitas* and nature, denies their real distinction from one another, it seems to be implied that a thing has *haecceitas* or 'thisness' by the fact that it exists. His theory is not the same as that of the Nominalists, since he postulates contraction of the nature by the 'ultimate reality'; but the fact that he speaks of 'ultimate reality' would seem to imply that a nature acquires this ultimate reality through existence, though it is not, says Scotus, existence itself.[4]

[1] *Ox.*, 2, 3, 6, no. 15.

[2] 2, 12, 5, nos. 1, 8, 13, 14.

[3] 7, 13, nos. 9 and 26.

[4] *Quaestiones in libros Metaph.*, 7, 13, no. 7.

CHAPTER XLVIII

SCOTUS—IV: NATURAL THEOLOGY

Metaphysics and God—Knowledge of God from creatures—Proof of God's existence—Simplicity and intelligence of God—God's infinity—The Anselmian argument—Divine attributes which cannot be philosophically demonstrated—The distinction between the divine attributes—The divine ideas—The divine will—Creation.

1. GOD is not, properly speaking, an object of metaphysical science, says Scotus,[1] in spite of the fact that metaphysics are the science of being, and God is the first being. A truth belongs properly to that science in which it is known *a priori*, from the principles of that science, and the metaphysician knows truths about God only *a posteriori*. God is, therefore, the proper object of theology, in which science He is known as He is in His essence, in Himself; He is the object of metaphysics only *secundum quid*, inasmuch as the philosopher comes to know God only in and through His effects.

This statement certainly does not mean that for Scotus the philosopher or metaphysician is unable to attain any certain knowledge of God. 'By our natural power (*ex naturalibus*) we can know some truths concerning God', says Scotus,[2] and he goes on to explain that many things (*multa*) can be known about God by the philosophers through a consideration of God's effects. By the natural power of reason one can conclude that God is one, supreme, good, but not that God is three in Persons.[3] Theology deals more properly with the divine Persons than with the essential attributes of God, for most of the essential attributes (*essentialia plurima*) can be known by us in metaphysics.[4] Accordingly, the statement that God is, strictly speaking, the object of theology rather than of metaphysics does not mean that Scotus excludes the study of God from metaphysics, since although God is not the primary object of metaphysics, He is none the less considered in metaphysics in the noblest way in which He can be studied in any natural science.[5] In the *De primo principio*[6] Scotus recapitulates the perfections which the philosophers have proved to belong to

[1] *Rep.*, Prol., 3, no. 1. [2] *Ibid.*, Prol., 3, no. 6. [3] *Ox.*, 1, 1, 2, no. 2.
[4] *Ox.*, Prol., 4, no. 32. [5] *Ibid.*, Prol., 4, no. 20. [6] E.g. 4, nos. 36, 37.

God and distinguishes them from other perfections, such as omnipotence and universal and special providence, which belong more properly to the *credibilia*, truths which have not been proved by the philosophers but which are believed by *Catholici*. These latter truths, says Scotus, will be considered in *sequenti* (*tractatu*) and the words have been added, *scilicet in Theorematibus*. That an attempt was made to disprove this identification of the 'following' treatise with the *Theoremata* and that this attempt was largely due to the at least apparent contradiction between the *Theoremata* and the *De primo principio* has already been mentioned in Chapter XLV, and, as I there explained, I propose to expose the natural theology of Scotus on the supposition that the *Theoremata* is not the authentic work of Scotus, with the proviso that, were the authenticity of the *Theoremata* ever to be satisfactorily proved, one would have to explain the apparent contradiction on some such line as that adopted by M. Gilson. In any case, however, Scotus has made it perfectly clear in his certainly authentic works that the philosopher can prove many truths about God by the light of natural reason, without any actual employmentof the data of revelation. Some of the points in regard to which Scotus restricted the scope of the unaided human intellect will be noted in the following pages; but it is important to note that Scotus was neither a sceptic nor an agnostic in regard to natural theology, and the *Theoremata*, even if authentic, would be quite insufficient to dispose of the clear and abundant evidence on this point which is afforded by the Commentaries on the *Sentences* and by the *De primo principio*.

2. Scotus certainly thought that the existence of God stands in need of rational proof and that this rational proof must be *a posteriori*. Of his use of the Anselmian argument I shall speak later.

First of all, man has no intuitive knowledge of God in this life, since the intuition of God is precisely that form of knowledge which places a man *extra statum viae*.[1] Our knowledge starts from the things of sense, and our natural conceptual knowledge of God is arrived at through reflection on the objects of experience.[2] By considering creatures as God's effects the human mind is able to form concepts which apply to God; but one must add that the concepts of God which are formed from creatures are imperfect,[3] in contrast, that is, with concepts based on the divine essence

[1] *Quodlibet*, 7, no. 8. [2] *Ox.*, 1, 3, 2, nos. 1 and 30. [3] *Ibid.*, Prol., 1, no. 17.

itself. It follows that our natural knowledge of God is indistinct and obscure, since it is not knowledge of God as immediately present to the intellect in His essence.[1]

Our natural knowledge of God rests on our capacity to form univocal concepts, as has been explained in the last chapter. Scotus affirms that 'creatures which impress their own ideas (*species*) on the intellect, can also impress the ideas of transcendent (attributes) which belong in common to them and to God';[2] but it would not be possible to proceed from a knowledge of creatures to the knowledge of God, were we not able to form from creatures univocal concepts. When the intellect has formed these concepts, it can combine them to form a composite quidditative idea of God. Just as the imagination can combine the images of mountain and gold to form the image of a golden mountain, so can the intellect combine the ideas of goodness, supreme and actuality to form the concept of a supremely good and actual being.[3] Needless to say, this comparison should not mislead us into thinking that for Scotus the combining activity of the mind in natural theology is exactly parallel to the combining work of imagination and fancy; the former activity is governed by the objective truth and apprehended logical necessity, whereas the imaginative construction of a golden mountain is 'imaginary', that is, arbitrary or the work of fancy.

3. How does Scotus prove the existence of God? In the Oxford Commentary[4] he states that the existence of the first cause is shown much more perfectly from the attributes (*passiones*) of creatures considered in metaphysics than from those which are considered by the natural philosopher. 'For it is a more perfect and immediate knowledge of the first being to know it as first or necessary being than to know it as first mover.' Scotus does not here deny that the natural philosopher can show that the fact of motion requires a first mover; but his point is that the argument from motion does not, of itself, transcend the physical order and arrive at the necessary being which is the ultimate total cause of its effects. The first mover, considered as such, is simply the cause of motion; it is not conceived as the cause of the being of all other things, but is a (necessary) hypothesis to explain the physical fact of motion. The argument from motion is thus very far from being Scotus's favourite proof. It may be noted in passing that if the

[1] *Rep.*, Prol., 3, 2, no. 4.
[2] *Ox.*, 1, 3, 2, no. 18.
[3] *Ibid.*
[4] Prol., 2 lateralis, no. 21.

Commentary on the *Physics*, which is now rejected as spurious, were authentic, the difficulty in accepting the *Theoremata* might perhaps be lessened. In the former work[1] the author makes clear his belief that the argument from motion does not, of itself, bring us to a recognisable concept of God, since it merely arrives at a first mover, without indicating the nature of the first mover. Thus if it could be maintained that the author of the *Theoremata* was speaking of natural philosophy when he said that it cannot be proved that God is living or intelligent, it would seem that the apparent contradiction between the *Theoremata* and Scotus's certainly authentic works could be resolved. However, as the *Questions on the Physics of Aristotle* is unauthentic and as the authenticity of the *Theoremata* has not been proved, it is hardly worth while pursuing the matter further. In any case it remains true that Scotus emphasised those proofs for the existence of God which are founded on *passiones metaphysicae*. Moreover, in the Oxford Commentary,[2] Scotus remarks that the proposition that mover and moved must be distinct 'is true only in corporeal things' and 'I also believe that (even) there it is not necessarily true', while 'I say at least that in regard to spiritual beings it is simply false . . .

In the *De primo principio*[3] Scotus argues from the fact of contingency to the existence of a first cause and a necessary being. That there are beings which can have being after not-being, which can come into existence, which are contingent, is clear; and such beings require a cause of their being, since they can neither cause themselves nor be caused by nothing (*nec a se nec a nihilo*). If A is the cause of the being of a contingent object, it must be itself either caused or uncaused. If it is itself caused, let B be the cause of A. But it is impossible to proceed to infinity; so there must ultimately be a cause which is itself uncaused. Scotus distinguishes clearly between the series of *essentialiter ordinata* and the series of *accidentaliter ordinata*, and he points out that what he is denying is not the possibility of an unending regress of successive causes, each of which, taken in itself, is contingent, but the possibility of an unending (vertical) series of simultaneous total causes. As he observes, even if we grant the possibility of an infinite series of successive causes, the whole chain requires an explanation, and this explanation must be outside the chain itself, since each member of the chain is caused, and so contingent. An infinite

[1] 3, 7. [2] 2, 25, *quaestio unica*, no. 12. [3] 3.

series of succeeding contingent beings cannot explain its own existence, since the whole series is contingent if each member is contingent: it is necessary to postulate a transcendent cause. 'The totality of ordered effects (*causatorum*) is itself caused; therefore (it has been caused) by some cause which does not belong to that totality.'[1] If, for example, one postulates that the human race goes back to infinity, there is an infinite succession of fathers and children. The father causes the child; but after the father's death the son continues to exist and continues to be contingent. An ultimate cause is required, not only of the son's being here and now, but also of the whole series of fathers and sons, since the infinite regress does not make the series necessary. The same principle must be extended to the universe of contingent beings in general: the universe of contingent beings requires an *actual* transcendent cause (itself uncaused). An infinite succession 'is impossible, except in virtue of some nature of infinite duration (*durante infinite*), on which the whole succession and every member of it depends'.[2]

Scotus then proceeds to show that the first cause in the essential order of dependence must exist actually and cannot be merely possible,[3] that it is necessary being, that is, that it cannot not exist[4] and that it is one.[5] There cannot be more than one necessary being. Scotus argues, for example, that if there were two beings with a common nature of necessary being, one would have to distinguish formally between the common nature and the individuality, which would be something other than necessary being. If it is answered that there is no such distinction in a necessary being, it follows that the two beings are indistinguishable and hence one. This argument, though based on Scotus's theory of the common nature and of individuation, reminds one of an analogous argument given by St. Anselm. Moreover, the one essential order of the universe postulates only one *primum effectivum*. Scotus then goes on to show that there is a first final cause, *primum finitivum*,[6] and a supreme being in the order of eminence,[7] and proceeds to show that the *primum effectivum*, the *primum finitivum* and the *primum eminens* (or *perfectissimum*) are identical.[8]

In the Oxford Commentary on the *Sentences*[9] Scotus argues in much the same way. We have to proceed from creatures to God

[1] *De primo principio*, 3, 3.
[2] *Ibid.*, 3, 4.
[3] *Ibid.*, 3, no. 5.
[4] *Ibid.*, 3, no. 6.
[5] *Ibid.*, 3, nos. 6–7.
[6] *Ibid.*, 3, no. 9.
[7] *Ibid.*, nos. 9–10.
[8] *Ibid.*, nos. 11–14.
[9] *Ox.*, 2, 2, nos. 10ff.

by considering the causal relation (in respect of either efficient or final causality) or the relation of *excessum* to *excedens* in the order of perfection. Contingent being, the *effectibile*, is caused by nothing or by itself or by another. As it is impossible for it to be caused by nothing or by itself, it must be caused by another. If that other is the first cause, we have found what we are seeking: if not, then we must proceed further. But we cannot proceed for ever in the vertical order of dependence. *Infinitas autem est impossibilis in ascendendo.*[1] Nor can we suppose that contingent beings cause one another, for then we shall proceed in a circle, without arriving at any ultimate explanation of contingency. It is useless to say that the world is eternal, since the eternal series of contingent beings itself requires a cause.[2] Similarly in the order of final causality there must be a final cause which is not directed to any more ultimate final cause,[3] while in the order of eminence there must be a most perfect being, a *suprema natura.*[4] These three are one and the same being. The first efficient cause acts with a view to the final end; but nothing other than the first being itself can be its final end. Similarly, the first efficient cause is not univocal with its effects, that is, it cannot be of the same nature, but must transcend them; and as first cause, it must be the 'most eminent' being.[5]

4. As the first being is uncaused, it cannot possess essential parts like matter and form nor can it possess accidents: it cannot, in short, be composed in any way but must be essentially simple.[6] It must be intelligent and possessed of will. The natural agents in the world which do not consciously act for an end do nevertheless act for an end; and this means that they do so by the power and knowledge of the agent which transcends them. If the natural agents of the world act teleologically, this supposes that the primary cause knows the end and wills it, since nothing can be directed to an end except in virtue of knowledge and will (as, we might say, the arrow is directed to an end by an archer who knows and wills the end). God loves Himself and wills Himself necessarily; but He does not will necessarily anything outside Himself, since nothing outside Himself is necessary to Him: He alone is necessary being. It follows that He causes His effects freely and not necessarily. God knows and understands from eternity all that He can produce; He has actual and distinct

[1] *Ox.*, 2, 2, no. 11. [2] *Ibid.*, nos. 14–15. [3] *Ibid.*, no. 17.
[4] *Ibid.*, no. 18. [5] *Ibid.* [6] *De primo principio*, 4, nos. 1–4.

understanding of every intelligible, and this understanding is identical with Himself (*idem sibi*).[1]

5. But Scotus gave his closest attention to the infinity of God. The simplest and most perfect concept of God which we can form is that of the absolutely infinite Being. It is simpler than the concept of goodness or the like, since infinity is not like an attribute or *passio* of the being of which it is predicated, but signifies the intrinsic mode of that being. It is the most perfect concept, since infinite being includes virtually infinite truth, infinite goodness and every perfection which is compatible with infinity.[2] It is true that every perfection in God is infinite, but 'it has its formal perfection from the infinity of the essence as its root and foundation'.[3] All the divine perfections are grounded in the divine essence, which is best described as the infinity of being: it is not correct, therefore, to state that for Scotus the divine essence consists in will. 'Although the will is formally infinite, it does not, however, include all intrinsic perfections formally in itself . . . but the essence alone includes all perfections in this way.'[4]

In the *Opus Oxoniense*[5] and in the *De primo principio*[6] Scotus gives a series of proofs of the divine infinity. Presupposing the compatibility of infinity with being Scotus takes as the text of his first argument Aristotle's words, *Primum movet motu infinito; ergo habet potentiam infinitam*, and argues that the conclusion is invalid if it is understood as following from motion which is infinite in duration, since length of duration does not make a thing more perfect, though it is valid if it is understood as following from the power to produce by motion infinite effects, that is, successively. God, as first efficient Cause, able to produce an infinity of effects, must be infinite in power. Moreover, as God possesses in Himself in a more eminent way the causality of all possible secondary causes, He must be infinite in Himself, *intensive*.[7] Secondly, God must be infinite since He knows an infinity of intelligible objects. This argument might seem to be a sheer *petitio principii*; but Scotus gives a somewhat singular reason for supposing that God knows an infinity of *intelligibilia*. 'Whatsoever things are infinite in potency, so that if they are taken one after the other they can have no end, are infinite in act, if they are together in act. But it is clear enough that intelligible objects are infinite in potency in

[1] *De primo principio*, 4, no. 14. [2] *Ox.*, 1, 2, 3, no. 17. [3] *Ibid.*, 4, 3, 1, no. 32.
[4] *Ibid.*, 4, 13, 1, no. 32. [5] 2, 2, nos. 25ff. [6] 4, nos. 15ff.
[7] Cf. *Ox.*, 1, 2, 2, nos. 25–9.

respect of the created intellect, and in the uncreated intellect all (the *intelligibilia*) which are successively intelligible by the created intellect are actually understood together. Therefore, there are there (in the uncreated intellect) an infinite number of actually apprehended objects.'[1] Thirdly, Scotus argues from the finality of the will. 'Our will can desire and love an object greater than any finite object . . . and what is more, there seems to be a natural inclination to love above all an infinite good. . . . It thus appears that in the act of loving we have experience of an infinite good; indeed, the will seems to find no perfect rest in any other object . . .' The infinite good must, therefore, exist.[2] The fourth argument of the Oxford Commentary[3] is to the effect that it is not incompatible with finite being that there should be a more perfect being, but that it is incompatible with the *ens eminentissimum* that there should be a more perfect being. But infinity is greater and more perfect than finitude, and infinity and being are compatible. The *ens eminentissimum* must, therefore, be infinite. The proof that infinity is compatible with being amounts to little more than saying that we can discern no incompatibility. In the *De primo principio*[4] Scotus also proves God's infinity from the fact that His intellect is identical with His substance, arguing that such identification is impossible in a finite being.

Having proved, to his satisfaction at least, God's infinity, Scotus is able to show that God must be one and one alone.[5]

6. In his discussion of the divine infinity Scotus introduces the so-called ontological argument of St. Anselm.[6] He has just remarked that the intellect, the object of which is being, finds no mutual repugnance between 'being' and 'infinite', and that it would be astonishing, supposing the two to be incompatible, if the intellect did not discern the incompatibility, 'when a discord in sound so easily offends the hearing'. If there is such an incompatibility, why does not the intellect 'shrink back' from the idea of the infinite, if it is incompatible with its own proper object, being? He then proceeds to state that the argument of St. Anselm in the first chapter of the *Proslogium* can be 'coloured' (*potest colorari*) and that it should be understood in this way: 'God is that than which, having been thought without contradiction, a greater cannot be thought without contradiction. That (the words) "without contradiction" must be added is clear, for that in the thought

[1] *Ox.*, 1, 2, 2, no. 30; cf. *De primo principio*, 15ff.
[2] *Ox.*, 1, 2, 2, no. 31.
[3] 1, 2, 2, nos. 31–2.
[4] 4, no. 21.
[5] *Ox.*, 1, 2, 3; *De primo principio*, 4, nos. 38–40.
[6] *Ox.*, 1, 2, 2, no. 32.

of which a contradiction is included (that is, involved), is unthinkable . . .' It has been asserted that since Scotus admits that the Anselmian argument must be 'coloured', he rejects it. But he obviously does not reject it without more ado. Why should he 'colour' it, except to use it? And in point of fact he does use it. First he tries to show that the idea of the *summum cogitabile* is without contradiction, i.e. that the essence or *esse quidditativum* is possible, and then he observes that if the *summum cogitabile* is possible, it must exist, that it must have *esse existentiae. Majus igitur cogitabile est, quod est in re quam quod est tantum in intellectu.* That which really exists is *majus cogitabile* than that which does not really exist but is merely conceived, inasmuch as that which really exists is 'visible' or capable of being intuited, and that which can be intuited is 'greater' than that which can be merely conceived or can be known by abstractive thought alone. It follows, then, that the *summum cogitabile* must really exist. Scotus is not saying that we have a natural intuition of God; he is giving a reason for the judgement that that which really exists is greater or more perfect than that which does not really exist extramentally.

There is no doubt, then, that Scotus makes use of the Anselmian argument. Two questions arise, therefore. First, in what does the *coloratio* of the argument consist? Secondly, how did Scotus think that his use of the argument was consistent with his clear assertion that we can demonstrate God's existence only *a posteriori*? First the *coloratio* consists in an attempt to show that the idea of the most perfect being is the idea of a possible being, and he does this primarily by observing that no contradiction is observable in the idea of the most perfect being. In other words, he anticipates Leibniz's attempt to show that the idea of God is the idea of a possible being, inasmuch as the idea does not involve any contradiction, and the idea of a being which does not involve a contradiction constitutes the idea of a possible being. On the other hand, Scotus did not consider that the fact that we cannot observe any contradiction in the idea of the most perfect being is a demonstrative proof of the fact that no contradiction is involved. We cannot show apodeictically and *a priori* that the most perfect being is possible, and that is why he states elsewhere that the Anselmian argument belongs to the proofs which amount to no more than *persuasiones probabiles*.[1] This supplies the answer to our second

[1] *Rep.*, 1, 2, 3, no. 8.

question. Scotus considered his use of the Anselmian argument to be compatible with his assertion that we can demonstrate God's existence only *a posteriori* because he did not regard the Anselmian argument as a demonstration, but only as a 'probable persuasion', a probable proof. He did not simply reject the argument as St. Thomas did; but he was dissatisfied with the argument as it stood and thought that it needed 'colouring'. On the other hand, he did not think that the 'colouring', the proof that the idea of God is the idea of a possible being, is a demonstrative proof, and so he put forward the argument as probable. He used it as an auxiliary argument to show what is involved or implied in the idea of God rather than as a strict demonstration of God's existence. It is as though he had said: 'This is the best we can make of the argument, and it has its uses if you accept the premisses; but I do not regard the argument as a demonstration. If a strict demonstration of God's existence is wanted, it will have to proceed *a posteriori*.'

7. Scotus did not consider that we can demonstrate by the natural reason all God's essential attributes. Thus in the *De primo principio*[1] he says that consideration of the attributes of omnipotence, immensity, omnipresence, truth, justice, mercy and providence directed to all creatures, to intelligent creatures in particular, will be postponed until the next treatise, as they are *credibilia*, that is, revealed objects of faith. It might well appear strange to read that omnipotence, for instance, cannot be philosophically demonstrated as a divine attribute, when Scotus does not hesitate to conclude God's infinity from His infinite power; but he distinguishes between omnipotence in the proper theological sense (*proprie theologice*), which cannot be demonstrated with certainty by philosophers, and infinite power (*potentia infinita*), which can be demonstrated by philosophers.[2] The distinction consists in this. God's power to produce every possible effect, immediately *or* mediately, can be proved philosophically, but not His power to produce all possible effects immediately. Even though the first cause possesses in itself *eminentius* the causality of the secondary cause, it does not necessarily follow, says Scotus, that the first cause can produce the effect of the secondary cause immediately, without the co-operation of the secondary cause, not because the causality of the first cause needs adding to, so to speak, but because the imperfection of the effect may require, so far as the philosopher can see, the causal operation of the finite cause as its

[1] 4, no. 37.

[2] *Ox.*, I, 42, *quaestio unica*, no. 2.

explanation. Scotus is thus not attacking the demonstrability of God's creative power: what he is saying is that the proposition, 'whatever the first efficient cause can do with the co-operation of a secondary cause, that it can do immediately by itself', is neither self-evident nor philosophically demonstrable, but is known by faith (*non est nota ex terminis neque ratione naturali, sed est tantum credita*). The objection that God's universal immediate causality would destroy the proper causality of creatures cannot be solved by reason alone.[1]

As to the divine immensity and omnipresence, Scotus's denial of the demonstrability of this attribute of God depends on his denial of St. Thomas's rejection of *actio in distans*, action at a distance. According to St. Thomas[2] *actio in distans* is impossible, while for Scotus the greater the efficacy of the agent, the greater its power to act at a distance. 'Therefore, since God is the most perfect agent, it cannot be concluded concerning Him through the nature of action that He is together with (essentially present to) any effect caused by Him, but rather that He is distant.'[3] It is difficult to see what *actio in distans* could possibly mean in regard to God; but, as far as Scotus is concerned, he is not denying that God is omnipresent or that omnipresence is a necessary attribute of God, but only that God's omnipresence is philosophically demonstrable and, in particular, that the supposed impossibility of *actio in distans* is a valid reason for showing that God is omnipresent.

Probably 'truth' must be taken together with mercy and justice, as meaning in the context much the same as justice. At least, if this suggestion of commentators is not accepted, it is extremely difficult to see what Scotus did mean, since truth and veracity are listed among the divine attributes which are known by the natural reason.[4] As to justice, Scotus sometimes seems to say that the divine justice can be known by the natural light of reason;[5] but when he denies that the justice of God is philosophically demonstrable he appears to mean that it cannot be proved that God rewards and punishes in the next life, since it cannot be proved strictly by the philosopher that the soul is immortal,[6] or that we cannot justify by our reason all the ways of God in regard to man. That God is merciful, in the sense of forgiving sins and forgoing

[1] Cf. *Rep.* 1, 42, 2, no. 4; *Quodlibet*, 7, nos. 4 and 18.
[2] *S.T.*, Ia, 8, 1, *ad* 3.
[3] *Rep.*, 1, 37, 2, nos. 6ff.
[4] Cf. *De primo principio*, 4, nos. 36ff; *Ox.*, Prol., 2, no. 10; 3, 23, no. 5; 3, 24, no. 22.
[5] Cf. *ibid.*, 4, 17, no. 7; *Rep.*, 4, 17, no. 7.
[6] Cf. *Ox.*, 4, 43, 2, no. 27.

the exaction of punishment, cannot be philosophically demonstrated. Finally, as to divine providence, when Scotus says this cannot be philosophically proved, he appears to mean, not that no providence at all can be demonstrated, but that immediate or special providential action on the part of God, without the employment of secondary causes, cannot be philosophically demonstrated. Scotus certainly held that divine creation, conservation and government of the world can be demonstrated.

8. Scotus rejected the theories of St. Thomas and Henry of Ghent concerning the absence in God of any distinction other than the real distinction between the divine Persons and postulated a formal objective distinction between the divine attributes. The *ratio formalis* of wisdom, for example, is not identical with the *ratio formalis* of goodness. Now, 'infinity does not destroy the *ratio* of that to which it is added'.[1] If, therefore, the formal character of the univocal concept of wisdom is not the same as the formal character of the univocal concept of goodness, infinite wisdom will be formally distinct from infinite goodness. It follows, then, that the divine attributes of wisdom and goodness will be formally distinct, independently of the human mind's operation. On the other hand, there can be no composition in God, nor any real distinction in the technical sense between the divine attributes. The distinction between the divine attributes must be, therefore, not a real distinction, but a *distinctio formalis a parte rei*, and the formula will be that the attributes are really or substantially identical (*in re*), but formally distinct. 'So I allow that truth is identical with goodness *in re*, but not, however, that truth is formally goodness.'[2] Scotus contends that the distinction between the divine essence and the divine attributes and between the attributes themselves does not impair the divine simplicity, since the attributes are not accidents of God, nor do they inform God as finite accidents inform finite substances. As infinite they are really identical with the divine essence, and God can be called Truth or Wisdom or Goodness; but the fact remains that the *rationes formales* of truth, wisdom and goodness are formally and objectively distinct.[3]

9. It has been maintained in the past that the divine ideas depend, according to Scotus, on God's free will, so that the exemplar ideas are God's arbitrary creation. But as a matter of fact Scotus explicitly teaches that it is the divine intellect which

[1] *Ox.*, 1, 8, 4, no. 17. [2] *Ibid.*, 1, 8, 4, no. 18. [3] *Ibid.*, nos. 19ff.

produces the ideas: 'the divine intellect, precisely as intellect, produces in God the *rationes ideales*, the ideal or intelligible natures'.[1] The divine essence, however, is the foundation of the ideas. 'God first knows His essence, and in the second instant He understands (*intelligit*) creatures by means of His essence, and then in that way the knowable object depends on the divine understanding in regard to its being known (*in esse cognito*), since it is constituted in its *esse cognito* by that understanding.'[2] The divine ideas do not, then, depend on the divine will. 'The divine intellect, as in some way, that is, logically prior to the act of the divine will, produces those objects in their intelligible being (*in esse intelligibili*), and so in respect of them it seems to be a merely natural cause, since God is not a free cause in respect of anything but that which presupposes in some way His will or an act of His will.'[3] Possibles are not produced by the divine omnipotence, but by the divine intellect, which produces them *in esse intelligibili*.[4]

The divine ideas are infinite in number, and they are substantially identical with the divine essence; but they are not formally identical with the divine essence:[5] they are necessary and eternal, but they are not formally necessary and eternal in precisely the same sense as the divine essence, since the divine essence has a certain logical priority. Again, 'although the divine essence was from eternity the exemplary cause of the stone in its intelligible being, yet by a certain order of priority the Persons were "produced" before the stone in its intelligible being . . . even though it is eternal.'[6] Logically speaking, the divine essence is imitable before the divine intellect apprehends it as imitable.[7] The ideas are participations or possible imitations of the divine essence, apprehended by the divine intellect, and it is because the divine essence is infinite, because it is imitable in an infinite number of ways, that the ideas are infinite, though the presence of the ideas does not compel God to create corresponding objects.[8]

10. Scotus did not teach that the divine will acts in a simply capricious and arbitrary manner, though this doctrine has been ascribed to him. 'Will in God is His essence really, perfectly and identically',[9] and the divine volition is one act in itself.[10] The divine will and the act of the divine will, which are one *in re*, cannot change, therefore, though it does not follow that what God

[1] *Ox.*, 1, 36, no. 4, cf. no. 6. [2] *Rep.*, 1, 36, 2, no. 33. [3] *Ox.*, 1, 3, 4, no. 20.
[4] *Ibid.*, 2, 1, 2, no. 6. [5] *Rep.*, 1, 36, 3, no. 27. [6] *Collationes*, 31, no. 5.
[7] *Ox.*, 1, 35, no. 8. [8] *Ibid.*, 1, 38, no. 5. [9] *Rep.*, 1, 45, 2, no. 7.
[10] *Ox.*, 1, 17, 3, no. 18.

wills eternally must necessarily exist eternally. 'The operation (of the will) is in eternity, and the production of *esse existentiae* is in time.'[1] Logically speaking, even in God understanding precedes will, and God wills most rationally (*rationabilissime*). Although there is, ontologically, but one act of the divine will, we can distinguish the primary act by which God wills the end or *finis*, Himself, the secondary act by which He wills what is immediately ordered to the end, for example, by predestinating the elect, the third act by which He wills those things which are necessary to attain this end (e.g. grace), and the fourth act by which He wills more remote means, such as the sensible world.[2] But although the divine understanding logically precedes the divine volition, the divine will does not need direction as though it could err or choose something unsuitable, and *in this sense* the divine will is its own rule. Scotus sometimes states, indeed, that the divine will wills because it wills and that no reason can be given; but he makes his meaning clear enough. After citing Aristotle to the effect that it is the mark of an uneducated man to seek a demonstrative reason for everything, Scotus argues that it is not only ultimate principles which cannot be demonstrated, but also contingent things, because contingent things do not follow from necessary principles. The idea of human nature in God is necessary; but why God willed human nature to be represented in this or that individual, at this or that time, is a question to which no answer can be given save that 'because He willed it to be, therefore it was good that it should be'.[3] Scotus's point is that contingent things cannot be deduced by necessary demonstrations, since they would be necessary, and not contingent, if they could be so deduced. If you ask, he says, why heat heats, the only answer is that heat is heat: so the only answer to the question why God willed a contingent thing is that He willed it.[4] Scotus is not denying that God acts for an end, Himself, that He acts 'most rationally'; but he wants to show the absurdity of seeking a necessary reason for what is not necessary. 'From a necessary (principle) there does not follow something contingent.'[5] The free choice of God is the ultimate reason of contingent things, and we cannot legitimately go behind God's free choice and seek a necessary reason determining that choice. God's intellect does not determine His creative work by necessary reasons, since creation is free, nor is He

[1] *Ox.*, 1, 39, no. 21, cf. *ibid.*, 2, 1, 2, no. 7. [2] *Ibid.*, 3, 32, no. 6.
[3] *Ibid.*, 2, 1, 2, no. 65. [4] *Ibid.*, 1, 8, 5, nos. 23f.; cf. *Quodlibet*, 16.
[5] *Rep.*, 1, 10, 3, no. 4.

determined by the goodness of objects, since the objects do not yet exist: rather are they good because He wills them to be. That God can create only what is an imitation of His essence and that He cannot, therefore, create anything evil, is understood.

Scotus thus insisted on God's freedom of will in regard to His operations *ad extra*; but he also maintained that though God loves Himself necessarily and cannot not will and love Himself, that love is none the less free. This theory certainly seems rather singular. That God's will is free in regard to finite objects other than Himself follows from the infinity of the divine will, which can have as its necessary object only an infinite object, God Himself; but that God should love Himself necessarily and freely at the same time would certainly appear, at first sight at least, to involve a contradiction. Scotus's position is as follows. Liberty belongs to the perfection of volition, and it must be present formally in God. As volition directed to the final end is the most perfect kind of volition, it must include what belongs to the perfection of volition. It must, therefore, be free. On the other hand, the divine will, identical with God, cannot but will and love the final end, God Himself. The principle of reconciliation of the two seemingly contradictory propositions is that necessity in the supreme act of the will does not take away, but rather postulates, what belongs to the perfection of will. 'The intrinsic condition of the power itself whether absolutely or in order to a perfect act is not incompatible with perfection in operation. But liberty is an intrinsic condition of the will absolutely or in order to the act of willing. Therefore liberty is compatible with a perfect possible condition in operation, and such a condition is necessity, especially when it is possible.'[1] Scotus gives an example to show what he means. 'If someone voluntarily hurls himself over a precipice (*voluntarie se praecipitat*) and, while falling, always continues to will it, he falls indeed necessarily by the necessity of natural gravity, and yet he freely wills that fall. So God, although He necessarily lives by His natural life, and that with a necessity which excludes all liberty, wills none the less freely that He should live by that life. Therefore, we do not place the life of God under necessity (i.e. we do not attribute necessity to God's life) if we understand by "life" life as loved by God by free will.'[2] Scotus appears to mean, then, that we can distinguish in God the natural necessity by which He loves Himself and His free ratification, as

[1] *Quodlibet*, 16, no. 8. [2] *Ibid.*, 16, no. 9; cf. *Rep.*, 1, 10, 3, nos. 3ff.

it were, of that necessity, so that necessary love of Himself and free love of Himself are not incompatible. One may think that this distinction is not particularly helpful; but in any case it is clear that Scotus's voluntaristic and libertarian doctrine does not imply that God could refrain from willing Himself or that His love for Himself is arbitrary. The truth of the matter is that Scotus attached so much value to liberty as a perfection of will that he was reluctant to exclude it even from those acts of will which he was compelled to regard as necessary. This will be apparent when we come to consider his doctrine concerning the human will.

11. Scotus maintained that God's power to create out of nothing is demonstrable by the natural light of reason. God as first efficient cause must be able to produce some effect immediately, since otherwise He would not be able to produce effects even mediately (taking as proved that He is *first* efficient cause). 'Therefore it is clear to the natural intellect that God can cause in such a way that something should be from Him (i.e. should have its being from God) without any element of itself being presupposed or any receptive element in which it is received. It is clear, then, to the natural reason that, although the Philosopher (Aristotle) did not say so, something can be proved to be capable of being caused by God in this way.' 'And I say that Aristotle did not affirm that God creates something in this way; but it does not thereby follow that the contrary (i.e. of Aristotle's opinion) cannot be known by the natural reason. . . .'[1] Moreover, it can be proved that God can create out of nothing.[2] But the relationship involved by creation is not mutual: the relation of the creature to God is a real relation, whereas the relation of God to the creature is a mental relation only (*relatio rationis*), since God is not essentially Creator and cannot be called Creator in the same sense in which He is called wise or good. He is really Creator; but His relationship to the creature is not a real relation, since He is not Creator by essence, in which case He would create necessarily, nor on the other hand can He receive an accidental relation.

As to the question whether creation in time can be proved, Scotus inclined to the opinion of St. Thomas, though he did not accept St. Thomas's reasons, that creation in time cannot be proved philosophically. The logical priority of *nihil* can be proved, 'since otherwise creation could not be admitted'; but it is not

[1] *Rep.*, 2, 1, 3, nos. 9–11; cf. *Ox.*, 2, 1, 2; *Collationes*, 13, no. 4.
[2] *Ox.*, 4, 1, 1, nos. 27ff.

necessary that logical priority should involve temporal priority. Scotus speaks, however, with hesitation. 'It does not seem to be necessary that *nihil* should precede the world temporally; but it seems sufficient if it precedes the world logically.'[1] In other words, Scotus rejected the opinion of St. Bonaventure that the impossibility of creation from eternity can be philosophically demonstrated, and he inclined to the opinion of St. Thomas that creation in time is also incapable of philosophic demonstration; but he speaks more hesitantly on the point than does St. Thomas.

[1] *Ox.*, 2, 1, 3, no. 19.

CHAPTER XLIX

SCOTUS—V: THE SOUL

The specific form of man—Union of soul and body—Will and intellect—Soul's immortality not strictly demonstrated.

1. THAT the rational soul is the specific form of man can be philosophically proved,[1] and the opinion of Averroes that the intellect is a separate principle is unintelligible. 'All philosophers, generally speaking, have included "rational" in the definition of man as his special *differentia*, understanding by "rational" that the intellectual soul is an essential part of man.' No philosopher of note denies this, 'although that accursed Averroes in his fiction *On the Soul*, which, however, is intelligible neither to himself nor to anyone else, affirms that the intellect is a certain separate substance, which can be joined to us by means of the *phantasmata*; a union which neither he himself nor any disciple of his has hitherto been able to explain, nor has he been able by means of that union to preserve (the truth that) man understands. For according to him man would not be formally anything else but a kind of superior irrational animal, more excellent than other animals in virtue of his type of irrational, sensitive soul.'[2]

That the rational soul is the form of man Scotus proves by an enthymeme. 'Man understands (*intelligit*, apprehends intellectually) formally and properly; therefore the intellectual soul is the proper form of man.'[3] The antecedent, he says, seems to be clear enough through the authority of Aristotle; but in case anyone wantonly denies it, a rational proof must be given. To understand properly (*intelligere proprie*) means to understand by an act of knowledge which transcends every kind of sensitive knowledge, and that man understands in this sense can be proved as follows. To exercise intellectual activity in the proper sense is, as remarked, to exercise an activity transcending the power of sense. Now, sensitive apprehension is an organic function, since each of the senses has a determinate kind of object, the object of the special sense in question. Thus vision is determined to the perception of colour, hearing to that of sound. But the intellect is not determined in this way: its object is being, and it is not bound to a bodily organ in the sense in which sensation is bound. It can

[1] *Ox.*, 4, 43, 2, nos. 4–5. [2] *Ibid.*, 4, 43, 2, no. 5. [3] *Ibid.*, 4, 43, 2, no. 6.

apprehend objects which are not immediately given to sensation, such as generic and specific relations. Intellectual cognition, therefore, transcends the powers of sense, and it follows that man can *intelligere proprie.*[1]

That the conclusion of the original enthymeme ('therefore the intellectual soul is the proper form of man') follows from the antecedent can be shown in two ways. Intellectual cognition, as a function of man, must be 'received' in something in man himself which is not extended and which is neither a part nor the whole of the corporeal organism. If it was received in something extended, it would be itself extended and a purely organic function, which it has been proved not to be. When Scotus talks about intellectual cognition being 'received', he means that it is not identical with our substance, since we are not always exercising the power of intellectual cognition; so it must be the act of some principle in us. But it cannot be the act of the material part of man: therefore it must be the act of a spiritual formal principle, and what can this be but the intellectual soul, the principle which has the power of exercising intellectual activity? Secondly, man is master of his voluntary acts, he is free, and his will is not determined to any one kind of appetible object. Therefore it transcends organic appetite, and its acts cannot be the acts of any material form. It follows that our free, voluntary acts are the acts of an intellectual form, and if our free acts are *our* acts, as they are, then the form of which they are the acts must be *our* form. The intellectual soul is, then, the form of man: it is his specific form, which differentiates man from the brutes.[2]

2. In man there is only one soul, though there is, as already mentioned, a form of corporeity. There are, as we also saw earlier, various 'formalities' in the one human soul, which, though not really distinct (separable) from one another, are distinct with a *distinctio formalis a parte rei*, since the intellectual, sensitive and vegetative activities are formally and objectively distinct; but they are formalities of the one rational soul of man. This one rational soul is, therefore, not only the principle of man's rational cognition, but it is also the principle of his sensitive activity and of his life. It gives *esse vivum*, and it is the formal principle by which the organism is a living organism:[3] it is the substantial form of man.[4] The soul is, therefore, a part of man, and it is only

[1] *Ox.*, 4, 43, 2, nos. 6–11.
[2] *Ibid.*, 4, 43, 2, no. 12.
[3] *Ibid.*, 2, 16, no. 6.
[4] *Ibid.*, 2, 1, 4, no. 25.

improperly that it can be called subsistent, since it is part of a substance rather than a substance by itself; it is the composite being, soul and body, which is a *per se unum*.[1] The soul in the state of separation from the body is not, properly speaking, a person.[2] The soul perfects the body only when the latter is properly disposed for it, and *this* soul has an aptitude for *this* body. This means, says Scotus,[3] that the soul cannot be individuated by the matter it informs, since the soul, that is, a particular soul, is infused into a body, and the creation of that soul is logically prior to its union with the body.

Scotus differs also from St. Thomas in holding that the rational soul does not confer *esse simpliciter*, but rather *esse vivum* and *esse sensitivum*: there is, as already mentioned, a form of corporeity. If the rational soul were to confer *esse simpliciter* on man, man could not really be said to die. Death involves the corruption of the 'entity' of man, and this implies that both soul and body have a reality of their own, that the being of man as man is his being as a *compositum*, not his being as a soul. If the soul conferred *esse simpliciter* and there were no other form in the body, the separation of soul from body would not mean a corruption of the being of man as man. For death to take place, man must have a being as *compositum*, a being distinct from that of his component parts, taken separately or together, for it is this being of man as a *compositum* which is corrupted at death. Moreover, St. Thomas, according to Scotus, contradicts himself. 'Elsewhere he says that the state of the soul in the body is more perfect than its state outside the body, since it is a part of the *compositum*'; yet at the same time he asserts that the soul confers, and therefore possesses, *esse simpliciter*, and that it is not less perfect merely by the fact that it does not communicate that *esse* to any thing other than itself. 'According to you the soul possesses the same *esse* totally in a state of separation which it possessed when united with the body . . . therefore it is in no way more imperfect by the fact that it does not communicate that *esse* to the body.'[4]

The soul is united to the body for the perfection of the whole man, who consists of soul and body. According to St. Thomas,[5] the soul is united to the body for the good of the soul. The soul is naturally dependent on the senses for its cognition, the *conversio ad phantasma* being natural to it,[6] and therefore the soul is united

[1] *Ox.*, 4, 12, 1, no. 19. [2] *Quodlibet*, 9, no. 7, and 19, no. 19. [3] *Ibid.*, 2, 3 ff.
[4] *Ox.*, 4, 43, 1, nos. 2–6. [5] *S.T.*, Ia, 89, 1. [6] Cf. *ibid.*, Ia, 84, 7.

to the body for the soul's good, in order that it may operate according to its nature. For Scotus, however, as we have already seen, the direction of the human intellect towards material things and its *de facto* dependence on the senses originate not so much in the nature of the human reason as such as in the present state of the soul, its condition in the body as wayfarer (with the alternative suggestion that sin may possibly be the responsible factor). St. Thomas would object that in this case its union with the body is for the good of the body, not of the soul, and that this is irrational, 'since matter is for the sake of form, and not conversely'. To such an objection Scotus's answer is that the soul is united to the body, not for the good of the body simply, but for the good of the composite being, man. It is man, the composite being, who is the term of the creative act, not soul taken by itself or body taken by itself, and the union of soul and body is effected in order that this composite being may be realised: the union exists, therefore, for the good of the whole man, *propter perfectionem totius*. The union of soul with body does not take place 'for the perfection of the body, nor for the perfection of the soul alone, but for the perfection of the whole which consists of these parts; and so although no perfection may accrue to this or that part which it would not have possessed without such a union, the union does not, however, take place in vain, since the perfection of the whole, which is principally intended by nature, could not be had except in that way.'[1]

3. Of Scotus's idea of human intellectual activity something has already been said in the chapter on knowledge; but a brief discussion must be given of his doctrine concerning the relation of will to intellect, as this has given rise to some misunderstanding concerning his general position.

The intellect is not, like the will, a free power. 'It is not in the power of the intellect to restrain its assent to the truths which it apprehends; for in so far as the truth of principles becomes clear to it from the terms or the truth of conclusions from principles, in so far must it give its assent on account of its lack of liberty.'[2] Thus if the truth of the proposition that the whole is greater than the part becomes clear to the intellect from the realisation of what a whole is and what a part is, or if the truth of the conclusion that Socrates is mortal becomes clear to the intellect from a consideration of the premisses that all men are mortal and that Socrates is a man, then the intellect is not free to withhold its consent to the

[1] *Ox.*, 4, 45, 2, no. 14.

[2] *Ibid.*, 2, 6, 2, no. 11.

proposition that the whole is greater than the part or the proposition that Socrates is mortal. The intellect is thus a *potentia naturalis*.

The will, however, is free, a *potentia libera*, and it is essentially free, its *ratio formalis* consisting more in its freedom than its character as appetite.[1] It is necessary to distinguish between will in the sense of a natural inclination and will as free, and it is only free will that is will in the proper sense; from which it follows that will is free of its very nature and that God could not, for example, create a rational will which would be *naturally* incapable of sinning.[2] By an elicited act of his free will, says Scotus, St. Paul willed 'to be dissolved and to be with Christ'; but this elicited act was contrary to his natural 'will', in the sense of natural inclination.[3] The two, therefore, are distinct, and this distinction is of importance when one considers man's desire of happiness or of his last end. The will as natural appetite or inclination to self-perfection necessarily desires happiness above all things, and since happiness or beatitude is, as a matter of concrete fact, to be found in God alone, there is in man a natural inclination to beatitude 'in particular', to God. But it does not follow that the will as free necessarily and perpetually desires the last end, nor that it necessarily elicits a conscious and deliberate act in regard to that object.[4] Scotus protests that he does not mean to imply that the will can choose misery *as such* or evil *as such*: 'I do not will beatitude' is not the same as 'I will the opposite of beatitude'; it means that I do not here and now elicit an act in its regard, not that I elicit a choice of its opposite, which cannot be an object of will. If I do elicit an act, however, that is, an act of willing beatitude, that act will be free, since every elicited act of the will is free.[5] Moreover, Scotus does not hesitate to draw the conclusion from his doctrine of the essential freedom of the will that the blessed in heaven will and love God freely.[6] He rejects, then, the doctrine of St. Thomas that when the *summum bonum* is clearly presented, the will chooses and loves it necessarily, and he even goes so far as to say that the blessed retain the power to sin. But when he says this, he does not mean to say any more than that the will as such remains free in heaven, since it is essentially free and heaven does not destroy its freedom: morally speaking, the blessed in heaven not only will not sin, but cannot sin, though this necessity is only *secundum*

[1] *Ox.*, 1, 17, 3, no. 5; 2, 25, no. 16. [2] *Ibid.*, 2, 23, nos. 8 and 7. [3] *Ibid.*, 3, 15, no. 37.
[4] Cf. *ibid.*, 4, 49, 10, no. 3; 2, 23, no. 8; 1, 1, 4, no. 16; *Collationes*, 16, no. 3.
[5] Cf. *Ox.*, 4, 49, 10, nos. 8f. [6] *Ox.*, 1, 1, 4, nos. 13ff.

quid, proceeding from the 'habit of glory' (*habitus gloriae*) and the inclination produced in the will, not from a physical determination of the will.[1] The will of the blessed is thus morally impeccable, though not physically impeccable. Scotus does not differ from St. Thomas as to the actual fact that the blessed will not sin and he is willing to say that they cannot sin, provided that 'cannot' is not understood in a sense which would imply that the essence of the will is in any way impaired.[2]

The intellect, then, is a *potentia naturalis*, the will a *potentia libera*, and, given Scotus's insistence on liberty as a perfection, his position in the controversy regarding the primacy of intellect over will or of will over intellect cannot be in doubt. Knowledge certainly precedes every elicited act of the will, since the will cannot exercise choice in regard to an entirely unknown object (Scotus was no 'irrationalist'), and it is difficult, he says, though not impossible, for the will not to incline itself to what is finally dictated by the practical reason; but, on the other hand, the will can command the intellect. Scotus does not mean, of course, that the will can command the intellect to assent to propositions which are seen to be false: the will does not add anything to the act of understanding as such,[3] nor is it the cause of the intellect's act.[4] But the will can co-operate mediately, as an efficient cause, by moving the intellect to attend to this or that intelligible object, to consider this or that argument.[5] It follows that 'the will, by commanding the intellect, is a superior cause in respect of its act. But the intellect, if it is the cause of volition (that is, as a partial cause, by supplying the knowledge of the object) is a cause subservient to the will'.[6]

Scotus gives other reasons for affirming the primacy of the will. The will is more perfect than the intellect since the corruption of the will is worse than the corruption of the intellect; to hate God is worse than not to know God or not to think of God. Again, sin means willing something evil, whereas to think of something evil is not necessarily a sin: it is only a sin when the will gives some consent to or takes some pleasure in the evil thought of.[7] Again, love is a greater good than knowledge, and love resides in the will,[8] while it is the will which plays the principal part in final beatitude, uniting the soul with God, possessing and enjoying God. Though both powers, intellect and will, are involved in beatitude,

[1] *Ox.*, 4, 49, 6, no. 9. [2] Cf. *Collatio*, 15. [3] *Rep.*, 2, 42, 4, no. 7.
[4] *Collationes*, 2, no 7. [5] *Rep.*, 1, 35, 1, no. 27.
[6] *Ox.*, 4, 49, *quaestio ex latere*, nos. 16 and 18. [7] *Ibid.*, no. 17. [8] *Ibid.*, no. 21.

the higher faculty, will, is the more immediate means of union with God.[1] Scotus thus rejected the Thomist doctrine of the primacy of the intellect and of the essence of beatitude and remained true to the tradition of the Augustinian-Franciscan School. It does not seem to be a matter of great moment, indeed, whether one adopts the Thomist or Scotist viewpoint, for both sides agree that beatitude, taken *extensive*, involves both powers; but it is necessary to explain Scotus's position, in order to show how foolish are accusations of irrationalism and of unmitigated voluntarism.

4. One might have expected, in view of Scotus's clear teaching, not only that the soul's intellectual activity transcends the powers of sense, but also that it can be proved philosophically to transcend the powers of sense and matter, that he would attempt to demonstrate the immortality of the human soul; but actually he did not believe that this truth can be strictly demonstrated in philosophy, and he criticised the proofs adduced by his predecessors. Of the three propositions, first that the rational soul is the specific form of man, secondly that the soul is immortal, and thirdly that the soul after death will not remain in a perpetual state of separation from the body (that is, that the body will rise again), the first is known by the natural light of reason, the error opposed to it, that of Averroes, being 'not only against the truth of theology, but also against the truth of philosophy' (that is, the Averroistic doctrine is not only against the truth as known by faith, but can also be philosophically refuted). 'But the other two (propositions) are not sufficiently known by the natural reason, although there are certain probable and persuasive arguments (*persuasiones probabiles*) for them. For the second, indeed, there are several more probable (arguments); hence the Philosopher seems to have held it *magis expresse*.' But for the third there are fewer reasons, and consequently the conclusion which follows from those reasons is not thereby sufficiently known through the natural reason.[2] Scotus's general position is, therefore, that we can prove philosophically that the rational soul is the specific form of man; but that we cannot prove demonstratively in philosophy either that the soul is immortal or that the body will rise again. The philosophical arguments for the soul's immortality have greater weight than those for the resurrection of the body, but they are none the less only probable arguments, the *a priori* arguments, namely those

[1] *Rep.*, 4, 49, 3, no. 7; *Ox.*, 4, 49, 3, nos. 5ff.

[2] *Ox.*, 4, 43, 2, no. 26.

based on the soul's nature, being better than the *a posteriori* arguments, for example, those based on the need for sanctions in a future life. The soul's immortality may be said to be morally provable, *ex inductione*, and it is certainly more probable, philosophically speaking, than its opposite; but the arguments adduced for it are not demonstrative and necessary arguments, enjoying absolute certainty.[1]

As regards the authority of Aristotle, Scotus declares that his opinion is not really clear. 'For he speaks in various ways in different places, and he had different principles, from some of which one opposite (one opinion) seems to follow, from others another. It is probable, then, that he was always doubtful about that conclusion, and at one time he would approach the one side, at another time the other, according as he was treating a matter which harmonised more with one side than with the other.'[2] In any case not all the assertions of the philosophers were proved by them by necessary reasons; but 'frequently they had only some probable persuasions (some probable and persuasive arguments) or the general opinion of preceding philosophers.'[3] The authority of Aristotle is, therefore, no certain argument for the soul's immortality.

As to the arguments adduced by St. Thomas and other Christian philosophers, these are not absolutely conclusive. In the *Summa Theologica*[4] St. Thomas argues that the human soul cannot be corrupted *per accidens*, in virtue of the corruption of the body, since it is a subsistent form, nor can it be corrupted *per se*, since *esse* belongs to a subsistent form in such a way that the natural corruption of the form would mean the separation of the form from itself. To this Scotus answers that St. Thomas is begging the question, since he presupposes that the soul of man is a *forma per se subsistens*, which is the very point which has to be proved. The proposition that the human soul is a form of this kind is accepted as an object of belief, but it is not known by natural reason.[5] If it be objected that this criticism is unfair, in view of the fact that St. Thomas has previously devoted an article (2) to showing that the human soul is an incorporeal and subsistent principle, Scotus retorts that though it can be shown that the rational soul in its intellectual activity does not use a corporeal organ and that its intellectual activity transcends the power of

[1] Cf. *Rep.*, 4, 43, 2, nos. 15ff. [2] *Ox.*, 4, 43, 2, no. 16. [3] *Ibid.*
[4] Ia, 75, 6. [5] *Ox.*, 4, 43, 2, no. 23.

sense, it does not necessarily follow that the rational soul does not depend, as regards its being, on the whole *compositum*, which is certainly corruptible.[1] In other words, the fact that the human soul does not employ a corporeal organ in its purely intellectual activity does not necessarily prove that it is not naturally dependent for its existence on the continued existence of the *compositum*. It would have to be demonstrated that a form which transcends matter in a certain operation is necessarily independent in regard to existence, and this, according to Scotus, has not been conclusively proved.[2]

In regard to the argument drawn from the desire of beatitude, which involves immortality, Scotus observes that if by desire is meant a natural desire in the strict sense, one which is simply the inclination of nature to some thing, then it is clear that a natural desire for a thing cannot be proved, unless the latter's natural possibility has first been proved: to assert the existence of a natural inclination towards a state, the possibility of which is still unknown, is to be guilty of a *petitio principii*. If, however, by natural desire is meant a natural desire in a wider sense, that is, an elicited desire which is in accordance with a natural inclination, it cannot be shown that the elicited desire is natural in this sense until it has been proved that there is a natural desire in the strict sense. It may be said that an object which becomes the object of an elicited desire immediately it is apprehended must be the object of a natural desire or inclination; but in this case one might as well argue that because a vicious man is immediately inclined to desire the object of his vice when he apprehends it, he has a natural inclination or a natural desire for it, whereas in point of fact nature is not of itself vicious, and certainly not in everybody. It is no good saying that an object which, directly it is apprehended, is the object of an elicited desire according to right reason is the object of a natural desire, since the whole question is to discover whether the desire for immortality is or is not in accordance with right reason: this cannot legitimately be taken for granted. Furthermore, if it is said that man has a natural desire for immortality because he naturally flees from death, and that therefore immortality is at least a possibility, one might equally well argue that a brute has a natural desire for immortality and that it can and does survive.[3]

It may be as well to recall the fact that Scotus is not saying that

[1] *Ox.*, 4, 43, 2, no. 18. [2] Cf. also *Rep.*, 4, 43, 2, no. 18. [3] *Ox.*, 4, 43, 2, nos. 29–31.

the arguments for immortality are not probable or persuasive, still less that they are worthless: he is saying that they are not, in his opinion, demonstrative. The argument from desire does not conclude, because if one is speaking of the biological inclination to avoid death or what leads to death, brutes also possess this inclination, while if one is speaking of an elicited, conscious desire, one cannot legitimately argue from the desire of immortality to the fact of immortality unless one has first shown that immortality is a possibility, that the human soul can survive the disintegration of the *compositum*. It is all very well to say that the sufferings of this life demand a counterpoise in another life; but it remains true that man is exposed to suffering in this life, just as he is capable of pleasure and joy in this life, by the very fact of his nature, so that exposure to suffering is natural, and we cannot argue without more ado that suffering must be counterbalanced by other-worldly happiness. As to the argument that there must be sanctions in an after life, and that an after life therefore exists, the argument is not valid until you have shown that God does actually reward and punish people in this way, and Scotus did not think that this can be proved purely philosophically.[1] The best argument for the immortality of the human soul may be that drawn from the intellect's independence of a corporeal organ, from its spiritual activity; but although Scotus thought that this proof constituted a highly probable argument, he did not consider that it was an absolutely conclusive argument, since it might be that the soul, which is created as part of the *compositum*, cannot exist except as part of the *compositum*.

[1] *Ox.*, 4, 43, 2, no. 27.

CHAPTER L

SCOTUS—VI: ETHICS

Morality of human acts—Indifferent acts—The moral law and the will of God—Political authority.

MY aim in this chapter is not to propound all the ethical doctrines of Scotus, but rather to show that the accusation which has been brought against him of teaching the purely arbitrary character of the moral law, as though it depended simply and solely on the divine will, is, in the main, an unjust accusation.

1. An act is naturally good (*naturaliter bonus*) when it possesses all that is required for its *esse naturale*, just as a body is beautiful when it possesses all those characteristics of size, colour, shape, etc., which befit the body itself and harmonise with one another. An act is morally good when it possesses all that is required, not by the nature of the act taken merely in itself, but by right reason (*recta ratio*). To enter the moral order at all an act must be free, for 'an act is neither praiseworthy nor blameworthy unless it proceeds from the free will'; but obviously this is required for both morally good and morally bad acts; something more than freedom is required for a morally good act and that is conformity with right reason.[1] 'To attribute moral goodness is to attribute conformity to right reason.'[2] Every morally good act must be objectively good, in the sense of having an object conformable to right reason; but no act is good on this count alone, save the love of God, which can in no circumstances be morally evil, just as no act is morally evil on account of its object alone, save hatred of God, which cannot be morally good in any circumstances.[3] It is impossible, for instance, to love God with a bad intention, since there would then be no love, just as it is impossible to hate God with a good intention. In other cases, however, 'the goodness of the will does not depend on the object alone, but on all the other circumstances, and chiefly on the end' (*a fine*), which holds the primary place among the 'circumstances' of the act.[4] But though the end holds the primary place among the circumstances of the act, an act is not morally good merely because the end is good:

[1] *Ox.*, 2, 40, *quaestio unica*, nos. 2–3. [2] *Ibid.*, 1, 17, 3, no. 14.
[3] *Rep.*, 4, 28, no. 6. [4] *Ox.*, 1, *distinctio ultima*, nos. 1 and 2.

the end does not justify the means. 'It is necessary that all the (requisite) circumstances should occur together in any moral act, for it to be morally good; the defect of any one circumstance is sufficient in order that (the act) should be morally bad':[1] 'evil things must not be done in order that good (results) may eventuate.'[2] For an act to be morally good, then, it must be free, and it must be objectively good and be done with the right intention, in the right way, and so on. If it possesses these circumstances, it will be in accordance with right reason.

2. Every human act, that is, every free act, is good or evil in some way, not only in the sense that every act, considered purely ontologically, i.e. as a positive entity, is good, but also in the sense that every act has an object which is either in accordance with right reason or contrary to it. But inasmuch as goodness of all the circumstances is required for a completely good moral act, it is possible, if some circumstance is deficient in the goodness it should have, for an act to be 'indifferent'. For example, in order for almsgiving to be a completely good moral act, to have full moral value, it must be done with a moral intention. Now, to give alms with a bad intention would make the act bad; but it is possible to give alms simply from an immediate inclination, for example, and such an act, says Scotus, can be called morally indifferent: it is neither a bad act nor is it a fully moral act.[3] In the admission of indifferent elicited acts (and Scotus insisted that he was not speaking of reflex acts like brushing away a fly from one's face)[4] Scotus adopted an opinion opposed to that of St. Thomas Aquinas; but in order to understand his opinion, it is important to realise that for Scotus 'the first practical principle is: God ought to be loved'.[5] A man is not obliged always to refer his act to God either actually or virtually, because, says Scotus, God has not laid us under this obligation, but unless this is done, the act will not be completely good morally. On the other hand, since we are not obliged so to refer every act, it does not follow that an act which is not so referred is an evil act. If it is incompatible with the love of God, it will be evil; but it can be compatible with the love of God without being referred to God either actually or virtually. In this case it is an indifferent act. Apparently Scotus thought that 'habitual' reference is not sufficient to give an act full moral value.

3. We have seen that a morally good act must be in accordance

[1] *Ox.*, 1, *distinctio ultima*, nos. 1 and 2.
[2] *Ibid.*, 4, 5, 2, no. 7.
[3] *Rep.*, 2, 41, no. 2.
[4] Cf. *Ox.*, 2, 41, no. 4.
[5] *Ibid.*, 4, 46, 1, no. 10.

with right reason. What, then, is the norm of right reason and of the morality of our actions? According to Scotus, 'the divine will is the cause of good, and so by the fact that He wills something it is good . . .'[1] This statement taken by itself naturally appears to imply that the moral law depends simply on the arbitrary will of God; but such was not Scotus's position, and he meant simply that what God wills is good because God of His very nature cannot will anything but what is good. Still, Scotus does make the moral law depend in one sense on the divine will, and his position must be made clear. Inasmuch as the divine intellect, considered as preceding an act of the divine will, perceives the acts which are in conformity with human nature, the eternal and immutable moral law is constituted in regard to its content; but it acquires obligatory force only through the free choice of the divine will. One can say, then, that it is not the content of the moral law which is due to the divine will, but the obligation of the moral law, its morally binding force. 'To command pertains only to the appetite or will.'[2] The intellect says that this is true or untrue, in the practical as in the speculative sphere, and though it inclines to action of a certain type, it does not dictate that one ought to act in that way. Scotus is not simply saying that obligation actually bears on human beings only because God has willed to create them, which would be obvious enough, since they could not be obliged if they did not exist; he is saying that the divine will is the fount of obligation. It seems to follow that if God had not chosen to impose obligation, morality would be a matter of self-perfection, in the sense that the intellect would perceive that a certain course of action is what befits human nature and would judge that it is reasonable and prudent to act in that way. One would have an ethic of the type represented by Aristotle's ethics. Actually, however, God has willed that course of action, and that will is reflected in moral obligation: to transgress the law is thus not simply irrational, it is sin in the theological sense of the word.

That the content of the moral law is not due simply to the arbitrary caprice or choice of God is made abundantly clear by Scotus. Speaking of the sin of Adam,[3] he observes: 'A sin which is a sin only because it is forbidden, is less of a sin formally than that which is evil in itself and not because it is forbidden. Now to eat of that tree was not more a sin, as far as the act was concerned,

[1] *Rep.*, 1, 48, *quaestio unica.* [2] *Ox.*, 4, 14, 2, no. 5.
[3] *Rep.*, 2, 22, *quaestio unica*, no. 3.

than to eat of another tree, but only because it was forbidden. But all sins which concern the ten commandments are formally evil not merely because they are forbidden, but because they are evil; therefore they are forbidden, since by the law of nature the opposite of any commandment was evil, and by natural reason a man can see that any of those precepts is to be observed.' Here Scotus states clearly that the ten commandments are not simply arbitrary precepts and that a man can discern their validity through the natural use of reason, a statement which should involve the conclusion that God Himself could not change them, not because He is subject to them, as it were, but because they are ultimately founded on His nature.

The difficulty arises, however, that God seems to have dispensed in some of the secondary precepts of the decalogue (the precepts of the second table). For example, He told the Israelites to despoil the Egyptians, and He commissioned Abraham to sacrifice his son Isaac. Scotus, discussing this matter, asks first whether all the ten commandments belong to the law of nature, and he proceeds to make a distinction. Those moral laws which are self-evident or which follow necessarily from self-evident practical principles belong to the natural law in the strictest sense, and in the case of these principles and conclusions no dispensation is possible. God could not, for example, permit a man to have other gods than Himself or to take His name in vain, as such acts would be quite incompatible with man's end, the love of God as God, which necessarily involves exclusive worship and reverence. On the other hand, a moral law may belong to the law of nature, not as following necessarily from self-evident principles, but as being in accordance with the primary, necessary and self-evident practical principles; and of this type are the commandments of the second table. In the case of these moral commandments God can dispense.[1] Scotus proceeds to argue, or to suggest the argument,[2] that even if the love of the neighbour belongs to the natural law in the strict sense, so that I am necessarily bound to will that my neighbour should love God, it does not necessarily follow that I should will that he should have this or that particular good. This does not, however, prevent Scotus from going on to say[3] that the precepts of the decalogue are binding in every state and that before the giving of the written law all men were bound to observe

[1] *Ox.*, 3, 37, *quaestio unica*, nos. 5–8. [2] *Ibid.*, 3, 37, *quaestio unica*, no. 11.
[3] *Ibid.*, 3, 37, *quaestio unica*, nos. 13–15.

them, 'because they were written interiorly in the heart, or perhaps by some external teaching given by God which parents learnt and handed on to their sons.' Moreover, he explains that the children of Israel did not really need any dispensation when they despoiled the Egyptians, since God, as supreme lord, transferred to the Israelites the goods of the Egyptians, so that the former did not take what was not their own. Nevertheless, Scotus's general position is that the first two commandments of the first table of the decalogue belong to the natural law in the strictest sense (about the third commandment, that concerning sabbath observance, he expresses doubt), whereas the precepts of the second table do not belong to the natural law in the strictest sense, though they do so belong in the wider sense. God can, then, dispense in the case of the precepts of the second table, though He cannot dispense in the case of commandments which belong strictly to the natural law. On this matter of dispensation Scotus's opinion is at variance with that of the Thomists, who do not allow that God can, properly speaking, dispense in the case of any of the precepts of the decalogue, since they all derive immediately or mediately from primary practical principles. The Thomists explain the apparent dispensations which troubled Scotus as instances of *mutatio materiae*, that is, in much the same way as Scotus himself explained the spoliation of the Egyptians by the Israelites.

There is no call to discuss such Scriptural passages here, as they do not enter into philosophy; but it should be observed that even if Scotus admits the possibility of dispensation in the case of some commandments, the fact that he refused to allow that possibility in regard to moral precepts which belong strictly to the natural law shows clearly that he did not regard the whole moral law as due simply to the arbitrary decision of the divine will. He may have thought that the inviolability of private property, and the consequent wrongness of stealing, were not so bound up with the natural law that no exceptions would be legitimate, even in 'hard cases'; but he certainly stated that if a moral precept belonged to the natural law in the strict sense, it was unalterable. It cannot be denied that Scotus makes remarks such as that the divine will is the first rule of rectitude and that 'whatever does not include a contradiction is not repugnant to the divine will absolutely speaking, so that whatever God does or may do will be right and just';[1] but he certainly did not think that God can, without

[1] *Rep.*, 4, 46, 4, no. 8.

contradiction, order or permit acts which are contrary to self-evident practical principles or principles necessarily following therefrom. Probably one should view in close connection Scotus's doctrine concerning moral obligation and that concerning the secondary precepts of the decalogue. The primary precepts are self-evident or are so intimately connected with self-evident principles that their obligatory character is obvious. The secondary precepts, however, are not immediately deducible from primary practical principles, even if their harmony with those principles and their immediate derivatives is evident. Their obligatory character is thus not self-evident or necessary, but depends on the divine will. Their content is not purely arbitrary, since their harmony and consonance with necessary principles is clear; but the connection is not so strict that God cannot make exceptions. If it is His will which so reinforces the natural harmony of the secondary precepts with necessary principles that the former become obligatory in the full moral sense, His will can also dispense.

It would seem, then, that Scotus occupies a position midway, if one may so put it, between St. Thomas and Ockham. He agrees with the former that there are moral principles which are unalterable and he does not teach that the entire moral law depends on the arbitrary decision of God's will. On the other hand he attributed a much greater degree of prominence to the divine will in the determination of the moral order than St. Thomas had done, and he appears to have held that obligation, at least in regard to certain commandments, depends on that will as distinct from the divine intellect. While, then, if we look at Scotus's philosophy by itself, we must allow that his moral doctrine is not that of arbitrary divine authoritarianism, we must also allow, if we look at the historical development of thought, that his moral doctrine helped to prepare the way for that of Ockham, in whose eyes the moral law, including the whole decalogue, is the arbitrary creation of the divine will.

4. As regards political authority, Scotus distinguishes it carefully from paternal authority,[1] and appears to suggest that it rests on free consent. 'Political authority . . . can be right by common consent and the choice of the community itself.'[2] Scotus speaks of people who see that they cannot get on without some authority and who agree together to commit the care of the community to

[1] *Rep.*, 4, 15, 4, nos. 10–11. [2] *Ox.*, 4, 15, 2, no. 7.

one person or to a community of persons, and either to one man for himself alone, so that his successor would have to be elected, or to one man for himself and his posterity.[1] Elsewhere[2] he speaks of many independent peoples who, 'in order to attain a continual state of peace, were able by the mutual consent of all to elect from among them one prince . . .'

Legitimate authority is one of the factors which are required in the legislators, the other factor being 'prudence', the ability to legislate in accordance with right reason.[3] The legislator must not pass laws for his private advantage, but for the common good, which is the end of legislation.[4] Moreover, the positive human law must not be in conflict either with the natural moral law or with the divine positive law. No more than St. Thomas Aquinas would Scotus have had any sympathy with the idea of despotic government or with that of the State as the fount of morality.

[1] *Ox.*, 4, 15, 2, no. 7.
[2] *Rep.*, 4, 15, 4, no. 11.
[3] *Ox.*, 4, 15, 2, no. 6.
[4] *Ibid.*, 4, 14, 2, no. 7.

CHAPTER LI

CONCLUDING REVIEW

Theology and philosophy—'Christian philosophy'—The Thomist synthesis—Various ways of regarding and interpreting mediaeval philosophy.

ANY general review of mediaeval philosophy must obviously be left to the conclusion of the next volume; but it may be worth while to indicate here some general aspects of the course of philosophy treated of in the present book, even though the omission of Ockhamism, which will be considered in the third volume, restricts the scope of one's reflections.

1. One can regard the development of philosophy in the Christian world from the days of the Roman Empire up to the thirteenth-century syntheses from the point of view of its relation to theology. In the first centuries of the Christian era there was scarcely any philosophy in the modern sense, in the sense, that is, of an autonomous science distinct from theology. The Fathers were aware, of course, of the distinction between reason and faith, between scientific conclusions and the data of revelation; but to distinguish reason and faith is not necessarily the same as to make a clear distinction between philosophy and theology. Christian apologists and writers who were anxious to show the reasonable character of the Christian religion, employed reason to show that there is, for example, but one God, and to that extent they may be said to have developed philosophical themes; but their aim was apologetic, and not primarily philosophic. Even those writers who adopted a hostile attitude towards Greek philosophy had to employ reason for apologetic purposes and they gave their attention to themes which are considered to belong to the province of philosophy; but though we can isolate those arguments and discussions which fall under the heading of philosophy, it would be idle to pretend that a Christian apologist of this kind was a professed philosopher; he may have borrowed from the philosophers to some extent, but he regarded 'philosophy' pretty well as a perverter of the truth and as a foe of Christianity. As to the Christian writers who adopted a predominantly favourable attitude to Greek philosophy, these tended to look on Greek philosophy as a preparation for Christian wisdom, the latter comprising not only the revealed

mysteries of faith but all truth about the world and human life looked at through the eyes of a Christian. Inasmuch as the Fathers not only applied reason to the understanding, correct statement and defence of the data of revelation, but also treated of themes which had been considered by Greek philosophers, they helped not only to develop theology, but also to provide material for the construction of a philosophy which would be compatible with Christian theology; but they were theologians and exegetes, not philosophers in the strict sense, save occasionally and incidentally; and even when they did pursue philosophic themes, they were rounding out, as it were, the total Christian wisdom rather than constructing a distinct philosophy or branch of philosophy. This is true even of St. Augustine, for although one can reconstruct a philosophy from his writings, he was above all a theologian and was not concerned to build up a philosophical system as such.

Fathers of the Church, like St. Gregory of Nyssa and St. Augustine, who in their writings utilised elements borrowed from neo-Platonism, found in neo-Platonism material which helped them in their development of a 'philosophy' of the spiritual life, to which, as Christians and saints, they paid much attention. It was only natural that they should speak of the soul, of its relation to the body, and of its ascent to God, in terms strongly reminiscent of Platonism and neo-Platonism; but since they could not (and in any case would not wish to) consider the soul's ascent to God in abstraction from theology and revelation, their philosophy, which concentrated so much on the soul and its ascent to God, was inevitably intertwined with and integrated into their theology. To treat St. Augustine's doctrine of illumination, for example, as a purely philosophic doctrine is not easy; it really ought to be looked at in the light of his general doctrine concerning the soul's relation to God and its ascent to God.

The general attitude of the Fathers set the tone, so to speak, for what we call 'Augustinianism'. St. Anselm, for instance, was a theologian, but he saw that the existence of the God who revealed the mysteries of the Christian religion needs in some way to be proved, and so he developed a natural theology, or helped towards the development of natural theology, though it would be a mistake to picture him as sitting down to elaborate a system of philosophy as such. *Fides quaerens intellectum* may, to speak rather crudely, work forwards or backwards. Working forwards from the data of revelation and applying reasoning to theological dogmas, in order to understand them as far as is possible, it produces Scholastic theology; working backwards, in the sense of considering the presuppositions of revelation, it develops the proofs of God's existence. But the mind at work in either case is really the mind of the theologian, even though in the second case it works within the province and with the methods of philosophy.

If the spirit of Augustinianism, born of the writings of the Fathers, was that of *fides quaerens intellectum*, it might also be called a spirit of *homo quaerens Deum*. This aspect of Augustinianism is especially marked in St. Bonaventure, whose thought was steeped so deeply in the affective spirituality of Franciscanism. A man may contemplate creatures, the world without and the world within, and discern their natures; but his knowledge is of little worth unless he discerns in nature the *vestigium Dei* and in himself the *imago Dei*, unless he can detect the operation of God in his soul, an operation which is itself hidden but is rendered visible in its effects, in its power. A number of 'Augustinians' no doubt maintained the doctrine of illumination, for example, out of conservatism and a respect for tradition; but in the case of a man like St. Bonaventure the retention of the doctrine was something much more than traditionalism. It has been said that of two doctrines, of which one attributes more to God and the other less, the Augustinian chooses the one which attributes more to God and less to the creature; but this is true only in so far as the doctrine is felt to harmonise with and express spiritual experience and in so far as it harmonises with and can be integrated into the general theological outlook.

If one understands the motto *fides quaerens intellectum* as expressing the spirit of Augustinianism and as indicating the place of philosophy in the mind of the Augustinian, it might be objected that such a description of Augustinianism is far too wide and that one might even have to class as Augustinians thinkers whom no one could reasonably call Augustinians. The passage from faith to 'understanding', to Scholastic theology on the one hand and to philosophy on the other hand, was ultimately the result of the fact that Christianity was given to the world as a revealed doctrine of salvation, not as a philosophy in the academic sense, nor even as a Scholastic philosophy. Christians believed first of all, and only afterwards, in the desire to defend, to explain and to understand what they believed, did they develop theology and, in subordination to theology, philosophy. In a sense this was the attitude not only of the early Christian writers and Fathers, but also of all those mediaeval thinkers who were primarily theologians. They believed first of all, and then they attempted to understand. This would be true of St. Thomas himself. But how could one call St. Thomas an Augustinian? Is it not better to confine the term 'Augustinian' to certain philosophical doctrines? Once one has done that, one has a means for distinguishing Augustinians from non-Augustinians: otherwise, one is involved in hopeless confusion.

There is a great deal of truth in this contention, and it must be admitted that in order to be able to discriminate between Augustinians and non-Augustinians in regard to the content of their philosophies, it is desirable to be clear first of all about what doctrines one is prepared to recognise as Augustinian and why; but I am speaking at present of the relation between theology and philosophy, and in regard to this point I maintain that, with an important qualification to be mentioned shortly, there is no essential difference in attitude between St. Augustine himself and the great theologian-philosophers of the thirteenth century. St. Thomas Aquinas certainly made a formal and methodological distinction between philosophy and theology, a distinction which was not clearly made by St. Gregory of Nyssa, St. Augustine, or St. Anselm; but the attitude of *fides quaerens intellectum* was none the less the attitude of St. Thomas. *On this point*, therefore, I should be willing to rank St. Thomas as an 'Augustinian'. In regard to doctrinal content one must adopt another criterion, it is true. St. Bonaventure too made a formal distinction between theology and philosophy, though he clung to and emphasised doctrines generally recognised as 'Augustinian', whereas St. Thomas rejected them, and in regard to these doctrines one can call the philosophy of Bonaventure 'Augustinian' and the philosophy of Thomas non-Augustinian. Again, St. Bonaventure, as we have seen, emphasised far more than St. Thomas the insufficiency of independent philosophy, so that it has even been said that the unity of Bonaventure's system must be sought on the theological and not on the philosophical level. All the same, St. Thomas himself did not believe that a purely independent philosophy would be, in actual fact and practice, completely satisfactory, and he, like St. Bonaventure, was primarily a theologian. There is a great deal to be said for M. Gilson's contention that for St. Thomas the sphere of philosophy is the sphere of *le révélable* (in the sense in which M. Gilson uses the term, and not, obviously enough, in every sense).

The 'important qualification' I mentioned above is this. Owing to the discovery of the complete Aristotle and his adoption by St. Thomas, so far as adoption was consistent with theological orthodoxy, St. Thomas provided the material for an independent philosophy. As I have suggested when treating of St. Thomas, the utilisation of the Aristotelian system helped philosophy to become self-conscious and to aspire after independence and autonomy. When philosophical material was comparatively scanty, as in the Patristic period and in the earlier centuries of the mediaeval era, there could be little question of an autonomous philosophy going its own way (it is not necessary to take the phenomenon of the *dialectici* very seriously); but once Aristotelianism, which appeared at least to be a complete philosophical system, elaborated independently of theology, had arrived on the scene and had won its right to be there, a parting of the ways was morally inevitable: philosophy had grown up, and would soon demand its birthright and wander out of the house. But this was by no means the intention of St. Thomas, who had meant to utilise Aristotelianism in the construction of a vast theologico-philosophical synthesis, in which theology should constitute the ultimate measuring-rod. Yet children, when they grow up, do not always behave exactly as their parents expected or wished. Bonaventure, Albert, Thomas utilised and incorporated an increasing amount of the new philosophical materials, and all the while they were rearing a child who would soon go his own way; but the three men, though differing from one another on many points of philosophical doctrine, were really at one in the ideal of a Christian synthesis. They belonged to the *Sancti*, not to the *philosophi*; and if one wishes to find a radical contrast between mediaeval thinkers in regard to their view of the relation between theology and philosophy, one should contrast not so much St. Anselm and St. Bonaventure on the one hand with St. Thomas on the other as St. Anselm, St. Bonaventure, St. Thomas and Scotus on the one hand with the Latin Averroists and, in the fourteenth century, the Ockhamist School on the other. The *philosophi* and radical Peripatetics stand over against the Fathers and theologians and *Sancti*.

2. What has already been said brings one to the question of 'Christian philosophy'. Can one speak of the 'Christian philosophy'

of the Middle Ages, and if so, in what sense? If philosophy is a legitimate and autonomous province of human study and knowledge ('autonomous' in the sense that the philosopher has his own method and subject-matter), it would appear that it is not and cannot be 'Christian'. It would sound absurd to speak of 'Christian biology' or 'Christian mathematics': a biologist or a mathematician can be a Christian, but not his biology or his mathematics. Similarly, it might be said, a philosopher can be a Christian, but not his philosophy. His philosophy may be true and compatible with Christianity; but one does not call a scientific statement Christian simply because it is true and compatible with Christianity. Just as mathematics can be neither pagan nor Moslem nor Christian, though mathematicians can be pagans or Moslems or Christians, so philosophy can be neither pagan nor Moslem nor Christian, though philosophers can be pagans or Moslems or Christians. The relevant question about a scientific hypothesis is whether it is true or false, confirmed by observation and experiment or refuted, not whether it is proposed by a Christian or a Hindoo or an atheist; and the relevant question about a philosophic doctrine is whether it is true or false, more or less adequate as an explanation of the facts it is supposed to explain, not whether it is expounded by a believer in Zeus, a follower of Mahomet or a Christian theologian. The most that the phrase 'Christian philosophy' can legitimately mean is a philosophy compatible with Christianity; if it means more than that, one is speaking of a philosophy which is not simply philosophy, but which is, partly at least, theology.

This is a reasonable and understandable point of view, and it certainly represents one aspect of St. Thomas's attitude towards philosophy, an aspect expressed in his formal distinction between theology and philosophy. The philosopher starts with creatures, the theologian with God; the philosopher's principles are those discerned by the natural light of reason, the theologian's are revealed; the philosopher treats of the natural order, the theologian primarily of the supernatural order. But if one adheres closely to this aspect of Thomism, one is placed in a somewhat difficult position. St. Bonaventure did not think that any satisfactory metaphysic can be achieved save in the light of the Faith. The philosophic doctrine of exemplary ideas, for example, is closely linked up with the theological doctrine of the Word. Is one to say, then, that St. Bonaventure had no philosophy properly speaking, or is one to sort out the theological elements from the philosophical elements? And if so, does not one run the risk of constructing a 'Bonaventurian philosophy' which St. Bonaventure himself would hardly have recognised as an adequate expression of his thought and intentions? Is it not perhaps simpler to allow that St. Bonaventure's idea of philosophy *was* that of a Christian philosophy, in the sense of a general Christian synthesis such as earlier Christian writers endeavoured to achieve? An historian is entitled to adopt this point of view. If one speaks simply as a philosopher who is convinced that philosophy either stands on its own feet or is not philosophy at all, one will not admit the existence of a 'Christian philosophy'; or, in other words, if one speaks simply as a 'Thomist', one will be forced to criticise any other and different conception of philosophy. But if one speaks as an historian, looking on from outside, as it were, one will recognise that there were two conceptions of philosophy, the one that of St. Bonaventure, the conception of a Christian philosophy, the other that of St. Thomas and Scotus, the conception of a philosophy which could not properly be called Christian, save in the sense that it was compatible with theology. From this point of view one can say that St. Bonaventure, even though he made a formal distinction between theology and philosophy, continued the tradition of the Fathers, whereas with St. Thomas philosophy received a charter. In this sense Thomism was 'modern' and looked forward to the future. As a system of self-sufficient philosophy Thomism can enter into competition and discussion with other philosophies, because it can prescind from dogmatic theology altogether, whereas a Christian philosophy of the Bonaventurian type can hardly do so. The true Bonaventurian could, of course, argue with modern philosophers on particular points, the proofs of God's existence, for example; but the total system could hardly enter the philosophical arena on equal terms, precisely because it is not simply a philosophical system but a Christian synthesis.

Yet is there not a sense in which the philosophies of St. Augustine and St. Bonaventure and St. Albert and St. Thomas can all be called Christian? The problems which they discussed were in large measure set by theology, or by the necessity of defending Christian truth. When Aristotle argued to the existence of an unmoved mover, he was answering a problem set by metaphysics (and by physics); but when St. Anselm and St. Bonaventure and St. Thomas proved God's existence, they were showing the rational foundation for the acceptance of a revelation in which they already believed. St. Bonaventure was concerned also to show God's immanent activity within the soul; and even though St. Thomas employed Aristotle's own argument, he was not answering simply an abstract problem nor was he interested simply in showing that there is an unmoved mover, an ultimate cause of motion; he was interested in proving the existence of God, a Being who meant a great deal more to St. Thomas than an unmoved mover. His arguments can naturally be considered in themselves and, from the philosophic standpoint, they must be so considered; but he approached the question from the viewpoint of a theologian, looking on the proof of God's existence as a *praeambulum fidei*. Moreover, although St. Thomas certainly spoke of philosophy or metaphysics as the science of being as being, and though his declaration that the rational knowledge of God is the highest part of philosophy, that to which other parts lead, can certainly be regarded as suggested by Aristotle's words, in his *Summae* (which are of the greatest importance from the philosophical, as well as from the theological standpoint) he follows the order suggested by theology, and his philosophy fits closely into his theology, making a synthesis. St. Thomas did not approach philosophical problems in the spirit of a professor of the Parisian faculty of arts; he approached them in the spirit of a Christian theologian. Moreover, in spite of his Aristotelianism and in spite of his repetition of Aristotelian statements, I think it can be maintained that for St. Thomas philosophy is not so much a study of being in general as a study of God, God's activity and God's effects, so far as the natural reason will take us; so that God is the centre of his philosophy as of his theology, the same God, though attained in different ways. I have suggested earlier on that St. Thomas's formal charter to philosophy meant that philosophy would in the end go her own way, and I think that this is true; but that is not to say that St. Thomas envisaged or desired the 'separation' of philosophy from theology. On the contrary, he attempted a great synthesis, and he attempted it as a Christian theologian who was also a philosopher; he would doubtless have considered that what would have appeared to him as the vagaries and errors of philosophers in later centuries were largely due to those very causes in view of which he declared revelation to be morally necessary.

3. More chapters have been devoted to the philosophy of St. Thomas Aquinas than to any other philosopher, and rightly so,

since Thomism is unquestionably the most imposing and comprehensive synthesis considered in this book. I may have emphasised those aspects of Thomism which are of non-Aristotelian origin, and one should, I think, bear these aspects in mind, lest one forget that Thomism is a synthesis and not simply a literal adoption of Aristotelianism; but none the less Thomism *can*, of course, be regarded as the culminating process of a movement in the Christian West towards the adoption and utilisation of Greek philosophy as represented by Aristotle. Owing to the fact that philosophy in the time of the Fathers meant, to all intents and purposes, neo-Platonism, to utilise Greek philosophy meant, for the Fathers, to utilise neo-Platonism: St. Augustine, for instance, did not know much of the historic system of Aristotle, as distinct from neo-Platonism. Moreover, the spiritual character of neo-Platonism appealed to the mind of the Fathers. That the categories of neo-Platonism should continue to dominate Christian thought in the early Middle Ages was only natural, in view of the fact that the Fathers had utilised them and that they were consecrated through the prestige attaching to the writings of the Pseudo-Dionysius, believed to be St. Paul's convert. Furthermore, even when the *corpus* of Aristotle's writings had become available in Latin translations from the Greek and the Arabic, the differences between Aristotelianism proper and neo-Platonism proper were by no means clearly recognised: they could not be clearly recognised so long as the *Liber de causis* and the *Elementatio theologica* were ascribed to Aristotle, especially when the great Moslem commentators had themselves drawn copiously on neo-Platonism. That Aristotle had criticised Plato was, of course, perfectly clear from the *Metaphysics*; but the precise nature and scope of the criticism was not so clear. The adoption and utilisation of Aristotle did not mean, therefore, the negation and rejection of all neo-Platonism, and though St. Thomas recognised that the *Liber de causis* was not the work of Aristotle, one can regard his interpretation of Aristotle in a manner consonant with Christianity, not merely as an interpretation *in meliorem partem* (which it was, from the viewpoint of anyone who is both a Christian and an historian), but also as following from the general conception of Aristotle in his time. St. Bonaventure certainly thought that Aristotle's criticism of Plato involved a rejection of exemplarism (and in my opinion St. Bonaventure was quite right); but St. Thomas did not think so, and he interpreted Aristotle accordingly. One might be tempted to think that St. Thomas was simply whitewashing Aristotle; but one should not forget that 'Aristotle' for St. Thomas meant rather more than Aristotle means to the modern historian of Greek philosophy; he was, to a certain extent at least, an Aristotle seen through the eyes of commentators and philosophers who were themselves not pure Aristotelians. Even the radical Aristotelians by intention, the Latin Averroists, were not pure Aristotelians in the strict sense. If one adopts this point of view, one will find it easier to understand how Aristotle could appear to St. Thomas as 'the Philosopher', and one will realise that when St. Thomas baptised Aristotelianism he was not simply substituting Aristotelianism for neo-Platonism, but that he was completing that process of absorbing Greek philosophy which had begun in the early days of the Christian era. In a sense we can say that neo-Platonism, Augustinianism, Aristotelianism and the Moslem and Jewish philosophies came together and were fused in Thomism, not in the sense that selected elements were juxtaposed mechanically, but in the sense that a true fusion and synthesis was achieved under the regulating guidance of certain basic ideas. Thomism, in the fullest sense, is thus a synthesis of Christian theology and Greek philosophy (Aristotelianism, united with other elements, or Aristotelianism, interpreted in the light of later philosophy) in which philosophy is regarded in the light of theology and theology itself is expressed, to a considerable extent, in categories borrowed from Greek philosophy, particularly from Aristotle.

I have asserted that Thomism is a synthesis of Christian theology and Greek philosophy, which might seem to imply that Thomism in the narrower sense, that is, as denoting simply the Thomist philosophy, is a synthesis of Greek philosophy and that it is nothing else but Greek philosophy. In the first place, it seems preferable to speak of Greek philosophy rather than of Aristotelianism, for the simple reason that St. Thomas's philosophy was a synthesis of Platonism (using the term in a wide sense, to include neo-Platonism) and of Aristotelianism, though one should not forget that the Moslem and Jewish philosophers were also important influences in the formation of his thought. In the first volume of my history I have argued that Plato and Aristotle should be regarded as complementary thinkers, in some respects at least, and that a synthesis is needed. St. Thomas Aquinas achieved this synthesis. We cannot speak of his philosophy, therefore, as simply Aristotelianism; it is rather a synthesis of

Greek philosophy, harmonised with Christian theology. In the second place, Thomism is a real synthesis and is not a mere juxtaposition of heterogeneous elements. For example, St. Thomas did not take over the Platonic-Plotinian-Augustinian tradition of exemplary ideas and merely juxtapose it with the Aristotelian doctrine of substantial form: he gave each element its ontological status, making the substantial form subordinate to the exemplary idea, and explaining in what sense one is entitled to speak of 'ideas' in God. Again, if he adopted the (originally) Platonic notion of participation, he did not employ it in a manner which would conflict with the Aristotelian elements of his metaphysic. St. Thomas went beyond the Aristotelian hylomorphism and discerned in the real distinction between essence and existence a profounder application of the principle of potentiality and act. This distinction enabled him to use the Platonic notion of participation to explain finite being, while at the same time his view of God as *ipsum esse subsistens* rather than as mere unmoved mover enabled him to use the idea of participation in such a way as to throw into relief the idea of creation, which was to be found neither in Plato nor in Aristotle. Needless to say, St. Thomas did not take participation, in the full sense, as a premiss; the complete idea of participation could not be obtained until God's existence had been proved, but the material for the elaboration of that idea was provided by the real distinction between essence and existence.

4. Some of the viewpoints adopted in this book may appear to be somewhat inconsistent; but one must remember that it is possible to adopt different viewpoints in regard to the history of mediaeval philosophy, or indeed in regard to the history of philosophy in any epoch. Apart from the fact that one will naturally adopt a different viewpoint and interpret the development of philosophy in a different light according as one is a Thomist, a Scotist, a Kantian, an Hegelian, a Marxist or a Logical Positivist, it is possible even for the same man to discern different principles or modes of interpretation, none of which he would be willing to reject as totally illegitimate and yet for none of which he would be prepared to claim complete truth and adequacy.

Thus it is possible, and from certain viewpoints perfectly legitimate, to adopt the linear or progressive mode of interpretation. It is possible to view the absorption and utilisation of Greek philosophy by Christian thinkers as starting practically from zero in the early years of the Christian era, as increasing through the thought of the Fathers up to the Scholasticism of the early Middle Ages, as being suddenly, comparatively speaking, enriched through the translations from the Arabic and the Greek, and as developing through the thought of William of Auvergne, Alexander of Hales, St. Bonaventure and St. Albert the Great, until it reached its culmination in the Thomist synthesis. According to this line of interpretation it would be necessary to regard the philosophy of St. Bonaventure as a stage in the development of Thomism, and not as a parallel and heterogeneous philosophy. One would regard the achievement of St. Thomas, not so much as an adoption of Aristotle in place of Augustine or of neo-Platonic Platonism, but rather as a confluence and synthesis of the various currents of Greek philosophy, and of Islamic and Jewish philosophy, as well as of the original ideas contributed by Christian thinkers. Mediaeval philosophy before St. Thomas one would regard, not as 'Augustinianism' as opposed to Aristotelianism, but as pre-Thomist Scholasticism or as the Scholasticism of the earlier Middle Ages. This line of interpretation seems to me to be perfectly legitimate, and it has the very great advantage of not leading to a distorted idea of Thomism as pure Aristotelianism. It would even be possible and legitimate to look on Thomism as an Aristotelianised Platonism rather than as a Platonised Aristotelianism. What has been said of the 'synthetic' character of Thomism and of its relation to Greek, and Islamic, philosophy in general rather than to Aristotelianism in particular supports this line of interpretation, which was also suggested by what was said in the first volume of this history concerning the complementary character of the Platonic and Aristotelian philosophies.

On the other hand, if one follows this line of interpretation exclusively, one runs the risk of missing altogether the rich variety of mediaeval philosophy and the individuality of the different philosophers. The spirit of St. Bonaventure was not the same as that of Roger Bacon nor the same as that of St. Thomas, and French historians like M. Gilson have done us a great service in drawing attention to and throwing into relief the peculiar genius of individual thinkers. This 'individualisation' of mediaeval philosophers is all the more to be welcomed in view of the fact that the Christian thinkers shared a common theological background, so that their philosophical differences were expressed within a comparatively restricted field, with the result that mediaeval philosophy might seem to consist of a series of repetitions on salient points and a series of differences on relatively insignificant points. If one said simply that St. Bonaventure postulated a special illumination and that St. Thomas rejected it, the difference between them would not present so much interest as it does if St. Bonaventure's theory of illumination is linked up with his total thought and if St. Thomas's denial of any special illumination is seen against the background of his system in general. But one cannot depict the total thought of Bonaventure or the general system of Thomas without setting in relief the peculiar spirit of each thinker. It may very well be true that M. Gilson, as I suggested earlier in this book, has exaggerated the differences between St. Bonaventure and St. Thomas, and that it is possible to look on St. Bonaventure's philosophy as a stage in the evolution of Thomism rather than as a parallel and different philosophy; but it is also possible for different men to have different conceptions of what philosophy is, and if a man does not accept the Thomist point of view, he will probably be no more inclined to look on Bonaventure as an incomplete Thomas than a Platonist would be inclined to look on Plato as an incomplete Aristotle. It is, I think, a mistake to insist so much on the linear type of interpretation that one rules out as illegitimate the type of interpretation represented by M. Gilson or, conversely, so to insist upon the individual characteristics and spirits of different thinkers as to lose sight of the general evolution of thought towards a complete synthesis. Narrowness of vision can hardly produce adequate understanding.

Again, while it is possible to view the development of mediaeval philosophy as a development towards the Thomist synthesis and to regard pre-Thomist philosophies as stages in that development, and while it is possible to concentrate more on the peculiarities of different philosophies and the individual geniuses of different thinkers, it is also possible to see and to throw into relief different general lines of development. Thus it is possible to distinguish different types of 'Augustinianism' instead of being content with one portmanteau word; to distinguish, for example, the typically Franciscan Augustinianism of St. Bonaventure from the Aristotelianised Augustinianism of Richard of Middleton or the Avicennian Augustinianism of Henry of Ghent and, in a certain measure, of Duns Scotus. It is possible to trace the respective influences on mediaeval thought of Avicenna, Averroes and Avicebron, and to attempt a corresponding classification. Hence phrases such as *augustinisme avicennisant*, *augustinisme avicebronisant*, *avicennisme latin*, of which French historians have made use. An investigation of such influences is certainly of value; but the classification produced by such an investigation cannot be regarded as a *complete* and entirely adequate classification of mediaeval philosophies, since insistence on the influence of the past tends to obscure original contributions, while it depends largely on what points of his philosophy one happens to have in mind whether one classes a philosopher as falling under the influence of Avicenna or Averroes or Avicebron.

Again, one can regard the development of mediaeval philosophy in regard to the relation of Christian thought to 'humanism', to Greek thought and culture and science in general. Thus if St. Peter Damian was a representative of the negative attitude towards humanism, St. Albert the Great and Roger Bacon represented a positive attitude, while from the political point of view Thomism represents a harmonisation of the natural and humanistic with the supernatural which is absent in the characteristic political theory of Giles of Rome. St. Thomas, again, through the greater part he attributes to human activity in knowledge and action compared with some of his predecessors and contemporaries, may be said to represent a humanistic tendency.

In fine, mediaeval philosophy can be considered under several aspects, each of which has its own justification, and it ought to be so considered if one is to attain anything like an adequate view of it; but any more extensive treatment of mediaeval philosophy in general must be reserved until the conclusion of the next volume, when the philosophy of the fourteenth century has been discussed. In the present volume the great synthesis of St. Thomas naturally and rightly occupies the central position, though, as we have seen, mediaeval philosophy and the philosophy of St. Thomas are not synonymous. The thirteenth century was the century of speculative thought, and the century was exceptionally rich in speculative thinkers. It was the century of original thinkers, whose thought had not yet become hardened into the dogmatic traditions of philosophical Schools. But though the great thinkers of the thirteenth century differed from one another in their philosophical doctrines and criticised one another, they did so against a background of commonly accepted metaphysical principles. One must distinguish criticism concerning the application of accepted metaphysical principles from criticism of the very foundations of metaphysical systems. The former was practised by all the great speculative thinkers of the Middle Ages; but the latter did not appear until the fourteenth century. I have concluded this volume with a consideration of Duns Scotus, who, from the chronological point of view, stands at the juncture of the thirteenth and fourteenth centuries; but even if one can discern in his philosophy the faint beginnings of the more radical spirit of criticism which was to characterise the Ockhamist movement of the fourteenth century, his criticism of his contemporaries and predecessors did not involve a denial of the metaphysical principles commonly accepted in the thirteenth century. Looking back on the Middle Ages, we may tend to see in the system of Scotus a bridge between the two centuries, between the age of St. Thomas and the age of Ockham; but Ockham himself certainly did not see in Scotus a kindred spirit, and I think that even if Scotus's philosophy did prepare the way for a more radical criticism his system must be regarded as the last of the great mediaeval speculative syntheses. It can hardly be denied, I think, that certain of Scotus's opinions in rational psychology, in natural theology and in ethics look forward, as it were, to the Ockhamist critique of metaphysics and the peculiar Ockhamist view of the nature of the moral law; but if one considers Scotus's philosophy in itself, without reference to a future which we know but he did not, we are forced to realise that it was just as much a metaphysical system as any of the great systems of the thirteenth century. It seemed to me, then, that Scotus's place was in this volume rather than in the next. In the next volume I hope to treat of fourteenth-century philosophy, of the philosophies of the Renaissance and of the revival of Scholasticism in the fifteenth and sixteenth centuries.

APPENDIX I

Honorific titles applied in the Middle Ages to philosophers treated of in this volume.

RHABANUS MAURUS:	Praeceptor Germaniae.
ABELARD:	Peripateticus Palatinus.
ALAN OF LILLE:	Doctor universalis.
AVERROES:	Commentator.
ALEXANDER OF HALES:	Doctor irrefragibilis.
ST. BONAVENTURE:	Doctor seraphicus.
ST. ALBERT THE GREAT:	Doctor universalis.
ST. THOMAS AQUINAS:	Doctor angelicus and Doctor communis.
ROGER BACON:	Doctor mirabilis.
RICHARD OF MIDDLETON:	Doctor solidus.
RAYMOND LULL:	Doctor illuminatus.
GILES OF ROME:	Doctor fundatissimus.
HENRY OF GHENT:	Doctor solemnis.
DUNS SCOTUS:	Doctor subtilis.

APPENDIX II

A SHORT BIBLIOGRAPHY

General Works on Mediaeval Philosophy

BRÉHIER, E. Histoire de la philosophie: tome 1, l'antiquité et le moyen âge. Paris, 1943.

CARLYLE, R. W. & A. J. A History of Mediaeval Political Theory in the West. 4 vols. London, 1903–22.

DEMPF, A. Die Ethik des Mittelalters. Munich, 1930.
Metaphysik des Mittelalters. Munich, 1930.

DE WULF, M. Histoire de la philosophie médiévale. 3 vols. Louvain, 1934–47 (6th edition). English translation of first two vols. by E. C. Messenger, London, 1935–8 (3rd edition).

GEYER, B. Die patristische und scholastische Philosophie. Berlin, 1928. (This is the second volume of the revised edition of Ueberweg.)

GILSON, E. La philosophie au moyen âge. Paris, 1944 (2nd edition, revised and augmented). English translation, 1936.
L'esprit de la philosophie médiévale. 2 vols. Paris, 1944 (2nd edition).
Études de philosophie médiévale. Strasbourg, 1921.
The Unity of Philosophical Experience. London, 1938.
Reason and Revelation in the Middle Ages. New York, 1939.

GRABMANN, M. Die Philosophie des Mittelalters. Berlin, 1921.
Mittelalterliches Geistesleben. 2 vols. Munich, 1926 and 1936.

GRUNWALD, G. Geschichte der Gottesbeweise im Mittelalter bis zum Ausgang der Hochscholastik. Münster, 1907.
(Beiträge zur Geschichte der Philosophie und Theologie des Mittelalters, 6, 3.)

HAURÉAU, B. Histoire de la philosophie scolastique. 3 vols. Paris, 1872–80.

HAWKINS, D. J. B. A Sketch of Mediaeval Philosophy. London, 1946.

LOTTIN, O. Psychologie et morale aux XIIe et XIIIe siècles. Tome 1: Problèmes de Psychologie. Louvain, 1942. Tome 2: Problèmes de Morale. 1948.
Le droit naturel chez S. Thomas d'Aquin et ses prédécesseurs. Bruges, 1931 (2nd edition).

PICAVET, F. Esquisse d'une histoire générale et comparée des philosophies médiévales. Paris, 1907 (2nd edition).
Essais sur l'histoire générale et comparée des théologies et des philosophies médiévales. Paris, 1913.

ROMEYER, B. La philosophie chrétienne jusqu'à Descartes. 3 vols. Paris, 1935–7.

RUGGIERO, G. DE. La filosofia del cristianesimo. 3 vols. Bari.

STÖCKL, A. Geschichte der Philosophie des Mittelalters. 3 vols. Mainz, 1864–6.

VIGNAUX, P. La pensée au moyen âge. Paris, 1938.

Chapter II: The Patristic Period

(*a*) *Texts: General collections of*

Migne (edit.), Patrologia Graeca. Paris.

Migne (edit.), Patrologia Latina. Paris.

Die griechischen christlichen Schriftsteller der ersten drei Jahrhunderte. Leipzig.

Corpus scriptorum ecclesiasticorum Latinorum. Vienna.

Ante-Nicene Christian Library, Translations of the writings of the Fathers down to A.D. 325. Edinburgh.

A Library of the Fathers (English translations). Oxford.

Ancient Christian Writers: the works of the Fathers in Translation. Westminster, Maryland, U.S.A., 1946 (edit. J. Quasten and J. C. Plumpe).

(*b*) *Particular Texts*

ARISTIDES. Apology. In *Zwei griechische Apologeten*, J. Geffcken. Leipzig, 1907.

Apology. In *Texte und Untersuchungen*, IV. E. Hennecke (edit.). Leipzig, 1893.

ARNOBIUS. Libri 7 adversus gentes. Appended to *Lactantii opera omnia* (L. C. Firmiani). Paris, 1845.

ATHENAGORAS. Apology. In *Zwei griechische Apologeten*. J. Geffcken. Leipzig, 1907.

Libellus pro Christianis and Oratio de resurrectione cadaverum in *Texte und Untersuchungen*, IV. E. Schwartz (edit.). Leipzig, 1891.

CLEMENT OF ALEXANDRIA. The Exhortation to the Greeks, etc. G. W. Butterworth (edit.). London, 1919.

EUSEBIUS. The Proof of the Gospel (*Demonstratio Evangelica*). 2 vols. W. J. Ferrar (edit.). London, 1920.

GREGORY OF NYSSA, ST. The Catechetical Oration of St. Gregory of Nyssa. J. H. Srawley (edit.). London, 1917.

La Création de l'homme. J. Laplace and J. Daniélou. Paris, 1943.

HIPPOLYTUS. Philosophumena. 2 vols. F. Legge (edit.). London, 1921.

IRENAEUS, ST. The Treatise of Irenaeus of Lugdunum against the Heresies. F. R. Montgomery Hitchcock (edit.). London, 1916.

JUSTIN MARTYR, ST. The Dialogue with Trypho. A. L. Williams (edit.). London, 1930.

LACTANTIUS. Opera omnia. L. C. Firmiani. Paris, 1843.

MINUCIUS FELIX. The Octavius of Minucius Felix. J. H. Freese (edit.). London (no date).

ORIGEN. Homélies sur la Genèse. L. Doutreleau (edit.). Paris, 1943.
Origen on First Principles. G. W. Butterworth (edit.). London, 1936.

TATIAN. Oratio ad Graecos. In *Texte und Untersuchungen*, IV. E. Schwartz (edit.). Leipzig, 1888.

TERTULLIAN. Tertullian concerning the Resurrection of the Flesh. A. Souter (edit.). London, 1922.
Tertullian against Praxeas. A. Souter (edit.). London, 1920.
Tertullian's Apology. J. E. B. Mayer (edit.). Cambridge, 1917.

Other Works

ARNOU, R. De 'platonismo' Patrum. Rome, 1935.

BALTHASAR, HANS VON. Présence et pensée. Essai sur la philosophie religieuse de Grégoire de Nysse. Paris, 1943.

BARDY, G. Clément d'Alexandrie. Paris, 1926.

BAYLIS, H. J. Minucius Felix. London, 1928.

DANIÉLOU, J. Platonisme et théologie mystique. Essai sur la doctrine spirituelle de saint Grégoire de Nysse. Paris, 1944.

DIEKAMP, F. Die Gotteslehre des heiligen Gregor von Nyssa. Münster, 1896.

ERMONI, V. Saint Jean Damascène. Paris, 1904.

FAIRWEATHER, W. Origen and the Greek Patristic Philosophy. London, 1901.

FAYE, E. DE. Gnostiques et gnosticisme. Paris, 1925 (2nd edition).

HITCHCOCK, F. R. MONTGOMERY. Irenaeus of Lugdunum. Cambridge, 1914.

LEBRETON, J. Histoire du dogme de la Trinité. Paris, 1910.

MONDÉSERT, C. Clément d'Alexandrie. Lyons, 1944.

MORGAN, J. The Importance of Tertullian in the development of Christian dogma. London, 1928.

PICHON, R. Étude sur les mouvements philosophiques et religieux sous le règne de Constantin. Paris, 1903.

PRESTIGE, G. L. God in Patristic Thought. London, 1936.

PUECH, A. Histoire de la littérature grecque chrétienne depuis les origines jusqu'à la fin du IVe siècle. 3 vols. Paris, 1928–30.

RIVIÈRE, J. Saint Basile, évêque de Césarée. Paris, 1930.

THAMIN, R. Saint Ambroise et la morale chrétienne au IVe siècle. Paris, 1895.

Chapters III–VIII: St. Augustine

Texts

Patrologia Latina (Migne), vols. 32–47.
Corpus scriptorum ecclesiasticorum latinorum, vols. 12, 25, 28, 33, 34, 36, 40, 41–4, 51–3, 57, 58, 60, 63 . . .
City of God. 2 vols. (Everyman Edition). London, 1945.
Confessions. F. J. Sheed. London, 1943.
The Letters of St. Augustine. W. J. Sparrow-Simpson (edit.). London, 1919.

Studies on Augustine

BARDY, G. Saint Augustin. Paris, 1946 (6th edition).
BOURKE, V. J. Augustine's Quest of Wisdom. Milwaukee, 1945.
BOYER, C. Christianisme et néo-platonisme dans la formation de saint Augustin. Paris, 1920.
L'idée de vérité dans la philosophie de saint Augustin. Paris, 1920.
Essais sur la doctrine de saint Augustin. Paris, 1932.
COMBES, G. La doctrine politique de saint Augustin. Paris, 1927.
FIGGIS, J. N. The Political Aspects of St. Augustine's City of God. London, 1921.
GILSON, E. Introduction à l'étude de saint Augustin. Paris, 1943 (2nd edition).
GRABMANN, M. Der göttliche Grund menschlicher Wahrheitserkenntnis nach Augustinus and Thomas von Aquin. Cologne, 1924.
Die Grundgedanken des heiligen Augustinus über Seele und Gott. Cologne, 1929 (2nd edition).
HENRY, P. L'extase d'Ostie. Paris, 1938.
HESSEN, J. Augustins Metaphysik der Erkenntnis. Berlin, 1931.
LE BLOND, J. M. Les conversions de saint Augustin. Paris, 1948.
MARTIN, J. La doctrine sociale de saint Augustin. Paris, 1912.
Saint Augustin. Paris, 1923 (2nd edition).
MAUSBACH, J. Die Ethik des heiligen Augustinus. 2 vols. Freiburg, 1929 (2nd edition).
MESSENGER, E. C. Evolution and Theology. London, 1931. (For Augustine's theory of *rationes seminales*.)
MUÑOZ VEGA, P. Introducción a la síntesis de San Augustin. Rome, 1945.
PORTALIÉ, E. Augustin, saint. Dictionnaire de théologie catholique, vol. I. Paris, 1902.
SWITALSKI, B. Neoplatonism and the Ethics of St. Augustine. New York, 1946.

Publications for 15th centenary of St. Augustine

A Monument to St. Augustine. London, 1930.

Aurelius Augustinus. Cologne, 1930.

S. Agostino. Milan, 1931.

Études sur S. Augustin. *Archives de Philosophie*, vol. 7, cahier 2. Paris, 1930.

Religion y Cultura. XV Centenario de la Muerte de San Augustin. Madrid, 1931.

Mélanges augustiniens. Paris, 1930.

Miscellanea agostiniana. 2 vols. Rome, 1930–1.

Chapter IX: The Pseudo-Dionysius

Texts

Patrologia Graeca, vols. 3–4.

Dionysius the Areopagite on the Divine Names and the Mystical Theology. C. E. Rolt (edit.). London, 1920.

Chapter X: Boethius, Cassiodorus, Isidore

Texts

Patrologia Latina (Migne); vols. 63–4 (Boethius), 69–70 (Cassiodorus), 81–4 (Isidore).

BOETHIUS. The Theological Tractates and The Consolation of Philosophy. H. F. Stewart and E. K. Rand (edit.). London, 1926.

De Consolatione Philosophiae. A. Fortescue (edit.). London, 1925.

Studies

BARRETT, H. M. Boethius: Some Aspects of his Times and Work. Cambridge, 1940.

PATCH, H. R. The Tradition of Boethius, a Study of his Importance in Medieval Culture. New York, 1935.

RAND, E. K. Founders of the Middle Ages; ch. 5, Boethius the Scholastic. Harvard U.P., 1941.

Chapter XI: The Carolingian Renaissance

Texts

Patrologia Latina (Migne); vols. 100–1 (Alcuin), 107–12 (Rhabanus Maurus).

Studies

BUXTON, E. M. WILMOT. Alcuin. London, 1922.

LAISTNER, M. L. W. Thought and Letters in Western Europe, A.D. 500–900. London, 1931.

TAYLOR, H. O. The Mediaeval Mind, vol. 1. London, 1911.

TURNAU, D. Rabanus Maurus praeceptor Germaniae. Munich, 1900.

Chapters XII–XIII: John Scotus Eriugena

Texts

Patrologia Latina (Migne); vol. 122.

Selections (in English) in *Selections from Mediaeval Philosophers*, vol. 1, by R. McKeon. London, 1930.

Studies

BETT, H. Johannes Scotus Eriugena, a Study in Mediaeval Philosophy. Cambridge, 1925.

CAPPUYNS, M. Jean Scot Erigène, sa vie, son œuvre, sa pensée. Paris, 1933.

SCHNEIDER, A. Die Erkenntnislehre des Johannes Eriugena im Rahmen ihrer metaphysischen und anthropologischen Voraussetzungen. 2 vols. Berlin, 1921–3.

SEUL, W. Die Gotteserkenntnis bei Johannes Skotus Eriugena unter Berücksichtigung ihrer neo-platonischen und augustinischen Elemente. Bonn, 1932.

Chapter XIV: The Problem of Universals

Texts

Patrologia Latina (Migne); vols. 105 (Fredegisius), 139 (Gerbert of Aurillac), 144–5 (St. Peter Damian), 158–9 (St. Anselm), 160 (Odo of Tournai), 163 (William of Champeaux), 178 (Abelard), 188 (Gilbert de la Porrée), 199 (John of Salisbury), 175–7 (Hugh of St. Victor).

B. GEYER. Die philosophischen Schriften Peter Abelards. 4 vols. Münster, 1919–33.

Selections from Abelard in *Selections from Mediaeval Philosophers*, vol. 1, by R. McKeon. London, 1930.

Studies

BERTHAUD, A. Gilbert de la Porrée et sa philosophie. Poitiers, 1892.

CARRÉ, M. H. Realists and Nominalists. Oxford, 1946.

COUSIN, V. Ouvrages inédits d'Abélard. Paris, 1836.

DE WULF, M. Le problème des universaux dans son évolution historique du IXe au XIIIe siècle. Archiv für Geschichte der Philosophie, 1896.

LEFÈVRE, G. Les variations de Guillaume de Champeaux et la question des universaux. Lille, 1898.

OTTAVIANO, C. Pietro Abelardo, La vita, le opere, il pensiero. Rome, 1931.

PICAVET, F. Gerbert ou le pape philosophe. Paris, 1897.
Roscelin philosophe et théologien, d'après la légende et d'après l'histoire. Paris, 1911.

REINERS, J. Der aristotelische Realismus in der Frühscholastik. Bonn, 1907.
Der Nominalismus in der Frühscholastik. Münster, 1910 (Beiträge, 8, 5).

REMUSAT, C. DE. Abaelard. 2 vols. Paris, 1845.

SICKES, J. G. Peter Abaelard. Cambridge, 1932.

Chapter XV: St. Anselm of Canterbury

Texts

Patrologia Latina (Migne); vols. 158–9.

Studies

BARTH, K. Fides quaerens intellectum. Anselms Beweis der Existenz Gottes im Zusammenhang seines theologischen Programms. Munich, 1931.

FISCHER, J. Die Erkenntnislehre Anselms von Canterbury. Münster, 1911 (Beiträge, 10, 3).

FILLIÂTRE, C. La philosophie de saint Anselme, ses principes, sa nature, son influence. Paris, 1920.

GILSON, E. Sens et nature de l'argument de saint Anselme, in *Archives d'histoire doctrinale et littéraire du moyen âge*, 1934.

KOYRÉ, A. L'idée de Dieu dans la philosophie de saint Anselme. Paris, 1923.

LEVASTI, A. Sant' Anselmo, Vita e pensiero. Bari, 1929.

Chapter XVI: The School of Chartres

Texts

Patrologia Latina (Migne); vols. 199 (John of Salisbury, containing also fragments of Bernard of Chartres, columns 666 and 938), 90 (William of Conches's *Philosophia*, among works of Bede).

JANSSEN, W. Der Kommentar des Clarembaldus von Arras zu Boethius De Trinitate. Breslau, 1926.

BARACH, C. S. & WROBEL, J. Bernardus Silvestris, De mundi universitate libri duo. Innsbruck, 1896.

WEBB, C. C. J. Metalogicon. Oxford, 1929.
Policraticus. 2 vols. Oxford, 1909.

Studies

CLERVAL, A. Les écoles de Chartres au moyen âge du Ve au XVIe siècle. Paris, 1895.

FLATTEN, H. Die Philosophie des Wilhelm von Conches. Coblenz, 1929.

SCHARSCHMIDT, C. Joannes Saresberiensis nach Leben und Studien, Schriften und Philosophie. Leipzig, 1862.

WEBB, C. C. J. John of Salisbury. London, 1932.

Chapter XVII: The School of St. Victor

Texts

Patrologia Latina (Migne); vols. 175–7 (Hugh), 196 (Richard and Godfrey).

Studies

EBNER, J. Die Erkenntnislehre Richards von Sankt Viktor. Münster, 1917 (Beiträge, 19, 4).

ETHIER, A. M. Le De Trinitate de Richard de Saint-Victor. Paris, 1939.

KILGENSTEIN, J. Die Gotteslehre des Hugo von Sankt Viktor. Würzburg, 1897.

MIGNON, A. Les origines de la scolastique et Hugues de Saint-Victor. 2 vols. Paris, 1895.

OSTLER, H. Die Psychologie des Hugo von Sankt Viktor. Münster, 1906 (Beiträge, 6, 1).

VERNET, F. Hugues de Saint-Victor. Dictionnaire de théologie catholique, vol. 7.

Chapter XVIII: Dualists and Pantheists

ALPHANDÉRY, P. Les idées morales chez les hétérodoxes latins au début du XIIIe siècle. Paris, 1903.

BROEKX, E. Le catharisme. Louvain, 1916.

CAPELLE, G. C. Autour du décret de 1210: III, Amaury de Bène, Étude sur son panthéisme formel. Paris, 1932 (Bibliothèque thomiste, 16).

RUNCIMAN, S. The Mediaeval Manichee. Cambridge, 1947.

THÉRY, G. Autour du décret de 1210: I, David de Dinant, Étude sur son panthéisme matérialiste. Paris, 1925 (Bibliothèque thomiste, 6).

Chapter XIX: Islamic Philosophy

Texts

ALFARABI. Alpharabius de intelligentiis, philosophia prima. Venice, 1508.

Alfarabis philosophische Abhandlungen, aus dem arabischen übersetzt. Fr. Dieterici. Leiden, 1892.

Alfarabi über den Ursprung der Wissenschaften. Cl. Baeumker. Münster, 1933.

Alfarabius de Platonis Philosophia. Edited by F. Rosenthal and R. Walzer. Plato Arabus, vol. 2. London, Warburg Institute, 1943.

ALGAZEL. Alagazel's Metaphysics, a Mediaeval Translation. Toronto, 1933.

AVICENNA. Avicennae Opera. Venice, 1495–1546.

Avicennae Metaphysices Compendium. Rome, 1926 (Latin).

AVERROES. Aristotelis opera omnia, Averrois in ea opera commentaria. 11 vols. Venice.
Die Epitome der Metaphysik des Averroës. S. Van den Bergh. Leiden, 1924.
Accord de la religion et de la philosophie, traité d'Ibn Rochd (Averroes), traduit et annoté. L. Gauthier. Algiers, 1905.

Studies: General

BOER, T. J. DE. History of Philosophy in Islam. Translated by E. R. Jones. London, 1903.
CARRA DE VAUX, B. Les penseurs d'Islam. 5 vols. Paris, 1921–6.
GAUTHIER, L. Introduction à l'étude de la philosophie musulmane. Paris, 1923.
MUNK, S. Mélanges de philosophie juive et arabe. Paris, 1927.
O'LEARY, DE LACY. Arabic Thought and its place in History. London, 1922.
The Legacy of Islam. T. Arnold and A. Guillaume (edit.). Oxford, 1931.

Particular

ALONSO, M. Teologia de Averroes. Madrid-Granada, 1947.
ASÍN Y PALACIOS, M. Algazel: Dogmatica, moral, ascética. Saragossa, 1901.
CARRA DE VAUX, B. Gazali. Paris, 1902.
Avicenne. Paris, 1900.
GAUTHIER, L. La théorie d'Ibn Rochd sur les rapports de la religion et de la philosophie. Paris, 1909.
Ibn Roschd (Averroès). Paris, 1948.
GOICHON, A. M. Introduction à Avicenne. Paris, 1933.
La distinction de l'essence et de l'existence d'après Ibn Sīnā (Avicenna). Paris, 1937.
La philosophie d'Avicenne. Paris, 1944.
HORTEN, M. Die Metaphysik des Averroës. Halle, 1912.
KLEINE, W. Die Substanzlehre Avicennas bei Thomas von Aquin. Fribourg, 1933.
RENAN, E. Averroès et l'averroisme. Paris, 1869 (3rd edition).
SALIBA, D. Étude sur la métaphysique d'Avicenne. Paris, 1927.
SMITH, M. Al-Ghazālī, the Mystic. London, 1944.
SWEETMAN, J. W. Islam and Christian Theology, vol. 1. London 1945.
WENSINCK, A. J. La Pensée de Ghazzālī. Paris, 1940.

Chapter XX: Jewish Philosophy

Texts

Avencebrolis Fons Vitae, ex arabico in latinum translatus ab Johanne Hispano et Dominico Gundissalino. Münster, 1892–5.

MAIMONIDES. Le guide des égarés, traité de théologie et de philosophie. 3 vols. Paris, 1856–66.

Studies

GUTTMANN, J. Die Philosophie des Judentums. Munich, 1933.
HUSIK, I. A History of Mediaeval Jewish Philosophy. New York, 1918.
LEVY, L. G. Maïmonide. Paris, 1932 (2nd edition).
MUNK, S. Mélanges de philosophie juive et arabe. Paris, 1927.
MUNZ, J. Moses ben Maimon, sein Leben und seine Werke. Frankfurt am M., 1912.
ROHNER, A. Das Schöpfungsproblem bei Moses Maimonides, Albertus Magnus und Thomas von Aquin. Münster, 1913 (Beiträge, 11, 5).
ROTH, L. Spinoza, Descartes and Maimonides. Oxford, 1924.

Chapter XXI: The Translations

See the bibliography in M. De Wulf's *Histoire de la philosophie médiévale*, vol. 2, 6th French edition. (In the English translation by Dr. E. C. Messenger the bibliography and the sections by A. Pelzer on the translations have been abridged.) See also B. Geyer's *Die patristische und scholastische Philosophie* (1928), pp. 342–51, with the corresponding bibliography, p. 728.

Chapter XXII: Introduction (to Thirteenth Century)

BONNEROT, J. La Sorbonne, sa vie, son rôle, son œuvre à travers les siècles. Paris, 1927.
DENIFLE, H. and CHATELAIN, A. Chartularium Universitatis Parisiensis. 4 vols. Paris, 1889–97.
Auctuarium Chartularii Universitatis Parisiensis. 2 vols. Paris, 1894–7.
Les universités françaises au moyen âge. Paris, 1892.
GLORIEUX, P. Répertoire des maîtres en théologie de Paris au XIIIe siècle. 2 vols. Paris, 1933–4.
GRABMANN, M. I divieti ecclesiastici di Aristotele sotto Innocenzo e Gregorio IX. Rome, 1941.
LITTLE, A. G. The Grey Friars in Oxford. Oxford, 1892.
RASHDALL, H. The Universities of Europe in the Middle Ages. New edition, edited by F. M. Powicke and A. B. Emden. 3 vols. Oxford, 1936.
SHARP, D. E. Franciscan Philosophy at Oxford in the Thirteenth Century. Oxford, 1936.

Texts *Chapter XXIII: William of Auvergne*

Opera. 2 vols. Paris, 1674.

Studies

BAUMGARTNER, M. Die Erkenntnislehre des Wilhelm von Auvergne. Münster, 1895 (Beiträge, 2, 1).

MASNOVO, A. Da Guglielmo d'Auvergne a San Tommaso d'Aquino. Milan, vol. 1 (1930 and 1945); vol. 2 (1934 and 1946); vol. 3 (1945).

Texts *Chapter XXIV: Robert Grosseteste and Alexander of Hales*

Die philosophischen Werke des Robert Grosseteste, Bischof von Lincoln. L. Baur. Münster, 1912 (Beiträge, 9).

THOMSON, S. H. The Writings of Robert Grosseteste, Bishop of Lincoln, 1175–1253. Cambridge, 1940 (Bibliographical).

Doctoris irrefragabilis Alexandri de Hales, O.M. Summa Theologica. 3 vols. Quaracchi, 1924–30.

Studies

BAUR, L. Die Philosophie des Robert Grosseteste. Münster, 1917 (Beiträge, 18, 4–6).

For Alexander of Hales, see introduction to Quaracchi critical edition (*supra*).

Text *Chapters XXV–XXIX: St. Bonaventure*

Opera omnia. 10 vols. Quaracchi, 1882–1902.

Studies

BISSEN, J. M. L'exemplarisme divin selon saint Bonaventure. Paris, 1929.

DE BENEDICTIS, M. M. The Social Thought of Saint Bonaventure. Washington, 1946.

GILSON, E. The Philosophy of St. Bonaventure. London, 1938.

GRÜNEWALD, S. Franziskanische Mystik. Versuch zu einer Darstellung mit besonderer Berücksichtigung des heiligen Bonaventura. Munich, 1931.

LUTZ, E. Die Psychologie Bonaventuras. Münster, 1909 (Beiträge, 6, 4–5).

LUYCKX, B. A. Die Erkenntnislehre Bonaventuras. Münster, 1923 (Beiträge, 23, 3–4).

O'DONNELL, C. M. The Psychology of St. Bonaventure and St. Thomas Aquinas. Washington, 1937.

ROBERT, P. Hylémorphisme et devenir chez S. Bonaventure. Montreal, 1936.

ROSENMÖLLER, B. Religiöse Erkenntnis nach Bonaventura. Münster, 1925 (Beiträge, 25, 3–4).

Texts *Chapter XXX: St. Albert the Great*

Opera Omnia. A Borgnet. 38 vols. Paris, 1890–9. (See also G. Meersseman. Introductio in opera omnia beati Alberti Magni, O.P. Bruges, 1931.)

De vegetalibus. C. Jessen. Berlin, 1867.

De animalibus. H. Stradler. Münster, 1916 (Beiträge, 15–16).

Studies

ARENDT, W. Die Staats- und Gesellschaftslehre Alberts des Grossen nach den Quellen daargestellt. Jena, 1929.

BALES, H. Albertus Magnus als Zoologe. Munich, 1928.

FRONOBER, H. Die Lehre von der Materie und Form nach Albert dem Grossen. Breslau, 1909.

GRABMANN, M. Der Einfluss Alberts des Grossen auf das mittelalterliche Geistesleben, in *Mittelalterliches Geistesleben*, vol. 2. Munich, 1936.

LIERTZ, R. Der selige Albert der Grosse als Naturforscher und Lehrer. Munich, 1931.

REILLY, G. C. Psychology of St. Albert the Great compared with that of St. Thomas. Washington, 1934.

SCHEEBEN, H. C. Albertus Magnus. Bonn, 1932.

SCHMIEDER, K. Alberts des Grossen Lehre von natürlichem Gotteswissen. Freiburg im/B., 1932.

SCHNEIDER, A. Die Psychologie Alberts des Grossen. Münster, 1903–6 (Beiträge, 4, 5–6).

Texts *Chapters XXXI–XLI: St. Thomas Aquinas*

Opera omnia (Leonine edition). Rome, 1882. So far 15 vols. have been published.

Opera omnia (Parma edition). 25 vols. Parma, 1852–73. Reprint, New York, 1948.

Opera omnia (Vivès edition). 34 vols. Paris, 1872–80.

The English Dominican Fathers have published translations of the *Summa theologica*, the *Summa contra Gentiles*, and the *Quaestiones disputatae*. London (B.O.W.) There is a volume of selections (in English) in the Everyman Library, London.

Basic Writings of St. Thomas Aquinas, edit. A. Pegis. 2 vols. New York, 1945.

Bibliography

BOURKE, V. J. Thomistic Bibliography, 1920–40. St. Louis Mo, U.S.A., 1945.

GRABMANN, M. Die echten Schriften des heiligen Thomas von Aquin. Münster, 1920.

(2nd edition) Die Werke des heiligen Thomas von Aquin. Münster, 1931.

MANDONNET, P. Des écrits authentiques de St. Thomas. Fribourg (Switzerland), 1910 (2nd edition).

MANDONNET, P. and DESTREZ, J. Bibliographie thomiste. Paris, 1921.

Life

CHESTERTON, G. K. St. Thomas Aquinas. London, 1933, 1947.

DE BRUYNE, E. St. Thomas d'Aquin, Le milieu, l'homme, la vision du monde. Brussels, 1928.

GRABMANN, M. Das Seelenleben des heiligen Thomas von Aquin. Munich, 1924.

General Studies

D'ARCY, M. C. Thomas Aquinas. London, 1931.

DE BRUYNE, E. See above.

GILSON, E. Le Thomisme. Paris, 1944 (5th edition).
English translation, *The Philosophy of St. Thomas Aquinas*. Cambridge, 1924, 1930, 1937.

LATTEY, C. (editor). St. Thomas Aquinas. London, 1924. (Cambridge Summer School Papers.)

MANSER, G. M. Das Wesen des Thomismus. Fribourg (Switzerland), 1931.

MARITAIN, J. St. Thomas Aquinas. London, 1946 (3rd edition).

OLIGIATI, F. A Key to the Study of St. Thomas. Translated by J. S. Zybura. St. Louis (U.S.A.), 1925.

PEILLAUBE, E. Initiation à la philosophie de S. Thomas. Paris, 1926.

RIMAUD, J. Thomisme et méthode. Paris, 1925.

SERTILLANGES, A. D. Foundations of Thomistic philosophy.
Translated by G. Anstruther. London, 1931.
S. Thomas d'Aquin. 2 vols. Paris, 1925. (4th edition).

VANN, G. Saint Thomas Aquinas. London, 1940.

Metaphysics

FINANCE, J. DE. Être et agir dans la philosophie de S. Thomas. Bibliothèque des Archives de philosophie. Paris, 1945.

FOREST, A. La structure métaphysique du concret selon S. Thomas d'Aquin. Paris, 1931.

GILSON, E. L'Être et l'essence. Paris, 1948.

GRABMANN, M. Doctrina S. Thomae de distinctione reali inter essentiam et esse ex documentis ineditis saeculi XIII illustrata. Rome, 1924. (Acta hebdomadae thomisticae.)

HABBEL, J. Die Analogie zwischen Gott und Welt nach Thomas von Aquin und Suarez. Fribourg (Switzerland), 1929.

MARC, A. L'idée de l'être chez S. Thomas et dans la scolastique postérieure. Paris, 1931. (Archives de philosophie, 10, 1.)

PIEPER, J. Die Wirklichkeit und das Gute nach Thomas von Aquin. Münster, 1934.

RÉGNON, T. DE. La métaphysique des causes d'après S. Thomas et Albert le Grand. Paris, 1906.

ROLAND-GOSSELIN, M. D. Le 'De ente et essentia' de S. Thomas d'Aquin. Paris, 1926. (Bibliothèque thomiste, 8.)

SCHULEMANN, G. Das Kausalprinzip in der Philosophie des heiligen Thomas von Aquin. Münster, 1915 (Beiträge, 13, 5).

WÉBERT, J. Essai de métaphysique thomiste. Paris, 1926.

And see General Studies.

Natural Theology

GARRIGOU-LAGRANGE, R. God: His Existence and His Nature. 2 vols. Translated by B. Rose. London, 1934–6.

PATTERSON, R. L. The Concept of God in the Philosophy of Aquinas. London, 1933.

ROLFES, E. Die Gottesbeweise bei Thomas von Aquin und Aristoteles. Limburg a.d. Lahn, 1927 (2nd edition).

And see General Studies.

Cosmology

BEEMELMANNS, F. Zeit und Ewigkeit nach Thomas von Aquin. Münster, 1914 (Beiträge, 17, 1).

CHOISNARD, P. Saint Thomas d'Aquin et l'influence des astres. Paris, 1926.

CORNOLDI, G. M. The Physical System of St. Thomas. Translated by E. H. Dering. London, 1895.

MARLING, J. M. The Order of Nature in the Philosophy of St. Thomas Aquinas. Washington, 1934.

And see General Studies.

Psychology

LOTTIN, O. Psychologie et morale aux XIIe et XIII siècles. Tome 1 Problèmes de Psychologie. Louvain, 1942.

MONAHAN, W. B. The Psychology of St. Thomas Aquinas. London, no date.

O'MAHONY, L. E. The Desire of God in the Philosophy of St. Thomas Aquinas. London, 1929.

PEGIS, A. C. St. Thomas and the Problem of the Soul in the Thirteenth Century. Toronto, 1934.

And see General Studies.

Knowledge

GRABMANN, M. Der göttliche Grund menschlicher Wahrheitserkenntnis nach Augustinus und Thomas von Aquin. Cologne, 1924.

HUFNAGEL, A. Intuition und Erkenntnis nach Thomas von Aquin. Cologne, 1924.

MARÉCHAL, J. Le point de départ de la métaphysique. Cahier 5; Le thomisme devant la philosophie critique. Louvain, 1926.

MEYER, H. Die Wissenschaftslehre des Thomas von Aquin. Fulda, 1934.

NOEL, L. Notes d'épistémologie thomiste. Louvain, 1925.

PÉGHAIRE, J. Intellectus et Ratio selon S. Thomas d'Aquin. Paris, 1936.

RAHNER, K. Geist in Welt. Zur Metaphysik der endlichen Erkenntnis bei Thomas von Aquin. Innsbruck, 1939.

ROMEYER, B. S. Thomas et notre connaissance de l'esprit humain. Paris, 1928 (Archives de philosophie, 6, 2).

ROUSSELOT, P. The Intellectualism of St. Thomas. Translated by Fr. James, O.S.F.C. London, 1935.

TONQUÉDEC, J. DE. Les principes de la philosophie thomiste. La critique de la connaissance. Paris, 1929 (Bibliothèque des Archives de philosophie).

VAN RIET, G. L'épistémologie thomiste. Louvain, 1946.

WILPERT, P. Das Problem der Wahrheitssicherung bei Thomas von Aquin. Münster, 1931 (Beiträge, 30, 3).

Moral Theory

GILSON, E. S. Thomas d'Aquin. (Les moralistes chrétiens.) Paris, 1941 (6th edition).

LEHU, L. La raison règle de la moralité d'après St. Thomas d'Aquin. Paris, 1930.

LOTTIN, O. Le droit naturel chez S. Thomas et ses prédécesseurs. Bruges, 1926.

PIEPER, J. Die ontische Grundlage des Sittlichen nach Thomas von Aquin. Münster, 1929.

ROUSSELOT, P. Pour l'histoire du problème de l'amour au moyen âge. Münster, 1908 (Beiträge, 6, 6).

SERTILLANGES, A. D. La Philosophie Morale de S. Thomas d'Aquin. Paris, 1942 (new edition).

Political Theory

DEMONGEOT, M. Le meilleur régime politique selon S. Thomas. Paris, 1928.

GRABMANN, M. Die Kulturphilosophie des heiligen Thomas von Aquin. Augsburg, 1925.

KURZ, E. Individuum und Gemeinschaft beim heiligen Thomas von Aquin. Freiburg im/B., 1932.

MICHEL, G. La notion thomiste du bien commun. Paris, 1932.

ROCCA, G. DELLA. La politica di S. Tommaso. Naples, 1934.

ROLAND-GOSSELIN, B. La doctrine politique de S. Thomas d'Aquin. Paris, 1928.

Aesthetic Theory

DE WULF, M. Études historiques sur l'esthétique de S. Thomas d'Aquin. Louvain, 1896.

DYROFF, A. Über die Entwicklung und den Wert der Aesthetik des Thomas von Aquino. Berlin, 1929 (Festgabe Ludwig Stern).

MARITAIN, J. Art and Scholasticism. London, 1930.

Controversies

EHRLE, F. Der Kampf um die Lehre des heiligen Thomas von Aquin in den ersten fünfzig Jahren nach seinem Tode. In *Zeitschrift für katholische Theologie*, 1913.

Chapter XLII: Latin Averroism: Siger of Brabant

Texts

BAEUMKER, C. Die Impossibilia des Siger von Brabant. Münster, 1898 (Beiträge, 2, 6).

BARSOTTI, R. Sigeri de Brabant. De aeternitate mundi. Münster, 1933 (Opuscula et Textus, 13).

DWYER, W. J. L'Opuscule de Siger de Brabant 'De Aeternitate Mundi'. Louvain, 1937.

GRABMANN, M. Die Opuscula De summo bono sive de vita philosophi und De sompniis des Boetius von Dacien. In *Mittelalterliches Geistesleben*, vol. 2. 1936.
Neuaufgefundene Werke des Siger von Brabant und Boetius von Dacien. (Proceedings of the Academy of Munich, Philosophy.) 1924.

MANDONNET, P. Siger de Brabant et l'averroïsme latin. (Les Philosophes Belges, 6.) Louvain, 1908, 1911.

STEGMÜLLER, F. Neugefundene Quaestionen des Sigers von Brabant. In *Recherches de théologie ancienne et médiévale*, 1931.

VAN STEENBERGHEN, F. Siger de Brabant d'après ses œuvres inédits. (Les Philosophes Belges, 12.) Louvain, 1931.

Studies

BAEUMKER, C. Zur Beurteilung Sigers von Brabant. In *Philosophisches Jahrbuch*, 1911.

MANDONNET, P. See above (Les Philosophes Belges, 6–7).

OTTAVIANO, C. S. Tommaso d'Aquino, Saggio contro la dottrina avveroistica dell'unita dell'intelletto. Lanciano, 1930.

SASSEN, F. Siger de Brabant et la double vérité. *Revue néo-scolastique*, 1931.

VAN STEENBERGHEN, F. Les œuvres et la doctrine de Siger de Brabant. Brussels, 1938.
See above (Les Philosophes Belges, 12–13).
Aristote en Occident. Louvain, 1946.

Chapter XLIII: Franciscan Thinkers

1. *Bacon: Texts*

BREWER, J. S. Fratris Rogeri Baconi opera quaedam hactenus inedita. London, 1859.

BRIDGES, J. H. The Opus Maius of Roger Bacon, 2 vols. Oxford, 1897.
Supplementary volume. Oxford, 1900.

BURKE, R. B. The Opus Maius of Roger Bacon. 2 vols. (English). Philadelphia, 1928.

RASHDALL, H. Fratris Rogeri Baconi Compendium studii theologiae. Aberdeen, 1911.

STEELE, R. Opera hactenus inedita Rogeri Baconi. 16 fascicules so far published. Oxford, 1905–40.

Studies

BAEUMKER, C. Roger Bacons Naturphilosophie. Münster, 1916.

CARTON, R. La synthèse doctrinale de Roger Bacon. Paris, 1929.
L'expérience mystique de l'illumination intérieure chez Roger Bacon. Paris, 1924.
L'expérience physique chez Roger Bacon, contribution à l'étude de la méthode et de la science expérimentale au XIIIe siècle. Paris, 1924.

CHARLES, E. Roger Bacon, sa vie, ses ouvrages, ses doctrines. Paris, 1861.

LITTLE, A. G. Roger Bacon, Essays contributed by various writers. Oxford, 1914.

2. *Matthew of Aquasparta: Texts*

Quaestiones disputatae de fide et de cognitione. Quaracchi, 1903.

A. Daniels (Beiträge, 8, 1–2; Münster, 1909) gives extracts from the Commentary on the *Sentences*.

Studies

LONGPRÉ, E. Matthieu d'Aquasparte. *Dictionnaire de théologie catholique*, vol. 10. 1928.

3. *Peter John Olivi: Texts*

B. Jansen. Petri Johannis Olivi Quaestiones in 2 librum Sententiarum. 3 vols. Quaracchi, 1922–6.

Petri Joannis Provencalis Quodlibeta. Venice, 1509.

Studies

CALLAEY, F. Olieu ou Olivi. *Dictionnaire de théologie catholique*, vol. 11. 1931.

JANSEN, B. Die Erkenntnislehre Olivis. Berlin, 1931.

Die Unsterblichkeitsbeweise bei Olivi und ihre philosophiegeschichtliche Bedeutung. In *Franziskanische Studien*. 1922.

Quonam spectet definitio Concilii Viennensis de anima. In *Gregorianum*, 1920.

4. *Roger Marston: Texts*

Fratris Rogeri Marston, O.F.M., Quaestiones disputatae. Quaracchi, 1932.

Studies

BELMOND, S. La théorie de la connaissance d'après Roger Marston. In *France franciscaine*, 1934.

GILSON, E. Roger Marston, un cas d'augustinisme avicennisant. In *Archives d'histoire doctrinale et littéraire du moyen âge*, 1932.

JARRAUX, L. Pierre Jean Olivi, sa vie, sa doctrine. In *Études franciscaines*, 1933.

PELSTER, F. Roger Marston, ein englischer Vertreter des Augustinismus. In *Scholastik*, 1928.

5. *Richard of Middleton: Texts*

Quodlibeta. Venice, 1509; Brescia, 1591.

Supra quatuor libros Sententiarum. 4 vols. Brescia, 1591.

Study

HOCEDEZ, E. Richard de Middleton, sa vie, ses œuvres, sa doctrine. Paris, 1925.

6. *Raymond Lull: Texts*

Opera omnia, I. Salzinger. 8 vols. Mainz, 1721–42.

Obras de Ramón Lull. Palma, 1745.

O. Keicher (see below) has published the *Declaratio Raymundi* in the Beiträge series.

Studies

BLANES, F. SUREDA. El beato Ramón Lull, su época, su vida, sus obras, sus empresas. Madrid, 1934.

CARRERAS Y ARTAU, T. & J. Historia de la Filosofia Española. Filosofia Christiana de los Siglos XIII al XIV. Vols. 1 and 2. Madrid, 1939–43.
KEICHER, O. Raymundus Lullus und seine Stellung zur arabischen Philosophie. Münster, 1909 (Beiträge, 7, 4–5).
LONGPRÉ, E. Lulle. In *Dictionnaire de théologie catholique*, vol. 9.
OTTAVIANO, C. L'ars compendiosa de Raymond Lulle. Paris, 1930.
PEERS, E. A. Fool of Love; the Life of Ramon Lull. London, 1946.
PROBST, J. H. Caractère et origine des idées du bienheureux Raymond Lulle. Toulouse, 1912.
La mystique de Raymond Lull et l'Art de Contemplation. Münster, 1914 (Beiträge, 13, 2–3).

Chapter XLIV: Giles of Rome and Henry of Ghent

1. *Giles of Rome: Texts*

Ancient editions. See Ueberweg-Geyer, Die patristische und scholastische Philosophie, pp. 532–3.
HOCEDEZ, E. Aegidii Romani Theoremata de esse et essentia, texte précedé d'une introduction historique et critique. Louvain, 1930.
KOCH, J. Giles of Rome; Errores Philosophorum. Critical Text with Notes and Introduction. Translated by J. O. Riedl. Milwaukee, 1944.
SCHOLZ, R. Aegidius Romanus, de ecclesiastica potestate. Weimar, 1929.

Studies

BRUNI, G. Egidio Romano e la sua polemica antitomista. In *Rivista di filosofia neoscolastica*, 1934.
HOCEDEZ, E. Gilles de Rome et saint Thomas. In *Mélanges Mandonnet*. Paris, 1930.
Gilles de Rome et Henri de Gand. In *Gregorianum*, 1927.

2. *Henry of Ghent: Texts*

Summa theologica. 2 vols. Paris, 1520; 3 vols. Ferrara, 1646.
Quodlibeta, 2 vols. Paris, 1518; Venice, 1608.

Studies

HOCEDEZ, E. Gilles de Rome et Henri de Gand. In *Gregorianum*, 1927.
PAULUS, J. Henri de Gand. Essai sur les tendances de sa métaphysique. Paris, 1938.

Chapters XLV–L: John Duns Scotus

Texts

WADDING, L. Opera Omnia. Lyons, 1639. 12 vols.
Opera Omnia (2nd edition). Paris (Vivès), 1891–5. 26 vols.

B. J. D. Scoti Commentaria Oxoniensia (on the first and second books of the *Sentences*). Quaracchi, 1912–14. 2 vols.

Tractatus de Primo Principio. Quaracchi, 1910.

MULLER, P. M., O.F.M. Tractatus de Primo Principio. Editionem curavit Marianius. Freiburg im/B., 1941.

The critical edition of Scotus's works is yet to come.
Cf. *Ratio criticae editionis operum omnium J. Duns Scoti Relatio a Commissione Scotistica exhibita Capitulo Generali Fratrum Minorum Assisii A.D.* 1939 *celebrato.* Rome, 1939.

For a summary of recent controversy and articles on the works of Scotus, as on his doctrine, cf.:

BETTONI, E., O.F.M. Vent'anni di Studi Scotisti (1920–40). Milan, 1943.

Studies

BELMOND, S., O.F.M. Essai de synthèse philosophique du Scotisme. Paris, Bureau de 'la France Franciscaine'. 1933.
Dieu. Existence et Cognoscibilité. Paris, 1913.

BETTONI, E., O.F.M. L'ascesa a Dio in Duns Scoto. Milan, 1943.

DE BASLY, D., O.F.M. Scotus Docens ou Duns Scot enseignant la philosophie, la théologie, la mystique. Paris, 'La France Franciscaine'. 1934.

GILSON, E. Avicenne et le point de départ de Duns Scot. Archives d'histoire doctrinale et littéraire du moyen âge, vol. 1, 1927.
Les seize premiers Theoremata et la pensée de Duns Scot. Archives d'histoire doctrinale et littéraire du moyen âge. 1937–8.

GRAJEWSKI, M. J., O.F.M. The Formal Distinction of Duns Scotus. Washington, 1944.

HARRIS, C. Duns Scotus. Oxford, 1927. 2 vols. (Makes copious use of the unauthentic *De Rerum Principio*.)

HEIDEGGER, M. Die Kategorien — und Bedeutungslehre des Duns Scotus. Tübingen, 1916.

KRAUS, J. Die Lehre des J. Duns Skotus von der Natura Communis. Fribourg (Switzerland), 1927.

LANDRY, B. Duns Scot. Paris, 1922.

LONGPRÉ, E., O.F.M. La philosophie du B. Duns Scot. Paris, 1924. (Contains a reply to Landry's work.)

MESSNER, R., O.F.M. Schauendes und begriffliches Erkennen nach Duns Skotus. Freiburg im/B., 1942.

MINGES, P., O.F.M. Der angeblich exzessive Realismus des Duns Skotus. 1908 (Beiträge, 8, 1).

J. Duns Scoti Doctrina Philosophica et Theologica quoad res praecipuas proposita et exposita. Quaracchi. 1930. 2 vols. (Cites spurious writings; but a very useful work.)

PELSTER, F. Handschriftliches zu Skotus mit neuen Angaben über sein Leben. Franzisk. Studien, 1923.

ROHMER, J. La finalité morale chez les théologiens dès saint Augustin à Duns Scot. Paris, 1939.

INDEX OF NAMES

(The principal references are printed in heavy figures. References followed by an asterisk refer to the Appendices)

INDEX OF SUBJECTS

A HISTORY OF PHILOSOPHY

VOLUME III

OCKHAM TO SUÁREZ

BY

FREDERICK COPLESTON, S.J.

CONTENTS

CONTENTS

APPENDICES

FOREWORD

THE first part of this volume is concerned with the philosophy of the fourteenth century. A good deal in the history of the philosophical thought of this period is still obscure, and no definitive account of it can be written until we have at our disposal a much greater number of reliable texts than are at present available. However, in publishing the account contained in this volume I am encouraged by the thought that the learned Franciscan scholar, Father Philotheus Boehner, who is doing so much to shed light on the dark places of the fourteenth century, was so kind as to read the chapters on Ockham and to express appreciation of their general tone. This does not mean, of course, that Father Boehner endorses all my interpretations of Ockham. In particular he does not agree with my view that analysis discloses two ethics implicitly contained in Ockham's philosophy. (This view is in any case, as I hope I have made clear in the text, a conjectural interpretation, developed in order to account for what may seem to be inconsistencies in Ockham's ethical philosophy.) And I do not think that Father Boehner would express himself in quite the way that I have done about Ockham's opinions on natural theology. I mention these differences of interpretation only in order that, while thanking Father Boehner for his kindness in reading the chapters on Ockham, I may not give the impression that he agrees with all that I have said. Moreover, as proofs were already coming in at the time the chapters reached Father Boehner, I was unable to make as extensive a use of his suggestions as I should otherwise wish to have done. In conclusion I should like to express the hope that when Father Boehner has published the texts of Ockham which he is editing he will add a general account of the latter's philosophy. Nobody would be better qualified to interpret the thought of the last great English philosopher of the Middle Ages.

CHAPTER I

INTRODUCTION

Thirteenth century—Fourteenth century contrasted with thirteenth—Philosophies of the Renaissance—Revival of Scholasticism.

1. In the preceding volume I traced the development of mediaeval philosophy from its birth in the pre-mediaeval period of the early Christian writers and Fathers through its growth in the early Middle Ages up to its attainment of maturity in the thirteenth century. This attainment of maturity was, as we have seen, largely due to that fuller acquaintance with Greek philosophy, particularly in the form of Aristotelianism, which took place in the twelfth century and the early part of the thirteenth. The great achievement of the thirteenth century in the intellectual field was the realization of a synthesis of reason and faith, philosophy and theology. Strictly speaking, of course, one should speak of 'syntheses' rather than of 'a synthesis', since the thought of the thirteenth century cannot legitimately be characterized with reference to one system alone; but the great systems of the period were, in spite of their differences, united by the acceptance of common principles. The thirteenth century was a period of positive constructive thinkers, of speculative theologians and philosophers, who might criticize one another's opinions in regard to this or that problem, but who at the same time were agreed in accepting fundamental metaphysical principles and the mind's power of transcending phenomena and attaining metaphysical truth. Scotus, for example, may have criticized St. Thomas's doctrines of knowledge and of analogy in certain points; but he criticized it in what he regarded, rightly or wrongly, as the interests of objectivity of knowledge and of metaphysical speculation. He considered that St. Thomas had to be corrected or supplemented in certain points; but he had no intention of criticizing the metaphysical foundations of Thomism or of undermining the objective character of philosophic speculation. Again, St. Thomas may have thought that more must be allowed to the unaided power of the human reason than was allowed to it by St. Bonaventure; but neither of these theologian-philosophers

doubted the possibility of attaining certain knowledge concerning the metaphenomenal. Men like St. Bonaventure, St. Thomas, Giles of Rome, Henry of Ghent and Duns Scotus were original thinkers; but they worked within the common framework of an ideal synthesis and harmony of theology and philosophy. They were speculative theologians and philosophers and were convinced of the possibility of forming a natural theology, the crown of metaphysics and the link with dogmatic theology; they were uninfected by any radical scepticism in regard to human knowledge. They were also realists, believing that the mind can attain an objective knowledge of essences.

This thirteenth-century ideal of system and synthesis, of harmony between philosophy and theology, can be viewed perhaps in relation to the general framework of life in that century. Nationalism was growing, of course, in the sense that the nation-States were in process of formation and consolidation; but the ideal of a harmony between papacy and empire, the supernatural and natural focuses of unity, was still alive. In fact, one can say that the ideal of harmony between papacy and empire was paralleled, on the intellectual plane, by the ideal of harmony between theology and philosophy, so that the doctrine as upheld by St. Thomas of the indirect power of the papacy in temporal matters and of the State's autonomy within what was strictly its own sphere was paralleled by the doctrine of the normative function of theology in regard to philosophy together with the autonomy of philosophy in its own sphere. Philosophy does not draw its principles from theology, but if the philosopher reaches a conclusion which is at variance with revelation, he knows that his reasoning is at fault. Papacy and empire, especially the former, were unifying factors in the ecclesiastical and political spheres, while the pre-eminence of the university of Paris was a unifying factor in the intellectual sphere. Moreover, the Aristotelian idea of the cosmos was generally accepted and helped to lend a certain appearance of fixity to the mediaeval outlook.

But though the thirteenth century may be characterized by reference to its constructive systems and its ideal of synthesis and harmony, the harmony and balance achieved were, at least from the practical standpoint, precarious. Some ardent Thomists would be convinced, no doubt, that the synthesis achieved by St. Thomas should have been universally accepted as valid and ought to have been preserved. They would not be prepared to admit that the balance and harmony of that synthesis were intrinsically precarious. But they would be prepared, I suppose, to admit that in practice it was scarcely to be expected that the Thomist synthesis, once achieved, would win universal and lasting acceptance. Moreover, there are, I think, elements inherent in the Thomist synthesis which rendered it, in a certain sense, precarious, and which help to explain the development of philosophy in the fourteenth century. I want now to illustrate what I mean.

The assertion that the most important philosophical event in mediaeval philosophy was the discovery by the Christian West of the more or less complete works of Aristotle is an assertion which could, I think, be defended. When the work of the translators of the twelfth century and of the early part of the thirteenth made the thought of Aristotle available to the Christian thinkers of western Europe, they were faced for the first time with what seemed to them a complete and inclusive rational system of philosophy which owed nothing either to Jewish or to Christian revelation, since it was the work of a Greek philosopher. They were forced, therefore, to adopt some attitude towards it: they could not simply ignore it. Some of the attitudes adopted, varying from hostility, greater or less, to enthusiastic and rather uncritical acclamation, we have seen in the preceding volume. St. Thomas Aquinas's attitude was one of critical acceptance: he attempted to reconcile Aristotelianism and Christianity, not simply, of course, in order to avert the dangerous influence of a pagan thinker or to render him innocuous by utilizing him for 'apologetic' purposes, but also because he sincerely believed that the Aristotelian philosophy was, in the main, true. Had he not believed this, he would not have adopted philosophical positions which, in the eyes of many contemporaries, appeared novel and suspicious. But the point I want to make at the moment is this, that in adopting a definite attitude towards Aristotelianism a thirteenth-century thinker was, to all intents and purposes, adopting an attitude towards *philosophy*. The significance of this fact has not always been realized by historians. Looking on mediaeval philosophers, especially those of the thirteenth century, as slavish adherents of Aristotle, they have not seen that Aristotelianism really meant, at that time, philosophy itself. Distinctions had already been drawn, it is true, between theology and philosophy; but it was the full appearance of Aristotelianism on the scene which showed the mediaevals the power and scope, as it were, of philosophy. Philosophy, under the guise of Aristotelianism, presented itself to their gaze as something which was not merely theoretically but also in historical fact independent of theology. This being so, to adopt an attitude towards Aristotelianism was, in effect, to adopt an attitude, not simply towards Aristotle as distinguished, for example, from Plato (of whom the mediaevals really did not know very much), but rather towards philosophy considered as an autonomous discipline. If we regard in this light the different attitudes adopted towards Aristotle in the thirteenth century, one obtains a profounder understanding of the significance of those differences.

(i) When the integral Aristotelians (or 'Latin Averroists') adopted the philosophy of Aristotle with uncritical enthusiasm and when they acclaimed Aristotle as the culmination of human genius, they found themselves involved in difficulties with the theologians. Aristotle held, for example, that the world was uncreated, whereas theology affirmed that the world had a beginning through divine creation. Again, Aristotle, as interpreted by Averroes, maintained that the intellect is one in all men and denied personal immortality whereas Christian theology maintained personal immortality. In face of these obvious difficulties the integral Aristotelians of the faculty of arts at Paris contended that the function of philosophy is to report faithfully the tenets of the philosophers. Therefore there was no contradiction involved in saying at the same time that philosophy, represented by Aristotle; taught the eternity of the world and the unicity of the human soul, while truth, represented by theology, affirmed the creation of the world in time and each man's possession of his individual rational soul.

This plea on the part of the integral Aristotelians or 'Averroists' that they were simply reporting the tenets of Aristotle, that is, that they were acting simply as historians, was treated by the theologians as a mere subterfuge. But, as I remarked in my second volume, it is difficult to ascertain what the mind of the Averroists really was. If, however, they really meant to do no more than report the opinions of past thinkers, and if they were sincere in affirming the truth of Christian revelation and theology, it would seem that their attitude must have been more or less this. Philosophy represents the work of the human reason reflecting on the natural order. Reason, personified by Aristotle, tells us that in the natural course of events time could have had no beginning and that the intellect would naturally be one in all men. That time had no beginning would thus be a philosophical truth; and the same must be said of monopsychism. But theology, which deals with the supernatural order, assures us that God by His divine power created the world in time and miraculously gave to each individual man his own immortal intellectual soul. It is not that something can be a fact and not a fact at the same time: it is rather that something would be a fact, were it not for God's miraculous intervention which has ensured that it is not a fact.

In regard to creative activity the position is, of course, exactly the same whether the integral Aristotelians of the faculty of arts at Paris were simply reporting Aristotle's teaching as they interpreted it, without reference to its truth or falsity, or whether they were affirming it as true. For in either case they did not add anything, at any rate not intentionally. It was the philosophers of the faculty of theology who were the productive and creative thinkers inasmuch as they felt compelled to examine Aristotelianism critically and, if they accepted it in the main, to rethink it critically. But the point I am trying to make is rather this. The position adopted by the integral Aristotelians implied a radical separation between theology and philosophy. If their own account of their activity is to be taken at its face value, they equated philosophy with history, with reporting the opinions of former philosophers. Philosophy understood in this sense is obviously independent of theology, for theology cannot affect the fact that certain opinions have been held by certain thinkers. If, on the other hand, the theologians were right in thinking that the integral Aristotelians really meant to assert the truth of the offending propositions, or if these propositions were asserted as propositions which would have been true, had not God intervened, the same conclusion concerning philosophy's complete independence of theology is implied. As the philosopher would be concerned merely with the natural course of events, he would be justified in drawing conclusions which conflicted with theological doctrine, since he would simply be asserting what would have been the case, had the natural course of events prevailed. Theology could tell us that a conclusion reached by philosophy did not represent the facts; but the theologian would not be justified in saying that the philosopher's reasoning was wrong simply because the conclusion at which he arrived was theologically unacceptable. We may learn from theology that the natural course of events has not been followed in some particular case; but that would not affect the question what the natural course of events is or would have been.

The most obviously salient features of the integral Aristotelianism or 'Averroism' of the thirteenth century were its slavish adherence to Aristotle and the rather desperate devices adopted by its adherents to square their position with the demands of theological orthodoxy. But implicit in integral Aristotelianism was a sharp separation between philosophy and theology, and an assertion of the former's complete independence. It is true that one should not over-emphasize this line of thought. The separation between theology and philosophy which was implicit in fourteenth-century Ockhamism did not derive from thirteenth-century 'Averroism'. But the appearance on the scene of the Aristotelian system in the thirteenth century was the factor which made it possible to give serious attention to the question of synthesis or separation, precisely because it led to the emergence of something which could be either synthesized or separated.

(ii) St. Thomas Aquinas recognized the distinction between philosophy and theology, in regard to both method and subject-matter. As I pointed out in the last volume, he took this distinction seriously. Though theology tells us that the world did not exist from eternity but had a beginning, no philosopher, according to St. Thomas, has ever adequately demonstrated this fact. The alleged proofs of the world's eternity are invalid, but so are the alleged proofs of the statement that the world did not exist from eternity. In other words, philosophy has not succeeded in solving the question whether the world was or was not created from eternity, though revelation does give us the answer to the question. This is an example of the real distinction which exists between philosophy and theology. On the other hand, St. Thomas certainly did not think that the philosopher could arrive, by valid rational argument, at any conclusion incompatible with Christian theology. If a philosopher arrives at a conclusion which contradicts, explicitly or implicitly, a Christian doctrine, that is a sign that his premisses are false or that there is a fallacy somewhere in his argument. In other words, theology acts as an external norm or as a kind of signpost, warning the philosopher off a cul-de-sac or blind alley. But the philosopher must not attempt to substitute data of revelation for premisses known by the philosophic reason. Nor can he make explicit use of dogma in his arguments. For philosophy is intrinsically autonomous.

In practice, this attitude meant that the philosopher who adopted it philosophized in the light of the faith, even if he did not make formal and explicit use of the faith in his philosophy. The maintenance of this attitude was, moreover, facilitated by the fact that the great thinkers of the thirteenth century were primarily theologians: they were theologian-philosophers. At the same time, once philosophy was recognized as an intrinsically autonomous discipline, it was only to be expected that it should tend in the course of time to go its own way and that it should, as it were, chafe at its bonds and resent its position as handmaid of theology. And indeed, once it had become a normal proceeding for philosophers to be primarily, and even exclusively, philosophers, it was natural that philosophy's alliance with theology should tend to disappear. Furthermore, when the philosophers had no firm belief in revelation, it was only to be expected that the positions of theology and philosophy should be reversed, and that philosophy should tend to subordinate theology to herself, to incorporate the subject-matter of theology in philosophy or even to exclude theology altogether. These developments lay, indeed, well in the future; but they may be said, without absurdity at least, to have had their remote origin in the appearance of the Aristotelian system on the scene in the early thirteenth century.

These remarks are not intended to constitute an evaluation of the Aristotelian philosophy; they are meant to be a historical interpretation of the actual course of development taken by philosophic thought. No doubt, they are somewhat too summary and do not allow for the complexity of philosophic development. Once philosophy had been recognized as an autonomous discipline, that process of self-criticism which would seem to be essential to philosophy set in, and, not unnaturally, the criticism, as it grew, undermined the foundations of the synthesis achieved in the thirteenth century. That is one of the reasons why I spoke of that synthesis as 'precarious'. Whatever one may think of the truth or falsity of Aristotelian metaphysics, for example, it was not to be expected that philosophic thought should stop at a particular point: criticism was, from the practical standpoint, inevitable. But there is a second factor to bear in mind. Once a closely-knit theological-philosophical synthesis had been achieved, in which philosophical terms and categories were used for the expression of theological truths, it was not unnatural that some minds should feel that faith was in danger of being rationalized and that Christian theology had become unduly contaminated with Greek and Islamic metaphysics. Such minds might feel that the mystical rather than the philosophical approach was what was needed, especially in view of the wrangling of the Schools on points of theoretical rather than of primarily religious significance and interest. This second line of thought would also tend to dissolve the thirteenth-century synthesis, though the approach was different from that of thinkers who concentrated on philosophical problems and undermined the synthesis by extensive and far-reaching criticism of the philosophic positions characteristic of that synthesis. We shall see how both lines of thought manifested themselves in the fourteenth century.

(iii) To turn to a different field, namely that of political life and thought. It would obviously be absurd to suggest that there was ever anything but a precarious harmony and balance between the ecclesiastical and civil powers in the Middle Ages: no profound knowledge of mediaeval history is required to be well aware of the constantly recurring disputes between pope and emperor and of the quarrels between popes and kings. The thirteenth century was enlivened by these disputes, especially by those between the emperor Frederick II and the Holy See. Nevertheless, although both parties sometimes made extravagant claims in their own favour, the quarrels were, so to speak, family quarrels: they took place within that mediaeval framework of papacy and empire which found a theoretical expression in the writings of Dante. Moreover, as far as the commonly held political theory was concerned, the distinction between the two powers was recognized. St. Thomas Aquinas who, living in Paris, was more concerned with kingdoms than with the empire, recognized the intrinsically autonomous character of temporal sovereignty, though he naturally also recognized the indirect power of the Church in temporal affairs which follows from the recognition of the superiority of the supernatural function of the Church.[1] If one keeps to the plane of theory, one can speak, therefore, of a balance or harmony between the two powers in the thirteenth century, provided that one does not obscure the fact that in practical life the harmony was not so very apparent. The plain fact is that those popes who entertained grandiose ambitions in regard to temporal power were unable to realize those ambitions, while

[1] The use of the phrase 'indirect power' involves an interpretation of Thomas's doctrine.

emperors who wished to do exactly as they chose without paying any attention to the Holy See were also unable to fulfil their desires. Triumphs on either side were temporary and not lasting. A certain balance, of a somewhat precarious nature, was therefore achieved.

At the same time, however, national kingdoms were becoming consolidated and the centralized power of national monarchs gradually increased. England had never been subject, in any practical sense, to the mediaeval emperor. Moreover, the empire was primarily a German affair; France, for instance, was independent; and the course taken by the dispute between Boniface VIII and Philip the Fair of France at the close of the thirteenth century showed clearly enough the position of France in relation both to the Holy See and to the empire. This growth of national kingdoms meant the emergence of a factor which would eventually destroy the traditional balance of papacy and empire. In the fourteenth century we witness the reflection, on the plane of theory, of the civil authority's growing tendency to assert its independence of the Church. The emergence of the strong national States, which became such a prominent feature of post-mediaeval Europe, began in the Middle Ages. They could hardly have developed in the way they did without the centralization and consolidation of power in the hands of local monarchs; and the process of this centralization and consolidation of power was certainly not retarded by the humiliation to which the papacy was exposed in the fourteenth century through the 'Babylonish captivity', when the popes were at Avignon (1305–77), and through the succeeding calamity of the 'Great Schism', which began in 1378.

The Aristotelian theory of the State could be, and was, utilized within the framework of the two-powers scheme by a thirteenth-century thinker like St. Thomas. This facilitated the theoretical recognition of the State as an intrinsically autonomous society, though it had to be supplemented by a Christian idea of the end of man and of the status and function of the Church. This 'addition' was not, however, simply an addition or juxtaposition; for it profoundly modified, by implication at least, the Greek outlook on the State. Conversely, by emphasizing the Aristotelianism in mediaeval political theory the position of the State could be stressed in such a way as practically to reverse the typical mediaeval conception of the proper relation between the two powers. We can see an example of this in the fourteenth century in the political theory of Marsilius of Padua. To say this is not to say, however, that Marsilius's theory was due to the Aristotelian philosophy: it was due much more, as we shall see later, to reflection on concrete historical events and situations. But it does mean that the Aristotelian theory of the State was a double-edged weapon; and that it not only could be but was utilized in a manner foreign to the mind of a theologian-philosopher like Aquinas. Its use represented, indeed, the growing political consciousness; and the phases of its use expressed the phases of the growth of that consciousness in concrete historical development.

2. If the thirteenth century was the period of creative and original thinkers, the fourteenth century may be called, in contrast, the period of Schools. The Dominicans naturally tended to adhere to the doctrines of St. Thomas Aquinas: and a series of injunctions by various Dominican Chapters encouraged them to do so. A number of works on the texts of St. Thomas appeared. Thus, at the request of Pope John XXII, Joannes Dominici composed an *Abbreviatio* or compendium of the *Summa theologica*, which he finished in 1331, while another Dominican, Benedict of Assignano (d. 1339), wrote a *Concordance*, in which he tried to show how the doctrine of the *Summa theologica* harmonized with that of St. Thomas's commentary on the *Sentences*. Then there were the commentators on, or interpreters of, St. Thomas, Dominicans like Hervaeus Natalis (d. 1323), who wrote a *Defensa doctrinae D. Thomae* and attacked Henry of Ghent, Duns Scotus and others, or John of Naples (d. 1330). But it was the fifteenth century, with John Capreolus (*c.* 1380–1444), rather than the fourteenth century, which was distinguished for achievement in this field. Capreolus was the most eminent commentator on St. Thomas before Cajetan (1468–1534).

Besides the Thomists there were the Scotists, who formed a rival school to the former, though Duns Scotus was not, in the fourteenth century, the official Doctor of the Franciscans in the same way that St. Thomas was the official Doctor of the Dominicans. In addition, there were the Hermits of St. Augustine, who followed the teaching of Giles of Rome. Henry of Ghent also had his followers, though they did not form a compact school.

In the fourteenth century these groups together with those who followed other thirteenth-century thinkers more or less closely represented the *via antiqua*. They lived on the thought of the preceding century. But at the same time there arose and spread in the fourteenth century a new movement, associated for ever with the name of William of Ockham. The thinkers of this new movement, the *via moderna*, which naturally possessed all the charm of 'modernity', opposed the realism of the earlier schools and became known as the 'nominalists'. This appellation is in some respects not very apposite, since William of Ockham, for example, did not deny that there are universal concepts in some sense; but the word is universally employed and will doubtless continue to be employed. There is not much point, then, in attempting to change it, though a better name is 'terminists'. The logicians of the new movement gave great attention to the logical status and function of terms. It is true that they strongly opposed and criticized the realism of earlier philosophers, particularly that of Duns Scotus; but it would be an over-simplification of their anti-realism to say that it consisted in attributing universality to 'names' or words alone.

It would, however, be a grossly inadequate description if one contented oneself with saying that the fourteenth-century nominalists attacked the realism of the thirteenth-century philosophers. The nominalist movement possessed a significance and an importance which cannot be adequately expressed by reference to one particular controversy. It constituted the wedge which was driven between theology and philosophy, and which broke apart the synthesis achieved in the thirteenth century. The nominalist spirit, if one may so speak, was inclined to analysis rather than to synthesis, and to criticism rather than to speculation. Through their critical analysis of the metaphysical ideas and arguments of their predecessors the nominalists left faith hanging in the air, without (so far as philosophy is concerned) any rational basis. A broad generalization of this sort has, of course, the defects attaching to such generalizations; it does not apply to all thinkers who were influenced by nominalism; but it indicates the result of the more extreme tendencies in the movement.

Philosophy can hardly live without the analytic and critical spirit: at least, critical analysis is one of the 'moments' of philosophic thought, and it is natural that it should follow a period of constructive synthesis. As we have seen, the spirit was present, to a certain extent, in the thought of Duns Scotus, who maintained, for example, that the proofs of the soul's immortality are not absolutely conclusive and that a number of the divine attributes often held to be demonstrable cannot really be demonstrated. But it must be noted that Scotus was a metaphysician who argued as a metaphysician. It is true that he was, like other mediaeval metaphysicians, a logician; but the logician had not, with him, begun to take the place of the metaphysician: his system belongs to the group of thirteenth-century metaphysical syntheses. In the fourteenth century, however, a change can be observed. Metaphysics, while not abandoned, tends to give place to logic; and questions which were formerly treated as metaphysical questions are treated primarily as logical questions. When William of Ockham tackles the subject of universals, he places the emphasis on the logical aspects of the question, on the *suppositio* and *significatio terminorum* rather than on the ontological aspects. Ockham seems to have been convinced of his fidelity to the exigencies of the Aristotelian logic; and one can even say that it was in the name of the Aristotelian logic, or of what he regarded as such, that Ockham criticized the metaphysics of predecessors like Duns Scotus and Thomas Aquinas. One can, of course, devote oneself to logical studies without troubling about metaphysics, and some of the Oxford logicians of the fourteenth century seem to have done so. But one can also go on to criticize metaphysical arguments and proofs in the name of logic, and this is what Ockham did. As we shall see, he to all intents and purposes undermined the natural theology and metaphysical psychology of his predecessors. In his opinion, the alleged proofs or demonstrations of God's attributes or of the spirituality and immortality of the soul either rest on principles the truth of which is not self-evident or terminate in conclusions which do not strictly follow from the relevant premisses. Ockham admitted, indeed, that some metaphysical arguments are 'probable'; but this simply illustrates the tendency in the fourteenth century to substitute probable arguments for demonstrations.

This substitution of probable arguments was connected, of course, with the nominalist tendency to doubt or to deny the validity of inferring from the existence of one thing the existence of another. Ockham stressed the primacy of intuition of the existent individual thing. In regard to a thing's existence the first question to ask, then, is whether we intuit it as existent. In the case of the spiritual soul, for example, Ockham would deny that we have any such intuition. The question then arises whether we can argue with certainty to the existence of the spiritual soul from the intuitions we do have. Ockham did not think this possible. He did not indeed make a purely phenomenalistic analysis of causality: he used the principle himself in metaphysics: but the later 'extremists', like Nicholas of Autrecourt, did give such an analysis. The result was that they questioned our knowledge of the existence of material substance, and probably also of the spiritual soul. In fact, no logical inference from the existence of one thing to the existence of another could amount to a 'demonstration' or cogent proof. In this way the whole metaphysical system of the thirteenth century was discredited.

This thoroughgoing criticism of the preceding metaphysical systems obviously involved a breach in the synthesis of theology and philosophy which had been a characteristic of those systems. St. Thomas, for example, even if he treated the philosophical arguments for the existence of God in works which were only in part philosophical, as distinct from theological, was certainly convinced that valid metaphysical arguments can be given for God's existence. These arguments belong to the *praeambula fidei*, in the sense that the acceptance of divine revelation logically presupposes the knowledge that a God exists who is capable of revealing Himself, a knowledge which can be gained in abstraction from theology. But if, as a number of the fourteenth-century philosophers believed, no cogent proof or demonstration of God's existence can be given, the very existence of God has to be relegated to the sphere of faith. Two consequences follow. First of all, theology and philosophy tend to fall apart. Of course, this consequence might be avoided, were the whole idea of philosophic 'proof' to be revised, but if the choice lies between demonstration and faith, and if the demonstrability of the 'preambles' of faith is denied, the consequence can scarcely be avoided. Secondly, if the important problems of traditional metaphysics, problems which linked philosophy with theology and religion, are relegated to the sphere of faith, philosophy tends to take on more and more a 'lay' character. This consequence did not become very apparent with Ockham himself, since he was a theologian as well as a philosopher, but it became more apparent with certain other fourteenth-century thinkers, like Nicholas of Autrecourt, who belonged to the faculty of arts.

To say that a thirteenth-century philosopher like St. Thomas was preoccupied with 'apologetics' would be untrue and anachronistic. None the less, though not preoccupied with apologetics in the way some Christian thinkers of a later age have been, he was certainly concerned with the relation between philosophy and revelation. Alive to the contemporary currents of thought and to the controversies of his time, he was prepared neither to reject the new Aristotelian metaphysics in the name of Christian tradition nor to pursue philosophic reflection without any regard to its bearing on Christian theology. He was careful to synthesize dogmatic theology on the one hand with his philosophy on the other, and to show the link between them. When we come to William of Ockham in the fourteenth century however, we find a marked absence of any concern for 'apologetics'. We find, indeed, a theologian who considered that his predecessors had obscured or overlaid Christian truths with false metaphysics; but we find also a philosopher who was quite content to apply his principles in a logical and consistent manner, without appearing to care, or perhaps fully to realize, the implications in regard to the synthesis between theology and philosophy. Truths which he believed but which he did not think could be philosophically proved he relegated to the sphere of faith. By assigning to the sphere of faith the truth that there exists an absolutely supreme, infinite, free, omniscient and omnipotent Being, he snapped the link between metaphysics and theology which had been provided by Aquinas's doctrine of the provable *praeambula fidei*. By making the moral law dependent on the free divine choice he implied, whether he realized it or not, that without revelation man can have no certain knowledge even of the present moral order established by God. The best that man could do, unaided by revelation, would presumably be to reflect on the needs of human nature and human society and follow the dictates of his practical reason, even though those dictates might not represent the divine will. This would imply the possibility of two ethics, the moral order established by God but knowable only by revelation, and a provisional and second-class natural and non-theological ethic worked out by the human reason without revelation. I do not mean to say that Ockham actually drew this conclusion from his authoritarian conception of the moral law; but it was, I think, implicit in that conception. To make these observations is not of itself, of course, to make a statement either in favour of or against the validity of Ockham's philosophical arguments; but it is as well to draw attention to the lack of apologetic preoccupations in Ockham. He was a theologian and a philosopher and a political and ecclesiastical pamphleteer; but he was not an 'apologist', not even in the senses in which Aquinas can reasonably be called an 'apologist', and still less in the modern sense of the word.

Some philosophers in the fourteenth century endeavoured to bridge the threatening gap between theology and philosophy by extending Henry of Ghent's theory of 'illumination'. Thus Hugolino of Orvieto (d. 1373), a Hermit of St. Augustine, distinguished certain degrees of illumination, and maintained that Aristotle, for example, was enlightened by a special divine illumination which enabled him to know something of God and of certain of His attributes. Others, however, turned to mysticism and concentrated their attention on a speculative treatment of the relation of the world to God and, in particular, of the relation of the human soul to God. This movement of speculative mysticism, the chief representative of which was the German Dominican Meister Eckhart, was, as we shall see later, very far from being simply a reaction to the arid wranglings of the Schools or a flight from scepticism to the safe haven of piety; but it was, none the less, a feature of the fourteenth century, quite distinct from the more academic philosophy of the universities.

An important feature of fourteenth-century university life, particularly at Paris, was the growth of science. Something will be said about this later on, though only a brief treatment of this theme can be expected in a history of philosophy. The development of mathematical and scientific studies by such fourteenth-century figures as Nicholas of Oresme, Albert of Saxony and Marsilius of Inghen is generally associated with the Ockhamist movement; and thus it is regarded as a feature of the fourteenth, as contrasted with the thirteenth, century. There is certainly truth in this contention, not so much because William of Ockham showed any particular interest in empirical science or because the fourteenth-century scientists accepted all the Ockhamist positions as because the Ockhamist philosophy should, of its very nature, have favoured the growth of empirical science. William of Ockham had a strong belief in the primacy of intuition, that is, in the primacy of intuition of the individual thing: all real knowledge is ultimately founded on intuitive knowledge of individual existents. Moreover, the only adequate ground for asserting a causal relation between two phenomena is observation of regular sequence. These two theses tend of themselves to favour empirical observation and a fresh approach to scientific questions. And in point of fact we do find that the leading figures in fourteenth-century science were associated in some way, though sometimes rather loosely, with the 'modern way'.

At the same time one is not justified in asserting without qualification that a rudimentary appreciation of physical science was peculiar to the fourteenth century, as contrasted with the thirteenth, or that the scientific studies associated with the Ockhamist movement were the direct progenitors of Renaissance science. Already in the thirteenth century interest had been taken in the Latin translations of Greek and Arabic scientific works, and original observations and experiments had been made. We have only to think of men like Albert the Great, Peter of Maricourt and Roger Bacon. In the following century criticism of Aristotle's physical theories coupled with further original reflection and even experiment led to the putting forward of new explanations and hypotheses in physics; and the investigations of the physicists associated with the Ockhamist movement passed in the fifteenth century to northern Italy. The science of the universities of northern Italy certainly influenced the great scientists of the Renaissance, like Galileo; but it would be a mistake to think that Galileo's work was nothing but a continuation of 'Ockhamist' science, though it would be also a mistake to think that it was not influenced by the latter. For one thing, Galileo was able to achieve his results only through a use of mathematics which was unknown in the fourteenth century. This use was facilitated by the translation, at the time of the Renaissance, of works by Greek mathematicians and physicists; and Galileo was stimulated to apply mathematics to the solution of problems of motion and mechanics in a way for which the mediaeval scientists did not possess the necessary equipment. The use of mathematics as the special means of disclosing the nature of physical reality led to a transformation in physical science. The old way of common-sense observation was abandoned in favour of a very different approach. Though it may sound strange to say so, physical science became less 'empirical': it was set free not only from Aristotelian physical theories but also from the common-sense idea of an observational method which had tended to prevail among earlier physicists. It is true that some continuity can be observed between thirteenth- and fourteenth-century science, and between fourteenth-century science and that of the Renaissance; but that does not alter the fact that in the last period a revolution in physical science took place.

3. Mention of the Renaissance of the fifteenth and sixteenth centuries probably still conjures up for some minds the idea of a sudden and abrupt transition and awakening, when the learning and literature of the ancient world were made available, when education began, when men began to think for themselves after the intellectual slavery of the Middle Ages, when the invention of printing made the wide dissemination of books at last possible, when the discovery of new lands broadened men's horizons and opened up new sources of wealth, and when the discovery of gunpowder conferred an inestimable blessing upon mankind.

Such a view is, of course, a considerable exaggeration. As far as the recovery of ancient literature, for example, is concerned, this began centuries before the Italian Renaissance; while in regard to thinking for oneself, it does not require a very profound knowledge of mediaeval philosophy to realize that there was plenty of original thinking in the Middle Ages. On the other hand, one should not emphasize the element of continuous transition so much that one implies that the Renaissance does not form a recognizable period or that its achievements were negligible. It is a question of looking at the matter in the light of our present knowledge of the Middle Ages and of correcting false impressions of the Renaissance, and not a question of suggesting that the word 'Renaissance' is a mere word, denoting no reality. Something more on this subject will be said at a later stage; at the moment I wish to confine myself to a few introductory remarks on the philosophies of the Renaissance.

When one looks at mediaeval philosophy, one certainly sees variety; but it is a variety within a common pattern, or at least it is a variety set against a common and well-defined background. There was certainly original thought; but none the less one gets the impression of a common effort, of what one may call teamwork. The thirteenth-century philosophers criticized one another's opinions; but they accepted not only the same religious faith but also, for the most part, the same metaphysical principles. One thus obtains the impression of a philosophical development which was carried on by men of independent minds but which was at the same time a common development, to which the individual philosophers made their several contributions. Even in the fourteenth century the *via moderna* was so widespread a movement as to grow in the course of time into a more or less hardened 'school', taking its place along with Thomism, Scotism and Augustinianism.

When one looks at Renaissance philosophy, however, one is faced at first sight with a rather bewildering assortment of philosophies. One finds for instance Platonists, Aristotelians of various kinds, anti-Aristotelians, Stoics, sceptics, eclectics and philosophers of nature. One can separate the philosophies into various general currents of thought, it is true, even if it is rather difficult to know to which current one should assign a particular thinker; but the over-all impression is one of a pullulating individualism. And this impression is, in many respects, correct. The gradual breakdown of the framework of mediaeval society and the loosening of the bonds between men which helped to produce a more or less common outlook; the transition to new forms of society, sometimes separated from one another by religious differences; the new inventions and discoveries; all this was accompanied by a marked individualism in philosophic reflection. The feeling of discovery, of adventure, was in the air; and it was reflected in philosophy. To say this is not to retract what I have already said about the inadequacy of regarding the Renaissance as without roots in the past. It had its roots in the past and it passed through several phases, as we shall see later; but this does not mean that a new spirit did not come into being at the time of the Renaissance, though it would be more accurate to say that a spirit which had manifested itself to a certain extent at an earlier date showed an outburst of vitality at the time of the Renaissance. For example, the recovery of the classical literature had started at a much earlier date, within the Middle Ages, as has already been remarked; but historians, while rightly emphasizing this fact, have also rightly pointed out that in regard to the Renaissance the important point is not so much that numbers of fresh texts were made available as that the texts were read in a new light. It was a question of appreciating the texts and the thought therein contained for themselves and not just as possible sources of Christian edification or disedification. The bulk of Renaissance thinkers, scholars and scientists were, of course, Christians; and it is as well to remember the fact; but none the less the classical revival, or perhaps rather the Renaissance phase of the classical revival, helped to bring to the fore a conception of autonomous man or an idea of the development of the human personality which, though generally Christian, was more 'naturalistic' and less ascetic than the mediaeval conception. And this idea favoured the growth of individualism. Even among writers who were devout

Christians one can discern the conviction that a new age for man was beginning. This conviction was not due simply to classical studies, of course; it was due to the complex of historical changes which were taking place at the Renaissance.

It was at the time of the Renaissance that the works of Plato and Plotinus were translated, by Marsilius Ficinus; and in the earlier phase of the period an attempt was made to form a philosophical synthesis of Platonic inspiration. The Platonic philosophers were, for the most part, Christians; but, very naturally, Platonism was looked on as a kind of antithesis to Aristotelianism. At the same time another group of humanists, influenced by the Latin classical literature, attacked the Aristotelian logic and Scholastic abstractions in the name of good taste, realism and the feeling for the concrete, rhetoric and literary exposition. A new idea of education by means of classical literature rather than by abstract philosophy was taking shape. Polite and humanistic scepticism was represented by Montaigne, while Justus Lipsius revived Stoicism and Pierre Gassendi Epicureanism. The Aristotelians of the Renaissance, apart from the Scholastics, were meanwhile divided among themselves into the Averroists and those who favoured the interpretation of Aristotle given by Alexander of Aphrodisias. These latter favoured an interpretation of Aristotle's psychology which led to the denial of human immortality, even the impersonal immortality admitted by the Averroists. Pomponazzi, the chief figure of this group, drew the conclusion that man has a purely terrestrial moral end. At the same time he professed to be a believing Christian and so had to make a rigid division between theological and philosophical truth.

The philosophies which took the form of revivals of classical thought tended to accustom people to an idea of man which had no very obvious connection with Christianity and which was sometimes frankly naturalistic, even if the authors of these naturalistic pictures of man were generally Christians. An analogous process of development went on in regard to the philosophy of nature. Whereas certain forms of Oriental thought would scarcely favour the study of nature, owing to the notion that the phenomenal world is illusion or mere 'appearance', Christian philosophy favoured in a sense the investigation of nature, or at least set no theoretical bar to it, because it regarded the material world not only as real but also as the creation of God, and so as worthy of study. At the same time the emphasis laid by a Christian theologian, philosopher and saint like Bonaventure on the religious orientation of man led to a natural concentration on those aspects of the material world which could be most easily looked on not only as manifestations of God but also as means to elevate the mind from the material to the spiritual. The saint was not particularly interested in studying the world for its own sake: he was much more interested in detecting in it the mirror of the divine. Nevertheless, Christian philosophy, apart from this natural concentration of interest, was not radically hostile to the study of the world; and in the case of thirteenth-century philosophers like St. Albert the Great and Roger Bacon we find a combination of the spiritual outlook with an interest in the empirical study of nature. In the fourteenth century we find this interest in scientific studies growing, in association with the Ockhamist movement and favoured by the rift which was introduced into the thirteenth-century synthesis of theology and philosophy. The way was being prepared for a philosophy of nature which, while not necessarily anti-Christian, emphasized nature as an intelligible totality governed by its own immanent laws. It might perhaps be better to say that the way was being gradually prepared for the scientific study of nature, which was in the course of time, though only at a later period, to shed the name of 'natural philosophy' or 'experimental philosophy' and to become conscious of itself as a separate discipline, or set of disciplines, with its own method or methods. But at the time of the Renaissance we find a number of philosophies of nature arising which stand apart from the development of physical science as such, in that they are characterized by a marked speculative trait which sometimes manifested itself in fanciful and bizarre ideas. These philosophies varied from the Christian and strongly Platonic or neo-Platonic philosophy of a Nicholas of Cusa to the pantheistic philosophy of a Giordano Bruno. But they were marked by common characteristics, by a belief, for example, in nature as a developing system which was infinite, or potentially infinite, and which was regarded either as the created infinite, mirroring the uncreated and divine infinite, or as itself in some sense divine. God was certainly not denied; but the emphasis was placed, in varying degrees with different philosophers, on nature itself. Nature tended to be looked on as the macrocosm and man as the microcosm. This was, indeed, an old idea, going back to Greek times; but it represented a change of emphasis from that characteristic of the mediaeval outlook. In other words, there was a tendency to regard nature as an autonomous system, even though nature's dependence on God was not denied. The bizarre and fantastic aspects of some of these philosophies may tend to make one impatient of them and their authors; but they are of importance in that they marked the rise of a new direction of interest and because of the fact that they formed a kind of mental background against which the purely scientific study of nature could go forward. Indeed, it was against the background of these philosophies, which were the ancestors of philosophies like those of Spinoza and Leibniz, rather than against the background of fourteenth-century Ockhamism, that the great advances of the scientific phase of the Renaissance were achieved. Not infrequently the philosophers anticipated speculatively hypotheses which the physicists were to verify or confirm. Even Newton, it may be remembered, looked upon himself as a philosopher.

When we turn to the Renaissance scientists, we find them interested primarily in knowledge for its own sake. But at the same time it was a characteristic of some Renaissance thinkers to emphasize the practical fruits of knowledge. The new scientific discoveries and the opening up of the new world naturally suggested a contrast between a knowledge of nature, gained by study of her laws and making possible a use of nature for man's benefit, and the older abstract discipline which seemed devoid of practical utility. Study of final causes gets one nowhere; study of efficient causes enables one to control nature and to extend man's dominion over nature. The best-known expression of this outlook is to be found in the writings of Francis Bacon (d. 1626), who, though often assigned to 'modern philosophy', may reasonably be assigned to the Renaissance period. (Distinctions of this sort are to a certain extent a matter of personal choice, of course.) It would be a mistake to father this sort of attitude on the great scientific figures; but it is an attitude which has come to dominate a great part of the modern mentality. One can detect it even in some of the political thinkers of the Renaissance. Machiavelli (d. 1527), for example, neglecting theoretical problems of sovereignty and of the nature of the state in favour of 'realism' wrote his *Prince* as a text for princes who wanted to know how to conserve and augment their power.

Finally, one has to consider the great scientific figures, like Kepler and Galileo, who laid the foundations of the classical science of the modern era, the Newtonian science, as it is often known. If the first phase of the Renaissance was that of Italian humanism, the last was that of the growth of modern science. This development came to exercise a profound influence not only on philosophy but also on the modern mentality in general. But of this influence it will be more proper to speak in other volumes.

4. Martin Luther was very strongly anti-Aristotelian and anti-Scholastic; but Melanchthon, his most eminent disciple and associate, was a humanist who introduced into Lutheran Protestantism a humanistic Aristotelianism set to the service of religion. The Reformers were naturally much more concerned with religion and theology than with philosophy; and men like Luther and Calvin could hardly be expected to have very much sympathy with the predominantly aesthetic attitude of the humanists, even though Protestantism stressed the need for education and had to come to terms with humanism in the educational field.

However, though humanism, a movement which was unsympathetic to Scholasticism, began in Catholic Italy, and though the greatest figures of humanism in northern Europe, Erasmus above all, but also men like Thomas More in England, were Catholics, the late Renaissance witnessed a revival of Scholasticism, a brief treatment of which I have included in the present volume. The centre of this revival was, significantly, Spain, a country which was not much affected either by the religious upheavals and divisions which afflicted so much of Europe or, indeed, by Renaissance philosophy. The revival came at the end of the fifteenth century, with Thomas de Vio (d. 1534), known as Cajetan, De Sylvestris (d. 1520) and others; and in the sixteenth century we find two principal groups, the Dominican group, represented by writers like Francis of Vitoria (d. 1546), Dominic Soto (d. 1560), Melchior Cano (d. 1566), and Dominic Báñez (d. 1640), and the Jesuit group, represented, for example, by Toletus (d. 1596), Molina (d. 1600), Bellarmine (d. 1621), and Suárez (d. 1617). The most important of these late Scholastics is probably Suárez, of whose philosophy I shall give a more extended treatment than in the case of any of the others.

The themes treated by the Renaissance Scholastics were for the most part those themes and problems already set by preceding mediaeval Scholasticism; and if one looks at the extensive works of Suárez, one finds abundant evidence of the author's very wide knowledge of preceding philosophies. The rise of Protestantism naturally led the Scholastic theologians to discuss relevant theological problems which had their repercussions in the field of philosophy; but the Scholastics were not much affected by the characteristically Renaissance philosophies. A thinker like Suárez bears more resemblance to the theologian-philosophers of the thirteenth century than to the intellectual free-lances of the Renaissance. Yet, as we shall see later, contemporary movements influenced Suárez in two ways at least. First, the old philosophical method of commenting on a text was abandoned by him in his *Metaphysical Disputations* for a continuous discussion in a more modern, even if, it must be confessed, somewhat prolix style. Philosophy came to be treated, not in predominantly or largely theological works, but in separate treatises. Secondly, the rise of national states was reflected in a fresh development of political theory and of the philosophy of law, of a much more thorough character than anything produced by mediaeval Scholasticism. In this connection one thinks naturally of the study of international law by the Dominican Francis of Vitoria and of Suárez' treatise on law.

PART I
THE FOURTEENTH CENTURY

CHAPTER II

DURANDUS AND PETRUS AUREOLI

James of Metz—Durandus—Petrus Aureoli—Henry of Harclay—The relation of these thinkers to Ockhamism.

1. One is naturally inclined to think that all the theologians and philosophers of the Dominican Order in the late Middle Ages followed the teaching of St. Thomas Aquinas. In 1279 those who did not embrace Thomism were forbidden by the Chapter of Paris to condemn it, and in 1286 the same Chapter enacted that non-Thomists should be removed from their chairs. In the following century the Chapters of Saragossa (1309) and of Metz (1313) made it obligatory to accept the teaching of St. Thomas (who was not canonized until 1323). But these enactments did not succeed in making all Dominicans conform. Leaving out of account Meister Eckhart, whose philosophy will be discussed in the chapter on speculative mysticism, one may mention among the dissentients James of Metz, though his two commentaries on the *Sentences* of Peter Lombard, which seem to have been composed the one before 1295 and the other in 1302, antedated the official imposition of Thomism on members of the Order.

James of Metz was not an anti-Thomist in the sense of being an opponent of St. Thomas's teaching in general; nor was he a philosophic revolutionary; but he did not hesitate to depart from the teaching of St. Thomas and to question that teaching when he saw fit. For example, he did not accept the Thomist view of matter as the principle of individuation. It is form which gives unity to the substance and so constitutes it; and we must accordingly recognize form as the principle of individuation, since individuality presupposes substantiality. James of Metz appears to have been influenced by thinkers like Henry of Ghent and Peter of Auvergne. Thus he developed Henry's idea of the 'modes of being' (*modi essendi*). There are three modes of being, that of substance, that of real accident (quantity and quality) and that of relation. The modes are distinct from one another; but they are not things which together with their foundations make up composite beings. Thus relation is a mode of being which relates a substance or an absolute accident to the term of the relation: it is not itself a thing. Most relations, like similarity, for example, or equality, are mental: the causal relation is the only 'real' relation, independent of our thought. James was something of an eclectic; and his divagations from the teaching of St. Thomas called forth criticism and reproof from the pen of Hervé Nédellec,[1] a Dominican who published a *Correctorium fratris Jacobi Metensis*.

2. Durandus (Durand de Saint-Pourçain) was much more of an *enfant terrible* than was James of Metz. Born between 1270 and 1275, he entered the Dominican Order and did his studies at Paris, where he is supposed to have followed the lectures of James of Metz. At the beginning of the first edition of his commentary on the *Sentences* he laid down the principle that the proper procedure in speaking and writing of things which do not touch the Faith is to rely on reason rather than on the authority of any Doctor however famous or grave. Armed with this principle Durandus proceeded on his way, to the displeasure of his Dominican colleagues. He then published a second edition of his commentary, omitting the offending propositions; but nothing was gained thereby, for the first edition continued in circulation. The Dominican Chapter of Metz condemned his peculiar opinions in 1313, and in 1314 a commission presided over by Hervé Nédellec censured 91 propositions taken from the first edition of Durandus's commentary. The latter, who was at this time a lecturer at the papal court of Avignon, defended himself in his *Excusationes*; but Hervé Nédellec pursued the attack in his *Reprobationes excusationum Durandi* and followed it up by attacking Durandus's teaching at Avignon. In 1316 the Dominican General Chapter at Montpellier, considering that a 'remedy' should be provided for this shocking state of affairs, drew up a list of 235 points on which Durandus had differed from the teaching of St. Thomas. In 1317 Durandus became Bishop of Limoux, being translated to Puy in 1318 and finally to Meaux in 1326. Strengthened by his episcopal position, he published, sometime after 1317, a third edition of his commentary on the *Sentences*, in which he returned, in part, to the positions he had once retracted. One can safely assume that he had always continued to hold the theories in question. As a matter

[1] i.e. Hervaeus Natalis, who became Master-General of the Dominicans in 1318.

of fact, though possessed of an independent spirit in regard to St. Thomas's teaching, Durandus was not a revolutionary. He was influenced by the doctrine of Henry of Ghent, for example, while on some points he spoke like an Augustinian. In 1326, when Bishop of Meaux, he was a member of the commission which censured 51 propositions taken from William of Ockham's commentary on the *Sentences*. He died in 1332.

One of Durandus's opinions which offended his critics concerned relations. For Durandus, as for James of Metz, relation is a *modus essendi*, a mode of being. Henry of Ghent, as we have seen, had distinguished three modes of being, that of a substance, that of an absolute accident (quantity and quality) which inheres in a substance, and that of a relation. A relation was regarded by Henry as being a kind of internal tendency of a being towards another being. As far as the real being of a relation is concerned, then, it is reducible to the being of a substance or of a real accident; and the Aristotelian categories are to be regarded as comprising substance, quantity, quality, relation, and the six subdivisions of relation. This doctrine of the three basic modes of being was adopted by James of Metz and Durandus. As the modes of being are really distinct, it follows that the relation is really distinct from its foundation. On the other hand, as the relation is simply the foundation or subject in its relatedness to something else,[1] it cannot properly be a 'thing' or 'creature'; at least, it cannot enter into composition with its foundation.[2] There is a real relation only when a being related to another possesses an objective, internal exigency for this relatedness. This means that there is a real relation, so far as creatures are concerned, only when there is real dependence; and it follows therefore that the causal relation is the only real relation in creatures.[3] Similarity, equality and all relations other than the causal relation are purely conceptual; they are not real relations.

Durandus applied this doctrine to knowledge. The act of knowing is not an absolute accident which inheres in the soul, as St. Thomas thought; it is a *modus essendi* which does not add anything to the intellect or make it more perfect. 'It must be said

[1] The relation is a *modus essendi ad aliud, qui est ipse respectus relationis.* 1 *Sent.* (A), 33, 1.

[2] *Relatio est alia res a suo fundamento, et tamen non facit compositionem. Ibid.*

[3] *Relata realia ex natura sui fundamenti habent inter se necessariam coexigentiam ratione fundamenti. Ibid.* (A), 31, 1. *In creaturis realis relatio requirit dependentiam in relato. Ibid.* (A), 30, 2.

that sensation and understanding do not imply the addition to the sense and the intellect of anything real which enters into composition with them.'[1] Sensation and understanding are immanent acts which are really identical with the sense and the intellect. Why did Durandus hold this? Because he considered that to maintain that the soul, when it enters into cognitive relation with an object, receives accidents by way of addition is to imply that an external object can act on a spiritual principle or a non-living object on a living subject, a view which he calls 'ridiculous'. Durandus's thought on this matter is clearly of Augustinian inspiration. For example, one of the reasons why St. Augustine maintained that sensation is an act of the soul alone was the impossibility of a material thing acting on the soul. The object is a *conditio sine qua non*, but not a cause, of knowledge; the intellect itself is the cause.

From this theory of knowledge as a relation Durandus drew the conclusion that the whole apparatus of cognitive *species*, in the sense of accidental forms, can be dispensed with. It follows also that it is unnecessary to postulate an active intellect which is supposed to abstract these *species*. Similarly, Durandus got rid of 'habits' in the intellect and will, and he followed the Augustinian tradition in denying any real distinction between intellect and will.

The principal reason why Durandus got into trouble over his doctrine of relations was its application to the doctrine of the Trinity. In the first edition of his commentary on the *Sentences*[2] he asserted that there is a real distinction between the divine essence or nature and the divine relations or Persons, though in the second passage referred to he speaks with some hesitation. This opinion was condemned by the commission of 1314 as 'entirely heretical'. Durandus tried to explain away his assertions, but Hervé Nédellec drew attention to his actual words. In the Avignon *Quodlibet* he admitted that one could not properly speak of a real distinction between the divine nature and the divine internal relations: the latter are *modi essendi vel habendi essentiam divinam* and the distinction is only *secundum quid*. A renewed attack by Hervé Nédellec followed this change, and in the final edition of the commentary Durandus proposed another view.[3] There are, he says, three possible theories. First, essence and relation, though not two things, differ in that they are not the

[1] *Quaestio de natura cognitionis* (ed. J. Koch), p. 18.
[2] 1 *Sent.* (A), 13, 1, and 33, 1.
[3] 1 *Ibid.* (C), 33, 1.

same 'adequately and convertibly'. Secondly, essence and relation differ as thing and 'mode of possessing the thing'. This was the view of Henry of Ghent, James of Metz and, formerly, of Durandus himself. Thirdly, essence and relation differ *formaliter ex natura rei,* although they are identically the same thing. Durandus adopts this third view, that of Scotus, though he adds that he does not understand what *formaliter* means unless this view contains the other two. The first view is included, in that essence and relation, while they are the same thing, are not the same thing 'adequately and convertibly'. The second view is also included, namely that essence and relation differ as *res et modus habendi rem.* In other words, Durandus's opinion did not undergo any very startling change.

It used to be said that Durandus was a pure conceptualist in regard to universals and that he thus helped to prepare the way for Ockhamism. But it is now clear that he did not deny that there was some real foundation in things for the universal concept. He held, indeed, that it is 'frivolous to say that there is universality in things, for universality cannot be in things, but only singularity';[1] but the unity of nature which is thought by the intellect as being common to a multiplicity of objects exists really in things, though not as an objective universal. Universality belongs to concepts, but the nature which is conceived by the intellect as a universal exists really in individual things.

Durandus certainly rejected a considerable number of theories which had been maintained by St. Thomas. We have seen that he denied the doctrines of *species* and of habits or dispositions, and the real distinction between intellect and will. Moreover, in regard to the immortality of the soul he followed Scotus in saying that it is not demonstrable; or, at least, that it is difficult to demonstrate in a rigorous manner. But, as already mentioned, he was not a revolutionary even if he was an independent and critical thinker. His psychology was largely Augustinian in character and inspiration, while even his doctrine of relations was founded on that of Henry of Ghent. And in regard to universals he did not reject the position maintained by the mediaeval Aristotelians. In other words, the former picture of Durandus as a closely-related predecessor of William of Ockham has had to be abandoned, though it is true, of course, that he employed the principle of economy, known as 'Ockham's razor'.

[1] 2 *Sent.*, 3, 7, 8.

3. Petrus Aureoli (Pierre d'Auriole) entered the Order of Friars Minor and studied at Paris. After having lectured at Bologna (1312) and Toulouse (1314) he returned to Paris where he received the doctorate of theology in 1318. In 1321 he became Archbishop of Aix-en-Provence. He died shortly afterwards, in January 1322. His first philosophical work was the uncompleted *Tractatus de principiis naturae*, which dealt with questions of natural philosophy. His main work, a commentary on the *Sentences* of Peter Lombard, was published in two successive editions. We have also his *Quodlibeta*.

Petrus Aureoli takes his stand firmly on the statement that everything which exists is, by the very fact that it exists, an individual thing. Speaking of the dispute concerning the principle of individuation, he asserts that in reality there is no question at all to discuss, 'since every thing, by the very fact that it exists, exists as an individual thing' (*singulariter est*).[1] Conversely, if anything is common or universal or can be predicated of a plurality of objects, it is shown by that very fact to be a concept. 'Therefore to seek for something whereby an extramental object is rendered individual is to seek for nothing.'[2] For this is tantamount to asking in what way an extramental universal is individualized, when in point of fact there is no such thing as an extramental universal which could be individualized. The metaphysical problem of individuation is thus no problem at all. There is no universal outside the mind. But this does not mean that God cannot create a number of individuals of the same species; and we know, in fact, that He has done so. Material things have forms, and certain of these forms possess a quality which we call 'likeness' (*similitudo*). If it is asked what sort of a thing (*quale quid*) Socrates is, the answer is that he is a man: there is a quality of likeness in Socrates and Plato of such a kind that though there is nothing in Socrates which is in Plato, there is not in Plato anything to which there cannot be a likeness in Socrates. 'I and you are not the same; but I can be such as you are. So the Philosopher says that Callias, by generating Socrates, generates a similar being.'[3] The extramental foundation of the universal concept is this quality of likeness. Petrus Aureoli does not deny, then, that there is an objective foundation for the universal concept: what he does deny is that there is any common

[1] 2 *Sent.*, 9, 3, 3, p. 114, a A. Pagination is given according to the 1596 edition (Rome).

[2] *Ibid.*

[3] *Ibid.*, p. 115, a F.

reality which exists extramentally. As to immaterial forms, these can also be alike. Hence there is no reason why several angels should not belong to the same species.

The intellect, as active, assimilates to itself this likeness and, as passive, is assimilated to it, thus conceiving the thing, that is, producing an 'objective concept' (*conceptus obiectivus*). This concept is intramental, of course, and, as such, it is distinct from the thing; but on the other hand it is the thing as known. Thus Petrus Aureoli says that when the intellectual assimilation takes place 'the thing immediately receives *esse apparens*'. If the assimilation is clear, the thing will have a clear *esse apparens* or phenomenal existence; if the assimilation is obscure, the *esse apparens* will be obscure. This 'appearance' is in the intellect alone.[1] 'From the fact that a thing produces an imperfect impression of itself in the intellect, there arises the generic concept, by which the thing is conceived imperfectly and indistinctly, while from the fact that the same thing produces a perfect impression of itself in the intellect there arises the concept of (specific) difference, by which the thing is conceived in its specific and distinct existence.'[2] The 'objective' diversity of concepts is the result of the formal diversity of the impression made by one and the same object on one and the same mind. 'Therefore if you ask in what the specific unity of humanity consists, I say that it consists in humanity, not in animality, but in humanity as conceived. And in this way it is the same as the objective concept of man. But this unity exists in potency and inchoately in the extramental thing, inasmuch as the latter is capable of causing in the intellect a perfect impression like to the impression caused by another thing.'[3]

Every extramentally existing thing is individual; and it is 'nobler' to know it directly in its unique individuality than to know it by means of a universal concept. The human intellect, however, cannot grasp directly and primarily, the thing in its incommunicable individuality, though it can know it secondarily, by means of the imagination: primarily and immediately it apprehends the form of the material thing by means of a universal concept.[4] But to say that the intellect knows the thing 'by means of a universal concept' does not mean that there is a *species intelligibilis* in the Thomist sense which acts as a *medium quo* of

[1] 2 *Sent.*, 3, 2, 4, p. 30, c F.
[2] *Ibid.*, p. 66, b D.
[3] *Ibid.*, 9, 2, 3, p. 109, b A B.
[4] *Ibid.*, 11, 4, 2, pp. 142–5.

knowledge. 'No real form is to be postulated as existing subjectively in the intellect, or in the imagination . . . but that form which we are conscious of beholding when we know the rose as such or the flower as such is not something real impressed subjectively on the intellect, or on the imagination; nor is it a real subsistent thing; it is the thing itself as possessing *esse intentionale*. . . .'[1] Petrus Aureoli thus dispenses with the *species intelligibilis* as *medium quo* of knowledge and insists that the intellect knows the thing itself directly. This is one reason why Étienne Gilson can say that Petrus Aureoli 'admits no other reality than that of the knowable object' and that his solution does not consist of eliminating the *species intelligibilis* in favour of the concept, but in suppressing even the concept.[2] On the other hand, the thing which is known, that is, the object of knowledge, is the extramental thing as possessing *esse intentionale* or *esse apparens*; and it acquires this *esse intentionale* through 'conception' (*conceptio*). The thing as possessing *esse intentionale* is thus the concept (that is to say, the 'objective concept' as distinguished from the 'subjective concept' or psychological act as such); and it follows that the concept is the object of knowledge. 'All understanding demands the placing of a thing in *esse intentionali*', and this is the *forma specularis*.[3] 'The thing posited in *esse apparenti* is said to be conceived by the act of the intellect, indeed, it is the intellectual concept; but a concept remains within the conceiver, and is (owes its being to) the conceiver. Therefore the thing as appearing depends effectively on the act of the intellect, both in regard to production and in regard to content.'[4] Dr. B. Geyer can say, then, that 'the *species*, the *forma specularis*, is thus, according to Aureoli, no longer the *medium quo* of knowledge, as with Thomas Aquinas, but its immediate object'.[5] But, even if Petrus Aureoli may speak on occasion as though he wished to maintain a form of subjective idealism, he insists, for example, that 'health as conceived by the intellect and health as it is present extramentally are one and the same thing in reality (*realiter*), although they differ in their mode of being, since in the mind health has *esse apparens et intentionale*, while extramentally, in the body, it has *esse existens et reale*. . . . They differ in mode of being (*in modo essendi*), although they are one and the same thing.'[6]

[1] 1 *Sent.*, 9, 1, p. 319, a B.
[2] *La philosophie au moyen âge*, p. 632.
[3] 1 *Sent.*, 9, 1, p. 320, a B.
[4] *Ibid.*, p. 321, b B C.
[5] *Die patristische und scholastische Philosophie*, p. 526.
[6] 1 *Sent.*, 9, 1, p. 321, a D E.

'Hence it is clear that things themselves are conceived by the mind, and that that which we intuit is not another *forma specularis*, but the thing itself as having *esse apparens*; and this is the mental concept or objective idea (*notitia obiectiva*).'[1]

Knowledge, for Petrus Aureoli, is rooted in the perception of the concrete, of actually existing things. But a thing as known *is* the thing as having *esse apparens et intentionale*; it *is* the concept. According to the degree of clarity in the knowledge of the thing there arises a generic or specific concept. Genera and species, considered as universals, do not, however, exist extramentally, and are to be regarded as 'fabricated' by the mind. Petrus Aureoli may thus be called a 'conceptualist' inasmuch as he rejects any extramental existence on the part of universals; but he cannot rightly be called a 'nominalist', if 'nominalism' is taken to involve a denial of the objective similarity of natures. This is not to say, however, that he does not speak, more or less frequently, in an ambiguous and even inconsistent fashion. His idea of logic may be said to favour nominalism in that the logician is said to deal with words (*voces*). 'Therefore the logician considers them ("second intentions"), not as *entia rationis*, for it belongs to the metaphysician to decide about real being and conceptual being, but in so far as they are reduced to speech. . . .'[2] But, though the doctrine that logic is concerned with words (*voces*) may seem, if taken by itself, to favour nominalism, Petrus Aureoli adds that the logician is concerned with words as expressing concepts. 'The word, as well as the concept (*ut expressiva conceptus*), is the subject-matter of logic.'[3] In his logic, says Petrus Aureoli, Aristotle always implies that he is considering words as expressing concepts.[4] Moreover, speech, which expresses concepts, is the subject of truth and falsity: it is the sign of truth and falsity (*voces enim significant verum vel falsum in ordine ad conceptum*).[5] The theory of the *suppositio*, as formed in the terministic logic, may be implied in Petrus Aureoli's idea of logic; but he was not a 'nominalist' in metaphysics. It is true that he emphasized the qualitative similarity of things rather than the similarity of nature or essence; but he does not seem to have denied essential similarity as the foundation of the specific concept: rather did he presuppose it.

We have seen that for Petrus Aureoli conceptual knowledge is of the extramental thing in its likeness to other things rather than

[1] 1 *Sint.*, 9, 1, p. 321, b B.
[2] *Ibid.*, 23, 2, p. 539, a F–b A.
[3] *Prologus in Sent.*, 5, p. 66, a D.
[4] *Ibid.*, a F.
[5] *Ibid.*, a E.

of the thing precisely as individual. But it is better, he insists, to know the individual thing in its individuality than to know it by means of a universal concept. If the human intellect in its present state knows things rather *per modum abstractum et universalem* than precisely in their individuality, this is an imperfection. The individual thing can make an impression on the senses in such a way that there is sense-knowledge or intuition of the individual thing as individual; but the material thing cannot make an impression of this sort on the immaterial intellect; its form is known abstractly by the intellect, which cannot directly and immediately attain the individual thing as individual. But this does not alter the fact that an intellectual intuition or knowledge of the individual thing as individual would be more perfect than abstract and universal knowledge. 'For the knowledge which attains to the thing precisely as the thing exists is more perfect than knowledge which attains to the thing in a manner in which the thing does not exist. But it is clear that a universal thing does not exist, except in individual things and through individual things, as the Philosopher says against Plato, in the seventh book of the *Metaphysics*. . . . It is quite clear that science, which apprehends essences (*quidditates*), does not apprehend things precisely as they exist . . . but knowledge of this precise individual is knowledge of the thing as it exists. Therefore, it is nobler to know the individual thing as such (*rem individuatam et demonstratam*) than to know it in an abstract and universal way.'[1] It follows that even if the human intellect cannot have that perfect knowledge of individual things which must be attributed to God, it should approach as near thereto as possible by keeping in close contact with experience. We should adhere to 'the way of experience rather than to any logical reasonings, since science arises from experience'.[2] Petrus Aureoli also stressed inner experience of our psychic acts, and he frequently appeals to inner experience or introspection to support his statements about knowledge, volition and psychic activity in general. He shows a strong 'empiricist' bent in his treatment of universals, in his insistence on keeping close to experience, and in his interest in natural science, which is shown by the examples he takes from Aristotle and his Islamic commentators; but

[1] 1 *Sent.*, 35, 4, 2, p. 816, b C–E.

[2] *Prologus in Sent.*, prooemium, 3, p. 25, a F. Petrus Aureoli is here arguing that it is possible for an act of intuition to exist in the absence of the object. This view was also held by Ockham. The remark about keeping close to experience is incidental in the context; but it is none the less significant and enuntiates a principle.

Dreiling's investigation led him to conclude that 'the empiricist tendency of Aureoli has a centripetal rather than a centrifugal direction and is turned towards the psychic life more than towards external nature'.[1]

Mention of Petrus Aureoli's appeals to introspection or inner experience leads one on to discuss his idea of the soul. First of all, it can be proved that the soul is the form of the body, in the sense that the soul is an essential part of man which together with the body makes up man. Indeed, 'no philosopher ever denied this proposition'.[2] But it cannot be proved that the soul is the form of the body in the sense that it is simply the forming and termination of matter (*formatio et terminatio materiae*) or that it makes the body to be a body. 'This has not yet been demonstrated, either by Aristotle or by the Commentator or by any other Peripatetic.'[3] In other words, it can be proved, according to Petrus Aureoli, that the soul is an essential part of man and that it is the principal part (*pars principalior*) of man; but it cannot be proved that it is simply that which makes matter to be a human body or that its relation to the body is analogous to the shape of a piece of copper. If a piece of copper is shaped into a statue, its figure may be called a form; but it is no more than the termination (*terminatio*) or figure of the copper; it is not a distinct nature. The human soul, however, is a distinct nature.

Now, Petrus Aureoli declared that a substantial form is simply the actuation of matter (*pura actuatio materiae*) and that, together with matter, it composes one simple nature.[4] It follows that if the human soul is a distinct nature and is not simply the actuation of matter, it is not a form in the same way and in the same sense that other forms are forms. 'I say, therefore, in answer to the question that it can be demonstrated that the soul is the form of the body and an essential part of us, though it is not the actuation and perfection of the body in the way that other souls are.'[5] The spiritual soul of man and the soul or vital principle of a plant, for example, are not forms in a univocal sense.

On the other hand, the Council of Vienne (1311–12) had just laid down that the intellectual or rational soul of man is 'truly, *per se* and essentially the form of the body'. So, after asserting that the human soul is not the form of the body in the same sense in which other forms which inform matter are forms, Petrus

[1] *Der Konzeptualismus . . . des Franziskanererzbischofs Petrus Aureoli*, p. 197.
[2] 2 *Sent.*, 16, 1, 1, p. 218, b.
[3] *Ibid.*, p. 219, a B.
[4] *Ibid.*, 12, 2, 1, p. 174, b D.
[5] *Ibid.*, 15, 1, 1, p. 223, a F.

Aureoli goes on to say that 'the ninth decree of the sacred Council of Vienne' has asserted the opposite, namely that 'the soul is the form of the body, just like other forms or souls'.[1] In face of this embarrassing situation Petrus Aureoli, while adhering to his position that it cannot be proved that the human soul is the form of the body in the same way that other souls are forms, declares that though this cannot be proved, it is nevertheless known by faith. He makes a comparison with the doctrine of the Trinity. This doctrine cannot be philosophically proved, but it has been revealed and we accept it on faith.[2] He allows that it cannot be demonstrated that the human soul is *not* the form of the body in the same sense that other souls are the forms of their respective matters; but he refuses to allow that it can be demonstrated that the soul *is* the form of the body in this sense. He obviously thought that reason inclines one to think that the human soul and the souls of brutes or plants are forms in an equivocal sense; and he remarks that the teaching of the Saints and Doctors of the Church would not lead one to expect the doctrine laid down by the Council; but, none the less, he accepts the Council's doctrine, as he understands it, and draws a strange conclusion. 'Although it cannot be demonstrated that the soul is the form of the body in the way that other forms (are forms of their respective matters), yet it must be held, as it seems to me, that, just as the shape of wax is the form and perfection of wax, so the soul is simply the actuation and forming of the body in the same way as other forms. And just as no cause is to be sought why from the wax and its shape there results one thing, so no cause is to be sought why from the soul and body there results one thing. Thus the soul is simply the act and perfection of matter, like the shape of the wax . . . I hold this conclusion precisely on account of the decision of the Council, which, according to the apparent sense of the words, seems to mean this.'[3]

The Fathers of the Council would have been startled to hear this interpretation put on their words; but, as he interpreted the Council's decision in this way and accepted it in this sense, Petrus Aureoli obviously found himself in considerable difficulty on the subject of the human soul's immortality. 'Faith holds that the soul is separated (i.e. outlives the body); but it is difficult to see how this can be done if the soul is assumed to be like other forms, simply the actuation of matter. I say, however, that just as God

[1] 2 *Sent.*, 15, 1, 2, p. 223, b A–C. [2] *Ibid.*, b E–F. [3] *Ibid.*, p. 224, b D–F.

can separate accidents from the subject (i.e. substance), although they are no more than actuations of the subject, so He can miraculously separate the soul, although it is simply the actuation of matter.'[1] It is, indeed, necessary to say that in forms or 'pure perfections' there are degrees. If the form is extended, it can be affected (and so corrupted) by a natural extended agent; but if the form is unextended, then it cannot be affected (and so corrupted) by a natural extended agent. Now the human soul, although it is *pura perfectio materiae*, cannot be affected (i.e. corrupted) by a natural extended agent; it can be 'corrupted' only by God. This is not, however, a very satisfactory answer to the difficulty which Petrus Aureoli created for himself by his interpretation of the Council of Vienne; and he declares that our minds are not capable of understanding how the soul is naturally incorruptible if it is what the Council stated it to be.[2]

Petrus Aureoli obviously did not think that the natural immortality of the human soul can be philosophically demonstrated; and he seems to have been influenced by the attitude adopted by Duns Scotus in this matter. Various arguments have been produced to prove that the human soul is naturally immortal; but they are scarcely conclusive.[3] Thus some people have argued 'from the proportion of the object to the power' or faculty. The intellect can know an incorruptible object. Therefore the intellect is incorruptible. Therefore the substance of the soul is incorruptible. But the reply might be made that in this case the eye would be incorruptible (presumably because it sees the incorruptible heavenly bodies) or that our intellect must be infinite and uncreated because it can know God, who is infinite and uncreated. Again, others argue that there is a 'natural desire' to exist for ever and that a natural desire cannot be frustrated. Petrus Aureoli answers, like Scotus though more summarily, that the brutes too desire to continue in existence inasmuch as they shun death. The argument, if valid, would thus prove too much. Others, again, argue that justice requires the rewarding of the good and the punishment of the wicked in another life. 'This argument is moral and theological, and moreover, it is not conclusive.' For it might be answered that sin is its own punishment and virtue its own reward.

Petrus Aureoli proceeds to give some arguments of his own; but

[1] 2 *Sent.*, 15, 1, 2, p. 226, a E–F.
[2] *Ibid.*, p. 226, a F–b B.
[3] *Ibid.*, 19, 1, p. 246, b D.

he is not very confident as to their probative force. 'Now I give my arguments, but I do not know if they are conclusive.'[1] First of all, man can choose freely, and his free choices are not affected by the heavenly bodies nor by any material agent. Therefore the principle of this operation of free choice also is unaffected by any material agent. Secondly, we experience in ourselves immanent, and therefore spiritual operations. Therefore the substance of the soul is spiritual. But the material cannot act on the spiritual or destroy it. Therefore the soul cannot be corrupted by any material agent.

If man is truly free, it follows, according to Petrus Aureoli, that a judgment concerning a future free act is neither true nor false. 'The opinion of the Philosopher is a conclusion which has been thoroughly demonstrated, namely that no singular proposition can be formed concerning a future contingent event, concerning which proposition it can be conceded that it is true and that its opposite is false, or conversely. No proposition of the kind is either true or false.'[2] To deny this is to deny an obvious fact, to destroy the foundation of moral philosophy and to contradict human experience. If it is now true that a certain man will perform a certain free act at a certain future time, the act will necessarily be performed and it will not be a free act, since the man will not be free to act otherwise. If it is to be a free act, then it cannot now be either true or false that it will be performed.

To say this may appear to involve a denial of the 'law' that a proposition must be either true or false. If we are going to say of a proposition that it is not true, are we not compelled to say that it is false? Petrus Aureoli answers that a proposition receives its determination (that is, becomes true or false) from the being of that to which it refers. In the case of a contingent proposition relating to the future that to which the proposition refers has as yet no being: it cannot, therefore, determine the proposition to be either true or false. We can say of a given man, for example, that on Christmas day he will either drink wine or not drink wine, but we cannot affirm separately either that he will drink wine or that he will not drink wine. If we do, then the statement is neither true nor false: it cannot become true or false until the man actually drinks wine on Christmas day or fails to do so. And Petrus Aureoli appeals to Aristotle in the *De Interpretatione* (9) in support of his view.

[1] 2 *Sent.*, 19, 1, p. 247, a. [2] 1 *Sent.*, 38, 3, p. 883, b C–D.

As to God's knowledge of future free acts, Petrus Aureoli insists that God's knowledge does not make a proposition concerning the future performance or non-performance of such acts either true or false. For example, God's foreknowledge of Peter's denial of his Master did not mean that the proposition 'Peter will deny his Master' was either true or false. Apropos of Christ's prophecy concerning Peter's threefold denial Petrus Aureoli observes: 'therefore Christ would not have spoken falsely, even had Peter not denied Him thrice'.[1] Why not? Because the proposition, 'you will deny Me thrice', could not be either true or false Aureoli does not deny that God knows future free acts; but he insists that, although we cannot help employing the word 'foreknowledge' (*praescientia*), there is no foreknowledge, properly speaking, in God.[2] On the other hand, he rejects the view that God knows future free acts as present. According to him, God knows such acts in a manner which abstracts from past, present and future; but we cannot express the mode of God's knowledge in human language. If the problem of the relation of future free acts to God's knowledge or 'foreknowledge' of them is raised, the problem 'cannot be solved otherwise than by saying that foreknowledge does not make a proposition concerning a future contingent event a true proposition';[3] but this does not tell us what God's 'foreknowledge' is positively. 'We must bear in mind that the difficulty of this problem arises either from the poverty of human language, which cannot express statements save by propositions referring to present, past and future time, or from the condition of our mind, which is always involved in time (*qui semper est cum continuo et tempore*).'[4] Again, 'it is very difficult to find the right way of expressing the knowledge which God has of the future. . . . No proposition in which a reference is made to the future expresses the divine foreknowledge properly: indeed, such a proposition is, strictly speaking, false. . . . But we can say that it (a contingent event) was eternally known to God by a knowledge which neither was distant from that event nor preceded it', although our understanding is unable to grasp what this knowledge is in itself.[5]

It should be noted that Petrus Aureoli is not embracing the opinion of St. Thomas Aquinas, for whom God, in virtue of His eternity, knows all things as present. He admits that God knows

[1] 1 *Sent.*, 38, 3, p. 888, a B. [2] *Ibid.*, p. 889, b A. [3] *Ibid.*, 39, 3, p. 901, a C.
[4] *Ibid.*, a F–b A. [5] *Ibid.*, p. 902, a F–b B.

all events eternally; but he will not allow that God knows them as present; he objects to any introduction of words like 'present', 'past' and 'future' into statements concerning God's knowledge, if these statements are meant to express the actual mode of God's knowledge. What it comes to, then, is that Petrus Aureoli affirms God's knowledge of future free acts and at the same time insists that no proposition relating to such future acts is either true or false. Exactly how God knows such acts we cannot say. It is perhaps needless to add that Petrus Aureoli rejects decisively any theory according to which God knows future free acts through the determination or decision of His divine will. In his view a theory of this kind is incompatible with human freedom. Thomas Bradwardine, whose theory was directly opposed to that of Petrus Aureoli, attacked him on this point.

Petrus Aureoli's discussion of statements concerning God's knowledge which involve a reference, explicit or implicit, to time serves as an illustration of the fact that mediaeval philosophers were not so entirely blind to problems of language and meaning as might perhaps be supposed. The language used about God in the Bible forced upon Christian thinkers at a very early date a consideration of the meaning of the terms used; and we find the mediaeval theories of analogical predication worked out as a response to this problem. The precise point which I have mentioned in connection with Petrus Aureoli should not be taken as an indication that this thinker was conscious of a problem to which other mediaeval philosophers were blind. Whether one is satisfied or not with mediaeval discussions and solutions of the problem, one could not justifiably claim that the mediaevals did not even suspect the existence of the problem.

4. Henry of Harclay, who was born about 1270, studied and taught in the university of Oxford, where he became Chancellor in 1312. He died at Avignon in 1317. He has sometimes been spoken of as a precursor of Ockhamism, that is to say of 'nominalism'; but in reality the type of theory concerning universals which he defended was rejected by Ockham as unduly realist in character. It is quite true that Henry of Harclay refused to allow that there is any common nature existing, as common, in members of the same species, and he certainly held that the universal concept as such is a production of the mind; but his polemics were directed against Scotist realism, and it was the Scotist doctrine of the *natura communis* which he rejected. The nature of any given man

is his individual nature, and it is in no way 'common'. However, existent things can be similar to one another, and it is this similarity which is the objective foundation of the universal concept. One can speak of abstracting something 'common' from things, if one means that one can consider things according to their likeness to one another. But the universality of the concept, its predicability of many individuals, is superimposed by the mind: there is nothing objectively existing in a thing which can be predicated of any other thing.

On the other hand, Henry evidently thought of the universal concept as a confused concept of the individual. An individual man, for example, can be conceived distinctly as Socrates or Plato, or he may be conceived 'confusedly' not as this or that individual, but simply as 'man'. The similarity which makes this possible is, of course, objective; but the genesis of the universal concept is due to this confused impression of individuals, while the universality, formally considered, of the concept is due to the work of the mind.

5. It is clear enough that the three thinkers, some of whose philosophical ideas we have considered in this chapter, were not revolutionaries in the sense that they set themselves against the traditional philosophical currents in general. For example, they did not manifest any marked preoccupation with purely logical questions and they did not show that mistrust of metaphysics which was characteristic of Ockhamism. They were, indeed, in varying degrees critical of the doctrine of St. Thomas. But Henry of Harclay was a secular priest, not a Dominican; and in any case he showed no particular hostility towards Thomism, though he rejected St. Thomas's doctrine concerning the principle of individuation, affirmed the older theory of a plurality of formal principles in man and protested against the attempt to make a Catholic of the 'heretical' Aristotle. Again, Petrus Aureoli was a Franciscan, not a Dominican, and he was not under any obligation to accept the teaching of St. Thomas. Of these three philosophers, then, it is only Durandus whose departures from Thomism might be called 'revolutionary'; and, even in his case, his opinions can be called 'revolutionary' only in regard to his position as a Dominican and to the obligation on the members of his Order of following the teaching of St. Thomas, the Dominican Doctor. In this restricted sense he might be called a revolutionary: he was certainly independent. Hervé Nédellec, the Dominican theologian who wrote

against Henry of Ghent and James of Metz, conducted a prolonged warfare against Durandus, while John of Naples and Peter Marsh (Petrus de Palude), both Dominicans, drew up a long list of points on which Durandus had offended against the teaching of Aquinas.[1] Bernard of Lombardy, another Dominican, also attacked Durandus; but his attack was not sustained like that of Hervé Nédellec; he admired and was partly influenced by Durandus. A sharp polemic (the *Evidentiae Durandelli contra Durandum*) came from the pen of Durandellus who was identified for a time with Durandus of Aurillac but who may have been, according to J. Koch, another Dominican, Nicholas of St. Victor.[2] But, as we have seen, Durandus did not turn against or reject the thirteenth-century tradition as such: on the contrary, his interests were in metaphysics and in psychology much more than in logic, and he was influenced by speculative philosophers like Henry of Ghent.

But, though one can hardly call Durandus or Petrus Aureoli a precursor of Ockhamism, if by this one means that the shift of emphasis from metaphysics to logic, coupled with a critical attitude towards metaphysical speculation as such, is a feature of their respective philosophies, yet it is probably true that in a broad sense they helped to prepare the way for nominalism and that they can be called, as they often have been called, transition-thinkers. It is perfectly true that Durandus, as has already been mentioned, was a member of the commission which censured a number of propositions taken from Ockham's commentary on the *Sentences*; but though this fact obviously manifests his personal disapproval of Ockham's teaching it does not prove that his own philosophy had no influence at all in favouring the spread of Ockhamism. Durandus, Petrus Aureoli and Henry of Harclay all insist that only individual things exist. It is true that St. Thomas Aquinas held precisely the same; but Petrus Aureoli drew from it the conclusion that the problem of a multiplicity of individuals within the same species is no problem at all. Quite apart from the question whether there is or is not such a problem, the resolute denial that there is a problem facilitates, I think, the taking of further steps on the road to nominalism which Petrus Aureoli himself did not take. After all, Ockham regarded his theory of universals as simply the logical conclusion of the truth that only individuals exist. Again, though it can be said with truth that Durandus's assertion that universality

[1] On this subject see J. Koch: *Durandus de S. Porciano O.P.*, in *Beiträge zur Gesch. des Mittelalters*, 26, 1, pp. 199 ff., Münster i. W., 1927.

[2] *Ibid.*, pp. 340–69.

belongs only to the concept and Petrus Aureoli's and Henry of Harclay's assertions that the universal concept is a fabrication of the mind and that universality has *esse obiectivum* only in the concept do not constitute a rejection of moderate realism, yet the tendency shown by Petrus Aureoli and Henry of Harclay to explain the genesis of the universal concept by reference to a confused or less clear impression of the individual does facilitate a breakaway from the theory of universals maintained by Thomas Aquinas. Further, cannot one see in these thinkers a tendency to wield what is known as 'Ockham's razor'? Durandus sacrificed the Thomist cognitive *species* (that is 'species' in its psychological sense) while Petrus Aureoli often made use of the principle *pluralitas non est ponenda sine necessitate* in order to get rid of what he regarded as superfluous entities. And Ockhamism belonged, in a sense, to this general movement of simplification. In addition, it carried further that spirit of criticism which one can observe in James of Metz, Durandus and Petrus Aureoli. Thus I think that while historical research has shown that thinkers like Durandus, Petrus Aureoli and Henry of Harclay cannot be called 'nominalists', there are aspects of their thought which enable one to link them in some degree to the general movement of thought which facilitated the spread of Ockhamism. Indeed, if one accepted Ockham's estimation of himself as a true Aristotelian and if one looked on Ockhamism as the final overthrow of all vestiges of non-Aristotelian realism, one could reasonably regard the philosophers whom we have been considering as carrying a step further the general anti-realist movement which culminated in Ockhamism. But it would be necessary to add that they were still more or less moderate realists and that in the eyes of the Ockhamists they did not proceed far enough along the anti-realist path. Ockham certainly did not regard these thinkers as 'Ockhamists' before their time.

CHAPTER III

OCKHAM (1)

Life—Works—Unity of thought.

1. WILLIAM OF OCKHAM was probably born at Ockham in Surrey, though it is possible that he was simply William Ockham and that his name had nothing to do with the village. The date of his birth is uncertain. Though usually placed between 1290 and 1300, it is possible that it took place somewhat earlier.[1] He entered the Franciscan Order and did his studies at Oxford, where he began the study of theology in 1310. If this is correct, he would have lectured on the Bible from 1315 to 1317 and on the *Sentences* from 1317 to 1319. The following years, 1319–24, were spent in study, writing and Scholastic disputation. Ockham had thus completed the studies required for the *magisterium* or doctorate; but he never actually taught as *magister regens*, doubtless because early in 1324 he was cited to appear before the pope at Avignon. His title of *inceptor* (beginner) is due to this fact that he never actually taught as doctor and professor; it has nothing at all to do with the founding of a School.[2]

In 1323 John Lutterell, former Chancellor of Oxford, arrived at Avignon where he brought to the attention of the Holy See a list of 56 propositions taken from a version of Ockham's commentary on the *Sentences*. It appears that Ockham himself, who appeared at Avignon in 1324, presented another version of the commentary, in which he had made some emendations. In any case the commission appointed to deal with the matter did not accept for

[1] As he seems to have been ordained subdeacon in February 1306, he was most probably born before 1290; according to P. Boehner, about 1280.

[2] P. Boehner follows Pelster in interpreting *inceptor* in the strict sense, that is to say, as meaning someone who had fulfilled all the requirements for the doctorate, but who had not taken up his duties as an actual professor. If this interpretation is accepted it is easy to explain how the *Venerabilis Inceptor* could sometimes be called *doctor*, and even *magister*; but the word *inceptor* should not, I think, be so explained as to imply that the man to whom it was applied was, or might be, an actual doctor. The word was used for a candidate for the doctorate, a 'formed bachelor', and though Ockham was qualified to take the doctorate, he does not appear to have actually taken it. As to his honorific title, *Venerabilis Inceptor*, the first word was applied to him as founder of 'nominalism', while the second, as we have seen, referred simply to his position at the time his studies at Oxford came to an end. Incidentally, there is no evidence whatever that he ever studied at Paris or took the doctorate there.

condemnation all the propositions complained of by Lutterell: in its list of 51 propositions it confined itself more or less to theological points, accepting 33 of Lutterell's propositions and adding others of its own. Some propositions were condemned as heretical, others, less important, as erroneous but not heretical; but the process was not brought to a final conclusion, perhaps because Ockham had in the meantime fled from Avignon. It has also been conjectured that the influence of Durandus, who was a member of the commission, may have been exerted in Ockham's favour, on one or two points at least.

At the beginning of December 1327 Michael of Cesena, the Franciscan General, arrived at Avignon, whither Pope John XXII had summoned him, to answer for his attacks on the papal Constitutions concerning evangelical poverty. At the instance of the General Ockham interested himself in the poverty dispute, and in May 1328 Michael of Cesena, who had just been re-elected General of the Franciscans, fled from Avignon, taking with him Bonagratia of Bergamo, Francis of Ascoli and William of Ockham. In June the pope excommunicated the four fugitives, who joined the Emperor Ludwig of Bavaria at Pisa and went with him to Munich. Thus there began Ockham's participation in the struggle between emperor and pope, a struggle in which the emperor was also assisted by Marsilius of Padua. While some of Ockham's polemics against John XXII and his successors, Benedict XII and Clement VI, concerned theological matters, the chief point of the whole dispute was, of course, the right relation of the secular to the ecclesiastical power, and to this point we shall return.

On October 11th, 1347, Ludwig of Bavaria, Ockham's protector, suddenly died, and Ockham took steps to reconcile himself with the Church. It is not necessary to suppose that his motives were merely prudential. A formula of submission was prepared but it is not known if Ockham actually signed it or whether the reconciliation was ever formally effected. Ockham died at Munich in 1349, apparently of the Black Death.

2. The commentary on the first book of the *Sentences* was written by Ockham himself, and the first edition of this *Ordinatio*[1] seems to have been composed between 1318 and 1323. The commentaries on the other three books of the *Sentences* are *reportationes*, though they also belong to an early period. Boehner

[1] The word *ordinatio* was used to denote the text or the part of a text which a mediaeval lecturer actually wrote or dictated with a view to publication.

thinks that they were composed before the *Ordinatio*. The *Expositio in librum Porphyrii*, the *Expositio in librum Praedicamentorum*, the *Expositio in duos libros Elenchorum* and the *Expositio in duos libros Perihermenias* appear to have been composed while Ockham was working on his commentary on the *Sentences* and to have antedated the first *Ordinatio* though not the *Reportatio*. The text of these logical works, minus the *In libros Elenchorum*, in the 1496 Bologna edition is entitled *Expositio aurea super artem veterem*. The *Expositio super octo libros Physicorum* was composed after the commentary on the *Sentences* and before the *Summa totius logicae*, which was itself composed before 1329. As to the *Compendium logicae*, its authenticity has been questioned.

Ockham also composed *Summulae in libros Physicorum* (or *Philosophia naturalis*) and *Quaestiones in libros Physicorum*. As to the *Tractatus de successivis*, this is a compilation made by another hand from an authentic work of Ockham, namely the *Expositio super libros Physicorum*. Boehner makes it clear that it can be used as a source for Ockham's doctrine. 'Almost every line was written by Ockham, and in this sense the *Tractatus de successivis* is authentic.'[1] The authenticity of the *Quaestiones diversae: De relatione, de puncto, de negatione*, is also doubtful.

Theological works by Ockham include the *Quodlibeta VII*, the *Tractatus de Sacramento Altaris* or *De Corpore Christi* (which seems to contain two distinct treatises) and the *Tractatus de praedestinatione et de praescientia Dei et de futuris contingentibus*. The authenticity of the *Centiloquium theologicum* or *summa de conclusionibus theologicis* has not been proved. On the other hand, the arguments adduced to prove that the work is unauthentic do not appear to be conclusive.[2] To Ockham's Munich period belong among other works the *Opus nonaginta dierum*, the *Compendium errorum Ioannis papae XXII*, the *Octo quaestiones de potestate papae*, the *An princeps pro suo succursu, scilicet guerrae, possit recipere bona ecclesiarum, etiam invito papa*, the *Consultatio de causa matrimoniali* and the *Dialogus inter magistrum et discipulum de imperatorum et pontificum potestate*. The last-named work is Ockham's chief political publication. It consists of three parts, composed at different times. But it has to be used with care,

[1] *Tractatus de successivis*, edit. Boehner, p. 29.

[2] See E. Iserloh: *Um die Echtheit des Centiloquium; Gregorianum*, 30 (1949), 78–103.

as many opinions for which Ockham does not make himself responsible are canvassed in it.

3. Ockham possessed an extensive knowledge of the work of the great Scholastics who had preceded him and a remarkable acquaintance with Aristotle. But even though we can discern anticipations in other philosophers of certain theses of Ockham, it would appear that his originality is incontestable. Though the philosophy of Scotus gave rise to certain of Ockham's problems and though certain of Scotus's views and tendencies were developed by Ockham, the latter constantly attacked the system of Scotus, particularly his realism; so that Ockhamism was a strong reaction to, rather than a development of, Scotism. No doubt Ockham was influenced by certain theories of Durandus (those on relations, for example) and Petrus Aureoli; but the extent of such influence, such as it was, does little to impair Ockham's fundamental originality. There is no adequate reason for challenging his reputation as the fountainhead of the terminist or nominalist movement. Nor is there, I think, any cogent reason for representing Ockham as a mere Aristotelian (or, if preferred, as a mere would-be Aristotelian). He certainly tried to overthrow Scotist realism with the help of the Aristotelian logic and theory of knowledge, and further he regarded all realism as a perversion of true Aristotelianism; but he also endeavoured to rectify the theories of Aristotle which excluded any admission of the liberty and omnipotence of God. Ockham was not an 'original' thinker in the sense of one who invented novelties for the sake of novelty, though his reputation as a destructive critic might lead one to suppose that he was; but he was an original thinker in the sense that he thought out his problems for himself and developed his solutions thoroughly and systematically.

The question has been raised and discussed[1] whether or not Ockham's literary career must be regarded as falling into two more or less unconnected parts and, if so, whether this indicates a dichotomy in his character and interests. For it might seem that there is little connection between Ockham's purely logical and philosophical activities at Oxford and his polemical activities at Munich. It might appear that there is a radical discrepancy between Ockham the cold logician and academic philosopher and Ockham the impassioned political and ecclesiastical controversialist. But such a supposition is unnecessary. Ockham was an

[1] See, for example, Georges de Lagarde (cf. *Bibliog.*), IV, pp. 63–6; V, pp. 7 ff.

independent, bold and vigorous thinker, who showed a marked ability for criticism; he held certain clear convictions and principles which he was ready to apply courageously, systematically and logically; and the difference in tone between his philosophical and polemical works is due rather to a difference in the field of application of his principles than to any unreconciled contradiction in the character of the man. No doubt his personal history and circumstances had emotional repercussions which manifested themselves in his polemical writings; but the emotional overtones of these writings cannot conceal the fact that they are the work of the same vigorous, critical and logical mind which composed the commentary on the *Sentences*. His career falls into two phases, and in the second phase a side of Ockham manifests itself which had no occasion to show itself in the same way during the first phase; but it seems to me an exaggeration to imply that Ockham the logician and Ockham the politician were almost different personalities. It is rather that the same personality and the same original mind manifested itself in different ways according to the different circumstances of Ockham's life and the different problems with which he was faced. One would not expect the exile of Munich, his Oxford career cut short and the ban of excommunication on his head, to have treated the problems of Church and State in exactly the same way that he treated the problem of universals at Oxford; but on the other hand one would not expect the exiled philosopher to lose sight of logic and principle and to become simply a polemical journalist. If one knew sufficient of Ockham's character and temperament, the apparent discrepancies between his activities in the two phases would, I think, seem quite natural. The trouble is that we really know very little of Ockham the man. This fact prevents one from making any categorical assertion that he was not a kind of split or double personality; but it seems more sensible to attempt to explain the different aspects of his literary activity on the supposition that he was not a split personality. If this can be done, then we can apply Ockham's own razor to the contrary hypothesis.

As we shall see, there are various elements or strands in Ockham's thought. There are the 'empiricist' element, the rationalist and logical elements, and the theological element. It does not seem to me very easy to synthesize all the elements of his thought; but perhaps it might be as well to remark immediately that one of Ockham's main preoccupations as a philosopher was to purge

Christian theology and philosophy of all traces of Greek necessitarianism, particularly of the theory of essences, which in his opinion endangered the Christian doctrines of the divine liberty and omnipotence. His activity as a logician and his attack on all forms of realism in regard to universals can thus be looked on as subordinate in a sense to his preoccupations as a Christian theologian. This is a point to bear in mind. Ockham was a Franciscan and a theologian: he should not be interpreted as though he were a modern radical empiricist.

CHAPTER IV

OCKHAM (2)

Ockham and the metaphysic of essences—Peter of Spain and the terminist logic—Ockham's logic and theory of universals—Real and rational science—Necessary truths and demonstration.

1. AT the end of the last chapter I mentioned Ockham's preoccupation as a theologian with the Christian doctrines of the divine omnipotence and liberty. He thought that these doctrines could not be safeguarded without eliminating the metaphysic of essences which had been introduced into Christian theology and philosophy from Greek sources. In the philosophy of St. Augustine and in the philosophies of the leading thirteenth-century thinkers the theory of divine ideas had played an important part. Plato had postulated eternal forms or 'ideas', which he most probably regarded as distinct from God but which served as models or patterns according to which God formed the world in its intelligible structure; and later Greek philosophers of the Platonic tradition located these exemplary forms in the divine mind. Christian philosophers proceeded to utilize and adapt this theory in their explanation of the free creation of the world by God. Creation considered as a free and intelligent act on God's part, postulates in God an intellectual pattern or model, as it were, of creation. The theory was, of course, constantly refined; and St. Thomas took pains to show that the ideas in God are not really distinct from the divine essence. We cannot help using language which implies that they are distinct; but actually they are ontologically identical with the divine essence, being simply the divine essence known by God as imitable externally (that is, by creatures) in different ways. This doctrine was the common doctrine in the Middle Ages up to and including the thirteenth century, being considered necessary in order to explain creation and to distinguish it from a purely spontaneous production. Plato had simply postulated universal subsistent forms; but though the Christian thinkers, with their belief in divine providence extending to individuals, admitted ideas of individuals in God, they retained the originally Platonic notion of universal ideas. God creates man, for example, according to His universal idea of human nature. From

this it follows that the natural moral law is not something purely arbitrary, capriciously determined by the divine will: given the idea of human nature, the idea of the natural moral law follows.

Correlative to the theory of universal ideas in God is the acceptance of some form of realism in the explanation of our own universal ideas. Indeed, the former would never have been asserted without the latter; for if a class-word like 'man' were devoid of any objective reference and if there were no such thing as human nature, there would be no reason for ascribing to God a universal idea of man, that is, an idea of human nature. In the second volume of this work an account has been given of the course of the controversy concerning universals in the Middle Ages up to the time of Aquinas; and there it was shown how the early mediaeval form of ultra-realism was finally refuted by Abelard. That only individuals exist came to be the accepted belief. At the same time the moderate realists, like Aquinas, certainly believed in the objectivity of real species and natures. If *X* and *Y* are two men, for example, they do not possess the same individual nature; but none the less each possesses his own human nature or essence, and the two natures are similar, each nature being, as it were, a finite imitation of the divine idea of human nature. Duns Scotus proceeded further in the realist direction by finding a formal objective distinction between the human nature of *X* and the *X*-ness of *X* and between the human nature of *Y* and the *Y*-ness of *Y*. Yet, though he spoke of a 'common nature', he did not mean that the actual nature of *X* is individually the same as the actual nature of *Y*.

William of Ockham attacked the first part of the metaphysic of essences. He was, indeed, willing to retain something of the language of the theory of divine ideas, doubtless largely out of respect for St. Augustine and tradition; but he emptied the theory of its former content. He thought of the theory as implying a limitation of the divine freedom and omnipotence, as though God would be governed, as it were, and limited in His creative act by the eternal ideas or essences. Moreover, as we shall see later, he thought that the traditional connection of the moral law with the theory of divine ideas constituted an affront to the divine liberty: the moral law depends ultimately, according to Ockham, on the divine will and choice. In other words, for Ockham there is on the one hand God, free and omnipotent, and on the other hand creatures, utterly contingent and dependent. True, all orthodox Christian thinkers of the Middle Ages held the same; but the point is that according to Ockham the metaphysic of essences was a non-Christian invention which had no place in Christian theology and philosophy. As to the other part of the metaphysic of essences Ockham resolutely attacked all forms of 'realism', especially that of Scotus, and he employed the terminist logic in his attack; but, as we shall see, his view of universals was not quite so revolutionary as is sometimes supposed.

Mention will be made later of Ockham's answer to the question, in what sense is it legitimate to speak of ideas in God; at present I propose to outline his logical theory and his discussion of the problem of universals. It must be remembered, however, that Ockham was a gifted and acute logician with a love for simplicity and clarity. What I have been saying about his theological preoccupations should not be taken to mean that his logical inquiries were simply 'apologetic': I was not trying to suggest that Ockham's logic can be waved aside as informed by interested and extrinsic motives. It is rather that in view of some of the pictures which have been given of Ockham it is as well to bear in mind the fact that he *was* a theologian and that he did have theological preoccupations: remembrance of this fact enables one to form a more unified view of his intellectual activity than is otherwise possible.

2. I have said that Ockham 'employed the terminist logic'. This was not a tendentious statement, but it was meant to indicate that Ockham was not the original inventor of the terminist logic. And I wish to make some brief remarks about its development before going on to outline Ockham's own logical theories.

In the thirteenth century there naturally appeared a variety of commentaries on the Aristotelian logic and of logical handbooks and treatises. Among English authors may be mentioned William of Shyreswood (d. 1249), who composed *Introductiones ad logicam,* and among French authors Lambert of Auxerre and Nicholas of Paris. But the most popular and influential work on logic was the *Summulae logicales* of Peter of Spain, a native of Lisbon, who taught at Paris and later became Pope John XXI. He died in 1277. At the beginning of this work we read that 'dialectic is the art of arts and the science of sciences' which opens the way to the knowledge of the principles of all methods.[1] A similar statement of the fundamental importance of dialectic was

[1] Ed. Bochenski, p. 1.

made by Lambert of Auxerre. Peter of Spain goes on to say that dialectic is carried on only by means of language, and that language involves the use of words. One must begin, then, by considering the word, first as a physical entity, secondly as a significant term. This emphasis on language was characteristic of the logicians and grammarians of the faculty of arts.

When Peter of Spain emphasized the importance of dialectic, he meant by 'dialectic' the art of probable reasoning; and in view of the fact that some other thirteenth-century logicians shared this tendency to concentrate on probable reasoning as distinct from demonstrative science on the one hand and sophistical reasoning on the other, it is tempting to see in their works the source of the fourteenth-century emphasis on probable arguments. No doubt there may have been a connection; but one must remember that a thinker like Peter of Spain did not abandon the idea that metaphysical arguments can give certainty. In other words, Ockham was doubtless influenced by the emphasis placed by the preceding logicians on dialectic or syllogistic reasoning leading to probable conclusions; but that does not mean that one can father on his predecessors his own tendency to look on arguments in philosophy, as distinct from logic, as probable rather than demonstrative arguments.

A number of the treatises in Peter of Spain's *Summulae logicales* deal with the Aristotelian logic; but others deal with the 'modern logic' or logic of terms. Thus in the treatise headed *De suppositionibus* he distinguishes the *significatio* from the *suppositio* of terms. The former function of a term consists in the relation of a sign to the thing signified. Thus in the English language the term 'man' is a sign, while in the French language the term 'homme' has the same sign-function. But in the sentence 'the man is running' the term 'man', which already possesses its *significatio*, acquires the function of standing for (*supponere pro*) a definite man, whereas in the sentence 'man dies' it stands for all men. One must thus, says Peter, distinguish between *significatio* and *suppositio*, inasmuch as the latter presupposes the former.

Now, this logic of terms, with its doctrine of signs and of 'standing-for', undoubtedly influenced William of Ockham, who took from his predecessors much of what one might call his technical equipment. But it does not follow, of course, that Ockham did not develop the terminist logic very considerably. Nor does it follow that Ockham's philosophical views and the use to which he put the terminist logic were borrowed from a thinker like Peter of Spain. On the contrary, Peter was a conservative in philosophy and was very far from showing any tendency to anticipate Ockham's 'nominalism'. To find the antecedents of the terminist logic in the thirteenth century is not the same thing as attempting to push back the whole Ockhamist philosophy into that century: such an attempt would be futile.

The theory of supposition was, however, only one of the features of fourteenth-century logic. I have given it special mention here because of the use made of it by Ockham in his discussion of the problem of universals. But in any history of mediaeval logic prominence would have to be given to the theory of consequences or of the inferential operations between propositions. In his *Summa Logicae*[1] Ockham deals with this subject after treating in turn of terms, propositions and syllogisms. But in the *De puritate artis logicae*[2] of Walter Burleigh the theory of consequences is given great prominence, and the author's remarks on syllogistics form a kind of appendix to it. Again, Albert of Saxony in his *Perutilis Logica* treats syllogistics as part of the general theory of consequences, though he follows Ockham in starting his treatise with a consideration of terms. The importance of this development of the theory of consequences in the fourteenth century is the witness it bears to the growing conception of logic as formalistic in character. For this feature of the later mediaeval logic reveals an affinity, which was for long disregarded or even unsuspected, between mediaeval and modern logic. Research into the history of mediaeval logic has not indeed yet reached the point at which an adequate account of the subject becomes possible. But further lines for reflection and research are indicated in Father Boehner's little work, *Mediaeval Logic*, which is mentioned in the Bibliography. And the reader is referred to this work for further information.

3. I turn now to Ockham's logic, with special attention to his attack on all realist theories of universals. What has been said in the preceding section will suffice to show that the ascription to Ockham of various logical words and notions should not necessarily be taken to imply that he invented them.

(i) There are various kinds of terms, traditionally distinguished from one another. For example, some terms refer directly to a

[1] Edited by P. Boehner, O.F.M. The Franciscan Institute, St. Bonaventure, N.Y. and E. Nauwelaerts, Louvain. *Pars prima*, 1951.

[2] Edited by P. Boehner, O.F.M. *Ibid.*, 1951.

reality and have a meaning even when they stand by themselves. These terms ('butter', for instance) are called categorematic terms. Other terms, however, like 'no' and 'every' acquire a definite reference only when standing in relation to categorematic terms, as in the phrases 'no man' and 'every house'. These are called syncategorematic terms. Again, some terms are absolute, in the sense that they signify a thing without reference to any other thing, while other terms are called connotative terms, because, like 'son' or 'father', they signify an object considered only in relation to some other thing.

(ii) If we consider the word 'man', we shall recognize that it is a conventional sign: it signifies something or has a meaning, but that this particular word has that particular meaning or exercises that particular sign-function is a matter of convention. This is easily seen to be the case if we bear in mind the fact that in other languages 'homme' and 'homo' are used with the same meaning. Now, the grammarian can reason about words as words, of course; but the real material of our reasoning is not the conventional but the natural sign. The natural sign is the concept. Whether we are English and use the word 'man' or whether we are French and use the word 'homme', the concept or logical significance of the term is the same. The words are different, but their meaning is the same. Ockham distinguished, therefore, both the spoken word (*terminus prolatus*) and the written word (*terminus scriptus*) from the concept (*terminus conceptus* or *intentio animae*), that is, the term considered according to its meaning or logical significance.

Ockham called the concept or *terminus conceptus* a 'natural sign' because he thought that the direct apprehension of anything causes naturally in the human mind a concept of that thing. Both brutes and men utter some sounds as a natural reaction to a stimulus; and these sounds are natural signs. But 'brutes and men utter sounds of this kind only to signify some feelings or some accidents present in themselves', whereas the intellect 'can elicit qualities to signify any sort of thing naturally'.[1] Perceiving a cow results in the formation of the same idea or 'natural sign' (*terminus conceptus*) in the mind of the Englishman and of the Frenchman though the former will express this concept in word or writing by means of one conventional sign, 'cow', while the latter will express it by means of another conventional sign, 'vache'. This treatment of signs was an improvement on that given by

[1] 1 *Sent.*, 2, 8, Q.

Peter of Spain, who does not seem to give sufficient explicit recognition to the identity of logical significance which may attach to corresponding words in different languages.

To anticipate for a moment, one may point out that when Ockham is called a 'nominalist', it is not meant, or should not be meant, that he ascribed universality to words considered precisely as *termini prolati* or *scripti*, that is, to terms considered as conventional signs: it was the natural sign, the *terminus conceptus*, of which he was thinking.

(iii) Terms are elements of propositions, the term standing to the proposition as *incomplexum* to *complexum*; and it is only in the proposition that a term acquires the function of 'standing for' (*suppositio*). For example, in the statement 'the man is running' the term 'man' stands for a precise individual. This is an instance of *suppositio personalis*. But in the statement 'man is a species' the term 'man' stands for all men. This is *suppositio simplex*. Finally, in the statement '*Man* is a noun' one is speaking of the word itself. This is *suppositio materialis*. Taken in itself the term 'man' is capable of exercising any of these functions; but it is only in a proposition that it actually acquires a determinate type of the functions in question. *Suppositio*, then, is 'a property belonging to a term, but only in a proposition'.[1]

(iv) In the statement 'man is mortal' the term 'man', which is, as we have seen, a sign, stands for things, that is, men, which are not themselves signs. It is, therefore, a term of 'first intention' (*primae intentionis*). But in the statement 'species are subdivisions of genera' the term 'species' does not stand immediately for things which are not themselves signs: it stands for class-names, like 'man', 'horse', 'dog', which are themselves signs. The term 'species' is thus a term of second intention (*secundae intentionis*). In other words, terms of second intention stand for terms of first intention and are predicated of them, as when it is said that 'man' and 'horse' are species.

In a broad sense of 'first intention' syncategorematic terms may be called first intentions. Taken in themselves, they do not signify things; but when conjoined with other terms they make those other terms stand for things in a determinate manner. For example, the term 'every' cannot by itself stand for definite things; but as qualifying the term 'man' in the sentence 'every man is mortal' it makes the term 'man' stand for a definite set of things.

[1] *Summa totius logicae*, 1, 63.

In the strict sense of 'first intention', however, a term of first intention is an 'extreme term' in a proposition, one, that is, which stands for a thing which is not a sign or for things which are not signs. In the sentence 'arsenic is poisonous', the term 'arsenic' is both an 'extreme term' and one which stands in the proposition for something which is not itself a sign. A term of second intention, strictly understood, will thus be a term which naturally signifies first intentions and which can stand for them in a proposition. 'Genus', 'species' and 'difference' are examples of terms of second intention.[1]

(v) Ockham's answer to the problem of universals has been already indicated in effect: universals are terms (*termini concepti*) which signify individual things and which stand for them in propositions. Only individual things exist; and by the very fact that a thing exists it is individual. There are not and cannot be existent universals. To assert the extramental existence of universals is to commit the folly of asserting a contradiction; for if the universal exists, it must be individual. And that there is no common reality existing at the same time in two members of a species can be shown in several ways. For example, if God were to create a man out of nothing, this would not affect any other man, as far as his essence is concerned. Again, one individual thing can be annihilated without the annihilation or destruction of another individual thing. 'One man can be annihilated by God without any other man being annihilated or destroyed. Therefore there is not anything common to both, because (if there were) it would be annihilated, and consequently no other man would retain his essential nature.'[2] As to the opinion of Scotus that there is a formal distinction between the common nature and the individuality, it is true that he 'excelled others in subtlety of judgment';[3] but if the alleged distinction is an objective and not purely mental distinction, it must be real. The opinion of Scotus is thus subject to the same difficulties which were encountered by older theories of realism.

Whether the universal concept is a quality distinct from the act of the intellect or whether it is that act itself is a question of but secondary importance: the important point is that 'no universal is anything existing in any way outside the soul; but everything which is predicable of many things is of its nature in the mind, whether subjectively or objectively; and no universal belongs to

[1] *Quodlibet*, 4, 19. [2] 1 *Sent.*, 2, 4, D. [3] *Ibid.*, 2, 6, B.

the essence or quiddity of any substance whatever'.[1] Ockham does not appear to have attached very great weight to the question whether the universal concept is an accident distinct from the intellect as such or whether it is simply the intellect itself in its activity: he was more concerned with the analysis of the meaning of terms and propositions than with psychological questions. But it is fairly clear that he did not think that the universal has any existence in the soul except as an act of the understanding. The existence of the universal consists in an act of the understanding and it exists only as such. It owes its existence simply to the intellect: there is no universal reality corresponding to the concept. It is not, however, a fiction in the sense that it does not stand for anything real: it stands for individual real things, though it does not stand for any universal thing. It is, in short, a way of conceiving or knowing individual things.

(vi) Ockham may sometimes imply that the universal is a confused or indistinct image of distinct individual things; but he was not concerned to identify the universal concept with the image or phantasm. His main point was always that there is no need to postulate any factors other than the mind and individual things in order to explain the universal. The universal concept arises simply because there are varying degrees of similarity between individual things. Socrates and Plato are more similar to one another than either is to an ass; and this fact of experience is reflected in the formation of the specific concept of man. But we have to be careful of our way of speaking. We ought not to say that 'Plato and Socrates agree (share) in something or in some things, but that they agree (are alike) by some things, that is, by themselves and that Socrates agrees with (*convenit cum*) Plato, not in something, but by something, namely himself'.[2] In other words, there is no nature common to Socrates and Plato, *in* which they come together or share or agree; but the nature which is Socrates and the nature which is Plato are alike. The foundation of generic concepts can be explained in a similar manner.

(vii) The question might well be raised how this conceptualism differs from the position of St. Thomas. After all, when Ockham says that the notion that there are universal things corresponding to universal terms is absurd and destructive of the whole philosophy

[1] 1 *Sent.*, 2, 8, Q.

[2] *Ibid.*, 2, 6, E E. *Respondeo quod conveniunt (Socrates et Plato) aliquibus, quia seipsis, et quod Socrates convenit cum Platone non in aliquo sed aliquo, quia seipso.*

of Aristotle and of all science,[1] St. Thomas would agree. And it was certainly St. Thomas's opinion that while the natures of men, for example, are alike there is no common nature considered as a thing in which all individual men have a share. But it must be remembered that St. Thomas gave a metaphysical explanation of the similarity of natures; for he held that God creates things belonging to the same species, things, that is, with similar natures, according to an idea of human nature in the divine mind. Ockham, however, discarded this theory of divine ideas. The consequence was that for him the similarities which give rise to universal concepts are simply similarities, so to speak, of fact: there is no metaphysical reason for these similarities except the divine choice, which is not dependent on any divine ideas. In other words, although St. Thomas and William of Ockham were fundamentally at one in denying that there is any *universale in re*, the former combined his rejection of ultra-realism with the Augustinian doctrine of the *universale ante rem*, whereas the latter did not.[2]

Another, though less important, difference concerns the way of speaking about universal concepts. Ockham, as we have seen, held that the universal concept is an act of the understanding. 'I say that the first intention as well as the second intention is truly an act of the understanding, for whatever is saved by the fiction can be saved by the act.'[3] Ockham appears to be referring to the theory of Petrus Aureoli, according to which the concept, which is the object appearing to the mind, is a 'fiction'. Ockham prefers to say that the concept is simply the act of the understanding. 'The first intention is an act of the understanding signifying things which are not signs. The second intention is the act signifying first intentions.'[4] And Ockham proceeds to say that both first and second intentions are truly real entities, and that they are truly qualities subjectively existent in the soul. That they are real entities, if they are acts of the understanding, is clear; but it seems rather odd perhaps to find Ockham calling them qualities. However, if his various utterances are to be interpreted as consistent with one another, he cannot be supposed to mean that universal concepts are qualities really distinct from the acts of understanding. 'Everything which is explained through positing something distinct from the act of understanding can be explained without positing such a distinct thing.'[5] In other words, Ockham

[1] *Expositio aurea*, 3, 2, 90, R. [2] See vol. II, p. 154. [3] *Quodlibet*, 4, 19.
[4] *Ibid.* [5] *Summa totius logicae*, I, 12.

is content to talk simply about the act of the understanding; and he applies the principle of economy to get rid of the apparatus of abstracting *species intelligibiles*. But though there is certainly a difference between the theory of Aquinas and that of Ockham in this respect, it must be remembered that Aquinas insisted strongly that the *species intelligibilis* is not the object of knowledge: it is *id quo intelligitur* and not *id quod intelligitur*.[1]

4. We are now in a position to consider briefly Ockham's theory of science. He divides science into two main types, real science and rational science. The former (*scientia realis*) is concerned with real things, in a sense to be discussed presently, while the latter (*scientia rationalis*) is concerned with terms which do not stand immediately for real things. Thus logic, which deals with terms of second intention, like 'species' and 'genus', is a rational science. It is important to maintain the distinction between these two types of science: otherwise concepts or terms will be confused with things. For example, if one does not realize that Aristotle's intention in the *Categories* was to treat of words and concepts and not of things, one will interpret him in a sense quite foreign to his thought. Logic is concerned with terms of second intention, which cannot exist *sine ratione*, that is, without the mind's activity; it deals, therefore, with mental 'fabrications'. I said earlier that Ockham did not much like speaking of universal concepts as fictions or fictive entities; but the point I then had in mind was that Ockham objected to the implication that what we know by means of a universal concept is a fiction and not a real thing. He was quite ready to speak of terms of second intention, which enter into the propositions of logic, as 'fabrications', because these terms do not refer directly to real things. But logic, which is rational science, presupposes real science; for terms of second intention presuppose terms of first intention.

Real science is concerned with things, that is, with individual things. But Ockham also says that 'real science is not always of things as the objects which are immediately known'.[2] This might seem to be a contradiction; but Ockham proceeds to explain that any science, whether real or rational, is only of propositions.[3] In other words, when he says that real science is concerned with things, Ockham does not mean to deny the Aristotelian doctrine that science is of the universal; but he is determined to hold to the other Aristotelian doctrine that it is only individuals which exist.

[1] Cf. *S.T.*, 1, 76, 2, *ad* 4; 1, 85, 2. [2] 1 *Sent.*, 2, 4, M. [3] *Ibid.*

Real science, then, is concerned with universal propositions; and he gives as examples of such propositions 'man is capable of laughter' and 'every man is capable of training'; but the universal terms stand for individual things, and not for universal realities existing extramentally. If Ockham says, then, that real science is concerned with individual things by means of terms (*mediantibus terminis*), he does not mean that real science is unconnected with actual existents which are individual things. Science is concerned with the truth or falsity of propositions; but to say that a proposition of real science is true is to say that it is verified in all those individual things of which the terms of the proposition are the natural signs. The difference between real and rational science consists in this, that 'the parts, that is, the terms of the propositions known by real science stand for things, which is not the case with the terms of propositions known by rational science, for these terms stand for other terms'.[1]

5. Ockham's insistence on individual things as the sole existents does not mean, therefore, that he rejects science considered as a knowledge of universal propositions. Nor does he reject the Aristotelian ideas of indemonstrable principles and of demonstration. As regards the former, a principle may be indemonstrable in the sense that the mind cannot but assent to the proposition once it grasps the meaning of the terms, or it may be indemonstrable in the sense that it is known evidently only by experience. 'Certain first principles are not known through themselves (*per se nota* or analytic) but are known only through experience as in the case of the proposition "all heat is calefactive".'[2] As to demonstration, Ockham accepts the Aristotelian definition of demonstration as a syllogism which produces knowledge; but he proceeds to analyse the various meanings of 'know' (*scire*). It may mean the evident understanding of truth; and in this sense even contingent facts, such as the fact that I am now sitting, can be known. Or it may mean the evident understanding of necessary, as distinct from contingent, truths. Or, thirdly, it may mean 'the understanding of one necessary truth through the evident understanding of two necessary truths; . . . and it is in this sense that "knowing" is understood in the aforementioned definition'.[3]

This insistence on necessary truths must not be taken to mean that for Ockham there can be no scientific knowledge of contingent things. He did not think, indeed, that an affirmative and assertoric

[1] 1 *Sent.*, 2, 4, O. [2] *Summa totius logicae*, 3, 2. [3] *Ibid.*

proposition concerning contingent things and referring to present time (that is, in relation to the speaker) can be a necessary truth; but he held that affirmative and assertoric propositions which include terms standing for contingent things can be necessary, if they are, or can be considered as equivalent to, negative or hypothetical propositions concerning possibility.[1] In other words, Ockham regarded necessary propositions including terms standing for contingent things as equivalent to hypothetical propositions, in the sense that they are true of each thing for which the subject-terms stands *at the time of the existence of that thing*. Thus the proposition, 'every *X* is *Y*' (where *X* stands for contingent things and *Y* for possessing a property) is necessary if considered as equivalent to 'if there is an *X*, it is *Y*' or 'if it is true to say of anything that it is an *X*, it is also true to say of it that it is *Y*'.

Demonstration for Ockham is demonstration of the attributes of a subject, not of the existence of the subject. We cannot demonstrate, for example, that a certain kind of herb exists; but we may be able to demonstrate the proposition that it has a certain property. True, we can know by experience that it has this property, but if we merely know the fact because we have experienced it, we do not know the 'reason' of the fact. If, however, we can show from the nature of the herb (knowledge of which presupposes experience, of course) that it necessarily possesses this property, we have demonstrative knowledge. To this sort of knowledge Ockham attached considerable importance: he was very far from being a despiser of the syllogism. 'The syllogistic form holds equally in every field.'[2] Ockham did not mean by this, of course, that all true propositions can be proved syllogistically; but he considered that in all matters where scientific knowledge is obtainable syllogistic reasoning holds good. In other words, he adhered to the Aristotelian idea of demonstrative 'science'. In view of the fact that Ockham is not infrequently called an 'empiricist' it is as well to bear in mind the 'rationalist' side of his philosophy. When he said that science is concerned with propositions he did not mean that science is entirely divorced from reality or that demonstration is incapable of telling us anything about things.

[1] *Summa totius logicae*, 3, 2.

[2] 1 *Sent.*, 2, 6, D.

CHAPTER V

OCKHAM (3)

Intuitive knowledge—God's power to cause intuitive 'knowledge' of a non-existent object—Contingency of the world-order—Relations—Causality—Motion and time—Conclusion.

1. SCIENCE, according to Ockham, is concerned with universal propositions, and syllogistic demonstration is the mode of reasoning proper to science in the strict sense: an assent in science is an assent to the truth of a proposition. But this does not mean that for Ockham scientific knowledge is *a priori* in the sense of being a development of innate principles or ideas. On the contrary, intuitive knowledge is primary and fundamental. If we consider, for example, the proposition that the whole is greater than the part, we shall recognize that the mind assents to the truth of the proposition as soon as it apprehends the meaning of the terms; but this does not mean that the principle is innate. Without experience the proposition would not be enunciated; nor should we apprehend the meaning of the terms. Again, in a case where it is possible to demonstrate that an attribute belongs to a subject it is by experience or intuitive knowledge that we know that there is such a subject. Demonstration of a property of man, for example, presupposes an intuitive knowledge of men. 'Nothing can be known naturally in itself unless it is known intuitively.'[1] Ockham is here arguing that we cannot have a natural knowledge of the divine essence as it is in itself, because we have no natural intuition of God; but the principle is a general one. All knowledge is based on experience.

What is meant by intuitive knowledge? 'Intuitive knowledge (*notitia intuitiva*) of a thing is knowledge of such a kind that one can know by means of it whether a thing is or not; and if it is, the intellect immediately judges that the thing exists and concludes evidently that it exists, unless perchance it is hindered on account of some imperfection in that knowledge.'[2] Intuitive knowledge is thus the immediate apprehension of a thing as existent, enabling the mind to form a contingent proposition concerning the existence of that thing. But intuitive knowledge is also knowledge of such

[1] I *Sent.*, 3, 2, F.

[2] *Prol. Sent.*, I, 2.

a kind that 'when some things are known, of which the one inheres in the other or is locally distant from the other or is related in some other way to the other, the mind straightway knows, by virtue of that simple apprehension of those things, whether the thing inheres or does not inhere, whether it is distant or not, and so with other contingent truths. . . . For example, if Socrates is really white, that apprehension of Socrates and whiteness by means of which it can be known evidently that Socrates is white is intuitive knowledge. And, in general, every simple apprehension of a term or of terms, that is, of a thing or things, by means of which some contingent truths, especially concerning the present, can be known, is intuitive knowledge.'[1] Intuitive knowledge is thus caused by the immediate apprehension of existent things. The concept of an individual thing is the natural expression in the mind of the apprehension of that thing, provided that one does not interpret the concept as a *medium quo* of knowledge. 'I say that in no intuitive apprehension, whether sensitive or intellectual, is the thing placed in any state of being which is a medium between the thing and the act of knowing. That is, I say that the thing itself is known immediately without any medium between itself and the act by which it is seen or apprehended.'[2] In other words, intuition is immediate apprehension of a thing or of things leading naturally to the judgment that the thing exists or to some other contingent proposition about it, such as 'it is white'. The guarantee of such judgments is simply evidence, the evident character of the intuition, together with the natural character of the process leading to the judgment. 'I say, therefore, that intuitive knowledge is proper individual knowledge . . . because it is naturally caused by one thing and not by another, nor can it be caused by another thing.'[3]

It is clear that Ockham is not speaking simply of sensation: he is speaking of an intellectual intuition of an individual thing, which is caused by that thing and not by anything else. Moreover, intuition for him is not confined to intuition of sensible or material things. He expressly says that we know our own acts intuitively, this intuition leading to the formation of propositions like 'there is an understanding' and 'there is a will'.[4] 'Aristotle says that nothing of those things which are external is understood, unless first it falls under sense; and those things are only sensibles according to him.

[1] *Prol. Sent.*, 1, 2.
[2] 1 *Sent.*, 27, 3, K.
[3] *Quodlibet*, 1, 13.
[4] *Ibid.*, 1, 14.

And this authority is true in regard to those things; but in regard to spirits it is not.'[1] As intuitive knowledge precedes abstractive knowledge, according to Ockham, we can say, using a later language, that for him sense-perception and introspection are the two sources of all our natural knowledge concerning existent reality. In this sense one can call him an 'empiricist'; but on this point he is no more of an 'empiricist' than any other mediaeval philosopher who disbelieved in innate ideas and in purely *a priori* knowledge of existent reality.

2. We have seen that for Ockham intuitive knowledge of a thing is caused by that thing and not by any other thing. In other words, intuition, as immediate apprehension of the individual existent, carries its own guarantee. But, as is well known, he maintained that God could cause in us the intuition of a thing which was not really there. 'Intuitive knowledge cannot be caused naturally unless the object is present at the right distance; but it could be caused supernaturally.'[2] 'If you say that it (intuition) can be caused by God alone, that is true.'[3] 'There can be by the power of God intuitive knowledge (*cognitio intuitiva*) concerning a non-existent object.'[4] Hence among the censured propositions of Ockham's we find one to the effect that 'intuitive knowledge in itself and necessarily is not more concerned with an existent than with a non-existent thing, nor does it regard existence more than non-existence'. This is doubtless an interpretative summary of Ockham's position; and since it appears to contradict his account of the nature of intuitive knowledge as distinct from abstractive knowledge (in the sense of knowledge which abstracts from the existence or non-existence of the things for which the terms in the proposition stand), the following remarks may help to make his position clearer.

(i) When Ockham says that God could produce in us intuition of a non-existent object, he is relying on the truth of the proposition that God can produce and conserve immediately whatever He normally produces through the mediation of secondary causes. For example, the intuition of the stars is normally and naturally produced in us by the actual presence of the stars. To say this is to say that God produces in us intuitive knowledge of the stars by means of a secondary cause, namely the stars themselves. On Ockham's principle, then, God could produce this intuition directly, without the secondary cause. He could not do this if it

[1] *Quodlibet*, 1, 14. [2] 2 *Sent.*, 15, E. [3] *Quodlibet*, 1, 13. [4] *Ibid.*, 6, 6.

would involve a contradiction; but it would not involve a contradiction. 'Every effect which God causes through the mediation of a secondary cause He can produce immediately by Himself.'[1]

(ii) But God could not produce in us evident knowledge of the proposition that the stars are present when they are not present; for the inclusion of the word 'evident' implies that the stars really are present. 'God cannot cause in us knowledge such that by it a thing is seen evidently to be present although it is absent, for that involves a contradiction, because such evident knowledge means that it is thus in fact as is stated by the proposition to which assent is given.'[2]

(iii) Ockham's point seems to be, then, that God could cause in us the act of intuiting an object which was not really present, in the sense that He could cause in us the physiological and psychological conditions which would normally lead us to assent to the proposition that the thing is present. For example, God could produce immediately in the organs of vision all those effects which are naturally produced by the light of the stars. Or one can put the matter this way. God could not produce in me the actual vision of a present white patch, when the white patch was not present; for this would involve a contradiction. But He could produce in me all the psycho-physical conditions involved in seeing a white patch, even if the white patch was not really there.

(iv) To his critics, Ockham's choice of terms seemed to be confusing and unfortunate. On the one hand, after saying that God cannot cause evident knowledge that a thing is present when it is not present, he adds that 'God can cause a "creditive" act by which I believe that an absent is present', and he explains that 'that "creditive" idea will be abstractive, not intuitive'.[3] This seems to be fairly plain sailing, if it can be taken as meaning that God could produce in us, in the absence of the stars, all the psycho-physical conditions which we would naturally have in the presence of the stars, and that we would thereby have a knowledge of what the stars are (so far as this can be obtained by sight), though the knowledge could not properly be called 'intuition'. On the other hand, Ockham seems to speak of God as being able to produce in us 'intuitive knowledge' of a non-existent object, though this knowledge is not 'evident'. Moreover, he does not seem to mean simply that God could produce in us intuitive knowledge of the nature of the object; for he allows that 'God can produce an

[1] *Quodlibet*, 6, 6. [2] *Ibid.*, 5, 5. [3] *Ibid.*

assent which belongs to the same species as that evident assent to the contingent proposition, "this whiteness exists", when it does not exist'.[1] If God can properly be said to be capable of producing in us assent to a proposition affirming the existence of a non-existent object, and if this assent can properly be called not only a 'creditive act' but also 'intuitive knowledge', then one can only suppose that it is proper to speak of God as capable of producing in us intuitive knowledge which is not in fact intuitive knowledge at all. And to say this would seem to involve a contradiction. To qualify 'intuitive knowledge' by the words 'not evident' would appear to amount to a cancellation of the former by the latter.

Possibly these difficulties are capable of being cleared up satisfactorily, from Ockham's point of view, I mean. For example, he says that 'it is a contradiction that a chimera be seen intuitively'; but 'it is not a contradiction that that which is seen is nothing in actuality outside the soul, so long as it can be an effect or was at some time an actual reality'.[2] If God had annihilated the stars, He could still cause in us the act of seeing what had once been, so far as the act is considered subjectively, just as He could give us a vision of what will be in the future. Either act would be an immediate apprehension, in the first case of what has been and in the second case of what will be. But, even then, it would be peculiar to imply that if we assented to the proposition, 'these things exist *now*', the assent could be produced by God, unless one were willing to say that God could deceive us. Presumably this was the point to which exception was taken by Ockham's theological opponents, and not the mere assertion that God could act directly on our sense organs. However, it must be remembered that Ockham distinguished evidence, which is objective, from certitude as a psychological state. Possession of the latter is not an infallible guarantee of possession of the former.

(v) In any case one must remember that Ockham is not speaking of the natural course of events. He does not say that God acts in this way as a matter of fact: he simply says that God could act in this way in virtue of His omnipotence. That God is omnipotent was not, however, for Ockham a truth which can be philosophically proved: it is known only by faith. If we look at the matter from the purely philosophical point of view, therefore, the question of God's producing in us intuitions of non-existent objects simply does not come up. On the other hand, what Ockham has to say

[1] *Quodlibet*, 5, 5.

[2] *Ibid.*, 6, 6.

on the matter admirably illustrates his tendency, as a thinker with marked theological preoccupations, to break through, as it were, the purely philosophic and natural order and to subordinate it to the divine liberty and omnipotence. It illustrates, too, one of his main principles, that when two things are distinct there is no absolutely necessary connection between them. Our act of seeing the stars, considered as an act, is distinct from the stars themselves: it can therefore be separated from them, in the sense that divine omnipotence could annihilate the latter and conserve the former. Ockham's tendency was always to break through supposedly necessary connections which might seem to limit in some way the divine omnipotence, provided that it could not be shown to his satisfaction that denial of the proposition affirming such a necessary connection involved the denial of the principle of contradiction.

3. Ockham's insistence on intuitive knowledge as the basis and source of all our knowledge of existents represents, as we have seen, the 'empiricist' side of his philosophy. This aspect of his thought may also be said to be reflected in his insistence that the order of the world follows the divine choice. Scotus had made a distinction between God's choice of the end and His choice of the means, as though one could speak significantly of God 'first' willing the end and 'then' choosing the means. Ockham, however, rejected this way of speaking. 'It does not seem to be well said that God wills the end before that which is (ordered) to the end, because there is not there (in God) such a priority of acts, nor are there (in God) such instants as he postulates.'[1] Apart from the anthropomorphisms of such language it seems to impair the utter contingency of the order of the world. The choice of the end and the choice of the means are both utterly contingent. This does not mean, of course, that we have to picture God as a sort of capricious superman, liable to alter the world-order from day to day or from moment to moment. On the supposition that God has chosen a world-order, that order remains stable. But the choice of the order is in no way necessary: it is the effect of the divine choice and of the divine choice alone.

This position is intimately associated, of course, with Ockham's concern for the divine omnipotence and liberty; and it may appear out of place to speak of it as in any way reflecting the 'empiricist' aspect of his philosophy, since it is the position of a theologian.

[1] 1 *Sent.*, 41, 1, E.

But what I meant was this. If the order of the world is entirely contingent on the divine choice, it is obviously impossible to deduce it *a priori*. If we want to know what it is, one must examine what it is in fact. Ockham's position may have been primarily that of a theologian; but its natural effect would be to concentrate attention on the actual facts and to discourage any notion that one could reconstruct the order of the world by purely *a priori* reasoning. If a notion of this kind makes its appearance in the pre-Kantian continental rationalism of the classical period of 'modern' philosophy, its origin is certainly not to be looked for in fourteenth-century Ockhamism: it is to be associated, of course, with the influence of mathematics and of mathematical physics.

4 Ockham's tendency, then, was to split up the world, as it were, into 'absolutes'. That is to say, his tendency was to split up the world into distinct entities, each of which depends on God but between which there is no necessary connection: the order of the world is not logically prior to the divine choice, but it is logically posterior to the divine choice of individual contingent entities. And the same tendency is reflected in his treatment of relations. Once granted that there exists only individual distinct entities and that the only kind of distinction which is independent of the mind is a real distinction in the sense of a distinction between separate or separable entities, it follows that if a relation is a distinct entity, distinct, that is, from the terms of the relation, it must be really distinct from the terms in the sense of being separate or separable. 'If I held that a relation were a thing, I should say with John (Scotus) that it is a thing distinct from its foundation, but I should differ (from him) in saying that every relation differs really from its foundation . . . because I do not admit a formal distinction in creatures.'[1] But it would be absurd to hold that a relation is really distinct from its foundation. If it were, God could produce the relation of paternity and confer it on someone who had never generated. The fact is that a man is called a 'father' when he has generated a child; and there is no need to postulate the existence of a third entity, a relation of paternity, linking father to child. Similarly Smith is said to be like Brown because, for example, Smith is a man and Brown is a man or because Smith is white and Brown is white: it is unnecessary to postulate a third entity, a relation of similarity, in

[1] 2 *Sent.*, 2, H.

addition to the 'absolute' substances and qualities; and if one does postulate a third entity, absurd conclusions result.[1] Relations are names or terms signifying absolutes; and a relation as such has no reality outside the mind. For example, there is no order of the universe which is actually or really distinct from the existent parts of the universe.[2] Ockham does not say that a relation is identical with its foundation. 'I do not say that a relation is really the same as its foundation; but I say that a relation is not the foundation but only an "intention" or concept in the soul, signifying several absolute things.'[3] The principle on which Ockham goes is, of course, the principle of economy: the way in which we speak about relations can be analysed or explained satisfactorily without postulating relations as real entities. This was, in Ockham's view, the opinion of Aristotle. The latter would not allow, for example, that every mover is necessarily itself moved. But this implies that relations are not entities distinct from absolute things; for, if they were, the mover would receive a relation and would thus be itself moved.[4] Relations are thus 'intentions' or terms signifying absolutes; though one must add that Ockham restricts the application of this doctrine to the created world: in the Trinity there are real relations.

This theory naturally affected Ockham's view of the relation between creatures and God. It was a common doctrine in the Middle Ages among Ockham's predecessors that the creature has a real relation to God, although God's relation to the creature is only a mental relation. On Ockham's view of relations, however, this distinction becomes in effect null and void. Relations can be analysed into two existent 'absolutes'; and in this case to say that between creatures and God there are different kinds of relation is simply to say, so far as this way of speaking is admissible, that God and creatures are different kinds of beings. It is perfectly true that God produced and conserves creatures and that the latter could not exist apart from God; but this does not mean that the creatures are affected by a mysterious entity called an essential relation of dependence. We conceive and speak about creatures as essentially related to God; but what actually exists is God on the one hand and creatures on the other, and there is no need to postulate any other entity. Ockham distinguishes various senses in which 'real relation' and 'mental relation' can be understood;[5]

[1] Cf. *Expositio aurea*, 2, 64, V.
[2] 1 *Sent.*, 30, 1, S.
[3] *Ibid.*, 30, 1, R.
[4] *Expositio aurea*, 2, 64, R.
[5] 1 *Sent.*, 30, 5.

and he is willing to say that the relation of creatures to God is a 'real' and not a 'mental' relation, if the statement is taken to mean, for example, that a stone's production and conservation by God is real and does not depend on the human mind. But he excludes any idea of there being any additional entity in the stone, in addition, that is, to the stone itself, which could be called a 'real relation'.

One particular way in which Ockham tries to show that the idea of real relations distinct from their foundations is absurd deserves special mention. If I move my finger, its position is changed in regard to all the parts of the universe. And, if there are real relations distinct from their foundation, 'it would follow that at the movement of my finger the whole universe, that is, heaven and earth, would be at once filled with accidents'.[1] Moreover, if, as Ockham says, the parts of the universe are infinite in number, it would follow that the universe is peopled with an infinite number of fresh accidents whenever I move my finger. This conclusion he considered absurd.

For Ockham, then, the universe consists of 'absolutes', substances and absolute accidents, which can be brought into a greater or lesser local approximation to one another, but which are not affected by any relative entities called 'real relations'. From this it would seem to follow that it is futile to think that one could read off, as it were, a mirror of the whole universe. If one wants to know anything about the universe, one must study it empirically. Very possibly this point of view should be regarded as favouring an 'empiricist' approach to knowledge of the world; but it does not follow, of course, that modern science actually developed against a mental background of this sort. Nevertheless, Ockham's insistence on 'absolutes' and his view of relations may reasonably be said to have favoured the growth of empirical science in the following way. If the creature is regarded as having a real essential relation to God, and if it cannot be properly understood without this relation being understood, it is reasonable to conclude that the study of the way in which creatures mirror God is the most important and valuable study of the world, and that a study of creatures in and for themselves alone, without any reference to God, is a rather inferior kind of study, which yields only an inferior knowledge of the world. But if creatures are 'absolutes', they can perfectly well be studied without any

[1] 2 *Sent.*, 2, G.

reference to God. Of course, as we have seen, when Ockham spoke of created things as 'absolutes' he had no intention of questioning their utter dependence on God; his point of view was very much that of a theologian; but none the less, if we can know the natures of created things without any advertence to God, it follows that empirical science is an autonomous discipline. The world can be studied in itself in abstraction from God, especially if, as Ockham held, it cannot be strictly proved that God, in the full sense of the term 'God', exists. In this sense it is legitimate to speak of Ockhamism as a factor and stage in the birth of the 'lay spirit', as M. de Lagarde does. At the same time one must remember that Ockham himself was very far from being a secularist or modern 'rationalist'.

5. When one turns to Ockham's account of causality one finds him expounding the four causes of Aristotle. As to the exemplary cause, which, he says, Seneca added as a fifth type of cause, 'I say that strictly speaking nothing is a cause unless it is a cause in one of the four ways laid down by Aristotle. So the idea or exemplar is not strictly a cause; though, if one extends the name "cause" to (cover) everything the knowledge of which is presupposed by the production of something, the idea or exemplar is a cause in this sense; and Seneca speaks in this extended sense.'[1] Ockham accepts, then, the traditional Aristotelian division of causes into the formal, material, final and efficient causes; and he affirms that 'to any type of cause there corresponds its own (type of) causation'.[2]

Moreover, Ockham did not deny that it is possible to conclude from the characteristics of a given thing that it has or had a cause; and he himself used causal arguments. He did, however, deny that the simple knowledge (*notitia incomplexa*) of one thing can provide us with the simple knowledge of another thing. We may be able to establish that a given thing has a cause; but it does not follow that we thereby gain a simple and proper knowledge of the thing which is its cause. The reason of this is that the knowledge in question comes from intuition; and the intuition of one thing is not the intuition of another thing. This principle has, of course, its ramifications in natural theology; but what I want to emphasize at the moment is that Ockham did not deny that a causal argument can have any validity. It is true that for him two things are always really distinct when the concepts of the two things are distinct, and that when two things are distinct God could create

[1] 1 *Sent.*, 35, 5, N. [2] 2 *Sent.*, 3, B.

the one without the other; but, given empirical reality as it is, one can discern causal connections.

But, though Ockham enumerates four causes in the traditional manner and though he does not reject the validity of causal argument, his analysis of efficient causality has a marked 'empiricist' colouring. In the first place he insists that, though one may know that a given thing has *a* cause, the only way in which we can ascertain that this definite thing is the cause of that definite thing is by experience: we cannot prove by abstract reasoning that *X* is the cause of *Y*, where *X* is one created thing and *Y* is another created thing. In the second place the experiential test of a causal relation is the employment of the presence and absence methods or the method of exclusion. We are not entitled to assert that *X* is the cause of *Y*, unless we can show that when *X* is present *Y* follows and that when *X* is absent, whatever other factors may be present, *Y* does not follow. For example, 'it is proved that fire is the cause of heat, since, when fire is there and all other things (that is, all other possible causal factors) have been removed, heat follows in a heatable object which has been brought near (the fire) . . . (Similarly) it is proved that the object is the cause of intuitive knowledge, for when all other factors except the object have been removed intuitive knowledge follows'.[1]

That it is by experience we come to know that one thing is the cause of another is, of course, a common-sense position. So, for the matter of that, is Ockham's idea of the test which should be applied in order to ascertain whether *A*, *B* or *C* is the cause of *D* or whether we have to accept a plurality of causes. If we find that when *A* is present *D* always follows, even when *B* and *C* are absent, and that when *B* and *C* are present but *A* is absent *D* never follows, we must take it that *A* is the cause of *D*. If, however, we find that when *A* alone is present *D* never follows, but that when *A* and *B* are both present *D* always follows, even though *C* is absent, we must conclude that both *A* and *B* are causal factors in the production of *D*. In calling these positions common-sense positions I mean that they are positions which would naturally commend themselves to ordinary common sense and that there is nothing revolutionary about either position in itself: I do not mean to suggest that from the scientific point of view the matter was adequately stated by Ockham. It does not need very much reflection to see that there are cases in which the supposed cause

[1] 1 *Sent.*, 1, 3, N.

of an event cannot be 'removed', in order to see what happens in its absence. We cannot, for example, remove the moon and see what happens to the movement of the tides in the absence of the moon, in order to ascertain whether the moon exercises any causal influence on the tides. However, that is not the point to which I really want to draw attention. For it would be absurd to expect an adequate treatment of scientific induction from a thinker who was not really concerned with the matter and who showed comparatively little interest in matters of pure physical science; especially at a time when science had not attained that degree of development which would appear to be required before reflection on scientific method can really be valuable. The point to which I draw attention is rather this, that in his analysis of efficient causality Ockham shows a tendency to interpret the causal relation as invariable or regular sequence. In one place he distinguishes two senses of cause. In the second sense of the word an antecedent proposition may be called a 'cause' in relation to the consequent. This sense does not concern us, as Ockham expressly says that the antecedent is not the cause of the consequent in any proper sense of the term. It is the first sense which is of interest. 'In one sense it (cause) means something which has another thing as its effect; and in this sense that can be called a cause on the positing of which another thing is posited and on the non-positing of which that other thing is not posited.'[1] In a passage like this Ockham seems to imply that causality means regular sequence and does not seem to be talking simply of an empirical test which should be applied to ascertain whether one thing is actually the cause of another thing. To state without more ado that Ockham reduced causality to regular succession would be incorrect; but he does seem to show a tendency to reduce efficient causality to regular succession. And, after all, to do so would be very much in harmony with his theological view of the universe. God has created distinct things; and the order which prevails between them is purely contingent. There are regular sequences as a matter of fact; but no connection between two distinct things can be said to be necessary, unless one means by necessary simply that the connection, which depends on God's choice, is always observable in fact. In this sense one can probably say that Ockham's theological outlook and his tendency to give an empiricist account of efficient causality went hand in hand. However, as God has

[1] 1 *Sent.*, 41, 1, F.

created things in such a way that a certain order results, we can predict that the causal relations we have experienced in the past will be experienced in the future, even though God by the use of His absolute power *could* interfere with the order. This theological background is, of course, generally absent from modern empiricism.

6. It is clear that Ockham utilized his razor in his discussion of causality, just as in that of relations in general. He utilized it too in his treatment of the problem of motion. Indeed, his use of the razor or principle of economy was often connected with the 'empiricist' side of his philosophy, inasmuch as he wielded the weapon in an effort to get rid of unobservable entities the existence of which was not, in his opinion, demanded by the data of experience (or taught by revelation). His tendency was always towards the simplification of our view of the universe. To say this is not to say, of course, that Ockham made any attempt to reduce things to sense-data or to logical constructions out of sense-data. Such a reduction he would doubtless have regarded as an over-simplification. But, once granted the existence of substance and absolute accidents, he made an extensive use of the principle of economy.

Employing the traditional Aristotelian division of types of movement, Ockham asserts that neither qualitative alteration nor quantitative change nor local motion is anything positive in addition to permanent things.[1] In the case of qualitative alteration a body acquires a form gradually or successively, part after part, as Ockham puts it; and there is no need to postulate anything else but the thing which acquires the quality and the quality which is acquired. It is true that the negation of the simultaneous acquisition of all the parts of the form is involved; but this negation is not a thing; and to imagine that it is is to be misled by the false supposition that to every distinct term or name there corresponds a distinct thing. Indeed, if it were not for the use of abstract words like 'motion', 'simultaneity', 'succession', etc., the problems connected with the nature of motion would not create such difficulty for people.[2] In the case of quantitative change it is obvious, says Ockham, that nothing is involved save 'permanent things'. As to local motion, nothing need be postulated except a body and its place, that is, its local situation. To be moved locally 'is first to have one place, and afterwards, without any other thing being postulated, to have another place, without any intervening state

[1] 2 *Sent.*, 9, C, D, E. [2] *Tractatus de successivis*, ed. Boehner, p. 47.

of rest, . . . and to proceed thus continuously. . . . And consequently the whole nature of motion can be saved (explained) by this without anything else but the fact that a body is successively in distinct places and is not at rest in any of them.'[1] In the whole of his treatment of motion, both in the *Tractatus de successivis*[2] and in the commentary on the *Sentences*[3] Ockham makes frequent appeal to the principle of economy. He does the same when dealing with sudden change (*mutatio subita*, that is, substantial change), which is nothing in addition to 'absolute' things. Of course, if we say that 'a form is acquired by change' or 'change belongs to the category of relation', we shall be tempted to think that the word 'change' stands for an entity. But a proposition like 'a form is lost and a form is gained through sudden change' can be translated into a proposition like 'the thing which changes loses a form and acquires a form together (at the same moment) and not part after part'.[4]

The principle of economy was invoked too in Ockham's treatment of place and time. Expounding the Aristotelian definitions,[5] he insists that place is not a thing distinct from the surface or surfaces of the body or bodies in regard to which a certain thing is said to be in a place; and he insists that time is not a thing distinct from motion. 'I say that neither time nor any *successivum* denotes a thing, either absolute or relative, distinct from permanent things; and this is what the Philosopher means.'[6] In whichever of the possible senses one understands 'time', it is not a thing in addition to motion. 'Primarily and principally "time" signifies the same as "motion", although it connotes both the soul and an act of the soul, by which it (the soul or mind) knows the before and after of that motion. And so, presupposing what has been said about motion, and (presupposing) that the statements are understood. . ., it can be said that "time" signifies motion directly and the soul or an act of the soul directly; and on this account it signifies directly the before and after in motion.'[7] As Ockham expressly says that the meaning of Aristotle in the whole of this chapter about time is, in brief, this, that 'time' does not denote

[1] *Tractatus de successivis*, ed. Boehner, p. 46.

[2] This treatise is a compilation; but it is a compilation from Ockham's authentic writings. See p. 45.

[3] 2, 9.

[4] Cf. *Tractatus de successivis*, ed. Boehner, pp. 41–2.

[5] For the Aristotelian definitions of place and time see, for example, the first volume of this history, *Greece and Rome*, pp. 321–2.

[6] 2 *Sent.*, 12 D.

[7] *Tractatus de successivis*, ed. Boehner, p. 111.

any distinct thing outside the soul beyond what 'motion' signifies,[1] and as this is what he himself held, it follows that in so far as one can distinguish time from motion it is mental, or, as Ockham would say, a 'term' or 'name'.

7. As a conclusion to this chapter one can remind oneself of three features of Ockham's 'empiricism'. First, he bases all knowledge of the existent world on experience. We cannot, for example, discover that *A* is the cause of *B*, or that *D* is the effect of *C*, by *a priori* reasoning. Secondly, in his analysis of existent reality, or of the statements which we make about things, he uses the principle of economy. If two factors will suffice to explain motion, for example, one should not add a third. Lastly, when people do postulate unnecessary and unobservable entities, it is not infrequently because they have been misled by language. There is a striking passage on this matter in the *Tractatus de successivis*.[2] 'Nouns which are derived from verbs and also nouns which derive from adverbs, conjunctions, prepositions, and in general from syncategorematic terms . . . have been introduced only for the sake of brevity in speaking or as ornaments of speech; and many of them are equivalent in signification to propositions, when they do not stand for the terms from which they derive; and so they do not signify any things in addition to those from which they derive. . . . Of this kind are all nouns of the following kind: negation, privation, condition, perseity, contingency, universality, action, passion, . . . change, motion, and in general all verbal nouns deriving from verbs which belong to the categories of *agere* and *pati*, and many others, which cannot be treated now.'

[1] *Tractatus de successivis*, ed. Boehner, p. 119. [2] *Ibid*., p. 37.

CHAPTER VI

OCKHAM (4)

The subject-matter of metaphysics—The univocal concept of being —The existence of God—Our knowledge of God's nature—The divine ideas—God's knowledge of future contingent events—The divine will and omnipotence.

1. OCKHAM accepts the statement of Aristotle that being is the subject of metaphysics; but he insists that this statement must not be understood as implying that metaphysics, considered in a wide sense, possesses a strict unity based on its having one subject-matter. If Aristotle and Averroes say that being is the subject of metaphysics, the statement is false if it is interpreted as meaning that all the parts of metaphysics have being as their subject-matter. The statement is true, however, if it is understood as meaning that 'among all the subjects of the different parts of metaphysics being is first with a priority of predication (*primum primitate praedicationis*). And there is a similarity between the question, what is the subject of metaphysics or of the book of categories and the question who is the king of the world or who is the king of all Christendom. For just as different kingdoms have different kings, and there is no king of the whole (world), though sometimes these kings may stand in a certain relation, as when one is more powerful or richer than another, so nothing is the subject of the whole of metaphysics, but here the different parts have different subjects, though these subjects may have a relation to one another.'[1] If some people say that being is the subject of metaphysics, while others say that God is the subject of metaphysics, a distinction must be made, if both statements are to be justified. Among all the subjects of metaphysics God is the primary subject as far as primacy of perfection is concerned; but being is the primary subject as far as primacy of predication is concerned.[2] For the metaphysician, when treating of God, considers truths like 'God is good', predicating of God an attribute which is primarily predicated of being.[3] There are, then, different branches of metaphysics, or different metaphysical sciences with different subjects. They have a certain relationship to one another, it is

[1] *Prol. Sent.*, 9, N. [2] *Ibid.* [3] *Ibid.*, D, D.

true; and this relationship justifies one in speaking of 'metaphysics' and in saying, for example, that being is the subject-matter of metaphysics in the sense mentioned, though it would not justify one's thinking that metaphysics is a unitary science, that is, that it is numerically one science.

2. In so far as metaphysics is the science of being as being it is concerned not with a thing but with a concept.[1] This abstract concept of being does not stand for a mysterious something which has to be known before we can know particular beings: it signifies all beings, not something in which beings participate. It is formed subsequently to the direct apprehension of existing things. 'I say that a particular being can be known, although those general concepts of being and unity are not known.'[2] For Ockham being and existing are synonymous: essence and existence signify the same, though the two words may signify the same thing in different ways. If 'existence' is used as a noun, then 'essence' and 'existence' signify the same thing grammatically and logically; but if the verb 'to be' is used instead of the noun 'existence', one cannot simply substitute 'essence', which is a noun, for the verb 'to be', for obvious grammatical reasons.[3] But this grammatical distinction cannot properly be taken as a basis for distinguishing essence and existence as distinct things: they are the same thing. It is clear, then, that the general concept of being is the result of the apprehension of concrete existing things; it is only because we have had direct apprehension of actual existents that we can form the general concept of being as such.

The general concept of being is univocal. On this point Ockham agrees with Scotus, so far as the use of the word 'univocal' is concerned. 'There is one concept common to God and creatures and predicable of them':[4] 'being' is a concept predicable in a univocal sense of all existent things.[5] Without a univocal concept we could not conceive God. We cannot in this life attain an intuition of the divine essence; nor can we have a simple 'proper' concept of God; but we can conceive God in a common concept predicable of Him and of other beings.[6] This statement must, however, be properly understood. It does not mean that the univocal concept of being acts as a bridge between a direct apprehension of creatures and a direct apprehension of God. Nor does it mean that one can form the abstract concept of being and

[1] 3 *Sent.*, 9, T.
[2] 1 *Sent.*, 3, 1, E.
[3] *Quodlibet*, 2, 7; *Summa totius logicae*, 3, 2.
[4] 1 *Sent.*, 2, 9, P.
[5] *Ibid.*, X.
[6] *Ibid.*, P.

deduce therefrom the existence of God. The existence of God is known in other ways, and not by an *a priori* deduction. But without a univocal concept of being one would be unable to conceive the existence of God. 'I admit that the simple knowledge of one creature in itself leads to the knowledge of another thing in a common concept. For example, by the simple knowledge of a whiteness which I have seen I am led to the knowledge of another whiteness which I have never seen, inasmuch as from the first whiteness I abstract a concept of whiteness which refers indifferently to them both. In the same way from some accident which I have seen I abstract a concept of being which does not refer more to that accident than to substance, nor to the creature more than to God.'[1] Obviously, my seeing a white patch does not assure me of the existence of any other white patch; nor did Ockham ever imagine that it could do so. To say that it could would be in flagrant contradiction with his philosophical principles. But, according to him, my seeing a white patch leads to an idea of whiteness which is applicable to other white patches when I see them. Similarly, my abstraction of the concept of being from apprehended existent beings does not assure me of the existence of any other beings. Yet unless I had a common concept of being I could not conceive of the existence of a being, God, which, unlike white patches, cannot be directly apprehended in this life. If, for example, I have no knowledge of God already and then I am told that God exists, I am able to conceive His existence in virtue of the common concept of being, though this does not mean, of course, that I have a 'proper' concept of the divine being.

Ockham was very careful to state his theory of the univocal concept of being in a way which would exclude any pantheistic implication. We must distinguish three types of univocity. In the first place a univocal concept may be a concept which is common to a number of things which are perfectly alike. In the second place a univocal concept may be a concept common to a number of things which are like in some points and unlike in other points. Thus man and ass are alike in being animals; and their matters are similar, though their forms are different. Thirdly, a univocal concept may mean a concept which is common to a plurality of things which are neither accidentally nor substantially alike; and it is in this way that a concept common to God and the creature is univocal, since they are alike neither substantially nor

[1] 3 *Sent.*, 9, R.

accidentally.[1] In regard to the contention that the concept of being is analogous and not univocal, Ockham observes that analogy can be understood in different ways. If by analogy is meant univocity in the third sense mentioned above, then the univocal concept of being may, of course, be called 'analogous';[2] but, since being as such is a concept and not a thing, there is no need to have recourse to the doctrine of analogy in order to avoid pantheism. If by saying that there can be a univocal concept of being predicable of God as well as of creatures, one meant to imply either that creatures are modes, as it were, of a being identified with God, or that God and creatures share in being, as something real in which they participate, then one would be forced either into accepting pantheism or into reducing God and creatures to the same level; but the doctrine of univocity does not imply anything of the kind, since there is no reality corresponding to the term 'being' when it is predicated univocally. Or, rather, the corresponding reality is simply different beings which are simply conceived as existing. If one considered these beings separately, one would have a plurality of concepts, for the concept of God is not the same as the concept of the creature. And in this case the term 'being' would be predicated equivocally, not univocally. Equivocation does not belong to concepts but to words, that is, to spoken or written terms. As far as the concept is concerned, when we conceive a plurality of beings we either have one concept or a number of concepts. If a word corresponds to one concept, it is used univocally; if it corresponds to several concepts, it is used equivocally. There is, then, no room for analogy, either in the case of concepts or in that of spoken or written words. 'There is no analogical predication, as contradistinguished from univocal, equivocal and denominative predication.'[3] In fact, as denominative (that is, connotative) predication is reducible to univocal or to equivocal predication, one must say that predication must be either univocal or equivocal.[4]

3. But, though God can be conceived in some way, can it be philosophically shown that God exists? God is indeed the most perfect object of the human intellect, the supreme intelligible reality; but He is certainly not the first object of the human intellect in the sense of being the object which is first known.[5] The primary object of the human mind is the material thing or embodied nature.[6]

[1] 3 *Sent.*, 9, Q. [2] *Ibid.*, R. [3] *Ibid.*, E. [4] *Expositio aurea*, 2, 39, V.
[5] 1 *Sent.*, 3, 1, D. [6] *Ibid.*, F.

We possess no natural intuition of the divine essence; and the proposition that God exists is not a self-evident proposition as far as we are concerned. If we imagine someone enjoying the vision of God and making the statement 'God exists', the statement may seem to be the same as the statement 'God exists' made by someone in this life who does not enjoy the vision of God. But though the two statements are verbally the same, the terms or concepts are really different; and in the second case it is not a self-evident proposition.[1] Any natural knowledge of God must, therefore, be derived from reflection on creatures. But can we come to know God from creatures? And, if so, is this knowledge certain knowledge?

Given Ockham's general position in regard to the subject of causality, one could hardly expect him to say that God's existence can be proved with certainty. For if we can only know of a thing that it has *a* cause, and if we cannot establish with certainty by any other way than by actual experience that *A* is the cause of *B*, we could not establish with certainty that the world is caused by God, if the term 'God' is understood in a recognized theistic sense. It is not very surprising, then, to find Ockham criticizing the traditional proofs of God's existence. He did not do so in the interests of scepticism, of course, but rather because he thought that the proofs were not logically conclusive. It does not follow, however, that once given his attitude scepticism, agnosticism or fideism, as the case might be, would not naturally follow.

As the authenticity of the *Centiloquium theologicum* is doubtful, it would scarcely be appropriate to discuss the treatment of the 'first mover' argument which is given by the author of that work. It is sufficient to say that the author refuses to allow that the basic principle of this Aristotelian-Thomist argument is either self-evident or demonstrable.[2] In fact, there are exceptions to the principle, inasmuch as an angel, and the human soul too, moves itself; and such exceptions show that the alleged principle cannot be a necessary principle and that it cannot form a basis for any strict proof of God's existence, especially as it cannot be proved that an infinite regress in the series of movers is impossible. The argument may be a probable argument in the sense that it is more probable that there is a first unmoved mover than that there is no such first unmoved mover; but it is not a certain argument. This criticism follows the line already suggested by Scotus; and even

[1] 1 *Sent.*, 3, 4, D, F.

[2] This principle is that whatever is moved is moved by another (*quidquid movetur ab alio movetur*).

if the work in which it occurs is not a work of Ockham, the criticism would seem to be in harmony with Ockham's ideas. Moreover, there can be no question of his having accepted St. Thomas's *manifestior via* as a certain argument for God's existence, as distinct from the existence of a first mover in a general sense. The first mover might be an angel or some being less than God, if we mean by 'God' an infinite, unique and absolutely supreme being.[1]

The proof from finality also goes by the board. Not only is it impossible to prove that the universe is ordered to one end, God,[2] but it cannot even be proved that individual things act for ends in a way which would justify any certain argument to God's existence. In the case of things which act without knowledge and will, all that we are warranted in saying is that they act because of a natural necessity: it makes no sense to say that they act 'for' an end.[3] Of course, if one presupposes God's existence, one can then speak of inanimate things as acting for ends, that is, for ends determined by God, who created their natures;[4] but if a statement is based on the presupposition of God's existence, it cannot itself be used to prove God's existence. As to agents endowed with intelligence and will, the reason for their voluntary actions is to be found in their own wills; and it cannot be shown that all wills are moved by the perfect good, God.[5] In fine, it is impossible to prove that there is in the universe an immanent teleological order, the existence of which makes it necessary to assert God's existence. There is no order distinct from 'absolute' natures themselves; and the only way in which one could prove God's existence would be as efficient cause of the existence of finite things. Is it, however, possible to do so?

In the *Quodlibet* Ockham states that one must stop at a first efficient cause and not proceed to infinity: but he adds immediately that this efficient cause might be a heavenly body, since 'we know by experience that it is the cause of other things'.[6] He says expressly not only that 'it cannot be proved by the natural reason that God is the immediate efficient cause of all things', but also that it cannot be proved that God is the mediate efficient cause of any effect. He gives as one reason of this the impossibility of proving that there exist any things other than corruptible things. It cannot be proved, for instance, that there is a spiritual and immortal soul in man. And the heavenly bodies can cause

[1] Cf. *Quodlibet*, 7, 22–3. [2] *Ibid.*, 4, 2.
[3] *Summulae in libros physicorum*, 2, 6.
[4] 2 *Sent.*, 3, NN; *Quodlibet*, 4, 1. [5] 1 *Sent.*, 1, 4, E. [6] *Quodlibet*, 2, 1.

corruptible things, without its being possible to prove that the heavenly bodies themselves are caused by God.

However, in the commentary on the *Sentences*, Ockham gives his own version of the proof from efficient causality. It is better, he says, to argue from conservation to conserver rather than from product to producer. The reason for this is that 'it is difficult or impossible to prove against the philosophers that there cannot be an infinite regress in causes of the same kind, of which one can exist without the other'.[1] For example, Ockham does not think that it can be strictly proved that a man does not owe his total being to his parents, and they to their parents, and so on indefinitely. If it is objected that even in the case of an infinite series of this kind the infinite series would itself depend for its production on a being intrinsic to the series, Ockham answers that 'it would be difficult to prove that the series would not be possible unless there were one permanent being, on which the whole infinite series depended'.[2] He therefore prefers to argue that a thing which comes into being (that is, a contingent thing) is conserved in being as long as it exists. It can then be asked whether the conserver is itself dependent for its conservation or not. But in this case we cannot proceed to infinity, because an infinite number of *actual* conservers is, says Ockham, impossible. It may be possible to admit an infinite regress in the case of beings which exist one after the other, since in this case there would not be an actually existent infinity; but in the case of actual conservers of the world here and now, an infinite regress would imply an actual infinity. That an actual infinity of this sort is impossible is shown by the arguments of philosophers and others, which are 'reasonable enough' (*satis rationabiles*).

But even though reasonable arguments can be adduced for the existence of God as first conserver of the world, the unicity of God cannot be demonstrated.[3] It can be shown that there is some ultimate conserving being in *this* world; but we cannot exclude the possibility of there being another world or other worlds, with its or their own relatively first beings. To prove that there is a first efficient cause which is more perfect than *its* effects is not the same thing as proving the existence of a being which is superior to every other being, unless you can first prove that every other being is the effect of one single cause.[4] The unicity of God is known with certainty only by faith.

[1] 1 *Sent.*, 2, 10, O. [2] *Ibid.* [3] *Quodlibet*, 1, 1. [4] 1 *Sent.*, 35, 2, C.

In answer, therefore, to the question whether Ockham admitted any philosophical proof of God's existence one must first make a distinction. If by 'God' one means the absolutely supreme, perfect, unique and infinite being, Ockham did not think that the existence of such a being can be strictly proved by the philosopher. If, on the other hand, one means by 'God' the first conserving cause of this world, without any certain knowledge about the nature of that cause, Ockham did think that the existence of such a being can be philosophically proved. But, as this second understanding of the term 'God' is not all that is usually understood by the term, one might just as well say, without further ado, that Ockham did not admit the demonstrability of God's existence. Only by faith do we know, as far at least as certain knowledge is concerned, that the supreme and unique being in the fullest sense exists. From this it would seem to follow, as historians have argued, that theology and philosophy fall apart, since it is not possible to prove the existence of the God whose revelation is accepted on faith. But it does not follow, of course, that Ockham himself was concerned to separate theology from philosophy. If he criticized the traditional proofs of God's existence, he criticized them from the point of view of a logician, and not in order to break apart the traditional synthesis. Moreover, though it may be tempting to a modern philosopher to depict Ockham as assigning to theological propositions a purely 'emotional' significance by relegating a large number of the propositions of traditional metaphysics to dogmatic theology, this would be an inaccurate interpretation of his position. When he said, for example, that theology is not a science, he did not mean that theological propositions are not informative propositions or that no theological syllogism can be a correct piece of reasoning: what he meant was that since the premisses of theological arguments are known by faith the conclusions too fall within the same sphere, and that since the premisses are not self-evident the arguments are not scientific demonstrations in the strict sense of 'scientific demonstration'. Ockham did not deny that a probable argument can be given for God's existence. What he denied was that the existence of God as the unique absolutely supreme being can be philosophically 'demonstrated'.

4. If the existence of God as the absolutely supreme being cannot be strictly proved by the natural reason, it is obvious that it cannot be proved that there is an infinite and omnipotent being, creator of all things. But the question may be raised whether,

given the concept of God as the absolutely supreme being, it can then be demonstrated that God is infinite and omnipotent. Ockham's answer to this question is that attributes like omnipotence, infinity, eternity or the power to create out of nothing cannot be demonstrated to belong to the divine essence. His reason for saying this is a technical one. *A priori* demonstration involves the use of a middle term to which the predicate in question belongs in a prior manner. But in the case of an attribute like infinity there can be no middle term to which infinity belongs; and so there can be no demonstration that God is infinite. It may be said that concepts like infinity or the power of creating out of nothing can be demonstrated to belong to the divine essence by using their definitions as middle terms. For example, one can argue in this way. Anything which can produce something from nothing is capable of creating. But God can produce something from nothing. Therefore God can create. A syllogism of this kind, says Ockham, is not what is meant by a demonstration. A demonstration in the proper sense increases knowledge; but the syllogism just mentioned does not increase knowledge, since the statement that God produces or can produce something from nothing is precisely the same as the statement that God creates or can create. The syllogism is useless unless one knows the meaning of the term 'create'; but if we know the meaning of the term 'create' we know that the statement that God can produce something from nothing is the statement that God can create. Thus the conclusion which is professedly demonstrated is already assumed: the argument contains the fallacy of begging the question.[1]

On the other hand, there are some attributes which can be demonstrated. We can argue, for example, as follows. Every being is good: but God is a being: therefore God is good. In a syllogism of this sort there is a middle term, a concept common to God and creatures. But the term 'good' must here be understood as a connotative term, as connoting a relation to the will, if the argument is to be a demonstration. For if the term 'good' is not taken as a connotative term, it is simply synonymous with the term 'being'; and in this case we learn nothing at all from the argument. No attribute can be demonstrated to belong to a subject, unless the conclusion of the demonstration is *dubitabilis*, that is, unless one can significantly raise the question whether the

[1] *Prol. Sent.*, 2, D, D.

attribute is to be predicated of the subject or not. But if the term 'good' is taken not as a connotative term but as synonymous with 'being', we could not know that God is a being and significantly raise the question whether God is good. It is not required, of course, that the attribute predicated of a subject should be really distinct from a subject. Ockham rejected the Scotist doctrine of a formal distinction between the divine attributes, and maintained that there is no distinction. But we do not possess an intuition of the divine essence; and though the realities represented by our concepts of the divine essence and attributes are not distinct we can argue from one concept to another provided that there is a middle term. In the case of concepts common to God and creatures there is a middle term.

But in our knowledge of God's nature what is it precisely that constitutes the term of our cognition? We do not enjoy intuitive knowledge of God, which it is beyond the scope of the human intellect to attain by its own efforts. Nor can there be any natural 'abstractive' knowledge of God as He is in Himself, since it is impossible for us by our natural powers to have an abstractive knowledge of something in itself without an intuitive knowledge of that thing. It follows, therefore, that in our natural state it is impossible for us to know God in such a way that the divine essence is the immediate and sole term of the act of knowing.[1] Secondly, we cannot in our natural state conceive God in a simple concept, proper to Him alone. For 'no thing can be known by us through our natural powers in a simple concept proper to itself, unless the thing is known in itself. For otherwise we could say that colour can be known in a concept proper to colours by a man born blind.'[2] But, thirdly, God can be conceived by us in connotative concepts and in concepts which are common to God and creatures, like being. As God is a simple being, without any internal distinction save that between the three divine Persons, proper quidditative concepts (*conceptus quidditativi*) would be convertible; and so they would not be distinct concepts. If we can have distinct concepts of God, this is due to the fact that our concepts are not proper quidditative concepts of God. They are not convertible because they are either connotative concepts, like the concept of infinity which connotes the finite negatively, or concepts common to God and creatures, like the concept of wisdom. It is only a proper quidditative concept which corresponds

[1] 1 *Sent.*, 2, 9, P. [2] *Ibid.*, R.

to a single reality. A connotative concept connotes a reality other than the subject of which it is predicated; and a common concept is predicable of other realities than the one of which it is in fact predicated. Moreover, the common concepts which we predicate of God are due to a reflection on other realities than God and presuppose them.

An important consequence follows. If we have, as we do have, distinct concepts of God, a simple being, our conceptual knowledge of the divine nature is a knowledge of concepts rather than a knowledge of God as He is. What we attain is not the divine essence but a mental representation of the divine essence. We can form, it is true, a composite concept which is predicable of God alone; but this concept is a mental construction; we cannot have a simple concept proper to God which would adequately mirror the divine essence. 'Neither the divine essence . . . nor anything intrinsic to God nor anything which is really God can be known by us without something other than God being involved as object.'[1] 'We cannot know in themselves either the unity of God . . . or His infinite power or the divine goodness or perfection; but what we know immediately are concepts, which are not really God but which we use in propositions to stand for God.'[2] We know the divine nature, then, only through the medium of concepts; and these concepts, not being proper quidditative concepts, cannot take the place of an immediate apprehension of the essence of God. We do not attain a reality (*quid rei*), but a nominal representation (*quid nominis*). This is not to say that theology is not true or that its propositions have no meaning; but it is to say that the theologian is confined to the sphere of concepts and mental representation and that his analyses are analyses of concepts, not of God Himself. To imagine, for example, as Scotus did, that because we conceive divine attributes in distinct concepts these attributes are formally distinct in God is to misunderstand the nature of theological reasoning.

The foregoing inadequate account of what Ockham has to say on the subject of our knowledge of the divine nature really belongs to an account of his theological rather than of his philosophical ideas. For if the existence of God as the absolutely supreme being cannot be firmly established by the philosopher, it is obvious that the philosopher cannot give us any certain knowledge of God's nature. Nor can the theologian's reasoning, according to Ockham,

[1] 1 *Sent.*, 3, 2, F.

[2] *Ibid.*, M.

give us certain knowledge of God's nature. As far as the analysis of concepts goes, an unbeliever could perform the same analysis as is performed by the believing theologian. What gives us certain knowledge of the truth of theological propositions is not the theologian's reasoning as such, nor his demonstrations, so far as demonstration is possible for him, but God's revelation accepted on faith. The theologian can reason correctly from certain premisses; but so can the unbeliever. The former, however, accepts the premisses and the conclusions on faith; and he knows that the propositions are true, that is, that they correspond to reality. But he knows this by faith; and his knowledge is not, in the strict sense, 'science'. For there is no intuitive knowledge lying at the basis of his reasoning. Ockham did not intend to question the truth of theological dogmas: he set out to examine the nature of theological reasoning and theological concepts, and he treated his problems from the point of view of a logician. His theological nominalism was not, in his own mind, equivalent to agnosticism or scepticism: it was rather, in intention at any rate, a logical analysis of a theology which he accepted.

But though Ockham's discussion of our knowledge of God's nature belongs more properly to the theological than to the philosophical sphere, it has its place in a discussion of his philosophy, if only for the reason that in it he deals with matters which preceding mediaeval philosophers had considered to fall within the metaphysician's competence. Similarly, though the philosopher as such could scarcely, in Ockham's eyes, establish anything with certainty about the divine 'ideas', this topic had been a salient feature of the traditional mediaeval metaphysics, and Ockham's treatment of it is closely linked with his general philosophic principles. It is desirable, therefore, to say something about it here.

5. In the first place there cannot be any plurality in the divine intellect. The divine intellect is identical with the divine will and the divine essence. We may speak about 'the divine will', 'the divine intellect' and 'the divine essence'; but the reality referred to is one single and simple being. Hence, talk about the 'divine ideas' cannot be taken to refer to realities in God which are in any way distinct either from the divine essence or from one another. If there were a distinction at all, it would be a real distinction; and a real distinction cannot be admitted. In the second place,

it is quite unnecessary, and also misleading, to postulate divine ideas as a kind of intermediary factor in creation. Apart from the fact that if the divine ideas are in no way distinct from the divine intellect, which is itself identical with the divine essence, they cannot be an intermediary factor in creation, God can know creatures and create them without the intervention of any 'ideas'.[1] Ockham makes it clear that in his opinion the theory of ideas in God is simply a piece of anthropomorphism. It also involves a confusion between *quid rei* and *quid nominis*.[2] The upholders of the theory would certainly admit that there is not a real distinction either between the divine essence and the divine ideas or between the ideas themselves but that the distinction is a mental distinction; yet they talk as though the distinction of ideas in God were prior to the production of creatures. Moreover, they postulate in God ideas of universals, which as a matter of fact do not correspond to any reality. In fine, Ockham applies the principle of economy to the theory of divine ideas in so far as this theory implies that there are ideas in God which are distinct from creatures themselves, whether the ideas are interpreted as real or as mental relations. It is unnecessary to postulate such ideas in God to explain either His production of or His knowledge of creatures.

In one sense, therefore, Ockham may be said to have rejected the theory of divine ideas. But this does not mean that he was prepared to declare that St. Augustine was in error or that there was no acceptable interpretation of the theory. On the contrary, as far as verbal acceptance was concerned, he must be said to have accepted the theory. But the meaning which he attaches to the statements he makes has to be clearly understood, if he is not to be judged guilty of flagrant self-contradiction. He asserts, for instance, that there is an infinite number of distinct ideas; and this assertion appears at first hearing to be in obvious contradiction with his condemnation of any ascription of distinct ideas to God.

In the first place, the term 'idea' is a connotative term. It denotes directly the creature itself; but it connotes indirectly the divine knowledge or knower. 'And so it can be predicated of the creature itself that it is an idea but not of the knowing agent nor of the knowledge, since neither the knowledge nor the knower is

[1] Cf. 1 *Sent.*, 35, 5, C.

[2] In other words, Ockham considered that the upholders of the theory had been misled by language, confusing words or names with things.

an idea or pattern.'[1] We can say, then, that the creature itself is the idea. 'The ideas are not in God subjectively and really; but they are in Him only objectively, that is, as certain things which are known by Him, for the ideas are the things themselves which are producible by God.'[2] In other words, it is quite sufficient to postulate God on the one hand and creatures on the other hand: the creatures as known by God are the 'ideas', and there are no other ideas. The creature as known from eternity by God can be considered as the pattern or exemplar of the creature as actually existent. 'The ideas are certain known patterns (*exempla*); and it is by reference to them that the knower can produce something in real existence. . . . This description does not fit the divine essence itself, nor any mental relation; but the creature itself. . . . The divine essence is not an idea . . . (Nor is the idea either a real or a mental relation) . . . Not a real relation, since there is no real relation on God's part to the creature; and not a mental relation, both because there is no mental relation of God to the creature to which the name "idea" could be given and because a mental relation cannot be the exemplar of the creature, just as an *ens rationis* cannot be the exemplar of a real being.'[3] But if creatures themselves are the ideas, it follows that 'there are distinct ideas of all makable things, as the things themselves are distinct from one another'.[4] And thus there are distinct ideas of all the essential and integral parts of producible things, like matter and form.[5]

On the other hand, if the ideas are the creatures themselves, it follows that the ideas are of individual things, 'since individual things alone are producible outside (the mind) and no others'.[6] There are, for example, no divine ideas of genera; for the divine ideas are creatures makable by God, and genera cannot be produced as real existents. It follows, too, that there are no ideas of negations, privations, evil, guilt and the like, since these are not and cannot be distinct things.[7] But, as God can produce an infinity of creatures, we must say that there is an infinite number of ideas.[8]

Ockham's discussion of the theory of divine ideas illuminates both the general mediaeval outlook and his own mentality. The respect for St. Augustine in the Middle Ages was too great for it to be possible for a theologian simply to reject one of his main theories. We find, then, the language of the theory being retained

[1] 1 *Sent.*, 35, 5, E. [2] *Ibid.*, G. [3] *Ibid.*, E. [4] *Ibid.*, G.
[5] *Ibid.* [6] *Ibid.* [7] *Ibid.* [8] *Ibid.*

and used by Ockham. He was willing to speak of distinct ideas and of these ideas as patterns or exemplars of creation. On the other hand, using the principle of economy and determined to get rid of anything which might seem to come between the omnipotent Creator and the creature so as to govern the divine will, he pruned the theory of all Platonism and identified the ideas with creatures themselves as producible by God and as known by God from eternity as producible. From the philosophical point of view he fitted the theory to his general philosophy by eliminating universal ideas, while from the theological point of view he safeguarded, as he thought, the divine omnipotence and eliminated what he considered to be the contamination of Greek metaphysics. (Having identified the ideas with creatures he was able, however, to observe that Plato acted rightly in neither identifying the ideas with God nor placing them in the divine mind.) This is not to say, of course, that Ockham's use of the language of the Aristotelian theory was insincere. He postulated the theory, in so far as it could be taken to mean simply that creatures are known by God, for one of the main traditional reasons, namely that God creates rationally and not irrationally.[1] But at the same time it is clear that in Ockham's hands the theory was so purged of Platonism that to all intents and purposes it was rejected in its original form. Abelard, while rejecting ultra-realism, had retained the theory of universal ideas in God, largely out of respect for St. Augustine; but Ockham eliminated these universal divine ideas. His version of the theory of ideas is thus consistent with his general principle that there are only individual existents and with his constant attempt to get rid of any other factors which could be got rid of. It might be said, of course, that to speak of producible creatures as known by God from all eternity ('things were ideas from eternity; but they were not actually existent from eternity')[2] is to admit the essence of the theory of ideas; and this is, in fact, what Ockham thought and what justified him, in his opinion, in appealing to St. Augustine. But it is perhaps questionable if Ockham's theory is altogether consistent. As he would not confine God's creative power in any way, he had to extend the range of 'ideas' beyond the things actually produced by God; but to do this is, of course, to admit that the 'ideas' cannot be identified with creatures that have existed, do exist and will exist; and to admit this is to come very close to the Thomist theory, except that no ideas of universals

[1] Cf. 1 *Sent.*, 35, 5, E. [2] *Ibid.*, M.

are admitted. The conclusion that should probably be drawn is not that Ockham made an insincere use of the language of a theory which he had really discarded, but rather that he sincerely accepted the theory, though he interpreted it in such a way as to fit in with his conviction that only individuals exist or can exist and that universal concepts belong to the level of human thought and are not to be attributed to God.

6. When it comes to discussing the divine knowledge Ockham shows a marked and, indeed, very understandable reluctance to make assertions concerning a level of cognition which lies entirely outside our experience.

That God knows, besides Himself, all other things cannot be proved philosophically. Any proof would rest principally on God's universal causality; but, apart from the fact that it cannot be proved by means of the principle of causality that a cause knows its immediate effect, it cannot be proved philosophically that God is the immediate cause of all things.[1] Probable arguments can be given for saying that God knows some things other than Himself; but the arguments are not conclusive. On the other hand, it cannot be proved that God knows nothing other than Himself; for it cannot be proved that every act of cognition depends on its object.[2] Nevertheless, though it cannot be philosophically proved that God is omniscient, that is, that He knows not only Himself but also all other things as well, we know by faith that He is.

But, if God knows all things, does this mean that He knows future contingent events, in the sense of events which depend on free wills for their actuality? 'I say to this question that it must be held without any doubt that God knows all future contingent events with certainty and evidence. But it is impossible for any intellect in our present state to make evident either this fact or the manner in which God knows all future contingent events.'[3] Aristotle, says Ockham, would have said that God has no certain knowledge of any future contingent events for the following reason. No statement that a future contingent event depending on free choice will happen or will not happen is true. The proposition that it either will or will not happen is true; but neither the statement that it will happen nor the statement that it will not happen is true. And if neither statement is true, neither statement can be known. 'In spite of this reason, however, we must hold that God evidently knows all future contingents. But the way (in which

[1] 1 *Sent.*, 35, 2, D. [2] *Ibid.* [3] *Ibid.*, 38, 1, L.

God knows them) I cannot explain.'[1] But Ockham goes on to say that God does not know future contingent events as present to Him,[2] or by means of ideas as media of knowledge, but by the divine essence itself, although this cannot be proved philosophically. Similarly in the *Tractatus de praedestinatione et de praescientia Dei et de futuris contingentibus*[3] Ockham states: 'So I say that it is impossible to express clearly the way in which God knows future contingent events. However, it must be held that He does (know them), though contingently.' By saying that God knows future contingent facts 'contingently' Ockham means that God knows them as contingent and that His knowledge does not make them necessary. He goes on to suggest that 'the divine essence is intuitive knowledge which is so perfect and so clear that it is itself evident knowledge of all past and future events, so that it knows which part of a contradiction will be true and which part false'.[4]

Thus Ockham affirms that God does not merely know that, for example, I shall choose tomorrow either to go for a walk or to stop at home and read; He knows which alternative is true and which false. This affirmation is not one that can be proved philosophically: it is a theological matter. As to the mode of God's knowledge, Ockham does not offer any suggestion beyond saying that the divine essence is such that God does know future contingent facts. He does not have recourse to the expedient of saying that God knows which part of a disjunctive proposition concerning a future contingent event is true because He determines it to be true: he very sensibly admits that he cannot explain how God knows future contingent events. It is to be noted, however, that Ockham is convinced that one part of a disjunctive proposition concerning such an event is true, and that God knows it as true. This is the important fact from the purely philosophical point of view: the relation of God's knowledge of future free events to the theme of predestination does not concern us here. It is an important fact because it shows that Ockham did not admit an exception to the principle of excluded middle. Some fourteenth-century philosophers did admit an exception. For Petrus Aureoli, as we have seen, propositions which either affirm or deny that a definite contingent event will happen in the future are neither true nor false.

[1] 1 *Sent.*, 38, 1, M.

[2] St. Thomas held that future contingent events are present to God in virtue of His eternity and that He knows them as present.

[3] Ed. Boehner, p. 15.

[4] *Ibid.*

Petrus Aureoli did not deny that God knows future contingent events; but he maintained that as God's knowledge does not look forward, as it were, to the future, it does not make an affirmative or a negative statement which concerns a definite free act in the future either true or false. One can say, then, that he admitted an instance of a 'three-valued' logic, though it would, of course, be an anachronism to depict him as elaborating such a logic. This is not the case, however, with William of Ockham, who does not admit any propositions to be neither true nor false. He rejected Aristotle's arguments designed to show that there are such propositions, though there are one or two passages which seem at first sight to support Aristotle's point of view. Moreover, in the *Summa totius logicae*[1] Ockham expressly states, in opposition to Aristotle, that propositions about future contingent events are true or false. Again, in the *Quodlibet*[2] he maintains that God can reveal knowledge of affirmative propositions concerning future contingent events, because such propositions are true. God made revelations of this sort to the prophets; though precisely how it was done 'I do not know, because it has not been revealed to me.' One cannot say, then, that Ockham admitted an exception to the principle of excluded middle. And because he did not admit an exception he was not faced with the problems of reconciling the admission with the divine omniscience.

7. If the terms 'will', 'intellect' and 'essence' are understood in an absolute sense, they are synonymous. 'If some name were used to signify precisely the divine essence and nothing else, without any connotation of anything else whatever, and similarly if some name were used to signify the divine will in the same manner, those names would be simply synonymous names; and whatever was predicated of the one could be predicated of the other.'[3] Accordingly, if the terms 'essence' and 'will' are taken absolutely, there is no more reason to say that the divine will is the cause of all things than that the divine essence is the cause of all things: it comes to the same thing. However, whether we speak of the 'divine essence' or of the 'divine will', God is the immediate cause of all things, though this cannot be demonstrated philosophically.[4] The divine will (or the divine essence) is the immediate cause of all things in the sense that without the divine causality no effect would follow, even though all other conditions and dispositions were present. Moreover, the power of God is unlimited, in the

[1] 2, 32. [2] 4, 4. [3] 1 *Sent.*, 45, 1, C. [4] *Ibid.*, G.

sense that He can do all that is possible. But to say that God cannot do what is intrinsically impossible is not to limit God's power; for it makes no sense to speak of doing or making what is intrinsically impossible. However, God can produce every possible effect, even without a secondary cause; He could, for instance, produce in the human being an act of hatred of Himself, and if He were to do so He would not sin.[1] That God can produce every possible effect, even without the concurrence of a secondary cause, cannot be proved by the philosopher; but it is none the less to be believed.

The divine omnipotence cannot, then, be philosophically proved. But once it is assumed as an article of faith the world appears in a special light. All empirical causal relations, that is, all regular sequences, are seen as contingent, not only in the sense that causal relations are matters for experiential verification and not for *a priori* deduction, but also in the sense that an external agent, namely God, can always produce *B* without employing *A* as secondary cause. Of course, in all mediaeval systems of thought the uniformity and regularity of natural processes were regarded as contingent, inasmuch as the possibility of God's miraculous intervention was admitted by all Christian thinkers. But the metaphysic of essences had conferred on Nature a comparative stability of which Ockham deprived it. With him relations and connections in nature were really reduced to the co-existence or successive existence of 'absolutes'. And in the light of the divine omnipotence, believed on faith, the contingency of relations and of order in nature was seen as the expression of the all-powerful will of God. Ockham's view of nature, taken in isolation from its theological background, might reasonably be regarded as a stage on the path to a scientific view of nature through the elimination of the metaphysical; but the theological background was not for Ockham himself an irrelevant excrescence. On the contrary, the thought of the divine omnipotence and liberty pervaded, explicitly or implicitly, his whole system; and in the next chapter we shall see how his convictions on this matter influenced his moral theory.

[1] 1 *Sent.*, 42, 1, G

CHAPTER VII

OCKHAM (5)

That an immaterial and incorruptible soul is the form of the body cannot be philosophically proved—The plurality of really distinct forms in man—The rational soul possesses no really distinct faculties—The human person—Freedom—Ockham's ethical theory.

1. JUST as Ockham criticized the traditional proofs of God's existence, so also did he criticize a number of the proofs advanced by his predecessors in psychology. We experience acts of understanding and willing; but there is no compelling reason to attribute these acts to an immaterial form or soul. We experience these acts as acts of the form of the body; and, as far as experience takes us, we might reasonably conclude that they are the acts of an extended and corporeal form.[1] 'Understanding by intellectual soul an immaterial and incorruptible form which is wholly in the whole and wholly in every part (of the body), it cannot be known evidently either by arguments or by experience that there is such a form in us or that the activity of understanding belongs to a substance of this kind in us, or that a soul of this kind is the form of the body. I do not care what Aristotle thought about this, for he seems to speak always in an ambiguous manner. But these three things we hold only by faith.'[2] According to Ockham, then, we do not experience the presence of an immaterial and incorruptible form in ourselves; nor can it be proved that the acts of understanding which we do experience are the acts of such a form. And even if we could prove that the acts of understanding which we experience are the acts of an immaterial substance, it would not follow that this substance is the form of the body. And if it cannot be shown by philosophic reasoning or by experience that we possess immaterial and incorruptible souls, it obviously cannot be shown that these souls are created directly by God.[3] Ockham does not say, of course, that we do not possess immortal souls: what he says is that we cannot prove that we possess them. That we do possess them is a revealed truth, known by faith.

2. But though Ockham accepted on faith the existence of an

[1] *Quodlibet*, 1, 12. [2] *Ibid.*, 1, 10. [3] *Ibid.*, 2, 1.

immaterial and incorruptible form in man, he was not prepared to say that this form informs matter directly. The function of matter is to support a form; and it is clear that the matter of the human body has a form. But the corruptibility of the human body shows that it is not an incorruptible form which informs matter immediately. 'I say that one must postulate in man another form in addition to the intellectual soul, namely a sensitive form, on which a natural agent can act by way of corruption and production.'[1] This sensitive form or soul is distinct from man's intellectual soul and, unless God wills otherwise, it perishes with the body.[2] There is only one sensitive form in an animal or in a man; but it is extended in such a way that 'one part of the sensitive soul perfects one part of matter, while another part of the same soul perfects another part of matter'.[3] Thus the part of the sensitive soul which perfects the organ of sight is the power of seeing, while the part which perfects the organ of hearing is the power of hearing.[4] In this sense, then, we can speak of sensitive powers which are really distinct from one another; for 'the accidental dispositions which are of necessity required for the act of seeing are really distinct from the dispositions which are of necessity required for the act of hearing'.[5] This is clear from the fact that one can lose the power of sight, for example, without losing the power of hearing. But if we mean by 'powers' forms which are the eliciting principles of the various acts of sensation, there is no need to postulate really distinct powers corresponding to the various organs of sense: the principle of economy can be applied. The one eliciting principle is the sensitive form or soul itself, which is extended throughout the body and works through the different sense-organs.

In one place Ockham speaks as follows. 'According to the opinion which I consider the true one there are in man several substantial forms, at least a form of corporeity and the intellectual soul.'[6] In another place he says that though it is difficult to prove that there are or are not several substantial forms in man, 'it is proved (that there are) in the following way, at least in regard to the intellectual soul and the sensitive soul, which are distinct in man'.[7] His remark about the difficulty of proof is explained in the *Quodlibet*,[8] where he says that it is difficult to prove that the sensitive and intellectual souls are distinct in man 'because it cannot be proved from self-evident propositions'. But this does

[1] 2 *Sent.*, 22, H. [2] *Quodlibet*, 2, 10. [3] 2 *Sent.*, 26, E. [4] *Ibid.*
[5] *Ibid.*, D. [6] *Ibid.*, 9, C C. [7] 4 *Sent.*, 7, F. [8] 2, 10.

not prevent his going on to offer arguments based on experience, such as the argument that we can desire a thing with the sensitive appetite, while at the same time we turn away from it with the rational will. As to the fact that in one place he seems to insist on the intellectual soul and the form of corporeity, whereas in another place he seems to insist on the presence in man of intellectual and sensitive souls, the apparent inconsistency seems to be explicable in terms of the two contexts. In any case Ockham clearly maintained the existence in man of three distinct forms. He argues not only that the intellectual soul and the sensitive soul are distinct in man,[1] but also that the sensitive soul and the form of corporeity are really distinct both in men and brutes.[2] In maintaining the existence of a form of corporeity in man Ockham was, of course, continuing the Franciscan tradition; and he gives the traditional theological argument, that the form of corporeity must be postulated in order to explain the numerical identity of Christ's dead body with His living body, though he gives other arguments as well.

In saying that there is in man a form of corporeity and in maintaining that the intellectual soul does not inform prime matter directly Ockham was continuing, then, a traditional position, in favour of which he rejected that of St. Thomas. Moreover, though he maintained the doctrine of the plurality of substantial forms, he did not deny that man, taken in his totality, is a unity. 'There is only one total being of man, but several partial beings.'[3] Nor did he deny that the intellectual soul is the form of the body, though he did not think that this can be proved philosophically. Hence it can hardly be said that Ockham contradicted the teaching of the Council of Vienne (1311), since the Council did not assert that the rational or intellectual soul informs prime matter directly. The majority of the members of the Council themselves held the doctrine of the form of corporeity; and when they declared that the rational soul informs the body directly they left the question entirely open whether or not the body which is informed by the rational soul is constituted as a body by its own form of corporeity or not. On the other hand, the Council had clearly intended to defend the unity of the human being against the implications of Olivi's psychological theories;[4] and it is at least questionable whether Ockham's teaching satisfied this demand.

[1] *Quodlibet*, 2, 10; 2 *Sent.*, 22, H.
[2] *Ibid.*, 2, 10.
[3] *Quodlibet*, 2, 11.
[4] See vol. II of this history, pp. 451-3.

It must be remembered that for Ockham a real distinction meant a distinction between things which can be separated, at least by the divine power: he rejected the Scotist doctrine of formal objective distinctions, that is, of objective distinctions between different 'formalities' of one and the same thing, which cannot be separated from one another. When discussing the question whether the sensitive soul and the intellectual soul are really distinct in man, he remarks that the sensitive soul of Christ, though always united to the Deity, remained where God pleased during the time between Christ's death and the resurrection. 'But whether it remained with the body or with the intellectual soul God alone knows; yet both can well be said.'[1] If, however, the sensitive form is really separable from man's rational form and from his body, it is difficult to see how the unity of man can be preserved. It is true, of course, that all the mediaeval Christian thinkers would have admitted that the rational soul is separable from the body: they obviously could not do otherwise. And it might be argued that to assert the separability of the sensitive from the rational soul does not impair man's unity any more than does the assertion that man's rational soul is separable from his body. However, one is entitled to say at least that Ockham's doctrine of the real distinction between the sensitive and rational souls in man makes it harder to safeguard the unity of man than does Scotus's doctrine of the formal distinction. Ockham, of course, disposed of Scotus's formal distinction by means of the principle of economy, and he supported his theory of the real distinction between the sensitive and rational souls by an appeal to experience. It was, indeed, for similar reasons that Scotus maintained the formal distinction; but he seems to have realized better than Ockham the fundamental unity of man's intellectual and sensitive life. In certain respects he appears to have been less influenced by Aristotle than was Ockham, who envisaged the possibility at any rate of the rational soul's being united to the body more as a mover than as a form, though, as we have seen, he accepted on faith the doctrine that the intellectual soul is the form of the body.

3. Though Ockham asserted the existence in man of a plurality of forms, really distinct from one another, he would not admit a real distinction between the faculties of a given form. We have already seen that he refused to allow that the sensitive soul or form possesses powers which are really distinct from the sensitive

[1] *Quodlibet*, 2, 10.

soul itself and from one another, unless by 'powers' one means simply accidental dispositions in the various sense-organs. He also refused to allow that the rational soul or form possesses faculties which are really distinct from the rational soul itself and from one another. The rational soul is unextended and spiritual; and it cannot have parts or ontologically distinct faculties. What is called the intellect is simply the rational soul understanding, and what we call the will is simply the soul willing. The rational soul produces acts; and the intellectual power or faculty 'does not signify only the essence of the soul, but it connotes the act of understanding. And similarly in the case of the will.'[1] In one sense, then, intellect and will are really distinct, that is, if we are taking them as connotative terms; for an act of understanding is really distinct from an act of willing. But if we are referring to that which produces the acts, intellect and will are not really distinct. The principle of economy can be applied in the elimination of really distinct faculties or principles.[2] There is one rational soul, which can elicit different acts. As to the existence of an active intellect distinct from the passive intellect there is no compelling reason for accepting it. The formation of universal concepts, for example, can be explained without postulating any activity of the intellect.[3] Nevertheless, Ockham is prepared to accept the active intellect on account of the authority 'of the saints and philosophers',[4] in spite of the fact that the arguments for its existence can be answered and that in any case no more than probable arguments can be given.

4. In asserting a plurality of substantial forms in man and in denying at the same time that intellect and will are really distinct faculties Ockham remained faithful to two features of the Franciscan tradition. But the doctrine of the plurality of forms in man traditionally meant an acceptance of the form of corporeity in addition to the one human soul, not a breaking-up, as it were, of the soul into distinct forms in Ockham's sense of distinction. His substitution of the real distinction, involving separability, for Scotus's formal objective distinction was scarcely compatible with the assertion of the unity of the human being. Yet in discussing human personality Ockham insisted on this unity. The person is a *suppositum intellectuale*, a definition which holds good for both created and uncreated persons.[5] A *suppositum* is 'a complete

[1] 2 *Sent.*, 24, L. [2] *Ibid.*, K. [3] *Ibid.*, 25, O.
[4] *Ibid.*, A A. [5] 1 *Sent.*, 25, J.

being, incommunicable by identity, incapable of inhering in anything, and not supported (*sustentatum*) by anything'.[1] The words 'a complete being' exclude from the class of *supposita* all parts, whether essential or integral, while the words 'incommunicable by identity' exclude the divine essence, which, though a complete being, is 'communicated' identically to the divine Persons. The phrase 'incapable of inhering in anything' excludes accidents, while 'not supported (Ockham means "taken up" or "assumed") by anything' excludes the human nature of Christ, which was assumed by the second Person and is consequently not a person. In the commentary on the *Sentences* Ockham defines 'person' as 'an intellectual and complete nature, which is neither supported (*nec sustentatur*, is not assumed) by anything else nor is able, as a part, to form with another thing one being'.[2] In the case of the three divine Persons each *suppositum intellectuale* or Person is constituted by the divine essence and a relation.[3]

The human person, then, is the total being of man, not the rational form or soul alone. It is in virtue of the rational form that a human being is a *suppositum intellectuale* as distinct from any other kind of *suppositum*; but it is the whole man, not the rational form alone, which constitutes the human person. Ockham, therefore, maintains with St. Thomas that the human soul in the state of separation from the body after death is not a person.[4]

5. One of the principal characteristics of a rational creature is freedom.[5] Freedom is the power 'by which I can indifferently and contingently produce an effect in such a way that I can cause or not cause that effect, without any difference in that power having been made'.[6] That one possesses this power cannot be proved by *a priori* reasoning, but 'it can, however, be known evidently through experience, that is, through the fact that every man experiences that however much his reason dictates something his will can will it or not will it'.[7] Moreover, the fact that we blame and praise people, that is, that we impute to them the responsibility for their actions, or for some of their actions, shows that we accept freedom as a reality. 'No act is blameworthy unless it is in our power. For no one blames a man born blind, for he is blind by sense (*caecus sensu*). But if he is blind by his own act, then he is blameworthy.'[8]

[1] *Quodlibet*, 4, 11.
[2] 3 *Sent.*, 1, B; cf. 1 *Sent.*, 23, 1, C.
[3] 1 *Sent.*, 25, 1, J.
[4] *Ibid.*, 23, 1, C.
[5] *Ibid.*, 1, 3, U.
[6] *Quodlibet*, 1, 16.
[7] *Ibid.*
[8] 3 *Sent.*, 10, H.

According to Ockham, the will is free to will or not to will happiness, the last end; it does not will it necessarily. This is clear in regard to the last end considered in the concrete, that is to say, God. 'No object other than God can satisfy the will, because no act which is directed to something other than God excludes all anxiety and sadness. For, whatever created object may be possessed, the will can desire something else with anxiety and sadness.'[1] But that the enjoyment of the divine essence is possible to us cannot be proved philosophically; it is an article of faith.[2] If then we do not know that the enjoyment of God is possible, we cannot will it. And even if we know by faith that it is possible, we can still will it or not will it, as is clear from experience. What is more, we do not will necessarily even perfect happiness in general. For the intellect may believe that perfect happiness is not possible for man and that the only condition possible for us is the one in which we actually find ourselves. But if the intellect can believe that perfect happiness is impossible, it can dictate to the will that it should not will something which is impossible and incompatible with the reality of human life. And in this case the will is able not to will what the intellect says that it should not will. The judgment of the intellect is, indeed, erroneous; but though 'the will does not necessarily conform to the judgment of the reason, it can conform with the judgment of the reason, whether that judgment be right or erroneous'.[3]

In emphasizing the freedom of the will in the face of the judgment of the intellect Ockham was following in the common tradition of the Franciscan philosophers. But it may be remarked that his view on the will's freedom even in regard to the willing of happiness in general (*beatitudo in communi*) fitted in very much with his ethical theory. If the will is free to will or not to will happiness, it would scarcely be possible to analyse the goodness of human acts in terms of a relation to an end which is necessarily desired. And in point of fact Ockham's ethical theory was, as we shall see presently, markedly authoritarian in character.

It is only to be expected that Ockham would insist that the will is free to elicit an act contrary to that to which the sensitive appetite is strongly inclined.[4] But he admitted, of course, the existence of habits and inclinations in the sensitive appetite and in the will.[5] There is some difficulty, he says, in explaining how it

[1] 1 *Sent.*, 1, 4, S.
[2] *Ibid.*, E.
[3] *Ibid.*, 1, 6, P.
[4] 3 *Sent.*, 10, D.
[5] Cf. 3 *Sent.*, 4, M; 3 *Sent.*, 10, D; 4 *Sent.*, 12, C.

is that habits are formed in a free power like the will as a result of repeated acts of the sensitive appetite; but that they are formed is a matter of experience. 'It is difficult to give the cause why the will is more inclined not to will an object which causes pain in the sensitive appetite.' The cause cannot be found in a command of the intellect, because the intellect can equally well say that the will should will that object as that it should not will it. But 'it is obvious through experience that even if the intellect says that death should be undergone for the sake of the State, the will is naturally, so to speak, inclined to the contrary'. On the other hand, we cannot simply say that the cause of the will's inclination is pleasure in the sensitive appetite. For, 'however intense may be the pleasure in the sensitive appetite, the will can, in virtue of its freedom, will the opposite'. 'And so I say that there does not seem to be any other cause for the will's natural inclination except that such is the nature of the matter; and this fact becomes known to us through experience.'[1] In other words, it is an undoubted fact of experience that the will is inclined to follow the sensitive appetite; but it is difficult to give a satisfactory theoretical explanation of the fact, though this does not alter the nature of the fact. If we indulge the sensitive appetite in a certain direction, a habit is formed, and this habit is reflected in what we can call a habit in the will, and this habit grows in strength if the will does not react sufficiently against the sensitive appetite. On the other hand, it remains in the will's power to act against habit and inclination, even if with difficulty, because the will is essentially free. A human act can never be attributed simply to habit and inclination; for it is possible for the will to choose in a manner contrary to the habit and inclination.

6. A created free will is subject to moral obligation. God is not, and cannot be, under any obligation; but man is entirely dependent upon God, and in his free acts his dependence expresses itself as moral obligation. He is morally obliged to will what God orders him to will and not to will what God orders him not to will. The ontological foundation of the moral order is thus man's dependence on God, as creature on Creator; and the content of the moral law is supplied by the divine precept. 'Evil is nothing else than to do something when one is under an obligation to do the opposite. Obligation does not fall on God, since He is not under any obligation to do anything.'[2]

[1] 3 *Sent.*, 13, U.

[2] 2 *Sent.*, 5, H.

This personal conception of the moral law was closely connected with Ockham's insistence on the divine omnipotence and liberty. Once these truths are accepted as revealed truths, the whole created order, including the moral law, is viewed by Ockham as wholly contingent, in the sense that not only its existence but also its essence and character depend on the divine creative and omnipotent will. Having got rid of any universal idea of man in the divine mind, Ockham was able to eliminate the idea of a natural law which is in essence immutable. For St. Thomas man was contingent, of course, in the sense that his existence depends on God's free choice; but God could not create the particular kind of being which we call man and impose on him precepts irrespective of their content. And, though he considered, for exegetic reasons connected with the Scriptures, that God can dispense in the case of certain precepts of the natural law, Scotus was fundamentally of the same mind as St. Thomas.[1] There are acts which are intrinsically evil and which are forbidden because they are evil: they are not evil simply because they are forbidden. For Ockham, however, the divine will is the ultimate norm of morality: the moral law is founded on the free divine choice rather than ultimately on the divine essence. Moreover, he did not hesitate to draw the logical consequences from this position. God concurs, as universal creator and conserver, in any act, even in an act of hatred of God. But He could also cause, as total cause, the same act with which He concurs as partial cause. 'Thus He can be the total cause of an act of hatred of God, and that without any moral malice.'[2] God is under no obligation; and therefore He could cause an act in the human will which would be a morally evil act if the man were responsible for it. If the man were responsible for it, he would commit sin, since he is obliged to love God and not hate Him; but obligation, being the result of divine imposition, cannot affect God Himself. 'By the very fact that God wills something, it is right for it to be done. . . . Hence if God were to cause hatred of Himself in anyone's will, that is, if He were to be the total cause of the act (He is, as it is, its partial cause), neither would that man sin nor would God; for God is not under any obligation, while the man is not (in the case) obliged, because the act would not be in his own power.'[3] God can do anything or order anything which does not involve logical contradiction. Therefore, because,

[1] On Scotus's moral theory, see vol. II of this history, pp. 545–50.

[2] 2 *Sent.*, 19, P.

[3] 4 *Sent.*, 9, E–F.

according to Ockham, there is no natural or formal repugnance between loving God and loving a creature in a way which has been forbidden by God, God could order fornication. Between loving God and loving a creature in a manner which is illicit there is only an extrinsic repugnance, namely the repugnance which arises from the fact that God has actually forbidden that way of loving a creature. Hence, if God were to order fornication, the latter would be not only licit but meritorious.[1] Hatred of God, stealing, committing adultery, are forbidden by God. But they could be ordered by God; and, if they were, they would be meritorious acts.[2] No one can say that Ockham lacked the courage to draw the logical conclusions from his personal theory of ethics.

Needless to say, Ockham did not mean to suggest that adultery, fornication, theft and hatred of God are legitimate acts in the present moral order; still less did he mean to encourage the commission of such acts. His thesis was that such acts are wrong because God has forbidden them; and his intention was to emphasize the divine omnipotence and liberty, not to encourage immorality. He made use of the distinction between the absolute power (*potentia absoluta*) of God, by which God could order the opposite of the acts which He has, as a matter of fact, forbidden, and the *potentia ordinata* of God, whereby God has actually established a definite moral code. But he explained the distinction in such a way as to make it clear not only that God could have established another moral order but that He could at any time order what He has actually forbidden.[3] There is no sense, then, in seeking for any more ultimate reason of the moral law than the divine *fiat*. Obligation arises through the encounter of a created free will with an external precept. In God's case there can be no question of an external precept. Therefore God is not obliged to order any kind of act rather than its opposite. That He has ordered this and forbidden that is explicable in terms of the divine free choice; and this is a sufficient reason.

The authoritarian element in Ockham's moral theory is, very naturally, the element which has attracted the most attention. But there is another element, which must also be mentioned. Apart from the fact that Ockham analyses the moral virtues in dependence on the Aristotelian analysis, he makes frequent use of the Scholastic concept of 'right reason' (*recta ratio*). Right reason is depicted as the norm, at least the proximate norm, of

[1] 3 *Sent.*, 12, AAA. [2] 2 *Sent.*, 19, O. [3] Cf. *Opus nonaginta dierum*, c. 95.

morality. 'It can be said that every right will is in conformity with right reason.'[1] Again, 'no moral virtue, nor any virtuous act, is possible unless it is in conformity with right reason; for right reason is included in the definition of virtue in the second book of the *Ethics*'.[2] Moreover, for an act to be virtuous, not only must it be in accordance with right reason but it must also be done because it is in accordance with right reason. 'No act is perfectly virtuous unless in that act the will wills that which is prescribed by right reason because it is prescribed by right reason.'[3] For if one willed that which is prescribed by right reason simply because it is pleasant or for some other motive, without regard to its being prescribed by right reason, one's act 'would not be virtuous, since it would not be elicited in conformity with right reason. For to elicit an act in conformity with right reason is to will what is prescribed by right reason on account of its being so prescribed.'[4] This insistence on motive was not, of course, a sudden outbreak of 'puritanism' on Ockham's part: Aristotle had insisted that for an act to be perfectly virtuous it must be done for its own sake, that is, because it is the right thing to do. We call an act just, he says, if it is what the just man would do; but it does not follow that a man is just, that is, that he has the virtue of justice, simply because he does the act which the just man would do in the circumstances. He has to do it as the just man would do it; and this includes doing it because it is the just thing to do.[5]

Right reason, then, is the norm of morality. A man may be mistaken in what he thinks is the dictate of right reason; but, even if he is mistaken, he is obliged to conform his will to what he believes to be prescribed by right reason. In other words, conscience is always to be followed, even if it is an erroneous conscience. A man may, of course, be responsible for his having an erroneous conscience; but it is also possible for him to be in 'invincible ignorance', and in this case he is not responsible for his error. In any case, however, he is bound to follow what happens to be the judgment of his conscience. 'A created will which follows an invincibly erroneous conscience is a right will; for the divine will wills that it should follow its reason when this reason is not blameworthy. If it acts against that reason (that is, against an

[1] 1 *Sent.*, 41, K.

[2] 3 *Sent.*, 12, NN. For the reference to Aristotle's *Ethics*, cf. *Nicomachean Ethics*, 1107, a.

[3] 3 *Sent.*, 12, CCC.

[4] *Ibid.*, CCC–DDD.

[5] Cf. *Nicomachean Ethics*, 1105, a b.

invincibly erroneous conscience), it sins. . . .'[1] A man is morally obliged to do what he in good faith believes to be right. This doctrine, that one is morally obliged to follow one's conscience, and that to follow an invincibly erroneous conscience, so far from being a sin, is a duty, was not a new doctrine in the Middle Ages; but Ockham expressed it in a clear and unequivocal manner.

It would seem, then, at least at first sight, that we are faced with what amounts to two moral theories in Ockham's philosophy. On the one hand there is his authoritarian conception of the moral law. It would appear to follow from this conception that there can be only a revealed moral code. For how otherwise than through revelation could man know a moral code which depends entirely on God's free choice? Rational deduction could not give us knowledge of it. On the other hand there is Ockham's insistence on right reason, which would seem to imply that reason can discern what is right and what is wrong. The authoritarian conception of morality expresses Ockham's conviction of the freedom and omnipotence of God as they are revealed in Christianity, while the insistence on right reason would seem to represent the influence on his thought of Aristotle's ethical teaching and of the moral theories of his mediaeval predecessors. It might seem, then, that Ockham presents one type of ethical theory in his capacity as theologian and another type in his capacity as philosopher. It has thus been maintained that in spite of his authoritarian conception of the moral law Ockham promoted the growth of a 'lay' moral theory represented by his insistence on reason as the norm of morality and on the duty of doing what one in good faith believes to be the right thing to do.

That there is truth in the contention that two moral theories are implicit in Ockham's ethical teaching can hardly, I think, be denied. He built on the substructure of the Christian-Aristotelian tradition, and he retained a considerable amount of it, as is shown by what he says about the virtues, right reason, natural rights and so on. But he added to this substructure a superstructure which consisted in an ultra-personal conception of the moral law; and he does not seem fully to have realized that the addition of this superstructure demanded a more radical recasting of the substructure than he actually carried out. His personal conception of the moral law was not without precedents in Christian

[1] 3 *Sent.*, 13, O.

thought; but the point is that in the twelfth and thirteenth centuries a moral theory had been elaborated in close association with metaphysics, which ruled out any view of the moral law as dependent simply and solely on the divine will. In retaining a good deal of the former moral theory, while at the same time asserting an authoritarian interpretation of the moral law, Ockham was inevitably involved in difficulties. Like other Christian mediaeval thinkers he accepted, of course, the existence of an actual moral order; and in his discussion of such themes as the function of reason or the existence of natural rights[1] he implied that reason can discern the precepts, or at least the fundamental precepts, of the moral law which actually obtains. At the same time he insisted that the moral order which actually obtains is due to the divine choice, in the sense that God could have established a different moral order and that He could even now order a man to do something contrary to the moral law which He has established. But, if the present moral order is dependent simply and solely on the divine choice, how could we know what it is save through God's revelation? It would seem that there can be only a revealed ethic. Yet Ockham does not appear to have said that there can be only a revealed ethic: he seems to have thought that men, without revelation, are able to discern the moral law in some sense. In this case they can presumably discern a prudential code or a set of hypothetical imperatives. Without revelation men could see that certain acts fit human nature and human society and that other acts are harmful; but they could not discern an immutable natural law, since there is no such immutable natural law, nor could they know, without revelation, whether the acts they thought right were really the acts ordered by God. If reason cannot prove conclusively God's existence, it obviously cannot prove that God has ordered this rather than that. If, therefore, we leave Ockham's theology out of account, it would seem that we are left with a non-metaphysical and non-theological morality, the precepts of which cannot be known as necessary or immutable precepts. Hence perhaps Ockham's insistence on the following of conscience, even an erroneous conscience. Left to himself, that is, without revelation, man might perhaps elaborate an ethic of the Aristotelian type; but he could not discern a natural law of the type envisaged by St. Thomas, since Ockham's authoritarian conception of the moral law, coupled with his 'nominalism', would rule this out.

[1] On this subject, see the following chapter.

In this sense, then, one is probably justified in saying that two moralities are implicit in Ockham's teaching, namely an authoritarian ethic and a 'lay' or non-theological ethic.

It is one thing, however, to say that the two ethical systems are implicit in Ockham's moral teaching; and it is another thing to suggest that he intended to promote an ethic divorced from theology. One could say with far more justice that he intended the very opposite; for he evidently considered that his predecessors had obscured the doctrines of the divine omnipotence and liberty through their theories of an immutable natural law. As far as the interpretation of Ockham's own mind is concerned, it is clear that it is the personal side of his moral theory which has to be stressed. One has only to look at a passage like the following wherein he says that the reason why an act elicited contrary to the dictate of conscience is a wrong act is that 'it would be elicited contrary to the divine precept and the divine will which wills that an act should be elicited in conformity with right reason'.[1] In other words, the ultimate and sufficient reason why we ought to follow right reason or conscience is that God wills that we should do so. Authoritarianism has the last word. Again, Ockham speaks of an act 'which is intrinsically and necessarily virtuous *stante ordinatione divina*'.[2] In the same section he says that 'in the present order (*stante ordinatione quae nunc est*) no act is perfectly virtuous unless it is elicited in conformity with right reason'. Such remarks are revealing. A necessarily virtuous act is only relatively so, that is, if God has decreed that it should be virtuous. Given the order instituted by God, it follows logically that certain acts are good and others bad; but the order itself is dependent on God's choice. It possesses a certain stability, and Ockham did not imagine that God is constantly changing His orders, so to speak; but he insists that its stability is not absolute.

One can, then, sum up Ockham's position on more or less the following lines. The human being, as a free created being which is entirely dependent on God, is morally obliged to conform his will to the divine will in regard to that which God commands or prohibits. Absolutely speaking, God could command or prohibit any act, provided that a contradiction is not involved. Actually God has established a certain moral law. As a rational being man can see that he ought to obey this law. But he may not know what God has commanded; and in this case he is morally obliged to do

[1] 3 *Sent.*, 13, C. [2] *Ibid.*, 12, CCC.

what he honestly believes to be in accordance with God's commands. To act otherwise would be to act contrary to what is believed to be the divine ordinance; and to do this is to sin. It is not clear what Ockham thought of the moral situation of the man who has no knowledge of revelation, or even no knowledge of God's existence. He appears to imply that reason can discern something of the present moral order; but, if he did mean this, it is difficult to see how this idea can be reconciled with his authoritarian conception of morality. If the moral law is dependent simply on the divine choice, how can its content be known apart from revelation? If its content can be known apart from revelation, how can it be dependent simply on the divine choice? It would seem that the only way of escaping this difficulty is to say that what can be known apart from revelation is simply a provisional code of morality, based on non-theological considerations. But that Ockham actually had this notion clearly in mind, which would imply the possibility of a purely philosophic and second-rank ethic, as distinct from the divinely-imposed and obligatory ethic, I should not care to affirm. He thought in terms of the ethical code commonly accepted by Christians, though he went on to assert that it was dependent on the free divine choice. Very probably he did not clearly realize the difficulties created by his authoritarian conception.

CHAPTER VIII

OCKHAM (6)

The dispute on evangelical poverty, and the doctrine of natural rights—Political sovereignty is not derived from the spiritual power—The relation of the people to their ruler—How far were Ockham's political ideas novel or revolutionary?—The pope's position within the Church.

1. It would be a mistake to suppose that Ockham was a political philosopher in the sense of a man who reflects systematically on the nature of political society, sovereignty and government. Ockham's political writings were not written to provide an abstract political theory; they were immediately occasioned by contemporary disputes involving the Holy See, and Ockham's immediate object was to resist and denounce what he regarded as papal aggression and unjustified absolutism; he was concerned with relations between pope and emperor and between the pope and the members of the Church rather than with political society and political government as such. Ockham shared in the respect for law and custom and in the dislike for arbitrary and capricious absolutism which were common characteristics of the mediaeval philosophers and theologians: it would be wrong to suppose that he set out to revolutionize mediaeval society. It is true, of course, that Ockham was led to lay down general principles on the relations of Church and State and on political government; but he did this mainly in the course of conducting controversies on concrete and specific points of dispute. For example, he published the *Opus nonaginta dierum* about the year 1332 in defence of the attitude of Michael of Cesena in regard to the dispute on evangelical poverty. Pope John XXII had condemned as heretical a doctrine on evangelical poverty which was held by many Franciscans and had deprived Michael of his post as General of the Franciscan Order. Counterblasts from Michael, who, together with Bonagratia of Bergamo and Ockham had taken refuge with the emperor, Ludwig of Bavaria, elicited from the pope the bull *Quia vir reprobus* (1329) in which Michael's doctrines were again censured and the Franciscans were rebuked for daring to publish tracts criticizing papal pronouncements. Ockham retaliated by subjecting the bull to

close scrutiny and trenchant criticism in the *Opus nonaginta dierum*. This publication was occasioned, therefore, not by any purely theoretical consideration of the position of the Holy See, but by a concrete dispute, that concerning evangelical poverty; it was not composed by a political philosopher in hours of cool reflection but by a participant in a heated controversy. Ockham criticized the papal pronouncements as themselves heretical and was able to refer to the erroneous opinion of John XXII concerning the beatific vision. He was thus writing primarily as a theologian.

But though Ockham wrote the *Opus nonaginta dierum* for the specific purpose of defending his Franciscan colleagues against papal condemnation, and though he devoted a good deal of his attention to discovering heresies and errors in the pope's pronouncements, he discussed the poverty question in the manner which one would expect of a philosopher, a man accustomed to close and careful reasoning. The result is that one can find in the work Ockham's general ideas on, for example, the right of property, though it must be confessed that it is not easy to settle the question exactly which of the opinions discussed are Ockham's own opinions, since he writes in a much more restrained and impersonal manner than one might expect in a polemical writer involved in a heated controversy.

Man has a natural right to property. God gave to man the power to dispose of the goods of the earth in the manner dictated by right reason, and since the Fall right reason shows that the personal appropriation of temporal goods is necessary.[1] The right of private property is thus a natural right, willed by God, and, as such, it is inviolable, in the sense that no one can be despoiled of this right by an earthly power. The State can regulate the exercise of the right of private property, the way in which property is transferred in society, for example; but it cannot deprive men of the right against their will. Ockham does not deny that a criminal, for instance, can legitimately be deprived of his freedom to acquire and possess property; but the right of property, he insists, is a natural right which does not depend in its essence on the positive conventions of society; and without fault on his own part or some reasonable cause a man cannot be forcibly deprived of the exercise of the right, still less of the right itself.

Ockham speaks of a right (*ius*) as being a legitimate power

[1] *Opus nonaginta dierum*, c. 14.

(*potestas licita*), a power in conformity with right reason (*conformis rationi rectae*), and he distinguishes legitimate powers which are anterior to human convention from those which depend on human convention. The right of private property is a legitimate power which is anterior to human convention, since right reason dictates the institution of private property as a remedy for the moral condition of man after the Fall. Inasmuch as a man is permitted to own property and use it and to resist anyone who tries to wrest his property from him, he has a right to private property, for that permission (*licentia*) comes from the natural law. But not all natural rights are of the same kind. There are, first, natural rights which are valid until a contrary convention is made. For example, the Roman people have, according to Ockham, the right to elect their bishop: this follows from the fact that they are under an obligation to have a bishop. But the Roman people may cede this right of election to the Cardinals, though the right of the Roman people must again be exercised if for any reason election by the Cardinals becomes impossible or impracticable. Conditional natural rights of this sort are examples of what Ockham calls rights flowing from the natural law understood in the third sense.[1] Secondly, there are natural rights which obtained in the state of humanity before the Fall, though 'natural right' in this sense means simply the consequence of a perfection which once existed and no longer exists; it is conditional on a certain state of human perfection. Thirdly, there are rights which share in the immutability of moral precepts, and the right of private property is one of these rights. In the *Breviloquium* Ockham declares that 'the aforementioned power of appropriating temporal things falls under a precept and is reckoned to belong to the sphere of morality (*inter pure moralia computatur*)'.

But a further distinction is required. There are some natural rights in the third sense named (Ockham's *primus modus*) which are so bound up with the moral imperative that nobody is entitled to renounce them, since renunciation of the right would be equivalent to a sin against the moral law. Thus everyone has the duty of preserving his own life, and he would sin against the moral law by starving himself to death. But if he is obliged to maintain his life, he has a right to do so, a right which he cannot renounce. The right of private property, however, is not of this kind. There is, indeed, a precept of right reason that temporal

[1] *Dialogus*, 22, 6.

goods should be appropriated and owned by men; but it is not necessary for the fulfilment of the precept that every individual man should exercise the right of private property, and he can, for a just and reasonable cause, renounce all rights to the possession of property. Ockham's main point in this connection is that the renunciation must be voluntary, and that when it is voluntary it is legitimate.

Pope John XXII had maintained that the distinction between merely using temporal things and having the right to use them was unreal. His principle was that 'he who, without a right, uses something uses it unjustly'. Now, the Franciscans were admittedly entitled to use temporal things like food and clothing. Therefore they must have a right over them, a right to use them, and it was unreal to pretend that it was the Holy See which possessed all these things without the Franciscans having any right at all. The reply was made that it is quite possible to renounce a right to property and at the same time to use legitimately those things of which the ownership has been renounced. The Franciscans renounced all rights of property, even the right of use: they were not like tenants who, without owning a field, have the right to use it and enjoy its fruits, but they enjoyed simply a 'precarious' use of temporal things over which they had no property rights at all. We must distinguish, says Ockham, between *usus iuris*, which is the right of using temporal things without the right over their substance, and *usus facti*, which springs from a mere permission to use the things of another, a permission which is at any moment revocable.[1] The pope had said that the Franciscans could not use food, for example, legitimately without at the same time having a right to do so, without, that is to say, possessing the *usus iuris*; but this is not true, said Ockham; the Franciscans have not the *usus iuris* but only the *usus facti*; they have the *usus nudus* or mere use of temporal things. Mere permission to use them does not confer a right to use them, for the permission is always revocable. The Franciscans are *usuarii simplices* in a strict sense; their use of temporal things is permitted or tolerated by the Holy See, which possesses both the *dominium perfectum* and the *dominium utile* (or, in Ockham's phrase, *usus iuris*) over these things. They have renounced all property rights whatsoever, and this is true evangelical poverty, after the example of Christ and the Apostles, who neither individually nor in common possessed

[1] Cf. *Opus nonaginta dierum*, c. 2.

any temporal things (an opinion which John XXII declared to be heretical).

The actual dispute concerning evangelical poverty does not concern the history of philosophy; but it has been mentioned in order to show how Ockham's preoccupation with a concrete dispute led him to institute an inquiry concerning rights in general and the right of property in particular. His main point was that the right of private property is a natural right, but that it is a right which a man may voluntarily renounce, and that this renunciation may even include the right of use. From the philosophical point of view the chief interest of the discussion lies in the fact that Ockham insisted on the validity of natural rights which are anterior to human conventions, especially in view of the fact that he made the natural law dependent on the divine will. It may appear a gross inconsistency to say on the one hand that the natural law depends on the divine will and on the other hand that there are certain natural rights which share in the fixity of the natural law, and when Ockham asserts, as he does, that the natural law is immutable and absolute he would seem to be underlining the self-contradiction. It is true that, when Ockham asserts the dependence of the moral law on the divine will, he refers primarily to the possibility that God might have created a moral order different from the one He has actually instituted, and, if this were all that he meant, self-contradiction might be avoided by saying that the moral law is absolute and unalterable in the present order. But Ockham meant more than that; he meant that God can dispense from the natural law, or order acts contrary to the natural law, even when the present moral order has been constituted. It may be that the idea of the moral law's dependence on the divine will is more evident in the commentary on the *Sentences* than in Ockham's political works and that the idea of the immutability of the moral law is more evident in the political works than in the commentary on the *Sentences*; but the former idea appears, not only in the commentary, but also in the political works. In the *Dialogus*, for example, he says that there can be no exception from the precepts of the natural law in the strict sense 'unless God specially excepts someone'.[1] The same theme recurs in the *Octo quaestionum decisiones*,[2] and in the *Breviloquium*. The most one can say, then, by way of apology for Ockham, in regard to his consistency or lack of it, is that for him the natural law is

[1] *Dialogus*, 1, 3, 2, 24.

[2] 1, 13.

unalterable, given the present order created by God, unless God intervenes to alter it in any particular instance. As a pure philosopher Ockham speaks on occasion as though there were absolute moral laws and human rights; but as a theologian he was determined to maintain the divine omnipotence as he understood it; and as he was theologian and philosopher in one it was scarcely possible for him to reconcile the absolute character of the moral law with his interpretation of the divine omnipotence, an omnipotence known by revelation but unprovable by the philosopher.

2. The dispute about evangelical poverty was not the only dispute in which Ockham was engaged; he was also involved in a dispute between the Holy See and the emperor. In 1323 Pope John XXII attempted to intervene in an imperial election, maintaining that papal confirmation was required, and when Ludwig of Bavaria was elected, the pope denounced the election. But in 1328 Ludwig had himself crowned at Rome, after which he declared the Avignon Pope to be deposed and appointed Nicholas V. (This antipope, however, had to make his submission in 1330, when Ludwig had departed for Germany.) The quarrel between pope and emperor lasted on after the death of John XXII in 1334 through the reign of Benedict XII into that of Clement VI, during whose pontificate Ockham died in 1349.

The immediate point at issue in this dispute was the emperor's independence of the Holy See; but the controversy had, of course, a greater importance than that attaching to the question whether or not an imperial election required papal confirmation; the broader issue of the proper relation between Church and State was inevitably involved. Further, the question of the right relation of sovereign to subjects was also raised, though it was raised primarily in regard to the pope's position in the Church. In this controversy Ockham stoutly supported the independence of the State in relation to the Church and in regard to the Church itself he strongly attacked papal 'absolutism'. His most important political work is the *Dialogus*, the first part of which was composed in the reign of John XXII. The *De potestate et iuribus romani imperii*, written in 1338 during the reign of Benedict XII, was subsequently incorporated in the *Dialogus* as the second treatise of the third part. The first treatise of the third part, the *De potestate papae et cleri*, was written with the purpose of dissociating its author from Marsilius of Padua, and it elicited from the latter the *Defensor minor*. The *Octo quaestionum decisiones super potestatem summi pontificis* was directed, partly at least, against the *De iure regni et imperii* of Leopold of Babenberg, while in the *Breviloquium de principatu tyrannico* Ockham gave a clear exposition of his political views. His last work, *De pontificum et imperatorum potestate*, was a diatribe against the Avignon papacy. Other polemical works include the *Compendium errorum papae*, an early publication which sums up Ockham's grievances against John XXII, and the *An princeps pro suo succursu, scilicet guerrae, possit recipere bona ecclesiarum, etiam invito papa*, which was written perhaps between August 1338 and the end of 1339 and was designed to show that Edward III of England was justified in taking subsidies from the clergy, even contrary to the pope's wishes or directions, in his war against the French.

Turning first to the controversy concerning the relations between Church and State one can remark that for the most part Ockham's thought moved within the older mediaeval political outlook. In other words, he gave little consideration to the relation of national monarch to emperor, and he was more concerned with the particular relations between pope and emperor than between Church and State in general. In view of his position as a refugee at the court of Ludwig of Bavaria this was only to be expected, though it is true, of course, that he could not discuss the immediate issue which interested him personally without extending his attention to the wider and more general issue. And, if one looks at Ockham's polemics from the point of view of their influence and in regard to the historical development of Europe, one can say that he did, in effect, concern himself with the relations of Church and State, for the position of the emperor in relation to a national monarch like the king of England was little more than a certain pre-eminence of honour.

In maintaining a clear distinction between the spiritual and temporal powers Ockham was not, of course, propounding any revolutionary theory. He insisted that the supreme head in the spiritual sphere, namely the pope, is not the source of imperial power and authority, and also that papal confirmation is not required in order to validate an imperial election. If the pope arrogates to himself, or attempts to assume, power in the temporal sphere, he is invading a territory over which he has no jurisdiction. The authority of the emperor derives, not from the pope, but from his election, the electors standing in the place of the people. There can be no doubt but that Ockham regarded political power as deriving from God through the people, either immediately, in the event of the people directly choosing a sovereign, or mediately, if the people have agreed, explicitly or implicitly, to some other way of transmitting political authority. The State needs a government and the people cannot avoid choosing a sovereign of some kind, whether emperor, monarch or magistrates; but in no case is the authority derived from, or dependent on, the spiritual power. That Ockham did not intend his denial of the pope's supreme power in temporal matters to apply only in favour of the emperor is made abundantly clear; for example, by the *An princeps pro suo succursu*. All legitimate sovereigns enjoy authority which is not derived from the pope.

3. But, as we have already seen, if Ockham supported the independence of temporal princes in relation to the Church, so far as temporal matters were concerned, he did not reject the temporal authority of the papacy in order to support political absolutism. All men are born free, in the sense that they have a right to freedom, and, though the principle of authority, like the principle of private property, belongs to the natural law, they enjoy a natural right to choose their rulers. The method of choosing a ruler and of transmitting authority from one ruler to his successor depends on human law, and it is obviously not necessary that every successive ruler should be elected; but the fundamental freedom of man to choose and appoint the temporal authority is a right which no power on earth can take from him. The community can, of course, of its own free will establish a hereditary monarchy; but in this case it voluntarily submits itself to the monarch and his legitimate successors, and if the monarch betrays his trust and abuses his authority, the community can assert its freedom by deposing him. 'After the whole world spontaneously consented to the dominion and empire of the Romans, the same empire was a true, just and good empire'; its legitimacy rested on its free acceptance by its subjects.[1] Nobody should be placed over the community except by its choice and consent; every people and State is entitled to elect its head if it so wills.[2] If there were any people without a ruler in temporal affairs, the pope would have neither the duty nor the power of appointing rulers for that people, if they wished to appoint their own ruler or rulers.[3]

4. These two important points, namely the independence of the

[1] *Dialogus*, 2, 3, 1, 27.
[2] *Opus nonaginta dierum*, 2, 4.
[3] *Ibid.*, 2, 3, 2, 6.

temporal power and the freedom of the people to settle their own form of government if they so choose, were not in themselves novelties. The idea of the two swords, for example, represented the common mediaeval outlook, and when Ockham protested against the tendency of certain popes to arrogate to themselves the position and rights of universal temporal monarchs, he was simply expressing the conviction of most mediaeval thinkers that the spiritual and temporal spheres must be clearly distinguished. Again, all the great mediaeval theologians and philosophers believed in natural rights in some sense and would have rejected the notion that princes possess absolute and unrestricted power. The mediaevals had a respect for law and custom and thoroughly disliked arbitrary power; and the idea that rulers must govern within the general framework of law expressed the general mediaeval outlook. It is difficult to say exactly how St. Thomas Aquinas regarded the problem of the derivation of the sovereign's authority; but he certainly thought of it as limited, as having a definite purpose, and he certainly considered that subjects are not bound to submit to tyrannical government. He recognized that some governments do, or may, derive their authority immediately from the people (ultimately from God); and, though there is no very clear indication that he regarded all governments as necessarily deriving their authority in this manner, he maintained that there can be a resistance to tyranny which is justified and is not to be accounted sedition. A ruler has a trust to fulfil, and if he does not fulfil it but abuses his trust, the community is entitled to depose him. There is good reason, then, for saying, as has been said, that in regard to dislike of arbitrary power and in regard to insistence on law, the principles of Ockham did not substantially differ from those of St. Thomas.

However, even though Ockham's insistence on the distinction of the spiritual and temporal powers and on the fundamental rights of subjects in a political community was not novel, still less revolutionary, if considered as expressing abstract principles, it does not follow that the manner in which he conducted his controversy with the papacy was not part of a general movement which can be called revolutionary. For the dispute between Ludwig of Bavaria and the papacy was one incident in a general movement of which the dispute between Philip the Fair and Boniface VIII had been an earlier symptom; and the direction of the movement, if looked at from the point of view of concrete historical development, was towards the complete independence of the State from the Church, even in spiritual matters. Ockham's thought may have moved within the old categories of papacy and empire, but the gradual consolidation of centralized national States was leading to a breakdown of the balance between the two powers and to the emergence of a political consciousness which found partial expression in the Reformation. Moreover, Ockham's hostility to papal absolutism even within the spiritual sphere, when viewed in the light of his general remarks on the relation of subjects to rulers, was bound to have implications in the sphere of political thought as well. I now turn to his ideas on the pope's position within the Church; though it is worth while noticing beforehand that, though Ockham's ideas on Church government concerned the ecclesiastical sphere and heralded the Conciliar Movement which was to be proximately occasioned by the Great Schism (1378–1417), these ideas were also part of the wider movement which ended in the disintegration of mediaeval Christendom.

5. It is entirely unnecessary to say more than a few words on the subject of Ockham's polemic against the position of the pope within the Church, as this subject belongs to Church history, not to the history of philosophy; but, as already mentioned, the further implications of his ideas on the subject make it desirable to say something about them. Ockham's main contention was that papal absolutism within the Church was unjustified, that it was detrimental to the good of Christendom, and that it should be checked and limited.[1] The means which Ockham suggested for limiting papal power was the establishment of a General Council. Possibly drawing on his experience and knowledge of the constitutions of the mendicant Orders he envisaged religious corporations such as parishes, chapters and monasteries sending chosen representatives to provincial synods. These synods would elect representatives for the General Council, which should include layfolk as well as clergy. It is to be noted that Ockham did not look on the General Council as an organ of infallible doctrinal pronouncements, even if he thought that it was more likely to be right than the pope alone, but as a limitation to and a check on papal absolutism: he was concerned with ecclesiastical politics, with constitutionalizing the papacy, rather than with purely theological matters. He did not deny that the pope is the successor

[1] Ockham did not deny papal supremacy as such; he rejected what he called 'tyrannical' supremacy.

of St. Peter and the Vicar of Christ, nor did he wish, in principle, to destroy the papal government of the Church; but he regarded the Avignon papacy as going beyond its brief, so to speak, and as being unfit to govern without decisive checks and limitations. No doubt he held heterodox opinions; but his motive in making these suggestions was that of combating the actual exercise of arbitrary and unrestrained power, and that is why his ideas on the constitutionalization of the papacy had implications in the political sphere, even if his ideas, when looked at in relation to the immediate future, must be regarded as heralding the Conciliar Movement.

CHAPTER IX

THE OCKHAMIST MOVEMENT: JOHN OF MIRECOURT AND NICHOLAS OF AUTRECOURT

The Ockhamist or nominalist movement—John of Mirecourt—Nicholas of Autrecourt—Nominalism in the universities—Concluding remarks.

1. THE phrase 'Ockhamist Movement' is perhaps something of a misnomer. For it might be understood as implying that William of Ockham was the sole fountainhead of the 'modern' current of thought in the fourteenth century and that the thinkers of the movement all derived their ideas from him. Some of these thinkers, like the Franciscan Adam Wodham or Goddam (d. 1358), had indeed been pupils of Ockham, while others, like the Dominican Holkot (d. 1349), were influenced by Ockham's writings without, however, having actually been his pupils. But in some other cases it is difficult to discover how far a given philosopher owed his ideas to Ockham's influence. However, even if from one point of view it may be preferable to speak of the 'nominalist movement' rather than of the 'Ockhamist Movement', it cannot be denied that Ockham was the most influential writer of the movement; and it is only just that the movement should be associated with his name. The names 'nominalism' and 'terminism' were used synonymously to designate the *via moderna*; and the salient characteristic of terminism was the analysis of the function of the term in the proposition, namely the doctrine of *suppositio* or standing-for. As has already been indicated, the theory of *suppositio* can be found in logicians before Ockham; in the writings of Peter of Spain, for example; but it was Ockham who developed the terminist logic in that conceptualist and 'empiricist' direction which we have come to associate with nominalism. One is justified, therefore, in my opinion, in speaking of the 'Ockhamist Movement', provided that one remembers that the phrase is not meant to imply that Ockham was the direct source of all the developments of that movement.

The development of the terminist logic forms one of the aspects of the movement. In this connection one may mention Richard Swineshead and William Heytesbury, both of whom were associated with Merton College, Oxford. The latter, whose logical writings enjoyed a wide circulation, became chancellor of the university of Oxford in 1371. Another popular logician of the fourteenth century was Richard Billingham. But the technical logical studies of the nominalists and of those influenced by the nominalist movement were frequently associated, as were those of Ockham himself, with a destructive attack on the traditional metaphysics, or rather on the proofs offered in the traditional metaphysics. Sometimes these attacks were based on the view that the traditional lines of proof did not amount to more than probable arguments. Thus according to Richard Swineshead the arguments which had been employed to prove the unicity of God were not demonstrations but dialectical arguments, that is to say, arguments which did not exclude the possibility of the opposite being true or which could not, in the language of the time, be reduced to the principle of contradiction. Sometimes emphasis was placed on our supposed inability to know any substance. If we can have no knowledge of any substance, argued Richard Billingham, we cannot prove the existence of God. Monotheism is a matter of faith, not of philosophical proof.

The relegation of propositions like 'God exists', where the term 'God' is understood as denoting the supreme unique Being, to the sphere of faith does not mean that any philosopher doubted the truth of these propositions: it simply means that he did not think that such propositions can be proved. Nevertheless, this sceptical attitude in regard to metaphysical arguments was doubtless combined, in the case of different philosophers, with varying degrees of insistence on the primacy of faith. A lecturer or professor in the faculty of arts might question the validity of metaphysical arguments on purely logical grounds, while a theologian might also be concerned to emphasize the weakness of the human reason, the supremacy of faith and the transcendent character of revealed truth. Robert Holkot, for example, postulated a 'logic of faith', distinct from and superior to natural logic. He certainly denied the demonstrative character of theistic arguments. Only analytic propositions are absolutely certain. The principle of causality, employed in traditional arguments for God's existence, is not an analytic proposition. From this it follows that philosophical arguments for God's existence cannot amount to more than probable arguments. Theology, however, is superior to philosophy; and in the sphere of dogmatic theology we can see the operation of a logic which is superior to the natural logic employed in philosophy. In particular, that the principle of contradiction is transcended in theology is clear, thought Holkot, from the doctrine of the Trinity. My point is, then, not that the theologians who were influenced by the nominalist criticism of metaphysical 'demonstrations' did not support their criticism by an appeal to logic, but rather that this relative scepticism in philosophy must not be taken without more ado as involving a sceptical attitude towards theological statements considered as statements of fact or as a conscious relegation of dogmatic theology to the sphere of conjecture.

Acceptance of this or that nominalist position did not mean, of course, that a given thinker adopted all the positions maintained by William of Ockham. John of Rodington (d. 1348), for example, who became Provincial of the English Franciscans, doubted the demonstrative character of arguments for God's unicity: but he rejected the notion that the moral law depends simply on the divine will. John of Bassolis (d. 1347), another Franciscan, also questioned the demonstrative character of metaphysical proofs for God's existence, unicity and infinity; but he combined this critical attitude with an acceptance of various Scotist positions. Scotism was naturally a powerful influence in the Franciscan Order, and it produced philosophers like Francis of Meyronnes (d. *c.* 1328), Antoine André (d. *c.* 1320), the *Doctor dulcifluus*, and Francis de Marcia, the *Doctor succinctus*. It is only to be expected, then, that we should find the Scotist and Ockhamist lines of thought meeting and mingling in thinkers like John of Ripa, who lectured at Paris in the early part of the second half of the fourteenth century, and Peter of Candia (d. 1410). Further, in some cases where a thinker was influenced both by the writings of St. Augustine and by Ockhamism, it is not always easy to judge which influence was the stronger on any given point. For example, Thomas Bradwardine (*c.* 1290–1349) appealed to St. Augustine in support of his doctrine of theological determinism; but it is difficult to say how far he was influenced by Augustine's writings taken by themselves and how far he was influenced in his interpretation of Augustine by the Ockhamist emphasis on the divine omnipotence and the divine will. Again, Gregory of Rimini (d. 1358), who became General of the Hermits of St. Augustine, appealed to Augustine in support of his doctrines of the primacy of intuition and the 'sign' function of universal terms. But there is difficulty in deciding to what extent he simply adopted Ockhamist positions and then tried to cover them with the mantle of St. Augustine because he himself was a member of the Augustinian Order, and to what extent he really believed that he found in St. Augustine's writings positions which had been suggested to him by Ockham's philosophy. The Dominican Robert Holkot even tried to show that some of his clearly Ockhamist tenets were really not alien to the mind of St. Thomas Aquinas.

Enough has been said to show that Ockhamism or nominalism, which was associated particularly with the secular clergy, penetrated deeply into the religious Orders. Its influence was felt not only in the Franciscan Order, to which Ockham himself had belonged, but also in the Dominican and other Orders. At the same time, of course, the traditional lines of thought were still maintained, especially in an Order which possessed an official Doctor, as the Dominican Order possessed St. Thomas. Take, for example, the Hermits of St. Augustine, who looked on Giles of Rome as their Doctor. We have seen that Gregory of Rimini, who was General of the Order from 1357 until 1358, was influenced by Ockhamism; but Thomas of Strasbourg, who preceded Gregory as General (1345–1357), had tried to protect the Order from nominalist influence in the name of fidelity to Giles of Rome. In point of fact it did not prove possible to keep out or stamp out the influence of nominalism; but the fact that the Order possessed an official Doctor doubtless encouraged a certain moderation in the degree to which the more extreme nominalist positions were accepted by the sympathizers with the *via moderna*.

One common factor among the nominalists or Ockhamists was, as we have seen, the emphasis they laid on the theory of *suppositio*, the analysis of the different ways in which the terms in a proposition stand for things. It is obvious, however, that one is justified in speaking about 'nominalism' or, if preferred, conceptualism only in the case of philosophers who, like Ockham, maintained that a general term or class-name stands in the proposition for individual things, and for individual things alone. Together with this doctrine, namely that universality belongs only to terms in their logical function, the nominalists also tended to maintain that only those propositions which are reducible to the principle of contradiction are absolutely certain. In other words, they held that the truth of a statement is not absolutely certain unless the opposite cannot be stated without contradiction. Now, no statement of a causal relationship can, they thought, be a statement of this kind. In other words, their theory of universals led the nominalists to an empiricist analysis of the causal relation. Moreover, in so far as the inference from phenomena to substance was an inference from effect to cause, this analysis affected also the nominalist view of the substance-accident metaphysic. If, then, on the one hand only analytic propositions, in the sense of propositions reducible to the principle of contradiction, are absolutely certain, while on the other hand statements about causal relations are empirical or inductive generalizations which enjoy at best only a very high degree of probability, it follows that the traditional metaphysical arguments, resting on the employment of the principle of causality and on the substance-accident metaphysic, cannot be absolutely certain. In the case, then, of statements about God's existence, for example, the nominalists maintained that they owed their certainty not to any philosophical arguments which could be adduced in their favour but to the fact that they were truths of faith, taught by Christian theology. This position naturally tended to introduce a sharp distinction between philosophy and theology. In one sense, of course, a sharp distinction between philosophy and theology had always been recognized, namely in the sense that a distinction had always been recognized between accepting a statement as the result simply of one's own process of reasoning and accepting a statement on divine authority. But a thinker like Aquinas had been convinced that it is possible to prove the 'preambles of faith', such as the statement that a God exists who can make a revelation. Aquinas was also convinced, of course, that the act of faith involves supernatural grace; but the point is that he recognized as strictly provable certain truths which are logically presupposed by the act of faith, even if in most actual cases supernatural faith is operative long before a human being comes to understand, if he ever does advert to or understand, the proofs in question. In the nominalist philosophy, however, the 'preambles of faith' were not regarded as strictly provable, and the bridge between philosophy and theology (so far, that is, as one is entitled to speak of a 'bridge' when faith demands supernatural grace) was thus broken. But the nominalists were not concerned with 'apologetic' considerations. In the Christian Europe of the Middle Ages apologetics were not a matter of such concern as they became for theologians and Catholic philosophers of a later date.

In the foregoing summary of the positions of the nominalists I have used the word 'nominalist' to mean the thoroughgoing nominalist or the thinker who developed the potentialities of nominalism or the 'ideal' nominalist, the nominalist *pur sang*. I have remarked earlier that not all those thinkers who were positively affected by the Ockhamist movement and who may in certain respects be called 'nominalists' adopted all the positions of Ockham. But it will be of use, I hope, to give some account of the philosophical ideas of two thinkers associated with the movement, namely John of Mirecourt and Nicholas of Autrecourt, the latter of whom particularly was an extremist. Acquaintance with the philosophy of Nicholas of Autrecourt is an effective means, if further means are still needed, of dispelling the illusion that there was no variety of opinions in mediaeval philosophy about important topics. After outlining the thought of these two men I shall conclude the chapter with some remarks on the influence of nominalism in the universities, especially in the new universities which were founded in the latter part of the fourteenth century and during the fifteenth.

2. John of Mirecourt, who seems to have been a Cistercian (he was called *monachus albus*, 'the white monk'), lectured on the *Sentences* of Peter Lombard at the Cistercian College of St. Bernard in Paris. Of these lectures, which were given in 1344–5, there exist two versions. As a number of his propositions were immediately attacked, John of Mirecourt issued an explanation and justification of his position; but none the less some 41 propositions were condemned in 1347 by the chancellor of the university and the faculty of theology. This led to the publication by John of another work in defence of his position. These two 'apologies', the first explaining or defending 63 suspected propositions, the second doing the same for the 41 condemned propositions, have been edited by F. Stegmüller.[1]

Two types of knowledge are distinguished by John of Mirecourt; and he distinguishes them according to the quality of our assent to different propositions. Sometimes our assent is 'evident', which means, he says, that it is given without fear, actual or potential, of error. At other times our assent is given with fear, actual or potential, of error, as, for example, in the case of suspicion or of opinion. But it is necessary to make a further distinction. Sometimes we give an assent without fear of error

[1] *Recherches de théologie ancienne et médiévale* (1933), pp. 40-79, 192-204.

because we see clearly the evident truth of the proposition to which we assent. This happens in the case of the principle of contradiction and of those principles and conclusions which are ultimately reducible to the principle of contradiction. If we see that a proposition rests upon or is reducible to the principle of contradiction, we see that the opposite of that proposition, its negation that is to say, is inconceivable and impossible. At other times, however, we give an assent without fear of error to propositions the truth of which is not intrinsically evident, though it is assured in virtue of irrefutable testimony. The revealed truths of faith are of this kind. We know, for example, only by revelation that there are three Persons in one God.

Leaving out of account the revealed truths of faith we have, then, so far, propositions to which we assent without fear of error because they are reducible to the primary self-evident principle, the principle of contradiction, and propositions to which we assent with fear of error (for example, 'I think that that object in the distance is a cow'). Assents of the first kind are called by John of Mirecourt *assensus evidentes*, assents of the second kind *assensus inevidentes*. But we must now distinguish two kinds of *assensus evidentes*. First of all, there are evident assents in the strictest and most proper meaning of the phrase. Assent of this kind is given to the principle of contradiction, to principles which are reducible to the principle of contradiction and to conclusions which rest upon the principle of contradiction. In the case of such propositions we have *evidentia potissima*. Secondly, there are assents which are indeed given without fear of error but which are not given in virtue of the proposition's intimate connection with the principle of contradiction. If I give my assent to a proposition based on experience (for example, 'there are stones') I give it without fear of error but I give it in virtue of my experience of the external world, not in virtue of the proposition's reducibility to the principle of contradiction. In the case of such proposition we have, not *evidentia potissima*, but *evidentia naturalis*. John of Mirecourt defines this 'natural evidence' as the evidence by which we give our assent to a thing's existence without any fear of error, this assent being brought about by causes which naturally necessitate our assent.

The above account of John's doctrine on human assents comes from his first apology. He is there explaining the 44th proposition, which had been made an object of attack. The proposition runs as follows: 'It has not been demonstratively proved from propositions which are self-evident or which possess an evidence reducible by us to the certitude of the primary principle that God exists, or that there is a most perfect being, or that one thing is the cause of another thing, or that any created thing has a cause without this cause having its own cause and so on to infinity, or that a thing cannot as a total cause produce something nobler than itself, or that it is impossible for something to be produced which is nobler than anything which (now) exists.' In particular, then, the proofs of God's existence do not rest on self-evident propositions or on propositions which we are capable of reducing to the principle of contradiction, which is the primary self-evident principle. John's adversaries interpreted his doctrine as meaning that no proof of God's existence is of such a kind that it compels assent once it is understood, and that we are not certain, so far as philosophy goes, of God's existence. In answer John observes that the proofs of God's existence rest on experience and that no proposition which is the result of experience of the world is reducible by us to the principle of contradiction. It is clear from his teaching in general, however, that he made one exception to this general rule, namely in the case of the proposition which asserts the existence of the thinker or speaker. If I say that I deny or even doubt my own existence I am contradicting myself, for I cannot deny or even doubt my existence without affirming my existence. On this point John of Mirecourt followed St. Augustine. But this particular proposition stands by itself. No other proposition which is the result of sense-experience, or experience of the external world, is reducible by us to the principle of contradiction. No proposition of this kind, then, enjoys *evidentia potissima*. But John denied that he meant that all such propositions are doubtful. They do not enjoy *evidentia potissima* but they enjoy *evidentia naturalis*. Although propositions founded on experience of the external world are not evident in the same way as the principle of contradiction is evident, 'it does not follow from this that we must doubt about them any more than about the first principle. From this it is clear that I do not intend to deny any experience, any knowledge, any evidence. It is even clear that I hold altogether the opposite opinion to those who would say that it is not evident to them that there is a man or that there is a stone, on the ground that it might appear to them that these things are so without their being really so. I do not mean to deny that these things are evident to us and known by us, but only that they are not known to us by the supreme kind of knowledge (*scientia potissima*).'

Analytic propositions, that is to say propositions which are reducible by analysis to the self-evident principle of contradiction, are thus absolutely certain, and this absolute certainty attaches also to each one's affirmation of his own existence. Apart from this last affirmation all propositions which are the result of and express experimental knowledge of the world enjoy only 'natural evidence'. But what does John of Mirecourt mean by 'natural evidence'? Does this mean simply that we spontaneously give our assent in virtue of a natural unavoidable propensity to assent? If so, does it or does it not follow that the propositions to which we give this kind of assent are certain? John admits that error is possible in the case of some empirical propositions: he could hardly do otherwise. On the other hand he asserts that 'we cannot err in many things (propositions) which accord with our experiences'. Again, he could hardly say anything else, unless he were prepared to admit that his adversaries had interpreted his doctrine correctly. But it seems to be clear that John of Mirecourt accepted the Ockhamist doctrine that sensitive knowledge of the external world could be miraculously caused and conserved by God in the absence of the object. This theme was treated by him at the beginning of his commentary on the *Sentences*. It is probably safe to say, then, that for him 'natural evidence' meant that we naturally assent to the existence of what we sense, though it would be possible for us to be in error, if, that is to say, God were to work a miracle. There is no contradiction in the idea of God working such a miracle. If, therefore, we use the word 'certain' in the sense not only of feeling certain but also of having objective and evident certainty, we are certain of the principle of contradiction and of propositions reducible thereto and each one is certain of his own existence, the infallible character of the intuition of one's own existence being shown by the connection of the proposition affirming one's own existence with the principle of contradiction; but we are not certain of the existence of external objects, however certain we may *feel*. If we care to bring in Descartes' hypothetical 'evil genius', we can say that for John of Mirecourt we are not certain of the existence of the external world, unless God assures us that it exists. All proofs, then, of God's existence which rest upon our knowledge of the external world are uncertain; at least they are not 'demonstrative', in the sense of being reducible to the principle of contradiction or of resting on it. In his first apology John openly says that the opposite of the proposition 'God exists' implies a contradiction; but he goes on to observe that a proposition of this kind does not enjoy the evidence which attaches to the first principle. Why not? Because we arrive at the knowledge expressed in such propositions by reflection on the data of sense-experience, in which we can err, although 'we cannot err in many things (propositions) which accord with our experiences'. Does he mean that we can err in particular empirical judgments, but that we cannot err in regard to a conclusion like the existence of God which follows on the totality of sense-experience rather than on particular empirical judgments? In this case what of the possibility of our having sense-experience when no object is present? This is, no doubt, a limiting possibility and we have no reason to suppose that it is an actuality so far as the totality of sense-experience is concerned; but none the less it remains a possibility. I do not see how the traditional proofs of God's existence can have more than moral certainty or, if you like, the highest degree of probability on John's premisses. In his apology he may make an attempt to justify his position by having it both ways; but it seems clear that for him the proofs of God's existence cannot be demonstrative in the sense in which he understands demonstrative. Leaving out of account the question whether John was right or wrong in what he said, he would have been more consistent, I think, if he had openly admitted that for him the proofs of God's existence, based on sense-experience, are not absolutely certain.

The principle of causality, according to John of Mirecourt, is not analytic; that is to say, it cannot be reduced to the principle of contradiction or be shown to depend upon it in such a way that the denial of the principle of causality involves a contradiction. On the other hand it does not follow that we have to doubt the truth of the principle of causality: we have 'natural evidence', even if we have not got *evidentia potissima*. Again the question arises exactly what is meant by 'natural evidence'. It can hardly mean objectively irrefutable evidence, for if the truth of the principle of causality were objectively so clear that it could not possibly be denied and that its opposite was inconceivable, it would surely follow that its evidence is reducible to the evidence of the principle of contradiction. When John speaks of 'causes naturally necessitating assent', it looks very much as though he meant that, though we can conceive the possibility of the principle of causality not being true, we are obliged by nature to think and act in the concrete as though it were true. From this it would appear to follow that for all practical purposes the proofs of God's existence which rest on the validity of the principle of causality are 'evident', but that none the less we can conceive of their not being cogent. Perhaps this means little more than that the proofs of God's existence cannot compel assent in the same way as a mathematical theorem, for example, can compel assent. John's opponents understood him as meaning that one cannot prove God's existence and that God's existence is therefore uncertain; but when he denied that the proofs are demonstrative he was using the word 'demonstrative' in a special sense, and, if his apology represents his real teaching, he did not mean to say that we must be sceptical concerning God's existence. There can, indeed, be little question of his having intended to teach scepticism; but on the other hand it is clear that he did not regard the proofs of God's existence as possessing the same degree of cogency which St. Thomas would have attributed to them.

In criticizing in this way the proofs of God's existence John of Mirecourt showed himself to be a thinker who had his place in the Ockhamist movement. He showed the same thing by his doctrine concerning the moral law. Proposition 51, as contained in the first apology, runs as follows. 'God can cause any act of the will in the will, even hatred of Himself; I doubt, however, whether anything which was created in the will by God alone would be hatred of God, unless the will conserved it actively and effectively.' According to the way of speaking common among the Doctors, says John, hatred of God involves a deformity in the will, and we must not allow that God could, as total cause, cause hatred of Himself in the human will. Absolutely speaking, however, God could cause hatred of Himself in the will, and if He did so, the man in question would not hate God culpably. Again, in the second apology the 25th condemned proposition is to the effect that 'hatred of the neighbour is not demeritorious except for the fact that it has been prohibited by God'. John proceeds to explain that he does not mean that hatred of the neighbour is not contrary to the natural law; he means that a man who hates his neighbour runs the risk of eternal punishment only because God has prohibited hatred of the neighbour. In regard to the 41st proposition of the first apology John similarly observes that nothing can be 'demeritorious' unless it is prohibited by God. It can, however, be contrary to the moral law without being demeritorious.

Needless to say, John of Mirecourt had no intention of denying our duty to obey the moral law; his aim was to emphasize the supremacy and omnipotence of God. Similarly he seems, though extremely tentatively, to have favoured the opinion of St. Peter Damian that God could bring it about that the world should never have been, that is to say, that God could bring it about that the past should not have happened. He allows that this undoing of the fact cannot take place *de potentia Dei ordinata*; but, whereas one might well expect him to appeal to the principle of contradiction in order to show that the undoing of the past is absolutely impossible, he says that this absolute impossibility is not evident to him. 'I was unwilling to lay claim to knowledge which I did not possess' (first apology, proposition 5). He does not say that it is possible for God to bring it about that the past should not have happened; he says that the impossibility of God's doing this is not evident to him. John of Mirecourt was always careful in his statements.

He shows a similar care in the way he hedges over those statements which appear to teach theological determinism and which may betray the influence of Thomas Bradwardine's *De Causa Dei*. According to John, God is the cause of moral deformity, of sin that is to say, just as He is the cause of natural deformity. God is the cause of blindness by not supplying the power of vision; and He is the cause of moral deformity by not supplying moral rectitude. John qualifies this statement, however, by observing that it is perhaps true that while a natural defect can be the total cause of natural deformity, a moral defect is not the total cause of moral deformity because moral deformity (sin), in order to exist, must proceed from a will (first apology, proposition 50). In his commentary on the *Sentences*[1] he first observes that it seems to him possible to concede that God is the cause of moral deformity, and then remarks that the common teaching of the Doctors is the very opposite. But they say the opposite since, in their eyes, to say that God is the cause of sin is to say that God acts sinfully, and that it is impossible for God to act sinfully is clear to John too. But it does not follow from this, he insists, that God cannot be the cause of moral deformity. God causes the moral deformity by not

[1] 2, 3, concl. 3.

supplying moral rectitude; but the sin proceeds from the will, and it is the human being who is guilty. Therefore, if John says that God is not the total cause of sin, he does not mean that God causes the positive element in the act of the will while the human being causes the privation of right order: for him God can be said to cause both, though the privation of right order cannot be realized except in and through a will. The will is the 'effective' cause, not God, though God can be called the 'efficacious' cause in that He wills efficaciously that there should be no rectitude in the will. Nothing can happen unless God wills it, and if God wills it, He wills it efficaciously, for His will is always fulfilled. God causes the sinful act even in its specification as a sinful act of a certain kind; but He does not cause it sinfully.

John considered that the real distinction between accidents and substances is known only by faith. 'I think that except for the faith many would perhaps have said that everything is a substance.'[1] Apparently he affirmed (at least he was understood as affirming) that 'it is probable, as far as the natural light of reason is concerned, that there are no accidents distinct from substance, but that everything is a substance; and except for the faith, this would be or could be probable' (43rd proposition of first apology). For example, 'it can be said with probability that thinking or willing is not something distinct from the soul, but that it is the soul itself' (proposition 42). John defends himself by saying that the reasons for affirming a distinction between substance and accident have more force than the reasons which can be given for denying a distinction; but he adds that he does not know if the arguments for affirming it can rightly be called demonstrations. It is clear that he did not think that these arguments amounted to demonstrations; he accepted the distinction as certain only on faith.

It is difficult to ascertain with any degree of certainty precisely what John of Mirecourt's personal opinions actually were, owing to the way in which he explains away in his apologies what he had said in his lectures on the *Sentences*. When John protests that he is simply retailing other people's opinions or when he remarks that he is merely putting forward a possible point of view without affirming that it is true, is he thoroughly sincere or is he being diplomatic? One can scarcely give any definite answer. However, I turn now to an even more extreme and thoroughgoing adherent of the new movement.

[1] 1 *Sent.*, 19, concl. 6, *ad* 5.

3. Nicholas of Autrecourt, who was born about the year 1300 in the diocese of Verdun, studied at the Sorbonne between 1320 and 1327. In due course he lectured on the *Sentences*, on Aristotle's *Politics*, etc. In 1338 he obtained a Prebend's stall in the Cathedral of Metz. Already in his introductory lecture on the *Sentences* of Peter Lombard, Nicholas had indicated his departure from the thought of previous philosophers, and a continuation of this attitude resulted in a letter from Pope Benedict XII to the Bishop of Paris on November 21st, 1340, in which the latter was instructed to see that Nicholas, together with certain other offenders, put in a personal appearance at Avignon within a month. The pope's death led to a postponement of the investigation of Nicholas's opinions; but after the coronation of Clement VI on May 19th, 1342, the matter was taken up again. The new pope entrusted the examination of Nicholas's opinions to a commission under the presidency of Cardinal William Curti, and Nicholas was invited to explain and defend his ideas. He was given the opportunity of defending himself in the pope's presence, and his replies to the objections brought against his doctrine were taken into account. But when it became clear what the verdict would be Nicholas fled from Avignon; and it is possible, though not certain, that he took refuge for the time being at the court of Ludwig of Bavaria. In 1346 he was sentenced to burn his writings publicly at Paris and to recant the condemned propositions. This he did on November 25th, 1347. He was also expelled from the teaching body of the university of Paris. Of his later life little is known, save for the fact that he became an official of the Cathedral of Metz on August 6th, 1350. Presumably he lived 'happily ever after'.

Of Nicholas's writings we possess the first two letters of a series of nine which he wrote to the Franciscan Bernard of Arezzo, one of his principal critics, and a large part of a letter which he wrote to a certain Aegidius (Giles). We also possess a letter from Aegidius to Nicholas. In addition, the lists of condemned propositions contain excerpts from other letters of Nicholas to Bernard of Arezzo together with some other fragments. All these documents have been edited by Dr. Joseph Lappe.[1] We possess also a treatise by Nicholas which begins *Exigit ordo executionis* and which is referred to as the *Exigit*. It has been edited by J. R. O'Donnell, together with Nicholas's theological writing *Utrum visio creaturae*

[1] *Beiträge zur Geschichte der Philosophie des Mittelalters*, VI, 2. References to 'Lappe' in the following account of Nicholas's philosophy are references to this edition, dated 1908.

rationalis beatificabilis per Verbum possit intendi naturaliter.[1] There is further a note by John of Mirecourt about Nicholas's doctrine on causality.[2]

At the beginning of his second letter to Bernard of Arezzo Nicholas remarks that the first principle to be laid down is that 'contradictions cannot be true at the same time'.[3] The principle of contradiction, or rather of non-contradiction, is the primary principle, and its primacy is to be accepted both in the negative sense, namely that there is no more ultimate principle, and in the positive sense, namely that the principle positively precedes and is presupposed by every other principle. Nicholas is arguing that the principle of non-contradiction is the ultimate basis of all natural certitude, and that while any other principle which is put forward as the basis of certitude is reducible to the principle of non-contradiction, the latter is not reducible to any other principle. If any principle other than the principle of non-contradiction is proposed as the basis of certitude, that is, if a principle which is not reducible to the principle of non-contradiction is proposed as the basis of certitude, the proposed principle may appear to be certain but its opposite will not involve a contradiction. But in this case the apparent certitude can never be transformed into genuine certitude. It is only the principle of non-contradiction which bears its own guarantee on its face, so to speak. The reason why we do not doubt the principle of non-contradiction is simply that it cannot be denied without contradiction. In order, then, for any other principle to be certain, its denial must involve a contradiction. But in that case it is reducible to the principle of non-contradiction, in the sense that it is certain in virtue of that principle. The principle of non-contradiction must therefore be the primary principle. It is to be remarked that it is not the truth of the principle of non-contradiction which is in question but its primacy. Nicholas tries to show that any genuine certitude rests ultimately on this principle, and he does it by showing that any principle which did not rest on, or was not reducible to, the principle of non-contradiction would not be genuinely certain.

Any certitude which we have in the light of the principle of non-contradiction is, says Nicholas, genuine certitude, and not even the divine power could deprive it of this character. Further, all genuinely certain propositions possess the same degree of evidence.

[1] *Mediaeval Studies*, vol. 1, 1939, pp. 179–280. References to the *Exigit* in the following pages are references to this edition.

[2] Lappe, p. 4.

[3] *Ibid*, 6*, 33.

It makes no difference whether a proposition is immediately or mediately reducible to the principle of non-contradiction. If it is not reducible to the principle of non-contradiction, it is not certain; and if it is reducible, it is equally certain, whether it is immediately or mediately reducible. In geometry, for example, a proposition is not less certain because it happens to be the conclusion of a long chain of reasoning, provided that it is rightly demonstrated in the light of the primary principle. Apart from the certitude of faith there is no other certitude than the certitude of the principle of non-contradiction and of propositions which are reducible to that principle.

In a syllogistic argument, then, the conclusion is certain only if it is reducible to the principle of non-contradiction. What is the necessary condition of this reducibility? The conclusion, says Nicholas, is reducible to the primary principle only if it is identical with the antecedent or with a part of what is signified by the antecedent. When this is the case it is impossible to affirm the antecedent and deny the conclusion or to deny the conclusion and affirm the antecedent without contradiction. If the antecedent is certain, the conclusion is also certain. For example, in the inference 'all *X*'s are *Y*, therefore this *X* is *Y*' the conclusion is identical with part of what is signified by the antecedent. It is impossible, without contradiction, to affirm the antecedent and deny the conclusion. That is, if it is certain that all *X*'s are *Y*, it is certain that any particular *X* is *Y*.

How does this criterion of certitude affect factual knowledge? Bernard of Arezzo maintained that because God can cause an intuitive act in the human being without the co-operation of any secondary cause we are not entitled to argue that a thing exists because it is seen. This view was similar to that of Ockham, though Bernard apparently did not add Ockham's qualification that God could not produce in us evident assent to the existence of a non-existent thing, since this would involve a contradiction. Nicholas maintained, though, that Bernard's view led to scepticism, for on his view we should have no means of achieving certitude concerning the existence of anything. In the case of immediate perception the act of perception is not a sign from which we infer the existence of something distinct from the act. To say, for example, that I perceive a colour is simply to say that the colour appears to me: I do not see the colour and then infer its existence. The act of perceiving a colour and the act of being aware that I perceive a colour are one and the same act: I do not perceive a colour and then have to find some guarantee that I actually do perceive a colour. Immediate cognition is its own guarantee. A contradiction would be involved in saying that a colour appears and at the same time that it does not appear. In his first letter to Bernard, Nicholas says, therefore, that in his opinion 'I am evidently certain of the objects of the five senses and of my acts.'[1] Against what he regarded as scepticism, then, Nicholas maintained that immediate cognition, whether it takes the form of sense-perception or of perception of our interior acts, is certain and evident; and he explained the certitude of this knowledge by identifying the direct act of perception and the self-conscious awareness of this act of perception. In this case a contradiction would be involved in affirming that I have an act of perception and in denying that I am aware that I have an act of perception. The act of perceiving a colour is the same as the appearing of the colour to me, and the act of perceiving the colour is identical with the act of being aware that I perceive a colour. To say that I perceive a colour and to say that the colour does not exist or that I am not aware that I perceive a colour would involve me in a contradiction.

Nicholas thus admitted as certain and evident not only analytic propositions but also immediate perception.[2] But he did not think that from the existence of one thing we can infer with certainty the existence of another thing. The reason why we cannot do this is that in the case of two things which are really different from one another it is possible without logical contradiction to affirm the existence of the one thing and deny the existence of the other. If *B* is identical either with the whole of *A* or with part of *A*, it is not possible without contradiction to affirm the existence of *A* and deny that of *B*; and if the existence of *A* is certain the existence of *B* is also certain. But if *B* is really distinct from *A* no contradiction is involved in affirming *A*'s existence and yet at the same time denying the existence of *B*. In the second letter to Bernard of Arezzo Nicholas makes the following assertion. 'From the fact that something is known to exist it cannot be inferred evidently, with, that is, evidence reducible to the first principle or to the certitude of the first principle, that another thing exists.'[3]

[1] Lappe, 6*, 15–16.

[2] Cf. *Exigit*, p. 235.

[3] Lappe, 9*, 15–20.

Bernard of Arezzo tried to counter Nicholas's assertion by what he evidently regarded as common-sense examples to the contrary. For instance, there is a white colour. But a white colour cannot exist without a substance. Therefore there is a substance. The conclusion of this syllogism is, said Bernard, certain. Nicholas's answer was on the following lines. If it is assumed that whiteness is an accident, and if it is assumed that an accident inheres in a substance and cannot exist without it, the conclusion is indeed certain. In the first place, however, the example would be irrelevant to the discussion. For what Nicholas asserted was that one cannot infer with certainty the existence of one thing from the existence of another. In the second place the assumptions that whiteness is an accident and that an accident necessarily inheres in a substance render the argument hypothetical. If whiteness is an accident and if an accident necessarily inheres in a substance, then, given this whiteness, there is a substance in which it inheres. But Nicholas would not admit that there is any compelling reason why these assumptions should be accepted. Bernard's argument conceals its assumptions. It does not show that one can argue with certainty from the existence of one thing to the existence of another thing, for Bernard has assumed that whiteness inheres in a substance. The fact that one sees a colour warrants one's concluding that a substance exists, only if one has assumed that a colour is an accident and that an accident necessarily inheres in a substance. But to assume this is to assume what has to be proved. Bernard's argument is therefore a concealed vicious circle.

Nicholas commented in a similar manner on another example brought by Bernard in order to show that one can argue with certainty from the existence of one thing to the existence of another thing. Fire is applied to tow, and there is no obstacle; therefore there will be heat. Either, said Nicholas, the consequent is identical with the antecedent or with part of it or it is not. In the first case the example would be irrelevant. For the argument would not be an argument from the existence of one thing to the existence of another thing. In the second case there would be two different propositions of which the one could be affirmed and the other denied without contradiction. 'Fire is applied to tow and there is no obstacle' and 'there will not be heat' are not contradictory propositions. And if they are not contradictory propositions the conclusion cannot be certain with the certitude which comes from reducibility to the first principle. Yet this, as has been agreed, is the only certitude.

From this position of Nicholas, that the existence of one thing cannot with certainty be inferred from that of another, it follows that no proposition which asserts that because *A* happens *B* will happen or that because *B* exists *A* exists, where *A* and *B* are distinct things, is or can be certain. Apart, then, from the immediate perception of sense-data (colours, for example) and of our acts no empirical knowledge is or can be certain. No causal argument can be certain. We doubtless believe in necessary connections in nature; but logic cannot detect them, and propositions which state them cannot be certain. What, then, is the reason of our belief in causal connections? Nicholas apparently explained this in terms of the experience of repeated sequences which gives rise to the expectation that if *B* has followed *A* in the past it will do so again in the future. Nicholas, it is true, affirmed that we cannot have probable knowledge that *B* will follow *A* in the future, unless we have evident certitude that at some time in the past *B* has followed *A*; but he did not mean that we cannot have probable knowledge that *B* will follow *A* in the future, unless we have evident certitude in the past of a necessary causal connection between *A* and *B*. What he meant, in terms of his own example in his second letter to Bernard, was that I cannot have probable knowledge that if I put my hand to the fire it will become warm, unless I have evident certitude of warmth in my hand having followed my putting my hand to the fire in the past. 'If it was once evident to me when I put my hand to the fire that I became warm, it is now probable to me that if I put my hand to the fire I should become warm.'[1] Nicholas considered that repeated experience of the coexistence of two things or of the regular sequence of distinct events increases the probability, from the *subjective* point of view, of similar experiences in the future; but repeated experience does not add anything to the objective evidence.[2]

It is clear that Nicholas considered that the possibility of God acting immediately as a causal agent, without, that is, using any secondary cause, rendered it impossible to argue with absolute certainty from the existence of one created thing to the existence of another created thing. He also argued against Bernard that on the principles enunciated by the latter it would be equally

[1] Lappe, 13*, 9–12. [2] *Exigit*, p. 237.

impossible. But the main interest of Nicholas's discussion of causality lies in the fact that he did not simply argue from the universally admitted doctrine of the divine omnipotence (universally admitted as a theological doctrine at any rate) but approached the question on a purely philosophical level.

It is to be noted that Nicholas did not deny that we can have certitude concerning the coexistence of appearances of *A* and *B*. All that is required is that we should actually have the two perceptions at once. But he did deny that one can infer with certainty the existence of the non-apparent from the existence of an appearance. He would not allow, then, that one can infer with certainty the existence of any substance. In order to know with certainty the existence of any material substance we should have either to perceive it directly, intuitively, or to infer its existence with certainty from the appearances or phenomena. But we do not perceive material substances, according to Nicholas. If we did, even the uneducated (the *rustici*) would perceive them. And this is not the case. Moreover, we cannot infer their existence with certainty, for the existence of one thing cannot be logically deduced from the existence of another thing.

In his ninth letter to Bernard, Nicholas asserted that 'these inferences are not evident: there is an act of understanding: therefore there is an intellect; there is an act of willing: therefore there is a will'.[1] This statement suggests that according to Nicholas we have no more certainty of the soul's existence as a substance than we have of material substances. Elsewhere, however, he states that 'Aristotle never had evident knowledge of any substance other than his own soul, understanding by "substance" something different from the objects of our five senses and from our formal experience.'[2] Again, 'we have no certitude concerning a substance joined to matter other than our soul'.[3] Statements like this have led some historians to conclude that Nicholas admitted that we have certitude about the knowledge of the soul as a spiritual substance. They accordingly interpret his remarks about our not being entitled to infer the existence of the intellect from the existence of acts of understanding and the existence of the will from the existence of acts of volition as an attack on the faculty psychology. This is certainly a possible interpretation, though it might be considered odd if Nicholas directed his attack simply against the theory of distinct faculties

[1] Lappe, 34*, 7–9. [2] *Ibid.*, 12*, 20–3. [3] *Ibid.*, 13*, 19–20.

which had already been subjected to criticism by William of Ockham, for example. But the *Exigit*[1] seems to imply, though it does not say so clearly, that we have no direct awareness of the soul. And in this case it would appear to follow, on Nicholas's premisses, that we have no natural knowledge of the soul's existence as a substance. The statement that Aristotle had no certain knowledge of any substance other than his own soul may be analogous to the assertion in the fifth letter to Bernard of Arezzo that we do not know with certainty that there is any efficient cause other than God. For his general position shows that in Nicholas's opinion we have no natural or philosophical certain knowledge that even God is an efficient cause. It is true that if the parallel between the two statements is pushed, it would seem to follow that Aristotle, according to Nicholas, enjoyed the certainty of faith about the existence of his soul as a spiritual substance; and Nicholas cannot possibly have meant to say this. But it is not necessary to interpret his remarks so strictly. However, it is difficult to be sure whether he did or did not make an exception in favour of our knowledge of our own souls from his general view that we have no certain knowledge of the existence of substances considered as distinct from phenomena.

It is evident that in his critique of causality and substance Nicholas anticipated the position of Hume; and the similarity is all the more striking if he did in fact deny that we have any certain knowledge of the existence of any substance, material or spiritual. But Dr. Weinberg is undoubtedly right, I think, in pointing out that Nicholas was not a phenomenalist. Nicholas thought that one cannot infer with certainty the existence of a non-apparent entity from the existence of phenomena; but he certainly did not think this means that one can infer its non-existence. In the sixth letter to Bernard he laid it down that 'from the fact that one thing exists, it cannot be inferred with certainty that another thing does not exist'.[2] Nicholas did not say that only phenomena exist or that affirmations of the existence of metaphenomenal entities are nonsensical. All he said was that the existence of phenomena does not enable us to infer with certainty the existence of the metaphenomenal or non-apparent. It is one thing to say, for example, that we are unable to prove that there is anything in a material object other than what appears to the senses, and it is another thing to say that there actually is no substance. Nicholas was not

[1] p. 225. [2] Lappe, 31*, 16–17.

a dogmatic phenomenalist. I do not mean to imply by this that Hume was a dogmatic phenomenalist, for he was not, whatever objections his (and Nicholas's) critical analyses of causality and substance may be open to. My point is simply that one must not conclude from Nicholas's denial of the demonstrability of the existence of substances that he actually denied the existence of all substances or said that their non-existence could be proved.

It is obvious enough that Nicholas's critique of causality and substance had important repercussions in regard to his attitude towards the traditional philosophical theology. Although Nicholas does not say so in clear and explicit terms, it would seem to follow from his general principles that it is not possible to prove the existence of God as efficient cause. In the fifth letter to Bernard he remarks that God may be the sole efficient cause, since one cannot prove that there is any natural efficient cause. But to say that God may be the sole efficient cause is not to say that He is the sole efficient cause or, indeed, that He can be proved to be an efficient cause at all. Nicholas meant merely that for all we know or can establish to the contrary God may be the sole efficient cause. As to our being able to prove that God actually is efficient cause, this is excluded by the general principle that we cannot infer with certainty the existence of one thing from the existence of another thing.

The causal or cosmological argument for God's existence could not, then, be a demonstrative argument on Nicholas's premisses. Nor could St. Thomas's fourth or fifth arguments be admitted as proofs yielding certain conclusions. We cannot, says Nicholas in the fifth letter to Bernard, prove that one thing is or is not nobler than another thing. Neither inspection of one thing nor comparison of two or more things is able to prove a hierarchy of degrees of being from the point of view of value. 'If anything whatever is pointed out, nobody knows evidently that it may not exceed all other things in value.'[1] And Nicholas does not hesitate to draw the conclusion that if by the term 'God' we understand the noblest being, nobody knows with certainty whether any given thing may not be God. If, then, we cannot establish with certainty an objective scale of perfection, St. Thomas's fourth argument obviously cannot be considered a demonstrative argument. As to the argument from finality, St. Thomas's fifth argument, this is ruled out by Nicholas's statement in the same letter that 'no one

[1] Lappe, 33*, 12–14.

knows evidently that one thing is the end (that is, final cause) of another'.[1] One cannot establish by inspection or analysis of any one thing that it is the final cause of another thing, nor is there any way of demonstrating it with certainty. We see a certain series of events, but final causality is not demonstrable.

Nicholas did, however, admit a probable argument for God's existence. Assuming as probable that we have an idea of the good as a standard for judging about the contingent relations between things,[2] and assuming that the order of the universe is such that it would satisfy a mind operating with the criterion of goodness and fitness, we can argue first that all things are so interconnected that one thing can be said to exist for the sake of another and secondly that this relationship between things is intelligible only in the light of the hypothesis that all things are subjected to an ultimate end, the supreme good or God. It might well appear that an argument of this kind would be no more than an entirely unfounded hypothesis, and that it could not, on Nicholas's own principles, amount to a probable argument. But Nicholas did not deny that we can have some sort of evidence enabling us to form a conjectural hypothesis which may be more or less probable, though it may not be certain as far as we are concerned. It might be true; it might even be a necessary truth; but we could not know that it was true, though we could believe it to be true. Besides theological belief, that is, faith in revealed truths, there is room for a belief which rests on arguments that are more or less probable.

Nicholas's probable argument for God's existence was part of the positive philosophy which he put forward as probable. It is not, in my opinion, worth while going into this philosophy in any detail. Apart from the fact that it was proposed as a probable hypothesis, its various parts are by no means always consistent with one another. One may mention, however, that for Nicholas the corruptibility of things is probably inconsistent with the goodness of the universe. Positively expressed this means that things are probably eternal. In order to show that this supposition cannot be ruled out by observation Nicholas argued that the fact that we see *B* succeeding *A* does not warrant our concluding that *A* has ceased to exist. We may not see *A* any more, but we do not see that *A* does not exist any more. And we cannot establish by reasoning that it does not any longer exist. If we could, we could establish by reasoning that nothing exists which is not observed,

[1] Lappe, 33*, 18–19. [2] *Exigit*, p. 185.

and this we cannot do. The Aristotelian doctrine of change is by no means certain. Moreover, the corruption of substances can be explained much better on an atomistic hypothesis than on Aristotelian principles. Substantial change may mean simply that one collocation of atoms is succeeded by another, while accidental change may mean the addition of fresh atoms to an atomic complex or the subtraction of some atoms from that complex. It is probable that the atoms are eternal and that precisely the same combinations occur in the periodic cycles which eternally recur.

As to the human soul, Nicholas maintained the hypothesis of immortality. But his suggestions on this matter are closely connected with a curious explanation of knowledge. As all things are eternal, it may be supposed that in knowledge the soul or mind enters into a temporary union with the object of knowledge. And the same can be said of imagination. The soul enters into a state of conjunction with images, but the images themselves are eternal. This hypothesis throws light, in Nicholas's opinion, on the nature of immortality. We may suppose that to good souls noble thoughts come after death, while to bad souls come evil thoughts. Or we may suppose that good souls enter into union with a better collection of atoms and are disposed to better experiences than they received in their previous embodied states, while evil souls enter into union with worse atoms and are disposed to receive more evil experiences and thoughts than in their previous embodied states. Nicholas claimed that this hypothesis allowed for the Christian doctrine of rewards and punishments after death; but he added a prudential qualification. His statements were, he said, more probable than the statements which had for a long time seemed probable. None the less, someone might turn up who would deprive his own statements of probability; and in view of this possibility the best thing to do is to adhere to the Biblical teaching on rewards and punishments. This line of argument was called in the *Articles of Cardinal Curti* a 'foxy excuse' (*excusatio vulpina*).[1]

Nicholas's positive philosophy was obviously at variance on some points with Catholic theology. And indeed Nicholas did not hesitate to say that his statements were more probable than the contradictory assertions. But one must interpret this attitude with some care. Nicholas did not state that his doctrines were true and the opposite doctrines false: he said that if the propositions which

[1] Lappe, 39*, 8.

were contradictory to his own were considered simply in regard to their probability, that is, as probable conclusions of reason, they were less probable than his own statements. For example, the theological doctrine that the world has not existed from eternity is for him certainly true, if it is considered as a revealed truth. But if one attends simply to the philosophical arguments which can be adduced in favour of its truth, one must admit, according to Nicholas, that they are less probable than the philosophical arguments which can be adduced in favour of the contradictory proposition. One is not entitled, however, to conclude that the contradictory proposition is not true. For all we know it may even be a necessary truth. Probability has to be interpreted in terms of the natural evidence available to us at any given moment, and a proposition may be for us more probable than its contradictory even though it is in fact false and its contradictory true. Nicholas did not propose a double-truth theory; nor did he deny any defined doctrines of the Church. What his subjective attitude was is a matter about which we cannot be sure. Pierre d'Ailly asserted that a number of Nicholas's propositions were condemned out of envy or ill-will; and Nicholas himself maintained that some statements were attributed to him which he did not hold at all or which he did not hold in the sense in which they were condemned. It is difficult to judge how far one is justified in taking his protestations at their face-value and how far one should assume that his critics were justified in dismissing these protestations as 'foxy' excuses. There can be little doubt, I think, that he was sincere in saying that the philosophy which he put forward as 'probable' was untrue in so far as it conflicted with the teaching of the Church. At least there is no real difficulty in accepting his sincerity on this point, since apart from any other consideration it would have been quite inconsistent with the critical side of his philosophy if he had regarded the conclusions of his positive philosophy as certain. On the other hand, it is not so easy to accept Nicholas's protestation that the critical views expounded in his correspondence with Bernard of Arezzo were put forward as a kind of experiment in reasoning. His letters to Bernard hardly give that impression, even if the possibility cannot be excluded that the explanation which he offered to his judges represented his real mind. After all, he was by no means the only philosopher of his time to adopt a critical attitude towards the traditional metaphysics, even if he went further than most.

It is, however, quite clear that Nicholas meant to attack the philosophy of Aristotle and that he considered his own positive philosophy to be a more probable hypothesis than the Aristotelian system. He declared that he was himself very astonished that some people study Aristotle and the Commentator (Averroes) up to a decrepit old age and forsake moral matters and the care of the common good in favour of the study of Aristotle. They do this to such an extent that when the friend of truth rises up and sounds a trumpet to rouse the sleepers from slumber they are greatly afflicted and rush upon him like armed men to deadly combat.[1]

Mention of 'moral matters' and of the 'common good' leads one to inquire what Nicholas's ethical and political teaching was. We have not much to go upon here. But it seems clear that he maintained the Ockhamist theory of the arbitrary character of the moral law. There is a condemned proposition of his to the effect that 'God can order a rational creature to hate Him, and that the rational creature merits more by obeying this precept than by loving God in obedience to a precept. For he would do so (that is, hate God) with greater effort and more against his inclination.'[2] As to politics, Nicholas is said to have issued a proclamation that whoever wanted to hear lectures on Aristotle's *Politics* together with certain discussions about justice and injustice which would enable a man to make new laws or to correct laws already in existence, should repair to a certain place where he would find Master Nicholas of Autrecourt, who would teach him all these things.[3] How far this proclamation constitutes evidence of Nicholas's serious concern for the common welfare and how far it is the expression of a love of notoriety it is difficult to say.

I have given an account of the philosophical ideas of John of Mirecourt and Nicholas of Autrecourt in a chapter on the 'Ockhamist Movement'. Is this procedure justified? Nicholas's positive philosophy, which he put forward as probable, was certainly not the philosophy of William of Ockham; and in this respect it would be quite wrong to call him an 'Ockhamist'. As to his critical philosophy, it was not the same as that of Ockham, and Nicholas cannot be properly called an 'Ockhamist', if by this term is meant a disciple of Ockham. Moreover, the tone of Nicholas's writing is different from that of the Franciscan theologian. None the less, Nicholas was an extreme representative of that critical movement of thought which was a prominent feature of fourteenth-century

[1] Cf. *Exigit*, pp. 181–2. [2] Lappe, 41*, 31–4. [3] *Ibid.*, 40*, 26–33.

philosophy and which finds expression in one aspect of Ockhamism. I have indicated earlier that I use the term 'Ockhamist Movement' to denote a philosophical movement which was characterized, in part, by a critical attitude towards the presuppositions and arguments of the traditional metaphysics, and if the term is used in this sense, one can, I think, justifiably speak of John of Mirecourt and Nicholas of Autrecourt as belonging to the Ockhamist movement.

Nicholas of Autrecourt was not a sceptic, if by this term we mean a philosopher who denies or questions the possibility of attaining any certain knowledge. He maintained that certainty is obtainable in logic and in mathematics and in immediate perception. In modern terms he recognized as certain both analytic propositions (the propositions which are now sometimes called 'tautologies') and basic empirical statements, though one must add the proviso that for Nicholas we can have evident immediate knowledge without that knowledge being expressed in a proposition. On the other hand, propositions involving the assertion of a causal relation in the metaphysical sense or propositions based on an inference from one existent to another he regarded not as certain propositions but rather as empirical hypotheses. One must not, however, turn Nicholas into a 'logical positivist'. He did not deny the significance of metaphysical or theological statements: on the contrary, he presupposed the certitude of faith and admitted revelation as a source of absolute certainty.

4. I announced my intention of concluding this chapter with some remarks on the influence of the new movement in the universities, especially in the universities which were founded in the latter part of the fourteenth century and during the fifteenth.

In 1389 a statute was passed at the university of Vienna requiring of students in the faculty of arts that they should attend lectures on the logical works of Peter of Spain, while later statutes imposed a similar obligation in regard to the logical works of Ockhamist authors like William Heytesbury. Nominalism was also strongly represented in the German universities of Heidelberg (founded in 1386), Erfurt (1392) and Leipzig (1409) and in the Polish university of Cracow (1397). The university of Leipzig is said to have owed its origin to the exodus of nominalists from Prague, where John Hus and Jerome of Prague taught the Scotist realism which they had learnt from John Wycliffe (*c.* 1320–84). Indeed, when the Council of Constance condemned the theological errors of John Hus in 1415, the nominalists were quick to argue that Scotist realism had also been condemned, though this was not actually the case.

In the first half of the fifteenth century a rather surprising revival of the philosophy of St. Albert the Great took place. The nominalists seem to have left Paris early in the century, partly owing to the conditions brought about by the Hundred Years War, though Ehrle was doubtless correct in connecting the revival of 'Albertism' with the return of the Dominicans to Paris in 1403. They had left the city in 1387. The supremacy of Albertism did not last very long, however, because the nominalists returned in 1437 after the city had been liberated from the English. On March 1st, 1474, King Louis XI issued a decree prohibiting the teaching of nominalism and ordering the confiscation of nominalist books; but in 1481 the ban was withdrawn.

In the fifteenth century, then, nominalism was strongly entrenched at Paris, Oxford and many German universities; but the older traditions continued to hold their ground in certain places. This was the case in the university of Cologne, which was founded in 1389. At Cologne the doctrines of St. Albert and St. Thomas were in possession. After the condemnation of John Hus the Prince Electors asked the university to adopt nominalism on the ground that the more old-fashioned realism easily led to heresy, even though it was not evil in itself. But in 1425 the university replied that while it remained open to anyone to adopt nominalism if he chose, the doctrines of St. Albert, St. Thomas, St. Bonaventure, Giles of Rome and Duns Scotus were above suspicion. In any case, said the university, the heresies of John Hus did not spring from philosophical realism but from the theological teaching of Wycliffe. Further, if realism were forbidden at Cologne the students would leave the university.

With the university of Cologne one must associate that of Louvain, which was founded in 1425. The statutes of 1427 required of candidates for the doctorate that they should take an oath never to teach the doctrines of Buridan, Marsilius of Inghen, Ockham or their followers; and in 1480 professors who expounded Aristotle in the light of the Ockhamist theories were threatened with suspension from office.

The adherents of the 'ancient way', therefore, were by no means completely routed by the nominalists. Indeed, in the middle of the fourteenth century realism gained a foothold at Heidelberg.

Moreover, they could boast of some eminent names. Chief among them was John Capreolus (*c.* 1380–1444), a Dominican who lectured for a time at Paris and later at Toulouse. He set out to defend the doctrines of St. Thomas against the contrary opinions of Scotus, Durandus, Henry of Ghent and all adversaries in general, including the nominalists. His great work, which was completed shortly before his death at Rodez and which earned for him the title of *Princeps thomistarum*, was the *Libri IV defensionum theologiae divi Thomae de Aquino*. Capreolus was the first of the line of distinguished Dominican Thomists and commentators on St. Thomas, which included at a later period men like Cajetan (d. 1534) and John of St. Thomas (d. 1644).

In the Italian universities a current of Averroistic Aristotelianism was represented at Bologna in the first half of the fourteenth century by thinkers like Thaddaeus of Parma and Angelo of Arezzo and passed to Padua and Venice where it was represented by Paul of Venice (d. 1429), Cajetan of Thiene (d. 1465), Alexander Achillini (d. 1512) and Agostino Nipho (d. 1546). The first printed edition of Averroes appeared at Padua in 1472. Something will be said later, in connection with the philosophy of the Renaissance, about the controversy between those who followed Averroes' interpretation of Aristotle and those who adhered to the interpretation given by Alexander of Aphrodisias, and about the condemnation of 1513. The Averroists have been mentioned here simply as an illustration of the fact that the *via moderna* should not be regarded as having swept all before it in the fourteenth and fifteenth centuries.

Nevertheless, nominalism possessed that attraction which comes from modernity and freshness, and it spread widely, as we have seen. A notable figure among fifteenth-century nominalists was Gabriel Biel (*c.* 1425–95), who taught at Tübingen and composed an epitome of Ockham's commentaries on the *Sentences* of Peter Lombard. Biel's work was a methodical and clear exposition of Ockhamism, and though he did not pretend to be more than a follower and exponent of Ockham he exercised a considerable influence. Indeed, the Ockhamists at the universities of Erfurt and Wittenberg were known as *Gabrielistae*. It is perhaps interesting to note that Biel did not interpret Ockham's moral theory as meaning that there is no natural moral order. There are objects or ends besides God which can be chosen in accordance with right reason, and pagan philosophers like Aristotle, Cicero and Seneca were able to accomplish morally good and virtuous acts. In virtue of his 'absolute power' God could, indeed, command acts opposed to the dictates of the natural reason; but this does not alter the fact that these dictates can be recognized without revelation.

5. Finally one may recall that the Ockhamist Movement or nominalism had various aspects. On the purely logical side it was partly a development of the logic of terms and of the theory of *suppositio* as found in pre-Ockhamist logicians like Peter of Spain. This terminist logic was used by William of Ockham in order to exclude all forms of realism. The problem of universals was treated from a logical rather than an ontological point of view. The universal is the abstract term considered according to its logical content, and this term stands in the proposition for individual things, which are the only things which exist.

This terminist logic had not of itself any sceptical consequences in regard to knowledge, nor did Ockham regard it as having any such consequences. But together with the logical aspect of nominalism one must take into account the analysis of causality and the consequences of this analysis in regard to the epistemological status of empirical hypotheses. In the philosophy of a man like Nicholas of Autrecourt we have seen a sharp distinction drawn between analytic or formal propositions, which are certain, and empirical hypotheses, which are not and cannot be certain. With Ockham this view, so far as he held it, was closely connected with his insistence on the divine omnipotence: with Nicholas of Autrecourt the theological background was very much less in evidence.

We have seen, too, how the nominalists (some more than others) tended to adopt a critical attitude towards the metaphysical arguments of the older philosophers. This attitude was fully explicit in an extremist like Nicholas of Autrecourt, since it was made to rest on his general position that one cannot infer with certainty the existence of one thing from the existence of another thing. Metaphysical arguments are probable rather than demonstrative.

But, whatever one may be inclined to think on one or two cases, this critical attitude in regard to metaphysical speculation was practically always combined with a firm theological faith and a firm belief in revelation as a source of certain knowledge. This firm belief is particularly striking in the case of Ockham himself. His view that it is possible to have what would be, from the psychological point of view, intuition of a non-existent thing and his theory about the ultimate dependence of the moral law on the divine choice were not expressions of scepticism but of the tremendous emphasis he placed on the divine omnipotence. If one attempts to turn the nominalists into rationalists or even sceptics in the modern sense, one is taking them out of their historical setting and severing them from their mental background. In the course of time nominalism became one of the regular currents in Scholastic thought; and a theological chair of nominalism was erected even in the university of Salamanca.

But nominalism suffered the fate of most philosophical schools of thought. It obviously began as something new; and whatever one's opinion concerning the various tenets of the nominalists may be, it can hardly be denied that they had something to say. They helped to develop logical studies and they raised important problems. But in the course of time a tendency to 'logic-chopping' showed itself, and this can perhaps be connected with their reserved attitude towards metaphysics. Logical refinements and exaggerated subtlety tended to drain off the energies of the later nominalists; and when philosophy received a fresh impetus at the time of the Renaissance this impetus did not come from the nominalists.

CHAPTER X

THE SCIENTIFIC MOVEMENT

Physical science in the thirteenth and fourteenth centuries—The problem of motion; impetus and gravity—Nicholas Oresme; the hypothesis of the earth's rotation—The possibility of other worlds —Some scientific implications of nominalism; and implications of the impetus theory.

1. For a long time it was widely supposed that there was no respect for experience in the Middle Ages and that the only ideas on science which the mediaevals possessed were adopted uncritically from Aristotle and other non-Christian writers. Science was assumed to have started again, after centuries of almost complete quiescence, at the time of the Renaissance. Then it was found that a considerable interest had been taken in scientific matters during the fourteenth century, that some important discoveries had been made at that time, that various theories had been fairly widely held which did not derive from Aristotle and that certain hypotheses which were usually associated with the Renaissance scientists had been proposed in the late Middle Ages. At the same time a better knowledge of late mediaeval philosophy suggested that the scientific movement of the fourteenth century should be connected with Ockhamism or nominalism, largely on the ground that Ockham and those who belonged more or less to the same movement of thought insisted on the primacy of intuition or of immediate experience in the acquisition of factual knowledge. It was not that Ockham himself was thought to have shown much interest in scientific matters; but his insistence on intuition as the only basis of factual knowledge and the empiricist side of his philosophy were thought to have given a powerful impetus to scientific interests and investigations. This view of the matter could be fitted into the traditional outlook inasmuch as Ockham and the nominalists were supposed to have been resolute anti-Aristotelians.

It is not at all my intention to attempt to deny that there is truth in this interpretation of the facts. Although Ockham cannot possibly be called simply 'anti-Aristotelian' without qualification, since in some matters he regarded himself as the true interpreter of Aristotle, his philosophy was in certain important respects undoubtedly at variance with Aristotle's, and it is clear that some thinkers who belonged to the nominalist movement were extremely hostile to Aristotelianism. Moreover, it is probably true to say that Ockhamist insistence on experience as the basis of our knowledge of existent things favoured the growth of empirical science. It may be difficult to assess an epistemological theory's positive influence on the growth of science; but it is reasonable to think that the doctrine of the primacy of intuition would naturally encourage such growth rather than discourage it. Moreover, if one assumes that causes cannot be discovered by *a priori* theorizing but that recourse must be had to experience in order to discover them, this assumption is calculated to turn the mind towards the investigation of the empirical data. No doubt, it can be said with justice that science does not consist in 'intuition' or in merely observing the empirical data; but the point is not that Ockhamism provided a theory of scientific method but rather that it helped to create an intellectual climate which facilitated and tended to promote scientific research. For by directing men's minds to the facts or empirical data in the acquisition of knowledge it at the same time directed them away from passive acceptance of the opinions of illustrious thinkers of the past.

But though it would be improper to discount the connection of fourteenth-century science with Ockhamism it would be equally improper to attribute its growth to Ockhamism as a sufficient cause. In the first place it is not clear to what extent one can legitimately speak of the fourteenth-century physicists as 'Ockhamists', even if one uses the term in a wide sense. One of the leading figures who took an interest in physical theories was John Buridan, who was for a time rector of the university of Paris and died about 1360. This theologian, philosopher and physicist was influenced by the terminist logic and by certain views which were held by Ockham; but he was by no means an unqualified nominalist. Apart from the fact that in his official capacity as rector he was associated with the condemnation of nominalist theories in 1340 he maintained, for example, in his writings that it is possible to prove the existence of one thing from the existence of another thing and that consequently it is possible to prove the existence of God. Albert of Saxony was rather more of an Ockhamist. Rector of the university of Paris in 1353 he became in 1365 the first rector of the university of Vienna. In the same year he was appointed bishop of Halberstadt. He died in that post in 1390. In logic he followed Ockham; but he was certainly not an extreme adherent of the *via moderna*. It is true that he held that the certitude given by experience cannot be absolute; but it would appear that his view of the hypothetical character of empirical statements was due more to the conviction that God can miraculously 'interfere' with the natural order than to any other consideration. Marsilius of Inghen (d. 1396), who was rector of the university of Paris in 1367 and 1371 and first rector of the university of Heidelberg in 1386, was indeed, a declared adherent of the *via moderna*; but he seems to have tempered the nominalist position on universals with a dose of realism, and he thought that the metaphysician can prove the existence and unicity of God. As for Nicholas Oresme, who taught at Paris and died as bishop of Lisieux in 1382, he was much more of a physicist than a philosopher, though he had, of course, theological and philosophical interests.

One can say then, I think, that the leading figures in the scientific movement of the fourteenth century had in most cases affiliations with the Ockhamist Movement. And if one is going to use the term 'nominalist' to denote those who adopted the Ockhamist or terminist logic, one can call them 'nominalists'. But it would be a mistake to suppose that they all adhered to Ockham's views on metaphysics; and it would be still more of a mistake to suppose that they shared the extremist philosophical position of a thinker like Nicholas of Autrecourt. Indeed, Buridan and Albert of Saxony both attacked Nicholas. It is fairly clear, however, that the *via moderna* in philosophy did stimulate, though it did not cause, the scientific developments of the fourteenth century.

That the nominalist movement cannot be accounted the sufficient cause of the growth of science in the fourteenth century is clear from the fact that fourteenth-century science was to a considerable extent a continuation of and growth from thirteenth-century science. I have mentioned that modern research has brought to light the reality of scientific progress in the fourteenth century. But research is also bringing to light the scientific investigations which were pursued in the thirteenth century. These investigations were stimulated mainly by the translations of Greek and Arabic scientific works; but they were none the less real. Mediaeval science was doubtless primitive and rudimentary if we compare it with the science of the post-Renaissance era; but there is no longer any excuse for saying that there was no science in the Middle Ages outside the fields of theology and philosophy. Not only was there a scientific development in the Middle Ages but there was also a continuity in some degree between the science of the late Middle Ages and the science of the Renaissance. It would be foolish to belittle the achievements of the Renaissance scientists or to make out that their hypotheses and discoveries were all anticipated in the Middle Ages. But it is also foolish to depict Renaissance science as being without historical antecedents and parentage.

In the thirteenth century a number of thinkers had insisted on the need for observation or 'experience' in scientific study. In the preceding volume of this history mention was made in this connection of St. Albert the Great (1206–80), Peter of Maricourt (exact dates unknown), Robert Grosseteste (*c.* 1175–1253) and of Roger Bacon (*c.* 1212–after 1292). Peter of Maricourt, who stimulated Bacon's interest in scientific matters, is notable for his *Epistola de magnete*, which was utilized by William Gilbert in the second half of the sixteenth century. Grosseteste wrote on optics and tried to improve the theory of refraction contained in Greek and Arabic writings. Optics constituted also one of Bacon's special interests. The Silesian scientist, mathematician and philosopher Witelo wrote on the same subject in his *Perspectiva*. This work was composed in dependence on the writings of the Islamic scientist Alhazen; and Kepler later supplied some developments on Witelo's ideas in his *Ad Vitellionem paralipomena* (1604). The Dominican Theodoric of Freiberg (d. *c.* 1311) developed a theory in explanation of the rainbow on an experimental basis, which was adopted by Descartes;[1] and another Dominican, Jordanus Nemorarius, made discoveries in mechanics.

But though the thirteenth-century physicists insisted on the need for observation in scientific research, and though a man like Roger Bacon was quick to see the practical purposes to which scientific discoveries could be put, they were by no means blind to the theoretical aspects of scientific method. They did not regard science as consisting in the mere accumulation of empirical data; nor did they concentrate simply on real or imagined practical results. They were interested in explaining the data. Aristotle had held that scientific knowledge is obtained only when one is in a position to show how the observed effects follow from their

[1] Theodoric's explanation of the shape of the bow was correct, though he failed to explain the colours.

causes; and for Grosseteste and Bacon this meant in large part being able to give a mathematical deduction of the effects. Hence the great emphasis placed by Bacon on mathematics as the key to other sciences. Furthermore, whereas Aristotle had not given any very clear indication how a knowledge of the 'causes' is to be actually obtained, Grosseteste and Bacon showed how the elimination of explanatory theories which are incompatible with the facts helped one to arrive at this knowledge. In other words, they saw not only that an explanatory hypothesis could be arrived at by examining the common factors in different instances of the phenomenon under investigation, but also that it is necessary to verify this hypothesis by considering what results should follow if the hypothesis were true and by then experimenting in order to see if these expectations are actually fulfilled.

Fourteenth-century science was therefore not an entirely new development: it was a continuation of the scientific work of the preceding century, just as this work was itself a continuation of the scientific studies made by Greek and Arab physicists and mathematicians. But in the fourteenth century other problems came into prominence, especially the problem of motion. And the consideration of this problem in the fourteenth century might have suggested a conception of scientific hypotheses which, had it been subsequently accepted by Galileo, might have gone a long way towards preventing the latter's clash with the theologians.

2. In Aristotle's account of motion a distinction was made between natural and unnatural motion. An element like fire is naturally light and its natural tendency is to move upwards towards its natural place, while earth is heavy and has a natural movement downwards. But one can take a naturally heavy thing and throw it upwards, a stone, for example; and so long as the stone is moving upwards its motion is unnatural. Aristotle considered that this unnatural motion requires an explanation. The obvious answer to the question why the stone moves upwards is that it is thrown upwards. But once the stone has left the hand of the person who throws it it continues to move upwards for some time. Aristotle's answer to the question why this happens was that the person who throws the stone and so starts it on its upward course moves not only the stone but also the surrounding air. This air moves the air higher up and each portion of the air which is moved carries the stone with it until the successive movements of portions of air become so weak that the stone's natural tendency to downward

motion is able at length to reassert itself. The stone then begins to move towards its natural place.

This account of unnatural or violent motion was rejected by William of Ockham. If it is the air which moves a flying arrow, then if two arrows meet in flight we shall have to say that at that moment the same air is causing movements in opposite directions; and this cannot be the case.[1] On the other hand, one cannot suppose that a stone which is thrown upwards continues to move in virtue of some power or quality imparted to it. There is no empirical evidence of the existence of any such quality distinct from the projectile. If there were such a quality it could be conserved by God apart from the projectile; but it would be absurd to suppose that this can be done. Local motion does not involve anything beyond a 'permanent thing' and the term of the motion.[2]

Ockham thus rejected the idea of a quality impressed on the projectile by the agent as an explanation of motion; and to this extent he may be said to have anticipated the law of inertia. But the physicists of the fourteenth century were not content to say that a thing moves because it is in motion: they preferred to adopt the theory of impetus, which had been put forward by Philoponus in the early part of the sixth century and which had been already adopted by the Franciscan Peter John Olivi (*c.* 1248–98), who spoke of the impulse (*impulsus*) or 'inclination' that is given to the projectile by the moving agent. This quality or energy in virtue of which a stone, for example, continues to move after it has left the hand of the thrower until it is overcome by the resistance of the air and the weight of the stone was called *impetus* by the fourteenth-century physicists. They supported the theory empirically, in that they maintained that it was better adapted than the Aristotelian theory for 'saving the appearances'. For example, John Buridan held that Aristotle's theory of motion was unable to explain the movement of a spinning top, whereas this could be explained on the impetus theory. The spinning top, he said, stays in one place; it does not leave its place, which could then be filled by air which would move the top. But though the fourteenth-century physicists attempted to support the impetus theory empirically or to verify it, they did not confine themselves to purely physical considerations but introduced philosophical questions stated in the traditional categories. For example, in his *Abbreviationes super VIII libros physicorum* Marsilius of Inghen

[1] 2 *Sent.*, 18, J.

[2] *Ibid.*, 9, E.

raised the question, to what category or *praedicamentum* should impetus be assigned. He did not supply any very definite answer to this question; but he clearly thought that there are different kinds of impetus. For some projectiles move upwards, others downwards, some straight forwards, others in a circle. Again, although Albert of Saxony declared that the question whether impetus is a substance or an accident is a question for the metaphysician rather than for the physicist, he himself asserted that it is a quality, that is to say an accident. In any case it is clear that these physicists regarded impetus as something distinct from and impressed upon the projectile or moving body: they did not follow William of Ockham in his denial of any such distinct reality.

An interesting application of the impetus theory was made in regard to the movement of the heavenly bodies. In his commentary on the *Metaphysics*[1] Buridan maintained that God imparted to the heavenly bodies an original impetus which is the same in kind as the impetus in virtue of which terrestrial bodies move. There is no need to suppose that the heavenly bodies are made of a special element (the quintessence or fifth element), which can only move with a circular motion. Nor is it necessary to postulate Intelligences of the spheres to account for the spheres' movements. Motion on earth and motion in the heavens can be explained in the same way. Just as a man imparts an impetus to the stone which he throws into the air, so God imparted impetus to the heavenly bodies when He created them. The reason why the latter continue to move while the stone eventually falls to the earth is simply that the stone encounters resistance whereas the heavenly bodies do not. The impetus of the stone is gradually overcome by the air's resistance and the force of gravity; and the operation of these factors results in the stone's eventually moving towards its natural place. But although the heavenly bodies are not composed of some special matter of their own these factors do not operate in their case: gravity, in the sense of a factor which makes a body tend towards the earth as its natural place, operates only in regard to bodies within the terrestrial sphere.

This theory of impetus was adopted, to all intents and purposes, by Albert of Saxony, Marsilius of Inghen and Nicholas Oresme. The first-named, however, tried to give a clear account of what is meant by gravity. He made a distinction between the centre of gravity in a body and the centre of its volume. These are not

[1] 12, 9.

necessarily the same. In the case of the earth they are different, as the earth's density is not uniform; and when we talk about the 'centre of the earth' in connection with gravity it is the earth's centre of gravity which is meant. The tendency of a body to move towards its natural place may, then, be taken to mean its tendency to unite its own centre of gravity with the earth's centre of gravity or 'the centre of the earth'. A body's 'gravity' means this tendency. It is noteworthy that this 'explanation' is a physical account: it is not an account in terms of 'ultimate causes' but a positive account of what happens or is thought to happen.

3. The wider implications of the impetus theory will be briefly discussed later in this chapter. At the moment I wish to mention one or two other developments connected with problems of motion.

Nicholas Oresme, who was one of the most independent and outstanding of the mediaeval physicists, made several discoveries in the sphere of dynamics. He found, for example, that when a body moves with a uniformly increasing velocity the distance which it travels is equal to the distance travelled in the same time by a body which moves with a uniform velocity equal to that attained by the first body at the middle instant of its course. Furthermore, he tried to find a way of expressing successive variations of intensity which would make it easy to understand and compare them. The way he suggested was that of representing them by means of graphs, making use of rectangular co-ordinates. Space or time would be represented by a straight base line. On this line Nicholas erected vertical lines, the length of which corresponded to the position or the intensity of the variable. He then connected the ends of the vertical lines and so was able to obtain a curve which represented the fluctuations in intensity. This geometrical device obviously prepared the way for further mathematical developments. But to depict Nicholas as the founder of analytic geometry, in the sense of ascribing to him the developments of Descartes, would be an exaggeration. For the geometrical presentation suggested by Nicholas had to be superseded by the substitution of numerical equivalents. This does not mean, however, that his work was not of importance and that it did not represent an important stage in the development of applied mathematics. He does not appear, however, to have realized very clearly the difference between symbol and reality. Thus in his treatise *De uniformitate et difformitate intensionum* he implies that heat of varying intensity is actually composed of geometrical particles of pyramidal structure, a notion which recalls to mind the statement in Plato's *Timaeus* that the particles of fire possess pyramidal form, as pyramids have 'the sharpest cutting edges and the sharpest points in every direction'.[1] Indeed, in the treatise *Du ciel et du monde*,[2] he shows plainly enough his predilection for Plato.

One of the problems discussed by Nicholas was that of the earth's movement. The matter had apparently already been discussed at an earlier date, for Francis of Meyronnes, a Scotist who wrote early in the fourteenth century, asserts that 'a certain doctor' maintained that if it was the earth which moved rather than the heavens it would be a 'better arrangement' (*melior dispositio*). Albert of Saxony dismissed as insufficient the arguments offered in favour of the hypothesis that the earth rotates daily on its axis; but Nicholas Oresme, who discussed the hypothesis at some length, gave it a more favourable reception, even if in the end he preferred not to accept it.

In his treatise *Du ciel et du monde* Nicholas maintained first of all that direct observation cannot afford a proof that the heaven or firmament rotates daily while the earth remains at rest. For the appearances would be precisely the same if it were the earth and not the heaven which rotated. For this and other reasons 'I conclude that one could not show by any experience that the heaven was moved with a daily motion and the earth was not moved in this way.'[3] As to other arguments adduced against the possibility of the earth's daily rotation, replies can be made to them all. For example, from the fact that parts of the earth tend to their 'natural place' with a downward movement it does not follow that the earth as a whole cannot rotate: it cannot be shown that a body as a whole may not have one simple movement while its parts have other movements.[4] Again, even if the heaven does rotate, it does not necessarily follow that the earth is at rest. When a mill-wheel rotates, the centre does not remain at rest, except for a mathematical point which is not a body at all.[5] As to arguments drawn from the Scriptures, one must remember that the Scriptures speak according to a common mode of speech and that they are not necessarily to be regarded as making a scientific statement in some particular case. From the statement in the Bible that the sun was stopped in its course[6] one is no more entitled to draw the

[1] *Timaeus*, 56a. [2] 62d., p. 280
[3] 140a, p. 273. References are to the edition by A. D. Menut and A. J. Denomy.
[4] 140d–141a, p. 275. [5] 141b, p. 276. [6] *Josue*, 10, 13

scientific conclusion that the heaven moves and that the earth does not than one is entitled to draw from phrases like 'God repented' the conclusion that God can actually change His mind like a human being.[1] In view of the fact that it is sometimes said or implied that this interpretation of the relevant Scriptural assertions was invented by theologians only when the Copernican hypothesis had been verified and could no longer be rejected, it is interesting to note the clear statement of it by Nicholas Oresme in the fourteenth century.

Furthermore, one can give positive reasons in support of the hypothesis that the earth rotates. For example, it is reasonable to suppose that a body which receives influence from another body should itself move to receive this influence, like a joint being roasted at the fire. Now, the earth receives heat from the sun. It is reasonable, then, to suppose that the earth moves in order to receive this influence.[2] Again, if one postulates the rotation of the earth one can 'save the appearances' much better than on the opposite hypothesis, since if one denies the earth's movement one has to postulate a great number of other movements in order to explain the empirical data.[3] Nicholas draws attention to the fact that Heraclitus Ponticus (Heraclides of Pontus) had put forward the hypothesis of the earth's movement; so it was not a new idea. Nevertheless, he himself ends by rejecting this hypothesis, 'notwithstanding the reasons to the contrary, for they are conclusions which are not evidently conclusive'.[4] In other words, he is not prepared to abandon the common opinion of the time for a hypothesis which has not been conclusively proved.

Nicholas had a critical mind and he was certainly no blind adherent of Aristotle. He saw that the problem was one of 'saving the appearances'; and he asked which hypothesis would account for the empirical data in the most economical manner. It appears to me to be fairly clear that, in spite of his eventual acceptance of the commonly held opinion, he considered the hypothesis of the earth's daily rotation on its axis to meet all requirements better than the opposite hypothesis. The same could not be said about Albert of Saxony, however, who rejected the theory of the earth's rotation on the ground that it did not save the appearances. Like Francis of Meyronnes, he seems to have thought that the theory claimed that all the movements of

[1] 141d–142a, pp. 276–7.
[2] 142b, p. 277.
[3] 143c–d, p. 278.
[4] 144b, p. 279.

the heavenly bodies could be eliminated if the earth were regarded as rotating; and he pointed out that the movements of the planets could not be eliminated in this way. Buridan also rejected the theory of the earth's rotation, though he discussed it quite sympathetically. It was Nicholas Oresme who saw clearly that the theory would only eliminate the diurnal rotation of the 'fixed' stars and would still leave the planets in motion. Some of the reasons he proposed in favour of the theory were good reasons, but others were not; and it would be an extravagance to depict Nicholas as having given a clearer and profounder exposition of the hypothesis of the earth's movement than the astronomers of the Renaissance, as Pierre Duhem was inclined to do. It is obvious, however, that men like Albert of Saxony and Nicholas Oresme can properly be called the precursors of the Renaissance physicists, astronomers and mathematicians. In so calling them Duhem was quite justified.

4. One of the questions discussed in the *Du ciel et du monde* is whether there could be other worlds besides this one. According to Nicholas, neither Aristotle nor anyone else has shown that God could not create a plurality of worlds. It is useless to argue from the unicity of God to the unicity of the world: God is not only one and unique but also infinite, and if there were a plurality of worlds none of them would be, as it were, outside the divine presence and power.[1] Again, to say that if there were another world, the element of earth in the other world would be attracted to this earth as to its natural place is no valid objection: the natural place of the element of earth in the other world would be in the other world and not in this.[2] Nicholas concludes, however, that although no sufficient proofs have been adduced by Aristotle or anyone else to show that there could not be other worlds in addition to this one, there never has been, is not and never will be any other corporeal world.[3]

5. The existence of a certain interest in scientific study during the thirteenth century has been mentioned earlier in this chapter; and the conclusion was then drawn that the scientific work of the succeeding century cannot be ascribed simply to the association of some of the fourteenth-century physicists with the Ockhamist movement. It is true, of course, that certain philosophical positions maintained by Ockham himself or by other followers of the *via moderna* were calculated to influence the conceptions of

[1] 38b–c, p. 243. [2] 38a–b, p. 243. [3] 39b–c, p. 244.

scientific method and of the status of physical theories. The combination of a 'nominalist' or conceptualist view of universals with the thesis that one cannot argue with certainty from the existence of one thing to the existence of another thing would naturally lead to the conclusion that physical theories are empirical hypotheses which can be more or less probable but which cannot be proved with certainty. Again, the emphasis laid by some philosophers on experience and observation as the necessary basis of our knowledge of the world might well encourage the view that the probability of an empirical hypothesis depends on the extent of its verification, that is, on its ability to explain or account for the empirical data. One might perhaps be tempted to suggest that the philosophy of the nominalist movement could have led to the conclusion that physical theories are empirical hypotheses which involve a certain amount of 'dictation' to nature and *a priori* construction, but which depend for their probability and utility on the extent to which they can be verified. A theory is constructed on the basis of empirical data, it might have been said, but it is a mental construction on the basis of those data. Its object, however, is to explain the phenomena, and it is verified in so far as it is possible to deduce from it the phenomena which are actually observed in ordinary life or which are obtained by artificial and purposive experiment. Moreover, that explanatory theory will be preferable which succeeds in explaining the phenomena with the least number of assumptions and presuppositions and which thus best satisfies the principle of economy.

But it is one thing to say that conclusions of this sort might have been suggested by the new movement in philosophy during the fourteenth century, and it is another thing to say that they were actually drawn. On the one hand, philosophers like Ockham do not seem to have shown any particular interest in questions of scientific theory and method as such, while on the other hand the physicists appear to have been more interested in their actual scientific research and speculations than in reflection on the underlying theory and method. This is, after all, only what one would expect. Reflection on scientific method and theory can hardly reach a high degree of development until physical science has itself progressed to a considerable extent and has reached a stage which prompts and stimulates reflection on the method employed and its theoretical presuppositions. We certainly do find in the thought of the fourteenth-century physicists some elements of the scientific theory which might have been suggested by contemporary philosophical developments. For example, Nicholas Oresme clearly regarded the function of any hypothesis about the world's rotation as being that of 'saving the appearances' or accounting for the observable data, and he clearly regarded as preferable the hypothesis which best satisfied the principle of economy. But the fourteenth-century physicists did not make in any very clear manner that kind of distinction between philosophy and physical science which the philosophy of the Ockhamist movement would appear to facilitate. As we have seen, the affiliations of the several physicists with the nominalist movement in philosophy were not by any means always as close as has sometimes been imagined. Moreover, the use of the principle of economy, as found in the physical speculations of Nicholas Oresme, for example, was already known in the thirteenth century. Robert Grosseteste, for instance, realized quite well that the more economical hypothesis is to be preferred to the less economical. He also realized that there is something peculiar about a mathematical explanation in astronomical physics, in that it does not provide knowledge of causes in a metaphysical sense. One has, then, to be careful in ascribing to the exclusive influence of the Ockhamist movement ideas in fourteenth-century science which, in the abstract, might perhaps have been the result of that movement. The idea of a scientific theory involving *a priori* mental construction could hardly arise except in a post-Kantian intellectual climate; and even the idea of physical theories as being concerned with 'saving the appearances' does not seem to have received special attention from or to have been specially developed by fourteenth-century nominalists.

It is true, however, that one can see a new view of the world coming to birth in the fourteenth century and that this was facilitated by the adoption of the theory of impetus in the explanation of movement. As we have seen, according to this theory celestial dynamics were explained on the same principle as terrestrial dynamics. Just as a stone continues to move after it has left the hand of the thrower, because a certain impetus has been imparted to it, so the celestial bodies move in virtue of an impetus originally imparted to them by God. On this view the first mover, God, appears as efficient rather than as final cause. By saying this I do not mean to imply that men like Nicholas Oresme and Albert of Saxony denied that God is final as well as efficient cause: I mean rather that the impetus theory which they adopted facilitated a shift of emphasis from the Aristotelian idea of God causing the movements of the heavenly bodies by 'drawing' them as final cause to the idea of God as imparting at creation a certain impetus in virtue of which these bodies, encountering no resistance, continued to move. This view might easily suggest that the world is a mechanical or quasi-mechanical system. God set the machine going, as it were, when He created it, after which it continues working on its own without further divine 'interference' save the activity of conservation and concurrence. If this idea were developed, God's function would appear to be that of a hypothesis for explaining the source of movement in the universe. And it would be natural to suggest that consideration of final causes should be excluded from physical science in favour of consideration of efficient causes, as Descartes, for example, insisted.

It must be repeated that I am not attempting to father all the ideas mentioned above on the physicists of the fourteenth century. They were concerned with the problem of motion as a particular problem rather than with drawing broad conclusions from it. And they were certainly not deists. None the less, one can see in the adoption of the impetus theory a step on the road towards a new conception of the material world. Or it might be better to say that it was a step on the road towards the development of physical science as distinct from metaphysics. It facilitated the growth of the idea that the material world can be considered as a system of bodies in motion in which impetus or energy is transmitted from body to body while the sum of energy remains constant. But it is one thing to state that the world, as considered by the physicist, can be regarded in this light, and it is another thing to say that the physicist, in his capacity as physicist, can give an adequate account of the world as a whole. When Descartes later insisted on the exclusion of consideration of final causes by what we would call the physical scientist and the astronomer, he did not say (nor did he think) that consideration of final causes has no place in philosophy. And the physicist-philosophers of the fourteenth century certainly did not say anything of the kind. It is conceivable that reflection on their scientific theories could have prompted them to make a clearer distinction between the world of the physicist and the world of the philosopher than they actually did; but in point of fact the idea that there is a rigid distinction between science and philosophy was an idea of much later growth. Before this idea could develop, science itself had to attain a very much richer and fuller development. In the thirteenth and fourteenth centuries we see the beginnings of empirical science in Christian Europe but only the beginnings. Still, it is as well to realize that the foundations of modern science were laid in mediaeval times. And it is as well also to realize that the development of empirical science is in no way alien in principle to the Christian theology which formed the mental background in the Middle Ages. For if the world is the work of God it is obviously a legitimate and worth-while object of study.

CHAPTER XI

MARSILIUS OF PADUA

Church and State, theory and practice—Life of Marsilius—Hostility to the papal claims—The nature of the State and of law—The legislature and the executive—Ecclesiastical jurisdiction—Marsilius and 'Averroism'—Influence of the Defensor pacis.

1. THE standard political idea of the Middle Ages was the idea of the two swords, of Church and Empire as two intrinsically independent Powers. In other words, the normal mediaeval theory, as presented by St. Thomas, was that Church and State were distinct societies, the former being concerned with man's supernatural well-being and his attainment of his last end, the latter with man's temporal well-being. As man has but one final end, a supernatural end, the Church must be considered superior to the State in point of value and dignity; but that does not mean that the Church is a glorified State enjoying direct jurisdiction in the temporal affairs of particular States, for, on the one hand, the Church is not a State and, on the other hand, each of them, the Church and the State, is a 'perfect' society.[1] All authority of man over man comes ultimately from God; but God wills the existence of the State as well as that of the Church. States existed before the Church, and the institution of the Church by Christ did not abrogate the State or subordinate the State, in the conduct of its own affairs, to the Church.

This view of Church and State is part and parcel of the harmonious philosophical structure achieved in the thirteenth century and associated especially with the name of St. Thomas Aquinas. But it is obvious enough that in practice a harmony of two Powers is inherently unstable, and in point of fact the disputes between papacy and empire, Church and State, loom large on the stage of mediaeval history. The Byzantine emperors had not infrequently attempted to interfere in purely doctrinal questions and to settle these questions by their own decisions; the western emperors did not attempt to usurp the teaching function of the Church, but they

[1] A 'perfect' society is a self-sufficing society, possessing in itself all the means required for attaining its end.

frequently quarrelled with the papacy over questions of jurisdiction, investiture and so forth, and we find first one side, then the other, gaining ground or giving ground, according to circumstances and according to the personal strength and vigour of the leaders on either side and their personal interest in advancing and maintaining practical claims. But we are not concerned here with the inevitable frictions and practical disputes between popes and emperors or kings: we are concerned only with the wider issues of which these practical disputes were, in part, the symptoms. (I say 'in part' because in the concrete historical life of the Middle Ages disputes between Church and State were in practice inevitable, even when no fundamentally conflicting theories about the relations of the two Powers were involved.) Whether one calls these wider issues 'theoretical' or 'practical' depends largely on one's point of view; it depends, I mean, on whether or not one regards political theory as simply an ideological reflection of concrete historical developments. I do not think, however, that any simple answer to the question is feasible. It is an exaggeration to say that theory is always simply the pale reflection of practice, exercising no influence on practice; and it is an exaggeration to say that political theory is never the reflection of actual practice. Political theory both reflects and influences practice, and whether one should emphasize the active or the passive element can be decided only by unprejudiced examination of the case under discussion. One cannot legitimately affirm *a priori* that a political theory like that of Marsilius of Padua, a theory which emphasized the independence and sovereignty of the State and which formed the antithesis to Giles of Rome's theoretical justification of the attitude of Pope Boniface VIII, was no more than the pale reflection of economic and political changes in the concrete life of the later Middle Ages. Nor is one entitled to affirm *a priori* that theories like that of Marsilius of Padua were the chief factor responsible for the practical disturbance of the harmonious balance between the Powers in so far as there ever was a harmonious balance in the sphere of practice—and for the emergence of sharply defined national entities with claims which amounted to that of complete autonomy. If one states either of these positions *a priori*, one is stating a theory which itself needs justification, and the only justification which could possibly be given would have to take the form of an examination of the actual historical data. In my opinion there are elements of truth in both theories; but it is not possible in a history of philosophy adequately to discuss the problem how far a given political theory was an ideological epiphenomenon of concrete historical changes or how far it played a part in actively influencing the course of history. In what follows, then, I wish to outline the ideas of Marsilius of Padua without committing myself to any decided opinion concerning the actual influence of these ideas or their lack of it. To form a decided opinion in virtue of a preconceived general theory is not, I think, a proper proceeding; and to discuss an actual example in sufficient detail is not possible in a general work. If, then, I expound Marsilius' ideas in a rather 'abstract way', this should not be taken to mean that I discount the influence of actual historical conditions in the formation of these ideas. Nor should incidental remarks concerning the influence of historical conditions on Marsilius' thought be taken to mean that I subscribe to the Marxist thesis concerning the nature of political theory. I do not believe in general *a priori* principles of interpretation to which the facts of history have to be fitted; and this holds for the anti-Marxist as well as for the Marxist theories.

2. It is uncertain in what year Marsilius of Padua was born. It would seem that he gave himself to the study of medicine; but in any case he went to Paris, where he was rector of the university from September 1312 until May 1313. The subsequent course of events is by no means clear. It appears that he returned to Italy and studied 'natural philosophy' with Peter of Abano from 1313 to the end of 1315. He may then have visited Avignon, and it appears from bulls of 1316 and 1318 that he was offered benefices at Padua. At Paris he worked on the *Defensor pacis*, with the collaboration of his friend John of Jandun, the book being finished on June 24th, 1324. His enmity towards the papacy and the 'clericals' must have begun at a considerably earlier date, of course; but in any case the book was denounced, and in 1326 Marsilius of Padua and John of Jandun fled from Paris and took refuge at Nuremberg with Ludwig of Bavaria, whom Marsilius accompanied to Italy, entering Rome in his entourage in January 1327. In a papal bull of April 3rd, 1327, Marsilius and John were denounced as 'sons of perdition and fruits of malediction'. The presence of Marsilius at his court was an obstacle to the success of Ludwig's attempts at reconciliation, first with John XXII, then with Benedict XII; but Ludwig had a high opinion of the author of the *Defensor pacis*. The Franciscan group did not share this opinion, and

Ockham criticized the work in his *Dialogus*, a criticism which led to the composition of the *Defensor minor*. Marsilius also published his *De iurisdictione imperatoris in causis matrimonialibus*, which was designed to serve the emperor in a practical difficulty concerning the projected marriage of his son. Marsilius maintained that the emperor could, on his own authority, dissolve an existing marriage and also dispense from the impediment of consanguinity. These two works were composed about 1341–2. A discourse of Clement VI, dated April 10th, 1343, asserts that the 'heresiarchs', Marsilius of Padua and John of Jandun, were both dead; but the exact date of Marsilius' death is unknown. (John of Jandun died considerably earlier than Marsilius.)

3. In his book on Marsilius of Padua[1] Georges de Lagarde finds the key to his mentality, not in a passion for religious reformation nor in a passion for democracy, but in an enthusiastic love for the idea of the lay State or, negatively, in a hatred of ecclesiastical interference in State affairs, that is to say, in a hatred of the doctrines of papal supremacy and of independent ecclesiastical jurisdiction. This is, I think, quite true. Possessed by an ardent enthusiasm for the autonomous State, the idea of which he supported by frequent references to Aristotle, Marsilius set out to show that the papal claims and the ecclesiastical jurisdiction laid down in the Canon Law involve a perversion of the true idea of the State and that they have no foundation in the Scriptures. His examination of the natures of Church and State and of their mutual relations leads him to a theoretical reversal of hierarchy of Powers: the State is completely autonomous and supreme.

But Marsilius was not simply pursuing an abstract theory. It appears that at one time he permitted himself to be lured from the quiet paths of science by the invitations of the Duke of Verona, Can Grande della Scala, and by Matteo Visconti of Milan. In any case his sympathies lay with the Ghibelline party, and he considered that the papal policy and claims were responsible for the wars and miseries of northern Italy. He lays at the door of the popes, who have disturbed the peace with their excommunications and interdicts, the responsibility for the wars, the violent deaths of thousands of the faithful, the hatred and contention, the moral corruption and crimes, the devastated cities and uncared for countryside, the churches abandoned by their pastors, and the

[1] *Naissance de l'esprit laïque;* Cahier II, *Marsile de Padoue.*

whole catalogue of evils which afflict the Italian City-States.[1] He may, no doubt, have exaggerated the situation: but the point I wish to make is that Marsilius was not simply theorizing in the abstract; his starting-point was a concrete historical situation, and his interpretation of this concrete situation reflected itself in his political theory. Similarly, in his account of the State as it ought to be we see an idealized reflection of the contemporary north-Italian republic, just as the Platonic and Aristotelian political theories were, to a greater or less extent, the idealization of the Greek City-State. The ideal of the empire, which is so prominent in Dante's political thought, is without any real effect on Marsilius' thought.

When, therefore, in the first *Dictio* of the *Defensor pacis* Marsilius discusses the nature of the State and draws on the teaching of Aristotle, it must be remembered that his thought is not moving in the purely abstract sphere but that it reflects his interpretation of and his enthusiasm for the Italian City-State. It may even be that the more abstract passages and the more Aristotelian parts are due to the influence of his collaborator, John of Jandun. Again, when in the second *Dictio* he discusses the Scriptural foundation, or lack of foundation, of the papal claims and of the independent ecclesiastical jurisdiction demanded by the Canon Law, it must be remembered that there is no real evidence that he had ever studied Civil Law and that his knowledge of Canon Law and of papal pronouncements did not, in spite of what some writers have maintained, amount to much more than knowledge of a Collection of Canons of the pseudo-Isidore and the bulls of Boniface VIII, Clement V and John XXII. He may have been acquainted with the Decree of Gratian; but the passages which are adduced as evidence of a knowledge of Gratian are too vague to serve as a proof of anything which could truly be called 'knowledge'. When Marsilius fulminated against the papal claims, he had primarily in mind the papal supremacy as conceived by Boniface VIII and those who shared his outlook. This is not to say, of course, that Marsilius did not deliver a general attack on the Church and its claims; but it is as well to remember that this attack had its roots in enmity towards the specific claims of specific ecclesiastics. When one reads in the third and concluding *Dictio* the summary of Marsilius' position, one should bear in mind both the historical situation which gave rise to and was reflected in

[1] *Def. pacis*, 2, 26, 19.

his theoretical statements and the abstract theory which, though historically conditioned, had its influence in inculcating a certain general mentality and outlook.

4. The first *Dictio* begins with a quotation from Cassiodorus in praise of peace. The quotations from classical writers and from the Bible cause perhaps a first impression of abstraction and antiquity; but very soon, after remarking that Aristotle has described almost all the causes of strife in the State, Marsilius remarks that there is another cause, which neither Aristotle nor any of his contemporaries or predecessors saw or could see.[1] This is a covert reference to Marsilius' particular reason for writing; and thus the actuality of the book makes itself felt at once, despite the borrowings from former writers.

The account of the nature of the State as a perfect or self-sufficing community which is brought into being for the sake of life but exists for the sake of the good life,[2] and the account of the 'parts' of the State[3] depend on Aristotle; but Marsilius adds an account of the priestly 'part' or order.[4] The priesthood is, then, part of the State, and though Christian revelation has corrected error in teaching and provided a knowledge of the salutary truth, the Christian priesthood remains none the less a part of the State. Marsilius' fundamental 'Erastianism' is thus asserted very early in the *Defensor pacis*.

Leaving out of account the cases where God directly appoints the ruler, one can reduce the different types of government to two fundamental types, government which exists by consent of the subjects and government which is contrary to the will of the subjects.[5] The latter type of government is tyrannical. The former type does not necessarily depend on election; but a government which depends on election is superior to a government which does not depend on election.[6] It may be that non-hereditary rule is the best form of elective government, but it does not follow that this form of government is best suited for any particular State.

Marsilius' idea of law, which next comes up for discussion in the *Defensor pacis*, involved a change from the attitude of thirteenth-century thinkers like St. Thomas. In the first place law has its origin, not in the positive function of the State, but in the need of preventing quarrels and strife.[7] Statute law is also rendered

[1] 1, 3. [2] 1, 4. [3] 1, 5. [4] 1, 5–6.
[5] 1, 9.5. [6] 1, 9, 7. [7] 1, 5, 7.

necessary with a view to preventing malice on the part of judges and arbiters.[1] Marsilius gives, indeed, several definitions of law. For example, law is the knowledge or doctrine or universal judgment concerning the things which are just and useful to the State's life.[2] But knowledge of these matters does not really constitute law unless a coercive precept is added touching their observance. In order that there should be a 'perfect law' there must be knowledge of what is just and useful and of what is unjust and harmful; but the mere expression of such knowledge is not law in the proper sense unless it is expressed as a precept backed up by sanctions.[3] Law is, therefore, a preceptive and coercive rule, fortified by sanctions applicable in this life.[4]

It would seem to follow from this that law concerns the objectively just and useful, that is to say, what is just and useful in itself, with a logical priority to any positive enactment and that Marsilius implicitly accepts the idea of natural law. So he does to a certain extent. In the second *Dictio*[5] he distinguishes two meanings of natural law. First, it may mean those statutes of the legislator on the rightness and obligatory character of which practically all people agree; for example that parents are to be honoured. These statutes depend on human institution; but they are called natural laws inasmuch as they are enacted by all nations. Secondly, 'there are certain people who call "natural law" the dictate of right reason in regard to human acts, and natural law in this sense they subsume under divine law'. These two senses of natural law, says Marsilius, are not the same; the phrase is used equivocally. In the first case natural law denotes the laws which are enacted in all nations and are practically taken for granted, their rightness being recognized by all: in the second case it denotes the dictates of right reason, which include dictates not universally recognized. From this it follows that 'certain things are licit according to human law which are not licit according to divine law, and conversely'.[6] Marsilius adds that licit and illicit are to be interpreted according to divine rather than human law when the two conflict. In other words, he does not simply deny the existence of natural law in the sense in which St. Thomas would understand it; but he pays little attention to the concept. His philosophy of law represents a transition stage on the way to the rejection of natural law in St. Thomas's sense.

That there is a shift of emphasis and a change in attitude is

[1] 1, 11. [2] 1, 10, 3. [3] 1, 10, 5. [4] 2, 8, 5. [5] 12, 7–8. [6] 2, 12, 9.

clear from the fact, already indicated, that Marsilius was unwilling to apply the word 'law' in a strict sense to any precept which is not fortified by sanctions applicable in this life. It is for this reason that he refused to allow that the law of Christ (*Evangelica Lex*) is law properly speaking: it is rather a speculative or operative doctrine, or both.[1] He speaks in the same strain in the *Defensor minor*.[2] Divine law is compared with the prescriptions of a doctor, it is not law in the proper sense. As natural law in the sense of the Thomist philosophy is expressly said by Marsilius to be reckoned under divine law, it, too, cannot be said to be law in the same sense that the law of the State is law. Thus, although Marsilius does not deny outright the Thomist conception of natural law, he implies that the standard type of law is the law of the State, and his doctrine points towards the conclusion that the law of the State is autonomous and supreme. As Marsilius subordinated Church to State, it would seem that he tended towards the idea that it is the State alone which can judge whether or not a given law is consonant with the divine law and is an application of it; but, on the other hand, as he reserved the name of law in the proper sense to the positive law of the State and refused it to divine law and to natural law in the Thomist sense, one might equally well say that his thought tended towards the separation of law and morality.

5. Law in the proper sense being human law, the law of the State, who precisely is the legislator? The legislator or first efficient cause of law is the people, the totality of citizens, or the more weighty part (*pars valentior*) of the citizens.[3] The more weighty part is estimated according to quantity and quality of persons: it does not necessarily mean a numerical majority, but it must, of course, be legitimately representative of the whole people. It can be understood either in accordance with the actually obtaining customs of States or it may be determined according to the opinions expressed by Aristotle in the sixth book of the *Politics*.[4] However, since there are practical difficulties in the way of the multitude's drawing up the laws, it is suitable and useful that the drawing up of laws should be entrusted to a committee or commission, which will then propose the laws for acceptance or rejection by the legislator.[5] These ideas of Marsilius reflect in large part the theory, if not always the practice, of the Italian republics.

The next point for consideration is the nature, origin and scope

[1] 2, 9, 3. [2] 1, 4. [3] 1, 12, 3. [4] 1, 12, 4. [5] 1, 13, 8.

of executive power in the State, the *pars principans*. The office of the prince is to direct the community according to the norms set by the legislator; his task is to apply and enforce the laws. This subordination of the prince to the legislator is best expressed when the executive power is conferred on each successive prince by election. Election is, in itself at least, preferable to hereditary succession.[1] In each State there should be a supreme executive power, though it does not necessarily follow that this power should be in the hands of one man.[2] Supremacy means that all other powers, executive or judicial, must be subordinate to the prince; but the supremacy is qualified by the assertion that if the prince transgresses the laws or fails seriously in the duties of his office he should be corrected, or if necessary removed from office, by the legislator or by those appointed by the legislature for this task.[3]

Marsilius' dislike of tyranny and his preference for the election of the executive reflect his concern with the well-being of the Italian City-State, while the concentration of supreme executive and judicial power in the hands of the prince reflects the general consolidation of power in the European States. It has been maintained that Marsilius envisaged a clear separation of powers; but though he separated the executive from the legislative power, he subordinated the judiciary to the executive. Again, it is true that he admitted in a sense the sovereignty of the people; but the later theory of the social contract has no clear explicit foundation in Marsilius' political theory. The subordination of the executive power to the legislature is supported by practical considerations touching the good of the State rather than by a philosophic theory of the social contract.

6. In discussing the nature of the State Marsilius has in view, of course, his coming attack on the Church. For example, the concentration of executive and judicial power, without exception, in the hands of the prince is designed to deprive the Church of all 'natural' foundations to its claims. It remains to be seen if the Church can support her claims from the data of revelation; and this subject is considered in the second part of the *Defensor pacis*. The transition from the first to the second part[4] consists of the statements that the State can function and that its parts can discharge their proper tasks only if the State is in a condition of peace and tranquillity; that it cannot be in this condition if the prince is interfered with or suffers aggression; and that the Church

[1] 1, 15, 3; cf. 1, 16. [2] 1, 17, 2, [3] 1, 18. [4] 1, 19.

has in fact disturbed the peace by its interference with the rights of the Holy Roman Emperor and of other persons.

After considering various definitions or meanings of the words 'Church', 'temporal', 'spiritual', 'judge' and 'judgment' Marsilius proceeds to argue[1] that Christ claimed no temporal jurisdiction when He was in this world but subjected Himself to the civil power, and that the Apostles followed Him in this. The priesthood, then, has no temporal power. Marsilius goes on in the following chapters to minimize the 'power of the keys' and sacerdotal jurisdiction. As to heresy, the temporal legislator may make it a crime with a view to securing the temporal well-being of the State; but to legislate on this point and to exercise coercion belongs to the State, not to the Church.[2]

After an excursus on absolute poverty, from which he draws the conclusion that Church endowments remain the property of the donor, so that the Church has only the use of them,[3] Marsilius proceeds to attack the divine institution of the papacy. It would be out of place to enter upon a discussion of Marsilius' attempt to disprove the papal claims by reference to the Scriptures; nor does space permit any detailed consideration of his conciliar theory, but it is important to note, first that Marsilius assumes that the Scriptures alone are the rule of faith, and secondly that decisions of General Councils are not regarded by him as having any coercive force unless ratified by the temporal legislator. Canon Law is dismissed as having no weight. A historical treatment of papal encroachments leads up to a consideration of the dispute between John XXII and Ludwig of Bavaria.[4] Mention is made of the state of affairs in Italy and of the excommunication of Matteo Visconti.

In the third part Marsilius gives a brief summary of the conclusions he has reached in the *Defensor pacis*. He makes it quite clear that he is primarily concerned, not with the furtherance of democracy nor with any particular form of government, but rather with the rejection of papal supremacy and ecclesiastical jurisdiction. Moreover, the whole course of the work shows that Marsilius was not content simply with rejecting ecclesiastical interference in temporal matters; he went on to subordinate the Church to the State in all matters. His position was not that of one protesting against the encroachments of the Church on the sphere of the State while admitting the Church as a 'perfect society', autonomous in spiritual affairs: on the contrary, his position was

[1] 2, 4. [2] 2, 10. [3] 2, 14. [4] 2, 26.

frankly 'Erastian' and, at the same time, of a revolutionary character. Previté-Orton is obviously quite correct when he says that, in spite of disproportions in the work, there is unity of purpose and idea in the *Defensor pacis*. 'Everything is subordinated to the main aim, that of the destruction of papal and ecclesiastical power.' In the first part of the work, that which deals with the nature of the State, those themes are discussed and those conclusions are drawn which will serve as foundation for the second part. On the other hand, Marsilius was not animated by a hatred against papal supremacy and ecclesiastical jurisdiction for hatred's sake: as we have seen, his actual starting-point was what he regarded as the deplorable condition of northern Italy. He speaks on occasion about the empire, of course, and he apparently envisages the emperor as ratifying decisions of General Councils; but he was interested above all in the City-State or republic, which he considered to be supreme and autonomous in matters spiritual and temporal. There is, indeed, some excuse for regarding him as a forerunner of Protestantism; his attitude towards the Scriptures and towards the papacy shows as much; but it would be a great mistake to regard his attack on the papacy and on ecclesiastical jurisdiction as having proceeded from religious convictions or zeal. One can, of course, admit that in the course of his writing Marsilius became a 'religious controversialist'; but his religious controversy was undertaken, not for the sake of religion, but in the interests of the State. What characterizes him is his conception of the completely autonomous State. He admitted divine law, it is true; but he also admitted that human law may conflict with divine law, and in this case all subjects of the State, clerics and laymen, must obey human law, though one passage, mentioned earlier, seems to imply that if a law of the State obviously contradicts the law of Christ, the Christian should follow the latter. But since the Church, according to Marsilius, has no fully independent authority to interpret the Scriptures, it would scarcely be possible for the Christian to appeal to the teaching of the Church. In spite of its roots in contemporary history Marsilius' political theory looks forward to conceptions of the nature and function of the State which are modern in character, and which have scarcely brought happiness to mankind.

7. It has been maintained that Marsilius' political theory is 'Averroistic' in character. Speaking of the *Defensor pacis* Étienne Gilson remarks that it is 'as perfect an example of political

Averroism as one could wish'.[1] This Averroism consists in the application to politics of the Averroistic dichotomy between the sphere of faith and the sphere of reason. Man has two ends, a natural end, which is served by the State, utilizing the teaching of philosophy, and a supernatural end, served by the Church, utilizing the data of revelation. As the two ends are distinct, the State is completely independent, and the Church has no title to interfere in political affairs. However, although Gilson stresses the Averroism of John of Jandun, he admits that the *Defensor pacis* is due principally to Marsilius of Padua and that what one actually knows of the Averroism of Marsilius 'does not go beyond an application of the theoretic separation of reason and faith to the domain of politics, where he transmutes it into a strict separation of the spiritual and the temporal, of the Church and the State'.[2]

Maurice De Wulf, on the other hand, held that any collaboration of John of Jandun in the *Defensor pacis* has to be excluded, on the ground of the work's unity of plan and homogeneity of style, and was of the opinion that, although Marsilius had been in contact with Averroistic circles, he was influenced much more by the political writings of Aristotle.[3] The Church is not a true society, at least it is not a 'perfect society' since it has no temporal sanctions at its disposal wherewith to enforce its laws. The Church is little more than an association of Christians who find their true unity in the State; and, though the priesthood is of divine institution, the Church's task, as far as this world is concerned, is to serve the State by creating the moral and spiritual conditions which will facilitate the work of the State.

De Wulf's view of the matter, apart from his rejection of any collaboration on the part of John of Jandun, seems to me to be more in accordance with the tone and spirit of the *Defensor pacis* than the idea that the work is of specifically Averroistic inspiration. Marsilius thought that the Church's claims and activity hindered and disturbed the peace of the State, and he found in the Aristotelian conception of the autonomous and self-sufficing State the key to the solution of the problem, provided that the Church was subordinated to the State. It seems to me that Marsilius was animated much more by regard for what he considered to be the welfare of the State than by theoretical considerations concerning

[1] *La philosophie au moyen âge* (1944), p. 592.
[2] *Ibid.*, p. 691
[3] *Histoire de la philosophie médiévale*, tome III (1947), p. 142.

the end of man. Nevertheless, this in no way excludes an Averroistic influence on Marsilius' thought and, after all, Averroism was, or professed to be, integral Aristotelianism. Averroes was regarded as the 'Commentator'. Marsilius was influenced by Peter of Abano and was in touch with John of Jandun; and both of these men were animated by the Averroistic veneration for Aristotle. There was really no homogeneous doctrine or set of doctrines which one can call 'Averroism'; and if it is true that 'Averroism' was less a doctrine than an attitude, one can perfectly well admit the 'Averroism' of Marsilius without being thereby compelled to conclude that his inspiration was derived from the Averroists rather than from Aristotle.

8. The *Defensor pacis* was solemnly condemned on April 27th, 1327; but it does not appear that the work was really studied by Marsilius' contemporaries, even by those who wrote against it, though Clement VI affirmed that he, when a cardinal, had submitted the work to a profound examination and had discovered therein 240 errors. Clement VI made this assertion in 1343, and we do not possess his publication. In 1378 Gregory XI renewed the condemnations of 1327; but the fact that the majority of the copies of manuscripts were made at the beginning of the fifteenth century seems to confirm the supposition that the *Defensor pacis* was not widely circulated in the fourteenth century. Those who wrote against the work in the fourteenth century tended to see in it little more than an attack on the independence of the Holy See and the immunity of the clergy: they did not realize its historical importance. In the following century the Great Schism naturally gave an impetus to the diffusion of Marsilius' theories; and these ideas exercised their long-term influence more as a 'spirit' than as precisely the ideas of Marsilius of Padua. It is significant that the first printed edition of the *Defensor pacis* was published in 1517 and that the work was apparently utilized by Cranmer and Hooker.

CHAPTER XII

SPECULATIVE MYSTICISM

Mystical writing in the fourteenth century—Eckhart—Tauler—Blessed Henry Suso—Ruysbroeck—Denis the Carthusian—German mystical speculation—Gerson.

1. ONE is accustomed perhaps to think of the sixteenth century, the century of the great Spanish mystics, as the period which was particularly distinguished for mystical writings. It may, indeed, well be that the works of St. Teresa and St. John of the Cross are the supreme achievements of mystical theology, the theoretical exposition, so far as this is possible, of the experimental knowledge of God; but we must remember that there had been writers on mysticism from early Christian times. We have only to think of St. Gregory of Nyssa and of the Pseudo-Dionysius in the Patristic age, of St. Bernard and of Hugh and Richard, of St. Victor in the twelfth century, and of St. Bonaventure and St. Gertrude in the thirteenth century. And in the fourteenth and fifteenth centuries there was a remarkable flowering of mystical writings. This fact is attested by the works of writers like Eckhart (1260–1327), Tauler (*c.* 1300–61), Bl. Henry Suso (*c.* 1295–1366), Ruysbroeck (1293–1381), St. Catherine of Siena (1347–80), Richard Rolle of Hampole (*c.* 1300–49), Walter Hilton (d. 1396), John Gerson (1363–1429), Denis the Carthusian (1402–71), St. Catherine of Bologna (1413–63) and St. Catherine of Genoa (1447–1510). It is with these mystical writings of the fourteenth and early part of the fifteenth centuries that I am concerned in this chapter; but I am concerned with them only in so far as they seem to be relevant to the history of philosophy; I am not concerned with mystical theology as such. This means that I shall confine my attention to philosophic speculation which appears to have been influenced by reflection on the mystical life; and this in turn means in effect that special consideration will be given to two themes, namely the relation of finite being in general and that of the human soul in particular to God. More concretely, it is writers like Eckhart rather than writers like Richard Rolle whose thought will be discussed. In a work on mystical theology as such, attention would have to be paid to writers who cannot be dealt

with here; but in a work on the history of philosophy, attention can be paid only to those who can reasonably be thought of as 'philosophers' according to some traditional or normal use of the term. I do not mean to imply, however, that the writers whom I propose to discuss in this chapter were primarily interested in theory. Even Eckhart, who was much more given to speculation than Henry Suso, for example, was deeply concerned with the practical intensification of religious life. This practical orientation of the mystical writers is shown partly by their use of the vernacular. Eckhart used both German and Latin, his more speculative work being in the latter language; Henry Suso also used both languages; Tauler preached in German; Ruysbroeck wrote in Flemish; and we possess a large collection of Gerson's French sermons, though he wrote mainly in Latin. A profound affective piety, issuing in a desire to draw others to closer union with God, is characteristic of these mystics. Their analyses of the mystical life are not so detailed and complete as those of the later Spanish mystical writers; but they form an important stage in the development of mystical theology.

One might reasonably be inclined to see in the flowering of mystical writing in the fourteenth century a reaction against logical and abstract metaphysical studies, against what some people call 'objective thinking', in favour of the one thing needful, salvation through union with God. And that there was such a reaction seems to be true enough. On the one hand there were the older philosophical traditions and schools; on the other hand there was the *via moderna*, the nominalist movement. The wranglings of the schools could not transform the heart; nor did they bring a man nearer to God. What more natural, then, than that the religious consciousness should turn to a 'philosophy' or pursuit of wisdom which was truly Christian and which looked to the work of divine grace rather than to the arid play of the natural intellect? The remarks of Thomas à Kempis on this matter are well known and have often been quoted. For example, 'I desire to feel compunction rather than to know its definition'; 'a humble rustic who serves God is certainly better than a proud philosopher who, neglecting himself, considers the movement of the heavens'; 'what is the use of much quibbling about hidden and obscure matters, when we shali not be reproved at the Judgment for being ignorant of them?'; 'and what do genera and species matter to us!'[1] Thomas

[1] *Imitation of Christ*, I, I; I, 2; I, 3.

à Kempis (1380–1471) belonged to the Brethren of the Common Life, an association founded by Gerard Groot (1340–84), who had been strongly influenced by the ideas of Ruysbroeck. The Brethren were of importance in the educational field, and they devoted special attention to the religious and moral upbringing of their charges.

But it was not only Scholastic aridities and academic wranglings about abstract questions which influenced, by way of reaction, the mystical writers; some of them seem to have been influenced by the Ockhamist tendency to deny the validity of the traditional natural theology and to relegate all knowledge of God, even of His existence, to the sphere of faith. The answer to this was found by the mystics, or by some of them, in an extension of the idea of experience. Thus, though Henry Suso did not deny the validity of a philosophical approach to God, he tried to show that there is a certitude based on interior experience, when this accords with the revealed truths of faith. And, indeed, had not Roger Bacon, who insisted so much on the experimental method in the acquisition of knowledge, included spiritual experience of God under the general heading of experience? The mystics in their turn saw no reason for confining 'experience' to sense-experience or to consciousness of one's internal acts.

From the philosophical point of view, however, the chief point of interest concerning the mystical writers is their speculative rationalization of religious experience, particularly their pronouncements concerning the relation of the soul to God and, in general, of creatures to God. As is not uncommon with mystical writers of earlier and also later times, some of them made statements which were certainly bold and which were likely to arouse the hostile attention of theologians who regarded the literal sense of such statements. The chief offender in this respect was Eckhart, a number of whose propositions were subsequently condemned, though Henry Suso, his disciple, defended his orthodoxy. There has also been controversy concerning statements made by Ruysbroeck and Gerson. In what follows I shall give particular, if brief, consideration to this speculative aspect of the mystics' writings. Though certain statements, especially in Eckhart's case, are unorthodox if understood in an absolutely literal sense, I do not consider that the writers in question had any intention of being unorthodox. Many of their suspect propositions can be paralleled in earlier writers and are to be seen in the light of the neo-Platonic tradition. In any case I consider that the attempt which has been made in certain quarters to find a new 'German theology' in Eckhart and his disciples is a vain attempt.

2. Meister Eckhart was born about 1260 at Hochheim near Gotha. Joining the Dominican Order he studied and then lectured at Paris. After having been Provincial of Saxony and later Vicar-General of the Order, he returned to Paris in 1311, where he lectured until 1314. From Paris he moved to Cologne; and it was the archbishop of that city who in 1326 instituted an inquiry into Eckhart's doctrine. Eckhart appealed to the Holy See; but in 1329, two years after his death, 28 propositions taken from his later Latin writings were condemned by Pope John XXII.

In the *Quaestiones Parisienses*[1] Eckhart raises the question whether in God being (*esse*) and understanding (*intelligere*) are the same. His answer is, of course, in the affirmative; but he proceeds to maintain[2] that it is not because God is that He understands, but that He is because He is intellect and understanding. Understanding or intellection is 'the foundation of His being' or existence. St. John did not say: 'In the beginning was being, and God was being'; he said: 'In the beginning was the Word, and the Word was with God, and the Word was God.' So, too, Christ said: 'I am the Truth.' Moreover, St. John also says that all things were made through the Word; and the author of the *Liber de càusis* accordingly concludes that 'the first of created things is being'. It follows that God, who is creator, is 'intellect and understanding, but not being or existence' (*non ens vel esse*). Understanding is a higher perfection than being.[3] In God, then, there is neither being nor existence, formally speaking, since God is the cause of being. Of course, if one likes to call understanding 'being', it does not matter; but in this case it must be understood that being belongs to God because He is understanding.[4] 'Nothing which is in a creature is in God save as in its cause, and it is not there formally. And so, since being belongs to creatures, it is not in God save as in its cause; and thus there is not being in God but the purity of being.'[5] This 'purity of being' is understanding. God may have said to Moses, 'I am who am'; but God was then speaking like someone whom one meets in the dark and questions as to his identity, and who, not wishing to reveal himself, answers, 'I am who I am.'[6] Aristotle observed that the power of vision must

[1] Ed. A. Dondaine, O.P., 1936, p. 1.
[2] p. 3.
[3] p. 5.
[4] p. 7.
[5] *Ibid.*
[6] pp. 7–8.

itself be colourless, if it is to see every colour. So God, if He is the cause of all being, must Himself be above being.[1]

In making *intelligere* more fundamental than *esse* Eckhart certainly contradicted St. Thomas; but the general notion that God is not being, in the sense that God is super-being or above being, was a commonplace of the neo-Platonic tradition. The doctrine can be found in the writings of the Pseudo-Dionysius, for example. As we have seen, Eckhart cites the author (in a remote sense) of the *Liber de causis*, namely Proclus; and it is very likely that he was influenced by Theodoric (or Dietrich) of Freiberg (*c.* 1250–*c.* 1311), another German Dominican, who made copious use of Proclus, the neo-Platonist. The neo-Platonic side of the teaching of Albert the Great lived on in the thought of Dominicans like Theodoric of Freiberg, Berthold of Moosburg and Meister Eckhart, though it must be added that what for St. Albert was a relic, as it were, of the past, became for some later thinkers a principal and exaggerated element of their thought. In his (unpublished) commentary on Proclus' *Elementatio theologica* Berthold appealed expressly to Albert the Great.

It has been held that, after having maintained in his earlier works that God is *intelligere* and not *esse*, Eckhart changed his view and later maintained that God is *esse*. This was the opinion of Maurice De Wulf, for example. Others, however, like M. Gilson, will not admit a change of doctrine on Eckhart's part. That Eckhart declared that God is *esse*, existence, is certain. Thus, in the *Opus tripartitum*[2] his first proposition is, *Esse est Deus.* 'God and existence are the same.'[3] And he alludes to the words in the book of Exodus, 'I am who am.' 'God alone is properly speaking being (*ens*), one, true and good.'[4] 'To anyone who asks concerning God what or who He is, the reply is: Existence.'[5] That this sounds like a change of front can hardly be denied; but Gilson argues that Eckhart always emphasized the unity of God and that for him real unity is the property of intelligent being alone; so that the supreme unity of God belongs to Him because He is, above all things, intellect, *intelligere*. Eckhart was certainly understood as seeking a unity in God transcending the distinction of Persons; and one of the condemned propositions (24) runs as follows. 'Every distinction is alien to God, whether in Nature or in Persons. Proof: the Nature itself is one, this one thing, and any

[1] p. 9.
[2] *Prologus generalis;* ed. H. Bascour, O.S.B., 1935.
[3] p. 12.
[4] p. 21.
[5] p. 22.

of the Persons is one and the same thing as the Nature.' The statement and condemnation of this proposition means, of course, that Eckhart was understood by the theologians who examined his writings as teaching that the distinction of Persons in the Godhead is logically posterior to the unity of Nature in such a way that unity transcends trinity. Henry Suso defended Eckhart by observing that to say that each of the divine Persons is identical with the divine Nature is the orthodox doctrine. This is perfectly correct. The examining theologians, however, understood Eckhart to mean that the distinction of Persons from one another is a secondary 'stage', as it were, in the Godhead. But I am not concerned with the orthodoxy or unorthodoxy of Eckhart's trinitarian doctrine: I wish merely to draw attention to the emphasis he laid on the unity of the Godhead. And it is Gilson's contention that this perfect unity belongs to God, according to Eckhart's constant opinion, in virtue of God's being primarily *intelligere*. The pure divine essence is *intelligere*, which is the Father, and it is from the fecundity of this pure essence that there proceed the Son (*vivere*) and the Holy Spirit (*esse*).

The truth of the matter seems to be that there are various strands in Eckhart's thought. When he comments on the words, 'I am who am', in the *Expositio libri Exodi*, he observes that in God essence and existence are the same and that the identity of essence and existence belongs to God alone. In every creature essence and existence are distinct, and it is one thing to ask about the existence of a thing (*de annitate sive de esse rei*) and another to ask about its quiddity or nature. But in the case of God, in whom existence and essence are identical, the fit reply to anyone who asks who or what God is, is that God exists or is. 'For existence is God's essence.'[1] This doctrine is obviously the Thomist doctrine, learnt and accepted by the Dominican. But in the very passage mentioned Eckhart speaks of the 'emanation' of Persons in the Godhead and uses the very neo-Platonic expression *monas monadem gignit*. Moreover, the tendency to find in God a unity without distinction, transcending the distinction of Persons, a tendency to which I have referred above, is also of neo-Platonic inspiration, as is also the doctrine that God is above being. On the other hand, the notion that *intelligere* is the supreme divine perfection seems to be original: in the Plotinian scheme the One is

[1] Meister Eckhart, *Die lateinischen Werke: erster Band*, fasc. 2, pp. 98–100, Stuttgart-Berlin, 1938.

above intellect. Probably it is not possible to harmonize these different strands perfectly; but it is not necessary to suppose that when Eckhart stressed the identity of existence and essence in God he was consciously renouncing his 'former' view that God is *intelligere* rather than *esse*. In the *Expositio libri Genesis* he says: 'the nature of God is intellect, and for Him to be is to understand'; *natura Dei est intellectus, et sibi esse est intelligere.*[1]

However, whether he changed his opinion or not, Eckhart made some rather bold statements in connection with the characterization of God as existence, *esse*. For example, 'outside God there is nothing, inasmuch as it would be outside existence'.[2] God is creator but He does not create 'outside' Himself. A builder makes a house outside himself, but it is not to be imagined that God threw, as it were, or created creatures outside Himself in some infinite space or vacuum.[3] 'Therefore God created all things, not to stand outside Himself or near and beside Himself, like other craftsmen, but He called (them) from nothingness, that is, from non-existence, to existence, which they found and received and had in Him. For He Himself is existence.'[4] There is nothing outside the first cause; for to be outside the first cause would mean being outside existence; since the first cause is God, and God is being and existence. The doctrine that 'outside' God there is nothing is certainly susceptible of an orthodox interpretation: if, that is to say, it is taken as tantamount to the denial of the creature's independence of God. Moreover, when Eckhart declares that, though creatures have their specific natures from their forms, which make them this or that kind of being, their *esse* does not proceed from the form but from God, he might seem to be simply insisting on the facts of divine creation and divine conservation. But he goes further than this and declares that God is to the creature as act to potency, as form to matter, and as *esse* to *ens*, implying apparently that the creature exists by the existence of God. Similarly he says that nothing so lacks distinction as that which is constituted and that from which and through which and by which it is constituted and subsists; and he concludes that nothing so lacks distinction (*nihil tam indistinctum*) as the one God or Unity and the multiplicity of creatures (*creatum numeratum*).

[1] Meister Eckhart, *Die lateinischen Werke: erster Band*, fasc. 1, p. 52, Stuttgart-Berlin, 1937.
[2] *Opus tripartitum, Prologus generalis;* ed. H. Bascour, O.S.B., p. 18.
[3] *Ibid.*, p. 16. [4] *Ibid.*

Now, if these propositions are taken in isolation, it is no wonder that Eckhart should be regarded as teaching a form of pantheism. But there is no justification for taking these texts in isolation, if we wish, that is to say, to discover what Eckhart meant. He was accustomed to use antinomies, to state a thesis and give reasons for it, and then to state an antithesis and give reasons for it. Obviously both sets of statements must be taken into consideration if Eckhart's meaning and intention are to be understood. For example, in the case in point the thesis is that nothing is so distinct from the created as God is. One of the reasons given is that nothing is so distant from anything as is the opposite of that thing. Now, 'God and the creature are opposed as the One and Unnumbered is opposed to number, the numbered and the numerable. Therefore nothing is so distinct (as God) from any created being.' The antithesis is that nothing is so 'indistinct' from the creature as God is; and reasons are given for saying this. It is pretty clear that Eckhart's line of thought was as follows. It is necessary to say that God and creatures are utterly different and opposed; but if one *simply* says this, one is implying what is not true; at least one is stating what is not the whole truth; for the creature exists only by and through God, without whom it is nothing at all.

For an understanding of Eckhart's antinomies one can profitably consult Otto Karrer's *Meister Eckhart*,[1] where he cites texts and appends explanatory notes. Karrer may endeavour in an exaggerated manner to assimilate Eckhart's teaching to that of St. Thomas, but his remarks serve to correct an exaggerated view of Eckhart's departures from St. Thomas. For example, Eckhart states that God alone is and that creatures are nothing and also that God is not being; that all creatures are God and also that all creatures are nothing; that no things are so unlike as Creator and creature and that no things are so like as Creator and creature; that God is in all things and also that God is above all things; that God is in all things as their being and also that God is outside all things. That God alone is and that creatures are nothing means simply that in comparison with God creatures are as nothing. In the Augustinian *Soliloquies*[2] occurs the statement that 'only of the Immortal can one really say that He is', and St. Anselm asserts[3] that in a certain sense God alone is. The statement that all creatures are God refers primarily to their eternal presence in God,

[1] Munich, 1926. [2] 1, 29. [3] *Proslog.*, 27, and *Monol.*, 31.

in the divine intellect, while the statement that they are nothing means that they are nothing apart from God. The doctrine that God and creatures are both like and unlike implies the theory of analogy and it has its roots in the Pseudo-Dionysian *Divine Names.*[1] St. Thomas affirmed[2] that the creature is like God but that God should not be said to be like the creature. God as immanent is in all things by 'power, presence and essence', but He is also above all things, or transcends all things, since He is their creator out of nothing and in no way depends on them. Thus, in his ninth German sermon[3] Eckhart says: 'God is in all creatures . . . and yet He is above them.' In other words, there is no adequate reason for finding pantheism in his thought, even though a considerable number of statements, taken in isolation, would seem to imply that he was a pantheist. What draws one's attention in his thought is the bold way in which he juxtaposes his theses and antitheses rather than the isolated statements, which are frequently commonplaces of mediaeval philosophy and can be discovered in Augustine or the Pseudo-Dionysius or the Victorines or even St. Thomas. As Karrer observes, one can find apparent antinomies even in St. Thomas. For instance, in the *Summa theologica*[4] St. Thomas says that God is above all things (*supra omnia*) and yet in all things (*in omnibus rebus*); that God is in things and yet that all things are in God; that nothing is distant from God and yet that things are said to be distant from God. One condemned proposition of Eckhart begins, 'all creatures are one pure nothingness'; and to say that his intentions were not heterodox is not, of course, to question the legitimacy of the ecclesiastical action which was taken, since it is obvious enough that the propositions in question could easily be misinterpreted, and what was condemned was the proposition as it stood taken in its literal or natural sense but not necessarily as the author understood and meant it. The proposition in question was condemned as 'badly sounding, rash and suspected of heresy', and Rome could hardly judge of it in any other way when it was presented for theological comment and judgment. To realize this, one has only to read the following passage in the fourth German sermon.[5] 'All creatures are a pure nothing. I do not say that they are little or something; they are a pure nothing.' But he goes on to

[1] 9, 6.
[2] *Summa theologica*, 1, 4, 3, *ad* 4.
[3] Meister Eckhart, *Die deutschen Werke: erster Band, Meister Eckhart's Predigten*, fasc. 2, p. 143.
[4] 1, 8, 1, *ad* 1 ff.
[5] *Op. cit.*, fasc. 1, pp. 69–70.

explain what he means. 'All creatures have no being, as their being depends on the presence of God. If God turned away from creatures for one moment, they would be reduced to nothing.' The historian of philosophy, however, is concerned with the author's intended meaning, not with the theological 'note' to be attached to isolated propositions; and it is, I think, to be regretted that some historians have apparently allowed the boldness of some of Eckhart's propositions to blind them both to the general context and meaning and to the history of the propositions in question.

Eckhart also made some strange statements concerning the act of creation. In the *Expositio libri Genesis* he says, with reference to the statement that God created 'in the beginning', that this 'beginning' is the 'now' of eternity, the indivisible 'now' (*nunc*) in which God is eternally God and the eternal emanation of the divine Persons takes place.[1] He goes on to say that if anyone asks why God did not create the world before He did, the answer is that He could not do so; and He could not do so because He creates the world in the same 'now' in which He is eternally God. It is false to imagine that God awaited, as it were, a moment in which to create the world. To put the matter crudely, in the same 'now' in which God the Father exists and generates His coeternal Son He also creates the world. At first hearing at least this sounds as though Eckhart meant to teach that creation is from eternity, that it is coeternal and bound up with the generation of the Son. Indeed, the first three condemned propositions show clearly that the examining theologians understood him in this sense.

It may be, of course, that Eckhart meant the eternity of creation to refer to the object of the creative act, the actual world, and not only to the act of creation as it is in God. This is certainly the natural interpretation of many of the statements he makes. But in this case are we also to take with absolute literalness his statement that 'creation' and every work of God is simultaneously perfected and finished in the very beginning of creation?[2] If so, would not this imply that there is no time and that the Incarnation, for instance, took place at the beginning of creation? It seems to me that Eckhart was thinking of creation as the work of God who is not in time. God created in the beginning, he says, 'that is, in Himself', since God Himself is the *Principium*.[3] For God there is

[1] Meister Eckhart, *Die lateinischen Werke; erster Band*, fasc. 1, p. 50, Stuttgart-Berlin, 1937.

[2] *Opus tripartitum, Prologi*, p. 18; ed. H. Bascour, O.S.B.

[3] *Ibid.*, p. 14.

no past or future; for Him all things are present. So He may rightly be said to have completed His work at the moment of creation. God is the beginning and end of all things, 'the first and the last'; and since God is eternal, existing in one eternal 'now', He must be conceived as eternally creating all things in that eternal 'now'. I am not suggesting that Eckhart's statements, taken as they stand, were correct from the theological point of view; but he seems to me to have been looking at the creation of the world from what one might call God's point of view and to have been insisting that one should not imagine that God created the world 'after' a time in which there was no world. As to the connection of creation with the generation of the Son, Eckhart was thinking of the words of St. John:[1] 'All things were made by him (the Word): and without him was made nothing that was made.' Coupling these words with the statement contained in the first verse of the first chapter of Genesis, 'In the beginning God created heaven and earth', and understanding 'beginning' with reference to God, that is to say, as referring to God's eternal 'now', he says that God created the world simultaneously with the generation of the Son, by whom 'all things were made'. This would certainly seem to imply that there was no beginning of time and to amount to a denial of creation in time; but in the *Expositio libri Genesis*,[2] after referring to the Platonic Ideas or *rationes rerum* and saying that the Word is the *ratio idealis*, he goes on to quote Boethius and says that God created all things *in ratione et secundum rationem idealem*. Again, the 'beginning' in which God created heaven and the earth is the *intellectus* or *intelligentia*. It is possible, then, that Eckhart did not mean that the object of the creative act, the actual world, is eternal, but rather that God eternally conceived and willed creation in and through the Word. This, in any case, is what he later said he had meant. 'Creation, indeed, and every act of God is the very essence of God. Yet it does not follow from this that if God created the world from eternity, the world on this account exists from eternity, as the ignorant think. For creation in the passive sense is not eternal, just as the created itself is not eternal.'[3] Eckhart obviously utilized sayings like that of St. Albert the Great: 'God created from eternity, but the created is not from eternity,'[4] and of St. Augustine: 'In the eternal Word dost Thou

[1] 1, 3. [2] *Die lateinischen Werke: erster Band*, fasc. 1, pp. 49–50.
[3] Cf. Daniels, *Eine lateinische Rechtfertigungsschrift des Meister Eckhart*, p. 10, n. 8. *Beiträge*, 23, 5, Münster i.W., 1923.
[4] Commentary on the *Celestial Hierarchy* of the Pseudo-Dionysius, 4.

speak eternally all that Thou speakest; and yet not all exists at once and from eternity that Thou effectest in speaking.'[1]

We seem perhaps to have strayed far from Eckhart the mystic. But the mystic aims at union with God, and it is not unnatural that a speculative mystic like Eckhart should emphasize the immanence of God in creatures and their dwelling in God. He did not deny God's transcendence; he affirmed it. But he certainly used exaggerated expressions and ambiguous expressions in stating the relations of creatures in general to God. A like boldness and proneness to exaggeration can be seen in his statements concerning the relation of the human soul in particular to God. In the human soul there is an element, which he called *archa* and which is uncreated. This element is the intelligence.[2] In virtue of *intelligere* the soul is deiform, since God Himself is *intelligere*. But the supreme mystical union with God does not take place through the activities of love and knowledge, which are activities of the soul and not the essence of the soul: it takes place in the innermost recess of the soul, the 'spark' or *scintilla animae*, where God unites the soul to Himself in a hidden and ineffable manner. The intellect apprehends God as Truth, the will as the Good: the essence of the soul, however, its citadel (*bürgelin*), is united with God as *esse*. The essence of the soul, also called its 'spark' (*vünkelin* or *scintilla*) is simple; it is on it that the image of God is stamped; and in the mystical union it is united with God as one and simple, that is to say, with the one simple divine essence transcending the distinction of Persons.[3] Eckhart thus preaches a mystical union which reminds one of Plotinus' 'flight of the alone to the Alone', and one can see the parallelism between his psychology and his metaphysic. The soul has a simple, unitary ground or essence and God has a simple essence transcending the distinction of Persons: the supreme mystical union is the union of the two. But this doctrine of a ground of the soul which is superior to the intelligence as a power does not necessarily mean that the soul's presence is not, in a higher sense, intellect. Nor does the doctrine that the ground of the soul is united with God as *esse* necessarily mean that the *esse* is not *intelligere*. In other words, I do not think that the mystical teaching of Eckhart necessarily contradicts Gilson's view that the statement that God is *esse* involves no break with the earlier statements that God is *intelligere*. The Sermons seem to make it

[1] *Conf.*, 11, 7. [2] Cf. twelfth German sermon, pp. 197–8. Cf. p. 189, n. 3.
[3] Cf. Meister Eckhart, *Die deutschen Werke: erster Band, Meister Eckhart's Predigten*, fasc. 1, pp. 24–45. Stuttgart-Berlin, 1936.

clear that Eckhart did not change his opinion. He speaks of the ground of the soul as intellect.

Of the union mystically effected between God and the soul Eckhart speaks in an extremely bold way. Thus in the German sermon on the text, 'the just shall live for evermore; and their reward is with the Lord',[1] he declares that 'we are wholly transformed and changed into God'. And he goes on to say that, just as the bread is changed into the Body of Christ, so is the soul changed into God in such a way that no distinction remains. 'God and I we are one. By knowledge I take God into myself; by love I enter into God.' Just as fire changes wood into itself, 'so we are transformed into God'. So too in the following sermon[2] Eckhart says that just as the food which I eat becomes one with my nature so do we become one with the divine nature.

Not unnaturally, statements of this kind did not pass unnoticed. The statement that there is something uncreated in the soul was censured, and the statement that we are wholly transformed into God in a manner similar to that of the transformation of bread into Christ's Body was condemned as heretical. In his self-justification Eckhart admitted that it is false to say that the soul or any part of it is uncreated; but he protested that his accusers had overlooked his having declared that the supreme powers of the soul were created in and with the soul.[3] In point of fact Eckhart had implied that there is something uncreated in the soul, and it is not to be wondered at that his words led to trouble; but he maintained that by 'uncreated' he meant 'not created *per se*, but concreated' (with the soul). Moreover, he had said not that the soul is uncreated but that if the whole soul were essentially and totally intellect, it would be uncreated. It is, however, difficult to see how he could maintain this, unless by 'intellect' he meant the ground of the soul, which is the image of God. In this case he may have meant that the soul, if totally and essentially the image of God (*imago Dei*), would be indistinguishable from the Word. This seems to be its probable meaning.

As to the statement that 'we are transformed and changed into God', Eckhart admits that it is an error.[4] Man, he says, is not the 'image of God, the unbegotten Son of God; but he is (made) to the image of God'. He goes on to say that just as many hosts on many altars are turned into the one Body of Christ, though the accidents

[1] *Wisdom* 6, 16; *op. cit.*, fasc. 2, pp. 99–115.
[2] *Op. cit.*, p. 119.
[3] Daniels, p. 5, n. 4; p. 17, n. 6.
[4] Daniels, p. 15, n. 1.

of each host remain, so 'we are united to the true Son of God, members of the one head of the Church who is Christ'. In other words, he admits that his original statements were exaggerated and incorrect, and that the comparison of the union of the soul with God to transubstantiation is an analogy, not a parallel. As a matter of fact, however, though Eckhart's statements in his sermons concerning mystical union with God were obviously *male sonantes* as they stood, they are by no means exceptional among mystical writers, even among some whose orthodoxy has never seriously been called in question. Phrases like man becoming God or the transformation of the soul into God can be found in the works of writers of unquestioned orthodoxy. If the mystic wishes to describe the mystical union of the soul with God and its effects, he has to make use of words which are not designed to express any such thing. For example, in order to express the closeness of the union, the elevation of the soul and the effect of the union on the soul's activity, he employs a verb like 'transform' or 'change into'. But 'change into' denotes such processes as assimilation (of food), consumption of material by fire, production of steam from water, heat from energy, and so on, whereas the mystical union of the soul with God is *sui generis* and really requires an altogether new and special word to describe it. But if the mystic coined a brand new word for this purpose, it would convey nothing at all to anyone who lacked the experience in question. Therefore he has to employ words in more or less ordinary use, even though these words inevitably suggest pictures and parallels which do not strictly apply to the experience he is attempting to describe. There is nothing to be surprised at, then, if some of the mystic's statements, taken literally, are inadequate or even incorrect. And if the mystic is also theologian and philosopher, as Eckhart was, inexactitude is likely to affect even his more abstract statements, at least if he attempts to express in theological and philosophical statements an experience which is not properly expressible, employing for this purpose words and phrases which either suggest parallels that are not strict parallels or already possess a defined meaning in theology and philosophy.

Moreover, Eckhart's thought and expression were influenced by a number of different sources. He was influenced, for example, by St. Thomas, by St. Bonaventure, by the Victorines, by Avicenna, by the Pseudo-Dionysius, by Proclus, by the Christian Fathers. He was, too, a deeply religious man who was primarily interested in man's attitude to and experience of God: he was not primarily a systematic philosopher, and he never systematically thought through and rendered consistent the ideas and phrases which he had found in various authors and the ideas which occurred to him in his own meditations on the Scriptures. If, then, it is asked whether certain statements made by Eckhart are theologically orthodox when taken in isolation and according to their 'natural' meaning, the answer can hardly be any other than a negative answer. Eckhart lived at a time when exactitude and accuracy of expression were expected; and the fact that he made his bold and exaggerated statements in sermons, the hearers of which might easily misunderstand his real intentions, renders the theological censure of certain propositions easily understandable. On the other hand, if it is asked whether Eckhart intended to be heterodox and whether he intended to found a 'German theology', the answer must also be in the negative. Disciples like Henry Suso warmly defended the Master against charges of heresy; and a man like Suso would never have done this had he seen any reason to doubt Eckhart's personal orthodoxy. To my mind it seems absurd either to make of Eckhart a 'German thinker' in revolt against Catholic orthodoxy or to attack the theologians who took exception to certain of his statements as though there were nothing in these statements to which they were entitled to take exception.

3. John Tauler was born at Strasbourg about the year 1300 and entered the Dominican Order at an early age. He did his studies at Paris; but it is clear that he was already more attracted to the mystical writers and to the writers influenced by neo-Platonism than to the logical investigations of contemporary philosophers or the purely abstract metaphysical speculations of the Schoolmen. He is famous as a preacher rather than as a theologian or a philosopher, and his preaching seems to have been especially concerned with the reformation and deepening of the spiritual life of religious and clergy. At the time of the Black Death he ministered heroically to the sick and dying. His writings present an orthodox Catholic and Christocentric mysticism, in distinction from the heretical and pantheistic mystical doctrines which were strenuously propagated at the time by various associations. He died in the city of his birth in the year 1361.

In Tauler's writings we find the same psychological doctrine of the 'spark' or 'foundation' of the soul as in the writings of Eckhart. The image of God resides in this apex or highest part of the soul, and it is by retreating within himself, transcending images and figures, that a man finds God. If a man's 'heart' (*Gemüt*) is turned towards this foundation of the soul, that is to say, if it is turned towards God, his faculties of intellect and will function as they ought; but if his 'heart' is turned away from the foundation of the soul, from the indwelling God, his faculties, too, are turned away from God. In other words, between the foundation of the soul and the faculties Tauler finds a link, *das Gemüt*, which is a permanent disposition of the soul in regard to its foundation or apex or 'spark'.

Tauler not only utilized the writings of St. Augustine, St. Bonaventure and the Victorines, but also those of the Pseudo-Dionysius; and he seems to have read some Proclus. He was also strongly influenced by Eckhart's teaching. But, whereas Eckhart not infrequently spoke in such a way that his orthodoxy was called in question, it would be superfluous to raise any such question in regard to Tauler, who insists on the simple acceptance of revealed truths and whose thought is constantly Christocentric in character.

4. Henry Suso was born at Constance about the year 1295. He entered the Dominican Order and did his studies at Constance (perhaps partly at Strasbourg), after which he went to Cologne. There he made the personal acquaintance of Eckhart, for whom he retained a lasting admiration, affection and loyalty. Returning to Constance he spent some years there, writing and practising extraordinary mortifications and penances; but at the age of forty he began an apostolic life of preaching not only in Switzerland but also in Alsace and the Rhineland. In 1348 he changed his convent at Constance for that at Ulm (driven thereto by calumnies) and it was at Ulm that he died in January, 1366. He was beatified by Gregory XVI in 1831.

Suso's chief concern as writer was to make known the soul's path to the highest union with God: he was above all a practical mystical writer. The more speculative part of his thought is contianed in *The Little Book of Truth* (*Büchlein der Wahrheit*) and in the last eight chapters of his autobiography. *The Little Book of Eternal Wisdom* (*Büchlein der ewigen Weisheit*) is a book of practical mysticism. Suso wrote a Latin version of it, the *Horologium Sapientiae*, which is not a translation but a development. Some letters and at least two certainly authentic sermons have also been preserved.

Suso warmly defended Eckhart against the charge of confusing God and creatures. He himself is perfectly clear and decisive about the distinction between them. He says indeed that creatures are eternally in God and that, as in God, they are God; but he carefully explains what he means by this. The ideas of creatures are eternally present in the divine mind; but these ideas are identical with the divine essence; they are not forms distinct from one another or from the divine essence. Further, this being of creatures in God is quite distinct from the being of creatures outside God: it is only through creation that 'creatures' exist. One cannot attribute creatureliness to creatures as they are in God. However, 'the creatureliness of any nature is nobler and more useful to it than the being which it has in God'.[1] In all this Suso was not saying anything different from what St. Thomas had taught. Similarly he expressly teaches that creation is a free act of God.[2] He certainly uses the Pseudo-Dionysian (that is to say, neo-Platonic) idea of the overflowing of the divine goodness; but he is careful to observe that this overflowing takes place as a necessary process only within the Godhead, where it is 'interior, substantial, personal, natural, necessary without compulsion, eternal and perfect'.[3] The overflowing in creation is a free act on God's part and is distinct from the eternal procession of the divine Persons. There is, then, no question of pantheism in Suso's thought.

A similar freedom from pantheistic tendencies is clear in Suso's doctrine of the soul's mystical union with God. As with Eckhart and Tauler, the mystical union is said to take place in the 'essence' of the soul, the 'spark' of the soul. This essence or centre of the soul is the unifying principle of the soul's powers, and it is in it that the image of God resides. Through the mystical union, which takes place by supernaturally impressed knowledge and love, this image of God is further actualized. This actualization is called the 'birth of God' (*Gottesgeburt*) or 'birth of Christ' (*Christusgeburt*) in the soul, by means of which the soul is made more like to and more united with the Deity in and through Christ. Suso's mysticism is essentially Christocentric. He speaks of the soul's 'sinking into' God; but he emphasizes the fact that there is not, and never can be, a complete ontological identification of the ground or essence of the soul with the divine Being. Man remains man, even if he becomes deiform: there is no pantheistic absorption of the creature

[1] *Book of Truth*, 332, 16.
[2] *Vita*, 21–4, p. 178.
[3] *Ibid.*, 178, 24–179, 7.

in God.[1] As I have said, Suso was strongly influenced by Eckhart, but he was always careful to bring his teaching into clear harmony with the doctrines of Catholic Christianity. It would, indeed, be preferable to say that his mystical teaching sprang from the Catholic tradition of spirituality, and that, as far as Eckhart is concerned, Suso interpreted the latter's teaching in an orthodox sense.

It has been said that Suso's thought differed from Eckhart's in regard to its direction. Eckhart preferred to start with God: his thought moved from the simple divine essence to the Trinity of Persons, especially to the Word or *Logos*, in which he saw the archetype of creation, and so to creatures in the Word. The union of the soul with God appeared to him as a return of the creature to its dwelling-place in the Word, and the highest mystical experience of the soul is the union of its centre with the simple centre or essence of the Godhead. Suso, however, was less speculatively inclined. His thought moved from the human person to the latter's dynamic union with Christ, the God-Man; and he emphasized strongly the place of the Humanity of Christ in the ascent of the soul to God. In other words, though he often used more or less the same phrases that Eckhart used, his thought was less neo-Platonic than Eckhart's, and he was more strongly influenced than was Eckhart by the affective spirituality and the Christocentric 'bride-mysticism' of St. Bernard.

5. John Ruysbroeck was born in 1293 at the village of Ruysbroeck near Brussels. After some years spent at the latter city he became Prior of the Augustinian convent of Groenendael (Green Valley) in the forest of Soignes near Brussels. He died in 1381. His writings include *The Adornment of the Spiritual Marriage* and *The Book of the Twelve Beguines*. He wrote in Flemish.

Ruysbroeck, who was strongly influenced by the writings of Eckhart, insists on the original presence of the creature in God and on the return to that state of unity. One can distinguish in man a threefold unity.[2] 'The first and highest unity of man is in God.' Creatures depend on this unity for their being and preservation, and without it they would be reduced to nothing. But this relationship to God is essential to the creature and it does not, of itself, make a man really good or bad. The second unity is also natural: it is the unity of man's higher powers inasmuch as these spring from the unity of his mind or spirit. This fundamental

[1] Cf. *Vita*, 50 and 51, p. 176.

[2] *Adornment*, 2, 2.

unity of spirit is the same as the first type of unity, the unity which depends on God; but it is considered in its activity rather than in its essence. The third unity, also natural, is the unity of the senses and of the bodily activities. If in regard to the second natural unity the soul is called 'spirit', in regard to the third it is called 'soul', that is, as vital principle and principle of sensation. The 'adornment' of the soul consists in the supernatural perfection of the three unities; the first through the moral perfection of the Christian; the second through the theological virtues and the gifts of the Holy Spirit; the third through mystical and inexpressible union with God. The highest unification is 'that most high unity in which God and the loving spirit are united without intermediary'.

Like Eckhart Ruysbroeck speaks of 'the most high and super-essential Unity of the Divine Nature'. The words recall the writing of the Pseudo-Dionysius. With this supreme Unity the soul, in the highest activity of the mystical life, can become united. But the union transcends the power of reason; it is accomplished by love. In it the ground of the soul is, as it were, lost in the ineffable abyss of the Godhead, in the Essential Unity to which 'the Persons, and all that lives in God, just give place'.[1]

Not unnaturally, Ruysbroeck's doctrine was attacked, particularly by Gerson. However, that he did not intend to teach pantheism Ruysbroeck made clear in *The Mirror of Eternal Salvation* and in *The Book of the Twelve Beguines*. He was defended by Jan van Schoonhoven (d. 1432), himself a mystic, and Denis the Carthusian did not hesitate to borrow from his writings.

6. Denis the Carthusian, who was born at Rychel in 1402 and died as a Carthusian of Roermond in 1471, does not belong chronologically to the period which is being treated in the first part of this work. For the sake of convenience, however, I shall say a few words about him here.

The 'ecstatic Doctor' had done his higher studies at Cologne, and, for a mystical writer, he was surprisingly interested in Scholastic themes. He composed commentaries on the *Sentences* of Peter Lombard and on Boethius, as well as on the writings of the Pseudo-Dionysius, and he wrote a summary of the orthodox faith according to the works of St. Thomas, a manual of philosophy and theology (*Elementatio philosophica et theologica*) and other theological works. In addition, there are his purely ascetical and mystical treatises. It is clear that he was at first a devoted

[1] *Adornment*, 3, 4.

follower of St. Thomas; and his hostility not only towards the nominalists but also towards the Scotists seems to have continued throughout his life. But he gradually moved from the camp of the Thomists to that of the followers of St. Albert, and he was much influenced by the writings of the Dominican Ulric of Strasbourg (d. 1277), who had attended St. Albert's lectures at Cologne. Not only did Denis reject the real distinction between essence and existence, which he had at first defended; but he also abandoned the Thomist view of the rôle of the 'phantasm' in human knowledge. Denis restricted the necessity of the phantasm to the lower levels of knowledge and maintained that the soul can know without recourse to the phantasm its own activity, angels and God. Our knowledge of the divine essence, however, is negative; the mind comes to realize clearly the incomprehensibility of God. In this emphasis on negative but immediate knowledge of God Denis was influenced by the Pseudo-Dionysius and by the writings of Ulric of Strasbourg and other followers of St. Albert. The Carthusian Doctor is a remarkable example of the combination of mystical with Scholastic interests.

7. The German mystics of the Middle Ages (I include Ruysbroeck, although he was a Fleming) drew their mysticism from its roots in the Christian Faith. It is not a question of enumerating sources, of showing the influence of the Fathers, of St. Bernard, of the Victorines, of St. Bonaventure or of trying to minimize the neo-Platonic influences on expression and even on idea, but of realizing the mystics' common belief in the necessity of supernatural grace which comes through Christ. The Humanity of Christ may play a larger part in the thought of Suso, for example, than in that of Eckhart; but the latter, in spite of all his exaggerations, was first and foremost a Christian. There is, then, no real support for the attempt which has been made to discover in the writings of the German mediaeval mystics like Eckhart, Tauler and Suso a 'German mysticism', if by this is meant a mysticism which is not Catholic but one proceeding from 'blood and race'.

On the other hand, the German mystics of the fourteenth century do represent an alliance of Scholasticism and mysticism which gives them a stamp of their own. Grabmann remarked that the combination of practical mysticism and of speculation is ultimately a continuation of St. Anselm's programme, *Credo, ut intelligam*. However, although the speculation of the German mystics grew out of the currents of thought which had inspired the mediaeval Scholastics and which had been systematized in various ways in the thirteenth century, their speculation must be seen in the light of their practical mysticism. If it was partly the circumstances of the education of this or that mystical writer which moulded the framework of his speculation and influenced his choice of theoretic ideas, it was also partly his practical mystical life and his reflection on his spiritual experience which influenced the direction of his speculation. It would be a mistake to think that the doctrine of the *scintilla animae*, the spark of the soul or the essence or ground or apex of the soul, was no more than a stock idea which was adopted mechanically from predecessors and passed on from mystic to mystic. The term *scintilla conscientiae* or *synderesis* occurs in St. Jerome[1] and it reappears in, for example, St. Albert the Great, who means by it a power existing in all men which admonishes them of the good and opposes evil. St. Thomas, who refers to St. Jerome,[2] speaks of synderesis metaphorically, as the *scintilla conscientiae.*[3] The mystics certainly meant something else than synderesis when they spoke of the spark or ground of the soul; but, even granting that, practically all the expressions by which they characterized the ground of the soul were already to be found, according to Denifle, in the writings of Richard of St. Victor. No doubt Denifle's contention is true; but the German mystics made the idea of the ground or spark of the soul one of their leading ideas, not simply because they found it in the writings of a revered predecessor, but because it fitted in with their experience of a mystical union with God transcending the conscious play of acts of intelligence and will. As found in their predecessors, the idea doubtless suggested to them this close union; but their meditation on the idea went hand in hand with their experience.

Possibly certain German writers have gone too far in finding in the combination of speculation with practical mysticism a distinguishing mark of the German mystics. It serves to differentiate them from some mystics, it is true, who were more or less innocent of theoretic speculations; but a similar combination can be seen in the case of the Victorines in the twelfth century and, indeed, in that of Gerson himself, though Gerson had scant sympathy for the line of speculation adopted by Eckhart and Ruysbroeck, as he interpreted it at least. However, there is an added characteristic which is connected with the fact that Eckhart, Tauler and Suso were all members of the Dominican Order, the

[1] *P.L.*, 25, 22 AB. [2] *De Veritate*, 16, 1, obj. 1. [3] *Ibid.*, 17, 2, *ad* 3.

Order of Friars Preachers. They disseminated mystical doctrine in their sermons, and attempted, as I have already mentioned, to deepen in this way the general spiritual life, particularly among religious. No doubt one could make a similar observation about St. Bernard, for example, but, particularly in the case of Eckhart, there is a speculative flavour and framework, due to the intervening development of mediaeval philosophy, which is not to be found in St. Bernard's sermons. Moreover, the Germans are more 'rugged', less flowery. The German speculative mysticism is so closely connected with Dominican preaching that it enables one to speak, in this sense, of the 'German mysticism' of the Middle Ages, provided that one does not mean to imply that the German Dominicans were attempting to establish a German religion or a German *Weltanschauung*.

8. John Gerson, who was born in 1363, succeeded Peter d'Ailly as chancellor of the university of Paris in 1395.[1] He has been accounted a nominalist; but his adoption of certain nominalist positions did not proceed from adherence to the nominalist philosophy. He was a theologian and mystical writer rather than a philosopher; and it was in the interests of faith and of theology that he tended in certain matters towards nominalist doctrine. Gerson's chancellorship fell in the period of the Great Schism (1378–1417) and he took a prominent part in the work of the Council of Constance. Much distressed not only at the state of the Church, but also at the condition of university studies and the propagation of doctrines which had, it seemed to him, led to or facilitated the rise of theories like those of Hus, he sought to apply a remedy, not through a dissemination of nominalism as such but through a recall of men to the right attitude towards God. The conflict of systems of philosophy and the curiosity and pride of theologians had, he thought, been responsible for much evil. In his *De modis significandi propositiones quinquaginta* Gerson maintained that the various branches of study had become confused to the detriment of truth, logicians trying to solve metaphysical problems by the *modus significandi* proper to logic, metaphysicians and logicians endeavouring to prove revealed truths or to solve theological problems by methods which are not fitted for dealing with the object of theology. This confusion, thought Gerson, had led to a state of anarchy in the intellectual world and to untrue

[1] Gerson died in 1429. For chronological details, see *La vie et les œuvres de Gerson* by P. Glorieux (Archives d'histoire doctrinale et littéraire du moyen âge, t. 18, pp. 149–92; Paris, 1951).

conclusions. Furthermore, the pride of the Scholastic theologians had engendered curiosity and the spirit of novelty or singularity. Gerson published two lectures *Contra vanam curiositatem in negotio fidei*, against vain curiosity in the matter of faith, in which he drew attention to the part played in Scholastic disputes by love of one's own opinions, envy, the spirit of contention and contempt for the uneducated and the uninitiated. The root fault is the pride of the natural reason which endeavours to exceed its bounds and to solve problems which it is incapable of solving.

It is from this angle that one should regard Gerson's attack on realism. The notion of ideas in God involves a confusion, first of logic with metaphysics, and then of metaphysics with theology. Secondly, it implies that God is not simple, since the realists tend to speak of these *rationes ideales* in God as though they were distinct; and some even speak as though creatures pre-existed in God, that is to say, as though the divine ideas were creatures existing in God. Thirdly, the doctrine of divine ideas, employed in explaining creation, serves only to limit the divine freedom. And why do philosophers and theologians limit the divine freedom? From a desire of understanding that which cannot be understood, a desire which proceeds from pride. The thinkers of the Platonic tradition also speak of God, not primarily as free, but as the Good, and they utilize the principle of the natural tendency of goodness to diffuse itself in order to explain creation. But by doing so they tend to make creation a necessary effect of the divine nature. Again, realist metaphysicians and theologians insist that the moral law in no way depends on the divine will, thus restricting the divine liberty, whereas in point of fact 'God does not will certain actions because they are good; but they are good because He wills them, just as others are bad because He prohibits them.'[1] 'Right reason does not precede the will, and God does not decide to give law to a rational creature because He has first seen in His wisdom that He ought to do so; it is rather the contrary which takes place.'[2] It follows that the moral law is not immutable. Gerson adopted this Ockhamist position in regard to the moral law because he considered that it was the only position consonant with God's liberty. The Platonizing philosophers and theologians, he thought, had abandoned the principle of belief, of humble subjection, for the pride of the understanding. Moreover, he did not fail to draw attention to the realist aspects of the thought of John Hus and of Jerome of

[1] *Opera*, 3, col. 13. [2] *Ibid.*, col. 26.

Prague; and he drew the conclusion that the pride of the understanding manifested by the realists leads in the end to open heresy.

Thus Gerson's attack on realism, though it involved him in some positions which were actually held by the nominalists, proceeded rather from religious preoccupations than from any particular enthusiasm for the *via moderna* as such. 'Repent and believe the Gospel'[1] was the text on which Gerson built his two lectures against vain curiosity in the matter of faith. The pride which had invaded the minds of university professors and lecturers had made them oblivious to the need for repentance and to the simplicity of faith. This point of view is obviously more characteristic of a man whose concern is the soul's attitude towards God than of a man who is passionately interested in academic questions for their own sake. Gerson's hostility towards the metaphysics and theology of the realists certainly bears some analogy to Pascal's hostility towards those who would substitute for the God of Abraham and Isaac and Jacob the 'God of the philosophers'.

If we look at the matter from this point of view, it is not surprising to find Gerson expressing his amazement that the Franciscans had abandoned St. Bonaventure for *parvenus* in the intellectual world. St. Bonaventure's *Itinerarium mentis in Deum* he regarded as a book beyond all praise. On the other hand, if we consider Gerson's hostility towards realism, his attacks on Ruysbroeck and his attempt to connect realism with the heresies of John Hus and Jerome of Prague, his enthusiasm for St. Bonaventure might well appear somewhat startling when it is remembered that St. Bonaventure laid great stress on the Platonic doctrine of ideas in its Augustinian form and roundly condemned Aristotle for 'execrating' the ideas of Plato. Gerson's conviction was that the theologians of his time had neglected the Bible and the Fathers, the true sources of theology, in favour of pagan thinkers and of importations from metaphysics which impaired the simplicity of faith. He regarded, however, the Pseudo-Dionysius as the disciple and convert of St. Paul, and considered the Dionysian writings to form part of the well-spring of true wisdom. St. Bonaventure he revered as a man who had consistently drunk of these undefiled waters and who had concerned himself above all with the true wisdom, which is the knowledge of God through Jesus Christ.

In spite, then, of his attack on realism, Gerson's mystical doctrine was deeply influenced by the teaching of the

[1] *St. Mark* 1, 15.

Pseudo-Dionysius. M. André Combes, in his most interesting study of Gerson's relation to the writings and thought of the Pseudo-Dionysius,[1] after showing the authenticity of the *Notulae super quaedam verba Dionysii de Caelesti Hierarchia* and arguing that the work should precede the first lecture against 'vain curiosity' in the *Opera* of Gerson, makes it clear that Gerson was never simply a 'nominalist' and that his ideas were never simply identical with those of Peter d'Ailly (1350–1420), his 'master'. In fact, as M. Combes has shown, Gerson borrowed from the Pseudo-Dionysius not merely an arsenal of terminology, but also the important doctrine of the 'return'. Creatures proceed from God and return to God. How is this return accomplished? By each nature performing those acts which are proper to it. Strictly speaking, says Gerson (in his *Sermo de die Jovis sancta*), it is only the rational creature who returns to God, though Boethius said that all things return to their beginning or principle. But the important point about Gerson's doctrine of the 'return' is the emphasis he lays on the fact that it does not mean an ontological merging of the creature with God. As he regarded the Pseudo-Dionysius as a personal disciple of St. Paul, he was convinced that the Dionysian teaching was perfectly 'safe'. But, realizing that it could be misinterpreted, he considered that the theologian must elucidate the Areopagite's true meaning; and he himself utilized the writings of Hugh of St. Victor and of St. Albert the Great. From this two relevant and important points emerge. First, Gerson by no means condemned or rejected the Scholastic theology as such, which he considered necessary for the right interpretation of the Scriptures, of the Fathers and of St. Paul's disciple. Secondly, when he attacked Ruysbroeck, he was not attacking him for drawing on the teaching of the Pseudo-Dionysius but for misinterpreting and perverting that doctrine. Of course, we know that the Pseudo-Dionysius was not a disciple of St. Paul and that he drew copiously on Proclus; but the point is that Gerson interpreted the Pseudo-Dionysius as if he were not a Platonist. This explains how he could show at the same time a marked hostility towards the Platonizers and a marked predilection for the Pseudo-Dionysius.

Gerson accepted the threefold division of theology given by the Pseudo-Dionysius, symbolic theology, theology in the proper sense, and mystical theology. The threefold division is to be found in St. Bonaventure's *Itinerarium mentis in Deum*;[2] but Gerson

[1] *Jean Gerson, Commentateur Dionysien*, Paris, 1940. [2] 1, 7.

seems to have drawn the distinction from the Pseudo-Dionysius' writings rather than from St. Bonaventure: at least he consulted the former and cites him as his authority. Mystical theology, he says, is the experimental knowledge of God, in which love, rather than the abstract speculative intellect, is at work, though the highest intellectual function is also involved. The *intelligentia simplex* and the *synderesis* or highest affective power are operative in mystical experience, which is not a rejection but a realization of the highest powers of the soul. Mystical union affects the foundation of the soul; but it is a union which does not dissolve the human personality in the Godhead. Mystical theology, at least if it is understood as mysticism itself rather than as the theory of mysticism, is the crown of theology, because it approaches nearest to the beatific vision, which is the final end of the soul.

The presence of this threefold division in Gerson's thought helps to make it clear that, while emphasizing the primacy of mystical theology, he did not reject theology in the ordinary sense. Nor did he reject philosophy. Whether his bent of mind might have led him to reject all but mystical theology had it not been for the Pseudo-Dionysius, St. Bonaventure and St. Albert is another and not very profitable question. He certainly laid stress on the Scriptures and the teaching of the Fathers and he certainly thought that theologians would do well to pay more attention to those sources; he certainly thought, moreover, that speculative theology contaminated by unwarranted importations from suspect philosophers encouraged pride and vain curiosity; but there is no real evidence for saying either that he rejected all Scholastic development of Scriptural and Patristic teaching or that he rejected a philosophy which observed its due limits. In some ways Gerson is the most interesting representative of the movement of speculative mysticism in the late Middle Ages. He shows us that the movement was primarily inspired by the desire for remedying the evils of the time and for deepening men's religious life: it was by no means a mere counter-blast to nominalist scepticism. As for Gerson's own nominalism, it is truer to say that he adopted and exploited certain nominalist positions in the service of his own primary aim rather than that he was a nominalist. To say that Gerson was a nominalist philosopher who at the same time happened to be a mystic would be to give a false impression of his aims, his theoretical position and his spirit.

PART II
THE PHILOSOPHY OF THE RENAISSANCE

CHAPTER XIII
THE REVIVAL OF PLATONISM

The Italian Renaissance—The northern Renaissance—The revival of Platonism.

1. THE first phase of the Renaissance was the humanistic phase which began in Italy and spread to northern Europe. But it would be absurd to speak as if the Renaissance was a historical period with such clearly-defined temporal limits that one could give the exact dates of its beginning and end. In so far as the Renaissance means or involved a rebirth of literature and a devotion to classical learning and style it may be said to have begun as early as the twelfth century, the century in which John of Salisbury, for example, had declaimed against barbarity in Latin style, the century which saw the humanism of the School of Chartres. It is true that the great theologians and philosophers of the thirteenth century were more concerned with *what* was said and with exactitude of statement than with literary style and grace of expression; but it should not be forgotten that a St. Thomas Aquinas could write hymns which are remarkable for their beauty and that in the same period in which Duns Scotus was composing his somewhat bold and unstylistic commentaries Dante was creating one of the greatest achievements of the Italian language. Dante (1265–1321) certainly wrote from the standpoint of a mediaeval; but in the same century in which Dante died, the fourteenth century, we find Petrarch (1304–74) not only setting himself against the cult of Aristotelian dialectic and promoting the revival of the classical, especially the Ciceronian, style but also favouring through his vernacular sonnets the growth of the spirit of humanistic individualism. Boccaccio (1313–75) also belonged to the fourteenth century; and at the end of the century, in 1396, Manuel Chrysoloras (d. 1415), the first real teacher of classical Greek in the West, began lecturing at Florence.

The political conditions in Italy favoured the growth of the humanistic Renaissance, inasmuch as princely, ducal and ecclesiastical patrons were able to spend large sums of money on the purchase and copying of manuscripts and on the foundation of libraries; and by the time the Renaissance made itself felt in northern Europe the greater part of the Greek and Latin classics had been recovered and made known. But the Italian Renaissance was by no means confined to the recovery and dissemination of texts. A most important feature was the rise of a new style and ideal of education, represented by teachers like Vittorino da Feltre (1378–1446) and Guarino of Verona (1370–1460). The humanistic educational ideal at its best was that of developing the human personality to the full. Ancient literature was regarded as the chief means of education; but moral training, development of character, physical development and awakening of the aesthetic sensibility were not neglected; nor was the ideal of liberal education regarded as in any way incompatible with the acceptance and practice of Christianity.[1] This, however, was the humanistic ideal at its best. In practice the Italian Renaissance became associated to a certain extent with a growth of moral or amoral individualism and with the pursuit of fame; while in the later stages of the Renaissance the cult of classical literature degenerated into 'Ciceronianism', which meant the substitution of the tyranny of Cicero for that of Aristotle. The exchange was scarcely a change for the better. Moreover, while a man like Vittorino da Feltre was a convinced and devout Christian, many figures of the Renaissance were influenced by a spirit of scepticism. While it would be ridiculous to belittle the achievements of the Italian Renaissance at its best, other aspects were symptomatic of the disintegration rather than of the enrichment of the preceding cultural phase. And the degenerate phase of 'Ciceronianism' was no improvement on the broader outlook fostered by a theological and philosophical education.

2. In the Italian Renaissance the ideas of self-development and self-culture were marked features: it was, in large part, an individualistic movement, in the sense that the ideal of social and moral reform was not conspicuous: indeed, some of the humanists were 'pagan' in outlook. The ideal of reform, when it came, did not spring from the Renaissance as such, which was predominantly cultural, aesthetic and literary in character. In northern Europe,

[1] The *De liberorum educatione*, published in 1450 by Aeneas Sylvius Piccolomini, later Pope Pius II, was taken in large part from Quintilian's *De Oratore*, which had been discovered in 1416, and from an educational work attributed to Plutarch.

however, the literary Renaissance was allied with efforts to achieve moral and social reformation, and there was a greater emphasis on popular education. The northern Renaissance lacked much of the splendour of the Italian Renaissance and it was less 'aristocratic' in character; but it was more obviously allied with religious and moral purposes and, arising at a later date than the Italian movement, it tended to merge with the Reformation, at least if 'Reformation' is understood in a very broad sense and not merely in the sectarian sense. But though both movements had their peculiar strong points, both tended to lose their original inspiration in the course of time, the Italian movement degenerating into 'Ciceronianism', the northern movement tending to pedantry and 'grammaticism', divorced from a living appreciation of the humanistic aspects of classical literature and culture.

Among the scholars associated with the Renaissance in northern Europe one may mention Rudolf Agricola (1443–85), Hegius (1420–95), who was for a time headmaster of a school at Deventer founded in the fourteenth century by the Brethren of the Common Life, and Jacob Wimpfeling (1450–1528), who made of the university of Heidelberg a centre of humanism in western Germany. But the greatest figure of the northern Renaissance was Erasmus (1467–1536), who promoted the study of Greek and Latin literature, including the Scriptures and the writings of the Fathers, and gave a great impetus to the development of humanistic education. In Great Britain there were ecclesiastics like William of Waynflete (*c.* 1395–1486), St. John Fisher (1459–1535), who brought Erasmus to Cambridge, John Colet (*c.* 1467–1519), who founded St. Paul's School in 1512, and Thomas Linacre (*c.* 1460–1524); and laymen like St. Thomas More (1478–1535). Winchester College was founded in 1382 and Eton in 1440.

The Reformers stressed the need of education; but they were led by religious motives rather than by devotion to the humanistic ideal as such. John Calvin (1509-64), who had studied the humanities in France, drew up an educational curriculum for the schools of Geneva and, since he was religious autocrat of the city, he was able to enforce a system of education on Calvinistic lines. But the most humanistically-minded of the famous continental reformers was Philip Melanchthon (1497–1560), the foremost disciple of Martin Luther (1483–1546). In 1518 Melanchthon became professor of Greek at the university of Wittenberg. The humanism of the Reformers, which was hindered rather than promoted by the religious tenets of strict Protestantism, was not, however, their own discovery; it was derived from the impetus of the Italian Renaissance. And in the Counter-Reformation the humanistic ideal was prominent in the educational system developed by the Society of Jesus, which was founded in 1540 and produced the *Ratio Studiorum* in a definite form in 1599.

3. Through the interest and enthusiasm which it aroused for the literature of Greece and Rome the humanistic phase of the Renaissance not unnaturally inspired a revival of ancient philosophy in its various forms. Of these revived philosophies one of the most influential was Platonism or, to speak more accurately, neo-Platonism. The most remarkable centre of Platonic studies in Italy was the Platonic Academy of Florence, founded by Cosimo de' Medici under the influence of George Gemistus Plethon (d. 1464) who arrived in Italy from Byzantium in 1438. Plethon was an enthusiastic adherent of the Platonic or neo-Platonic tradition, and he composed in Greek a work on the difference between the Platonic and Aristotelian philosophies. His main work, of which only parts have survived, was his *νόμων συγγραφή*. A kindred spirit was John Argyropoulos (d. 1486), who occupied the chair of Greek at Florence from 1456 until 1471, when he left for Rome, where he numbered Reuchlin among his pupils. One must also mention John Bessarion of Trebizond (1395–1472), who was sent from Byzantium together with Plethon to take part in the Council of Florence (1438–45), at which he laboured to achieve the reunion of the Eastern Church with Rome. Bessarion, who became a cardinal, composed among other works an *Adversus calumniatorem Platonis*, in which he defended Plethon and Platonism against the Aristotelian George of Trebizond, who had written a *Comparatio Aristotelis et Platonis* in answer to Plethon.

It must not be thought that these Platonists were all determined haters of Scholasticism. John Argyropoulos translated into Greek St. Thomas Aquinas's *De ente et essentia*, and Bessarion too had a great respect for the Angelic Doctor. For these Platonists it was not so much a question of setting one philosopher against another, Plato against Aristotle, as of renewing a Platonic, or rather neo-Platonic, view of reality which would unite in itself the valuable elements of pagan antiquity and yet at the same time be Christian. It was the religious side of neo-Platonism, as well as its philosophy of beauty and harmony, which particularly appealed to the Platonists and what they particularly disliked in Aristotelianism was the tendency to naturalism which they detected therein. Plethon looked to the renewal of the Platonic tradition for a renewal of life or a reform in Church and State; and if his enthusiasm for Platonism led him into an attack on Aristotle which even Bessarion considered to be somewhat immoderate, it was what he regarded as the spirit of Platonism and its potentialities for spiritual, moral and cultural renewal which inspired him, rather than a purely academic interest in, for example, the Platonic affirmation and the Aristotelian denial of the theory of Ideas. The Platonists considered that the world of the humanistic Renaissance would greatly benefit in practice by absorbing such a doctrine as that of Man as the microcosm and as the ontological bond between the spiritual and the material.

One of the most eminent scholars of the neo-Platonic movement was Marsilius Ficinus (1433–1499). As a young man he composed two works, the *De laudibus philosophiae* and the *Institutiones platonicae* and these were followed in 1457 by the *De amore divino* and the *Liber de voluptate*. But in 1458 his father sent him to Bologna, to study medicine. Cosimo de' Medici, however, recalled him to Florence and had him taught Greek. In 1462 Marsilius translated the Orphic Hymns and in the following years he translated, at Cosimo's request, the Dialogues and Epistles of Plato and works by Hermes Trismegistus, Iamblichus (*De Secta Pythagorica*), Theo of Smyrna (*Mathematica*) and others. In 1469 appeared the first edition of his commentary on Plato's *Symposium* and commentaries on the *Philebus*, the *Parmenides* and the *Timaeus*. In 1474 he published his *De religione christiana* and his most important philosophical work, the *Theologia platonica*. In the following year appeared the commentary on the *Phaedrus* and the second edition of the commentary on the *Symposium*. The translations of and commentaries on the *Enneads* of Plotinus were published in 1485 and 1486; and in 1489 the *De triplici vita*, Marsilius' last work. Marsilius was an indefatigable worker, and in his translations he aimed above all at literal fidelity to the original: even though he sometimes made mistakes in his translation, there can be no doubt of the benefit he conferred on the men of his age.[1]

Marsilius Ficinus became a priest when he was forty years old, and he dreamed of drawing atheists and sceptics to Christ by

[1] For some remarks on the value of Marsilius' translations of Plato and Plotinus, see J. Festugière, *La philosophie de l'amour de Marsile Ficin*, Appendix I, pp. 141–52.

means of the Platonic philosophy. In his commentary on the *Phaedrus* he declares that the love spoken of by Plato and that spoken of by St. Paul are one and the same, namely the love of the absolute Beauty, which is God. God is both absolute Beauty and the absolute Good; and on this theme Plato and Dionysius the Areopagite (the Pseudo-Dionysius) are in accord. Again, when Plato insisted that we are 'reminded of' eternal objects, the Ideas, by the sight of their temporal and material imitations, was he not saying the same as St. Paul when the latter declares that the invisible things of God are understood by means of creatures? In the *Theologia platonica* the universe is depicted according to the neo-Platonic spirit as a harmonious and beautiful system, consisting of degrees of being which extend from corporeal things up to God, the absolute Unity or One. The place of man as the bond between the spiritual and the material is emphasized; and, though Marsilius thought of Aristotelianism as springing from the same philosophical tradition and inspiration as Platonism, he insisted, both as Christian and as Platonist, on the immortality and divine vocation of the human soul. He naturally adopted leading ideas from St. Augustine, developing the Platonic theory of Ideas (or better, Forms) in an Augustinian sense and insisting on Illumination. We learn nothing save in and through God, who is the light of the soul.

A strongly-marked syncretistic element appears in Marsilius' philosophy, as in that of other Platonists like Plethon. It is not only Plato, Plotinus, Iamblichus and Proclus whose thought is synthesized with that of St. John, St. Paul and St. Augustine, but also Hermes Trismegistus[1] and other pagan figures make their appearance as bearers of the spiritual movement which sprang from an original primitive revelation of the beauty and harmoniously ordered and graded system of reality. Marsilius Ficinus, like other Christian Platonists of the Italian Renaissance, was not only personally captivated by Platonism (in a very wide sense), but he also thought that those minds which had become alienated from Christianity could be brought back to it by being led to view Platonism as a stage in divine revelation. In other words, there was no need to choose between the beauty of classical

[1] In the Greco-Roman world a considerable literature, dealing with religious, theosophical, philosophical, medical, astrological and alchemist topics became known as the Hermetic literature. It was attributed in some way to, or placed under the patronage of, the 'thrice-great Hermes', who was the Egyptian god Thoth, identified by the Greeks with Hermes.

thought on the one hand and Christianity on the other; one could enjoy both. One could not, however, enjoy the Platonic-Christian heritage if one fell a victim to Aristotelianism as interpreted by those who set Aristotle against Plato, understood him in a naturalistic sense and denied the immortality of the human soul.

The best-known member of the circle which was influenced by Marsilius Ficinus was probably John Pico della Mirandola (1463–94). John possessed a knowledge of both Greek and Hebrew, and when twenty-four years old he planned to defend at Rome 900 theses against all comers, his object being to show how Hellenism and Judaism (in the form of the Cabbala) can be synthesized in a Platonic-Christian system. The disputation was, however, forbidden by the ecclesiastical authorities. John's tendency to syncretism showed itself also in the composition of an (unfinished) work, *De concordia Platonis et Aristotelis*.

John Pico della Mirandola was strongly influenced by the 'negative theology' of neo-Platonism and the Pseudo-Dionysius. God is the One; but He is above being rather than being.[1] He is indeed all things, in the sense that He comprises in Himself all perfections; but He comprises these perfections in His undivided unity in an ineffable manner which exceeds our understanding.[2] As far as we are concerned, God is in darkness; we approach Him philosophically by denying the limitations of creaturely perfections. Life is one perfection; wisdom is another perfection. Think away the particularity and limitations of these and all other perfections and 'that which remains is God'. This is not to be understood pantheistically, of course; God is the One, transcending the world which He has created.

The world is a harmonious system, consisting of beings belonging to different levels of reality; and John Pico della Mirandola speaks of God as having desired to create someone to contemplate the nature of the world, to love its beauty and to admire its greatness. 'Therefore, all things having been already completed (as Moses and Timaeus testify), He took thought finally to produce man.'[3] But God did not assign to man a fixed and peculiar place in the universe or laws which he was unable to contravene. 'I placed thee in the middle of the world, that thence thou mightest see more easily all that is in the world. We made thee neither a heavenly being nor an earthly being, neither mortal nor immortal,

[1] Cf. *De ente et uno*, 4. [2] *Ibid.*, 5.
[3] *Oratio de hominis dignitate*, ed. E. Garin, p. 104.

in order that thou, as the free and sovereign artificer of thyself, mightest mould and sculpture thyself in the form which thou shouldest prefer. Thou wilt be able to degenerate to (the level of) the lower things, the brutes; thou wilt be able, according to thy will, to be reborn into the (level of) the higher things, the divine.'[1] Man is the microcosm; but he has the gift of freedom, which enables him to descend or to ascend. John was, therefore, hostile to the determinism of the astrologers, against whom he wrote his *In astrologiam libri XII*. His view of man, moreover, is a Christian view. There are three 'worlds' within the world or universe; the infralunar world, 'which brutes and men inhabit'; the celestial world, 'in which the planets shine'; and the super-celestial world, 'the abode of the angels'. But Christ, through the Passion, has opened to man the way into the super-celestial world, the way even to God Himself.[2] Man is the head and synthesis of the lower creation, and Christ is the head of the human race.[3] He is also, as divine Word, the 'beginning in which God made heaven and earth'.[4]

In his work against the astrologers John Pico della Mirandola opposed the magical conception of nature. In so far as astrology involved a belief in the harmonious system of nature and in the interrelatedness of all events, it was, whether true or false, a rational system. But it was not rationally grounded, and it involved, moreover, the belief that every earthly event was determined by the heavenly bodies and the belief that he who possessed a knowledge of certain symbols could by the right use of those symbols influence things. It was against the deterministic view of human actions and against the belief in magic that John set himself. Events are causally governed; but the causes are to be looked for in the natures and forms of the various things in the world, not in the stars, and a magical knowledge and use of symbol is ignorant superstition.

Finally one may mention that John's enthusiasm for Plato and his fondness for citing not only Greek and Islamic authors but also Oriental figures did not mean that he was without any appreciation of Aristotle. As already mentioned, he wrote a work on the agreement of Plato and Aristotle, and in the *Prooemium* to the *De ente et uno* he asserts his belief in this agreement. In the fourth chapter of this work he remarks, for instance, that those who think that Aristotle did not realize, as Plato did, that being is subordinate to

[1] *Oratio de hominis dignitate*, p. 106.
[2] *Heptaplus*, ed. E. Garin, pp. 186–8. [3] *Ibid.*, p. 220. [4] *Ibid.*, p. 244.

the One and does not include God 'have not read Aristotle', who expressed this truth 'much more clearly than Plato'. Whether John interpreted Aristotle correctly is, of course, another question; but he was certainly no fanatical anti-Aristotelian. As to the Scholastics, he cites them and he speaks of St. Thomas as 'the splendour of our theology'.[1] John was far too much of a syncretist to be exclusive.

In the last years of his life John Pico della Mirandola was influenced by Savonarola (1452–98), who also influenced the former's nephew, John Francis Pico della Mirandola (1469–1533). In his *De praenotionibus* John Francis discussed the criteria of divine revelation, finding the chief criterion in an 'inner light'. In regard to philosophy as such he did not follow his uncle's example of attempting to reconcile Aristotle and Plato: on the contrary, he sharply attacked the Aristotelian theory of knowledge in his *Examen vanitatis doctrinae gentium et veritatis Christianae disciplinae*. He argued that the Aristotelian bases his philosophy on sense-experience, which is supposed to be the source even of those most general principles which are employed in the process of proof. But sense-experience informs one about the conditions of the percipient subject rather than about objects themselves, and the Aristotelian can never proceed from his empiricist basis to a knowledge of substances or essences.

Among other Platonists one may mention Leo Hebraeus (*c.* 1460–*c.* 1530), a Portuguese Jew who came to Italy and wrote *Dialoghi d'amore* on the intellectual love of God whereby one apprehends beauty as the reflection of absolute Beauty. His views on love in general gave an impetus to the Renaissance literature on this subject, while his idea of the love of God in particular was not without influence on Spinoza. John Reuchlin (1455–1522) may also be mentioned here. This learned German, who not only was a master of the Latin and Greek languages but also introduced into Germany and promoted the study of Hebrew, studied in France and Italy, where, at Rome, he came under the influence of John Pico della Mirandola. In 1520 he became professor of Hebrew and Greek at Ingolstadt; but in 1521 he moved to Tübingen. Looking on the function of philosophy as the winning of happiness in this life and the next, he had little use for the Aristotelian logic and philosophy of nature. Strongly attracted by the Jewish Cabbala, he considered that a profound knowledge of the divine mysteries

[1] *Heptaplus*, p. 222.

is to be obtained from that source; and he combined his enthusiasm for the Cabbala with an enthusiasm for neo-Pythagorean number-mysticism. In his view Pythagoras had drawn his wisdom from Jewish sources. In other words, Reuchlin, though an eminent scholar, fell a victim to the attractions of the Cabbala and of the fantasies of number-mysticism; and in this respect he is more akin to the German theosophists and occultists of the Renaissance than to the Italian Platonists. However, he was certainly influenced by the Platonic circle at Florence and by John Pico della Mirandola, who also thought highly of Pythagoreanism, and on this account he can be mentioned in relation with Italian Platonism.

It is clear that the revived Platonism of Italy might just as well, or better, be called neo-Platonism. But the inspiration of Italian Platonism was not primarily an interest in scholarship, in distinguishing, for example, the doctrines of Plato from those of Plotinus and in critically reconstituting and interpreting their ideas. The Platonic tradition stimulated and provided a framework for the expression of the Renaissance Platonists' belief in the fullest possible development of man's higher potentialities and in their belief in Nature as the expression of the divine. But though they had a strong belief in the value and possibilities of the human personality as such they did not separate man either from God or from his fellow-men. Their humanism involved neither irreligion nor exaggerated individualism. And though they had a strong feeling for Nature and for beauty, they did not deify Nature or identify it with God. They were not pantheists. Their humanism and their feeling for Nature were characteristic of the Renaissance; but for a pantheistic view of Nature we have to turn to other phases of Renaissance thought and not to the Florentine Academy nor, in general, to Italian Platonism. Nor do we find in the Italian Platonists an individualism which discards the ideas of Christian revelation and of the Church.

CHAPTER XIV

ARISTOTELIANISM

Critics of the Aristotelian logic—Aristotelianism—Stoicism and scepticism.

1. THE Scholastic method and the Aristotelian logic were made objects of attack by a number of humanists. Thus Laurentius Valla or Lorenzo della Valle (1407–57) attacked the Aristotelian logic as an abstruse, artificial and abstract scheme which is able neither to express nor to lead to concrete and real knowledge. In his *Dialecticae disputationes contra Aristotelicos* he carried on a polemic against what he regarded as the empty abstractions of the Aristotelian-Scholastic logic and metaphysic. The Aristotelian logic, in Valla's opinion, is sophistry, depending largely on linguistic barbarism. The purpose of thought is to know things, and knowledge of things is expressed in speech, the function of words being to express in determinate form insight into the determinations of things. Many of the terms employed in the Aristotelian logic, however, do not express insight into the concrete characteristics of things, but are artificial constructions which do not express reality at all. A reform of speech is needed, and logic must be recognized as subordinate to 'rhetoric'. The orators treat all subjects much more clearly and in a profounder and sublimer manner than the confused, bloodless and dry dialecticians.[1] Rhetoric is not for Laurentius Valla simply the art of expressing ideas in beautiful or appropriate language; still less is it the art of persuading others 'rhetorically'; it denotes the linguistic expression of real insight into concrete reality.

Paying more attention to the Stoics and Epicureans than to Plato and Aristotle, Laurentius Valla maintained in his *De voluptate* that the Epicureans were right in emphasizing human striving after pleasure and happiness. But as a Christian he added that the complete happiness of man is not to be found in this life. Faith is necessary for life. For instance, man is conscious of freedom; but human freedom, according to Valla in his *De libero arbitrio*, is, as far as the natural light of reason can see, incompatible with the divine omnipotence. Their reconciliation is a mystery which must be accepted on faith.

[1] *De voluptate*, 1, 10.

Laurentius Valla's ideas on logic were taken up by Rudolf Agricola (1443–85) in his *De inventione dialectica*; and a somewhat similar view was maintained by the Spanish humanist Luis Vives (1492–1540). But Vives also deserves mention for his rejection of any slavish adherence to the scientific, medical or mathematical ideas of Aristotle and for his insistence that progress in science depends on direct observation of phenomena. In his *De anima et vita* he demanded recognition of the value of observation in psychology: one should not be content with what the ancients said about the soul. He himself treated in an independent way of memory, affections, etc., and stated, for example, the principle of association.

The importance of 'rhetoric' as a general science was strongly emphasized by Marius Nizolius (1488–1566 or 1498–1576), the author of a famous *Thesaurus Ciceronianus*. In philosophical writings like the *Antibarbarus philosophicus sive de veris principiis et vera ratione philosophandi contra pseudophilosophos* he rejected all undue deference to former philosophers in favour of independence of judgment. Philosophy in the narrow sense is concerned with the characteristics of things and comprises physics and politics, while rhetoric is a general science which is concerned with the meaning and right use of words. Rhetoric thus stands to other sciences as soul to body; it is their principle. It does not mean for Nizolius the theory and art of public speaking; it is the general science of 'meaning', and it is independent of all metaphysics and ontology. Rhetoric shows, for instance, how the meaning of general words, of universal terms, is independent of, or does not demand, the objective existence of universals. The universal term expresses a mental operation by which the human mind 'comprehends' all individual members of a class. There is no abstraction, in the sense of a mental operation whereby the mind apprehends the metaphysical essence of things in the universal concept; rather does the mind express in a universal term its experience of individuals of the same class. In the deductive syllogism the mind does not reason from the general or universal to the particular but rather from the whole to the part; and in induction the mind passes from the parts to the whole rather than from particulars to the universal. In 1670 Leibniz republished Nizolius' *De veris principiis et vera ratione philosophandi contra pseudophilosophos*, praising the author's attempt to free the general forms of thought from ontological presuppositions but criticizing his inadequate notion of induction. Even if, however, Nizolius did attempt to purify logic from metaphysics and to treat it from the linguistic point of view, it seems to me that his substitution of *comprehensio* for *abstractio* and of the relation of part to whole for the relation of particular to universal contributed very little, if anything, to the discussion concerning universals. That it is individuals alone which exist would have been agreed to by all mediaeval anti-realists; but it is not enlightening to say that universals are collective terms which arise by a mental act called *comprehensio*. What is it which enables the mind to 'comprehend' groups of individuals as belonging to definite classes? Is it simply the presence of similar qualities? If this is what Nizolius meant, he cannot be said to have added anything which was not already present in terminism. But he did insist that for factual knowledge we have to go to things themselves and that it is useless to look to formal logic for information about the nature or character of things. In this way his logical views contributed to the growth of the empiricist movement.

The artificial character of the Aristotelian-Scholastic logic was also insisted on by the famous French humanist Petrus Ramus or Pierre de la Ramée (1515–72), who became a Calvinist and perished in the massacre of St. Bartholomew's Eve. True logic is a natural logic; it formulates the laws which govern man's spontaneous and natural thinking and reasoning as expressed in correct speech. It is thus the *ars disserendi* and is closely allied with rhetoric. In his *Institutionum dialecticarum libri III* Petrus Ramus divided this natural logic into two parts, the first concerning 'discovery' (*De inventione*), the second dealing with the judgment (*De iudicio*). As the function of natural logic is to enable one to answer questions concerning things, the first stage of the process of logical thought consists in discovering the points of view or categories which will enable the inquiring mind to solve the question raised. These points of view or categories (Ramus calls them *loci*) include original or underived categories like cause and effect and derived or secondary categories like genus, species, division, definition, etc. The second stage consists in applying these categories in such a way that the mind can arrive at the judgment which answers the question raised. In his treatment of the judgment Petrus Ramus distinguishes three stages; first, the syllogism; secondly, the system, the forming, that is to say, of a systematic chain of conclusions; and thirdly, the bringing of all sciences and knowledge into relation with God. Ramus' logic consisted, therefore, of two main sections, one concerning the concept, the other concerning the judgment; he had little new to offer and as his ideal was that of deductive reasoning, he was unable to make any very positive contribution to the advance of the logic of discovery. His lack of real originality did not, however, prevent his logical writings winning widespread popularity, especially in Germany, where Ramists, anti-Ramists and semi-Ramists carried on a lively controversy.

Men like Laurentius Valla, Nizolius, and Petrus Ramus were strongly influenced by their reading of the classics, especially of Cicero's writings. In comparison with Cicero's orations the logical works of Aristotle and the Scholastics seemed to them dry, abstruse and artificial. In the speeches of Cicero, on the other hand, the natural logic of the human mind was expressed in relation to concrete questions. They stressed, therefore, 'natural' logic and its close association with rhetoric or speech. They certainly contrasted the Platonic dialectic with the Aristotelian logic; but in the formation of their ideas on logic, which should be regarded as expressing a humanistic reaction against Scholasticism, Cicero was actually of greater importance than Plato. Their emphasis on rhetoric, however, coupled with the fact that they retained in practice a good deal of the outlook of the formal logician, meant that they did little to develop the method or logic of science. It is true that one of their watchwords was 'things' rather than abstract concepts; and in this respect they may be said to have encouraged the empiricist outlook; but, in general, their attitude was aesthetic rather than scientific. They were humanists, and their projected reform of logic was conceived in the interests of humanism, that is, of cultured expression and, at a deeper level, of the development of personality, rather than in the interests of empirical science.

2. Turning from the opponents of the Aristotelian-Scholastic logic to the Aristotelians themselves, one may mention first one or two scholars who promoted the study of the writings of Aristotle and opposed the Italian Platonists. George of Trebizond (1395–1484), for instance, translated and commented on a number of Aristotle's works and he attacked Plethon as the would-be founder of a new neo-Platonic pagan religion. Theodore of Gaza (1400–78), who, like George of Trebizond, became a convert to Catholicism, was also an opponent of Plethon. He translated works of Aristotle and Theophrastus; and in his ὅτι ἡ φύσις οὐ βουλεύεται he

discussed the question whether the finality which exists according to Aristotle in nature is really to be ascribed to nature. Hermolaus Barbarus (1454–93) also translated works by Aristotle and commentaries by Themistius. Aristotelian scholars of this sort were for the most part opponents of Scholasticism as well as of Platonism. In the opinion of Hermolaus Barbarus, for example, St. Albert, St. Thomas and Averroes were all philosophical 'barbarians'.

The Aristotelian camp became divided between those who interpreted Aristotle according to the mind of Averroes and those who interpreted him according to the mind of Alexander of Aphrodisias. The difference between them which most excited the attention of their contemporaries was that the Averroists maintained that there is only one immortal intellect in all men while the Alexandrists contended there is no immortal intellect in man. As both parties thus denied personal immortality they excited the hostility of the Platonists. Marsilius Ficinus, for example, declared that both parties did away with religion by denying immortality and divine providence. At the fifth Lateran Council (1512–17) the doctrines of both Averroists and Alexandrists concerning man's rational soul were condemned. In the course of time, however, the former greatly modified the theologically objectionable aspects of Averroism, which tended to become a matter of scholarship rather than of any strict adherence to Averroes's peculiar philosophical ideas.

The centre of the Averroist party was at Padua. Nicoletto Vernias, who lectured at Padua from 1471 to 1499, at first maintained the Averroistic doctrine of one immortal reason in all men; but later on he abandoned his theologically unorthodox view and defended the position that each man has an individual immortal rational soul. The same is true of Agostino Nipho or Augustinus Niphus (1473–1546), a pupil of Vernias and author of commentaries on Aristotle, who first defended the Averroistic doctrine in his *De intellectu et daemonibus* and then later abandoned it. In his *De immortalitate animae*, written in 1518 against Pomponazzi, he maintained the truth of the Thomist interpretation of Aristotle's doctrine against the interpretation given by Alexander of Aphrodisias. One may also mention Alexander Achillini (1463–1512), who taught first at Padua and afterwards at Bologna, and Marcus Antonius Zimara (1460–1532). Achillini declared that Aristotle must be corrected where he differs from the orthodox teaching of the Church, while Zimara, who commented on both Aristotle and Averroes, interpreted the latter's doctrine concerning the human intellect as referring to the unity of the most general principles of knowledge which are recognized by all men in common.

The most important figure of the Alexandrist group was Pietro Pomponazzi (1462–1525), a native of Mantua, who taught successively at Padua, Ferrara and Bologna. But if one wishes to represent Pomponazzi as a follower of Alexander of Aphrodisias, one must add that it was the Aristotelian elements of Alexander's teaching which exercised a distinctive influence on him, rather than Alexander's own developments of Aristotle's doctrine. The aim Pomponazzi seems to have had in mind was to purify Aristotle of non-Aristotelian accretions. That is why he attacked Averroism, which he regarded as a perversion of genuine Aristotelianism. Thus in his *De immortalitate animae* (1516) he takes his stand on the Aristotelian idea of the soul as the form or entelechy of the body and uses it not only against the Averroists but also against those who, like the Thomists, try to show that the human soul is naturally separable from the body and immortal. His main point is that the human soul, in its rational as in its sensitive operations, depends on the body; and in support of his argument and of the conclusion he draws from it he appeals, in accordance with Aristotle's practice, to the observable facts. This is not to say, of course, that Aristotle drew the same conclusion from the observable facts that Pomponazzi drew; but the latter followed Aristotle in appealing to empirical evidence. It was largely because of its incompatibility with the observable facts that he rejected the Averroistic hypothesis concerning the rational soul of man.

Pomponazzi argued that it is an empirically supported fact that all knowledge originates in sense-perception and that human intellection always needs an image or phantasm. In other words, even those intellectual operations which transcend the power of animals are nevertheless dependent on the body; and there is no evidence to show that while the sensitive soul of the animal is intrinsically dependent on the body man's rational soul is only extrinsically dependent. It is perfectly true that the human soul can exercise functions which the animal soul is incapable of exercising; but there is no empirical evidence to show that those higher functions of the human soul can be exercised apart from the body. The human mind, for instance, is certainly characterized by the power of self-consciousness; but it does not possess this power in the way that an independent intelligent substance would possess it, namely as a power of direct and immediate intuition of itself; the human mind knows itself only in knowing something other than itself.[1] Even the beasts enjoy some self-knowledge. 'Nor must we deny that the beasts know themselves. For it seems to be altogether stupid and irrational to say that they do not know themselves, when they love themselves and their species.'[2] Human self-consciousness transcends the rudimentary self-consciousness of the brutes; but it is none the less dependent on the soul's union with the body. Pomponazzi did not deny that intellection is itself non-quantitative and non-corporeal; on the contrary, he affirmed it;[3] but he argued that the human soul's 'participation in immateriality' does not involve its separability from the body. His main objection against the Thomists was that they in his view asserted both that the soul is and that it is not the form of the body. He considered that they did not take seriously the Aristotelian doctrine which they professed to accept; they endeavoured to have it both ways. The Platonists were at least consistent, even if they paid scant attention to the facts of psychology. Pomponazzi's own theory, however, can scarcely be considered immune from inconsistency. While rejecting a materialistic view of the rational soul,[4] he yet refused to allow that one can argue from the immaterial character of the soul's intelligent life to its capacity for existing in a state of separation from the body. Nor is it easy to understand precisely what was meant by phrases like 'participation in immateriality' or *immaterialis secundum quid*. Possibly Pomponazzi's view, if translated into more modern terms, would be that of epiphenomenalism. In any case, his main point was that investigation of the empirical facts does not permit one to state that the human soul possesses any mode of cognition or volition which it can exercise in independence of the body and that its status as form of the body precludes its natural immortality. In order to possess natural immortality its relation to the body would have to be that accepted by the Platonists, and for the truth of the Platonic theory there is no empirical evidence. To this Pomponazzi added some considerations deduced from his acceptance of the notion of a hierarchy of beings. The human rational soul stands midway in the scale; like the lower souls it is

[1] *De immortalitate animae*, 10; *Apologia*, 1, 3.
[2] *Ibid.*
[3] *De immortalitate animae*, 9.
[4] Cf. *Ibid.*, 9–10.

the form of the body, though unlike them it transcends matter in its higher operations; like the separate Intelligences it understands essences, though unlike them it can do so only in and with reference to the concrete particular.[1] It depends for its materials of knowledge on the body, though in its use of the material supplied by sense-perception it transcends matter.

The inconsistency of Pomponazzi's doctrine has been mentioned above; and I do not see how this inconsistency can be denied. It must be remembered, however, that he demanded the fulfilment of two conditions before he would recognize the soul's immortality as rationally established.[2] First of all it must be shown that the intelligence as such, in its nature as intelligence, transcends matter. Secondly it must be shown that it is independent of the body in its acquisition of the materials of knowledge. The first position Pomponazzi accepted; the second he regarded as contrary to the empirical facts. The soul's natural immortality cannot, therefore, be proved by mere reason, since, in order for it to be proved, *both* positions would have to be established.

Pomponazzi also gave consideration to the moral objections which were brought against his doctrine, namely that it was destructive of morality by denying sanctions in the future life, by confining the operation of divine justice to the present life, in which it is obviously not always fulfilled, and, most important of all, by depriving man of the possibility of attaining his last end. As regards the first point Pomponazzi argued that virtue is in itself preferable to all other things and that it is its own reward. In dying for his country or in dying rather than commit an act of injustice or sin a man gains virtue. In choosing sin or dishonour in place of death a man does not win immortality, except perhaps an immortality of shame and contempt in the mind of posterity, even if the coming of inevitable death is postponed a little longer.[3] It is true that many people would prefer dishonour or vice to death if they thought that death ended all; but this shows simply that they do not understand the true nature of virtue and vice.[4] Moreover, this is the reason why legislators and rulers have to have recourse to sanctions. In any case, says Pomponazzi, virtue is its own reward, and the essential reward (*praemium essentiale*), which is virtue itself, is diminished in proportion as the accidental reward (*praemium accidentale*, a reward extrinsic to

[1] On the human mind's knowledge of the universal, see, for example, *Apologia*, 1, 3.

[2] *De immortalitate animae*, 4. [3] *Ibid.*, 14. [4] *Ibid.*

virtue itself) is increased. This is presumably a clumsy way of saying that virtue is diminished in proportion as it is sought with a view to obtaining something other than virtue itself. In regard to the difficulty about divine justice, he asserts that no good action ever goes unrewarded and no vicious action unpunished, since virtue is its own reward and vice its own punishment.[1]

As regards the end of man or purpose of human existence, Pomponazzi insists that it is a moral end. It cannot be theoretical contemplation, which is vouchsafed to few men; nor can it consist in mechanical skill. To be a philosopher or to be a house-builder is not within the power of all;[2] but to become virtuous is within everyone's power. Moral perfection is the common end of the human race; 'for the universe would be completely preserved (*perfectissime conservaretur*) if all men were zealous and perfectly moral, but not if all were philosophers or smiths or house-builders'.[3] This moral end is sufficiently attainable within the bounds of mortal life: the idea of Kant that the attainment of the complete good of man postulates immortality was foreign to the mind of Pomponazzi. And to the argument that man has a natural desire for immortality and that this desire cannot be doomed to frustration, he answers that in so far as there is really a natural desire in man not to die, it is in no way fundamentally different from the animal's instinct to shun death, while if an elicited or intellectual desire is meant, the presence of such a desire cannot be used as an argument for immortality, for it has first to be shown that the desire is not unreasonable. One can conceive a desire for all sorts of divine privileges; but it does not follow that such a desire will be fulfilled.[4]

In his *De naturalium effectuum admirandorum causis sive de incantationibus* (generally known as the *De incantationibus*) Pomponazzi endeavours to give a natural explanation of miracles and wonders. He makes a great deal of astral influences; but his astrological explanations are, of course, naturalistic in character, even if they are erroneous. He also accepted a cyclic theory of history and historical institutions, a theory which he apparently applied even to Christianity itself. But in spite of his philosophical ideas Pomponazzi reckoned himself a true Christian. Philosophy, for example, shows that there is no evidence for the immortality of the human soul; on the contrary, it would lead us to postulate the soul's mortal character; but we know by revelation that the

[1] *De immortalitate animae*, 13–14. [2] *Ibid.*, 14. [3] *Ibid.* [4] *Ibid.*, 10.

human soul is immortal. As already mentioned, Pomponazzi's doctrine concerning the soul's mortality was condemned at the fifth Lateran Council and he was attacked in writing by Niphus and others; but he was never involved in any more serious trouble.

Simon Porta of Naples (d. 1555), in his *De rerum naturalibus principiis, De anima et mente humana*, followed Pomponazzi's doctrine concerning the mortality of the human soul; but not all the latter's disciples did so. And we have seen that the Averroist school also tended to modify its original position. Finally we find a group of Aristotelians who can be classified neither as Averroists nor as Alexandrists. Thus Andrew Cesalpino (1519–1603) tried to reconcile the two parties. He is perhaps chiefly remarkable for his botanical work; in 1583 he published a *De plantis libri XVI*. Jacobus Zabarella (1532–89), though a devoted Aristotelian, left many important questions undecided. For instance, if one accepts the eternity of motion and of the world, one can accept an eternal first mover; but if one denies the eternity of motion and of the world, one has no adequate philosophical reason for accepting an eternal first mover. In any case it cannot be demonstrated that the heaven itself is not the supreme being. Similarly, if one regards the soul's nature as form of the body, one will judge it to be mortal; but if one regards its intellectual operations, one will see that it transcends matter. On the other hand, the active intellect is God Himself, using the human passive intellect as an instrument; and the question whether the human soul is immortal or not is left undecided as far as philosophy is concerned. Zabarella was succeeded in his chair at Padua by Caesar Cremoninus (1550–1631) who also refused to allow that one can argue with certainty from the movement of the heaven to the existence of God as mover. In other words the idea of Nature as a more or less independent system was gaining ground; and, indeed, Cremoninus insisted on the autonomy of physical science. He based his own scientific ideas, however, on those of Aristotle and rejected the newer ideas in physics, including the Copernican astronomy. He is said to have been the friend of Galileo who refused to look through a telescope in case he should find it necessary to abandon the Aristotelian astronomy.

The influence of Pomponazzi was strongly felt by Lucilius Vanini (1585–1619), who was strangled and burnt as a heretic at Toulouse. He was the author of an *Amphitheatrum aeternae providentiae* (1615) and of a *De admirandis naturae reginae deaeque mortalium arcanis libri quatuor* (1616). He seems to have embraced a kind of pantheism, though he was accused of atheism, which he was said to have dissembled in his first work.

Apart from the work done by scholars in connection with the text of Aristotle, it cannot, I think, be said that the Aristotelians of the Renaissance contributed much that was valuable to philosophy. In the case of Pomponazzi and kindred figures they may be said to have encouraged a 'naturalistic' outlook; but the growth of the new physics can scarcely be attributed to the influence of the Aristotelians. It was made possible very largely by mathematical developments, and it grew in spite of, rather than because of, the Aristotelians.

In northern Europe Philip Melanchthon (1497–1560), although an associate and collaborator of Martin Luther, who was a determined enemy of Scholastic Aristotelianism, distinguished himself as a humanist. Educated in the spirit of the humanistic movement, he then fell under Luther's influence and rejected humanism; but the fact that this narrowness of outlook did not last very long shows that he was always a humanist at heart. He became the leading humanist of the early Protestant movement and was known as the *Praeceptor Germaniae* because of his educational work. For the philosophy of Aristotle he had a lively admiration, though as a thinker he was somewhat eclectic, his ideal being that of moral progress through the study of classical writers and of the Gospels. He had little interest in metaphysics, and his idea of logic, as given in his logical text-books, was influenced by that of Rudolf Agricola. Aristotle he interpreted in a nominalistic sense; and, though he freely utilized Aristotle in his *Commentarius de anima* (in which ideas drawn indirectly from Galen also make their appearance) and in his *Philosophiae moralis epitome* and *Ethicae doctrinae elementa*, he endeavoured to bring Aristotelianism into harmony with revelation and to supplement it by Christian teaching. A salient aspect of Melanchthon's teaching was his doctrine of innate principles, particularly moral principles, and of the innate character of the idea of God, both of which are intuited by means of the *lumen naturale*. This doctrine was opposed to the Aristotelian view of the mind as a *tabula rasa*.

Melanchthon's utilization of Aristotle was influential in the Lutheran universities, though it did not commend itself to all Protestant thinkers, and there occurred some lively disputes, among which may be mentioned the week's debate at Weimar in

1560 between Flacius and Strigel on freedom of the will. Melanchthon maintained the freedom of the will; but Flacius (Illyricus) considered that this doctrine, supported by Strigel, was at variance with the true theory of original sin. In spite of Melanchthon's great influence there was always a certain tension between rigid Protestant theology and the Aristotelian philosophy. Luther himself did not deny all human freedom; but he did not consider that the freedom left to man after the Fall is sufficient to enable him to achieve moral reform. It was only natural, then, that controversy should arise between those who deemed themselves genuine disciples of Luther and those who followed Melanchthon in his Aristotelianism, which was somewhat of a strange bedfellow for orthodox Lutheranism. In addition, of course, there were, as has been mentioned earlier, the disputes between the Ramists, anti-Ramists and semi-Ramists.

3. Among other revivers of ancient philosophical traditions one may mention Justus Lipsius (1547–1606), author of a *Manuductio ad stoicam philosophiam* and a *Physiologia Stoicorum*, who revived Stoicism, and the famous French man of letters, Michel de Montaigne (1533–92), who revived Pyrrhonic scepticism. In his *Essais* Montaigne revived the ancient arguments for scepticism; the relativity of sense-experience, the impossibility of the intellect's rising above this relativity to the sure attainment of absolute truth, the constant change in both object and subject, the relativity of value-judgments, and so on. Man is, in fine, a poor sort of creature whose boasted superiority to the animals is, to a great extent, a vain and hollow pretension. He should, therefore, submit himself to divine revelation, which alone gives certainty. At the same time Montaigne came to attribute considerable importance to the idea of 'nature'. Nature gives to each man a dominant type of character which is fundamentally unchangeable; and the task of moral education is to awaken and preserve the spontaneity and originality of this endowment of nature rather than to attempt to mould it into a stereotyped pattern by the methods of Scholasticism. But Montaigne was no revolutionary; he thought rather that the form of life embodied in the social and political structure of one's country represents a law of nature to which one should submit oneself. The same is true of religion. The theoretical basis of any given religion cannot be rationally established; but the moral consciousness and obedience to nature form the heart of religion, and these will only be

injured by religious anarchy. In this practical conservatism Montaigne was, of course, faithful to the spirit of Pyrrhonic scepticism, which found in the consciousness of one's ignorance an added reason for adhering to traditional social, political and religious forms. A sceptical attitude in regard to metaphysics in general might seem calculated to lead to an emphasis on empirical science; but, as far as Montaigne himself was concerned, his scepticism was rather that of a cultivated man of letters, though he was influenced too by the moral ideal of Socrates and by the Stoic ideals of tranquillity and of obedience to nature.

Among Montaigne's friends was Pierre Charron (1541–1603), who became a lawyer and later a priest. In his *Trois vérités contre tous les athées, idolâtres, juifs, Mohamétans, hérétiques et schismatiques* (1593) he maintained that the existence of one God, the truth of the Christian religion and the truth of Catholicism in particular are three proved truths; but in his main work, *De la sagesse* (1601), he adopted from Montaigne a sceptical position, though he modified it in the second edition. Man is unable to reach certainty concerning metaphysical and theological truths; but human self-knowledge, which reveals to us our ignorance, reveals to us also our possession of a free will by which we can win moral independence and dominion over the passions. The recognition and realization of the moral ideal is true wisdom, and this true wisdom is independent of dogmatic religion. 'I desire that one should be a good man without paradise and hell; these words are, in my view, horrible and abominable, "if I were not a Christian, if I did not fear God and damnation, I should do this or that".'[1]

Another Pyrrhonist was Francis Sanchez (*c.* 1552–1632), a Portuguese by birth, who studied at Bordeaux and in Italy and taught medicine first at Montpellier and afterwards at Toulouse. In his *Quod nihil scitur*, which appeared in 1580, Sanchez maintained that the human being can know nothing, if the word 'know' is understood in its full sense, that is to say, as referring to the perfect ideal of knowledge. God alone, who has created all things, knows all things. Human knowledge is based either on sense-perception or on introspection. The former is not reliable, while the latter, though assuring us of the existence of the self, can give no clear idea of it; our knowledge of the self is indefinite and indeterminate. Introspection gives us no picture of the self, and without a picture or image we can have no clear idea. On the other hand

[1] *De la sagesse*, 2, 5, 29.

though sense-perception provides us with definite images, these images are far from giving a perfect knowledge of things. Moreover, as the multiplicity of things forms a unified system, no one thing can be perfectly known unless the whole system is known; and this we cannot know.

But though Sanchez denied that the human mind can attain perfect knowledge of anything, he insisted that it can attain an approximate knowledge of some things and that the way to do so is through observation rather than through the Aristotelian-Scholastic logic. The latter makes use of definitions which are purely verbal, and syllogistic demonstration presupposes principles the truth of which is by no means clear. Of the leading sceptics Sanchez probably came nearest to anticipating the direction which philosophy and science were to take; but he was prevented by his sceptical attitude from making positive and constructive suggestions. For example, his strictures on the old deductive logic would lead one to expect a clear emphasis on the empirical investigation of nature; but his sceptical attitude in regard to sense-perception was a hindrance to his making any valuable positive contribution to the development of natural philosophy. The scepticism of these Renaissance thinkers was doubtless a symptom of the period of transition between mediaeval thought and the constructive systems of the 'modern' era; but in itself it was a blind alley.

CHAPTER XV

NICHOLAS OF CUSA

Life and works—The influence of Nicholas's leading idea on his practical activity—The coincidentia oppositorum*—'Instructed ignorance'—The relation of God to the world—The 'infinity' of the world—The world-system and the soul of the world—Man, the microcosm; Christ—Nicholas's philosophical affiliations.*

1. NICHOLAS OF CUSA is not an easy figure to classify. His philosophy is frequently included under the heading 'mediaeval philosophy', and there are, of course, some good reasons for doing this. The background of his thought was formed by the doctrines of Catholicism and by the Scholastic tradition, and he was undoubtedly strongly influenced by a number of mediaeval thinkers. It was possible, then, for Maurice De Wulf to say of him, when outlining his ideas in the third volume of his history of mediaeval philosophy, that 'in spite of his audacious theories he is only a continuer of the past',[1] and that he 'remains a mediaeval and a Scholastic'.[2] On the other hand, Nicholas lived in the fifteenth century and for some thirty years his life overlapped that of Marsilius Ficinus. Moreover, although one can emphasize the traditional elements in his philosophy and push him back, as it were, into the Middle Ages, one can equally well emphasize the forward-looking elements of his thought and associate him with the beginnings of 'modern' philosophy. But it seems to me preferable to see in him a transition-thinker, a philosopher of the Renaissance, who combined the old with the new. To treat him simply as a mediaeval thinker seems to me to involve the neglect of those elements in his philosophy which have clear affinities with the philosophical movements of thought at the time of the Renaissance and those elements which reappear at a later date in the system of a thinker like Leibniz. Yet even if one decides to classify Nicholas of Cusa as a Renaissance philosopher, there still remains the difficulty of deciding to which Renaissance current of thought his philosophy should be assigned. Is he to be associated with the Platonists on the ground that he was influenced by the neo-Platonic tradition? Or does his view of Nature as in some

[1] p. 207. [2] p. 211.

sense 'infinite' suggest rather that he should be associated with a philosopher like Giordano Bruno? There are doubtless grounds for calling him a Platonist, if one understands the term in a sufficiently generous way; but it would be peculiar if one included him in the same chapter as the Italian Platonists. And there are doubtless grounds for calling him a philosopher of Nature; but he was before all things a Christian, and he was no pantheist like Bruno. He in no way deified Nature. And he cannot be classified with the scientists, even if he was interested in mathematics. I have therefore adopted the solution of giving him a chapter to himself. And this is, in my opinion, what he deserves. Though having many affiliations, he stands more or less by himself.

Nicholas Kryfts or Krebs was born at Cusa on the Moselle in 1401. Educated as a boy by the Brothers of the Common Life at Deventer, he subsequently studied at the universities of Heidelberg (1416) and Padua (1417–23) and received the doctorate in Canon Law. Ordained priest in 1426, he took up a post at Coblenz; but in 1432 he was sent to the Council of Basle on the business of the Count von Manderscheid, who wanted to become bishop of Trier. Becoming involved in the deliberations of the Council, Nicholas showed himself a moderate adherent of the conciliar party. Later, however, he changed his attitude to the position of the papacy and fulfilled a number of missions on behalf of the Holy See. For example, he went to Byzantium in connection with the negotiations for the reunion of the Eastern Church with Rome, which was accomplished (temporarily) at the Council of Florence. In 1448 he was created cardinal and in 1450 he was appointed to the bishopric of Brixen, while from 1451 to 1452 he acted as Papal Legate in Germany. He died in the August of 1464 at Todi in Umbria.

In spite of his ecclesiastical activities Nicholas wrote a considerable number of works, of which the first important one was the *De concordantia catholica* (1433–4). His philosophical writings include the *De docta ignorantia* and the *De coniecturis* (1440), the *De Deo abscondito* (1444) and the *De quaerendo Deum* (1445), the *De Genesi* (1447), the *Apologia doctae ignorantiae* (1449), the *Idiotae libri* (1450), the *De visione Dei* (1453), the *De possest* (1460), the *Tetralogus de non aliud* (1462), the *De venatione sapientiae* (1463) and the *De apice theoriae* (1464). In addition he composed works on mathematical subjects, like the *De transmutationibus geometricis* (1450), the *De mathematicis complementis* (1453) and the *De mathematica perfectione* (1458), and on theological subjects.

2. The thought of Nicholas of Cusa was governed by the idea of unity as the harmonious synthesis of differences. On the metaphysical plane this idea is presented in his idea of God as the *coincidentia oppositorum*, the synthesis of opposites, which transcends and yet includes the distinct perfections of creatures. But the idea of unity as the harmonious reconciliation or synthesis of opposites was not confined to the field of speculative philosophy: it exercised a powerful influence on Nicholas's practical activity, and it goes a long way towards explaining his change of front in regard to the position in the Church of the Holy See. I think that it is worth while to show how this is the case.

At the time when Nicholas went to the Council of Basle and published his *De concordantia catholica* he saw the unity of Christendom threatened, and he was inspired by the ideal of preserving that unity. In common with a number of other sincere Catholics he believed that the best way of preserving or restoring that unity lay in emphasizing the position and rights of General Councils. Like other members of the conciliar party, he was encouraged in this belief by the part played by the Council of Constance (1414–18) in putting an end to the Great Schism which had divided Christendom and caused so much scandal. He was convinced at that time of the natural rights of popular sovereignty not only in the State but also in the Church; and, indeed, despotism and anarchy were always abhorrent to him. In the State the monarch does not receive his authority directly and immediately from God, but rather from or through the people. In the Church, he thought, a General Council, representing the faithful, is superior to the pope, who possesses only an administrative primacy and may for adequate reasons be deposed by a Council. Though he maintained the idea of the empire, his ideal was not that of a monolithic empire which would override or annul the rights and duties of national monarchs and princes: it was rather that of a federation. In an analogous manner, though he was a passionate believer in the unity of the Church, he believed that the cause of this unity would be better served by a moderate conciliar theory than by an insistence on the supreme position of the Holy See. By saying this I do not mean to imply that Nicholas did not at that time believe that the conciliar theory was theoretically justified or that he supported it only for practical reasons, because he considered that the Church's unity would thus be best preserved and that ecclesiastical reform would stand a better chance of being realized if the supremacy of General Councils was recognized. But these practical considerations certainly weighed with him. Moreover, a 'democratic' view of the Church as a harmonious unity in multiplicity, expressed juridically in the conciliar theory, undoubtedly possessed a strong attraction for him. He aimed at unity in the Church and in the State and between Church and State; but the unity at which he aimed, whether in the Church or in the State, or between Church and State, was not a unity resulting from the annulment of differences.

Nicholas came to abandon the conciliar theory and to act as a champion of the Holy See. This change of view was certainly the expression of a change in his theoretical convictions concerning the papacy as a divine institution possessing supreme ecclesiastical authority and jurisdiction. But at the same time he was certainly influenced by the conviction that the cause which he had at heart, namely the unity of the Church, would not in fact be promoted by belittling the position of the pope in the Church. He came to think that an effective implementation of the conciliar theory would be more likely to result in another schism than in unity, and he came to look on the supreme position of the Holy See as the expression of the essential unity of the Church. All the limited authorities in the Church receive their authority from the absolute or sovereign authority, the Holy See, in a manner analogous to the way in which finite, limited beings receive their being from the absolute infinite, God.

This change of view did not involve the acceptance of extravagant theories, like those of Giles of Rome. Nicholas did not envisage, for example, the subordination of State to Church, but rather a harmonious and peaceful relation between the two powers. It was always at reconciliation, harmony, unity in difference that he aimed. In this ideal of unity without suppression of differences he is akin to Leibniz. It is true that Nicholas's attempts to secure harmonious unity were by no means always successful. His attempts to secure harmony in his own diocese were not altogether felicitous; and the reunion of the Eastern Church with Rome, in which he co-operated, was of brief duration. But Leibniz's somewhat unpractical, and sometimes indeed superficial, plans and ideals of unity were also unrealized in practice.

3. God is, for Nicholas, the *coincidentia oppositorum*, the synthesis of opposites in a unique and absolutely infinite being. Finite things are multiple and distinct, possessing their different natures and qualities while God transcends all the distinctions and oppositions which are found in creatures. But God transcends these distinctions and oppositions by uniting them in Himself in an incomprehensible manner. The distinction of essence and existence, for example, which is found in all creatures, cannot be in God as a distinction: in the actual infinite, essence and existence coincide and are one. Again, in creatures we distinguish greatness and smallness, and we speak of them as possessing attributes in different degrees, as being more or less this or that. But in God all these distinctions coincide. If we say that God is the greatest being (*maximum*), we must also say that He is the least being (*minimum*), for God cannot possess size or what we ordinarily call 'greatness'. In Him *maximum* and *minimum* coincide.[1] But we cannot comprehend this synthesis of distinctions and oppositions. If we say that God is the *complicatio oppositorum et eorum coincidentia*,[2] we must realize that we cannot have a positive understanding of what this means. We come to know a finite thing by bringing it into relation to or comparing it with the already known: we come to know a thing by means of comparison, similarity, dissimilarity and distinction. But God, being infinite, is like to no finite thing; and to apply definite predicates to God is to liken Him to things and to bring Him into a relation of similarity with them. In reality the distinct predicates which we apply to finite things coincide in God in a manner which surpasses our knowledge.

4. It is clear, then, that Nicholas of Cusa laid emphasis on the *via negativa*, the way of negation in our intellectual approach to God. If the process of getting to know or becoming acquainted with a thing involves bringing the hitherto unknown thing into relation with, or comparing it with, the already known, and if God is unlike every creature, it follows that the discursive reason cannot penetrate God's nature. We know of God what He is not rather than what He is. In regard, therefore, to positive knowledge of the divine nature our minds are in a state of 'ignorance'. On the other hand, this 'ignorance' of which Nicholas speaks is not the ignorance of someone who has no knowledge of God or who has never made the effort to understand what God is. It is, of course, the result of human psychology and of the limitations

[1] *De docta ignorantia*, 1, 4. [2] *Ibid.*, 2, 1.

which necessarily affect a finite mind when confronted by an infinite object which is not an empirically given object. But, in order to possess a real value it must be apprehended as the result of these factors, or at any rate as the result of the infinity of God and the finitude of the human mind. The 'ignorance' in question is not the result of a refusal to make an intellectual effort or of religious indifference: it proceeds from the realization of God's infinity and transcendence. It is thus 'learned' or 'instructed ignorance'. Hence the title of Nicholas's most famous work, *De docta ignorantia*.

It may appear inconsistent to stress the 'negative way' and at the same time to affirm positively that God is the *coincidentia oppositorum*. But Nicholas did not reject the 'affirmative way' altogether. For example, since God transcends the sphere of numbers He cannot be called 'one' in the sense in which a finite thing, as distinct from other finite things, is called 'one'. On the other hand, God is the infinite Being and the source of all multiplicity in the created world; and as such He is the infinite unity. But we cannot have a positive understanding of what this unity is in itself. We do make positive affirmations about God, and we are justified in doing so; but there is no positive affirmation about the divine nature which does not need to be qualified by a negation. If we think of God in terms simply of ideas drawn from creatures our notion of Him is less adequate than the realization that He transcends all our concepts of Him: negative theology is superior to positive or affirmative theology. Superior to both, however, is 'copulative' theology by which God is apprehended as the *coincidentia oppositorum*. God is rightly recognized as the supreme and absolutely greatest Being: He cannot be greater than He is. And as the greatest Being He is perfect unity.[1] But we can also say of God that He cannot be smaller than He is. We can say, therefore, that He is the *minimum*. In fact, He is both the greatest and the smallest in a perfect *coincidentia oppositorum*. All theology is 'circular', in the sense that the attributes which we rightly predicate of God coincide in the divine essence in a manner which surpasses the understanding of the human mind.[2]

The lowest stage of human knowledge is sense-perception. The senses by themselves simply affirm. It is when we come to the level of reason (*ratio*) that there is both affirmation and denial. The discursive reason is governed by the principle of contradiction,

[1] *De docta ignorantia*, I, 5.

[2] *Ibid.*, I, 21.

the principle of the incompatibility or mutual exclusion of opposites; and the activity of the reason cannot bring us to anything more than an approximate knowledge of God. In accordance with his fondness for mathematical analogies Nicholas compares the reason's knowledge of God to a polygon inscribed in a circle. However many sides one adds to the polygon it will not coincide with the circle, even though it may approximate more and more to doing so. What is more, our knowledge of creatures also is only approximate, for their 'truth' is hidden in God. In fine, all knowledge by means of the discursive reason is approximate, and all science is 'conjecture'.[1] This theory of knowledge was developed in the *De coniecturis*; and Nicholas explained that the highest possible natural knowledge of God is attained not by discursive reasoning (*ratio*) but by intellect (*intellectus*), a superior activity of the mind. Whereas sense-perception affirms and reason affirms and denies, intellect denies the oppositions of reason. Reason affirms *X* and denies *Y*, but intellect denies *X* and *Y* both disjunctively and together; it apprehends God as the *coincidentia oppositorum*. This apprehension or intuition cannot, however, be properly stated in language, which is the instrument of reason rather than of intellect. In its activity as intellect the mind uses language to suggest meaning rather than to state it; and Nicholas employs mathematical analogies and symbols for this purpose. For example, if one side of a triangle is extended to infinity, the other two sides will coincide with it. Again, if the diameter of a circle is extended to infinity the circumference will coincide in the end with the diameter. The infinite straight line is thus at the same time a triangle and a circle. Needless to say, Nicholas regarded these mathematical speculations as no more than symbols; the mathematical infinite and the absolutely infinite being are not the same, though the former can both serve as a symbol for the latter and constitute an aid to thought in metaphysical theology.[2]

The leading ideas of the *De docta ignorantia* were resumed in the writings which compose the *Idiotae*, and in the *De venatione sapientiae* Nicholas reaffirmed his belief in the idea of 'learned' or 'instructed ignorance'. In this work he reaffirmed also the doctrine contained in the *De non aliud*. God cannot be defined by other terms: He is His own definition. Again, God is not other than anything else, for He defines everything else, in the sense that He alone is the source and conserver of the existence of all things.[3] Nicholas

[1] *De docta ignorantia*, 1, 3. [2] *Ibid.*, 1, 12. [3] *De venatione sapientiae*, 14.

also reaffirmed the central idea which he had developed in the *De possest*. 'God alone is *Possest*, because He is in act what He can be.'[1] He is eternal act. This idea he took up again in the *De apice theoriae*, his last work, in which God is represented as *posse ipsum*, the absolute power which reveals itself in creatures. The emphasis laid on this idea has suggested to students of Nicholas's works a change of view on the part of the author. And there is, indeed, a good deal to be said in favour of this interpretation. Nicholas says expressly in *De apice theoriae* that he once thought that the truth about God is found better in darkness or obscurity than in clarity and he adds that the idea of *posse*, of power or being able, is easy to understand. What boy or youth is ignorant of the nature of *posse*, when he knows very well that he can eat, run and speak? And if he were asked whether he could do anything, carry a stone, for example, without the power to do so, he would judge such a question to be entirely superfluous. Now, God is the absolute *posse ipsum*. It would appear, then, that Nicholas felt the need of counterbalancing the negative theology on which he had formerly laid such stress. And we may say perhaps that the idea of *posse*, together with other positive ideas like that of light, of which he made use in his natural theology, expressed his conviction of the divine immanence, while the emphasis on negative theology represented rather his belief in the divine transcendence. But it would be wrong to suggest that Nicholas abandoned the negative for the affirmative way. He makes it quite clear in his last work that the divine *posse ipsum* is in itself incomprehensible and that it is incommensurable with created power. In the *Compendium*,[2] which he wrote a year before the *De apice theoriae*, Nicholas says that the incomprehensible Being, while remaining always the same, shows Himself in a variety of ways, in a variety of 'signs'. It is as though one face appeared in different ways in a number of mirrors. The face is one and the same, but its appearances, which are all distinct from itself, are various. Nicholas may have described the divine nature in various ways, and he may very well have thought that he had overdone the way of negation; but it does not seem that there was any fundamental change in his point of view. God was always for him transcendent, infinite and incomprehensible, even though He was also immanent and even though Nicholas may have come to see the desirability of bringing this aspect of God into greater prominence.

[1] *De venatione sapientiae*, 13.

[2] 8.

5. In speaking of the relation between God and the world Nicholas used phrases which have suggested to some readers a pantheistic interpretation. God contains all things; He is *omnia complicans*. All things are contained in the divine simplicity, and without Him they are nothing. God is also *omnia explicans*, the source of the multiple things which reveal something of Him. *Deus ergo est omnia complicans, in hoc quod omnia in eo; est omnia explicans, in hoc quia ipse in omnibus.*[1] But Nicholas protested that he was no pantheist. God contains all things in that He is the cause of all things: He contains them *complicative*, as one in His divine and simple essence. He is in all things *explicative*, in the sense that He is immanent in all things and that all things are essentially dependent on Him. When he states that God is both the centre and the circumference of the world[2] he is to be interpreted neither in a pantheistic nor in an acosmistic sense. The world is not, says Nicholas, a limited sphere with a definite centre and circumference. Any point can be taken and considered as the world's centre, and it has no circumference. God, then, can be called the centre of the world in view of the fact that He is everywhere or omnipresent and the circumference of the world in that He is nowhere, that is, by local presence. Nicholas was certainly influenced by writers like John Scotus Eriugena, and he employed the same type of bold phrases and statements which Meister Eckhart had employed. But in spite of a strong tendency to acosmism, as far as the literal meaning of some of his statements is concerned, it is clear that he insisted strongly on the distinction between the finite creature and the infinite Godhead.

In phrases which recall to mind the doctrine of John Scotus Eriugena Nicholas explains that the world is a theophany, a 'contraction' of the divine being. The universe is the *contractum maximum* which came into existence through emanation from the *absolutum maximum*.[3] Every creature is, as it were, a created God or God created (*quasi Deus creatus*).[4] Nicholas even goes so far as to say that God is the absolute essence of the world or universe, and that the universe is that very essence in a state of 'contraction' (*Est enim Deus quidditas absoluta mundi seu universi. Universum vero est ipsa quidditas contracta*).[5] Similarly, in the *De coniecturis*[6] Nicholas declares that to say that God is in the world is also to say that the world is in God, while in the *De visione Dei*[7] he speaks of

[1] *De docta ignorantia*, 2, 3. [2] *Ibid.*, 2, 11. [3] *Ibid.*, 2, 4.
[4] *Ibid.*, 2, 2. [5] *Ibid.*, 2, 4. [6] 2, 7. [7] 12.

God as invisible in Himself but visible *uti creatura est*. Statements of this sort certainly lend themselves to a pantheistic interpretation; but Nicholas makes it clear on occasion that it is a mistake to interpret them in this way. For example, in the *De coniecturis*[1] he asserts that 'man is God, but not absolutely, since he is man. He is therefore a human God (*humanus est igitur Deus*).' He goes on to assert that 'man is also the world' and explains that man is the microcosm or 'a certain human world'. His statements are bold, it is true; but by saying that man is God, though not absolutely, he does not appear to mean more than other writers meant when they called man the image of God. It is clear that Nicholas was deeply convinced of the world's nothingness apart from God and of its relation to God as a mirror of the divine. The world is the *infinitas contracta* and the *contracta unitas*.[2] But this does not mean that the world is God in a literal sense; and in the *Apologia doctae ignorantiae* Nicholas explicitly rejects the charge of pantheism. In the *explicatio Dei* or creation of the world unity is 'contracted' into plurality, infinity into finitude, simplicity into composition, eternity into succession, necessity into possibility.[3] On the plane of creation the divine infinity expresses or reveals itself in the multiplicity of finite things, while the divine eternity expresses or reveals itself in temporal succession. The relation of creatures to the Creator surpasses our understanding; but Nicholas, according to his wont, frequently provides analogies from geometry and arithmetic, which, he believed, made things a bit clearer.

6. But though the world consists of finite things it is in a sense infinite. For example, the world is endless or indeterminate in respect of time. Nicholas agrees with Plato that time is the image of eternity,[4] and he insists that since before creation there was no time we must say that time proceeded from eternity. And if time proceeded from eternity it participates in eternity. 'I do not think that anyone who understands denies that the world is eternal, although it is not eternity.'[5] 'Thus the world is eternal because it comes from eternity and not from time. But the name "eternal" belongs much more to the world than to time since the duration of the world does not depend on time. For if the motion of the heaven and time, which is the measure of motion, were to cease, the world would not cease to exist.'[6] Nicholas thus makes a distinction between time and duration, though he does not develop the

[1] 2, 14. [2] *De docta ignorantia*, 2, 4. [3] *Ibid.*
[4] *De venatione sapientiae*, 9. [5] *De ludo globi*, 1. [6] *Ibid.*

theme. Time is the measure of motion, and it is thus the instrument of the measuring mind and depends on the mind.[1] If motion disappeared, there would be no time; but there would still be duration. Successive duration is the copy or image of the absolute duration which is eternity. We can conceive eternity only as endless duration. The duration of the world is thus the image of the divine eternity and can be called in some sense 'infinite'. This is a curious line of argument, and it is not easy to see precisely what is meant; but presumably Nicholas meant, in part at least, that the world's duration is potentially endless. It is not the absolute eternity of God, but it has not of itself any necessary limits.

The universe is one, unbounded by any other universe. It is, therefore, in some sense spatially 'infinite'. It is without any fixed centre, and there is no point which one could not choose to regard as the world's centre. There is, of course, no absolute 'up' or 'down' either. The earth is neither the centre of the world nor its lowest and least honourable part; nor has the sun any privileged position. Our judgments in these matters are relative. Everything in the universe moves, and so does the earth. 'The earth, which cannot be the centre, cannot be without any motion.'[2] It is smaller than the sun, but it is larger than the moon, as we know from observation of eclipses.[3] Nicholas does not appear to say explicitly that the earth rotates round the sun, but he makes it clear that both the sun and the earth move, together with all the other bodies, though their velocities are not the same. The fact that we do not perceive the earth's motion is no valid argument against its motion. We perceive motion only in relation to fixed points; and if a man in a boat on a river were unable to see the banks and did not know that the water itself was moving he would imagine that the boat was stationary.[4] A man stationed on the earth may think that the earth is stationary and that the other heavenly bodies are in motion, but if he were on the sun or the moon or Mars he would think the same of the body on which he was stationed.[5] Our judgments about motion are relative: we cannot attain 'absolute truth' in these astronomical matters. In order to compare the movements of the heavenly bodies we have to do so in relation to selected fixed points; but there are no fixed points in actuality. We can, therefore, attain only an approximate or relative knowledge in astronomy.

[1] *De ludo globi*, 2.
[2] *De docta ignorantia*, 2, 11.
[3] *Ibid.*, 2, 12.
[4] *Ibid.*
[5] *Ibid.*

7. The idea of a hierarchy of levels of reality from matter, through organisms, animals and man, up to pure spirits was a leading feature both of Aristotelianism and of the Platonic tradition. But Nicholas, while retaining this idea, laid particular emphasis on the individual thing as a unique manifestation of God. In the first place, no two individual things are exactly alike. By saying this Nicholas did not mean to deny the reality of species. The Peripatetics, he says,[1] are right in saying that universals do not actually exist: only individual things exist, and universals as such belong to the conceptual order. None the less members of a species have a common specific nature which exists in each of them in a 'contracted' state, that is to say, as an individual nature.[2] No individual thing, however, realizes fully the perfection of its species; and each member of a species has its own distinct characteristics.[3]

In the second place, each individual thing mirrors the whole universe. Every existent thing 'contracts' all other things, so that the universe exists *contracte* in every finite thing.[4] Moreover, as God is in the universe and the universe in God, and as the universe is in each thing, to say that everything is in each thing is also to say that God is in each thing and each thing in God. In other words, the universe is a 'contraction' of the divine being, and each finite thing is a 'contraction' of the universe.

The world is therefore a harmonious system. It consists of a multiplicity of finite things; but its members are so related to one another and to the whole that there is a 'unity in plurality'.[5] The one universe is the unfolding of the absolute and simple divine unity, and the whole universe is reflected or mirrored in each individual part. According to Nicholas, there is a soul of the world (*anima mundi*); but he rejects the Platonic view of this soul. It is not an actually existent being distinct from God on the one hand and from the finite things in the world on the other hand. If the soul of the world is regarded as a universal form containing in itself all forms, it has no separate existence of its own. The forms exist actually in the divine Word, as identical with the divine Word, and they exist in things *contracte*,[6] that is, as the individual forms of things. Nicholas evidently understood the Platonists as teaching that universal forms exist in a soul of the world, which is distinct from God, and this view he rejected. In

[1] *De docta ignorantia*, 2, 6. [2] *Ibid.*; cf. *De coniecturis*, 21, 3.
[3] *De docta ignorantia*, 3, 1. [4] *Ibid.*, 2, 5. [5] *Ibid.*, 2, 6. [6] *Ibid.*, 2, 9.

the *Idiotae*[1] he says that what Plato called the 'soul of the world' Aristotle called 'nature', and he adds that in his opinion the 'soul of the world' or 'nature' is God, 'who works all things in all things'. It is clear, then, that although Nicholas borrowed from Platonism the phrase 'soul of the world' he did not understand by this an existent being distinct from God and intermediate between God and the world. In his cosmology there is no intermediary stage in creation between the actual infinite, God, and the potential infinite, the created world.

8. Although each finite thing mirrors the whole universe, this is particularly true of man who combines in himself matter, organic life, sensitive animal life and spiritual rationality. Man is the microcosm, a little world, embracing in himself the intellectual and material spheres of reality.[2] 'We cannot deny that man is called the microcosm, that is, a little world'; and just as the great world, the universe, has its soul, so has man his soul.[3] The universe is mirrored in every part, and this is true analogously of man, who is the little universe or world. The nature of man is mirrored in a part like the hand, but it is mirrored more perfectly in the head. So the universe, though mirrored in every part, is mirrored more perfectly in man. Therefore man can be called a 'perfect world, although he is a little world and a part of the great world'.[4] In fact, as uniting in himself attributes which are found separately in other beings man is a finite representation of the divine *coincidentia oppositorum.*

The universe is the *concretum maximum,* while God is the *absolutum maximum,* absolute greatness. But the universe does not exist apart from individual things; and no individual thing embodies all the perfections of its species. The absolute greatness is thus never fully 'contracted' or rendered 'concrete'. We can conceive, however, a *maximum contractum* or *concretum* which would unite in itself not only the various levels of created existence, as man does, but also the Godhead itself together with created nature, though this union 'would exceed all our understanding'.[5] But though the mode of union is a mystery, we know that in Christ divine and human nature have been united without confusion of natures or distinction of persons. Christ, then, is the *maximum concretum.* He is also the *medium absolutum,* not only in the sense that in Him there is a unique and perfect union of the

[1] 3, 13. [2] *De docta ignorantia,* 3, 3. [3] *De ludo globi,* 1.
[4] *Ibid.* [5] *De docta ignorantia,* 3, 2.

uncreated and the created, of the divine and human nature, but also in the sense that He is the unique and necessary means by which human beings can be united to God.[1] Without Christ it is impossible for man to achieve eternal happiness. He is the ultimate perfection of the universe,[2] and in particular of man, who can realize his highest potentialities only through incorporation with Christ. And we cannot be incorporated with Christ or transformed into His image save through the Church, which is His body.[3] The *Dialogus de pace seu concordantia fidei* shows that Nicholas was by no means narrow in his outlook and that he was quite prepared for concessions to the Eastern Church for the sake of unity; but his works in general by no means suggest that he favoured sacrificing the integrity of the Catholic faith in order to obtain external unity, profoundly concerned though he was about unity and deeply conscious of the fact that such unity could be obtained only through peaceful agreement.

9. It is clear enough that Nicholas of Cusa made copious use of the writings of preceding philosophers. For example, he often quotes the Pseudo-Dionysius; and it is obvious that he was strongly influenced by the latter's insistence on negative theology and on the use of symbols. He knew, too, the *De divisione naturae* of John Scotus Eriugena, and though Eriugena's influence on his thought was doubtless less than that exercised by the Pseudo-Dionysius (whom he thought of, of course, as the disciple of St. Paul) it is reasonable to suppose that some of his bold statements on the way in which God becomes 'visible' in creatures were prompted by a reading of the ninth-century philosopher's work. Again, Nicholas was certainly influenced by the writings of Meister Eckhart and by the latter's use of startling antinomies. Indeed, a great deal of Nicholas's philosophy, his theory of *docta ignorantia*, for example, his idea of God as the *coincidentia oppositorum*, his insistence on the world as a divine self-manifestation and as the *explicatio Dei*, his notion of man as the microcosm, can be regarded as a development of earlier philosophies, particularly those belonging in a wide sense to the Platonic tradition and those which may be classed as in some sense 'mystical'. His fondness for mathematical analogies and symbolism recalls not only the writings of Platonists and Pythagoreans in the ancient world but also those of St. Augustine and other Christian writers. It is considerations of this sort which provide much justification for those who would

[1] *De visione Dei*, 19–21. [2] *Ibid.*, 21. [3] *De docta ignorantia*, 3, 12.

class Nicholas of Cusa as a mediaeval thinker. His preoccupation with our knowledge of God and with the world's relation to God points backward, it might be maintained, to the Middle Ages. His whole thought moves, some historians would say, in mediaeval categories and bears the imprint of mediaeval Catholicism. Even his more startling utterances can be paralleled in the case of writers whom everyone would class as mediaevals.

On the other hand, it is possible to go to the opposite extreme and to attempt to push Nicholas forward into the modern period. His insistence on negative theology, for example, and his doctrine of God as the *coincidentia oppositorum* can be assimilated to Schelling's theory of the Absolute as the vanishing-point of all differences and distinctions, while his view of the world as the *explicatio Dei* can be regarded as a foretaste of Hegel's theory of Nature as God-in-His-otherness, as the concrete manifestation or embodiment of the abstract Idea. His philosophy can, that is to say, be considered as an anticipation of German idealism. In addition it is obvious that Nicholas's idea of the mirroring of the universe in each finite thing and of the qualitative difference which exists between any two things reappeared in the philosophy of Leibniz.

It can hardly be denied, I think, that there is truth in both these conflicting points of view. Nicholas's philosophy undoubtedly depended on or utilized to a great extent preceding systems. On the other hand, to point out the similarities between certain aspects of his thought and the philosophy of Leibniz is by no means to indulge in far-fetched analogies. When it comes to connecting Nicholas of Cusa with post-Kantian German speculative idealism the links are clearly more tenuous, and there is more chance of anachronistic assimilations; but it is true that interest in his writings began to show itself in the nineteenth century and that this was largely due to the direction taken in that century by German thought. But if there is truth in both points of view, that is all the more reason, I think, for recognizing in Nicholas a transition-thinker, a figure of the Renaissance. His philosophy of Nature, for example, certainly contained elements from the past, but it represented also the growing interest in the system of Nature and what one may perhaps call the growing feeling for the universe as a developing and self-unfolding system. Nicholas's idea of the 'infinity' of the world influenced other Renaissance thinkers, especially Giordano Bruno, even though Bruno developed

Nicholas's ideas in a direction which was alien to the latter's mind and convictions. Again, however much Nicholas's theory of Nature as the *explicatio Dei* may have been dependent on the Platonic or neo-Platonic tradition, we find in that theory an insistence on the individual thing and on Nature as a system of individual things, none of which are exactly alike, that looks forward, as has already been mentioned, to the Leibnizian philosophy. Furthermore, his rejection of the idea that anything in the world can properly be called stationary and of the notions of any absolute 'centre' or 'up' and 'down' links him with the cosmologists and scientists of the Renaissance rather than with the Middle Ages. It is perfectly true, of course, that Nicholas's conception of the relation of the world to God was a theistic conception; but if Nature is looked on as a harmonious system which is in some sense 'infinite' and which is a developing or progressive manifestation of God, this idea facilitates and encourages the investigation of Nature for its own sake and not simply as a stepping-stone to the metaphysical knowledge of God. Nicholas was not a pantheist, but his philosophy, in regard to certain aspects at least, can be grouped with that of Bruno and other Renaissance philosophers of Nature; and it was against the background of these speculative philosophies that the scientists of the Renaissance thought and worked. One may remark in this connection that Nicholas's mathematical speculations provided a stimulus for Leonardo da Vinci.

In conclusion we may perhaps remind ourselves that though Nicholas's idea of the infinite system of Nature was developed by philosophers like Giordano Bruno and though these speculative natural philosophies formed a background for and stimulus to the scientific investigation of Nature, Nicholas himself was not only a Christian but also an essentially Christian thinker who was preoccupied with the search for the hidden God and whose thought was definitely Christocentric in character. It was in order to illustrate this last point that in dealing with his theory of man as the microcosm I mentioned his doctrine of Christ as the *maximum contractum* and the *medium absolutum*. In his humanistic interests, in his insistence on individuality, in the value he attached to fresh mathematical and scientific studies, and in the combination of a critical spirit with a marked mystical bent he was akin to a number of other Renaissance thinkers; but he continued into the Renaissance the faith which had animated and inspired the great thinkers of the Middle Ages. In a sense his mind was steeped in the new ideas which were fermenting at the time; but the religious outlook which permeated his thought saved him from the wilder extravagances into which some of the Renaissance philosophers fell.

CHAPTER XVI

PHILOSOPHY OF NATURE (I)

General remarks—Girolamo Cardano—Bernardino Telesio—Francesco Patrizzi—Tommaso Campanella—Giordano Bruno—Pierre Gassendi.

1. In the last chapter mention was made of the link between Nicholas of Cusa's idea of Nature and the other philosophies of Nature which appeared at the time of the Renaissance. Nicholas's idea of Nature was theocentric; and in this aspect of his philosophy he stands close to the leading philosophers of the Middle Ages; but we have seen how in his thought the idea of Nature as an infinite system, in which the earth occupies no privileged position, came to the fore. With a number of other Renaissance thinkers there arose the idea of Nature considered as a self-sufficient unity, as a system unified by all-pervading forces of sympathy and attraction and animated by a world-soul, rather than, as with Nicholas of Cusa, as an external manifestation of God. By these philosophers Nature was regarded practically as an organism, in regard to which the sharp distinctions, characteristic of mediaeval thought, between living and non-living and between spirit and matter, lost their meaning and application. Philosophies of this type naturally tended to be pantheistic in character. In certain respects they had an affinity with aspects of the revived Platonism or neo-Platonism of the Renaissance; but whereas the Platonists laid emphasis on the supernatural and on the soul's ascent to God, the philosophers of Nature emphasized rather Nature itself considered as a self-sufficient system. This is not to say that all the Renaissance thinkers who are usually regarded as 'natural philosophers' abandoned Christian theology or looked on themselves as revolutionaries; but the tendency of their thought was to loosen the bonds which bound nature to the supernatural. They tended to 'naturalism'.

It is, however, rather difficult to make general judgments about those Renaissance thinkers whom historians are accustomed to classify as 'natural philosophers' or 'philosophers of Nature'; or perhaps one should say rather that it is dangerous to do so. Among the Italians, for example, one can certainly find affinities between the philosophy of Giordano Bruno and the German romantic philosophy of the nineteenth century. But 'romanticism' is not exactly a characteristic which one would naturally attribute to the thought of Girolamo Fracastoro (1483–1553), who was physician to Pope Paul III and who wrote on medical subjects, as well as composing a work on astronomy, the *Homocentricorum seu de stellis liber* (1535). In his *De sympathia et antipathia rerum* (1542) he postulated the existence of 'sympathies' and 'antipathies' between objects, that is, of forces of attraction and repulsion, to explain the movements of bodies in their relations to one another. The names 'sympathy' and 'antipathy' may appear perhaps to be symptomatic of a romantic outlook; but Fracastoro explained the mode of operation of these forces by postulating *corpuscula* or *corpora sensibilia* which are emitted by bodies and enter through the pores of other bodies. Applying this line of thought to the problem of perception, he postulated the emission of *species* or images which enter the percipient subject. This theory obviously renewed the mechanical theories of perception put forward in ancient times by Empedocles, Democritus and Epicurus, even though Fracastoro did not adopt the general atomistic theory of Democritus. A view of this kind emphasizes the passivity of the subject in its perception of external objects, and in his *Turrius sive de intellectione* (published 1555) he says that understanding (*intellectio*) is but the representation of an object to the mind, the result of the reception of a *species* of the object. From this he drew the conclusion that understanding is probably purely passive. It is true that he also postulated a special power, which he named *subnotio*, of experiencing or apprehending the various impressions of a thing as a totality possessing relations which are present in the object itself or as a meaningful whole. So one is not entitled to say that he denied any activity on the part of the mind. He did not deny the mind's reflective power nor its power to construct universal concepts or terms. Moreover, the use of the term *species* was obviously derived from the Aristotelian-Scholastic tradition. None the less, Fracastoro's theory of perception has a strongly marked 'naturalistic' character. Perhaps it is to be associated with his interests as a medical man.

Fracastoro was a physician, while Cardano was a mathematician and Telesio possessed a wide interest in scientific matters. But though a man like Telesio stressed the need for empirical investigation and research in science he certainly did not confine himself to hypotheses which could be empirically verified but advanced philosophical speculations of his own. It is not always easy to decide whether a given Renaissance thinker should be classified as a philosopher or a scientist: a number of philosophers of the time were interested in science and in scientific investigation, while the scientists were by no means always averse to philosophic speculation. However, those whose personal scientific work was of importance in the development of scientific studies are very reasonably classed as scientists, while those who are noteworthy rather for their speculation than for their personal contribution to scientific studies are classed as philosophers of Nature, even though they may have contributed indirectly to scientific advance by anticipating speculatively some of the hypotheses which the scientists attempted to verify. But the union of philosophic speculation with an interest in scientific matters, sometimes combined with an interest in alchemy and even in magic, was characteristic of the Renaissance thinkers. They had a profound belief in the free development of man and in his creative power and they sought to promote human development and power by varied means. Their minds delighted in free intellectual speculation, in the development of fresh hypotheses and in the ascertaining of new facts about the world; and the not uncommon interest in alchemy was due rather to the hope of thus extending man's power, control and wealth than to mere superstition. With the necessary qualifications one can say that the Renaissance spirit expressed a shift of emphasis from the other-worldly to the this-worldly, from transcendence to immanence, and from man's dependence to man's creative power. The Renaissance was a time of transition from a period in which the science of theology formed the mental background and stimulated men's minds to a period in which the growth of the particular natural sciences was to influence more and more the human mind and human civilization; and some at least of the Renaissance philosophies were fertilizing agents for the growth of science rather than systems of thought which one could be expected to treat very seriously as philosophies.

In this chapter I propose to deal briefly with some of the Italian philosophers of Nature and with the French philosopher, Pierre Gassendi. In the next chapter I shall treat of German philosophers of Nature, excluding Nicholas of Cusa, who has been considered separately.

2. Girolamo Cardano (1501–76) was a mathematician of note

and a celebrated physician, who became professor of medicine at Pavia in 1547. A typically Renaissance figure he combined his mathematical studies and the practice of medicine with an interest in astrology and a strong bent towards philosophical speculation. His philosophy was a doctrine of hylozoism. There is an original, indeterminate matter, filling all space. In addition it is necessary to postulate a principle of production and movement, which is the world-soul. The latter becomes a factor in the empirical world in the form of 'warmth' or light; and from the operation of the world-soul in matter empirical objects are produced, all of which are en-souled and between which there exist relations of sympathy and antipathy. In the process of the world's formation the heaven, the seat of warmth, was first separated from the sublunary world, which is the place of the wet and the cold elements. Cardano's enthusiasm for astrology was expressed in his conviction that the heavens influence the course of events in the sublunary world. Metals are produced in the interior of the earth through the mutual reactions of the three elements of earth, water and air; and not only are they living things but they all tend towards the form of gold. As for what are normally called living things, animals were produced from worms, and the forms of worms proceed from the natural warmth in the earth.

This view of the world as an animate organism or as a unified system animated by a world-soul obviously owed a good deal to the *Timaeus* of Plato, while some ideas, like those of indeterminate matter and of 'forms', derived from the Aristotelian tradition. It might be expected perhaps that Cardano would develop these ideas in a purely naturalistic direction, but he was not a materialist. There is in man an immortal rational principle, *mens*, which enters into a temporary union with the mortal soul and the body. God created a definite number of these immortal souls, and immortality involves metempsychosis. In this view of the immortal mind as something separable from the mortal soul of man one can see the influence of Averroism; and one can probably see the same influence in Cardano's refusal to admit that God created the world freely. If creation was due simply and solely to the divine choice, there was no reason or ground for creation: it was a necessary process rather than the result of God's choice.

But there was more in Cardano's philosophy than a mere antiquarianism or a patching-together of elements taken from different philosophies of the past to make a hylozoistic and animistic system. It is clear that he laid great emphasis on the idea of natural law and on the unity of Nature as a law-governed system; and in this respect his thought was in tune with the scientific movement of the Renaissance, even though he expressed his belief in natural law in terms of ideas and theories taken from philosophies of the past. This conviction in regard to the reign of law comes out clearly in his insistence that God has subjected the heavenly bodies, and bodies in general, to mathematical laws and that the possession of mathematical knowledge is a form of true wisdom. It is represented even by his belief in 'natural magic', for the power of magic rests on the unity of all that is. Naturally, the sense in which words can be said to 'be' and to belong to the realm of causes needs a far clearer analysis than Cardano attempted; but the interest in magic which was one of the characteristics of some of the Renaissance thinkers expresses their belief in the causal system of the universe, even though to us it may seem fantastic.

3. A hylozoistic theory was also maintained by Bernardino Telesio (1509–88) of Cosenza in Calabria, the author of *De natura rerum iuxta propria principia* and the founder of the *Academia Telesiana* or *Cosentina* at Naples. According to Telesio, the fundamental causes of natural events are the warm and cold elements, the opposition between which is concretely represented by the traditional antithesis between heaven and earth. In addition to these two elements Telesio postulated a third, passive matter, which becomes distended or rarefied through the activity of the warm and compressed through the activity of the cold element. In the bodies of animals and men there is present the 'spirit', a fine emanation of the warm element, which passes throughout the body by means of the nerves though it is properly situated in the brain. This idea of 'spirit' goes back to the Stoic theory of the *pneuma* which was itself derived from the medical schools of Greece, and it reappears in the philosophy of Descartes under the name 'animal spirits'.

The 'spirit', which is a kind of psychological substance, can receive impressions produced by external things and can renew them in the memory. The spirit has thus the function of receiving sense-impressions and of anticipating future sense-impressions; and analogical reasoning from case to case is grounded in sense-perception and memory. Reasoning begins, then, with sense-perception and its function is to anticipate sense-perception, in that its conclusions or anticipations of future experience must be empirically verified. Telesio does not hesitate to draw the conclusion that *intellectio longe est sensu imperfectior.*[1] He interpreted geometry, for example, in the light of this theory, namely as a sublimated form of analogical reasoning based on sense-perception. On the other hand, he admitted the idea of empty space, which is not a thing but rather the system of relations between things. Places are modifications of this general order or system of relations.

The fundamental natural drive or instinct in man is that of self-preservation. This is the ruling instinct in animals as well, and even in anorganic matter, which is non-living only in a comparative sense, as is shown by the omnipresence of motion, a symptom of life. (Indeed, all things are gifted with 'perception' in some degree, an idea which was later developed by Leibniz.) It was in terms of this fundamental instinct that Telesio analysed man's emotional life. Thus love and hate are feelings directed respectively towards that which promotes and that which hinders self-preservation, while joy is the feeling attendant on self-preservation. The cardinal virtues, prudence, for example, and fortitude, are all various forms in which the fundamental instinct expresses itself in its fulfilment, whereas sadness and kindred emotions reflect a weakening of the vital impulse. We have here an obvious anticipation of Spinoza's analysis of the emotions.

Telesio did not think, however, that man can be analysed and explained exclusively in biological terms. For man is able to transcend the biological urge to self-preservation: he can even neglect his own happiness and expose himself freely to death. He can also strive after union with God and contemplate the divine. One must postulate, therefore, the presence in man of a *forma superaddita*, the immortal soul, which informs body and 'spirit', and which is capable of union with God.

The professed method of Telesio was the empirical method; for he looked to sense-experience for knowledge of the world and regarded reasoning as little more than a process of anticipating future sense-experience on the basis of past experience. He may thus be regarded as having outlined, even if somewhat crudely, one aspect of scientific method. At the same time he propounded a philosophy which went far beyond what could be empirically verified by sense-perception. This point was emphasized by

[1] *De rerum natura*, 8, 3.

Patrizzi, to whom I shall turn next. But the combination of a hostility towards Scholastic abstractions not only with an enthusiasm for immediate sense-experience but also with insufficiently-grounded philosophical speculations was not uncharacteristic of Renaissance thought, which was in many respects both rich and undisciplined.

4. Although Francesco Patrizzi (1529–97) observed that Telesio did not conform in his philosophical speculations to his own canons of verification he himself was much more given to speculation than was Telesio, the essence of whose philosophy may very possibly lie in its naturalistic aspect. Born in Dalmatia Patrizzi ended his life, after many wanderings, as professor of the Platonic philosophy at Rome. He was the author of *Discussionum peripateticarum libri XV* (1571) and *Nova de universis philosophia* (1591), in addition to a number of other works, including fifteen books on geometry. A determined enemy of Aristotle, he considered that Platonism was far more compatible with Christianity and that his own system was eminently adapted for winning heretics back to the Church. He dedicated his *Nova philosophia* to Pope Gregory XIV. Patrizzi might thus very well have been treated in the chapter on the revival of Platonism; but he expounded a general philosophy of Nature, and so I have chosen to deal briefly with his thought here.

Patrizzi had recourse to the ancient light-theme of the Platonic tradition. God is the original and uncreated light, from which proceeds the visible light. This light is the active, formative principle in Nature, and as such it cannot be called wholly material. Indeed, it is a kind of intermediary being which constitutes a bond between the purely spiritual and the purely material and inert. But besides light it is necessary to postulate other fundamental factors in Nature. One of these is space, which Patrizzi describes in a rather baffling manner. Space is subsistent existence, inhering in nothing. Is it, then, a substance? It is not, says Patrizzi, an individual substance composed of matter and form, and it does not fall within the category of substance. On the other hand it is a substance in some sense; for it inheres in nothing else. It cannot therefore be identified with quantity. Or, if it is, it is not to be identified with any quantity which falls under the category of quantity: it is the source and origin of all empirical quantity. Patrizzi's description of space reminds one rather of that given by Plato in the *Timaeus*. It cannot be called anything definite. It is neither purely spiritual; nor is it on the other hand a corporeal substance: rather is it 'incorporeal body', abstract extension which precedes, logically at least, the production of distinct bodies and which can be logically constructed out of *minima* or points. The idea of the *minimum*, which is neither great nor small but is potentially either, was utilized by Giordano Bruno. Space is filled, according to Patrizzi, by another fundamental factor in the constitution of the world, namely 'fluidity'. Light, warmth, space and fluidity are the four elementary factors or principles.

Patrizzi's philosophy was a curious and bizarre amalgam of neo-Platonic speculation and an attempt to explain the empirical world by reference to certain fundamental material or quasi-material factors. Light was for him partly the visible light, but it was also a metaphysical principle or being which emanates from God and animates all things. It is the principle of multiplicity, bringing the multiple into existence; but it is also the principle of unity which binds all things into a unity. And it is by means of light that the mind is enabled to ascend to God.

5. Another strange mixture of various elements was provided by Tommaso Campanella (1568–1639), a member of the Dominican Order and author of the famous political Utopia, the *City of the Sun* (*Civitas solis*, 1623), in which he proposed, whether seriously or not, a communistic arrangement of socicty obviously suggested by Plato's *Republic*. Campanella spent a very considerable portion of his life in prison, mainly on account of charges of heresy; but he composed a number of philosophical works, including *Philosophia sensibus demonstrata* (1591), *De sensu rerum* (1620), *Atheismus triumphatus* (1631) and *Philosophia universalis seu metaphysica* (1637). In politics he upheld the ideal of a universal monarchy under the spiritual headship of the pope and the temporal leadership of the Spanish monarchy. The very man who had to undergo a term of imprisonment on the accusation of conspiring against the king of Spain lauded the Spanish monarchy in his *De monarchia hispanica* (1640).

Campanella was strongly influenced by Telesio, and he insisted on the direct investigation of Nature as the source of our knowledge about the world. He tended also to interpret reasoning on the same lines as those laid down by Telesio. But the inspiration of his thought was different. If he emphasized sense-perception and the empirical study of Nature, he did so because Nature is, as he put it, the living statue of God, the mirror or image of God.

There are two main ways of coming to a knowledge of God, first the study with the aid of the senses of God's self-revelation in Nature, and secondly the Bible. That Nature is to be regarded as a manifestation of God was, of course, a familiar theme in mediaeval thought. We have only to think of St. Bonaventure's doctrine of the material world as the *vestigium* or *umbra Dei*; and Nicholas of Cusa, who influenced Campanella, had developed this line of thought. But the Renaissance Dominican laid stress on the actual observation of Nature. It is not primarily a question of finding mystical analogies in Nature, as with St. Bonaventure, but rather of reading the book of Nature as it lies open to sense-perception.

That God's existence can be proved was a matter of which Campanella felt quite certain. And the way he set about proving it is interesting, if only because of its obvious affinity with the teaching of Descartes in the seventeenth century. Arguing against scepticism, Campanella maintained that we can at least know that we do not know this or that, or that we doubt whether this or that is the case. Moreover, in the act of doubting one's own existence is revealed. On this point Campanella is a kind of link between St. Augustine with his *Si fallor, sum*, and Descartes, with his *Cogito, ergo sum*. Again, in the consciousness of one's own existence there is also given the consciousness of what is other than oneself: in the experience of finitude is given the knowledge that other being exists. In love, too, is given the consciousness of the existence of the other. (Perhaps Descartes might have adopted and utilized this point of view to advantage.) I, therefore, exist, and I am finite; but I possess, or can possess, the idea of the infinite reality. This idea cannot be my own arbitrary construction or indeed my construction at all: it must be the effect of God's operation in me. Through reflection on the idea of infinite and independent being I see that God actually exists. In this way knowledge of my own existence as a finite being and knowledge of God's existence as infinite being are closely linked. But it is possible also for man to have an immediate contact with God, which affords the highest possible knowledge open to man and at the same time involves love of God; and this loving knowledge of God is the best way of knowing God.

God is the Creator of all finite beings, and these are composed, according to Campanella, of being and not-being, the proportion of not-being increasing as one descends the scale of perfection. This is certainly a very peculiar way of speaking; but the main idea was derived from the Platonic tradition and was not Campanella's invention. The chief attributes (*primalitates*) of being are power, wisdom and love; and the more not-being is mixed with being, the weaker is the participation in these attributes. As one descends the scale of perfection, therefore, one finds an increasing proportion of impotence or lack of power, of unwisdom and of hatred. But every creature is animate in some sense, and nothing is without some degree of perception and feeling. Moreover, all finite things together form a system, the precondition of which is provided by space; and they are related to one another by mutual sympathies and antipathies. Everywhere we find the fundamental instinct of self-preservation. But this instinct or drive is not to be interpreted in a narrowly and exclusively egoistic sense. Man, for example, is a social being, adapted to life in society. Furthermore, he is able to rise above love of self in the narrow sense to love of God, which expresses his tendency to return to his origin and source.

We come to recognize the primary attributes of being through reflection on ourselves. Every man is aware that he can act or that he has some power (*posse*), that he can know something and that he wills or has love. We then ascribe these attributes of power, wisdom and love to God, the infinite being, in the highest possible degree, and we find them in non-human finite things in varying degrees. This is an interesting point because it illustrates Campanella's tendency to imply that we interpret Nature on an analogy with ourselves. In a sense all knowledge is knowledge of ourselves. We perceive the effects of things on ourselves, and we find ourselves limited and conditioned by things other than ourselves. We attribute to them, therefore, activities and functions analogous to those we perceive in ourselves. Whether this point of view is consistent with Campanella's insistence, under the influence of Telesio, on direct sense-knowledge of Nature is perhaps questionable; but the justification for our interpretation of Nature on an analogy with ourselves he found in the doctrine of man as the microcosm. If man is the microcosm or little world, the world in miniature, the attributes of being as found in man are also the attributes of being in general. If this way of thinking really represents Campanella's mind, it is open to the obvious objection that the theory of man as the microcosm should be a conclusion and not a premiss. But Campanella started, of course, from the view that God is revealed in every creature as in a mirror. If this point of view is adopted, it follows that knowledge of the being best known to us is the key to the knowledge of being in general.

6. The most celebrated of the Italian philosophers of Nature is Giordano Bruno. Born at Nola near Naples in 1548 (hence sometimes called 'the Nolan') he entered the Dominican Order at Naples; but in 1576 he laid aside the habit at Rome after he had been accused of holding heterodox opinions. He then began a life of wandering which took him from Italy to Geneva, from Geneva to France, from France to England, where he gave some lectures at Oxford, from England back again to France and then to Germany. Returning rashly to Italy, he was arrested by the Venetian Inquisition in 1592, and in the following year he was handed over to the Roman Inquisition and spent some years in prison. Finally, as he continued to stand by his opinions, he was burned at Rome on February 17th, 1600.

Bruno's writings include *De umbris idearum* (1582) and the following works in dialogue form: *La cena de le ceneri* (1584), *Della causa, principio e uno* (1584), *De l'infinito, universo e mondi* (1584), *Spaccio della bestia trionfante* (1584), *Cabala del cavallo pegaseo con l'agguiunta dell'asino cillenico* (1585) and *Degl' eroici furori* (1585). Among his other works are three Latin poems, published in 1591, the *De triplici minimo et mensura ad trium speculativarum scientiarum et multarum activarum artium principia libri V*, the *De monade, numero et figura, secretioris nempe physicae, mathematicae et metaphysicae elementa* and the *De immenso et innumerabilibus, seu de universo et mundis libri VIII*.

The starting-point and the terminology of Bruno's thought were furnished, very naturally, by preceding philosophies. He took over the neo-Platonic metaphysical' scheme, as mediated by the Italian Platonists and by Nicholas of Cusa. Thus in his *De umbris idearum* he represented Nature with its multiplicity of beings as proceeding from the divine super-substantial unity. There is a hierarchy in Nature from matter upwards to the immaterial, from darkness to light; and Nature is intelligible in so far as it is the expression of the divine ideas. Human ideas, however, are simply shadows or reflections of the divine ideas, though human knowledge is capable of advancement and deepening in proportion as the mind moves upwards from the objects of sense-perception towards the divine and original unity, which in itself, however, is impenetrable by the human intellect.

But this traditional scheme formed little more than the

background of Bruno's thought, against which his own philosophy developed. Though neo-Platonism had always represented the world as a divine 'emanation' or creation and as the reflection of God, it had always stressed the divine transcendence and incomprehensibility. But the inner movement of Bruno's speculation was towards the idea of the divine immanence, and so towards pantheism. He never achieved a complete conciliation of the two points of view; nor did he ever carry through a definite exclusion of one point of view in favour of the other.

In his *Della causa, principio e uno* Bruno asserts God's transcendence and incomprehensibility and His creation of things which are distinct from Him. 'From the knowledge of all dependent things we cannot infer any other knowledge of the first cause and principle than by the rather inefficacious way of traces (*de vestigio*). . . . So that to know the universe is like knowing nothing of the being and substance of the first principle. . . . Behold, then, about the divine substance, both because of its infinity and because of its being extremely remote from its effects . . . we can know nothing save by way of traces, as the Platonists say, or by remote effects, as the Peripatetics say. . . .'[1] The interest soon shifts, however, to the principles and causes in the world, and Bruno brings into prominence the idea of the world-soul as the immanent causal and moving agent. The primary and principal faculty of the world-soul is the universal intellect, which is 'the universal physical efficient agent' and 'the universal form' of the world.[2] It produces natural forms in the world, while our intellects produce universal ideas of these forms. It is the universal form of the world in that it is everywhere present and animates everything. Leather as leather or glass as glass, says Bruno, is not in itself animate in the ordinary sense; but it is united to and informed by the world-soul and it has, as matter, the potentiality of forming part of an organism. Matter, in the sense of Aristotle's 'first matter', is indeed, considered from one point of view, a formless and potential substrate; but considered as the fountain-head and source of forms it cannot be regarded as an unintelligible substrate; ultimately pure matter is the same thing as pure act. Bruno used Nicholas of Cusa's doctrine of the *coincidentia oppositorum* in regard to the world. Starting with the assertion of distinctions he went on to show their relative character. The world consists of distinct things and factors, but in the end it is seen to be 'one, infinite,

[1] *Dialogo secondo, Opere*, I, pp. 175–6.

[2] *Ibid.*, p. 179.

immobile' (that is, incapable of local motion), one being, one substance.[1] The idea, taken over from Nicholas of Cusa, that the world is infinite is supported by arguments in the *De l'infinito, universo e mondi*. 'I call the universe *tutto infinito*, because it has no margin, limit or surface; I do not call the universe *totalmente infinito*, because any part that we take is finite, and of the innumerable worlds which it contains each is finite. I call God *tutto infinito* because He excludes of Himself all limits and because each of His attributes is one and infinite; and I call God *totalmente infinito* because He is wholly in the whole world and infinitely and totally in each of its parts, in distinction from the infinity of the universe which is totally in the whole but not in the parts, if indeed, in reference to the infinite, they can be called parts.'[2]

Here Bruno draws a distinction between God and the world. He also speaks of God, using the phrases of Nicholas of Cusa, as being the infinite *complicatamente e totalmente* whereas the world is the infinite *explicatamente e non totalmente*. But the tendency of his thought is always to weaken these distinctions or to synthesize the 'antitheses'. In the *De triplici minimo* he speaks of the *minimum* which is found on the mathematical, physical and metaphysical planes. The mathematical *minimum* is the *monas* or unit; the physical *minimum* is the atom or monad, indivisible and in some sense animate, and immortal souls are also 'monads'. Nature is the harmonious self-unfolding system of atoms and monads in their interrelations. Here we have a pluralistic view of the universe, conceived in terms of monads, each of which is in some sense gifted with perception and appetition; and this aspect of Bruno's philosophy anticipates the monadology of Leibniz. But we have already noted his remark that one can hardly speak of 'parts' in relation to the infinite world; and the complementary aspect of his philosophy is represented by his idea of finite things as accidents or *circonstanzie* of the one infinite substance. Again, God is called *Natura naturans* in so far as He is considered in distinction from His manifestations, while He is called *Natura naturata* when considered in His self-manifestation. Here we have the monistic aspect of Bruno's thought which anticipated the philosophy of Spinoza. But as has been already remarked, Bruno never positively abandoned pluralism in favour of monism. It is reasonable to say that the tendency of his thought lay in the

[1] *Dialogo quinto*, pp. 247 ff.

[2] *Dialogo primo*, p. 298.

direction of monism; but in actual fact he continued to believe in the transcendent God. He considered, however, that philosophy deals with Nature and that God in Himself is a subject which can be properly treated only in theology, above all by the method of negative theology. One is not justified, then, in stating roundly that Bruno was a pantheist. One can say, if one likes, that his mind tended to move away from the categories of neo-Platonism and of Nicholas of Cusa in the direction of a greater insistence on the divine immanence; but there is no real reason for supposing that his retention of the doctrine of the divine transcendence was a mere formality. His philosophy may be a stage on the road from Nicholas of Cusa to Spinoza; but Bruno himself did not travel to the end of that road.

But Bruno's thought was not inspired simply by the neo-Platonic tradition interpreted in a pantheistic sense; it was also deeply influenced by the astronomical hypothesis of Copernicus. Bruno was not a scientist, and he cannot be said to have contributed to the scientific verification of the hypothesis; but he developed speculative conclusions from it with characteristic boldness, and his ideas acted as a stimulus on other thinkers. He envisaged a multitude of solar systems in limitless space. Our sun is simply one star among others, and it occupies no privileged position: still less does the earth. Indeed, all judgments about position are, as Nicholas of Cusa said, relative; and no one star or planet can be called the centre of the universe in an absolute sense. There is no centre, and there is no absolute up or down. Moreover, from the fact that the earth is inhabited by rational beings we are not entitled to draw the conclusion that it is unique in dignity or that it is the centre of the universe from the valuational point of view: for all we know, the presence of life, even of rational beings like ourselves, may not be confined to this planet. The solar systems rise and perish, but all together they form one developing system, indeed one organism animated by the world-soul. Bruno did not confine himself to maintaining that the earth moves and that judgments of position are relative: he linked up the Copernican hypothesis of the earth's movement round the sun with his own metaphysical cosmology. He thus entirely rejected the geocentric and anthropocentric conception of the universe both from the astronomical point of view and in the wider perspective of speculative philosophy. In his system it is Nature considered as an organic whole which stands in the centre of the picture, and not terrestrial human beings who are *circonstanzie* or accidents of the one living world-substance, even if from another point of view each is a monad, mirroring the whole universe.

In some early writings Bruno dealt with questions concerning memory and logic under the influence of the doctrines of Raymond Lull (d. 1315). We can distinguish ideas in the universal intelligence, in the physical order as forms and in the logical order as symbols or concepts. The task of a developed logic would be to show how the plurality of ideas emerge from the 'one'. But though he may be regarded as in some sense a link between Lull and Leibniz, Bruno is best known for his doctrines of the infinite world-substance and of monads and for his speculative use of the Copernican hypothesis. In regard to the first doctrine he probably exercised some influence upon Spinoza, and he was certainly acclaimed as a prophet by later German philosophers like Jacobi and Hegel. In regard to the theory of monads, which is more apparent in his later works, he certainly anticipated Leibniz in some important points, even though it seems improbable that Leibniz received any substantial direct influence from Bruno in the formation of his ideas.[1] Bruno adopted and utilized many ideas taken from Greek, mediaeval and Renaissance thinkers, especially from Nicholas of Cusa; but he possessed an original mind with a strong speculative bent. His ideas were often far-fetched and fantastic and his thought undisciplined, though he was certainly capable of methodical thinking when he chose; and he played the rôle not only of philosopher but also of poet and seer. We have seen that he cannot be called a pantheist in an unqualified manner; but this does not mean that his attitude towards Christian dogmas was either favourable or respectful. He aroused the disapproval and hostility not only of Catholic theologians but also of Calvinists and Lutherans, and his unhappy end was due not to his championship of the Copernican hypothesis, nor to his attacks on Aristotelian Scholasticism, but to his apparent denial of some central theological dogmas. He did make an attempt to explain away his unorthodoxy by reference to a kind of 'double-truth' theory; but his condemnation for heresy was perfectly understandable, whatever one may think of the physical treatment meted out to him. His ultimate fate has, of course, led some writers to attribute to him a greater philosophic importance than

[1] See note on p. 268.

he possesses; but though some of the encomia which have sometimes been lavished upon him in an uncritical manner were exaggerated, he nevertheless remains one of the leading and most influential thinkers of the Renaissance.

7. The date of Pierre Gassendi's death, 1655, coupled with the fact that he carried on a controversy with Descartes, offers a very good reason for considering his philosophy at a later stage. On the other hand, his revival of Epicureanism justifies one, I think, in including it under the general heading of Renaissance philosophy.

Born in Provence in 1592, Pierre Gassendi studied philosophy there at Aix. Turning to theology, he lectured for a time on the subject and was ordained priest; but in 1617 he accepted the chair of philosophy at Aix, where he expounded more or less traditional Aristotelianism. His interest in the discoveries of the Renaissance scientists, however, led his thought into other paths, and in 1624 there appeared the first book of his *Exercitationes paradoxicae adversus Aristotelicos*. He was at this time a canon of Grenoble. The work was to have been composed of seven books; but, apart from a portion of the second book, which appeared posthumously in 1659, no more than the first book was written. In 1631 he published a work against the English philosopher Robert Fludd (1574–1637), who had been influenced by Nicholas of Cusa and Paracelsus, and in 1642 his objections against Descartes's system were published.[1] In 1645 he was appointed professor of mathematics at the Collège Royal in Paris. While occupying this post he wrote on some physical and astronomical questions, but he is best known for the works which he wrote under the influence of the Epicurean philosophy. His treatise *De vita, moribus et doctrina Epicuri libri VIII* appeared in 1647, and this was followed in 1649 by the *Commentarius de vita, moribus et placitis Epicuri seu animadversiones in decimum librum Diogenis Laertii*. This was a Latin translation of and commentary on the tenth book of Diogenes Laërtius's *Lives of the Philosophers*. In the same year he published his *Syntagma philosophiae Epicuri*. His *Syntagma philosophicum* was published posthumously in the edition of his works (1658). In addition he wrote a number of *Lives*, of Copernicus and Tycho Brahe for example.

Gassendi followed the Epicureans in dividing philosophy into logic, physics and ethics. In his logic, which includes his theory

[1] They are the fifth in the series of objections published in the works of Descartes.

of knowledge, his eclecticism at once becomes apparent. In company with many other philosophers of the time he insisted on the sense-origin of all our natural knowledge: *nihil in intellectu quod non prius fuerit in sensu.* And it was from an empiricist standpoint that he criticized Descartes. But although he spoke as if the senses were the only criterion of evidence he also admitted, as one might well expect of a mathematician, the evidence of the deductive reason. As to his 'physics', this was clearly a combination of very different elements. On the one hand, he revived the Epicurean atomism. Atoms, possessing size, shape and weight (interpreted as an inner propensity to movement) move in empty space. According to Gassendi, these atoms come from a material principle, the substrate of all becoming, which, with Aristotle, he described as 'prime matter'. With the help of atoms, space and motion he gave a mechanistic account of Nature. Sensation, for example, is to be explained mechanically. On the other hand, man possesses a rational and immortal soul, the existence of which is revealed by the facts of self-consciousness and by man's power of forming general ideas and apprehending spiritual objects and moral values. Moreover, the system, harmony and beauty of Nature furnish a proof of the existence of God, who is incorporeal, infinite and perfect. Man, as a being who is both spiritual and material and who can know both the material and the spiritual, is the microcosm. Finally, the ethical end of man is happiness, and this is to be understood as absence of pain in the body and tranquillity in the soul. But this end cannot be fully achieved in this life; it can be perfectly attained only in the life after death.

The philosophy of Gassendi may be regarded as an adaptation of Epicureanism to the requirements of Christian orthodoxy. But there is no good reason for saying that the spiritualistic side of his philosophy was inspired simply by motives of diplomatic prudence and that he was insincere in his acceptance of theism and of the spirituality and immortality of the soul. It may well be that the historical importance of his philosophy, so far as it possesses historical importance, lies in the impulse it gave to a mechanistic view of Nature. But this does not alter the fact that his philosophy, considered in itself, is a curious amalgam of Epicurean materialism with spiritualism and theism and of a rather crude empiricism with rationalism. His philosophizing exercised a considerable influence in the seventeenth century, but it was too unsystematic, too much of a patchwork, and too unoriginal to exercise any lasting influence.

CHAPTER XVII

PHILOSOPHY OF NATURE (2)

Agrippa von Nettesheim—Paracelsus—The two Van Helmonts—Sebastian Franck and Valentine Weigel—Jakob Böhme—General remarks.

In this chapter I propose to outline the ideas not only of men like Paracelsus, who are naturally labelled philosophers of Nature, but also of the German mystic, Jakob Böhme. The latter would possibly be more accurately classified as a theosophist than as a philosopher; but he certainly had a philosophy of Nature, which in some respects resembles that of Bruno. Böhme was doubtless much more religiously-minded than Bruno, and to classify him as a philosopher of Nature may involve placing the accent in the wrong place; but, as we have already seen, the term 'Nature' often meant a great deal more for a Renaissance philosopher than the system of empirically-given distinct things which are capable of being investigated systematically.

1. The theme of microcosm and macrocosm, which is prominent in the Italian philosophies of Nature, occupies a prominent place in the German philosophies of the Renaissance. A feature of the neo-Platonic tradition, it became one of the cardinal points in the system of Nicholas of Cusa, and his profound influence on Giordano Bruno has already been mentioned. His influence was naturally also felt by the German thinkers. Thus according to Heinrich Cornelius Agrippa von Nettesheim (1486–1535) man unites in himself the three worlds, namely the terrestrial world of the elements, the world of the heavenly bodies and the spiritual world. Man is the ontological bond between these worlds, and this fact explains his ability to know all three worlds: man's range of knowledge depends on his ontological character. Further, the harmonious unity of the three worlds in man, the microcosm, reflects the harmonious unity which exists between them in the macrocosm. Man has his soul, and the universe possesses its soul or spirit (*spiritus mundi*), which is responsible for all production. There are, indeed, sympathies and antipathies between distinct things; but they are due to the presence in things of immanent vital principles which are effluences from the *spiritus mundi*.

Finally, the affinities and connections between things and the presence in them of latent powers form the basis for the magical art: man can discover and utilize these powers in his service. In 1510 Agrippa von Nettesheim published his *De occulta philosophia* and though he decried the sciences, including magic, in his *Declamatio de vanitate et incertitudine scientiarum* (1527), he republished the work on occultism in a revised form in 1533. Like Cardano, he was a physician and, like Cardano again, he was interested in magic. It is not an interest which one would associate with modern doctors; but the combination of medicine with magic in an earlier age is understandable. The physician was conscious of powers and healing properties of herbs and minerals and of his ability to utilize them to a certain extent. But it does not follow that he had a scientific understanding of the processes which he himself employed; and it is hardly to be wondered at if he was attracted by the idea of wresting nature's secrets from her by occult means and employing the hidden powers and forces thus discovered. Magic would appear to him as a kind of extension of 'science', a short-cut to the acquisition of further knowledge and skill.

2. This view of the matter is borne out by the example of that strange figure, Theophrastus Bombast von Hohenheim, commonly known as Paracelsus. Born at Einsiedeln in 1493, he was for a time professor of medicine at Basle. He died at Salzburg in 1541. Medical science, which promotes human happiness and well-being, was for him the highest of the sciences. It depends, indeed, on observation and experiment; but an empirical method does not by itself constitute medicine a science. The data of experience must be systematized. Furthermore, the true physician will take account of other sciences like philosophy, astrology and theology; for man, with whom medical science is concerned, participates in three worlds. Through his visible body he participates in the terrestrial world, the world of the elements, through his astral body in the sidereal world and through his immortal soul (the *mens* or *Fünklein*) in the spiritual and divine world. Man is thus the microcosm, the meeting-place of the three worlds which compose the macrocosm; and the physician will have to take this into account. The world at large is animated by its immanent vital principle, the *archeus*, and an individual organism like man develops under the impulse of its own vital principle. Medical treatment should consist essentially in stimulating the activity of the

archeus, a principle which obviously embodies the truth that the task of the physician is to assist nature to do her work. Indeed, Paracelsus put forward some perfectly sensible medical views. Thus he laid considerable emphasis on the individual and on individual factors in the treatment of disease; no disease, he thought, is ever found in exactly the same form or runs precisely the same course in any two individuals. For the matter of that, his idea that the physician should widen his field of view and take other sciences into account was by no means devoid of value. For it means essentially that the physician should consider man as a whole and should not confine his attention exclusively to physical symptoms and causes and treatment.

In some respects, then, Paracelsus was an enlightened theorist; and he attacked violently the medical practice of the time. In particular, he had no use for slavish adherence to the teaching of Galen. His own methods of procedure were highly empirical, and he can hardly be called a scientific chemist, even though he was interested in chemical specifics and drugs but he had at least an independent mind and an enthusiasm for the progress of medicine. With this interest in medicine, however, he combined an interest in astrology and in alchemy. Original matter consists of or contains three fundamental elements or substances, sulphur, mercury and salt. Metals are distinguished from one another through the predominance of this element rather than that; but since they all consist ultimately of the same element it is possible to transform any metal into any other metal. The possibility of alchemy is thus a consequence of the original constitution of matter.

Although Paracelsus may have tended to mix up philosophical speculation with 'science' and also with astrology and alchemy in a fantastic manner, he drew a sharp distinction between theology on the one hand and philosophy on the other. The latter is the study of Nature, not of God Himself. Yet Nature is a self-revelation of God; and we are thus able to attain to some philosophical knowledge of Him. Nature was originally present in God, in the 'great mystery' or 'divine abyss'; and the process by which the world is built up is one of differentiation, that is, of the production of distinctions and oppositions. We come to know only in terms of oppositions. For example, we come to know joy in its opposition to sorrow, health in its opposition to sickness. Similarly, we come to know good only in opposition to evil and God only in opposition to Satan. The term of the world's development will be the absolute division between good and evil, which will constitute the last judgment.

3. Paracelsus' ideas were developed by the Belgian chemist and physician, John Baptist van Helmont (1577–1644). The two primary elements are water and air, and the fundamental substances, namely sulphur, mercury and salt, proceed from water and can be transmuted into water. Van Helmont made a real discovery, however, when he realized that there are gases which are different from atmospheric air. He discovered that what he called *gas sylvestre* (carbon dioxide), which is emitted by burning charcoal, is the same as the gas given off by fermenting must. He is, therefore, of some importance in the history of chemistry. Further, his interest in this science, combined with his interests in physiology and medicine, prompted him to experiment in the application of chemical methods in preparing drugs. In this matter he carried on the work of Paracelsus. Van Helmont was much more of a careful experimenter than Paracelsus had been; but he shared the latter's belief in and enthusiasm for alchemy. In addition, he took up and developed Paracelsus' vitalistic theory. Each organism has its own general *archeus* or *aura vitalis*, on which are dependent the *archei* of the different parts or members of the organism. Not content with the vital principles, however, he also postulated a power of movement, which he called *blas*. This is of various kinds. There is, for instance, a *blas* peculiar to the heavenly bodies (*blas stellarum*) and another which is found in man, the relation between the *blas humanum* and the human *archeus* being left rather obscure.

John Baptist van Helmont did indeed indulge in speculations about the Fall and its effects on human psychology; but he was concerned primarily with chemistry, medicine and physiology, to which one must add alchemy. His son, however, Francis Mercury Van Helmont (1618–99), with whom Leibniz was acquainted,[1] developed a monadology according to which there are a finite number of imperishable monads. Each monad may be called corporeal in so far as it is passive, and spiritual in so far as it is active and endowed with some degree of perception. The inner sympathies and attractions between monads cause groups of them to form complex structures, each of which is governed by a central monad. In man, for example, there is a central monad, the soul,

[1] It seems probable that at any rate the term 'monad' was adopted by Leibniz from the younger Van Helmont or through a reading of Bruno suggested by Van Helmont.

which rules the whole organism. This soul shares in the imperishable character of all monads; but it cannot achieve the perfection of its development in one lifetime, that is to say, in the period in which it is the controlling and directing power in one particular set or series of monads. It therefore enters into union with other bodies or sets of monads until it has perfected itself. It then returns to God, who is the *monas monadum* and the author of the universal harmony of creation. The mediator between God and creatures is Christ.

The younger Van Helmont regarded his philosophy as a valuable antidote to the mechanistic interpretation of Nature, as represented by Descartes (in regard to the material world) and by the philosophy of Thomas Hobbes. His monadology was a development of Bruno's ideas, though it was doubtless also influenced by the vitalistic doctrines of Paracelsus and the elder Van Helmont. It is obvious that it anticipated in many respects the monadology of a much more talented man, Leibniz, though it would appear that Leibniz arrived independently at his fundamental ideas. There was, however, a second link between Van Helmont and Leibniz, and that was a common interest in occultism and alchemy, though in Leibniz's case this interest was perhaps simply one way in which his insatiable curiosity showed itself.

4. The German mystical tradition found a continuation in Protestantism with men like Sebastian Franck (1499–1542) and Valentine Weigel (1533–88). The former, however, would not normally be called a philosopher. At first a Catholic, he became a Protestant minister, only to abandon his charge and lead a restless and wandering life. He was hostile not only to Catholicism but also to official Protestantism. God is the eternal goodness and love which are present to all men, and the true Church, he thought, is the spiritual company of all those who allow God to operate within them. Men like Socrates and Seneca belonged to the 'Church'. Redemption is not a historical event, and doctrines like those of the Fall and the redemption by Christ on Calvary are no more than figures or symbols of eternal truths. This point of view was obviously theological in character.

Valentine Weigel, however, attempted to combine the mystical tradition with the philosophy of Nature as found in Paracelsus. He followed Nicholas of Cusa in teaching that God is all things *complicite* and that the distinctions and oppositions which are found in creatures are one in Him. But to this he added the curious notion that God becomes personal in and through creation, in the sense that He comes to know Himself in and through man, in so far as man rises above his egotism and shares in the divine life. All creatures, including man, receive their being from God, but all have an admixture of not-being, of darkness, and this explains man's power of rejecting God. The being of man tends necessarily towards God, turning to its source and origin and ground; but the will can turn away from God. When this happens, the resulting inner tension is what is known as 'hell'.

Accepting from Paracelsus the division of the universe into three worlds, the terrestrial, the sidereal or astral and the heavenly, Weigel also accepted the doctrine of the astral body of man. Man has a mortal body, which is the seat of the senses, but he has also an astral body, which is the seat of reason. In addition he has an immortal soul or part to which belongs the *Fünklein* or *Gemüt*, the *oculus intellectualis* or *oculus mentis*. This is the recipient of supernatural knowledge of God, though this does not mean that the knowledge comes from without; it comes from God present in the soul, knowing Himself in and through man. And it is in the reception of this knowledge, and not in any external rite or in any historical event, that regeneration consists.

It is clear, then, that Weigel attempted a fusion of Nicholas of Cusa's metaphysic and Paracelsus' philosophy of Nature with a religious mysticism which owed something to the tradition represented by Meister Eckhart (as is shown by the use of the term *Fünklein*, the spark of the soul) but which was strongly coloured by an individualistic and anti-ecclesiastical type of Protestant piety and which also tended in a pantheistic direction. In some respects his philosophy puts one in mind of themes of later German speculative idealism, though in the case of the latter the markedly religious and pietistic element of Weigel's thought was comparatively absent.

5. The man who attempted in a much more complete and influential manner to combine the philosophy of Nature with the mystical tradition as represented in German Protestantism was that remarkable figure, Jakob Böhme. Born in 1575 at Altseidenberg in Silesia, he at first tended cattle, though he received some education at the town-school at Seidenberg. After a period of wandering he settled at Görlitz in 1599, where he pursued the trade of a shoemaker. He married and attained a considerable degree of prosperity, which enabled him to retire

from his shoemaking business though he subsequently took to making woollen gloves. His first treatise, *Aurora*, was written in 1612, though it was not then published. Indeed, the only works which were published in his lifetime were some devotional writings, which appeared at the beginning of 1624. His *Aurora* was, however, circulated in manuscript, and while this brought him a local reputation it also brought upon him from the Protestant clergy a charge of heresy. His other works include, for example, *Die drei Prinzipien des göttlichen Wesens*, *Vom dreifachen Leben der Menschen*, *Von der Gnadenwahl*, *Signatura rerum* and *Mysterium magnum*. An edition of his works was published at Amsterdam in 1675, considerably later than the year of Böhme's death, which occurred in 1624.

God considered in Himself is beyond all differentiations and distinctions: He is the *Ungrund*,[1] the original ground of all things: He is 'neither light, nor darkness, neither love nor wrath, but the eternal One', an incomprehensible will, which is neither evil nor good.[2] But if God is conceived as the *Ungrund* or Abyss, 'the nothing and the all',[3] the problem arises of explaining the emergence of multiplicity, of distinct existent things. First of all Böhme postulates a process of self-manifestation within the inner life of God. The original will is a will to self-intuition, and it wills its own centre, which Böhme calls the 'heart' or 'eternal mind' of the will.[4] Thus the Deity discovers itself; and in the discovery there arises a power emanating from the will and the heart of the will, which is the moving life in the original will and in the power (or second will) that arises from, but is identical with, the heart of the original will. The three movements of the inner life of God are correlated by Böhme with the three Persons of the Trinity. The original will is the Father; the heart of the will, which is the Father's 'discovery and power', is the Son; and the 'moving life' emanating from Father and Son is the Holy Spirit. Having dealt with these obscure matters in a very obscure way Böhme goes on to show how Nature came into being as an expression or manifestation of God in visible variety. The impulse of the divine will to self-revelation leads to the birth of Nature as it exists in God. In this ideal or spiritual state Nature is called the *mysterium magnum*. It emerges in visible and tangible form in the actual world, which is external to God and is animated by the *spiritus mundi*. Böhme

[1] *Von der Gnadenwahl*, 1, 3.
[2] *Ibid.*, 1, 3–5.
[3] *Ibid.*, 1, 3.
[4] *Ibid.*, 1, 9–10.

proceeds to give a spiritual interpretation of the ultimate principles of the world and of the various elements, including Paracelsus' sulphur, mercury and salt.

As Böhme was convinced that God in Himself is good and that the *mysterium magnum* is also good, he found himself confronted with the task of explaining the evil in the actual world. His solution of this problem was not always the same. In the *Aurora* he maintained that only what is good proceeds from God; but there is a good which remains steadfast (Christ) and a good which falls away from goodness, typified by Satan. The end of history is, therefore, the rectification of this falling-away. Later, however, Böhme stated that the external manifestation of God must be expressed in contraries, which are natural concomitants of life. The *mysterium magnum*, when it unfolds itself in visible variety, expresses itself in contrary qualities:[1] light and darkness, good and evil, are correlative. There is, then, a dualism in the world. Christ reconciled man to God, but it is possible for men to refuse salvation. Finally, Böhme tried to relate evil to a movement in the divine life, which he called the wrath of God. The end of history will then be the triumph of love, involving the triumph of the good.

Böhme's ideas were derived in part from a number of different sources. His meditations on the Scriptures were coloured by the mysticism of Kaspar von Schwenckfeld (1490–1561) and of Valentine Weigel; and we find in his writings a deep piety and an insistence on the individual's relation to God. For the idea of a visible and unified authoritative Church he had evidently little sympathy: he laid all the emphasis on personal experience and inner light. This aspect of his thought would not by itself entitle him to be called a philosopher. So far as he can properly be called a philosopher, the name is justified mainly by his having grappled with two problems of theistic philosophy, namely the problem of the relation of the world to God and the problem of evil. Böhme was obviously no trained philosopher, and he was aware of the inadequacy and obscurity of his language. Moreover, he evidently picked up terms and phrases from his friends and from his reading, which derived mainly from the philosophy of Paracelsus, but which he used to express the ideas fermenting in his own mind. None the less, even though the shoemaker of Görlitz was no trained philosopher, he can be said to have carried on the speculative tradition coming from Meister Eckhart and Nicholas of Cusa

[1] Cf. *Von der Gnadenwahl*, 8, 8.

through the German philosophers of Nature, particularly Paracelsus, a tradition which he impregnated with a strong infusion of Protestant piety. Yet even if one makes due allowance for the handicaps under which he laboured, and even though one has not the slightest intention of questioning his deep piety and the sincerity of his convictions, it may be doubted whether his obscure and oracular utterances throw much light on the problems with which he dealt. No doubt the obscurity is broken through from time to time by rays of light; but his thought as a whole is unlikely to commend itself to those who are not theosophically inclined. It might be said, of course, that Böhme's obscure utterances represent the attempt of a higher kind of knowledge to express itself in inadequate language. But if one means by this that Böhme was struggling to convey solutions to philosophical problems, it has yet to be shown that he actually possessed those solutions. His writings leave one in considerable doubt at any rate whether this could properly be affirmed.

But to cast doubt upon the philosophical value of Böhme's utterances is not to deny their influence. He exercised an influence on men like Pierre Poiret (1646–1719) in France, John Pordage (1607–81) and William Law (1686–1761) in England. More important, however, is his influence on post-Kantian German idealism. Böhme's triadic schemes and his idea of the self-unfolding of God reappear, indeed, in Hegel, though minus Böhme's intense piety and devotion; but it was probably Schelling who, in the later phase of his philosophical development, was most influenced by him. For the German idealist drew on Böhme's theosophy and on his ideas about creation and the origin of evil. Schelling was led to Böhme partly by Franz von Baader (1765–1841), who had himself been influenced by Saint-Martin (1743–1803), an opponent of the Revolution who had translated Böhme's *Aurora* into French. There are always some minds for whom Böhme's teaching possesses an appeal, though many others not unnaturally fail to share this sympathy.

6. We have seen how the Renaissance philosophies of Nature varied considerably in tone and emphasis, ranging from the professedly empiricist theories of some of the Italian philosophers to the theosophy of a Jakob Böhme. We find, indeed, a common emphasis on Nature as the manifestation of the divine and as a revelation of God which is deserving of study. But whereas in one philosophy the accent may be laid predominantly on the empirical

study of Nature itself as given to the senses, in another the accent may be laid on metaphysical themes. For Bruno Nature was an infinite system which can be studied in itself, so to speak; and we saw how he championed enthusiastically the Copernican hypothesis. Yet Bruno was above all things a speculative philosopher. And with Böhme we find the emphasis laid on theosophy and on man's relation to God. It is desirable, indeed, to speak of 'accent' and 'emphasis', since the philosophers not infrequently combined an interest in empirical problems with a bent for somewhat ill-grounded speculations. Furthermore, they often combined with these interests an interest in alchemy, in astrology and in magic. They express the feeling for Nature which was one characteristic of the Renaissance; but in their study of Nature they were inclined to take attractive short-cuts, whether by bold and often bizarre philosophical speculations or by means of occultism or by both. The philosophies of Nature acted as a kind of background and stimulus to the scientific study of Nature; but for the actual development of the sciences other methods were required.

CHAPTER XVIII

THE SCIENTIFIC MOVEMENT OF THE RENAISSANCE

General remarks on the influence of science on philosophy—Renaissance science; the empirical basis of science, controlled experiment, hypothesis and astronomy, mathematics, the mechanistic view of the world—The influence of Renaissance science on philosophy.

1. WE have seen that even in the thirteenth century there was a certain amount of scientific development and that in the following century there was an increased interest in scientific problems. But the results of scholarly researches into mediaeval science have not been such as to necessitate any substantial change of view in regard to the importance of Renaissance science. They have shown that interest in scientific matters was not so alien to the mediaeval mind as has been sometimes supposed, and they have shown that the Aristotelian physics and the Ptolemaic astronomy did not possess that firm and universal hold on the mind of the mediaeval physicist with which they have often been credited; but all this does not alter the fact that science underwent a remarkable development at the time of the Renaissance and that this development has exercised a profound influence on European life and thought.

It is not the business of the historian of philosophy to give a detailed account of the discoveries and achievements of the Renaissance scientists. The reader who desires to acquaint himself with the history of science as such must obviously turn to the relevant literature on the subject. But it would be impossible to by-pass the development of science at the time of the Renaissance, if for no other reason than that it exercised a powerful influence upon philosophy. Philosophy does not pursue an isolated path of its own, without any contact with other factors of human culture. It is simply an undeniable historical fact that philosophic reflection has been influenced by science both in regard to subject-matter and also in regard to method and aims. In so far as philosophy involves reflection on the world philosophic thought will obviously be influenced in some way by the picture of the world that is painted by science and by the concrete achievements of science. This is likely to be the case in some degree in all phases of philosophic development. As to scientific method, when the use of a certain method is seen to lead to striking results it is likely that the thought will occur to some philosophers that the adoption of an analogous method in philosophy might also produce striking results in the way of established conclusions. And this thought is one which actually did influence certain philosophers of the Renaissance period. When, however, it is seen that philosophy does not develop in the same way as science, the realization of the fact is likely to give rise to the question whether the prevalent conception of philosophy should not be revised. Why is it, as Kant asked, that science progresses and that universal and necessary scientific judgments can be made and are made (or seemed to Kant to be made), while philosophy in its traditional form does not lead to comparable results and does not seem to progress in the way that science progresses? Is not our whole conception of philosophy wrong? Are we not expecting of philosophy what philosophy of its very nature cannot give? We should expect of philosophy only what it can give, and in order to see what it can give we have to inquire more closely into the nature and functions of philosophic thought. Again, as the particular sciences develop, each with its particular method, reflection will naturally suggest to some minds that these sciences have successively wrested from philosophy her various chosen fields. It may very understandably appear that cosmology or natural philosophy has given way to physics, the philosophy of the organism to biology, philosophical psychology to scientific psychology, and perhaps even moral philosophy to sociology. In other words, it may appear that for all factual information about the world and existent reality we must turn to direct observation and to the sciences. The philosopher, it may appear, cannot increase our knowledge of things in the way that the scientist can, though he may still perform a useful function in the province of logical analysis. And this is, roughly, what a considerable number of modern philosophers think. It is also possible, of course, to accept the idea that all that can be definitely known falls within the province of the sciences and yet at the same time to maintain that it is the special function of philosophy to raise those ultimate problems which cannot be answered by the scientist or in the way that the scientist answers his problems. And then one gets a different conception, or different conceptions, of philosophy.

Again, as science develops, reflection on the methods of science will also develop. Philosophers will be stimulated to analyse scientific method and to do for induction what Aristotle did for syllogistic deduction. And so we get the reflections of Francis Bacon at the time of the Renaissance and of John Stuart Mill in the nineteenth century and of many other philosophers in more recent times. Thus the concrete progress of the sciences may lead to the development of a new field of philosophic analysis, which could not have been developed apart from actual scientific studies and achievements, since it takes the form of reflection on the method actually used in science.

Further, one can trace the influence of a particular science on a particular philosopher's thought. One can trace, for example, the influence of mathematics on Descartes, of mechanics on Hobbes, the rise of historical science on Hegel or of biology and the evolutionary hypothesis on Bergson.

In the foregoing sketchy remarks I have strayed rather far from the Renaissance and have introduced philosophers and philosophical ideas which will have to be discussed in later volumes of this history. But my object in making these remarks was simply the general one of illustrating, even if in an inevitably inadequate manner, the influence of science upon philosophy. Science is not, of course, the only extra-philosophical factor which exercises an influence upon philosophic thought. Philosophy is influenced also by other factors in human culture and civilization. So, too, is science for the matter of that. Nor is one entitled to conclude from the influence of science and other factors upon philosophy that philosophic thought is itself powerless to exercise any influence upon other cultural elements. I do not think that this is in fact the case. But the point which is relevant to my present purpose is the influence of science upon philosophy, and it is for this reason that I have stressed it here. Before, however, anything very definite can be said about the influence of Renaissance science in particular on philosophic thought something must be said about the nature of Renaissance science, even though I am only too conscious of the handicaps under which I labour in attempting to discuss the matter.

2. (i) The 'vulgar' notion of the cause which brought about the flowering of Renaissance science is still, I suppose, that at that period men began for the first time, since the beginning of the Middle Ages at any rate, to use their eyes and to investigate

Nature for themselves. Direct observation of the facts took the place of reliance on the texts of Aristotle and other ancient writers, and theological prejudice gave place to immediate acquaintance with the empirical data. Yet only a little reflection is needed to realize the inadequacy of this view. The dispute between Galileo and the theologians is considered, perhaps inevitably, as the representative symbol of the struggle between direct recourse to the empirical data on the one hand and theological prejudice and Aristotelian obscurantism on the other. But it is obvious that ordinary observation will not suffice to convince anyone that the earth moves round the sun: ordinary observation would suggest the contrary. The heliocentric hypothesis doubtless 'saved the appearances' better than the geocentric hypothesis did; but it was a hypothesis. Moreover, it was a hypothesis which could not be verified by the type of controlled experiment which is possible in some other sciences. It was not possible for astronomy to advance very much on the basis of observation alone; the use of hypothesis and of mathematical deduction were also required. It argues, then, a short-sighted view of the achievements of Renaissance science if one ascribes those achievements simply to observation and experiment. As Roger Bacon, the thirteenth-century Franciscan, had insisted, astronomy requires the aid of mathematics.

Yet every science is based in some way on observation and has some connection with the empirical data. It is obvious that a physicist who sets out to ascertain the laws of motion starts in a sense with observed movements; for it is the laws exemplified by movements which he wishes to ascertain. And if the laws which he eventually formulates are entirely incompatible with the observed movements, in the sense that if the laws were true the observed movements would not happen, he knows that he will have to revise his theory of motion. The astronomer does not proceed without any reference at all to empirical data: the chemist starts with the empirical data and makes experiments with existent things: the biologist would not get very far if he paid no attention to the actual behaviour of organisms. The development of physics in comparatively recent times, as interpreted by Eddington, for example, may tend to give the impression that science is not concerned with anything so plebeian as empirical data and that it is a pure construction of the human mind which is imposed upon Nature and constitutes the 'facts'; but unless one is dealing with pure mathematics, from which one cannot expect factual information about the world, one can say that every science rests ultimately on a basis of observation of the empirical data. When a science reaches a high degree of development, the empirical basis may not be so immediately obvious; but it is there none the less. The scientist does not set out to evolve a purely arbitrary theory: rather does he set out to 'explain' phenomena and, where possible, he will test or verify his theory, mediately if not immediately.

The connection of scientific theory with the empirical data is probably always obvious in the case of some sciences, whereas in the case of other sciences it may become far from obvious as the science reaches a high degree of development. But it is likely to be insisted on in the earlier stages of the development of any science, and this is especially the case when explanatory theories and hypotheses are put forward which conflict with long established notions. Thus at the time of the Renaissance, when the Aristotelian physics were being discarded in favour of fresh scientific conceptions, appeal was frequently made to the empirical data and to 'saving the appearances'. We have seen how the philosophers of Nature often stressed the need for the empirical study of the facts, and it scarcely needs pointing out that medicine and anatomy, not to speak of technology and geography, would not have made the progress which they actually did make in the sixteenth and seventeenth centuries without the aid of empirical investigation. One cannot construct a useful map of the world or give a valid account and explanation of the circulation of the blood by purely *a priori* reasoning.

The results of actual observation may be seen particularly in the advance of anatomy and physiology. Leonardo da Vinci (1452–1519), the great artist who was also deeply interested in scientific and mechanical problems and experiments, was gifted with a remarkable flair for anticipating future discoveries, inventions and theories. Thus he anticipated speculatively the discovery of the circulation of the blood, which was made by William Harvey about 1615; and in optics he anticipated the undulatory theory of light. He is also well known for his plans for flying-machines, parachutes and improved artillery. But it is his anatomical observation which is relevant in the present context. The results of this observation were portrayed in a large number of drawings; but as they were not published they did not exercise the influence which they might have done. The influential book in this connection was the *De fabrica humani corporis* (1543) by Andreas Vesalius, in which he recorded his study of anatomy. This work was of considerable importance for the development of anatomy, since Vesalius did not set out to find evidence in support of traditional theories but was concerned to observe for himself and to record his observations. The book was illustrated, and it also contained accounts of experiments made by the author on animals.

(ii) The discoveries in anatomy and physiology by men like Vesalius and Harvey were naturally powerful influences in undermining men's trust in traditional theories and assertions and in directing their minds to empirical investigation. The fact that the blood circulates is a commonplace for us; but it was not by any means a commonplace then. The ancient authorities, like Galen and Hippocrates, knew nothing of it. But the scientific advance of the Renaissance cannot be ascribed simply to 'observation' in the narrow sense: one has to take into account the increased use of controlled experiment. For example, in 1586 Simon Stevin published the account of a deliberately contrived experiment with leaden balls, which refuted Aristotle's assertion that the velocity of falling bodies is proportional to the weight of the bodies. Again, William Gilbert, who published his *De magnete* in 1600, confirmed by experiment his theory that the earth is a magnet possessing poles which are near its geographical poles, though not coincident with them, and that it is to these magnetic poles that the needle of the compass is attracted. He took a spherical loadstone and observed the behaviour or a needle or a piece of iron wire placed on it in successively different positions. On each occasion he marked on the stone the direction in which the wire came to rest, and by completing the circles he was able to show that the wire or needle always came to rest pointing to the magnetic pole.

It was Galileo Galilei (1564–1642), however, who was the foremost exponent of the experimental method among the Renaissance scientists. Born at Pisa, he studied at the university of that city, exchanging the study of medicine, with which he started, for the study of mathematics. After lecturing at Florence he became professor of mathematics first at Pisa (1589) and then at Padua (1592), occupying this last place for eighteen years. In 1610 he went to Florence as mathematician and philosopher to the Grand Duke of Tuscany and as *mathematicus primarius* in the university, though he was free from the obligation of giving courses of lectures in the university. In 1616 began the celebrated affair with the Inquisition about his astronomical views, which ended with Galileo's formal recantation in 1633. The great scientist was indeed held in detention for a time; but his scientific studies were not stopped, and he was able to continue working until he became blind in 1637. He died in 1642, the year in which Isaac Newton was born.

Galileo's name is universally associated with astronomy; but his work was also of great importance in the development of hydrostatics and mechanics. For example, whereas the Aristotelians maintained that it was a body's shape which decided whether it would sink or float in water, Galileo tried to show experimentally that Archimedes was right in saying that it was the density or specific gravity of a body, and not its shape, which determined whether it would sink or float. He also tried to show experimentally that it was not simply the body's density which decided the matter but rather its density as relative to that of the fluids in which it was placed. Again, while at Pisa he confirmed by experiment the discovery already made by Stevin that bodies of different weight take the same time to fall a given distance and that they do not, as the Aristotelians thought, reach the ground at different times. He also endeavoured to establish experimentally the law of uniform acceleration, which had indeed been anticipated by other physicists, according to which the speed of a body's fall increases uniformly with the time, and the law that a moving body, unless acted upon by friction, the resistance of the air or gravity, continues to move in the same direction at a uniform speed. Galileo was especially influenced by his conviction that Nature is essentially mathematical, and hence that under ideal conditions an ideal law would be 'obeyed'. His relatively crude experimental results suggested a simple law, even if they could hardly be said to 'prove' it. They also tended to suggest the falsity of the Aristotelian notion that no body would move unless acted upon by an external force. Indeed, Galileo's discoveries were one of the most powerful influences which discredited the Aristotelian physics. He also gave an impetus to technical advance by, for example, his plans for a pendulum clock, which was later constructed and patented by Huygens (1629–95), and by his invention, or reinvention, of the thermometer.

(iii) Mention of controlled experiment should not be taken to imply that the experimental method was widely practised from the beginning of the sixteenth century. On the contrary, it is the comparative rarity of clear cases in the first half at any rate of the century which makes it necessary to draw attention to it as something which was just beginning to be understood. Now, it is clear that experiment, in the sense of deliberately contrived experiment, is inseparable from the use of tentative hypotheses. It is true that one might devise an experiment simply to see what happens; but in actual practice controlled experiment is devised as a means of verifying a hypothesis. To perform an experiment is to put a question to Nature, and asking that particular question normally presupposes some hypothesis. One would not drop balls of different weight from a tower in order to see whether they do or do not hit the ground at the same time, unless one wished to confirm a preconceived hypothesis or unless one envisaged two possible hypotheses and desired to discover which was correct. It would be wrong to suppose that all Renaissance scientists had a clear conception of the hypothetical character of their theories: but that they used hypotheses is clear enough. It is most obvious in the case of astronomy, to which I now turn.

Nicholas Copernicus (1473–1543), the famous and learned Polish ecclesiastic, was by no means the first to realize that the apparent movement of the sun from east to west is no conclusive proof that it does actually move in this way. As we have seen, this fact had been clearly realized in the fourteenth century. But whereas the fourteenth-century physicists had confined themselves to developing the hypothesis of the earth's daily rotation on its axis, Copernicus argued on behalf of the hypothesis that the rotating earth also rotates round a stationary sun. He thus substituted the heliocentric for the geocentric hypothesis. This is not to say, of course, that he discarded the Ptolemaic system entirely. In particular, he retained the old notion that the planets move in circular orbits, though he supposed that these were 'eccentric'. In order to make his heliocentric hypothesis square with the appearances, he then had to add a number of epicycles. He postulated less than half the number of circles postulated by the Ptolemaic system of his time, and he thus simplified it; but he went about matters in much the same way as his predecessors had done. That is to say, he made speculative additions in order to 'save the appearances'.

There can be little doubt that Copernicus was convinced of the truth of the heliocentric hypothesis. But a Lutheran clergyman called Andreas Osiander (1498–1552), to whom the manuscript of Copernicus' *De revolutionibus orbium cœlestium* had been entrusted by Georg Joachim Rheticus of Wittenberg, took it upon himself to substitute a new preface for that written by Copernicus. In this new preface Osiander made Copernicus propose the heliocentric theory as a mere hypothesis or mathematical fiction. In addition he omitted the references to Aristarchus which Copernicus had made; and this omission brought upon Copernicus charges of dishonest plagiarism. Luther and Melanchthon thoroughly disapproved of the new hypothesis; but it did not excite any pronounced opposition on the part of the Catholic authorities. Osiander's preface may have contributed to this, though it must also be remembered that Copernicus had circulated privately his *De hypothesibus motuum coelestium commentariolus* without arousing hostility. It is true that the *De revolutionibus*, which was dedicated to Pope Paul III, was put on the Index in 1616 (*donec corrigatur*), as objections were raised against some sentences which represented the heliocentric hypothesis as a certainty. But this does not alter the fact that the work did not arouse opposition on the part of Catholic ecclesiastical circles when it was first published. In 1758 it was omitted from the revised Index.

Copernicus' hypothesis did not immediately find enthusiastic adherents, however, apart from the Wittenberg mathematicians, Reinhold and Rheticus. Tycho Brahe (1546–1601) opposed the hypothesis and invented one of his own, according to which the sun circles round the earth, as in the Ptolemaic system, while Mercury, Venus, Mars, Jupiter and Saturn circle round the sun in epicycles. The first real improvement on Copernicus' theory was made by John Kepler (1571–1630). Kepler, who was a Protestant, had been convinced by Michael Mästlin of Tübingen that the Copernican hypothesis was true, and he defended it in his *Prodromus dissertationum cosmographicarum seu mysterium cosmographicum*. The work contained, however, Pythagorean speculations concerning the geometrical plan of the world, and Tycho Brahe characteristically suggested that the young Kepler should give more attention to sound observation before indulging in speculation. But he took Kepler as his assistant, and after his patron's death Kepler published the works in which he enunciated his famous three laws. These works were the *Astronomia nova* (1609), the *Epitome astronomiae copernicanae* (1618) and the *Harmonices mundi* (1619). The planets, said Kepler, move in ellipses having the sun as one focus. The radius sector of the ellipse sweeps out equal areas in equal times. Moreover, we can compare mathematically the times required by the various planets to complete their respective orbits by the use of the formula that the square of the time taken by any planet to complete its orbit is proportional to the cube of its distance from the sun. In order to explain the movement of the planets Kepler postulated a motive force (or *anima motrix*) in the sun which emits rays of force, rotating with the sun. Sir Isaac Newton (1642–1727) later showed that this hypothesis was unnecessary, for in 1666 he discovered the law of the inverse square, that the sun's gravitational pull on a planet which is n times the earth's distance from the sun is $1/n^2$ times the pull at the earth's distance, and in 1685 he at last found himself in a position to work out the mathematical calculations which agreed with the demands of observation. But though Newton showed that the movements of the planets can be explained without postulating Kepler's *anima motrix*, the latter had made a most important contribution to the advance of astronomy by showing that the movements of all the then known planets could be accounted for by postulating a number of ellipses corresponding to the number of planets. The old paraphernalia of circles and epicycles could thus be dispensed with. The heliocentric hypothesis was thus greatly simplified.

On the observational side the advance of astronomy was greatly promoted by the invention of the telescope. The credit for the practical invention of the telescope must be given, it seems, to one of two Dutchmen in the first decade of the seventeenth century. Galileo, hearing of the invention, made an instrument for himself. (A Jesuit, Father Scheiner, constructed an improved instrument by embodying a suggestion made by Kepler, and Huygens introduced further improvements.) By using the telescope Galileo was enabled to observe the moon, which revealed itself as having mountains; and from this he concluded that the moon consists of the same sort of material as the earth. He was also able to observe the phases of Venus and the satellites of Jupiter, his observations fitting in very well with the heliocentric, but not with the geocentric, hypothesis. Furthermore, he observed the existence of sunspots, which were also seen by Scheiner. The existence of varying sunspots showed that the sun consisted of changeable matter, and this fact further discredited the Aristotelian cosmology. In general the telescopic observations made by Galileo and others provided empirical confirmation of the Copernican hypothesis. Indeed, observation of the phases of Venus showed clearly the superiority of the heliocentric to the geocentric hypothesis, since they were inexplicable in terms of the Ptolemaic scheme.

Perhaps one should say something at this point about the deplorable clash between Galileo and the Inquisition. Its importance as evidence of the Church's supposed hostility towards science has often been greatly exaggerated. Indeed, the fact that it is to this particular case that appeal is almost always made (the case of Bruno was quite different) by those who wish to show that the Church is the enemy of science should by itself be sufficient to cast doubt on the validity of the universal conclusion which is sometimes drawn from it. The action of the ecclesiastical authorities does not, it is true, reflect credit on them. One could wish that they had all realized more clearly the truth, suggested by Galileo himself in a letter of 1615, envisaged by Bellarmine and others at the time, and clearly affirmed by Pope Leo XIII in his encyclical letter *Providentissimus Deus*, that a Biblical passage like *Josue* 10, 12–13 can be taken as an accommodation to the ordinary way of speaking and not as an assertion of a scientific fact. We all speak of the sun as moving, and there is no reason why the Bible should not employ the same way of speaking, without one's being entitled to draw therefrom the conclusion that the sun rotates round a stationary earth. Moreover, even though Galileo had not proved the truth of the Copernican hypothesis beyond question, he had certainly shown its superiority to the geocentric hypothesis. This fact is not altered by his having laid particular stress on an argument based on a mistaken theory about the ebb and flow of the tides in his *Dialogo sopra i due massimi sistemi del mondo*, the work which precipitated a serious clash with the Inquisition. On the other hand, Galileo obstinately refused to recognize the hypothetical character of his theory. Given his naïvely realist view of the status of scientific hypotheses, it might perhaps have been difficult for him to recognize it; but Bellarmine pointed out that the empirical verification of a hypothesis does not necessarily prove its absolute truth, and if Galileo had been ready to recognize this fact, which is familiar enough today, the whole unfortunate episode with the Inquisition could have been avoided. However, Galileo not only persisted in maintaining the non-hypothetical character of the Copernican hypothesis but was also needlessly provocative into the bargain. Indeed, the clash of personalities played a not unimportant part in the affair. In fine, Galileo was a great scientist, and his opponents were not great scientists. Galileo made some sensible remarks about the interpretation of the Scriptures, the truth of which is recognized today and might well have been recognized more clearly by the theologians involved in the case. But the fault was by no means all on one side. In regard to the status of scientific theories Bellarmine's judgment was better than Galileo's, even though the latter was a great scientist and the former was not. If Galileo had had a better understanding of the nature of scientific hypotheses, and if the theologians in general had not taken up the attitude which they did in regard to the interpretation of isolated Biblical texts, the clash would not have occurred. It did occur, of course, and in regard to the superiority of the heliocentric over the geocentric hypothesis Galileo was undoubtedly right. But no universal conclusion can legitimately be drawn from this case about the Church's attitude to science.

(iv) It is clear that in the astronomy of the Renaissance hypothesis as well as observation played an indispensable rôle. But the fruitful combination of hypothesis and verification, both in astronomy and in mechanics, would not have been possible without the aid of mathematics. In the sixteenth and seventeenth centuries mathematics made considerable progress. A notable step forward was taken when John Napier (1550–1617) conceived the idea of logarithms. He communicated his idea to Tycho Brahe in 1594, and in 1614 he published a description of the general principle in his *Mirifici logarithmorum canonis descriptio*. Shortly afterwards the practical application of the principle was facilitated by the work of Henry Briggs (1561–1630). In 1638 Descartes published an account of the general principles of analytic geometry, while in 1635 Cavalieri, an Italian mathematician, published a statement of the 'method of indivisibles', which had already been used in a primitive form by Kepler. This was, in essence, the first statement of the calculus of infinitesimals. In 1665–6 Newton discovered the binomial theorem, though he did not publish his discovery until 1704. This hesitation in publishing results led to the celebrated dispute between Newton and Leibniz and their respective supporters about priority in discovering the differential and integral calculi. The two men discovered the calculus independently, but although Newton had written a sketch of his ideas in

1669 he did not actually publish anything on the matter until 1704, whereas Leibniz began publication in 1684. These elaborations of the calculus were, of course, much too late to be utilized by the great scientists of the Renaissance, and a man like Galileo had to rely on older and clumsier mathematical methods. But the point is that his ideal was that of developing a scientific view of the world in terms of mathematical formulae. He may be said to have combined the outlook of a mathematical physicist with that of a philosopher. As a physicist he tried to express the foundations of physics and the observed regularities of Nature in terms of mathematical propositions, so far as this was possible. As a philosopher he drew from the success of the mathematical method in physics the conclusion that mathematics is the key to the actual structure of reality. Though partly influenced by the nominalist conception of causality and the nominalist substitution of the study of the behaviour of things for the traditional search for essences, Galileo was also strongly influenced by the mathematical ideas of Platonism and Pythagoreanism; and this influence predisposed him to believe that the objective world is the world of the mathematician. In a well-known passage of his work *Il saggiatore* (6) he declared that philosophy is written in the book of the universe but that 'it cannot be read until we have learnt the language and understood the characters in which it is written. It is written in mathematical language, and its characters are triangles, circles and other geometrical figures, without which it is impossible to understand a single word.'

(v) This aspect of Galileo's idea of Nature expressed itself in a mechanistic view of the world. Thus he believed in atoms and explained change on the basis of an atomist theory. Again, he maintained that qualities like colour and warmth exist as qualities only in the sensing subject: they are 'subjective' in character. Objectively they exist only in the form of the motion of atoms; and they can thus be explained mechanically and mathematically. This mechanistic conception of Nature, based on an atomist theory, was also maintained by Pierre Gassendi, as we saw earlier. It was further developed by Robert Boyle (1627–91), who believed that matter consists of solid particles, each possessing its own shape, which combine with one another to form what are now termed 'molecules'. Finally Newton argued that if we knew the forces which act upon bodies, we could deduce the motions of those bodies mathematically, and he suggested that the ultimate atoms or particles are themselves centres of force. He was concerned immediately only with the movements of certain bodies; but in the preface to his *Philosophiae naturalis principia mathematica* he put forward the idea that the movements of all bodies could be explained in terms of mechanical principles and that the reason why natural philosophers had been unable to achieve this explanation was their ignorance of the active forces in nature. But he took care to explain that it was his purpose to give only 'a mathematical notion of those forces, without considering their physical causes or seats'. Hence when he showed that 'the force' of gravity which causes an apple to fall to the ground is identical with 'the force' which causes the elliptical movements of the planets, what he was doing was to show that the movements of planets and falling apples conform to the same mathematical law. Newton's scientific work enjoyed such a complete success that it reigned supreme, in its general principles that is to say, for some two hundred years, the period of the Newtonian physics.

3. The rise of modern science or, better, of the classical science of the Renaissance and post-Renaissance periods naturally had a profound effect on men's minds, opening up to them new vistas of knowledge and directing them to new interests. No sensible man would wish to deny that the scientific advance of the sixteenth and seventeenth centuries was one of the most important and influential events in history. But it is possible to exaggerate its effect on the European mind. In particular, it is, I think, an exaggeration to imply that the success of the Copernican hypothesis had the effect of upsetting belief about man's relation to God, on the ground that the earth could no longer be regarded as the geographical centre of the universe. That it did have this effect is not infrequently implied, and one writer repeats what another has said on the subject; but any necessary connection between the revolution in astronomy and a revolution in religious belief has yet to be demonstrated. Further, it is a mistake to suppose that the mechanical view of the universe either was or ought logically to have been a bar to religious belief. Galileo, who considered that the application of mathematics to the world is objectively ensured, believed that it was ensured by God's creation of the world as a mathematically intelligible system. It was divine creation which guaranteed the parallelisms between mathematical deduction and the actual system of Nature. Robert Boyle also was convinced of divine creation. And that Newton

was a man of firm piety is well known. He even conceived absolute space as the instrument by which God is omnipresent in the world and embraces all things in His immanent activity. It is true, of course, that the mechanistic view of the world tended to promote deism, which brings in God simply as an explanation of the origin of the mechanical system. But it must be remembered that even the old astronomy, for example, can be regarded as a mechanical system in a sense: it is a mistake to suppose that the scientific advance of the Renaissance suddenly cut away, as it were, the link between the world and God. The mechanical-mathematical view naturally involved the elimination from physics of the consideration of final causes; but, whatever the psychological effect of this change on many minds may have been, the elimination of final causes from physics did not necessarily involve a denial of final causality. It was a consequence of the advance in scientific method in a particular field of knowledge; but this does not mean that men like Galileo and Newton regarded physical science as the sole source of knowledge.

I want to turn, however, to the influence of the new science on philosophy, though I shall confine myself to indicating two or three lines of thought without attempting at this stage to develop them. As a preliminary, one may remind oneself of the two elements of scientific method, namely the observational and inductive side and the deductive and mathematical side.

The first aspect of scientific method, namely observation of the empirical data as a basis for induction, for discovering causes, was stressed by Francis Bacon. But as his philosophy will form the subject of the next chapter I shall say no more about him here. What I want to do at the moment is to draw attention to the connection between the emphasis laid by Francis Bacon on observation and induction in scientific method and the classical British empiricism. It would certainly be quite wrong to regard classical empiricism as being simply the philosophical reflection of the place occupied by observation and experiment in Renaissance and post-Renaissance science. When Locke asserted that all our ideas are based on sense-perception and introspection he was asserting a psychological and epistemological thesis, the antecedents of which can be seen in mediaeval Aristotelianism. But it can legitimately be said, I think, that a powerful impetus was given to philosophical empiricism by the conviction that the contemporary scientific advances were based on actual observation of the empirical data. The scientific insistence on going to the observable 'facts' as a necessary basis for explanatory theory found its correlative and its theoretical justification in the empiricist thesis that our factual knowledge is ultimately based on perception. The use of observation and experiment in science, and indeed the triumphant advance of science in general, would naturally tend, in the minds of many thinkers, to stimulate and confirm the theory that all our knowledge is based on perception, on direct acquaintance with external and internal events.

It was, however, the other aspect of scientific method, namely the deductive and mathematical aspect, which most influenced the continental 'rationalist' philosophy of the post-Renaissance period. The success of mathematics in the solution of scientific problems naturally enhanced its prestige. Not only was mathematics clear and exact in itself, but in its application to scientific problems it also made clear what had formerly been obscure. It appeared as the highroad to knowledge. It is understandable that the certainty and exactitude of mathematics suggested to Descartes, himself a talented mathematician and the chief pioneer in the field of analytic geometry, that an examination of the essential characteristics of the mathematical method would reveal the right method for use in philosophy also. It is understandable also that under the influence of mathematics as a model several of the leading philosophers on the Continent believed that they could reconstruct the world, as it were, in an *a priori* deductive manner with the aid of certain fundamental ideas analogous to the definitions and axioms of mathematics. Thus a mathematical model provided the framework of Spinoza's *Ethica more geometrico demonstrata*, though it scarcely provided its content.

We have seen how the development of astronomy and of mechanics at the time of the Renaissance promoted the growth of a mechanical view of the world. This outlook was reflected in the field of philosophy. Descartes, for example, considered that the material world and its changes can be explained simply in terms of matter, identified with geometrical extension, and motion. At creation God placed, as it were, a certain amount of motion or energy in the world, which is transmitted from body to body according to the laws of mechanics. Animals can be considered as machines. Descartes himself did not apply these mechanistic analogies to the human being as a whole, but some later French thinkers did. In England Thomas Hobbes, who objected against

Descartes that thought is an activity of bodies and that the activity of bodies is motion, believed that just as the behaviour of inanimate bodies can be deduced from certain fundamental ideas and laws so the behaviour of human societies, which are simply organizations of bodies, can be deduced from the properties of these organized groupings of bodies. Mechanics thus furnished a partial model for Descartes and a more complete model for Hobbes.

The foregoing remarks are intentionally brief and summary: they are designed only to indicate some of the lines on which the development of science influenced philosophic thought. Names of philosophers have been introduced who will be treated of in the next volume; and it would be out of place to say more about them here. It may be as well, however, to point out in conclusion that the philosophic ideas which have been mentioned reacted in turn on science. For example, Descartes' conception of organic bodies may have been crude and inadequate, but it probably helped to encourage scientists to investigate the processes and behaviour of organic bodies in a scientific manner. A hypothesis need not be completely true in order to bear fruit in some particular direction.

CHAPTER XIX

FRANCIS BACON

English philosophy of the Renaissance—Bacon's life and writings—The classification of the sciences—Induction and 'the idols'.

1. THE first outstanding philosopher of the post-mediaeval period in England was Francis Bacon: it is his name which is for ever associated with the philosophy of the Renaissance in Great Britain. With the exception of St. Thomas More and Richard Hooker, whose political ideas will be briefly considered in the next chapter, the other British philosophers of the Renaissance merit little more than bare mention. It should, however, be emphasized that the general tone of philosophical thinking in the English universities at the time of the Renaissance was conservative. The Aristotelian-Scholastic logical tradition persisted for many years, especially at Oxford, and it formed the background of John Locke's university education in the seventeenth century. Latin works of logic, like the *Institutionum dialecticarum libri IV* of John Sanderson (1587–1602) or the *Logicae libri V de praedicabilibus* of Richard Crakanthorpe (1569–1624), began to give place to works in the vernacular like *The rule of reason, containing the arte of logique* (1552) by Thomas Wilson or *The philosopher's game* (1563) and the *Arte of reason rightly termed Witcraft* (1573) of Ralph Lever; but such works contained nothing much in the nature of novelty. Sir William Temple (1533–1626) defended the Ramist logic; but he was attacked by Everard Digby (1550–92), who wrote a refutation of Ramism in the name of Aristotelianism. Sir Kenelm Digby (1603–65), who became a Catholic in Paris, where he was acquainted with Descartes, endeavoured to combine the Aristotelian metaphysics with the corpuscular theory of matter. Everard Digby, though an Aristotelian in logic, was influenced by the neo-Platonic ideas of Reuchlin. Similarly, Robert Greville, Lord Brooke (1608–43), was influenced by the Platonic Academy of Florence; and in *The Nature of Truth* he maintained a doctrine of the divine light which helped to prepare the way for the group of Cambridge Platonists. Ideas of Cardinal Nicholas of Cusa and of Paracelsus were represented by Robert Fludd (1574–1637), who

travelled extensively on the Continent and was influenced by the continental Renaissance. In his *Philosophia Mosaica* he depicted God as the synthesis in identity of opposites. In Himself God is incomprehensible darkness; but considered in another aspect He is the light and wisdom which manifests itself in the world, which is the *explicatio Dei*. The world manifests in itself the twofold aspect of God, for the divine light is manifested in, or is the cause of, warmth, rarefaction, light, love, goodness and beauty, while the divine darkness is the origin of cold, condensation, hate and unloveliness. Man is a microcosm of the universe, uniting in himself the two aspects of God which are revealed in the universe. There is in man a constant strife between light and darkness.

2. The leading figure of the philosophy of the Renaissance in England was, however, a thinker who turned consciously against Aristotelianism and who did so not in favour of Platonism or of theosophy but in the name of scientific and technical advancement in the service of man. The value and justification of knowledge, according to Francis Bacon, consists above all in its practical application and utility; its true function is to extend the dominion of the human race, the reign of man over nature. In the *Novum Organum*[1] Bacon calls attention to the practical effects of the invention of printing, gunpowder and the magnet, which 'have changed the face of things and the state of the world; the first in literature, the second in warfare; the third in navigation'. But inventions such as these did not come from the traditional Aristotelian physics; they came from direct acquaintance with nature herself. Bacon certainly represents 'humanism' in the sense that he was a great writer; but his emphasis on man's dominion over nature by means of science distinguishes him sharply from the Italian humanists, who were more concerned with the development of the human personality, while his insistence on going direct to nature, on the inductive method, and his mistrust of speculation distinguish him from the neo-Platonists and the theosophists. Though he did not make positive contributions to science himself and though he was far more influenced by Aristotelianism than he realized, Bacon divined in a remarkable way the technical progress which was to come, a technical progress which, he was confident, would serve man and human culture. This vision was present, in a limited sense, to the minds of the alchemists; but Bacon saw that it was a scientific knowledge of nature, not alchemy

[1] I, 129.

or magic or fantastic speculation, which was to open up to man the path of dominion over nature. Bacon stood not only chronologically but also, in part at least, mentally on the threshold of a new world revealed by geographical discovery, the finding of fresh sources of wealth and, above all, by the advance in natural science, the establishment of physics on an experimental and inductive basis. It must be added, however, that Bacon had, as we shall see, an insufficient grasp and appreciation of the new scientific method. That is why I stated that he belonged mentally 'in part at least' to the new era. However, the fact remains that he did look forward to the new era of scientific and technical achievement: his claim to be a herald or *buccinator* of that era was justified, even if he over-estimated his power of vision.

Francis Bacon was born in 1561 in London. After studying at Cambridge he spent two years in France with the British ambassador and then took up the practice of law. In 1584 he entered Parliament and enjoyed a successful career which culminated in his appointment as Lord Chancellor in 1618 and the reception of the title Baron Verulam. He was created Viscount of St. Albans in 1621; but in the same year he was accused of accepting bribes in his judicial capacity. Found guilty he was sentenced to deprivation of his offices and of his seat in Parliament, a large fine and imprisonment in the Tower. In actual fact, however, he was released from the Tower after a few days and payment of the fine was not exacted. Bacon admitted that he had accepted presents from litigants, though he claimed that his judicial decisions had not been influenced thereby. His claim may or may not be valid; one cannot know the truth about this matter; but in any case it would be an anachronism to expect of a judge in the reigns of Elizabeth and James I precisely the same standard of behaviour which is demanded today. This is not to defend Bacon's behaviour, of course; and the fact that he was brought to trial bears witness to contemporary realization of the fact that his behaviour was improper. But it must be added at the same time that his fall was not brought about simply by a disinterested desire for pure justice on the part of his opponents: partly at least he was the victim of political intrigue and jealousy. In other words, though it is true that Bacon was not a man of profound moral integrity, he was not a wicked man or an iniquitous judge. His reception of presents, as also his behaviour towards Essex, has sometimes been presented in a grossly exaggerated light. It is quite incorrect to regard him as an example of a sort of 'split personality', a man who combined in himself the two irreconcilable characters of the disinterested philosopher and the egoistic politician who cared nothing for the demands of morality. He was by no means a saint like Thomas More; but neither was he an instance of Jekyll and Hyde. His death occurred on April 9th, 1626.

Of the Advancement of Learning appeared in 1606 and the *De sapientia veterum* in 1609. Bacon planned a great work, the *Instauratio magna*, of which the first part, the *De dignitate et augmentis scientiarum*, appeared in 1623. This was a revision and extension of *The Advancement of Learning*. The second part, the *Novum organum*, had appeared in 1620. This had its origin in the *Cogitata et visa* (1607); but it was never completed, a fate which overtook most of Bacon's literary plans. In 1622 and 1623 he published parts of his projected *Historia naturalis et experimentalis ad condendam philosophiam: sive phenomena universi*. The *Sylva sylvarum* and the *New Atlantis* were published posthumously. Numerous other writings include essays and a history of Henry VII.

3. According to Bacon[1] 'that division of human learning is most true which is derived from the threefold faculty of the rational soul'. Taking memory, imagination and reason to be the three faculties of the rational soul, he assigns history to memory, poetry to imagination and philosophy to reasoning. History, however, comprises not only 'civil history', but also 'natural history', and Bacon remarks that 'literary history' should be attended to.[2] Philosophy falls into three main divisions; the first being concerned with God (*de Numine*), the second with nature and the third with man. The first division, that concerned with God, is natural or rational theology; it does not comprise 'inspired or sacred theology', which is the result of God's revelation rather than of man's reasoning. Revealed theology is, indeed, 'the haven and sabbath of all human contemplations',[3] and it is a province of knowledge (*scientia*), but it stands outside philosophy. Philosophy is the work of the human reason, nature being known directly (*radio directo*), God indirectly by means of creatures (*radio refracto*), and man by reflection (*radio reflexo*). Bacon's division of human learning or knowledge according to the faculties of the rational soul is unhappy and artificial; but when he comes to determine the main divisions of philosophy he divides them according to objects: God, nature and man.

[1] *De augmentis scientiarum*, 2, 1. [2] *Ibid.*, 2, 4. [3] *Ibid.*, 3, 1.

The divisions of philosophy, he says,[1] are like the branches of a tree which are united in a common trunk. This means that there is 'one universal science, which is the mother of the rest' and is known as 'first philosophy'. This comprises both fundamental axioms, like *quae in eodem tertio conveniunt, et inter se conveniunt*, and fundamental notions like 'possible' and 'impossible', 'being' and 'not-being', etc. Natural theology, which is the knowledge of God that can be obtained 'by the light of nature and the contemplation of created things'[2] treats of God's existence and of His nature, but only so far as this is manifested in creatures; and it has as its appendix *doctrina de angelis et spiritibus*. The philosophy of nature Bacon divides into speculative and operative natural philosophy. Speculative natural philosophy is subdivided into *physics* (*physica specialis*) and metaphysics. Metaphysics, as part of natural philosophy, must be distinguished, Bacon says,[3] from first philosophy and natural theology, to neither of which does he give the name 'metaphysics'. What, then, is the difference between physics and metaphysics? It is to be found in the types of causes with which they are respectively concerned. Physics treats of efficient and material causes, metaphysics of formal and final causes. But Bacon presently declares that 'inquiry into final causes is sterile and, like a virgin consecrated to God, produces nothing'.[4] One can say, then, that metaphysics, according to him, is concerned with formal causes. This was the position he adopted in the *Novum organum*.

One is naturally tempted to interpret all this in Aristotelian terms and to think that Bacon was simply continuing the Aristotelian doctrine of causes. This would be a mistake, however, and Bacon himself said that his readers should not suppose that because he used a traditional term he was employing it in the traditional sense. By 'forms', the object of metaphysics, he meant what he called 'fixed laws'. The form of heat is the law of heat. Actually there is no radical division between physics and metaphysics. Physics started with examining specific types of matter or bodies in a restricted field of causality and activity; but it goes on to consider more general laws. Thus it shades off into metaphysics, which is concerned with the highest or widest laws of nature. Bacon's use of Aristotelian terminology is misleading. Metaphysics is for him the most general part of what might otherwise be called physics. Moreover, it is not directed to

[1] *De augmentis scientiarum*, 3, 1. [2] *Ibid.*, 2. [3] *Ibid.*, 4. [4] *Ibid.*, 5.

contemplation but to action. We seek to learn the laws of nature with a view to increasing human control over bodies.

Speculative natural philosophy consisting, then, of physics and metaphysics, what is operative natural philosophy? It is the application of the former; and it falls into two parts, mechanics (by which Bacon means the science of mechanics) and magic. Mechanics is the application of physics in practice, while magic is applied metaphysics. Here again Bacon's terminology is apt to mislead. By 'magic' he does not mean, he tells us, the superstitious and frivolous magic which is as different from true magic as the chronicles about King Arthur are different from Caesar's commentaries: he means the practical application of the science of 'hidden forms' or laws. It is improbable that youth could be suddenly and magically restored to an old man; but it is probable that a knowledge of the true natures of assimilation, bodily 'spirits', etc., could prolong life or even partly restore youth 'by means of diets, baths, unctions, the right medicines, suitable exercises and the like'.[1]

The 'appendix' of natural philosophy is mathematics.[2] Pure mathematics comprises geometry, which treats of continuous abstract quantity, and arithmetic, which treats of discrete abstract quantity. 'Mixed mathematics' comprises perspective, music, astronomy, cosmography, architecture, etc. Elsewhere,[3] however, Bacon remarks that astronomy is rather the noblest part of physics than a part of mathematics. When astronomers pay exclusive attention to mathematics they produce false hypotheses. Even if Bacon did not reject outright the heliocentric hypothesis of Copernicus and Galileo, he certainly did not embrace it. Apologists for Bacon point out that he was convinced that the appearances could be saved either on the heliocentric or on the geocentric hypothesis and that the dispute could not be settled by mathematical and abstract reasoning. Doubtless he did think this; but that does not alter the fact that he failed to discern the superiority of the heliocentric hypothesis.

The third main part of philosophy is the part dealing with man. It comprises *philosophia humanitatis* or anthropology and *philosophia civilis* or political philosophy. The former treats first of the human body and is subdivided into medicine, cosmetics, athletics and *ars voluptuaria*, including, for example, music considered from a certain point of view. Secondly it treats of the human soul,

[1] *De augmentis scientiarum*, 5. [2] *Ibid.*, 6. [3] *Ibid.*, 4.

though the nature of the rational, divinely created and immortal soul (*spiraculum*) as distinct from the sensitive soul is a subject which belongs to theology rather than to philosophy. The latter is, however, able to establish the fact that man possesses faculties which transcend the power of matter. Psychology thus leads on to a consideration of logic, *doctrina circa intellectum*, and ethics, *doctrina circa voluntatem*.[1] The parts of logic are the *artes inveniendi, judicandi, retinendi et tradendi*. The most important subdivision of the *ars inveniendi* is what Bacon calls 'the interpretation of nature', which proceeds *ab experimentis ad axiomata, quae et ipsa nova experimenta designent*.[2] This is the *novum organum*. The art of judging is divided into induction, which belongs to the *novum organum*, and the syllogism. Bacon's doctrine concerning the *novum organum* will be considered presently, as also his theory of the 'idols' which forms one of the topics comprised under the heading of the doctrine of the syllogism. In passing it may be mentioned that apropos of pedagogy, which is an 'appendix' of the *ars tradendi*, Bacon observes, 'Consult the schools of the Jesuits: for nothing that has been practised is better than these.'[3] Ethics deals with the nature of human good (*doctrina de exemplari*), not only private but also common, and with the cultivation of the soul with a view to attaining the good (*doctrina de georgica animi*). The part dealing with the common good does not treat of the actual union of men in the State but with the factors which render men apt for social life.[4] Finally *philosophia civilis*[5] is divided into three parts, each of which considers a good which accrues to man from civil society. *Doctrina de conversatione* considers the good which comes to man from association with his fellows (*solamen contra solitudinem*); *doctrina de negotiis* considers the help man receives from society in his practical affairs; and the *doctrina de imperio sive republica* considers the protection from injury which he obtains through government. Or one can say that the three parts consider the three types of prudence; *prudentia in conversando, prudentia in negotiando* and *prudentia in gubernando*. Bacon adds[6] that there are two *desiderata* in the part dealing with government, namely a theory concerning the extension of rule or empire and a science of universal justice, the *de justitia universali sive de fontibus iuris*.

In the ninth and last book of the *De augmentis scientiarum*

[1] *De augmentis scientiarum*, 5, 1. [2] *Ibid.*, 2. [3] *Ibid.*, 6, 4.
[4] *Ibid.*, 7, 2. [5] *Ibid.*, 8, 1. [6] *Ibid.*, 8, 3.

Bacon touches briefly on revealed theology. Just as we are bound to obey the divine law, he says, even when the will resists; so we are obliged to put faith in the divine word even when reason struggles against it. 'For, if we believe only those things which are agreeable to our reason, we assent to things, not to their Author' (that is to say, our belief is based on the evident character of the propositions in question, not on the authority of God revealing). And he adds that 'the more improbable (*absonum*, discordant) and incredible a divine mystery is, so much the more honour is paid to God through believing, and so much the nobler is the victory of faith'. This is not to say, however, that reason has no part to play in Christian theology. It is used both in the attempt to understand the mysteries of faith, so far as this is possible, and in drawing conclusions from them.

Bacon's outline of philosophy in the *De augmentis scientiarum* is on the grand scale and comprises a very extensive programme. He was undoubtedly influenced by traditional philosophy, probably to a greater extent than he realized; but I have already pointed out that the use of Aristotelian terms by Bacon is no sure guide to the meaning he gave them. And in general one can see a new philosophical outlook taking shape in his writings. In the first place, he eliminated from physics consideration of final causality, on the ground that the search for final causes leads thinkers to be content with assigning specious and unreal causes to events when they ought to be looking for the real physical causes, knowledge of which alone is of value for extending human power. In this respect, says Bacon,[1] the natural philosophy of Democritus was more solid and profound than the philosophies of Plato and Aristotle, who were constantly introducing final causes. It is not that there is no such thing as final causality; and it would be absurd to attribute the origin of the world to the fortuitous collision of atoms, after the manner of Democritus and Epicurus. But this does not mean that final causality has any place in physics. Furthermore, Bacon did not assign to metaphysics a consideration of final causality in the Aristotelian sense. Metaphysics was for him neither the study of being as being nor a contemplation of unmoving final causes: it is rather the study of the most general principles or laws or 'forms' of the material world, and this study is undertaken in view of a practical end. His conception of philosophy was to all intents and purposes naturalistic and

[1] *De augmentis scientiarum*, 3, 4.

materialistic. This does not mean that Bacon affirmed atheism or that he denied that man possesses a spiritual and immortal soul. It does mean, however, that he excluded from philosophy any consideration of spiritual being. The philosopher may be able to show that a first Cause exists; but he cannot say anything about God's nature, the consideration of which belongs to theology. Similarly, the subject of immortality is not one which can be treated philosophically. Bacon thus made a sharp division between theology and philosophy, not simply in the sense that he made a formal distinction between them but also in the sense that he accorded full liberty to a materialistic and mechanistic interpretation of Nature. The philosopher is concerned with what is material and with what can be considered from the mechanistic and naturalistic point of view. Bacon may have spoken on occasion in more or less traditional terms about natural theology, for example, but it is clear that the real direction of his thought was to relegate the immaterial to the sphere of faith. Moreover, in spite of his retention of the Aristotelian term 'first philosophy', he did not understand by it precisely what the Aristotelians had understood by it: for him first philosophy was the study of the axioms which are common to the different sciences and of various 'transcendental' concepts considered in their relations to the physical sciences. In a broad sense, Bacon's conception of philosophy was positivistic in character, provided that this is not taken to imply a rejection of theology as a source of knowledge.

4. I turn now to the second part of the *Instauratio magna*, which is represented by the *Novum organum sive indicia vera de interpretatione naturae*. In this work Bacon's philosophical attitude is most clearly revealed. 'Knowledge and human power come to the same thing', for 'nature cannot be conquered except by obeying her'.[1] The purpose of science is the extension of the dominion of the human race over nature; but this can be achieved only by a real knowledge of nature; we cannot obtain effects without an accurate knowledge of causes. The sciences which man now possesses, says Bacon,[2] are useless for obtaining practical effects (*ad inventionem operum*) and our present logic is useless for the purpose of establishing sciences. 'The logic in use is of more value for establishing and rendering permanent the errors which are based on vulgar conceptions than for finding out the truth; so that it is more harmful than useful.'[3] The syllogism consists of

[1] I, 3. [2] I, 11. [3] I, 12.

propositions; and propositions consist of words; and words express concepts. Thus, if the concepts are confused and if they are the result of over-hasty abstraction, nothing which is built upon them is secure. Our only hope lies in true *induction*.[1] There are two ways of seeking and finding the truth.[2] First, the mind may proceed from sense and from the perception of particulars to the most general axioms and from these deduce the less general propositions. Secondly it may proceed from sense and the perception of particulars to immediately attainable axioms and thence, gradually and patiently, to more general axioms. The first way is known and employed; but it is unsatisfactory, because particulars are not examined with sufficient accuracy, care and comprehensiveness and because the mind jumps from an insufficient basis to general conclusions and axioms. It produced *anticipationes naturae*, rash and premature generalizations. The second way, which has not yet been tried, is the true way. The mind proceeds from a careful and patient examination of particulars to the *interpretatio naturae*.

Bacon does not deny, then, that some sort of induction had been previously known and employed; what he objected to was rash and hasty generalization, resting on no firm basis in experience. Induction starts with the operation of the senses; but it requires the co-operation of mind, though the mind's activity must be controlled by observation. Bacon may have lacked an adequate notion of the place and importance of hypothesis in scientific method; but he saw clearly that the value of conclusions based on observation depend on the character of that observation. This led him to say that it is useless to attempt to graft the new on to the old; we must start again from the beginning.[3] He does not accuse the Aristotelians and Scholastics of neglecting induction entirely but rather of being in too much of a hurry to generalize and to draw conclusions. He thought of them as being more concerned with logical consistency, with ensuring that their conclusions followed in due form from their premisses, than with giving a sure foundation to the premisses on the truth of which the conclusions depended. Of the logicians he says[4] that 'they seem to have given scarcely any serious consideration to induction; they pass it over with a brief mention and hurry on to the formulas of disputation'. He, on the other hand, rejects the syllogism on the ground that induction must take its rise in the observation of

[1] 1, 14. [2] 1, 19 ff. [3] 1, 31. [4] *Instauratio magna, distributio operis.*

things, of particular facts or events, and must stick to them as closely as possible. The logicians wing their way at once to the most general principles and deduce conclusions syllogistically. This procedure is admittedly very useful for purposes of disputation; but it is useless for purposes of natural and practical science. 'And so the order of demonstration is reversed';[1] in induction we proceed in the opposite direction to that in which we proceed in deduction.

It might appear that Bacon's insistence on the practical ends of inductive science would itself tend to encourage the drawing of over-hasty conclusions. This was not his intention at least. He condemns[2] the 'unreasonable and puerile' desire to snatch at results which, 'as an Atlanta's apple, hinders the race'. In other words, the establishment of scientific laws by the patient employment of the inductive method will bring greater light to the mind and will prove of more utility in the long run than unco-ordinated particular truths, however immediately practical the latter may seem to be.

But to attain a certain knowledge of nature is not so easy or simple as it may sound at first hearing, for the human mind is influenced by preconceptions and prejudices which bear upon our interpretation of experience and distort our judgments. It is necessary, then, to draw attention to 'the idols and false notions' which inevitably influence the human mind and render science difficult of attainment unless one is aware of them and warned against them. Hence Bacon's famous doctrine of 'the idols'.[3] There are four main types, the idols of the tribe, the idols of the cave or den, the idols of the market-place and the idols of the theatre. 'The doctrines of the idols stands to the interpretation of nature as the doctrine of sophistical arguments stands to common logic.'[4] Just as it is useful for the syllogistic dialectician to be aware of the nature of sophistical arguments, so it is useful for the scientist or natural philosopher to be aware of the nature of the idols of the human mind, that he may be on his guard against their influence.

The 'idols of the tribe' (*idola tribus*) are those errors, the tendency to which is inherent in human nature and which hinder objective judgment. For example, man is prone to rest content with that aspect of things which strikes the senses. Apart from the

[1] *Instauratio magna, distributio operis.*
[2] *Ibid.*
[3] *Novum organum*, I, 38–68.
[4] *Ibid.*, I, 40.

fact that this tendency is responsible for the neglect of investigation into the nature of those things which, like air or the 'animal spirits', are not directly observable, 'sense is in itself weak and misleading'. For the scientific interpretation of nature it is not enough to rely on the senses, not even when they are supplemented by the use of instruments; suitable experiments are also necessary. Then, again, the human mind is prone to rest in those ideas which have once been received and believed or which are pleasing to it and to pass over or reject instances which run counter to received or cherished beliefs. The human mind is not immune from the influence of the will and affections: 'for what a man would like to be true, to that he tends to give credence'. Further, the human mind is prone to indulge in abstractions; and it tends to conceive as constant what is really changing or in flux. Bacon thus draws attention to the danger of relying on appearances, on the untested and uncriticized data of the senses; to the phenomenon of 'wishful thinking'; and to the mind's tendency to mistake abstractions for things. He also draws attention to man's tendency to interpret nature anthropomorphically. Man easily reads into nature final causes 'which proceed from the nature of man rather than from that of the universe'. On this matter one may recall what he says in his work *Of the Advancement of Learning* (2) concerning the introduction of final causes into physics. 'For to say that the hairs of the eyelids are for a quickset and fence about the sight; or that the firmness of the skins and hides of living creatures is to defend them from the extremities of heat or cold; or that the clouds are for watering of the earth' is 'impertinent' in physics. Such considerations 'stay and slug the ship from farther sailing, and have brought this to pass, that the search of the physical causes hath been neglected and passed in silence'. Although Bacon says, as we have seen, that final causality 'is well inquired and collected in metaphysics', it is pretty clear that he regarded notions like the above as instances of man's tendency to interpret natural activity on an analogy with human purposeful activity.

The 'idols of the den' (*idola specus*) are the errors peculiar to each individual, arising from his temperament, education, reading and the special influences which have weighed with him as an individual. These factors lead him to interpret phenomena according to the viewpoint of his own den or cave. 'For each one has (in addition to the aberrations of human nature in general) a certain individual cave or cavern of his own, which breaks and distorts the light of nature.' Bacon's language designedly recalls Plato's parable of the cave in the *Republic*.

The 'idols of the market-place' (*idola fori*) are errors due to the influence of language. The words used in common language describe things as commonly conceived; and when an acute mind sees that the commonly accepted analysis of things is inadequate, language may stand in the way of the expression of a more adequate analysis. Sometimes words are employed when there are no corresponding things. Bacon gives examples like *fortuna* and *primum mobile*. Sometimes words are employed without any clear concept of what is denoted or without any commonly recognized meaning. Bacon takes as an example the word 'humid', *humidum*, which may refer to various sorts of things or qualities or actions.

The 'idols of the theatre' (*idola theatri*) are the philosophical systems of the past, which are nothing better than stage-plays representing unreal worlds of man's own creation. In general there are three types of false philosophy. First there is 'sophistical' philosophy, the chief representative of which is Aristotle, who corrupted natural philosophy with his dialectic. Secondly, there is 'empirical' philosophy, based on a few narrow and obscure observations. The chemists are the chief offenders here: Bacon mentions the philosophy of William Gilbert, author of *De magnete* (1600). Thirdly there is 'superstitious' philosophy, characterized by the introduction of theological considerations. The Pythagoreans indulged in this sort of thing, and, more subtly and dangerously, Plato and the Platonists.

Bad demonstrations are the allies and support of the 'idols': 'by far the best demonstration is experience'.[1] But it is necessary to make a distinction. Mere experience is not enough; it may be compared to a man groping his way in the dark and clutching at anything which offers, in the hope that he will eventually take the right direction. True experience is planned: it may be compared to the activity of a man who first lights a lamp and sees the way clearly.[2] It is not a question of simply multiplying experiments, but of proceeding by an orderly and methodically inductive process.[3] Nor is true induction the same thing as *inductio per enumerationem simplicem*, which is 'puerile' and leads to precarious conclusions which are arrived at without sufficient examination and often with a total neglect of negative instances.[4]

[1] I, 70. [2] I, 83. [3] I, 100. [4] I, 105.

Bacon seems to have thought, wrongly, that the only form of induction known to the Aristotelians was perfect induction or induction 'by simple enumeration', in which no serious attempt was made to discover a real causal connection. But it is undeniable that insufficient consideration had been paid to the subject of inductive method.

What, then, is true induction, positively considered? Human power is directed to or consists in being able to generate a new form in a given nature. From this it follows that human science is directed to the discovery of the forms of things.[1] 'Form' does not here refer to the final cause: the form or formal cause of a given nature is such that, 'given the form, the nature infallibly follows'.[2] It is the law which constitutes a nature. 'And so the form of heat or the form of light is the same thing as the law of heat or the law of light.'[3] Wherever heat manifests itself it is fundamentally the same reality which manifests itself, even if the things in which heat manifests itself are heterogeneous; and to discover the law governing this manifestation of heat is to discover the form of heat. The discovery of these laws or forms would increase human power. For example, gold is a combination of various qualities or natures, and whoever knew the forms or laws of these various qualities or natures could produce them in another body; and this would infallibly result in the transformation of that body into gold.[4]

The discovery of forms in this sense, that is, of the eternal and unchangeable forms or laws, belongs, however, to metaphysics, to which, as has already been mentioned, the consideration of 'formal causes' properly belongs. Physics are concerned with efficient causes or with the investigation of concrete bodies in their natural operation rather than with the possible transformation of one body into another through a knowledge of the forms of simple natures. The physicist will investigate 'concrete bodies as they are found in the ordinary course of nature'.[5] He will investigate what Bacon calls the *latens processus*, the process of change which is not immediately observable but needs to be discovered. 'For example, in every generation and transformation of bodies inquiry must be made as to what is lost and flies away, what remains and what is added; what is dilated and what is contracted; what is united and what is separated; what is continued and what is cut off; what impels and what hinders; what

[1] 2, 1. [2] 2, 4. [3] 1, 17. [4] 2, 5. [5] *Ibid.*

dominates and what succumbs; and much else besides. Nor are these things to be investigated only in the generation and transformation of bodies but also in all other alterations and motions . . .'[1] The process of natural change depends on factors which are not immediately observed by the senses. The physicist will also investigate what Bacon calls the *latens schematismus*, the inner structure of bodies.[2] 'But the thing will not on that account be reduced to the atom, which presupposes the vacuum and unchanging matter (both of which are false) but to true particles, as they may be found to be.'[3]

We have thus the investigation of the eternal and changeless forms of simple natures, which constitutes metaphysics, and the investigation of the efficient and material causes and of the *latens processus* and *latens schematismus* (all of which relate to 'the common and ordinary course of nature, not to the fundamental and eternal laws'), which constitutes physics.[4] The purpose of both is, however, increase of man's power over nature; and this cannot be fully attained without a knowledge of the ultimate forms.

The problem of induction is, therefore, the problem of the discovery of forms. There are two distinct stages. First, there is the 'eduction' of axioms from experience; and, secondly, there is the deduction or derivation of new experiments from the axioms. In more modern language we should say that a hypothesis must first be formed on the basis of the facts of experience, and then observations which will test the value of the hypothesis must be deduced from the hypothesis. This means, says Bacon, that the primary task is to prepare a 'sufficient and good natural and experimental history', based on the facts.[5] Suppose that one desires to discover the form of heat. First of all one must construct a list of cases in which heat is present (*instantiae convenientes in natura calidi*); for example, the rays of the sun, the striking of sparks from flint, the interior of animals, or nasturtium when chewed. Then we shall have a *tabula essentiae et praesentiae*.[6] After this a list should be made of cases which are as much as possible alike to the first but in which heat is nevertheless absent. For example, 'the rays of the moon and of the stars and of comets are not found to be warm to the sense of touch'.[7] In this way *a tabula declinationis sive absentiae in proximo* will be constructed. Finally what Bacon calls a *tabula graduum* or *tabula comparativae* must be made of cases in which the nature whose form is being investigated

[1] 2, 6. [2] 2, 7. [3] 2, 8. [4] 2, 9. [5] 2, 10. [6] 2, 11. [7] 2, 12.

is present in varying degrees.[1] For example, the heat of animals is increased by exercise and by fever. These tables having been constructed, the work of induction really begins. By comparing the instances we must discover what is always present when a given nature (heat, for example) is present; what is always absent when it is absent; and what varies in correspondence with the variations of that 'nature'.[2] First of all, we shall be able to exclude (as the form of a given nature) what is not present in some instance in which that nature is present or which is present in an instance in which the nature is absent or which does not vary in correspondence with the variations of that nature. This is the process of *rejectio* or *exclusio*.[3] But it simply lays the foundations of true induction, which is not completed until a positive affirmation is arrived at.[4] A provisional positive affirmation is arrived at by comparing the positive 'tables'; and Bacon calls this provisional affirmation a *permissio intellectus* or *interpretatio inchoata* or *vindemiatio prima*.[5] Taking heat as an example, he finds the form of heat in motion or, more exactly, in *motus expansivus, cohibitus, et nitens per partes minores*, expanding and restrained motion which makes its way through the smaller parts.

However, in order to render the provisional affirmation certain further means have to be employed; and the rest of the *Novum organum*[6] is devoted to the first of these, which Bacon calls the way of *praerogativae instantiarum*, privileged cases or instances. One class of privileged case is that of unique cases, *instantiae solitariae*. These are cases in which the nature under investigation is found in things which have nothing in common save their participation in that nature. The plan of the *Novum organum* demands that after treating of the *praerogativae instantiarum* Bacon should go on to treat first of seven other 'helps to the intellect' in true and perfect induction and then of the *latentes processus* and *latentes schematismi* in nature; but in actual fact he gets no further than the completion of his treatment of the *praerogativae instantiarum*.

In the *Nova Atlantis*, which also is an unfinished work, Bacon pictures an island in which is situated Solomon's House, an institute devoted to the study and contemplation 'of the works and creatures of God'. Bacon is informed that 'the purpose of our foundation is the knowledge of the causes and motions and inner virtues in nature and the furthest possible extension of the limits

[1] 2, 13. [2] 2, 15. [3] 2, 16–18. [4] 2, 19. [5] 2, 20. [6] 2, 21 ff.

of human dominion'. He is then told of their researches and inventions, among which figure submarines and aeroplanes. All this illustrates Bacon's conviction concerning the practical function of science. But though he performed experiments himself he cannot be said to have contributed much personally to the practical realization of his dreams. He certainly exerted himself to find a patron able and willing to endow a scientific institute of the type of which he dreamed, but he met with no success. This lack of immediate success should not, however, be taken as an indication that Bacon's ideas were unimportant, still less that they were silly. The Scholastic, and in general the metaphysician, will lay much more emphasis on and attach much more value to 'contemplation' (in the Aristotelian sense) than Bacon did; but the latter's insistence on the practical function of science, or of what he called 'experimental philosophy', heralded a movement which has culminated in modern technical civilization, rendered possible by those laboratories and institutes of research and applied science which Bacon envisaged. He vehemently attacked the English universities, for which, in his opinion, science meant at the best mere learning and at the worst mere play with words and obscure terms, and he looked on himself, with his idea of fruitful knowledge, as the herald of a new era. So indeed he was. There has been a strong tendency to depreciate Francis Bacon and to minimize his importance; but the influence of his writings was considerable, and the outlook which he represented has entered profoundly into the western mind. Perhaps it is only fitting, if one can say so without being misunderstood, that the most recent systematic and appreciative study of his philosophy is the work of an American. For my own part I find Bacon's outlook inadequate, if it is considered as a comprehensive philosophy; but I do not see how one can legitimately deny its importance and significance. If one looks upon him as a metaphysician or as an epistemologist, he scarcely bears favourable comparison with the leading philosophers of the classical modern period; but if one looks upon him as the herald of the scientific age he stands in a place by himself.

One of the reasons why Bacon has been depreciated is, of course, his failure to attribute to mathematics that importance in physics which it actually possessed. And it would be difficult, I think, even for his most ardent admirer to maintain successfully that Bacon had a proper understanding of the sort of work which was being accomplished by the leading scientists of his day.

Furthermore, he implies that right use of the inductive method would put all intellects more or less on the same level, as though 'not much is left to acuteness and strength of talent'.[1] It is difficult, he says, to draw a perfect circle without a pair of compasses, but with it anyone can do so. A practical understanding of the true inductive method serves a function analogous to that of the pair of compasses. It was a weakness in Bacon that he did not fully realize that there is such a thing as scientific genius and that its rôle cannot be adequately supplied by the use of a quasi-mechanical method. No doubt he distrusted the illegitimate employment of imagination and fantasy in science, and rightly so; but there is considerable difference between the great scientist who divines a fruitful hypothesis and the man who is capable of making experiments and observations when he has been told on what lines to work.

On the other hand, Bacon was by no means blind to the use of hypothesis in science, even if he did not attach sufficient importance to scientific deduction. In any case the deficiencies in Bacon's conception of method ought not to prevent one giving him full credit for realizing the fact that a 'new organ' was required, namely a developed logic of inductive method. Not only did he realize the need and make a sustained attempt to supply it, but he also anticipated a great deal of what his successor in this matter was to say in the nineteenth century. There are, of course, considerable differences between Bacon's philosophy and that of J. S. Mill. Bacon was not an empiricist in the sense in which Mill was an empiricist, for he believed in 'natures' and in fixed natural laws; but his suggestions as to inductive method contain essentially the canons later formulated by Mill. Bacon may not have made any profound study of the presuppositions of induction. But, then, if induction requires a 'justification', it was certainly not supplied by Mill. Bacon obviously did not solve all problems of induction, nor did he give a final and adequate logical systematization of scientific method; but it would be absurd to expect or to demand that he should have done so. With all his shortcomings the author of the *Novum organum* occupies one of the most important positions in the history of inductive logic and of the philosophy of science.

[1] *Novum organum*, 1, 61.

CHAPTER XX

POLITICAL PHILOSOPHY

General remarks—Niccolò Machiavelli—St. Thomas More—Richard Hooker—Jean Bodin—Joannes Althusius—Hugo Grotius.

1. We have seen that political thought at the close of the Middle Ages still moved, to a great extent, within the general framework of mediaeval political theory. In the political philosophy of Marsilius of Padua we can certainly discern a strong tendency to the exaltation of the self-sufficiency of the State and to the subordination of Church to State; but the general outlook of Marsilius, as of kindred thinkers, lay under the influence of the common mediaeval dislike of absolutism. The conciliar movement aimed at the constitutionalization of ecclesiastical government; and neither Ockham nor Marsilius had advocated monarchic absolutism within the State. But in the fifteenth and sixteenth centuries we witness the growth of political absolutism; and this historical change was naturally reflected in political theory. In England we witness the rise of the Tudor absolutism, which began with the reign of King Henry VII (1485–1509), who was able to establish centralized monarchic power at the close of the Wars of the Roses. In Spain the marriage of Ferdinand and Isabella (1469) united the kingdoms of Aragon and Castile and laid the foundation for the rise of the Spanish absolutism which reached its culmination, so far as imperialistic glory was concerned, in the reign of Charles V (1516–56), who was crowned emperor in 1520 and abdicated in 1556 in favour of Philip II (d. 1598). In France the Hundred Years War constituted a set-back to the growth of national unity and the consolidation of the central power; but when in 1439 the Estates agreed to direct taxation by the sovereign for the purpose of supporting a permanent army, the foundation of monarchic absolutism was laid. When France emerged from the Hundred Years War in 1453, the way was open for the establishment of the absolute monarchy which lasted until the time of the Revolution. Both in England, where absolutism was comparatively short-lived, and in France, where it enjoyed a long life, the rising class of merchants favoured the centralization of power at the expense of

the feudal nobility. The rise of absolutism meant the decay of the feudal society. It meant also the inauguration of a period of transition between mediaeval and 'modern' conceptions of the State and of sovereignty. However, later developments can be left out of account here; it is with the Renaissance that we are concerned; and the Renaissance period was the period in which monarchic absolutism arose in an obvious manner.

This does not mean, of course, that the political theories of the Renaissance period were all theories of monarchic despotism. Catholics and Protestants were at one in regarding the exercise of sovereign power as divinely limited. For example, the famous Anglican writer, Richard Hooker, was strongly influenced by the mediaeval idea of law as divided into eternal, natural and positive law, while a Catholic theorist like Suárez insisted strongly on the unchangeable character of natural law and the indefeasibility of natural rights. The theory of the divine right of kings, as put forward by William Barclay in his *De regno et regali potestate* (1600), by James I in his *Trew Law of Free Monarchies* and by Sir Robert Filmer in his *Patriarcha* (1680), was not so much a theoretical reflection of practical absolutism as an attempt to support a challenged and passing absolutism. This is especially true of Filmer's work, which was largely directed against both Catholic and Protestant opponents of royal absolutism. The theory of the divine right of kings was not really a philosophical theory at all. Philosophers like the Calvinist Althusius and the Catholic Suárez did not regard monarchy as the sole legitimate form of government. Indeed, the theory of the divine right of kings was a passing phenomenon, and it was eminently exposed to the type of ridicule with which John Locke treated it.

But though the consolidation of centralized power and the growth of royal absolutism did not necessarily involve the acceptance of absolutism on the plane of political theory, they were themselves the expression of the felt need for unity in the changing economic and historical circumstances; and this need for unity was indeed reflected in political theory. It was reflected notably in the political and social philosophy of Machiavelli who, living in the divided and disunited Italy of the Renaissance, was peculiarly sensible to the need for unity. If this led him, in one aspect of his philosophy, to emphasize monarchic absolutism, the emphasis was due, not to any illusions about the divine right of kings, but to his conviction that a strong and stable political unity could be secured only in this way. Similarly, when at a later date Hobbes supported centralized absolutism in the form of monarchic government he did not do so out of any belief in the divine right of monarchs or in the divine character of the principle of legitimacy, but because he believed that the cohesion of society and national unity could be best secured in this way. Moreover, both Machiavelli and Hobbes believed in the fundamental egoism of individuals; and a natural consequence of this belief is the conviction that only a strong and unfettered central power is capable of restraining and overcoming the centrifugal forces which tend to the dissolution of society. In the case of Hobbes, whose philosophy will be considered in the next volume of this history, the influence of his system in general on his political theory in particular has also to be taken into account.

The growth of royal absolutism in Europe was also, of course, a symptom of, and a stimulant to, the growth of national consciousness. The rise of the nation-States naturally produced more prolonged reflection on the nature and basis of political society than had been given to this subject during the Middle Ages. With Althusius we find a use of the idea of contract, which was to play so prominent a part in later political theory. All societies, according to Althusius, depend on contract, at least in the form of tacit agreement, and the State is one of the types of society. Again, government rests on agreement or contract, and the sovereign has a trust to fufil. This contract theory was accepted also by Grotius, and it played a part in the political philosophies of the Jesuits Mariana and Suárez. The theory may be employed, of course, in different ways and with different purposes. Thus Hobbes used it to defend absolutism whereas Althusius employed it in defence of the conviction that political sovereignty is, of necessity, limited. But in itself the theory involves no particular view as to the form of government, though the idea of promise or agreement or contract as the basis of organized political society and of government might seem to stress the moral basis and the moral limitations of government.

The rise of absolutism naturally led to further reflection on the natural law and on natural rights. On this matter Catholic and Protestant thinkers were at one in continuing more or less the typical mediaeval attitude. They believed that an unchangeable natural law exists which binds all sovereigns and all societies and that this law is the foundation of certain natural rights. Thus the appeal to natural rights was allied with a belief in the limitation of sovereign power. Even Bodin, who wrote his *Six livres de la république* with a view to strengthening the royal power, which he considered to be necessary in the historical circumstances, had nevertheless a firm belief in natural law and in natural rights, particularly in the rights of private property. For the matter of that, not even the upholders of the divine right of kings imagined that the monarch was entitled to disregard the natural law: indeed, it would have constituted a contradiction had they done so. The theory of natural law and natural rights could not be asserted without a limitation on the exercise of political power being at the same time implied; but it did not involve an acceptance of democracy.

The Reformation naturally raised new issues in the sphere of political theory, or at least it set these issues in a fresh light and rendered them in certain respects more acute. The salient issues were, of course, the relation of Church to State and the right of resistance to the sovereign. The right of resistance to a tyrant was recognized by mediaeval philosophers, who had a strong sense of law; and it was only natural to find this view perpetuated in the political theory of a Catholic theologian and philosopher like Suárez. But the concrete circumstances in those countries which were affected by the Reformation set the problem in a new light. Similarly, the problem of the relation of Church to State took a new form in the minds of those who did not understand by 'Church' the super-national body the head of which is the pope as Vicar of Christ. One cannot conclude, however, that there was, for example, one clearly defined Protestant view on the right of resistance or one clearly defined Protestant view of the relation of Church to State. The situation was much too complicated to allow of such clearly defined views. Owing to the actual course taken by religious history we find different groups and bodies of Protestants adopting different attitudes to these problems. Moreover, the course of events sometimes led members of the same confession to adopt divergent attitudes at different times or in different places.

Both Luther and Calvin condemned resistance to the sovereign; but the attitude of passive obedience and submission came to be associated with Lutheranism, not with Calvinism. The reason for this was that in Scotland and in France Calvinists were at odds with the government. In Scotland John Knox stoutly defended resistance to the sovereign in the name of religious reform, while in France the Calvinists produced a series of works with the same theme. The best known of these, the *Vindiciae contra tyrannos* (1579), the authorship of which is uncertain, represented the view that there are two contracts or covenants, the one between people and sovereign, the other between the people together with the sovereign and God. The first contract creates the State; the second makes the community a religious body or Church. The point of bringing in this second contract was to enable the author to maintain the people's right not only of resistance to a ruler who tries to enforce a false religion but also of bringing pressure to bear on a 'heretical' ruler.

Owing to historical circumstances, then, some groups of Protestants seemed to those who favoured the idea of submission to the ruler in religious matters to be akin to the Catholics, that is to say, to be maintaining not only the distinction of Church and State but also the superiority of the former to the latter. And to a certain extent this was indeed the case. When ecclesiastical power was combined with secular power, as when Calvin ruled at Geneva, it was a simple matter to preach obedience to the sovereign in religious matters; but in Scotland and France a different situation obtained. John Knox found himself compelled to depart from the attitude of Calvin himself, and in Scotland the Calvinist body by no means considered itself obliged to submit to a 'heretical' sovereign. When, in France, the author of the *Vindiciae contra tyrannos* introduced the idea of the contract, he did so in order to find a ground for corporate Huguenot resistance and, ultimately, for bringing pressure to bear on ungodly rulers; he did not do so in order to support 'private judgment' or individualism or toleration. The Calvinists, in spite of their bitter hostility to the Catholic religion, accepted not only the idea of revelation but also that of invoking the aid of the civil power in establishing the religion in which they believed.

The Reformation thus led to the appearance of the perennial problem of the relation of Church and State in a new historical setting; but, as far as the Calvinists were concerned, there was some similarity at least between the solution they gave to the problem and the solution given by Catholic thinkers. Erastianism or the subordination of Church to State, was indeed a different solution; but neither Calvinists nor Erastians believed in the dissociation of religion from politics. Moreover, it would be a mistake to confuse either the limitations placed by Calvinists on the civil power or the Erastian subordination of Church to State with an assertion of 'democracy'. One could scarcely call the Scottish Presbyterians or the French Huguenots 'democrats', in spite of their attacks on their respective monarchs, while Erastianism could be combined with a belief in royal absolutism. It is true, of course, that religious movements and sects arose which did favour what may be called democratic liberalism; but I am speaking of the two most important of the Reformers, Luther and Calvin, and of the more immediate effects of the movements they inaugurated. Luther was by no means always consistent in his attitude or teaching; but his doctrine of submission tended to strengthen the power of the State. Calvin's teaching would have had the same effect but for historical circumstances which led to a modification of Calvin's attitude by his followers and to a forcing of Calvinists in certain countries into opposition to the royal power.

2. Niccoló Machiavelli (1469–1527) is celebrated for his attitude of indifference towards the morality or immorality of the means employed by the ruler in the pursuit of his political purpose, which is the preservation and increase of power. In *The Prince* (1513), which he addressed to Lorenzo, Duke of Urbino, he mentions such good qualities as keeping faith and showing integrity and then observes that 'it is not necessary for a prince to have all the good qualities I have enumerated, but it is very necessary that he should appear to have them'.[1] If, says Machiavelli, the prince possesses and invariably practises all these good qualities, they prove injurious, though the appearance of possessing these qualities is useful. It is a good thing to appear to be merciful, faithful, humane, religious and upright, and it is a good thing to be so in reality; but at the same time the prince ought to be so disposed that he is able to act in a contrary way when circumstances require. In fine, in the actions of all men, and especially of princes, it is results which count and by which people judge. If the prince is successful in establishing and maintaining his authority, the means he employs will always be deemed honourable and will be approved by all.

It has been said that in *The Prince* Machiavelli was concerned simply to give the mechanics of government, that he prescinded from moral questions and wished simply to state the means by which political power may be established and maintained. No

[1] *The Prince*, 18.

doubt this is true; but the fact remains that he obviously considered the ruler entitled to use immoral means in the consolidation and preservation of power. In the *Discourses* he makes it quite clear that in his opinion it is legitimate in the sphere of politics to use an immoral means in order to attain a good end. It is true that the end which Machiavelli has in mind is the security and welfare of the State; but, quite apart from the immoral character of the implied principle that the end justifies the means, the obvious difficulty arises that conceptions of what is a good end may differ. If morality is to be subordinated to political considerations, there is nothing but the actual possession of power to prevent political anarchy.

This does not mean that Machiavelli had any intention of counselling widespread immorality. He was perfectly well aware that a morally degraded and decadent nation is doomed to destruction; he lamented the moral condition of Italy as he saw it and he had a sincere admiration for the civic virtues of the ancient world. Nor do I think that one is entitled to state without any qualification that he explicitly rejected the Christian conception of virtue for a pagan conception. It is perfectly true that he says in the *Discourses*[1] that the Christian exaltation of humility and contempt of the world has rendered Christians weak and effeminate; but he goes on to say that the interpretation of the Christian religion as a religion of humility and love of suffering is an erroneous interpretation. Still, one must admit that a statement of this kind, when taken in connection with Machiavelli's general outlook, approaches very nearly to an explicit repudiation of the Christian ethic. And if one also takes into account his doctrine of the amoral prince, a doctrine which is at variance with the Christian conscience, whether Catholic or Protestant, one can hardly refrain from allowing that Nietzsche's reading of Machiavelli's mind was not without foundation. When, in *The Prince*,[2] Machiavelli remarks that many men have thought that the world's affairs are irresistibly governed by fortune and God, and when he goes on to say that, although he is sometimes inclined to that opinion, he considers that fortune can be resisted, implying that virtue consists in resisting the power which governs the world, it is difficult to avoid the impression that 'virtue' meant for him something different from what it means for the Christian. He admired strength of character and power to achieve one's ends: in the

[1] 2, 2. [2] 25.

prince he admired ability to win power and keep it: but he did not admire humility and he had no use for any universal application of what Nietzsche would call the 'herd morality'. He took it for granted that human nature is fundamentally egoistic; and he pointed out to the prince where his best interests lay and how he could realize them. The fact of the matter is that Machiavelli admired the unscrupulous though able potentate as he observed him in contemporary political or ecclesiastical life or in historical examples; he idealized the type. It was only through such men, he thought, that good government could be assured in a corrupt and decadent society.

The last sentence gives the key to the problem of the apparent discrepancy between Machiavelli's admiration for the Roman Republic, as manifested in the *Discourses on the First Ten Books of Titus Livius* and the monarchical doctrine of *The Prince*. In a corrupt and decadent society in which man's natural badness and egoism have more or less free scope, where uprightness, devotion to the common good, and the religious spirit are either dead or submerged by license, lawlessness and faithlessness, it is only an absolute ruler who is able to hold together the centrifugal forces and create a strong and unified society. Machiavelli was at one with the political theorists of the ancient world in thinking that civic virtue is dependent on law; and he considered that in a corrupt society reformation is possible only through the agency of an all-powerful lawgiver. 'This is to be taken for a general rule that it happens rarely, or not at all, that any republic or kingdom is either well-ordered at the beginning or completely reformed in regard to its old institutions, if this is not done by one man. It is thus necessary that there should be one man alone who settles the method and on whose mind any such organization depends.'[1] An absolute legislator is necessary, therefore, for the founding of a State and for the reform of a State; and in saying this Machiavelli was thinking primarily of contemporary Italian States and of the political divisions of Italy. It is law which gives birth to that civic morality or virtue which is required for a strong and unified State, and the promulgation of law requires a legislator. From this Machiavelli drew the conclusion that the monarchic legislator may use any prudent means to secure this end and that, being the cause of law and of civic morality, he is independent of both so far as is required for the fulfilment of his political function. The

[1] *Discourses*, 1, 9, 2.

moral cynicism expressed in *The Prince* by no means constitutes the whole of Machiavelli's doctrine; it is subordinate to the final purpose of creating or of reforming what he regarded as the true State.

But, though Machiavelli regarded the absolute monarch or legislator as necessary for the foundation or reformation of the State, absolute monarchy was not his ideal of government. In the *Discourses*[1] he roundly asserts that, in respect of prudence and constancy, the people have the advantage and are 'more prudent, more steady and of better judgment than princes'.[2] The free republic, which was conceived by Machiavelli on the model of the Roman Republic, is superior to the absolute monarchy. If constitutional law is maintained and the people have some share in the government, the State is more stable than if it is ruled by hereditary and absolute princes. The general good, which consists, according to Machiavelli, in the increase of power and empire and in the preservation of the liberties of the people,[3] is regarded nowhere but in republics; the absolute monarch generally has regard simply for his private interests.[4]

Machiavelli's theory of government may be somewhat patchwork and unsatisfactory in character, combining, as it does, an admiration for the free republic with a doctrine of monarchic despotism; but the principles are clear. A State, when once well-ordered, will hardly be healthy and stable unless it is a republic; this is the ideal; but in order that a well-ordered State should be founded or in order that a disordered State should be reformed, a monarchic legislator is necessary in practice. Another reason for this necessity is the need for curbing the power of the nobles, for whom Machiavelli, contemplating the Italian political scene, had a particular dislike. They are idle and corrupt, and they are always enemies of civil government and order;[5] they maintain bands of mercenaries and ruin the country. Machiavelli also looked forward to a prince who would liberate and unify Italy, who would 'heal her wounds and put an end to the ravaging and plundering of Lombardy, to the swindling and taxing of the kingdom of Naples and of Tuscany'.[6] In his view the papacy, not having sufficient strength to master the whole of Italy but being strong enough to prevent any other Power from doing so, was responsible for the division of Italy into principalities, with the result that the weak

[1] I, 58, 61. [2] *Ibid.*, 8. [3] *Ibid.*, I, 29, 5.
[4] *Ibid.*, 2, 2, 3. [5] *Ibid.*, I, 55, 7–11. [6] *The Prince*, 26.

and disunited country was a prey for the barbarians and for anyone who thought fit to invade it.[1]

Machiavelli, as historians have remarked, showed his 'modernity' in the emphasis he laid on the State as a sovereign body which maintains its vigour and unity by power-politics and an imperialistic policy. In this sense he divined the course of historical development in Europe. On the other hand he did not work out any systematic political theory; nor was he really concerned to do so. He was intensely interested in the contemporary Italian scene; he was an ardent patriot; and his writings are coloured through and through by this interest; they are not the writings of a detached philosopher. He also over-estimated the part played in historical development by politics in a narrow sense; and he failed to discern the importance of other factors, religious and social. He is chiefly known, of course, for his amoral advice to the prince, for his 'Machiavellianism'; but there can be little doubt that the principles of state-craft he laid down have not infrequently, even if regrettably, been those actually operative in the minds of rulers and statesmen. But historical development is not conditioned entirely by the intentions and deeds of those who occupy the limelight on the political stage. Machiavelli was clever and brilliant; but he can scarcely be called a profound political philosopher.

On the other hand, one must remember that Machiavelli was concerned with actual political life as he saw it and with what is actually done rather than with what ought to be done from the moral point of view. He expressly disclaims any intention of depicting ideal States[2] and he remarks that if a man lives up consistently to the highest moral principles in political life, he is likely to come to ruin and, if he is a ruler, to fail to preserve the security and welfare of the State. In the preface to the first book of the *Discourses*, he speaks of his new 'way', which, he claims, has been hitherto left untrodden. His method was one of historical induction. From a comparative examination of cause-effect sequences in history, ancient and recent, with due allowance for negative instances, he sought to establish certain practical rules in a generalized form. Given a certain purpose to be achieved, history shows that a certain line of action will or will not lead to the achievement of that purpose. He was thus immediately concerned with political mechanics; but his outlook implied a certain philosophy of history.

[1] *Discourses*, I, 12, 6–8.

[2] Cf. *The Prince*, 15.

It implied, for example, that there is repetition in history and that history is of such a nature that it affords a basis for induction. Machiavelli's method was not, of course, altogether new. Aristotle, for example, certainly based his political ideas on an examination of actual constitutions and he considered not only the ways in which States are destroyed but also the virtues which the ruler should pretend to have if he is to be successful.[1] But Aristotle was much more concerned than Machiavelli with abstract theory. He was also primarily interested in political organizations as the setting for moral and intellectual education, whereas Machiavelli was much more interested in the actual nature and course of concrete political life.

3. A very different type of thinker was St. Thomas More (1478–1535), Lord Chancellor of England, who was beheaded by Henry VIII for refusing to acknowledge the latter as supreme head of the Church in England. In his *De optimo reipublicae statu deque nova insula Utopia* (1516) he wrote, under the influence of Plato's *Republic*, a kind of philosophical novel describing an ideal State on the island of Utopia. It is a curious work, combining a sharp criticism of contemporary social and economic conditions with an idealization of the simple moral life, which was scarcely in harmony with the more worldly spirit of the time. More was unacquainted with *The Prince*; but his book was in part directed against the idea of statecraft represented in Machiavelli's work. It was also directed against the growing spirit of commercial exploitation. In these respects it was a 'conservative' book. On the other hand More anticipated some ideas which reappear in the development of modern socialism.

In the first book of his *Utopia* More attacks the destruction of the old agricultural system through the enclosure of land by wealthy and wealth-seeking proprietors. Desire of gain and wealth leads to the conversion of arable land into pasture, in order that sheep may be reared on a wide scale and their wool sold in foreign markets. All this greed for gain and the accompanying centralization of wealth in the hands of a few leads to the rise of a dispossessed and indigent class. Then, with a view to keeping this class in due subjection, heavy and fearful punishments are decreed for theft. But the increased severity of the criminal law is useless. It would be much better to provide the means of livelihood for the indigent, since it is precisely want which drives these people to

[1] Cf. *Politics*, 5, 11.

crime. The government, however, does nothing: it is busily engaged in diplomacy and wars of conquest. War necessitates extortionate taxation, and, when war is over, the soldiers are thrown into a community which is already unable to support itself. Power-politics thus aggravates the economic and social evils.

In contrast with an acquisitive society More presents an agricultural society, in which the family is the unit. Private property is abolished, and money is no longer used as a means of exchange. But More did not depict his Utopia as a republic of uneducated peasants. The means of livelihood are assured to all, and the working hours are reduced to six hours a day, in order that the citizens may have leisure for cultural pursuits. For the same reason a slave class sees to the harder and more burdensome work, the slaves consisting partly of condemned criminals, partly of captives of war.

It is sometimes said that More was the first to proclaim the ideal of religious toleration. It must be remembered, however, that in sketching his Utopia he prescinded from the Christian revelation and envisaged simply natural religion. Divergent views and convictions were to be tolerated for the most part, and theological strife was to be avoided; but those who denied God's existence and providence, the immortality of the soul and sanctions in the future life would be deprived of capacity to hold any public office and accounted as less than men. The truths of natural religion and of natural morality might not be called in question, whatever a man might think privately, for the health of the State and of society depended on their acceptance. There can be little doubt that More would have regarded the Wars of Religion with horror; but he was certainly not the type of man who asserts that it is a matter of indifference what one believes.

More had no use at all for the dissociation of morals from politics, and he speaks very sharply of statesmen who rant about the public good when all the time they are seeking their own advantage. Some of his ideas, those concerning the criminal code, for example, are extremely sensible, and in his ideals of security for all and of reasonable toleration he was far ahead of his time. But though his political ideal was in many respects enlightened and practical, in some other respects it can be regarded as an idealization of a past co-operative society. The forces and tendencies against which he protested were not to be stayed in their development by any

Utopia. The great Christian humanist stood on the threshold of a capitalistic development which was to run its course. Yet in due time some at any rate of his ideals were to be fulfilled.

4. More died before the Reformation in England had taken a definite form. In *The Laws of Ecclesiastical Polity* by Richard Hooker (1553–1600) the problem of Church and State finds its expression in the form dictated by religious conditions in England after the Reformation. Hooker's work, which had its influence on John Locke, was written in refutation of the Puritan attack on the established Church of England; but its scope is far wider than that of the ordinary controversial writing of the time. The author treats first of law in general, and on this matter he adheres to the mediaeval idea of law, particularly to that of St. Thomas. He distinguishes the eternal law, 'that order which God before all ages hath set down with Himself for Himself to do all things by',[1] from the natural law. He then proceeds to distinguish the natural law as operative in non-free agents, which he calls 'natural agents', from the natural law as perceived by the human reason and as freely obeyed by man.[2] 'The rule of voluntary agents on earth is the sentence that reason giveth concerning the goodness of those things which they are to do.'[3] 'The main principles of reason are in themselves apparent';[4] that is to say, there are certain general moral principles the obligatory character of which is immediately apparent and evident. A sign of this is the general consent of mankind. 'The general and perpetual voice of men is as the sentence of God Himself. For that which all men have at all times learned Nature herself must needs have taught; and God being the author of Nature, her voice is but His instrument.'[5] Other more particular principles are deduced by reason.

In addition to the eternal law and the natural law there is human positive law. The natural law binds men as men and it does not depend on the State;[6] but human positive law comes into being when men unite in society and form a government. Owing to the fact that we are not self-sufficient as individuals 'we are naturally induced to seek communion and fellowship with others'.[7] But societies cannot exist without government, and government cannot be carried on without law; 'a distinct kind of law from that which hath been already declared'.[8] Hooker teaches that there are two foundations of society; the natural inclination of man to

[1] I, 2. [2] I, 3. [3] I, 8. [4] *Ibid.*
[5] *Ibid.* [6] I, 10. [7] *Ibid.* [8] *Ibid.*

live in society, and 'an order expressly or secretly agreed upon, touching the manner of their union in living together. The latter is that which we call the law of a common weal, the very soul of a politic body, the parts whereof are by law animated, held together, and set on work in such actions as the common good requireth.'[1]

The establishment of civil government thus rests upon consent, 'without which consent there were no reason that one man should take upon him to be lord or judge over another'.[2] Government is necessary; but Nature has not settled the kind of government or the precise character of laws, provided that the laws enacted are for the common good and in conformity with the natural law. If the ruler enforces laws without explicit authority from God or without authority derived in the first instance from the consent of the governed, he is a mere tyrant. 'Laws they are not therefore which public approbation hath not made so', at least through 'Parliaments, Councils, and the like assemblies'.[3] How, then, does it come about that whole multitudes are obliged to respect laws in the framing of which they had no share at all? The reason is that 'corporations are immortal: we were then alive in our predecessors, and they in their successors do live still'.[4]

Finally there are 'the laws that concern supernatural duties',[5] 'the law which God Himself hath supernaturally revealed'.[6] Thus Hooker's theory of law in general follows the theory of St. Thomas, with the same theological setting or, rather, with a like reference of law to its divine foundation, God. Nor does he add anything particularly new in his theory of the origin of political society. He introduces the idea of contract or agreement; but he does not represent the State as a purely artificial construction; on the contrary, he speaks explicitly of man's natural inclination to society, and he does not explain the State and government simply in terms of a remedy for unbridled egoism.

When he comes to treat of the Church, Hooker distinguishes between truths of faith and Church government, which is 'a plain matter of action'.[7] The point he tries to develop and defend is that the ecclesiastical law of the Church of England is in no way contrary to the Christian religion or to reason. It ought, therefore, to be obeyed by Englishmen, for Englishmen are Christians and, as Christians, they belong to the Church of England. The assumption is that Church and State are not distinct societies, at least not when the State is Christian. Hooker did not, of course, deny

[1] 1, 10. [2] *Ibid.* [3] *Ibid.* [4] *Ibid.* [5] 1, 15. [6] 1, 16. [7] 3, 3.

that Catholics and Calvinists were Christians; but he assumed in a rather naïve fashion that the Christian faith as a whole requires no universal institution. He also assumed that ecclesiastical government was more or less a matter of indifference, a view which would commend itself, for different reasons, neither to Catholics nor to Calvinists.

Hooker is remarkable principally for his continuation of the mediaeval theory and divisions of law. In his political theory he was obviously not an upholder of the divine right of kings or of monarchic despotism. On the other hand, he did not propose his doctrine of consent or contract in order to justify rebellion against the sovereign. Even if he had considered rebellion justified, he would hardly have laboured such a point in a book designed to show that all good Englishmen should conform to the national Church. In conclusion one may remark that Hooker writes for the most part with remarkable moderation of tone, if, that is to say, one bears in mind the prevailing atmosphere of contemporary religious controversy. He was essentially a man of the *via media* and no fanatic.

5. Jean Bodin (1530–96), who had studied law at the university of Toulouse, endeavoured to make a close alliance between the study of universal law and the study of history in his *Methodus ad facilem historiarum cognitionem* (1566). After dividing history into three types he says: 'let us for the moment abandon the divine to the theologians, the natural to the philosophers, while we concentrate long and intently upon human actions and the rules governing them'.[1] His leading interest is revealed by the following statement in his *Dedication*. 'Indeed, in history the best part of universal law lies hidden; and what is of great weight and importance for the best appraisal of legislation—the custom of the peoples, and the beginnings, growth, conditions, changes and decline of all States—are obtained from it. The chief subject matter of this *Method* consists of these facts, since no rewards of history are more ample than those usually gathered about the governmental form of states.' The *Method* is remarkable for its strongly marked tendency to the naturalistic interpretation of history. For example, he treats of the effects of geographical situation on the physiological constitution, and so on the habits, of peoples. 'We shall explain the nature of peoples who dwell to the north and to the south, then of those who live to the east

[1] *Preamble.*

and to the west.'[1] This sort of idea reappears later in the writings of philosophers like Montesquieu. Bodin also evolved a cyclical theory of the rise and fall of States. But the chief importance of Bodin consists in his analysis of sovereignty. Originally sketched in chapter 6 of the *Methodus*, it is treated at greater length in the *Six livres de la république* (1576).[2]

The natural social unit, from which the State arises, is the family. In the family Bodin included not simply father, mother and children, but also servants. In other words he had the Roman conception of the family, with power residing in the *paterfamilias*. The State is a secondary or derived society, in the sense that it is 'a lawful government of several households, and of their common possessions, with sovereign power'; but it is a different kind of society. The right of property is an inviolable right of the family; but it is not a right of the ruler or the State, considered, that is to say, as ruler. The ruler possesses sovereignty; but sovereignty is not the same thing as proprietorship. It is clear, then, that for Bodin, as he says in the *Methodus*,[3] 'the State is nothing else than a group of families or fraternities subjected to one and the same rule'. From this definition it follows that 'Ragusa or Geneva, whose rule is comprised almost within its walls, ought to be called a State' and that 'what Aristotle said is absurd—that too great a group of men, such as Babylon was, is a race, not a State'.[4] It is also clear that for Bodin sovereignty is essentially different from the power of the head of a family and that a State cannot exist without sovereignty. Sovereignty is defined as 'supreme power over citizens and subjects, unrestrained by law'.[5] It involves the power to create magistrates and define their offices; the power to legislate and to annul laws; the power to declare war and make peace; the right of receiving appeals; and the power of life and death. But, though it is clear that sovereignty is distinct from the power of the head of a family, it is not at all clear how sovereignty comes into being, what ultimately gives the sovereign his title to exercise sovereignty and what is the foundation of the citizen's duty of obedience. Bodin apparently thought that most States come into existence through the exercise of force; but he did not consider that force justifies itself or that the possession of physical power *ipso facto* confers sovereignty on its possessor. What does confer legitimate sovereignty is, however, left obscure.

Sovereignty is inalienable and indivisible. Executive functions

[1] 5. [2] Enlarged Latin edition, 1584. [3] 6. [4] *Ibid.* [5] *Republic*, 1, 8.

and powers can, of course, be delegated, but sovereignty itself, the possession of supreme power, cannot be parcelled out, as it were. The sovereign is unrestrained by law, and he cannot limit his sovereignty by law, so long as he remains sovereign, for law is the creation of the sovereign. This does not mean, of course, that the sovereign is entitled to disregard the divine authority or the natural law; he cannot, for instance, expropriate all families. Bodin was insistent on the natural right of property, and the communistic theories of Plato and More drew sharp criticism from his pen. But the sovereign is the supreme fount of law and has ultimate and full control over legislation.

This theory of sovereignty must give the impression that Bodin believed simply in royal absolutism, especially if one speaks of the sovereign as 'he'. But though he certainly wished to strengthen the position of the French monarch, since he felt that this was necessary in the historical circumstances, his theory of sovereignty is not in itself bound up with monarchic absolutism. An assembly, for example, can be the seat of sovereignty. Forms of government may differ in different States; but the nature of sovereignty remains the same in all those States, if they are well-ordered States. Moreover, there is no reason why a monarch should not delegate a great deal of his power and govern 'constitutionally', provided that it is recognized that this governmental arrangement depends on the will of the monarch, if, that is to say, sovereignty rests with the monarch. For it does not necessarily follow that because a State happens to have a king, the latter is sovereign. If the king is really dependent on an assembly or parliament, he cannot be called a sovereign in the strict sense.

As historians have pointed out, however, Bodin was by no means always consistent. It was his intention to increase the prestige and insist on the supreme power of the French monarch; and it followed from his theory of sovereignty that the French monarch should be unrestricted by law. But it followed from his theory of natural law that there might be cases when the subject would be not only justified in disobeying a law promulgated by the sovereign but also morally obliged to do so. Moreover, he even went so far as to state that taxation, as it involves an interference with property, requires the assent of the Estates, though the latter, according to the theory of sovereignty, depend for their existence on the sovereign. Again, he recognized certain *leges imperii* or constitutional limitations on the power of the king. In other words, his desire to emphasize the monarch's supreme and sovereign power was at variance with his inclination towards constitutionalism and led him into contradictory positions.

Bodin emphasized the philosophical study of history and he certainly made a sustained attempt to understand history; but he was not altogether free from the prejudices and superstitions of his time. Though he rejected astrological determinism, he nevertheless believed in the influence of the heavenly bodies on human affairs and he indulged in speculations concerning numbers and their relations to governments and States.

In conclusion it may be mentioned that in his *Colloquium heptaplomeres*, a dialogue, Bodin pictures people of different religions living together in harmony. In the midst of historical events which were not favourable to peace among the members of different confessions he supported the principle of mutual toleration.

6. Bodin had given no very clear account of the origin and foundation of the State; but in the philosophy of the Calvinist writer Joannes Althusius (1557–1638) we find a clear statement of the contract theory. In Althusius' opinion a contract lies at the basis of every association or community of men. He distinguishes various types of community; the family, the *collegium* or corporation, the local community, the province and the State. Each of these communities corresponds to a natural need in man; but the formation of any definite community rests upon an agreement or contract whereby human beings agree to form an association or community for their common good in respect of specified purposes. In this way they become *symbiotici*, living together as sharers in a common good. The family, for instance, corresponds to a natural need in man; but the foundation of any definite family rests on a contract. So it is with the State. But a community, in order to attain its purpose, must have a common authority. So we can distinguish a second contract between the community and the administrative authority, a contract which is the foundation of the duties pertaining to either party.

There is a further important point to be made. As each type of community corresponds to a definite human need, the constitution of a wider or more extensive community does not annul or abolish the narrower community: rather is the wider community constituted by the agreement of a number of narrower communities, which themselves remain in existence. The local community, for example, does not annul the families or the corporations composing it; it owes its existence to their agreement and its purpose is distinct from theirs. They are not, therefore, swallowed up by the wider community. Again, the State is immediately constituted by the agreement of provinces rather than directly by a contract between individuals, and it does not render the provinces superfluous or useless. From this a certain federation logically follows. Althusius was far from considering the State as resting on a contract whereby individuals handed over their rights to a government. A number of associations, which, of course, ultimately represent individuals, agree together to form the State and agree on a constitution or law regulating the attainment of the common purpose or good for which the State is formed.

But, if the State is one among a number of communities or associations, what is its distinguishing and peculiar mark? As in Bodin's political theory it is sovereignty (*ius maiestatis*); but, unlike Bodin, Althusius declared that sovereignty rests always, necessarily and inalienably, with the people. This does not mean, of course, that he envisaged direct government by the people; through the law of the State, a law itself resting on agreement, power is delegated to the administrative officers or magistrates of the State. Althusius contemplated a supreme magistrate, who might, of course, though not necessarily, be a king, and 'ephors' who would see that the constitution was observed. But the theory does involve a clear assertion of popular sovereignty. It also involves the right of resistance, since the power of the ruler rests on a contract, and if he is faithless to his trust or breaks the contract, power reverts to the people. When this happens, the people may appoint another ruler, though this will be done in a constitutional manner.

Althusius assumed, of course, the sanctity of contracts, resting on the natural law; and the natural law itself he regarded, in the traditional manner, as resting on divine authority. It was Grotius, rather than Althusius, who re-examined the idea of natural law. But Althusius' political theory is remarkable for its assertion of popular sovereignty and the use made of the idea of contract. As a Calvinist he insisted on the right of resistance to the ruler; but it must be added that he had no idea of religious freedom or of a State which would be officially indifferent to forms of religion. Such a notion was no more acceptable to the Calvinist than to the Catholic.

7. The chief work of Hugo Grotius or Huig de Groot (1583–1645) is his famous *De iure belli ac pacis* (1625). In the *Prolegomena*

to that work[1] he represents Carneades as holding that there is no such thing as a universally obligatory natural law, 'because all creatures, men as well as animals, are impelled by nature towards ends advantageous to themselves'. Each man seeks his own advantage; human laws are dictated simply by consideration of expediency; they are not based upon or related to a natural law, for the latter does not exist. To this Grotius replies that 'man is, to be sure, an animal, but an animal of a superior kind', and 'among the traits characteristic of man is an impelling desire for society, that is, for the social life, not of any and every sort, but peaceful and organized according to the measure of his intelligence. . . . Stated as a universal truth, therefore, the assertion that every animal is impelled by nature to seek only its own good cannot be conceded.'[2] There is a natural social order, and it is the maintenance of this social order which is the source of law. 'To this sphere of law belong the abstaining from that which is another's . . . the obligation to fulfil promises . . .'[3] Furthermore, man is possessed of the power of judging 'what things are agreeable or harmful (as to both things present and things to come) and what can lead to either alternative'; and 'whatever is clearly at variance with such judgment is understood to be contrary also to the law of nature, that is, to the nature of man'.[4]

The nature of man is thus the foundation of law. 'For the very nature of man, which even if we had no lack of anything would lead us into the mutual relations of society, is the mother of the law of nature.'[5] The natural law enjoins the keeping of promises; and as the obligation of observing the positive laws of States arises from mutual consent and promise, 'nature may be considered, so to say, the great-grandmother of municipal law'. In point of fact, of course, individuals are by no means self-sufficient; and expediency has a part to play in the institution of positive law and subjection to authority. 'But just as the laws of each State have in view the advantage of that State, so by mutual consent it has become possible that certain laws should originate as between all States or a great many States; and it is apparent that the laws thus originating had in view the advantage, not of particular States, but of the great society of States. And this is what is called the law of nations, whenever we distinguish that term from the law of nature.'[6] But it is not simply a question of

[1] 5.
[2] *De iure belli ac pacis*, 6.
[3] *Ibid.*, 8.
[4] *Ibid.*, 9.
[5] *Ibid.*, 16.
[6] *Ibid.*, 17.

expediency: it is also a question of natural justice. 'Many hold, in fact, that the standard of justice which they insist upon in the case of individuals within the State is inapplicable to a nation or the ruler of a nation.'[1] But, 'if no association of men can be maintained without law . . . surely also that association which binds together the human race, or binds many nations together, has need of law; this was perceived by him who said that shameful deeds ought not to be committed even for the sake of one's country'.[2] It follows that 'war ought not to be undertaken except for the enforcement of rights; when once undertaken, it should be carried on only within the bounds of law and good faith'.[3]

Grotius is convinced, then, that 'there is a common law among nations, which is valid alike in peace and war'.[4] We have, therefore, the natural law, the municipal law or positive law of States, and the law of nations. In addition, Grotius, a believing Protestant, admits the positive Christian law. 'This, however—contrary to the practice of most men—I have distinguished from the law of nature, considering it as certain that in that most holy law a greater degree of moral perfection is enjoined upon us than the law of nature, alone and by itself, would require.'[5]

Historians generally attribute to Grotius an important rôle in the 'freeing' of the idea of natural law from theological foundations and presuppositions and in naturalizing it. In this respect, it is said, he was much closer than were the Schoolmen to Aristotle, for whom he had a great admiration. It is certainly true to some extent that Grotius separated the idea of natural law from the idea of God. 'What we have been saying would have a degree of validity even if we should concede that which cannot be conceded without the utmost wickedness, that there is no God, or that the affairs of men are of no concern to Him.'[6] But he proceeds to say that the law of nature, 'proceeding as it does from the essential traits implanted in man, can nevertheless rightly be attributed to God, because of His having willed that such traits exist in us'.[7] And he quotes Chrysippus and St. John Chrysostom in support. Moreover he defines the law of nature as follows. 'The law of nature is a dictate of right reason which points out that an act, according as it is or is not in conformity with rational nature, has in it a quality of moral baseness or moral necessity; and that, in consequence, such an act is either forbidden or enjoined by the

[1] *De iure belli ac pacis*, 21. [2] *Ibid.*, 23. [3] *Ibid.*, 25. [4] *Ibid.*, 28.
[5] *Ibid.*, 50. [6] *Prolegomena*, 11. [7] *Ibid.*, 12.

author of nature, God.'[1] Among his references on this matter he refers to Thomas Aquinas and Duns Scotus, whose remarks, he says, are by no means to be slighted. While, then, it may be true to say that, as a historical fact, Grotius' treatment of the idea of natural law contributed to the 'naturalization' of the idea inasmuch as he was treating law, not as a theologian, but as a lawyer and philosopher of law, it is wrong to suggest that Grotius made any radical break with the position of, say, St. Thomas. What seems to impress some historians is his insistence on the fact that an act enjoined or forbidden by the natural law is enjoined or forbidden by God because it is, in itself, obligatory or wrong. The natural law is unchangeable, even by God.[2] It is not right or wrong because of God's decision that it should be right or wrong. But the notion that the moral quality of acts permitted, enjoined or forbidden by the natural law depends on God's arbitrary *fiat* was certainly not that of St. Thomas. It represents, more or less, the Ockhamist view; but it is in no way necessarily bound up with the attribution of an ultimate metaphysical and 'theological' foundation to the natural law. When Grotius points out[3] the difference between the natural law and 'volitional divine law', he is making a statement with which St. Thomas would gave agreed. It seems to me that it is Grotius' 'modernity', his careful and systematic treatment of law from the standpoint of a lay lawyer and philosopher, which is responsible for the impression that he made a bigger break with the past than he actually did.

In his *Prolegomena*[4] Grotius says, 'I have made it my concern to refer the proofs of things touching the law of nature to certain fundamental conceptions which are beyond question, so that no one can deny them without doing violence to himself'. In the first book[5] he asserts that *a priori* proof, which 'consists in demonstrating the necessary agreement or disagreement of anything with a rational and social nature', is 'more subtle' than *a posteriori* proof, though the latter is 'more familiar'. But later in his work,[6] when treating of the causes of doubt in moral questions, he remarks that 'what Aristotle wrote is perfectly true, that certainty is not to be found in moral questions in the same degree as in mathematical science'. To this statement Samuel Pufendorf took exception.[7] I do not think, therefore, that one ought to lay great

[1] 1, 1, 10, 1. [2] 1, 1, 10, 5. [3] 1, 1, 10, 2. [4] 39.
[5] 1, 1, 12, 1. [6] 2, 23, 1. [7] *De jure naturae et gentium*, 1, 2, 9–10.

stress on Grotius' place in the movement of philosophical thought which was characterized by emphasis on deduction, an emphasis due to the influence of the success of mathematical science. No doubt he did not escape this influence; but the doctrine that there are self-evident principles of natural morality was by no means new.

'The State', says Grotius,[1] 'is a complete association of free men, joined together for the enjoyment of rights and for their common interests.' The State itself is the 'common subject' of sovereignty, sovereignty being the power 'whose actions are not subject to the legal control of another, so that they cannot be rendered void by the operation of another human will'.[2] The 'special subject is one or more persons, according to the laws and customs of each nation'.[3] Grotius proceeds to deny the opinion of Althusius (who is not named, however) that sovereignty always and necessarily resides in the people. He asks why it should be supposed that the people should be incapable of transferring sovereignty.[4] Though sovereignty is in itself indivisible, in the sense that it means something definite, the actual exercise of sovereign power can be divided. 'It may happen that a people, when choosing a king, may reserve to itself certain powers but may confer the others on the king absolutely.'[5] Divided sovereignty may have its disadvantages, but so has every form of government; 'and a legal provision is to be judged not by what this or that man considers best, but by what accords with the will of him with whom the provision originated'.[6]

As to resistance or rebellion against rulers, Grotius argues that it is quite incompatible with the nature and purpose of the State that the right of resistance should be without limitation. 'Among good men one principle at any rate is established beyond controversy, that if the authorities issue any order that is contrary to the law of nature or to the commandments of God, the order should not be carried out';[7] but rebellion is a different matter. However, if in the conferring of authority the right of resistance was retained or if the king openly shows himself the enemy of the whole people or if he alienates the kingdom, rebellion, that is, resistance by force, is justified.

Grotius teaches that a just war is permissible; but he insists that 'no other just cause for undertaking war can there be excepting

[1] 1, 1, 14, 1. [2] 1, 3, 7, 1. [3] 1, 3, 7, 3. [4] 1, 3, 8, 1.
[5] 1, 3, 17, 1. [6] 1, 3, 17, 2. [7] 1, 4, 1, 3.

injury received'.[1] It is permissible for a State to wage war against another State which has attacked it, or in order to recover what has been stolen from it, or to 'punish' another State, that is, if the other State is obviously infringing the natural or divine law. But preventive war may not be waged unless there is moral certainty that the other State intends attack;[2] nor may it be waged simply for advantage's sake,[3] nor to obtain better land,[4] nor out of a desire to rule others under the pretext that it is for their good.[5] War should not be waged in cases of doubt as to its justice,[6] and, even for just causes, it should not be undertaken rashly:[7] it should only be undertaken in cases of necessity,[8] and peace should always be kept in view.[9] In the actual conduct of war what is permissible can be viewed either absolutely, in relation to the law of nature, or in relation to a previous promise, in relation, that is, to the law of nations.[10] Discussion of the permissible in war with reference to a previous promise is discussion concerning good faith among enemies; and Grotius insists that good faith is always to be kept, because 'those who are enemies do not in fact cease to be men'.[11] For example, treaties should be scrupulously observed. The law of nature binds, of course, all men as men: the law of nations 'is the law which has received its obligatory force from the will of all nations, or of many nations'.[12] It is distinct, therefore, from the law of nature and rests on promise and on custom. 'The law of nations, in fact,' as Dio Chrysostom well observes, 'is the creation of time and custom. And for the study of it the illustrious writers of history are of the greatest value to us.'[13] In other words, custom, consent and contract between States give rise to an obligation just as promises between individuals give rise to an obligation. In the absence of any international authority or tribunal or court of arbitration war between States necessarily takes the place of litigation between individuals; but war should not be waged if it can be avoided by arbitration or conferences (or even lot, says Grotius); and if it cannot be avoided, if, that is to say, it proves to be necessary for the enforcement of rights, it should be waged only within the bounds of good faith and with a scrupulous attention to proper procedure analogous to that observed in judicial processes. It is obvious that Grotius considered 'public war' not as a justifiable instrument of policy, imperialistic ambition or territorial greed, but as something which cannot be avoided in the

[1] 2, 1, 1, 4. [2] 2, 22, 5. [3] 2, 22, 6. [4] 2, 23, 8. [5] 2, 22, 12. [6] 2, 23, 6. [7] 2, 24. [8] 2, 24, 8. [9] 3, 25, 2. [10] 3, 1, 1. [11] 3, 19, 1, 2. [12] 1, 1, 14, 1. [13] 1, 1, 14, 2.

absence of an international tribunal capable of rendering war as unnecessary as law-courts have rendered 'private war'. Nevertheless, just as individuals enjoy the right of self-defence, so do States. There can be a just war; but it does not follow that every means is legitimate even in a just war. The 'law of nations' must be observed.

Grotius was a humanist, a humanitarian and a learned man; he was also a convinced Christian. He desired the healing of the rifts between Christians; and he defended toleration in regard to the different confessions. His great work, *De iure belli ac pacis*, is remarkable, not only for its systematic and its humanitarian character, but also for its dispassionate freedom from bigotry. Its spirit is well expressed in a remark he makes about the Schoolmen. The latter, he says, 'furnish a praiseworthy example of moderation; they contend with one another by means of arguments—not, in accordance with the practice which has lately begun to disgrace the calling of letters, with personal abuse, base offspring of a spirit lacking self-mastery'.[1]

In this chapter I have avoided discussion of treatises on political theory by Scholastic writers, since I propose to treat of Renaissance Scholasticism in the next part of this work. But it may be as well to draw attention here to the fact that Scholastic authors formed an important channel whereby the mediaeval philosophy of law was transmitted to men like Grotius. This is particularly true of Suárez. In addition, the treatments of the 'law of nations' and of war by Vitoria and Suárez were not without influence on non-Scholastic writers of the Renaissance and post-Renaissance periods. One does not wish to depreciate the importance of a man like Grotius, but it is as well to realize the continuity which existed between mediaeval thought and the political and legal theories of the Renaissance period. Moreover, an understanding of the Scholastic philosophies of law helps one to avoid attributing to Grotius and kindred thinkers a degree of 'secularization' of thought which is not, in my opinion, present in their writings. The notion that the Scholastics in general made the natural law dependent on the arbitrary divine will naturally inclines those who hold it to regard a man like Grotius as one who humanized and secularized the concept of natural law. But the notion is incorrect and is based either on ignorance of Scholasticism in general or on an assumption that the peculiar ideas of some of the nominalist school represented the common views of Scholastic philosophers.

[1] *Prolegomena*, 52.

PART III

SCHOLASTICISM OF THE RENAISSANCE

CHAPTER XXI

A GENERAL VIEW

The revival of Scholasticism—Dominican writers before the Council of Trent; Cajetan—Later Dominican writers and Jesuit writers—The controversy between Dominicans and Jesuits about grace and free will—The substitution of 'philosophical courses' for commentaries on Aristotle—Political and legal theory.

1. ONE might perhaps have expected that the life and vigour of Aristotelian Scholasticism would have been finally sapped by two factors, first the rise and spread of the nominalist movement in the fourteenth century and secondly the emergence of new lines of thought at the time of the Renaissance. Yet in the fifteenth and sixteenth centuries there occurred a remarkable revival of Scholasticism, and some of the greatest names in Scholasticism belong to the period of the Renaissance and the beginning of the modern era. The chief centre of this revival was Spain, in the sense that most, though not all, of the leading figures were Spaniards. Cajetan, the great commentator on the writings of St. Thomas, was an Italian but Francis of Vitoria, who exercised a profound influence on Scholastic thought, was a Spaniard, as were also Dominic Soto, Melchior Cano, Dominic Báñez, Gabriel Vásquez and Francis Suárez. Spain was comparatively untouched either by the ferment of Renaissance thought or by the religious dissensions of the Reformation; and it was only natural that a renewal of studies which was carried through predominantly, though not, of course, exclusively, by Spanish theologians should take the form of a revivification, prolongation and development of Scholasticism.

This renewal of Scholastic thought is associated with two religious Orders in particular. First in the field were the Dominicans, who produced noted commentators on St. Thomas like Cajetan and De Sylvestris and eminent theologians and philosophers like Francis of Vitoria, Dominic Soto, Melchior Cano and Dominic Báñez. Indeed, the first stage of the revival of

Scholasticism, namely the stage which preceded the Council of Trent, was in a special degree the work of the Order of Preachers. The Council of Trent began in 1545, and it gave a powerful impulse to the renewal of Scholastic thought. The Council was primarily concerned, of course, with theological doctrines, questions and controversies, but the handling and discussion of these themes involved also a treatment of philosophical matters, in the sense at least that the theologians who assisted at the Council or who discussed the subjects which arose in the Council were necessarily involved to some extent in philosophical discussions. The work of the Dominicans in commenting on the works of St. Thomas and in elucidating and developing his thought was thus reinforced by the impulse contributed by the Council of Trent to the promotion of Scholastic studies. A further enrichment of life was given to Scholasticism by the Society of Jesus, which was founded in 1540 and which is especially associated with the work of the so-called Counter-Reformation, inaugurated by the Council. The Society of Jesus not only made a most important general contribution to the deepening and extension of intellectual life among Catholics through the foundation of numerous schools, colleges and universities but it also played a signal part in the theological and philosophical discussions and controversies of the time. Among the eminent Jesuits of the sixteenth century and the early part of the seventeenth we find names like Toletus, Molina, Vásquez, Lessius, St. Robert Bellarmine and, above all, Francis Suárez. I do not mean to imply that other Orders did not also play a part in the renewal of Scholasticism. There were well-known writers, like the Franciscan, Lychetus, who belonged to other Orders. But it remains true that the two bodies of men who did most for Scholastic thought at the time of the Renaissance were the Dominicans and the Jesuits.

2. Of the Scholastics who died before or shortly after the beginning of the Council of Trent one may mention, for example, Petrus Niger (d. 1477), author of *Clypeum thomistarum*, Barbus Paulus Soncinas (d. 1494), author of an *Epitome Capreoli*, and Dominic of Flanders (d. 1500), who published among other works *In XII libros metaphysicae Aristotelis quaestiones*. These three were all Dominicans. So also was Chrysostom Javelli (*c.* 1470–*c.* 1545) who was named Chrysostomus Casalensis after his birthplace. He lectured at Bologna and composed commentaries on the principal works of Aristotle; *Compendium logicae isagogicum*,

In universam naturalem philosophiam epitome, In libros XII metaphysicorum epitome, In X ethicorum libros epitome, In VIII politicorum libros epitome, Quaestiones super quartum meteorum, super librum de sensu et sensato, super librum de memoria et reminiscentia. He also defended Aquinas's exposition of Aristotle in *Quaestiones acutissimae super VIII libros physices ad mentem S. Thomae, Aristotelis et Commentatoris decisae* and in *Quaestiones super III libros de anima, super XII libros metaphysicae.* In addition he wrote *In Platonis ethica et politica epitome* and a *Christiana philosophia seu ethica*, besides publishing a refutation of Pomponazzi's arguments to show that the human soul is naturally mortal. This last theme he took up again in his *Tractatus de animae humanae indeficientia in quadruplici via, sc. peripatetica, academica, naturali et christiana.* He also wrote on the thorny subject of predestination.

Mention should also be made of Francis Sylvester de Sylvestris (*c.* 1474–1528), known as Ferrariensis, who lectured at Bologna and published *Quaestiones* on Aristotle's *Physics* and *De anima*, *Annotationes* on the *Posterior Analytics* and a commentary on St. Thomas's *Summa contra Gentiles.* But a much more important writer was Cajetan.

Thomas de Vio (1468–1534), commonly known as Cajetan, was born at Gaeta and entered the Dominican Order at the age of sixteen. After studying at Naples, Bologna and Padua he lectured in the university of Padua; and it was there that he composed his treatise on Aquinas's *De ente et essentia.* Subsequently he lectured for a time at Pavia, after which he held various high offices in his Order. In 1508 he was elected Master-General, and in this post he gave constant attention to promoting higher studies among the Dominicans. He was created a cardinal in 1517, and from 1518 to 1519 he was papal legate in Germany. In 1519 he was appointed Bishop of Gaeta. His numerous works include commentaries on the *Summa theologica* of St. Thomas, on the *Categories*, *Posterior Analytics* and *De anima* of Aristotle, and on the *Praedicabilia* of Porphyry, as well as his writings *De nominum analogia*, *De subiecto naturalis philosophiae*, *De conceptu entis*, *De Dei infinitate* and the already-mentioned *De ente et essentia.* Although Cajetan took part in theological and philosophical controversy he wrote with admirable calm and moderation. He was, however, accused of obscurity by Melchior Cano, who was more influenced than Cajetan by contemporary humanism and care for literary style.

In his *De nominum analogia* Cajetan developed a view of analogy which has exercised a considerable influence among Thomists. After insisting[1] on the importance of the rôle which analogy plays in metaphysics he goes on to divide analogy into three main kinds. (i) The first kind of analogy, or of what is sometimes called analogy, is 'analogy of inequality'.[2] Sensitive or animal life, for example, is found in a higher degree of perfection in men than in brutes; and in this sense they are 'unequally' animals. But this does not alter the fact, says Cajetan, that animality is predicated univocally of men and brutes. Corporeity is nobler in a plant than in a metal; but plants and metals are bodily things in a univocal sense. This type of analogy is called 'analogy', therefore, only by a misuse of the term. (ii) The second kind of analogy is analogy of attribution,[3] though the only type of this kind of analogy which Cajetan recognized was analogy of extrinsic attribution. An animal, for example, is called healthy because it possesses health formally, while food and medicine are called healthy only because they preserve or restore health in something other than themselves, an animal, for instance. This example may, however, be misleading. Cajetan did not assert that finite things are good, for example, only in the sense in which food is called healthy: he was well aware that each finite thing has its own inherent goodness. But he insisted that if finite things are called good precisely because of their relationship to the divine goodness as their efficient, exemplary or final cause, they are being called good only by extrinsic denomination. And he thought that when an analogous term is predicated of *A* only because of a relationship which *A* has to *B*, of which alone the analogous term is formally predicated, the predication is called analogous only on sufferance, as it were. Analogy in the proper and full sense occurs only in the case of the third kind of analogy. (iii) This third kind of analogy is analogy of proportionality.[4]

Analogy of proportionality can be either metaphorical or non-metaphorical. If we speak of a 'smiling meadow' this is an instance of metaphorical analogy; 'and sacred Scripture is full of this kind of analogy'.[5] But there is analogy of proportionality in the proper sense only when the common term is predicated of both analogates without the use of metaphor. If we say that there is an analogy between the relation of God's activity to His being and the relation of man's activity to his being, there is analogy of proportionality, since an imperfect similarity is asserted as holding

[1] Ch. 1. [2] *Ibid.* [3] Ch. 2. [4] Ch. 3. [5] *Ibid.*

between these two 'proportions' or relations; but activity is attributed formally and properly to both God and man. Again, we can predicate wisdom of God and man, meaning that an analogy holds between the relation of the divine wisdom to the divine being and the relation of man's wisdom to his being, and we do so without using the word 'wisdom' metaphorically.

According to Cajetan, this kind of analogy is the only kind which obtains between creatures and God; and he made a valiant effort[1] to show that it is capable of yielding a real knowledge of God. In particular, he tried to show that we can argue by analogy from creatures to God without committing the fallacy of equivocation. Suppose an argument like the following. Every pure perfection which is found in a creature exists also in God. But wisdom is found in human beings and it is a pure perfection. Therefore wisdom is found in God. If the word 'wisdom' in the minor premiss means human wisdom, the syllogism involves the fallacy of equivocation, because the word 'wisdom' in the conclusion does not mean human wisdom. In order to avoid this fallacy one must employ the word 'wisdom' neither univocally nor equivocally, that is, neither in one simple sense nor in two distinct senses, but in a sense which contains both uses *proportionaliter*. The conception 'father', for example, as predicated analogously of God and man contains both uses. It is true that we obtain a knowledge of wisdom, for instance, through an acquaintance with human wisdom and then apply it analogously to God; but, says Cajetan,[2] we should not confuse the psychological origin of a concept with its precise content when it is used analogously.

Apart from the obscurity of Cajetan's account of analogy, it is clear, I think, that to lay down rules for the term in order to avoid the fallacy of equivocation is not the same thing as to show that we are objectively justified in using the term in this way. It is one thing to say, for example, that if we assert that there is some similarity between the relation of the divine wisdom to the divine being and the relation of man's wisdom to his being we must not use the term 'wisdom' either univocally or equivocally; but it is another thing to show that we are entitled to speak at all of the divine wisdom. How could this possibly be shown if the only analogy which obtains between creatures and God is analogy of proportionality? It is difficult to see how this kind of analogy can be of any value at all in regard to our knowledge of God, unless the

[1] Ch. 10. [2] Ch. 11.

analogy of intrinsic attribution is presupposed. Cajetan had doubtless much of value to say on the wrong uses of analogy; but I venture to doubt whether his restriction of analogy, as applied to God and creatures, to analogy of proportionality represents the view of St. Thomas. And it is perhaps a little difficult to see how his position does not lead in the end to agnosticism.

Cajetan criticized Scotism on many occasions, though always politely and temperately. Still more did he criticize the 'Averroism' of his day. But it is worth noting that in his commentary on the *De anima* of Aristotle he allowed that the Greek philosopher had really held the opinion attributed to him by the Averroists, namely that there is only one intellectual and immortal soul in all men and that there is no individual or personal immortality. Cajetan certainly rejected both the Averroist thesis, that there is only one intellectual and immortal soul in all men, and the Alexandrist thesis, that the soul is naturally mortal. But he apparently came to think that the immortality of the human soul cannot be philosophically demonstrated though probable arguments can be adduced to show that it is immortal. In his commentary on the *Epistle to the Romans*,[1] he explicitly says that he has no philosophic or demonstrative knowledge (*nescio* is the word he uses) of the mystery of the Trinity, of the immortality of the soul, of the Incarnation 'and the like, all of which, however, I believe'. If he was ready to couple the immortality of the soul with the mystery of the Trinity in this way, he cannot have thought that the former is a philosophically demonstrable truth. Moreover, in his commentary on *Ecclesiastes*[2] he says explicitly that 'no philosopher has yet demonstrated that the soul of man is immortal: there does not appear to be a demonstrative argument; but we believe it by faith, and it is in agreement with probable arguments' (*rationibus probabilibus consonat*). One can understand, then, his objection to the proposed decree of the fifth Lateran Council (1513) calling upon professors of philosophy to justify the Christian doctrine in their lectures. In Cajetan's opinion this was the task of theologians and not of philosophers.

3. Among the later Dominican writers of the period one can mention first Francis of Vitoria (1480–1546), who lectured at Salamanca and composed commentaries on the *Pars prima* and on the *Secunda secundae* of Aquinas's *Summa theologica*. But he is best known for his political and juridical ideas, and these will be

[1] 9, 23. [2] 3, 21.

treated later. Dominic Soto (1494–1560), who also lectured at Salamanca, published, among other works, commentaries on Aristotle's logical writings and his *Physics* and *De anima*, as well as on the fourth book of the *Sentences* of Peter Lombard. Melchior Cano (1509–60) is justly celebrated for his *De locis theologicis*, in which he endeavoured to establish the sources of theological doctrine in a systematic and methodic manner. Bartholomew of Medina (1527–81), Dominic Báñez (1528–1604) and Raphael Ripa or Riva (d. 1611) were also outstanding Dominican theologians and philosophers.

Among the Jesuit writers an eminent name is that of Francis Toletus (1532–96), who was a pupil of Dominic Soto at Salamanca and afterwards lectured at Rome, where he was created cardinal. He published commentaries on the logical works of Aristotle and on his *Physics*, *De anima* and *De generatione et corruptione*, as well as on St. Thomas's *Summa theologica*. A set of learned commentaries on Aristotle were published by a group of Jesuit writers, known as the *Conimbricenses* from their connection with the university of Coimbra in Portugal. The chief member of this group was Peter de Fonseca (1548–99), who composed commentaries on the *Metaphysics*, as well as publishing *Institutiones dialecticae* and an *Isagoge philosophica* or introduction to philosophy. Among other Jesuit theologians and philosophers mention should be made of Gabriel Vásquez (*c.* 1551–1604), who lectured chiefly at Alcalá and Rome, and Gregory of Valentia (1551–1603). Both these men published commentaries on the *Summa theologica* of St. Thomas. Leonard Lessius (1554–1623), however, who lectured at Douai and Louvain, wrote independent works like his *De iustitia et iure ceterisque virtutibus cardinalibus* (1605), *De gratia efficaci, decretis, divinis libertate arbitrii et praescientia Dei conditionata disputatio apologetica* (1610), *De providentia Numinis et animae immortalitate* (1613), *De summo bono et aeterna beatitudine hominis* (1616) and *De perfectionibus moribusque divinis* (1620).

The Franciscan Lychetus (d. 1520) commented on the *Opus Oxoniense* and the *Quodlibeta* of Scotus. It was not until 1593, however, that the latter was declared the official Doctor of the Franciscan Order. Giles of Viterbo (d. 1532), an Augustinian, composed a commentary on part of the first book of the *Sentences* of Peter Lombard. And one must not omit to mention the group of professors associated with the university of Alcalá, founded by Cardinal Ximenes in 1489, who are known as the *Complutenses*,

The leading member of the group was Gaspar Cardillo de Villalpando (1537–81), who edited commentaries on Aristotle in which he tried to establish critically the actual meaning of the text.

4. Perhaps this is the place to say a few words about the famous controversy which broke out in the sixteenth century between Dominican and Jesuit theologians concerning the relation between divine grace and human free will. I do not wish to say much on the subject, as the controversy was primarily of a theological character. But it ought to be mentioned, I think, as it has philosophical implications.

Leaving out of account preliminary stages of the controversy one can start by mentioning a famous work by Luis de Molina (1535–1600), a Jesuit theologian who lectured for many years at the university of Evora in Portugal. This work, entitled *Concordia liberi arbitrii cum gratiae donis, divina praescientia, providentia, praedestinatione et reprobatione*, was published at Lisbon in 1589. In it Molina affirmed that 'efficacious grace', which includes in its concept the free consent of the human will, is not intrinsically different in nature from merely 'sufficient grace'. Grace which is merely sufficient is grace which is sufficient to enable the human will to elicit a salutary act, if the will were to consent to it and co-operate with it. It becomes 'efficacious', if the will does in fact consent to it. Efficacious grace is thus the grace with which a human will does in fact freely co-operate. On the other hand, if God exercises universal and particular providence, He must have infallible knowledge of how any will would react to any grace in any set of circumstances; and how can He know this if an efficacious grace is efficacious in virtue of the will's free consent? In order to answer this question Molina introduced the concept of *scientia media*, the knowledge by which God knows infallibly how any human will, in any conceivable set of circumstances, would react to this or that grace.

It is quite clear that Molina and those who agreed with him were concerned to safeguard the freedom of the human will. Their point of view may perhaps be expressed by saying that we start from what is best known to us, namely human freedom, and that we must explain the divine foreknowledge and the action of grace in such a way that the freedom of the will is not explained away or tacitly denied. If it did not seem fanciful to introduce such considerations into a theological dispute, one might perhaps suggest that the general humanistic movement of the Renaissance was reflected to some extent in Molinism. In the course of the controversy Molinism was modified by Jesuit theologians like Bellarmine and Suárez, who introduced the idea of 'congruism'. 'Congruous' grace is a grace which is congruous with or suited to the circumstances of the case and obtains the free consent of the will. It is opposed to 'incongruous' grace, which for some reason or other is not suited to the circumstances of the case, in that it does not obtain the free consent of the will, though in itself it is 'sufficient' to enable the will to make a salutary act. In virtue of the *scientia media* God knows from eternity what graces would be 'congruous' in regard to any will in any circumstances.

Molina's adversaries, of whom the most important was the Dominican theologian Báñez, started from the principle that God is the cause of all salutary acts and that God's knowledge and activity must be prior to and independent of the human will's free act. They accused Molina of making the power of divine grace subordinate to the human will. According to Báñez, efficacious grace is intrinsically different from merely sufficient grace, and it obtains its effect by reason of its own intrinsic nature. As for Molina's *scientia media* or 'intermediate knowledge', this is a mere term without any corresponding reality. God knows the future free acts of men, even conditional future free acts, in virtue of His predetermining decrees, by which He decides to give the 'physical premotion' which is necessary for any human act. In the case of a salutary act this physical premotion will take the form of efficacious grace.

Báñez and the theologians who agreed with him thus began with metaphysical principles. God, as first cause and prime mover, must be the cause of human acts in so far as they have being. Báñez, it must be emphasized, did not deny freedom. His view was that God moves non-free agents to act necessarily and free agents, when they act as free agents, to act freely. In other words God moves every contingent agent to act in a manner conformable to its nature. According to the Bannezian view, one must begin with assured metaphysical principles and draw the logical conclusions. The Molinist view, according to the Bannezians, was unfaithful to the principles of metaphysics. According to the Molinists on the other hand, it was very difficult to see how the Bannezians could retain human freedom in anything except in name. Moreover, if the idea of a divine concurrence which is logically prior to the free act and which infallibly brings about a certain act was admitted, it was very difficult to see how one is to avoid making God responsible for sin. The Molinists did not think that the distinctions introduced by their opponents in order to avoid the conclusion that God is responsible for sin were of any substantial use for this purpose. *Scientia media* was admittedly a hypothesis; but it was preferable to make this hypothesis rather than to suppose that God knows the future free acts of men in virtue of His predetermining decrees.

The dispute between the Dominicans and the Jesuits induced Pope Clement VIII to set up a special Congregation in Rome to examine the points at issue. The Congregation is known as the *Congregatio de auxiliis* (1598–1607). Both parties had full opportunity to state their respective cases; but the end of the matter was that both opinions were permitted. At the same time the Jesuits were forbidden to call the Dominicans Calvinists, while the Dominicans were told that they must not call the Jesuits Pelagians. In other words, the different parties could continue to propound their own ways of reconciling God's foreknowledge, predestination and saving activity with human freedom, provided that they did not call each other heretics.

5. Cajetan was the first to take Aquinas's *Summa theologica* as a theological text-book instead of the *Sentences* of Peter Lombard; and both Dominicans and Jesuits looked on St. Thomas as their Doctor. Aristotle was still regarded as 'the Philosopher'; and we have seen that Renaissance Scholastics continued to publish commentaries on his works. At the same time there was gradually effected a separation of philosophy from theology more systematic and methodic than that which had generally obtained in the mediaeval Schools. This was due partly to the formal distinction between the two branches of study which had already been made in the Middle Ages and partly, no doubt, to the rise of philosophies which owed nothing, professedly at least, to dogmatic theology. We find, then, the gradual substitution of philosophical courses for commentaries on Aristotle. Already with Suárez (d. 1617) we find an elaborate discussion of philosophical problems in separation from theology; and the order of treating metaphysical themes and problems which had been adopted by Suárez in his *Disputationes metaphysicae* exercised an influence on later Scholastic method. In the freer style of philosophical writing which was inaugurated by Suárez one can doubtless see the influence of Renaissance humanism. I said earlier in this chapter that Spanish Scholasticism was

comparatively unaffected by the Renaissance. But one must make an exception, I think, in regard to literary style. Suárez was, it must be admitted, a diffuse writer; but his work on metaphysics did a great deal to break through the former tradition of writing philosophy in the form of commentaries on Aristotle.

The eminent Dominican theologian and philosopher John of St. Thomas (1589–1644) published his *Cursus philosophicus* before his *Cursus theologicus*, and, to take another Dominican example, Alexander Piny issued a *Cursus philosophicus thomisticus* in 1670. The Carmelite Fathers of Alcalá published a *Cursus artium* in 1624, which was revised and added to in later editions. Among the Jesuits, Cardinal John de Lugo (1583–1660) left an unpublished *Disputationes metaphysicae*, while Peter de Hurtado de Mendoza published *Disputationes de universa philosophia* at Lyons in 1617 and Thomas Compton-Carleton a *Philosophia universa* at Antwerp in 1649. Similarly, both Rodrigo de Arriaga and Francis de Oviedo published philosophical courses, the former at Antwerp in 1632 and the latter at Lyons in 1640. A *Cursus philosophicus* by Francis Soares appeared at Coimbra in 1651, and a *Philosophia peripatetica* by John-Baptist de Benedictis at Naples in 1688. Similar philosophical courses were written by Scotists. Thus John Poncius and Bartholomew Mastrius published respectively a *Cursus philosophicus ad mentem Scoti* (1643) and a *Philosophiae ad mentem Scoti cursus integer* (1678). Among writers belonging to other religious Orders Nicholas of St. John the Baptist, a Hermit of St. Augustine, published his *Philosophia augustiniana, sive integer cursus philosophicus iuxta doctrinam sancti Patris Augustini* at Geneva in 1687, while Celestino Sfondrati, a Benedictine, published a *Cursus philosophicus sangallensis* (1695–9).

In the course of the seventeenth century, then, *Cursus philosophici* tended to take the place of the former commentaries on Aristotle. This is not to say, however, that the former custom was abandoned. Sylvester Maurus (1619–87), for example, a Jesuit theologian and philosopher, published a commentary on Aristotle in 1668. Nor is one entitled to conclude from the change in the method of philosophic writing that the Scholastics of the Renaissance and of the seventeenth century were profoundly influenced by the new scientific ideas of the time. The Franciscan Emmanuel Maignan, who published a *Cursus philosophicus* at Toulouse in 1652, complained that the Scholastics of his time devoted themselves to metaphysical abstractions and subtleties and that some of them, when their opinions on physics were challenged in the name of experience and experiment, replied by denying the testimony of experience. Maignan himself was considerably influenced by Cartesianism and atomism. Honoré Fabri (*c.* 1607–88), a Jesuit writer, laid particular emphasis on mathematics and physics; and there were, of course, other Scholastics who were alive to the ideas of their time. But if one takes the movement of the Renaissance and post-Renaissance philosophy as a whole, it is fairly obvious that Scholasticism lay somewhat apart from the main line of development and that its influence on non-Scholastic philosophers was restricted. This is not to say that it had no influence; but it is obvious that when we think of Renaissance and post-Renaissance philosophy we do not think primarily of Scholasticism. Generally speaking, the Scholastic philosophers of the period failed to give sufficient attention to the problems raised by, for example, the scientific discoveries of the time.

6. There was, however, at least one department of thought in which the Renaissance Scholastics were deeply influenced by contemporary problems and in which they exercised a considerable influence. This was the department of political theory. I shall say something more in detail later about Suárez' political theory; but I want to make some general remarks here concerning the political theory of the Scholastics of the Renaissance.

The problem of the relation between Church and State did not, as we have already seen, come to an end with the close of the Middle Ages. Indeed, it was in a sense intensified by the Reformation and by the claim of some rulers to possess jurisdiction even in matters of religion. As far as the Catholic Church was concerned a doctrine of full submission to the State was impossible: it was precluded by the position accorded to the Holy See and by the Catholic idea of the Church and her mission. The Catholic theologians and philosophers, therefore, felt called upon to lay down the principles by which the relations between Church and State should be governed. Thus Cardinal Robert Bellarmine maintained in his work on the papal power[1] that the pope, while not possessing a direct power over temporal affairs, possesses an indirect power. Temporal interests must give way to spiritual interests, if a clash arises. This theory of the pope's indirect power in temporal affairs did not mean that Bellarmine regarded the civil ruler as the pope's vicar—the theory excluded any such

[1] *De summo pontifice*, 1581; enlarged as *De potestate summi pontificis*, 1610.

idea; it was simply the consequence of applying the theological doctrine that man's end is a supernatural end, namely the beatific vision of God. The theory was also maintained by Francis Suárez in his *Defensio fidei catholicae* (1613), written against King James I of England.

But though Bellarmine and Suárez rejected the idea that the civil ruler is a vicar of the pope, they did not accept the theory that he derives his sovereignty directly from God, as was asserted by the upholders of the theory of the divine right of kings. And the fact that Suárez argued against this theory in his *Defensio fidei catholicae* was one of the reasons why James I had the book burned. Both Bellarmine and Suárez maintained that the civil ruler receives his power immediately from the political community. They held, indeed, that the civil ruler receives his authority ultimately from God, since all legitimate authority comes ultimately from Him; but it is derived immediately from the community.

One might be perhaps tempted to think that this theory was inspired by the desire to minimize the royal power at a time when the centralized and powerful monarchies of the Renaissance were very much in evidence. What better way of taking the wind out of the sails of the royalists could be devised than that of maintaining that though the monarch's power does not come from the pope it does not come directly from God either, but from the people? What better way of exalting the spiritual power could be found than that of asserting that it is the pope alone who receives his authority directly from God? But it would be a great mistake to regard the Bellarmine-Suárez theory of sovereignty as being primarily a piece of ecclesiastical propaganda or politics. The idea that political sovereignty is derived from the people had been put forward as early as the eleventh century by Manegold of Lautenbach; and the conviction that the civil ruler has a trust to fulfil and that if he habitually abuses his position he may be deposed was expressed by John of Salisbury in the twelfth, Aquinas in the thirteenth, and Ockham in the fourteenth century. Writers like Bellarmine and Suárez simply inherited the general outlook of the earlier Scholastic theologians and philosophers, though the fact that they gave a more formal and explicit statement of the theory that political sovereignty derives from the people was doubtless largely due to reflection on the concrete historical data of their time. When Mariana (d. 1624), the Spanish Jesuit, made his unfortunate statements about the use of tyrannicide as a remedy for political oppression (some of his remarks were interpreted as a defence of the murder of Henry III of France, and this caused his *De rege et regis institutione*, 1599, to be burned by the French Parliament) his principle was simply the principle of the legitimacy of resistance against oppression, which had been commonly accepted in the Middle Ages, though Mariana's conclusions were misguided.[1]

The Renaissance Scholastics were not, however, concerned simply with the position of the civil ruler in regard to the Church on the one hand and the political community on the other: they were concerned also with the origin and nature of political society. As far as Suárez is concerned, it is clear that he regarded political society as resting essentially on consent or agreement. Mariana, who derived the power of the monarch from a pact with the people, regarded the origin of political society as following a state of nature which preceded government; and the main step on the road to organized States and governments he found in the institution of private property. Suárez cannot be said to have followed Mariana in the latter hypothesis of a state of nature. But he found the origin of the State in voluntary consent, on the part of heads of families at least, though he evidently thought that such associations between men had occurred from the beginning.

Suárez may, then, be said to have held a double-contract theory, one contract being between the heads of families, the other between the society so formed and its ruler or rulers. But if one says this, one must realize that the contract theory as held by Suárez did not imply the artificial and conventional character either of political society or of government. His political theory, as we shall see more clearly later, was subordinate to his philosophy of law, in which he maintained the natural character of political society and political government. If we want to know Suárez' political theory, we have to turn primarily to his great treatise *De legibus*, which is above all things a philosophy of law. The idea of natural law, which goes back to the ancient world and which was given a metaphysical foundation by the philosophers of the Middle Ages, is essential to that philosophy and forms the background of his political theory. Political society is natural to man, and government is necessary for society; and as God is the Creator of human

[1] The then General of the Jesuits prohibited the teaching by members of the Order of Mariana's doctrine on tyrannicide.

nature both society and government are willed by God. They are not, therefore, purely arbitrary or conventional human contrivances. On the other hand, though Nature requires political society, the formation of determinate political communities normally depends on human agreement. Again, though Nature demands that any society should have some governing principle, Nature has not fixed any particular form of government or designated any particular individual as ruler. In certain instances God has directly designated a ruler (Saul, for instance, or David); but normally it rests with the community to determine the form of government.

The theory that political society rests on some sort of agreement was not altogether new, and one can find anticipations of it even in the ancient world. In the Middle Ages John of Paris, in his *Tractatus de potestate regia et papali* (c. 1303), presupposed a state of nature and held that though primitive men probably did not make any definite contract they were persuaded by their more rational fellows to live together under common law. And Giles of Rome in the thirteenth century had put forward a contract theory as one of the possible explanations of the foundation of political society. With Mariana in the sixteenth century the theory became explicit. In the same century the Dominican Francis of Vitoria implied a contract theory, and he was followed by the Jesuit Molina, though neither made any very explicit statement of the theory. Thus there was a growing tradition of the social contract theory; and Suárez' statement of it must be seen in the light of that tradition. In the course of time, however, the theory became divorced from the mediaeval philosophy of law. This philosophy was taken over, as we have seen, by Richard Hooker, and from him it passed, in a watered-down form, to Locke. But in Hobbes, Spinoza and Rousseau it is conspicuous by its absence, even if the old terms were sometimes retained. There is, then, a very great difference between the contract theory of Suárez and that of Rousseau, for example. And for this reason it may be misleading to speak of a contract theory in Suárez, if, that is to say, one understands by the term the sort of theory held by Rousseau. There was some historical continuity, of course; but the setting, atmosphere and the interpretation of the theory had undergone a fundamental change in the intervening period.

Another problem with which some of the Renaissance Scholastics concerned themselves was that of the relations between individual States. Already at the beginning of the seventh century St. Isidore of Seville in his curious encyclopaedic work, the *Etymologies*, had spoken of the *ius gentium* and of its application to war, making use of texts of Roman lawyers. Again, in the thirteenth century St. Raymund of Peñafort examined the topic of the right of war in his *Summa poenitentiae*, while in the second half of the fourteenth century there appeared works like the *De bello* of John of Legnano, a professor of the university of Bologna. Far better known, however, is Francis of Vitoria (1480–1546). It was very largely to him that the revival of theology in Spain was due, as was testified by pupils like Melchior Cano and Dominic Soto, while the Spanish humanist, Vivés, writing to Erasmus, praised Vitoria highly and spoke of his admiration for Erasmus and his defence of him against his critics. But it is for his studies on international law that Vitoria is known to the world at large.

Vitoria looked on different States as forming in some sense one human community, and he regarded the 'law of nations' as being not merely an agreed code of behaviour but as having the force of law, 'having been established by the authority of the whole world'.[1] His position seems to have been more or less as follows. Society could not hold together without laws the infringement of which renders transgressors liable to punishment. That such laws should exist is a demand of the natural law. There have therefore grown up a number of principles of conduct, for example the inviolability of ambassadors, on which society as a whole is agreed, since it is realized that principles of this kind are rational and for the common good. They are derivable in some way from the natural law and they must be reckoned to have the force of law. The *ius gentium* consists of prescriptions for the common good in the widest sense, which either belong directly to the natural law or are derivable in some way from it. 'What natural reason has established among all nations is called the *ius gentium*.'[2] According to Vitoria, the law of nations confers rights and creates obligations. Sanctions, however, can be applied only through the instrumentality of princes. But it is clear that his conception of international law leads to the idea of an international authority, though Vitoria does not say so.

Applying his ideas to war and to the rights of the Indians in regard to the Spaniards, Vitoria in the *De Indis* makes it clear that in his opinion physical power by itself confers no right to annex the property of others and that Christian missionary zeal confers no

[1] *De potestate civili*, 21. [2] *Ibid.*

title to make war on the heathen. As regards slavery he adopted the usual position of theologians of the time, namely that slavery is legitimate as a penal measure (corresponding to modern penal servitude). But this concession must not be taken to imply that the Scholastic theologians and philosophers simply accepted the contemporary customs in regard to slavery. The example of the Jesuit Molina is interesting in this matter. Not content with theorizing in his study he went down to the port at Lisbon and questioned the slave-traders. As a result of these frank conversations he declared that the slave-trade was simply a commercial affair and that all the talk about exalted motives, like that of converting the slaves to Christianity, was nonsense.[1] But though he condemned the slave-trade, he admitted the legitimacy of slavery as a penal measure, when, for example, criminals were sent to the galleys in accordance with the penal customs of the time.

Suárez developed the idea of the 'law of nations'. He pointed out that it is necessary to make a distinction between the law of nations and the natural law. The former prohibits certain acts for a just and sufficient reason, and so it can be said to render certain acts wrong, but the natural law does not make acts wrong but prohibits certain acts because they are wrong. That treaties should be observed, for example, is a precept of the natural law rather than of the law of nations. The latter consists of customs established by all, or practically all, nations; but it is unwritten law, and this fact distinguishes it from civil law. Although, for instance, the obligation to observe a treaty once it has been made proceeds from the natural law, the precept that an offer of a treaty, when made for a reasonable cause, should be accepted is not a matter of strict obligation proceeding from the natural law; nor is there any written law about the matter. The precept is an unwritten custom which is in harmony with reason, and it belongs to the 'law of nations'.

The rational basis of the *ius gentium* is, according to Suárez, the fact that the human race preserves a certain unity in spite of the division of mankind into separate nations and States. Suárez did not consider a world-State to be practicable or desirable; but at the same time he saw that individual States are not self-sufficing in a complete sense. They need some system of law to regulate their relations with one another. Natural law does not provide sufficiently for this need. But the conduct of nations has introduced

[1] Cf. *De iustitia*, 1, 2, disp. 34–5.

certain customs or laws which are in accord with the natural law, even though they are not strictly deducible from it. And these customs or laws form the *ius gentium*.

It has been said, not unreasonably, that Vitoria's idea of all nations as forming in some sense a world-community and of the *ius gentium* as law established by the authority of the whole world looked forward to the possible creation of a world-government, whereas Suárez' idea of the *ius gentium* looked forward rather to establishment of an international tribunal which would interpret international law and give concrete decisions without being itself a world-government, which Suárez did not regard as practicable.[1] However this may be, it is clear that in much of their political and legal philosophy the Renaissance Scholastics showed a grasp of concrete problems and a readiness to handle them in a 'modern' way. Men like Vitoria, Bellarmine and Suárez all maintained that political sovereignty is in some sense derived from the people; and they maintained the right of resistance to a ruler who acts tyrannically. Although they naturally thought in terms of contemporary forms of government, they did not consider that the actual form of government is a matter of prime importance. At the same time the fact that their conception of political society and of law was founded on a clear acceptance of the natural moral law constituted its great strength. They systematized and developed mediaeval legal and political philosophy and transmitted it to the seventeenth century. Grotius, for example, was certainly indebted to the Scholastics. Some people would maintain, I suppose, that the legal and political theory of the Renaissance Scholastics constituted a stage in the development from a predominantly theological outlook to a positivist outlook; and as a historical judgment this may be true. But it does not follow that the later secularization of the idea of natural law and its subsequent abandonment to all intents and purposes constituted a philosophical advance in any but a chronological sense.

[1] Cf. *The Catholic Conception of International Law* by J. B. Scott, Ch. XIII.

CHAPTER XXII

FRANCIS SUÁREZ (1)

Life and works—The structure and divisions of the Disputationes metaphysicae—*Metaphysics as the science of being—The concept of being—The attributes of being—Individuation—Analogy—God's existence—The divine Nature—Essence and existence—Substance and accident—Modes—Quantity—Relations*—Entia rationis—*General remarks—Étienne Gilson on Suárez.*

1. FRANCIS SUÁREZ (1548–1617), known as *Doctor eximius*, was born at Granada and studied canon law at Salamanca. He entered the Society of Jesus in 1564 and in due course began his professional career by teaching philosophy at Segovia. Afterwards he taught theology at Avila, Segovia, Valladolid, Rome, Alcalá, Salamanca and Coimbra. Suárez, who was an exemplary and holy priest and religious, was also very much the student, scholar and professor; and his whole adult life was devoted to lecturing, study and writing. He was an indefatigable writer, and his works fill twenty-three volumes in the earlier editions and twenty-eight volumes in the Paris edition of 1856–78. A large number of these works were, of course, concerned with theological questions; and for present purposes his most important writings are the two volumes of *Disputationes metaphysicae* (1597) and his great work *De legibus* (1612). One may also mention his *De Deo uno et trino* (1606) and the *De opere sex dierum* (published posthumously in 1621).

Suárez was convinced that a theologian ought to possess a firm grasp and profound understanding of the metaphysical principles and foundations of speculation. He says explicitly that no one can become a perfect theologian unless he has first laid the firm foundations of metaphysics. Accordingly, in his *Disputationes metaphysicae* he set out to give a complete and systematic treatment of Scholastic metaphysics; and, indeed, the work was the first of its kind. It was incomplete in the sense that metaphysical psychology was omitted; but this was supplied in the *Tractatus de anima* (published posthumously in 1621). Suárez abandoned the order adopted by Aristotle in his *Metaphysics*[1] and divided the

[1] The importance of this change is not diminished, of course, by the fact that we know that Aristotle's *Metaphysics* was not 'a book' but a collection of treatises.

matter systematically into fifty-four disputations, subdivided into sections; though at the beginning he provided a table showing where the themes treated of in the successive chapters of Aristotle's *Metaphysics* were dealt with in his own work. In this work the author's astounding erudition is clearly expressed in his discussions of, or references and allusions to, Greek, Patristic, Jewish, Islamic and Scholastic authors and to Renaissance thinkers like Marsilius Ficinus and Pico della Mirandola. Needless to say, however, Suárez does not confine himself to the historical recital of opinions; his object is always the attainment of a positive and objective answer to the problems raised. He may be prolix, but he is certainly systematic. As an example of a competent non-Scholastic judgment of the work one may quote the following sentence. 'All the important Scholastic controversies are in this work lucidly brought together and critically examined and their results combined in the unity of a system.'[1]

In the present chapter I shall be concerned mainly with the *Disputationes metaphysicae*. In the next chapter I shall treat of the contents of the *Tractatus de legibus ac Deo legislatore in X libros distributus*. This last work summarized and systematized Scholastic legal theories, and in it the author presented his own development of Thomist legal and political theory. In this connection one must mention also Suárez' *Defensio fidei catholicae et apostolicae adversus Anglicanae sectae errores, cum responsione ad apologiam pro iure fidelitatis et praefationem monitoriam Serenissimi Jacobi Angliae Regis* (1613). In this book Suárez maintained Bellarmine's theory of the indirect power of the pope in temporal affairs and argued against the notion, dear to James I of England, that temporal monarchs receive their sovereignty immediately from God. As I remarked in the last chapter, James I had the book burned.

2. Before going on to outline some of Suárez' philosophical ideas I want to say something about the structure and arrangement of the *Disputationes metaphysicae*.

In the first disputation (or discussion) Suárez considers the nature of first philosophy or metaphysics, and he decides that it can be defined as the science which contemplates being as being. The second disputation deals with the concept of being, while disputations 3 to 11 inclusive treat of the *passiones entis* or

[1] M. Frischeisen-Köhler and W. Moog: *Die Philosophie der Neuzeit bis zum Ende des XVIII Jahrhunderts*, p. 211; vol. III of F. Ueberweg's *Grundriss der Geschichte der Philosophie*, 12th edition.

transcendental attributes of being. Unity in general is the theme of the fourth disputation, while individual unity and the principle of individuation are dealt with in the fifth. The sixth disputation treats of universals, the seventh of distinctions. After considering unity Suárez passes to truth (disputation 8) and falsity (9), while in disputations 10 and 11 he treats of good and evil. Disputations 12 to 27 are concerned with causes; disputation 12 with causes in general, disputations 13 and 14 with the material cause, disputations 15 and 16 with the formal cause, disputations 17 to 22 with efficient causality, and disputations 23 and 24 with final causality, while exemplary causality is the subject of disputation 25. Finally, disputation 26 deals with the relations of causes to effects and disputation 27 with the mutual relations of the causes to one another.

The second volume begins with the division of being into infinite and finite being (disputation 28). Infinite or divine being is treated in the next two disputations, God's existence in disputation 29 and His essence and attributes in disputation 30. In disputation 31 Suárez goes on to consider finite created being in general, and in the following disputation he considers the distinction of substance and accidents in general. Disputations 33 to 36 contain Suárez' metaphysics of substance, and disputations 37 to 53 deal with the various categories of accidents. The last disputation of the work, 54, deals with *entia rationis*.

As has already been indicated, Suárez' *Disputationes metaphysicae* mark the transition from commentaries on Aristotle to independent treatises on metaphysics and to *Cursus philosophici* in general. It is true that one can discern among Suárez' predecessors, as for example with Fonseca, a growing tendency to shake off the bonds imposed by the commentary method; but it was Suárez who really originated the new form of treatment. After his time the *Cursus philosophici* and independent philosophical treatises became common, both inside and outside the Jesuit Order. Moreover, Suárez' decision not to include rational psychology in metaphysics but to treat it on its own and consider it as the highest part of 'natural philosophy'[1] had its influence on succeeding writers like Arriaga and Oviedo, who assigned the theory of the soul to physics rather than to metaphysics.[2]

One feature of Suárez' *Disputationes metaphysicae* which should

[1] *Disp. metaph.*, I, 2, nn. 19–20.
[2] This classification of psychology was in accordance with Aristotle's remarks in his *De Anima*.

be noticed is that no separation is made in this work between general and special metaphysics. The later distinction between ontology or general metaphysics on the one hand and special metaphysical disciplines like psychology, cosmology and natural theology on the other hand has commonly been ascribed to the influence of Christian Wolff (1679–1754), the disciple of Leibniz, who wrote separate treatises on ontology, cosmology, psychology natural theology, etc. But further investigation into the history of Scholasticism in the second half of the seventeenth century has shown that the distinction between general and special metaphysics and the use of the word 'ontology' to describe the former antedate the writings of Wolff. Jean-Baptiste Duhamel (1624–1706) used the word 'ontology' to describe general metaphysics in his *Philosophia vetus et nova* or *Philosophia universalis* or *Philosophia Burgundica* (1678). This is not to say, however, that Wolff's division of the philosophical disciplines was not of great influence or that the continued use of the word 'ontology' for general metaphysics is not to be ascribed primarily to him.

3. Metaphysics, says Suárez,[1] has as its *obiectum adequatum* being in so far as it is real being. But to say that the metaphysician is concerned with being as being is not the same thing as saying that he is concerned with being as being in complete abstraction from the ways in which being is concretely realized, that is to say, in complete abstraction from the most general kinds of being or *inferiora entis*. After all, the metaphysician is concerned with real being, with being as including in some way the *inferiora entis secundum proprias rationes*.[2] He is concerned, therefore, not only with the concept of being as such but also with the transcendental attributes of being, with uncreated and created, infinite and finite being, with substance and accidents, and with the types of causes. But he is not concerned with material being as such: he is concerned with material things only in so far as knowledge of them is necessary in order to know the general divisions and categories of being.[3] The fact is that the concept of being is analogous, and so it cannot be properly known unless the different kinds of being are clearly distinguished.[4] For instance, the metaphysician is primarily concerned with immaterial, not with material substance; but he has to consider material substance in so far as knowledge of it is necessary in order to distinguish it from immaterial substance and

[1] *Disp.*, 1, 1, 24. [2] 1, 2, 11. [3] 1, 2, 24. [4] *Ibid.*

in order to know the metaphysical predicates which belong to it precisely as material substance.[1]

With Suárez, then, as Suarezians at any rate would maintain, the fundamental metaphysical attitude of Thomism persists unchanged. The Aristotelian idea of 'first philosophy' as the study or science of being as being is maintained. But Suárez emphasizes the fact that by being he means real being; the metaphysician is not concerned simply with concepts. Again, though he is concerned primarily with immaterial reality, he is not so exclusively concerned with it that he has nothing to say of material reality. But he considers material reality only from the metaphysical point of view, not from the point of view of a physicist or of a mathematician; Suárez accepted the Aristotelian doctrine of the degrees of abstraction. Again, we may note that Suárez emphasized the analogical character of the concept of being; he would not allow that it is univocal. Lastly, as to the purpose of metaphysics, Suárez is convinced that it is the contemplation of truth for its own sake;[2] he remains in the serene atmosphere of the Aristotelian *Metaphysics* and of St. Thomas and is unaffected by the new attitude towards knowledge which manifested itself in a Francis Bacon.

4. In the second disputation Suárez treats of the concept of being; and he declares that 'the proper and adequate formal concept of being as such is one' and that 'it is different from the formal concepts of other things'.[3] As he goes on to say that this is the common opinion and reckons among its defenders 'Scotus and all his disciples', it might seem that he is making the concept of being univocal and not analogical. It is necessary, then, to say something about Suárez' view on this matter.

In the first place the formal concept of being is one, in the sense that it does not signify immediately any particular nature or kind of thing: it does not signify a plurality of beings according as they differ from one another, but 'rather in so far as they agree with one another or are like to one another'.[4] The concept of being is really distinct from the concept of substance or the concept of accident: it abstracts from what is proper to each.[5] It will not do to say that there is a unity of word alone, for the concept precedes the word and its use.[6] Moreover, 'to the formal concept of being there corresponds an adequate and immediate objective concept, which does not expressly signify either substance or accident, either God

[1] *Disp.*, 1, 2, 5. [2] 1, 4, 2. [3] 2, 1, 9.
[4] 2, 1, 9. [5] 2, 1, 10. [6] 2, 1, 13.

or creature: it signifies them all in so far as they are in some way like to one another and agree in being.'[1] Does this mean that in a created substance, for instance, there is a form of being which is actually distinct from the form or forms which make it a created substance in particular? No, abstraction does not necessarily require a distinction of things or forms which actually precedes the abstraction: it is sufficient if the mind considers objects, not as each exists in itself, but according to its likeness to other things.[2] In the concept of being as such the mind considers only the likeness of things, not their differences from one another. It is true that a real being is such by its own being which is inseparable from it, that is to say, it is true that a thing's being is intrinsic to it; but this simply means that the concept of being as such does not include its 'inferiors'.

Suárez admits, then, that a concept of being can be formed which is strictly one; and on this matter he ranges himself with Scotus against Cajetan. But he emphasizes the fact that this concept is the work of the mind and that 'as it exists in the thing itself, it is not something actually distinct from the inferiors in which it exists. This is the common opinion of the whole School of St. Thomas.'[3] Why, then, does he insist that the concept of being represents reality? If it represents reality, in what does being as such consist and how does it belong to its inferiors? Does it not seem that if the concept of being as such represents reality, it must represent something in the inferiors, that is, in existent beings, which is distinct from that intrinsic entity or beingness which is peculiar to each? And, if this is not so, does it not follow that the concept of being as such does not represent reality?

Suárez distinguishes 'being' understood as a participle, that is to say, as signifying the act of existing, from 'being' understood as a noun, that is to say, as signifying what has a real essence, whether it actually exists or not. A 'real essence' is one which does not involve any contradiction and which is not a mere construction of the mind. Now, 'being' understood as a participle gives rise to one concept 'common to all actually existent beings, since they are like to one another and agree in actual existence' and this holds good both for the formal and for the objective concepts.[4] We can also have one concept of being understood as a noun, provided that the concept simply abstracts from, and does not exclude, actual existence.

[1] *Disp.*, 2, 2, 8. [2] 2, 2, 15. [3] 2, 3, 7. [4] 2, 4, 4.

It does not appear to me that the repetition of this statement of our ability to form one concept of being provides a very adequate answer to the difficulties which can be raised; but I wish now to indicate why Suárez does not call this concept a univocal concept.

In order that a concept should be univocal, it is not sufficient that it should be applicable in the same sense to a plurality of different inferiors which have an equal relationship to one another.[1] Suárez, therefore, demanded more for a univocal concept than that it should be one concept; he demanded that it should apply to its inferiors in the same way. We can, indeed, form a formal concept of being which is one and which says nothing about the differences of the inferiors; but no inferior is, so to speak, outside being. When the concept of being is narrowed down (*contrahitur*) to concepts of different kinds of being, what is done is that a thing is conceived more expressly,[2] according to its own mode of existence, than it is by means of the concept of being.[3] This does not mean, however, that something is added to the concept of being as though from outside. On the contrary, the concept of being is made more express or determinate. In order that the inferiors should be properly conceived as beings of a certain kind, the concept of being must indeed be contracted: but this means making more determinate what was already contained in the concept. The latter cannot, therefore, be univocal.

5. In the third disputation Suárez proceeds to discuss the *passiones entis in communi*, the attributes of being as such. There are only three such attributes, namely unity, truth and goodness.[4] These attributes do not, however, add anything positive to being. Unity signifies being as undivided; and this undividedness adds to being simply a denial of division, not anything positive.[5] Truth of knowledge (*veritas cognitionis*) does not add anything real to the act itself, but it connotes the object existing in the way that it is represented by the judgment as existing.[6] But truth of knowledge is found in the judgment or mental act and is not the same as *veritas transcendentalis*, which signifies the being of a thing with connotation of the knowledge or concept of the intellect, which represents, or can represent, the thing as it is.[7] This conformity of the thing to the mind must be understood primarily of a relation to the divine mind, and only secondarily of conformity to the

[1] 2, 2, 36; 39, 3, 17. [2] *expressius, per maiorem determinationem.* [3] 2, 6, 7. [4] 3, 2, 3. [5] *Disp.*, 4, 1–2. [6] 8, 2, 9. [7] 8, 7, 25.

human mind.[1] As to goodness, this means the perfection of a thing, though it also connotes in another thing an inclination to or capacity for the aforesaid perfection. This connotation, however, does not add to the thing which is called good anything absolute; nor is it, properly speaking, a relation.[2] None of the three transcendental attributes of being, then, adds anything positive to being.

6. In the fifth disputation Suárez considers the problem of individuation. All actually existing things—all things which can exist 'immediately'—are singular and individual.[3] The word 'immediately' is inserted in order to exclude the common attributes of being, which cannot exist immediately, that is to say, which can exist only in singular, individual beings. Suárez agrees with Scotus that individuality adds something real to the common nature; but he rejects Scotus' doctrine of the *haecceitas* 'formally' distinct from the specific nature.[4] What, then, does individuality add to the common nature? 'Individuality adds to the common nature something which is mentally distinct from that nature, which belongs to the same category, and which (together with the nature) constitutes the individual metaphysically, as an individual *differentia* contracting the species and constituting the individual.'[5] Suárez remarks that to say that what is added is mentally distinct from the specific nature is not the same thing as saying that it is an *ens rationis*; he has already agreed with Scotus that it is *aliquid reale*. In answer, then, to the question whether a substance is individuated by itself Suárez replies that if the words 'by itself' refer to the specific nature as such, the answer is in the negative, but that, if the words 'by itself' mean 'by its own entity or being', the answer is in the affirmative. But it must be added that the thing's entity or being includes not only the *ratio specifica* but also the *differentia individualis*, the two being distinguished from one another by a mental distinction. Suárez emphasizes the fact that he is speaking of created things, not of the divine substance; but among created things he applies the same doctrine to both immaterial and material substances. From this it follows that he rejects the Thomist view of *materia signata* as the only principle of individuation.[6] In the case of a composite substance, composed, that is to say, of matter and form, 'the adequate principle of individuation is this matter and this form in union, the form being the chief principle and sufficient by itself for the composite, as an individual

[1] 8, 7, 28–9. [2] 10, 1, 12. [3] 5, 1, 4. [4] 5, 2, 8–9. [5] 5, 2, 16. [6] 5, 3.

thing of a certain species, to be considered numerically one. This conclusion . . . agrees with the opinion of Durandus and Toletus; and Scotus, Henry of Ghent and the Nominalists do not hold anything substantially different' (*in re non dissentiunt*).[1] It is perfectly true that because our knowledge is founded on experience of sensible things, we often distinguish individuals according to their several 'matters' or according to the accidents, like quantity, which follow on the possession of matter; but if we are considering a material substance in itself, and not in relation simply to our mode of cognition, its individuality must be primarily ascribed to its principal constitutive element, namely the form.[2]

7. Having dealt at length with the doctrine of causes Suárez comes in disputation 28 to the division of being into infinite being and finite being. This division is fundamental; but it can be made 'under different names and concepts'.[3] For example, being can be divided into *ens a se* and *ens ab alio*, into necessary being and contingent being, or into being by essence and being by participation. But these and similar divisions are equivalent, in the sense that they are all divisions of being into God and creatures and exhaust being, as it were.

The question then arises whether being is predicated equivocally, univocally or analogically of God and creatures. Suárez notes[4] that a doctrine of equivocation is wrongly attributed to Petrus Aureoli. The Scotist doctrine, that 'being signifies immediately one concept which is common to God and creatures and which is therefore predicated of them univocally, and not analogically',[5] Suárez rejects. But if being is predicated analogically of God and creatures, is the analogy in question the analogy of proportionality alone, as Cajetan taught, or the analogy of proportionality together with the analogy of attribution, as Fonseca, for example, considered? According to Suárez, the analogy in question cannot be the analogy of proportionality, for 'every true analogy of proportionality includes an element of metaphor', whereas 'in this analogy of being there is no metaphor'.[6] It must be, therefore, analogy of attribution, and, indeed, intrinsic attribution. 'Every creature is being in virtue of a relation to God, inasmuch as it participates in or in some way imitates the being (*esse*) of God, and, as having being, it depends essentially on God, much more than an accident depends on a substance.'[7]

[1] 5, 6, 15. [2] 5, 6, 17. [3] 28, 1, 6. [4] 28, 3, 1.
[5] 28, 3, 2. [6] 28, 3, 11. [7] 28, 3, 16.

8. In the following disputation (29) Suárez considers the question whether God's existence can be known by reason, apart from revelation. First of all he examines the 'physical argument', which is to all intents and purposes the argument from motion as found in Aristotle. Suárez' conclusion is that this argument is unable to demonstrate the existence of God. The principle on which the argument is founded, namely 'every thing which is moved is moved by another' (*omne quod movetur ab alio movetur*), he declares to be uncertain. Some things appear to move themselves, and it might be true of the motion of the heaven that the latter moves itself in virtue of its own form or of some innate power. 'How, then, can a true demonstration, proving God's existence, be obtained by the aid of uncertain principles?'[1] If the principle is rightly understood, it is more probable (*probabilius*) than its opposite, but all the same, 'by what necessary or evident argument can it be proved from this principle that there is an immaterial substance?'[2] Even if it can be shown that a mover is required, it does not follow that there is not a plurality of movers, still less that the mover is immaterial pure act. Suárez' point is that one cannot prove the existence of God as immaterial uncreated substance and pure act by arguments drawn from 'physics'. In order to show that God exists it is necessary to have recourse to metaphysical arguments.

First of all it is necessary to substitute for the principle *omne quod movetur ab alio movetur* the metaphysical principle *omne quod fit, ab alio fit.*[3] The truth of the principle follows from the evident truth that nothing can produce itself. On the basis of this metaphysical principle one can argue as follows.[4] 'Every being is either made or not made (uncreated). But not all beings in the universe can be made. Therefore there is necessarily some being which is not made, but which is uncreated.' The truth of the major premiss can be made evident in this way. A made or produced being is produced by 'something else'. This 'something else' is itself either made or not made. If the latter, then we already have an uncreated being. If the former, then that on which the 'something else' depends for existence is itself either made or not made. In order to avoid an infinite regress or a 'circle' (which would obtain if one said that *A* was made by *B*, *B* by *C*, and *C* by *A*), it is necessary to postulate an uncreated being. In his discussion of the impossibility of an infinite regress[5] Suárez distinguishes *causae per*

[1] 20, 1, 7. [2] 29, 1, 8. [3] 29, 1, 20. [4] 29, 1, 21. [5] 29, 1, 25–40.

se subordinatae and *causae per accidens subordinatae*; but he makes it clear that he considers an infinite regress impossible even in the case of the latter. He adopts, then, a different opinion from that of St. Thomas. But he remarks that even if one accepts the possibility of an infinite regress in the series of *causae per accidens subordinatae*, this does not affect the main line of the argument, for the infinite series would be eternally dependent on a higher extrinsic cause. If it were not, there would be no causality or production at all.

This argument, however, does not immediately show that God exists: it has still to be shown that there is only one uncreated being. Suárez argues first of all that 'although individual effects, taken and considered separately, do not show that the maker of all things is one and the same, the beauty of the whole universe and of all things which are in it, their marvellous connection and order sufficiently show that there is one first being by which all things are governed and from which they derive their origin'.[1] Against the objection that there might be several governors of the universe Suárez argues that it can be shown that the whole sensible world proceeds from one efficient cause. The cause or causes of the universe must be intelligent; but several intelligent causes could not combine to produce and govern the one systematically united effect unless they were subordinated to a higher cause using them as organs or instruments.[2] There is, however, another possible objection. Might there not be another universe, made by another uncreated cause? Suárez allows that the creation of another universe would not be impossible, but he observes that there is no reason to suppose that there is another universe. Still, given the possibility, the argument from the universe to the unicity of God holds good, strictly speaking, only for those things which are capable of being known by human experience and reasoning. He concludes, therefore, that an *a priori* proof of the unicity of uncreated being must be given.

The *a priori* proof is not, Suárez notes, *a priori* in the strict sense: it is impossible to deduce God's existence from its cause, for it has no cause. 'Nor, even if it had, is God known by us so exactly and perfectly that we can apprehend Him by means of His own principles, so to speak.'[3] Nevertheless, if something about God has been already proved *a posteriori*, we may be in a position to argue *a priori* from one attribute to another.[4] 'When it has been proved

[1] 29, 2, 7. [2] 29, 2, 21. [3] 29, 3, 1. [4] *Ibid.*

a posteriori that God is necessary self-existent being (*ens a se*), it can be proved *a priori* from this attribute that there cannot be any other necessary self-existent being, and consequently it can be proved that God exists.'[1] In other words, Suárez' argument is that it can be proved that there must be *a* necessary being and that it can then be shown conclusively that there cannot be more than *one* necessary being. How does he show that there can be only one necessary being? He argues that, in order that there may be a plurality of beings having a common nature, it is necessary that the individuality of each should be in some way (*aliquo modo*) outside the essence of the nature. For, if individuality was essential to the nature, the latter would not be multipliable. But in the case of uncreated being it is impossible for its individuality to be in any way distinct from its nature, for its nature is existence itself, and existence is always individual. The foregoing argument is the fourth which Suárez considers.[2] Later on[3] he remarks that 'although some of these arguments which have been considered do not perhaps, when taken separately, so convince the intellect that a froward or ill-disposed man cannot find ways of evading them, none the less all the arguments are most efficacious, and, especially if they are taken together, they abundantly prove the aforesaid truth'.

9. Suárez proceeds to consider the nature of God. He points out at the beginning of disputation 30 that the question of God's existence and the question of God's nature cannot be entirely isolated from one another. He also repeats his observation that, although our knowledge of God is *a posteriori*, we can in some cases argue *a priori* from one attribute to another. After these preliminary remarks he proceeds to argue that God is perfect being, possessing in Himself, as creator, all the perfections which He is capable of communicating. But He does not possess them all in the same way. Those perfections which do not of themselves contain any limitation or imperfection, God possesses 'formally' (*formaliter*). A perfection like wisdom, for example, though it exists in human beings in a finite or imperfect manner, does not include in its formal concept any limitation or imperfection, and it can be predicated formally of God, *salva analogia, quae inter Deum et creaturam semper intercedit.*[4] Perfections of this sort exist 'eminently' (*eminenter*) in God, for creaturely wisdom as such cannot be predicated of God; but there is, none the less, a formal

[1] 29, 3, 2. [2] 29, 3, 11. [3] 29, 3, 31. [4] 30, 1, 12.

analogous concept of wisdom which can be predicated formally, though analogously, of God. In the case, however, of perfections which involve inclusion of the being possessing them in a certain category these can be said to be present in God only *modo eminenti*, and not formally.

In succeeding sections Suárez argues that God is infinite,[1] pure act and without any composition,[2] omnipresent,[3] immutable and eternal, yet free,[4] one,[5] invisible,[6] incomprehensible,[7] ineffable,[8] living, intelligent and self-sufficient substance.[9] He then considers the divine knowledge[10] and the divine will[11] and the divine power.[12] In the section on the divine knowledge Suárez shows that God knows possible creatures and existent things and then remarks that the question of God's knowledge of conditional future contingent events cannot be properly treated without reference to theological sources, even though it is a metaphysical question, 'and so I entirely omit it'.[13] But he allows himself the remark that if statements like, 'if Peter had been here, he would have sinned' have a determinate truth, this truth cannot be unknown to God. That they have determinate truth is 'much more probable' (*multo probabilius*) than that they have not, in the sense that Peter in the example given would either have sinned or not have sinned and that, though we cannot know which would have happened, God can know it. However, as Suárez omits any further treatment of this matter in his metaphysical disputations, I too omit it.

10. Coming to the subject of finite being, Suárez treats first of the essence of finite being as such, of its existence, and of the distinction between essence and existence in finite being. He first outlines the arguments of those who hold the opinion that existence (*esse*) and essence are really distinct in creatures. 'This is thought to be St. Thomas's opinion, which, understood in this sense, has been followed by almost all the early Thomists.'[14] The second opinion mentioned by Suárez is that the creature's existence is 'formally' distinguished from its nature, as a mode of that nature. 'This opinion is attributed to Scotus.'[15] The third opinion is that essence and existence in the creature are distinguished only mentally (*tantum ratione*). This opinion, says Suárez,[16] was held by Alexander of Hales and others, including the nominalists. It is

[1] 30, 2. [2] 30, 3–5. [3] 30, 7. [4] 30, 8–9
[5] 30, 10. [6] 30, 11. [7] 30, 12. [8] 30, 13.
[9] 30, 14. [10] 30, 15. [11] 30, 16. [12] 30, 17.
[13] 30, 15, 33. [14] 31, 1, 3. [15] 31, 1, 11. [16] 31, 1, 12.

the opinion he himself defends, provided that 'existence' is understood to mean actual existence and 'essence' actually existing essence. 'And this opinion, if so explained, I think to be quite true.'[1] It is impossible, Suárez states, for anything to be intrinsically and formally constituted as a real and actual being by something distinct from it. From this it follows that existence cannot be distinguished from essence as a mode which is distinct from the essence or nature *ex natura rei*.[2] The right view is this.[3] If the terms 'existence' and 'essence' are understood to refer respectively to actual being (*ens in actu*) and potential or possible being (*ens in potentia*), then there is, of course, a real distinction; but this distinction is simply that between being and not-being, since a possible is not a being and its potentiality for existence is simply logical potentiality, that is, the idea of it does not involve a contradiction. But if 'essence' and 'existence' are understood to mean, as they should be understood to mean in the present controversy, actual essence and actual existence, the distinction between them is a mental distinction with an objective foundation (*distinctio rationis cum fundamento in re*). We can think of the natures or essences of things in abstraction from their existence, and the objective foundation for our being able to do so is the fact that no creature exists necessarily. But the fact that no creature exists necessarily does not mean that when it exists its existence and essence are really distinct. Take away the existence, so to speak, and you cancel the thing altogether. On the other hand, a denial of the real distinction between essence and existence does not, Suárez argues, lead to the conclusion that the creature exists necessarily.

Existence and essence together form an *ens per se unum*; but this composition is a 'composition' in an analogical sense. For it is only really distinct elements that can together form a real composition. The union of essence and existence to form an *ens per se unum* is called a 'composition' only in a sense analogous to the sense in which the union of matter and form, two really distinct elements, is called a composition.[4] Moreover, the union of essence and existence differs from that of matter and form in this point also, that the former is found in all creatures, whereas the latter is confined to bodies. Composition out of matter and form is a physical composition and forms the basis of physical change, whereas composition out of essence and existence is a metaphysical

[1] 31, 1, 13. [2] 31, 6, 9. [3] 31, 6, 13–24. [4] 31, 13, 7.

composition. It belongs to the being of a creature, whether spiritual or material. The statement that it is a *compositio rationis* does not contradict the statement that it belongs to the being of a creature, for the reason why it belongs to the being of a creature is not the mental character of the distinction between essence and existence but rather the objective foundation of this mental distinction, namely the fact that the creature does not exist necessarily or of itself (*a se*).

Suárez considers the objection that it follows or seems to follow from his view that the existence of the creature is not received in a potential and limiting element and that consequently it is perfect and infinite existence. If, it is said, existence is not an act which is received in a potential element, it is unreceived, and consequently it is subsistent existence. But, says Suárez,[1] the existence of a creature is limited by itself, by its entity, and it does not need anything distinct from itself to limit it. Intrinsically it is limited by itself; extrinsically or *effective* it is limited by God. One can distinguish two kinds of limitation or contraction, namely metaphysical and physical. 'Metaphysical limitation (*contractio*) does not require an actual real distinction between the limited and limiting factors, but a distinction of concepts with some objective foundation is sufficient; and so we can admit (if we wish to use the language of many people) that essence is made finite and is limited with a view to existence and, conversely, that existence is rendered finite and limited by being the act of a particular essence.'[2] As to physical limitations, an angel does not need any intrinsic principle of limitation other than its simple substance, while a composite substance is limited by its intrinsic component factors or principles. This is equivalent to saying that a composite substance also is limited by itself, since it is not something distinct from those intrinsic component factors taken together in their actuality.

Suárez' view is, then, this. 'Because existence is nothing else than essence constituted in act, it follows that, just as actual essence is formally limited by itself, or by its own intrinsic principles, so also created existence has its limitation from the essence, not because essence is a potentiality in which existence is received, but because existence is in reality nothing else but the actual essence itself.'[3] A great deal has been written in Scholastic circles about the dispute between Suárez and his Thomist

[1] 31, 13, 18. [2] *Ibid.* [3] *Ibid.*

opponents on the subject of the distinction between essence and existence; but, whichever side is right, it should at least be clear that Suárez had no intention whatsoever of impairing, so to speak, the contingent character of the creature. The creature is created and contingent, but what is created is an actual essence, that is to say, an existent essence, and the distinction between the essence and its existence is only mental, though this mental distinction is grounded on and made possible by the creature's contingent character. Both Thomists and Suarezians agree, of course, about the creature's contingent character. Where they differ is in the analysis of what it means to be contingent. When the Thomists say that there is a real distinction between essence and existence in the creature, they do not mean that the two factors are separable in the sense that either or both of them could preserve actuality in isolation; and when the Suarezians say that the distinction is a *distinctio rationis cum fundamento in re*, they do not mean that the creature exists necessarily, in the sense that it cannot not exist. However, I do not propose to take sides in the controversy; nor shall I introduce reflections which, in the context of contemporary philosophy in Great Britain, might suggest themselves.

11. Passing to the subject of substance and accident, Suárez remarks[1] that the opinion that the division between substance and accident is a sufficient proximate division of created being is 'so common, that it has been received by all as if it were self-evident. Therefore it needs an explanation rather than a proof. That among creatures some things are substances and others accidents is clear from the constant change and alteration of things.' But being is not predicated univocally of substance and accidents: it is predicated analogically. Now, many people, like Cajetan, think that the analogy in question is the analogy of proportionality alone; 'but I think that the same must be said in this connection as has been said concerning being as common to God and to creatures, namely that there is here no analogy of proportionality, properly speaking, but only analogy of attribution'.[2]

In creatures primary substance (that is, existent substance, as distinguished from the universal or *substantia secunda*) is the same thing as a *suppositum*;[3] and a *suppositum* of rational nature is a person.[4] But Suárez discusses the question whether 'subsistence' (*subsistentia*), which makes a nature or essence a created *suppositum*,

[1] 32, 1, 4. [2] 32, 2, 12. [3] 34, 1, 9. [4] 34, 1, 13.

is something positive, distinct from the nature. According to one opinion existence and subsistence are the same; and that which being a *suppositum* adds to a nature is consequently existence. 'This opinion is now frequently met with among modern theologians.'[1] But Suárez cannot agree with this theory, as he does not believe that existence is really distinct from the actual nature or essence. 'Actual essence and its existence are not really distinct. Therefore, in so far as subsistence is distinct from actual essence, it must be distinct from the existence of that essence.'[2] Therefore being a *suppositum* or having subsistence, which makes a thing independent of any 'support' (that is, which makes a thing a substance) cannot, in so far as it is something added to an actual essence or nature, be the same thing as existence. What, if anything, does subsistence add to an actual essence or nature? Existence as such simply means having actual being: that a being exists does not, of itself, determine whether it exists as a substance or as an accident. 'But subsistence denotes a determinate mode of existing',[3] namely existing as a substance, not inhering in a substance as an accident inheres in a substance. Therefore subsistence does add something. But what it adds is a mode of existing, a way of existing, not existence itself; it determines the mode of existence and gives to the substance its completion *in ratione existendi*, on the level of existence. Having subsistence or being a *suppositum* adds, therefore, to an actual essence or nature a mode (*modus*), and *subsistentia* differs modally (*modaliter*) from the nature of which it is the subsistence as a thing's mode differs from the thing itself.[4] The composition between them is, then, the composition of a mode with the thing modified.[5] Created subsistence is thus 'a substantial mode, finally terminating the substantial nature and constituting a thing as *per se* subsistent and incommunicable'.[6]

12. Here we meet Suárez' idea of 'modes', of which he makes extensive use. For example, he says that probably 'the rational soul, even while joined to the body, has a positive mode of subsistence, and, when it is separated (from the body), it does not acquire a new positive mode of existence, but it is simply deprived of the positive mode of union with the body'.[7] In man, then, not only is there a 'mode' whereby soul and body are conjoined but the soul, even while in the body, also has its own mode of partial

[1] 34, 4, 8. [2] 34, 4, 16. [3] 34, 4, 24. [4] 34, 4, 33.
[5] 34, 4, 39. [6] 34, 5, 1. [7] 34, 5, 33.

subsistence; and what happens at death is that the mode of union disappears, though the soul retains its own mode of subsistence. In purely material substances both form and matter have their own modes, in addition to the mode of union; but it is the 'partial mode' (*modus partialis*) of the matter alone which is conserved after separation of form and matter. The form of a purely material substance does not, like the human soul, which is the form of the body, preserve any mode of subsistence after the corruption of the substance.[1] A material form has not got its own mode of existence or partial subsistence,[2] but matter has. It follows that God could conserve matter without any form.[3]

13. In his detailed treatment of the different kinds of accidents Suárez gives a good deal of attention to the subject of quantity. First of all, the opinion that quantity is really distinct from material substance must be accepted. 'For although it may not be possible to demonstrate its truth sufficiently by natural reason, it is nevertheless shown to be true by the principles of theology, especially on account of the mystery of the Eucharist. Indeed, the natural reason, enlightened by this mystery, understands that this truth is more in agreement and conformity with the natures themselves of things (than the opposite opinion). Therefore the first reason for this opinion is that in the mystery of the Eucharist God separated quantity from the substances of bread and wine. . .'[4] This distinction must be a real distinction, for, if the distinction were only modal, quantity could not exist in separation from that of which it is a mode.

Considerations taken from the theology of the Eucharist appear also in Suárez' treatment of the formal effect of quanity (*effectus formalis quantitatis*), which he finds in the quantitative extension of parts as apt to occupy place. 'In the body of Christ in the Eucharist besides the substantial distinction of parts of matter there is also a quantitative extension of parts. For, although the parts of that body are not actually extended in place, they are none the less so extended and ordered in relation to one another that, if they were not supernaturally prevented, they would have to possess actual extension in place. This (first) extension they receive from quantity, and it is impossible for them to be without it if they are not without quantity.'[5]

14. As to relations, Suárez maintains that there are in creatures real relations which constitute a special category.[6] But a real

[1] 34, 5, 35. [2] 34, 5, 42. [3] 34, 5, 36. [4] 40, 2, 8. [5] 40, 4, 14. [6] 47, 1.

relation, although it signifies a real form, is not something actually distinct from every absolute form: it is in reality identified with an absolute form which is related to something else.[1] To take an example. In the case of two white things the one thing has to the other a real relation of similarity. But that real relation is not something really distinct from the thing's whiteness: it is the whiteness itself (considered as an 'absolute form') as similar to the whiteness of another thing. This denial of a real distinction between the relation and its subject[2] does not, says Suárez, contradict the assertion that real relations belong to a category of their own, for 'the distinction between categories is sometimes only a *distinctio rationis cum aliquo fundamento in re*, as we shall say later in regard to action, passion and other categories'.[3]

It is only real relations which can belong to the category of relation; for mental relations (*relationes rationis*) are not real beings and cannot, therefore, belong to the category *ad aliquid*.[4] But it does not follow that all real relations belong to the category of relation. If there are two white things, the one is really like the other; but if one of them is destroyed or ceases to be white, the real relation of similarity also ceases. There are, however, says Suárez, some real relations which are inseparable from the essences of their subjects. For example, it belongs to the essence of an existent creature that it depends on the Creator: 'it does not seem that it can be conceived or exist without a transcendental relation to that on which it depends. It is in this relation that the potentiality and imperfection of a created being as such seem especially to consist.'[5] Again, 'matter and form have a true and real mutual relationship essentially included in their own being; and so the one is defined by its relation to the other'.[6] These relations, called by Suárez *relationes transcendentales*, are not mental relations; they are real; but they cannot disappear while the subject remains, as predicamental relations (that is, relations belonging to the category of relation) can disappear. A predicamental relation is an accident acquired by a thing which is already constituted in its essential being; but a transcendental relation is, as it were (*quasi*), a *differentia* constituting and completing the essence of that thing of which it is affirmed to be a relation.[7] The

[1] 47, 2, 22.
[2] The opinion that there is always a real distinction between a real relation and its foundation is 'the opinion of the old Thomists', like Capreolus and Cajetan (47, 2, 2).
[3] 47, 2, 22. [4] 47, 3, 3. [5] 47, 3, 12. [6] 47, 3, 11. [7] 47, 4, 2.

definition of a predicamental relation is 'an accident, the whole being of which is *ad aliud esse, seu ad aliud se habere, seu aliud respicere*'.[1] This definition might seem to cover also transcendental relations; but 'I think that transcendental relations are excluded by the phrase, *cuius totum esse est esse ad aliud*, if it is understood in the strict sense explained at the end of the preceding section. For those beings which include a transcendental relation are not so related to another thing that their whole being consists simply in a relation to that other thing.'[2] Suárez goes on to argue that a predicamental relation requires a subject, a foundation (for example, the whiteness of a white thing) and a term of the relation.[3] But a transcendental relation does not require these three conditions. For example, 'the transcendental relation of matter to form has no foundation, but it is intimately included in matter itself'.[4]

The two examples of transcendental relation given above, namely the relation of creature to Creator and of matter and form to one another, should not lead one to suppose that, for Suárez, there is a 'mutual' relation between the creature and the Creator. There is a real relation to the Creator on the part of the creature but the Creator's relation to the creature is a *relatio rationis*.[5] The nominalists hold that[6] God acquires real relations in time, not in the sense that God acquires new perfections but in the sense, for example, that God is really Creator and, as creation took place in time, God becomes related to creatures in time. But Suárez rejects the opinion.[7] If the relation were real, God would acquire an accident in time which is an absurd idea; and it is useless to say that the relation would *assistere Deo*, and not *inesse Deo* (a distinction attributed to Gilbert de la Porrée), for the relation must be in a subject and, if it is not in the creature, it must be in God.

15. Suárez' final disputation (54) is devoted to the subject of *entia rationis*. He tells us that, although he has said in the first disputation that *entia rationis* are not included in the special subject-matter of metaphysics, he thinks that the general principles concerning this topic should be considered. The topic cannot be properly treated except by the metaphysician, even if it belongs to his subject-matter *quasi ex obliquo et concomitanter*.[8]

After distinguishing various possible meanings of the phrase *ens rationis*, Suárez says that, properly speaking, it signifies 'that

[1] 47, 5, 2. [2] 47, 6, 5. [3] 47, 6–9. [4] 47, 4, 2.
[5] 47, 15, 6. [6] 47, 15, 16. [7] 47, 15, 17–28. [8] 54, *introd.*

which has being objectively only in the mind' or 'that which is thought of as being by the mind, although it has no being in itself'.[1] Blindness, for example, has no positive being of its own, though it is 'thought of' as if it were a being. When we say that a man is blind, we do not mean that there is anything positive in the man to which the word 'blindness' is given; we mean that he is deprived of vision. But we think of this deprivation as if it were a being, says Suárez. A purely mental relation is another example of an *ens rationis*. So is a chimera or purely imaginative construction, which cannot have being apart from the mind. Its being consists in being thought or imagined.

Three reasons can be assigned why we form these *entia rationis*. First of all, the human intellect tries to know negations and privations. These are nothing in themselves; but the mind, which has being as its object, cannot conceive that which is in itself nothing except *ad modum entis*, that is, as if it were being. Secondly, our intellect, being imperfect, has sometimes, in its endeavour to know something which it cannot know as it exists in itself, to introduce relations which are not real relations by comparing it to something else. The third reason is the mind's power to construct composite ideas which cannot have an objective counterpart outside the mind, though the ideas of the parts correspond to something extramental. For example, we can construct the idea of a horse's body with a man's head.

There can be no concept of being common to real beings and to *entia rationis*, for existence (*esse*) cannot be intrinsically participated in by the latter. To 'exist' only in the mind is not to exist (*esse*), but to be thought or mentally constructed. Therefore *entia rationis* cannot be said to possess essence. This distinguishes them from accidents. Nevertheless, an *ens rationis* is called *ens* in virtue of 'some analogy' to being, since it is founded in some way on being.[2]

Entia rationis are caused by the intellect conceiving that which has no real act of being as if it were a being.[3] The senses, appetite and will are not causes of *entia rationis*, though the imagination can be; and in this respect 'the human imagination shares in some way the power of the reason', and perhaps it never forms them save with the co-operation of reason.[4]

The three types of *entia rationis* are negations, privations and (purely mental) relations. A negation differs primarily from a

[1] 54, 1, 6. [2] 54, 1, 9. [3] 54, 2, 15. [4] 54, 2, 18.

privation in that, while a privation signifies the lack of a form in a subject naturally apt to possess that form, a negation signifies the lack of a form without there being any natural aptitude to possess that form.[1] For example, blindness is a privation; but a man's lack of wings is a negation. According to Suárez[2] imaginary space and imaginary time, conceived without any 'subject', are negations. The logical relations of, for example, genus and species, subject and predicate, antecedent and consequent, which are 'second intentions', are purely mental and so *entia rationis*, though they are not gratuitously formed but have some objective foundation.[3]

16. In the multitudinous pages of the *Disputationes metaphysicae* Suárez pursues the problems considered into their various ramifications, and he is careful to distinguish the different meanings of the terms employed. He shows himself to be an analytic thinker, in the sense that he is not content with broad generalizations, hasty impressions or universal conclusions based on an insufficient study of the different aspects of the problem at issue. He is thorough, painstaking, exhaustive. One cannot, of course, expect to find in his work an analysis which will satisfy all the demands made by modern analysts: the terms and ideas in which he thought were for the most part traditional in the Schools and were taken for granted. One might, indeed, take various points out of Suárez' writings and express them in the more fashionable terms of today. For example, his observations that to 'exist' only in the mind is not really to exist at all but to be thought or mentally constructed could be translated into a distinction between different types of sentences analysed in reference to their logical meaning as distinct from their grammatical form. One has, however, to take a past thinker in his historical setting, and if Suárez is seen in the light of the philosophical tradition to which he belonged, there can be no doubt that he possessed the gift of analysis in an eminent degree.

That Suárez possessed an analytic mind would hardly, I think, be denied. But it has been maintained that he lacked the power of synthesis. He became immersed in a succession of problems, it is sometimes said, and he gave such a careful consideration to the manifold ways in which these problems had been treated and solved in history that he was unable to see the wood for the trees. Moreover, his great erudition inclined him to eclecticism. He

[1] 54, 5, 7. [2] 54, 5, 23. [3] 54, 6, 8–9.

borrowed a view here and an opinion there, and the result was a patchwork rather than a system. His critics would not, I think, suggest that he was a superficial eclectic, since it needs no very close acquaintance with his writings to see that he was very far from being superficial; but they do suggest that he was an eclectic in a sense which is incompatible with possessing the gift of synthesis.

The accusation that a given philosopher was not a system-builder is not an accusation which is likely to carry much weight in contemporary philosophical circles. Provided that the accusation does not rest on the fact that the philosopher in question expounded a number of mutually incompatible theses, many modern philosophers would comment, 'so much the better'. However, leaving this aspect of the matter out of account one can ask whether the accusation is in fact true. And in the first place one can ask in what sense Suárez was an eclectic.

That Suárez was an eclectic in some sense seems to me undeniable. He had an extremely extensive knowledge of former philosophies, even if, as is only to be expected, he was sometimes mistaken in his assertions or interpretations. And he could hardly possess this knowledge without being influenced by the opinions of the philosophers he studied. But this does not mean that he accepted other people's opinions in an uncritical manner. If, for example, he accepted the opinion of Scotus and Ockham that there is a confused intellectual intuition of the individual thing, which logically precedes abstraction, he did so because he thought that it was true. And if he questioned the universal applicability of the principle *quidquid movetur ab alio movetur* he did not do so because he was a Scotist or an Ockhamist (he was neither) but because he considered that the principle, considered as a universal principle, is in fact questionable. Moreover, if Suárez was an eclectic, so was Aquinas. The latter did not simply accept Aristotelianism in its entirety; if he had done so, he would have occupied a far less important position in the development of mediaeval philosophy and would have shown himself to be devoid of any spirit of philosophical criticism. Aquinas borrowed from Augustine and other thinkers, as well as from Aristotle. And there is no cogent reason why Suárez should not have followed his example by utilizing what he considered valuable in philosophers who lived at a later date than Aquinas. Of course, if the accusation of eclecticism means simply that Suárez departed from the teaching of St. Thomas on a number of points, he was certainly an eclectic. But the relevant philosophical question would be not so much whether Suárez departed from Aquinas's teaching as whether he was objectively justified in doing so.

That Aquinas was also in some sense an eclectic would presumably be admitted by all. What philosopher is not in some sense an eclectic? But some would still maintain that there is this big difference between the philosophy of St. Thomas and that of Suárez. The former rethought all the positions which he adopted from others and developed them, welding these developments, together with his own original contributions, into a powerful synthesis with the aid of certain fundamental metaphysical principles. Suárez on the other hand juxtaposed various positions and did not create a synthesis.

The truth of this accusation is, however, extremely doubtful. In his preface (*Ad lectorem*) to the *Disputationes metaphysicae* Suárez says that he intends to play the part of philosopher in such a way as to have always before his eyes the truth that 'our philosophy ought to be Christian and the servant of divine theology' (*divinae Theologiae ministram*). And if one regards his philosophical ideas in this light, one can see a synthesis clearly emerging from the mass of his pages. For Aristotle, in the *Metaphysics* at least, God was simply the first unmoved mover: His existence was asserted in order to explain motion. The Christian philosophers, like St. Augustine, introduced the idea of creation, and St. Thomas attempted to weld together Aristotelianism and creationism. Beneath, as it were, the Aristotelian distinction of matter and form St. Thomas discerned the more fundamental distinction of essence and existence, which runs through all finite being. Act is limited by potentiality, and existence, which stands to essence as act to potentiality, is limited by essence. This explains the finitude of creatures. Suárez, however, was convinced that the utter dependence which logically precedes any distinction of essence and existence is itself the ultimate reason of finitude. There is absolute being, God, and there is participated being. Participation in this sense means total dependence on the Creator. This total dependence or contingency is the reason why the creature is limited or finite.[1] Suárez did not explain finitude and contingency in terms of the distinction between existence and essence: he explained this distinction, in the sense, that is, in which he

[1] 31, 13, 18.

accepted it, in terms of a finitude which is necessarily bound up with contingency.

It is sometimes said that Suarezianism is an 'essential' philosophy or a philosophy of essence rather than a philosophy of existence, like Thomism. But it would seem difficult to find a more 'existential' situation than the situation of utter dependence which Suárez finds to be the ultimate characteristic of every being other than God. Moreover, by refusing to admit a 'real' distinction between essence and existence in the creature Suárez avoided the danger of turning existence into a kind of essence. Cancel the creature's existence, and its essence is cancelled too. The Thomist would say the same, of course; but this fact suggests perhaps that there is not so great a difference between the Thomist 'real' distinction and the Suarezian conceptual distinction with an objective foundation as might be supposed. The difference lies perhaps rather in the fact that the Thomist appeals to the metaphysical principle of the limitation of act by potentiality, which suggests a view of existence that seems strange to many minds, whereas Suárez founds his distinction simply on creation. The view is at any rate arguable that he carried the 'purification' of Greek philosophy a stage further by bringing the concept of creation and of utter dependence which creation spells more into the centre of the picture. Again, whereas St. Thomas laid stress on the Aristotelian argument from motion in proving God's existence, Suárez, like Scotus, preferred a more metaphysical and less 'physical' line of thought, precisely because the existence of creatures is more fundamental than their movement and because God's creation of finite being is more fundamental than His concurrence in their activity.

There are, moreover, many other ideas in the philosophy of Suárez which follow in some way from, or are connected with, his fundamental idea of dependence or 'participation'. Dependent being is necessarily finite, and as finite it is capable of acquiring further perfection. If it is a spiritual being it can do this freely. But as dependent it needs the divine concurrence even in the exercise of its freedom. And as utterly dependent on God it is subject to the divine moral law and is necessarily ordered to God. Again, as finite perfectible being the free creature is capable not only of acquiring perfection by its own activity, with the divine concurrence, but of receiving a perfection which lifts it above its natural life; as dependent spiritual being it is, as it were, malleable by God and possesses a *potentia obedientialis* for the reception of grace. Further, finite being is multipliable in diverse species and in a plurality of individuals in one species. And in order to explain the multipliability of individuals in a species it is not necessary to introduce the idea of matter as principle of individuation, with all the remnants of 'unpurified' Platonism attaching to that Aristotelian idea.

It has not been my intention in this last section of the present chapter to give my own views on the matters raised, and I do not wish to be understood in this sense. My intention has been rather that of showing that there is a Suarezian synthesis, that the key to it is the idea of 'participation' or dependence in being, and that it was this idea above all which must, Suárez was convinced, be the distinguishing mark of a Christian philosophy. To say this is not, of course, to suggest in any way that the idea is absent from Thomism. Suárez regarded himself as a follower of St. Thomas; and Suarezians do not set Suárez against St. Thomas. What they believe is that Suárez carried on and developed the work of St. Thomas in building up a metaphysical system in profound harmony with the Christian religion.

That the *Disputationes metaphysicae* exercised a wide influence in post-Renaissance Scholasticism scarcely needs saying. But they penetrated also into the Protestant universities of Germany, where they were studied by those who preferred Melanchthon's attitude towards philosophy to that of Luther. Indeed, the *Disputationes metaphysicae* served as a text-book of philosophy in a large number of German universities in the seventeenth century and part of the eighteenth. As for the leading post-Renaissance philosophers, Descartes mentions the work in his reply to the fourth set of objections, though apparently he did not know it at all well. But Leibniz tells us himself that he read the work as if it were a novel while he was still a youth. And Vico studied Suárez for a whole year. Again Suárez' idea of analogy is mentioned by Berkeley in his *Alciphron.*[1] At the present time the *Disputationes metaphysicae* are a living force primarily in Spain, where Suárez is considered one of the greatest, if not the greatest, of the national philosophers. To the modern world at large he is known rather for his *De legibus*, to which I shall turn in the next chapter.

17. Reference has been made in the preceding section to the contention that the metaphysics of Suárez is an essentialist, as

[1] 4, 20.

contrasted with an existentialist, metaphysics. In *Being and Some Philosophers* Professor Étienne Gilson argues that Suárez, following Avicenna and Scotus but proceeding further in the same direction, lost sight of Aquinas's vision of being as the concrete act of existing and tended to reduce being to essence. And Suárez begot Christian Wolff who refers with approval to the Spanish Jesuit in his *Ontologia*. Finally Suárez' influence has corrupted large tracts of neo-Scholasticism. Modern existentialism has protested in the name of existence against the essentialist philosophy. Kierkegaard reacted strongly against the system of Hegel, who is to be numbered, so one gathers, among the spiritual descendants of Suárez. But modern existentialism has no true realization of existence. The consoling conclusion emerges, therefore, that St. Thomas Aquinas is the one true metaphysician.

That the position and character of the analysis of the concept of being which is found in many neo-Scholastic text-books of metaphysics are very largely due to the influence of Suárez can hardly be denied. Nor can it well be denied, I think, that Suárez influenced Wolff and that a number of neo-Scholastic writers were influenced, indirectly at least, by Wolff. But the issues raised by Professor Gilson in his discussion of 'essentialist' metaphysics as contrasted with 'existentialist' metaphysics are so wide and far-reaching that they cannot, in my opinion, be properly treated in the form of a note to Suárez' philosophy. At the close of my *History of Philosophy* I hope to return to the subject in the course of considering the development of western philosophy as a whole. Meanwhile, it must suffice to have drawn the reader's attention to Gilson's estimate of Suárez' philosophy, which can be found in *L'être et l'essence* and *Being and Some Philosophers*, both of which books are listed in the Bibliography.

CHAPTER XXIII

FRANCIS SUÁREZ (2)

Philosophy of law and theology—The definition of law—Law (lex) *and right* (ius)*—The necessity of law—The eternal law—The natural law—The precepts of the natural law—Ignorance of natural law—The immutability of the natural law—The law of nations—Political society, sovereignty and government—The contract theory in Suárez—The deposition of tyrants—Penal laws—Cessation of human laws—Custom—Church and State—War.*

1. SUÁREZ' philosophy of law was based on that of St. Thomas Aquinas; but it must, none the less, be judged an original creative development, if one bears in mind its amplitude, thoroughness and profundity. In the philosophy of law Suárez was the mediator between the mediaeval conception of law, as represented by Thomism, and the conditions prevailing at the time he wrote. In the light of those conditions he elaborated a legal philosophy and in connection therewith a political theory which in scope and completeness went beyond anything attained in the Middle Ages and which exercised a profound influence. There can be no doubt that Grotius was seriously indebted to Suárez, even if he did not acknowledge this indebtedness clearly. That he did not do so can be easily understood, if one bears in mind, on the one hand, Suárez' doctrine of political authority and of the right to resist, and on the other hand Grotius' dependence on the King of France at the time that he wrote his *De iure belli ac pacis*.

In his preface to the *De legibus ac Deo legislatore* (1612) Suárez observes that no one need be surprised to find a professional theologian embarking on a discussion of law. The theologian contemplates God, not only as He is in Himself, but also as man's last end. This means that he is concerned with the way of salvation. Now, salvation is attained by free acts and moral rectitude; and moral rectitude depends to a great extent on law considered as the rule of human acts. Theology, then, must comprise a study of law; and, being theology, it is necessarily concerned with God as lawgiver. It may be objected that the theologian, while legitimately giving his attention to divine law, should abstain from concerning himself with human law. But all law derives its authority ultimately from God; and the theologian is justified in treating all types of law, though he does so from a higher point of view than that of the moral philosopher. For example, the theologian considers natural law in its relation of subordination to the supernatural order, and he considers civil law or human positive law with a view to determining its rectitude in the light of higher principles or with a view to making clear the obligations bearing on the conscience in regard to civil law. And Suárez appeals, in the first place, to the example of St. Thomas.

2. Suárez begins by giving a definition of law (*lex*) taken from St. Thomas. 'Law is a certain rule and measure, according to which one is induced to act or is restrained from acting.'[1] He goes on, however, to observe that the definition is too broad. For example, as no mention of obligation is made, no distinction is drawn between law and counsel. It is only after a discussion of the various conditions requisite for law that Suárez finally gives his definition of it as 'a common, just and stable precept, which has been sufficiently promulgated'.[2] Law, as it exists in the legislator, is the act of a just and upright will binding an inferior to the performance of a particular act;[3] and it must be framed for a community. Natural law relates to the community of mankind;[4] but human laws may properly be enacted only for a 'perfect' community.[5] It is also inherent in the nature of law that it be enacted for the common good, though this must be understood in relation to the actual subject-matter of the law, not in relation to the subjective intentions of the legislator, which is a personal factor.[6] Furthermore, it is essential to law that it should prescribe what is just, that is, that it should prescribe acts which can be justly performed by those whom the law affects. It follows from this that a law which is unjust or unrighteous is not, properly speaking, a law at all, and it possesses no binding force.[7] Indeed, an unrighteous law cannot be licitly obeyed, though in cases of doubt as to the righteousness of the law the presumption is in favour of the law. Suárez observes that in order for a law to be just three conditions must be observed.[8] First, it must be enacted, as already mentioned, for the common good, not for private advantage. Secondly, it must be enacted for those in regard to whom the legislator has authority to legislate, that is, for those who are his subjects. Thirdly, law must not proportion

[1] *De legibus*, 1, 1, 1; cf. St. Thomas, *S.T.*, Ia, IIae, 90, 1.
[2] *De legibus*, 1, 12, 5. [3] *Ibid.*, 1, 5, 24. [4] *Ibid.*, 1, 6, 18. [5] *Ibid.*, 1, 6, 21.
[6] *Ibid.*, 1, 7, 9. [7] *Ibid.*, 1, 9, 11. [8] *Ibid.*, 1, 9, 13.

burdens unequally, in an inequitable manner. The three phases of justice which must characterize the law in regard to its form are, then, legal justice, commutative justice and distributive justice.[1] Law must also, of course, be practicable, in the sense that the acts it enjoins must be practicable.

3. What is the relation between law (*lex*) and right (*ius*)? Strictly speaking, *ius* denotes 'a certain moral power which every man has, either over his own property or with respect to what is due to him'.[2] Thus the owner of a thing has a *ius in re* in regard to that thing actually possessed, while a labourer, for example, has a right to his wages, *ius ad stipendium*. In this sense of the word *ius* is distinct from *lex*. But the term *ius* is often used, says Suárez, in the sense of 'law'.

4. Are laws necessary? Law is not necessary, if by 'necessity' is understood absolute necessity. God alone is a necessary being in an absolute sense, and God cannot be subject to law.[3] But, given the creation of rational creatures, law must be said to be necessary in order that the rational creature may live in a manner befitting his nature. A rational creature is capable of choosing well or ill, rightly or wrongly; and it is susceptible of moral government. In fact, moral government, which is effected through command, is connatural to the rational creature. Given, therefore, rational creatures, law is necessary. It is irrelevant, says Suárez,[4] to argue that a creature may receive the grace of impeccability; for the grace in question does not involve the creature's removal from the state of subjection to law but brings it about that the creature obeys the law without fail.

5. Suárez' treatment of the eternal law is contained in the second book of the *De legibus*.[5] This law is not to be understood as a rule of right conduct imposed by God upon Himself:[6] it is a law of action in regard to the things governed. In regard to all things, irrational as well as rational? The answer depends on the degree of strictness in which the word 'law' is understood. It is true that all irrational creatures are subject to God and are governed by Him; but their subjection to God can be called 'obedience' only in a metaphorical sense, and the law by which God governs them is called a 'law' or 'precept' only metaphorically. In the strict sense, then, 'eternal law' has reference only to rational creatures.[7] It is the moral or human acts of rational creatures which form the

[1] *De legibus*, 1, 9, 13. [2] *Ibid.*, 1, 2, 5. [3] *Ibid.*, 1, 3, 2. [4] *Ibid.*, 1, 3, 3.
[5] Chapters 1–4. [6] *De legibus*, 2, 2, 5. [7] *Ibid.*, 2, 2, 13.

proper subject-matter of the eternal law, 'whether the latter commands their performance, prescribes a particular mode of acting, or prohibits some other mode'.[1]

The eternal law is 'a free decree of the will of God, who lays down the order to be observed; either generally, by the separate parts of the universe with respect to the common good . . . or else specifically, by intellectual creatures in their free actions'.[2] It follows that the eternal law, as a freely established law, is not absolutely necessary. This would be inconsistent with the eternity of the law only if nothing which is free could be eternal. The eternal law is eternal and immutable; but it is none the less free.[3] One can, however, distinguish law as it exists in the mind and will of the legislator from law as externally established and promulgated for the subjects. In the first phase the eternal law is truly eternal; but in the second phase it did not exist from eternity, because the subjects did not exist from eternity.[4] This being the case, one must conclude that actual promulgation to subjects is not the essence of eternal law. It is sufficient, for the eternal law to be called 'law', that it should have been made by the legislator to become effective at the proper time. In this respect the eternal law differs from other laws, which are not complete laws until they have been promulgated.[5]

Inasmuch as all created right reason partakes in 'the divine light which has been shed upon us', and inasmuch as all human power comes ultimately from God, all other law is a participation in the eternal law and an effect thereof.[6] It does not follow, however, that the binding force of human law is divine. Human law receives its force and efficacy directly from the will of a human legislator. It is true that the eternal law does not actually bind unless it is actually promulgated; and it is true that it is actually promulgated only through the medium of some other law, divine or human; but, in the case of human law, the obligation to observe it is caused proximately by this human law as enacted and promulgated by legitimate human authority, though fundamentally and mediately it proceeds from the eternal law.[7]

6. Turning to the subject of natural law, Suárez criticizes the opinion of his fellow-Jesuit, Father Vásquez, that rational nature and the natural law are the same. Suárez observes that, although rational nature is indeed the foundation of the objective goodness

[1] *De legibus*, 2, 2, 15. [2] *Ibid.*, 2, 3, 6. [3] *Ibid.*, 2, 3, 4. [4] *Ibid.*, 2, 1, 5. [5] *Ibid.*, 2, 1, 11. [6] *Ibid.*, 2, 4, 5. [7] *Ibid.*, 2, 4, 8–10.

of the moral acts of human beings, it does not follow that it should be called 'law'. Rational nature may be called a 'standard'; but the term 'standard' is a term of wider extension than the term 'law'.[1] There is, however, a second opinion, according to which rational nature, considered as the basis of the conformity or non-conformity of human acts with itself, is the basis of natural rectitude, while natural reason, or the power of rational nature to discriminate between acts in harmony with itself and acts not in harmony with itself, is the law of nature.[2] So far as this opinion means that the dictates of right reason, considered as the immediate and intrinsic rule of human acts, is the natural law, it may be accepted. In the strictest sense, however, the natural law consists in the actual judgment of the mind; but the natural reason or the natural light of reason may also be called natural law, for we think of men as permanently retaining that law in their minds, even though they may not be engaged in any specific act of moral judgment. In other words, the question how natural law should be defined is partly a terminological question.[3]

As to the relation of the natural law to God, there are two extreme positions, which are opposed to one another. According to the first opinion, ascribed to Gregory of Rimini, the natural law is not a preceptive law in the proper sense; for it does not indicate the will of a superior but simply makes clear what should be done, as being intrinsically good, and what should be avoided, as being intrinsically evil. The natural law is thus a demonstrative law rather than a preceptive law; and it does not derive from God as legislator. It is, so to speak, independent of God, that is, of God considered as moral legislator. According to the second opinion, however, which is ascribed to William of Ockham, God's will constitutes the whole basis of good and evil. Actions are good or evil simply and solely in so far as they are ordered or prohibited by God.

Neither of these opinions is acceptable to Suárez. 'I hold that a middle course should be taken, this middle course being, in my judgment, the opinion held by St. Thomas and common to the theologians.'[4] In the first place, the natural law is a preceptive and not merely a demonstrative law; for it does not merely indicate what is good or evil, but it also commands and prohibits. But it does not follow from this that the divine volition is the total cause of the good or evil involved in the observance or transgression of the natural law. On the contrary, the divine volition presupposes

[1] *De legibus*, 2, 5, 6. [2] *Ibid.*, 2, 5, 9. [3] *Ibid.*, 2, 5, 14. [4] *Ibid.*, 2, 6, 5.

the intrinsic moral character of certain acts. It is repugnant to reason to say, for example, that hatred of God is wrong simply and solely because it is prohibited by God. The divine volition presupposes a dictate of the divine reason concerning the intrinsic character of human acts. God is, indeed, the author of the natural law; for He is Creator and He wills to bind men to observe the dictates of right reason. But God is not the arbitrary author of the natural law; for He commands some acts because they are intrinsically good and prohibits other acts because they are intrinsically evil. Suárez does not, of course, mean to imply that God is, as it were, governed by a law which is external to His nature. What he means is that God (to speak anthropomorphically) could not help seeing that certain acts are in harmony with rational nature and that certain acts are morally incompatible with rational nature, and that God, seeing this, could not fail to command the performance of the former and prohibit the performance of the latter. It is true that the natural law, taken simply in itself, reveals what is intrinsically good and evil, without any explicit reference to God; but the natural light of reason none the less makes known to man the fact that actions contrary to the natural law are necessarily displeasing to the author and governor of nature. As to the promulgation of the natural law, 'the natural light is of itself a sufficient promulgation'.[1]

7. In the discussion of this matter in the *De legibus*, there is, I think, a certain prolixity and even a certain lack of clarity and exactitude. It is certainly clear that Suárez rejected the authoritarian ethical theory of William of Ockham and that, fundamentally, his own theory follows that of St. Thomas; but it does not seem to me to be made as clear as one could wish in what precise sense the term 'good' is being used. Suárez does, however, clarify the matter somewhat when he discusses the question what is the subject-matter dealt with by natural law.

He distinguishes various types of precepts which belong to the natural law.[2] First of all, there are general and primary principles of morality, such as 'one must do good and shun evil'. Secondly, there are principles which are more definite and specific, like 'God must be worshipped' and 'one must live temperately'. Both these types of ethical propositions are self-evident, according to Suárez. Thirdly, there are moral precepts which are not immediately self-evident but which are deduced from self-evident propositions and

[1] *De legibus*, 2, 6, 24.

[2] *Ibid.*, 2, 7, 5.

become known through rational reflection. In the case of some of these precepts, like 'adultery is wrong', their truth is easily recognized; but in the case of some other precepts, like 'usury is unjust' and 'lying can never be justified', more reflection is required in order to see their truth. Nevertheless, all these types of ethical propositions pertain to the natural law.

But if the natural law enjoins that good must be done, and if all righteous and licit acts are good acts, does it not seem to follow that the natural law enjoins the performance of all acts which are righteous and licit? Now, the act of contracting marriage is a good act. Is it, then, enjoined by the natural law? On the other hand, living according to the counsels of perfection is good. For example, it is good to embrace perpetual chastity. Is it, then, enjoined by the natural law? Certainly not; a counsel is not a precept. But why not? Suárez, developing a distinction made by St. Thomas, explains that, if virtuous acts are considered individually, not every such act falls under a natural precept. He mentions the counsels and contracting marriage.[1] One can also say[2] that all virtuous acts, in respect of the manner in which they should be performed, fall under the natural law, but that, in regard to their actual performance, they are not all absolutely prescribed by the natural law. It might, however, have been simpler to say that the natural law enjoins, not simply the doing of what is good, but the doing of good and the avoidance of evil, in the sense that what is prescribed absolutely is the doing of something good when its omission or the doing of something else would be evil. But the terms 'good' and 'evil' would still need some further clarificatory analysis. Some of the apparent confusion in Suárez' treatment of natural law seems to be due to his using the phrase 'natural law' both in a narrower sense, to mean the law based on human nature as such, and also in a wide sense, to include 'the law of grace'.[3] To embrace the evangelical counsels is certainly not made a matter of obligation by the essential propensities and requirements of human nature: but the life of the counsels is offered to the individual for a supernatural end, and it could become a matter of obligation only if God absolutely commanded an individual to embrace it or if he or she could achieve his or her last end only by embracing it.

Possibly the following may make Suárez' position a little clearer. An act is good if it is in accordance with right reason; and an act is evil if it is not in accordance with right reason. If doing a

[1] *De legibus*, 2, 7, 11. [2] *Ibid.* [3] Cf. *Ibid.*, 2, 8, 1.

certain act averts a man from his last end, that act is evil and is not in accordance with right reason, which enjoins that the means necessary to the attainment of the last end shall be taken. Now, every concrete human act, that is, every concrete deliberate free act, is in the moral order and is either good or bad: it is either in accordance or not in accordance with right reason.[1] The natural law enjoins, therefore, that every concrete human act should be good and not evil. But to say this is not the same thing as to say that every possible good act should be done. This would scarcely be possible; and in any case omitting to do one good act does not necessarily involve doing a bad act. To take a rather trivial example. If taking some exercise is indispensable for my health and the proper fulfilment of my work, it is in accordance with right reason that I should take some exercise. But it does not follow that I ought to go for a walk; for I might also play golf or swim or do gymnastic exercises. Again, it might be a good thing for a man to become a friar; but it does not follow that he is doing evil if he does not become a friar. He might marry, for example; and to marry is to do a good act, even if, abstractly speaking at least, to become a friar is better. What the moral law enjoins is to do good *and* not to do evil: it does not always order which good act is to be done. The natural law prohibits all evil acts, since the avoidance of evil is necessary for morality; but it does not order all good acts, for to do a particular good act is not always necessary. From the obligation of never sinning there follows the positive obligation of acting well; but this positive obligation is conditional ('if a free act is to be done'), not simply absolute. 'It is a general obligation of doing good, when some act has to be done; and this obligation can be fulfilled by acts which are not absolutely enjoined. Therefore, it is not all good acts which, by virtue of the natural law, fall under a precept.'[2]

8. As to possible ignorance of the natural law, Suárez maintains that no one can be ignorant of the primary or most general principles of the natural law.[3] It is possible, however, to be ignorant of particular precepts, even of those which are self-evident or easily deducible from self-evident precepts. But it does not follow that such ignorance can be guiltless, not at least for any considerable length of time. The precepts of the Decalogue are of this character. Their binding force is so easily recognizable that no

[1] *Tractatus de bonitate et malitia humanorum actuum*, 9, 3, 10.
[2] *De Religione, pars secunda*, 1, 7, 3.
[3] *De legibus*, 2, 8, 7.

one can remain in ignorance of it for any considerable length of time without guilt. However, invincible ignorance is possible in regard to those precepts knowledge of which requires greater reflection.

9. Are the precepts of the natural law immutable? Before the question can be profitably discussed, it is necessary to make a distinction.[1] It is possible for a law to become intrinsically defective by becoming harmful instead of useful or irrational instead of rational. It is also possible for a law to be changed by a superior. Again, both intrinsic change and extrinsic change can affect either the law itself or some particular case or application. For instance, a superior might abolish the law as such or he might relax it or dispense from it in some particular case. Suárez first considers intrinsic change; and he maintains[2] that, properly speaking, the natural law cannot undergo any change, either in regard to its totality or in regard to particular precepts, so long as human nature endures, gifted with reason and free will. If rational nature were abolished, natural law would also be abolished in regard to its concrete existence, since it exists in man or flows from human nature. As natural law flows from human nature, as it were, it cannot become injurious with the course of time; nor can it become irrational if it is grounded in self-evident principles. Apparent instances of intrinsic change in particular cases are due simply to the fact that the general terms in which a natural precept is customarily stated do not adequately express the natural precepts themselves. For instance, if a man has lent me a knife and demands it back, I ought to restore to him what is his property; but if he has become a homicidal maniac and I know that he wants to use the knife to murder someone, I ought not to restore it. This does not mean, however, that the precept that deposits should be restored on demand has undergone an intrinsic change in this case; it simply means that the precept, so stated, is an inadequate statement of what is contained in or involved by the precept itself. Similarly, the precept of the Decalogue, 'thou shalt not kill', really includes many conditions which are not explicitly mentioned; for example, 'thou shalt not kill on thine own authority and as an aggressor'.[3]

Can the natural law be changed by authority? Suárez maintains that 'no human power, even though it be the papal power, can abrogate any proper precept of the natural law' (that is, any

[1] *De legibus*, 2, 13, 1. [2] *Ibid.*, 2, 13, 2. [3] *Ibid.*, 2, 13, 8.

precept properly belonging to the natural law), 'nor truly and essentially restrict such a precept, nor grant a dispensation from it'.[1] A difficulty may seem to arise in regard to property. According to Suárez,[2] nature has conferred on men in common dominion over things, and consequently every man has the power to use those things which have been given in common. It might seem, then, that the institution of private property and of laws against theft either constitute an infringement of the natural law or indicate that the natural law is subject, in some cases at least, to human power. Suárez answers that the law of nature did not positively forbid the division of common property and its appropriation by individuals; the institution of common dominion was 'negative', not positive. Positively considered, the natural law ordains that no one should be prevented from making the necessary use of common property as long as it is common, and that, after the division of property, theft is wrong. We have to distinguish[3] between preceptive laws and the law concerning dominion. There is no preceptive law of nature that things should always be held in common; but there are preceptive laws relating to conditions which are to a certain extent subject to human power. Nature did not divide goods among private individuals; but the private appropriation of goods was not forbidden by natural law. Private property may, therefore, be instituted by human agency. But there are preceptive laws of nature relating to common ownership and to private ownership; and these preceptive laws are not subject to human agency. The power of the State to confiscate property when there is just cause (as in certain criminal cases) must be understood as provided for in the preceptive laws of nature.

In other words, Suárez will not admit that the natural law is subject to human power. At the same time he maintained that Nature gave the things of the earth to all men in common. But it does not follow, he tells us, either that the institution of private property is against the natural law or that it constitutes a change in the natural law. Why not? A matter may fall under the natural law either in a negative sense or in a positive sense (through positive prescription of an action). Now, common ownership was a part of natural law only in a negative sense, in the sense, that is to say, that by virtue of the natural law all property was to be held in common unless men introduced a different provision. The introduction of private property was thus not against the natural law

[1] *De legibus*, 2, 14, 8. [2] *Ibid.*, 2, 14, 16. [3] *Ibid.*, 2, 14, 19.

nor did it constitute a change in any positive precept of the natural law.

However, even if men cannot change or dispense from the natural law, has not God the power to do so? In the first place, if God can dispense from any of the precepts of the Decalogue, it follows that He can abrogate the whole law and order those acts which are forbidden by the natural law. Dispensation from the law prohibiting an act would render that act permissible; but, if God can render an otherwise prohibited act permissible, why could He not prescribe it? 'This was the opinion supported by Occam, whom Pierre d'Ailly and Andreas a Novocastro followed.'[1] The opinion is, however, to be rejected and condemned. The commands and prohibitions of God in respect of the natural law presuppose the intrinsic righteousness of the acts commanded and the intrinsic wickedness of the prohibited acts. The notion that God could command man to hate Him is absurd. Either God would be commanding man to hate an object worthy of love or He would have to render Himself worthy of hatred; but either supposition is absurd.

What, then, of Scotus' opinion, that a distinction must be drawn between the precepts of the First Table of the Decalogue and those of the Second Table and that God can dispense in regard to the latter? Suárez observes that, in a sense, it is inaccurate to say that God, according to Scotus, can dispense in the case of certain precepts of the natural law, since Scotus would not allow that all the precepts of the Decalogue belong, at least in the strictest sense, to the natural law. But Suárez rejects the opinion that the precepts of the Second Table do not strictly belong to the natural law. 'The arguments of Scotus, indeed, are not convincing.'[2]

Suárez maintains, then, that God cannot dispense in regard to any of the Commandments. He appeals to St. Thomas, Cajetan, Soto and others.[3] All the Commandments involve one intrinsic principle of justice and obligation. The apparent cases of dispensation of which we read in the Old Testament were not really cases of dispensation at all. For example, when God told the Hebrews to despoil the Egyptians, He was not acting as legislator and giving them a dispensation to steal. He was either acting as supreme lord and transferring dominion over the goods in question from the Egyptians to the Hebrews; or He was acting as supreme judge and awarded the Hebrews proper wages for their work, wages which had been withheld by the Egyptians.[4]

[1] *De legibus*, 2, 15, 3. [2] *Ibid.*, 2, 15, 12. [3] *Ibid.*, 2, 15, 16. [4] *Ibid.*, 2, 15, 20.

10. Suárez goes on to distinguish the natural law from 'the law of nations' (*ius gentium*). In Suárez' opinion, the *ius gentium* does not prescribe any acts as being of themselves necessary for right conduct, nor does it forbid anything as being of itself and intrinsically evil: such prescriptions and prohibitions pertain to the natural law, and not to the *ius gentium*.[1] The two are not, therefore, the same. The *ius gentium* 'is not only indicative of what is evil but also constitutive of evil'.[2] Suárez means that the natural law prohibits what is intrinsically evil whereas the *ius gentium* considered precisely as such does not prohibit intrinsically evil acts (for these are already forbidden by natural law) but prohibits certain acts for a just and sufficient reason and renders the performance of those acts wrong. From this it follows that the *ius gentium* cannot possess the same degree of immutability as the natural law possesses.

The laws of the *ius gentium* are, therefore, positive (not natural) and human (not divine) laws. In this case, however, does it differ from civil law? It is not sufficient merely to say that civil law is the law of one State, while the *ius gentium* is common to all peoples; for a mere difference between greater and less does not constitute a specific difference.[3] Suárez' opinion is that 'the precepts of the *ius gentium* differ from those of the civil law in that they are not established in written form'; they are established through the customs of all or nearly all nations.[4] The *ius gentium* is thus unwritten law; and it is made up of customs belonging to all, or practically all, nations. It can, indeed, be understood in two ways. A particular matter can pertain to the *ius gentium* either because it is a law which the various peoples and nations ought to observe in their relations with each other or because it is a set of laws which individual States observe within their own borders and which are similar and so commonly accepted. 'The first interpretation seems, in my opinion, to correspond most properly to the actual *ius gentium* as distinct from the civil law.'[5]

Of the *ius gentium* understood in this sense Suárez gives several examples. For example, as far as natural reason is concerned it is not indispensable that the power of avenging an injury by war should belong to the State, for men could have established some other means of avenging injury. But the method of war, which is 'easier and more in conformity with nature', has been adopted by custom and is just.[6] 'In the same class I place slavery.' The

[1] *De legibus*, 2, 17, 9.
[2] *Ibid.*, 2, 19, 2.
[3] *Ibid.*, 2, 19, 5.
[4] *Ibid.*, 2, 19, 6.
[5] *Ibid.*, 2, 19, 8.
[6] *Ibid.*

institution of slavery (as a punishment for the guilty) was not necessary from the standpoint of natural reason; but, given this custom, the guilty are bound to submit to it, while the victors may not inflict a more severe punishment without some special reason. Again, though the obligation to observe treaties once they have been made proceeds from the natural law, it is a matter pertaining to the *ius gentium* that offers of treaties, when duly made and for a reasonable cause, should not be refused. To act in this way is, indeed, in harmony with natural reason; but it is more firmly established by custom and the *ius gentium*, and so acquires a special binding force.

The rational basis of this kind of *ius gentium* is the fact that the human race, however much it may be divided into different nations and States, preserves a certain unity, which does not consist simply in membership of the human species, but is also a moral and political unity, as it were (*unitatem quasi politicam et moralem*). This is indicated by the natural precept of mutual love and mercy, which extends to all, 'even foreigners'.[1] A given State may constitute a perfect community, but, taken simply by itself, it is not self-sufficient but requires assistance through association and relationship with other States. In a certain sense, then, different States are members of a universal society; and they need some system of law to regulate their relations with one another. Natural reason does not provide sufficiently for this need; but the habitual conduct of nations has introduced certain laws which are in accordance with nature, even if they are not strictly deducible from the natural law.

St. Thomas asserted in the *Summa theologica*[2] that the precepts of the *ius gentium* are conclusions drawn from principles of the natural law and that they differ from precepts of the civil law, which are determinations of the natural law, not general conclusions from it. Suárez interprets this as meaning that the precepts of the *ius gentium* are general conclusions of the natural law, 'not in an absolute sense and by necessary inference, but in comparison with the specific determination of civil and private law'.[3]

11. In the third book of the *De legibus* Suárez turns to the subject of positive human law. He asks first whether man possesses the power to make laws or whether the making of laws by man spells tyranny; and his treatment of this question involves consideration of the State and of political authority.

[1] *De legibus*, 2, 19, 9. [2] Ia, IIae, 95, 4. [3] *De legibus*, 2, 20, 2.

Man is a social animal, as Aristotle said, and he has a natural desire to live in community.[1] The most fundamental natural society is, indeed, the family; but the family, though a perfect community for purposes of domestic or 'economic' government, is not self-sufficing. Man stands in further need of a political community, formed by the coalition of families. This political community is necessary, both for the preservation of peace between individual families and for the growth of civilization and culture.

Secondly, in a perfect community (Suárez is here speaking of the political community) there must be a governing power. The truth of this principle would seem to be self-evident, but it is confirmed by analogy with other forms of human society, like the family.[2] Moreover, as St. Thomas indicates,[3] no body can endure unless it possesses some principle the function of which is to provide for the common good. The institution of civil magistracy is thus necessary.

Thirdly, a human magistracy, if it is supreme in its own sphere, has the power to make laws in its own sphere, that is to say, civil or human laws. A civil magistracy is a necessity in a State; and the establishment of laws is one of the most necessary acts of a civil magistracy, if it is to fulfil its governmental and regulative function in the life of the State.[4] This power to make laws belongs to the magistracy which possesses supreme jurisdiction in the State: it is an essential factor in political sovereignty.

The State and political sovereignty are thus natural institutions, in the sense that nature demands their establishment. It may be true that empires and kingdoms have often been established through tyranny and force; but historical facts of this kind are examples of human abuse of power and strength, not of the essential nature of political sovereignty.[5] As to St. Augustine's opinion, that the domination of one man over another is due to the state of affairs brought about by sin, this is to be understood, says Suárez,[6] of that form of dominion which is accomplished by servitude and the exercise of coercion. Without sin there would be no exercise of coercion and no slavery; but there still would be government; at least, 'in so far as directive power is concerned, it would seem probable that this would have existed among men even in the state of innocence'.[7] In this matter Suárez follows St. Thomas.[8] In the *De opere sex dierum*[9] Suárez says that since

[1] *De legibus*, 3, 1, 3. [2] *Ibid.*, 3, 1, 4. [3] *De regimine principum*, 1, 1.
[4] *De legibus*, 3, 1, 6. [5] *Ibid.*, 3, 1, 11. [6] *Ibid.*, 3, 1, 12. [7] *Ibid.*
[8] For St. Augustine's opinion see Vol. II of this history, pp. 88–9. [9] 5, 7, 6.

human society is a result not of human corruption but of human nature itself, it appears that men would have been united in a political community even in the state of innocence, had that state continued to exist. Whether there would have been one political community or more is not a question which one can answer. All one can say is that if all men had continued to live in Paradise, there could have been one single political community. Suárez goes on to say that there would have been no servitude in the state of innocence but there would have been government, as this is required for the common good.[1]

But the fact that civil magistracy and government are necessary and that the supreme magistracy in a State has power to make laws, does not mean that the power to make laws is conferred directly and immediately on any individual or group of individuals. On the contrary, 'this power, viewed solely according to the nature of things, resides, not in any individual man, but rather in the whole body of mankind'.[2] All men are born free; and nature has not conferred immediately upon any man political jurisdiction over another.

When, however, it is said that the power of making laws was conferred by Nature immediately upon mankind ('the multitude of mankind'), this must not be understood as meaning that the power was conferred on men regarded simply as an aggregate, without any moral union. We must understand mankind as meaning men gathered together by common consent 'into one political body through one bond of fellowship and for the purpose of aiding one another in the attainment of a single political end'.[3] If regarded in this way, men form 'a single mystical body' which needs a single head.[4]

It is to be added that the power in question does not reside in mankind in such a way that it is one power residing in all existent men, with the consequence that they would all form one single political community. 'On the contrary, that would scarcely be possible, and much less would it be expedient.'[5] It seems, then, that the power of making laws, if it existed in the whole assemblage of mankind, did so only for a brief time: mankind began to be divided into distinct political communities 'soon after the creation of the world'. Once this division had begun to take place, the power to make laws resided in the several political communities.

[1] *De legibus*, 5, 7, 11.
[2] *Ibid.*, 3, 2, 3.
[3] *Ibid.*, 3, 2, 4.
[4] *Ibid.*
[5] *Ibid.*, 3, 2, 5.

This power comes from God as its primary source.[1] But how does He confer it? In the first place, it is given by God 'as a characteristic property resulting from nature'. In other words, God does not confer the power by any special act which is distinct from the act of creation. That it results from nature means that natural reason shows that the exercise of the power is necessary for the preservation and proper government of the political community, which is itself a natural society. In the second place, the power does not manifest itself until men have formed a political community. Therefore the power is not conferred by God without the intervention of will and consent on the part of men, that is to say, on the part of those men who, by consent, form themselves together into a perfect society or State. However, once they have formed the community the power is resident therein. It is rightly said, then, to have been immediately conferred by God. Suárez adds[2] that the power does not reside in a given political community in such a way that it cannot be alienated by the consent of that community or forfeited by way of just punishment.

12. It is clear that Suárez regarded political society as originating, essentially, in consent. That a greater or less number of States may have actually originated in other ways is a historical accident, not affecting the essence of the State. But if, to this extent, Suárez may be said to have proposed a theory of the 'social contract', this does not mean that he regarded political society as a purely artificial society, a creation of enlightened egoism. On the contrary, as we have seen, he found the ultimate origin of political society in human nature, that is, in the social character and needs of the human being. The formation of political society is a necessary expression of human nature, even if the formation of a given political community must be said to rest essentially on consent, since nature has not specified what particular communities are to be formed.

Much the same is to be said about his theory of sovereignty or, to restrict oneself to the actual point discussed, the power of making laws which appertains to sovereignty. Nature has not specified any particular form of government, says Suárez;[3] the determination of the form of government depends on human choice. It would be extremely difficult for the whole community as such to make laws directly, and practical considerations point to monarchy

[1] *De legibus*, 3, 3, 4. [2] *Ibid.*, 3, 3, 7. [3] *Ibid.*, 3, 4, 1.

as the best form of government, though it is as a rule expedient, given man's character, 'to add some element of common government'.[1] What this element of common government is to be, depends on human choice and prudence. In any case, whoever holds the civil power, this power has been derived, either directly or indirectly, from the people as a community. Otherwise it could not be justly held.[2] In order that sovereignty may justly be vested in a given individual, 'it must necessarily be bestowed upon him by the consent of the community'.[3] In certain cases God has conferred power directly, as on Saul; but such cases are extraordinary and, as far as regards the mode of imparting power, supernatural. In the case of hereditary monarchy the just possessor derived power from the commonwealth.[4] As to royal power obtained through unjust force, the king in this case possesses no true legislative power, though in the course of time the people may come to give their consent to and acquiesce in his sovereignty, thus rendering it legitimate.[5]

Thus, just as Suárez holds that the formation of a given political community depends on human consent, so he holds that the establishment of a certain government depends on the consent of the political community which confers the sovereignty. He may therefore be said to maintain, in a sense, the double-contract theory. But, just as he holds that the formation of political communities is a requirement of nature, so he holds that the establishment of some government is required by nature. He may tend to lay more emphasis on the idea of consent; indeed, he speaks explicitly of a 'pact or agreement' between the king and the kingdom;[6] but political authority and sovereignty are nevertheless necessary for the proper preservation and government of mankind. Political authority is derived ultimately from God, on whom all dominion depends; but the fact that it is conferred on a definite individual derives from a grant on the part of the State itself: 'the principate itself is derived from men'.[7] In other words, political sovereignty is not in itself simply a matter of convention or agreement, for it is necessary for human life; but the conferring of sovereignty on certain individuals does depend on agreement.

It may be noted in passing that Suárez thought in terms of the monarchic state of his time. The mediaeval idea of the imperial power plays little part in his political theory. In his *Defence of the*

[1] *De legibus*, 3, 4, 1. [2] *Ibid.*, 3, 4, 2. [3] *Ibid.* [4] *Ibid.*, 3, 4, 3.
[5] *Ibid.*, 3, 4, 4. [6] *Ibid.*, 3, 4, 5. [7] *Ibid.*, 3, 4, 5.

Catholic and Apostolic Faith[1] Suárez expressly denies that the emperor has universal temporal jurisdiction over all Christians. It is probable, he says, that the emperor never did possess this power; and, even if he did, he has certainly lost it. 'We assume that there are, besides the emperor, a number of temporal kings, like the kings of Spain, France and England, who are entirely independent of the emperor's jurisdiction.'[2] On the other hand, Suárez evidently did not think that a world-State and a world-government were practical possibilities. History shows that there never has been a truly world-wide government. It does not exist, never did exist, and never could have existed.[3] Suárez maintained as we have seen, that the existence of a single political community for all men is morally impossible and that, even if possible, it would be highly inexpedient.[4] If Aristotle was right, as he was, in saying that it is difficult to govern a very large city properly, it would be far more difficult to govern a world-State.

13. What implications did Suárez draw from his doctrine of the pact between monarch and kingdom? Did he hold in particular that the citizens have a right to depose a tyrannical monarch, one who violates his trust?

According to Suárez,[5] the transfer of sovereignty from the State to the prince is not a delegation but a transfer or unlimited bestowal of the whole power which resided in the community. The prince, then, may delegate the power, if he so chooses: it is granted to him absolutely, to be exercised by him personally or through agents, as he thinks most expedient. Moreover, once the power has been transferred to the monarch, he is the vicar of God; and obedience to him is obligatory, according to the natural law.[6] In fact, the transference of power to the monarch makes him superior even to the State which conferred the power, since the State has subjected itself to the monarchy by making the transference.

The monarch cannot, then, be deprived of his sovereignty, since he has acquired ownership of his power. But Suárez immediately adds the qualification, 'unless perchance he lapses into tyranny, on which ground the kingdom may wage a just war against him'.[7] There are two sorts of tyrants.[8] There is the tyrant who has usurped the throne by force and unjustly; and there is the legitimate prince who rules tyrannically in the use he makes of his power. In regard to the first kind of tyrant, the whole State or any

[1] 3, 5, 7. [2] *Ibid.* [3] *De legibus*, 3, 4, 7. [4] *Ibid.*, 3, 2, 5.
[5] *Ibid.*, 3, 4, 11. [6] *Ibid.*, 3, 4, 6. [7] *Ibid.*
[8] *Defence of the Catholic and Apostolic Faith*, 6, 4, 1.

part of it has the right to revolt against him, for he is an aggressor. To revolt is simply to exercise the right of self-defence.[1] As to the second type of tyrant, namely the legitimate prince who rules tyrannically, the State as a whole may rise against him, for it must be supposed that the State granted him the power on condition that he should govern for the common good and that he might be deposed if he lapsed into tyranny.[2] It is, however, a necessary condition for the legitimacy of such a revolt that the king's rule should be manifestly tyrannical and that the norms pertaining to a just war should be observed. Suárez refers to St. Thomas on this matter.[3] But it is only the whole State which is entitled to rise against a legitimate monarch acting tyrannically; for he cannot, without more ado, be an aggressor against all individual citizens in the way that the unjust usurper is an aggressor. This is not to say, however, that an individual who is the subject of actual tyrannical aggression on the part of a legitimate monarch may not defend himself. But a distinction must be drawn between self-defence and defence of the State.

In his *Defence of the Catholic and Apostolic Faith*[4] Suárez considers the particular question of tyrannicide. A legitimate monarch may not be slain by private authority on the grounds that he rules tyrannically. This is the doctrine of St. Thomas,[5] Cajetan and others. A private individual who kills on his own authority a legitimate monarch who acts tyrannically is a murderer. He does not possess the requisite jurisdiction.[6] As to self-defence, a private individual may not kill the legitimate monarch simply in order to defend his private possessions; but if the monarch tyrannically threatens the citizen's life, he may defend himself, even if the monarch's death results, though regard for the common welfare might, in certain circumstances, bind him in charity to refrain from slaying the monarch, even at the cost of his own life.

In the case of a tyrannical usurper, however, it is licit for the private individual to kill him provided that no recourse can be had to a superior authority and provided that the tyranny and injustice of the usurper's rule are manifest. Other conditions added by Suárez[7] are that tyrannicide is a necessary means for the liberation of the kingdom; that no agreement has been freely entered upon by the usurper and the people; that tyrannicide will not leave the State afflicted with the same or greater evils than

[1] *De triplici virtute theologica; de caritate*, 13, 8, 2. [2] *Ibid.*
[3] *De regimine principum*, 1, 6. [4] 6, 4. [5] *De regimine principum*, 1, 6.
[6] *Defence*, 6, 4, 4. [7] *Ibid.*, 6, 4, 8–9.

before; and that the State does not expressly oppose private tyrannicide.

Suárez thus affirms the right of resistance, which logically follows from his doctrine of the origin and transference of sovereignty. He certainly in no way encouraged unnecessary revolts; but it is easily understandable that his work on the Catholic Faith was most obnoxious to James I of England, who believed in the divine right of kings and the principle of legitimacy.

14. In the fourth book of the *De legibus* (*De lege positiva canonica*) Suárez considers canon law; and in the fifth book he treats *de varietate legum humanarum et praesertim de poenalibus et odiosis.* In connection with penal laws he raises the question of their binding force in conscience. First of all, it is possible for the human legislator to make laws which bind in conscience, even though a temporal penalty for transgression is attached.[1] But do such laws bind in conscience when the legislator has not expressly stated his intention of binding the consciences of his subjects? In Suárez' opinion[2] a law which contains a precept binds in conscience unless the legislator has expressed or made clear his intention not to bind the conscience. (Whether the law binds under pain of mortal or venial sin depends on the matter of the law and other circumstances.) Suárez draws the logical conclusion that just taxation laws bind in conscience, 'like the law in Spain taxing the price of wheat'.[3] It is possible, however, for there to be penal laws which do not bind in conscience in regard to the act to be performed. Whether a law is of this kind, that is, whether a law is merely penal, depends on the intention of the legislator. This intention need not necessarily be expressed in so many words, for it may be made clear by tradition and custom.[4] When a penal law does not actually command or prohibit an act but simply states, for example, that if someone exports wheat he will be fined, it can be presumed to be merely penal unless it is clear from some other consideration that it was meant to bind in conscience.

A human penal law can oblige subjects in conscience to undergo the penalty, even before judicial sentence; but only if the penalty is one that the subject can licitly inflict on himself and provided that it is not so severe or repugnant to human nature that its voluntary performance cannot be reasonably demanded.[5] But

[1] *De legibus*, 5, 3, 2.
[2] *Ibid.*, 5, 3, 6.
[3] *Ibid.*, 5, 3, 10.
[4] *Ibid.*, 5, 4, 8.
[5] *Ibid.*, 5, 5, 15.

it does not follow that all penal laws do so oblige in actual fact. If a penal law simply threatens a penalty, it does not oblige the transgressor to undergo the penalty before sentence, whatever the penalty may be:[1] the legislator's intention to oblige the transgressor in conscience to undergo the penalty on his own initiative must be made clear. As to the obligation to undergo the penalty inflicted by judicial sentence, Suárez holds that if some action or co-operation on the part of the guilty man is necessary for the execution of the penalty, he is bound in conscience to perform that act or give that co-operation, provided that the law which he has broken is a just law and that the penalty in question is not immoderate.[2] In this matter, however, common sense has to be used. No one, for example, is obliged to execute himself.[3]

As already mentioned, Suárez considered that taxation laws, if they are just, bind in conscience. He maintained that 'the laws by which such taxes are ordered to be paid, even if no penalty is attached, certainly cannot be called purely penal'.[4] They therefore bind in conscience; and just taxes must be paid in full, even if they have not been demanded, from oversight, for example, unless the legislator's intention to pass a purely penal taxation law is made clear. Regarded in themselves, taxation laws are true moral laws binding in conscience.[5] As for unjust taxation laws, they never bind in conscience, either before or after the demand for the payment of the tax.[6]

15. The sixth book of the *De legibus* is concerned with the interpretation, cessation and change of human laws. It is not always necessary that a law should be revoked by the sovereign before it can be disobeyed licitly. Apart from the fact that a law enjoining anything wrong, anything impossible of fulfilment or anything devoid of any utility is unjust and null from the start,[7] a law may cease to be valid and binding because the adequate end, both intrinsic and extrinsic of the law, has ceased to exist.[8] For example, if a law is passed imposing a tax solely with a view to obtaining money for a specific object, the law lapses, as regards its binding force, when the purpose has been achieved, even if the law has not been revoked. But if the end of a law is not purely extrinsic but is also intrinsic (for example, if a good act is indeed commanded with a view to some specific end but in such a way that the legislator would command that act irrespective of the

[1] *De legibus*, 5, 6, 4. [2] *Ibid.*, 5, 10, 8. [3] *Ibid.*, 5, 10, 12. [4] *Ibid.*, 5, 13, 4. [5] *Ibid.*, 5, 13, 9. [6] *Ibid.*, 5, 18, 12. [7] *Ibid.*, 6, 9, 3. [8] *Ibid.*, 6, 9, 10.

specific end), it cannot, of course, be taken for granted that the law lapses simply because the specified end has been achieved.

16. Suárez writes at length of unwritten law or custom, a matter to which he devotes the seventh book (*De lege non scripta quae consuetudo appellatur*). Custom, considered as a juridical factor, is introduced in default of law: it is unwritten law. But it is only common or public custom which can establish law (that is, custom regarded as law), not private custom, which is the custom of one person or of an imperfect community.[1] Moreover, a custom, to establish law, must be morally good: a custom which is intrinsically evil establishes no law.[2] But the distinction between morally good and bad customs is not the same as that between reasonable and unreasonable customs: a custom might be good in itself, that is, considered simply as a custom, while at the same time it might be unreasonable and imprudent if regarded juridically, namely as establishing law.[3]

For the establishment of a custom a perfect community is required:[4] but it is not necessary for its establishment that it should be observed by literally the whole of the community; it is sufficient if the greater part of the community observes it.[5] How is it established? By a repetition of certain public acts by the people.[6] These acts must, of course, be voluntary acts. The reason for this is that the acts which establish a custom are of effect in doing so only in so far as they manifest the consent of the people.[7] They must, therefore, be voluntary: a custom cannot be validly established by acts done under compulsion or from grave or unjust fear.[8] But it does not follow that the consent of the prince is not necessary for the valid establishment of custom or consuetudinary law. This consent may, however, be given in different ways; either by express consent, or by antecedently permitting the introduction of a custom or by contemporaneous or subsequent confirmation, or by the prince doing nothing to check the custom when he has become aware of it.[9] Tacit consent, then, on the part of the sovereign can be sufficient.

Legitimate custom may have various different effects. It may establish a law; it may serve to interpret an existent law; or it may abrogate a law.[10] As regards the first effect, ten years are necessary and sufficient to establish a legal custom.[11] As to the abrogation of law through custom, a twofold will, the will of the people and the

[1] *De legibus*, 7, 3, 8–10. [2] *Ibid.*, 7, 6, 4. [3] *Ibid.*, 7, 6, 7. [4] *Ibid.*, 7, 9, 3.
[5] *Ibid.*, 7, 9, 12. [6] *Ibid.*, 7, 10, 1. [7] *Ibid.*, 7, 12, 1. [8] *Ibid.*, 7, 12, 10.
[9] *Ibid.*, 7, 13, 6. [10] *Ibid.*, 7, 14, 1. [11] *Ibid.*, 7, 15, 2.

will of the prince, is necessary for the attainment of this effect,[1] though a tacit consent on the prince's part can suffice. Custom can even establish penal law.[2] A custom of ten years' standing is required for the abrogation of civil law; but in the case of canon law a period of forty years is required for a custom to be prescriptive against a law.[3]

In the eighth book of the *De legibus* (*De lege humana favorabili*) Suárez deals with privilege, and in the ninth and tenth books with divine positive law. Passing over these topics I propose to say something on Suárez' view of the relation of Church to State.

17. In his *Defence of the Catholic and Apostolic Faith* Suárez discusses and rejects the view that the pope possesses not only supreme spiritual power but also supreme civil power with the consequence that no purely temporal sovereign possesses supreme power in temporal affairs. He appeals to utterances of popes, and then goes on to argue[4] that no just title can be discovered whereby the pope possesses direct jurisdiction in temporal affairs over all Christian States. And without a just title he cannot possess such jurisdiction. There is no evidence that either divine or human law has conferred such jurisdiction on the pope. Suárez recognized, of course, the temporal jurisdiction of the pope as temporal ruler over the Papal States; but he refused to regard other temporal sovereigns as mere vicars of the Holy See. In other words Church and State are distinct and independent societies, even though the end for which the Church exists is higher than that for which the State exists.

But, although the pope does not possess direct or primary civil jurisdiction over temporal sovereigns, he possesses a directive power over them, not merely as individuals but also as sovereigns. In virtue of his spiritual jurisdiction the pope possesses the power of directing temporal princes with a view to a spiritual end.[5] 'By directive power we do not understand simply the power of advising, warning or requesting; for these are not peculiar to superior authority; but we mean a strict power of obliging.'[6] Temporal monarchs are the spiritual subjects of the pope; and the pope's spiritual authority includes the power of directing the monarch in the use of his temporal authority, 'if in any matter he deviates from right reason, or from faith, justice or charity'.[7] This involves an indirect power on the part of the pope over temporal affairs.

[1] *De legibus*, 7, 18, 5. [2] *Ibid.*, 7, 16, 3. [3] *Ibid.*, 7, 18, 12.
[4] *Defence*, 3, 5, 11. [5] *Ibid.*, 3, 22, 1. [6] *Ibid.* [7] *Ibid.*, 3, 22, 5.

There may occur a clash between spiritual good and temporal convenience or expediency; and on such occasions the temporal sovereign must yield to the spiritual.[1] The pope should not attempt to usurp direct temporal jurisdiction; but in cases where it is necessary for spiritual good he may interfere, in virtue of his indirect power.

Suárez thus maintained the doctrine of the pope's indirect, though not direct, jurisdiction in the temporal sphere. He also maintained that the pope possesses 'coercive power over temporal princes who are incorrigibly wicked, and especially over schismatics and stubborn heretics'.[2] For directive power without coercive power is inefficacious. This power extends not only to the infliction of spiritual punishments like excommunication but also to the infliction of temporal punishments, such as, in case of necessity, deposition from the throne.[3] As to heathen monarchs, even if the pope does not possess the power to punish them, he has the power to free their Christian subjects from allegiance to them, if the Christians are in danger of moral destruction.[4]

18. Finally something may be said on the subject of Suárez' doctrine concerning war.

War is not intrinsically evil: there can be a just war. Defensive war is permitted; and sometimes it is even a matter of obligation.[5] But certain conditions have to be observed in order that a war should be just. First of all, the war must be waged by a legitimate power; and this is the supreme sovereign.[6] But the pope has the right to insist that matters of dispute between Christian sovereigns should be referred to himself, though the sovereigns are not bound to secure the pope's authorization before making war, unless the pope has expressly said that they must do so.[7]

The second condition for a just war is that the cause of making war should be just. For example, the suffering of a grave injustice which cannot be repaired or avenged in any other way is a just cause for war.[8] A defensive war should be attempted; but before an offensive war is begun, the sovereign should estimate his chances of victory and should not begin the war if he is more likely to lose than to win it.[9] The reason for this proviso is that otherwise the prince would incur the obvious risk of inflicting great injuries on his State. (By 'offensive war' Suárez means, not an 'aggressive war', but a just war freely undertaken. It is

[1] *Defence*, 3, 22, 7. [2] *Ibid.*, 3, 23, 2. [3] *Ibid.*, 3, 23, 10.
[4] *Ibid.*, 3, 23, 22. [5] *De triplici virtute theologica; de caritate*, 13, 1, 4.
[6] *Ibid.*, 13, 2, 4. [7] *Ibid.*, 13, 2, 5. [8] *Ibid.*, 13, 4, 1. [9] *Ibid.*, 13, 4, 10.

legitimate to declare war freely in order to repair injuries suffered or to defend the innocent.)

The third condition for a just war is that the war must be properly conducted and that due proportion must be observed throughout its course and in victory. Before beginning a war the prince is bound to call the attention of the sovereign of the other State to the existence of a just cause of war and to ask for adequate satisfaction. If the other offers adequate reparation for the injury done, he is bound to accept it; if he nevertheless attacks, the war will be unjust.[1] During the conduct of the war it is legitimate to inflict on the enemy all losses necessary for the attainment of victory, provided that these losses do not involve intrinsic injury to innocent persons.[2] Finally, after the winning of victory the prince may inflict upon the conquered enemy such penalties as are sufficient for a just punishment; and he may demand compensation for all losses his State has suffered, including those suffered through the war.[3] Indeed, after the war 'certain guilty individuals among the enemy may also be put to death with justice'.[4]

As to the 'innocent', 'it is implicit in the natural law that the innocent include children, women, and all unable to bear arms', while, according to the *ius gentium*, ambassadors are included, and, among Christians, by positive law, religious and priests. 'All other persons are considered guilty; for human judgment looks upon those able to take up arms as having actually done so.'[5] Innocent persons as such may never be slain, for the slaying of them is intrinsically evil; but if victory cannot be achieved without the 'incidental' slaying of the innocent, it is legitimate to slay them.[6] Suárez means that it is legitimate, for example, to blow up a bridge or to storm a town, if such acts are necessary for victory, even though the attacker has reason to think that these acts will involve the death of some innocent persons 'incidentally'. It would not, however, be legitimate to do such acts with the purpose of killing innocent people.

A question in connection with war discussed by Suárez[7] is the question how far the soldiers partaking in it are morally obliged to ascertain whether it is a just or unjust war. His answer, briefly stated, is as follows. Regular soldiers who are subjects of a prince are not bound to make careful investigation before obeying the summons to war: they can assume that the war is just, unless the

[1] *De triplici virtute theologica; de caritate*, 13, 7, 3.
[2] *Ibid.*, 13, 7, 6.
[3] *Ibid.*, 13, 7, 7.
[4] *Ibid.*
[5] *Ibid.*, 13, 7, 10.
[6] *Ibid.*, 13, 7, 15.
[7] *Ibid.*, 13, 6, 8–12.

contrary is evident. If they have simply speculative doubts about the justice of the war, they should disregard these doubts; but if the soldiers have practical and convincing reasons for thinking that the justice of the war is extremely doubtful they should make further inquiries. As to mercenaries who are not subjects of the prince who proposes to make war, Suárez argues that, although the common opinion seems to be that they are bound to inquire into the justice of war before enlisting, he himself finds no difference in actual fact between subjects and non-subjects. The general principles are, (*a*) that if the doubt which arises about the justice of a war is purely negative, it is probable that soldiers may enlist without making any further inquiry; and (*b*) that if the doubt is positive, and if both sides advance plausible arguments, those about to enlist should inquire into the truth. If they cannot discover the truth, let them aid him who is probably in the right. In practice 'inquiry' for an ordinary soldier means consulting 'prudent and conscientious men' but if the soldiers form an organized body, they can leave the inquiry and decision to their commander. As to the sovereign who wishes to make war, he is bound, of course, to inquire diligently into the justice of his cause; and he may not go to war if the other side is more probably in the right, let alone if it is morally certain that justice rests with the other side.[1]

[1] *De triplici virtute theologica; de caritate*, 13, 6, 2.

CHAPTER XXIV

A BRIEF REVIEW OF THE FIRST THREE VOLUMES

Greek philosophy; the pre-Socratic cosmologies and the discovery of Nature, Plato's theory of Forms and idea of God, Aristotle and the explanation of change and movement, neo-Platonism and Christianity—The importance for mediaeval philosophy of the discovery of Aristotle—Philosophy and theology—The rise of science.

1. In the first volume of this *History of Philosophy* I dealt with the philosophy of Greece and Rome. If one regards Greek philosophy as starting in the sixth century B.C. and ending with Justinian's closing of the Athenian Academy in A.D. 529, one can say that it lasted for about a thousand years and that it formed a definite period of philosophic thought with certain more or less well-defined phases.

(i) According to the traditional division, the first phase was that of pre-Socratic philosophy; and it has been customary to depict this phase as characterized predominantly by cosmological speculation. This view has, of course, the authority of Socrates in the *Phaedo*; and Aristotle, who interpreted the thought of previous philosophers largely in terms of his own theory of causes, speaks of the early Greek philosophers as busying themselves with the 'material cause' and of thinkers like Empedocles and Anaxagoras as considering the source of motion or efficient cause. I think that this view of pre-Socratic philosophy, namely that it was predominantly, though certainly not exclusively, cosmological in character, is obviously reasonable and sound. One can express it perhaps by saying that the pre-Socratic philosophers discovered 'Nature', that is, they formed the idea of a cosmos, an organized physical system governed by law. That the cosmos was looked on as divine in some sense, and that one can discern in the theories of the pre-Socratics mythical elements, the connection of which with older cosmogonies can be traced, is true; but there is a world of difference between the mythical cosmogonies and the cosmologies of the pre-Socratic philosophers. There is connection, but there is also difference. The play of imagination and phantasy began to retreat before the reflective work of the mind, based to some degree on empirical data.

It is, I think, important to remember that the pre-Socratic cosmologists represent a pre-scientific phase of thought. There was then no distinction between philosophy and the empirical sciences; nor, indeed, could there have been. The empirical sciences had to attain a certain stage of development before the distinction could well be made; and we may recall that even after the time of the Renaissance 'natural philosophy' or 'experimental philosophy' was used as a name for what we would call 'physical science'. The early Greek philosophers aimed simply at understanding the nature of the world, and their attention was centred on certain problems which aroused their interest and curiosity or, as Aristotle puts it, 'wonder'. Some of these problems were certainly what we would call 'scientific problems', in the sense that they can be profitably dealt with only by the use of scientific method, though the pre-Socratics tried to solve them by the only means in their power, namely by reflection on casual observations and by speculation. In some instances they made brilliant guesses which anticipated scientific hypotheses of a much later date. Anaximander appears to have put forward an evolutionary hypothesis about man's origin, while the atomic theory of Leucippus and Democritus is a notable example of a speculative anticipation of a later scientific hypothesis. According to Aristotle, men first felt wonder at the more obvious things and later raised difficulties and questions about more important matters; and he mentions questions about the sun and the moon and the stars and about the generation of the universe. This statement by Aristotle is worth reflecting on. The 'wonder' of which he speaks was the fountainhead of both philosophy and science. But in the beginning they were not distinguished, and it is only in terms of a later distinction to which we have become thoroughly accustomed, that we classify questions about the sun and moon and stars as scientific questions. It is obvious enough to us that if we wish to learn about the stars, for example, we have to turn to the astronomer for information: we would hardly go to the speculative philosopher for our information. Similarly, we do not think that questions about the physical constitution of matter or about the mechanism of vision (a subject in which Empedocles, for example, interested himself) can be answered by means of arm-chair reflection.

If I were to rewrite the sections about the pre-Socratics in my first volume, I would wish, I think, to give more attention to these aspects of their thought, namely the fact that a number of the questions which they raised were what we would regard as scientific questions and that a number of the theories which they put forward were speculative anticipations of later scientific hypotheses. At the same time it would be incorrect to suggest that the pre-Socratics were nothing but would-be scientists who lacked the method and the requisite technical means for pursuing their real vocation. One might perhaps say something like this about Thales and Anaximenes; but it would be a strange thing to say about Parmenides or even, I think, about Heraclitus. It seems to me that the pre-Socratics, or some of them at least, raised a number of problems which have generally been considered properly philosophical problems. Heraclitus, for example, appears to have raised moral problems which cannot be answered by empirical science. And it is arguable that the drive behind the intellectual activity of some of them was the desire to 'explain' the universe by reducing multiplicity to unity and by discovering the nature of 'ultimate reality', and that they had this drive in common with later speculative philosophers.

I do not think, then, that one is justified in interpreting the pre-Socratics as nothing more than speculative forerunners of science. To do this is to be guilty of a rather cavalier and hasty generalization. At the same time it is only right to draw attention to the fact that some of the main questions which they raised were not questions which can be answered in the way in which the pre-Socratics (unavoidably) tried to answer them. And in this sense it is true to say that they were forerunners of science. It is, I think, also true to say that they were predominantly 'cosmologists' and that a good deal of the field of their cosmological speculation has now been taken over, as it were, by science. But though one can say if one likes that their assumption that Nature is an organized cosmos was a scientific hypothesis, one can just as well say that it was a philosophic hypothesis which lies at the root of all scientific work and research.

(ii) If the early cosmologists discovered Nature, the Sophists, Socrates and Plato discovered Man. It is true, of course, that this statement is inaccurate and exaggerated in at any rate two ways. In the first place, Man was not discovered by the Sophists or by Socrates in the sense that a hitherto unknown island is discovered by an explorer. Nor, for the matter of that, was Nature discovered in this sense by the pre-Socratics. And in the second place, pre-Socratic philosophers, like the Pythagoreans, had theories about

Man, just as Plato had theories about Nature. None the less at the time of Socrates there occurred a shift in philosophic interest and emphasis. And that is why some historians say, and are able to make out a reasonable case for saying, that Greek philosophy began with Socrates. In their view, pre-Socratic philosophy should be regarded as primitive science, not as philosophy at all. Philosophy began with the Socratic ethical analysis. This is not my view of the situation; but it is an arguable position.

But it is not my purpose to say anything further here about the shift of interest from Nature to Man. That there was such a shift of interest in the case of Socrates would not be denied; and I dwelt on this theme in my first volume. What I want to do now is to draw attention to a topic which I did not sufficiently emphasize in that volume, namely the part played by analysis in the philosophies of Socrates and Plato. It might be better, however, to say that I wish now to emphasize the part played by analysis in the philosophy of Plato, since it is an obvious enough fact that Socrates was concerned with analysis. (In saying this I am assuming the truth of the view, represented in my first volume, that Socrates did not invent the theory of Forms or Ideas.)

It seems to me that Plato's theory of values was based very largely on an analysis of ethical propositions and value-statements. And though statements of this kind do seem to me to imply belief in the objectivity of values in some sense, it does not follow that values possess the kind of objectivity which Plato appears to have attributed to them. If one may borrow the language of Husserl, one can say perhaps that Plato carried on a phenomenological analysis of 'essences' without observing the *epoche*, thus confusing descriptive phenomenology with metaphysics. Again, it is a feature of Plato's thought that he drew attention to the differences in logical meaning between different types of sentences. He saw, for example, that in some sentences names are used which do not denote any definite individual thing and that there is a sense in which such sentences can be true even if there are no individual things in existence which correspond to those names. On this basis he developed his theory of Forms in so far as it was extended to generic and specific terms. In doing so he was misled by language and confused logic with metaphysics.

In saying this I am very far from suggesting that Plato's idea of the Good and his theory of exemplarism were worthless and that his theory of Forms was no more than the result of a confusion of logic with metaphysics. His remarks about the Good, obscure though they may be, scarcely lend support to the notion that he postulated the Good simply and solely because he was misled by our use of the word 'good'. But the fact remains that Plato's dialectical and logical approach to the metaphysics of 'Forms' or 'Ideas' is open to very serious objections; and in my first volume I did not, I think, bring out sufficiently either the element of 'linguistic analysis' in Plato's philosophy or his confusion of logic with metaphysics.

But it is possible, I think, to place too much emphasis on the theory of Forms or Ideas in Plato's thought. There is no real evidence, so far as I know, that he ever abandoned this theory; indeed, it seems to me that the available evidence prohibits any such supposition. But at the same time I think that it is true to say that the idea of mind or soul came to play an increasingly important part in Plato's thought. The subject of Plato's theology is notoriously obscure; but it is at least clear that he was the real founder of natural theology. That he attached great importance to the idea of a divine Mind or Soul in the universe is made obvious in the *Laws*; and it is equally clear from the *Timaeus*, even if one has to allow for the 'mythical' character of the contents of that dialogue. This is not to say, of course, that Plato had any clear theistic philosophy: if he had, he certainly did not reveal the fact to his readers. If one means by 'God' the God of Judaeo-Christian monotheism, the evidence would suggest that Plato arrived by different lines of thought at two aspects of God; but it does not suggest, or at least it gives us no solid ground for asserting, that Plato combined those two aspects of Deity, attributing them to one personal Being. Thus the Good may be said to represent what the Christian philosopher calls 'God' under the aspect of exemplary cause, though it does not follow, of course, that Plato would have called the Good 'God'. And the Demiurge of the *Timaeus* and the divine Mind or Soul of the *Laws* may be said to represent God under the aspect of efficient cause, provided that one understands by efficient cause in this connection not a Creator in the full sense but an explanatory cause of the intelligible structure of the empirical world and of the orderly movements of the heavenly bodies. But there is no compelling evidence that Plato ever identified the Good with the being represented by the Demiurge of the *Timaeus*. Nevertheless it is clear that if his theory of Forms was his answer to one problem, his doctrine of a divine Mind or Soul was his answer to another problem; and it would appear that this latter doctrine came to occupy a more important position in his thoughts as time went on.

(iii) In regard to Aristotle, one must emphasize, I think, his attempt to give a rational account of the world of experience and, in particular, his preoccupation with the business of rendering observable change and movement intelligible. (It should be remembered that 'movement' did not mean for Aristotle simply locomotion: it included also quantitative and qualitative change.) One certainly ought not to eliminate or to brush aside the Platonic elements or the metaphysical elements in Aristotle's philosophy, as though they were simply relics of a Platonist phase in his development which he forgot to discard; but it is significant that the God of the *Metaphysics*, the first unmoved mover, was postulated as an explanation of movement in terms of final causality. The God of the *Metaphysics* tends to appear as an astronomical hypothesis.

If one bears in mind Aristotle's preoccupation with the explanation of change and movement, it becomes much easier to account for his radical criticism of the Platonic theory of Forms. As I have already said, Plato's theory certainly lies open to serious objections on logical grounds, and I doubt if his approach to the theory can stand up to criticism, however much value one may wish to attribute to the theory considered in itself and revised. On the other hand, several of Aristotle's criticisms seem to be singularly unimpressive as they stand. Aristotle tended to assume that what Plato was getting at in his theory of Forms was what he, Aristotle, understood by 'forms'; and he then objected that Plato's Forms did not fulfil the function which his own forms fulfilled and that consequently the Platonic theory was absurd. This line of criticism is not a happy one, since it rests on the assumption that Plato's theory was supposed to fulfil the same function which Aristotle's theory of formal causality was intended to fulfil. But if, as I have suggested, one bears in mind Aristotle's preoccupation with the explanation of change and movement and his 'dynamic' outlook, his hostility towards the Platonic theory becomes understandable. His fundamental objection was that the theory was too 'metaphysical'; it was useless, he thought, for explaining the mixture, as it were, of change and stability which we find in things: it was not a hypothesis which had its roots in the empirical data or which was capable of contributing to the explanation of the empirical data or which was verifiable. I do not wish to suggest that

Aristotle was a positivist. But if the word 'metaphysical' is understood as it sometimes is today, namely as referring to altogether unverifiable and gratuitous hypotheses, it is clear that Aristotle considered the Platonic theory to be too 'metaphysical'. I certainly do not think that the theory of exemplary causality has no explanatory function; but it can hardly possess any such function except in connection with the idea of a divine being capable of an activity of which the God of Aristotle's *Metaphysics* was not capable. If one looks at the matter from Aristotle's point of view, one can easily understand his attitude to the Platonic theory. One can also understand how St. Bonaventure in the Middle Ages was able to look on Aristotle as a natural philosopher but not as a metaphysician.

(iv) Plato's Demiurge formed the empirical world, conferring on it an intelligible pattern according to an external exemplar or model: Aristotle's God was the ultimate explanation, as final cause, of movement. For neither of them was God the creator, in the full sense, of empirical beings. The nearest the Greek philosophers came to the idea of creation and to a consideration of the problem of finite existence as such was in neo-Platonism.

But the point about neo-Platonism which I wish to emphasize here is its character as the synthesis of Greek philosophic thought and as a system in which philosophy, ethics and religion were combined. It presented itself as a 'way of salvation', even if as a highly intellectual way of salvation which could appeal only to comparatively few minds. In pre-Socratic Pythagoreanism we can already discern the conception of philosophy as a way of salvation, though this aspect of Pythagoreanism may have tended to retreat into the background in proportion as the mathematical studies of the School developed. With Socrates and his theory of virtue as knowledge one can see clearly the idea of philosophy as a way of salvation, and in the thought of Plato the idea is also prominent, though it tends to be overshadowed by the logical and mathematical aspects of his philosophy. Plato was, of course, no pragmatist; but it does not require any great knowledge of his writings in order to realize the importance he attached to the possession of truth for the life of the individual and for society in general. But it is in the later phases of Platonism, especially in neo-Platonism, that the idea of philosophy as a way of salvation becomes so obvious. One has only to think of Plotinus' doctrine of the ethical and religious ascent of man, culminating in ecstatic union with the One. When Porphyry expounded neo-Platonism as a Greek and supposedly intellectually superior rival to Christianity, he was able to do this because in neo-Platonism Greek philosophy had taken on the character of a religion. Stoicism and Epicureanism were both presented as ways of salvation; but though the Stoic ethic certainly possessed a striking nobility, neither system was of a sufficiently high intellectual order to enable it to play the part in the final stages of Greek thought which was actually played by neo-Platonism.

The fact that early Christian writers borrowed terms and ideas from neo-Platonism may tend to make one emphasize the continuity between Greek and Christian thought. And this was the line I took in my first and second volumes. I have no intention of renouncing the validity of this line of thought now; but it is as well to emphasize the fact that there was also a sharp break between Greek and Christian thought. A neo-Platonist like Porphyry realized very clearly the difference between a philosophy which attached little importance to history and for which the idea of an incarnate God was unthinkable and a religion which attached a profound importance to concrete historical events and which was founded on belief in the Incarnation. Moreover, the Christian acceptance of Christ as the Son of God and of a divine revelation in history meant that for the Christian philosophy as such could not be the way of salvation. Christian writers like Clement of Alexandria interpreted philosophy in the literal sense as 'love of wisdom' and regarded Greek philosophy, especially Platonism in a wide sense, as a preparation for Christianity which fulfilled for the Greek world a function analogous to that fulfilled for the Jews by the Law and the Prophets. One is therefore struck by the friendly attitude shown towards Greek philosophy by a Clement of Alexandria as contrasted with the attitude shown by a Tertullian. But if one considers the former attitude a little more closely one will see its implications, namely that the rôle of Greek philosophy has been taken over in a definite manner by the Christian religion. And in point of fact when philosophy really developed in the Christian mediaeval world it tended to be 'academic', a matter for universities and professional logicians. No Christian philosopher really looked on philosophy as a way of salvation; and when mediaeval thinkers are reproached with paying too much attention to logical subtleties it is often forgotten that for them philosophy could not well be anything else than an 'academic' pursuit. When in the modern era one finds the conception of philosophy as a 'way of salvation' showing itself again the conception usually originates either in a disbelief in Christian theology and the desire to find a substitute or, if it is shown by Christian thinkers, in the desire to find an acceptable approach to those who are no longer Christians. The believing Christian looks to religion to be the inspiration of his life and his guide to conduct rather than to philosophy, however interested he may be in the latter.

2. In my second volume I traced the history of philosophy in the Christian world up to the end of the thirteenth century, though I included John Duns Scotus (d. 1308), whose philosophy belongs rather with the great thirteenth-century systems than with the *via moderna* of the fourteenth century. The volume thus covered the Patristic period, the early mediaeval period and the period of constructive metaphysical thinking on the grand scale. The next period, that is to say, the late mediaeval period, has been sketched in the first part of the present volume.

This fourfold division of Christian philosophic thought from the beginning of the Christian era to the close of the Middle Ages is a traditional division, and it is, I think, justified and useful. But it is possible to make an even simpler division by saying that mediaeval philosophy falls into two main periods, the period preceding and the period following the introduction of the Aristotelian *corpus* to western Christendom. In any case I think that it is hardly possible to exaggerate the philosophic importance of this event, namely of the rediscovery of Aristotle. I am speaking primarily as a historian. Philosophers may differ in their evaluations of Aristotelian theories, but there is, I think, no ground for dispute concerning the importance of the rediscovery of Aristotle, considered as a historical event. Apart from the system of John Scotus Eriugena, of which little notice was taken, the early mediaevals possessed nothing which we should be likely to call a philosophical system; and in particular they had no intimate knowledge of any system which owed nothing to Christianity. But the rediscovery of Aristotle and the translation of the leading Islamic thinkers in the second half of the twelfth century and the first part of the thirteenth brought to the knowledge of the Christian mediaeval thinkers for the first time a developed system which was the work of a pagan philosopher and which owed nothing to Christianity. Aristotle therefore naturally tended to mean for them 'philosophy'. It is a great mistake to allow the obstinacy with which some Renaissance Scholastics clung to the physical and scientific ideas of Aristotle to make one think of the discovery of Aristotle as a philosophical disaster. In the Middle Ages Aristotle was, indeed, known as 'the philosopher', and he was so named because his system was for the mediaevals 'philosophy' to all intents and purposes. But his system meant for them 'philosophy' not so much because it was Aristotelian, in the sense in which we distinguish Aristotelianism from Platonism, Stoicism, Epicureanism or neo-Platonism, as because it was the one great system of philosophy of which they possessed an extensive knowledge. It is important to realize this fact. If we speak, for example, of the attempt of St. Thomas to reconcile Aristotelianism with Christian theology, one will realize the nature of the situation better if one makes the experiment of substituting the word 'philosophy' for the word 'Aristotelianism'. When some of the theologians in the thirteenth century adopted a hostile attitude to Aristotle and regarded his philosophy as being in many respects an intellectual menace, they were rejecting independent philosophy in the name of the Christian faith. And when St. Thomas adopted in great measure the Aristotelian system, he was giving a charter to philosophy. He should not be regarded as burdening Christian thought with the system of a particular Greek philosopher. The deeper significance of his action was that he recognized the rights and position of philosophy as a rational study distinct from theology.

It is as well, too, to remind oneself of the fact that the utilization of the new learning in a constructive manner was due to men like St. Thomas and Duns Scotus who were primarily theologians. The rediscovery of Aristotle raised the problem of the relation between theology and philosophy in a form far more acute than it had previously assumed in the Middle Ages. And the only people in the thirteenth century who made a serious attempt to cope with the problem constructively were the theologians. Those professors of the faculty of arts who are often known as the 'Latin Averroists' tended to accept the entire philosophy of Aristotle, as it stood or as interpreted by Averroes, in a slavish manner. And when taxed with the fact that some of Aristotle's doctrines were incompatible with Christian theology, they answered that the philosopher's business is simply to report philosophical opinions. If they were sincere in giving this answer, they equated philosophy with the history of philosophy. If they were not sincere, they accepted

Aristotle in an uncritical and slavish manner. In either case they adopted no constructive attitude. Theologians like St. Thomas on the other hand endeavoured to synthesize Aristotelianism, which, as I have said, meant to all intents and purposes 'philosophy', with the Christian religion. This was not, however, a mere attempt to force Aristotle into a Christian mould, as some critics imagine: it involved a rethinking and development of the Aristotelian philosophy. St. Thomas's work was not a work of ignorant distortion but of original construction. He did not assume the truth of Aristotelianism because it was Aristotelianism and then try to force it into a Christian mould. He was convinced that Aristotelianism, in its main lines, was the result of sound reasoning; and when he attacked the monopsychistic doctrine of the Averroists he attacked it partly on the ground that Averroes had, in his opinion, misinterpreted Aristotle and partly on the ground that monopsychism was false and that it could be shown to be false by philosophic reasoning. It is the second ground which is the most important. If a philosophical theory was incompatible with Christian theology, St. Thomas believed that it was false. But he was well aware that from the philosophic point of view it is not sufficient to say that a theory is false because it is incompatible with Christianity. He was also aware that it is not sufficient to argue that it rested on a misinterpretation of Aristotle. His primary task was to show that the theory rested on bad or inconclusive reasoning. In other words, his rethinking of Aristotelianism was a philosophic rethinking: it did not simply take the form of confronting Aristotelian and supposedly Aristotelian theories with Christian theology and eliminating or changing theories which were incompatible with that theology without any philosophical argument. He was quite prepared to meet both the integral Aristotelians and the anti-Aristotelians on their own ground, namely on an appeal to reasoning. In so doing he developed philosophy as a separate branch of study, separate, that is, from theology on the one hand and from a mere reporting of the words of Aristotle on the other.

One can say, then, that it was due to the rediscovery of Aristotle coupled with the work of the thirteenth-century theologian-philosophers that mediaeval philosophy attained adult stature. Knowledge of the metaphysical and physical works of Aristotle widened the mediaevals' conception of philosophy, which could no longer be looked upon as more or less equivalent to dialectic.

Aristotelianism was thus a fecundating principle of prime importance in the growth of mediaeval philosophy. It is doubtless regrettable that Aristotelian science, especially Aristotelian astronomy, should have come to be accorded the degree of respect which it won for itself in certain quarters; but this does not alter the fact that Aristotle the philosopher was very far from being a paralysing weight and burden round the necks of the mediaeval thinkers. Without him mediaeval philosophy would scarcely have been able to advance as rapidly as it did. For study of the works of Aristotle not only raised the general standard of philosophic thinking and analysis but also greatly extended the field of study of the mediaeval philosophers. For example, knowledge of Aristotle's psychological and epistemological theories led to a prolonged reflection on these themes. And when Aristotle's general position was accepted, as by St. Thomas, new problems arose or old problems were rendered more acute. For if there are no innate ideas and our ideas are formed in dependence on sense-perception, the question arises, how is metaphysics possible, in so far as metaphysics involves thinking and speaking of beings which transcend matter. And what meaning can be attached to terms descriptive of transcendent beings? St. Thomas was aware of these problems and of their origin and he gave some consideration to them, while Scotus also was aware of the need for providing some theoretical justification of metaphysics. Again it is arguable that Aristotle's 'empiricism' was one of the influences which gave rise in the fourteenth century to lines of criticism which tended to undermine the metaphysical systems which had themselves been built on Aristotle's ideas. In fine, whatever one's estimation of the value of Aristotle's theories may be, it is hardly possible to deny the fact that the mediaevals' knowledge of his philosophy acted as a most powerful and wide-ranging influence in stimulating philosophic thought in the Middle Ages. When his ideas came to have a deadening effect on thought, this was due simply to the fact that the living and creative movement of thought which had originally been stimulated by his writings had spent itself, for the time being at least.

But if one emphasizes the importance of Aristotelianism for mediaeval philosophy, one must also remember that the theologian-philosophers of the thirteenth century deepened it considerably from the metaphysical point of view. Aristotle himself was concerned to explain the *how* of the world, that is to say, certain features of the world, especially change or becoming or 'movement'. With a philosopher like St. Thomas, however, there was a shift of emphasis: the problem of the *that* of the world, the problem that is, of the existence of finite beings, became primary. It is perfectly true, of course, as M. Gilson has shown with his customary lucidity, that the Judaeo-Christian doctrine of creation directed attention to this subject; and this obviously took place long before the time of St. Thomas. But the latter gave expression to the primacy of this problem for the Christian metaphysician in his theory of the distinction between essence and existence (or rather in his use of the distinction, since he did not invent it). It is possible, therefore, to call the philosophy of St. Thomas an 'existential' philosophy in a sense in which one can hardly call Aristotle's philosophy 'existential'.

3. The mediaevals always had some knowledge of the Aristotelian logic. And at the time when philosophy meant for most people little more than logic or dialectic it was perfectly understandable that philosophy should be widely regarded as being, in a famous phrase, 'the handmaid of theology'. Logic, according to Aristotle's own view, is an instrument of reasoning, and in the early Middle Ages there was not very much outside the theological sphere to which this instrument could be applied. Although, then, a distinction was drawn between faith and reason, that is, between truths accepted on authority and believed by faith and truths which were accepted as the result of demonstration, the problem of the relation of philosophy to theology was not acute. But when the Aristotelian system as a whole became known in the Christian universities the province of philosophy was extended far beyond the sphere of dialectic. The rise of natural or philosophic theology (which had, of course, its roots in the writings of St. Anselm) and of natural philosophy or cosmology, together with metaphysical psychology, introduced the idea of philosophy as a branch of study distinct from theology and from what would now be called 'science'. It followed, therefore, that Christian thinkers had to give their attention to the proper relation of philosophy to theology.

St. Thomas's views on this matter have been outlined in the second volume of this history, and I do not propose to repeat them here. Let it be sufficient to recall that he gave a charter to philosophy and recognized its intrinsic independence. Naturally, St. Thomas, as a believing Christian, was convinced that a philosophic theory which was incompatible with Christianity was false, for he was far from entertaining the absurd idea that two contradictory propositions could be true at the same time. But, given the truth of Christianity, he was convinced that it could always be shown that a philosophic proposition which was incompatible with Christianity was the result of bad or specious arguments. Philosophers as individual thinkers might go wrong in their reasoning and contradict revealed truth; but philosophy itself could not do so. There is no such thing as an infallible philosopher; but, if there were, his conclusions would always be in harmony with revealed truth, though he would arrive at his conclusions independently of the data of revelation.

This was, of course, a very tidy and convenient view of the relation of philosophy to theology. But one must remark in addition that according to St. Thomas the metaphysician, while unable to demonstrate the revealed mysteries of Christianity, like the Trinity, is able to demonstrate or establish with certainty the 'preambles of faith', such as the existence of a God capable of revealing truths to men. In the fourteenth century, however, as we have seen in the first part of the present volume, a number of philosophers began to question the validity of proofs which St. Thomas had accepted as valid proofs of the 'preambles of faith', that is, as demonstrations of the rational foundations of faith. Their right to criticize any given proof could hardly be questioned legitimately; for analysis and criticism are essential to philosophy. If a philosopher thought, for example, that the principle *omne quod movetur ab alio movetur* could not bear the weight laid on it in St. Thomas's first argument for God's existence, he had every right to say so. On the other hand, if a philosopher questioned the validity of all the proofs for God's existence, it was hardly possible to maintain the close relation between philosophy and theology asserted by St. Thomas, and the problems of the rationality of faith became acute. But no really serious consideration was given to this problem in the fourteenth century. A theologian-philosopher like William of Ockham could question the validity of metaphysical proofs for God's existence without going on to inquire seriously either what the true nature of arguments for God's existence is or what is the rational ground of our belief in God if His existence cannot be demonstrated in the traditional manner. Partly because so many of the leading 'nominalists' were themselves theologians, partly because the general mental background was still provided by Christianity, and partly because the attention of many philosophers was absorbed in logical and analytic problems (and, in Ockham's case, in political and ecclesiastical polemics) the problems raised by the nominalist criticism of traditional metaphysics were not fully grasped or sufficiently discussed. Theology and philosophy were tending to fall apart, but the fact was not clearly recognized.

4. In the first part of the present volume we saw how the *via moderna* spread in the fourteenth and fifteenth centuries. We also saw how in the fourteenth century there were anticipations at least of a new scientific outlook, which developed with striking rapidity at the time of the Renaissance. If the pre-Socratic philosophers discovered Nature, in the sense that they formed the idea of a cosmos or law-governed system, the Renaissance scientists discovered Nature in the sense that they developed the use of scientific method in the discovery of the 'laws' which actually govern natural events. To speak of laws governing Nature may well be open to objection; but the point is not that this or that language was used at the time or that this or that language ought to be used but rather that the Renaissance scientists developed the scientific study of Nature in a way in which it had never been developed before. This meant that physical science attained adult stature. It may have been often known as 'natural philosophy' or 'experimental philosophy', but, terminology apart, the fact remains that through the work of the Renaissance scientists science came to occupy a place of its own alongside theology and philosophy. And with the growth of modern science a great change has gradually taken place in the common estimation of what 'knowledge' is. In the Middle Ages theology and philosophy were universally regarded as 'sciences'; the great figures in university life were the theologians and the philosophers; and it was they who in general estimation were the possessors of knowledge. In the course of time, however, scientific knowledge in the modern sense has come to be popularly regarded as the norm and standard of knowledge; and in many countries neither theologians nor philosophers would be commonly regarded as possessing 'knowledge' in the sense in which scientists are thought to possess it. This attitude towards knowledge has arisen only gradually, of course, and its growth has been fostered by the development of applied and technical science. But the plain fact is that whereas in the Middle Ages philosophy was to all intents and purposes the sole representative of 'scientific'

knowledge outside the sphere of theology, in the post-Renaissance world rival claimants have arisen which in the estimation of many people have wrested from philosophy the title to represent knowledge at all. To mention this view of the matter in connection with Renaissance science is, of course, to anticipate, and it would be inappropriate to discuss the matter at length here. But I have mentioned it in order to show the great importance of the scientific development of the Renaissance period or, rather, one of the ways in which it was important for philosophy. If one can find in the rediscovery of Aristotle a dividing-line in mediaeval philosophy, one can also find in the growth of Renaissance science a dividing-line in the history of European thought.

In view of the fact that the older histories of philosophy were inclined to neglect mediaeval philosophy, of which they knew little, and practically to jump from Aristotle to Descartes, later historians have very rightly emphasized the continuity between Greek philosophy and Christian thought and between mediaeval philosophy and that of the post-Renaissance period. That Descartes, for example, was dependent on Scholasticism for many of his philosophical categories and ideas, that the mediaeval theory of natural law was utilized by Hooker and passed from him in a diluted form to Locke, and that the latter was more dependent on Aristotelianism than he probably realized are now matters of common knowledge among historians. But it is, I think, a mistake so to emphasize the element of continuity that the elements of novelty and change are slurred over. The climate of thought in the post-Renaissance world was not the same as that prevailing in the Middle Ages. The change was due, of course, to a number of different factors working together; but the rise of science was certainly not the least important of those factors. The development of science made it much easier than it formerly had been to consider the world from a point of view which had no obvious connection with theology. If one compares, for instance, St. Bonaventure or even St. Thomas with a philosopher like Descartes one finds at once a considerable difference of outlook and interest, in spite of the fact that all three men were believing Catholics. St. Bonaventure was principally interested in creatures in their relationship to God, as *vestigia Dei*, or in man's case, as the *imago Dei*. St. Thomas, owing to his Aristotelianism, shows a greater interest in creatures from a purely philosophical point of view; but he was above all things a theologian and it is obvious that his primary interest was that of a theologian and a specifically Christian thinker. In the case of Descartes, however, we find an outlook which, though it was the attitude of a man who was a Christian, was what one may call 'neutral' in character. In the post-Renaissance period there were, of course, philosophers who were atheists or at any rate non-Christian: one has only to think of some of the figures of the French Enlightenment. But my point is that after the Middle Ages philosophy tended to become 'lay' in character. A man like Descartes was certainly a good Christian; but one would hardly think of his philosophy as a specifically Christian philosophy, in spite of the influence of his religious beliefs on his philosophic thought. The rise of humanism at the time of the Renaissance, followed by the growth of science, produced fresh interests and lines of thought which, though not necessarily incompatible with theology, could be pursued without any obvious association with or relation to it. This is clear enough in the case of science itself, and the growth of science reacted on philosophy. Or perhaps it is better to say that both the science and the philosophy of the time manifested the growth of the new outlook and fostered it.

But if one stresses the difference between the mediaeval and Renaissance worlds in the climate of thought, it is necessary to qualify this emphasis by drawing attention to the gradual and in large part continuous evolution of the new outlook. A comparatively early mediaeval thinker like St. Anselm was chiefly interested in understanding the faith: for him the primacy of faith was obvious, and what we might call his philosophizing was largely an attempt to understand by the use of reason what we believe. *Credo, ut intelligam.* In the thirteenth century the rediscovery of Aristotelianism greatly widened the interests and horizons of Christian thinkers. Acceptance of Aristotle's physics, however erroneous many of his scientific theories may have been, paved the way for a study of the world for its own sake so to speak. A professional theologian like St. Thomas was naturally not interested in developing what we would call science, not because of any hostility towards such studies but because his interests lay elsewhere. But by the rediscovery of Aristotle and the translations of Greek and Arabic scientific works the ground was prepared for scientific advance. Already in the thirteenth century, and still more in the fourteenth century, we can see the beginning of a scientific investigation of Nature. The ferment of Renaissance philosophy, with its mixture of philosophic speculation and scientific hypothesis, further prepared the way for the rise of Renaissance science. One can say, then, that the rediscovery of Aristotle in the Middle Ages was the remote preparation for the rise of science. But one can, of course, go further still and say that the Christian doctrine of the world's creation by God provided a theological preparation for the advance of science. For if the world is a creation, and if matter is not evil but good, the material world is obviously worth scientific investigation. But scientific investigation could not develop until the right method was found; and for that Christian Europe had to wait many centuries.

The foregoing remarks may possibly sound like an endorsement of Auguste Comte's doctrine of the three stages, as though I meant to say that the theological stage was followed by the philosophical and the philosophical by the scientific stage, in the sense that the later stage supplanted the former, both *de facto* and *de iure*. In regard to the historical facts it has been argued that the development of Greek thought proceeded in the very opposite direction to that demanded by Comte's theory.[1] For the movement was from a primitive 'scientific' stage through metaphysics to theology, rather than from theology through metaphysics to science. However, the development of thought in western Christianity can be used to a certain extent in support of Comte's theory, in so far as the historical facts are concerned. For it might be argued that the primacy of theology was succeeded by a stage characterized by 'lay' philosophical systems, and that this stage has been succeeded by a positivist stage. An interpretation of this sort is certainly open to the objection that it is based on aspects of the development of thought which have been selected in order to support a preconceived theory. For it is clear that the development of Scholastic philosophy did not simply follow the development of Scholastic theology: to a great extent the two developed together. Again, the rise of science in the post-Renaissance world was contemporaneous with a succession of philosophic systems. However, it does seem that at any rate a plausible case can be made out in favour of Comte's interpretation of western thought since the beginning of Christianity. It makes some sense at least to distinguish the Age of Faith, the Age of Reason and the Age of Science, if one is speaking of climates of thought. In the Middle

[1] On this subject *The Christian Challenge to Philosophy* by W. H. V. Reade (London, 1951) can profitably be consulted.

Ages religious faith and theology shaped the climate of thought; at the time of the 'Enlightenment' wide sections of the intellectual public placed their trust in 'reason' (though the use of the word 'reason' in this connection stands in need of careful analysis); and in the modern world a positivist climate of thought prevails in a number of countries if one understands 'positivist' and 'positivism' in a wide sense. Yet even if a plausible case can be made out for Comte's theory from the historical point of view, it certainly does not follow that the succession of stages, in so far as there actually was a succession of stages, constitutes a 'progress' in any but a temporal sense of the word 'progress'. In one period theology may be the paramount branch of study and in another period science; but a change in the climate of thought from a theological to a scientific period does not mean that theology is false or that a scientific civilization is an adequate realization of the potentialities of human culture.

It is, however, fairly obvious now that science cannot disprove the validity of faith or of theological beliefs. Physics, for example, has nothing to say about the Trinity or about the existence of God. If many people have ceased to believe in Christianity, this does not show that Christianity is false. And, in general, the relation of science to religion and theology is not one of acute tension: the tension which in the last century was often alleged to exist between them does not really exist at all. The theoretical difficulty arises rather in regard to the relation of philosophy to theology. And this tension existed in germ once philosophy had attained to adult stature. It did not become obvious as long as the leading philosophers were also theologians; but once the rise of science had directed men's thought in fresh directions and philosophers were no longer primarily theologians the tension was bound to become apparent. As long as philosophers thought that they were able to build up a true metaphysical system by a method of their own, the tension tended to take the form of a tension between divergent conclusions and propositions. But now that a considerable number of philosophers believe that the philosopher has no method of his own the employment of which is capable of adding to human knowledge, and that all factual knowledge is derivable from immediate observation and from the sciences, the problem is rather one concerning the rational foundations of faith. In this sense we are back in the situation created in the fourteenth century by the nominalist criticism of traditional metaphysics, though the nature of the problem is clearer now than it was then. Is there such a thing as a valid metaphysical argument? Can there be metaphysical knowledge and, if so, what sort of knowledge is it? Have we 'blind' faith on the one hand and scientific knowledge on the other, or can metaphysics supply a kind of bridge between them? Questions of this sort were implicit in fourteenth-century nominalist criticism, and they are still with us. They have been rendered all the more acute, on the one hand by the constant growth of scientific knowledge since the time of the Renaissance and, on the other hand, by the succession of metaphysical systems in the post-Renaissance and modern worlds, leading to a prevailing mistrust of metaphysics in general. What is the rôle of philosophy? What is its proper relation to science? What is its proper relation to faith and religious belief?

These questions cannot be further developed or discussed now. My object in raising them is simply that of suggesting various points for reflection in considering the later development of philosophic thought. In the next volume I hope to treat of 'modern' philosophy from Descartes to Kant inclusive, and in connection with Kant we shall be faced with an explicit statement regarding these questions and their solution.

APPENDIX I

Honorific titles applied to philosophers treated of in this volume.

DURANDUS:	Doctor modernus, *later* Doctor resolutissimus.
PETRUS AUREOLI:	Doctor facundus.
WILLIAM OF OCKHAM:	Venerabilis inceptor.
ANTOINE ANDRÉ:	Doctor dulcifluus
FRANCIS DE MARCIA:	Doctor succinctus.
JOHN OF MIRECOURT:	Monachus albus.
GREGORY OF RIMINI:	Doctor authenticus.
JOHN RUYSBROECK:	Doctor admirabilis.
DENIS THE CARTHUSIAN:	Doctor ecstaticus.
JOHN GERSON:	Doctor christianissimus.
JAKOB BÖHME:	Philosophus teutonicus.
FRANCIS SUÁREZ:	Doctor eximius.

APPENDIX II

A SHORT BIBLIOGRAPHY

General Works

Boehner, Ph., O.F.M. *Medieval Logic.* Manchester, 1952.

Bréhier, E. *La philosophie du moyen âge*, nouvelle édition corrigée. Paris, 1949.

Histoire de la philosophie. tome 1, *L'antiquité et le moyen âge.* Paris, 1943. (A treatment of Renaissance philosophy is included in this volume.)

Burckhardt, J. *The Civilization of the Renaissance.* London, 1944.

Carlyle, R. W. and A. J. *A History of Mediaeval Political Theory in the West.* 6 vols. London, 1903–36.

Cassirer, E. *Individuum und Kosmos in der Philosophie der Renaissance.* Berlin, 1927.

Copleston, F. C. *Mediaeval Philosophy.* London, 1952.

Crombie, A. C. *Augustine to Galileo. The History of Science, A.D. 400–1650.* London, 1952. (Unfortunately this work appeared when the present volume was already in proof.)

Curtis, S. J. *A Short History of Western Philosophy in the Middle Ages.* London, 1950.

Dempf, A. *Die Ethik des Mittelalters.* Munich, 1930.

Metaphysik des Mittelalters. Munich, 1930.

De Wulf, M. *Histoire de la philosophie médiévale.* tome 3, *Aprés le treizième siècle.* Louvain, 1947 (6th edition).

Dilthey, W. *Gesammelte Schriften*, vol. 2 (for Renaissance). Berlin and Leipzig, 1919.

Frischeisen-Köhler, M. and Moog, W. *Die Philosophie der Neuzeit bis zum Ende des XVIII Jahrhunderts.* Berlin, 1924. (This is the third volume of the revised Ueberweg and covers the Renaissance period.)

Geyer, B. *Die patristische und scholastische Philosophie.* Berlin, 1928. (This is the second volume of the revised edition of Ueberweg.)

Gilson, É. *La philosophie au moyen âge.* Paris, 1944. (2nd edition, revised and augmented.)

The Unity of Philosophical Experience. London, 1938.

Being and Some Philosophers. Toronto, 1949.

L'être et l'essence. Paris, 1948.

Grabmann, M. *Die Philosophie des Mittelalters.* Berlin, 1921.

Mittelalterliches Geistesleben. 2 vols. Munich, 1926 and 1936.

Hauréau, B. *Histoire de la Philosophie scolastique.* 3 vols. Paris, 1872–80.

Hawkins, D. J. B. *A Sketch of Mediaeval Philosophy.* London, 1946.

Hirschberger, J. *Geschichte der Philosophie. I, Altertum und Mittelalter.* Freiburg i. B., 1949.

Picavet, F. *Esquisse d'une histoire générale et comparée des philosophies médiévales.* Paris, 1907 (2nd edition).

Essais sur l'histoire générale et comparée des théologies et des philosophies médiévales. Paris, 1913.

Poole, R. L. *Illustrations of the History of Medieval Thought and Learning.* London, 1920 (2nd edition).

Romeyer, B. *La philosophie chrétienne jusqu'à Descartes.* 3 vols. Paris, 1935–7.

Ruggiero, G. de. *La filosofia del Cristianesimo.* 3 vols. Bari.

Rinascimento, Riforma e Contrariforma. Bari, 1937.

Vignaux, P. *La pensée au moyen âge.* Paris, 1938.

Chapter II: Durandus and Petrus Aureoli

Texts

Durandus

In 4 libros Sententiarum. Various sixteenth-century editions (of 3rd redaction), beginning with the Paris edition of 1508.

Durandi de S. Porciano O.P. Quaestio de natura cognitionis et Disputatio cum anonymo quodam necnon Determinatio Hervaei Natalis O.P. J. Koch (edit.). Münster, 1929; 2nd edition 1929 (Opuscula et textus, 6).

Durandus de S. Porciano, Tractatus de habitibus. Quaestio 4: De subiectis habituum, addita quaestione critica anonymi cuiusdam. J. Koch (edit.). Münster, 1930 (Opuscula et textus, 8).

Petrus Aureoli

In 4 libros Sententiarum. Rome, 1596.

Studies

Dreiling, R. *Der Konzeptualismus in der Universalienfrage des Franziskanererzbischofs Petrus Aureoli (Pierre d'Auriole).* Münster, 1913 (Beiträge, 11, 6.)

Koch, J. *Jakob von Metz, O.P.* Archives d'histoire doctrinale et littéraire du moyen âge, 1929–30 (pp. 169–232).

Durandus de Sancto Porciano O.P. Forschungen zum Streit um Thomas von Aquin zu Beginn des 14 Jahrhunderts, Erster Teil, Literargeschichtliche Grundlegung. Münster, 1927 (Beiträge 26, 1).

Kraus, J. *Die Universalienlehre des Oxforder Kanzlers Heinrich von Harclay in ihrer Mittelstellung zwischen skotistischen Realismus und ockhamistischen Nominalismus.* Divus Thomas (Fribourg, Switzerland), vol. 10 (1932), pp. 36–58 and 475–508 and vol. 11 (1933), pp. 288–314.

Pelster, F. *Heinrich von Harclay, Kanzler von Oxford, und seine Quästionen.* Miscellanea F. Ehrle, vol. 1, pp. 307–56. Rome, 1924.

Teetaert, A. *Pierre Auriol.* Dictionnaire de théologie catholique, vol. 12, cols. 1810–81. Paris, 1934.

Chapters III–VIII: William of Ockham

Texts

Super quattuor libros sententiarum subtilissimae quaestiones. Lyons, 1495.

Quodlibeta septem. Paris, 1487; Strasbourg, 1491.

Expositio aurea et admodum utilis super artem veterem. Bologna, 1496.

Summa totius logicae. Paris, 1948, and other editions, especially: *Summa Logicae. Pars prima.* Ph. Boehner, O.F.M. (edit.). St. Bonaventure, New York, and Louvain, 1951.

Summulae in libros Physicorum. Bologna, 1495 and other editions.

Quaestio prima principalis Prologi in primum librum sententiarum cum interpretatione Gabrielis Biel. Ph. Boehner, O.F.M. (edit.). Paderborn, 1939.

The Tractatus de successivis, attributed to William Ockham. Ph. Boehner, O.F.M. (edit.). St. Bonaventure (New York), 1944.

The Tractatus de praedestinatione et de praescientia Dei et de futuris contingentibus of William Ockham. Ph. Boehner, O.F.M. (edit.). St. Bonaventure (New York), 1945. (This edition also contains a 'Study on the Mediaeval Problem of a Three-valued logic' by the editor.)

Ockham: Selected Philosophical Writings. Ph. Boehner, O.F.M. (edit.). London, 1952.

Gulielmi de Occam Breviloquium de potestate papae (critical edition). L. Baudry (edit.). Paris, 1937.

Gulielmi de Ockham Opera politica, vol. 1. J. O. Sikes (edit.). Manchester, 1940.

Studies

Abbagnano, N. *Guglielmo di Ockham.* Lanciano, 1931.

Amann, E. *Occam.* Dictionnaire de théologie catholique, vol. 11, cols. 864–904. Paris, 1931.

Baudry, L. *Guillaume d'Occam. Sa vie, ses œuvres, ses idées sociales et politiques. I, L'homme et les œuvres.* Paris, 1949.

Boehner, Ph., O.F.M. *Ockham's Theory of Truth.* Franciscan Studies, 1945, pp. 138–61.

Ockham's Theory of Signification. Franciscan Studies, 1946, pp. 143–70.

Carré, H. M. *Realists and Nominalists* (pp. 101–25). Oxford, 1946.

Giacón, C. *Guglielmo di Occam.* 2 vols. Milan, 1941.

Guelluy, R. *Philosophie et théologie chez Guillaume d'Ockham.* Louvain, 1947.

Hamann, A., O.F.M. *La doctrine de l'église et de l'état chez Occam.* Paris, 1942.

Hochstetter, E. *Studien zur Metaphysik und Erkenntnislehre des Wilhelms von Ockham.* Berlin, 1937.

Lagarde, G. de *Naissance de l'esprit laïque au déclin du moyen âge.*
Cahier IV: *Ockham et son temps.* 1942.
V: *Ockham. Bases de départ.* 1946.
VI: *Ockham. La morale et le droit.* 1946.

Martin, G. *Wilhelm von Ockham. Untersuchungen zur Ontologie der Ordnungen.* Berlin, 1949.

Moody, E. A. *The Logic of William of Ockham.* London, 1935.

Vignaux, P. *Nominalisme.* Dictionnaire de théologie catholique, vol. 11, cols. 748–84. Paris, 1931.

Zuidema, S. U. *De Philosophie van Occam in zijn Commentaar op de Sententiën.* 2 vols. Hilversum, 1936.

Chapter IX: The Ockhamist Movement: John of Mirecourt and Nicholas of Autrecourt.

Texts

John of Mirecourt

Birkenmaier, A. *Ein Rechtfertigungsschreiben Johanns von Mirecourt.* Münster, 1922 (Beiträge, 20, 5).

Stegmüller, F. *Die zwei Apologien des Jean de Mirecourt.* Recherches de théologie ancienne et médiévale 1933, pp. 40–79, 192–204.

Nicholas of Autrecourt

Lappe, J. *Nikolaus von Autrecourt.* Münster, 1908 (Beiträge, 6, 1). (This contains correspondence between Nicholas and Bernard of Arezzo and between Nicholas and Giles.)

O'Donnell, J. R. *Nicholas of Autrecourt.* Mediaeval Studies, 1 (1939), pp. 179–280. (This contains an edition of the *Exigit.*)

Studies

Lang, A. *Die Wege der Glaubensbegründung bei den Scholastikern des 14 Jahrhunderts.* Münster, 1931 (Beiträge, 30, 1–2).

Lappe, J. See above.

Michalski, C. *Les courants philosophiques à Oxford et à Paris pendant le XIVe siècle.* Bulletin de l'Académie polonaise des Sciences et des Lettres, 1920 (separately, Cracow, 1921).

Les sources du criticisme et du scepticisme dans la philosophie du XIVe siècle. Cracow, 1924.

Michalski, C. *Le criticisme et le scepticisme dans la philosophie du XIVe siècle.* Bulletin de l'Académie polonaise des Sciences et des Lettres, 1925 (separately, Cracow, 1926).

Les courants critiques et sceptiques dans la philosophie du XIVe siècle. Cracow, 1927.

O'Donnell, J. R. *The Philosophy of Nicholas of Autrecourt and his appraisal of Aristotle.* Mediaeval Studies, 4 (1942) pp. 97–125.

Ritter, G. *Studien zur Spätscholastik*, 2 vols. Heidelberg, 1921–2.

Vignaux, P. *Nominalisme.* Dictionnaire de théologie catholique, vol. 11, cols. 748–84. Paris, 1931.

Nicholas d'Autrecourt, ibid., cols. 561–87.

Weinberg, J. R. *Nicholas of Autrecourt. A Study in 14th-century Thought.* Princeton, 1948.

Chapter X: The Scientific Movement

Texts

Buridan

Johannis Buridani Quaestiones super libros quattuor de coelo et mundo. A. E. Moody (edit.). Cambridge (Mass.), 1942.

Quaestiones super octo libros physicorum Aristotelis. Paris, 1509.

In metaphysicen Aristotelis quaestiones. Paris, 1480, 1518.

Summulae logicae. Lyons, 1487.

Quaestiones et decisiones physicales insignium virorum Alberti de Saxonia, Thimonis, Buridani. Paris, 1516, 1518. (Contains Buridan's *Quaestiones in libros de Anima* and his *Quaestiones* on Aristotle's *Parva naturalia.*)

Albert of Saxony

Quaestiones super artem veterem. Bologna, 1496.

Quaestiones subtilissimae Alberti de Saxonia super libros Posteriorum. Venice, 1497.

Logica. Venice, 1522.

Sophismata Alberti de Saxonia. Paris, 1489.

Quaestiones in libros de coelo et mundo. Pavia, 1481.

Subtilissimae quaestiones super octo libros physicorum. Padua, 1493.

Quaestiones in libros de generatione (contained in work mentioned last under *Buridan*).

Marsilius of Inghen

Quaestiones Marsilii super quattuor libros sententiarum. Strasbourg, 1501.

Abbreviationes super VIII libros. Venice, 1521.

Egidius cum Marsilio et Alberto de generatione. Venice, 1518.

Nicholas of Oresme

Maistre Nicole Oresme: Le livre du ciel et du monde. A. D. Menut and A. J. Denomy (edit.). Mediaeval Studies, 1941 (pp. 185–280), 1942 (pp. 159–297), 1943 (pp. 167–333). (This Text and Commentary has been published separately. Date unstated.)

Studies

Bochert, E. *Die Lehre von der Bewegung bei Nicolaus Oresme.* Münster, 1934 (Beiträge, 31, 3).

Duhem, P. *Le syèstme du monde: histoire des doctrines cosmologiques de Platon à Copernic.* 5 vols. Paris, 1913–17.

Études sur Léonard de Vinci. 3 vols. Paris, 1906–13.

Haskins, C. H. *Studies in the History of Mediaeval Science.* Cambridge (Mass.), 1924.

Heidingsfelder, G. *Albert von Sachsen.* Münster, 1926 (Beiträge 22, 3–4).

Maier, A. *Das Problem der intensiven Grösse in der Scholastik.* Leipzig, 1939.

Die Impetustheorie der Scholastik. Vienna, 1940.

An der Grenzen von Scholastik und Naturwissenschaft. Studien zur Naturphilosophie des 14 Jahrhunderts. Essen, 1943.

Die Vorläufer Galileis im 14 Jahrhundert. Rome, 1949.

Michalski, C. *La physique nouvelle et les différents courants philosophiques au XIVe siècle.* Bulletin de l'Académie polonaise des Sciences et des Lettres, 1927 (separately, Cracow, 1928).

Moody, E. A. *John Buridan and the Habitability of the Earth.* Speculum, 1941, pp. 415–25.

Ritter, G. *Studien zur Spätscholastik.* Vol 1, *Marsilius von Inghen und die okkamistischc Schule in Deutschland.* Heidelberg, 1921.

Sarton, G. *Introduction to the History of Science.* 3 vols. Washington, 1927–48.

Thorndike, L. *A History of Magic and Experimental Science.* Vols. 3–4, *The fourteenth and fifteenth centuries.* New York, 1934.

Chapter XI: Marsilius of Padua

Texts

The Defensor Pacis of Marsilius of Padua. C. W. Previté-Orton (edit.). Cambridge, 1928.

Marsilius von Padua, Defensor Pacis. R. Scholz (edit.). Hannover, 1933.

Studies

Checchini, A. and Bobbio, N. (edit.). *Marsilio da Padova, Studi raccolti nel VI centenario della morte.* Padua, 1942.

Gewirth, A. *Marsilius of Padua. The Defender of Peace.* Vol. 1, *Marsilius of Padua and Medieval Political Philosophy.* New York, 1951.

Lagarde, G. de *Naissance de l'esprit laïque au déclin du moyen âge.* Cahier II: *Marsile de Padoue.* Paris, 1948.

Previté-Orton, C. W. *Marsiglio of Padua.* Part II: *Doctrines.* English Historical Review, 1923, pp. 1–18.

Chapter XII: Speculative Mysticism

Texts

Eckhart

Meister Eckhart. Die deutschen und lateinischen Werke herausgegeben im Auftrage der Deutschen Forschungsgemeinschaft. Stuttgart, 1936 (in course of publication).

Magistri Eckhardi Opera latina auspiciis Instituti Sanctae Sabinae ad codicum fidem edita. Leipzig.

I. *Super oratione dominica.* R. Klibansky (edit.). 1934.

II. *Opus tripartitum: Prologi.* H. Bascour, O.S.B. (edit.). 1935.

III. *Quaestiones Parisienses.* A. Dondaine, O.P. (edit.). 1936.

Eine lateinische Rechtfertigungsschrift des Meister Eckhart. A. Daniels (edit.). Münster, 1923 (Beiträge, 23, 5).

Meister Eckhart. Das System seiner religiösen Lehre und Lebensweisheit. Textbuch aus den gedrückten und ungedrückten Quellen mit Einführung. O. Karrer (edit.). Munich, 1926.

Tauler

Die Predigten Taulers. F. Vetter (edit.). Berlin, 1910.

Sermons de Tauler. 3 vols. E. Hugueny, P. Théry and A. L. Corin (edit.). Paris, 1927, 1930, 1935.

Bl. Henry Suso

Heinrich Seuse. Deutsche Schriften. K. Bihlmeyer (edit.). 2 vols. Stuttgart, 1907.

L'œuvre mystique de Henri Suso. Introduction et traduction. 4 vols. B. Lavaud, O.P. Fribourg, Switzerland, 1946–7.

Blessed Henry Suso's Little Book of Eternal Wisdom. R. Raby (translator). London, 1866 (2nd edition).

The Life of Blessed Henry Suso by Himself. T. F. Knox (translator). London, 1865.

Ruysbroeck

Jan van Ruusbroec. Werke. Nach der Standardschrift von Groenendal herausgegeben von der Ruusbroec—Gesellschaft in Antwerpen. 2nd edition. 4 vols. Cologne, 1950.

Gerson

Johannis Gersonii opera omnia. 5 vols. M. E. L. Du Pin (edit.). Antwerp, 1706.

Jean Gerson, Commentateur Dionysien. Les Notulae super quaedam verba Dionysii de Caelesti Hierarchia. A. Combes. Paris, 1940.

Six Sermons français inédits de Jean Gerson. L. Mourin (edit.). Paris, 1946.

Studies

Bernhart, J. *Die philosophische Mystik des Mittelalters von ihren antiken Ursprungen bis zur Renaissance.* Munich, 1922.

Bizet, J. A. *Henri Suso et le déclin de la scolastique.* Paris, 1946.

Brigué, L. *Ruysbroeck.* Dictionnaire de théologie catholique, vol. 14, cols. 408–20. Paris, 1938.

Bühlmann, J. *Christuslehre und Christusmystik des Heinrich Seuse.* Lucerne, 1942.

Combes, A. *Jean de Montreuil et le chancelier Gerson.* Paris, 1942.

Connolly, J. L. *John Gerson, Reformer and Mystic.* Louvain, 1928.

Della Volpe, G. *Il misticismo speculativo di maestro Eckhart nei suoi rapporti storici.* Bologna, 1930.

Dempf, A. *Meister Eckhart. Eine Einführung in sein Werk.* Leipzig, 1934.

Denifle, H. *Das geistliche Leben. Deutsche Mystiker des 14 Jahrhunderts.* Salzburg, 1936 (9th edition by A. Auer).

Hornstein, X. de *Les grands mystiques allemands du XIVᵉ siècle. Eckhart, Tauler, Suso.* Lucerne, 1920.

Wautier D'Aygalliers, A. *Ruysbroeck l'Admirable.* Paris, 1923.

Chapter XIII: The Revival of Platonism

Texts

Erasmus. *Opera.* 10 vols. Leyden, 1703–6.

Letters. Latin edition by P. S. Allen, H. S. Allen, H. W. Garrod. 11 vols. Oxford, 1906–47.

Leone Ebreo. *The Philosophy of Love.* F. Friedeberg-Sealey and J. H. Barnes (translators). London, 1937.

Marsilii Ficini Opera. 2 vols. Paris, 1641.

Pico della Mirandola, G. *Opera omnia.* 2 vols. Basle, 1573.
The Renaissance Philosophy of Man (*Petrarca, Valla, Ficino, Pico, Pomponazzi, Vives*). E. Cassirer, P. O. Kristeller, J. H. Randall, Jr. (edit.). Chicago, 1948.

Studies

Burckhardt, J. *The Civilization of the Renaissance.* London, 1944.
Della Torre, A. *Storia dell' academia platonica di Firenze.* Florence, 1902.
Dress, W. *Die Mystik des Marsilio Ficino.* Berlin, 1929.
Dulles, A. *Princeps concordiae. Pico della Mirandola and the Scholastic Tradition.* Cambridge (Mass.), 1941.
Festugière, J. *La philosophie de l'amour de Marsile Ficin.* Paris, 1941.
Garin, E. *Giovanni Pico della Mirandola.* Florence, 1937.
Gentile, G. *Il pensiero italiano del rinascimento.* Florence, 1940 (3rd edit.).
Hak, H. *Marsilio Ficino.* Amsterdam, Paris, 1934.
Hönigswald, R. *Denker der italienischen Renaissance. Gestalten und Probleme.* Basle, 1938.
Taylor, H. O. *Thought and Expression in the Sixteenth Century.* New York, 1920.
Trinkaus, C. E. *Adversity's Noblemen: The Italian Humanists on Happiness.* New York, 1940.
Woodward, W. H. *Studies in Education during the Age of the Renaissance.* Cambridge, 1906.

Chapter XIV: Aristotelianism

Texts

Laurentius Valla. *Dialecticae disputationes contra Aristotelicos*, 1499. (*Opera.* Basle, 1540.)
Rudolf Agricola. *De inventione dialectica.* Louvain, 1515; and other editions.
Marius Nizolius. *De veris principiis et vera ratione philosophandi contra pseudophilosophos libri IV.* Parma, 1553 (edited by Leibniz under the title *Antibarbarus philosophicus*, Frankfurt, 1671 and 1674).
Petrus Ramus. *Dialecticae partitiones.* Paris, 1543.
Aristotelicae animadversiones. Paris, 1543.
Dialectique. Paris, 1555.
Alexander Achillini. *De universalibus.* Bologna, 1501.
De intelligentiis. Venice, 1508.
De distinctionibus. Bologna, 1518.

Pietro Pomponazzi. *Opera*. Basle, 1567.
Melanchthon. *Opera*. C. G. Bretschneider and H. E. Bindseil (edit.). 28 vols. Halle, 1824–60.
Supplementa Melanchthonia. Leipzig, 1910–
Montaigne. *Essais*. Numerous editions, the most complete being by F. Strowski, P. Gebelin and P. Villey (5 vols.), 1906–33.
Sanchez. *Tractatus philosophici*. Rotterdam, 1649.

Studies

Batistella, R. M. *Nizolio*. Treviso, 1905.
Cassirer, E., Kristeller, P. O. and Randall, J. H. (edit.). *The Renaissance Philosophy of Man (Petrarca, Valla, Ficino, Pico, Pomponazzi, Vives)*. Chicago, 1948.
Douglas, C. and Hardie, R. P. *The Philosophy and Psychology of Pietro Pomponazzi*. Cambridge, 1910.
Friedrich, H. *Montaigne*. Berne, 1949.
Giarratano, C. *Il pensiero di Francesco Sanchez*. Naples, 1903.
Graves, F. P. *Peter Ramus and the Educational Reformation of the 16th Century*. London, 1912.
Hönigswald, R. *Denker der italienischen Renaissance. Gestalten und Probleme*. Basle, 1938.
Moreau, P. *Montaigne, l'homme et l'œuvre*. Paris, 1939.
Owen, J. *The Sceptics of the Italian Renaissance*. London, 1893.
Petersen, P. *Geschichte der aristotelischen Philosophie im protestantischen Deutschland*. Leipzig, 1921.
Revista Portuguesa de Filosofia (1951; t. 7, fasc. 2). *Francisco Sanchez no IV Centenário do seu nascimento*. Braga, 1951. (Contains Bibliography of writings about Sanchez.)
Strowski, F. *Montaigne*. Paris, 1906.
Waddington, C. *De Petri Rami vita, scriptis, philosophia*. Paris, 1849.
Ramus, sa vie, ses écrits et ses opinions. Paris, 1855.

Chapter XV: Nicholas of Cusa

Texts

Nicolai de Cusa Opera Omnia iussu et auctoritate Academiae Heidelbergensis ad codicum fidem edita. Leipzig, 1932–
Opera. 3 vols. Paris, 1514. Basle, 1565.
Schriften, im Auftrag der Heidelberger Akademie der Wissenschaften in deutscher Uebersetzung herausgegeben von E. Hoffmann. Leipzig, 1936–
Philosophische Schriften. A. Petzelt (edit.). Vol. 1, Stuttgart, 1949.
De docta ignorantia libri tres. Testo latino con note di Paolo Rotta. Bari, 1913.

The Idiot. San Francisco, 1940.
Des Cardinals und Bischofs Nikolaus von Cusa wichtigste Schriften in deutscher Uebersetzung. F. A. Scharpff. Freiburg i. B., 1862.

Studies

Bett, H. *Nicholas of Cusa.* London, 1932.
Clemens, F. J. *Giordano Bruno und Nicolaus von Cues.* Bonn, 1847.
Gandillac, M. de *La philosophie de Nicolas de Cues.* Paris, 1941.
Gradi, R. *Il pensiero del Cusano.* Padua, 1941.
Jacobi, M. *Das Weltgebäude des Kard. Nikolaus von Cusa.* Berlin, 1904.
Koch, J. *Nicolaus von Cues und seine Umwelt.* 1948.
Mennicken, P. *Nikolaus von Kues.* Trier, 1950.
Rotta, P. *Il cardinale Niccolò di Cusa, la vita ed il pensiero.* Milan, 1928.
Niccolò Cusano. Milan, 1942.
Schultz, R. *Die Staatsphilosophie des Nikolaus von Kues.* Hain, 1948.
Vansteenberghe, E. *Le cardinal Nicolas de Cues.* Paris, 1920.
Autour de la docte ignorance. Münster, 1915 (Beiträge, 14, 2–4).

Chapters XVI–XVII: Philosophy of Nature

Texts

Cardano. *Hieronymi Cardani Mediolanensis philosophi et medici celeberrimi opera omnia.* 10 vols. Lyons, 1663.
Telesio. *De natura rerum iuxta propria principia.* Naples, 1586.
Patrizzi. *Discussiones peripateticae.* Basle, 1581.
Nova de universis philosophia. London, 1611.
Campanella. *Philosophia sensibus demonstrata.* Naples, 1590.
Prodromus philosophiae. Padua, 1611.
Atheismus triumphatus. Rome, 1630.
La città del sole. A Castaldo (edit.). Rome, 1910.
Bruno. *Opere italiane.* G. Gentile (edit.). Bari.
I. *Dialoghi metafisici.* 1907
II. *Dialoghi morali.* 1908.
Opera latine conscripta. I & II. Naples, 1880 and 1886.
III & IV. Florence, 1889 and 1891.
S. Greenberg. *The Infinite in G. Bruno. With a translation of Bruno's Dialogue: Concerning the Cause, Principle and One.* New York, 1950.
D. W. Singer. *G. Bruno: His Life and Thought. With a translation of*

Bruno's Work: On the Infinite Universe and Worlds. New York, 1950.

Gassendi. *Opera*. Lyons, 1658, Florence, 1727.

Paracelsus. *Four Treatises of Theophrastus von Hohenheim called Paracelsus*. H. E. Sigerist (edit.). Baltimore, 1941.

Paracelsus. *Selected Writings*. Edited with an Introduction by Jolande Jacobi. Translated by Norbert Guterman. London, 1951.

Van Helmont, J. B. *Opera*. Lyons, 1667.

Van Helmont, F. M. *Opuscula philosophica*. Amsterdam, 1690.
The paradoxical discourses of F. M. van Helmont. London, 1685.

Weigel. *Libellus de vita beata*. Halle, 1609.
Der güldene Griff. Halle, 1613.
Vom Ort der Welt. Halle, 1613.
Dialogus de christianismo. Halle, 1614.
Erkenne dich selbst. Neustadt, 1615.

Böhme. *Werke*. 7 vols. K. W. Schiebler (edit.). Leipzig, 1840–7 (2nd edition).
Works. C. J. Barber (edit.). London, 1909–

Studies

Blanchet, L. *Campanella*. Paris, 1920.

Boulting, W. *Giordano Bruno, His Life, Thought and Martyrdom*. London, 1914.

Cicuttini, L. *Giordano Bruno*. Milan, 1950.

Fiorentino, F. *Telesio, ossia studi storici sull 'idea della natura nel risorgimento italiano*. 2 vols. Florence, 1872–4.

Gentile, G. *Bruno e il pensiero del rinascimento*. Florence, 1920.

Greenberg, S. See under *Texts* (Bruno).

Hönigswald, R. *Denker der italienischen Renaissance. Gestalten und Probleme*. Basle, 1938.

McIntyre, J. L. *Giordano Bruno*. London, 1903.

Peip. A. *Jakob Böhme, der deutsche Philosoph*. Leipzig, 1850.

Penny, A. J. *Studies in Jakob Böhme*. London, 1912.
Introduction to the Study of Jacob Böhme's Writings. New York, 1901.

Sigerist, H. E. *Paracelsus in the Light of Four Hundred Years*. New York, 1941.

Singer, D. W. See under *Texts* (Bruno).

Stillman, J. M. *Theophrastus Bombastus von Hohenheim, called Paracelsus*. Chicago, 1920.

Troilo, E. *La filosofia di Giordano Bruno*. Turin, 1907.

Wessely, J. E. *Thomas Campanellas Sonnenstadt*. Munich, 1900.

Whyte, A. *Jacob Behmen: An Appreciation*. Edinburgh, 1895.

Chapter XVIII: The Scientific Movement of the Renaissance.

Texts

Leonardo da Vinci. *The Literary Works.* J. R. Richter (edit.). Oxford, 1939.
Copernicus. *Gesamtausgabe.* 4 vols.
Tycho Brahe. *Opera omnia.* Prague, 1611, Frankfurt, 1648.
Kepler. *Opera omnia.* 8 vols. Frankfurt, 1858–71.
Galileo. *Opere.* E. Albèri (edit.). Florence, 1842–56.
Le opere di Galileo Galilei. 20 vols. Florence, 1890–1907.
Dialogo sopra i due massimi systemi del mondo. Florence, 1632.
(English translation by T. Salusbury in *Mathematical Collections and Translations.* London, 1661.)
Dialogues concerning Two New Sciences. H. Crew and A. de Salvio (Translators). Evanston, 1939.

Studies

Aliotta, A. and Carbonara, C. *Galilei.* Milan, 1949.
Armitage, A. *Copernicus, the Founder of Modern Astronomy.* London, 1938.
Burtt, E. A. *The Metaphysical Foundations of Modern Physical Science.* New York, 1936.
Butterfield, H. *Origins of Modern Science.* London, 1949.
Dampier, Sir W. C. *A History of Science.* Cambridge, 1929 (4th edition, 1948).
A Shorter History of Science. Cambridge, 1944.
Dannemann, F. *Die Naturwissenschaften in ihrer Entwicklung und in ihrem Zusammenhange.* 4 vols. Leipzig, 1910–13.
Dreyer, J. L. E. *Tycho Brahe.* Edinburgh, 1890.
Duhem, P. *Études sur Léonard de Vinci.* Paris, 1906–13.
Les origines de la statique. Paris, 1905–6.
Fahie, J. J. *Galileo, his Life and Work.* London, 1903.
Grant, R. *Johann Kepler. A Tercentenary Commemoration of his Life and Work.* Baltimore, 1931.
Jeans, Sir J. H. *The Growth of Physical Science.* Cambridge, 1947.
Koyré, A. *Études Galiléennes.* Paris, 1940.
McMurrich, J. P. *Leonardo da Vinci the Anatomist.* London, 1930.
Sedgwick, W. T. and Tyler, H. W. *A Short History of Science.* New York, 1917 (revised edition, 1939).
Stimson, D. *The Gradual Acceptance of the Copernican Theory of the Universe.* New York, 1917.
Strong, E. W. *Procedures and Metaphysics.* Berkeley, U.S.A., 1936.

Taylor, F. Sherwood. *A Short History of Science.* London, 1939.
Science Past and Present. London, 1945.
Galileo and Freedom of Thought. London, 1938.

Thorndike, L. *A History of Magic and Experimental Science.* 6 vols. New York, 1923–42.

Whitehead, A. N. *Science and the Modern World.* Cambridge, 1927 (Penguin, 1938).

Wolf, A. *A History of Science, Technology and Philosophy in the Sixteenth and Seventeenth Centuries.* London, 1935.

Chapter XIX: Francis Bacon

Texts

The Philosophical Works of Francis Bacon. J. M. Robertson (edit.). London, 1905.

Works. R. L. Ellis, J. Spedding and D. D. Heath (edit.). 7 vols. London, 1857–74.

Novum Organum. Edited with introduction and notes by T. Fowler. Oxford, 1889 (2nd edition).

The Advancement of Learning. London (Everyman Series).

R. W. Gibson. *Francis Bacon. A Bibliography.* Oxford, 1950.

Studies

Anderson, F. H. *The Philosophy of Francis Bacon.* Chicago, 1948.

Fischer, Kuno. *Francis Bacon und seine Schule.* Heidelberg, 1923 (4th edition).

Nichol, J. *Francis Bacon, his Life and Philosophy.* 2 vols. London and Edinburgh, 1901.

Sturt, M. *Francis Bacon, a Biography.* London, 1932.

Chapter XX: Political Philosophy

Texts

Machiavelli. *Le Opere di Niccolò Machiavelli.* 6 vols. L. Passerini and G. Milanesi (edit.). Florence, 1873–77.
Tutte le Opere storiche e letterarie di Niccolò Machiavelli. G. Barbèra (edit.). Florence, 1929.
Il Principe. L. A. Burd (edit.). Oxford, 1891.
The Prince. W. K. Marriott (translator). London, 1908 and reprints (Everyman Series).
The Discourse of Niccolò Machiavelli. 2 vols. L. J. Walker, S.J. (translator and editor). London, 1950.
The History of Florence. 2 vols. N. H. Thomson (translator). London, 1906.

Machiavelli (*contd.*) *The Works of Nicholas Machiavel.* 2 vols. E. Farneworth (translator). London, 1762. (2nd edition in 4 vols., 1775).

The Historical, Political and Diplomatic Writings of Niccolò Machiavelli. 4 vols. Boston and New York, 1891.

More. *Utopia* (Latin and English). J. H. Lupton (edit.). London, 1895. (There are many other versions, including an English text in the Everyman Series.)

L'Utopie ou le traité de la meilleure forme de gouvernement. Texte latine édite par M. Delcourt avec des notes explicatives et critiques. Paris, 1936.

The English Works. London, 1557. This text is being re-edited and two volumes appeared in 1931 (London), edited by W. E. Campbell and A. W. Reed.

There are various editions of the Latin works. For example, *Opera omnia latina*: Louvain, 1566.

Hooker. *Works.* 3 vols. J. Keble (edit.). Oxford, 1845 (3rd edition).

The Laws of Ecclesiastical Polity, Books I–V. Introduction by Henry Morley. London, 1888.

Bodin. *Method for the Easy Comprehension of History.* B. Reynolds (translator). New York, 1945.

Six livres de la république. Paris, 1566. Latin edition: Paris, 1584. English translation by R. Knolles: London, 1606.

Althusius. *Politica methodice digesta.* Herborn, 1603. Enlarged edition; Groningen, 1610. Modern edition by C. J. Friedrich. Cambridge (Mass.), 1932.

Grotius. *De iure belli ac pacis.* Washington, 1913 (edition of 1625). English translation by F. W. Kelsey and others. Oxford, 1925. (These two vols. together constitute No. 3 of 'The Classics of International Law.')

Studies

Allen, J. W. *A History of Political Thought in the Sixteenth Century.* London, 1928.

Baudrillart, H. *Jean Bodin et son temps.* Paris, 1853.

Burd, L. A. *Florence (II), Machiavelli.* (The Cambridge Modern History, vol. 1, ch. 6.) Cambridge, 1902.

Campbell, W. E. *More's Utopia and his Social Teaching.* London, 1930.

Chambers, R. W. *Thomas More.* London, 1935.

Chauviré, R. *Jean Bodin, auteur de la République.* Paris, 1914.

D'Entrèves, A. P. *Natural Law. An Introduction to Legal Philosophy.* London, 1951.

Figgis, J. N. *Studies of Political Thought from Gerson to Grotius.* Cambridge, 1923 (2nd edition).

Foster, M. B. *Masters of Political Thought.* Vol. 1, *Plato to Machiavelli* (Ch. 8, Machiavelli). London, 1942.

Gierke, O. von *Natural Law and the Theory of Society.* 2 vols. E. Barker (translator). Cambridge, 1934.

Johannes Althusius und die Entwicklung der naturrechtlichen Staatstheorien. Breslau, 1913 (3rd edition).

Gough, J. W. *The Social Contract. A Critical Study of its Development.* Oxford, 1936.

Hearnshaw, F. J. C. *The Social and Political Ideas of some Great Thinkers of the Renaissance and the Reformation.* London, 1925.

The Social and Political Ideas of some Great Thinkers in the Sixteenth and Seventeenth Centuries. London, 1926.

Meinecke, F. *Die Idee der Staatsräson.* (Ch. 1, Machiavelli.) Munich, 1929 (3rd edition).

Ritchie, D. G. *Natural Rights.* London, 1916 (3rd edition).

Sabine, G. H. *A History of Political Theory.* London, 1941.

Villari, P. *The Life and Times of Niccolò Machiavelli.* 2 vols. L. Villari (translator). London, 1892.

Vreeland, H. *Hugo Grotius.* New York, 1917.

Chapter XXI: (Scholasticism of the Renaissance) A General View

Texts

A number of titles of works are mentioned in the course of the chapter. Only a very few selected texts will be mentioned here. For fuller biographies the *Dictionnaire de théologie catholique* can be profitably consulted under the relevant names. The standard bibliographical work for writers of the Dominican Order between 1200 and 1700 is *Scriptores Ordinis Praedicatorum* by Quétif-Echard. A photolithographic reprint of the revised Paris edition of 1719–21 is being published by Musurgia Publishers, New York. For Jesuit authors consult Sommervogel-De Backer, *Bibliothèque de la compagnie de Jésus.* Liége, 1852ff.

Cajetan. *Thomas de Vio Cardinalis Caietanus. Scripta theologica.* Vol. 1, *De comparatione auctoritatis papae et concilii cum apologia eiusdem tractatus.* V. M. I. Pollet (edit.). Rome, 1936.

Thomas de Vio Cardinalis Caietanus (1469–1534); *Scripta philosophica:*

Cajetan (*contd.*) *Commentaria in Porphyrii Isagogen ad Praedicamenta Aristotelis.* I. M. Marega (edit.). Rome, 1934.

Opuscula oeconomico-socialia. P. N. Zammit (edit.). Rome, 1934.

De nominum analogia. De conceptu entis. P. N. Zammit (edit.). 1934.

Commentaria in de Anima Aristotelis. Y. Coquelle (edit.). Rome, 1938.

Caietanus . . . in 'De Ente et Essentia' Commentarium. M. H. Laurent (edit.). Turin, 1934.

Cajetan's commentary on Aquinas's *Summa theologica* is printed in the *Opera omnia* (Leonine edition) of St. Thomas.

Bellarmine. *Opera omnia.* 11 vols. Paris, 1870–91.

Opera oratoria postuma. 9 vols. Rome, 1942–8.

De controversiis. Rome, 1832.

Tractatus de potestate summi pontificis in rebus temporalibus. Rome, 1610.

Molina. *De Institia et Iure.* 2 vols. Antwerp, 1615.

Concordia liberi arbitrii cum gratiae donis, divina praescientia, providentia, praedestinatione et reprobatione. Paris, 1876.

Vitoria. *De Indis et de Iure Belli Relectiones.* E. Mys (edit.). Washington, 1917 (Classics of International Law, No. 7).

John of St. Thomas. *Cursus Philosophicus Thomisticus* (edit. Reiser). 3 vols. Turin, 1930–8.

Cursus philosophicus. 3 vols., Paris, 1883.

Joannis a Sancto Thoma O.P. Cursus theologici. Paris, Tournai, Rome, 1931 ff.

Studies

Barcía Trelles, C. *Francisco Suárez, Les théologiens espagnols du XVI siècle et l'école moderne du droit internationale.* Paris, 1933.

Brodrick, J. *The Life and Work of Blessed R. Cardinal Bellarmine.* 2 vols. London, 1928.

Figgis, J. N. See under bibliography for Suárez.

Fritz, G., and Michel, A. Article *Scolastique* (section III) in the Dictionnaire de théologie catholique, vol. 14, cols. 1715–25. Paris, 1939.

Giacón, C. *La seconda scolastica.* I, *I grandi commentatori di san Tommaso;* II, *Precedenze teoretiche ai problemi giuridici;* III, *I Problemi giuridico-politici.* Milan, 1944–50.

Littlejohn, J. M. *The Political Theory of the Schoolmen and Grotius.* New York, 1896.

Régnon, T. de *Bañes et Molina.* Paris, 1883.

Scott, J. B. *The Catholic Conception of International Law. Francisco de Vitoria, Founder of the Modern Law of Nations: Francisco Suárez, Founder of the Philosophy of Law in general and in particular of the Law of Nations.* Washington, 1934.

Smith, G. (edit.). *Jesuit Thinkers of the Renaissance. Essays presented to John F. McCormick, S.J.* Milwaukee, Wis., 1939.

Solana, M. *Historia de la Filosofia Española en el siglo XVI.* Madrid, 1940.

Stegmüller, F. *Geschichte des Molinismus. Band I, Neue Molinaschriften.* Münster, 1935 (Beiträge, 32).

Streitcher, K. *Die Philosophie der spanischen Spätscholastik an den deutschen Universitäten des siebzehnten Jahrhunderts* (in *Gesammelte Aufsätze zur Kulturgeschichte Spaniens*). Münster, 1928.

Vansteenberghe, E. Article *Molinisme* (and bibliography) in the Dictionnaire de théologie catholique, vol. 10, cols. 2094–2187. Paris, 1928.

Chapters XXII–XXIII: Francis Suárez

Texts

Opera. 28 vols. Paris, 1856–78.

Metaphysicarum Disputationum Tomi duo. Salamanca, 1597. (Many editions, up to that of Barcelona, 1883–4.)

Selections from Three Works of Francisco Suárez, S.J. (*De legibus, Defensio fidei catholicae. De triplici virtute theologica.*) 2 vols. Vol. 1, the Latin texts; Vol. 2, the translation. Oxford, 1944. (Classics of International Law, No. 20.)

Among bibliographies one can mention *Bibliografica Suareciana* by P. Mugica. Granada, 1948.

Studies

Aguirre, P. *De doctrina Francisci Suárez circa potestatem Ecclesiae in res temporales.* Louvain, 1935.

Alejandro, J. M. *La gnoseología del Doctor Eximio y la acusación nominalista.* Comillas (Santander), 1948.

Bouet, A. *Doctrina de Suárez sobre la libertad.* Barcelona, 1927.

Bouillard, R. Article *Suárez: théologie pratique.* Dictionnaire de théologie catholique, vol. 14, cols. 2691–2728. Paris, 1939.

Bourret, E. *De l'origine du pouvoir d'après Saint Thomas et Suárez.* Paris, 1875.

Breuer, A. *Der Gottesbeweis bei Thomas und Suárez. Ein wissenschaftlicher Gottesbeweis auf der Grundlage von Potenz und Aktverhältnis oder Abhängigkeitsverhältnis.* Fribourg (Switzerland), 1930.

Conde y Luque, R. *Vida y doctrinas de Suárez.* Madrid, 1909.

Dempf, A. *Christliche Staatsphilosophie in Spanien.* Salzburg, 1937.

Figgis, J. N. *Some Political Theories of the early Jesuits.* (Translations of the Royal Historical Society, XI. London, 1897.)

Studies of Political Thought from Gerson to Grotius. Cambridge, 1923 (2nd edition).

Political Thought in the Sixteenth Century. (The Cambridge Modern History, vol. 3, ch. 22). Cambridge, 1904.

Giacón, C. *Suárez.* Brescia, 1945.

Gómez Arboleya, E. *Francisco Suárez* (1548–1617). Granada, 1947.

Grabmann, M. *Die disputationes metaphysicae des Franz Suárez in ihrer methodischen Eigenart und Fortwirkung* (*Mittelalterliches Geistesleben*, vol. 1, pp. 525–60.). Munich, 1926.

Hellín, J. *La analogía del ser y el conocimiento de Dios en Suárez.* Madrid, 1947.

Iturrioz, J. *Estudios sobre la metafísica de Francisco Suárez, S.J.* Madrid, 1949.

Lilley, A. L. *Francisco Suárez. Social and Political Ideas of some Great Thinkers of the XVIth and XVIIth centuries.* London, 1926.

Mahieu, L. *François Suárez. Sa philosophie et les rapports qu'elle a avec la théologie.* Paris, 1921.

(Replies by P. Descoqs to this work are contained in *Archives de Philosophie*, vol. 2 (pp. 187–298) and vol. 4 (pp. 434–544). Paris, 1924 and 1926.)

Monnot, P. Article *Suárez: Vie et œuvres.* Dictionnaire de théologie catholique, vol. 14, cols. 2638–49. Paris, 1939.

Plaffert, F. *Suárez als Völkerrechtslehrer.* Würzburg, 1919.

Recaséns Siches, L. *La filosofía del Derecho en Francisco Suárez.* Madrid, 1927.

Regout, D. *La doctrine de la guerre juste de saint Augustin à nos jours* (pp. 194–230). Paris, 1934.

Rommen, H. *Die Staatslehre des Franz Suárez.* München-Gladbach, 1927.

Scorraille, R. de. *Francois Suárez de la Compagnie de Jésus.* 2 vols. Paris, 1911.

Scott, J. B. *The Catholic Conception of International Law. Francisco de Vitoria, Founder of the Modern Law of Nations: Francisco Suárez, Founder of the Modern Philosophy of Law in general and in particular of the Law of Nations.* Washington, 1934.

Werner, K. *Franz Suárez und die Scholastik der letzten Jahrhunderte.* 2 vols. Ratisbon, 1861 and 1889.

Zaragüeta, J. *La filosofía de Suárez y el pensamiento actual.* Granada, 1941.

Among the special issues of periodicals and collected articles devoted to the philosophy of Suárez one may mention the following:

Actas del IV centenario del nacimiento de Francisco Suárez, 1548–1948. 2 vols. Madrid, 1949–50. (Contains articles on Suárez' theological, philosophical and political ideas.)

Archives de philosophie, vol. 18. Paris, 1949.

Pensamiento, vol. 4, número extraordinario, Suárez en el cuarto centenario de su nacimiento (1548–1948). Madrid, 1948. (This number of *Pensamiento* contains valuable studies on the metaphysical, epistemological, political and legal ideas of Suárez.)

Razón y Fe, tomo 138, fascs. 1–4, July–October 1948. Centenario de Suárez, 1548–1948. Madrid, 1948. (Suárez is considered both as theologian and philosopher, but mainly as philosopher.)

The two following works deal mainly with theological aspects of Suárez' thought:

Estudios Eclesiasticos, vol. 22, nos. 85–6, April–September, 1948. Francisco Suárez en el IV centenario de su nacimiento. Madrid, 1948.

Miscelánea Comillas, IX. Homenaje al doctor eximio P. Francisco Suárez, S.J., en el IV centenario de su nacimiento, 1548–1948. Comillas (Santander), 1948.

Among the works published in connection with the third centenary of Suárez' death (1917) one may mention:

Commemoración del tercer centenario del Eximio Doctor español Francisco Suárez, S.J. (1617–1917). Barcelona, 1923.

P. Franz Suárez, S.J. Gedenkblätter zu seinem dreihundertjährigen Todestag (25 September 1617). Beiträge zur Philosophie des P. Suárez by K. Six, etc. Innsbruck, 1917.

Rivista di Filosofia Neo-scolastica, X (1918).

Scritti vari publicati in occasione del terzo centenario della morte di Francesco Suárez, per cura del prof. Agostino Gemelli. Milan, 1918.

Rivière, E. M. and Scorraille, R. de *Suárez et son œuvre. À l'occasion du troisième centenaire de sa mort*, 1617–1917. Vol. 1, La bibliographie des ouvrages imprimés et inédits (E. M. Rivière). Vol. 2, *La Doctrine* (R. de Scorraille). Toulouse-Barcelona, 1918.

INDEX

(The principal references are printed in heavy figures. References followed by an asterisk refer to the Appendices or to a bibliographical note.)

5

6 BME
7 IND
8 CHI
9 G
0 R
1 H/C

2 M
3 RR
4 17
5 18
6 15
7 19
8 19
9 K
0 20
1 20

S S S B
S S B B
B B A A
A A A M
M M M M